The Legal Environment of Business

A Managerial Approach: Theory to Practice

Fourth Edition

©philsajonesen/Getty Images

Sean P. Melvin
Elizabethtown College

F. E. Guerra-Pujol
University of Central Florida

McGraw Hill

THE LEGAL ENVIRONMENT OF BUSINESS: A MANAGERIAL APPROACH: THEORY TO PRACTICE, FOURTH EDITION

Published by McGraw-Hill Education, 2 Penn Plaza, New York, NY 10121. Copyright © 2021 by McGraw-Hill Education. All rights reserved. Printed in the United States of America. Previous editions © 2018, 2015, and 2011. No part of this publication may be reproduced or distributed in any form or by any means, or stored in a database or retrieval system, without the prior written consent of McGraw-Hill Education, including, but not limited to, in any network or other electronic storage or transmission, or broadcast for distance learning.

Some ancillaries, including electronic and print components, may not be available to customers outside the United States.

This book is printed on acid-free paper.

2 3 4 5 6 7 8 9 LWI 24 23 22 21 20

ISBN 978-1-260-24780-0 (bound edition)
MHID 1-260-24780-5 (bound edition)
ISBN 978-1-264-08664-1 (loose-leaf edition)
ISBN 1-264-08664-4 (loose-leaf edition)

Executive Portfolio Manager: *Kathleen Klehr*
Product Developers: *Jaroslaw Szymanski; Allie Kukla*
Marketing Manager: *Claire McLemore*
Content Project Managers: *Lori Koetters; Angela Norris*
Buyer: *Laura Fuller*
Design: *Matt Diamond*
Content Licensing Specialist: *Beth Cray*
Cover Image: *philsajonesen/Getty Images*
Compositor: *SPi Global*

All credits appearing on page or at the end of the book are considered to be an extension of the copyright page.

Library of Congress Cataloging-in-Publication Data

Names: Melvin, Sean P., author. | Guerra-Pujol, F. E., author.
Title: The legal environment of business : a managerial approach : theory to practice / Sean P. Melvin, Elizabethtown College; F. E. Guerra-Pujol, University of Central Florida.
Description: Fourth edition. | New York, NY : McGraw-Hill Education, [2020] | Includes bibliographical references and index.
Identifiers: LCCN 2019044810 | ISBN 9781260247800 (hardcover) | ISBN 1260247805 (bound edition) | ISBN 9781264086641 (loose-leaf edition) | ISBN 1264086644 (loose-leaf edition)
Subjects: LCSH: Businesspeople—United States—Textbooks. | Commercial law—United States—Textbooks.
Classification: LCC KF390.B84 M45 2020 | DDC 346.7307—dc23
LC record available at https://lccn.loc.gov/2019044810

The Internet addresses listed in the text were accurate at the time of publication. The inclusion of a website does not indicate an endorsement by the authors or McGraw-Hill Education, and McGraw-Hill Education does not guarantee the accuracy of the information presented at these sites.

mheducation.com/highered

©philsajonesen/Getty Images

For Joanna, Sean, and Ally—always.

S.P.M.

For Sydjia, the love of my life.

F.E.G.P.

For our students: past, present, and future.

The Authors

about the authors

Courtesy of Sean P. Melvin

Sean P. Melvin is an associate professor of business law at Elizabethtown College (Pennsylvania), where he served as department chair for eight years, won the Delta Mu Delta Outstanding Teacher of the Year award, and received several Faculty Merit awards for teaching and scholarship. Prior to his appointment at Elizabethtown, he was an assistant professor of business at a large state university where he taught in both the undergraduate and MBA programs. Before his academic career, Professor Melvin was a corporate lawyer in a large Philadelphia-based law firm and went on to become vice president and general counsel at a publicly traded technology company.

Professor Melvin is the author or co-author of nine books (including five textbooks), has contributed scholarly and professional articles and case studies to over two dozen publications, and is a member of the Academy of Legal Studies in Business (ALSB). His article "Case Study of a Coffee War" was selected as Best International Case Study at the 86th annual ALSB conference.

Courtesy of F. E. Guerra-Pujol

F. E. Guerra-Pujol is a lecturer of business law at the University of Central Florida (UCF), a large state university located in Orlando, where he also serves as faculty editor of the *UCF Undergraduate Research Journal*. Prior to his appointment at UCF, he was an associate professor at the Pontifical Catholic University School of Law in Ponce, Puerto Rico, and practiced corporate and tax law with a large Latin American law firm. Professor Guerra-Pujol received his BA from UC Santa Barbara and his JD from Yale Law School.

Professor Guerra-Pujol has published refereed articles, book chapters, and other scholarly works and is a member of the Academy of Legal Studies in Business (ALSB). He is currently writing a book titled *Alternate Legal Worlds* exploring law from a science fiction perspective, and his work has been featured on Freakonomics Radio, Hacker News, and the website io9.

preface

©philsajonesen/Getty Images

Think of this textbook as a road map that guides you through the twists and turns of the laws that impact business entities, owners, and managers. This road map will help you understand ways in which business owners and managers can add value to their companies by using legal insight and strategy for business planning and for limiting liability. We have tailored the text, examples, cases, and teaching features to the needs of business students by providing concise explanations of law (theory) and then supplying the tools necessary for students to apply their knowledge in the business environment (practice).

MASTERING THE MATERIAL

The first step in mastering the material is to recognize that you must *internalize* the concepts presented in your courses. This requires more than a casual reading of assignments. For many years, we have asked students who earned an "A" in our courses to write a few sentences of advice to future students on how to internalize the material and achieve a top grade in the course. We offer you some of their collective wisdom:

- At the beginning of the course, match the syllabus with the textbook. Note the areas that the instructor is focused on by comparing the amount of coverage between topics. For example, if it appears from the syllabus that you will be spending several classes on constitutional law, that is an area that will undoubtedly be assessed (through an examination, project, etc.) and requires more intense study and review.
- The day before a class, study the assignment as follows: (1) read the major and minor headings in the textbook to get a general sense of what the material covers; (2) go back and read the text carefully, using a highlighter and pencil to mark important text and make notes in the margins; and (3) review the concept summaries, flowcharts, and self-checks to be sure you understand the material, and put question marks next to any concept you do not understand.
- The day of your class, if possible, take 15 minutes before your class to review the highlighted text, margin notes, and concept summaries.
- During class, be sure that your text is open and that your notes are tied to any assignments in the text. For example, suppose your instructor takes time to go over the concept of jurisdiction in some detail during class, draws a flowchart on the board, and goes over the self-check answers. This is a clear sign that jurisdiction will be assessed in some form (most commonly through an examination or quiz). In your notes on jurisdiction, indicate that the concept is important (and requires more intense study) and cross-reference it with page numbers in your textbook.
- As soon as possible after class (ideally, immediately after class but no later than that same evening), take 15 minutes to write out 10 note cards. First, write out five of the most important concepts covered in class that day. Second, write out five terms (words or short phrases) that were used by the instructor during class. This will give you a convenient and portable resource for reviewing.

Finally, we offer you the same advice for success in your course that we have offered our own students for more than a decade: The secret is that there is no secret. No methodology, advice, or review cards substitute for a sustained and diligent study of the material.

A NOTE TO THE INSTRUCTOR

The instructor's materials are based on a turnkey approach that provides a comprehensive set of course materials along with the textbook. These materials have been developed with an eye toward minimizing instructor preparation time while still allowing the instructor to tailor the course in a way that meets the unique needs of instructors and students alike. In addition to the traditional supplementary materials package that includes an Instructor's Manual, Test Bank, and PowerPoint slides, the instructor resources also include a robust package of online content including McGraw Hill's interactive exercises via Connect, quizzes, links to streaming videos, case updates, sample text-specific syllabi with alternatives for a variety of classroom circumstances, multiple formats, teaching notes, sample questions, and assignment sheets tied to the simulation materials and the Capstone case studies.

Sean P. Melvin
F. E. Guerra-Pujol

changes to this edition

©philsajonesen/Getty Images

The authors embrace a commitment to continuous improvement of the content, case selection, features, and approach embodied in this textbook. We are privileged to have candid reviews, suggestions, and guidance from over 100 business law professors from a wide variety of colleges and universities. Much of this fourth edition is based on specific feedback from our reviewers and students.

Chapter 1

- New Case: *South Dakota v. Wayfair Inc.* (2018)
- New material on precedent
- Update to Strategic Legal Solutions: The Big Picture
- Added Case Summary
- Added Key Point

Chapter 2

- New material on due process
- New Case: *Masterpiece Bakeshop, Ltd. v. Colorado Civil Rights Commission* (2018)
- New Case: *Trump v. Hawaii* (2018)
- New Case: *Carpenter v. United States* (2018)
- New Case: *Patel v. Zillow, Inc.* (2019)

Chapter 3

- Updated Table 3.1 on U.S. Supreme Court Acceptance Rate
- Added Concept Summary on precedent
- New Case: *Bristol-Myers Squibb Co. v. Superior Court of California* (2017)
- New Case: *Florida v. Georgia* (2018)

Chapter 4

- Updated Introduction and Learning Objectives
- Added section on Class Action Lawsuits
- New material on Class Action Fairness Act
- New Case: *In re Subway Sandwich Marketing and Sales Litigation*, T. Frank (2017)
- Updated Stages of Litigation
- New Case: *20/20 Financial Consulting, Inc. v. John Does* (2010)

- Updated FAA Section
- New Case: *Schein, Inc. v. Archer & White Sales, Inc.* (2019)
- New Strategy 101 feature: Online Dispute Resolution

Chapter 5

- Revised content and title
- Updated Business Ethics Defined
- Updated Moral Philosophy and Ethical Decisions
- New Ethical Decision-Making Process case study on Google
- New Case: *Brook Brothers Inc. v. Bubbles by Brooks, LLC* (2013)

Chapter 6

- Updated material on unilateral contracts (rewards)
- Streamlined material on Mailbox Rule
- New Key Point
- New summary table
- New Legal Strategy 101 feature

Chapter 7

- New Case: *Holder Construction v. Georgia Tech Facilities, Inc.* (2006)
- New Case: *Thomas v. Montelucia Villas, LLC* (2013)
- Revised material on anticipatory repudiation
- New Key Point
- Streamlined Remedies at Law section
- Revised Legal Strategy 101

Chapter 8

- Updated Battle of the Forms material
- New Case: *Accettura & Wozniak v. Vacationland, Inc.* (2018)
- New Case: *Hemlock Semiconductor Operations v. SolarWorld Industries Sachsen* (2017)
- New material: Statute of Frauds
- New material and new case: Cure
- New Critical Thinking questions
- Updated Legal strategy 101

Chapter 9
- New case: *Turner v. Wells* (2018)
- Revised Assumption of Duty section
- Updated Legal Implications in Cyberspace
- Updated and Legal/Ethical Discussion on Products Liability and Guns
- New End-of-Chapter case summaries
- Updated Legal Strategy 101

Chapter 10
- Updated Classification of Agents
- Added new section on Uber
- New Case: *Carroll Management Group, LLC v. A Carpet & Paint, LLC* (2015)
- Updated and streamlined ABC Test for Agency Status
- Updated Strategic Legal Solutions
- New material on Going-and-Coming Rule
- New material on liability of LLC managers
- New Key Point: Classification

Chapter 11
- Updated Employee-at-will Doctrine
- New Case: *McQueary v. The Pennsylvania State University* (2016)
- Updated Statutory Exceptions
- New Critical Thinking case questions
- Updated material on Whistleblower Statutes
- New material: Affordable Care Act
- Updated Legal Strategy 101

Chapter 12
- Updated Title VII material to account for new sex discrimination cases
- New Case: *Zarda v. Altitude Express* (2018)
- Updated Sexual Harassment, added Impact of the #MeToo Movement
- Updated Hostile Work Environment
- Updated flow chart: Title VII Analysis
- Streamlined Disparate Impact Theory material

Chapter 13
- Updated Choosing a Business Entitiy
- New Case: *Doctors Hospital at Renaissance v. Andrade* (2016)
- Added material on Personal Guarantees
- Updated Self-Check
- New Key Point
- Updated Legal Strategy 101

Chapter 14
- Updated Overview of LLCs and LLPs
- New Case: *Headfirst Baseball LLC v. Elwood* (2017)
- Updated Chapter Review Questions
- Revised Concept Summary: Dissociation
- New Key Point
- Updated Legal Strategy 101

Chapter 15
- Updated Fiduciary Duties section
- Revised Corporate Opportunity Doctrine
- Streamlined Financing section
- New Legal Strategy 101 feature

Chapter 16
- Updated Crowdfunding
- Updated Peer-to-Peer Lending
- New material: Process of a Public Offering
- Revised material on Regulation D Exemptions
- Revised table: Summary of Exemptions
- Revised table: Crowdfunding Regulation
- Streamlined Safe Harbors
- New material: Insider Trading
- New material: Personal Benefits Test
- New Case: *Digital Realty Trust v. Somers* (2018)
- New table: Insider Trading Theories
- New Legal Strategy 101

Chapter 17
- Updated Scope of Administrative Agency Power
- Updated Limits on Administrative Agencies
- Added Concept Summary: Limits on Administrative Agencies
- Updated Regulatory Flexibility Act
- Updated Legal Stategy 101 feature
- Updated : Net Neutrality

Chapter 18
- Updated Strategic Legal Solutions for Managers

- New material on Clean Air Act
- Updated Deepwater Horizon (BP) Oil Spill
- Added Critical Thinking questions to cases

Chapter 19

- Updated Monopoly Power and Rule of Reason
- Updated "Search Bias" Investigation against Google
- Updated Antitrust and Sports section
- New Critical Thinking case questions
- Updated Legal Strategy 101

Chapter 20

- Updated Bankruptcy Guidelines/Amounts
- Updated material on Bad Faith Filings
- Updated material on Power of Trustees
- Updated Preferential Transfers
- New Critical Thinking case questions
- Updated Legal Strategy 101

Chapter 21

- Updated coverage of Warranties
- Updated section on CFBP
- Updated section on Credit Transactions
- Added Key Points
- Updated Self-Check questions
- Added Critical Thinking questions to cases
- Updated Legal Strategy 101

Chapter 22

- Revised section on the *Park* Doctrine
- Updated Fourth Amendment and the Impact of Technology on Warrants Requirements
- Updated Fourth Amendment summary table
- New Case: *United States v. DeCoster* (2016)
- Updated Criminal Law and Business Entities
- Updated Criminal Procedure
- Updated Business Ethics feature: Enforcement of Insider Trading Laws

Chapter 23

- Revised Introduction and Learning Objectives
- New section on Types of Property Rights
- Revised Eminent Domain section
- New Key Term (transaction costs)
- New Case: *Jackson v. Wyndham Destinations, Inc.* (2019)
- New Case: *Casino Reinvestment Development Authority v. Birnbaum* (2019)

Chapter 24

- Revised Introduction and Learning Objectives
- Revised Trade Secrets section
- New Case: *IBM v. Johnson* (2009)
- Revised Trademarks section
- New Case: *Elliott v. Google, Inc.* (2017)
- New question for Business Ethics Perspective feature
- Updated First Amendment Concerns section
- Extended discussion of SCOTUS case *Matal v. Tam* (2017)
- New developments in the Washington Redskins trademark case
- Revised Copyright Law section
- New Criminal Sanctions for Infringement section
- Revised Defenses to Copyright Infringement Claims section
- Added reference to Google's PageRank Patent
- New Case: *Rentmeester v. Nike* (2019)
- New Case: *ConnectU v. Zuckerberg* (2008)

Chapter 25

- Updated section on Comity
- Updated "Foreign Official" and the FCPA
- Updated Enforcing Intellectual Property Rights
- Updated section on World Court and European Court of Justice

©philsajonesen/Getty Images

NEW CONNECT'S APPLICATION-BASED ACTIVITIES

New for the 4th edition are Application-Based Activities for Business Law. This digital feature provides students valuable practice using problem-solving skills to apply their knowledge to realistic scenarios. Students progress from understanding basic concepts to using their knowledge to analyze complex scenarios and solve problems. Application-Based Activities have been developed for the most-often-taught topics (as ranked by instructors) in the business law course. These unique activities are assignable and auto-gradable in Connect.

Chapter Features

Each chapter begins with *Learning Objectives* and a short overview that provides students with a map of the chapter. The *Learning Objectives* are a point-by-point checklist of the skills and learning goals that gives students a convenient study guide for previewing and reviewing material in the chapter.

Learning Objectives

After studying this chapter, students who have mastered the material will be able to:

1-1 Understand the broad definition and origins of law.
1-2 List and explain the purposes of the law.
1-3 Explain the importance and benefits of legal awareness for business owners and managers in creating a strategy and adding value to a company.
1-4 Articulate the role of counsel in legal decision making in a business context.
1-5 Recognize, explain, and give examples of sources of American law.
1-6 Understand the legal doctrine of stare decisis.
1-7 Classify the law into several broad categories.
1-8 Differentiate between the concepts of law and equity.
1-9 Identify and apply important equitable maxims.

Strategic Legal Solutions

Strategic Legal Solutions provides practical answers for legal problems faced by managers and business owners. *Strategic Legal Solutions* is structured in a problem and solution format that allows students to understand how a particular section's legal concepts may be used to solve real-world business problems.

STRATEGIC LEGAL SOLUTIONS

Developing Codes of Ethics and Conduct

PROBLEM: While many organizations may have a set of informal values and standards to which they aspire to adhere, such informal value systems may be too vague and thus not very helpful in a practical context.

STRATEGIC SOLUTION: Develop an effective code of ethics and code of conduct for your business organization. Such codes should be developed in cooperation with (and not exclusively by) the organization's human resource manager and legal counsel. Ideally, the entire organization, not just management, should play a role or have a say in the creation and periodic affirmation of such codes.

Depending on the organization, a code of ethics and code of conduct may be expressed in the same document. Here, they are examined separately.

For a code of ethics, consider the following guidelines:

- Identify the ethical values needed to comply with relevant laws and regulations.
- Identify the ethical values most relevant to the main activities in each area of your organization. For example, the chief financial officer may identify objectivity and accuracy as important values.

walkthrough

©philsajonesen/Getty Images

BUSINESS ETHICS PERSPECTIVE

Good Faith and the Nuclear Condition Option

Note that while the law imposes a good faith requirement on all contracting parties, as a practical matter the law may also protect those who are ostensibly acting in good faith but may have unethical motives. In some contracts, the parties agree to a conditional clause sometimes known as a *nuclear condition*, that is, a clause whereby one party may cancel the contract completely if a condition is not met to that party's subjective satisfaction. Consider the case in which the president of WidgetCo assigns Manager to purchase a piece of real estate. Manager enters into a contract with Owner for the sale of a piece of commercial real estate. Manager insists that the contract contain an "acceptable financing" clause as follows: "As a specific condition precedent to WidgetCo's obligation to close, the parties agree that WidgetCo must obtain financing for the transaction on terms and conditions acceptable to WidgetCo in WidgetCo's sole discretion." learns that WidgetCo is able to obtain financing on extremely favorable terms according to industry standards.

1. Given that the contract requires that any financing terms must be acceptable to WidgetCo, what are Manager's legal obligations to go through with the transaction? Does this differ from Manager's ethical obligations?
2. Is it possible for Manager to comply with the good faith requirement and still avoid the contract with Owner?
3. Recall the discussion of ethical decision-making models in Chapter 5, "Business Ethics, Corporate Social Responsibility, and Law." How could these models help guide Manager's course of action?
4. Assume that the president orders Manager to lie on the loan application, thereby ensuring that any financial institution will reject the loan application. Note that lying on a bank loan application is a crime. What are Manager's options at that point?

Business Ethics Perspective

The coverage of business ethics reflects its increasingly important place in the business world. In addition to Chapter 5, "Business Ethics, Corporate Social Responsibility, and Law," the textbook features logically placed boxes with discussion questions intended to help students understand ethical decision making in contemporary contexts.

Legal/Ethical Reflection and Discussion

This feature is strategically placed in parts of the text where the instructor may wish to have students reflect on the ethical dimension of a legal problem. It starts with a short narrative and ends with a series of questions that fundamentally ask students: What would *you* do?

LEGAL/ETHICAL REFLECTION AND DISCUSSION

Made in the USA

A manager for WidgetCo is approached by a foreign vendor who offers to supply widgets at a substantial discount from what his company is currently paying. When determining WidgetCo's course of action, consider both the moral minimum and the maximizing profits approaches to business ethics:

- Why should it matter whether the lower-priced widgets are not made in the USA?
- Why should it matter whether the foreign company is subject to the same quality-control and labor safety regulations as the current USA supplier?
- Why should it matter whether the lower-priced widgets are more (or less) likely to be faulty or substandard?
- Why should it matter whether faulty or substandard widgets could make the company's products more dangerous to users or to the environment?

CASE 3.2 Clemens v. McNamee, 615 F.3d 374 (5th Cir. 2010)

FACT SUMMARY In the summer of 2007, federal agents contacted Brian McNamee in connection with a federal investigation into the illegal manufacture and sale of performance-enhancing drugs in professional sports. McNamee was an athletic trainer who had worked for both the Toronto Blue Jays and the New York Yankees baseball clubs. After authorities convinced McNamee that they had sufficient evidence to convict him for injecting athletes with anabolic steroids, McNamee agreed to cooperate with investigators in exchange for immunity from prosecution. During an interview with investigators, McNamee admitted that he had administered steroids to all-star pitcher Roger Clemens in both Toronto and New York. McNamee repeated this allegation to Major League Baseball investigators and to a reporter during an interview with *Sports Illustrated*. In 2008, Clemens, a citizen of Texas, filed a defamation suit against McNamee, a citizen of New York, in federal court based on diversity of citizenship. The trial court dismissed the complaint due to lack of personal jurisdiction over McNamee because his alleged defamation contacts as required by the long-arm statute and due process. The court held that to support personal jurisdiction in a defamation claim, the forum must be the "focal point" of the story. Although the court acknowledged that the defamation may cause distress and damage to Clemens's reputation in Texas, it concluded that the alleged defamatory statement was inadequately directed to Texas to satisfy the minimum-contacts requirement.

WORDS OF THE COURT: Minimal Contacts and Injurious Effect "In support of jurisdiction, Clemens points to the harm he suffered in Texas and to McNamee's knowledge of the likelihood of such damage in the forum. Yet under [previous case law], Clemens has not made a prima facie showing that McNamee made statements in which Texas was the focal point: the statements did not concern activity in Texas; nor were they made in Texas or directed to Texas residents any more than residents of any state. As such, the district court did not err in dismissing Clemens' suit for lack of personal jurisdiction over McNamee."

Cases

The textbook uses a *hybrid* format to report case law rather than including lengthy excerpts from judicial opinions. Students are provided with (1) a summary of the facts; (2) a decision and opinion synopsis; (3) short excerpts from the actual opinion, called "Words of the Court," to help students understand a key point in the case; and (4) several case questions to facilitate discussion. Students will find this format useful for understanding legal cases in a business context.

x WALKTHROUGH

walkthrough

©philsajonesen/Getty Images

Self-Checks

Self-Check exercises offer students an opportunity to reinforce and apply the material being studied in the textbook. Students use black-letter law and cases to answer short hypothetical questions on a specific topic. *Self-Checks* appear in the textbook after important legal concepts and are always keyed to problems faced by business managers and owners. Answers to the *Self-Checks* are provided at the end of the chapter.

> **Self-Check** Source of Constitutional Authority
>
> What is the constitutional source of authority for each of the following laws?
>
> 1. A federal statute that makes it more difficult for businesses to qualify for protection under bankruptcy laws.
> 2. An increase in the federal corporate income tax.
> 3. A federal statute that adds criminal penalties for patent infringement.
> 4. A federal statute creating an agency to regulate ground shipping between states.
> 5. A federal statute that requires that 25 percent of federal government construction contracts be awarded to companies that are women- or minority-owned enterprises.
>
> *Answers to this Self-Check are provided at the end of the chapter.*

> **CONCEPT SUMMARY** Internet and E-mail Jurisdiction
>
> - Lower federal courts have applied different tests to determine whether online activities can generate sufficient "minimum contacts" for personal jurisdiction purposes, such as the *Zippo* sliding-scale test and the *Calder* effects test.
> - Under the *Zippo* sliding-scale test, there are minimum contacts when a defendant actively and repeatedly conducts business over the Internet, while there are no minimum contacts when a defendant merely posts information on a website that anyone can access. In the middle of this sliding scale, however, courts must consider the level and nature of the exchange of information on a case-by-case basis to determine whether there are minimum contacts.
> - Under the "effects test," the minimum contacts requirement is satisfied if it is reasonably *foreseeable* that the defendant's actions could have an *injurious effect* on a resident of the court's state.

Concept Summaries and Flowcharts

To help students with *reinforcing* and *reviewing* the application of the law in a business context, each major section within each chapter features a summary of the section. When a legal procedure is involved, flowcharts are used to summarize the process.

Other Textbook Features

Key Points briefly reinforce an important concept. *Legal Speak* presents instant definitions of important legal terms in the margins of the text.

> **KEY POINT**
>
> The primary purposes of the law are
> - To provide a system of order that defines conduct and consequences.
> - To promote equality and justice in society.
> - To provide a method for resolving disputes.
> - To promote good faith dealing among merchants.
> - To provide a degree of reliability in applying the law evenly.

> **Language of the Law**
>
> In order to maximize the value of interaction between business owners/managers and attorneys, a basic understanding of legal terminology is useful. Students studying business law face the task of learning legal syntax at the same time as they learn how to apply the legal doctrines in a business context. This is analogous to learning a complicated subject matter in a foreign language, yet it is manageable with careful study. Legal terms are sometimes referred to as *jargon* or *legalese*, but having a working knowledge of some common legal terminology is an important step to mastering the material. Although much of the language of the law has Latin roots, the terminology is primarily a combination of Latin, early and modern English, and French. The vocabulary of American law is drawn from the various cultures and events that shaped American history. To facilitate your understanding of legal expression, important legal terms are highlighted throughout the text, summarized at the end of each chapter, and also featured alphabetically in the glossary. The authoritative source for legal terms is *Black's Law Dictionary*, first published in 1891. There are also several websites that provide definitions and examples for legal terms.

> **LEGAL IMPLICATIONS IN CYBERSPACE**
>
> **Protections for Online Content Providers**
>
> Along with holding the actual tortfeasor liable in a defamation case, the law imposes certain liability upon the publisher of libelous statements as well. However, the law does not impose liability on the *distributor* of the publication (such as a bookstore or newsstand). For example, suppose a famous movie star is the subject of a gossip feature in a hypothetical tabloid called the *American Tattler*. The feature implies that the movie star was seen at a local restaurant and was so intoxicated that she could not control her conduct. In a lawsuit for defamation, the movie star proves that the story was false and that it led to her being fired by her movie studio. In terms of liability, both the author of the defamatory feature and the publication (*American Tattler*) may be liable for damages.
>
> However, the rules pertaining to publishers of online content in cyberspace are different. In our movie-star example, suppose that instead of the *American Tattler* publishing the defamatory feature, a gossip columnist hired by America Online (AOL) wrote the article for an AOL entertainment news board. There would be no doubt of the liability of the author, but would AOL be liable as the "publisher"?

Legal Implications in Cyberspace apply traditional legal concepts in the context of the Internet.

WALKTHROUGH   xi

walkthrough

©philsajonesen/Getty Images

End-of-Chapter Features

Each chapter ends with several features crafted to help students review and connect the different sections of the chapter by applying the material learned in the text in a practical way.

THEORY TO PRACTICE

PART I

Santiago Information Systems (Santiago) is a business based in Baltimore, Maryland, that purchases old computers, refurbishes them with new software and hardware parts, and sells them in bulk for about half the price of a new PC. For the past three years, Santiago has shipped approximately 40 percent of its inventory to the same client. The client is the Wilmington School District (Wilmington) in Wilmington, Delaware, and the school pays approximately $80,000 to Santiago for the computers per year. Santiago also visits each school to be sure that the computers are installed correctly and that the school district is satisfied with the order. Santiago has a website that gives contact information for the company, but the site is only partially interactive because users can transact business only by sending Santiago an e-mail via the website. Recently, Wilmington discovered that large shipments of Santiago's products were defective, and it has been unable to come to a resolution with Santiago over the matter.

1. If Wilmington wishes to sue Santiago, what court or courts would have jurisdiction over this matter?
2. What would be the best venue and why?
3. If a Delaware court decides that it does not have jurisdiction, how may that affect Wilmington's decision on whether or not to file a lawsuit?

PART II

Assume that one of Santiago's suppliers, Parts R Us (Parts), is headquartered in Union City, New Jersey, and has been shipping Santiago parts for approximately four years in a row. Last year, Parts sold approximately $7,000 in hardware to Santiago. In the past 10 years, Parts R Us has shipped to businesses in Maryland, New York, New Jersey, and Connecticut. Parts has also e-mailed advertisements to potential leads in each of the 50 states. Wilmington has determined that Parts provided the defective components used in the computer order described in Part I.

1. If Wilmington decides to file suit against Parts in Delaware, will a Delaware court have personal jurisdiction over Parts? Why or why not?
2. Suppose Parts has a website where customers can order products, pay for them via credit card, and have them delivered via a delivery service to any U.S. city. How does this affect your jurisdiction analysis?
3. If Parts's only contact with Delaware is via its website, what standard should the trial court apply to determine whether there are minimum contacts?

Legal Strategy 101: This feature challenges students to apply their legal knowledge in a strategic context. Each chapter reinforces the opening chapter's *Strategic Legal Solutions: The Big Picture* by posing a real-world legal/ethical dilemma that has a strategic dimension and offering questions/exercises to stimulate critical thinking and discussion.

Theory to Practice: Each chapter features a hypothetical legal problem faced by a manager that is related to specific material in that chapter. The hypothetical problem is followed by questions that connect the problem to several different sections in the chapter.

Manager's Challenge: This feature allows students to engage in writing or a group work assignment that sets forth a manager's task relating to the material in the chapter. Some challenges are designed for teams, others for individuals.

Key Terms: Key terms for students are boldfaced in the text and listed as a group at the end of the chapter with a definition and reference to the page number in the chapter where the term is first mentioned.

Case Summaries: Several brief case summaries are included, with a heading for each that indicates its general topic reference to the chapter and with questions about the case summary. These cases are intended to reinforce students' knowledge of how laws apply in different fact circumstances.

Chapter Review Questions and Answers: Several multiple choice questions designed to reinforce learning objectives are featured at the end of each chapter, along with answers and explanations.

©philsajonesen/Getty Images

walkthrough

Business Law Simulation Exercises

The textbook features three business law simulation exercises. In a simulation exercise, students are provided with facts, law, and cases related to a hypothetical business dispute and are assigned to analyze the material, understand the legal and ethical issues presented, and then work toward a resolution. The simulations are also excellent for review and reinforcement because the materials involve cases directly related to one or more topics covered in a particular unit of the textbook.

BUSINESS LAW SIMULATION EXERCISE 1

©philsajonesen/Getty Images

Restrictive Covenants in Contracts: Neurology Associates, LLP v. Elizabeth Blackwell, M.D.

Learning Objectives

After studying this simulation, students who have mastered the material will be able to:

1. Explain the legal doctrines that govern the use of restrictive covenants.
2. Interpret and apply the rules set forth in current case law.
3. Articulate a cogent argument for each party/side in the dispute.
4. Negotiate a tenable solution as an alternative to a judicial forum.

Chapters 6 and 7 provided you with a variety of legal doctrines and rules governing contract formation and performance and then illustrated how these doctrines and rules apply in the corporate sector context. This

- Part 3 is an assignment sheet that will be provided to you by your instructor to be used in conjunction with this simulation.

capstone case study 1
COFFEE WARS: STARBUCKS V. CHARBUCKS[1]

©philsajonesen/Getty Images

OVERVIEW AND OBJECTIVES

Two years after opening their family-owned coffee bean roastery, Jim and Annie Clark had become accustomed to long workweeks and bootstrap financing. By 1997, their Black Bear Micro Roastery was finally growing, and the Clarks were hopeful that their new specialty blend, Charbucks, would give their uniquely dark-roasted coffee bean a catchy name to remember. Soon after launching the new blend, Annie Clark received a phone call from an insistent in-house lawyer at coffee giant Starbucks that threatened the very existence of the Clarks' company. Starbucks claimed that the Charbucks name and label infringed on its trademark, and it demanded that the Clarks cease the use of the name Charbucks and that any existing products with that name be removed from supermarket shelves. But the Clarks insisted that they had been careful to design the label with Black Bear Micro Roastery logos and that the name was tied to the dark-roasting process and not to anything related to the name Starbucks. Despite their beliefs that no infringement had taken place, the Clarks entered into settlement negotiations to avoid the legal costs associated with defending a trademark lawsuit. After the settlement negotiations failed, Starbucks sued Black Bear Micro Roastery, and the stage was set for a coffee war that pitted a multinational powerhouse against a Main Street merchant. This case study emphasizes use of legal insight and business strategy, gives context for evaluating business ethics, and requires the application of trademark law.

Review Legal Concepts

Prior to reading the case, briefly review the following legal concepts that were covered in the textbook: legal insight and business strategy (Chapter 1); business, societal, and ethical contexts of law (Chapter 5); and

THE BLACK BEAR MICRO ROASTERY

Jim and Annie Clark were native New Englanders who shared a passion for coffee and an entrepreneurial spirit. After three years of research, they launched Black Bear Micro Roastery in 1995 with a mission of creating a unique methodology for roasting gourmet coffee beans through use of advanced technology and the "traditional Yankee work ethic." The company was situated in the lakes region of New Hampshire and targeted connoisseur coffee drinkers, primarily in the New England area, who appreciated the micro-roastery approach of producing small, high-quality batches of coffee beans. The beans were sold via mail order, from the Black Bear website, and through New England specialty stores and supermarkets. Eventually, Black Bear also sold its products through its own retail outlet and café in Portsmouth, New Hampshire.

True to their belief in the micro-roastery concept and their entrepreneurial courage, the Clarks invested their life savings in the company. In order to start the business, the couple sold many of their assets and refinanced the mortgage on their home for extra cash. They enlisted their teenage daughters as their labor force and committed to seven-day workweeks. The family business was the centerpiece of their family's livelihood.

As with many start-ups, business for Black Bear was slow and rocky at first. The price of green coffee beans had fluctuated unexpectedly, and the 1997 Teamsters strike at United Parcel Service had eaten into profit margins. Undeterred, Jim and Annie Clark kept the company going until it began to grow ever so slowly. In order to develop a niche in the gourmet coffee market, Black Bear began to develop unique blends with catchy names that were easy to remember. This included blends such as "Country French," "Kenya Safari," and "Mocha Java."

Capstone Case Studies

Capstone case studies center on the dilemmas of actual corporations that were faced with a corporate crisis involving legal and ethical issues. They are intended to help students connect several different legal and ethical concepts in a single case study. First, students reread concept summaries from specific chapters to reinforce their knowledge of specific legal issues. Second, students study a narrative of facts of the case, dynamics of the marketplace, and important trends of the time. Discussion questions are grouped by topical subject matter such as negligence, products liability, administrative agency regulation, and criminal law. Ethical decision-making questions are integrated into each case. The *Capstone Case Study* feature also provides a short exercise designed for use as a writing assignment, small group work, or class discussion.

online assignments and resources

NEW Connect's Business Law Application-Based Activities (ABAs) Application-Based Activities for Business Law provide students valuable practice using problem-solving skills to apply their knowledge to realistic scenarios. Students progress from understanding basic concepts to using their knowledge to analyze complex scenarios and solve problems. Application-Based Activities have been developed for the most-often-taught topics (as ranked by instructors) in the business law course. These unique activities are assignable and auto-gradable in Connect.

SmartBook® 2.0 Available within Connect, SmartBook 2.0 is an adaptive learning solution that provides personalized learning to individual student needs, continually adapting to pinpoint knowledge gaps and focus learning on concepts requiring additional study. SmartBook 2.0 fosters more productive learning, taking the guesswork out of what to study, and helps students better prepare for class. With the ReadAnywhere mobile app, students can now read and complete SmartBook 2.0 assignments both online and offline. For instructors, SmartBook 2.0 provides more granular control over assignments with content selection now available at the concept level. SmartBook 2.0 also includes advanced reporting features that enable instructors to track student progress with actionable insights that guide teaching strategies and advanced instruction, for a more dynamic class experience.

Writing Assignment As part of a larger set of learning activities that provide students with core course content as well as opportunities to practice the skills they need to develop, the new MH writing assignment toolset offers faculty the ability to assign a full range of writing assignments to students (both manual-scoring and auto-scoring) with just-in-time feedback. You may set up manually scored assignments in a way that students can

- automatically receive grammar and high-level writing feedback to improve their writing before they submit their project to you;
- run Originality checks and receive feedback on "exact matches" and "possibly altered text" that includes guidance to properly paraphrase, quote, and cite sources to improve the academic integrity of their writing before they submit their project to you.

The new writing assignment will also have features that allow you to assign milestone draft (optional), easily re-use your text and audio comments, build/score with your rubric, and review your own Originality report of student work. In addition, you may choose from a set of auto-scored, short-answer questions that allow you to add lower-stake writing activities to your course without adding significant grading and feedback to your workload; these promote critical thinking/conceptual understanding of course content and provide students with instantaneous feedback.

Interactives McGraw-Hill Connect's Interactives offer a variety of automatically graded exercises that require students to apply key concepts. Whether the assignment includes a click and drag, video case, or *decision generator*, these interactives provide instant feedback and progress tracking for students and detailed results for the instructor.

Instructor's Manual The Instructor's Manual is designed to be an effective course management tool and an integral part of the turnkey approach used throughout the supplementary material package. The features and format are intended to give instructors maximum flexibility to determine and produce high-quality course content. The Instructor's Manual also has a special "Day One" section addressing important fundamental course decisions for instructors who are new to the course.

Test Bank and Quizzes Our test bank and quizzes contain a variety of true/false, multiple-choice, and essay questions as well as scenario-based questions.

PowerPoint Presentation Slides This edition's revised PowerPoints contain an easy-to-follow lecture outline summarizing key points for every chapter.

Business Law Newsletter McGraw-Hill Education's monthly business law newsletter, *Proceedings,* is designed specifically with the business law educator in mind. *Proceedings* incorporates "hot topics" in business law, video suggestions, an ethical dilemma, teaching tips, and a "chapter key" cross-referencing newsletter topics with the various McGraw-Hill business law textbooks. *Proceedings* is emailed to business law instructors each month.

AACSB Statement McGraw-Hill Education is a proud corporate member of AACSB International. The authors of *The Legal Environment of Business,* 4th Edition, understand the importance and value of AACSB accreditation and recognize the curricula guidelines detailed in the AACSB standards for business accreditation by connecting selected questions in the test bank to the general knowledge and skill guidelines in the AACSB standards.

The statements contained in *The Legal Environment of Business,* 4th Edition, are provided only as a guide for the users of this textbook. The AACSB leaves content coverage and assessment within the purview of individual schools, the mission of the school, and the faculty. Although *The Legal Environment of Business,* 4th Edition, and the teaching package make no claim of any specific AACSB qualification or evaluation, we have within *The Legal Environment of Business,* 4th Edition, labeled selected questions according to the general knowledge and skill areas.

Tegrity: Lectures 24/7 Tegrity in Connect is a tool that makes class time available 24/7 by automatically capturing every lecture. With a simple one-click start-and-stop process, you capture all computer screens and corresponding audio in a format that is easy to search, frame by frame. Students can replay any part of any class with easy-to-use, browser-based viewing on a PC, Mac, iPod, or other mobile device.

Educators know that the more students can see, hear, and experience class resources, the better they learn. In fact, studies prove it. Tegrity's unique search feature helps students efficiently find what they need, when they need it, across an entire semester of class recordings. Help turn your students' study time into learning moments immediately supported by your lecture. With Tegrity, you also increase intent listening and class participation by easing students' concerns about note-taking. Using Tegrity in Connect will make it more likely you will see students' faces, not the tops of their heads.

Test Builder in Connect Available within Connect, Test Builder is a cloud-based tool that enables instructors to format tests that can be printed or administered within an LMS. Test Builder offers a modern, streamlined interface for easy content configuration that matches course needs, without requiring a download.
Test Builder allows you to:
- Access all test bank content from a particular title.
- Easily pinpoint the most relevant content through robust filtering options.
- Manipulate the order of questions or scramble questions and/or answers.
- Pin questions to a specific location within a test.
- Determine your preferred treatment of algorithmic questions.
- Choose the layout and spacing.
- Add instructions and configure default settings.

Test Builder provides a secure interface for better protection of content and allows for just-in-time updates to flow directly into assessments.

Assurance of Learning Ready Many educational institutions today are focused on the notion of assurance of learning, an important element of some accreditation standards. *The Legal Environment of Business* is designed specifically to support your assurance of learning initiatives with a simple, yet powerful, solution. Each test bank question for *The Legal Environment of Business* maps to a specific chapter learning objective listed in the text. You can use our test bank software, Test Builder, or Connect to easily query for learning objectives that directly relate to the learning objectives for your course. You can then use the reporting features of Test Builder to aggregate student results in similar fashion, making the collection and presentation of assurance of learning data simple and easy.

FOR INSTRUCTORS

You're in the driver's seat.

Want to build your own course? No problem. Prefer to use our turnkey, prebuilt course? Easy. Want to make changes throughout the semester? Sure. And you'll save time with Connect's auto-grading too.

65%
Less Time Grading

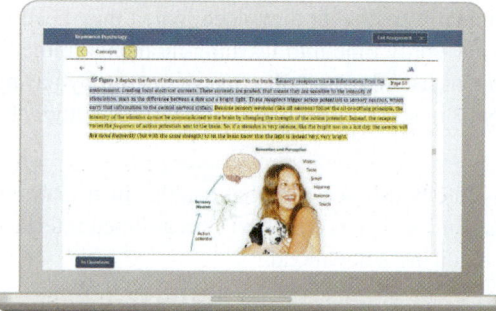

Laptop: McGraw-Hill; Woman/dog: George Doyle/Getty Images

They'll thank you for it.

Adaptive study resources like SmartBook® 2.0 help your students be better prepared in less time. You can transform your class time from dull definitions to dynamic debates. Find out more about the powerful personalized learning experience available in SmartBook 2.0 at **www.mheducation.com/highered/connect/smartbook**

Make it simple, make it affordable.

Connect makes it easy with seamless integration using any of the major Learning Management Systems—Blackboard®, Canvas, and D2L, among others—to let you organize your course in one convenient location. Give your students access to digital materials at a discount with our inclusive access program. Ask your McGraw-Hill representative for more information.

Padlock: Jobalou/Getty Images

Solutions for your challenges.

A product isn't a solution. Real solutions are affordable, reliable, and come with training and ongoing support when you need it and how you want it. Our Customer Experience Group can also help you troubleshoot tech problems—although Connect's 99% uptime means you might not need to call them. See for yourself at **status.mheducation.com**

Checkmark: Jobalou/Getty Images

FOR STUDENTS

Effective, efficient studying.

Connect helps you be more productive with your study time and get better grades using tools like SmartBook 2.0, which highlights key concepts and creates a personalized study plan. Connect sets you up for success, so you walk into class with confidence and walk out with better grades.

Study anytime, anywhere.

Download the free ReadAnywhere app and access your online eBook or SmartBook 2.0 assignments when it's convenient, even if you're offline. And since the app automatically syncs with your eBook and SmartBook 2.0 assignments in Connect, all of your work is available every time you open it. Find out more at www.mheducation.com/readanywhere

> "I really liked this app—it made it easy to study when you don't have your textbook in front of you."
>
> - Jordan Cunningham, Eastern Washington University

No surprises.

The Connect Calendar and Reports tools keep you on track with the work you need to get done and your assignment scores. Life gets busy; Connect tools help you keep learning through it all.

Calendar: owattaphotos/Getty Images

Learning for everyone.

McGraw-Hill works directly with Accessibility Services Departments and faculty to meet the learning needs of all students. Please contact your Accessibility Services office and ask them to email accessibility@mheducation.com, or visit www.mheducation.com/about/accessibility for more information.

Top: Jenner Images/Getty Images. Left: Hero Images/Getty Images. Right: Hero Images/Getty Images

acknowledgments

We owe a great deal of gratitude to our entire team at McGraw-Hill Education. Although many team members worked diligently with us in developing and strengthening this book over the course of more than a decade, there are a core of professionals who have provided extraordinary support and enthusiasm for the book for many years: Managing Director Tim Vertovec, Executive Portfolio Manager Kathleen Klehr, Product Developers Jaroslaw Szymanski and Allie Kukla, and Content Project Managers Lori Koetters and Angela Norris are exceptional in their creativity, insight, and work ethic.

Throughout the development of each edition of this book, we have been privileged to have the candid and valuable advice of our reviewers and focus groups. Our reviewers provided us with priceless suggestions, feedback, and constructive criticism. The depth and sincerity of their reviews indicate that they are a devoted group of teacher-scholars. The content of the book was greatly enhanced because of their efforts.

Hakim Adjoua
Columbus State Community College

Wayne Anderson
Missouri State University

Linda Axelrod
Metropolitan State University

David Berkowitz
Chapman University

Perry Binder
Georgia State University

Andrea Boggio
Bryant University

Eli Bortman
Babson College

Michael Bryant
Bryant University

Gretchen Carroll
Owens Community College

Darrell Cartwright
Jefferson State Community College

Anita Cava
University of Miami

Robert Cherry
Appalachian State University

Tracy Cole
Arkansas Tech University

Tom Collins
University of Wisconsin–Platteville

Angelo Corpora
Palomar College

Aquesha Daniels
Western Kentucky University

Rebecca Davis
University of Kentucky–Lexington

Glenn Doolittle
Santa Ana College

Craig Ehrlich
Babson College

Teressa Elliott
Northern Kentucky University

Tim Fogarty
Case Western Reserve University

Michael Fore
Eastern Kentucky University

John Geary
Appalachian State University

Wendy Gelman
Florida International University–Miami

John Gergacz
University of Kansas

Jeane Gohl-Noice
Parkland College

Marc Hall
Auburn University–Montgomery

R. Lainie W. Harris
Georgia Southern University

Eloise Hassell
University of North Carolina–Greensboro

Diane Hathaway
University of Cincinnati

Arlene Hibschweiler
State University of New York–Buffalo

Frederick Jones
Kennesaw State University

Susan Kendall
Arapahoe Community College

Cheryl Kirschner
Babson College

Stan Leasure
Missouri State University

Colleen Less
Johnson & Wales University

Christine Lewis
Auburn University–Montgomery

Mark Lewis
Arkansas State University

Janice Loutzenhiser
California State University–San Bernardino

Nancy Mansfield
Georgia State University

Ernest Mayo
Johnson & Wales University

Martha Novy-Broderick
University of Maine

Les Nunn
University of Southern Indiana

Tom Parrish
Liberty University

Steven Popejoy
University of Central Missouri

Brenda Rice
Ozarks Technical Community College

Alan Roline
University of Minnesota–Duluth

Steven Schamber
St. Louis Community College

Julie Shadoan
Western Kentucky University

Randy Skalberg
University of Minnesota–Duluth

Cheryl Staley
Lake Land College

Kurt Stanberry
University of Houston–Downtown

Connie Strain
Arapahoe Community College

Frank Sullivan
University of Nevada–Las Vagas

Greg Swan
Chandler-Gilbert Community College

Keith Swim
Texas A&M University

Daphyne Saunders Thomas
James Madison University

Mary Torma
Lorain County Community College

Michael Vasilou
DeVry University–Chicago

Glen Vogel
Hofstra University

Ronald Washburn
Bryant University

Mark Whitaker
Hampton University

Glynda White
College of Southern Nevada

Michael Wiggins
Georgia Southern University

Susan Willey
Georgia State University

LeVon Wilson
Georgia Southern University

John Wrieden
Florida International University–Miami

brief table of contents

UNIT ONE	**Fundamentals of the Legal Environment of Business 1**
	Chapter 1 Legal Foundations 2
	Chapter 2 Business and the Constitution 40
	Chapter 3 The American Judicial System, Jurisdiction, and Venue 76
	Chapter 4 Resolving Disputes: Litigation and Alternative Dispute Resolution 110
	Chapter 5 Business Ethics, Corporate Social Responsibility, and Law 140

UNIT TWO	**Law and Commerce 169**
	Chapter 6 Overview and Formation of Contracts 170
	Chapter 7 Contract Enforceability and Performance 206
	Chapter 8 Contracts for the Sale of Goods 246
	Chapter 9 Torts and Products Liability 282

UNIT THREE	**Regulation in the Workplace 327**
	Chapter 10 Agency 328
	Chapter 11 Employment Relationships and Labor Law 364
	Chapter 12 Employment Discrimination 406

UNIT FOUR	**Business Entities, Securities Regulation, and Corporate Governance 451**
	Chapter 13 Choice of Business Entity, Sole Proprietorships, and Partnerships 452
	Chapter 14 Limited Liability Companies and Limited Liability Partnerships 480
	Chapter 15 Corporations 500
	Chapter 16 Regulation of Securities, Corporate Governance, and Financial Markets 528

UNIT FIVE	**Regulatory Environment of Business 567**
	Chapter 17 Administrative Law 568
	Chapter 18 Environmental Law 598
	Chapter 19 Antitrust and Regulation of Competition 628
	Chapter 20 Creditors' Rights and Bankruptcy 652
	Chapter 21 Warranties and Consumer Protection Law 678
	Chapter 22 Criminal Law and Procedure in Business 708
	Chapter 23 Personal Property, Real Property, and Land Use Law 742
	Chapter 24 Intellectual Property 766
	Chapter 25 International Law and Global Commerce 810

CAPSTONE CASE STUDIES
1. Coffee Wars: Starbucks v. Charbucks   839
2. The Odwalla Juice Company Crisis   843
3. Fraud under the Arches: The McDonald's Game Piece Scandal   847

APPENDICES
  A. The Constitution of the United States of America   853
  B. Excerpts from the Sarbanes-Oxley Act of 2002   863

table of contents

\\ UNIT ONE
Fundamentals of the Legal Environment of Business

CHAPTER 1   Legal Foundations   2

Introduction to Law   3
   Purposes of Law   3
   Language of the Law   4
Legal Decisions in a Business Environment: Theory to Practice   4
   Legal Insight and Business Strategy   5
   Role of Counsel   5
Sources and Levels of American Law   7
   Constitutional Law   8
   Statutory Law   8
   Interpreting Statutes   9
Case 1.1: United States v. Ulbricht, 31 F. Supp. 3d 540 (S.D.N.Y. 2014)   10
   Finding Statutory Law   11
   Common Law   11
   Stare Decisis and Precedent   11
   Stare Decisis and Business   12
   Departing from Precedent   12
Case 1.2: South Dakota v. Wayfair, Inc., 138 S. Ct. 2080 (2018)   13
   Administrative Law   14
   Secondary Sources of Law   14
   Uniform Model Laws   15
   Restatements of the Law   16
Categories of Law   17
   Criminal Law versus Civil Law   18
   Substantive Law versus Procedural Law   18
   Law versus Equity   18
Case 1.3: Wilcox Investment, L.P. v. Brad Wooley Auctioneers, Inc., 454 S.W.3D 792 (Ark. Ct. App. 2015)   19
   Public Law versus Private Law   20
Strategic Legal Solutions: The Big Picture   21
   Overview   21
   Strategy #1—Noncompliance   21
   Strategy #2—Avoidance   22
   Strategy #3—Prevention   22
   Strategy #4—Value Creation (or "Legal Competitive Advantage")   23
   Summing Up   25
Key Terms   25
Chapter Review Questions   26
Theory to Practice   27
Manager's Challenge   27
Appendix to Chapter 1: A Business Student's Guide to Understanding Cases and Finding the Law   32

CHAPTER 2   Business and the Constitution   40

Structure of the Constitution: Federal Powers   41
   Structure of the Constitution   41
   Amendments   42
Overview of Federal Powers   42
   Article I—Congressional Powers   42
   Article II—Executive Powers   43
   Article III—Judicial Powers   43
Case 2.1: United States v. Alvarez, 567 U.S. 709 (2012)   44
   Separation of Powers   45
   Applying the Constitution: Standards of Judicial Review   45
   Rational Basis Review   46
   Intermediate-Level Scrutiny   46
   Strict Scrutiny   46
Case 2.2: Brown v. Entertainment Merchants Association, 564 U.S. 786 (2011)   47
   The Supremacy Clause and Preemption   47
Commerce Powers   48
   Application of Commerce Powers   48
   Interstate versus Intrastate Commercial Activity   48
Case 2.3: Gonzalez v. Raich, 545 U.S. 1 (2005)   48
   The Commerce Clause and Civil Rights   50
   Noncommercial Activity   51
   The Dormant Commerce Clause   51
Tax and Spend Powers   52
   Necessary and Proper Clause   52
Constitutional Protections   54
   The Bill of Rights and Business   54
   The First Amendment   55
   Limits on Free Speech   55
Case 2.4: Masterpiece Cakeshop, Ltd. v. Colorado Civil Rights Commission, 138 S. Ct. 1719 (2018)   55
   Commercial Speech   56
Case 2.5: R.J. Reynolds Tobacco Company v. Food and Drug Administration, 696 F.3d 1205 (D.C. Cir. 2012)   57
   Advertising and Obscenity Regulation   57
   Political Speech by Corporations   58

Case 2.6: Citizens United v. Federal Election Commission, 558 U.S. 310 (2010) 59
    The Fourth Amendment 60
    Exceptions 61
    Reasonableness Requirement 61
    Searches and Seizures 62
Case 2.7: United States v. Jones, 565 U.S. 400 (2012) 62
    Postscript: The USA PATRIOT Act 63
Due Process Protections 64
    Due Process 64
    Equal Protection 64
Postscript: The Right to Privacy 66
    Federal Statutes 66
    Workplace Privacy 66
Key Terms 67
Chapter Review Questions 68
Theory to Practice 68
Legal Strategy 101 69
Manager's Challenge 70

CHAPTER 3   The American Judicial System, Jurisdiction, and Venue   76

Role and Structure of the Judiciary 76
    State versus Federal Courts 77
    State Courts 77
    Federal Courts 79
How the Law Develops 83
Jurisdiction and Venue 84
    Jurisdiction and Business Strategy 85
    Overview of Jurisdiction 85
    Two-Part Analysis 85
    Subject Matter Jurisdiction: Authority over the Dispute 86
    Original versus Concurrent Jurisdiction 86
    Choice of Forum 87
    Jurisdiction over Property 88
    Personal Jurisdiction 88
    In-State Defendants 88
    Out-of-State Defendants 88
Case 3.1: Goodyear Dunlop Tires Operation v. Brown, 564 U.S. 915 (2011) 89
    Injurious Effect 90
Case 3.2: Clemens v. McNamee, 615 F.3d 374 (5th Cir. 2010) 91
    Physical Presence 91
    Voluntary 92
    Venue 93
Case 3.3: Franklin v. Facebook, No. 1:15-CV-00655 (N.D. Ga. 2015) 93
Internet Jurisdiction 95
    How the Law Develops in Real Time 95
International Jurisdiction in the Internet Age 98
    Country of Origin Standard 99
    Other Theories of Jurisdiction in Electronic Commerce 99
Key Terms 100
Chapter Review Questions 101
Theory to Practice 102
Legal Strategy 101 102
Manager's Challenge 103

CHAPTER 4   Resolving Disputes: Litigation and Alternative Dispute Resolution   110

Civil Litigation 111
Dispute Resolution and Business Planning 111
Class Action Lawsuits 111
    Class Action Fairness Act (CAFA) 112
Case 4.1: *In re* Subway Sandwich Marketing & Sales Practices Litigation, T. Frank, Objector, No. 16-1652 (7th Cir. 2017) 113
Stages of Litigation 114
    Prelawsuit: Demand and Prelitigation Settlement Negotiations 114
    Standing 115
    Statute of Limitations 115
    Pleadings Stage 115
    Complaint and Summons 115
    Answer 115
    Counterclaim 118
    Cross-Claim 118
    Motions 118
    Discovery Stage 118
    Scope, Timing, and Methods of Discovery 119
Case 4.2: 20/20 Financial Consulting, Inc. v. John Does 1–5, 2010 U.S. Dist. LEXIS 55343 (D.C. Colo. May 11, 2010) 119
    Pretrial Conference 122
    Trial 122
    Jury Selection and Opening Statements 123
    Testimony and Submission of Evidence 123
    Closing Arguments and Charging the Jury 123
    Deliberations and Verdict 123
    Posttrial Motions and Appeals 123
    Collecting the Judgment 124
Alternative Dispute Resolution 124
    Informal ADR 125
    Formal ADR 125
    Arbitration 126
    Legally Mandated Arbitration 126
    Federal Arbitration Act 127
Case 4.3: Henry Schein, Inc. v. Archer & White Sales, Inc., 139 S. Ct. 524 (2019) 128
    Employment and Labor Arbitration 129
Case 4.4: National Football League Management Council v. Brady, 820 F.3d 527 (2d Cir. 2016) 129

    Mediation 130
    Expert Evaluation 130
    Other Forms of ADR 131
Key Terms 132
Chapter Review Questions 133
Theory to Practice 134
Legal Strategy 101 134
Manager's Challenge 135

CHAPTER 5   Business Ethics, Corporate Social Responsibility, and Law 140

What is Ethics? 141
    Relationship between Ethics and Law 141
Business Ethics Defined 142
    Primary and Secondary Stakeholders 142
    Moral Minimum versus Maximizing Profits 142
Case 5.1: Ypsilanti Township v. General Motors Corporation, 506 N.W.2d 556, 201 Mich. App. 128 (1993) 144
Moral Philosophy and Ethical Decision Making 145
    Principles-Based Approach 145
    Religion 145
    Virtue 145
    Natural Law 145
    The Categorical Imperative 146
    Consequences-Based Approach 146
    Contract-Based Approach 147
Values Management and Challenges to Business Ethics 148
Common Traits of Effective Values Management 148
Strategic Advantages of Values Management 151
    Cultivation of Strong Teamwork and Productivity 152
    Clarity in Business Operations 152
    Public Image 152
    Staying the Ethical Course in Turbulent Times 152
Ethical Decision Making: A Manager's Paradigm 152
Ethical Decision-Making Case Studies 153
    Google's Project Maven 153
    Employee Stakeholders Assert Power 154
    Google's Project Maven: Questions for Discussion 154
    Facebook's Secret Psychology Experiment: The Law and Ethics of A/B Testing 155
    Public Outcry 155
    Ethical Analysis 156
    Facebook's Secret Psychology Experiment: Questions for Discussion 156
Corporate Social Responsibility 157
    The Narrow View: "Greed Is Good" 157
    The Moderate View: Just Follow the Law 158
    The Broad View: Good Corporate Citizenship 158

Case 5.2: Brooks Brothers Group, Inc. v. Bubbles by Brooks, LLC, Opposition No. 91205596 (T.T.A.B. July 11, 2013) 159
    CSR and Litigation 159
Landmark Case 5.3: Grimshaw v. Ford Motor Company, 119 Cal. App. 3d 757 (1981) 160
Key Terms 161
Chapter Review Questions 162
Theory to Practice 163
Legal Strategy 101 163
Manager's Challenge 164

\\ UNIT TWO
Law and Commerce 169

CHAPTER 6   Overview and Formation of Contracts 170

Definition of a Contract 171
Categories of Contracts 171
    Written versus Oral Contracts 171
    Bilateral versus Unilateral Contracts 171
Case 6.1: Augstein v. Leslie & NextSelection, Inc., 11 Civ. 7512 (HB), 2012 U.S. Dist. LEXIS 149517 (S.D.N.Y. Oct. 17, 2012) 172
    Express versus Implied versus Quasi-Contracts 173
    Other Categories 174
Sources of Contract Law 175
Contract Transactions 176
Contract Formation 178
    Offer 178
Landmark Case 6.2: Lucy v. Zehmer, 84 S.E.2d 516 (Va. 1954) 179
    Advertisements as an Offer 180
Case 6.3: Leonard v. PepsiCo, Inc., 210 F.3d 88 (2d Cir. 2000) [affirming lower court decision and reasoning in 88 F. Supp. 2d 116 (S.D.N.Y. 1999)] 181
    Acceptance 182
    Termination of an Offer 182
    Termination by Operation of Law 185
    When Acceptance Is Effective: The Mailbox Rule 185
    Silence as an Acceptance 187
    Insufficient Agreement 187
    Indefinite Terms 188
    Mistake 188
    Consideration 189
    Legal Detriment 190
    Amount and Type of Consideration 190
    Preexisting Duty Rule 191
    Bargained-for Exchange 191

    Past Consideration 191
    Promissory Estoppel 192
    Capacity 193
    Minors 193
    Mental Incompetents 193
Case 6.4: Sparrow v. Demonico, 461 Mass. 322 (2012) 194
    Legality 195
Key Terms 196
Chapter Review Questions 198
Theory to Practice 198
Legal Strategy 101 199
Manager's Challenge 200

CHAPTER 7   Contract Enforceability and Performance 206

Enforceability 206
    Genuineness of Assent 206
    Misrepresentation 207
    Fraudulent Misrepresentation 207
Case 7.1: Italian Cowboy Partners, Ltd. v. The Prudential Insurance Company of America, 341 S.W.3d 323 (Tex. 2011) 208
    Duress 210
    Undue Influence 210
    Unconscionability 210
    Statute of Frauds 211
Case 7.2: Holloway v. Dekkers & Twin Lakes Golf Course, 380 S.W.3d 315 (Tex. Ct. App. 2012) 212
    Interpretation Rules for Written Contracts 214
Nature and Effect of Conditions 215
    Categories of Conditions 215
Good Faith Performance and Discharge 217
    Substantial Performance 218
Landmark Case 7.3: Jacob & Youngs v. Kent, 129 N.E. 889 (N.Y. 1921) 219
Other Events of Discharge 220
    Mutual Consent 220
    Operation of Law 222
    Impossibility 222
    Impracticability 223
Case 7.4: Holder Construction Group v. Georgia Tech Facilities, Inc., 282 Ga. App. 796 (2006) 223
    Frustration of Purpose 224
Breach of Contract and Anticipatory Repudiation 225
    Anticipatory Repudiation 226
Case 7.5: Thomas v. Montelucia Villas, LLC, 302 P.3d 617 (Ariz. 2013) 227
Remedies at Law 228
    Compensatory Damages 228
    Consequential Damages 229
    Restitution 229
    Liquidated Damages 230

Equitable Remedies 230
    Specific Performance 230
    Injunctive Relief 231
    Reformation 231
Avoidance and Mitigation of Damages 231
    Clean Hands and Tender of Performance 232
Contracts Involving Rights of a Third Party 232
    Assignment 232
    Delegation 233
    Third-Party Beneficiaries 233
Case 7.6: Emmelyn Logan-Baldwin v. L.S.M. General Contractors, Inc., 942 N.Y.S.2d 718, 94 A.D.3d 1466 (N.Y. 2012) 234
Key Terms 235
Chapter Review Questions 237
Theory to Practice 238
Legal Strategy 101 239
Manager's Challenge 240

CHAPTER 8   Contracts for the Sale of Goods 246

Introduction to Article 2 of the UCC 247
    UCC Coverage and Definitions 247
    Function of the UCC 247
Agreement in a Sales Contract: Offer 248
    Offers with Open Terms 249
    Quantity 249
    Other Open Terms 249
    Firm Offers by Merchants 250
Agreement in Sales Contracts: Acceptance 250
    Battle of the Forms 250
    Nonmerchant Transactions 250
    Merchant Transactions 251
Case 8.1: Hebberd-Kulow Enterprises v. Kelomar, No. D066505, 2016 Cal. App. Unpub. LEXIS 696 (Jan. 27, 2016) 252
    Consideration 253
Statute of Frauds 254
Title and Allocation of Risk 256
    Title 256
    Risk of Loss 256
    Goods Picked Up by the Buyer 257
Performance of Sales Contracts 259
    Obligations of All Parties 259
    Seller's Obligations and Rights 259
    Perfect Tender 260
    Cure 260
Case 8.2: Accettura & Wozniak v. Vacationland, Inc., 2018 IL App (2d) 170972 (Sept. 28, 2018) 261
    Commercial Impracticability 263
Case 8.3: Hemlock Semiconductor Operations v. SolarWorld Industries Sachsen, 867 F.3d 692 (6th Cir. 2017) 263

Buyer's Rights and Obligations   264
  Buyer's Right of Inspection: Acceptance or Rejection   264
  Special Rules for Installment Contracts   265
Breach and Remedies in Sales Agreements   266
  Anticipatory Repudiation in the UCC   266
  Remedies Available to the Seller   267
  Goods in Hands of Seller   267
  Goods in Hands of Buyer   267
  Remedies Available to the Buyer   267
  Remedies Following Rejection of Goods   268
  Cover   268
  Lawsuit for Money Damages   268
  Specific Performance   269
  Remedies Following Acceptance of Nonconforming Goods   269
  Revocation of Acceptance   269
  Lawsuit for Money Damages   269
  Risk of Loss   269
Case 8.4: 3L Communications v. Merola d/b/a NY Telecom Supply, No. M2012-02163-COA-R3-CV, 2013 Tenn. App. LEXIS 589 (Sept. 6, 2013)   270
Contracts for International Sales of Goods   271
  U.N. Convention on Contracts for the International Sale of Goods   271
  Coverage and Major Provisions of CISG   272
  No Writing Required   272
  Offer and Acceptance   272
  Remedies   272
  INCO: International Chamber of Commerce Terms   272
Key Terms   273
Chapter Review Questions   275
Theory to Practice   275
Legal Strategy 101   276
Manager's Challenge   277

CHAPTER 9   Torts and Products Liability   282

Overview of Tort Law   283
Sources of Law   283
Categories of Torts   283
Intentional Business-Related Torts   284
  Defamation   284
  Public Figure Standard   284
Case 9.1: Turner v. Wells, 879 F.3d 1254 (11th Cir. 2018)   285
  Defenses to Defamation   286
  Truth   286
  Privilege Defenses   286
Case 9.2: Nelson v. Tradewind Aviation, 111 A.3d 887 (Conn. App. Ct. 2015)   287
  Trade Libel and Product Disparagement Laws   288
  Fraudulent Misrepresentation   289

False Imprisonment   291
Business Competition Torts   291
  Tortious Interference with Existing Contractual Relationship   291
  Tortious Interference with Prospective Advantage   293
Negligence   294
  Elements of Negligence   294
  Duty   295
Case 9.3: Yost v. Wabash College, Phi Kappa Psi Fraternity, 3 N.E.3d 509 (Ind. 2014)   297
  Breach of Duty   298
  Cause in Fact   299
  Proximate (Legal) Cause   300
Landmark Case 9.4: Palsgraf v. Long Island Railroad Co., 162 N.E. 99 (N.Y. Ct. App. 1928)   300
  Actual Damages   302
  Defenses to Negligence Claims   302
  Comparative Negligence   303
  Assumption of the Risk   303
Case 9.5: Zeidman v. Fisher, 980 A.2d 637 (Pa. Super. Ct. 2009)   303
Strict Liability Torts   304
  Abnormally Dangerous Activities   305
Products Liability   306
  Negligence   306
  Warranty   306
  Strict Liability   306
  Defining "Defect"   307
Case 9.6: Bunch v. Hoffinger Industries, 123 Cal. App. 4th 1278, 20 Cal. Rptr. 3d 780 (2004)   308
  Causation and Damages   311
  Seller's Defenses   311
Key Terms   312
Chapter Review Questions   313
Theory to Practice   314
Legal Strategy 101   315
Manager's Challenge   315
BUSINESS LAW SIMULATION EXERCISE 1 Restrictive Covenants in Contracts: Neurology Associates, LLP v. Elizabeth Blackwell, M.D.   320

\\ UNIT THREE
Regulation in the Workplace   327

CHAPTER 10   Agency   328

Definitions and Sources of Agency Law   328
Classification of Agents   329
  Employee Agents   329
  Employee Agents versus Independent Contractors: Direction and Control   329
  State Law   330

Case 10.1: Avanti Press v. Employment Department Tax Section, 274 P.3d 190 (Or. Ct. App. 2012)   331
    California's Independent Contractor Law   *332*
    IRS's Three-Prong Test   *333*
    Liability for Misclassification   *333*
Overview of an Agency Transaction   336
    Creation of an Agency Relationship   336
    Manifestations and Consent   *336*
    Control   *336*
    Formalities   *336*
Case 10.2: Bosse v. Brinker Restaurant Corp. d/b/a Chili's Grill and Bar, 2005 Mass. Super. LEXIS 372 (Aug. 1, 2005)   337
    Overlay of Agency Law with Other Areas of Law   338
Liability of the Principal for Acts of the Agent   339
    Authority   339
    Actual Authority   *339*
    Apparent Authority   *339*
Case 10.3: GGNSC Batesville, LLC d/b/a Golden Living Center v. Johnson, 109 So. 3d 562 (Miss. 2013)   339
    Ratification   *340*
    Agent's Contract Liability to Third Parties   341
    Fully Disclosed Agency   *341*
    Partially Disclosed Agency   *341*
    Undisclosed Agency   *342*
Case 10.4: Carroll Management Group, LLC v. A Carpet & Paint, LLC, 779 S.E.2d 26 (Ga. Ct. App. 2015)   342
    Tort Liability to Third Parties   343
    Physical Injury Requirement   *343*
    Scope of Employment   *343*
Case 10.5: Moradi v. Marsh USA, Inc., 219 Cal. App. 4th 886 (2013)   345
    Intentional Torts   *346*
    Negligent Hiring Doctrine   346
    Independent Contractors   *347*
Duties, Obligations, and Remedies of the Principal and Agent   348
    Agent's Duties to the Principal   348
    Loyalty   *348*
Case 10.6: SP Midtown, Ltd. v. Urban Storage, LP, Tex. App. LEXIS 3364 (May 8, 2008)   349
    Obedience   *350*
    Care   *350*
    Disclosure   *350*
    Accounting   *351*
    Principal's Remedies for Breach   351
    Rescission and Disgorgement   *352*
    Unauthorized Acts of Agents   *352*
Case 10.7: Romanelli v. Citibank, 60 A.D.3d 428 (N.Y. App. Div. 2009)   352

Duties and Obligations of the Principal to the Agent   353
    Agent's Remedies for Breach   354
Termination of the Agency Relationship   354
    Express Acts   354
    Operation of Law   356
Key Terms   357
Chapter Review Questions   358
Theory to Practice   358
Legal Strategy 101   359
Manager's Challenge   360

CHAPTER 11   Employment Relationships and Labor Law   364

Origins of Employment Regulation and Labor Law   365
Employment-At-Will Doctrine   365
    Express Contracts   365
    Labor Contracts   366
    Common Law Exceptions   366
    Implied Contracts   *366*
Case 11.1: Buttrick v. Intercity Alarms, 2009 Mass. App. Div. 97 (2009)   367
    Public Policy Exception   *368*
    Statutory Exceptions   369
    State Whistleblower Statutes   *369*
Case 11.2: McQueary v. The Pennsylvania State University, No. 2012-1804 (Pa. Ct. Com. Pl. Nov. 30, 2016)   370
    Federal Whistleblower Statutes   *371*
Employment Regulation   372
    Wages and Hours   372
    Minimum Wage, Maximum Hours, and Overtime   *372*
Case 11.3: Integrity Staffing Solutions v. Busk, 574 U.S. 27 (2014)   373
    Exempt Employees   374
Case 11.4: Madden v. Lumber One Home Center, 745 F.3d 899 (8th Cir. 2014)   375
    Misclassification   *376*
    Child Labor Laws   377
    State Wage and Hour Laws   378
    Retirement   378
    Regulation of Pensions and Retirement Accounts   *379*
    Social Security   379
    Health Care   379
    Patient Protection and Affordable Care Act of 2010 and Health Care and Education Reconciliation Act of 2010   *380*
    Sudden Job Loss   380
    Workplace Injuries   380
    Defenses to Workers' Compensation Claims   *381*

Intentional Actions or Recklessness of the Employer 381
   Course of Employment 381
   Regulation of Workplace Safety 381
   Occupational Safety and Health Administration 382
   Family and Medical Leave Act 383
   FMLA Scope and Coverage 383
   FMLA Protections 383
Case 11.5: Jaszczyszyn v. Advantage Health Physician Network, 504 F. App'x 440, 2012 WL 5416616 (6th Cir. Nov. 7, 2012) 384
   Key Employees 385
Employee Privacy 386
   Monitoring of E-Mail and Internet Usage 386
   Employer Liability 386
   Telephone and Voice Mail 386
   Drug and Alcohol Testing 387
   Americans with Disabilities Act Considerations 387
Case 11.6: Leonel v. American Airlines, Inc., 400 F.3d 702 (9th Cir. 2005) 387
   Polygraph Testing 388
Labor Unions and Collective Bargaining 388
   Labor Law 388
   Labor-Management Relations 389
   Labor Management Relations Act 389
   Labor-Management Reporting and Disclosure Act 389
   Union Formation 390
   Authorization Cards 390
   Election 390
   Certification 391
   Reform Efforts 391
   Collective Bargaining 391
   Good Faith Bargaining Requirements 392
   Grievances 392
   Strikes and Other Work Stoppages 392
   Poststrike Rehiring 392
Case 11.7: NLRB v. Midwestern Personnel Services, Inc., 322 F.3d 969 (7th Cir. 2003) 393
   Illegal Work Stoppages and Boycotts 395
   Lockouts and Replacement Workers 395
Key Terms 396
Chapter Review Questions 398
Theory to Practice 398
Legal Strategy 101 400
Manager's Challenge 401

CHAPTER 12 Employment Discrimination 406

Definition, Source of Law, and Statutory Origins 406
   Equal Employment Opportunity Commission (EEOC) 407
Federal Workplace Antidiscrimination Statutes 407

Title VII 408
   Protected Classes 408
   Sexual Orientation as a Protected Class 409
Case 12.1: Zarda v. Altitude Express, 883 F.3d 100 (2d Cir. 2018) 410
   Theories of Discrimination 411
   Disparate Treatment 411
Case 12.2: U.S. Equal Employment Opportunity Commission v. Abercrombie & Fitch Stores, Inc., 135 S. Ct. 2028 (2015) 412
   Mixed Motives 414
   Disparate Impact 415
Sexual Harassment 416
Case 12.3: Morris v. City of Colorado Springs d/b/a Memorial Health System, 666 F.3d 654 (10th Cir. 2012) 417
   Same Sex Harassment 418
   Vicarious Liability of Employers 418
   Strict Liability for Harassment by Supervisor 419
   Impact of the #MeToo Movement 419
   Remedies 423
Age Discrimination in Employment Act 424
   Substantially Younger Requirement 424
Americans with Disabilities Act 425
   Documented-Disability Requirement 425
   ADA Amendments Act of 2008 426
   "Regarded-as" Test 426
   Qualified Individual 427
Case 12.4: Samson v. Federal Express Corporation, 746 F.3d 1196 (11th Cir. 2014) 427
   Reasonable Accommodations 428
Equal Pay Act 428
   Lilly Ledbetter Fair Pay Act of 2009 429
Procedures for Asserting a Claim 430
Employer Defenses 431
   Business Necessity 431
   Faragher/Ellerth Defense 431
   Bona Fide Occupational Qualification 431
   Seniority 432
   Employee Misconduct 432
Affirmative Action Programs 432
   Legality 433
State Antidiscrimination Statutes 433
Case 12.5: Enriquez v. West Jersey Health Systems, 777 A.2d 365 (N.J. Super. Ct. App. Div. 2001) 434
Key Terms 435
Chapter Review Questions 436
Theory to Practice 437
Legal Strategy 101 437
Manager's Challenge 438
BUSINESS LAW SIMULATION EXERCISE 2
Employment Discrimination: John Falstaff v. Paul Revere Furniture Company 443

\\ UNIT FOUR
Business Entities, Securities Regulation, and Corporate Governance 451

CHAPTER 13   Choice of Business Entity, Sole Proprietorships, and Partnerships 452

Choosing a Business Entity   453
   Sole Proprietorships   454
   Termination   455
Case 13.1: Biller v. Snug Harbor Jazz Bistro of Louisiana, L.L.C., 99 So. 3d 730 (4th Cir. 2012)   455
   Partnerships   456
   General Partnerships   456
Case 13.2: Waddell v. Rustin, 2011 Tenn. App. LEXIS 377 (2011)   457
   Limited Partnerships   461
Case 13.3: Doctors Hospital at Renaissance v. Andrade, 493 S.W.3d 545 (Tex. 2016)   463
   Family Limited Partnerships   465
   Partner Dissociation and Dissolution of the Partnership   466
   Dissociation under the RUPA   466
Case 13.4: Robertson v. Mauro, LEXIS 91610 (D. Idaho, 2013)   467
   Withdrawal under the RULPA   468
   Other Events of Dissolution   469
   Franchises: A Method Rather Than an Entity   470
   Franchise Agreements   470
   FTC Regulation   470
   State Regulation   471
Key Terms   471
Chapter Review Questions   472
Theory to Practice   473
Legal Strategy 101   474
Manager's Challenge   475

CHAPTER 14   Limited Liability Companies and Limited Liability Partnerships 480

Overview of LLCS and LLPs   480
   Limited Liability Companies (LLCs)   482
   Formation   482
   Liability   485
   Taxation   485
   Capitalization   485
Case 14.1: AK-Feel, LLC v. NHAOCG, LLC, 62 A.3d 649 (Del. Ch. 2012)   486
   Management and Operation   486
   Dissolution, Dissociation, and Expulsion of Members   487
Case 14.2: Headfirst Baseball LLC v. Elwood, 239 F. Supp. 3d 7 (D.D.C. 2017)   488
   Limited Liability Partnerships (LLPs)   489
   Formation   489
   Liability   489
Case 14.3: Dillard Department Stores, Inc. v. Chargois & Ernster, 602 F.3d 610 (5th Cir. 2010)7   490
   Taxation   491
   Capitalization   491
   Management and Operation   492
Key Terms   493
Chapter Review Questions   493
Theory to Practice   494
Legal Strategy 101   494
Manager's Challenge   495

CHAPTER 15   Corporations 500

Corporate Entities   501
   Categories of Corporations   501
   Privately Held versus Publicly Held   501
   Other Categories   502
   Formation   502
   Preincorporation Activity: Liability of Promoters   503
Case 15.1: Branch v. Mullineaux, 2010 NY Slip Op 31850(U) (N.Y. Sup. Ct. July 15, 2010)   503
   Choice of State of Incorporation   504
   Capitalization   505
   Debt   505
   Equity   505
   Venture Capital Firms   505
   Public Offerings   505
   Initial Organizational Meeting   505
   Commencement of Business and Corporate Formalities   506
   Liability   506
   Personal Guarantees   507
   Taxation   507
   C Corporations   508
   S Corporations   508
Structure, Management, and Operation   509
   Shareholders   509
   Board of Directors   510
   Election of Directors   510
   Removal of Directors   511
   Meetings   511
   Committees   511
   Officers   511
   President   512
   Vice President   512
   Treasurer   512
   Secretary   512
   Fiduciary Duties of Officers and Directors   513
   Duty of Care   513
   Business Judgment Rule   514
Landmark Case 15.2: Smith v. Van Gorkom, 488 A.2d 858 (Del. 1985)   515
   Duty of Loyalty   516

Case 15.3: Ebenezer United Methodist Church v. Riverwalk Development Phase II, 45 A.3d 883 (Md. Ct. Spec. App. 2012) 517
    Breach-of-Fiduciary-Duty Lawsuits by Shareholders 519
    Limiting Director Liability 519
    Piercing the Corporate Veil 520
Case 15.4: Florence Cement Co. v. Vittraino, 292 Mich. App. 461 (2011) 521

Key Terms 521
Chapter Review Questions 522
Theory to Practice 523
Legal Strategy 101 523
Manager's Challenge 524

CHAPTER 16   Regulation of Securities, Corporate Governance, and Financial Markets   528

Fundamentals of the Securities Market 529
    Defining a Security 530
    Federal Securities Law 530
    Modern Application of the Howey *Test* 531
    Stock Market Games 532
    Crowdfunding 532
    Parties in the Securities Market 533
Categories of Securities 533
    Equity Instruments 533
    Common Stock 533
    Preferred Stock 534
    Debt Instruments 534
    Use of Bonds and Debentures 534
    Peer-to-Peer Lending 534
Securities Regulation 535
    Securities and Exchange Commission 535
    EDGAR 537
    The Securities Act of 1933 537
    The Process of a Public Offering 538
    Preregistration Documentation 538
    Registration 538
    Exemptions from Registration 539
    Regulation D: Private and Small Transactions 540
    Accredited Investors 540
    Rule 504: Smaller Offerings 540
    Rule 506: Larger Private Placements 540
    Regulation A: Large Exempt Offerings 541
    Disclosures Required 541
    Crowdfunding 542
    Liability for Violations 542
    Defenses and Safe Harbors 543
    Safe Harbors: The Private Securities Litigation Reform Act of 1995 543
    Materiality 544
    Bespeaks Caution Doctrine 544

Case 16.1: Kaufman v. Trump's Castle Funding, 7 F.3d 357 (3d Cir. 1993) 544
    The Securities Exchange Act of 1934 545
    Section 10b 545
    Insider Trading 546
Case 16.2: United States v. McGee, 763 F.3d 304 (3d Cir. 2014) 546
    Tipper-Tippee Liability 548
    Section 16 549
    Rule 10b-5 and Section 16 in Tandem 549
    Defenses 550
    Securities Litigation Uniform Standards Act of 1998 551
    Securities Regulation by States: Blue-Sky Laws 551
Regulation of Corporate Governance and Financial Markets 551
    The Sarbanes-Oxley (SOX) Act of 2002 553
    Reforms in the Accounting Industry 553
    Financial Reporting 553
    Corporate Governance 554
    Enforcement under SOX 554
    Emergency Escrow 554
    Substantial Penalties 555
    Whistleblowers 555
    Document Destruction Rules 555
    Conspiracy to Commit Fraud 555
    Congressional Response to the Financial Crisis 556
    Troubled Assets Relief Program (TARP) 556
    Financial Market Regulation 556
    Dodd-Frank Act of 2010 557
    Financial Stability Oversight Council 557
    Consumer Financial Protection Bureau 557
    Expanded SEC Jurisdiction and Enforcement 558
    Whistleblower Provisions 558
Case 16.3: Digital Realty Trust v. Somers, 138 S. Ct. 767 (2018) 558

Key Terms 559
Chapter Review Questions 561
Theory to Practice 561
Legal Strategy 101 562
Manager's Challenge 563

\\ UNIT FIVE
Regulatory Environment of Business   567

CHAPTER 17   Administrative Law   568

Definition, Function, and Sources of Administrative Law 569
    Primary Functions of Administrative Agencies 569
    Policymaking 569

  Investigation and Enforcement   *569*
  Licensing and Permitting   *570*
  Distribution of Federal Statutory Benefits to the Public   *570*
  Sources of Administrative Law   *570*
  U.S. Constitution   *570*
  Administrative Procedures Act (APA)   *570*
  Enabling Statutes   *570*
  Common Law   *572*
 Scope of Administrative Agency Power   *572*
  Rulemaking   *572*
  Agency Study and Research   *572*
  Notice: Publication of the Proposed Rule   *572*
  Public Comment   *573*
  Protection of Small Business Owners   *575*
  Revision or Final Publication   *575*
Case 17.1: Association of Private Sector Colleges and Universities v. Duncan and the U.S. Department of Education, 681 F.3d 427 (D.C. Cir. 2012)   *575*
  Judicial Challenges   *577*
  Enforcement, Licensing, and Inspection   *578*
Case 17.2: Trinity Marine Products v. Secretary of Labor Elaine Chao, 512 F.3d 198 (5th Cir. 2007)   *579*
  Adjudication   *580*
  Appeals   *580*
 Limits on Administrative Agencies   *581*
  Executive Branch   *581*
  Appointments Clause   *581*
  Direct Power   *581*
  Congress   *582*
  Judicial Review   *582*
  Statutory Interpretation by Agencies   *582*
  Applying the Arbitrary and Capricious Standard   *586*
Case 17.3: Van Hollen v. Federal Elections Commission, 811 F.3d 486 (D.C. Cir. 2016)   *586*
 Public Accountability   *588*
  Private Citizen Suits   *588*
  Federal Disclosure Statutes   *589*
  Freedom of Information Act (FOIA)   *589*
Case 17.4: Consumer Federation of America v. Department of Agriculture, 455 F.3d 283 (D.C. Cir. 2006)   *590*
  Government in the Sunshine Act   *591*
 Administrative Law at the State Level   *591*

Key Terms   *591*
Chapter Review Questions   *592*
Theory to Practice   *592*
Legal Strategy 101   *593*
Manager's Challenge   *594*

CHAPTER 18   Environmental Law   598

Impact of Environmental Law on Business   *599*
Origins and Sources of Environmental Law   *599*
 Government Enforcement   *599*
  Citizen Suit Provisions and Watchdog Groups   *600*
Case 18.1: Friends of the Earth v. Gaston Copper Recycling Corp., 629 F.3d 387 (4th Cir. 2011)   *601*
National Environmental Policy Act   *602*
  NEPA Coverage and Procedures   *602*
  Procedural Steps   *602*
The Clean Air Act   *604*
  Stationary Sources of Air Pollution   *604*
  Market-Based Approaches   *604*
  Economic Incentive Theory   *605*
  Mobile Sources of Air Pollution   *606*
  Tailpipe Emissions   *606*
  Fuel Economy Standards   *606*
  Performance Standards   *606*
  Fuel Composition and Distribution   *607*
Water Pollution Control   *607*
  The Clean Water Act   *607*
  Water Quality Regulation   *608*
  Permitting   *608*
  Liability for Oil Spills   *608*
  Deepwater Horizon *(BP) Oil Spill*   *609*
Case 18.2: *In re* Oil Spill by the Oil Rig "Deepwater Horizon" in the Gulf of Mexico, on April 20, 2010, MDL 2179, (E.D. La. Sept. 9, 2014)   *610*
  Drinking Water   *611*
Regulation of Solid Waste and Hazardous Materials Disposal   *612*
  Resource Conservation and Recovery Act   *612*
  Toxic Substances Control Act   *613*
Comprehensive Environmental Response Compensation and Liability Act   *614*
  Superfund   *614*
  Removal and Remedial Responses   *614*
  Liability of Principally Responsible Parties (PRPs)   *615*
  Consent Decrees   *615*
  Allocation of Liability   *616*
Case 18.3: Goodrich Corp. v. Town of Middlebury, 311 F.3d 154 (2d Cir. 2002)   *616*
  Defenses to Liability   *617*
  Secured Creditors   *617*
  Innocent Landowners   *617*
  Prospective Purchasers   *617*
Wildlife Protection   *620*

Key Terms   *620*
Chapter Review Questions   *621*
Theory to Practice   *622*
Legal Strategy 101   *622*
Manager's Challenge   *623*

CHAPTER 19   Antitrust and Regulation of Competition   628

Background, Purpose, and Source of Antitrust Law   *629*
Federal Statutes and Enforcement   *629*

Sherman Antitrust Act 629
    Per Se Standard versus Rule of Reason Standard 630
    Rule of Reason 631
    Two-Sided Markets 631
Case 19.1: Ohio v. American Express Co., 138 S. Ct. 2274 (2018) 632
    Per Se Sherman Act Violations: Restraints 633
    Horizontal Restraints 633
    Meeting of the Minds 634
    Price-Fixing 634
Landmark Case 19.2: Texaco, Inc. v. Dagher, et al., 547 U.S. 1 (2006) 635
    Market Allocation 635
    Boycotts 635
    Vertical Restraints 636
    Nonprice Restraints 636
    Tying Agreements 637
    Criminal Liability 637
Antitrust Law and Sports 638
Case 19.3: O'Bannon v. National Collegiate Athletic Association, 802 F.3d 1049 (9th Cir. 2015) 638
    Major League Baseball 639
Landmark Case 19.4: Flood v. Kuhn, 407 U.S. 258 (1972) 640
    Curt Flood Act of 1998 640
    National Football League 641
Monopolization 641
    Monopoly Power 641
    The *United States v. Microsoft* Case 642
    Intent to Monopolize 642
    Attempted Monopolization 642
Clayton Act 642
    Tying Arrangements and Exclusive Dealing 643
    Mergers and Acquisitions 643
Federal Trade Commission Act 643
Case 19.5: McWane, Inc. v. Federal Trade Commission, 783 F.3d 814 (11th Cir. 2015) 643
    Search Bias: FTC Investigates Google 645
Hart-Scott-Rodino Antitrust Improvements Act of 1976 645
Robinson-Patman Act 645
    Price Discrimination 645
    Defenses 645
Key Terms 646
Chapter Review Questions 646
Theory to Practice 647
Legal Strategy 101 647
Manager's Challenge 648

CHAPTER 20 Creditors' Rights and Bankruptcy 652

Creditors' Rights 653
    Unsecured Creditors 653
    Secured Creditors 654

Secured Transactions under Article 9 of the UCC 654
    Security Agreement 654
    Perfection 654
Real Estate 655
Sureties and Guarantors 655
    Personal Guaranties for Business Loans 656
Alternatives for Insolvent Borrowers 657
    Out of Existence 657
    Workouts 657
    Assignment for the Benefit of Creditors 658
    Assignment Agreement 658
    Distribution 658
Case 20.1: Akin Bay Company, LLC v. Von Kahle, 180 So. 3d 1180 (Fla. Ct. App. 2015) 659
Bankruptcy 660
    Automatic Stay 661
    Bankruptcy Trustee 661
Debtor's Options 663
    Chapter 7: Liquidation and Discharge 663
    Bankruptcy Petition 663
    Automatic Stay 663
    Order for Relief 663
    Appointment of Trustee 663
Case 20.2: Kelley v. Cypress Financial Trading Co., L.P., 518 B.R. 373 (N.D. Tex. 2014) 664
    Meeting of Creditors and Administering of the Estate 664
    Distribution and Discharge 665
    Chapter 11: Reorganization 666
    DIP Powers 666
    Reorganization Plan 666
    Chapter 13: Repayment Plan 667
    The Fraud Exception 667
Case 20.3: Sauer Inc. v. Lawson (*In re* Lawson), 791 F.3d 214 (1st Cir. 2015) 667
Bankruptcy Abuse Prevention and Consumer Protection Act 668
    Means Test 668
Case 20.4: Ransom v. FIA Card Services, 562 U.S. 61 (2011) 669
    Proof of Income 670
    Alimony and Support 670
    Credit Counseling 670
Key Terms 671
Chapter Review Questions 672
Theory to Practice 672
Legal Strategy 101 673
Manager's Challenge 674

CHAPTER 21 Warranties and Consumer Protection Law 678

Warranties 679
    Express Warranty 679
    Implied Warranties 679

Merchantability 679
  Fitness for a Particular Purpose 680
  Warranty Disclaimers and Limitations 680
Case 21.1: Birdsong v. Apple, Inc., 590 F.3d 955 (9th Cir. 2009) 681
  Magnuson-Moss Warranty–Federal Trade Commission Improvement Act 682
  Labeling Requirements 683
  Restrictions on Disclaimers and Limitations 683
  Consumer Product Safety Act 684
  Other CPSA Protections 685
Consumer Protection Law 685
  Consumer Financial Protection Bureau 685
  Consumer Reviews 686
False Advertising 686
  Bait and Switch 686
  Pricing 687
  Telemarketing 688
  Odometers 688
  State Statutes 688
  Lemon Laws 689
  Consumer Protection Statutes 689
Case 21.2: Vagias v. Woodmont Properties, 894 A.2d 68 (N.J. Super. Ct. 2006) 689
Food and Drug Safety 692
  FDA Regulations and Enforcement: Food Safety 692
Credit Transactions 692
  Consumer Credit Regulation 693
  Truth in Lending Act 693
Case 21.3: Palmer v. Champion Mortgage, 465 F.3d 24 (1st Cir. 2006) 694
  Other Federal Statutory Protections 695
  Home Mortgages 695
  Antidiscrimination 695
  Credit Cards 696
  Identity Theft 697
  Consumer Leases 698
  Credit Reports 698
Consumer Debt Collection 698
  FDCPA Requirements 699
  Enforcement 699
Case 21.4: U.S. Consumer Financial Protection Bureau v. Pressler & Pressler LLP, CFPB No. 2016-CFPB-0009 (Apr. 25, 2016) 699

Key Terms 700
Chapter Review Questions 702
Theory to Practice 702
Legal Strategy 101 703
Manager's Challenge 704

CHAPTER 22 Criminal Law and Procedure in Business 708

Origins and Sources of Criminal Law and Procedure 708
Modern Criminal Law: The Model Penal Code 709

Criminal Law Versus Criminal Procedure 709
  Criminal Law and Civil Law 709
  Burden of Proof 710
  General Principles of Criminal Law 710
  Criminal Liability 710
  Act Requirement 710
  Mental Requirement 711
  Defenses 711
  Types of Crimes 712
Criminal Law and Business Entities 712
  Individual Liability for Business Crimes 713
  Responsible Corporate Officers: The Park *Doctrine* 713
Case 22.1: United States v. DeCoster, 828 F.3d 626 (8th Cir. 2016) 714
White-Collar Crime 715
  Fraud 715
  Ponzi Schemes 716
  Conspiracy 717
  Racketeer Influenced and Corrupt Organizations Act (RICO) 717
  Insider Trading 718
  Bribery 720
  Obstruction of Justice 721
Case 22.2: Arthur Andersen LLP v. United States, 544 U.S. 696 (2005) 721
  Foreign Corrupt Practices Act (FCPA) 723
The Criminal Justice System 724
  Investigation 724
  Adjudication 724
Criminal Procedure 725
  Searches and Arrest 726
  Expectation of Privacy 726
  Plain View Doctrine 727
  Search Incident to Arrest 727
Case 22.3: Riley v. California, 573 U.S. 373 (2014) 728
  Searches of Business Premises 729
  Self-Incrimination 729
  Production of Business Records 731
  Trial 731
  Double Jeopardy 731
  Exclusionary Rule 731
Key Terms 735
Chapter Review Questions 736
Theory to Practice 736
Legal Strategy 101 737
Manager's Challenge 738

CHAPTER 23 Personal Property, Real Property, and Land Use Law 742

Types of Property Rights 743
Categories of Property 743
Tangible Property 743
  Personal Property 743

Personal Property: Rights of Ownership and Ownership by Possession 744
Found Articles 744

Case 23.1: Grande, as Personal Representative of the Estate of Robert A. Spann, v. Jennings, 278 P.3d 1287 (Ariz. Ct. App. 2012) 745

Adverse Possession 746
Good Faith Purchasers 746
Bailments 746

Case 23.2: Ziva Jewelry v. Car Wash Headquarters, 897 So.2d 1011 (Ala. 2004) 746

Leased Personal Property: UCC Article 2A 747

Real Property 748
Ownership Rights 749
Use and Enjoyment of the Land 749
Subsurface Rights 749
Water Rights 749
Airspace Rights 749

Landmark Case 23.3: Fontainebleau Hotel Corp. v. Forty-Five Twenty-Five, Inc., 114 So.2d 357 (Fla. Dist. Ct. App. 1959) 750

Forms of Real Property Ownership Interests 750
Fee Simple 751
Life Estate 751
Leasehold Estate 752
Easements 753
Adverse Possession 754
Open, Notorious, and Visible Possession 754
Exclusive and Actual Possession 754
Continuous Possession 754

Case 23.4: 2 North Street Corp. v. Getty Saugerties Corp., 68 A.D.3d 1392 (N.Y. App. Div. 2009) 755

Sale of Real Estate 755
Regulation of Commercial Land Use 756
Zoning Ordinances 756
Use Regulation 756
Enforcement and Appeals 756
Limits on Zoning Regulations 756
Environmental Regulation 757
Eminent Domain 757
Procedure 758
Public Use 758

Case 23.5: Kelo v. City of New London, 545 U.S. 469 (2005) 758

Key Terms 759
Chapter Review Questions 760
Theory to Practice 761
Legal Strategy 101 761
Manager's Challenge 762

CHAPTER 24 Intellectual Property 766

Trade Secrets and the Protection of Business Information 767
Trade Secret Protections 767

Misappropriation 767

Case 24.1: IBM v. Johnson, 629 F. Supp. 2d 321 (S.D.N.Y. 2009) 768

Criminal Sanctions 768
Exclusive Rights for Unlimited Duration 769

Trademarks, Service Marks, and Trade Dress 769
Trade Dress 770
Product Design 770
Trademarks as a Business Asset 771
Classifications of Trademarks 771
Arbitrary or Fanciful Marks 771
Suggestive Marks 772
Descriptive Marks 772

Case 24.2: *In re* Hershey Chocolate & Confectionery Corp., Serial No. 77809223 (T.T.A.B. June 28, 2012) 773

Generic Marks 774

Case 24.3: Elliott v. Google, Inc., 860 F.3d 1151 (9th Cir. 2017) 774

Case 24.4: People for the Ethical Treatment of Animals v. Doughney, 113 F. Supp. 2d 915 (E.D. Va. 2000) 775

Enforcing the Mark 776
Acquiring Rights 777
Applications and the USPTO 777
First Amendment Issues 777
Mark Maintenance 779
Policing the Mark 779
Trademark Infringement 780

Case 24.5: Mattel v. MCA Records, 296 F.3d 894 (9th Cir. 2002) 781

Trademark Dilution 782

Copyright Law: Protections of Original Expressions 783
Originality and Creativity Requirements 784
Durable Medium 785
Registration and Notice 785
Copyright Infringement 785
Direct Infringement 785
Indirect Infringement 786
Vicarious Infringement 786
Criminal Sanctions for Infringement 786
Defenses to Infringement Claims 787
Public Domain 787
First Sale 787
Fair Use 787
Purpose and Nature of the Use 788
Nature of the Work 788
Amount and Substantiality Used 788
Market Effect 788

Landmark Case 24.6: Metro-Goldwyn-Mayer Studios v. Grokster, Ltd., 545 U.S. 913 (2005) 791

Patents: Legal Protection of Inventions and Processes 793
Cost Considerations 794
Fundamentals of Patent Law 794
Patent Prosecution 794

Categories 795
Patent Duration 795
Patentability Standards 795
Novelty 795
Nonobviousness 796
Patentable Subject Matter 796
Requirements for Design Patents 796
Business Method Patents 796
Case 24.7: Alice Corporation Pty. Ltd. v. CLS Bank International, 573 U.S. 208 (2014) 797
Infringement, Notice, and Remedies 800
Literal Infringement 801
Equivalence 801
Notice and Enforcement 801
Remedies 801
Key Terms 802
Chapter Review Questions 804
Theory to Practice 804
Legal Strategy 101 805
Manager's Challenge 806

CHAPTER 25 International Law and Global Commerce 810

Definition, Sources, and Systems of International Law 811
Public Law versus Private Law 811
Sources of International Law 811
Treaties 811
Customs 811
Judicial Decisions 811
International Organizations 812
International Courts 812
Sovereign Immunity 813
Case 25.1: Butters v. Vance International, Inc., 225 F.3d 462 (4th Cir. 2000) 814
Legal Systems of Nations 815
Civil Law Systems 815
Common Law Systems 815
Religious-Based Legal Systems 815
Mixed Legal Systems 815
International Dispute Resolution 815
Arbitration 816
International Arbitration Forums 816
Ad Hoc Arbitration Rules 816
Alternatives to the ICC: The World Intellectual Property Organization 817
International Mediation 817
International Commercial Law 817
Foreign Corrupt Practices Act (FCPA) 817
Case 25.2: United States v. Esquenazi, 752 F.3d 912 (11th Cir. 2014) 818
U.N. Convention on Contracts for the International Sale of Goods (CISG) 820
Coverage and Major Provisions of the CISG 820
Case 25.3: Forestal Guarani S.A. v. Daros International, Inc., 613 F.3d 395 (3d Cir. 2010) 821
INCO: International Chamber of Commerce Terms 822
Enforcing Intellectual Property Rights Abroad 823
Comprehensive Agreements 823
Agreements on Trademarks 823
Agreement on Copyrights 824
Agreement on Patents 825
Key Terms 825
Chapter Review Questions 826
Theory to Practice 826
Legal Strategy 101 827
Manager's Challenge 828
BUSINESS LAW SIMULATION EXERCISE 3 Trademarks in Cyberspace: Cool Runnings v. BigBuy.com 832

\\ CAPSTONE CASE STUDIES

1. Coffee Wars: Starbucks v. Charbucks 839
2. The Odwalla Juice Company Crisis 843
3. Fraud under the Arches: The McDonald's Game Piece Scandal 847

\\ APPENDICES

A. The Constitution of the United States of America 853
B. Excerpts from the Sarbanes-Oxley Act of 2002 863

Glossary 865
Case Index 890
Subject Index 894

UNIT ONE   Fundamentals of the Legal Environment of Business

CHAPTER 1 Legal Foundations

APPENDIX TO CHAPTER 1 A Business Student's Guide to Understanding Cases and Finding the Law

CHAPTER 2 Business and the Constitution

CHAPTER 3 The American Judicial System, Jurisdiction, and Venue

CHAPTER 4 Resolving Disputes: Litigation and Alternative Dispute Resolution

CHAPTER 5 Business Ethics, Corporate Social Responsibility, and Law

CHAPTER 1
Legal Foundations

©philsajonesen/Getty Images

Learning Objectives

After studying this chapter, students who have mastered the material will be able to:

- **1-1** Understand the broad definition and origins of law.
- **1-2** List and explain the purposes of the law.
- **1-3** Explain the importance and benefits of legal awareness for business owners and managers in creating a strategy and adding value to a company.
- **1-4** Articulate the role of counsel in legal decision making in a business context.
- **1-5** Recognize, explain, and give examples of sources of American law.
- **1-6** Understand the legal doctrine of stare decisis.
- **1-7** Classify the law into several broad categories.
- **1-8** Differentiate between the concepts of law and equity.
- **1-9** Identify and apply important equitable maxims.

Undertaking the study of law may seem overwhelming. Legal doctrines and rules can be complex and difficult to navigate. Yet the law impacts many facets of our daily life both at home and at work. This textbook is designed to make studying the law more *manageable* by examining legal issues that are most commonly encountered in the business environment. In fact, studies have shown that business owners and managers who have a high level of legal insight create *value* for their business and recognize legal challenges as business planning opportunities. This legal awareness may be gained only by understanding important legal doctrines and processes.

Applying this knowledge allows managers to limit risk and incorporate the law into their business strategies. This chapter introduces students to the foundations of the law and explains why the application of legal doctrines is an important part of the business environment. Specifically, in this chapter students will learn

- How legal issues impact business planning and strategy.
- The foundations, definitions, and scope of various primary and secondary sources of law.
- Categories of law.

INTRODUCTION TO LAW

The term **law** has been defined in a variety of ways throughout recorded history. A generally accepted generic definition of the law is a *body of rules of action or conduct prescribed by controlling authority, and having legal binding force.*[1] When studying law in any context, it is important to think of the law in broad terms. While many equate the law with stacks of neatly bound volumes of codes in a library, this is only one component of a much larger body of law. Law may be set down in a written code as prescribed by an elected legislative body, but it also takes the form of judicial decisions and actions of government agencies. While there are many sources of American law, the common characteristic of the current state of law is that it creates *duties, obligations,* and *rights* that reflect accepted views of a given society. Much of the origins of the law dealt with issues related to ownership of property; however, modern legal doctrines have evolved into a relatively complex system of principles and protections. Most importantly, the law also provides a mechanism to resolve disputes arising from those duties and rights and allows parties to enforce promises in a court of law. Law is often classified by subject matter so that one refers to certain rules regarding agreements as *contract law,* while other laws that regulate certain rights of employees are referred to as *employment law*. **Jurisprudence**, roughly defined as the science and philosophy of law, defines several schools of thought that are used to describe various approaches to the appropriate function of law and how legal doctrines should be developed and applied. Most schools of jurisprudential thought center on how legal rights are recognized.

LO 1-1

Understand the broad definition and origins of law.

Purposes of Law

The most visible function of the law on a day-to-day basis is to provide for some system of order that defines rules of conduct and levies punishment or other consequences for the violation of those rules. However, there are many other purposes of recognizing a uniform system of laws. The origins of recorded law were initially a collection of rules of powerful tribal chieftains intended to perpetuate their domination and the power of their authority with little consideration for the rights of individuals. However, over the better part of three millennia, the purpose of law evolved substantially into ensuring consistency and fairness. In the United States, lawmakers have increasingly embraced legal mechanisms, such as antidiscrimination laws, to help promote equality and justice in society, in education, as well as in the workplace. The law also sets out a method for resolving disputes by providing a basis for deciding the legal interests and rights of the parties. For purposes of studying the impact of law on business, it is important to recognize that the law also serves as an important catalyst for commerce by promoting *good faith dealing* among merchants and consumers and giving some degree of *reliability* in applying the law evenly so that the law can be considered in business planning and commercial transactions.

LO 1-2

List and explain the purposes of the law.

For example, assume Clothing Manufacturing Corporation (CMC) orders 100 bales of wool from Woolpack, Inc., in anticipation of a large order for winter clothing from retail outlets. The laws that govern the various transactions that arise from the CMC-Woolpack agreement set a standard of good faith and provide both parties the confidence necessary to set the business process in motion (e.g., to begin making decisions related to financing, operations, and marketing). Moreover, the merchants may rely on the courts if either party needs to recoup any losses resulting from the other party's unlawful actions.

---

[1] *Black's Law Dictionary* (6th ed. 1990).

> **KEY POINT**
>
> The primary purposes of the law are
> - To provide a system of order that defines conduct and consequences.
> - To promote equality and justice in society.
> - To provide a method for resolving disputes.
> - To promote good faith dealing among merchants.
> - To provide a degree of reliability in applying the law evenly.

Language of the Law

In order to maximize the value of interaction between business owners/managers and attorneys, a basic understanding of legal terminology is useful. Students studying business law face the task of learning legal syntax at the same time as they learn how to apply the legal doctrines in a business context. This is analogous to learning a complicated subject matter in a foreign language, yet it is manageable with careful study. Legal terms are sometimes referred to as *jargon* or *legalese,* but having a working knowledge of some common legal terminology is an important step to mastering the material. Although much of the language of the law has Latin roots, the terminology is primarily a combination of Latin, early and modern English, and French. The vocabulary of American law is drawn from the various cultures and events that shaped American history. To facilitate your understanding of legal expression, important legal terms are highlighted throughout the text, summarized at the end of each chapter, and also featured alphabetically in the glossary. The authoritative source for legal terms is **Black's Law Dictionary**, first published in 1891. There are also several websites that provide definitions and examples for legal terms.

LEGAL DECISIONS IN A BUSINESS ENVIRONMENT: THEORY TO PRACTICE

LO 1-3 Explain the importance and benefits of legal awareness for business owners and managers in creating a strategy and adding value to a company.

While an in-depth understanding of the various areas of law is a vast undertaking requiring years of intensive study, the primary objective of this textbook is to cover a variety of legal topics that are most commonly encountered in the business environment. However, developing legal insight by understanding the fundamentals of legal theory and how they may impact business is only a first step in learning how legal decisions should be made in a business context. The second step involves learning to *apply* legal theories in practice and recognizing that having legal awareness may present opportunities for proactive business planning—empowering business owners and managers to limit liability, gain a competitive edge, and add value to the business. Relying exclusively on attorneys to drive the legal decision-making process in the context of business is expensive and involves the significant risk that a decision will be made without sufficient knowledge of business operations, objectives, and current economic realities. Instead, studies and research indicate that when managers work *cooperatively* with their attorneys, the results contribute to better strategic business decisions that add value to the business. For example, recognizing that having a code of conduct for employees and creating a standardized procedure for hiring new employees are issues that a good manager should view as essential, attorneys regularly play a part in ensuring compliance with applicable federal, state, and local laws. Later in this chapter, we will discuss a mechanism that business owners and managers may use to spot legal issues, apply an appropriate analysis, decide on alternative solutions, and plan a legal and ethical course of action that both limits liability and maximizes business opportunities.

> **KEY POINT**
>
> Learning to apply legal theories in practice and having legal awareness present opportunities for proactive business planning, empowering managers to limit liability, gain a competitive edge, and add value to the business.

Management teams with legal insight add value to their company by limiting liability and identifying opportunities. Eric Audras/PhotoAlto/PictureQuest

Legal Insight and Business Strategy

To understand the way various areas of the law impact business and the importance of having legal insight in a business context, let's examine a typical business planning process. Suppose that the management team at Indiana Printing Company (IPC) is planning to expand its existing business into new markets. The team is considering several options and will have to have a sufficient understanding of the legal risks and business opportunities associated with each option. Table 1.1 sets out possible options for IPC's expansion and some of the potential legal impacts for each option.

The list of legal issues in Table 1.1 is meant to be illustrative and not exhaustive. Indeed, issues regarding negligence, criminal law, administrative law, bankruptcy, consumer protection, agency, and many others may present themselves before, during, or after the transaction is complete.

LO 1-4

Articulate the role of counsel in legal decision making in a business context.

Role of Counsel

Although this textbook emphasizes understanding legal issues in the context of business decision making, this is not to suggest that an attorney's role in this process is diminished—quite the opposite. The content, features, and exercises contained in this textbook emphasize that working closely with a business attorney results in business opportunities, reduced costs, and limitation of risk and liability. Attorneys, particularly in a business context, may also be referred to as **counsel**. Business owners and managers work with counsel in one of two formats. For larger companies or companies that have extraordinary regulatory burdens (such as complying with securities or patent laws), counsel may very well be a part of the executive or midlevel management team. These attorneys are referred to as *in-house counsel* and usually have the title "general counsel" at the executive management level (e.g., vice president and general counsel). Depending on the size and complexity of the company, the

CHAPTER ONE | Legal Foundations 5

TABLE 1.1 — Expansion Options and Potential Legal Impacts

Option	Area of Law	Potential Legal Impact
Expansion through acquisition of another company. One common way to expand is to purchase an existing business entity through an acquisition of assets or of stock.	■ Contracts	■ Contract law governs negotiations and agreements for the acquisition.
	■ Property/environmental	■ If the acquisition involves any land purchase, real estate law (such as zoning) and environmental law must be considered.
	■ Employment and labor	■ The hiring of new employees by IPC (even former employees of the target company) or the layoff of IPC or target-company employees must be done in conformance with state and federal employment and labor laws.
	■ Tax	■ The transaction may create tax liability under local, state, and/or federal laws.
	■ Antitrust	■ If the acquisition results in IPC's gaining too much market share, federal antitrust laws must be considered and preacquisition approvals may be needed from the government.
Expansion through introducing and aggressively marketing a new product line. Expanding through marketing of a new product line generally involves raising sufficient capital to properly develop, manufacture, and go to market.	■ Securities law	■ Any solicitation by IPC to sell shares of its business to the public is highly regulated by securities law.
	■ Intellectual property	■ In order to maintain its competitive edge, IPC will need to put measures in place to help guarantee protection of ideas and processes by trade secret law; the final design may be protected by patent law.
	■ Administrative law	■ Federal regulatory agencies have guidelines for the advertising and labeling of products.
Expansion through aggressive integration of a highly interactive website and e-marketing campaigns, including international markets. In light of the growth in e-commerce, some companies find this to be the most cost-efficient method of expansion.	■ Jurisdiction	■ Website expansion may result in IPC's being subject to the jurisdiction of more out-of-state courts than under its previous business model.
	■ International law	■ IPC may be subject to international agreements and treaties regarding sales and intellectual property.

general counsel may also supervise one or more attorneys, usually with the title "associate counsel." Additionally, the general counsel may also serve as a corporate officer of the company, called the secretary, and be responsible for record keeping and complying with notice and voting requirements for the board of directors.[2] The general counsel is also responsible for selecting and supervising lawyers from outside law firms when a particular field of expertise is needed, such as a trial lawyer (also called a *litigator*).

The majority of companies, however, rely on attorneys employed by *law firms* for their legal needs. These attorneys devote a significant amount of their professional time

---

[2]The legal structure of corporations and other business entities is discussed in detail in Unit Three, "Regulation in the Workplace."

to advising businesses on issues such as formation, governance, labor and employment laws, regulatory agency compliance, legal transactions (such as an acquisition), intellectual property (such as trademarks or patents), and other legal issues important to business operations. These attorneys (known as *business lawyers* or *corporate lawyers*) rarely if ever appear in court or perform other tasks that are associated with lawyers in the minds of the general public. Indeed, the law has become increasingly complex and specialized. Therefore, it is not unusual that more than one attorney's advice is needed when facing a significant legal issue such as an employment discrimination lawsuit or when obtaining financing for a corporation from the general public through the sale of stock. Law firms vary greatly in size, from those that have one or just a few lawyers in a local or regional practice to firms that have hundreds of lawyers spread throughout the globe. In a business context, law firms bill clients based on an hourly rate that is tied to an individual lawyer's experience, her reputation in the field, and the market being served (with large cities that are the center of business operations having higher rates).

 Self-Check Role of Counsel

What advice might Adams seek from an attorney in the following situations?

1. Adams sells custom-designed T-shirts from his basement apartment. The business begins to turn a profit.
2. Adams wants to expand his T-shirt business by renting a kiosk in a local mall and hiring Baker.
3. Adams wants to obtain trademark protection for his products.
4. Baker offers Adams $50,000 to purchase the T-shirt business's name and assets.

Answers to this Self-Check are provided at the end of the chapter.

SOURCES AND LEVELS OF AMERICAN LAW

LO 1-5

Recognize, explain, and give examples of sources of American law.

American law is composed of a unique blend from various sources based on U.S. historical roots. Fundamentally, much of American law is derived from English legal doctrines that came with the English settlers of the colonies. In the West and Southwest, land once controlled by Mexico, there are strong Spanish influences, while in Louisiana, once French territory, French civil law roots are evident. Modern law in the United States regulating businesses and individuals is generally a combination of **constitutional law**, **statutory law**, **common law**, and **administrative law** (or *regulatory law*) at the federal, state, and local levels. These sources of law are known as *primary sources* of law and may sometimes work in conjunction with one another or independently. For example, law related to the protection of trade secrets[3] is composed from a variety of sources of law. Perhaps the most famous and profitable example of a trade secret is the recipe and process for making Coca-Cola. While most states have specific trade secret statutes that give legal recourse to a party who has suffered a loss as a result of the unlawful use of trade secrets, some do not. Does this mean that the company that owns the Coca-Cola

---

[3]Trade secret law, which is covered in detail in Chapter 24, "Intellectual Property," is the legal protection of certain confidential business information.

Legal Speak >))

Enumerated Powers
Article I, Section 8, of the U.S. Constitution names 17 specific powers granted to the federal government. These are known as *enumerated powers*.

recipe has no legal recourse against someone who steals its trade secret in those states where no *specific statutes* exist? The answer is no because even absent a specific statute, the law still provides the damaged party some recourse against the violator. This recourse is provided by court case history (called *common law,* discussed later), which provides guidance to the trial courts deciding trade secret disputes. Even in states that *do* have statutes related to trade secret protection, there is case law that helps courts apply the statute consistently.

Constitutional Law

Constitutional law is the foundation for all other law in the United States and is the supreme law of the land. It functions in tandem with other sources of law in three broad areas: (1) establishing a *structure* for federal and state governments (including qualifications for certain offices and positions), setting rules for amending the constitution, and granting specific *enumerated powers* to the different branches of government; (2) establishing the concept of *federalism,* allowing the federal and state governments shared powers; and (3) establishing individual *civil rights* and providing *procedural protections* for U.S. citizens from wrongful government actions.

Constitutional law is different from other sources of law primarily in terms of *permanence* and *preemption.* In terms of permanence, a constitution is thought to reflect the basic principles of a particular society and should be amended only in extraordinary cases and only when a majority of its constituents agree over a certain period of time. Preemption in this context means that constitutional law is supreme over all other sources of law such as federal and state statutes, treaties, and common law.

Constitutional law exists at both the federal and state levels because each state has its own constitution that is the highest source of law within the state's borders (so long as it is not inconsistent with federal law). States tend to amend their constitutions more frequently than is the case with the U.S. Constitution. Constitutional issues that impact businesses include Congress's powers to regulate interstate commerce; the creation of legal protections for intellectual property (such as patents and copyrights); the protection of certain forms of commercial speech from unwarranted government regulation; limitations on a state's authority to tax products and services in commerce; and powers of the executive, legislative, and judicial branches to regulate business activity. Congressional powers and other aspects of constitutional law are discussed in detail in Chapter 2, "Business and the Constitution."

Statutory Law

Statutes are written laws that are passed by the federal or a state legislature and then either approved or rejected by the executive branch. The U.S. Congress is the exclusive legislative body for the passage of federal law. When Congress is drafting a federal statute, but has not yet passed it or had the executive

The U.S. Congress is the exclusive legislative body for the passage of federal law. Jill Braaten/McGraw-Hill Education

branch's concurrence, it is known as a *bill*. On the *federal* level, the president is the executive and may either sign a bill into law (thereby adopting it as a statute) or veto (reject) the bill, in which case the bill becomes subject to the Congress's right to override the veto and make the bill into a statute with a two-thirds majority vote.

At the *state* level, the state legislature (called by different names in different states, such as the *General Assembly*) passes statutes that regulate such areas as motor vehicle laws, business corporation and partnership laws, and other traditional state matters. The governor (as executive) has authority to sign a state bill into law or to exercise other rights as laid out in the state constitution. Written laws at the *local* level are called **ordinances** (sometimes referred to as *local regulations*). Ordinances generally regulate issues such as zoning (regulating where certain businesses, such as factories, may be located) or impose health and safety regulations on local merchants such as restaurants.

Interpreting Statutes When interpreting statutes, courts initially apply the **plain meaning rule**. This means that if the words in the statute have clear and widely understood meanings, the court applies the statute in accordance with the rule. However, more complex statutes require further analysis, and courts look to two sources for guidance. The structure of the statute itself generally provides some indication of how the legislature intended it to be applied. The structure of the statute and the format of its mandates in a law are referred to as its **statutory scheme**. When interpreting statutes, courts also look to the records kept by the legislature, including the debates, committee and conference reports, and legislative findings of fact. These records are known as the statute's **legislative history** and may provide some indication of the intent of the legislative body that passed the statute. For example, in Chapter 2, "Business and the Constitution," we discuss the U.S. Supreme Court's ruling on the constitutionality of the Patient Protection and Affordable Care Act (commonly referred to as "Obamacare").[4] The act includes an individual mandate requiring individuals to be covered by health insurance by a certain date or face a penalty. The court analyzed the application of the mandate from multiple points of view and, using the act's statutory scheme and legislative history, it validated the individual mandate's constitutionality based on its application as a tax rather than as a penalty.

One of the biggest challenges courts face when interpreting a statute is applying the law in a context that did not exist at the time the statute became law. In Case 1.1, a federal trial court applies a 1986 law outlawing money laundering in the context of digital currency on the notorious (and now defunct) Silk Road online marketplace.

Henry II established English common law courts, called "King's Bench" courts, around 1178. 19th era/Alamy

---

[4] 26 U.S.C. § 5000A.

CASE 1.1 United States v. Ulbricht, 31 F. Supp. 3D 540 (S.D.N.Y. 2014)

FACT SUMMARY In February 2014, a federal Grand Jury indicted Ross Ulbricht, also known as Dread Pirate Roberts (Ulbricht), for, among other things, conspiracy to launder money obtained from illegal activities. Prosecutors alleged that Ulbricht was engaged in narcotics trafficking, computer hacking, and money laundering conspiracies by designing, launching, and administering a website called Silk Road as an online marketplace for illicit goods and services. Silk Road was designed to operate like eBay: (1) a seller would electronically post a good or service for sale; (2) a buyer would electronically purchase the item; (3) the seller would then ship or otherwise provide to the buyer the purchased item; (4) the buyer would provide feedback; and (5) the site operator (i.e., Ulbricht) would receive a portion of the seller's revenue as a commission. Ulbricht, as the alleged site designer, made the site available only to those using Tor, a software and network system that allows for anonymous, untraceable Internet browsing. He allowed payment only via bitcoin, an anonymous and untraceable form of digital currency. Thousands of transactions allegedly occurred over the course of nearly three years—sellers posted goods when available; and buyers purchased goods when desired.

Ulbricht filed a motion to dismiss the indictments based on a number of theories. Ulbricht argued that he could not be guilty of money laundering because the use of bitcoins did not fit into the statute's requirement that money laundered be a result of a "financial transaction." Since bitcoins are not monetary instruments, transactions involving bitcoins cannot form the basis for a money laundering conspiracy. He supported his argument by noting that the IRS has announced that it treats virtual currency as property and not as currency.

SYNOPSIS OF DECISION AND OPINION The U.S. district court ruled against Ulbricht. The court rejected Ulbricht's theory that use of bitcoins is not a financial transaction. The court noted that because bitcoins carry value and act as a medium of exchange, they fall into the meaning of financial transaction in the money laundering statute. Since bitcoins may be exchanged for legal tender, be it U.S. dollars, euros, or some other currency, they can be an instrument in money laundering.

WORDS OF THE COURT: Plain Meaning of the Statute "Put simply, 'funds' can be used to pay for things in the colloquial sense. Bitcoins can be either used directly to pay for certain things or can act as a medium of exchange and be converted into a currency which can pay for things. Indeed, the only value for Bitcoin lies in its ability to pay for things—it is digital and has no earthly form; it cannot be put on a shelf and looked at or collected in a nice display case. Its form is digital—bits and bytes that together constitute something of value. And they may be bought and sold using legal tender . . . The money laundering statute is broad enough to encompass use of Bitcoins in financial transactions. . . . Congress intended to prevent criminals from finding ways to wash the proceeds of criminal activity by transferring proceeds to other similar or different items that store significant value. . . . There is no doubt that if a narcotics transaction was paid for in cash, which was later exchanged for gold, and then converted back to cash, that would constitute a money laundering transaction . . . . One can money launder using Bitcoin."

Case Questions

1. Why did Ulbricht point out that the IRS treats bitcoins as property?
2. Does the fact that Ulbricht created Silk Road have any bearing on the court's decision?
3. *Focus on Critical Thinking:* Is the court interpreting the statute or filling in a gap that exists in a statute? If Congress had wanted to include digital currency in its definition of financial transactions, why didn't it do so by naming it specifically in the statute or in an amendment to the law? Did the court overreach in this case by trying to decipher the intent of Congress?

Aftermath: After a four-week trial, a jury found Ulbricht guilty on all counts, including money laundering. On May 29, 2015, Ulbricht was sentenced to life in prison and ordered to forfeit nearly $184 million.

Finding Statutory Law The official publication of federal statutory law is the United States Code (U.S.C.), which arranges all existing federal laws in a system organized by title and divided into chapters and sections. The legal community uses a special format, known as a **citation**, to express where a statutory law can be found. You'll note citations in the footnotes of each chapter of this text that identify a specific reference for the statutes being covered in the chapter. For example, later in this textbook, students will study a federal law called the Fair Labor Standards Act (also known, in part, as the "minimum wage" law) in detail. The citation for the law (listed in the footnote) is 29 U.S.C. § 201. This indicates that in order to find the Fair Labor Standards Act, we need to consult Title 29 of the United States Code and turn to section (abbreviated § in singular or §§ in plural) 201 for the first chapter of the statute. Although attorneys and judges often use specialized software and legal research services to find and understand statutes, an increasing amount of information about statutory resources and statutes themselves is available online for free. Note also that Appendix to Chapter 1 ("A Business Student's Guide to Understanding Cases and Finding the Law") provides information on using the Internet to find and apply statutory law.

State statutes have the same fundamental format and purpose as the U.S.C., but the actual term used to refer to state statutes varies from state to state. *Codes* or *consolidated statutes* are two common terms.

Commercial services also sell print and online versions of federal and state statutes in a unique format that includes annotations and short comments used to interpret the statutes correctly. Attorneys use these commercial services in performing legal research so that they can properly counsel their clients on the law.

Common Law

Common law is essentially law made by the courts. Although lawmaking is primarily the responsibility of state and federal legislatures, courts must fill in the gaps when a controversy arises that is not covered under existing law. Consider, for example, the impact of the Internet on the development of law. Settled laws related to contracts, jurisdiction, trespass, obscenity, and many other areas must be reconsidered in light of the widespread use of the Internet. Courts have to fill in the gaps to apply existing law to Internet use until the legislature can respond with statutory law aimed at resolving cyber-related disputes.

The U.S. system of common law is deeply rooted in British common law that developed over several centuries, beginning around 1066 when the Norman kings established uniform methods for resolving (mostly land) disputes in England. The largest industrialized nations using the common law in some form include the United States, the United Kingdom, Canada, Australia, and generally the former colonies of Britain. Other countries, such as Japan and France, use a *civil law* system that requires courts to adhere to a strict interpretation of a legislatively established code or regulation. While the general notion of *precedent* is recognized by civil law, its role is substantially reduced in a civil law system. The power of courts to establish law in matters not specifically addressed by the code is very limited in civil law countries. Legal systems and sources of law in foreign countries are covered in Chapter 25, "International Law and Global Commerce."

Stare Decisis and Precedent

The common law also includes the application of past judicial decisions to contemporary cases. The **doctrine of stare decisis**, one of the most important concepts in American law, is the principle that similar cases with similar facts and issues should have similar judicial outcomes. This allows individuals and businesses to have some degree of confidence that the law will remain reasonably constant from year to year and court to court.

LO 1-6

Understand the legal doctrine of stare decisis.

> **Legal Speak >))**
>
> **Appellate Courts**
> Courts that review the decisions of trial courts and have the authority to overturn decisions if they are inconsistent with the current state of the law. Trial courts, appellate courts, and other types of dispute resolution forums are covered in detail in Chapter 3, "The American Judicial System, Jurisdiction, and Venue."

The notion of applying the law of previous cases to current cases with substantially similar circumstances is called **precedent**. Precedent is created when an *appellate court* renders a decision, known as the *holding* of the case, absent a controlling statute. Should a similar fact situation later occur, all *lower courts,* such as trial courts, are bound to follow the appellate court's decision as long as no new statutory law has been enacted. This provides an element of predictability for lawyers and litigants when they are contemplating legal and business decisions and actions.

Precedent established in one state's court will have no bearing on the courts of other states. A state court facing an issue for the first time (known as a "case of first impression") might look to precedent created in other states for insight; however, nothing requires its adherence to the other states' decisions. Note that the court system and how appellate courts form precedent are topics covered in detail in Chapter 3, "The American Judicial System, Jurisdiction, and Venue."

Stare Decisis and Business

To understand the importance of stare decisis in the business environment, consider the opportunities for business planning that may benefit the company by understanding the legal impact of a certain course of action. Suppose that Jackson is a manager in charge of managing the acquisition of certain assets from another company. One important aspect of such a transaction is how the acquisition will be *taxed.* If Jackson's company enters into an agreement with Main Street Industries (MSI) to acquire certain assets from MSI, how will the transaction be treated by the Internal Revenue Service (IRS)?[5] This, of course, is a very important fact in determining the price of the transaction and planning for the allocation of the tax burden between the buyer and the seller. How can the parties structure the transaction to be sure that the taxation represents the parties' intent? Ultimately, because stare decisis is a deeply rooted concept that applies to all laws, Jackson need only learn how the IRS has treated similar transactions in the past and how courts have ruled on the IRS's interpretation and actions in applying the law. If a certain transaction has been taxed in a certain way in the past, the doctrine of stare decisis dictates that if Jackson structures her transaction in a similar fashion, her transaction will be taxed in the same way. With sufficient legal certainty about the taxation impact, the parties may now proceed with negotiations and structure a mutually acceptable agreement.

> **Legal Speak >))**
>
> **Case of First Impression**
> A case with issues that have never been litigated before in the court hearing it.

Departing from Precedent Strict adherence to precedent and the doctrine of stare decisis has a significant drawback: It doesn't allow for evolving societal standards of behavior or expectations. In one famous case, a state's highest court provided a memorable metaphor for departing from precedent:

> "Stare decisis is not an iron mold into which every utterance by a court, regardless of circumstances, parties, economic barometer and sociological climate, must be poured, and, where, like wet concrete, it must acquire an unyielding rigidity which nothing later can change."
>
> *Flagiello v. Pennsylvania Hospital, 208 A.2d 193 (Pa. 1965)*

On a case-by-case basis, courts sometimes justify departing from precedent on the basis that technological or societal changes render a particular precedent unworkable. In Case 1.2, the U.S. Supreme Court considers the question of when to abandon standing precedent based on economic and technological changes in the online marketplace.

---

[5]The IRS is the federal government's tax agency.

CASE 1.2 South Dakota v. Wayfair, Inc., 138 S. Ct. 2080 (2018)

FACT SUMMARY South Dakota, like many states, taxes the retail sales of goods and services in the state. Sellers are required to collect and remit the tax to the state, but if they do not, then in-state consumers are responsible for paying a use tax at the same rate. Under *National Bellas Hess, Inc. v. Department of Revenue of Illinois* and *Quill Corp. v. North Dakota,* South Dakota may not require a business that has no physical presence in the state to collect its sales tax. Consumer compliance rates are notoriously low, however, and it is estimated that *Bellas Hess* and *Quill* cause South Dakota to lose between $48 and $58 million annually. Concerned about the erosion of its sales tax base and corresponding loss of critical funding for state and local services, the South Dakota legislature enacted a law requiring out-of-state sellers to collect and remit sales tax "as if the seller had a physical presence in the State." The Act covers only sellers that, on an annual basis, deliver more than $100,000 of goods or services into the state or engage in 200 or more separate transactions for the delivery of goods or services into the state. Respondents, top online retailers with no employees or real estate in South Dakota, each meet the Act's minimum sales or transactions requirement but do not collect the state's sales tax. South Dakota filed suit in state court, seeking a declaration that the Act's requirements are valid and applicable to respondents and an injunction requiring respondents to register for licenses to collect and remit the sales tax. Respondents sought summary judgment arguing that the Act is unconstitutional. The trial court granted their motion. The state supreme court affirmed on the ground that *Quill* is controlling precedent. Respondents appealed to the U.S. Supreme Court.

SYNOPSIS OF DECISION AND OPINION The U.S. Supreme Court reversed the decision of the state supreme court and ruled in favor of South Dakota. The Court held that the previous precedent using the "physical presence" rule created in *Quill* was no longer workable due to the advances in the cyberspace marketplace. The Court pointed out that the physical presence rule has long been criticized as giving out-of-state sellers an advantage. Each year, it becomes further removed from economic reality and results in significant revenue losses to the states. These critiques underscore that the rule, both as first formulated and as applied today, is an outdated interpretation of the Commerce Clause.

WORDS OF THE COURT: Precedent "The *Quill* Court itself acknowledged that the physical presence rule is artificial at its edges. That was an understatement when *Quill* was decided; and when the day-to-day functions of marketing and distribution in the modern economy are considered, it is all the more evident that the physical presence rule is artificial in its entirety. Modern e-commerce does not align analytically with a test that relies on the sort of physical presence defined in *Quill*. In a footnote, *Quill* rejected the argument that title to a few floppy diskettes present in a State was sufficient to constitute a [physical presence]. But it is not clear why a single employee or a single house should create a [physical presence] while 'physical' aspects of pervasive modern technology should not. For example, a company with a website accessible in South Dakota may be said to have a physical presence in the State via the customers' computers. A website may leave cookies saved to the customers' hard drives, or customers may download the company's app onto their phones. Or a company may lease data storage that is permanently, or even occasionally, located in South Dakota. What may have seemed like a clear, bright-line tes[t] when *Quill* was written now threatens to compound the arbitrary consequences that should have been apparent from the outset. The dramatic technological and social changes of our increasingly interconnected economy mean that buyers are closer to most major retailers than ever before—regardless of how close or far the nearest storefront. Between targeted advertising and instant access to most consumers via any internet-enabled device, a business may be present in a State in a meaningful way without that presence being physical in the traditional sense of the term. A virtual showroom can show far more inventory, in far more detail, and with greater opportunities for

(continued)

consumer and seller interaction than might be possible for local stores. Yet the continuous and pervasive virtual presence of retailers today is, under *Quill,* simply irrelevant. This Court should not maintain a rule that ignores these substantial virtual connections to the State. . . .

Although we approach the reconsideration of our decisions with the utmost caution, *stare decisis* is not an inexorable command. Here, *stare decisis* can no longer support the Court's prohibition of a valid exercise of the States' sovereign power. . . . For these reasons, the Court concludes that the physical presence rule of *Quill* is unsound and incorrect.

The Court's decisions in *Quill Corp. v. North Dakota* and *National Bellas Hess, Inc. v. Department of Revenue of Ill.* should be, and now are, overruled."

Case Questions

1. What was the "physical presence" test?
2. Why did the Court overrule *Quill* and *National Bellas Hess*?
3. *Focus on Critical Thinking:* What other areas of the law might be affected by technology in the future?

Administrative Law

While statutory law stems from the authority of the legislature and common law is derived from the courts, administrative law is the source of law that authorizes the exercise of authority by *executive branch* agencies and *independent* government agencies. Members of the House and Senate can't be experts on all things and can't be expected to research the details of all matters before Congress. For efficiency, Congress creates administrative agencies to focus on particular areas, much like a large company creates departments and committees to streamline decision making. Federal administrative law is largely authorized by statutes and the Constitution, and rules for applying the law are articulated and carried out by *administrative agencies.* Pursuant to congressional mandates, these agencies are empowered to administer the details of federal statutes and have broad powers to impose regulations, make policy, and enforce the law in their designated areas of jurisdiction. State legislatures also are empowered to create administrative agencies to address state matters. For example, the U.S. Environmental Protection Agency (EPA) is charged with drafting regulations that carry out the broad mandates set by Congress in the Clean Air Act (among many others) to reduce air pollution. The EPA sets regulations and imposes restrictions on some industries to help accomplish that goal. The EPA is also empowered to enforce those regulations. Courts are highly deferential to agency decisions involving how and when an agency enforces a regulation. Detailed coverage of this source of law and administrative agencies is featured in Chapter 17, "Administrative Law."

Some of the specific types of laws that impact business owners and managers and are covered in this textbook are featured in Table 1.2.

Primary sources of law are applied consistent with a hierarchy in which one source may trump another source if the two sources conflict. This is called *preemption.* For example, think about where you're seated at this moment. What law applies to you? You're subject to the U.S. Constitution, U.S. treaties, federal statutory and administrative law, and federal common law. You're also in a state, so state constitutional, statutory, administrative, and common law apply to you. County, city, township, and other local laws might also apply. There is certainly a potential for conflict. Figure 1.1 illustrates the hierarchy of primary sources of federal and state law.

Secondary Sources of Law

When interpreting statutory law or applying judicially created law, courts also look to **secondary sources** of law. In the business context, the most important secondary sources

TABLE 1.2   Examples of Laws That Impact Business

Type of Law	Source(s)	Level(s)
Negligence (tort)	Statutory and common law	Primarily state
Employment discrimination	Primarily statutory and administrative	Primarily state and federal, some local
Copyright	Statutory and administrative	Federal
Contracts for sale of goods	Statutory	State
Contracts for services	Primarily common law	State
Bankruptcy	Statutory and administrative	Federal
Securities law (selling company stock to the public)	Statutory and administrative	Federal and state
Zoning ordinances	Statutory	Local
Taxes	Statutory and administrative	Federal, state, and local

of law are (1) the **Restatements of the Law**, a collection of uniform legal principles focused in a particular area of traditional state law, and (2) various sets of **model state statutes** drafted by legal experts as a model for state legislatures to adopt in their individual jurisdictions. The purpose behind these secondary sources of law is to increase the level of uniformity and fairness across courts in all 50 states. The secondary sources of law also feature commentary and examples to help guide courts in applying the law. However, secondary sources of law have *no independent authority* or legally binding effect. State legislatures and courts are free to adopt all, adopt part of, or reject secondary sources of law.

Uniform Model Laws

In 1892, the National Conference of Commissioners on Uniform State Laws (NCCUSL) was formed by the American Bar Association for the purpose of establishing uniform

FIGURE 1.1   Hierarchy of Primary Sources of Federal and State Law

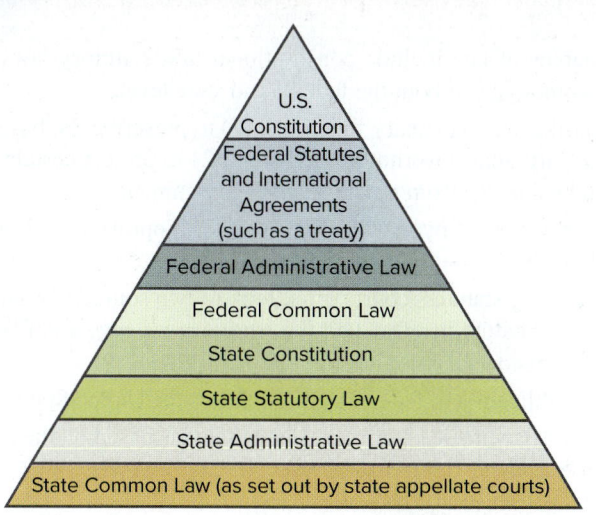

standards in areas of the law where national interests would be achieved through use of uniform laws. Imagine that a business in Delaware purchases goods from a seller in New York. While these goods are being shipped by truck via an independent trucking company, they are destroyed in an accident in New Jersey. Which state's law applies? Without a uniform set of laws, businesses would be required to know and apply the law in all 50 states and would be overwhelmed by excessive litigation. Uniform laws solve many such problems.

The primary focus of the model laws is commerce, and chief among these is the Uniform Commercial Code (UCC), which was drafted by the NCCUSL and has been adopted in some form by every state except Louisiana. The UCC provides a comprehensive set of rules and principles intended to increase reliability and predictability in business transactions. Although this textbook refers to several different sections of the UCC, extensive coverage is given to Article 2, which governs contracts for the sale of goods. The NCCUSL also created several uniform codes related to the formation and structure of business entities, such as the Uniform Partnership Act and the Model Business Corporation Act. The NCCUSL will, from time to time, revise these model acts, and the new model laws are referred to using the term *Revised* (e.g., the *Revised* Uniform Partnership Act).

Restatements of the Law

In the 1920s, the American Law Institute (ALI) was formed to reduce the undue complexity and growing uncertainty of judicial decisions by systematically publishing a *statement* of common law legal principles and rules in a given area of the law, such as torts. The ALI is composed of law professors, judges, and lawyers, and it has developed the *Restatements of the Law* in various legal categories. Explanatory notes and applicable examples accompany the restatements, and the restatements are continuously revised. When the ALI publishes a revision, the new version is referred to by the name and edition; thus, the second edition of the contracts restatement is called *Restatement (Second) of Contracts*. The areas covered by the restatements that are included in this textbook are contracts, property, agency, torts, and foreign relations law.

CONCEPT SUMMARY Sources of Law

Primary:

- Primary sources of law include constitutional law, statutory law, administrative law, and common law at both the federal and state levels.
- Constitutions have two primary functions: (1) to prescribe the basic structure and powers of a particular government body and (2) to protect certain rights of individuals and businesses from government encroachment.
- Statutory law is created by a legislative body and approved or disapproved by the executive branch.
- When interpreting statutes, courts often look to two sources for guidance: (1) the structure of the statute itself, called the *statutory scheme,* and (2) the records of the legislative history behind the statute.
- The official publication of federal statutory law is the United States Code (U.S.C.).
- Common law is law made by appellate courts and is based on the fundamentals of previous cases that have similar facts.

- Appellate courts create precedent, and under the doctrine of stare decisis, lower courts apply the precedent to new cases with similar facts.
- Precedent created in a state applies only in that state and has no binding authority in any other state.
- Administrative law is the source of law that regulates the exercise of authority by administrative agencies.
- Pursuant to congressional mandates, administrative agencies are empowered to administer the details of federal statutes and have broad powers to impose regulations, make policy, and enforce the law in their designated areas of jurisdiction.

Secondary:
- Secondary sources of law include the *Restatements of the Law* and sets of model statutes such as the Uniform Commercial Code (UCC).
- Secondary sources have no independent authority, nor are they legally binding.
- The *Restatements of the Law* are collections of uniform legal principles in a specific area of law that are designed to reduce the complexity of judicial decisions.
- Model statutes are drafted by legal experts, in hopes that they will be used or adopted by state legislatures so as to provide uniformity in laws between the states.

 Self-Check Sources of Law

What source(s) and level(s) of law governs the following business transactions?

1. American Hardware Supply enters into an agreement with a retail home improvement chain to supply the chain with certain inventory.
2. Whitney wishes to apply for a patent for a device he invented.
3. Marshall is considering raising money for his business by selling stock in the company.
4. Bio-Tech Inc. ran out of cash and cannot pay its debts as they come due. Management seeks protection from creditors.
5. Barnum wishes to bring his famous horse show into town and plans to stage it in a residential area of the city.

Answers to this Self-Check are provided at the end of the chapter.

CATEGORIES OF LAW

LO 1-7
Classify the law into several broad categories.

Because the body of American law is so vast and diverse, it is sometimes helpful to break down the law into broad categories based on classifications related to a particular legal function or a right afforded by law. It is important to note that these classifications are not mutually exclusive. One particular act or transaction may be classified in more than one legal category. For example, suppose that a party to a contract breaks her promise to the other party (an act known as a *breach of contract*). The remedy for the breach may depend on the legal classification of contracts as *civil law*. At the same time, one party may have rights classified as *substantive law*, which are derived from a source of *statutory law*.

Criminal Law versus Civil Law

Laws, primarily statutes, are either *criminal* or *civil* in nature. **Civil laws** are designed to compensate parties (including businesses) for losses as a result of another's conduct. These losses are known as **damages**. **Criminal laws** are designed to protect society, and the violation of criminal laws results in penalties to the violator such as fines or imprisonment. Criminal fines are paid to the government and do not reimburse the victim. Remember that these categories are not mutually exclusive. For instance, a driver who is intoxicated and injures a pedestrian in an accident has committed both a criminal act (driving while intoxicated), for which he can be prosecuted by authorities, and a civil wrong (negligence), for which the driver can be sued by the injured party to recover for any losses suffered as a result of the injury (medical bills, etc.). Criminal law as it relates to business is discussed in Chapter 22, "Criminal Law and Procedure in Business."

Substantive Law versus Procedural Law

Substantive laws provide individuals with rights and create certain duties. **Procedural laws** provide a structure and set out rules for pursuing substantive rights. For example, while state common law may provide an individual who has suffered losses due to the negligence of another the right to obtain restitution from the wrongdoer (substantive law), a state statute will prescribe the procedure for using legal means to actually collect the restitution (procedural law). This includes rules that govern court procedures such as how and when to file a lawsuit as well as the process for obtaining the restitution once a court has given the injured party a certain money award. Procedural law also sets out the steps the government must take if it needs to infringe on substantive rights. For example, if the police believe that a business owner is committing a nonviolent crime such as embezzlement or fraud, they may not simply barge into the owner's office without notice to search for and seize evidence. The Fourth Amendment to the U.S. Constitution protects citizens against unreasonable searches and seizures, a substantive right of privacy. The Fourth Amendment also specifies the procedural steps that must be taken to override the substantive rights in question in order to obtain a search warrant. These procedural steps require police to convince a judge or magistrate, through evidence of probable cause, that a crime is being committed, as well as provide evidence necessary to prove that crime is in the owner's possession.

LO 1-8

Differentiate between the concepts of law and equity.

Law versus Equity

Most modern American courts are combined courts of law and equity. However, we still use the terms *law* and *equity* when describing the appropriate *measure of judicial action* intended to compensate an injured party in a civil lawsuit. These measures are known as **remedies**.

Remedies at law generally take the form of *money damages:* A court orders the wrongdoer to pay another party a certain sum of money to compensate for any losses suffered as a result of the wrongdoer's conduct. However, in some cases, a party will not necessarily be fully or even partially compensated through money damages. In such a case, a court may award **equitable relief** instead of (or in addition to) a remedy at law. Most commonly, equitable relief can include an *injunction* or *restraining order* (a judicial order requiring a party to either perform or cease performing a certain activity) and *specific performance* (an order requiring a party to carry out her obligations as specified in a contract). Specific performance is available only if the goods contracted for are rare or one of a kind. To understand this concept in a business context, suppose that Maxwell enters into a valid written agreement with Book Barn to purchase a first edition of *The Old Man and the Sea,* autographed by Ernest Hemingway, for $25,000. Maxwell leaves the store to obtain

UNIT ONE | Fundamentals of the Legal Environment of Business a certified check from his bank. When he returns one hour later, the owner of Book Barn refuses to sell him the book because he has received a phone call from another buyer offering $30,000. In this case, Maxwell may file a lawsuit for Book Barn's failure to live up to the agreement (known as *breach of contract,* discussed in Chapter 7, "Contract Enforceability and Performance"), but he has not suffered an out-of-pocket loss because he never had the opportunity to present Book Barn with the check. However, Maxwell may seek a *remedy at equity* from a court, where he can request an injunction to prevent Book Barn from selling the book to another buyer until the court can hear the case. If Maxwell wins the case, he may seek an order of *specific performance* whereby the court orders Book Barn to transfer ownership of the book to Maxwell in exchange for the $25,000 price as specified in the agreement between the parties. Maxwell would likely be awarded these equitable remedies because the legal remedies available to him are not adequate to address his injury.

In Case 1.3, a state appellate court reviews a case that resulted in a remedy of specific performance.

CASE 1.3 Wilcox Investment, L.P. v. Brad Wooley Auctioneers, Inc., 454 S.W.3D 792 (Ark. Ct. App. 2015)

FACT SUMMARY Wilcox Investment Limited Partnership (Wilcox) entered into a contract with Brad Wooley Auctioneers, Inc. (Auctioneers) to market and sell approximately 333 acres of real property owned by Wilcox in Arkansas. It was to be an "absolute" auction, meaning that the property would be sold to the highest bidder regardless of price. As the date of the auction approached, Wilcox expressed reservations about the auction to Auctioneers but decided to go through with the auction because Auctioneers agreed to cancel the auction if the bidder turnout was low. Only four bidders attended the sale. Wilcox did not attend but was represented by two of his children and his attorney. According to Wilcox, Auctioneers agreed to postpone the sale. Auctioneers disputed that it agreed to halt the sale. In any case, Auctioneers started the bidding, and Shollmier was declared the highest bidder with a bid of $235,000. Wilcox, contending that the property was appraised in excess of $950,000, refused to complete the sale.

Shollmier sued Wilcox, asking the court for a remedy of specific performance to compel Wilcox to proceed with the sale. Auctioneers also filed suit to recover its commission. Wilcox argued that the sale was void because Shollmier engaged in collusion with Auctioneers during the bidding process. The jury found that Wilcox and Auctioneers entered into a contract to sell the real property at absolute auction to the highest bidder, that Shollmier was the highest bidder, and that Wilcox breached the auction contract and the purchase agreement. The court accordingly ordered Wilcox to convey the property to Shollmier. Wilcox appealed, arguing, in part, that specific performance was not an appropriate remedy.

SYNOPSIS OF DECISION AND OPINION The Court of Appeals of Arkansas affirmed the jury's verdict in favor of Shollmier and Auctioneers. The court reasoned that there was no evidence of collusion and rejected Wilcox's argument that the auction contract was void. The court held that Auctioneers had no duty to halt the auction and that Shollmier's bid was made in good faith and not in conjunction with Auctioneers. Because money is not an adequate remedy, specific performance is appropriate.

WORDS OF THE COURT: Specific Performance Appropriate "In his response . . . Wilcox argued that there was a disputed issue of whether the Auctioneers breached their duty by continuing the sale after perceiving collusion. . . . [The trial] court found that this issue was not material to Wilcox's claims against the Auctioneers but that it would be dispositive on Shollmier's claim for specific performance against Wilcox. We now know from the final judgment that the issue of collusion was impliedly

(continued)

resolved against Wilcox by the jury in finding that Wilcox breached the purchase agreement."

Case Questions

1. Why wasn't money an adequate remedy in this case?
2. What does Wilcox mean when he alleges that Shollmier engaged in collusion?
3. *Focus on Critical Thinking:* How could Wilcox have prevented the property from being sold below the appraised price at auction?

> **KEY POINT**
>
> When a remedy at law is inadequate, an injured party may also obtain a remedy at equity. When a remedy at law is fully sufficient to bring justice, equitable remedies are not permitted.

The term *equity* is also used in the context of common law rules that guide courts in deciding cases and controversies before them. These equity rules are called **equitable maxims**, and they are intended to be broad statements of rules that are based on notions of fairness and justice in applying the law. These doctrines are applied in suits seeking both legal and equitable damages. Table 1.3 summarizes the most commonly used maxims.

Public Law versus Private Law

LO 1-9

Identify and apply important equitable maxims.

Public laws are those derived from some government entity. Examples include statutes (legislature/executive) and administrative regulations (state or federal administrative agencies). **Private laws** are recognized as binding between two parties even though no specific statute or regulation provides for the rights of the parties. The most common example is a contract for services. For example, suppose Claude hires Pablo to paint a portrait of

TABLE 1.3 Equitable Maxims

Maxim	Rule	Example
Equity aids the vigilant	The law favors those who exercise vigilance in pursuing their claims and disfavors those who rest on their legal rights by failing to act to protect their rights in a reasonable period of time.	Statute of limitations imposes a deadline on when an aggrieved party must file a claim. After the deadline has passed, the party is barred from recovering any losses or damages.
Substance over form	Courts look to the intent of parties involved and adhere to a standard of good faith and fair play instead of applying the letter of the law in a way that would violate fundamental principles of fairness and consistency.	Blackwell signs an agreement that she is a limited partner. In substance, she acts like a general partner. Courts will treat her as a general partner despite what the parties call themselves.
Clean hands doctrine	Courts are guided in their decisions not only by the letter of the law but also on the basis that one seeking the aid of a court must come to the court with clean hands that are unstained by bad faith, misrepresentations, or deceit.	Kauffman fraudulently transfers stock to his brother to avoid paying a legal judgment entered against him. When a dispute arises with his brother, Kauffman sues to try and recover the stock. Kauffman is barred from recovering the stock because he committed fraud in transferring it to his brother in the first place.

Claude's wife. After it is complete, Claude thinks Pablo's painting is too abstract and refuses to pay for it. Although no specific public law exists that regulates this relationship, the agreement is still legally binding and the rules of the transaction are governed by the common law of contracts.

STRATEGIC LEGAL SOLUTIONS: THE BIG PICTURE

Law interacts with business in many different ways and on many different levels. In this section, we focus on the big picture, on the *strategic* nature of these complex and multifaceted interactions. In fact, because legal rules often have gaps or grey areas, because legal compliance is costly, and because laws are not always perfectly enforced, the legal environment of business in the real world is essentially a *strategic* environment.

Strategy is integrated throughout this textbook in a variety of ways. This overview is intended to introduce students to the intersection between law and strategy and to help them think of the law as part of business decision making rather than as a book of rules. "Strategic Legal Solutions" are featured in a problem/solution format and offer an in-depth discussion of specific legal issues and possible strategic solutions. "Strategy 101" is featured at the end of each chapter and helps students understand how strategic considerations may fit into the topics covered in the chapter.

Overview

Generally speaking, a strategy refers to a plan of action. Strategies are helpful when one is operating under conditions of uncertainty. For example, because of various real-world factors—such as limited resources, opportunistic behavior, and asymmetrical information—the legal environment is full of uncertainty: Laws are not always obeyed, nor are laws always enforced. This uncertainty regarding the level of legal compliance and the level of legal enforcement opens up many types of legal strategies, strategies business leaders often pursue as they compete for customers and market share.

For convenience, we will classify legal strategies into four major categories or "ideal types": (1) *noncompliance,* (2) *avoidance,* (3) *prevention,* and (4) *value creation* or "legal competitive advantage." Now, let's take a closer look at these four major forms of legal strategy below, illustrating each type of legal strategy with concrete examples.

Strategy #1—Noncompliance

One possible legal strategy in an uncertain and competitive environment is *noncompliance.* Simply put, noncompliance consists of openly disregarding or flouting the law. But why would a business firm ever openly choose noncompliance as its legal strategy? Why risk flouting the law? Put crudely, in cost-benefit terms, when the costs of compliance are greater than the costs of noncompliance, it might actually pay to break the law.

Consider the market for overnight delivery and other shipping services in New York City, a highly lucrative and competitive industry. Instead of fully complying with burdensome parking regulations, it's a "dirty little secret" that shipping companies like FedEx, UPS, and even the U.S. Postal Service have openly adopted a noncompliance strategy: These firms write the costs of parking infractions into their business model, paying

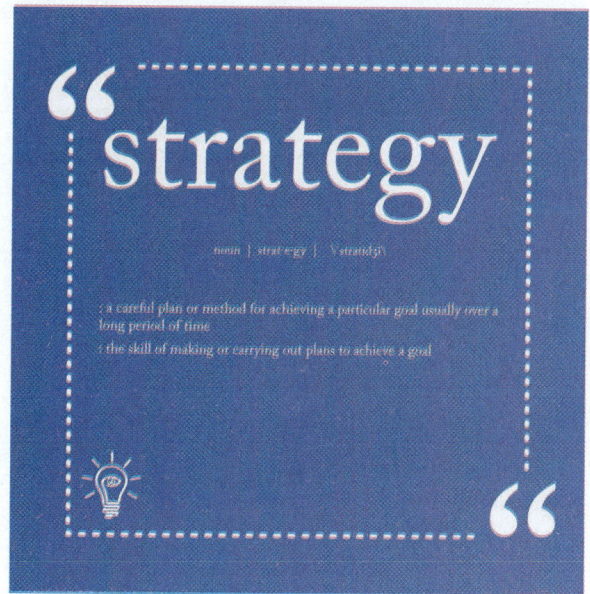

Definition of *strategy.* ©Dragana Gerasimoski/Shutterstock

"No parking" sign. StockSigns/Alamy

millions of dollars annually for the parking fines that their delivery trucks incur in New York City in order to effectively compete for the lucrative Gotham market.[6]

Critical Thinking Question: *In your opinion, is the noncompliance strategy always unethical?*

Strategy #2—Avoidance

When business firms decide to create legal loopholes or exploit grey areas in the law, they are essentially adopting an *avoidance* approach to law, a legal strategy that is very frequently used in the business world.

Before proceeding, notice that avoidance is technically not the same as noncompliance. Strictly speaking, the avoidance approach views legal compliance as a cost to be minimized; hence a company using an avoidance strategy takes steps to minimize its costs of legal compliance. By way of example, a familiar—and controversial—illustration of the avoidance approach is the decision to relocate overseas or outsource certain activities to another jurisdiction in order to avoid burdensome and costly local regulations.

Consider one of the biggest corporate megadeals of this decade: Pfizer's $160-billion merger with the Irish drug company Allergan. Pfizer, a U.S. company, was the world's 48th largest company before the merger. The parties structured this deal as a tax inversion; in other words, Pfizer will reconstitute itself as an Irish company in order to lower its U.S. tax burden.[7]

In sum, companies are likely to adopt an avoidance strategy when they see a law as a costly obstacle or burdensome impediment that is interfering with their desired business goals.

Critical Thinking Questions: *From an ethical perspective, what do you think of Pfizer's tax inversion strategy? Is an avoidance strategy unethical?*

Strategy #3—Prevention

Simply put, the *prevention* strategy consists of identifying potential legal risks to one's business and taking deliberate and proactive measures to minimize those risks *before* the risks materialize. In other words, business leaders adopting a preventive legal approach work directly with legal counsel in order to anticipate potential legal pitfalls their business may confront and then attempt to devise effective legal solutions ahead of time.

The widespread use of legal disclaimers in many types of consumer contracts provides a good example of the prevention strategy. For example, have you ever entered a spicy food contest? Increasingly,

Map of Ireland. Rainer Lesniewski/Shutterstock

---

[6]*See, e.g.,* Andrew J. Hawkins, *Parking Tickets: All in the Cost of Doing Business,* Crain's N.Y. Bus., May 26, 2013.

[7]*See, e.g.,* James Surowiecki, *Why Firms Are Fleeing,* The New Yorker, Jan. 11, 2016.

restaurateurs have used liability waivers to prevent any liability based on some physical injury that accompanies a potentially hazardous food item such as a "ghost pepper." According to the *Journal of Emergency Medicine,* one man was hospitalized for 23 days with a tear in his esophagus after participating in a ghost-pepper-eating contest.

At Mikey's Late Night Slice in Columbus, Ohio, the "Fiery Death with Hate Sausage" is a pizza loaded with a mix of the hottest peppers. However, customers can only try it once they've signed a three-page waiver outlining dangers and safety precautions, like how to wash skin and eyes, and agreeing to "disclaim, release and relinquish any and all claims, actions and lawsuits."[8]

Critical Thinking Exercise: *Do you use Facebook, Twitter, or Instagram (or some other social networking site)? Look up the "terms of use" of one of these websites and try to find at least one disclaimer or other limitation of liability clause.*

Strategy #4—Value Creation (or "Legal Competitive Advantage")

Last, but certainly not least, business leaders can use the law creatively and strategically not only to minimize costs and risks but also to create new sources of value as well as generate new streams of revenue. We refer to this form of legal strategy as *value creation* or "legal competitive advantage" to acknowledge that law can often be a source of competitive advantage.[9]

Need to sign a waiver when you order pizza?
FoodCollection

How can a business outperform its competitors? The concept of competitive advantage attempts to answer this fundamental question. Briefly, there are two types of business strategies a firm may follow in order to outperform its rivals. One strategy is lower cost. The other strategy is differentiation. Here, let's focus on the strategy of differentiation.

From a legal perspective, one major method of differentiating one's business and of creating durable forms of value is through intellectual property law. A great example of legal competitive advantage is Google's popular search engine algorithm, which was invented by Larry Page and Sergey Brin while they were graduate students at Stanford.

The original patent for their search engine algorithm (US 6,285,999) contains a detailed description of their first algorithm and also lists Stanford University as the "assignee" or legal owner of their important invention.[10] Subsequently, however, Larry Page and Sergey Brin left Stanford and founded their own private search-engine company. They also continued to refine and improve their search engine algorithm over the years, but now, instead of using patent law to protect their rights to their search-engine

---

[8] B. Parkin, *Want to Try Our Insanely Spicy Pizza with Hate Sausage: First Sign a Waiver,* Wall St. J., Jan. 27, 2018.

[9] *See generally* Michael E. Porter, *Competitive Advantage* (Free Press 1985).

[10] By the way, you can see their original "page rank" patent for yourself in Connect.

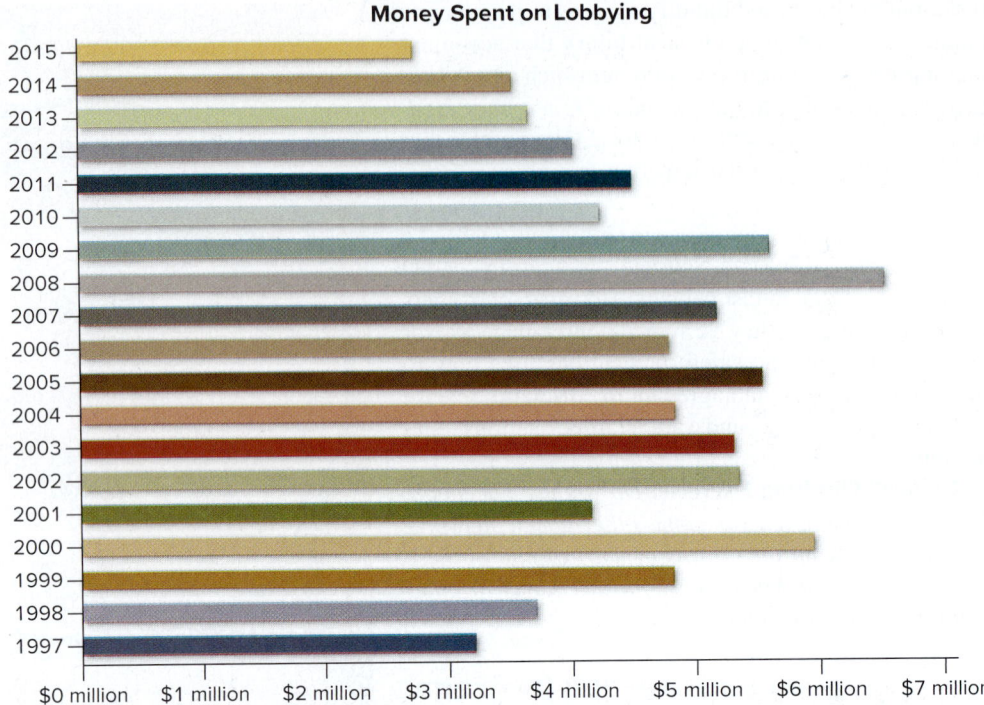

Money spent on lobbying by Disney. Sources: Adapted from Crockett, Zachary. "How Mickey Mouse Evades the Public Domain," Priceonomics, 7 January 2016; data from OpenSecrets.org

algorithm, they have opted to keep their world-famous algorithm a trade secret. In other words, no one but Larry Page and Sergey Brin knows the exact details of how the Google search engine works.

Another form of legal competitive advantage occurs through lobbying efforts (i.e., when companies lobby legislatures like the Congress to enact laws protecting their business from competition). One of the most egregious examples of this form of legal competitive advantage is the Walt Disney Company's efforts to protect its intellectual property rights in Mickey Mouse, perhaps the most iconic cartoon character of all time. Mickey is quite possibly the world's most famous personality; according to market researchers, his 97 percent recognition rate in the United States edges out even Santa Claus![11] *Forbes* has even dubbed him "the world's richest fictional billionaire," placing his estimated worth to Disney at $5.8 billion per year.

In any case, in the words of one commentator: "Disney has done everything in its power to make sure it retains the copyright on Mickey . . . Every time Mickey's copyright is about to expire, Disney spends millions lobbying Congress for extensions, and trading campaign contributions for legislative support. With crushing legal force, they've squelched anyone who attempts to disagree with them."[12]

The nearby chart will give you some idea as to how much of its resources Disney expends on lobbying efforts in order to maintain its competitive advantage.

Critical Thinking Question: *Have you ever created any form of intellectual property?*

---

[11] *See, e.g.,* Joseph Menn, *Whose Mouse Is It Anyway?,* L.A. Times, Aug. 22, 2008.

[12] Crockett, Zachary. "How Mickey Mouse Evades the Public Domain," *Priceonomics,* 7 January 2016.

Summing Up

A business firm's choice of legal strategy can have a tangible impact on the company's bottom line. As discussed above, there are many forms of legal strategy, including (1) non-compliance, (2) avoidance (e.g., the aggressive exploitation of loopholes), (3) prevention of legal risks, and (4) value creation, or long-term legal competitive advantage. Moreover, note that these legal strategies are not mutually exclusive. Many business firms use some mix of all of these various legal strategies, depending on the immediate challenges they confront and the opportunities they want to seize.

In fact, we expect the role of law and legal strategies in the business world to become even more sophisticated and creative as more and more board members of major publicly held corporations are lawyers or have formal legal training. One recent study, for example, found that 43 percent of U.S. companies had at least one lawyer on their board of directors in 2009, up from 24 percent in 2000.[13] We will discuss many more examples of legal strategy in future chapters.

---

[13]*See* Gillian Tett, "More U.S. Lawyers Move to Boardrooms," *Financial Times,* Feb. 21, 2013. *See also* Robert C. Bird, Paul Borochin, and John D. Knopf, *The Role of the Chief Legal Officer in Corporate Governance,* 34 J. Corp. Fin. 1 (2015).

KEY TERMS

Law p. 3   A body of rules of action or conduct prescribed by controlling authority and having legal binding force.

Jurisprudence p. 3   The science and philosophy of law that defines various approaches to the appropriate function of law and how legal doctrines should be developed and applied.

Black's Law Dictionary p. 4   The leading legal dictionary.

Counsel p. 5   Another term for *attorney.*

Constitutional law p. 7   The body of law interpreting state and federal constitutions.

Statutory law p. 7   The body of law created by the legislature and approved by the executive branch of state and federal government.

Common law p. 7   Law that has not been passed by the legislature but rather is made by the courts; based on the fundamentals of previous cases with similar facts.

Administrative law p. 7   Refers to both the law made by administrative agencies and the laws and regulations that govern the creation, organization, and operation of administrative agencies.

Ordinances p. 8   Local statutes passed by local legislatures.

Plain meaning rule p. 9   The principle that if the words in a statute have clear and widely understood meanings, the court applies the statute; used as the initial guideline in statutory interpretation to determine how a rule should be applied.

Statutory scheme p. 9   The structure of a statute and the format of its mandates.

Legislative history p. 9   The records kept by the legislature, including the debates, committee and conference reports, and legislative findings of fact used when creating a law, which can be used to show the legislature's intent.

Citation p. 10   The special format used by the legal community to express where a statute or case law can be found.

Doctrine of stare decisis p. 11   The principle that similar cases with similar facts under similar circumstances should have similar outcomes.

Precedent p. 11   Applying the law made in previous appellate court opinions to current cases with similar facts; binding on the trial courts.

Secondary sources p. 14   Sources of law that have no independent authority or legally binding effect but can be used to illustrate a point or clarify a legal issue.

Restatements of the Law p. 15   A collection of uniform legal principles focused in a particular area of the law, which contains statements of common law legal principles and rules in a given area of law.

Model state statutes p. 15   Statutes drafted by legal experts to be used as a model for state legislatures to adopt in their individual jurisdictions in order to increase the level of uniformity and fairness across courts in all states.

Civil laws p. 18   Laws designed to compensate parties for money lost as a result of another's conduct.

Damages p. 18   Money lost as a result of another's conduct.

Criminal laws p. 18   Laws designed to protect society that result in penalties to the violator such as fines or imprisonment.

Substantive laws p. 18   Laws that provide individuals with rights and create certain duties.

Procedural laws p. 18   Laws that provide a structure and set out rules for pursuing substantive rights.

Remedies p. 18   Judicial actions, which can be monetary or equitable, taken by courts that are intended to compensate an injured party in a civil lawsuit.

Equitable relief p. 18   Relief granted in the form of either specific performance ("do it") or an injunction ("stop doing it") when monetary damages are insufficient due to the unique or irreversible consequence of the breach.

Equitable maxims p. 20   Common law rules that guide courts in deciding cases and controversies and are intended to be broad statements of rules based on notions of fairness and justice.

Public laws p. 20   Laws derived from a government entity.

Private laws p. 20   Laws recognized as binding between two parties even though no specific statute or regulation provides for the rights of the parties.

CHAPTER REVIEW QUESTIONS

1. **Which of the following is an important purpose of the law in a business context?**
   a. Provides reliability.
   b. Promotes good faith among merchants.
   c. Protects individual rights.
   d. Both (a) and (b).

2. **BigCo is planning an acquisition of the assets of SmallCo and plans to hire SmallCo's management team. Which of the following areas of the law may have an impact on its acquisition planning?**
   a. Tax law
   b. Contracts
   c. Employment law
   d. All of the above

3. **Which of the following sources of law is created by a legislative body?**
   a. Constitutional
   b. Common law
   c. Statutory
   d. Administrative

4. **The notion of applying the law of previous cases to current cases with substantially similar facts is called _____.**
   a. Application
   b. Precedent
   c. Breach
   d. Comparison

5. **If a party has suffered damages as a result of another's conduct, but the money damages are not adequate to compensate the injured party, a court may provide _____ relief.**
   a. Equitable
   b. Legal
   c. Jury
   d. Preliminary

Answers and explanations are provided at the end of this chapter.

THEORY TO PRACTICE

Galaxy Inc. is a supplier of greeting cards, small gifts, tokens, and games appropriate for special occasions such as holidays and birthdays. Galaxy distributes its products primarily through large supermarket and drugstore chains. Increasingly, Galaxy has lost revenue to supermarkets that prefer to enter into the supplier market by manufacturing these products in a foreign country at a steep discount (instead of buying Galaxy's products) and selling them in their stores at a higher profit. In response to this, Galaxy's management team has begun to roll out a new business model whereby Galaxy will begin to retail its own products through newly created Galaxy retail stores. Jackson is a senior manager charged with overseeing the expansion efforts.

1. Suppose that Jackson intends to lease (rent) these new spaces for the Galaxy stores and hire new employees to staff them. What areas of the law may impact Jackson's planning process? Identify the source and level for each area of law.
2. What options does Jackson have for legal advice to guide his efforts? Would Galaxy use in-house or outside counsel? What is the role that counsel might play in these transactions?
3. Assume that Jackson also plans to acquire the assets of a smaller retail company in order to carry out this expansion. Jackson is concerned about the potential tax impact that may be triggered by the transaction. How can Jackson plan with certainty for a particular type of tax treatment? What legal doctrine allows him to rely on the law in the planning process?
4. Assume that Jackson enters into a contract with Holmes for Holmes to act as store manager in one location. After two weeks, Jackson fires Holmes for incompetence. Holmes believes that Jackson fired him in violation of an antidiscrimination law, but he keeps forgetting to file the appropriate paperwork and eight months pass by. Finally, Holmes gets around to filing a complaint. What equitable maxim would apply to Holmes's complaint? Does this maxim favor Holmes or Jackson?
5. As part of Galaxy's opening day celebrations, it provides sweet snacks for customers shopping at the store. Jackson places colorful warning labels on each snack package: "WARNING: These snacks contain nuts and other nut-based allergens." What strategy has Jackson used to reduce Galaxy's potential for liability?

MANAGER'S CHALLENGE

Midlevel managers are frequently involved with vendors, competitors, customers, and employees on a daily basis. This makes them invaluable sources for spotting and meeting legal challenges in the early stages. Suppose that in the Theory to Practice problem, Jackson, a senior manager, receives an e-mail from a competing company:

> Galaxy: You have stolen our trademark. We have the trademark rights for the Hobgoblin Necklace and you don't have our permission to use it. Yet, on a recent visit to one of your stores, you have Hobgoblin Necklaces for sale. Cease and desist or we will turn this matter over to our attorney.
> Signed,
> Necklace Emporium

Assume that you are a midlevel manager and that Jackson hands you the e-mail and informs you that, to his knowledge, Galaxy followed all proper legal procedures for the trademark. Using the strategies that you learned in Strategic Legal Solutions: The Big Picture, compose a two- to three-page memorandum addressed to Jackson that gives guidance on handling this legal challenge.

CASE SUMMARY 1.1 Sokoloff v. Harriman Estate Development Corp., 754 N.E.2d 184 (N.Y. 2001)

EQUITY AND FAIRNESS

Sokoloff purchased land in the Village of Sands Point and, in anticipation of building a home, hired Harriman to provide preconstruction services, including the creation of architectural and landscaping plans. Sokoloff paid Harriman a $10,000 retainer fee and a total of $55,000 for creating and filing the architectural plans with the village. However, when it came time to build the home, Harriman estimated the cost to be over $1.8 million. Sokoloff, finding this amount to be exorbitant, decided to get quotes from other builders, based on the plans he had Harriman design. However, Harriman said that the plans could not be used to construct the home unless he was the builder.

CASE QUESTIONS

1. Can Harriman withhold the plans from Sokoloff?
2. What legal theories or maxims would a court consider in deciding this case?
3. How should the court rule and why?

CASE SUMMARY 1.2 Jones v. R. R. Donnelley & Sons Co., 541 U.S. 369 (2004)

STATUTE OF LIMITATIONS

The U.S. Congress enacted a statute providing for a four-year statute of limitations for any cause of action arising out of an act of Congress enacted after 1990. Jones, an African-American employee of R. R. Donnelley & Sons Co. (Donnelley), was denied a transfer to one of Donnelley's other plants when his plant closed. Moreover, while an employee for Donnelley, Jones was subject to a hostile work environment and various acts of discrimination. Jones, an Illinois citizen, wishes to sue Donnelley for violating federal antidiscrimination statutes. It has been three years since Jones worked for Donnelley, and Illinois has a two-year statute of limitations.

CASE QUESTIONS

1. Which statute of limitations governs and why?
2. Will Jones be able to sue Donnelley?

CASE SUMMARY 1.3 Day v. Case Credit Corp., 2007 U.S. Dist. LEXIS 64045 (E.D. Ark. 2007)

CLEAN HANDS DOCTRINE

Case Credit Corp. (Case) finances the sale of farm equipment to farmers. Day bought farm equipment financed by Case, yet Day never actually signed the sales contract. Instead, an employee of Case forged Day's signature on the sales contract with higher prices in an effort to pocket the difference for himself. Case was aware of the forgery but did not make any effort to stop the employee or inform Day. When Day could not pay the loans back, Case filed suit to recover the farm equipment or compel payment.

CASE QUESTIONS

1. If the court applies the clean hands doctrine, will Case be able to recover the farm equipment because Day is unable to make the payments? Why or why not?
2. Are Case's hands clean? Why or why not?

CASE SUMMARY 1.4 Cargill v. Monfort of Colorado, Inc., 479 U.S. 104 (1986)

EQUITABLE RELIEF

Monfort, the nation's fifth largest beef packer, is concerned about a merger of the nation's second largest packer, Cargill, with the nation's third largest packer. Monfort believes that the merger will give Cargill almost 21 percent of the market, leaving Monfort with only 5 percent. Monfort believes this merger may result in a violation of federal antitrust laws and wishes to file suit to prevent it.

CASE QUESTION

If Monfort files suit and the merger is deemed to violate antitrust laws, what type of remedy will Monfort want to receive and why?

CASE SUMMARY 1.5 Arizona v. United States, 132 S. Ct. 2492 (2012)

CONSTITUTIONAL INTERPRETATION

In 2010, the State of Arizona passed the Support Our Law Enforcement and Safe Neighborhoods Act to address problems that the legislature contended were being created by the large number of unlawful immigrants living and working within the state's borders. Among other provisions, the law created state immigration offenses and expanded the authority of local police to enforce immigration laws by requiring individuals lawfully detained by the police (e.g., a traffic stop) to verify their citizenship. The law also provided criminal penalties for unauthorized aliens who sought or engaged in work within Arizona. The U.S. Department of Justice filed suit against Arizona seeking to invalidate the law on the basis that federal immigration statutes precluded individual states from enacting their own immigration laws. Arizona argued that weak and uneven enforcement of federal immigration laws necessitated state regulation and that the state law did not conflict with the federal law. The U.S. Court of Appeals ruled in favor of the United States, and the State of Arizona appealed to the U.S. Supreme Court.

CASE QUESTIONS

1. Who prevails and why?
2. If a federal law is ineffective, should a state have the right to legislate in that area without federal intervention?

CASE SUMMARY 1.6 *In re* the Appeal from the Civil Penalty Assessed for Violations of the Sedimentation Pollution Control Act, 379 S.E.2d 30 (1989)

PRECEDENT

This case arises from an assessment of a civil penalty against two landowners for violations of the Sedimentation Pollution Control Act of 1973, by the North Carolina Department of Natural Resources and Community Development (NRCD). While enlarging one of the subdivisions on the property, between October and December 1983, the owners disturbed approximately 2½ acres of land by grading, cutting, and filling, in order to construct a street to provide access to residential lots. Owners were assessed civil penalties for violations of the act. The trial court concluded that although the assessment was "not effected [sic] by error of law," the authority conferred by the statute allowed the secretary of NRCD to assess civil penalties in his "absolute discretion," and thus the statute constituted a legislative grant of judicial power prohibited by the North Carolina Constitution. A divided panel[14] of the North Carolina Court of Appeals upheld the trial court's judgment. In doing so, the panel disregarded another panel of the North Carolina Court of Appeals that had, in a previous case with the same issues, found that the NRCD has discretion to assess fines due to guidelines and limitations that exist in the act in question. The North Carolina Supreme Court heard the appeal.

CASE QUESTIONS

1. How is precedent created, and how is it applied in future cases?
2. When two separate panels of the same court hear different cases with similar issues, must the second panel follow the decision made by the first?
3. If precedent has been set by a state appellate panel, who has the power to overrule that precedent?

✓ Self-Check ANSWERS Role of Counsel

1. Laws related to start-up (incorporation), sales of goods (commercial law), ordinances such as zoning (basement location), and taxation of transactions and income.
2. *For business operations:* laws related to lease of a kiosk, credit transactions, and local licensing.
   For employees: labor laws (minimum wage, overtime) and employment discrimination.
3. Laws related to how to qualify for trademark protection, the process of registration, and enforcement of the mark.
4. Laws related to asset purchases, contracts, taxes, and trademarks.

Sources of Law

1. A contract issue governed by statutory (UCC) law at the state level.
2. A patent issue governed by statutory law at the federal level.
3. A securities issue governed by statutory and administrative law at the federal and state levels.
4. A bankruptcy issue governed by statutory and administrative law at the federal level.
5. A zoning issue governed by statutory law at the local level.

---

[14]Often, appellate court justices do not all sit on cases together. For efficiency, smaller groups, frequently called *panels,* may hear and decide cases.

CHAPTER REVIEW QUESTIONS: Answers and Explanations

1. **d.** In terms of a business context, the most important purposes of the law are reliability (using the law for planning) and good-faith dealing among merchants. Answer choice (c) is incorrect because, although it is true that the law protects individual rights, the question specifically relates to a business context.

2. **d.** An asset acquisition involves tax law (e.g., did the transaction create tax liability? and who pays?) and contracts (e.g., agreement of sale and others). Employment law also is important because the transaction involves hiring SmallCo employees.

3. **c.** Statutory law is created when a state or federal legislature passes a law and the executive either concurs or vetoes the legislation. Answer choices (a), (b), and (d) are wrong because they do not involve a legislative body.

4. **b.** Precedent springs from the doctrine of stare decisis and provides reliability that is so important in the law. Similar cases with similar facts should have similar outcomes. Answer choices (a), (c), and (d) are nonsensical.

5. **a.** Equitable relief is appropriate when an injured party cannot be compensated through money damages. Answer choice (b) is incorrect because legal damages are typically thought of as money awards. Answer choice (c) is incorrect because a jury can award both equitable and money relief. Answer choice (d) is unrelated to the concept of law or equity.

©philsajonesen/Getty Images

APPENDIX TO CHAPTER 1

A Business Student's Guide to Understanding Cases and Finding the Law

This textbook emphasizes ways in which business owners and managers can add value to their companies by using legal insight for business planning and limiting risk. Using a basic system for understanding court case opinions improves one's ability to grasp the impact of the law on business. Because much of the law is composed of cases and statutes, learning the fundamentals of how and where to find the law allows business owners and managers to work more effectively with counsel and empowers them to become better decision makers by using legal considerations as a part of their strategic planning.

Understanding Case Law: The SUR System

All of the legal cases in this textbook are reported in a unique format designed especially for business students. For each case, students are provided with a summary of the case facts and a synopsis of the court's decision and opinion. Students then read an actual excerpt from the case in the *words of the court* that is directly related to the legal point being covered in the text. All procedural language and parts of the opinion that are unrelated to the legal point have been edited out. This allows the reader to focus on one or two key points of law in the case. However, case law from other sources is likely to be a complete word-for-word reporting without any trustworthy explanation or summary. Understanding cases by reading the full text can be challenging even for attorneys. The *SUR system* provides business students with a systematic method for analyzing cases and helps the reader draw out essential information without getting bogged down in legal details.

SUR stands for *scan, understand, review*. Although this system is helpful for reading any complex or dense text, it is specifically tailored for reading legal cases. Not only will this method help students fully understand the cases contained in this text, but it is also useful for comprehending full-length cases found in other sources. Figures 1A.1, 1A.2, and 1A.3 illustrate how the SUR system is applied.

Scan the Case

Read the *headings* and *first two sentences* of each section of the case to the end of the opinion. Then read the *last three* sentences of the case. While scanning, use a pencil or highlighter to note names of the parties, the court that decided the case, and the final decision of the court.

Understand the Case

After scanning, begin to read (and reread when necessary) the case from the beginning. Use a pencil to circle important facts and legal terms. At this stage, many students find it useful to draw flowcharts and other summaries in order to understand a chain of facts more clearly. Look up legal terms using the online law dictionary listed in Table 1A.1 later in this appendix. Do your best to skip procedural language such as the standards of review for an appellate court or issues related to pretrial discovery or motions. While reading the fact summary in the beginning of the case, keep the following question in mind:

> ISSUE: What legal *issues* are being created by the party's actions? That is, what legal *question* will the court have to answer?

Once you begin reading the court's ruling, continue to mark potentially important phrases, paying special attention to the court's statement of the current law. Look for wording such as "the statute provides for" or

FIGURE 1A.1 Example of SUR System Using Case 1.1, *United States v. Ulbricht*

After the *Scan* stage, the text would appear as follows:

CASE 1.1 *United States v. Ulbricht*, 31 F. Supp. 3d 540 (S.D.N.Y. 2014)

FACT SUMMARY In February 2014, ==a federal Grand Jury indicted Ross Ulbricht==, also known as Dread Pirate Roberts (Ulbricht), for, among other things, ==conspiracy to launder money obtained from illegal activities.== Prosecutors alleged that Ulbricht was engaged in narcotics trafficking, computer hacking, and money laundering conspiracies by designing, launching, and administering a website called Silk Road as an online marketplace for illicit goods and services. Silk Road was designed to operate like eBay: (1) a seller would electronically post a good or service for sale; (2) a buyer would electronically purchase the item; (3) the seller would then ship or otherwise provide to the buyer the purchased item; (4) the buyer would provide feedback; and (5) the site operator (i.e., Ulbricht) would receive a portion of the seller's revenue as a commission. ==Ulbricht, as the alleged site designer, made the site available only to those using Tor, a software and network system that allows for anonymous, untraceable Internet browsing. He allowed payment only via bitcoin==, an anonymous and untraceable form of digital currency. Thousands of transactions allegedly occurred over the course of nearly three years—sellers posted goods when available; and buyers purchased goods when desired.

Ulbricht filed a motion to dismiss the indictments based on a number of theories. Ulbricht argued that he could not be guilty of money laundering because the ==use of bitcoins did not fit into the statute's requirement that money laundered be a result of a "financial transaction."== Since bitcoins are not monetary instruments, transactions involving bitcoins cannot form the basis for a money laundering conspiracy. He supported his argument by noting that the IRS has announced that it treats virtual currency as property and not as currency.

SYNOPSIS OF DECISION AND OPINION The U.S. district ==court ruled against Ulbricht.== The court rejected Ulbricht's theory that use of bitcoins is not a financial transaction. The court noted that because ==bitcoins carry value and act as a medium of exchange, they fall into the meaning of financial transaction in the money laundering statute.== Since bitcoins may be exchanged for legal tender, be it U.S. dollars, euros, or some other currency, they can be an instrument in money laundering.

WORDS OF THE COURT: Plain Meaning of Statute "Put simply, 'funds' can be used to pay for things in the colloquial sense. Bitcoins can be either used directly to pay for certain things or can act as a medium of exchange and be converted into a currency which can pay for things. Indeed, the only value for Bitcoin lies in its ability to pay for things—it is digital and has no earthly form; it cannot be put on a shelf and looked at or collected in a nice display case. Its form is digital—bits and bytes that together constitute something of value. And they may be bought and sold using legal tender . . . The money laundering statute is broad enough to encompass use of Bitcoins in financial transactions. . . . Congress intended to prevent criminals from finding ways to wash the proceeds of criminal activity by transferring proceeds to other similar or different items that store significant value. . . . There is no doubt that if a narcotics transaction was paid for in cash, which was later exchanged for gold, and then converted back to cash, that would constitute a money laundering transaction. . . . One can money launder using Bitcoin."

APPENDIX TO CHAPTER 1 | A Business Student's Guide to Understanding Cases and Finding the Law

FIGURE 1A.2

After the *Understand* stage, the text would look like this:

CASE 1.1 United States v. Ulbricht, 31 F. Supp. 3d 540 (S.D.N.Y. 2014)

FACT SUMMARY In February 2014, a federal Grand Jury indicted Ross Ulbricht, also known as Dread Pirate Roberts (Ulbricht), for, among other things, conspiracy to launder money obtained from illegal activities. Prosecutors alleged that Ulbricht was engaged in narcotics trafficking, computer hacking, and money laundering conspiracies by designing, launching, and administering a website called Silk Road as an online marketplace for illicit goods and services. Silk Road was designed to operate like eBay: (1) a seller would electronically post a good or service for sale; (2) a buyer would electronically purchase the item; (3) the seller would then ship or otherwise provide to the buyer the purchased item; (4) the buyer would provide feedback; and (5) the site operator (i.e., Ulbricht) would receive a portion of the seller's revenue as a commission. Ulbricht, as the alleged site designer, made the site available only to those using Tor, a software and network system that allows for anonymous, untraceable Internet browsing. He allowed payment only via bitcoin, an anonymous and untraceable form of digital currency. Thousands of transactions allegedly occurred over the course of nearly three years—sellers posted goods when available; and buyers purchased goods when desired.

Ulbricht filed a motion to dismiss the indictments based on a number of theories. Ulbricht argued that he could not be guilty of money laundering because the use of bitcoins did not fit into the statute's requirement that money laundered be a result of a "financial transaction." Since bitcoins are not monetary instruments, transactions involving bitcoins cannot form the basis for a money laundering conspiracy. He supported his argument by noting that the IRS has announced that it treats virtual currency as property and not as currency.

SYNOPSIS OF DECISION AND OPINION The U.S. district court ruled against Ulbricht. The court rejected Ulbricht's theory that use of bitcoins is not a financial transaction. The court noted that because bitcoins carry value and act as a medium of exchange, they fall into the meaning of financial transaction in the money laundering statute. Since bitcoins may be exchanged for legal tender, be it U.S. dollars, euros, or some other currency, they can be an instrument in money laundering.

WORDS OF THE COURT: Plain Meaning of Statute "Put simply, 'funds' can be used to pay for things in the colloquial sense. Bitcoins can be either used directly to pay for certain things or can act as a medium of exchange and be converted into a currency which can pay for things. Indeed, the only value for Bitcoin lies in its ability to pay for things—it is digital and has no earthly form; it cannot be put on a shelf and looked at or collected in a nice display case. Its form is digital—bits and bytes that together constitute something of value. And they may be bought and sold using legal tender . . . The money laundering statute is broad enough to encompass use of Bitcoins in financial transactions. . . . Congress intended to prevent criminals from finding ways to wash the proceeds of criminal activity by transferring proceeds to other similar or different items that store significant value. . . . There is no doubt that if a narcotics transaction was paid for in cash, which was later exchanged for gold, and then converted back to cash, that would constitute a money laundering transaction. . . . One can money launder using Bitcoin."

Annotations:

- Federal criminal statute
- Issue: Does use of bitcoins qualify as a financial transaction under money laundering statutes?
- Rule: Bitcoins can be an instrument for purposes of the money laundering statute.
- Analysis: Bitcoins carry value and act as a medium of exchange in the same way as currency.
- Conclusion: Money laundering statutes include the use of bitcoins.

FIGURE 1A.3

After the *Review* stage, the text would look like this:

CASE 1.1 United States v. Ulbricht, 31 F. Supp. 3d 540 (S.D.N.Y. 2014)

FACT SUMMARY In February 2014, a federal Grand Jury indicted Ross Ulbricht, also known as Dread Pirate Roberts (Ulbricht), for, among other things, conspiracy to launder money obtained from illegal activities. Prosecutors alleged that Ulbricht was engaged in narcotics trafficking, computer hacking, and money laundering conspiracies by designing, launching, and administering a website called Silk Road as an online marketplace for illicit goods and services. Silk Road was designed to operate like eBay: (1) a seller would electronically post a good or service for sale; (2) a buyer would electronically purchase the item; (3) the seller would then ship or otherwise provide to the buyer the purchased item; (4) the buyer would provide feedback; and (5) the site operator (i.e., Ulbricht) would receive a portion of the seller's revenue as a commission. Ulbricht, as the alleged site designer, made the site available only to those using Tor, a software and network system that allows for anonymous, untraceable Internet browsing. He allowed payment only via bitcoin, an anonymous and untraceable form of digital currency. Thousands of transactions allegedly occurred over the course of nearly three years—sellers posted goods when available; and buyers purchased goods when desired.

Ulbricht filed a motion to dismiss the indictments based on a number of theories. Ulbricht argued that he could not be guilty of money laundering because the use of bitcoins did not fit into the statute's requirement that money laundered be a result of a "financial transaction." Since bitcoins are not monetary instruments, transactions involving bitcoins cannot form the basis for a money laundering conspiracy. He supported his argument by noting that the IRS has announced that it treats virtual currency as property and not as currency.

SYNOPSIS OF DECISION AND OPINION The U.S. district court ruled against Ulbricht. The court rejected Ulbricht's theory that use of bitcoins is not a financial transaction. The court noted that because bitcoins carry value and act as a medium of exchange, they fall into the meaning of financial transaction in the money laundering statute. Since bitcoins may be exchanged for legal tender, be it U.S. dollars, euros, or some other currency, they can be an instrument in money laundering.

This case stands for the proposition that although electronic currency is not specifically mentioned in the money laundering statute, the fact that they carry value and can be exchanged for legal tender qualifies as a financial transaction in the context of money laundering statutes.

Annotations:
- Federal criminal statute
- Issue: Does use of bitcoins qualify as a financial transaction under money laundering statutes?
- Rule: Bitcoins can be an instrument for purposes of the money laundering statute.
- Analysis: Bitcoins carry value and act as a medium of exchange in the same way as currency.
- Conclusion: Money laundering statutes include the use of bitcoins.

"the only relief available under the statute" to alert you to important language. As you read and mark the text, keep in mind the following questions and jot down any related thoughts:

> RULE: What law *generally* applies to this situation, and are there any exceptions? What statute, common law, or other legal doctrine is applicable in this situation? What precedent exists? Courts often start the legal analysis section of their opinions by stating what the law is or by quoting from the statute at issue.
>
> ANALYSIS: How does the court apply the law to this set of facts? Are there any other factors that the court is considering when applying the law? Are there any legal exceptions or privileges that apply to these facts? Was it necessary to deviate from precedent?
>
> CONCLUSION: What was the court's answer to the question posed in the issue phases of this analysis?

Review the Case

Use a highlighter (some students may find it helpful to use a different color for reviewing than the color used for scanning) to go over the case one more time. Read the case at a reading speed that is halfway between scanning and comprehensive reading. Highlight sparingly, marking only what you find to be most important. Many students find it helpful to sketch out a flowchart or summary of the entire case. After reviewing the case, spot and note the answers to the issue, rule, analysis, and conclusion questions. Then put away the materials, and consider a final question: *What is the fundamental premise of this case?* Write out the answer in two or three sentences, and include it with the case notes for future use. Difficulty in answering that question may be remedied by going back to the *Understand* step and refining the issue, rule, and analysis. Remember that you may not look at the case again for several weeks or months until preparing for

TABLE 1A.1 Reliable Sources for Legal Research on the Internet

Website Name	Source	Description	URL*
Free and low-cost legal research	Georgetown University Law Center—Law Library	One of the very best tools for free and low-cost online research. The website provides an excellent overview, links to different types of free materials, and direct links to federal and state statutes and cases. It also summarizes the features and costs of less expensive databases.	http://guides.ll.georgetown.edu/home
Free Internet legal sources	University of Washington School of Law	Comprehensive offerings and an easy-to-use layout for finding the law. The site also provides an excellent brochure (in pdf) called "How to Research a Legal Problem: A Guide for Non-Lawyers."	https://guides.lib.uw.edu/law/guides
All Law: The Internet's premier law portal	Commercial website (primarily generates revenue through advertising)	Very simple layout and direct links that make this website efficient for locating federal or state statutes and cases.	www.alllaw.com/law/
Free legal advice	Commercial website (primarily generates revenue through advertising)	Comprehensive topical information arranged by legal topic (also contains advice related to insurance). However, the site is not useful for finding cases or specific statutes.	https://www.freeadvice.com/
Online law dictionary	Commercial website (primarily generates revenue through advertising)	Comprehensive law dictionary with search engine.	http://dictionary.law.com

an exam. The SUR system increases learning intensity and provides a document ready for use when you are studying the material later.

Finding the Law

The Internet has been the single most important force in providing unprecedented public access to the law. Cases, statutes, and topics on legal information are accessible online and largely free of charge. In addition to Internet services, several commercial services (such as Lexis-Nexis and Westlaw) provide special versions of case law that are enhanced with summaries, explanations, and a system that ties cases together based on legal topics. Table 1A.1, above, provides examples of reliable Internet sources for legal research. Table 1A.2 summarizes the four-step method illustrated in the discussion below. This method provides a systematic process for finding the law through either an Internet-based or a commercial service.

Step 1: Identify a Precise Legal Question

The first step in finding the law is to clearly identify a legal question to answer. Using your knowledge of the levels and sources of law covered in Chapter 1, "Legal Foundations," try to determine whether the question is best answered by a statute or a case. For example, suppose that Adams is an employee of Coats and Hats Co. (CHC), a business with 45 employees. One morning he informs his manager, Icahn, that he has been subpoenaed for jury duty in a state court and will need the next day off with pay. Because the company is performing a crucial inventory count that week, Adams is needed in the warehouse or, alternatively, a replacement will need to be hired. Icahn wants to know if CHC is legally obligated to permit Adams to take the time off necessary to serve on jury duty. If so, is the company legally responsible for paying Adams while he is on jury duty? Because the issue is related to employer obligations to employees when called for jury duty to a state court, Icahn would likely find guidance in a *state statute*.

Step 2: Strategize Based on Resources

Once you have determined the basic legal question and potential source of law, the strategy for tracking down the answer is necessarily based on resources. If

TABLE 1A.2	Sample Research Strategy Using Internet Sources: CHC-Adams Example	
Step 1	Identify precise legal question(s) and try to determine what source of law governs the issue(s).	Questions: 1. Is CHC required to permit Adams to take time off for jury duty in a state court? 2. If yes, is CHC obligated to pay Adams for the time he spends on jury duty? Sources: Look in the statutes of the state where CHC employs Adams.
Step 2	Strategize based on resources.	Use Georgetown's website: 1. Table of contents: Click on *Statutes and Codes: State Codes*. 2. Choose *State Research Guides* and then *Pennsylvania resources*. 3. Under "Electronic versions" choose *Free Web*, and use the free search engine for the Pennsylvania code. 4. Use the search engine to find a statute by entering "Jury Duty and Employer." 5. Click on the first result, and read the statute. Does it help resolve the question(s)?
Step 3	Find an application.	On the same web page (Pennsylvania resources) click on *Cases and Courts* to use the search engine for any cases involving employers/employees and time off for jury duty.
Step 4	Consult with counsel.	Provide Adams with time off for jury duty, but without pay. Hire a temporary worker for the warehouse (not permitted to discipline or terminate Adams). Icahn checks his plan with his counsel before implementing.

commercial research services are available to you, it may be advantageous to use them in order to get the maximum amount of information in the least amount of time. However, such services are typically very expensive and, therefore, are usually limited to law firms, large companies, and academic institutions. Government, municipal, college, and law school libraries have federal and state statutes in book form. However, finding specific information on the law in books or through commercial services may be difficult without extensive training in legal research. Most legal research by nonlawyers is accomplished through the Internet. Pick the appropriate legal website for your research (see Table 1A.1 for the best websites for finding the law). Depending on which site you choose, try to find a general explanation of the topic. Alternatively, use the legal website's search engine to narrow your search in finding the source. In the CHC-Adams hypothetical case, Icahn may wish to use a website that gives a general explanation on rights of employees, but certain issues he seeks may be too narrow for a general explanation. In this case, Icahn will be best off simply using the website's search engine to find the statute in the state in which CHC employs Adams. For example, if CHC is located in Pennsylvania, Icahn will go to the Georgetown Law Center website and follow these steps: (1) Select *Statutes and Codes/State Codes* from the table of contents on the left side to get to Pennsylvania resources and (2) find the free electronic version of the statutes and use the search engine to find any relevant statute. Use of the words "jury duty" may be too general, so narrowing it down with modifiers such as "jury duty and employer" helps to hone in on the answer.

A Word of Caution about Internet Sources

While the Internet has made the law more accessible to the public, it has also created an environment where information goes unchecked and unverified. The best sources for legal research are typically the sites maintained by law school libraries. For more general legal information, websites should be evaluated based on sponsorship (who maintains the website?), authority (are the authors of the information identified, and are they attorneys?), and longevity (how long has the website been in existence?). The websites listed in Table 1A.1 are authoritative, have special features designed for nonattorneys, and are time-tested.

Step 3: Find an Application

Once you have located a statute, learn how the statute was applied in a case. Use the website's search engine, which enables you to find cases by entering the name or citation of the statute. Through the search results, you can read how courts have applied the statute and learn whether any exceptions exist. For example, in the CHC-Adams case, Ichan can use the Georgetown Law Center website to find a case by selecting *Cases and Courts* from the Pennsylvania resources menu and entering terms in the search engine. This will allow him to read how courts have interpreted the statute, if necessary, and help him to understand how it applies to CHC.

Step 4: Consult with Counsel

It is dangerous to make any decision based on legal research by a nonattorney. Once a business owner or manager has a grasp of the issues, she should contact her counsel and discuss the issue and potential consequences of any decisions. The ability to find and understand the law in a business environment should be considered an *enhancement* to helping add value to a company through use of the law in business planning. It is not a substitute for working closely with an attorney. For example, in the CHC-Adams case, based on his research, Icahn is prepared to provide Adams with time off for jury duty (as required by statute), but he does not intend to pay him. He will need to hire a temporary worker for the warehouse because he is not permitted to terminate Adams for missing work due to jury duty. However, before implementing his plan, he plans to consult with his counsel and make any adjustments necessary.

CHAPTER 2
Business and the Constitution

©philsajonesen/Getty Images

Learning Objectives

After studying this chapter, students who have mastered the material will be able to:

2-1   Describe the purpose and structure of the Constitution.
2-2   List the major provisions of the first three articles of the Constitution.
2-3   Explain the role of judicial review in interpreting the Constitution.
2-4   Recognize the three standards of constitutional review and their application.
2-5   Understand the scope of Congress's powers under the Commerce Clause.
2-6   Describe constitutional restrictions on state regulation of commerce in the business environment.
2-7   Explain why Congress's tax and spend powers are an independent source of federal power.
2-8   Describe the main protections in the First Amendment and explain how they apply in the business environment.
2-9   Describe the main protections in the Fourth Amendment and explain how they apply in the business environment.
2-10 Identify limits imposed on government power by the Due Process and Equal Protection clauses of the Constitution.

The U.S. Constitution is the oldest national charter in continuous use in the world. Officially ratified on June 21, 1788, its longevity may be due to its brevity, flexibility, and relative simplicity: The U.S. Constitution is one of the shortest constitutions in the world. Because the Constitution establishes the basic structure of the federal government and sets forth fundamental rights and protections, business owners and business managers should be aware of how the Constitution works and how it has been interpreted by the courts. In this chapter students will learn

- The structure of the U.S. Constitution and its role in the American legal system.
- The specific powers granted to the three branches of the federal government under the Constitution.
- The main constitutional rights and protections afforded to individuals and business entities in the Bill of Rights and the Fourteenth Amendment.

40   UNIT ONE | Fundamentals of the Legal Environment of Business

STRUCTURE OF THE CONSTITUTION: FEDERAL POWERS

LO 2-1 Describe the purpose and structure of the Constitution.

The United States is a **federal system** in which a national government in Washington, D.C., coexists with state governments in each state. A key concept underlying the federal system is that the Constitution grants limited powers to the federal government: The powers of the federal government must be *specifically* granted by the U.S. Constitution. For example, Congress has the power to regulate interstate commerce because the Constitution specifically grants Congress the explicit power to regulate interstate and foreign commerce. The states, by contrast, retain the inherent power to protect the health, safety, and general welfare of their citizenry.[1]

The Constitution begins with a general preamble stating the Constitution's main objectives, including things such as justice, liberty, tranquility, and the common defense. The articles then set out the structure, powers, and procedures of the federal government. From a business perspective, it is important to note that Congress's powers to directly and exclusively regulate *bankruptcy, patents,* and *copyrights* are set out in Article I. Table 2.1, in the next section, provides a brief synopsis of the main provisions in each article of the Constitution.

Overall, the Constitution serves three general functions:

- It establishes a *structure* for the federal government; that is, it creates three coequal branches: the legislative branch, the executive branch, and the judicial branch.
- It delegates enumerated and limited *powers* to each coequal branch of the federal government.
- It provides *procedural protections* to citizens, persons, and business firms.

Structure of the Constitution

The U.S. Constitution is composed of a **preamble**, seven **articles**, and 27 **amendments**. The first three articles establish a system of government with three coequal branches: the **legislative branch**, the **executive branch**, and the **judicial branch**.

Notice how the structure of the federal government is divided into three coequal branches and how each branch is assigned a specific set of powers. The underlying rationale for this structure is that each branch may exercise its respective powers to ensure that the other branches do not exceed their authority under the Constitution. This method of dividing power among three coequal branches is commonly called the system of *checks and balances.* As famously explained by James Madison in Federalist Paper No. 51:

> Ambition must be made to counteract ambition. The interest of the man must be connected with the constitutional rights of the place. . . . If men were angels, no government would be necessary. If angels

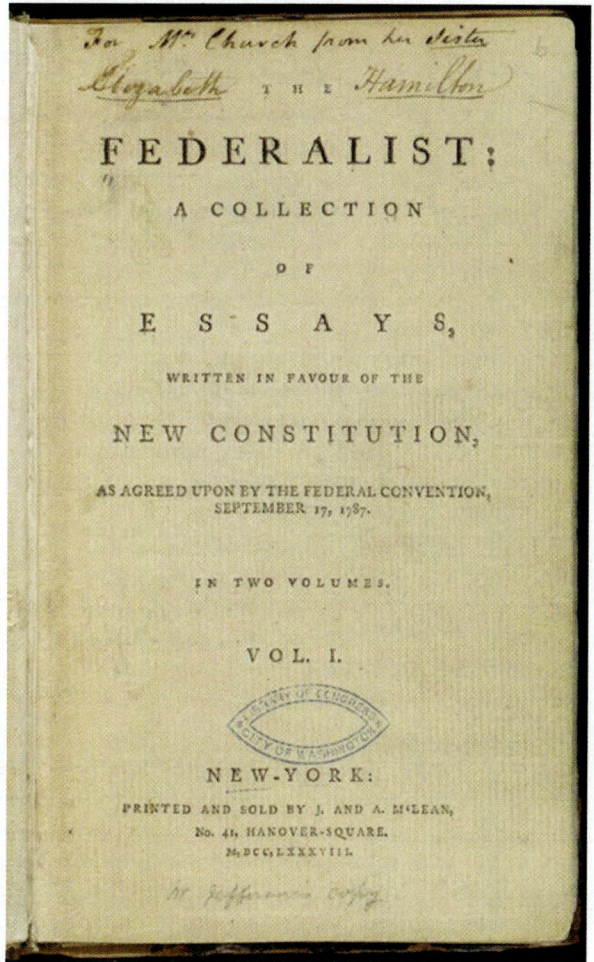

The *Federalist Papers,* a series of newspaper articles written in 1787 by Alexander Hamilton, James Madison, and John Jay in support of ratification of the Constitution, are still cited today when courts interpret the Constitution. AmericasLibrary.gov

---

[1] This inherent power of the state to protect its citizenry's health, safety, and general welfare is also referred to as the state's police powers.

were to govern men, neither external nor internal controls on government would be necessary. In framing a government which is to be administered by men over men, the great difficulty lies in this: you must first enable the government to control the governed; and in the next place oblige it to control itself.

Amendments

The Constitution has been *amended* (added to or changed) on several occasions since its ratification in 1788. The first 10 amendments to the Constitution, called the **Bill of Rights**, were ratified in 1791. In summary, the Bill of Rights recognizes the rights "of the people" regarding freedom of speech, religion, and assembly and establishes protections against random searches and seizures and other matters. (Including the first 10 amendments of the Bill of Rights, the Constitution has been amended 27 times!) Among the most important of these amendments, especially for business firms, are the First, Fourth, Fifth, and Fourteenth Amendments. The terms and scope of these amendments are discussed in detail later in this chapter.

OVERVIEW OF FEDERAL POWERS

LO 2-2

List the major provisions of the first three articles of the Constitution.

The powers granted to the three branches of the federal government in the Constitution are known as **enumerated powers**. The powers of the federal government are supposed to be *limited in scope,* and each act of the federal government must be authorized by one of the specific enumerated powers listed in the articles of the Constitution. Table 2.1 provides a brief overview of the articles in the Constitution.

> **KEY POINT**
>
> Although the Constitution grants explicit power to the federal government in certain matters, Congress may delegate various powers to state governments. For example, state governments have the right to define exempt-property standards in bankruptcy matters.

Article I—Congressional Powers

The primary authorization of constitutional powers is given to Congress in **Article I, Section 8** of the Constitution. Among the powers of Congress that generally impact business are (1) the power to *regulate commerce* (**Commerce Clause**); (2) the power to tax and the power to spend government funds (*tax and spend provisions*); and (3) the power to regulate *bankruptcy, patents, and copyrights.* In addition, Congress has a *general implied power* to make all laws necessary for carrying out its enumerated powers (**Necessary and Proper Clause**).

TABLE 2.1	Overview of Articles in the U.S. Constitution
Article I	Establishes the legislative branch (a bicameral Congress composed of the House of Representatives and the Senate); sets qualifications for members of Congress; grants congressional powers (lawmaking).
Article II	Establishes the executive branch (president); sets qualifications for the presidency; grants executive powers (enforcement of laws).
Article III	Establishes the judicial branch, including a Supreme Court; grants certain judicial powers.
Article IV	Establishes the relationship between the states and the federal government; describes the power of Congress over territories and the admission of new states into the Union.
Article V	Describes the process for amending the Constitution in the future.
Article VI	Establishes the Constitution and federal law as the supreme law of the land; authorizes the national debt (Congress may borrow money); requires public officials to take an oath to support the Constitution.
Article VII	Lists the requirements for ratification of the Constitution.

Article II—Executive Powers

The president is the chief executive of the United States and the commander-in-chief of the armed forces. Presidential powers that affect business include (1) the power to carry out laws made by Congress; (2) the power to enter into treaties (subject to Senate approval) and carry out foreign policy; and (3) the power to appoint federal officers and judges (also subject to Senate approval).

> **KEY POINT**
>
> The president not only appoints federal officers (with Senate approval) but has the power, in many cases, to unilaterally dismiss those same federal officers.

Executive orders have the force of law and are typically issued by the president as a method to carry out executive functions of government. Although there is no constitutional provision that explicitly permits executive orders, Congress may delegate some degree of discretionary power to the president to carry out a federal statute. In cases where there is no congressional delegation, courts have upheld the president's power to issue executive orders based on the general grant of constitutional power to the executive branch for carrying out federal laws. Executive orders may have an impact on business, especially if they concern areas such as employment law or immigration law. One example is President Obama's 2014 executive order on "Deferred Action for Parents of Americans and Lawful Permanent Residents" (DAPA), which deferred the deportation of certain persons living illegally in the United States.

A **presidential proclamation**, by contrast, is a statement issued by the president on a ceremonial occasion or to elaborate an issue of public or foreign policy. Presidential proclamations thus fall into two broad categories:

1. *Ceremonial* proclamations that designate special observances or celebrate national holidays and
2. *Substantive* proclamations, which usually involve the conduct of foreign affairs and other sworn executive duties, such as matters of international trade, the execution of set export controls, the establishment of tariffs, or the enforcement of federal immigration laws.

Article III—Judicial Powers

The federal judiciary adjudicates (decides) cases and controversies that fall within its authority. In addition to providing for the creation of federal courts, the Constitution also establishes the boundaries of **jurisdiction** of federal courts. Jurisdiction is the legal authority of a court to decide a case. Both the U.S. Constitution and individual state constitutions contain language that establishes jurisdiction for certain matters to be heard by certain courts. The concept of jurisdiction is discussed in detail in Chapter 3, "The American Judicial System, Jurisdiction, and Venue."

One of the central concepts in federal constitutional law is **judicial review**, the notion that federal courts have the power to invalidate state or federal laws that are inconsistent with the U.S. Constitution in some way. This authority, possibly the most important judicial power, is not enumerated in the Constitution. It was established by the Supreme Court in the landmark case of *Marbury v. Madison* in 1803. In *Marbury*, the Court ruled that (1) the Constitution is superior to federal and state statutes and (2) when there is a conflict between the

LO 2-3

Explain the role of judicial review in interpreting the Constitution.

The Congressional Medal of Honor. Tribune Content Agency LLC/Alamy

Constitution and a state or federal law, the Court has the authority to declare the challenged law as unconstitutional.[2]

Although *Marbury* was decided over 200 years ago, it is still considered good precedent, and federal and state courts regularly cite the case as a source of authority for the power to invalidate a law or governmental action that is in conflict with the Constitution. Over the better part of two centuries, the Supreme Court has further defined its self-declared power of judicial review, including the power of federal courts to review state court decisions to the extent that such decisions involve federal law or federal constitutional issues.

In Case 2.1, the U.S. Supreme Court exercises its power of judicial review to strike down a federal statute as unconstitutional.

CASE 2.1 United States v. Alvarez, 567 U.S. 709 (2012)

FACT SUMMARY The Stolen Valor Act of 2005 made it a federal crime to make false claims related to receiving military decoration or honors. The penalty for false claims about the Congressional Medal of Honor was enhanced to include up to one year in prison. The law was passed largely in response to media stories about various public officials who had exaggerated or lied about their military record during their campaigns or while in office. Xavier Alvarez was an individual who served as a member of a municipal water district board in Claremont, California. During one public meeting of the board, Alvarez introduced himself and included facts about his past, including that he had served as a Marine, been wounded, and received the Congressional Medal of Honor. None of these representations were true. Alvarez was charged with violating the Stolen Valor Act and pled guilty, but he reserved the right to challenge the constitutionality of the law based on the First Amendment upon appeal. The U.S. Court of Appeals for the Ninth Circuit struck the statute down as an unconstitutional infringement of free speech under the First Amendment. The government appealed to the U.S. Supreme Court, arguing that because Alvarez's statements were false, he was not entitled to First Amendment protection.

SYNOPSIS OF DECISION AND OPINION The U.S. Supreme Court ruled in favor of Alvarez and upheld the lower court's decision that the statute violated the First Amendment. The Court ruled that its previous decisions made clear that content-based restrictions on speech were presumed to be invalid and that it was the government's responsibility to demonstrate a compelling interest. The Court rejected the government's argument that false speech is not protected, and it pointed out several instances in which it had previously ruled that falsity alone does not make a statement fall automatically outside the protection of the First Amendment. The Court acknowledged that the government's interest in protecting the integrity of the Medal of Honor was beyond question. However, the Court's decision to strike the law down as unconstitutional was rooted in the failure of the government to provide evidence of a direct link between the statute and the injury to be prevented in protecting the government interest.

WORDS OF THE COURT: Judicial Review "The First Amendment requires that the Government's chosen restriction on the speech at issue be 'actually necessary' to achieve its interest. There must be a direct causal link between the restriction imposed and the injury to be prevented. The link

(continued)

---

[2]Because of its sweeping importance, *Marbury* has been subject to intense analysis, justification, and criticism. Some critics argue that the Supreme Court, in essence, gave the power of judicial review to itself. Most of the criticism of the *Marbury* opinion is derived from the fact that the Constitution does not expressly authorize the courts to invalidate congressional statutes and that such a power is not contemplated in any preratification debates or in advocacy publications such as the *Federalist Papers*.

between the Government's interest in protecting the integrity of the military honors system and the Act's restriction on the false claims of liars like respondent has not been shown. . . . It must be acknowledged that when a pretender claims the Medal to be his own, the lie might harm the Government by demeaning the high purpose of the award, diminishing the honor it confirms, and creating the appearance that the Medal is awarded more often than is true. Furthermore, the lie may offend the true holders of the Medal. . . . Yet these interests do not satisfy the Government's heavy burden when it seeks to regulate protected speech. The Government points to no evidence to support its claim that the public's general perception of military awards is diluted by false claims such as those made by Alvarez."

Case Questions

1. The dissenting justices argued that allowing First Amendment protection for statements that are lies was a dangerous and unwise path. They also concluded that the link between the statute and the government's interest was more than enough to satisfy any constitutional scrutiny. Are the dissenting arguments compelling? Why or why not?
2. Could Congress have crafted a different law that would have achieved its intended result but survived a constitutional challenge? How?
3. *Focus on Critical Thinking:* At what point do falsehoods become so serious as to warrant a restriction of the speaker's speech rights?

Separation of Powers

The Constitution's creation of three coequal branches and its enumeration of government powers are part of an overall framework that is designed to ensure that no one branch exceeds its constitutional authority. This elaborate system of checks and balances is based on a **separation of powers**, ensuring that no one branch becomes overly dominant over the other branches.

Table 2.2 lists some of the various powers that each branch has that act as a check on the other branches.

> **KEY POINT**
>
> Federal legislation or regulation must be authorized by a specific, enumerated power in the Constitution.

Applying the Constitution: Standards of Judicial Review

The U.S. Supreme Court has established three standards of judicial review in constitutional cases. In summary, when reviewing a government action for constitutional soundness (such as the passage or enforcement of a federal or state law), the Court classifies its action into one of three categories of scrutiny: (1) **rational basis** review, (2) **intermediate-level scrutiny**, or (3) **strict scrutiny**.

LO 2-4

Recognize the three standards of constitutional review and their application.

TABLE 2.2 Example of Constitutional Checks and Balances

Branch	Power	Power Checked
Executive	Veto	Congress's lawmaking authority
Legislative	Override veto with supermajority	President's veto authority
Legislative	Impeachment and removal	Presidential misconduct and federal judicial power
Judicial	Invalidate a law as unconstitutional	Congress's authority to make laws; the president's authority to enforce laws

Rational Basis Review Government actions in this category are subject to the lowest level or *least* amount of judicial review. In order for the court to uphold the action, the government need only show that (1) its action advanced a *legitimate* government objective (such as public welfare, health, or safety) and (2) the action was somehow related to the government's objective. Government actions that fall into this category include almost every economic regulation and tax-related law.

For example, suppose that Congress passes a law requiring all Internet service providers (ISPs) to be directly regulated by a new federal administrative agency. Further suppose that the law imposes a tax on the ISPs to fund the agency. MegaSearch is an ISP subject to the law and files suit contending the law is an unconstitutional exercise of congressional powers. Because the regulation is purely economic, a court will likely rule against MegaSearch and uphold the law as constitutional using the rational basis category so long as the government provides evidence that the law advances some legitimate government objective (such as consumer protection). If a state raises its toll fees for a state highway and cites rising maintenance costs, a similar presumption of legality applies.

Intermediate-Level Scrutiny Some actions are categorized as subject to intermediate-level scrutiny. Courts will uphold government actions as constitutional so long as the government can prove that (1) its action advances an important government objective (a higher level than the "legitimate" criterion used in the rational basis test) and (2) the action is *substantially related* to the government's objective.

A relatively small number of cases fall into this category. For example, courts have used this category in cases involving government action related to regulating the time, place, and manner of a political demonstration that is protected under the First Amendment. Suppose in the MegaSearch example discussed earlier that the management at MegaSearch organizes a protest against the law and applies for local permits to stage demonstrations opposing the law in several cities across the country. One city, Silicon Village, rejects the permit application because MegaSearch's proposed demonstration would block a high-volume traffic area and endanger both pedestrians and drivers. The village also points out that a public park located in the village would be a more appropriate venue. If MegaSearch sues the village for denying the company its First Amendment right to protest, a court would likely find the village's actions permissible under the intermediate-level scrutiny standard because the government's denial of the permit is substantially related to an important government objective (protection of drivers and pedestrians).

Strict Scrutiny When a government action impairs a fundamental constitutional right or is based on a "suspect" classification (i.e., race, national origin, or alienage), courts apply a *strict scrutiny* standard when deciding whether to uphold the government action. Courts will uphold the law only if (1) the government's objective is *compelling*, (2) the means chosen by the government to advance that objective are necessary to achieve that compelling end, and (3) no *less-restrictive alternatives* exist.

In the strict scrutiny category of judicial review, the government has the burden of persuasion. As a practical matter, when courts classify government actions as belonging in the strict scrutiny category, they are signaling that the government action is likely to be ruled unconstitutional. For example, continuing with the MegaSearch example, suppose the government passes a law that imposes a higher level of tax on ISPs that cater to Latino users by basing the tax assessment on the number of searches conducted using words and phrases in Spanish. Such a law would be a clear example of the government's use of a suspect classification (national origin) and, as such, it would be struck down under a strict scrutiny analysis.

In Case 2.2, the U.S. Supreme Court examines the constitutionality of a California statute regarding a limitation of First Amendment freedom of speech and applies the strict scrutiny standard.

CASE 2.2 Brown v. Entertainment Merchants Association, 564 U.S. 786 (2011)

FACT SUMMARY In 2005, California passed a law that banned the sale or rental of violent video games to anyone under age 18 and required warning labels beyond the existing Entertainment Software Ratings Board's voluntary rating system. The law covered games in which players had the options of killing, maiming, dismembering, or sexually assaulting characters that represent human beings. Entertainment Merchants Association (EMA), an association of companies in the video games business, sued the State of California, seeking to have the new law declared unconstitutional. The federal trial court concluded that the statute violated the First Amendment and prevented enforcement of the law. On appeal, the federal appellate court affirmed the decision of the trial court. California appealed to the U.S. Supreme Court.

SYNOPSIS OF DECISION AND OPINION The U.S. Supreme Court ruled in favor of the EMA and struck down the law as unconstitutional. The Court held that video games are considered speech, similar to plays and movies, and are therefore protected by the First Amendment despite the fact that some people find the video games offensive. Because the law restricted speech, the Court applied a strict scrutiny analysis to the statute and found that (1) California failed to meet its burden of proving a compelling government interest through the use of expert testimony and (2) the law was both too broad (i.e., it covered minors whose parents believed violent video games were harmless) and too narrow (i.e., it did not cover other forms of violent expression such as novels). Finally, the Court distinguished violence from obscenity by ruling that violent speech in this context was protected under the First Amendment.

WORDS OF THE COURT: Due Process and Freedom of Speech "Because the Act imposes a restriction on the content of protected speech, it is invalid unless California can demonstrate that it passes strict scrutiny—that is, unless it is justified by a compelling government interest and is narrowly drawn to serve that interest. The State must specifically identify an 'actual problem' in need of solving, and the curtailment of free speech must be actually necessary to the solution. . . . That is a demanding standard . . . [and] California cannot meet that standard. At the outset, it acknowledges that it cannot show a direct causal link between violent video games and harm to minors. . . . The State's evidence is not compelling. California relies primarily on the research of Dr. Craig Anderson and a few other research psychologists whose studies purport to show a connection between exposure to violent video games and harmful effects on children. These studies have been rejected by every court to consider them, and with good reason: They do not prove that violent video games *cause* minors to *act* aggressively (which would at least be a beginning). Instead, '[n]early all of the research is based on correlation, not evidence of causation, and most of the studies suffer from significant, admitted flaws in methodology.' They show at best some correlation between exposure to violent entertainment and minuscule real-world effects, such as children's feeling more aggressive or making louder noises in the few minutes after playing a violent game than after playing a nonviolent game. [. . .] Our cases have been clear that the obscenity exception to the First Amendment does not cover whatever a legislature finds shocking, but only depictions of 'sexual conduct.'"

Case Questions

1. Why did the Supreme Court apply the "strict scrutiny" standard to the California statute?
2. If the expert testimony had been conclusive and scientifically proven, would the Court's decision have been different? Why or why not?
3. *Focus on Critical Thinking:* Given the increase in mass shootings, should states be legislating this type of conduct, or should such conduct be solely a private issue to be decided on and enforced by parents or guardians?

The Supremacy Clause and Preemption

Because our federal system of government contemplates the coexistence of federal law with the various laws of the states, there are often conflicts between federal law and state law. Article VI of the U.S. Constitution provides that federal laws are always *supreme* to any conflicting state law. This is known as the **Supremacy Clause**, and it invalidates any state law that is in direct conflict with federal law. The power granted by the supremacy clause to override a state law is called **preemption**. In order for preemption to occur, the federal law must be directly in conflict with the state law to the point where the two laws cannot coexist. For example, in *Geier v. American Honda Motor Company,*[3] the U.S. Supreme Court held that a federal regulation giving auto manufacturers the choice between airbags or alternative methods of passenger safety restraints preempted a claim by an injured party against an auto manufacturer under a state common law doctrine based on failing to install airbags. The Court ruled that, because the injured party's case depended upon a claim that auto manufacturers had a legal duty to install airbags and the violation of that duty resulted in the injury, the state common law could not coexist with federal law that specifically allowed auto manufacturers who opted not to install airbags in favor of another type of restraint system.

COMMERCE POWERS

LO 2-5

Understand the scope of Congress's powers under the Commerce Clause.

The source of Congress's broadest power is the Commerce Clause in Article I, Section 8 of the Constitution, whereby Congress is granted the express power to "regulate Commerce . . . among the several States." Because almost every activity potentially affects commerce in some way, Congress has very broad powers to enact legislation under the Commerce Clause.

Application of Commerce Powers

Although Congress has exercised its commerce powers in various ways, the broad textual power to regulate all persons and products in the flow of interstate commerce is the fundamental source of Congress's commerce power.

Interstate versus Intrastate Commercial Activity Congress has the express authority to regulate (1) the channels of interstate commerce such as railways and highways; (2) the instrumentalities of interstate commerce, such as vehicles used in shipping products; and (3) articles moving in interstate commerce. Furthermore, even if an activity is a purely *intrastate* or local one (i.e., taking place within a single state's borders), Congress still has the power to regulate such local activity if the activity in the aggregate produces a *substantial economic effect* on interstate commerce.

For example, the U.S. Supreme Court has deferred to congressional regulation of a product that is cultivated for noncommercial purposes solely in one state, determining that such activity is sufficiently related to *interstate* commerce. In Case 2.3, the Court considers whether a state law legalizing purely local cultivation, processing, and use of marijuana affects interstate commerce.

CASE 2.3 Gonzalez v. Raich, 545 U.S. 1 (2005)

FACT SUMMARY In 1996, California voters approved a proposition legalizing the use of marijuana for medical purposes. The California legislature then adopted the Compassionate Use Act of 1996 to ensure that its residents had access to marijuana for medical use as an alternative to conventional medications. The law created an exemption from criminal prosecution for physicians, patients, and primary caregivers who possess or grow marijuana for medical use with the approval

(continued)

---

[3]529 U.S. 861 (2000).

48 UNIT ONE | Fundamentals of the Legal Environment of Business

and recommendation of a physician. Angel Raich and Diane Monson were patients diagnosed with a variety of medical conditions that were not alleviated through traditional methods and medications. As a result, physicians for each patient prescribed marijuana. Raich's physician testified that marijuana had been the only effective method to alleviate her symptoms and that discontinuing medical marijuana treatments would cause Raich excruciating pain and could very well prove fatal. In 2002, U.S. drug agents arrived at Monson's home and confiscated and destroyed her marijuana plants pursuant to a federal law called the Controlled Substances Act (CSA). Raich and Monson brought suit seeking to prevent federal law enforcement officials from enforcing the CSA in medical marijuana cases. They argued that enforcement of the CSA violated the Commerce Clause because the medical marijuana was cultivated and possessed within state borders and did not enter the stream of commerce. The trial court ruled in favor of the government, and the appellate court ruled that the noncommercial cultivation and possession of marijuana was *intra*state and thus was not intended to enter *inter*state commerce. The government appealed to the U.S. Supreme Court.

SYNOPSIS OF DECISION AND OPINION The U.S. Supreme Court ruled in favor of the government and held that the CSA was a valid exercise of congressional powers derived from the Commerce Clause. In analyzing the question of purely intrastate production and use of marijuana, the Court pointed out that Congress need only supply a rational basis for believing that locally cultivated marijuana would end up in interstate commerce. The Court held that congressional concerns about distinguishing between marijuana cultivated locally and marijuana grown elsewhere and the concerns about medicinal marijuana's contribution to illicit drug channels were rational and therefore constitutional.

WORDS OF THE COURT: Commerce Clause "The question before us, however, is not whether it is wise to enforce the statute in these circumstances; rather, it is whether Congress' power to regulate interstate markets for medicinal substances encompasses the portions of those markets that are supplied with drugs produced and consumed locally. Well-settled law controls our answer. . . . In assessing the scope of Congress' authority under the Commerce Clause, we stress that the task before us is a modest one. We need not determine whether respondents' activities, taken in the aggregate, substantially affect interstate commerce in fact, but only whether a 'rational basis' exists for so concluding. [. . .] Given the enforcement difficulties that attend distinguishing between marijuana cultivated locally and marijuana grown elsewhere, [citation omitted] and concerns about diversion into illicit channels, we have no difficulty concluding that Congress had a rational basis for believing that failure to regulate the intrastate manufacture and possession of marijuana would leave a gaping hole in the CSA. Thus . . . , when it enacted comprehensive legislation to regulate the interstate market in a fungible commodity, Congress was acting well within its authority to 'make all Laws which shall be necessary and proper' to regulate commerce . . . among the several States.' [. . .] That the regulation ensnares some purely intrastate activity is of no moment. As we have done many times before, we refuse to excise individual components of that larger scheme. . . . The congressional judgment that an exemption for such a significant segment of the total market would undermine the orderly enforcement of the entire regulatory scheme is entitled to a strong presumption of validity. Indeed, that judgment is not only rational, but 'visible to the naked eye.'"

Case Questions

1. Federal law expressly prohibits the cultivation, processing, distribution, and use of marijuana. Because a national market for marijuana cannot legally exist, why is this a Commerce Clause case?

2. Do you agree or disagree with the Court that locally grown and locally consumed crops can have an impact on interstate commerce?

3. *Focus on Critical Thinking:* The California law gave licensed physicians the legal authority to prescribe medical marijuana. Does this case give courts the right or power to substitute its judgment for the judgment of a trained physician?

The Commerce Clause and Civil Rights
An unorthodox use of the federal commerce power has been in the area of civil rights. Indeed, the Supreme Court's level of deference for use of congressional commerce powers reached its peak during the civil rights era. In the 1964 Civil Rights Act, for example, Congress used its commerce power to ban discrimination in places of public accommodation, such as privately owned restaurants and hotels, and in two important civil rights cases decided by the U.S. Supreme Court during this era, the Court ruled that the Civil Rights Act was a permissible application of Congress's commerce powers. In *Heart of Atlanta Motel v. United States*,[4] the Court made clear that a federal ban on racial discrimination in privately owned hotel and motel accommodations was a constitutionally permitted use of the commerce power. Specifically, the Court ruled that discrimination in private accommodations discouraged interstate travel. Moreover, in a companion case,[5] *Katzenbach v. McClung*,[6] the Court ruled that a privately owned local restaurant that was located far from any interstate highway and that had no appreciable business from interstate travelers was nevertheless subject to the reach of the federal statute because the restaurant

> **KEY POINT**
>
> Congress's broadest powers are derived from the Commerce Clause. Courts are highly deferential to congressional action in areas that affect interstate commerce.

President Lyndon Johnson (seated), seen here with Dr. Martin Luther King Jr., signed the Civil Rights Act in 1964. AP Images

---
[4]379 U.S. 241 (1964).

[5]Two cases with similar issues are often argued together. The Court publishes both opinions at the same time.

[6]379 U.S. 294 (1964).

purchased *some* food and paper supplies from out-of-state vendors. Because these purchases were of items that had moved in commerce, the Court ruled that Congress could properly exercise its power to regulate a restaurant whose business interests were primarily local.

Noncommercial Activity More recently, the U.S. Supreme Court has signaled some limits on Congress's commerce power. In cases where the activity is purely *noncommercial* (such as when Congress passes a criminal statute that is unrelated to commerce), the Court has used increased levels of scrutiny to be sure that the activity that Congress seeks to regulate has a sufficient nexus (connection) to some legitimate economic interest. In *United States v. Lopez,*[7] for example, the Court invalidated a federal statute on the basis that it was beyond the commerce powers of Congress. In *Lopez,* the Court struck down the Gun-Free School Zones Act of 1990, which made it a federal crime to possess a gun within a certain distance from a school. The Court concluded that the banning of firearms in local schools was a state police power and, therefore, more appropriately handled by state governments. The significance of this decision, however, remains to be seen. After the Court struck down the law in *Lopez,* Congress simply turned around and reenacted the same law, adding a finding of fact that gun possession in schools affected economic productivity by making it more difficult for students to obtain an education.

Five years after the *Lopez* case was decided, the U.S. Supreme Court invalidated another statute in *United States v. Morrison*[8] on the same grounds. In that case, the Court struck down the Violence Against Women Act (VAWA), which gave victims of gender-motivated violence the right to sue their abusers for money damages in federal court. Again, however, Congress brushed aside the Court's ruling and simply reauthorized the law, making exhaustive findings of fact that detailed the cumulative economic effect of gender-motivated crimes.

The Dormant Commerce Clause

May states regulate commerce that crosses into their state borders? Yes and no. The U.S. Supreme Court has inferred from the Commerce Clause significant restrictions on the police power of the states. Specifically, the Supreme Court has ruled that the mere existence of congressional commerce powers prohibits the states from *discriminating* against or *unduly burdening* interstate commerce.

As a general rule, a state is free to regulate commerce so long as (1) the state does not discriminate against or impose an undue burden on out-of-state businesses and (2) the state law promotes a *legitimate* objective, such as health, safety, or welfare. It is important to note that economic protectionism—state laws that promote the economic interest of its own citizens at the expense of out-of-state citizens—is not a legitimate state objective.

Suppose, for example, that in order to protect its local beef industry, the Texas state legislature imposes an inspection requirement and fee on all non-Texas-bred beef sold within Texas. The state legislature justifies this inspection and fee on the basis that the law is protecting the health of it citizens. A court would likely strike down the law because it discriminates against out-of-state ranchers. Moreover, the inspection fee and the inspection process could be viewed as imposing unreasonable burdens on interstate commerce.

LO 2-6

Describe constitutional restrictions on state regulation of commerce in the business environment.

---

[7]514 U.S. 549 (1995).
[8]529 U.S. 598 (2000).

> ## LEGAL/ETHICAL REFLECTION AND DISCUSSION
>
> In *Gonzalez v. Raich,* Justice Stevens, in the majority decision, wrote, "[O]ur cases have taught us that there are some unscrupulous physicians who overprescribe when it is sufficiently profitable to do so." He also wrote, "The likelihood that all such production (of marijuana) will promptly terminate when patients recover or will precisely match the patients' medical needs during their convalescence seems remote."
>
> Should such judicial speculation ever be part of a court's decision-making process?

LO 2-7

Explain why Congress's tax and spend powers are an independent source of federal power.

TAX AND SPEND POWERS

Article I, Section 8, Clause 1 of the Constitution states:

> The Congress shall have the Power To lay and collect Taxes, Duties, Imposts and Excises, to pay the Debts and provide for the common Defence and general Welfare of the United States; but all Duties, Imposts and Excises shall be uniform throughout the United States[.]

Congress thus has the textual power to impose taxes and to spend federal tax revenues in any way that promotes the common defense and general welfare of the United States. Further, the U.S. Supreme Court has, for the most part, been highly deferential to Congress in terms of what constitutes "general welfare" and under what circumstances Congress may exercise its taxing power and its decision-making power in allocating government spending.

Most importantly, because the power to tax is an enumerated power of Congress (i.e., because this power is granted to Congress in the text of the Constitution), it is an independent source of federal authority. As a result, the U.S. Supreme Court has ruled on several occasions that Congress may tax activities or property that it might not otherwise be authorized to regulate directly under any of its enumerated legislative powers.

By way of example, in perhaps the most far-reaching taxing power case ever decided, the U.S. Supreme Court ruled in *National Federation of Independent Business v. Sebelius,*[9] that the *individual mandate* contained in the Affordable Care Act (a requirement that individuals purchase health insurance) could be sustained as a tax, even though this requirement itself was outside of Congress's power to regulate commerce. Writing for five members of the Court, Chief Justice Roberts upheld the individual mandate under the general Article I power of Congress to impose taxes.

Specifically, the Court held that even though proponents of the Act consistently characterized the individual mandate as a penalty and not a tax, the penalty still operated as a tax. The Court reasoned that failure to purchase health insurance required a payment to the IRS and that individuals thus had the choice under the Act of paying a tax to the IRS instead of purchasing insurance. The Court also reaffirmed that Congress may seek to achieve regulatory goals through its taxing power that it might not be able to achieve under its other Article I powers. For their part, Justices Kennedy, Alito, Scalia, and Thomas dissented, arguing that the taxing power could not sustain the individual mandate because Congress lacked the power to impose the mandate in the first place.

Necessary and Proper Clause

Congress may also place *conditions* on the use of federal money by the states in order to achieve some national public policy objective. Congress generally cites the Necessary and Proper Clause as authorization to set conditions on federal spending. This ability to set

---
[9]567 U.S. 1 (2012).

conditions on the use of federal money has been a controversial method of congressional regulation because it falls outside the areas of *traditional* regulation. Also, state legislatures have objected to this type of regulation as a backdoor method for imposing laws on states that are outside Congress's enumerated powers. The U.S. Supreme Court, however, has generally upheld federal spending conditions that are tied to individual states' passing of certain laws that carry out congressionally established goals.

In *South Dakota v. Dole*,[10] for example, the Court deferred to Congress's ability to attach spending conditions on federal highway funds distributed to the states for repairing and building highways. Specifically, Congress had conditioned its transportation spending to a state's legal drinking age.[11] Unless a state passed a law to raise the legal drinking age to 21 by a certain date, it would lose 5 percent of its allotted highway funding from the federal government.

South Dakota and other states challenged the law as an unconstitutional intrusion by Congress into state affairs. The Court, however, sided with Congress, ruling that the drinking-age condition is constitutionally permissible under Congress's spending authority so long as the condition itself is not a violation of individual constitutional rights.

In upholding the federal law, the Court announced a four-part test for evaluating the constitutionality of conditions attached to federal spending programs: (1) the spending power must be exercised in pursuit of the general welfare, (2) grant conditions must be clearly stated, (3) the conditions must be related to a federal interest in the national program or project, and (4) the spending power cannot be used to induce states to do things that would themselves be unconstitutional. This case signaled an important victory for Congress, which now regularly uses spending conditions as a form of regulation for individuals and businesses.

 Self-Check Source of Constitutional Authority

What is the constitutional source of authority for each of the following laws?

1. A federal statute that makes it more difficult for businesses to qualify for protection under bankruptcy laws.
2. An increase in the federal corporate income tax.
3. A federal statute that adds criminal penalties for patent infringement.
4. A federal statute creating an agency to regulate ground shipping between states.
5. A federal statute that requires that 25 percent of federal government construction contracts be awarded to companies that are women- or minority-owned enterprises.

Answers to this Self-Check are provided at the end of the chapter.

CONCEPT SUMMARY *Structure and Nature of the Constitution: Federal Powers*

- Under the federal system used by the United States, the federal government has only limited powers to regulate individuals and businesses.
- These federal powers are specifically enumerated in the Constitution and are supposed to be limited in scope.

(continued)

---

[10]483 U.S. 203 (1987).

[11]At that time, 19 states permitted consumption of some or all alcoholic beverages before the age of 21.

- The enumerated powers of the federal legislative branch (Congress) include (1) the power to regulate commerce; (2) the power to tax and spend; (3) the power to regulate bankruptcy, patents, and copyrights; and (4) a general implied authority to make all laws necessary for carrying out its enumerated powers.
- The president is granted the power to (1) carry out laws made by Congress, (2) be the commander in chief of the armed forces, (3) enter into treaties and carry out foreign policy, and (4) appoint federal officers and judges.
- Federal courts are authorized to decide cases and controversies falling within federal jurisdiction.
- Congress's broadest power is derived from the Commerce Clause.
- Under the Commerce Clause, Congress has the authority to regulate (1) channels of interstate commerce such as railways and highways; (2) the instrumentalities of interstate commerce such as vehicles used in shipping; (3) the articles moving in interstate commerce; and (4) any activity that has substantial economic effect on interstate commerce, including activities that are not commercial in nature.
- The U.S. Constitution is composed of a preamble, seven articles, and 27 amendments, the first 10 of which are called the Bill of Rights.
- The first three articles of the Constitution establish a three-part system of government with three coequal branches: the legislative branch, the executive branch, and the judicial branch.
- This three-part structure is designed so that each of the branches exercises its respective powers to ensure that the other branches do not exceed their authority under the Constitution (referred to as *separation of powers* or a system of *checks and balances*).
- Under the Supremacy Clause, federal laws preempt (override) any conflicting state laws.
- Congress has the power to tax the citizenry and spend the federal government's money in any way that promotes the common defense and general welfare.

CONSTITUTIONAL PROTECTIONS

LO 2-8

Describe the main protections in the First Amendment and explain how they apply in the business environment.

In addition to creating the structure of the federal government and granting each branch of the federal government certain enumerated and limited powers, the Constitution also confers on persons and businesses many constitutional rights. Most of these rights are contained in the first 10 amendments to the Constitution (the Bill of Rights). From a business perspective, however, it is important to note that corporations and other business entities do *not* always receive the same level of constitutional protection as individuals.

The Bill of Rights and Business

The Bill of Rights contains many of the rights common in the American vernacular. Among these rights are freedom of speech, the press, religion, and expression (First Amendment); the right to keep and bear arms (Second Amendment); freedom from unreasonable government-conducted searches and seizures (Fourth Amendment); rights against self-incrimination and to a speedy jury trial by our peers (Fifth and Sixth Amendments); right to a jury trial in civil cases (Seventh Amendment); and freedom from cruel and unusual punishment (Eighth Amendment). Although all of these rights are important, the coverage in this textbook will focus on the Bill of Rights provisions that relate directly to business issues.

The First Amendment

The First Amendment begins with the words "Congress shall make no law" and then articulates several specific protections against government encroachment in the areas of religion, press, speech, assembly, and petition of grievances. The introductory phrase demonstrates that the framers originally intended the Constitution to function as a *limit* on the federal government. It was not until the passage of the Fourteenth Amendment in 1868 that these limitations were extended to state governments as well. In addition, in controversial cases like *Citizens United* and *Masterpiece Cakeshop* (the gay wedding cake case), the U.S. Supreme Court has broadened First Amendment protections for business owners in the area of free speech. We shall examine these leading cases below.

Limits on Free Speech   Although the U.S. Supreme Court has given broad protections to speech that involves political expression, the First Amendment is by no means absolute. Justice Oliver Wendell Holmes famously wrote that the First Amendment does not protect someone who falsely yells "Fire!" in a crowded theater. Courts have ruled that the government may place reasonable restrictions on the time, place, and manner of political expression in cases, for example, where public safety may be threatened. Likewise, the tort of defamation, a restriction on speech discussed in Chapter 9, "Torts and Products Liability," is another limitation on freedom of speech relevant to business.

Also, what happens when the speech and religion rights of business owners conflict with other compelling constitutional rights, such as the principle of equal protection of law? In Case 2.4, the gay wedding cake case, the Supreme Court tries to strike a balance between the speech rights of a small business owner and the rights of gays and lesbians to purchase goods and services free of discrimination.

CASE 2.4 Masterpiece Cakeshop, Ltd. v. Colorado Civil Rights Commission, 138 S. Ct. 1719 (2018)

FACT SUMMARY   Jack Phillips owns and operates a small bakery called Masterpiece Cakeshop, which is located in Lakewood, Colorado. In 2012 a gay couple, David Mullins and Charlie Craig, visited Masterpiece Cakeshop to order a wedding cake. The two men were going to be married in Massachusetts, which had recently legalized gay marriage, and they wanted to purchase a wedding cake for a reception to be held in Colorado. The baker, however, turned them down, saying that same-sex marriage was in conflict with his religious faith. The gay couple felt humiliated by the baker's refusal to serve them, so they filed a complaint with Colorado's Civil Rights Commission, saying that Mr. Phillips had violated a state law barring discrimination based on sexual orientation. The gay couple won before the state civil rights commission and in the state courts, but the baker appealed to the U.S. Supreme Court.

SYNOPSIS OF DECISION AND OPINION   The Supreme Court ruled in favor of the baker, but the Court's decision was a narrow one, leaving open the larger question of whether a business can discriminate against gays and lesbians based on rights protected by the First Amendment. Instead, the Court focused on the lack of neutrality in the initial proceedings before the Colorado Civil Rights Commission, which had ruled against the baker because some members of the panel had allegedly acted with "clear and impermissible hostility" to the baker's sincere religious beliefs.

WORDS OF THE COURT: Sincere Religious Beliefs   "[The baker] was entitled to a neutral decisionmaker who would give full and fair consideration to his religious objection . . . [but] the outcome of cases like this in other circumstances must

(continued)

await further elaboration in the courts, all in the context of recognizing that these disputes must be resolved with tolerance, without undue disrespect to sincere religious beliefs, and without subjecting gay persons to indignities when they seek goods and services in an open market."

Case Questions

1. Although the Supreme Court rendered a narrow ad hoc decision, why is *Masterpiece Cakeshop* such an important case?

2. Why do you think the Supreme Court decided to avoid or sidestep the larger question posed by this case?

3. *Focus on Critical Thinking:* The Colorado Court of Appeals had ruled that the baker's free speech and religious rights had not been violated because the baker was still free to say what he liked about same-sex marriage in other settings. Are you persuaded by this reasoning? Why or why not?

Commercial Speech The most common form of commercial speech—ways in which business entities communicate with the public—is *advertising* through print, television, radio, and the Internet. Traditionally, advertising has received little or no First Amendment protection, but the Supreme Court has gradually increased the constitutional protections for advertising.

In *Virginia State Board of Pharmacy v. Virginia Citizens Consumer Council*,[12] the U.S. Supreme Court held that purely commercial speech (speech with no political implications whatsoever) was entitled to partial First Amendment protection so long as the speech was truthful and concerned a lawful activity. In the *Virginia* case, the Court struck down a state law that prohibited pharmacists from advertising prices for prescription drugs. The Court rejected the state's contention that it had a substantial interest in ensuring that cut-rate prices that may be created by competition among pharmacies would not result in substandard service. Given that the information banned by the statute was limiting the free flow of information to consumers, the Court held that such regulation violated the First Amendment.

Four years after the *Virginia* case, the Court expanded its analytical framework for deciding when regulations of commercial speech are constitutional. Specifically, in *Central Hudson Gas v. Public Service Commission*,[13] the Court created a four-part test that subjects government restrictions on commercial speech to a form of intermediate-level scrutiny:

- *Part One:* So long as the commercial speech concerns lawful activities and is not misleading, the speech qualifies for protection under the First Amendment. If the speech is entitled to protection, then the government's regulation must pass the final three parts of the *Central Hudson* test in order for the restriction to be lawful.

- *Part Two:* The government must show that it has a *substantial government interest* in regulating the speech.

- *Part Three:* The government must demonstrate that the restriction *directly advances* the government's interest.

- *Part Four:* The government's restriction must be *not more extensive* than necessary (not too broad) to achieve the government's asserted interest.

In Case 2.5, a federal appellate court applies the *Central Hudson* framework to a regulation compelling speech by the tobacco industry.

---

[12] 425 U.S. 748 (1976).
[13] 447 U.S. 557 (1980).

CASE 2.5 R.J. Reynolds Tobacco Company v. Food and Drug Administration, 696 F.3d 1205 (D.C. Cir. 2012)

FACT SUMMARY The Family Smoking Prevention and Tobacco Control Act, passed in 2009, directed the secretary of the U.S. Department of Health and Human Services to issue regulations requiring that all cigarette packages manufactured or sold in the United States bear one of nine new textual warnings, as well as "color graphics depicting the negative health consequences of smoking." The Food and Drug Administration (FDA) initiated a rulemaking proceeding through which it selected the nine images that would accompany the statutorily prescribed warnings. Among those proposed by the FDA were images of a man exhaling cigarette smoke through a tracheotomy hole in his throat and a pair of diseased lungs next to a pair of healthy lungs. R.J. Reynolds and four other tobacco companies (RJR) challenged the rule, arguing that it would infringe on their commercial speech rights under the First Amendment. The trial court ruled in favor of RJR and the FDA appealed.

SYNOPSIS OF DECISION AND OPINION The U.S. Court of Appeals for the District of Columbia upheld the trial court's decision in favor of RJR. The court applied the *Central Hudson* test and ruled that the FDA had failed to supply any evidence that the rule, which restricted commercial speech, directly advanced a substantial government interest. The court ruled that the labels were not purely factual because they did not convey any warning information or offer any information about the impact of smoking. Rather, the images were intended to generate emotional responses. Therefore, the FDA could not meet its burden under the *Central Hudson* test with respect to how the graphic warnings directly advanced the government's interest.

WORDS OF THE COURT: Applying the *Central Hudson* Test "Under *Central Hudson*, the government must first show that its asserted interest is 'substantial.' If so, the Court must determine 'whether the regulation directly advances the governmental interest asserted, and whether it is not more extensive than is necessary to serve that interest.' . . . FDA has not provided a shred of evidence—much less the 'substantial evidence' required . . . showing that the graphic warnings will 'directly advance' its interest in reducing the number of Americans who smoke. FDA makes much of the 'international consensus' surrounding the effectiveness of large graphic warnings, but offers no evidence showing that such warnings have *directly caused* a material decrease in smoking rates in any of the countries that now require them."

Case Questions

1. Commercial speech is generally analyzed under intermediate-level scrutiny rather than under strict scrutiny. Do you think it is appropriate to treat commercial advertising differently than other forms of speech? Why or why not?
2. What did the FDA need to prove in order to prevail in this case?
3. *Focus on Critical Thinking:* Do professional athletes have a constitutional right to kneel during the national anthem? Why or why not?

Advertising and Obscenity Regulation Sometimes commercial speech runs afoul of governmental attempts to ban or regulate materials it deems obscene. However, obscenity regulation of commercial speech is subject to the same scrutiny as any other government regulation of commercial speech. For example, a federal appellate court ruled that a state agency's decision to effectively prohibit a corporation's use of a certain label on its beer products, which the agency deemed offensive, violated the business owner's commercial speech rights. In that case, *Bad Frog Brewery, Inc. v. N.Y. State Liquor Authority*,[14] the U.S. Court of Appeals for the Second Circuit held that the labels on the brewery's beer

---

[14]134 F.3d 87 (2d Cir. 1998).

A sign for a First Amendment Area in the Muir Woods National Monument park in Mill Valley, California. Ramin Talaie/Corbis/Getty Images

bottles, which depicted a cartoon frog making a vulgar gesture, were protected commercial speech under the First Amendment. In particular, the court ruled that the New York State Liquor Authority failed to demonstrate the agency's asserted interest of protecting children from vulgarity when it denied Bad Frog's application to use the labels in New York on the basis that the labels were offensive. Because the labels were not misleading and did not concern an unlawful activity, the labels were a protected form of commercial speech and any government regulation must conform with the requirements set out in the four-part *Central Hudson* case. Ruling in favor of Bad Frog, the court remarked that a state must demonstrate that its commercial speech limitation is part of a substantial effort to advance a valid state interest, "not merely the removal of a few grains of offensive sand from the beach of vulgarity."

Political Speech by Corporations

Another form of commercial speech occurs when corporations and other business entities fund political speech or engage in corporate advocacy of a particular candidate or political issue. May the government regulate such commercial speech under the same standards as the *Central Hudson* case? Generally, political speech by corporations is fully protected by the First Amendment.

In *First National Bank of Boston v. Bellotti*,[15] the U.S. Supreme Court created a new level of First Amendment protection for corporations engaged in *political* speech. Specifically, the Supreme Court struck down a Massachusetts state statute that prohibited corporations from using corporate assets to fund expenditures related to "influencing or affecting the vote on any question submitted to the voters" (known as a *ballot proposition*).[16] Although the Court recognized that some constitutional rights are not afforded to corporations, the Court ruled that freedom of corporate political speech is fully protected and that any attempt to regulate political speech by corporations would be subject to *strict scrutiny*. The Court also held that a corporation's freedom of speech is not limited to matters materially affecting its business. Rather, a business has a constitutionally protected right to communicate about any political matter consistent with the goal of the First Amendment: the free flow of information and debate. For the first time, the Court recognized that speech that is within the protection of the First Amendment does not lose its protection simply because the speaker is a corporation.

In Case 2.6, a case that attracted significant media and public attention, the U.S. Supreme Court considers whether the government may impose limits on political spending by corporations in *candidate elections*.

Legal Speak >))

Ballot Proposition
A question put to the voters during a state election to decide issues such as whether the state should impose a new income tax or whether the state should allow marijuana to be used for medicinal purposes. In some states, this is known as a *ballot initiative* or a *referendum*.

KEY POINT

Commercial speech in the form of advertising has partial First Amendment protection (i.e., is subject to intermediate-level scrutiny). Corporate *political* speech, however, has full First Amendment protection (i.e., is subject to strict scrutiny) under *Bellotti* and *Citizens United*.

---

[15] 435 U.S. 765 (1978).

[16] Also known in certain states as a *referendum* or *ballot initiative*.

CASE 2.6 Citizens United v. Federal Election Commission, 558 U.S. 310 (2010)

FACT SUMMARY In an attempt to regulate big money campaign contributions by corporations and labor unions in federal elections, Congress enacted the Bipartisan Campaign Reform Act in 2002 (commonly referred to as the "McCain-Feingold Act"), which imposed a wide variety of restrictions on "electioneering communications," including an outright ban on issue advocacy advertising or issue ads paid for by corporations and labor unions. Citizens United, a conservative nonprofit corporation, produced a 90-minute documentary called *Hillary: The Movie,* which criticized then-Senator Hillary Clinton and questioned her fitness for office. (Figure 2.1 depicts the poster art that Citizens United used to promote its political documentary.) The group planned to show the film on cable TV during the upcoming 2008 Democratic presidential primaries. Before releasing the film, Citizens United brought an action in the U.S. District Court for the District of Columbia against the Federal Election Commission (FEC), the agency in charge of enforcing federal election law. The U.S. district court ruled in favor of the FEC, and Citizens United appealed to the U.S. Supreme Court, arguing that the campaign reform finance law violated the First Amendment on its face and when applied to *Hillary: The Movie* and to the ads promoting the film.

SYNOPSIS OF DECISION AND OPINION The U.S. Supreme Court reversed the lower court and ruled in favor of Citizens United by a 5-4 vote. The Court ruled that political spending is a form of protected speech under the First Amendment and that the government may not prevent corporations or labor unions from spending money to support or denounce individual candidates in elections. Although this First Amendment right is not absolute—Congress may continue to restrict corporations from donating money directly to candidates—Congress may not prevent corporations from seeking to persuade the voting public through other means, including TV ads.

WORDS OF THE COURT: Protected Speech "The Court has recognized that First Amendment protection extends to corporations. . . . When Government seeks to use its full power, including the criminal law, to command where a person may get his or her information or what distrusted source he or she may not hear, it uses censorship to control thought. This is unlawful. The First Amendment confirms the freedom to think for ourselves. . . . Modern day movies, television comedies, or skits on Youtube.com might portray public officials or public policies in unflattering ways. Yet if a covered transmission during the blackout period creates the background for candidate endorsement or opposition, a felony occurs solely because a corporation, other than an exempt media corporation, has made the 'purchase, payment, distribution, loan, advance, deposit, or gift of money or anything of value' in order to engage in political speech. Speech would be suppressed in the realm where its necessity is most evident: in the public dialogue preceding a real election. Governments are often hostile to speech, but under our law and our tradition it seems stranger than fiction for our Government to make this political speech a crime. Yet this is the statute's purpose and design."

Case Questions

1. What if Citizens United had published a book criticizing Hillary Clinton? Does the McCain-Feingold Act apply to the publication of books?
2. Should corporations have constitutional rights?
3. *Focus on Critical Thinking:* A week after the U.S. Supreme Court announced its decision in the *Citizens United* case, President Obama publicly criticized the Court's decision in his annual State of the Union speech. (You can check out President Obama's criticism of the *Citizens United* decision here: https://www.youtube.com/watch?v=deGg41IiWwU.) Do you think President Obama's critique is correct or misguided?

| FIGURE 2.1 | *Hillary: The Movie* |

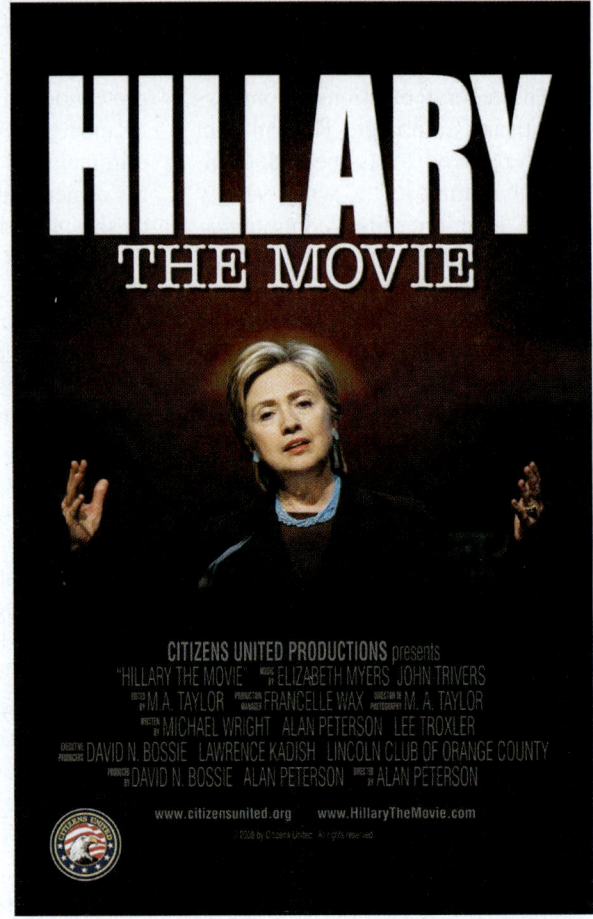

Poster for "Hillary: The Movie, a Citizens United Production."
Everett Collection, Inc./Alamy

The controversial ruling in the *Citizens United* case does not overturn the existing limits imposed by law on campaign contributions or the existing prohibition of direct corporate contributions to a candidate. These limits remain intact. Rather, the Supreme Court's ruling in *Citizens United* applies to *independent business expenditures* on political speech.

The Fourth Amendment

The **Fourth Amendment** of the U.S. Constitution states:

> The right of the people to be secure in their persons, houses, papers, and effects, against unreasonable searches and seizures, shall not be violated, and no Warrants shall issue, but upon probable cause, supported by Oath or affirmation, and particularly describing the place to be searched, and the persons or things to be seized.

Generally speaking, a search or seizure conducted by the government is illegal without a warrant from a judge or magistrate. Although the warrant requirement is most often thought of in the context of law enforcement, the Fourth Amendment covers all government agents.

LO 2-9

Describe the main protections in the Fourth Amendment and explain how they apply in the business environment.

To obtain a warrant, the government must first demonstrate **probable cause** to a judge or a magistrate that the proposed search or seizure is justified under the law. The judge or magistrate must then consider the *totality of circumstances* and determine whether to issue the warrant. The Fourth Amendment is generally enforced by courts under the Exclusionary Rule. Under the Exclusionary Rule, any evidence obtained in violation of the Fourth Amendment may be excluded from evidence in a criminal prosecution.

Exceptions Courts, however, have created many exceptions to the warrant requirement. The government, for example, does not need a warrant if there are "exigent circumstances" and if it is acting with probable cause and obtaining a warrant is impractical. Other well-established exceptions to the warrant requirement include consensual searches, searches incident to a valid arrest, seizures of items in plain view, and brief investigatory stops. Investigatory stops must be temporary and the questioning during the stop must be for a limited purpose and conducted in a manner necessary to fulfill the purpose.

Moreover, not every search or seizure raises a Fourth Amendment issue. The Fourth Amendment only protects against searches and seizures *conducted by the government* or pursuant to governmental direction. Surveillance and investigatory actions taken by private persons, such as private investigators, suspicious spouses, or nosy neighbors, are not governed by the Fourth Amendment.

Also, the Fourth Amendment does not apply against governmental action unless the target of the search can show that he or she has a reasonable expectation of privacy in the place to be searched or the thing to be seized. The U.S. Supreme Court has explained that what "a person knowingly exposes to the public, even in his own home or office, is not a subject of Fourth Amendment protection. . . ." But what one seeks to preserve as private, even in an area accessible to the public, may be constitutionally protected.

Applying this principle, the Court has ruled that individuals generally maintain a reasonable expectation of privacy in their bodies, clothing, and personal belongings. Likewise, homeowners possess a privacy interest that extends inside their homes and in the curtilage immediately surrounding the outside of their homes, but not in the "open fields" and "wooded areas" extending beyond the curtilage. Automobile owners have a reasonable expectation of privacy in the cars they own and drive, though the expectation of privacy is less than a homeowner's privacy interest in his or her home.

A business owner's expectation of privacy in commercial property is less than the privacy interest afforded to a private homeowner and is particularly attenuated in commercial property used in "closely regulated" industries, such as airports, railroads, restaurants, and liquor establishments, where business premises may be subject to regular administrative searches by state or federal agencies for the purpose of checking compliance with health, safety, or security regulations.

Public records, published phone numbers, and other matters readily accessible to the general public enjoy no expectation of privacy. Similarly, the Court has said that individuals do not possess an expectation of privacy in their personal characteristics. Thus, the police may require individuals to give handwriting samples and voice exemplars—as well as hair, blood, DNA, and fingerprint samples—without complying with the Fourth Amendment's warrant requirement.

Reasonableness Requirement With or without a warrant, searches and seizures conducted by the government must be reasonable. Generally speaking, a search or seizure conducted with a warrant is presumed reasonable, while warrantless searches and seizures are presumed unreasonable. In cases of warrantless searches and seizures, courts will try to balance the degree of intrusion on the individual's privacy with the need to promote governmental interests. Courts will examine the *totality of the circumstances* to determine if such a warrantless search or seizure was reasonable or justified.

Searches and Seizures The courts must determine what constitutes a *search* or a *seizure* under the Fourth Amendment.

Physical Searches A search occurs when a governmental employee or an agent of the government violates an individual's reasonable expectation of privacy. A dog-sniff inspection, for example, is invalid if the inspection violates one's reasonable expectation of privacy. Electronic surveillance is also considered a search under the Fourth Amendment.

Physical Seizures of Persons A seizure of a person, within the meaning of the Fourth Amendment, occurs when a person is not free to ignore the police and leave at will. Specifically, two elements must be present to constitute a seizure of a person. First, there must be a show of authority by the police officer or government agent. The presence of handcuffs or weapons, the use of forceful language, and physical contact are each a strong indicator of such authority. Second, the person being seized must submit to the authority. Thus, an individual who ignores an officer's request and walks away has not been seized for Fourth Amendment purposes.

Physical Seizures of Property A seizure of private property, within the meaning of the Fourth Amendment, occurs when there is some meaningful interference with an individual's possessory interests in the property, but in some circumstances, warrantless seizures of objects in plain view may not constitute seizures. Also, when executing a search warrant, an officer might be able to seize an item observed in plain view even if it is not specified in the warrant.

Electronic Searches and Seizures In recent years, the applicability of the Fourth Amendment to electronic searches and seizures has generated a significant amount of litigation and has received much attention from the courts. (See Case 2.7, *United States v. Jones*.) Many electronic search cases involve determining whether law enforcement can search a company-owned computer that an employee uses to conduct business. Although the case law is split, the majority of courts have held that employees do not have a legitimate expectation of privacy to information stored on a company-owned computer. In a recent case, for example, the U.S. Supreme Court did not find a reasonable expectation to privacy for personal text messages sent and received on an employer-owned pager.

CASE 2.7 United States v. Jones, 565 U.S. 400 (2012)

FACT SUMMARY Antoine Jones was the owner of the Levels Nightclub in Washington, D.C. The police suspected Jones of drug trafficking and asked a judge for a search warrant to attach a global positioning system (GPS) tracking device to the underside of Jones's Jeep. The judge granted the warrant, but the police exceeded the scope of the warrant in both geography and length of time. Using evidence obtained from the GPS device, Jones was eventually charged and convicted of participating in a criminal conspiracy. Jones appealed his conviction, arguing that 24-hour surveillance through a GPS tracker violates the Fourth Amendment's right against unreasonable search and seizure. The U.S. Court of Appeals for the District of Columbia overturned Jones's conviction, holding that the police action was an unlawful search because it violated Jones's reasonable expectation of privacy. The government appealed to the U.S. Supreme Court.

(continued)

SYNOPSIS OF DECISION AND OPINION The U.S. Supreme Court held that installing a GPS tracking device on a vehicle and then using the device to monitor the vehicle's movements constitutes a search under the Fourth Amendment. However, although the Court voted unanimously that placing a GPS device on a suspect's car is a search, the justices were split 5-4 regarding the fundamental reasons or rationale in support of the Court's ultimate conclusion. The majority held that by physically installing a GPS device on Jones's car, the police had committed a trespass against Jones's personal effects.

WORDS OF THE COURT: Physical Intrusions
"The Fourth Amendment provides in relevant part that '[t]he right of the people to be secure in their persons, houses, papers, and effects, against unreasonable searches and seizures, shall not be violated.' It is beyond dispute that a vehicle is an 'effect' as that term is used in the Amendment. . . . We hold that the Government's installation of a GPS device on a target's vehicle, and its use of that device to monitor the vehicle's movements, constitutes a 'search.' . . . It is important to be clear about what occurred in this case: The Government physically occupied private property for the purpose of obtaining information. We have no doubt that such a physical intrusion would have been considered a 'search' within the meaning of the Fourth Amendment when it was adopted. . . . The text of the Fourth Amendment reflects its close connection to property, since otherwise it would have referred simply to 'the right of the people to be secure against unreasonable searches and seizures'; the phrase 'in their persons, houses, papers, and effects' would have been superfluous."

Case Questions
1. In addition to vehicles, can you think of any other examples of personal effects that are protected under the Fourth Amendment? Does one have a reasonable expectation of privacy when driving or walking in plain view along public roads or sidewalks?
2. What if Jones had been driving a stolen vehicle? Would the placement of a GPS device on a stolen vehicle still constitute a search?
3. *Focus on Critical Thinking:* What if the police had monitored Jones's personal movements by operating a miniature unmanned aerial vehicle in public airspace (i.e., a small drone equipped with a high-resolution camera)? Would the police still need a warrant under this hypothetical scenario?

Postscript: The USA PATRIOT Act Following the September 11, 2001, terrorist attacks on the World Trade Center and the Pentagon, Congress enacted the "Uniting and Strengthening America by Providing Appropriate Tools Required to Intercept and Obstruct Terrorism Act" (called the *USA PATRIOT Act*). In brief, this legislation increases the ability of law enforcement agencies to search e-mail and telephonic communications as well as medical, financial, and library records.

One provision of the USA PATRIOT Act permits law enforcement to obtain access to stored voicemails by obtaining a basic search warrant rather than a surveillance warrant. Obtaining a search warrant requires a much lower evidentiary showing. In addition, a highly controversial provision of the USA PATRIOT Act includes permission for law enforcement to use so-called *sneak-and-peak* warrants. A sneak-and-peak warrant is a special warrant in which law enforcement can delay notifying the property owner about the warrant's issuance until after the search or seizure is conducted.

Section 505 of the USA PATRIOT Act also expanded the controversial use of National Security Letters. In brief, a National Security Letter is a secret administrative subpoena that requires certain persons, groups, organizations, or companies to provide documents or records about certain persons. These documents typically involve private telephone, e-mail, and financial records. A National Security Letter also imposes a *gag order,* meaning that the person or persons who receive the secret letter/subpoena may not disclose the existence of the National Security Letter.

Under the USA PATRIOT Act, law enforcement can use National Security Letters to investigate U.S. citizens, even when law enforcement does not think the individual under investigation has committed a crime. The Department of Homeland Security (DHS) and the Federal Bureau of Investigation (FBI) have used National Security Letters frequently. By issuing a National Security Letter, DHS, the FBI, and other governmental agencies are not required to first obtain a warrant or court order before conducting searches of records of persons under investigation.

DUE PROCESS PROTECTIONS

LO 2-10

Identify limits imposed on government power by the Due Process and Equal Protection clauses of the Constitution.

Due Process

Due process of law is a constitutional guarantee that is designed to protect both individuals and business firms from arbitrary decision making by the government. The concept of due process traces its origins to the Magna Carta, or "Great Charter," of 1215 A.D., which obligated the King of England to act in accordance with "the law of the land."

Today, this fundamental protection appears twice in the U.S. Constitution: in the **Due Process Clause** of the Fifth and Fourteenth Amendments, which prohibits the government from depriving persons of their life, liberty, or property in an arbitrary way. (The Fifth Amendment applies to the federal government, while the Fourteenth Amendment, which was enacted after the Civil War, applies to state governments.)

In brief, **due process of law** has two dimensions: one is procedural; the other is substantive. Procedural due process imposes certain *procedural* requirements on federal and state governments when they impair life, liberty, or property. At a minimum, procedural due process requires the government to give adequate notice, a fair and neutral hearing, and an opportunity to present evidence before any official action is taken that would deprive the life, liberty, or property of an individual or a business firm.

Substantive due process, by contrast, limits the *substantive* police power of the states to restrict individual liberty. These substantive due process rights require that laws enacted by the government be published for public inspection and be specific enough that a reasonable person would understand how the law applies. As a result, laws that are too vague or overly broad are unconstitutional under the substantive due process doctrine.

Many famous Supreme Court cases often have a due process aspect to them. By way of example, notice how the Supreme Court's narrow decision in Case 2.4, *Masterpiece Cakeshop, Ltd. v. Colorado Civil Rights Commission,* can be viewed in light of procedural due process. In addition, notice too the direct connection between due process and minors' free speech rights in Case 2.2, *Brown v. Entertainment Merchants Association.* Both cases are discussed earlier in this chapter.

The Magna Carta. David M. Rubenstein Collection/National Archives and Records Administration

Equal Protection

The Equal Protection Clause is part of the Fourteenth Amendment and prohibits state governments from denying their citizens equal protection of the laws.[17] Fundamentally, equal protection requires the government to treat people who are similarly situated equally. This requirement, however, does not mean that everyone must be

---

[17]Although the direct text of the clause applies to state governments, the U.S. Supreme Court has ruled that the federal government is also bound by the same rules of equal protection via the Fifth Amendment.

treated exactly the same. The government may create constitutionally permissive *categories* and may treat each category differently, but persons within each category must be treated the same.

For example, suppose that you attend a state college or university. Do all of the students pay the same tuition? Most likely the answer is no. In-state residents generally pay less tuition than out-of-state students because this difference can be justified by the fact that in-state students (or their parents) pay taxes that help support the school while out-of-state students' tax revenues stay in their home states. Accordingly, this classification between in-state and out-of-state students is permissible. A state college or university cannot, however, decide to charge different rates based on the students' different home states (one rate for Delaware, a second for California, a third for Iowa, etc.). Also, charging different rates based on race, religion, or national origin would not be constitutionally valid regardless of a student's state of residence.

Recall from our discussion earlier in this chapter that courts use a variety of levels of judicial review in constitutional cases: strict scrutiny, intermediate-level scrutiny, and rational basis review. When a government action (such as enacting a statute or enforcing a law or regulation) is based on a suspect classification, or if the action impairs a fundamental right protected in the Constitution, courts will apply the *strict scrutiny* standard of judicial review.

For example, courts have held that any government action based on race or national origin is automatically considered a *suspect* classification, thus triggering strict scrutiny. Courts have also held that government actions restricting the right to vote, access to the courts, or the right to travel from state to state are subject to the strict scrutiny standard as well.

Semi-suspect (also called *quasi-suspect*) classifications, by contrast, trigger so-called intermediate-level scrutiny. Courts have used this intermediate standard of review when government actions are based on gender or birth status (e.g., children born to unwed mothers). Lastly, recall from earlier in this chapter that economic or tax regulations are judged under the rational basis standard.

CONCEPT SUMMARY Constitutional Protections

- The Bill of Rights contains protections for citizens from unlawful or repressive acts by the government.
- Corporations and other business entities do not always receive the same level of constitutional protections as individuals.
- Traditionally, advertising had little or no First Amendment protection; however, the Supreme Court has gradually increased the constitutional protections related to advertising, allowing purely commercial speech to have partial First Amendment protection so long as it is truthful.
- Corporate *political* speech has full First Amendment protection.
- The Fourth Amendment prohibits unreasonable searches by the government.
- The Due Process Clause of the Fifth and Fourteenth Amendments protects individuals from being deprived of "life, liberty, or property" without due process of law.
- The right to equal protection does not necessarily mean that everyone must be treated exactly the same.

POSTSCRIPT: THE RIGHT TO PRIVACY

Although not explicitly mentioned in the Constitution, the right to *privacy* plays a central role in constitutional law. The U.S. Supreme Court formally recognized a constitutional right to privacy in 1965 in the landmark case of *Griswold v. Connecticut*.[18] This case involved a challenge to a state statute that criminalized (1) the use of contraceptives and (2) aiding or counseling others in their use. Dr. Griswold was convicted under this state statute for counseling married couples in the use of contraceptives at a local Planned Parenthood office. The U.S. Supreme Court, however, struck down the state statute as unconstitutional. The Court held that the First, Third, Fourth, Fifth, and Ninth Amendments created a constitutionally protected zone of privacy. The right of privacy recognized in *Griswold* was later extended to abortion rights in *Roe v. Wade*,[19] one of the most controversial U.S. Supreme Court decisions in American history. The *Roe* Court struck down as unconstitutional a state statute that banned all abortions under any circumstances. The Court recognized that a woman's right to privacy is fundamental under the Fourteenth Amendment. Thus, the government has only a limited right to regulate abortions and cannot completely outlaw abortion procedures and providers. Although the existence of a constitutional right of privacy has generated intense and emotional debate, the holdings in *Griswold* and *Roe* have become settled law.

Federal Statutes

In addition to the right of privacy afforded by the U.S. Supreme Court's interpretation of the Constitution, Congress has also legislated specific privacy rights, such as the Health Insurance Portability and Accountability Act (HIPAA), which regulates health care providers, health plans, and plan administrators in gathering, storing, and disclosing medical information about individuals. This federal law requires that specific policies and record-keeping practices be used in order to ensure the privacy of any medical information, such as diagnoses, tests, medications, and so forth. Congress has also sought to ensure certain privacy protections by mandating that government agencies allow only appropriate public and media access to agency records and reports under the Freedom of Information Act.

Workplace Privacy

Most privacy rights afforded by the U.S. Constitution do not extend to the workplace because courts have held that there is generally no reasonable expectation of privacy in the workplace. Nonetheless, privacy rights have become increasingly important to business owners and managers as Congress and state legislatures seek to clarify workplace privacy rights by statute in areas such as employee drug testing, searches of employee areas (such as lockers or desks) by employers, and electronic monitoring of e-mail and Internet usage. Statutes that regulate the workplace are covered in detail in Chapter 11, "Employment Relationships and Labor Law."

---

[18] 381 U.S. 479 (1965).
[19] 410 U.S. 113 (1973).

KEY TERMS

Federal system p. 41 System in which a national government coexists with state governments.

Preamble p. 41 The introductory part of the Constitution that states its broad objectives.

Articles p. 41 The main provisions of the Constitution that set out the government's structure, power, and procedures.

Amendments p. 41 Changes made to the Constitution since its ratification.

Legislative branch p. 41 Established under Article I of the Constitution; consists of the House of Representatives and the Senate.

Executive branch p. 41 Established under Article II of the Constitution; consists of the president and vice president.

Judicial branch p. 41 Established under Article III of the Constitution; consists of the Supreme Court and other federal courts.

Bill of Rights p. 42 The first 10 amendments to the Constitution that preserve the rights of the people from unlawful acts of government officials, establish and protect freedom of speech and religion, and so on.

Enumerated powers p. 42 Those powers that are explicitly granted to the three branches of government in the Constitution.

Article I, Section 8 p. 42 The main provision of the Constitution that enumerates the limited powers of Congress.

Commerce Clause p. 42 The constitutional clause giving Congress the exclusive power to regulate foreign commerce, interstate commerce, and commerce with the Indian Tribes.

Necessary and Proper Clause p. 42 The constitutional clause giving Congress the general implied authority to make laws necessary to carry out its other enumerated powers.

Executive order p. 43 An order made by the president and which carries the full force of law; issued to enforce or interpret federal statutes and treaties.

Presidential proclamation p. 43 Statement issued by the president on a ceremonial occasion or to elaborate an issue of public or foreign policy.

Jurisdiction p. 43 The legal authority that a court must have before it can hear a case.

Judicial review p. 43 The power of the judiciary to declare a legislative or executive act unconstitutional.

Separation of powers p. 45 The system of checks and balances created by the Constitution whereby the three branches have unique powers that allow them to resolve conflicts among themselves, thus ensuring no one branch exceeds its constitutional authority.

Rational basis p. 45 The lowest level of scrutiny applied by courts deciding constitutional issues through judicial review; upheld if the government shows that the law has a reasonable connection to achieving a legitimate and constitutional objective.

Intermediate-level scrutiny p. 45 The middle level of scrutiny applied by courts deciding constitutional issues through judicial review; upheld if the government shows that a regulation involves an important government objective that is furthered by substantially related means.

Strict scrutiny p. 45 The most stringent standard of scrutiny applied by courts deciding constitutional issues through judicial review when the government action is related to a fundamental right or is based on a suspect classification; upheld if the government shows a compelling need that justifies the law being enacted and no less restrictive alternatives exist.

Supremacy Clause p. 48 The constitutional clause that makes clear that federal law is always supreme to any state law that is in direct conflict.

Preemption p. 48 The concept that primary sources of law are applied consistent with a hierarchy and that a law higher in the hierarchy will overrule and make void a conflicting law lower in the hierarchy. Federal law preempts conflicting state law.

Fourth Amendment p. 60 Protects individual citizens' rights to be secure in their "persons, houses, papers and effects."

Probable cause p. 61 A reasonable amount of suspicion supported by circumstances sufficiently strong to justify a belief that a person has committed a crime.

Due Process Clause p. 64 The constitutional clause protecting individuals from being deprived of "life, liberty, or property" without due process of law.

Due process of law p. 64 The constitutional principle that the government must respect the legal rights that are owed to a person according to the law.

CHAPTER REVIEW QUESTIONS

1. "Judicial review" refers to:
   a. The case or controversy requirement of Article III of the Constitution.
   b. The overall system of checks and balances among the three branches of government.
   c. The three standards of review used by courts when applying constitutional law.
   d. The power of courts to invalidate laws inconsistent with the Constitution.
   e. The power of the executive branch to veto Supreme Court decisions.

2. In which of the following cases is a court most likely to apply "rational basis" review?
   a. A case involving an economic regulation.
   b. A case involving the right to vote.
   c. A case involving speech rights.
   d. A case involving a suspect classification such as race or national origin.
   e. A case involving a classification based on gender.

3. Regarding the right to "equal protection," which of the following statements is true?
   a. Laws must treat persons who are similarly situated equally.
   b. Laws may never make classifications, even when there is a compelling state interest.
   c. Laws must treat everyone exactly the same.
   d. Laws that invade a person's privacy are unconstitutional.
   e. Laws that are too broad or overly vague are unconstitutional.

4. Article I of the Constitution confers on the Congress the power to regulate interstate commerce. Which of the following statements about the Commerce Clause is true?
   I. The commerce power is an enumerated power of Congress.
   II. Congress's commerce power is generally interpreted by the courts very narrowly.
   III. Congress's commerce power limits the power of state governments to regulate commerce locally.
   a. I only
   b. II only
   c. I, II, and III
   d. I and II
   e. I and III

5. Which of the following statements regarding "commercial speech" like advertising is true?
   a. Commercial speech has absolute First Amendment protection like political speech because the Constitution states that Congress shall make no law abridging the freedom of speech.
   b. Commercial speech has full First Amendment protection (subject to strict scrutiny).
   c. Commercial speech has partial First Amendment protection (subject to rational basis review).
   d. Commercial speech has partial First Amendment protection (subject to intermediate-level scrutiny).
   e. Commercial speech has no First Amendment protection.

Answers and explanations are provided at the end of this chapter.

THEORY TO PRACTICE

Quick Courier Services (Quick) is a hypothetical company with 2,500 employees and contractors nationwide and with corporate headquarters in New York City. Quick provides courier services to businesses that require documents or packages to be delivered on a same-day basis. While most of the deliveries are made by car or van, Quick also employs several bicycle couriers to accommodate customers in large cities.

1. Assume that, after a rash of bicycle accidents in several cities nationwide, Congress enacts a federal statute prohibiting the use of bicycle couriers. The statute is intended to protect the safety of the public at large. Congress justifies the statute on the basis that couriers are inherently involved in commercial activity. What enumerated power is Congress using as the basis of its authority to enact this statute?

If Quick were to challenge the constitutionality of the statute, what would its probable legal theory be?

2. Suppose that, instead of an outright ban on bicycle couriers, Congress enacts a law prohibiting any companies that use bicycle couriers from receiving any money from federal grant programs or federal contracts. Does this new law change your analysis relating to congressional authority?

3. Assume that Quick also does business in Boston. Assume also that the Massachusetts legislature enacts a state law that imposes a registration requirement on all courier companies that are headquartered outside of Massachusetts's state borders. The registration requirement includes an annual fee that is not required of in-state couriers. Has Massachusetts infringed on Congress's constitutional authority? What is the standard used by courts to analyze such a law?

4. Assume further that the Occupational Safety and Health Administration (OSHA), a federal government agency, imposes an administrative fine on Quick without giving the company's officers adequate notice to provide evidence that no violation has occurred. How would the Due Process Clause protect Quick from OSHA's actions?

5. If OSHA wishes to search Quick's premises for evidence of an administrative violation, what constitutional amendment would govern the process? If the purpose of the search is to investigate a criminal conspiracy involving Quick's officers, how would that change your answer?

LEGAL STRATEGY 101

The Strategic Legal Battle for Equality

Today, we often take racial, gender, and religious equality for granted. But equality was not always the norm in our nation. In 1896, for example, the U.S. Supreme Court decided the controversial case of *Plessy v. Ferguson*.[20] The Court not only established the *separate but equal* doctrine in this infamous case; it also effectively ratified the evil of racial segregation in public schools as well as privately owned facilities.

Lawyers for the NAACP, however, devised an ingenious legal strategy to overturn this nefarious precedent. Instead of challenging the separate but equal doctrine directly, the NAACP decided to pursue an *equalization strategy*. Because segregated schools rarely received equal funding in many parts of our country, the NAACP filed lawsuits demanding that facilities provided for black students be made truly equal to those reserved for white students.

In addition, the NAACP adopted an incremental approach to legal change. It initially sought to equalize professional schools for graduate students, not all public schools for all children. Lawyers for the NAACP decided to pursue this indirect legal strategy for two reasons. First, they recognized that the Supreme Court

NAACP lawyers Thurgood Marshall, standing, and Charles Houston, right. Their client, Donald Gaines Murray, center, had been excluded from the University of Maryland law school. Pictorial Press Ltd/Alamy

would be reluctant to overturn one of its own decisions, and, secondly, they knew that those states that practiced segregation in graduate education would not be able to afford to maintain separate black professional schools that were truly equal in quality to those available to white students.[21]

---

[20] *Plessy v. Ferguson*, 163 U.S. 537 (1896).

[21] *See generally* Mark V. Tushnet, *The NAACP's Legal Strategy Against Segregated Education, 1925–1950* (University of North Carolina Press 1987).

Led by Charles Hamilton Houston and his former student and protégée, Thurgood Marshall (who would many years later be appointed the first African-American justice of the U.S. Supreme Court), the NAACP won several early cases using this legal strategy, including *Murray v. Maryland* (1936),[22] which resulted in the desegregation of the University of Maryland School of Law, and *Missouri ex rel. Gaines v. Canada* (1938),[23] in which the U.S. Supreme Court ordered the admission of a black student to the University of Missouri Law School.

Then, in 1950, the NAACP won cases that struck down Texas and Oklahoma laws requiring segregated graduate schools in *Sweatt v. Painter*[24] and *McLaurin v. Oklahoma*.[25] In those cases, a unanimous U.S. Supreme Court held that the Equal Protection Clause of the Fourteenth Amendment required those states to admit black students to their graduate and professional schools.

These decisions eventually paved the way for one of the NAACP's greatest legal victories in its storied history: *Brown v. Board of Education*,[26] decided in 1954. In this landmark decision, the U.S. Supreme Court repudiated the last vestiges of *Plessy,* holding that segregation in public education, even when the facilities are equal, violates the Equal Protection Clause of the Fourteenth Amendment as a matter of law.

CRITICAL THINKING QUESTION

Why did it take the U.S. Supreme Court so long to repudiate the doctrine of "separate but equal"? In your opinion, is the slow nature of judicial decision making a "bug" or a "feature" of our legal system?

---

[22]*Murray v. Maryland*, 169 Md. 478 (1936).
[23]*Missouri ex rel. Gaines v. Canada*, 305 U.S. 337 (1938).
[24]*Sweatt v. Painter*, 339 U.S. 629 (1950).
[25]*McLaurin v. Oklahoma*, 339 U.S. 637 (1950).

[26]*Brown v. Board of Education*, 347 U.S. 483 (1954).

MANAGER'S CHALLENGE

Assume you are a senior manager at Quick Courier Services (Quick), the hypothetical company in this chapter's Theory to Practice problem. You receive this e-mail from Quick's CEO:

> Quick is considering paying for full-page advertisements in *The New York Times, The Washington Post,* and other national newspapers to denounce the members of Congress who voted in favor of the national ban on bicycle couriers [see item (1) in the Theory to Practice problem]. However, I recently read about Congress considering a law that bans such advertisements if funded by a corporation.
>
> Before I contact our counsel, I would like a one- to two-page background memorandum addressing the question: May Congress ban our advertisements on the basis that they are funded by corporate money and not by individual voters or political committees? Why or why not? Is there any important case law to support your answer to this question?

See Connect for Manager's Challenge sample answers.

CASE SUMMARY 2.1 Trump v. Hawaii, 138 S. Ct. 2392 (2018)

EXECUTIVE POWER

A week after assuming office, President Donald J. Trump issued an executive order suspending the entry of all refugees to the United States for 120 days, barring Syrian refugees indefinitely, and blocking the entry of citizens from seven predominantly Muslim countries (Iran, Iraq, Libya, Somalia, Sudan, Syria, and Yemen) into the United States for 90 days. President Trump's controversial travel ban caused chaos at many U.S. airports and led to an avalanche of lawsuits. Instead of revoking the ban, President Trump eventually issued a revised travel ban in the form of a presidential proclamation on September 24, 2017. The new travel ban imposed restrictions on foreign nationals entering the United States from Chad, Iran, Libya, Somalia, Syria, and Yemen as well as from North Korea and Venezuela. Although the travel restrictions varied in their details, for the most part citizens of these countries were forbidden from entering the United States, and many of them were also barred from working, studying, or vacationing in the U.S. (Chad was later removed from the list.) "Making America Safe is my number one priority. We will not admit those into our country we cannot safely vet," President Trump tweeted just after he released the presidential proclamation. The State of Hawaii, several individuals, and a Muslim group challenged the constitutionality of the president's travel ban in federal court. They argued that the latest ban was tainted by religious animus and not adequately justified by national security concerns.

CASE QUESTIONS

1. In deciding whether the new travel ban is constitutional or not, does it matter that the new travel ban was issued as a presidential proclamation and not as an executive order?
2. What if the travel ban had been issued on September 12, 2001, a day after the 9/11 attacks? Should that fact, standing alone, be relevant in deciding whether the travel ban is constitutional?

CASE SUMMARY 2.2 Carpenter v. United States, 138 S. Ct. 2206 (2018)

SEARCH OF CELLPHONE LOCATION DATA

Timothy Ivory Carpenter was accused of participating in a series of brazen armed robberies of Radio Shacks in the Detroit area starting in 2010. According to the testimony of several witnesses, Mr. Carpenter planned the robberies, procured guns for his partners in crime, and served as a lookout, typically waiting in a stolen car across the street. To build their case against him, federal prosecutors also relied on four months of detailed records that they obtained from cellphone companies without a search warrant. The cellphone location records showed that Mr. Carpenter's phone had been nearby the Radio Shacks when several of the robberies occurred. Mr. Carpenter was then convicted of the robberies and sentenced to 116 years in prison.

CASE QUESTIONS

1. What if Mr. Carpenter were a spy for Russia or a terrorist plotting to bomb a national monument? Should the government be required to obtain a search warrant in cases involving foreign affairs or national security?
2. If an individual voluntarily enables the "location tracking" feature of his cellphone, does he really have a reasonable expectation of privacy in his cellphone data?

CASE SUMMARY 2.3 Cipollone v. Liggett Group, Inc., 505 U.S. 504 (1992)

PREEMPTION

Rose Cipollone began smoking at the age of 16 and eventually died from lung cancer caused by her smoking habit. Rose Cipollone's son brought suit against Liggett and other cigarette manufacturers for violation of several New Jersey consumer protection statutes, alleging that the tobacco companies were liable for his mother's death because the companies engaged in false advertising, fraudulently misrepresented the hazards of smoking, and were involved in a conspiracy to deprive the public of medical and scientific information about smoking. Liggett urged the court to dismiss the state law claims, contending that the claims relating to the manufacturer's advertising and promotional activities were preempted by two federal laws: (1) the Federal

Cigarette Labeling and Advertising Act of 1965 and (2) the Public Health Cigarette Smoking Act of 1969.

CASE QUESTIONS

1. What must be shown for a federal law to preempt state law?
2. Why would Congress want to preempt state laws regarding the advertising and promotion of tobacco products? Do you agree with its decision to do so? Why or why not?

CASE SUMMARY 2.4 State v. DeAngelo, 930 A.2d 1236 (N.J. 2007)

COMMERCIAL SPEECH

During a labor dispute, a local labor union engaged in a public protest of what it claimed were unfair labor practices of a local business. As part of its protest, union members displayed a 10-foot inflatable rat-shaped balloon on a public sidewalk in front of the business involved in the dispute. A municipal ordinance banned all public displays of "balloon or inflated" signs except in cases of a grand opening. The union challenged the ordinance in court as an unconstitutional ban on commercial speech.

CASE QUESTIONS

1. Is the ordinance constitutional, or is it a valid (content-neutral) "time, place, and manner" regulation?
2. What level of scrutiny will a court apply to the ordinance?
3. What if it were an election year and the labor union had placed the inflatable rat-shaped balloon in front of the local chapter of the Republican Party or Democratic Party to protest either party's political platform?

CASE SUMMARY 2.5 United States v. Alderman, 565 F.3d 641 (9th Cir. 2009)

COMMERCE CLAUSE

In 2002, Congress passed the Body Armor Act that made it illegal for anyone who has been convicted of a violent felony to possess body armor. Cedrick Alderman was convicted of violating the statute, and he then challenged the law's constitutionality during appeal. Alderman contended that Congress had exceeded its authority because the law was not sufficiently related to interstate commerce.

CASE QUESTIONS

1. Is the Body Armor Act constitutional?
2. If Alderman purchased the body armor in the state where it was manufactured, how did his purchase affect "interstate" commerce?
3. Suppose Congress enacts a prospective law prohibiting all private persons from purchasing or owning body armor in the future. In your opinion, would such a law be constitutional?

CASE SUMMARY 2.6 United States v. American Library Association, 539 U.S. 194 (2003)

NECESSARY AND PROPER CLAUSE

In an effort to increase Internet access for the public, Congress enacted legislation to create the E-Rate program, which provides discounted Internet rates, as well as the Library Services and Technology Act (LSTA), which provides financial grants to libraries.

At the same time, Congress also approved the Children's Internet Protection Act (CIPA). In brief, CIPA conditions the receipt of federal funds under the E-Rate program and the LSTA on libraries' purchase and installation of software that blocks obscene or pornographic material. A group of libraries and private citizens filed suit, claiming that connecting LSTA grant funds to CIPA compliance is unconstitutional.

CASE QUESTIONS

1. Is the condition requiring the purchase and installation of blocking software in order to qualify for discounts and grants constitutional?
2. Is the First Amendment at issue in this case? Explain your answer.
3. What regulations or restrictions, if any, may Congress impose on Internet communications?

CASE SUMMARY 2.7 State Farm Mutual v. Campbell, 538 U.S. 408 (2003)

DUE PROCESS AND PUNITIVE DAMAGES

Curtis Campbell was involved in a car accident in which one person was killed and another permanently disabled. State Farm, Campbell's insurer, investigated the accident and concluded that Campbell was negligent (i.e., at fault for the accident) but refused to settle a case brought by the injured parties for Campbell's $50,000 policy limit. Prior to trial, State Farm falsely told Campbell that (1) he was not liable in the case brought against him by the injured parties and (2) State Farm and Campbell's mutual interests were closely aligned, so hiring his own attorney was unnecessary. Based on State Farm's assurances, Campbell did not consult his own attorney. At trial, a jury found against both Campbell and State Farm. The jury awarded the plaintiffs $185,849, far more than the amount requested during pretrial settlement discussions. State Farm refused to pay any amount beyond the $50,000 policy limit, and its general counsel advised Campbell to sell his house to cover the excess award owed to the plaintiffs. Campbell then sued State Farm for bad faith, fraud, and intentional infliction of emotional distress. The jury found for Campbell, awarding him $2.6 million in compensatory damages, to compensate him for his actual losses, and $145 million in punitive damages. Consistent with a state statute limiting certain damage awards, the trial court reduced the awards to $1 million in compensatory damages and $25 million in punitive damages. An appellate court later reinstated the original $145 million punitive-damage award on the basis that the state's punitive-damage statute allowed larger damage awards if the defendant acted in a particularly reprehensible manner. State Farm appealed.

CASE QUESTIONS

1. When State Farm appealed the jury's punitive-damage award, it argued that such a disproportionately large punitive-damage award ($145 million) was a violation of the Due Process Clause. Do you agree or disagree?
2. The Due Process Clause, like all the protections in the Bill of Rights, is meant to apply to government agents, not to private parties. Should a civil jury be considered a government actor or a private actor under the Due Process Clause?
3. How can one determine what constitutes an excessive award of damages that violates a defendant's right to due process, compared to one that does not violate the Due Process Clause? Is this distinction clear?

CASE SUMMARY 2.8 Pagan v. Fruchey and Village of Glendale, 492 F.3d 766 (6th Cir. 2007)

APPLYING THE *CENTRAL HUDSON* TEST

The Village of Glendale, Ohio, enacted a local ordinance prohibiting anyone from parking a vehicle on a public road for the purpose of displaying it for sale. Christopher Pagan, a resident of Glendale, parked his car on a public street and posted a "For Sale" sign on the vehicle. A Glendale police officer warned Pagan to take down the sign or face a citation for violating the local ordinance. Pagan then filed suit against the Village of Glendale and Glendale's chief of police, Matt Fruchey, claiming that the ordinance was an unconstitutional infringement of Pagan's First Amendment commercial speech rights. The defendants asserted that Glendale had a substantial regulatory interest in traffic and pedestrian safety. The police chief testified as to his opinion regarding public safety, but Glendale did not present any empirical data or research at trial. After the trial court dismissed Pagan's claim, the U.S. Circuit Court of Appeals for the Sixth Circuit reversed the trial court's dismissal because there was not a sufficient nexus or connection between Glendale's asserted regulatory interest (public safety) and the local ordinance.

CASE QUESTIONS

1. Why didn't the appeals court give more weight to the police chief's opinion?
2. What types of data do you suppose the court wanted from Glendale to support the village's claim that the ordinance advanced its traffic safety interest?
3. Should commercial speech receive the same level of protection as political speech?

CASE SUMMARY 2.9 Patel v. Zillow, Inc., 915 F.3d 446 (7th Cir. 2019)

COMMERCIAL SPEECH

Vipul Patel is a property owner in the Chicago area who wants to sell his house. Zillow, Inc. (Zillow) is an online real estate database company that was founded in 2006 by Rich Barton and Lloyd Frink, former Microsoft executives and founders of the Microsoft spin-off Expedia. Zillow assigns a "Zestimate" to every listing in its real estate database, and each Zestimate is based on a computer-generated algorithm using public and user-submitted data. Mr. Patel alleges that the computer-generated Zestimate for his house is misleading and unfair because it is far below the fair market value of his home. He asked Zillow either to increase the Zestimate for his house or to remove the listing from its database altogether. When Zillow refused to take either step, Mr. Patel sued Zillow, alleging that Zillow's practice of listing and publicly posting property values without a license is fraudulent and constitutes an invasion of privacy. Among other things, Zillow argues in its defense that it is not breaking any laws and that it is simply exercising its right to free speech.

CASE QUESTIONS

1. Can data generated by a computer algorithm be a form of commercial speech? Why or why not?
2. Should the government regulate business firms like Zillow? Why or why not?

 Self-Check ANSWERS Source of Constitutional Authority

What is the constitutional source of authority for each of the following laws?

1. Article I, § 8: Congress's power to regulate bankruptcy laws.
2. Article I, § 8: Tax and spend powers.
3. Article I, § 8: Careful! This answer appears to be Congress's power to grant and regulate patents. But the fact that Congress is passing a criminal law would be outside the scope of the narrow patent power. Rather, this law is best thought of as Congress's authority to legislate under the Necessary and Proper Clause because the law is directly ancillary to the enumerated power (patents).
4. Article I, § 8: Congress's power to regulate interstate commerce.
5. Article I, § 8: Tax and spend power.

CHAPTER REVIEW QUESTIONS: Answers and Explanations

1. **d.** Judicial review refers to the inherent and general power of courts to declare unconstitutional those laws inconsistent with the Constitution. Answer choice (a) is incorrect because Article III does not refer to judicial review at all, (b) refers to the separation of powers, and (c) refers to the specific standards of review used by courts in constitutional cases. Answer choice (e) is incorrect because the president does not have the explicit power to veto Supreme Court decisions.

2. **a.** Rational basis review is most likely to be used in a case involving economic legislation. Answer choices (b), (c), and (d) all involve strict scrutiny, while answer choice (e) involves intermediate-level scrutiny.

3. **a.** Equal protection does not mean that everyone must be treated exactly the same, so (c) is incorrect. Answer choice (b) is also incorrect because constitutionally permissive (nonsuspect) categories or classifications may be created and the categories may be treated differently; however, those within each category must be treated the same. Answer choice (d) refers to the right to privacy, not equal protection, while answer choice (e) refers to due process.

4. **e.** The power to regulate commerce is an enumerated power because this power is explicitly provided to Congress in Article I of the Constitution. Moreover, the U.S. Supreme Court has interpreted this power very broadly (not narrowly) and has consistently ruled that the Commerce Clause does not allow the states to discriminate against or impose unreasonable burdens on interstate commerce.

5. **c.** In *Virginia State Board of Pharmacy*, the Supreme Court held that commercial speech was entitled to partial First Amendment protection, and in *Central Hudson*, the Court extended intermediate-level review to commercial speech cases.

CHAPTER 3

The American Judicial System, Jurisdiction, and Venue

©philsajonesen/Getty Images

Learning Objectives

After studying this chapter, students who have mastered the material will be able to:

3-1   Explain the role of the judiciary in the American legal system.
3-2   Distinguish between federal courts and state courts.
3-3   Identify the main duties of trial courts versus appellate courts.
3-4   Articulate how the law evolves through the adjudication of cases.
3-5   Differentiate between subject matter jurisdiction and personal jurisdiction.
3-6   Explain original jurisdiction and how state and federal courts may have concurrent jurisdiction.
3-7   Recognize the types of controversies over which federal courts have subject matter jurisdiction and those in which diversity jurisdiction applies.
3-8   Explain the role of long-arm statutes in determining personal jurisdiction.
3-9   Apply the minimum contacts test in both a traditional and an Internet setting.

The primary role of courts is to decide cases and resolve legal disputes. Court decisions may also shape or create legal doctrines that impact business. Business owners and managers should thus know how our court system works in practice, especially because the risk of litigation is always present in the business world.

In this chapter, students will learn

- The role and structure of the American judicial system.
- The function and legal authority of state and federal courts.
- How the law develops through court decisions.

In order for a court to render a binding decision, a court must have *jurisdiction* or legal authority over both the dispute itself (subject matter jurisdiction) and the parties in the case (personal jurisdiction).

Accordingly, students will also learn

- The circumstances under which a court has the legal authority to decide a case (jurisdiction).
- The appropriate location to resolve a dispute (venue).

ROLE AND STRUCTURE OF THE JUDICIARY

The American legal system is structured around a set of federal and state **courts** collectively known as the **judiciary**. The judiciary has two primary roles. First, courts *adjudicate* cases. In its adjudication role, a court resolves disputes. Second, courts are also charged with the responsibility of *judicial review*.[1] In its judicial review role, a court may review decisions of lower courts or the actions of the other branches of the government to determine whether these decisions and actions comply with existing law and with the Constitution.

State versus Federal Courts

The U.S. system of government is a "federal" system: It recognizes two distinct levels of government, state and federal. As a result, there are two levels of courts in this dual structure. One level, **state courts**, adjudicates cases arising under state statutes, state common law, or state constitutional law. In addition, state courts also may apply nonexclusive federal statutes as well as federal constitutional law. The other level, **federal courts**, is concerned primarily with national laws, federal constitutional issues, and other cases that are outside the purview of state courts.

It is important to note that not all courts have the *authority* to hear all cases. In order for a court, whether state or federal, to have the legal authority to hear a case, the court must have *jurisdiction* over the dispute and parties in the case. Proper venue also must be established. The concepts of jurisdiction and venue are discussed in detail later in this chapter.

LO 3-1
Explain the role of the judiciary in the American legal system.

LO 3-2
Distinguish between federal courts and state courts.

LO 3-3
Identify the main duties of trial courts versus appellate courts.

State Courts The majority of court cases filed in the United States are brought in state courts. All 50 states have two types of tribunals: **state trial courts** and **state appellate courts**.

State Trial Courts When one party alleges a breach of a legal duty or a violation of a legal right, the aggrieved party, called the **plaintiff**, may initiate in a trial court a civil action or lawsuit against the alleged wrongdoer, called the **defendant**. Trial courts

The American judiciary consists of a system of state and federal courts. Comstock/Getty Images

---
[1] Recall from Chapter 2, "Business and the Constitution," that the U.S. Supreme Court, in the landmark case of *Marbury v. Madison*, established the power of judicial review.

adjudicate cases through an established procedure in which both parties are able to present evidence, question witnesses, and articulate legal arguments about their case.[2]

The names of trial courts vary widely from state to state. However, all state trial courts have either *general authority* to hear a case or *limited authority* to hear a particular type of case. Courts of general authority are organized into geographic districts (often divided at the county level or by a set of contiguous counties)[3] and adjudicate many types of cases, including breach of contract, employment discrimination, personal injury, criminal cases, property disputes, and so forth. Courts of limited authority, by contrast, are often confined to a particular type of dispute such as family law matters (e.g., divorce, child custody, or adoption cases) or probate matters (e.g., wills and estates). Some states, notably Delaware, have courts devoted solely to issues relating to commercial law matters. In Delaware, these specialized courts are called *chancery courts*.

It is important to remember that state trial court decisions are binding *only* on the parties involved in the dispute. Trial court decisions do not set precedent for future disputes or parties. Only appellate courts set precedent.

> **KEY POINT**
>
> Inferior courts often do not maintain a permanent record of their trials. Some states simply record the trial and then erase the recording after the period for appeal has expired.
>
> State trial courts are courts of record, meaning that a court stenographer attends the trial and creates a permanent written transcript of the trial.

For minor matters and cases with a dollar value that is relatively low (typically less than $10,000, depending on the state), there are local courts known alternatively as municipal courts, small-claims courts, or justice-of-the-peace courts. Such courts provide local access to a court for the purpose of resolving relatively simple disputes on an expedited basis. These courts are typically referred to as *inferior* trial courts because states provide an automatic appeal for the losing party, usually to the state trial court. This appeal actually takes the form of a new trial, or **trial de novo**.

State trial courts are often divided into (1) courts that hear **civil cases**, in which one party seeks a remedy, such as an award of money damages, for a private wrong committed by another party, and (2) courts that hear **criminal cases**, in which the accused party is charged by the government of committing a crime.

Legal Speak >))

Trial de Novo
A form of appeal in which the appeals court conducts a new trial as if the original trial had never occurred.

State Appellate Courts

After a state trial court has rendered a decision, the losing party may file an appeal in a state appellate court. Appellate courts are primarily concerned with reviewing the decisions of trial courts. In some states, appeals to any appellate-level courts are *discretionary*. That is, the party requesting the appeal (known as the *petitioning* party or the *appellant*) files a document with the court requesting an appeal. Based on a variety of factors, the appellate court then decides whether to allow the appeal to be heard. In other states, the losing party has an automatic right of appeal to the appellate court. In either case, if the appellate court denies an appeal, the trial court ruling is *binding* on the parties in that case.[4]

Appellate judges determine whether the trial in the lower court was conducted in accordance with the legal rules and doctrines of that state. Appellate courts assess the lower court's decision by (1) reviewing lower court transcripts and rulings; (2) reading *briefs,* which are documents written by the attorneys for each side articulating legal reasons why their side should prevail; and (3) sometimes allowing the attorneys to engage in *oral*

---

[2]Note that the role of trial courts is examined in the context of a civil lawsuit, known as *litigation,* in the next chapter.

[3]In the United States, 48 states are divided into counties. Louisiana is divided into parishes, and Alaska is divided into boroughs.

[4]In extraordinary cases, a petitioning party sometimes has the right to appeal to a higher court if the intermediate appellate court denies the appeal.

argument, which requires the attorneys for the parties to appear in front of an appellate panel of judges to participate in a live question-and-answer session on the legal issues in the case.

The appellate court focuses on such issues as the rulings of the trial judges, the admission of evidence, jury selection, and other factors that may have affected the outcome of the case in the lower court. Note that appellate courts, except in some rare cases, do *not* consider new evidence in their review. Instead, the main job of appellate courts is to determine whether a legal error was made at the trial court level. In cases where the error is substantial enough, a court may reverse the decision of the trial court and **remand** the case back to the trial court.

Another major distinction between trial courts and appellate courts is that an appellate court decision sets *precedent* that is binding on all lower trial courts.[5] Because one of the primary purposes of the law is to provide some degree of reliability and uniformity in adjudicating cases, trial courts are required to follow the rulings of appellate courts. In most states, the highest appellate court is called the *state supreme court.*[6] A state supreme court's decision is final and binding on *all* courts situated in that state (including federal courts located in that state) on *all* issues involving state law.

States vary as to how state trial court and appellate judges are selected. Some states elect all trial and appellate judges as part of their general elections, while others use an appointment process whereby the governor appoints a judge, but the appointment is subject to review and rejection by the state legislature (typically the state senate). Some states use a hybrid method whereby local judges are elected and appellate court judges go through an appointment process.

Legal Speak >))

Remand
To send a case back to the lower court from which it came for further action consistent with the opinion and instructions of the higher court.

KEY POINT

Only appellate courts have the right to set binding precedent.

Federal Courts
The federal government operates a separate system of federal courts. Trial courts at the federal level are the **U.S. district courts**. Federal appellate courts are called the **U.S. courts of appeal**. Because the federal appellate courts are divided into circuits, these courts are frequently referred to as *circuit courts of appeal.* Finally, the **U.S. Supreme Court** not only has authority to review the decisions of the circuit courts; it also has authority to review decisions of state supreme courts that involve some issue of federal law.

U.S. District Courts
District courts serve the same primary trial function as state trial courts but address issues involving federal matters such as federal statutes, regulations, or constitutional issues. There are 94 districts in the United States, with at least one federal district court in every state and one for the District of Columbia. Federal district courts may also decide certain matters involving *state law* when the parties are from different states and the amount in controversy exceeds $75,000. These federal trial courts hear a variety of matters and render decisions that are binding only on the parties involved in the dispute. Some federal courts specialize in certain areas of law. They include the Bankruptcy Court, the Tax Court, and the Court of International Trade.

KEY POINT

When the parties are from different states and the amount in controversy exceeds $75,000, federal courts may decide state law cases (e.g., contract disputes), except in cases involving divorce, alimony, or child custody.

---

[5] Recall from Chapter 1, "Legal Foundations," that the concept of *precedent* springs from the doctrine of stare decisis.

[6] But not always: In the state of New York, the state's highest court is the New York Court of Appeals. The New York Supreme Court has two divisions, the trial division, which is the state's general trial court, and the appellate division, which is the state's intermediary appellate court.

U.S. Courts of Appeal There are 13 federal courts of appeal, each of which reviews the decisions of federal district courts in the state or several states within its circuit. Two exceptions are the Court of Appeals for the District of Columbia, which decides cases originating in Washington, D.C., and the Federal Circuit Court of Appeals, which decides a variety of exclusively federal issues such as patent, copyright, and trademark cases or cases where the United States is named as a defendant. The Federal Circuit is said to have national jurisdiction because its authority is not confined to one particular circuit. Just as with state appellate courts, federal circuit courts of appeal set precedent and their decisions are binding on all the states in that circuit. Figure 3.1 illustrates how the federal circuits are divided geographically.

U.S. Supreme Court The U.S. Constitution does not specify the number of justices who sit on the Supreme Court. Originally established at six members, one chief justice and five associate justices, the Court has ranged from a low of five members to a high of 10 members. It has remained at nine members since 1869.

The U.S. Supreme Court has both original and appellate jurisdiction. The Court's original jurisdiction is limited to cases involving ambassadors and other high public officials and those cases where the disputing parties are two states. In original jurisdiction cases, the Court operates as a trial court.

In addition to the Court's original jurisdiction and its appellate authority to decide any appeal from any U.S. circuit court of appeal, the Court also may exercise its appellate authority over state supreme courts when a federal issue is involved.

FIGURE 3.1 Map of the U.S. Circuits

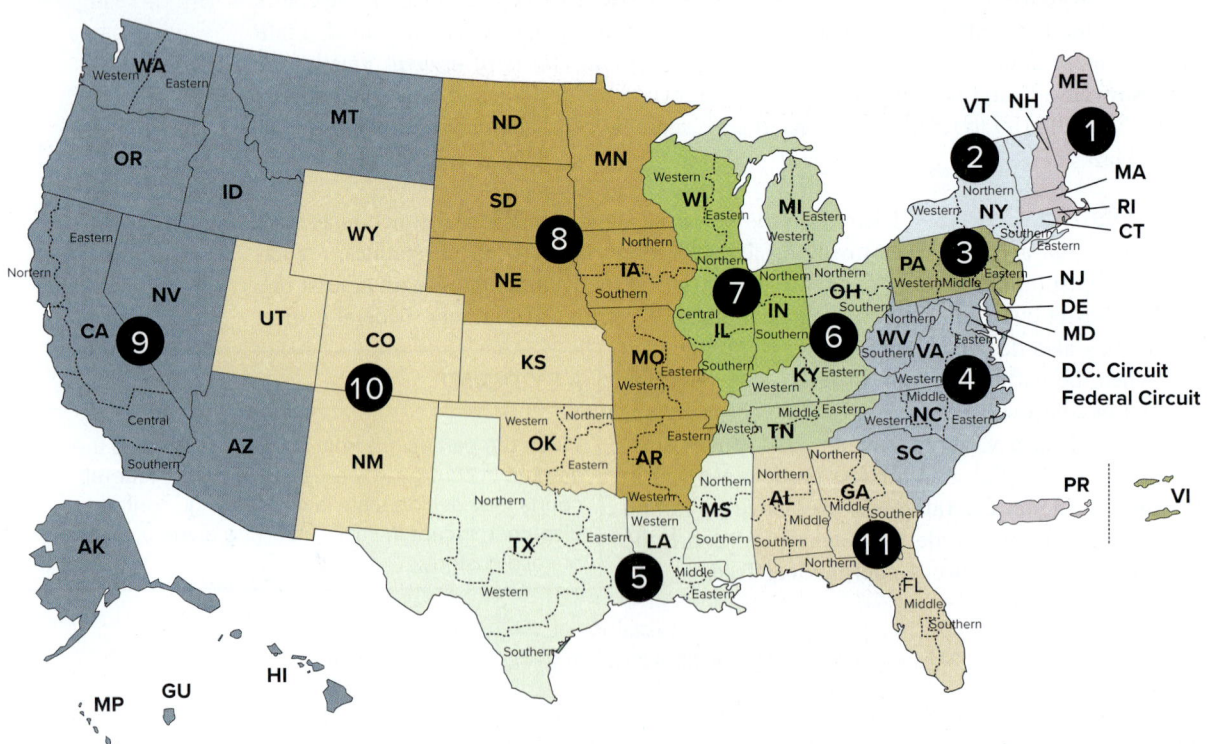

Source: www.uscourts.gov/courtlinks.

TABLE 3.1 U.S. Supreme Court Case Acceptance Rate

Term	Total Number of Cert. Petitions	Number of Cert. Petitions Granted	Acceptance Rate (0.01 = 1%)
2009	8,131	77	0.9%
2010	7,868	90	1.1
2011	7,685	66	0.9
2012	7,647	93	1.2
2013	7,586	76	1
2014	7,083	71	1
2015	6,536	81	1.2
2016	6,289	75	1.2
2017	6,229	78	1.3

Source: Journal of the Supreme Court of the United States.

Furthermore, the Court's appellate review is discretionary. An aggrieved party may petition the Court to review its appeal by presenting a petition for *writ of certiorari* that explains the basis for the appeal. Upon review, if four of the nine justices vote to hear the case, the parties in the case are then permitted to pursue the appeal before the Supreme Court. In practice, however, the odds of getting a case to the Court are very low. Typically, parties file between 6,000 and 8,000 petitions for a writ of certiorari per year, and the Court grants only about 1 percent of those requests. Table 3.1 illustrates the number of petitions filed versus the number of petitions granted by the Supreme Court from 2009 to 2014.

In addition to deciding some highly publicized and politically charged cases, the main work of the U.S. Supreme Court is to decide cases presenting legal issues that have generated conflicting opinions among the appellate circuit courts, referred to by the Court as a *conflict among the circuits* or a *circuit split*.

All federal judges are selected via the appointment process. The president nominates candidates for federal trial and appellate courts. The nominees are then subject to the review of the Senate. If the nominee is rejected, the president must nominate another candidate. Once confirmed, the nominee is sworn in as a federal judge and may be removed from office only by impeachment.

Legal Speak >))

Writ of Certiorari
A discretionary order issued by the Supreme Court granting a request to argue an appeal. A party filing for an appeal must file a petition for writ of certiorari.

CONCEPT SUMMARY *Role and Structure of the Judiciary*

- The roles of trial courts are to adjudicate disputes and resolve cases.
- The role of appellate courts is to review the decisions of trial courts.
- Both trial and appellate courts also have the power of judicial review: They may review the actions of the other branches of government to ensure they comply with existing legal and constitutional requirements.

(continued)

The Supreme Court of the United States. Photographs in the Carol M. Highsmith Archive, Library of Congress, Prints and Photographs Division.

- State courts generally handle matters dealing with state statutes, state common law, and state constitutional law. The majority of cases filed in the United States are filed in state courts.
- State trial courts with general authority hear a wide variety of cases. State trial courts with limited authority hear specific types of cases such as those involving family law or probate matters.
- There are two levels of state courts: (1) trial courts, where parties present their cases and evidence, and (2) appellate courts, which review the decisions of lower courts.
- Only appellate courts set precedent. The decisions of trial courts are binding only on the parties in the particular matter before the court.
- Federal trial courts are called *district courts*. Federal appellate courts are called *circuit courts of appeal*.
- The U.S. Supreme Court has both original and appellate jurisdiction.
- A *circuit split* occurs when two or more different federal circuit courts of appeal offer conflicting rulings on the same legal or constitutional issue.
- The U.S. Supreme Court is more likely to grant review of a case if the case presents a legal issue in which there is a circuit split, though the existence of a circuit split is only one of the factors the Court considers when deciding whether to grant review of a case.

HOW THE LAW DEVELOPS

LO 3-4
Articulate how the law evolves through the adjudication of cases.

The American legal system is a "common law" system: The law is interpreted and developed by courts in written decisions. When a decision is issued by an appellate court, it not only decides the individual case before the court; it also sets a precedent for lower courts to follow in future cases. Furthermore, because of our federal structure or dual system of government (state and federal), it can often be a daunting task—even for trained lawyers!—to figure out "what the law is" or what binding precedents apply in any given case.

As we saw in the previous section, trial courts may rule on certain points of law and render a decision, but in terms of precedent, a trial court decision is binding only on the parties to the case and on no one else. In other words, a trial court decision does not establish binding precedent. If, however, an appellate court affirms or reverses the decision of the trial court, the decision of the appellate court sets a precedent: From that point on, the appellate court's ruling on that particular point of law must be followed by the trial courts in the same jurisdiction in all future cases.

To further complicate matters, federal trial courts within a certain state (called *district courts*) may rule on *state law* issues in so-called diversity of citizenship cases (e.g., cases involving parties from different states and an amount in controversy in excess of $75,000).

Figure 3.2 illustrates the structure of state and federal courts.

Consider the following hypothetical case to illustrate how the law develops. Assume that in the imaginary U.S. state of Holmestown, no precedent exists on the following issue

FIGURE 3.2 Understanding State and Federal Courts

*Both the federal and state court systems include courts of special or limited jurisdiction. Examples include state family and probate courts and federal bankruptcy and tax courts.

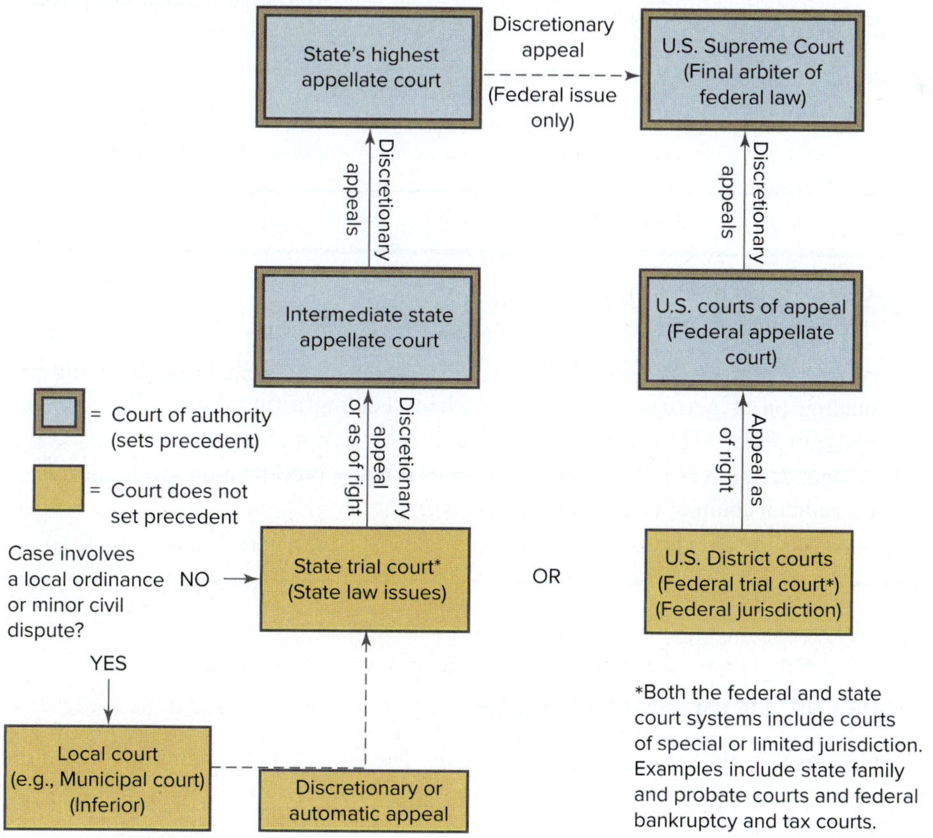

of state law: *Does an e-mail constitute a signed writing sufficient to satisfy a state statute that requires certain contracts to be in writing?* Further assume that two separate controversies have occurred simultaneously and two separate cases, each with different parties, have been filed.

Case Number	Court	Date	Ruling on Issue	Effect on Parties and Future Cases
Case 1	Holmestown state trial court	Jan. 10	*E-mail is sufficient.*	Binding only on parties in Case 1.
Case 2	Federal district court (federal trial) located in Holmestown Federal jurisdiction has been established	Jan. 15	*E-mail is not sufficient.*	Binding only on the parties in this case (Case 2). No effect on the parties in Case 1.
Case 3	Holmestown state appellate court	May 1	*E-mail is sufficient.*	Binding on all Holmestown state and federal trial courts in Holmestown. Case 1 decision is upheld, and its ruling is now applied in Holmestown state trial courts/federal trial courts in Holmestown from May 1 onward.
Case 4	Federal court of appeals that includes Holmestown in its circuit	June 1	Must follow Holmestown state appellate court's precedent set in Case 3 because it is an issue of state law: *E-mail is sufficient.*	If there are no federal issues, the court applies Holmestown state law as interpreted by Holmestown state appellate courts in Case 3. The court's decision is binding only on Holmestown, not on other states in the circuit.
Case 5	State supreme court of Holmestown	July 31	Denies appeal from losing party in Holmestown appellate court decision (Case 3).	Law as decided by the appellate court in Case 3 is settled and binding on all Holmestown courts. Precedent is undisturbed.

CONCEPT SUMMARY Precedent

- A **precedent** is a principle or rule established in a previous legal case that is either binding on or persuasive for a court when deciding a future case with similar issues or facts.
- A legal decision of a higher court becomes binding precedent on lower courts in the judicial chain of command.
- A court should not overturn a precedent unless there is a strong reason to do so.

LO 3-5

Differentiate between subject matter jurisdiction and personal jurisdiction.

JURISDICTION AND VENUE

Not all courts have the authority to hear all cases. The law sets out certain procedural rules that govern which courts may decide which cases. **Jurisdiction** is a court's authority to decide a particular case based on (1) who the parties are and (2) the subject matter of the dispute. **Venue** is a determination of the most appropriate *location* for litigating a dispute.

Jurisdiction and Business Strategy

Improvements in technology and in product and service delivery make jurisdiction and venue essential to business planning. As with all legal decisions that business owners and managers make, jurisdiction must be considered in a cost-benefit context. For example, consider a company like Facebook, with headquarters in northern California. Facebook now has over two billion active users all over the world. This means that Facebook could potentially be sued in any state and in other countries as well. With so many users worldwide, what can Facebook do to ensure that any lawsuit involving a Facebook user is litigated in northern California? For the answer to this question, keep reading. We will explore this issue in more depth later in the chapter and, in Case 3.3, examine an actual lawsuit brought against Facebook presenting the questions raised here.

For now, consider two hypothetical companies, Ultimate Widget Corporation (UWC) and Knock Off Stores, Inc. (Knock Off). Suppose UWC, a New York company, is considering suing Knock Off, a California company, over copyright infringement. UWC management must consider not only the merits of its potential lawsuit but also the costs involved in pursuing the suit. Specifically, UWC's management must consider (1) the total amount of the possible recovery from Knock Off, (2) the actual benefits UWC will reap from the prevention of Knock Off's copyright infringement, and (3) any alternate dispute resolution methods available. If Knock Off is a small company and not likely to steal any of UWC's customers or markets, it may not be worth the costs of litigation to sue Knock Off in California. Pursuing the infringement action would expose UWC to the expense of traveling to California, hiring local counsel in California, and losing productive hours of managers and other witnesses who would be required to travel to testify and be deposed for the case. However, if a New York court has jurisdiction over the dispute, this fact is likely to change the dynamics of the cost-benefit analysis for UWC because now the expenses of the suit are markedly lower.

> *Legal Speak >))*
>
> **Jurisdiction**
> An English word derived through the combination of two Latin words: *juris* ("of law" or "of right") and *dictio* ("speaking"). Thus, *jurisdiction* refers to a court's authority to *speak the law,* or render a decision in a legal dispute.

> **KEY POINT**
>
> The cost-benefit analysis involving jurisdictional restrictions may affect the managerial decision-making process when a company or individual contemplates filing a lawsuit. Litigating disputes in out-of-state courts increases the costs of litigation.

Overview of Jurisdiction

The origins of jurisdiction are found in the U.S. Constitution, specifically, the Due Process Clause of the Fifth and the Fourteenth Amendments. In essence, the Constitution prohibits the deprivation of a property interest (usually money damages) without a fair process. While the origins of jurisdiction lie in the Constitution, appellate courts and legislatures have also shaped the rules used by modern courts to analyze questions of jurisdiction.

> **LO 3-6**
> Explain original jurisdiction and how state and federal courts may have concurrent jurisdiction.

Two-Part Analysis

Jurisdiction requires a two-part analysis: A court must have both (1) **subject matter jurisdiction** and (2) **personal jurisdiction** (also known as *in personam jurisdiction*). Subject matter jurisdiction is the court's authority over the *dispute* between the parties, while personal jurisdiction is the court's authority over the *parties* involved in the dispute.

For example, suppose that Abel is employed by Auto Parts Company (APC) to drive a delivery vehicle. One morning, Abel is on a delivery, and due to his lack of care (called *negligence*[7]), he hits Cain, a pedestrian who is crossing the street in a designated public crosswalk located directly in front of the hotel where he has been staying. Cain is severely injured, and he considers filing a lawsuit against Abel to recover the losses he has suffered

---

[7]*Negligence,* the legal term for such lack of care, is discussed extensively in Chapter 9, "Torts and Products Liability."

from the incident. However, Cain discovers that Abel is without assets and, in the state where the incident has taken place, the law provides that APC is responsible for Abel's actions. Consequently, Cain decides to pursue a lawsuit against APC.

Initially, Cain must decide in *which* court to file the lawsuit. He probably will have some choice, but it will be a limited one. This is true because the court selected must have jurisdiction over this type of dispute (a negligence case) and over the defendant (APC). Cain will likely bring this suit in a *state* trial court because the jurisdiction of federal courts is limited. We will refer to the *Cain v. APC* case throughout this section to illustrate various aspects of jurisdiction and venue.

Subject Matter Jurisdiction: Authority over the Dispute

LO 3-7

Recognize the types of controversies over which federal courts have subject matter jurisdiction and those in which diversity jurisdiction applies.

Recall from the discussion at the beginning of this chapter that state and federal statutes define which courts have *general* jurisdiction and which have *limited* jurisdiction. State statutes give state trial courts subject matter jurisdiction on virtually all matters involving a state statute, state common law, or a state constitutional issue.

Federal district courts, by contrast, are limited by the Constitution and by federal statutes as to what types of cases they have authority to hear. In order for a federal court to have subject matter jurisdiction in a case, the issue must generally involve a **federal question** (e.g., some issue arising from the U.S. Constitution, a federal statute or regulation, or federal common law).

Federal courts have *exclusive* jurisdiction over all cases in which the United States is a **party** in the litigation. For example, a business that sues the Internal Revenue Service for a federal tax refund must pursue the matter in federal court because it involves the United States as a party named in the lawsuit.

Even if there is no federal question and the United States is not a party to the litigation, federal courts may have subject matter jurisdiction over cases involving parties from *two different states* (or one party from outside the United States), a situation known as **diversity of citizenship**.

An additional requirement in diversity-of-citizenship cases is that the amount in controversy must be more than $75,000. For example, if a dispute arises in which a business in New York sues a business in California for breach of contract for $80,000, the parties are said to be *diverse* and a federal court sitting in New York or California will be given subject matter jurisdiction in the case. Note that the amount-in-controversy requirement applies *only* when a court has jurisdiction via the diversity-of-citizenship requirement. In a diversity case, a federal court applies *state law* because the dispute involves issues governed by state statutes or state common law.

Recall the Cain-APC hypothetical case from the beginning of this section. Now assume that Cain is a resident of Massachusetts and that he is visiting Texas, where APC is headquartered, when the incident occurs. Cain is likely to prefer filing the lawsuit in his home state to avoid spending time and resources traveling to Texas to attend the trial. Assuming that Cain's injuries are sufficiently severe to warrant damages exceeding $75,000, Cain may consider filing suit in the federal district court in Massachusetts. That court has subject matter jurisdiction because the parties are diverse and the amount in controversy has been satisfied. However, that is only the first part of the jurisdiction analysis. Once it has been determined that the federal district court in Massachusetts has subject matter jurisdiction, Cain must also clear another substantial jurisdictional requirement: *personal jurisdiction*. We discuss personal jurisdiction in greater detail later in this chapter.

Original versus Concurrent Jurisdiction
Courts that are authorized to initially hear a case are said to have **original jurisdiction**. However, it is important to note that more than one court may have jurisdiction over the same case. This scenario is called

TABLE 3.2 Subject Matter Jurisdiction

Court	Requirements	Subject Matter Jurisdiction in Melvin Ventures Case?
Local court	Any case claiming *up to* $10,000 in damages	No
State trial court	Any case in *excess of* $10,000 in damages	Yes
State appellate court	Appeals from state trial court	No
Federal trial court	More than $75,000 in damages; diversity of citizenship	Yes

concurrent jurisdiction. State courts may have concurrent jurisdiction with other state courts or federal courts. For example, suppose that Melvin Ventures Co. alleges that one of its out-of-state vendors has breached a contract, causing $100,000 in damages. Melvin Ventures will have a choice of several forums for bringing a lawsuit against the vendor. Table 3.2 illustrates the various courts that may have concurrent jurisdiction in the case.

Choice of Forum

Choosing a forum (court location) to litigate a dispute when courts have concurrent jurisdiction is an important strategic choice. A party filing a lawsuit must take into account several factors:

- Costs — This factor includes travel costs, filing fees, and legal fees for local counsel (necessary for out-of-state lawsuits).
- Judges — The expertise and experience of the judge varies greatly based on the court. Local judges are typically not suited for complex business cases. State and federal judges have earned law degrees and typically have gained significant legal experience prior to becoming a judge.
- Juries — Juries may vary depending on the location and choice of the forum (e.g., a jury in a small town in Kansas versus a jury in New York City).
- Appeals — In many cases, the losing party in a local court case is entitled to an automatic appeal. Appeals from other courts are typically discretionary.
- Time — The amount of time that it takes to actually get to trial varies, depending on the court and the backlog of cases in the court. Local inferior courts often hear cases within a few weeks, while state trial courts and federal courts may take several months if not years to get a case ready for trial.

✓ **Self-Check** Subject Matter Jurisdiction

In the following cases, does a federal district court located in New Jersey have *subject matter* jurisdiction?

1. A New Jersey businessperson sues her in-state business partner for a breach of contract that resulted in $40,000 in losses.
2. The U.S. Environmental Protection Agency sues a New Jersey corporation for cleanup costs under a federal statute that regulates local waste disposal.

(continued)

3. A Pennsylvania resident sues a New Jersey corporation for an injury caused by the corporation's product; the injury has resulted in $90,000 of unpaid medical bills.
4. A New Jersey corporation is sued by a New Jersey resident under federal employment discrimination statutes.
5. A New Jersey resident sues the U.S. government in an appeal from the ruling of the U.S. Copyright Office.

Answers to this Self-Check are provided at the end of the chapter.

Legal Speak >))

Litigant
The generic term used to describe any party to a lawsuit.

Jurisdiction over Property
Courts may also exercise jurisdiction in a lawsuit based on property located within their jurisdictional boundaries. **In rem jurisdiction**[8] typically allows a court the authority to determine title to an object or real estate. **Quasi in rem jurisdiction** occurs when a court uses its in rem jurisdiction to compel a litigant to appear in court by attaching property that belongs to the litigant. This allows a court to obtain jurisdiction even if that court would normally have no personal jurisdiction over that party. For example, suppose that Molony, a resident of Florida, injures Trostle, a resident of Pennsylvania, during Trostle's vacation in Key West. If Trostle wishes to sue Molony in Pennsylvania, normally a Pennsylvania court would not have personal jurisdiction over Molony because he does not live there and the injury did not occur there. However, suppose that Molony owns a bed-and-breakfast in Pennsylvania. In that case, the Pennsylvania court could use its quasi in rem jurisdiction to compel Molony to appear in court and answer the negligence allegations—or Molony could face the seizure of his bed-and-breakfast to reimburse Trostle for any damages suffered as a result of Molony's negligence.

Personal Jurisdiction

Personal jurisdiction, called **in personam jurisdiction**, is a court's authority over the *parties* in a legal dispute. A party may be either an individual or a business entity such as a corporation. Since 1877, in the landmark case *Pennoyer v. Neff*,[9] the U.S. Supreme Court has articulated a framework for the exercise of personal jurisdiction by lower courts with the objective of providing *fairness* to the parties and complying with federal constitutional requirements related to due process. Of course, courts have modified this framework as necessary based on the realities of industrial and technological advances in society. This framework is used to determine jurisdiction over the defendant by a state's trial courts *and* the federal district courts within that state. Typically, analysis of personal jurisdiction focuses on the *conditions* of the controversy and the *actions* of the defendant.

In-State Defendants Personal jurisdiction is obtained by the courts when the business or individual is served with the complaint, initiating the lawsuit. The service of the complaint puts the business or individual on notice of being sued. Complaints are discussed in detail in Chapter 4, "Resolving Disputes: Litigation and Alternative Dispute Resolution."

LO 3-8

Explain the role of long-arm statutes in determining personal jurisdiction.

Out-of-State Defendants Courts use a two-prong test to determine whether they have personal jurisdiction over a party who does not reside in the state in which the court is located. First, the court's jurisdiction must be authorized by a **state long-arm statute** that grants the court specific authorization over the defendant due to the defendant's conduct or

---

[8]*In rem* is Latin for "against the matter (thing)" (Collins, *Latin,* 1e).
[9]95 U.S. 714 (1877).

other circumstances. As the name implies, long-arm statutes are intended to allow a court to "reach" into another state and exercise jurisdiction over a nonresident defendant. Typically, long-arm statutes[10] provide for jurisdiction if an out-of-state defendant (1) transacts business within the state's borders, or (2) commits a negligent act in that state that results in a loss to another party, or (3) owns property in the state.

The second prong requires a court to ensure that exercising jurisdiction over an out-of-state defendant meets the constitutional requirements of *fairness* and *due process*. This means that courts must consider the plight of the defendant who has been forced to defend a lawsuit in another state by taking into account the burden on the defendant. Courts examine two specific questions in deciding these fairness and due process issues.

Question No. 1: Does the defendant have some level of **minimum contacts** with the state, such as regularly shipping products to consumers in that state? If a defendant has continuous and systematic contact with a particular state, this will be sufficient to satisfy the minimum-contacts requirement.[11]

Question No. 2: Has the defendant *purposefully availed* himself by some affirmative act directed to that specific state? Whether a company has purposely availed itself in a state was addressed by the U.S. Supreme Court in *Asahi Metal Industry Co., Ltd. v. Superior Court of California*.[12] When a company performs "some act by which [the company] purposefully avails itself of the privilege of conducting activities within the forum State, thus invoking the benefits and protections of its laws," then the availment test is met.

In Case 3.1, the U.S. Supreme Court applies the minimum contacts test.

LO 3-9

Apply the minimum contacts test in both a traditional and an Internet setting.

CASE 3.1 Goodyear Dunlop Tires Operation v. Brown, 564 U.S. 915 (2011)

FACT SUMMARY Two 13-year-old boys from North Carolina, Matthew Helms and Julian Brown, had traveled to France to participate in a soccer tournament. The two boys were involved in a bus wreck outside Paris on their way back to the airport and died from injuries suffered in the accident. The parents of the boys believed the accident was due to a defective tire manufactured by a foreign subsidiary of the Goodyear Tire and Rubber Company (Goodyear USA) and sued the parent company and three of its foreign subsidiaries in a state court in North Carolina. Goodyear USA did not challenge personal jurisdiction, but the foreign subsidiaries argued that the North Carolina courts lacked jurisdiction over them and moved to dismiss the complaint for lack of personal jurisdiction. The trial court denied the motion, and the North Carolina Court of Appeals affirmed the trial court's decision in favor of Brown, ruling that a small percentage of tires manufactured by the foreign subsidiaries had entered the North Carolina market and that was sufficient minimum contacts. The Goodyear foreign subsidiaries then appealed to the U.S. Supreme Court.

SYNOPSIS OF DECISION AND OPINION The U.S. Supreme Court reversed the decision of the appellate court and ruled in favor of Goodyear. The Court concluded that specific jurisdiction was lacking in this case because the foreign subsidiaries' contacts with North Carolina were too limited. In addition, the Court also ruled that general jurisdiction over the foreign subsidiaries did not exist either. Specifically, the Court held that general jurisdiction is available to hold a corporation answerable for all claims within a state only if the corporation's

(continued)

---

[10] Many states base their long-arm statutes on a model act called the Uniform Interstate and International Procedure Act.
[11] *International Shoe v. Washington*, 326 U.S. 310 (1945).
[12] 480 U.S. 102 (1987).

contacts with the forum state are so continuous and systemic as to render the corporation "at home" in the forum state.

WORDS OF THE COURT: Continuous and Systematic Contacts

"The Due Process Clause of the Fourteenth Amendment sets the outer boundaries of a state tribunal's authority to proceed against [an out-of-state] defendant. The canonical opinion in this area remains *International Shoe*, in which we held that a State may authorize its courts to exercise personal jurisdiction over an out-of-state defendant if the defendant has 'certain minimum contacts with [the State] such that the maintenance of the suit does not offend "traditional notions of fair play and substantial justice."' . . . North Carolina is not a forum in which it would be permissible to subject petitioners to [personal] jurisdiction. [The foreign subsidiaries of Goodyear USA] are in no sense at home in North Carolina. Their attenuated connections to the State . . . fall far short of 'the continuous and systematic general business contacts' necessary to empower North Carolina to entertain suit against them on claims unrelated to anything that connects them to the State."

Case Questions

1. Why didn't the parents of the boys in this case initiate their lawsuit against the foreign subsidiaries of Goodyear USA in a French court?
2. Does this decision mean that the boys' parents are without any legal recourse against Goodyear's foreign subsidiaries?
3. The parent company in this case is Goodyear USA, an Ohio corporation with its principal place of business in the state of Ohio. Would the courts in North Carolina have personal jurisdiction over Goodyear USA in this case? Why or why not?
4. What if the executives of Goodyear's foreign subsidiaries had attended a business retreat in North Carolina? Would their presence in North Carolina allow a state court to exercise personal jurisdiction over the foreign subsidiaries in this case?
5. *Focus on Critical Thinking:* Why does the Court refer to the Due Process Clause in this decision? Also, should courts automatically deem a foreign subsidiary to share the "home" of its parent corporation for purposes of establishing personal jurisdiction over the foreign subsidiary?

Legal Speak >))

Defamation
Discussed in detail in Chapter 9, "Torts and Products Liability," defamation is an intentional act of making an untrue public statement about a party that causes some loss to be suffered by the defamed party.

Injurious Effect Another important consideration that courts explore in a personal jurisdiction analysis is whether it was reasonably *foreseeable* that the defendant's actions would have an *injurious effect* on a resident of the court's state. This question is usually applied in the context of a dispute involving some *intentional* act by the defendant that results in an injury to an individual or business entity located in the court's state. For example, in *Calder v. Jones*,[13] the U.S. Supreme Court ruled that a California court had jurisdiction over a Florida corporation in a defamation case filed by the actress Shirley Jones against a tabloid, the *National Enquirer*. Despite the fact that the tabloid had no physical presence or other contacts with California, the Court reasoned that jurisdiction was proper because the defendant knew, or should have known, that the defamatory article would have an injurious effect on the actress in California, where she lived and worked. This became known as the *effects test* and is now an important part of a personal jurisdiction analysis. Note, however, that courts apply the effects test narrowly and, thus far, only to cases involving intentional injurious acts (such as defamation).[14]

---

[13] 465 U.S. 783 (1984).

[14] The Court also applied the effects test in *Keeton v. Hustler Magazine*, 465 U.S. 770 (1984). The case involved a libel claim filed by Kathy Keeton in federal district court in New Hampshire. Keeton chose New Hampshire believing it to be a forum favorable to her case. *Hustler*'s only contact with the state was the circulation of copies of its magazine in New Hampshire. The Supreme Court held that a "regular circulation of magazines in the forum State is sufficient to support an assertion of jurisdiction in this case because of the potential for the injurious effect to be felt in New Hampshire."

In Case 3.2, a federal court uses an injurious effect analysis in a defamation case filed by a professional athlete.

CASE 3.2 Clemens v. McNamee, 615 F.3d 374 (5th Cir. 2010)

FACT SUMMARY In the summer of 2007, federal agents contacted Brian McNamee in connection with a federal investigation into the illegal manufacture and sale of performance-enhancing drugs in professional sports. McNamee was an athletic trainer who had worked for both the Toronto Blue Jays and the New York Yankees baseball clubs. After authorities convinced McNamee that they had sufficient evidence to convict him for injecting athletes with anabolic steroids, McNamee agreed to cooperate with investigators in exchange for immunity from prosecution. During an interview with investigators, McNamee admitted that he had administered steroids to all-star pitcher Roger Clemens in both Toronto and New York. McNamee repeated this allegation to Major League Baseball investigators and to a reporter during an interview with *Sports Illustrated*. In 2008, Clemens, a citizen of Texas, filed a defamation suit against McNamee, a citizen of New York, in federal court based on diversity of citizenship. The trial court dismissed the complaint due to lack of personal jurisdiction over McNamee because his alleged defamatory statements were made outside Texas. Clemens appealed to the Court of Appeals.

SYNOPSIS OF DECISION AND OPINION The Court of Appeals for the Fifth Circuit upheld the trial court's ruling in favor of McNamee and affirmed the dismissal of Clemens's defamation complaint. The court rejected Clemens's contention that jurisdiction was proper in a Texas court because he suffered harm from the defamation in Texas. The court analyzed McNamee's contacts with Texas in the context of the defamation claim and concluded that McNamee did not have sufficient minimum contacts as required by the long-arm statute and due process. The court held that to support personal jurisdiction in a defamation claim, the forum must be the "focal point" of the story. Although the court acknowledged that the defamation may cause distress and damage to Clemens's reputation in Texas, it concluded that the alleged defamatory statement was inadequately directed to Texas to satisfy the minimum-contacts requirement.

WORDS OF THE COURT: Minimal Contacts and Injurious Effect "In support of jurisdiction, Clemens points to the harm he suffered in Texas and to McNamee's knowledge of the likelihood of such damage in the forum. Yet under [previous case law], Clemens has not made a prima facie showing that McNamee made statements in which Texas was the focal point: the statements did not concern activity in Texas; nor were they made in Texas or directed to Texas residents any more than residents of any state. As such, the district court did not err in dismissing Clemens' suit for lack of personal jurisdiction over McNamee."

Case Questions

1. Why is due process relevant to the outcome of this case?
2. What is the practical implication of this decision? Does it mean that Clemens cannot bring suit for defamation in any court?
3. *Focus on Critical Thinking:* Why didn't Clemens sue McNamee in New York? Suppose that McNamee claimed that he had injected Clemens with steroids in Texas. Would this admission change the outcome of this case? How?

Physical Presence The physical presence of an out-of-state party in a particular state is generally an automatic basis for jurisdiction over the defendant by both that state's courts *and* federal trial courts within that state. In a business context, physical presence may include having an office, agent, or personnel (such as a sales team) located within the court's jurisdiction.

Many states have also passed specific statutes that give state courts personal jurisdiction over out-of-state residents who operate motor vehicles within the state for the narrow

| FIGURE 3.3 | Facebook's Forum Selection Clause |

"You will resolve any claim, cause of action or dispute . . . you have with us arising out of or relating to [these terms of service] or Facebook exclusively in the U.S. District Court for the Northern District of California or a state court located in San Mateo County, and you agree to submit to the personal jurisdiction of such courts for the purpose of litigating all such claims."

purposes of allowing a victim of an auto accident to pursue a claim against an out-of-state driver.

Voluntary A court also has personal jurisdiction if the parties agree to litigate in a specific court. Voluntary personal jurisdiction applies when a nonresident party agrees to the jurisdiction of a particular court in a certain state. This voluntary jurisdiction is often done through a *forum selection clause* written in a contract between the parties. A forum selection clause is a contractual agreement that obligates the parties to litigate any dispute arising out of the contract in a particular court named in the clause. Essentially, the parties are agreeing to a forum *ahead of time* so that if any litigation involving that particular contract is instituted, both parties are obligated to litigate the dispute in a predetermined court. As an example, Figure 3.3 restates the forum selection clause set forth in Facebook's terms of service. Note that later in this section, in Case 3.3, a federal trial court interprets and applies Facebook's forum selection clause.

The leading case involving a forum selection clause is *Carnival Cruise Lines v. Shute*, 499 U.S. 585 (1991), in which the U.S. Supreme Court upheld a federal court's ruling that dismissed a personal injury claim by a resident of the state of Washington who had been a passenger on a Carnival Cruise Lines ship and had fallen during a guided tour of the ship. The Court concluded that the passenger ticket was a contract between the passenger and Carnival Cruise Lines and that the ticket contained a forum selection clause whereby the parties agreed to litigate any disputes in Miami, Florida (where Carnival's headquarters is located).

Recall our *Cain v. APC* hypothetical case introduced earlier in the chapter. Suppose that Cain files his lawsuit in a federal district court in Massachusetts. In addition to establishing subject matter jurisdiction, he must also meet the court's standards for personal jurisdiction over APC. In this case, given the fact that the incident took place in Texas, it may be difficult for Cain to demonstrate APC's connection with Massachusetts unless APC owns property, maintains an office, regularly sends personnel to Massachusetts, or has some other regular and systematic connection with the state. In its jurisdiction analysis of the Cain versus APC matter, a federal court would first look to the Massachusetts long-arm statute and then to the constitutional requirements of due process and fairness, including APC's level of minimum contacts and purposeful availment in Massachusetts.

CONCEPT SUMMARY *Jurisdiction*

	Federal Trial Courts	State Trial Courts
Personal Jurisdiction	1. Residents and business entities located in the state where the federal trial court sits; or	1. Residents and business entities located in the state; or

(continued)

	Federal Trial Courts	**State Trial Courts**
	2. Nonresidents with *minimum contacts* with the state in which the federal trial court sits; or	2. Nonresidents owning property in the state; or
	3. Nonresidents owning property in the state in which the federal trial court sits; or	3. Nonresidents with *minimum contacts* with the state according to state long-arm statute; or
	4. Voluntary	4. Voluntary
Subject Matter Jurisdiction	1. Federal question; or 2. United States is a party; or 3. Diversity of citizenship exists and amount in controversy exceeds $75,000 (amount required only in diversity cases)	State law matters (statutes, common law, state constitutional issues)

Venue

While jurisdiction requires an analysis of whether a court has legal authority over a particular case, venue is a legal concept that defines the most appropriate *location* for the dispute to be heard. Two or more courts will sometimes have jurisdiction over the very same matter, but it might be more appropriate from a fairness perspective for the case to be heard in a particular location. Many states have venue rules to determine where a case may be heard. Typically, state statutes provide that venue in a civil case is where the defendant resides or is headquartered, while in a criminal case the venue is ordinarily where the crime was committed. While changes in venue for civil cases are rare, in high-profile criminal cases a defense attorney may ask for a *change of venue* to help select a jury from outside the area where the crime was committed, under the theory that the out-of-area jury will be more impartial and less influenced by the media.

To understand how venue may be important in a business context, suppose two Florida-based companies, Beta and Alpha, are involved in a breach of contract dispute in which Beta sues Alpha. The transaction involves an order that took place over a website based in Florida, and the order was shipped from Alpha's warehouse in Georgia to Beta's branch office in South Carolina. Although a number of state and federal courts may have jurisdiction over a dispute in this case, a Florida court may decide that Florida is the best *venue* for the dispute to be litigated because both parties have their principal office located there and assumedly it is the most convenient forum for the parties. It is likely that the witnesses and records are in Florida as well. Note, however, that a state court cannot unilaterally declare that venue exists in *another* jurisdiction. Courts apply venue statutes to determine whether or not *their* court is the most appropriate venue.

In Case 3.3, a federal trial court orders a transfer of venue based on a forum selection clause.

CASE 3.3 Franklin v. Facebook, No. 1:15-CV-00655 (N.D. Ga. 2015)

FACT SUMMARY Ricky Franklin received a series of unsolicited text messages from Facebook on his cell phone. (For example, one unsolicited text message read: "Today is Sara Glenn's birthday. Reply to post on her Timeline or reply to post 'Happy Birthday!'") Franklin sued Facebook in the U.S. District Court for the Northern District of Georgia, alleging that Facebook violated the

(continued)

Telephone Consumer Protection Act (TCPA), a federal law enacted in 1991, as well as Georgia law. In response to Franklin's complaint, Facebook filed a Motion to Transfer Venue, requesting the district court to enforce the forum selection clause in Facebook's terms of service, which every Facebook user must agree to when creating a Facebook account, and to transfer the case to the federal district court in Northern California. Specifically, Facebook argued Franklin was contractually bound to Facebook's terms of service, which includes a forum selection clause requiring "any claim, cause of action or dispute (claim)" against Facebook must be brought exclusively in either "the U.S. District Court for the Northern District of California or a state court located in San Mateo County." Franklin opposed Facebook's motion to transfer, arguing that his choice of forum was entitled to greater weight and that the forum selection clause in Facebook's terms of service was inapplicable to his case because his complaint was not based on his own use of Facebook but rather on the transmission of unsolicited text messages.

SYNOPSIS OF DECISION AND OPINION The U.S. District Court for the Northern District of Georgia ruled in favor of Facebook and granted the motion to transfer. The court ruled that the forum selection clause in Facebook's terms of service was valid and applied to the facts of this case.

WORDS OF THE COURT: Presumptive Validity of the Forum Selection Clause "[Facebook's terms of service] governs the legal relationship between Defendant [Facebook] and millions of users of its website and related services. Because of this, the forum selection clause contained in [Facebook's terms of service] has been addressed by numerous courts in actions involving Defendant. The Court cannot identify a single instance where any federal court has struck down [Facebook's terms of service] as an impermissible contract of adhesion induced by fraud or overreaching or held the forum selection clause now at issue to be otherwise unenforceable due to public policy considerations. [Here, the court cites several other federal district court cases involving Facebook's forum selection clause.] The Court finds the reasoning of these cases persuasive, declines to depart from the great weight of persuasive authority on this question, and accordingly finds that Plaintiff [Ricky Franklin] has failed to overcome the presumptive validity of the forum selection clause on the basis of fraud, overreaching, or contravention of public policy."

Case Questions

1. Are forum selection clauses always enforceable? Put another way, under what situations will a court *not* enforce a forum selection clause?

2. Franklin had alleged in his complaint that the text messages he received from Facebook were unsolicited and thus not related to his own Facebook account. Given this allegation, did the court decide the case correctly?

3. In its order, the court refers to the "persuasive authority" of several district court decisions involving Facebook users in previous cases. Nevertheless, was the judge obligated as a matter of law to follow these previous decisions? Why or why not?

4. *Focus on Critical Thinking:* What if Franklin had posted the following "status update" on his Facebook account right after signing up for Facebook for the first time:

> I, Ricky Franklin, hereby agree to every provision in Facebook's terms of use, except for the forum selection clause. I do not agree to the forum selection clause because I live in Georgia and I want a court in Georgia to resolve any dispute I may have with Facebook in the future.

If Facebook had chosen not to deactivate or suspend Franklin's account after he had posted such a message to his Facebook account, would the forum selection clause still have been enforceable?

INTERNET JURISDICTION

How do the principles of personal jurisdiction and minimum contacts apply to websites and e-mails? That is, if you send an e-mail to someone in another state, or if you do business over the Internet with someone in another state, would the courts in the other state have personal jurisdiction over you? Internet and e-mail jurisdiction is an area of law that is still developing.

How the Law Develops in Real Time

Today, almost anything can be bought, sold, or exchanged online. The Internet allows any business to reach consumers worldwide, build brand recognition, and maximize revenue. Almost all businesses have their own websites, and the online activities of a business or individual might include sending e-mails and text messages or engaging in video conferencing. Additional online activities might include sponsored ads on Google, Facebook, or other popular websites.

Because online activities are now so commonplace, business owners and managers must consider whether their various activities on the Internet could confer personal jurisdiction in courts in far-off locations. Simply put, is sending an e-mail or a text message sufficient to establish personal jurisdiction? What about a blog post or a YouTube video?

Ideally, one could look to legislation (such as state long-arm statutes) or court decisions for guidance on these issues. But most state long-arm statutes were enacted decades ago, before the Internet was commercialized in the mid-1990s. As such, the U.S. Supreme Court has yet to decide a personal jurisdiction case involving e-mail or purely Internet activities.

Meanwhile, lower courts are divided on the issue of Internet jurisdiction. Some courts have ruled that having a physical presence in the forum state is not necessary when continuous electronic communications are conducted between the parties and the out-of-state party is engaged in an ongoing business relationship with parties located in the forum state. For example, in *Costar Realty Information v. Meissner*,[15] a district court held that e-mails directed into Maryland, coupled with other activities, established personal jurisdiction over an Arizona-based defendant. Although the defendant had never entered Maryland, it had contracted to use the local plaintiff's database and services, it had communicated with the plaintiff via e-mail and telephone, and it had repeatedly accessed the plaintiff's Maryland-based servers.

At the same time, other courts have reached the opposite conclusion, holding that e-mail communications alone are insufficient to establish personal jurisdiction. For instance, a week after *Costar Realty* was decided by a district court in Maryland, the Fourth Circuit Court of Appeals (which encompasses Maryland) affirmed a trial court's dismissal for lack of personal jurisdiction over two nonresident defendants in the case of *Consulting Engineers Corp. v. Geometric Ltd.*[16] The federal appellate court held that a handful of e-mails and telephone communications alone did not satisfy minimum contacts with the state of Virginia. Although the plaintiff argued that the out-of-state defendant had intentionally directed electronic communications into Virginia with the clear intent of transacting business there, the court rejected that broad application and looked instead at "the quality and nature of the contacts" to evaluate whether they met the standards for minimum contacts. The court held that even if the defendant had "reached out" to plaintiffs via e-mail in Virginia, that fact, coupled only with the e-mails and telephone calls, was insufficient to establish personal jurisdiction.

Given this divergence among the lower courts, the issue of Internet jurisdiction provides a real-time case study of how the law develops in response to rapid technological

---

[15]604 F. Supp. 2d 757 (D. Md. 2009).

[16]561 F.3d 273 (4th Cir. 2009).

change. First, let's recap what we already know about personal jurisdiction; then let's see how the lower courts have grappled with Internet jurisdiction cases. To begin with, courts have developed a standard three-prong test for establishing personal jurisdiction over an out-of-state defendant:

1. The defendant must have sufficient minimum contacts with the forum state;
2. The claim asserted against the defendant must arise out of those contacts; and
3. The exercise of jurisdiction must be fair and reasonable.

In Internet jurisdiction cases, courts tend to diverge over the first prong: when do online activities generate sufficient minimum contacts with the forum state? In fact, a **circuit split** currently exists among the federal courts of appeal as to this issue. The Fourth and Fifth Circuits, for example, have handed down opinions applying *Zippo*'s sliding-scale analysis.[17] On the other hand, cases from the Seventh and Ninth Circuits have rejected *Zippo* and applied the *Calder* effects test instead to determine whether online activities could subject a defendant to personal jurisdiction in the target forum,[18] while the Second Circuit has adopted a "totality test" instead.[19] Let's take a closer look at these tests.

The *Zippo* test was announced in the case of *Zippo Manufacturing Co. v. Zippo Dot Com, Inc.*[20] This test uses a three-point sliding scale to assess whether a defendant's online activities constitute minimum contacts. In summary, there are minimum contacts when a defendant's website or Internet presence is on the far end of the scale (e.g., when a defendant actively and repeatedly conducts business over the Internet). By contrast, there are no minimum contacts when a defendant is on the opposite end of the scale—situations in which the defendant merely posts information on a website that anyone can access. In the middle of the sliding scale—interactive websites in which users exchange information with a host computer—courts must consider the level and nature of the exchange of information on a case-by-case basis to determine whether there are minimum contacts. Figure 3.4 is an illustration of the *Zippo* sliding scale used by many courts to analyze minimum contacts via the Internet.

Under the alternative "effects test," by contrast, the minimum contacts requirement is satisfied if it is reasonably *foreseeable* that the defendant's actions could have an *injurious effect* on a resident of the court's state.

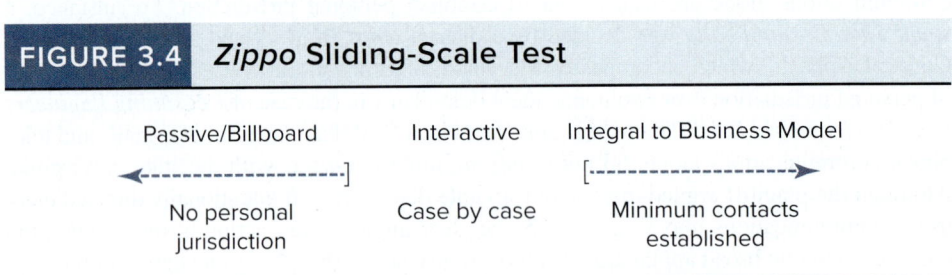

FIGURE 3.4 *Zippo* **Sliding-Scale Test**

[17] *See, e.g., Revell v. Lidov*, 317 F.3d 467 (5th Cir. 2002); *ALS Scan, Inc. v. Digital Serv. Consultants, Inc.*, 293 F.3d 707 (4th Cir. 2002).

[18] *See, e.g., Brayton Purcell, LLP v. Recordon & Recordon*, 606 F.3d 1124 (9th Cir. 2010); *Tamburo v. Dworkin*, 601 F.3d 693 (7th Cir. 2010).

[19] *See Grand River Enters. Six Nations, Ltd. v. Pryor*, 425 F.3d 158 (2d Cir. 2005).

[20] 952 F. Supp. 1119 (W.D. Pa. 1997).

The effects test originated in the case of *Calder v. Jones.*[21] Recall that *Calder* involved a lawsuit for defamation. Specifically, the U.S. Supreme Court ruled that a California court had personal jurisdiction over the *National Enquirer,* a Florida corporation, in a defamation case filed by Shirley Jones, an actress who lived in California. Despite the fact that the *Enquirer* had no physical presence in California, the Court reasoned that jurisdiction was proper because the *Enquirer* knew or should have known that its defamatory article would have an injurious effect on the actress in California, where she lived and worked.

Regardless of whether a particular jurisdiction follows the *Zippo* sliding-scale test, the *Calder* effects test, or an all-purpose totality test, in all cases courts will carefully consider any facts demonstrating how a website or e-mail/text message targets a particular forum. For instance, do the websites under consideration list specific jurisdictions where shipments will or will not be made? Does the website contain an end-user agreement that designates certain jurisdictions for legal actions? Is a specific mailing address or area code listed on the website or e-mail?

Jurisdictionally savvy business owners and managers should thus keep abreast of case law developments and consider conducting a strategic self-study or "self-audit" to determine where their online business transactions occur nationwide under the various legal tests. A strategic self-audit could prove helpful in predetermining jurisdictions where one's business is likely to be hauled into court.

Finally, although there is a circuit split regarding which test to apply, two facts remain clear: We should expect more and more cases involving wrongs committed over the Internet, and as these cases are decided and trickle upwards toward the U.S. Supreme Court, the law in this area will continue to develop.

CONCEPT SUMMARY Internet and E-mail Jurisdiction

- Lower federal courts have applied different tests to determine whether online activities can generate sufficient "minimum contacts" for personal jurisdiction purposes, such as the *Zippo* sliding-scale test and the *Calder* effects test.
- Under the *Zippo* sliding-scale test, there are minimum contacts when a defendant actively and repeatedly conducts business over the Internet, while there are no minimum contacts when a defendant merely posts information on a website that anyone can access. In the middle of this sliding scale, however, courts must consider the level and nature of the exchange of information on a case-by-case basis to determine whether there are minimum contacts.
- Under the "effects test," the minimum contacts requirement is satisfied if it is reasonably *foreseeable* that the defendant's actions could have an *injurious effect* on a resident of the court's state.

 Self-Check *Zippo* Standard

For the following, determine whether the court would have personal jurisdiction under the *Zippo* standard.

1. Scanner Corp., a Maryland-based corporation with its principal place of business in Baltimore, creates and markets copyrighted photos of models that are used as

(continued)

---

[21]465 U.S. 783 (1984).

background material on product packaging and picture frames. AP Picture Co. (AP) has wrongfully appropriated hundreds of Scanner's photos and published them on its website, where members can pay to download them. AP receives advertisement fees based on the amount of consumer traffic generated by the website. Scanner files suit in a Maryland court against AP and AP's Internet service provider, Megabites, a Georgia corporation with its principal place of business in Atlanta. Does the Maryland court have jurisdiction over Megabites?

2. Kristin, a resident of Hawaii, maintains a not-for-profit website from her home that offers information and opinions on commercial household movers. While the website does not charge for its usage, it does accept donations. Last summer, Kristin posted various derogatory and unflattering comments about Moving–U Inc. (MU), a New York corporation. In response to a user's question, Kristin asserted that MU was operating without the requisite legal authorization and insurance. If MU wishes to sue Kristin in a federal court in New York, does the court have personal jurisdiction over Kristin?

3. Natural Foods Inc. (Natural) is a Nevada-based firm that sells organic beef. Although it originally did business exclusively in Nevada through a small retail stand, Natural eventually created a website whereby customers throughout the United States could order beef to be shipped from Natural's ranch in Nevada to any city in the United States. When ordering, customers provide their billing and shipping addresses as well as credit card information and can sign up to receive newsletters. Johanna, a resident of Florida, orders beef via Natural's website and becomes sick after eating the product. Johanna sues Natural in a federal district court in Florida under a variety of legal theories. Does Natural have sufficient contacts for the Florida court to have personal jurisdiction over the company?

4. Big Bank Securities Inc. (BBS) is a Delaware corporation, with its principal place of business in New York. BBS trades various securities for its own benefit and for its clients. Cheyenne Securities Investors Inc. (CSI) is a Wyoming corporation providing portfolio management for various clients. A trader for CSI has contacted BBS through an instant-messaging program used by investors. CSI offers to sell $15 million in bonds to BBS in response to an earlier inquiry. BBS agrees to buy the bonds and sets a price and time for delivery of the bond instruments. The entire transaction is completed via the instant-messaging system. The next day CSI reneges on the sale, claiming it believes BBS has insider information. CSI has no offices or agents in New York. Would New York state courts have personal jurisdiction over a BBS versus CSI lawsuit for breach of contract?

Answers to this Self-Check are provided at the end of the chapter.

INTERNATIONAL JURISDICTION IN THE INTERNET AGE[22]

The Internet makes it easier than ever before for an individual or a business to engage in international transactions. While international commerce presents a substantial opportunity for a business's products or services to be advertised and sold to hundreds of millions of potential consumers worldwide, there are attendant legal risks that business owners and managers should be aware of. Even with the rapid movement toward global harmonization of laws and regulations, individual countries have their own political traditions, national cultures, and identities that may affect the way a country applies its laws and legal systems.

For example, suppose that Snow Sports Equipment (SSE) decides to expand its business to the European market. The owners of SSE set up an export chain whereby its products are

---
[22]Note that commercial jurisdiction in the general context of international law is discussed in detail in Chapter 25, "International Law and Global Commerce."

sold via a website with computers and servers located in an office in Boulder, Colorado, and then shipped from a leased warehouse in Prague, Czech Republic, to a retail store in Geneva, Switzerland. Which country's courts would have jurisdiction over any disputes involving the product? Also, which law would apply? U.S. law? European Union law? Swiss law? Czech law? Can a European consumer sue SSE in Europe under Swiss law or European law? (Note that the Czech Republic is an EU member state, but Switzerland is not.) This uncertainty and the inherent difficulty in determining which laws apply to an Internet transaction create challenges for business owners and managers. To some extent, these challenges can be addressed through the use of forum selection clauses and choice of law clauses in business contracts. Thus, effective business owners and managers will work with their business lawyers to anticipate and solve these challenges ahead of time, and some degree of cost-benefit analysis may be necessary to measure the risks of international trade versus the return on investment.

Country of Origin Standard

The governments of the United States, Canada, and the European Union have generally agreed to apply the law of the country in which the defendant's servers are *located*. This so-called **country of origin principle** provides courts an easy rule of thumb to determine the relevant choice of law. Yet some countries have adopted a *country of reception* approach that increases the risk to a business because, in theory, one would need to have a fundamental knowledge of the laws of each individual country where one conducts business online in order to reduce the risk of noncompliance.

Other Theories of Jurisdiction in Electronic Commerce

Consider a decision by Australia's highest court, issued in December 2002. The court ruled that American-based publisher Dow Jones could be sued in Australia for defamation based on an article that appeared on its website, even though Dow Jones has no presence in Australia and its website and infrastructure (such as the mainframe servers) are located in New Jersey. The plaintiff in the case, Joseph Gutnick, a wealthy Australian businessman, likely chose his home forum because of its convenience and Australia's relatively pro-plaintiff defamation laws. Dow Jones contended that the case should take place in the United States because that was where the article was uploaded to its computer servers (in New Jersey) and it was also the closest location to where the article was physically published (New York). The Australian court ruled against Dow Jones, reasoning that an online article is actually published where and when the article appears on the user's computer screen.

CONCEPT SUMMARY   Minimum Contacts on the Internet

- The *Zippo* standard is a sliding-scale approach for measuring the amount of a party's minimum contacts based on the interactivity of a website.
- Under the *Zippo* standard, passive websites that provide information and can be accessed by any Internet user do not— standing alone—provide a basis for personal jurisdiction.
- Websites used with some degree of interactivity are evaluated on a case-by-case basis: Websites that simply exchange information generally do not involve sufficient contacts for asserting personal jurisdiction, while websites involving subscription services may provide the basis for minimum contacts and purposeful availment.

(continued)

- Websites that are integral to the business model and are used consistently for commercial transactions generally constitute minimum contacts.
- E-mail communication between parties with an ongoing business relationship has been found to be sufficient minimum contacts by a limited number of courts.
- In international transactions conducted over the Internet, courts in the location of the website's servers will generally have jurisdiction over any disputes arising out of the use of the website under "the country of origin" approach.

KEY TERMS

Court p. 76 A judicial tribunal duly constituted for the hearing and adjudication of cases.

Judiciary p. 76 The collection of federal and state courts existing primarily to adjudicate disputes and charged with the responsibility of judicial review.

State courts p. 77 Courts that adjudicate matters dealing primarily with cases arising from state statutory, state common, or state constitutional law.

Federal courts p. 77 Courts that adjudicate matters dealing primarily with national laws, federal constitutional issues, and other cases (such as cases involving diversity jurisdiction).

State trial courts p. 77 The first courts at the state level before which the facts of a case are decided.

State appellate courts p. 77 State-level courts of precedent, concerned primarily with reviewing the decisions of trial courts.

Plaintiff p. 77 The party initiating a lawsuit.

Defendant p. 77 The party responding to a lawsuit and alleged by the plaintiff to have caused a wrongful act.

Trial de novo p. 78 A completely new trial.

Civil cases p. 78 Cases in which one party seeks a remedy, such as an award of money damages, for a private wrong committed by another party.

Criminal cases p. 78 Cases in which the accused party is charged by the government with committing a crime.

Remand p. 79 When an appellate court sends a case back to the lower court from which it came for further action consistent with the opinion and instructions of the higher court.

U.S. district courts p. 79 Trial courts at the federal level.

U.S. courts of appeal p. 79 The intermediate appellate courts in the federal system, frequently referred to as the *Circuit Courts of Appeal*. There are 13 circuits or geographical areas, each of which reviews the decisions of the federal district courts in the state or several states within its circuit.

U.S. Supreme Court p. 79 The highest federal court that not only reviews decisions of the lower federal courts but also reviews decisions of state courts that involve some issue of federal law.

Precedent p. 84 Applying the law made in previous appellate court opinions to current cases with similar facts; binding on the trial courts.

Jurisdiction p. 84 The legal authority that a court must have before it can hear a case.

Venue p. 84 A determination of the most appropriate court location for litigating a dispute.

Subject matter jurisdiction p. 85 The court's authority over the dispute between the parties.

Personal jurisdiction p. 85 The court's authority over the parties involved in the dispute.

Federal question p. 86 Some issue arising from the Constitution, a federal statute or regulation, or federal common law.

Party p. 86 A person or entity making or responding to a claim in a court.

Diversity of citizenship p. 86 Situation in which opposing parties in a lawsuit are citizens of different states or one party is a citizen of a foreign country; the case is placed under federal court jurisdiction if the amount in controversy exceeds $75,000 and does not involve a decree for divorce, alimony, or child custody.

Original jurisdiction p. 86 Jurisdiction that enables a court to be the trial court to hear the case. The case must be filed first in this court.

Concurrent jurisdiction p. 87 Situation in which two different courts each has subject matter jurisdiction to hear a case.

In rem jurisdiction p. 88   Jurisdiction over real or personal property when the property itself is the principal subject of the lawsuit.

Quasi in rem jurisdiction p. 88   Jurisdiction over real or personal property when the lawsuit has to do with personal liabilities not directly associated with the property.

In personam jurisdiction p. 88   Another term for *personal jurisdiction*.

State long-arm statutes p. 88   State statutes intended to allow a court to reach into another state and exercise jurisdiction over a nonresident defendant due to the defendant's activities or other conduct affecting the state in which the court sits.

Minimum contacts p. 89   A legal term for when it is appropriate for a court in one state (the forum state) to assert personal jurisdiction over a defendant from another state.

Circuit split p. 96   Occurs when two or more different federal circuit courts of appeal offer conflicting rulings on the same issue.

Country of origin principle p. 99   General agreement between the United States, Canada, and the European Union governments to apply the law of the country in which the defendant's servers are located.

CHAPTER REVIEW QUESTIONS

1. Which of the following is a major distinction between trial courts and appellate courts?
   a. Only appellate courts decide questions of constitutional law; trial courts interpret statutes.
   b. Only appellate courts set precedents that are binding on trial courts.
   c. Only trial courts have the power to remand cases up to appellate courts.
   d. Only trial court judges are elected; appellate court judges are appointed.
   e. Only appellate court judges are elected; trial court judges are appointed.

2. Diversity of citizenship is an example of what type of federal jurisdiction?
   a. Original jurisdiction
   b. Voluntary jurisdiction
   c. Personal jurisdiction
   d. Quasi in rem jurisdiction
   e. Subject matter jurisdiction

3. Which of the following scenarios illustrates the concept of voluntary jurisdiction? *(More than one answer might be literally true. Choose the best one.)*
   a. An out-of-state defendant who signs a contract containing a forum selection clause in which the parties agree to litigate any disputes in the designated forum state.
   b. An out-of-state defendant who knowingly makes a defamatory statement with the purpose of causing injury to the defamed person in that person's forum state.
   c. An out-of-state defendant who owns an interactive website accessible to users in the plaintiff's forum state.
   d. An out-of-state defendant who inherits property under a contested will.
   e. An out-of-state defendant who travels to the plaintiff's forum state.

4. Which of the following statements regarding the three scales of the *Zippo* standard is true?
   I. *Fully interactive websites always generate minimum contacts.*
   II. *Passive websites never generate minimum contacts.*
   III. *Websites that are integral to the website owner's business model always generate minimum contacts.*
   a. I and II
   b. II and III
   c. I, II, and III
   d. I only
   e. II only

5. Which of the following statements regarding minimum contacts in Internet jurisdiction cases is true?
   a. Most courts apply the totality test.
   b. Most courts apply the *Zippo* standard.
   c. Most courts follow the *Calder* effects test.
   d. Most courts apply a bright-line rule: Internet activity alone never generates sufficient minimum contacts consistent with due process.
   e. The lower courts are split on the issue of Internet jurisdiction; this area of law is still developing.

Answers and explanations are provided at the end of this chapter.

THEORY TO PRACTICE

PART I

Santiago Information Systems (Santiago) is a business based in Baltimore, Maryland, that purchases old computers, refurbishes them with new software and hardware parts, and sells them in bulk for about half the price of a new PC. For the past three years, Santiago has shipped approximately 40 percent of its inventory to the same client. The client is the Wilmington School District (Wilmington) in Wilmington, Delaware, and the school pays approximately $80,000 to Santiago for the computers per year. Santiago also visits each school to be sure that the computers are installed correctly and that the school district is satisfied with the order. Santiago has a website that gives contact information for the company, but the site is only partially interactive because users can transact business only by sending Santiago an e-mail via the website. Recently, Wilmington discovered that large shipments of Santiago's products were defective, and it has been unable to come to a resolution with Santiago over the matter.

1. If Wilmington wishes to sue Santiago, what court or courts would have jurisdiction over this matter?
2. What would be the best venue and why?
3. If a Delaware court decides that it does not have jurisdiction, how may that affect Wilmington's decision on whether or not to file a lawsuit?

PART II

Assume that one of Santiago's suppliers, Parts R Us (Parts), is headquartered in Union City, New Jersey, and has been shipping Santiago parts for approximately four years in a row. Last year, Parts sold approximately $7,000 in hardware to Santiago. In the past 10 years, Parts R Us has shipped to businesses in Maryland, New York, New Jersey, and Connecticut. Parts has also e-mailed advertisements to potential leads in each of the 50 states. Wilmington has determined that Parts provided the defective components used in the computer order described in Part I.

1. If Wilmington decides to file suit against Parts in Delaware, will a Delaware court have personal jurisdiction over Parts? Why or why not?
2. Suppose Parts has a website where customers can order products, pay for them via credit card, and have them delivered via a delivery service to any U.S. city. How does this affect your jurisdiction analysis?
3. If Parts's only contact with Delaware is via its website, what standard should the trial court apply to determine whether there are minimum contacts?

LEGAL STRATEGY 101

Forum Shopping

Forum shopping refers to a common strategic tactic by plaintiffs in civil litigation. It occurs when a strategic plaintiff selects the most favorable legal forum in which to initiate a lawsuit.

Forum shopping is often maligned and criticized, but it is a common legal strategy. In fact, forum shopping provides a good illustration of the *preventive* or risk-reduction legal strategy we saw at the end of Chapter 1: the proactive practice of anticipating potential legal risks to one's business and taking preventive measures to reduce or manage those risks.

By way of example, perhaps the single-greatest or looming legal risk that all businesses face is the threat of litigation, and a common legal strategy to address this risk is the use of well-drafted "forum selection clauses" in business agreements. Let's take a look at a real-world instance of this preventive legal strategy.

Consider a familiar website like Facebook. With over two billion active users, the threat of litigation is a daunting one. But to open a Facebook account in the first place, a user must agree to Facebook's *terms of service*. (You can check out Facebook's user agreement for yourself here: https://www.facebook.com/terms.) Among the many provisions in Facebook's user agreement is the following forum selection clause:

> You will resolve any claim, cause of action or dispute . . . you have with us arising out of or relating to this [user agreement] or Facebook exclusively in the U.S. District Court for the Northern District of California or a state court

Silicon Valley. KiskaMedia/Getty Images

located in San Mateo County, and you agree to submit to the personal jurisdiction of such courts for the purpose of litigating all such claims.

In other words, because Facebook's corporate headquarters are located in Menlo Park, California (in San Mateo County), and because the closest federal trial court is located in nearby San Jose, California (in next-door Santa Clara County), if a Facebook user ever wants to sue Facebook for any reason, he or she must do so in Facebook's "back yard," so to speak. Moreover, notice how this legal strategy not only helps a giant business firm like Facebook reduce its legal expenses by consolidating most of its litigation in northern California; it also guarantees Facebook "home court advantage" in cases involving out-of-state plaintiffs!

Yes, the law is supposed to be applied impartially, and yes, courts are supposed to be fair and neutral, but in close cases, the benefit of securing home court advantage cannot be underestimated, especially in jury trials. In sum, because the risk of litigation is a real one, business firms may take strategic measures—such as incorporating well-drafted "forum selection clauses" into their business agreements before any litigation ensues—in order to channel litigation toward a favorable legal forum or secure home court advantage in the event of litigation.

CRITICAL THINKING QUESTIONS

1. Is forum shopping ethical?
2. Should courts enforce forum selection clauses in business-to-consumer contracts like the Facebook user agreement described here? Why or why not?
3. Suppose Facebook did not have a forum selection clause in its user agreement. Would Facebook be subject to the jurisdiction of every state court in the United States because it has millions of users in every U.S. state?

MANAGER'S CHALLENGE

Managers are frequently involved in various aspects of business planning. Managers need to be aware not only of current trends that affect their industry but also of potential liability issues during the planning process. Assume that you are a midlevel manager at Santiago Information Systems (see the Theory to Practice problem). After settling with Wilmington in an out-of-court agreement, Santiago embarks on an expansion plan, and you receive the following e-mail from your senior manager:

> We are planning a very aggressive marketing campaign and extending our reach beyond institutions such as Wilmington by targeting individual consumers as well. This will include revamping and expanding the functionality of our website to include online ordering and the use of e-mail advertisements to selected consumer groups. Write a two- to three-page memorandum advising me of any potential liability associated with the website in terms of out-of-state clients, and make recommendations on how to limit any liability from the marketing plan related to revamping the website and using mass e-mail advertisements to selected consumers. Be sure to include any cost-benefit issues that may be applicable.

See Connect for Manager's Challenge sample answers.

CASE SUMMARY 3.1 Bickford v. Onslow Memorial Hospital Foundation, 855 A.2d 1150 (Me. 2004)

PERSONAL JURISDICTION

Bickford, a resident of Maine, received hospital bills over a period of several months from Onslow Memorial Hospital (Onslow), which had treated a relative of Bickford's ex-wife. Although Onslow eventually acknowledged that Bickford was not legally responsible for the bills, Onslow continued to pursue the debt through collection and reported the debt as delinquent to Bickford's credit agencies. Bickford filed suit against Onslow in a Maine state court, alleging a violation of several consumer protection laws. Onslow is located in North Carolina and does not own property or have any agents in Maine.

CASE QUESTION

1. Does the Maine court have personal jurisdiction over Onslow?

CASE SUMMARY 3.2 M/S Bremen v. Zapata Off-Shore Co., 407 U.S. 1 (1972)

JURISDICTION: FORUM SELECTION CLAUSE

Zapata, a Texas corporation, hired Unterweser, a German corporation, to provide a tugboat for pulling Zapata's oil rig. Unterweser prepared a contract, and Zapata signed the contract after having made several changes. The contract contained a forum selection clause requiring any disputes to be litigated in the International Commercial Court in London. Zapata had not altered that part of the contract. Unterweser's tugboat departed from Louisiana pulling Zapata's oil rig, but while the tugboat and rig were in international waters off the Gulf of Mexico, a storm arose that resulted in severe damage to the oil rig. Zapata instructed Unterweser to tow the rig to the nearest port, in Tampa, Florida. Zapata then filed a lawsuit in the federal district court in Tampa for $3.5 million against Unterweser.

CASE QUESTIONS

1. Does the court in Tampa have jurisdiction over Unterweser? Why or why not?
2. Will the forum selection clause be enforced? Why or why not?

CASE SUMMARY 3.3 Pennzoil v. Colelli, 149 F.3d 197 (3d Cir. 1998)

PURPOSEFUL AVAILMENT

Colelli & Associates (Colelli) is a manufacturing firm with its principal place of business in Ohio. Colelli was engaged in the manufacture and sale of a specialized oil well solvent, which it sold to several oil producers based in Ohio. Sixty percent of the oil produced by the Ohio producers was shipped to refineries in Pennsylvania, including a refinery owned and operated by Pennzoil Products Company (Pennzoil). Pennzoil, a corporation based in Nevada with refineries around the world, sued Colelli in a federal district court located in Pennsylvania on a product liability claim, contending that Colelli's solvent had damaged its Pennsylvania refinery. Colelli contested the court's jurisdiction because the company had no *direct* contact with Pennsylvania business owners and had no other contacts within Pennsylvania. Pennzoil argued that Colelli knew that its product was being used by Pennsylvania companies and had gained a substantial benefit by virtue of its product being used by Pennsylvania oil refineries such as Pennzoil's.

CASE QUESTION

1. Has Colelli purposefully availed itself in Pennsylvania to warrant personal jurisdiction? Why or why not?

CASE SUMMARY 3.4 World-Wide Volkswagen Corp. v. Woodson, 444 U.S. 286 (1980)

MINIMUM CONTACTS

The Robinsons, residents of New York, purchased a new Audi car from Seaway, a car dealership in New York. Seaway obtained this car from World-Wide Volkswagen, a New York corporation that is a regional distributor for Audi serving the New York, New Jersey, and Connecticut markets. While driving the car through Oklahoma, the Robinsons were severely injured in a car accident. The Robinsons brought a product liability lawsuit against both Seaway and World-Wide Volkswagen in a federal trial court in Oklahoma. World-Wide contended that the Oklahoma court did not have personal jurisdiction because World-Wide had no property, presence, or agents in Oklahoma.

CASE QUESTIONS

1. Does the court in Oklahoma have personal jurisdiction over World-Wide Volkswagen?
2. Because a car is inherently mobile and because the continental United States is connected by a network of national highways, do these facts mean that jurisdiction is appropriate in any state where a car has traveled?

CASE SUMMARY 3.5 Toys "R" Us, Inc. v. Step Two, S.A., 318 F.3d 446 (3d Cir. 2003)

MINIMUM CONTACTS VIA THE WEB

Toys "R" Us is a Delaware corporation headquartered in New Jersey that owns and operates retail stores worldwide. In 1999, it acquired Imaginarium Toy Centers, including the rights to various trademarks held by Imaginarium. Step Two, a corporation based in Spain, owns franchised toy stores operating under the Imaginarium name in several Spanish cities but does not maintain any offices or stores outside of Spain. Each corporation registered multiple e-mail addresses under the Imaginarium name. Step Two's sites were interactive and allowed users to purchase toys online, but the company would ship only within Spain. If a user signed up for Step Two's electronic newsletter, the user was prompted to enter personal information and was provided with a drop-down menu of various Spanish provinces where users were located. This menu did not accommodate mailing addresses within the United States, and Step Two maintains that it has never made a sale in the United States. Toys "R" Us claimed that it had evidence that a resident of New Jersey made two purchases via the website, but it conceded that these purchases were delivered to a Toys "R" Us employee in Spain, who then forwarded the items to the purchaser in New Jersey. Toys "R" Us filed a trademark infringement suit in a federal district court in New Jersey.

CASE QUESTIONS

1. Does the federal court in New Jersey have subject matter jurisdiction over this case?
2. Has Step Two purposefully availed itself in New Jersey, thus having the requisite minimum contacts? Why or why not?
3. Analyze this case under both the *Zippo* sliding-scale test and the *Calder* effects test. Describe the analysis and potential outcome under each. Which one is the correct test to use and why?

CASE SUMMARY 3.6 Office Depot, Inc. v. Zuccarini, 596 F.3d 696 (9th Cir. 2010)

JURISDICTION: *IN REM/QUASI IN REM*

In December 2000, Office Depot obtained a court judgment against John Zuccarini under the Anti-cybersquatting Consumer Protection Act of 1999 based on Zuccarini's registration of the domain name "offic-depot.com." Because Office Depot was unable to collect on the judgment, it eventually assigned the judgment to another company, DS Holdings (DSH). DSH registered the judgment in the district court for the Northern District of California and subsequently learned that Zuccarini owned more than 248 domain names registered with the company VeriSign, of which more than 190 were "dot-com" domain names. Targeting the dot-com domain names, DSH sought to levy and sell some of those names owned by Zuccarini. (The Anti-cybersquatting Consumer Protection Act states that jurisdiction over domain names shall be "in the judicial district in which the domain name registrar, domain name registry, or other domain name authority that registered or assigned the domain name is located. . . .") The district court appointed a receiver to take control of and auction off some of Zuccarini's domain names in order to satisfy the original judgment in the *Office Depot* case. DSH never claimed that the district court in the Northern District of California had personal jurisdiction over Zuccarini himself but instead argued that the court had *in rem* jurisdiction over his intangible property rights (i.e., his various "dot.com" domain names) located in the state of California. The district court ruled for DSH, and Zuccarini appealed to the Ninth Circuit Court of Appeals, contending that the Northern District of California was not a proper place to levy against his domain names and that the appointment of the receiver was therefore improper.

CASE QUESTIONS

1. Do *in rem* and *quasi in rem* jurisdiction apply to intangible property rights like domain names? Why or why not?
2. Which form of jurisdiction should apply to this case: *in rem* or *quasi in rem*?
3. Why can the court obtain jurisdiction allowing the seizure and sale of domain names without first obtaining personal jurisdiction over the defendant John Zuccarini?

CASE SUMMARY 3.7 Tempur-Pedic International v. Go Satellite Inc., 758 F. Supp. 2d 366 (N.D. Tex. 2010)

INTERNET JURISDICTION

Tempur-Pedic brought suit against Go Satellite in a federal court in Texas, alleging that Go Satellite infringed on Tempur-Pedic's registered trademark. The suit alleged that Go Satellite operated two websites that sold Tempur-Pedic brand mattresses without being an authorized dealer for Tempur-Pedic. Go Satellite asked the court to dismiss the claim because the Texas court had no personal jurisdiction over the company because it was based in Kentucky, did not own property in Texas, and had no sales force in Texas. Tempur-Pedic countered that Go Satellite's website was highly interactive, including the ability for consumers to purchase and pay online and to have a virtual chat with a customer service representative, and had, in fact, sold and shipped mattresses to consumers in Texas.

CASE QUESTIONS

1. What test or tests could the court apply to determine whether the website constitutes sufficient contacts to warrant personal jurisdiction in Texas?
2. Does the court have personal jurisdiction over Go Satellite? Why or why not?
3. Name some examples of "interactivity" that a court may consider when analyzing personal jurisdiction via the Internet.

CASE SUMMARY 3.8 Bristol-Myers Squibb Co. v. Superior Court of California, 137 S. Ct. 1773 (2017)

PERSONAL JURISDICTION

Several hundred individuals (678 persons in all) brought a massive lawsuit against the Bristol-Myers Squibb Company in a California state court, alleging that they all suffered negative side effects from the drug Plavix, which was manufactured by Bristol-Meyers in Puerto Rico. Only 86 of the plaintiffs, however, lived in California. The remaining 592 plaintiffs lived outside California, and only one percent of Bristol-Meyer's total revenues came from the sale of Plavix in California. Lawyers for Bristol-Meyers thus petitioned the court in California to dismiss the claims of the non-California plaintiffs for lack of personal jurisdiction.

CASE QUESTIONS

1. Do the California courts have general or specific jurisdiction over the claims of the 592 non-California plaintiffs?
2. What if the non-California plaintiffs can prove that they purchased Plavix in California?
3. Even if the non-California plaintiffs did not purchase any Plavix in California, what if they can prove that they had visited California while they were taking Plavix?

CASE SUMMARY 3.9 Florida v. Georgia, 138 S. Ct. 2502 (2018)

ORIGINAL JURISDICTION

In the southeastern United States, the Apalachicola-Chattahoochee-Flint (ACF) River Basin contains three major rivers, including the Chattahoochee River, which forms the state border between Georgia and Alabama, and the Flint River, which runs from northern Georgia until it meets with the Chattahoochee River at the southern edge of Georgia and Alabama. Both of these rivers then join together to become the Apalachicola River, which crosses into Florida's panhandle. Besides serving as a source of water for various municipal water systems in all three states, the ACF River Basin also provides significant quantities of water for agricultural irrigation. Population growth in Atlanta and severe regional droughts in 2011 and 2012, however, have reduced water flows from the ACF River Basin into the Florida panhandle. As a result, Florida sued Georgia in the U.S. Supreme Court, requesting a water allocation cap on Georgia. The Supreme Court assigned a special master to review Florida's complaint, and after a six-week trial, the special master ruled against Florida. Undaunted, Florida challenged the special master's ruling in the Supreme Court.

CASE QUESTIONS

1. Why does this case fall under the U.S. Supreme Court's original jurisdiction?
2. Why did the Supreme Court appoint a "special master" to hear this case in the first instance instead of deciding the merits of Florida's lawsuit itself?
3. Does the Congress have the power to enlarge or reduce the Supreme Court's original jurisdiction?

 Self-Check ANSWERS Subject Matter Jurisdiction

1. No. No diversity of citizenship and no federal issue involved.
2. Yes. The U.S. government agency is a party to the litigation.
3. Yes. Diversity of citizenship, with the amount in controversy exceeding $75,000.
4. Yes. Federal issue involving a federal statute.
5. Yes. The United States is a party to the litigation and a federal statute is at issue.

Zippo Standard

1. No. The court cannot exercise personal jurisdiction over Megabites. The company's conduct is strictly passive and, thus, not sufficient for an exercise of jurisdiction. *See generally ALS Scan, Inc. v. Digital Serv. Consultants, Inc.*, 293 F.3d 707 (4th Cir. 2002).
2. No. Regardless of the acceptance of donations or responses to user questions, New York courts would not have jurisdiction for defamatory comments made outside New York. The website in question can be accessed by anyone in the world, and there is no evidence that Kristin is targeting New York or availing herself of the opportunity to directly conduct business in New York. *See generally Best Van Lines, Inc. v. Walker*, 490 F.3d 239 (2d Cir. 2007).
3. Yes. Considering the interactivity of its website and the fact that consumers can purchase products from it, courts in Florida could exercise jurisdiction over Natural Foods.
4. Yes. A New York court would have jurisdiction because CSI is clearly attempting to do business in New York with BBS through the instant-messaging system. CSI knowingly contacted BBS in order to initiate the transaction, which culminated in the sale of $15 million in bonds; thus, CSI entered into New York to conduct business. *See generally Deutsche Bank Sec., Inc. v. Mont. Bd. of Invs.*, 850 N.E.2d 1140 (N.Y. 2006).

CHAPTER REVIEW QUESTIONS: Answers and Explanations

1. **b.** Trial court decisions are binding only on the parties to the case. Appellate court decisions are binding on lower courts in future cases. Answer choice (a) is incorrect because appellate courts also interpret statutes. Choice (c) is incorrect because appellate courts, not trial courts, have the power to remand cases. And choices (d) and (e) are incorrect because different states use different methods of selecting state trial and state appellate judges, while all federal judges must be appointed by the president and confirmed by the Senate.

2. **e.** Subject matter jurisdiction refers to a court's power to decide the legal claims presented by the parties to a case, and in the federal courts, there are two major types of subject matter jurisdiction: federal question jurisdiction and diversity of citizenship jurisdiction. Original jurisdiction (choice [a]) refers to the U.S. Supreme Court's constitutional power to hear certain cases in the first instance. Voluntary jurisdiction (choice [b]) refers to situations in which the parties agree to litigate in a specific court. Personal jurisdiction (choice [c]) refers to a court's power over the parties. Quasi in rem (choice [d]) refers to jurisdiction over land or personal property in certain cases.

3. **a.** A contract containing a forum selection clause is literally the textbook example of voluntary jurisdiction. Answer choice (b) is an example of the concept of injurious effects. Choice (c) refers to one of the scales of the *Zippo* standard, while jurisdiction in the scenario in choice (d) will depend on the state in which the will was made. Choice (e) refers to the concept of physical presence.

4. **b.** Under the *Zippo* sliding-scale standard, interactive websites are judged on a case-by-case basis.

5. **e.** The decisions of the lower courts diverge on the matter of minimum contacts in Internet jurisdiction cases, and, thus, this area of law is still developing. Answer choices (a), (b), (c), and (d) are wrong because of the word "most." In reality, different courts have applied different tests and standards to assess the level of contacts in Internet cases, but no court has applied a simple bright-line rule in Internet cases (e.g., a clear rule holding that Internet activity alone never generates sufficient minimum contacts consistent with due process).

CHAPTER 4
Resolving Disputes: Litigation and Alternative Dispute Resolution

©philsajonesen/Getty Images

Learning Objectives

After studying this chapter, students who have mastered the material will be able to:

4-1   Identify the ways in which civil litigation and dispute resolution inform business planning.
4-2   Explain how the Class Action Fairness Act impacts class action lawsuits.
4-3   Name the stages of litigation and identify the main features of each stage.
4-4   List the methods of alternative dispute resolution (ADR) and the potential advantages of using ADR.
4-5   Distinguish between arbitration and mediation and compare and contrast both methods of ADR.
4-6   Apply the legal standards under which an arbitration clause may be found invalid.
4-7   Provide an example of a hybrid form of alternative dispute resolution.

Litigation and alternative dispute resolution (ADR) are an essential part of business planning and strategy. It is inevitable that businesses will need to resolve disputes with their customers, other businesses, and local, state, or federal government agencies. Whether those disputes can be resolved without recourse to costly litigation will significantly affect the company's bottom line. It is therefore imperative that managers understand their options and the advantages and disadvantages of ordinary civil litigation versus alternative methods of dispute resolution. Accordingly, in this chapter students will learn

- The role of dispute resolution in business planning.
- The stages of civil litigation in resolving disputes.
- Methods of alternative dispute resolution.

CIVIL LITIGATION

Civil litigation refers to dispute resolution processes of civil (noncriminal) cases in public courts of law. (The term *litigation* is sometimes used as a synonym for *trial*, but in reality the scope of litigation is much broader and includes *pretrial* as well as *posttrial* events.) There are many varieties of business litigation, including contract and employment disputes and lawsuits relating to negligence, bankruptcy, and intellectual property issues as well. Moreover, the odds that a business firm will become involved in litigation continue to go up. According to the U.S. Bureau of Justice Statistics, the total number of civil cases filed in state and federal courts now exceeds 30 million cases annually.[1]

DISPUTE RESOLUTION AND BUSINESS PLANNING

LO 4-1
Identify the ways in which civil litigation and dispute resolution inform business planning.

Dispute resolution is a crucial part of business planning and strategy that requires a thoughtful cost-benefit analysis; that is, it is not a technical or purely legal matter to be delegated to attorneys. While legal counsel is an important source of information and advice, business managers and owners must make critical decisions regarding how to resolve a dispute. Furthermore, business managers and owners have an ever-increasing number of options to resolve disputes within and outside the legal system, and each option has advantages and disadvantages.

To illustrate how dispute resolution may be used in business planning, suppose that Classic Retail Outlets (CRO) enters into a contract with Sign Designs Company (SignCo). The contract calls for SignCo to design, manufacture, and install signage for several CRO locations. The parties agree on certain specifications and a payment of 50 percent at the time of signing the contract and 50 percent at the time of delivery. SignCo delivers a prototype of the new sign, but CRO management is unhappy with the design and claims that SignCo did not follow the specifications in the contract. SignCo agrees to work on a new prototype but delays the process for several months. Finally, SignCo submits a new prototype, but CRO again rejects the prototype, citing additional flaws in its design. In addition, so much time has passed that CRO has had to incur the expense of installing temporary signs.

In this hypothetical example, a dispute is brewing between CRO and SignCo. Yet at least two business problems still exist: (1) Despite the fact that 50 percent of the contract price has been paid to SignCo, CRO still needs a sign and has now expended more money than anticipated due to the temporary signs, and (2) SignCo has devoted significant time and materials to the project and may believe that CRO is being unreasonable in its expectations. Business owners and managers have a host of options for resolving such disputes. Therefore, CRO should consider the alternatives presented in Table 4.1 in deciding how to address this dispute.

CLASS ACTION LAWSUITS

LO 4-2
Explain how the Class Action Fairness Act impacts class action lawsuits.

A class action lawsuit is one in which a *group* of people with the same or similar injuries sue for damages that were caused by the *same* defendant. Typically, a class action lawsuit is centered on allegations of a defendant's (1) illegal conduct such as discriminatory employment practices, (2) involvement in an unlawful transaction such as consumer fraud, or (3) sale of a defective product such as a pharmaceutical drug or medical device. One type of class action lawsuit, known as a mass tort action, involves a massive accident, such as a train derailment where many people are injured.

Class action lawsuits are controversial. On one hand, it levels the playing field between well-funded corporations and individual consumers. For example, suppose that BigCo

---

[1] *State Court Caseload Statistics,* U.S. Bureau Just. Stat., http://www.bjs.gov/index.cfm?ty=tp&tid=30.

TABLE 4.1	Dispute Resolution Options for Classic Retail Outlets versus SignCo			
Action	**Potential Benefits**	**Potential Costs**	**Risks**	
Lawsuit Draft a formal Complaint against SignCo; file the Complaint in the appropriate court of law; and serve the Complaint, along with the summons, on SignCo.	Court-ordered resolution to have the deposit refunded and have SignCo pay additional damages to compensate CRO for the cost of the temporary signage.	Significant expenditures: legal fees, hard costs (such as travel and fees for experts), human resource costs when time must be devoted to litigation procedures, appellate costs.	1. Loss at trial or loss upon appeal. 2. Legal fees may be higher than the final judgment amount awarded. 3. Possible countersuit by SignCo. 4. Permanent damage to business relationship. 5. Potential for bad publicity.	
Arbitration If the contract between CRO and SignCo has an arbitration clause, submit the dispute to arbitration as per the arbitration clause in the contract.	Enforceable resolution to have the deposit refunded and have SignCo pay additional damages to compensate for the cost of the temporary signage.	Moderate range in legal fees, arbitration/mediation fees; limited human resource expenditures; no chance of appellate fees (if binding).	1. Loss at arbitration that may not be appealed (if binding). 2. Win in arbitration, but may still have to go to trial (if nonbinding). 3. Potential damage to business relationship.	
Informal settlement Cancel the contract, agree not to sue each other, and agree to a figure that (1) compensates CRO for the cost of the temporary signage and (2) allows a percentage of the total fee to compensate SignCo for time invested in the project.	1. Parties agree not to sue each other. 2. Potential exists to preserve the business relationship. 3. Time and talent are not used to prepare for dispute resolution methods.	Low range of legal fees, moderate human resource investment, no threat of litigation by SignCo.	Settlement negotiations may drag on, and CRO must find a new vendor.	
Revise contract, continue relationship Make contract expectations clearer, and revise payments that compensate both parties for the loss.	Transaction is completed (perhaps even at a profit), and business relationship is preserved.	Low range of legal fees, moderate human resources.	Potential litigation by SignCo and potential for the new contract to generate yet another dispute.	

imposes a $100 late fee on its customers that pay even one day late. Suppose further that this type of late fee charge is prohibited by a state consumer protection statute. As a practical matter, although the late fee charges are clearly illegal, each individual would suffer relatively minor damages—so minor, in fact, that individuals would hardly be in a position to pursue legal redress on their own given the time and resources necessary to file a lawsuit. Together, however, the value of the individual claims makes the possibility of legal action more realistic. Forming a class means that the defendants face a larger cumulative claim, while class members share expenses of litigation such as attorney fees or expert witness costs.

Class Action Fairness Act (CAFA)

At the same time, groups that advocate for business owners such as the U.S. Chamber of Commerce decry class actions as an abuse of the civil litigation system intended to benefit attorneys and provide little relief to the actual plaintiffs in the case. For example, in

Kamilewicz v. Bank of Boston Corporation,[2] a case that drew significant media attention, an appellate court affirmed a settlement in which the class members received one-time interest payments ranging from zero dollars to $8.76, while attorneys in the case were awarded a multimillion-dollar fee. In the wake of such high-profile class action settlements, Congress passed the Class Action Fairness Act (CAFA) of 2005. Fundamentally, the law provides federal courts with authority to scrutinize procedures for the review of class action settlements and changes the rules for evaluating settlements, often reducing attorney fees that are deemed excessive relative to the benefits afforded class members. The law also provides for more judicial oversight of coupon settlements (sometimes called script or voucher or nonpecuniary settlements), where class members are awarded a coupon for use with future purchases of a product.

In Case 4.1, an appellate court applies CAFA to a settlement involving the Subway Footlong sandwich.

CASE 4.1 *In re* Subway Sandwich Marketing & Sales Practices Litigation, T. Frank, Objector, No. 16-1652 (7th Cir. 2017)

FACT SUMMARY In January 2013 an Australian teenager measured his Subway Footlong sandwich and discovered it was only 11 inches long. He photographed the sandwich alongside a tape measure and posted the photo on his Facebook page. It went viral, and soon after a number of lawsuits were filed across the United States against Subway for damages and injunctive relief under state consumer-protection laws. The lawsuits were combined and several plaintiffs sought class action certification. During discovery, Subway established that their unbaked bread sticks are uniform, and the baked rolls rarely fall short of 12 inches. The minor variations that do occur are wholly attributable to the natural variability in the baking process and cannot be prevented. Nonetheless, Subway entered into a settlement agreement and implemented certain measures to ensure, to the extent practicable, that all Footlong sandwiches are at least 12 inches long. The settlement acknowledged, however, that even with these measures in place, some sandwich rolls will inevitably fall short due to the natural variability in the baking process. The parties also agreed to cap the fees of class counsel at $525,000. The settlement provided $500 for each of 10 class representatives (class members who allowed their name to be used as lead plaintiffs). However, Theodore Frank (Frank), one of the class members who received no payment, argued that the settlement enriched only the lawyers and provided no meaningful benefits to the class. The trial court preliminarily approved the settlement and Frank appealed.

SYNOPSIS OF DECISION AND OPINION The U.S. Court of Appeals for the Seventh Circuit reversed the decision of the trial court and ruled in favor of Frank. The court held that the procedures required by the settlement do not benefit the class in any meaningful way and act only to benefit the class action lawyers. They reasoned that because there were no identifiable benefits to class members, the class should not have been certified, and the settlement should not have been approved.

WORDS OF THE COURT: No Meaningful Relief "A class settlement that results in fees for class counsel but yields no meaningful relief for the class is 'no better than a racket.' If the class settlement does not provide 'effectual relief' to the class and its 'principal effect' is to 'induce the defendants to pay the class's lawyers enough to make them go away,' then the class representatives have failed in their duty . . . to 'fairly and adequately protect the interests of the class.' . . . 'No class action settlement that yields zero benefits for the class should be approved, and a class action that seeks only worthless benefits for the class should be dismissed out of hand.'"

(continued)

---

[2]100 F.3d 1348 (7th Cir. 1996).

Case Questions

1. Why do you think that the class representatives approved this settlement?
2. The plaintiff's counsel argued that the settlement did provide meaningful benefits to the class because Subway has bound itself to a set of procedures designed to achieve better bread-length uniformity. Is that a convincing argument? Why or why not?
3. *Focus on Critical Thinking:* Could there be *any* remedies that the court would find "meaningful"? If the Footlong sub was only 9", how would that impact the case? Is there a baseline as to how much a merchant can deceive a consumer?

CONCEPT SUMMARY *Class Action Lawsuits*

- A class action lawsuit is one in which a *group* of people with the same or similar injuries sue for damages that were caused by the *same* defendant.
- Class action lawsuits are controversial. On one hand, they level the playing field between well-funded corporations and individual consumers. Critics contend that class action suits benefit attorneys more than class members.
- Congress passed the Class Action Fairness Act (CAFA) that provides federal courts with authority to scrutinize procedures for the review of class action settlements and changes the rules for evaluating settlements, often reducing attorney fees that are deemed excessive relative to the benefits afforded class members.

LO 4-3

Name the stages of litigation and identify the main features of each stage.

STAGES OF LITIGATION

Litigation is most easily understood when broken down into stages. In the prelawsuit phase, the parties are typically attempting to negotiate a settlement and must also consider some of the requirements for filing a lawsuit such as standing and the statute of limitations. In the pleadings stage, the parties file documents laying out the details of the dispute. The parties then enter the discovery stage, where they gather evidence using various techniques such as depositions. During the pretrial conference and trial phase, the parties resolve any pretrial issues and adjudicate the dispute. In the posttrial phase, the parties decide whether to appeal the verdict and consider other posttrial issues such as collecting the judgment.

Prelawsuit: Demand and Prelitigation Settlement Negotiations

When a dispute arises between two parties, one party will typically make an informal demand of the other party in which the principals (or their attorneys) lay out the basics of the dispute and demand a certain action. This usually leads to informal discussions directly between the parties without third-party involvement. In some states, it is necessary to make a formal demand before filing suit. The demand is often followed by an informal prelitigation settlement discussion involving the parties and their lawyers. If the issues are relatively simple, this informal method can be a cost-effective way of resolving a dispute fairly. However, if the legal issues are more complex or the parties are antagonistic toward each other, the prelitigation discussion will simply act as notice that a party intends to file a lawsuit if an agreement cannot be reached.

> **KEY POINT**
>
> Negotiation is a form of alternative dispute resolution, or ADR (discussed later in this chapter), because successful prelitigation negotiations avoid the filing of a formal lawsuit.

Standing In order for one party (the plaintiff) to bring a civil lawsuit against another party (the defendant), the plaintiff must have **standing** to sue. Specifically, the plaintiff must show three things: (1) that she has suffered a harm or an *injury in fact;* (2) that her harm is *direct, concrete,* and *individualized;* and (3) that there is an appropriate *legal remedy* to redress her harm.

Statute of Limitations Even if standing can be established, the plaintiff also must file the lawsuit within a certain time limit called the **statute of limitations**. The statute of limitations is the time limit within which a lawsuit must be filed or the lawsuit will be barred forever. In most cases, this time limit begins when the plaintiff's injury occurs. For example, suppose a customer is injured after he slips on a puddle of spilled cappuccino at an EspressoCo coffee shop on July 1, 2015. If EspressoCo is located in a jurisdiction where the statute of limitations is set at two years, the customer must file his lawsuit related to the incident no later than July 1, 2017.

It may be helpful to think of the statute of limitations as an hourglass with, in this scenario, exactly two years' worth of sand in it. The hourglass is turned over and the sand begins to run the moment the customer is injured. Any lawsuit related to the injury must be filed before the last grain of sand falls.

The actual time limits of statutes of limitations vary from state to state and may also vary depending on the cause of action alleged. For example, breach of contract statutes run from as short as 3 years to as long as 15 years. Even within a state, some statutes differentiate between written and oral contracts and have different time limits for each type of contract.

The statute of limitations may be thought of as an hourglass with a limited amount of sand (time). Oleksandr Melnyk/123RF

Pleadings Stage

Complaint and Summons If informal attempts at resolution fail, formal action begins when the plaintiff initiates a lawsuit by filing a **complaint** with the local clerk of courts.[3] In summary, the complaint sets out the plaintiff's version of the facts of the case, the damages that have been suffered, and why the plaintiff believes that the defendant is legally responsible for those damages.

The filing of the complaint sets the pleadings stage in motion. During this stage, the plaintiff is typically required to serve the defendant with a **summons**, along with a copy of the plaintiff's complaint. The summons is a formal, written notification served to the defendant informing her that she has been named in a lawsuit and that she must file an answer within a certain period of time. In some cases, the summons and complaint may be served by certified mail to the defendant. In other cases, a deputy sheriff or process server must deliver the documents in person. Court procedures prescribe how the complaint should be served upon the defendant to ensure timely notice of the claims asserted by the plaintiff.

Figure 4.1 sets out a sample complaint for the hypothetical *CRO v. SignCo* dispute.

Answer Once the defendant is served with the complaint, she must either file a motion to dismiss (see Motions below) or provide a formal **answer** to the complaint within a

Legal Speak >))

Plaintiff
The party who initiates a lawsuit by filing a complaint in a court of law against one or more defendants, demanding some legal remedy from the court.

Defendant
The party sued in a civil lawsuit or the party charged with a crime in a criminal prosecution. In some types of cases (such as divorce), the defendant may be called the *respondent.*

---

[3]Although *clerk of courts* is a common title for the official designated to receive civil complaints, the actual title varies widely among the states.

CHAPTER FOUR | Resolving Disputes: Litigation and Alternative Dispute Resolution

FIGURE 4.1 Sample Complaint: *Classic Retail Outlets, Inc. v. Sign Designs Company*

Daniel J. Webster, Esquire
ID# 70665
1120 Liberty Place
Philadelphia, Pennsylvania 19124
Attorney for Plaintiffs

In the Pennsylvania Court of Common Pleas
Philadelphia County

CLASSIC RETAIL OUTLETS, INC. :
       Plaintiff, :
                   :
       v. :   **Complaint**
                   :   Civil Docket 20-2100
SIGN DESIGNS COMPANY :
       Defendant, :
                   :
_____ :

In this complaint, the plaintiff alleges as follows:

1. Plaintiff and defendant are both Pennsylvania business entities headquartered in Philadelphia, Pennsylvania.
2. Jurisdiction over the subject matter is proper under the Pennsylvania Code.
3. On July 1, 2019, plaintiff contracted with defendant for services related to the design and installation of exterior signage for several of plaintiff's retail outlet sites. The contract specified the appearance and features of the signs.
4. The contract called for plaintiff to pay $25,000 at the execution of the contract and $25,000 at the completion of defendant's services.
5. Plaintiff fulfilled its obligation under the contract by paying $25,000 to defendant on July 1, 2019.
6. On July 30, 2019, Troy Machir, a principal in the plaintiff company, met with Matthew Diller, a principal in the defendant company, to review a preliminary version of the designs that defendant had completed.
7. During that meeting, Machir expressed his dissatisfaction with the work done and pointed out several errors where defendant had failed to follow the specifications detailed in the original contract.
8. As a result of that meeting, Diller promised to begin the design process anew and adhere more closely to the specifications of the contract.
9. Over the next two months, Machir attempted to obtain another preliminary design from defendant by contacting Diller and others at the defendant company via telephone and e-mail.
10. Diller, nor anyone else at the defendant company, responded to these calls or e-mails.
11. On October 1, 2019, Machir met with Diller once again, and Diller presented a revised version of the design.
12. At that meeting, Machir expressed continued dissatisfaction with the design and again pointed out that the design was not consistent with the specifications in the contract.
13. In addition, Machir pointed out several instances where the problems identified at their July meeting were not remedied. Diller again promised to fix the problems.
14. On October 15, 2019, Diller informed Machir that the defendant company could not follow the specifications in the contract at the price agreed to and that an additional fee of $20,000 would be necessary to complete the work.
15. Because of the delay caused by the defendant, plaintiff has had to expend $20,000 to erect temporary signage at its retail outlet sites.
16. The failure of Defendant Company to design a sign according to the specifications of the contract is a failure to perform its obligations under their agreement and constitutes a breach of contract.

    WHEREFORE, plaintiffs request judgment in the amount of $25,000 as refund of the deposit, plus $20,000 for the necessary temporary signage, plus statutory interest, and any other damages the court deems appropriate.

Dated: 1st day of October, 2020.
By:_____
Daniel J. Webster, Esquire
Attorney for the Plaintiff

prescribed time frame (normally within 20 days). The answer responds to each paragraph of the complaint. Often, the answer is simply a device for the parties to understand what issues they agree on and what issues will be in dispute at trial.

Figure 4.2 shows an answer to CRO's complaint. Note how the numbered paragraphs correspond to those in the complaint and how the responses are very limited and general.

FIGURE 4.2 Sample Answer: *Classic Retail Outlets, Inc. v. Sign Designs Company*

Oliver W. Holmes, Esquire
ID# 40016
One Alpha Drive
Elizabethtown, Pennsylvania 17022
Attorney for Defendants

In the Pennsylvania Court of Common Pleas
of
Philadelphia County

CLASSIC RETAIL OUTLETS, INC. :
    Plaintiff,
:
v. :
:
SIGN DESIGNS COMPANY :
    Defendant,
:
_____ :

Answer
Civil Docket 20-2100

In this answer, the defendant responds to plaintiff's complaint as follows:

1. Admitted.
2. Admitted.
3. Admitted.
4. Admitted.
5. Admitted.
6. Defendant has insufficient information to admit or deny.
7. Defendant has insufficient information to admit or deny.
8. Defendant has insufficient information to admit or deny.
9. Defendant has insufficient information to admit or deny.
10. Denied. Diller contacted Plaintiff Company several times during this period.
11. Defendant has insufficient information to admit or deny.
12. Defendant has insufficient information to admit or deny.
13. Defendant has insufficient information to admit or deny.
14. Defendant has insufficient information to admit or deny.
15. Defendant has insufficient information to admit or deny.
16. Paragraph 16 is a conclusion of law to which no answer is required.

Defendant also denies any and all parts of the plaintiff's complaint not specifically mentioned in this Answer.

Dated: 20th day of October, 2020.
By:_____
Oliver W. Holmes, Esquire
Attorney for the Defendant

The defendant is required only to state her position regarding each paragraph, with no need to provide a specific defense at this stage. If the defendant does not answer on time, she is said to be in *default* and generally will automatically lose the case without the benefit of trial. This outcome is known as a *default judgment*.

Counterclaim   If the defendant believes that the plaintiff has caused her damages arising out of the *very same* set of facts as articulated in the complaint, the defendant may file a **counterclaim** when she files her answer. (In some states, the counterclaim is called a *countersuit*.) The counterclaim is similar to a complaint in that the defendant's allegations and theory of liability against the plaintiff are set out in the pleading. The plaintiff must now answer the counterclaim allegations made by the defendant within a prescribed time period.

Cross-Claim   The defendant also may file a **cross-claim** to bring a third party into the litigation as a new defendant. A cross-claim is filed when the defendant believes that a third party is either partially or fully liable for the damages that the plaintiff has suffered and, therefore, should be brought into the case as an indispensable party in the trial.

Motions

From the time the pleadings are filed, through discovery and trial, and even after the trial, the parties to the litigation may file **motions** with the court. A *motion* is a legal document filed by one party requesting the court to take some action pertaining to the litigation. Some of the more common motions are described in Table 4.2.

Discovery Stage

Once the initial pleadings are filed, most lawsuits move into the **discovery** stage, in which the parties attempt to collect evidence for trial. While it may make television shows and

TABLE 4.2   Motions Used during Litigation

Stage of Litigation	Motion	Request
Pretrial	To Dismiss	To dismiss a case because of a procedural defect such as a court's lack of jurisdiction, failure of the plaintiff to state a valid claim, a plaintiff's lack of standing, or expiration of the statute of limitations
Pretrial	For Summary Judgment	To enter judgment in the requesting party's favor without a trial because no issues of fact are presented in the case or the answer shows that there is no actual dispute and, thus, no jury trial is needed. The requesting party thus believes that it should win as a matter of law
Pretrial	To Compel Discovery	To issue a court order demanding that a party must comply with a lawful discovery request
Trial	To Dismiss for Mistrial	To stop the trial in progress and dismiss it because of some extraordinary circumstance resulting in prejudice against one side or the other (rare in civil litigation)
Trial	For a Directed Verdict	To stop the trial and dismiss it because the opposing party (usually the plaintiff) has not met its burden of proof
Posttrial	For Judgment as a Matter of Law*	To reverse the verdict of the jury because no reasonable jury could have heard the evidence presented at trial and rendered such a verdict

*Also called by some state courts a *judgment non obstante veredicto* (notwithstanding the verdict).

movies more interesting, surprise evidence may not be introduced at an actual trial. Discovery is the legal process for the orderly exchange of evidence. Each side has the right to know and examine the evidence that the other side has, including evidence that is both *inculpatory* and *exculpatory*.

Scope, Timing, and Methods of Discovery

The rules for exchanging information during discovery are set out in court procedures (called the *Rules of Civil Procedure*). Generally speaking, everything relevant to a dispute is discoverable, unless the information is protected by a legal privilege, such as confidential conversations between attorney and client. Furthermore, relevant information need not be admissible at trial so long as the discovery is reasonably calculated to lead to the discovery of admissible evidence.[4]

Despite this broad scope, discovery does have some important limits. An attorney's work product, including information gathered in preparation for trial, is not discoverable unless the information can no longer be acquired or cannot be obtained without undue hardship. (For example, if an attorney has interviewed a witness who has since died, then that interview would be subject to discovery. Likewise, if an attorney has interviewed a witness who has since moved to, or returned to, another country, then that interview is also discoverable.)

State and federal rules determine when discovery may commence. Usually these rules prohibit discovery for a specific number of days after the pleadings have been filed or require that a pretrial conference be held before discovery begins. Expedited discovery, subject to court approval, may be requested. This permits discovery to commence sooner than normally permitted under court rules. In Case 4.2, for example, a federal district court decides whether to permit expedited discovery of the identities of anonymous authors of online postings.

Legal Speak >))

Inculpatory Evidence Evidence that tends to prove a criminal offense or civil wrong.

Exculpatory Evidence Evidence that tends to prove innocence or nonliability.

CASE 4.2 20/20 Financial Consulting, Inc. v. John Does 1–5, 2010 U.S. Dist. LEXIS 55343 (D.C. Colo. May 11, 2010)

FACT SUMMARY After 20/20 Financial Consulting discovered allegedly defamatory statements about itself posted on various websites and blogs by anonymous authors, the firm conducted an unsuccessful preliminary investigation to discover the names of the authors from the operators of the websites and blogs. Subsequently, 20/20 filed suit naming five unknown authors as "John Doe" defendants and sought a court order to conduct expedited discovery in an attempt to establish the true identities of the authors. The rules that govern federal court procedures allow expedited discovery if the information obtained will make trial more efficient.

SYNOPSIS OF DECISION AND OPINION The U.S. District Court in Colorado found in favor of 20/20 and granted its request for expedited discovery. The court ruled that because the plaintiff had exhausted reasonable attempts to identify the defendants through nonjudicial means, 20/20 was entitled to use the tools of discovery in order to help it locate the anonymous authors of the alleged defamatory Internet posts. Because the court found that discovery would be the only practical way to ascertain the true identities of the defendants, it ruled that 20/20 should be given the opportunity to pursue its claim against the defendants in an efficient manner.

WORDS OF THE COURT: Expedited Discovery Appropriate "The court finds that good cause exists to permit Plaintiff to conduct expedited discovery to discover the identities of Defendants. Indeed, this case is largely analogous to [a previous case] where the court permitted expedited

(continued)

---

[4]*Turner v. Summit Treestands, LLC*, 2011 U.S. Dist. LEXIS 139146 (Dec. 5, 2011).

discovery to identify defendants allegedly engaged in copyright infringement by downloading and distributing the plaintiffs' recordings using an online media distribution system. There the court found that the plaintiffs had set forth good cause for expedited discovery because the 'Defendants must be identified before this suit can progress further.' Much like [the defendants in that case], Defendants here have engaged in anonymous online behavior, which will likely remain anonymous unless Plaintiff is able to ascertain their identities. And thus far, Plaintiff has been unsuccessful in its attempts to ascertain Defendants' identities through informal, pre-lawsuit investigation. Because it appears likely that Plaintiff will continue to be thwarted in its attempts to identify Defendants without the benefit of formal discovery mechanisms, the court finds that Plaintiff should be permitted to conduct expedited discovery."

Case Questions

1. Why will formal discovery be more effective than merely requesting the information informally?
2. From the standpoint of the operators of blogs and Internet chat rooms, how does the formal discovery process provide them with real and intangible protection?
3. *Focus on Critical Thinking:* In your opinion, would justice be better served if all or most civil cases proceeded directly to the trial stage without the need for costly discovery?

Discovery is accomplished primarily by four methods: depositions, interrogatories, requests for admissions, and requests for production.

Legal Speak >))

Subpoena
A court order compelling a person to testify or produce evidence in her possession.

Depositions **Depositions** are oral questions asked of either a party or a witness in the case. A deposition can be taken at a courthouse but is more commonly taken in the setting of a conference room at a law firm. Although there is a court reporter present to create a written record and the witnesses are under oath, no judge is present. Depositions may be taken from any person with relevant information pertaining to the case. This includes the opposing party as well as any witnesses. If the witness has relevant evidence, the party taking the deposition may request a subpoena *duces tecum* (or subpoena for production of evidence) from the court to compel the witness to bring such evidence to the deposition.

Along with providing an exchange of information and eliminating the possibility of surprise at trial, depositions also serve a valuable purpose during trial. If a witness gives testimony that differs from facts previously stated in his deposition, for example, the deposition may be used to discredit the witness and attack his testimony. Also, should a witness claim to have forgotten a fact or circumstance (remember that discovery takes place soon after the pleadings are filed while the actual trial may be conducted months or years later), his deposition may be introduced to refresh the witness's memory.

Interrogatories **Interrogatories** are written questions submitted to the opposing party that must be answered in writing. Only the actual *parties* to the litigation, however, are required to answer interrogatories. For example, suppose that a professor throws a piece of chalk at a student, hitting her in the eye and causing serious injury. Every student in the room may be required to answer questions at a deposition; however, only the professor and the injured student may be compelled to answer interrogatories. Generally, interrogatories involve questions regarding points on which the litigant does not have readily available knowledge. The litigant may have to review files, memorandums, transcripts, and so forth in order to properly answer the questions.

Request for Admissions While the first attempt to narrow the issues in dispute is through the defendant's answer, a **request for admissions** furthers the objective of determining which facts are in dispute (and, thus, must be proved at trial) and which facts both parties accept as true. For example, one party may request that the other party admit the existence and date of a certain contract. If the other party refuses to admit those facts, witnesses must be called at trial to prove the existence and date of the contract.

LEGAL/ETHICAL REFLECTION AND DISCUSSION

If a person is a witness to an incident, such as the brawl between singers Chris Brown and Drake at a New York City club,[5] or has pertinent evidence relating to a lawsuit, she may be required by the court to participate in a deposition and compelled to testify at trial. This means that the person may need to take time off from work, arrange for child care, or be otherwise inconvenienced. Witnesses, other than hired experts, and deposed parties do not get paid for their participation. Moreover, they are considered in contempt of court if they do not show up when ordered and may be penalized.

1. Should an injured party be able to compel a witness to testify at trial or participate in a deposition?
2. If a witness can prove a monetary hardship, should she be paid for her participation? Is this practical?
3. Interrogatories are required only of the parties to the lawsuit. Why is it impractical to require interrogatories for witnesses?
5. Would justice be affected if witness participation regarding trial testimony and depositions was voluntary?

Request for Production Requests for admissions (above) are narrow and are designed to help a party discover a specific fact in the case. In contrast, a **request for production** can be very wide in scope, so that such a request would cover all documents, memorandums, reports, notes, calendars, videotapes, audiotapes, e-mails, computer hard drives, and so on relevant to the case at hand. In a complex securities or banking fraud case or one in which many documents are involved, it is not uncommon for the parties to send truckloads of boxes containing materials requested by the opposing side.

KEY POINT

Unless protected by a legal privilege, all information relative to the case is subject to discovery.

 Self-Check Methods of Discovery

A delivery van for Read-a-Book Company is involved in a traffic accident with a car driven by Kagen. In her negligence suit against Read-a-Book, Kagen claims that she sustained a back injury in the accident and is now unable to work at full capacity in her job. The driver of the delivery van counters that he was driving safely and that it was Kagen who caused the accident. What discovery method or methods could be used to obtain the following pieces of evidence?

1. Statements from the passenger who was in Kagen's car at the time of the accident.
2. Copies of doctors' reports prepared by the physicians who treated Kagen's alleged injuries.
3. Copies of the hospital report showing Kagen's blood alcohol level when she was treated.

---

[5]*Chris Brown Injured After Getting into NYC Bar Brawl with Drake over Ex Rihanna*, N.Y. Daily News (June 15, 2012).

4. A report regarding the weather conditions at the time of the accident.
5. A written statement from Kagen in which she presents her version of the accident.
6. A written statement of Kagen's job description and responsibilities.
7. An oral statement of Kagen's ability to perform her job responsibilities after the accident, along with company videotapes of Kagen at her job after the accident.

Answers to this Self-Check are provided at the end of the chapter.

Pretrial Conference

Several weeks before trial, the parties will typically attend a **pretrial conference** with the judge. The conference is generally held between the attorneys for the parties and the judge in the case, and no court reporter is present. The purpose of the conference is to accomplish two objectives. The primary reason is to encourage *settlement*. A judge can often give a neutral face-value view of the case and facilitate some negotiations between the two sides or eliminate any obstacles that have blocked negotiations, such as one party's refusal to discuss settlement. Second, the court will resolve any outstanding motions, confirm that discovery is proceeding smoothly, and dispose of any procedural issues that have arisen during the pleadings or discovery stages.

Trial

If the case cannot be settled, the parties will eventually go to **trial**. Think of a trial as being like a novel. The opening statements are the prologue, laying the groundwork for what is to come; the testimony and submission of evidence are the body of the novel or story; and the closing arguments and the charging of the jury are the epilogue, summarizing what has happened and tying up loose ends.

Television personality Erin Andrews gets her day in court.
Mark Humphrey/Pool/Getty Images

The trial generally takes place in front of a judge as the *finder of law,* with the jury as the *finder of fact.* As the finder of law, the judge determines such important rulings as what evidence will be admitted, what witnesses may testify, what the jury will hear and not hear, and even what legal arguments the attorneys may present to the jury. The jury, as the finder of fact, determines whose version of the facts is more believable by examining the evidence and listening to the testimony of witnesses. In some cases, the judge will act as both the finder of fact and the finder of law at the same time. This is known as a **bench trial**.

Jury Selection and Opening Statements
The actual trial begins with **jury selection**. This is the process of asking potential jurors questions to reveal any prejudices that may affect their judgment of the facts. The questioning process is known as *voir dire*.[6] For a criminal trial, voir dire can be extensive and last for days or even weeks, depending on the case. However, in civil litigation the voir dire process is not as extensive, and the jury will usually be seated in relatively short order. After the jury has been selected, the attorneys present their theories of the case and what they hope to prove to the jury in their **opening statements**.

Testimony and Submission of Evidence
After the opening statements, the plaintiff's attorney asks questions, known as **direct examination**, of the witnesses on the plaintiff's list. After the plaintiff's attorney finishes questioning a witness, the defendant's attorney may conduct **cross-examination** of that witness. Cross-examination is composed of questions limited to issues that were brought out on direct examination. The same process is repeated for the defendant's witnesses. Each side also uses its witnesses to introduce relevant evidence. Witnesses may be called upon to authenticate documents, to verify physical evidence, or to provide expert testimony accompanied by charts or graphs shown to the jury.

Closing Arguments and Charging the Jury
Once the testimony is completed and the evidence has been submitted to the jury, each attorney sums up the case and tries to convince the jury that his version of the case is more compelling. This is known as **closing argument**. The judge then proceeds with the **charging of the jury**, by giving the jurors detailed instructions on how to work through the process of coming to a factual decision in the case. The judge will also inform the jury that the standard of proof in a civil case is **preponderance of the evidence**.

Deliberations and Verdict
After receiving the charge, jurors move to a private room and engage in **deliberations**. Although the jury is permitted to send questions to the judge or make other requests (such as a request to reexamine specific pieces of evidence), the jurors must deliberate alone. The jury's decision is the **verdict**. If, however, the jury cannot agree on a verdict, this outcome is referred to as a **hung jury**, and a new trial with a new jury must be held. Rules in state courts for civil litigation frequently do not require a unanimous verdict, so hung juries are less frequent in business cases.

Posttrial Motions and Appeals
As discussed earlier in this section, there may be posttrial motions in which the losing party tries to convince the original judge that the verdict was flawed. Finally, the losing party may appeal to a higher court. Appellate courts engage in judicial review to decide whether any errors were committed during the trial,

---

Legal Speak >))

Preponderance of the Evidence
The standard used to decide a civil case whereby the jury is to favor one party when the evidence is of greater weight and more convincing than the evidence that is offered in opposition to it (i.e., more likely than not). The preponderance standard is a substantially lower standard of proof than that used in a criminal case.[7]

---

[6] Pronounced "vwar deer," this is a permutation of a Latin word and a French word meaning "to speak the truth."

[7] The standard used in a criminal case is "beyond a reasonable doubt" and is discussed in detail in Chapter 22, "Criminal Law and Procedure in Business."

and they also have the power to *reverse* or *modify* the decisions of trial courts. Generally, an appeal will not succeed unless the losing party can show that one or more prejudicial legal errors affected the trial's outcome.

Collecting the Judgment Although the prevailing party may have received a court judgment stating what he is entitled to recover from the defendant, collecting a judgment may sometimes be difficult, especially if the defendant's assets are tied up in nonliquid forms, such as real estate, or are exempt from the claims of creditors through a bankruptcy filing. However, the law does afford the prevailing party some tools to collect the judgment. For example, some states allow a judgment to be collected through the garnishment of wages, whereby the defendant's employer is ordered by the court to pay part of the defendant's wages directly to the holder of the judgment. The holder of a judgment also becomes a creditor (typically called a *judgment creditor*) and has the right to pursue the defendant's assets to satisfy the debt owed. The rights and the regulation of creditors and debtors are discussed in detail in Chapter 20, "Creditors' Rights and Bankruptcy."

CONCEPT SUMMARY Stages of Litigation

Prelawsuit: Demand and Prelitigation Settlement Negotiations
   Standing
   Statute of Limitations
   Jurisdiction (discussed in Chapter 3)
Pleadings Stage
   Complaint and Summons
   Answer
   Counterclaim
   Cross-Claim
Motions
Discovery Stage
   Methods of Discovery
Pretrial Conference
Trial
   Jury Selection and Opening Statements
   Testimony and Submission of Evidence
   Closing Arguments and Charging the Jury
   Deliberations and Verdict
Posttrial Motions and Appeals
Collecting the Judgment

LO 4-4

List the methods of alternative dispute resolution (ADR) and the potential advantages of using ADR.

ALTERNATIVE DISPUTE RESOLUTION

Alternative dispute resolution (ADR) refers to nonjudicial methods by which disputes involving individuals or businesses are resolved outside of the federal or state court system through the help of third parties. The main methods of ADR include mediation and arbitration.

Recall the hypothetical dispute between Classic Retail Outlets (CRO) and SignCo at the beginning of this chapter. In this example, several forms of informal and formal dispute resolution may benefit CRO and SignCo. If CRO decides to file a lawsuit, the company's management will have to allocate significant resources in terms of legal fees and litigation costs. Equally as important, CRO assumes several risks, including the risk of losing at trial, but even if CRO prevails, it may end up paying more in legal costs than it hopes to recover from SignCo in court. Moreover, any litigation will likely result in the dissolution of the business relationship between CRO and SignCo. Aside from those costs, time is wasted that could be spent on more productive activities, such as securing new business or executing existing business activities.

Given these risks of litigation, some of the potential advantages of ADR over litigation are as follows:

- *Costs:* ADR could potentially cost a fraction of normal litigation costs. Depending on the location of the trial, trial attorneys may charge between $200 per hour (in smaller markets) to as much as $1,000 per hour in, for example, New York City. Although some of the more mundane work in litigation may be done by nonlawyer professionals (such as legal assistants or paralegals) at lower rates, legal fees accumulate quickly once a lawsuit is commenced and accelerate once discovery begins.
- *Preserving the business relationship:* Litigation is, by its nature, adversarial. Allegations and defenses may turn antagonistic and result in termination of a business relationship. ADR, particularly informal ADR (discussed next), is focused on preserving the business relationship as part of the dispute resolution process. Business owners and managers work carefully to build alliances among vendors, suppliers, retailers, advertisers, and many other businesses that add value. ADR can help preserve alliances and avoid unnecessary antagonism over a dispute.
- *Time:* The time spent in ADR is much less than the normal two- to three-year (or more) period normally associated with discovery, a civil jury trial, and possible appeal.
- *Expertise:* In some cases the parties may choose an industry expert to help resolve their dispute. When a case is before a jury, there is an uncontrollable risk that the jury may have a difficult time grasping the details of a complex case. Even a highly competent judge conducting a bench trial may not have the background to fully understand the technical details and terminology involved in certain industry disputes. For example, knowing how to generally use a computer is very different from understanding the complexities of programming computer codes.
- *Privacy:* ADR methods are usually conducted in private with no public record required. This, in turn, reduces the risk of accidental disclosure of confidential business information through public court records. The privacy factor is also helpful in avoiding any unwanted publicity in the matter.

Informal ADR

Informal ADR often involves the parties negotiating face-to-face or through intermediaries to arrive at a mutually agreeable solution without the use of a formal process. It can take the form of (1) a *settlement agreement,* whereby one party agrees to a payment in exchange for the other party's promise not to sue, or (2) an agreement to cancel a contract or to revise an existing contract to better reflect the parties' obligations and needs.

Formal ADR

The most common formal ADR methods are *arbitration, mediation,* and *expert evaluation.* Most state or federal courts require mediation or nonbinding arbitration prior to allowing certain civil lawsuits to go to trial. Typically, in a business context, ADR is invoked either via contract or by mutual agreement. In a contractual arrangement, the parties enter into a contract that contains a clause requiring the parties to submit any disputes to a specific alternative dispute resolution process (usually binding arbitration). These ADR clauses are commonly contained in contracts relating to employment, sale of goods, brokerage agreements (such as a stockbroker or online trading account), financing, and licenses to use software. By way of example, the Terms of Use of the popular social media website Instagram contains the following binding arbitration clause:

> . . . you agree that all disputes between you and Instagram . . . will be resolved by binding, individual arbitration under the American Arbitration Association's rules for arbitration of consumer-related disputes and you and Instagram hereby expressly waive trial by jury. . . .

In addition, many employment contracts require employees with job-related grievances to enter into binding arbitration and prohibit them from filing a civil lawsuit against the employer in a court of law. Should a work-related problem arise, employees often are surprised by such clauses, which they may have overlooked when signing the contract. Unless the terms of the arbitration clause are unfair, courts will enforce an arbitration award pursuant to such a clause.

Arbitration

LO 4-5

Distinguish between arbitration and mediation and compare and contrast both methods of ADR.

One of the most common forms of ADR is **arbitration**. During arbitration, an individual *arbitrator* (or a panel of arbitrators) conducts a hearing between the parties in the dispute. The hearing is similar to a court setting but is less formal because there is no discovery and the rules of evidence do not apply. Parties seeking arbitration typically apply for an arbitrator through an ADR agency. The largest arbitration provider in the United States is the American Arbitration Association (AAA).

When the AAA receives an application for arbitration, it appoints a *tribunal administrator,* who coordinates the case and informs the parties of the procedures and rules of arbitration. Next, an arbitrator who is mutually agreed upon by the parties is appointed to the case. The arbitrator functions much like a judge would in a standard trial and in some states even has the power of subpoena (the ability to demand certain documents or witnesses). For arbitration cases, although an attorney is not required, parties in a business dispute often opt to be represented by counsel. An arbitration hearing resembles a trial in that there are opening statements, both parties present limited evidence and call a predetermined number of witnesses, each party has the right of cross-examination, and both parties make closing arguments. Unless already mandated in a contract, at the beginning of the arbitration both parties agree to either binding or nonbinding arbitration. If binding, the arbitrator's decision is final unless both parties agree to have the case reopened.

LO 4-6

Apply the legal standards under which an arbitration clause may be found invalid.

Legally Mandated Arbitration When the parties agree to an arbitration clause in a contract, this is known as a *private* arbitration. Additionally, some states and federal courts require (either by statute or a court-imposed procedure) that certain civil lawsuits go to nonbinding arbitration before proceeding to trial. Although this type of arbitration is nonbinding (the losing party has the right of automatic appeal to the trial court), the idea is to encourage the parties to settle before trial. The key advantage of legally mandated arbitration is that each side is able to present the case to a neutral party and the arbitrator's decision can be used as a starting point for settlement negotiations.

Federal Arbitration Act

The Federal Arbitration Act[8] (FAA) is a statute that requires state and federal courts to enforce arbitration awards. Specifically, the FAA states that "a written provision of . . . a contract evidencing a transaction involving commerce to settle by arbitration a controversy thereafter arising out of such a contract . . . shall be valid, irrevocable, and enforceable, save upon such grounds as exists at law . . . for the revocation of any contract."[9]

Congress enacted this law because many state and federal courts had previously invalidated arbitration clauses or overturned arbitration awards. This hostile view of arbitration led Congress to enact the FAA in order to make clear that arbitration was preferred over litigation as a method of dispute resolution so long as the parties agreed to an arbitration clause.

In addition, the FAA also identifies the following four grounds when courts may *set aside* the award of an arbitrator:

1. The arbitration involves some degree of corruption or fraud.
2. The arbitrator has exhibited inappropriate bias.
3. The arbitrator has committed some gross procedural error (such as refusing to hear relevant evidence) that prejudices the rights of one party.
4. The arbitrator has exceeded her explicit powers or failed to use them to make an appropriate final award.

Although the FAA does not spell out any specific procedure or format for arbitration, it does provide a means for enforcing both arbitration clauses and the decisions of arbitrators through the use of federal courts. In Case 4.3, the U.S. Supreme Court applies the FAA in the context of an arbitration clause in a contract.

Kheng Guan Toh/123RF

---

[8] 9 U.S.C. §§ 1–16.
[9] U.S.C§ 2.

CASE 4.3 Henry Schein, Inc. v. Archer & White Sales, Inc., 139 S. Ct. 524 (2019)

FACT SUMMARY Archer and White (Archer) is a North Carolina–based business that distributes dental equipment. Archer entered into a distribution contract with Henry Schein, Inc. (Schein),[10] a dental equipment manufacturer. The contract contained the following arbitration clause:

> **Disputes.** This Agreement shall be governed by the laws of the State of North Carolina. Any dispute arising under or related to this Agreement (except for actions seeking injunctive relief and disputes related to trademarks, trade secrets, or other intellectual property of [Schein]), shall be resolved by binding arbitration in accordance with the arbitration rules of the American Arbitration Association. The place of arbitration shall be in Charlotte, North Carolina.

The relationship eventually soured, and Archer filed suit against Schein in a federal court in Texas alleging violations of federal and state antitrust law and seeking both money damages and injunctive relief. After Archer sued, Schein invoked the Federal Arbitration Act and asked the trial court to refer the parties' antitrust dispute to arbitration in accordance with the original distribution contract. However, the trial court ruled in favor of Archer based on precedent set out by the U.S. Court of Appeals for the 5th Circuit that recognizes an exception to arbitration agreements if the demand for arbitration is "wholly groundless." The appellate court affirmed the decision of the trial court. Schein appealed to the U.S. Supreme Court arguing that the contract's express incorporation of the American Arbitration Association's rules meant that an arbitrator—not the court—had to decide whether the defendant's argument for arbitration is wholly groundless.

SYNOPSIS OF DECISION AND OPINION The U.S. Supreme Court reversed the decision of the lower courts and ruled in favor of Schein. It held that the wholly groundless exception to arbitrability is inconsistent with the Federal Arbitration Act and because arbitration is a matter of contract, courts must enforce arbitration contracts according to their terms. The Court reasoned that parties to a contract may agree to have an arbitrator decide not only the merits of a particular dispute, but also gateway questions of arbitrability. When the parties' contract delegates gateway questions (e.g., is arbitration an appropriate forum) to an arbitrator, a court may not override the contract, even if the court thinks that the arbitrability claim is wholly groundless.

WORDS OF THE COURT: Exception Inconsistent with FAA "We conclude that the 'wholly groundless' exception is inconsistent with the text of the [FAA] and with our precedent. We must interpret the [FAA] as written, and the Act in turn requires that we interpret the contract as written. When the parties' contract delegates the arbitrability question to an arbitrator, a court may not override the contract. In those circumstances, a court possesses no power to decide the arbitrability issue. . . . That conclusion follows not only from the text of the FAA but also from precedent. We have held that a court may not 'rule on the potential merits of the underlying claim' that is assigned by contract to an arbitrator, 'even if it appears to the court to be frivolous.'"

Case Questions

1. Why do you suppose that the 5th Circuit Court of Appeals adopted the "wholly groundless" exception in the first place? Could the exception prevent frivolous arbitration claims?
2. Why was it important to Schein's argument that the contract expressly incorporated the American Arbitration Association's rules?
3. *Focus on Critical Thinking:* Why did the Court interpret the Federal Arbitration Act so strictly in this case? Should courts have more leeway when interpreting statutes?

---

[10]Although Archer originally entered into the contract with Pelton and Crane, Schein became the successor in interest. For purposes of clarity, we use Schein throughout the case summary.

Employment and Labor Arbitration Arbitration clauses are a central issue in the context of employment and labor disputes. In these types of disputes, courts are highly deferential to a decision rendered by an arbitrator because an arbitration clause is the product of negotiations between employer and employee. In *Gilmer v. Interstate/Johnson Lane Corporation*,[11] the U.S. Supreme Court held that the FAA applies to arbitration clauses contained in employment contracts even when an employee brings suit against an employer for violating federal antidiscrimination laws.

Labor unions negotiate a contract on behalf of their members called a collective bargaining agreement that frequently includes mandatory and binding arbitration. In *14 Penn Plaza LLC v. Pyett*,[12] the U.S. Supreme Court rejected a challenge by a union member to the legality of an arbitration clause in a union contract. The Court held that when a union negotiates an arbitration clause, it does not constitute an unconscionable or severable waiver of a union member's rights. In Case 4.4, a federal appellate court considers an appeal of a labor arbitration decision against star NFL quarterback Tom Brady surrounding a controversy dubbed by the media as "deflategate."

CASE 4.4 National Football League Management Council v. Brady, 820 F.3d 527 (2d Cir. 2016)[13]

FACT SUMMARY On January 18, 2015, the New England Patriots and the Indianapolis Colts played in the American Football Conference Championship Game at the Patriots' home stadium to determine which team would advance to Super Bowl XLIX. During the game, officials from the National Football League (League) were prompted by a complaint from a Colts player to test all of the game balls for inflation level. Of 11 balls used by the Patriots, all 11 were underinflated and measured below the acceptable range established by League rules. Of the 4 balls used by the Colts, each tested within the permissible range. The League retained a law firm to investigate the events, culminating in a 139-page report concluding that it was more probable than not that two Patriots equipment assistants were responsible for deflating the Patriots' game balls after the balls were examined by the referee.

The report also concluded that Patriots quarterback Tom Brady had been at least generally aware of the deflation, and that it was unlikely that an equipment assistant would deflate game balls without Brady's knowledge and approval. As a result of the report, the League notified Brady of his four-game suspension under the League's rules pursuant to its union contract governing players. Brady, through his union, appealed the suspension and asserted his union contract rights to an arbitration hearing. After 10 hours of testimony including a revelation that Brady had ordered his assistant to destroy the cell phone that he had been using since early November 2014, a period that included the AFC Championship Game and the initial weeks of the subsequent investigation, Brady's suspension was upheld by the arbitrator. On appeal, a federal trial court vacated the decision on the basis that Brady had not been provided adequate notice that the suspension was within the League's range of punishments. The League appealed.

SYNOPSIS OF DECISION AND OPINION The U.S. Court of Appeals for the Second Circuit reversed the trial court's decision, ruled in favor of the League, and instructed the lower court to confirm the arbitration award. The court held that Brady

(continued)

---

[11] 500 U.S. 20 (1991).
[12] 129 S. Ct. 1456 (2009).
[13] The full name of this case is *National Football League Management Council and National Football League v. National Football League Players Association, on its own behalf and on behalf of Tom Brady, and Tom Brady*. It was condensed for the sake of clarity.

had not met the high standard required for courts to vacate arbitration awards. This was particularly true when the arbitration was held pursuant to a union contract. The court rejected the trial court's conclusions about improper notice to Brady because it was outside the proper scope of a court's review in labor arbitration cases.

WORDS OF THE COURT: Deference to Arbitrator "The basic principle driving both our analysis and our conclusion is well established: a federal court's review of labor arbitration awards is narrowly circumscribed and highly deferential—indeed, among the most deferential in the law. Our role is not to determine for ourselves whether Brady participated in a scheme to deflate footballs or whether the suspension imposed by the [League] should have been for three games or five games or none at all. Nor is it our role to second-guess the arbitrator's procedural rulings. Our obligation is limited to determining whether the arbitration proceedings and award met the minimum legal standards . . . These standards do not require perfection in arbitration awards. Rather, they dictate that even if an arbitrator makes mistakes of fact or law, we may not disturb an award so long as he acted within the bounds of his bargained-for authority."

Case Questions

1. Why did the court reject the trial court's conclusions?
2. What standard *should* a court apply in deciding whether to vacate a labor arbitration award?
3. *Focus on Critical Thinking:* The union contract permits the League's commissioner to serve as sole arbitrator in a disciplinary suspension appeal. Could this impact the impartiality of the arbitration? Why would the players' union agree to that provision in its contract with the League?

Mediation

Another common form of ADR is **mediation**. Mediation is becoming increasingly common as a cost-efficient form of dispute resolution primarily because mediation is relatively informal and does not require as much time or preparation as arbitration. A mediator is typically appointed in much the same manner as an arbitrator. In fact, in addition to arbitration services, the American Arbitration Association also provides mediation services.

The mediator is often, though not required to be, an attorney who is specially trained in the art of negotiation and paid an hourly rate or fixed fee for a certain period of time (usually per day or per mediation session). The mediator's task is to facilitate discussion, listening to each party's grievances and arguments and ensuring communication between the parties. The mediator's goal is to defuse the antagonism between the two parties and focus on working toward a mutually beneficial solution. Note, however, that in mediation no final decision is rendered, so if the parties are unable to reach an agreement, they must resolve their dispute using another method.

Mediation is sometimes required by statute or court procedure before a dispute can be brought to trial. As with legally mandated arbitration, the goal of legally required mediation is to allow the parties the opportunity to settle the case. Because much of the antagonism that surrounds a legal dispute is dissipated by the mediator's efforts, the process can help parties to see the dispute in a more even-tempered fashion. The ultimate goal is to work toward a mutually satisfactory resolution.

KEY POINT

The primary difference between arbitration and other methods of ADR is that arbitration provides the parties with an actual decision on who prevails in the dispute.

Expert Evaluation

For parties involved in a business dispute in which the issues are complex or related to the intricacies of a certain industry or profession, **expert evaluation** (neutral fact-finding) by an independent expert who can then recommend a settlement is an attractive alternative. The **expert evaluator** first reviews documents and evidence provided by each party that give a full description of the events and circumstances leading to the claim and the resulting loss. The evaluator then follows up with questions and sometimes takes statements from witnesses, if necessary. Drawing on her range of experience and expertise in the industry, the evaluator gives her opinion on the merits, puts a value on the claim, or recommends a settlement amount. The goal of this process is to facilitate a negotiated settlement without the expense and time required in a trial.

Other Forms of ADR

In some cases, parties to a dispute want to have the opportunity to settle the case through mediation, but they also want some degree of certainty in the event the mediation fails to produce a settlement. In those circumstances, parties may use a hybrid of mediation and arbitration. In this hybrid form, sometimes known as **med-arb**, both parties first submit to mediation for a set period of time (perhaps two business days). If the mediation fails, the process then moves to binding arbitration. The goal is to reach an agreement with the least amount of formality possible. If the dispute cannot be settled during mediation, arbitration is available as an automatic fallback.

Summary jury trials are used primarily in federal courts but have occasionally been used by state courts when there are complex issues to be litigated. An abbreviated half- to full-day trial is conducted before a jury, usually after discovery has been completed. Time limits may be set regarding each facet of the summary trial. No live expert testimony is presented, and the attorneys primarily conduct the proceeding through oral argument. Typically, no record is kept. A sitting or retired judge conducts the trial and issues a nonbinding advisory opinion.

Businesses may also use an ADR method called a **mini-trial**. Here, a condensed version of the case is presented to the top management from both sides. A neutral party, often an expert in the subject matter of the dispute, conducts the trial. The primary purpose of the mini-trial is to allow the management from both sides to see and hear the facts and arguments, hopefully enabling them to engage in more fruitful negotiations and thus avoid litigation. The neutral party does not ordinarily render a decision but may be requested by the parties to provide his expert opinion as to the likelihood of the outcome should the matter proceed to trial.

LO 4-7

Provide an example of a hybrid form of alternative dispute resolution.

CONCEPT SUMMARY Alternative Dispute Resolution (ADR)

- The primary advantages of ADR are reductions in costs and time, the preservation of business relationships, the involvement of an expert neutral party, and privacy.
- ADR usually arises as a result of a contract between two parties that have agreed ahead of time to resolve any disputes using a certain ADR method, such as arbitration.
- The primary methods of ADR are arbitration, mediation, expert evaluation, or some hybrid of these three methods.
- In arbitration, the parties submit their dispute to one or more arbitrators and present evidence and limited witness testimony, and then a decision is made.
- Mediation is the attempt by a trained third party to bring the opposing parties to an agreement on the dispute by proposing possible solutions; however, no decision is made.
- The primary difference between arbitration and other methods of ADR is that arbitration provides the parties with a decision.

KEY TERMS

Civil litigation p. 111   A dispute resolution process in which the parties and their counsel argue their views of a civil controversy in a court of law.

Standing p. 115   Requirement that, to maintain a lawsuit against another party, the party asserting the claim must have suffered an injury in fact; the harm must be direct, concrete, and individualized; and an appropriate legal remedy must be available.

Statute of limitations p. 115   The time limit within which a lawsuit must be filed or the lawsuit will be barred forever *(ch. 4)*. State law that places a time limit on the enforcement of certain contracts in order to ensure diligent enforcement *(ch. 7)*.

Complaint p. 115   The first formal document filed with the local clerk of courts when the plaintiff initiates a lawsuit claiming legal rights against another.

Summons p. 115   Formal notification to the defendant that she has been named in the lawsuit and that her answer must be filed within a certain period of time.

Answer p. 115   Defendant's formal response to each paragraph of the complaint.

Counterclaim p. 118   A claim filed by a defendant who believes that the plaintiff has caused her damages arising out of the very same set of facts as articulated in the complaint.

Cross-claim p. 118   A claim filed by a defendant who believes that a third party is either partially or fully liable for the damages that the plaintiff has suffered and, therefore, should be involved as an indispensable party in the trial.

Motion p. 118   A request made by either party that asks the court to issue a certain order (such as a motion for summary judgment). Motions may be made before, during, and after the trial.

Discovery p. 118   Process for the orderly exchange of information and evidence between the parties involved in litigation prior to trial.

Deposition p. 120   Method of discovery in which a party or witness gives sworn testimony prior to trial.

Interrogatory p. 120   Method of discovery in which one party submits written questions to the opposing party to gather evidence prior to trial.

Request for admissions p. 120   A set of statements sent from one litigant to an adversary for the purpose of determining what facts are in dispute and which facts both parties accept as true.

Request for production p. 121   A request aimed at producing specific items to help one party discover some important fact in the case.

Pretrial conference p. 122   A meeting between the attorneys for the parties and the judge in the case several weeks prior to trial, with the objectives of encouraging settlement and resolving any outstanding motions or procedural issues that arose during the pleadings or discovery stage.

Trial p. 122   Stage of litigation that occurs when the case cannot be settled, generally taking place in front of a judge as the finder of law and with a jury as the finder of fact.

Bench trial p. 123   Trial without a jury, in which the judge is both the finder of law and the finder of fact.

Jury selection p. 123   The process of asking potential jurors questions to reveal any prejudices that may affect their judgment of the facts.

Opening statements p. 123   Attorneys' presentations of their theories of the case and what they hope to prove to the jury; made at the onset of the trial.

Direct examination p. 123   The first questioning of a witness during a trial, in which the witness is questioned by the attorney for the party presenting the witness.

Cross-examination p. 123   The opportunity for an attorney to ask questions in court, limited to issues brought out on direct examination, of a witness who has testified for the opposing party.

Closing arguments p. 123   Attorneys' summations of the case, during which each attorney tries to convince the jury to decide the case in her party's favor; occurs after testimony is completed and evidence has been submitted.

Charging of the jury p. 123   Instructions given from the judge to the jury explaining how to work through the process of coming to a factual decision in the case.

Preponderance of the evidence p. 123   The standard used to decide a civil case whereby the jury is to favor one party when the evidence is of greater weight and more convincing than the evidence that is offered in opposition to it (i.e., more likely than not). The preponderance standard is a substantially lower standard of proof than that used in a criminal case.

Deliberations p. 123   The process in which jurors discuss, in private, the testimony and evidence presented at trial and vote to reach their verdict.

Verdict p. 123   The final decision of a jury in a case.

Hung jury p. 123   A jury that cannot come to a consensus decision on which party should prevail in a case.

Arbitration p. 126   Method of alternative dispute resolution in which the parties present their sides of the dispute to one or more neutral parties who then render a decision; often involves a set of rules designed to move from dispute to decision quickly.

Mediation p. 130   Method of alternative dispute resolution in which a mediator attempts to settle a dispute by learning the facts of the matter and then negotiating a settlement between the two adverse parties.

Expert evaluation p. 130   Method of alternative dispute resolution in which an independent expert acts as the neutral fact-finder; particularly useful for parties involved in a business dispute where the issues are somewhat complex and related to the intricacies of a certain industry or profession.

Expert evaluator p. 130   The neutral fact-finder in expert evaluation who reviews documents and evidence provided by each party and draws on her range of experience and expertise in the industry to offer an opinion on the merits and value of the claim and recommend a settlement amount.

Med-arb p. 131   Method of alternative dispute resolution whereby the parties begin with mediation and agree to submit to arbitration if mediation fails in a fixed time period.

Summary jury trial p. 131   An abbreviated trial conducted before a jury and a sitting or retired judge at which attorneys present oral arguments without witness testimony and the decision is nonbinding.

Mini-trial p. 131   A condensed version of the case is presented to the top management from both sides, with an expert neutral party conducting the trial, allowing them to see and hear facts and arguments so more meaningful negotiations can take place.

CHAPTER REVIEW QUESTIONS

1. **The major formal phases of civil litigation occur in this order:**
    a. Pleadings stage, trial, posttrial
    b. Pleadings stage, settlement, trial, posttrial
    c. Pleadings stage, discovery stage, trial, posttrial
    d. Settlement, pleadings stage, trial, posttrial
    e. Pleadings stage, settlement, trial, posttrial

2. **If a plaintiff brings a civil lawsuit against a defendant for breach of contract, what burden of proof applies?**
    a. Preponderance of the evidence ("more likely than not")
    b. Probable cause
    c. Reasonable and fair
    d. Clear and convincing evidence
    e. Proof beyond a reasonable doubt

3. **The major methods of "discovery" before trial are**
    I. Depositions and Interrogatories
    II. Requests for Admission
    III. Requests for Production
    a. I only
    b. I and II
    c. II and III
    d. I and III
    e. I, II, and III

4. **Which of the following statements is always true about arbitration?**
    a. Arbitration does not produce a decision.
    b. The disputing parties must consent to the arbitrator's decision in cases involving binding arbitration.
    c. Arbitration is generally more costly and time-consuming than civil litigation.
    d. Federal courts may set aside arbitration awards that do not conform to law.
    e. The disputing parties are bound to the decision of the arbitrator if they agreed to binding arbitration beforehand.

5. **What is the main difference between arbitration and mediation?**
    a. Mediation is more formal than arbitration.
    b. Arbitration produces a decision; mediation does not.
    c. Mediation produces a decision; arbitration does not.
    d. Arbitration is designed to facilitate settlement.
    e. Arbitration awards are private and thus not subject to public scrutiny.

Answers and explanations are provided at the end of this chapter.

THEORY TO PRACTICE

Medical Instruments, Inc. (MII), required a larger warehouse for its facilities. MII located a 10,000-square-foot building in New Hampshire and signed a lease with Commercial Properties (CP) for one year with a right to renew for five one-year terms upon 60 days' notice. After the first renewal, CP sent back a new lease with substantially the same terms, except that the new lease had a mandatory arbitration clause that required any tenant to go through arbitration in CP's home state of California. MII signed the lease without objection. One month after taking occupancy, MII complained that a leak in the warehouse roof was allowing water to drip into a corner of the warehouse and that MII had to move its hardware equipment out of the warehouse to protect it from water damage. CP did not fix the leak until one month later, and MII suffered losses because its hardware was partially destroyed by the leak. MII also had additional out-of-pocket losses related to the expense of moving the equipment to another location.

1. If MII sues CP in a state trial court for the losses it incurred, what would CP's likely defense be?
2. Discuss the significance of the fact that the original lease did not have an arbitration clause but the new one did. Also, is it significant that the place of arbitration would require MII to travel to California? Do these facts give a court any reason to invalidate the arbitration clause?
3. What cases that you studied in this chapter help to support your arguments in Question 2?
4. Assume that *no* arbitration clause exists in the new lease. What are MII's options in pursuing damages if CP refuses to compensate MII for the losses it has incurred?
5. Assume that MII files a lawsuit against CP. As part of its case, MII wishes to show that CP had notice of the leak and failed to fix it for one month. What methods of discovery would be useful to obtain this information from CP?
6. Suppose that CP refuses to turn over all phone records and repair request forms to MII based on the fact that the information is confidential and cannot be disclosed in litigation. What standard will a court use to judge whether the information is a trade secret and therefore not subject to disclosure? What case supports your answer?

LEGAL STRATEGY 101

Online Dispute Resolution

A business may be engaged in hundreds of relatively low-cost transactions per year with various out-of-state vendors such as suppliers, shipping companies, office supply stores, contractors, and the like. When disputes arise, a business may be at a distinct disadvantage and bargaining position because the amount in controversy is too low to justify even the least-expensive form of alternative dispute resolution. However, over an extended period of time, these small losses add up to unnecessary liabilities, leaving managers with a difficult choice when faced with a dispute over a relatively low amount of money with an out-of-state vendor: (1) invest in a dispute resolution method despite the fact that the costs may very well exceed the benefits in that particular dispute or (2) allow the losses to accumulate and potentially seek favorable tax treatment for writing off bad debt.

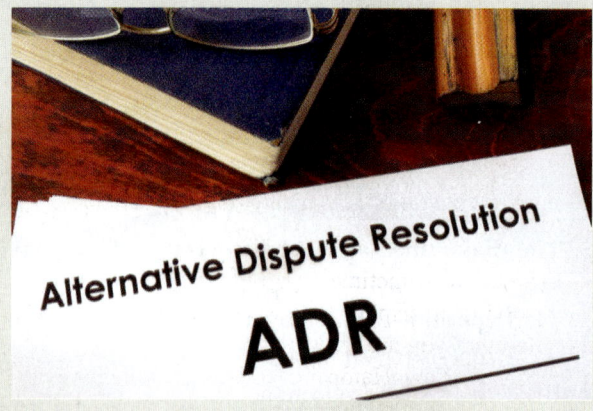

designer491/Alamy

Businesses are now capable of making small purchases from vendors across the globe and can do so quickly and conveniently. This renders traditional forms of ADR impracticable, given the reluctance to pay for an arbitrator or attorney and the fact that traveling to another location to settle a dispute often returns a sum less than the costs of travel. Online dispute resolution (ODR) has all of the advantages of traditional forms of ADR: The parties in question can avoid the expense and publicity of trial plus an agreement is usually reached much faster.

Online technology is ideal for low-cost transactional disputes such as a party seeking a refund for a defective product. Often these types of issues can be resolved using the technology alone. For example, blind-bidding sites like ClickandSettle.com and Cybersettle.com offer an automated service where parties individually enter the price they're willing to pay or receive. The software evaluates these numbers and then sends each party a fair price based on their initial demand.

Another form of ODR is more geared toward complex transactions. For example, Square Trade proposes prewritten resolutions. For example, if you received a damaged shipment of goods, Square Trade offers a standard menu of solutions such as (1) replacement with an undamaged good, (2) return for a full refund, or (3) keeping the merchandise with a partial refund. The parties may also fill in their own solution, but this guided approach helps the parties focus on a resolution to the dispute.

If direct negotiation fails to resolve the issue, Square Trade users can request a mediator for a $20 fee per participant plus a percentage fee if the dispute exceeds $1,000. At OnlineResolution.com, mediation fees range between $15 and $25. For disputes of more than $500, each participant pays $50 per hour, scaling up to $150 per party per hour, based on the value under dispute.

Option 1: Online Mediation. Online mediation is a logical first step to settling disputes. Like traditional forms of mediation, online mediation is generally nonbinding. Parties present their positions to a mediator who considers their arguments and attempts to negotiate a settlement. An advantage to online mediation is that dialogue is carried out via e-mail so participants can submit responses at their convenience and can think out their replies rather than engage in what may be an antagonistic live hearing.

Option 2: Online Arbitration. Online arbitration is similar to traditional arbitration, except that all communications take place using the Internet. The arbitrator convenes the arbitration via live webcast and issues a decision based on the evidence presented. In an online setting, all communications, including the presentation of evidence, is supplied in electronic form: text, image, audio, or video. Participants in online arbitration agree in advance to abide by the arbitrator's decision, and that the award may be enforced by an appropriate court. Following completion of the online arbitration, each participant typically completes a brief evaluation of the arbitrator and the process.

CRITICAL THINKING QUESTIONS

1. Use your favorite search engine to look up some online dispute firms. Are they competitively priced? Would it be more or less than filing a case in person?
2. Is it possible that even virtual ADR may be biased toward one side or the other? Explain.
3. Ultimately, doesn't online ADR depend on good faith of the parties? If one party refuses to abide by the decision, how do online ADR providers ensure that the parties abide by the rules?

MANAGER'S CHALLENGE

Managers are sometimes the first line of opportunity in resolving a dispute before it turns into litigation. Assume that you are an MII manager in charge of the property in New Hampshire described in this chapter's Theory to Practice. Write a two- to three-page memorandum to your senior manager that describes the relative advantages of ADR over litigation in the MII-CP dispute. Using Table 4.1, offer suggestions on how this particular dispute may be resolved.

See Connect for Manager's Challenge sample answers.

CASE SUMMARY 4.1 American Express v. Italian Colors Restaurant, 133 S. Ct. 2304 (2013)

ARBITRATION PROVISION IN CONTRACT

American Express (Amex) entered into agreements with Italian Colors Restaurant (ICR) and other merchants that accept American Express credit cards. The agreement contains an arbitration clause that requires that all disputes between Amex and ICR be resolved through arbitration and prohibits any claim from being arbitrated on a class action basis. Nonetheless, ICR and other merchants filed a class action suit against Amex, alleging violation of federal antitrust statutes. Amex moved to compel individual arbitration, but ICR argued that the clause was invalid because the cost of expert analysis necessary to prove their antitrust allegations would greatly exceed the maximum recovery for each individual merchant plaintiff. The trial court ruled in favor of Amex, but a federal court of appeals reversed the trial court's ruling and held that the clause was unenforceable because of the prohibitive cost structure. Amex appealed to the U.S. Supreme Court.

CASE QUESTIONS

1. Who prevails and why? Explain.
2. Was the waiver of class action arbitration by the merchants truly voluntary? Why or why not?
3. If the costs of experts exceed the potential recovery amount in the absence of a class action, doesn't the arbitration clause in this case have the effect of shielding Amex from antitrust laws?

CASE SUMMARY 4.2 Infinite Energy, Inc. v. Thai Heng Chang, 2008 WL 4098329 (N.D. Fla. 2008)

REQUEST FOR PRODUCTION

Chang was terminated from his employment at Infinite Energy, Inc., for allegedly leaking confidential information to competitors. Litigation ensued, and during discovery Infinite requested access to all of Chang's e-mail accounts. Although Chang turned over e-mails from his work account, he refused to turn over e-mails from his private e-mail account with Yahoo! Infinite claimed that the private e-mails were essential to its case, and Chang contended that the e-mails were confidential and unrelated to his employment and, therefore, not within the scope of discovery.

CASE QUESTIONS

1. Who prevails and why?
2. Is this information necessary for Infinite's case? Why or why not?

CASE SUMMARY 4.3 Hooters of America, Inc. v. Phillips, 173 F.3d 933 (4th Cir. 1999)

ARBITRATION CLAUSES AND PUBLIC POLICY

Annette Phillips began working as a bartender at a Hooters restaurant in South Carolina in 1989. Five years later, Hooters initiated an alternative dispute resolution program among its employees. As part of that program, the company conditioned eligibility for raises, transfers, and promotions upon an employee's signing an agreement to arbitrate employment-related disputes including, among other issues, discrimination or sexual harassment claims. The agreement provided for binding arbitration in accordance with a standard set of rules that were created and administered by Hooters. In 1994 and again in 1995,

Phillips signed the agreement but did not obtain a copy of the rules. In 1996, Phillips quit her job and refused to arbitrate based on the unfairness of the Hooters arbitration rules. Among the provisions she found to be unfair were

- The requirement that arbitrators be selected exclusively from a list provided by Hooters.
- Hooters's rights to expand the scope of the arbitration, to move for summary dismissal, and to record the proceeding without any similar rights for the employee.
- Hooters's unilateral authority to bring an arbitration award to court in order to vacate or modify the award if the company could show that the panel had exceeded its authority.

After Phillips notified Hooters that she intended to file suit for sexual harassment and employment discrimination, Hooters filed suit to compel arbitration. The district court ruled in favor of Phillips and held that the arbitration clause was unenforceable and void because it was not a true meeting of the minds required for an enforceable agreement between the parties and that the clause was void as a matter of public policy. Hooters appealed.

CASE QUESTIONS

1. Who prevails and why?
2. Why do you think that Hooters chose to include a mandatory arbitration clause in its employment contracts?
3. Had Phillips been provided a copy of the rules when she signed the employment contract, would this change your analysis? Why or why not?

CASE SUMMARY 4.4 AutoNation USA Corp. v. Leroy, 105 S.W.3d 190 (Tex. App. 2003)

ADR IN CONSUMER CONTRACTS

Leroy purchased a used car from AutoNation, a used-car dealer chain. All buyers entered into a purchase agreement, and those who financed their vehicles through AutoNation also signed a retail installment contract. The purchase agreement included an arbitration agreement, but the retail installment contract did not. Leroy alleged that she and all other customers who signed installment contracts were overcharged as a result of a computer error committed by AutoNation.

She filed a motion in a trial court to have her lawsuit certified as a class action. Although AutoNation argued that the arbitration clause in the purchase agreement controlled the case, the trial court certified the class action, ruling that because the installment contract had no arbitration agreement, the plaintiffs were free to pursue their remedy in court.

CASE QUESTION

1. Did the trial court rule correctly? Explain.

CASE SUMMARY 4.5 Brower v. Gateway, 246 A.2d 246 (N.Y. App. Div. 1998)

ENFORCEABILITY OF ARBITRATION CLAUSE

Brower purchased a computer from Gateway 2000 through a retail outlet. The computer box contained appropriate manuals and a document titled "Standard Terms and Conditions Agreement," which provided that the terms and conditions in the agreement would become binding if the consumer retained the computer for 30 days. Brower retained the product for more than 30 days. The Gateway agreement contained an arbitration clause mandating that any disputes arising out of the purchase be arbitrated before the International Chamber of Commerce (ICC). The ICC is situated in Europe, and its procedures require arbitration parties to pay an advance fee of $4,000, of which $2,000 is nonrefundable regardless of which party prevails. Brower filed suit against Gateway, alleging breach of warranty.

Gateway sought to have the suit dismissed from the court and to compel ICC arbitration in accordance with the terms of the Gateway agreement. Brower argued that the arbitration clause was unenforceable because, among other reasons, the ICC rules were too burdensome on the parties and prevented them from protecting their rights.

CASE QUESTIONS

1. Were the ICC rules too burdensome on the parties, preventing them from protecting their rights?
2. How would you rewrite Gateway's clause to be sure that it would be judged reasonable by the New York court?

CASE SUMMARY 4.6 Hickman v. Taylor, 329 U.S. 495 (1947)

INTERROGATORIES AND PRIVILEGED INFORMATION

On February 7, 1943, the tugboat *J.M. Taylor* sank while engaged in towing a car float of the Baltimore & Ohio Railroad across the Delaware River at Philadelphia. The incident resulted in the death of five crew members. Anticipating litigation, the owners of the tug hired a law firm, and their attorneys conducted interviews with survivors and other witnesses and also obtained statements from representatives of the estates of two of the deceased crew members. One claimant brought suit against the tug owner and, during discovery, sent the following interrogatory: "State whether any statements of the members of the crews of the tugs *J.M. Taylor* and *Philadelphia*—another tug helping to tow the car float—or of any other vessel were taken in connection with the towing of the car float and the sinking of the Tug *John M. Taylor*. Attach hereto exact copies of all such statements if in writing, and if oral, set forth in detail the exact provisions of any such oral statements or reports." The law firm claimed that the information requested was privileged attorney work product.

CASE QUESTIONS

1. Should the information gathered by the law firm be made available, or is an attorney's work product privileged and not subject to discovery?
2. If an attorney's work product is declared privileged in corporate-versus-individual cases, does this give a corporate defendant a tremendous advantage in a suit by an individual plaintiff? That is, can the corporate defendant create a veil of secrecy over all the pertinent facts it can collect after the claim arises by merely asserting that such facts have been gathered by its large staff of attorneys?
3. In its decision, the U.S. Supreme Court said, "Historically, a lawyer is an officer of the court and is bound to work for the advancement of justice while faithfully protecting the rightful interests of his clients. In performing his various duties, however, it is essential that a lawyer work with a certain degree of privacy, free from unnecessary intrusion by opposing parties and their counsel." Do you agree or disagree with this position? Why or why not?

Self-Check ANSWERS Methods of Discovery

1. A deposition.
2. An interrogatory or a separate motion for the production of documents.
3. An interrogatory or a separate motion for the production of documents.
4. An admission.
5. An interrogatory.
6. An interrogatory or a separate motion for the production of documents.
7. A subpoena *duces tecum* served on Aimee's employer for any video to be produced at the employer's deposition.

CHAPTER REVIEW QUESTIONS: Answers and Explanations

1. **c.** The major formal phases of civil litigation are pleadings, discovery, trial, and posttrial. Answer choices (a), (b), (d), and (e) are incorrect for two reasons: (1) they all omit the discovery phase of litigation and (2) settlement generally occurs out of court and is thus not a stage of litigation.

2. **a.** The standard of proof that applies to ordinary civil cases is "more likely than not" or preponderance of the evidence. Probable cause (choice [b]) refers to government searches and seizures. Reasonable and fair (choice [c]) is a made-up standard. Clear and convincing evidence (choice [d]) is a higher standard than mere preponderance, while proof beyond a reasonable doubt (choice [e]) is the standard used in criminal cases.

3. **e.** Depositions, interrogatories, requests for admission, and requests for production are all major methods of discovery in civil litigation.

4. **e.** Arbitration is binding when the parties to the arbitration have agreed to binding arbitration via contract or agreement beforehand. Answer choices (a) and (b) are wrong because arbitration (whether binding or nonbinding) always produces a decision and because consent to the arbitration award is not required in cases of binding arbitration. Answer choice (c) is incorrect because arbitration is generally far less costly and time-consuming than ordinary civil litigation, while answer choice (d) is wrong because "nonconformity to law" is not one of the four reasons for which a court may set aside an arbitration award under the Federal Arbitration Act.

5. **b.** The main difference between mediation and arbitration is that the latter produces a decision; mediation does not. Hence, answer choice (c) is wrong. Answer choice (a) is also incorrect because mediation is more informal than arbitration, while answer choices (d) and (e) are wrong because both mediation and arbitration are designed to facilitate settlement and because both of these methods of ADR are private.

CHAPTER 5

Business Ethics, Corporate Social Responsibility, and Law

©philsajonesen/Getty Images

Learning Objectives

After studying this chapter, students who have mastered the material will be able to:

5-1 Explain the relationship between ethics and law.
5-2 Articulate a working definition of business ethics in the context of primary and secondary stakeholders.
5-3 Identify the major theories of ethics from the field of moral philosophy.
5-4 Identify the main challenges to business ethics management and formulate a response to each challenge.
5-5 List the common traits of effective values management.
5-6 Develop a code of ethics.
5-7 Define values management and articulate several reasons why values management is important in business operations.
5-8 Employ an ethical decision-making paradigm used by managers to resolve ethical dilemmas.
5-9 Apply your knowledge of business ethics to recent case studies of companies facing ethical dilemmas.
5-10 Articulate the various views on corporate social responsibility and defend a particular view.

Although the law provides one set of boundaries for business operations, a concurrent set of boundaries—business ethics and principles of corporate social responsibility—is equally important to business owners and managers. While some critics argue that business ethics is an oxymoron and a recent phenomenon meant simply to fill popular and management literature, ethics affects almost every decision we make in both our personal lives and in a business context.

In this chapter, students will learn

- Major theories of ethics.
- The definition of business ethics and stakeholders.
- The challenges and strategic advantages of values management.
- Fundamentals of corporate social responsibility.

WHAT IS ETHICS?

How do you decide between right and wrong? Ethics is the set of *moral principles* or *core values* for deciding between right and wrong.

As a result, ethics apply to our everyday decisions. Have you ever received too much money back when you paid for something in a store? Have you ever been tempted to call in sick to work (or skip class) when you just wanted a day off? Each of these scenarios presents an ethical dilemma, and you must thus decide what to do in each case based on your core values and sense of ethics.

Relationship between Ethics and Law

LO 5-1

Explain the relationship between ethics and law.

A comprehensive understanding of law and ethics first starts with the overarching notion of justice. Broadly defined, justice is the maintenance or administration of what is fair. A popular depiction of justice since antiquity is captured in the image below. This symbol has three elements that are meant to embody fundamental notions of justice as an arbiter of legal disputes. First, justice should apply equally to all. To justice, it does not matter if the individual is rich or poor, famous or not. In a just system, legal principles apply equally to all parties regardless of their position in society or wealth. Second, justice has an enforcement mechanism to impose penalties and ensure compliance and fidelity to the law. A legal system that exists solely in theory without proper enforcement cannot adequately regulate behavior and exists as a fiction on paper rather than as a just and real system of law. You can have the best laws on the books, but without enforcement they will mean very little in practice. Third, justice equally considers opposing sides and weighs the merits of the competing arguments carefully and with due consideration. Just laws and outcomes must, therefore, balance competing interests to achieve a proportional outcome that is fair and balanced for the parties involved and those similarly situated.

As an ideal, the law strives to encode basic notions of justice and fairness. For example, laws cannot be just if they are not made widely available for public consumption. It would be unfair and unjust to expect someone to comply with a law that was not made publicly available. In a business setting, it would be unfair to be held accountable for an offense many years after the injurious action allegedly occurred. To avoid this scenario, laws called statutes of limitations place a time limit on the ability of plaintiffs to pursue legal claims such as breach of contract.

In an ideal system, the law should always strive to achieve justice to derive the right outcome. In practice, however, this does not always occur because the overlap between ethics and the law is not always perfect as illustrated in the figure below.

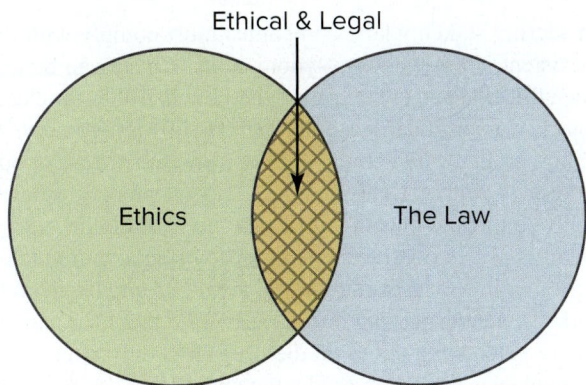

Relationship between ethics and the law

CHAPTER FIVE | Business Ethics, Corporate Social Responsibility, and Law

LO 5-2

Articulate a working definition of business ethics in the context of primary and secondary stakeholders.

BUSINESS ETHICS DEFINED

A useful working definition of **business ethics** is a *consciousness* of what is right or wrong in the workplace and a commitment to taking responsibility for an ethical course of action in business operations. In essence, when making a business decision, the main idea here is that one should consider the impact of one's decision on the owners, investors, employees, and customers of the business and also on the community at large (collectively known as *stakeholders*).

Primary and Secondary Stakeholders

Broadly speaking, business ethics embraces a broader constituency than just a business's owners and managers. To this end, in their planning and operations, many business entities have replaced the word *stockholder* with *stakeholder*. **Stakeholder** is an expansive term that includes a business entity's owners, investors, employees, customers, suppliers, and the wider community. In planning and decision making, many companies now consider both *primary stakeholders* and *secondary stakeholders*.

Although various commentators have given a wide variety of definitions for stakeholders, primary stakeholders are generally those who will feel a direct impact based on the decision. Secondary stakeholders are those who do not have any direct connection to the business but may suffer some adverse consequences in an indirect way. For example, during President Obama's first term in office, the Whirlpool Corporation, maker of Maytag and KitchenAid appliances, received $19 million in government stimulus funds intended to create jobs. Nevertheless, in 2010, Whirlpool announced that it was going to close its long-standing American plants in Fort Smith, Arkansas, and in Evansville, Indiana, resulting in approximately 2,100 jobs lost. This was only a part of a decision to cut 5,000 jobs in North America and Europe. Whirlpool shifted manufacturing from those two plants to facilities in Mexico, where workers earn approximately $4 per hour.

The primary stakeholders affected certainly include the fired workers and their families. Suppliers to the plants are also directly impacted, as are the cities of Fort Smith and Evansville, which no longer receive tax revenues from Whirlpool. Secondary stakeholders may include local businesses that are not patronized by the former employees, as well as their suppliers and other customers. In short, a worker who has lost her job likely won't be eating out as much. The restaurant may then need to adjust prices to compensate for lost business, thus affecting its customers. The restaurant may also need to lay off workers should business drop substantially. The mayor of Evansville stated that although the city stood to lose 1,000 jobs, he estimated that 10,000 people could be impacted by the plant closure. As this example shows, primary and secondary stakeholders are an important part of the social responsibility of a corporation, which is discussed in more detail later in this chapter.

Moral Minimum versus Maximizing Profits

In addition to considering stakeholders, companies must comply with the law. But ethics and law, while coexistent, are not always synonymous. An act can be legal without being ethical, while some ethical acts can be against the law. In 1955, for example, Rosa Parks, a working-class black woman, boarded a private bus in Montgomery, Alabama, and sat in the front of the bus in the "whites only" section. She was arrested, but her arrest highlighted the immorality of segregationist laws and social practices prevalent in the Deep South and eventually led to the enactment of new civil rights laws. One can thus argue that she acted ethically in breaking the law in order to bring attention to unethical policies.

At the other extreme, how can something be legal but unethical? When pharmaceutical companies market a new drug, they often inflate the price, in part because they have no competition due to patents they hold on the drug. It is only after the company's patent expires that other companies can begin producing and selling generic versions, usually at a dramatically lower price. Unfortunately, until the generic drugs appear, many people who might benefit from lower drug prices must use other, sometimes less effective, alternatives. As owners of the patent, the pharmaceutical companies are acting legally in setting their drug prices. Nevertheless, some people are harmed by the drug company's pricing policies. Assuming it is profitable and stable, the pharmaceutical company could adopt a "moral minimum" approach by lowering its profit margin—which might do good for a greater number of people—or it could instead maximize profits by maintaining high prices, which might deny relief to a part of society that it otherwise could help.

Businesses are confronted with such predicaments frequently. To minimize the risk of fines and lawsuits, companies must ensure that compliance with the law remains a priority. To maintain goodwill, attract customers and top-quality employees, and avoid adverse publicity, companies must also monitor their ethical conduct. The principles-based and consequences-based approaches discussed later in this chapter guide managers when they are making business decisions. In addition, viewed from a macro perspective, businesses generally follow either a **moral minimum** or **maximizing profits** ethical philosophy.

In summary, the moral minimum theory encourages a business to "do no harm" or, alternatively, "do the least possible harm." As long as the business remains profitable, the company strives to act as ethically as possible, even at the expense of some additional profits. By contrast, a company that follows a maximizing profits theory strives to make as much money as possible, as long as no laws are broken.

For example, suppose that a company is building a factory in a city, and it knows that the factory will produce exhaust fumes in large quantities. The Environmental Protection Agency (EPA) has established air quality standards that the company must adhere to. After extensive research, the company finds that it can spend $5 million to purchase and install equipment that will allow it to meet the EPA required standards exactly. This approach will reduce the pollution to a level that will not affect most of the city's citizens, but a small percentage of those with lung or breathing problems could experience increased discomfort. Through its research, the company also learns that for $8 million it can install equipment that will far exceed the minimum standards. This will provide the cleanest and healthiest environment for the entire city, creating no impact on the city's air quality. Either choice results in a legal decision by the company. If the company chooses a moral minimum approach, it will spend the $8 million to do no harm, while a maximizing profits approach will save the company $3 million but put some people at risk.

LEGAL/ETHICAL REFLECTION AND DISCUSSION

Made in the USA

A manager for WidgetCo is approached by a foreign vendor who offers to supply widgets at a substantial discount from what his company is currently paying. When determining WidgetCo's course of action, consider both the moral minimum and the maximizing profits approaches to business ethics:

- Why should it matter whether the lower-priced widgets are not made in the USA?

- Why should it matter whether the foreign company is subject to the same quality-control and labor safety regulations as the current USA supplier?

- Why should it matter whether the lower-priced widgets are more (or less) likely to be faulty or substandard?

- Why should it matter whether faulty or substandard widgets could make the company's products more dangerous to users or to the environment?

In Case 5.1, General Motors is sued for closing one of its plants in Michigan, a business decision that was detrimental to some of its employees and to the community where the plant was located.

CASE 5.1 Ypsilanti Township v. General Motors Corporation, 506 N.W.2d 556, 201 Mich. App. 128 (1993)

FACT SUMMARY General Motors Corporation (GMC) operated two plants in Ypsilanti Township, Michigan (Ypsilanti). From 1975 to 1988, GMC took advantage of 11 tax abatements, which lowered or eliminated taxes owed on real estate, provided for in a Michigan state statute to encourage business owners to create and maintain jobs in the state. As part of the tax abatement application process, GMC would consistently represent that its plants offered local residents nearly 13,000 jobs. In 1991, GMC announced that it was consolidating its operations and closing one of the Ypsilanti plants. More than 4,000 jobs were lost. Ypsilanti sued GMC for breach of promise and for misrepresentation. The lower court ruled in favor of Ypsilanti, finding that GMC's promises were binding and that allowing GMC to close the plant would result in unfairness and would impose an extreme burden on Ypsilanti residents.

SYNOPSIS OF DECISION AND OPINION The Michigan Court of Appeals reversed the lower court and found for GMC. The court found that the promises of long-term relationships and the expectation of continued operations based on receipt of the tax abatements were not legally binding on GMC.

WORDS OF THE COURT: Corporate Promises "First, the mere fact that a corporation solicits a tax abatement and persuades a municipality with assurances of jobs cannot be evidence of a promise. The very purpose of tax abatement legislation is to induce companies to locate and to continue business enterprises in the municipality. . . . The fact that a manufacturer uses hyperbole and puffery in seeking an advantage or concession does not necessarily create a promise. For example, statements such as 'We're partners' and 'We look forward to growing together' were found not to constitute a promise to keep a collective bargaining agreement in force for the foreseeable future so as to create [a binding promise generating] a continuing duty of the employer to honor an expired agreement. . . . It has never been held that an abatement carries a promise of continued employment."

Case Questions

1. When GMC closed the Ypsilanti plant, almost 20 percent of Ypsilanti's population became unemployed overnight. Who were the primary and secondary stakeholders affected?
2. How would you describe GMC's actions from a maximizing profits or a moral minimum perspective?
3. *Focus on Critical Thinking:* GMC was found to have the legal right to close the plant. Was its action ethical? Why or why not?

CONCEPT SUMMARY Business Ethics

- Business ethics consists of recognizing right or wrong in the workplace and taking responsibility for an ethical course of action in business operations.
- Business ethics requires that primary and secondary stakeholders be identified and considered when companies are making business decisions.
- The moral minimum theory of business ethics encourages a business to "do no harm" or, alternatively, "do the least possible harm."
- A company that follows a maximizing profits theory strives to make as much profit as possible, as long as no laws are broken.

MORAL PHILOSOPHY AND ETHICAL DECISION MAKING

Where do our ethics come from? Ethics may come from many sources, including family, church, school, community norms, and moral reasoning. All these factors help shape one's personal beliefs about right and wrong. Here, we shall review some major theories of ethics from the field of moral philosophy.

Certain moral philosophies may influence one's moral judgments and preferred solutions to ethical dilemmas. **Morals** are generally accepted *standards* of right and wrong in a given society or community. These standards may be based on the law, one's religion, one's personal belief systems, or some combination of all three. The term **ethics** refers to having a *conscious system* in place for solving moral dilemmas. Individual approaches to thinking ethically may be based on several broad sources of ethical standards that stem from certain historical theories of morality. Although a close examination of moral philosophy is outside the scope of this textbook, it is essential to understand the main theoretical approaches to ethics and morality. In summary, there are three major ethical traditions: principles, consequences, and contracts.

LO 5-3
Identify the major theories of ethics from the field of moral philosophy.

Principles-Based Approach

The principles-based approach to ethics encompasses a large family of diverse moral theories, including theories based on religion, virtue, natural law, and universal moral duties. What these theories have in common is that they are all based on general or universal moral principles.

Religion   Ethical decisions that are made according to a set of established principles or standards such as *religious tenets* or codes—for example, the Koran (Islamic canonical law) or the Old Testament (Judeo-Christian tradition)—employ a principles-based approach. These religious-based principles establish duties and are not subject to exceptions, but they may be tempered by other religious principles such as mercy and justice.

Virtue   Another principles-based approach to ethics is called *virtue ethics,* a tradition that goes back to Aristotle.[1] This ethical theory evaluates conduct based on whether it promotes good moral character. Moreover, according to Aristotle, for a person to become virtuous, she can't simply study what virtue *is;* she must actually do virtuous deeds.

Natural Law   In addition to religious-based principles, some philosophers claim that humans have certain *inherent* moral rights and duties that spring from their ability to reason and choose freely what they do with their lives. *Natural law* theory is a moral philosophy that certain rights and moral values are timeless and universal and discoverable through human reason or, as the U.S. Declaration of Independence (1776) famously states

> We hold these truths to be self-evident, that all men are created equal, that they are endowed by their Creator with certain unalienable Rights, that among these are Life, Liberty and the pursuit of Happiness.

Historically, natural law refers to the use of reason to deduce universal and timeless rules of moral behavior. Although the natural law tradition goes back to the ancient Greeks and Romans, medieval theologian Thomas Aquinas (1225–1274) developed the most well-known theory of natural law. According to Aquinas, (1) natural law is given by God, (2) it is authoritative over all human beings, and (3) it is knowable through the use of reason.[2]

---

[1] Aristotle, *Nicomachean Ethics* (T.H. Irwin trans., Hackett Publishing Company 1999).

[2] For a comprehensive overview of natural law theory, *see* Leo Strauss, *Natural Right and History* (University of Chicago Press 1950).

The Categorical Imperative The great Prussian-born philosopher Immanuel Kant (1724–1804) developed a form of principles-based ethics, which he called *duty-based* ethics, in his famous and oft-cited work *The Critique of Practical Reason.* According to Kant, one should act morally because it is the right thing to do, without any ulterior motive. In particular, Kant's approach to ethics is based on an inherent notion that humans should act from a sense of duty to human dignity. Kant theorized that *rights* imply *duties* and that the duty to respect the rights of others is paramount in acting morally. In the words of Kant

> Act in such a way that you treat humanity, whether in your own person or in the person of any other, always at the same time as an end and never merely as a means to an end.

Moreover, the idea of the *categorical imperative* is a central theme in Kant's work. In summary, the categorical imperative is a moral test to help individuals decide right from wrong. Specifically, when considering whether a given action is right or wrong in the moral sense, Kant would ask, "What if everybody took that same action?" This Kantian question is sometimes called a *universalization* test. If everyone should act the same way (e.g., if everyone should tell the truth or keep their promises), then the action (promise-keeping; truth-telling) is moral. Kant further believed that the answers to this universal moral test are unconditional and absolute.

Consequences-Based Approach

This approach emphasizes that the ethical course of action is the one that provides the greatest good (happiness) for the greatest number of people and has the least harmful consequences for the majority of the community. The approach stems from the **utilitarian** stream of moral philosophy.[3] Under this model, an action is ethically sound if it produces positive results or the least harm for the most people. Simply put, the course of action that results in the most benefits for the most individuals is the most ethical. By contrast, if an action impacts the majority of community members in a negative way, it is inherently unethical. Business owners and managers who employ a consequences-based approach seek to produce the greatest balance of good over harm for all who are affected, including owners, employees, customers, investors, and the community at large. Critics of utilitarianism argue that this approach amounts to using a mathematical formula to decide matters of morality.

LEGAL/ETHICAL REFLECTION AND DISCUSSION

The Trolley Problem

Do you kill one person to save five?

The *trolley problem* is a famous thought experiment in ethics.[4] Imagine a runaway trolley barreling down a railway track. The trolley's brakes are not working, and ahead, on the tracks, there are five workers. The trolley is headed straight for them. You are standing next to a lever. If you pull this lever, the trolley will switch to a side track and the five workers will be saved. However, you notice there is one person on the side track.

You thus have two options: (1) Do nothing, and the trolley kills the five people on the main track, or (2) pull the lever, diverting the trolley onto the side track, where it will kill one person. What should you do? What are the results of your decision using a principles, consequences, and contact-based approach?

---

[3] The founder of utilitarianism is the famous 18th-century philosopher Jeremy Bentham.

[4] Philosopher Philippa Foot is credited with inventing this famous hypothetical. *See* F. E. Guerra-Pujol, *Trolley Problems,* 63 Drake L. Rev. 101 (2014).

Contract-Based Approach

Harvard philosopher John Rawls (1921–2002) developed a contract-based theory of ethics in his influential book *A Theory of Justice* (1971). His approach is considered a contractarian one because Rawls imagines a world in which people must negotiate their own ethical rules and principles for themselves. What makes Rawls's particular theory so original and famous, however, is his notion of the Original Position, a hypothetical situation in which everyone negotiates from behind a *veil of ignorance*. This veil blinds people to all facts about themselves:

> . . . no one knows his place in society, his class position or social status, nor does anyone know his fortune in the distribution of natural assets and abilities, his intelligence, strength, and the like. I shall even assume that the parties do not know their conceptions of the good or their special psychological propensities. The principles of justice are chosen behind a veil of ignorance.[5]

According to Rawls, ignorance of these details about oneself will lead people to negotiate a set of ethical principles that are fair to all. Why? Because if no one knows what his ultimate position in society will be, people negotiating from behind the veil of ignorance are not going to privilege any one class of people; instead, they will develop ethical rules and principles that treat all fairly. In particular, Rawls claims that individuals in the Original Position should adopt a *maximin* strategy that maximizes the prospects of the least well-off: "They are the principles that rational and free persons concerned to further their own interests would accept in an initial position of equality as defining the fundamentals of the terms of their association."[6]

CONCEPT SUMMARY Moral Philosophy and Ethical Decision Making

- Ethics addresses how one should act in a given situation and comprises the systematic set of rules used to guide decision making and choice of action when one is confronted with a moral dilemma.
- Morals are generally accepted *standards* of right and wrong in a given society or community. These standards may be based on law, religion, personal belief systems, moral reasoning, or some combination of these.
- In a principles-based approach to ethical decision making, decisions are made according to a set of established principles or standards, such as religious tenets or codes, natural law, or moral principles like the categorical imperative.
- A consequences-based approach to ethical decision making emphasizes that the ethical course of action is the one that provides the most good (happiness) for the greatest number of people.
- A contract-based or Rawlsian approach to ethical decision making imagines what ethical rules people would agree to if they could negotiate these rules ahead of time, from behind a veil of ignorance.

---

[5]John Rawls, *A Theory of Justice* (1971), p.11.

[6]John Rawls, *A Theory of Justice* (1971), p.11.

> **Self-Check** Business Ethics: Principles-Based, Consequences-Based, or Contract-Based Approach
>
> For each of the following, decide whether the action or decision best reflects the principles-based approach, the consequences-based approach, or the contract-based approach.
>
> 1. A new code of conduct and code of ethics, written by management and disseminated to the entire corporate workforce, requires mandatory compliance by all employees.
> 2. A company introduces a new approved drug that cures 80 percent of those who take it, has no negative or positive effect on 10 percent of those who take it, and has a negative effect on 10 percent of those who take it.
> 3. Believing that corporations should be good corporate citizens, a start-up encourages its employees to donate to their preferred charities and promises to match every dollar of every donation if the start-up goes public in the future.
>
> *Answers to this Self-Check are provided at the end of the chapter.*

LO 5-4

Identify the main challenges to business ethics management and formulate a response to each challenge.

VALUES MANAGEMENT AND CHALLENGES TO BUSINESS ETHICS

Business ethics in the workplace emphasizes prioritizing moral values for the organization and ensuring that employee and manager behaviors are aligned with those values. This approach is known as **values management**. Yet, despite evidence that embracing business ethics promotes profitability and contributes to sound public policy, some business cultures are resistant to values management programs.

A useful approach to consider when deciding whether a manager or a company is acting in an ethical manner is to apply a "broadcast news test." Ask yourself, "How would I feel if the business decision was announced to the public on social media or the local and national news?" How would your family and friends react to the decision? In today's social media environment, very little goes unnoticed or unreported, so it might be even more appropriate to ask how one would feel if a video of a major decision went viral. Table 5.1 lists common challenges and possible responses to business ethics and values management.

LO 5-5

List the common traits of effective values management.

LO 5-6

Develop a code of ethics.

COMMON TRAITS OF EFFECTIVE VALUES MANAGEMENT

One way business organizations implement values management is by developing codes of ethics and an ethical vision to guide the decisions and behavior of their employees and managers. (Think of Google's famous "Don't be evil" policy.) Such values management programs can also include extensive training and monitoring protocols, depending on the organization's command structure, but at a minimum, every business organization should consider developing a code of ethics to provide guidance in ethical dilemmas.

Although ethicists have various views on how an ideal ethical organization should operate, all effective values management programs share certain common traits:

- Management articulates a clear vision of ethics and moral integrity through all levels of the organization.
- Management's vision of ethics and integrity is implemented at all levels of the decision-making process of the organization.

TABLE 5.1 Challenges and Realities in Business Ethics

Challenge	Reality
Business ethics is unnecessary because it asserts the obvious: Act ethically.	The value of a code of ethics to an organization is its priority and focus with respect to certain ethical values in the company. Dishonesty takes a variety of forms. If an organization is confronting varying degrees of dishonesty (including more common examples such as office supply theft) or deceit in the workplace, a priority on honesty is very timely—and honesty should be listed in that organization's code of ethics.
Complying with the law is an organization's sole guide for ethical conduct.	While the law may operate as a baseline for ethical decision making, unethical acts may operate within the limits of the law (e.g., withholding information from superiors, casting revenue in favorable terms with a dubious basis for the projection, and spreading rumors). Illegal conduct sometimes has its genesis in unethical behavior that has gone unnoticed.
Ethics can't be managed.	Management inherently incorporates a value system. Strategic priorities (maximizing profit, expanding market share, cutting costs, etc.) can be very strong influences on ethical decision making. Workplace regulations and rules directly influence behaviors in a manner that improves the general good and/or minimizes potential harm to stakeholders.
Ethics is about philosophy and has little to do with the day-to-day realities of running a business.	Business ethics is a management discipline with a programmatic approach that includes several practical tools. Ethics management programs have practical applications in other areas of management as well.
Business ethics cannot be taught. It is religion and not management.	Altering people's values isn't the objective of an organizational ethics program. Managing values and conflict among them is the primary objective.

- The reward systems, policies, and practices of the organization are aligned with management's vision of ethics and integrity.
- Above all, responsibility is seen as individual rather than collective in that individuals are encouraged to assume personal responsibility for the actions and decisions of the organization.

STRATEGIC LEGAL SOLUTIONS

Developing Codes of Ethics and Conduct

PROBLEM: *While many organizations may have a set of informal values and standards to which they aspire to adhere, such informal value systems may be too vague and thus not very helpful in a practical context.*

STRATEGIC SOLUTION: *Develop an effective code of ethics and code of conduct for your business organization. Such codes should be developed in cooperation with (and not exclusively by) the organization's human resource manager and legal counsel. Ideally, the entire organization, not just management, should play a role or have a say in the creation and periodic affirmation of such codes.*

Depending on the organization, a code of ethics and code of conduct may be expressed in the same document. Here, they are examined separately.

For a code of ethics, consider the following guidelines:

- Identify the ethical values needed to comply with relevant laws and regulations.
- Identify the ethical values most relevant to the main activities in each area of your organization. For example, the chief financial officer may identify objectivity and accuracy as important values.

(continued)

- Identify the ethical values most relevant to your organization's employees and workplace. Consider which of these issues are ethical in nature, for example, issues relating to fairness and honesty.
- Identify the ethical values that might be most important to your organization's primary and secondary stakeholders, including employees, clients, customers, suppliers, lenders, and members of the local community.

Examples of ethical values may include

- *Trustworthiness:* Honesty, integrity, promise-keeping, loyalty.
- *Respect:* Autonomy, privacy, dignity, courtesy, tolerance, acceptance.
- *Responsibility:* Accountability, pursuit of excellence.
- *Caring:* Compassion, consideration, giving, sharing, kindness.
- *Justice and fairness:* Procedural fairness, impartiality, consistency, equity, equality, due process.
- *Civic virtue and citizenship:* Law abiding, community service, protection of the environment.

Codes of ethics are general guidelines to promote ethical decision making. *Codes of conduct,* by contrast, are specific rules stating what actions are prohibited in the workplace. Examples of topics typically addressed by codes of conduct may include policies relating to dress codes, illegal drug use, antidiscrimination, sexual harassment, confidentiality rules, rules against accepting personal gifts from third parties as a result of a company role or action, other conflict-of-interest rules, compliance with applicable laws and regulations, not using the organization's property for personal use, and reporting illegal or questionable activity.

Managers should also think beyond these traditional legalistic expectations. It is important to identify what's ethically sensitive in your particular organization as well. Codes of conduct should be integrated into the various areas of the organization, including personnel matters, such as job descriptions and performance appraisal forms, management-by-objectives expectations, standard forms, checklists, budget report format, and other relevant control instruments to ensure conformance with the code of conduct. An effective code of conduct also contains examples of appropriate behavior.

As with any management practice, the best outcome is behavior that is consistent with the organization's values and ethical vision. The best ethical values and intentions are meaningless unless they generate fair and just behaviors in the workplace. All levels of employees in a company need to react to business situations in a fair and consistent manner.

Complaints and lawsuits frequently arise when employees, job applicants, or customers are treated, or are perceived as being treated, unfairly. One of the primary benefits of a code of ethics and a code of conduct is that such codes provide employees with rules and ideals that they can universally follow. When a company is dealing with a diverse population of employees, common sense is not always common and the concept of right and wrong is not always easily agreed upon. Written codes can provide a central source of inspiration and guidance to ensure uniform conduct. That is why practices that generate lists of ethical values, or codes of ethics, must also generate policies, procedures, and training that translate those values into appropriate behaviors.

LEGAL/ETHICAL REFLECTION AND DISCUSSION

The Penn State Saga

In 2011, the Pennsylvania State University community was stunned by multiple charges of child molestation committed by former assistant football coach Jerry Sandusky. Sandusky had used Penn State's facilities, with permission, for a children's charity organization with which he was affiliated. Soon after the initial charges were filed, allegations of perjury and failure to report the situation were brought against Penn State

(continued)

management. Joe Paterno, the legendary head football coach, was found to have been aware of the situation. Penn State's athletic program motto is "Success with Honor." The football program had never been charged with a severe NCAA rules violation, and the program enjoyed a high graduation rate. A subsequent investigation showed that Coach Paterno did in fact report the incidents to his superiors but had not taken any independent action. As a result of intense media coverage, a former university vice president and the former athletic director were implicated in a cover-up, along with the university president, Graham Spanier. Spanier and Paterno were fired. On June 22, 2012, Jerry Sandusky was convicted of 45 of 48 counts of sexual assault involving 10 boys. In addition, many of Sandusky's victims filed civil lawsuits against Penn State for damages. On October 28, 2013, Penn State University reached settlements with 26 of Sandusky's victims, costing the university a total of $59.7 million.

Not all victims settled with Penn State. One victim (identified only as "Victim 9" in court documents) sued Penn State on November 21, 2013, citing that the victim had been unable to reach a settlement with the institution, and in a separate case involving another victim ("Victim 6"), a U.S. district court judge in Philadelphia ruled on November 6, 2013, in favor of the university, stating that Penn State could not legally be held liable for Sandusky's actions simply because he was employed there. The judge stated that Victim 6 failed "to explain how molestation was the kind of act that Penn State employed Sandusky to perform." But on April 9, 2015, Penn State trustees voted to approve a confidential settlement with "one or more" victims from the child sexual abuse scandal involving Jerry Sandusky.

By 2019, the amount that Penn State paid as a result of the Sandusky child abuse scandal topped out at $220 million. Only $30 million, or just under a third of the expenditures, were reimbursed by insurance carriers. Thirty-three victims received a total of $63.1 million. Former assistant coach Mike McQueary, who was fired by Penn State soon after he helped uncover the abuse, received a $14.1 million judgment as a whistleblower (the McQueary case is covered in more detail in Chapter 11, Employment Relationships and Labor Law). The rest of the money was paid out for fines, attorney fees, and investigation costs. The NCAA brought sanctions against the university including fines, restrictions on postseason play, a reduction in football scholarships, and university-wide probation.[7]

1. Paterno said that he fulfilled his responsibility by reporting what he knew to the university management. Could he have done more? Should he have done more? If so, what specific steps should he have taken?
2. Who are the primary and secondary stakeholders in this dilemma?
3. Once the university administration became aware of the Sandusky allegations, what specific actions should it have taken?
4. Is it fair for current Penn State student-athletes to be affected by incidents that they had nothing to do with and that happened before many of them entered the university?
5. Did Paterno and the university management demonstrate a commitment to their stated expectation, "Success with Honor"?
6. Was the cover-up intended to preserve the university's reputation? Is that a justification for the university's failure to act? Are there ever any circumstances in which a cover-up is ethical? Can any ethical theory justify the university's failure to act?
7. Initially, the NCAA stripped Penn State's football team of 112 wins as part of their sanctions. The NCAA reversed their position three years later and restored the wins. Did the NCAA act ethically in restoring the wins? Why or why not?

STRATEGIC ADVANTAGES OF VALUES MANAGEMENT

As we have seen thus far, when business owners and managers identify and prioritize their organization's ethical values and establish associated policies and procedures to encourage or reward ethical behavior, they are engaged in values management.

---

[7]C. Thompson, *Penn State's costs in the Jerry Sandusky scandal have hit $220 million; where'd the money go?* PennLive (April 17, 2019).

LO 5-7

Define values management and articulate several reasons why values management is important in business operations.

Values management is also crucial in other management practices, such as management of a diverse workforce, total quality management, and strategic planning. Moreover, there are both business and public benefits to values management because managing values in the workplace legitimizes managerial actions, strengthens the coherence and balance of the organization's culture, improves trust in relationships between individuals and groups, supports greater consistency in standards and qualities of products, and cultivates greater sensitivity to the impact of the enterprise's values and messages. Indeed, companies that have embraced a values management system often report strategic advantages as well.

Cultivation of Strong Teamwork and Productivity

Values management may help align employee behaviors with the ethical values of the organization's top-level management. Sometimes an organization finds surprising disparity between its preferred values and the values actually reflected by behaviors in the workplace. Ongoing attention and dialogue regarding values in the workplace promote openness, integrity, and community, which are critical ingredients of team-building in the workplace. Employees who feel strong alignment between their values and those of the organization tend to react with higher levels of motivation and performance.

Clarity in Business Operations

Setting ethical standards also gives an organization's employees context for executing business operations. Context, in turn, lends more clarity to strategic planning by identifying preferred values and ensuring that organizational behaviors are aligned with those values. This effort includes identifying values, developing written policies and procedures to align behaviors with preferred values, and then training all personnel about these policies and procedures. These standards can also be used as a framework for performance, reliability, measurement, and feedback. A comprehensive values management program may also be used in managing and promoting workplace diversity and in considering the values and perspectives of different stakeholders.

Public Image

Aligning individual behaviors with an organization's values is also critical to developing effective marketing and public relations programs. By devoting consistent and serious attention to values management, a business organization is able to portray itself in a positive light to the public. People see such organizations as valuing people more than profits and as striving to operate with the utmost integrity.

> **KEY POINT**
>
> Values management has many strategic advantages.

Staying the Ethical Course in Turbulent Times

The global financial crisis that began in 2008 and the instability over Britain's exit from the European Union (referred to as "Brexit") provide recent examples of turbulent times in the corporate and financial sectors. Strong leadership in values management can, in principle, provide guidance to managers and employees, especially during times of economic turbulence and unpredictable change.

LO 5-8

Employ an ethical decision-making paradigm used by managers to resolve ethical dilemmas.

ETHICAL DECISION MAKING: A MANAGER'S PARADIGM

It is not uncommon for business ethics to be portrayed as a matter of resolving conflicts in which one option appears to be the clear choice. Case studies that present situations where an employee is faced with whether or not to lie, steal, cheat, abuse another, break terms of a

FIGURE 5.1 Ethical Decision Making

1. Define the dilemma → How and when did the dilemma occur? What were the underlying reasons for the conflict?

2. Identify impact → Which primary and secondary stakeholders will be affected? How will these stakeholders be affected?

3. Apply standards → What is the legal impact of the dilemma? What values and ethical principles has the organization set out for guidance? What are the consequences of action or inaction?

4. Develop choices and discuss impact with various constituencies → Which choice results in the most benefit to stakeholders? Will any of the choices result in harm to stakeholders? What are the level and severity of the harms? Which choice upholds the values of the organization?

5. Implement, evaluate, and monitor → How can this decision be implemented with greatest attention to all stakeholders? Under what circumstances are you willing to make an exception to your decision? How could this company avoid this dilemma in the future?

contract, and so on are too simplistic. Ethical dilemmas faced by managers are often complex, with no clear ethical choice. The use of a paradigm in the flowchart (see Figure 5.1) can help business owners and managers apply ethical decision making more consistently.

ETHICAL DECISION-MAKING CASE STUDIES

Business ethics cannot be studied in a vacuum. The principles and theories that are discussed in this chapter are useful only if they are understood in a business context. Study the following two well-known cases in some detail, and apply the concepts that have been covered thus far. Use the ethical decision-making flowchart in Figure 5.1 to assess and discuss the ethical challenges presented in these two cases. Several questions for discussion are included at the end of each case study. The first case involves a values conflict between stakeholder groups. The second case involves a major public company[8] that conducted a secret and controversial social psychology experiment on its own users.

LO 5-9

Apply your knowledge of business ethics to recent case studies of companies facing ethical dilemmas.

Google's Project Maven

The announcement by Google in June 2018 that it would not seek another contract for its work providing artificial intelligence (AI) for a U.S. Department of Defense project was a culmination of months of internal struggle that pitted shareholder interests against stakeholder interests. However, after a backlash from employees and other stakeholders, Google updated its CSR strategy to include specific policies on AI research. These policies include a specific prohibition of deploying Google technologies that "cause or are likely to cause overall harm." Nor will Google participate in developing "[w]eapons or other technologies whose principal purpose or implementation is to cause or directly facilitate injury to people."[9]

---

[8] A publicly held company is one whose stock is bought and sold in public markets. Regulation of public companies and markets is discussed in detail in Chapter 16, "Regulation of Securities, Corporate Governance, and Financial Markets."

[9] Sundar Pichai, *AI at Google: Our Principles,* Google (2018), www.blog.google/technology/ai/ai-principles/.

Google headquarters. Uladzik Kryhin/Shutterstock

The origins of Google's AI controversy began in September 2017 after its management team announced that Google was awarded a contract for $28M to work with the Pentagon on a program dubbed "Project Maven." The project required Google to develop and support AI algorithms that the Department of Defense used to analyze footage from military drones. It was touted by Google as "a large government program that will result in improved safety for citizens and nations through faster identification of evils such as violent extremist activities and human right abuses." According to *The New York Times,* two sets of e-mails reveal that Google's senior leadership was enthusiastically supportive of Project Maven primarily because it would help pave the way for larger Pentagon contracts. Privately, though, the e-mails showed a deep concern about how the company's involvement would be perceived. Google's chief AI scientist urged colleagues in an internal e-mail to avoid "any mention or implication of AI" in public statements about the Pentagon contract and warned that it may become "red meat to the media" and ultimately damage Google.[10]

Employee Stakeholders Assert Power News of the Pentagon contract and Google's AI efforts fueled an extraordinary internal debate and protest. Employees feared that the partnership would pivot toward developing weaponry and other offensive tech. Its top technical talent complained that the Pentagon contract betrayed its principles, while profit-oriented officials at Google worried that the protests would damage its chances to secure more business from the Defense Department. Several AI scientists resigned in protest, while others called for the company to cancel the Maven contract. The growing protests resulted in a petition signed by about 4,000 employees who demanded a clear policy stating that neither Google nor its contractors will ever build warfare technology. Google was faced with the classic CSR dilemma: profits for shareholders versus well-being of stakeholders.

Google's Project Maven: Questions for Discussion

1. Given Google's reaction to the petition and protests, which CSR strategy did Google follow to resolve its dilemma? Explain.
2. Employees are one set of stakeholders impacted by Google's decision. What other stakeholders might have been involved and what were their interests? Did all stakeholders have the same interests?
3. What did Google's chief scientists mean by warning her colleagues of AI being "red meat to the media"? How could the use of the term *AI* damage Google? Explain.
4. Critics of the protests and of Google's reaction point out that Google's actions will ultimately make no difference to society because plenty of other tech companies are waiting to fill Google's shoes with a Pentagon contract. Does that strike you as convincing? Explain.

---

[10]Scott Shane et al., *How a Pentagon Contract Became an Identity Crisis for Google,* N.Y. Times, May 30, 2018.

Facebook's Secret Psychology Experiment: The Law and Ethics of A/B Testing

Over a billion users around the world have Facebook accounts. For a week in January 2012, many of those users (over 689,000 users in all) were experimented on without their knowledge or any meaningful consent.

Researchers at Facebook, as well as Cornell University and UCSF (the University of California, San Francisco), conducted a massive social psychological experiment on hundreds of thousands of Facebook users by tinkering with their individual News Feeds—the continuous stream of status updates, photos, and news articles that appears on each user's Facebook account. Facebook secretly altered the algorithm that determines what content shows up in each user's News Feed. Some people were shown mostly positive or happy News Feeds; others were shown mostly negative or sadder-than-average News Feeds. Facebook was studying an important psychological phenomenon called "emotional contagion."

Facebook eventually published its research results in the *Proceedings of the National Academy of the Sciences* in June 2014.[11] The researchers working with Facebook claimed to have found evidence of "emotional contagion"; that is, by modifying the Facebook News Feed to contain slightly more positive or more negative postings, they were able to observe a small but statistically significant impact on users' posting habits. In particular, if you see lots of positive posts on Facebook, you are marginally more likely to post something positive yourself.

But was this experiment ethical or even legal?

Facebook did not inform its users of the experiment ahead of time or allow any of them to opt out of the experiment. Legally speaking, Facebook does ask people for a generalized consent in its "Data Use Policy" agreement when people sign up, specifically saying that it may use the information it receives about each user for data analysis, testing, research, and service improvement. Many consider this user agreement, however, to be a weak form of consent and argue that Facebook should provide its users the option to opt out from these experiments.

Nor did Facebook submit its experiment to an Institutional Review Board (an independent ethics committee that requires scientific experiments to abide by consent and safety standards) for pre-approval. Instead, the social giant considered its experiment just another A/B test, which most tech companies and start-ups engage in on a regular basis. (The essence of A/B testing is to separate an otherwise undifferentiated community based on a single factor and then evaluate the behavior of one group against another. Online, this usually means silently redirecting visitors to a landing page programmed to display variations on a sales pitch, and then noticing which approach results in more clicks on the primary call-to-action button. In stores, it can mean shelving the same items differently across otherwise identical Walmart stores, playing upbeat or downbeat background music on alternate weeks at Starbucks, or experimenting with the color and size of the lettering on the value menu at McDonald's.)

Public Outcry The study generated a huge public outcry and produced a lot of negative publicity for Facebook. The *Proceedings of the National Academy of the Sciences* published an "Editorial Expression of Concern," and one law professor (James Grimmelmann, University of Maryland) argued that the actions of Facebook were

---

[11] Adam D. I. Kramer, Jamie E. Guillory & Jeffrey T. Hancock, *Experimental Evidence of Massive-Scale Emotional Contagion Through Social Networks*, 111 Proc. Nat'l Acad. Sci. 8788 (2014).

"illegal, immoral, and mood-altering." In addition, the Electronic Privacy Information Center (EPIC) filed a formal complaint with the Federal Trade Commission on July 3, 2014, claiming that Facebook had broken the law when it conducted the study on the emotions of its users without their knowledge or consent. In its complaint, EPIC alleged that Facebook had deceived its users by secretly conducting a psychological experiment on their emotions: "At the time of the experiment, Facebook did not state in the Data Use Policy that user data would be used for research purposes. Facebook also failed to inform users that their personal information would be shared with researchers."

Although Sheryl Sandburg, Facebook's COO, issued a half-hearted apology on behalf of Facebook, stating that the study "was part of ongoing research companies do to test different products" and that it "was poorly communicated and for that [lack of] communication we apologize," it's not clear whether Facebook and other major websites like Google and OkCupid continue to engage in this practice on a regular basis.

Ethical Analysis One way of deciding whether A/B testing is ethical is to focus on whether there is a risk of harm when a test is done. For example, if Facebook wants to know which shade of blue to use in its user interface, it might use A/B testing to try a few shades and measure users' responses. This is ethical because no user is harmed, especially if the only result is that the service better serves users.

Other uses of A/B testing might be unethical. Consider a study in which users are incited to commit violent acts against immigrants in order to test the psychology of racism in an online environment. Such a study would have to be unethical because it generates significant risk of harm.

So the question is not whether A/B testing is always ethical or unethical, but rather where should companies like Facebook draw the line between ethical and unethical uses. Where would you draw this line?

One possible solution is to consider the risks of each test on a case-by-case basis. Specifically, where the risks are minimal, A/B testing (even without consent) might not be ethically objectionable, as in the shades-of-blue example. But at the same time, where the risks are extremely high or there are significant risks to nonparticipants, as in the immigrant-violence example, the test is most likely unethical even with consent from participants.[12]

Where exactly to draw this line, and what processes a company should use to avoid stepping over the line, is left to the reader.

Facebook's Secret Psychology Experiment: Questions for Discussion

1. Is Facebook an ethical company? Explain.
2. Did Facebook's purposeful manipulation of users' News Feeds create any substantial risk of harm to those users? Why or why not?
3. Should online experiments be strictly regulated by the government, or would strict regulation be counterproductive?
4. As a matter of ethics, should Facebook give its users the option to opt out of A/B testing in the future? What ethical theory do you think is relevant to this example?

---

[12]This analysis is borrowed from Ed Felten, *On the Ethics of A/B Testing,* Freedom to Tinker (July 8, 2014), https://freedom-to-tinker.com/blog/felten/on-the-ethics-of-ab-testing/.

5. Christian Rudder, the president of OkCupid, an online dating site, defended Facebook's actions by pointing out the prevalence of A/B testing in the online world: "*Guess what, everybody: if you use the Internet, you're the subject of hundreds of experiments at any given time, on every site. That's how websites work.*" Is this argument morally compelling or persuasive? Why or why not?

CORPORATE SOCIAL RESPONSIBILITY

While business ethics may be thought of as an application of ethics to the corporate sector and may be useful as a paradigm for determining responsibility in business dealings, corporate social responsibility (CSR) involves a broader-based identification of important business and social issues and a critique of business organizations and practices.

In summary, there are three schools of thought that define CSR in practice: the narrow view, the moderate view, and the broad view.

LO 5-10

Articulate the various views on corporate social responsibility and defend a particular view.

The Narrow View: "Greed Is Good"

Nobel Prize–winning economist Milton Friedman proposed that the only responsibility a business has is to maximize shareholder wealth (the maximizing profits theory).[13] Moreover, in his classic condemnation of the broad view of corporate social responsibility, Friedman further argued that managers who pursue social initiatives with corporate funds are violating their fiduciary duties to the owners of the corporation. This narrow view of CSR thus emphasizes a corporation's ethical duties to its shareholders. While individuals are free to act morally and behave in a socially responsible manner on their own time and

Corporate social responsibility includes the notion of recognizing the importance of good corporate citizenship and partnering with the community. Jack Star/PhotoLink/Getty Images

[13]Milton Friedman, *The Social Responsibility of Business Is to Increase Its Profits*, N.Y. Times Mag. (Sept. 13, 1970).

with their own resources, managers are responsible solely to the shareholders to make as much profit as legally possible. As for society's well-being, the argument goes, the "invisible hand" of the market will end up producing the most benefits overall to society. According to Adam Smith's famous "invisible hand" metaphor, the common good is best served when people and businesses pursue not the common good, but rather their self-interest.

The Moderate View: Just Follow the Law

Advocates of a more moderate view of CSR emphasize the role that the government and regulatory agencies play in setting the outer limits of corporate social responsibility. According to this moderate or "government hand" view, it is the government's job to establish legal and regulatory guidelines for business because the government already represents the aggregate moral views of the public. Under this view, a business's ethical responsibility is to comply with the law and pursue objectives that are legal. The regulatory hands of the law and the political process, rather than Adam Smith's invisible hand, provide the basis for ethical decision making.

The Broad View: Good Corporate Citizenship

Business organizations committed to a broad view of CSR aim to achieve commercial success in ways that honor ethical values and respect people, communities, and the natural environment in a sustainable manner while recognizing the interests of stakeholders. Stakeholders include investors, customers, employees, business partners, local communities, the environment, and society at large. The broad view of CSR also involves the notion of "corporate citizenship," which means a business should strive to promote the economic, legal, ethical, and philanthropic social responsibilities expected of it by its stakeholders.

Furthermore, the broadest view of CSR is that corporations have a social responsibility and that profitability is secondary (the moral minimum theory). Indeed, some business ethicists argue that corporations are allowed to exist only because they can serve some public good. Thus, these ethicists often invoke a set of societal expectations with the idea that corporations should conduct their business on such terms. Their starting point is socially defined goals rather than business objectives. Others, however, argue that CSR is in the public's interest and a company's self-interest *and* that a company does well by employing socially responsible principles in its business operations. In this way, CSR may be thought of as a form of enlightened self-interest because the long-term prosperity of a firm depends not on short-term profits but on societal well-being.

In any case, an integral part of the broad CSR perspective is the focus on what some ethicists call the *triple bottom line*. Essentially, the triple bottom line emphasizes not only the conventional creation of economic value (profits), but also a company's creation (or destruction) of environmental and social value. The triple-bottom-line approach thus places a great deal more pressure on managers to perform, as it is not uncommon that these three sets of bottom-line issues conflict. It is not enough, then, for managers to aggressively pursue a social agenda; they must also not lose sight of financial goals or environmental performance.

In Case 5.2, the U.S. Trademark Trial and Appeal Board (TTAB), an administrative court of the U.S. Patent and Trademark Office (USPTO), heard a case involving a trademark owner's opposition to another company's trademark application. It is an example of a business reforming its actions by integrating a CSR strategy.

CASE 5.2 Brooks Brothers Group, Inc. v. Bubbles by Brooks, LLC, Opposition No. 91205596 (T.T.A.B. July 11, 2013)

FACT SUMMARY Amy Brooks, a cancer survivor from Minnesota, started her small home-based business Bubbles by Brooks, which specializes in making soap and skin care products handcrafted and designed to reduce irritation as cancer patients go through therapy. Her sales at the time of this case amounted to a little less than $100,000 a year.

When Amy applied for a federal trademark for her business name, Brooks Brothers, the large clothing retailer, opposed her registration at the U.S. Trademark Office. The retailer's lawyers stated that "[although] 'Brooks' may be your surname, it does not give you the right to infringe on the Brooks Brothers trademark or otherwise compete with Brooks Brothers."

After a year of legal wrangling, Brooks Brothers withdrew its opposition to Amy's federal trademark application, and she was finally able to register her mark.

SYNOPSIS OF DECISION AND OPINION The Trademark Trial and Appeal Board dismissed the case before reaching a decision in light of the settlement agreed upon by both parties.

Amy was fortunate to secure pro bono legal representation from a large law firm in her area that was willing to litigate on her behalf. During the proceedings, the law firm's attorneys working on her behalf filed a lengthy motion to the court requesting a ruling in Amy's favor. Facing a potentially adverse ruling, and a lengthy and potentially embarrassing case, Brooks Brothers settled and withdrew their opposition to Amy's use and application of the trademark "Bubbles by Brooks."

WORDS OF THE COURT: Settled "In view of the stipulation filed June 13, 2013, the opposition is dismissed. . . ."

Case Questions

The Federal Rules of Civil Procedure, which govern the rules for federal litigation, state that the rules "should be construed, administered, and employed by the court and the parties to secure the just, speedy, and inexpensive determination of every action and proceeding."

1. In light of the Federal Rules of Civil Procedure, do parties have an ethical duty to refrain from lengthy litigation in certain cases?
2. Which CSR approach did the opposer, Brooks Brothers, adopt in this case? How did this approach backfire from a strategic perspective?
3. Which CSR approach would you have chosen and why?
4. *Focus on Critical Thinking:* Use your favorite search engine to find any websites or documents related to Brooks Brothers' commitment to CSR. How does it comport with their actions in this case? Should it be amended? Explain.

CSR and Litigation

Some companies apply a CSR lens when dealing with litigation. This approach may limit abusive litigation strategies initiated by lawyers who might be overly aggressive in their advocacy. For example, Walmart has specific internal CSR guidelines that instruct its attorneys to behave ethically during litigation and to

- Honor the spirit, intent, and requirements of all rules of civil procedure and rules of professional conduct.
- Conduct themselves in a manner that enhances and preserves the dignity and integrity of the system of justice.

- Adhere to the principles and rules of conduct that further the truth-seeking process so that disputes will be resolved in a just, dignified, courteous, and efficient manner.
- Make reasonable responses to discovery request[s] and not interpret them in an artificially restrictive manner so as to avoid disclosure of relevant and non-privileged information.
- Make good faith efforts to resolve disputes concerning pleadings and discovery.
- Agree to reasonable requests for extension of time and waiver of procedural formalities when doing so will not adversely affect Walmart's legitimate rights.
- Prepare and submit discovery requests that are limited to those requests reasonably necessary for the prosecution or defense of an action and not for the purpose of placing an undue burden or expense on another party.[14]

In Landmark Case 5.3, a state appellate court decides a product liability issue in the context of a dangerous design flaw. The flaw was known to management and was ignored because the costs of repair were thought to be significantly more than the costs of compensating injured victims. This case is thus frequently cited by CSR advocates as an example of the failing of both the narrow "invisible hand" and moderate "government hand" approaches.

LANDMARK CASE 5.3 Grimshaw v. Ford Motor Company, 119 Cal. App. 3d 757 (1981)

FACT SUMMARY In an effort to add a more fuel-efficient car to its line of automobiles, Ford designed the Pinto. During the design phase, Ford engineers became concerned that the placement of the gas tank was unsafe and subject to puncturing and rupturing at low-impact speeds. Crash tests confirmed this dangerous design flaw, and engineers recommended halting production until a more safe solution was developed. However, Ford's management overruled the engineers and pushed the Pinto into the manufacturing phase. There was evidence that Ford considered the design alternatives too expensive and decided that the proposed fix would have a higher overall cost than the risk of liability from lawsuits as a result of injuries to its customers. Richard Grimshaw, a passenger in a Pinto, was injured when the gas tank erupted in a low-speed crash. The jury found Ford liable for Grimshaw's injuries and awarded him $125 million. The trial court reduced the award to $3.5 million pursuant to a California state statute.

SYNOPSIS OF DECISION AND OPINION The California appellate court upheld the jury's verdict and the $3.5 million award. The court pointed out that the dangerous design flaw carried with it the severe risk of injury and that the evidence showed that Ford would have had to spend only $15.30 per car to have made the Pinto safer.

WORDS OF THE COURT: Corporate Malice "[T]here was substantial evidence that Ford's management decided to proceed with the production of the Pinto with knowledge of test results revealing design defects which rendered the fuel tank extremely vulnerable on rear impact at low speeds and endangered the safety and lives of the occupants. Such conduct constitutes corporate malice."

Case Questions

1. Which view of CSR do you believe Ford's managers had when making the Pinto decision?

(continued)

---

[14]Christopher J. Whelan & Neta Ziv, *Law Firm Ethics in the Shadow of Corporate Social Reponsibility*, 26 Geo. J. Leg. Ethics 153, 172–73 (2013) (citing Walmart Legal Dep't, *Outside Counsel Guidelines* 7 (Sept. 2010)).

2. Suppose that the changes necessary to make the design safer would have cost Ford $1,000 per car, instead of $15 per car as the plaintiff alleged. Would this fact have changed the outcome of the case?

3. *Focus on Critical Thinking:* Given the fact that Ford's sales plummeted after this lawsuit was filed, could it be argued that the invisible hand actually worked here?

CONCEPT SUMMARY *Values Management, Corporate Challenges, and Corporate Social Responsibility*

- Companies that practice a moral minimum ethical philosophy strive to act as ethically as possible as long as they remain profitable. These companies are said to follow a broad view of corporate social responsibility (i.e., "good corporate citizenship").
- Companies that practice a maximizing profits ethical philosophy strive to maximize their revenues, viewing ethics and corporate social responsibility as secondary to increasing shareholder wealth. These companies are said to follow a narrow view regarding corporate social responsibility (i.e., "greed is good").
- Companies that follow a moderate view of corporate social responsibility (i.e., "just follow the law") look primarily to statutes and regulations for guidance in their decision-making process.
- Values management consists of prioritizing moral values for the organization and ensuring that behaviors are aligned with those values.
- Values management has many strategic benefits; managing values in the workplace legitimizes managerial actions, strengthens the coherence and balance of the organization's culture, improves trust in relationships between individuals and groups, supports greater consistency in standards and the quality of products, and cultivates greater sensitivity to the impact of the enterprise's values and messages.
- Values management may help to align employee behaviors with the ethical values favored by the organization's top-level management. Behavior in the workplace often conflicts with preferred ethical values, so management must be vigilant.
- Developing written policies and procedures to align behaviors with preferred values and communicating such policies and procedures to all personnel are essential.

KEY TERMS

Business ethics p. 142   Recognizing right and wrong business behavior and acting responsibly toward the business's stakeholders.

Stakeholder p. 142   Any individual or entity affected by a business's operations, including the business's owners, investors, employees, customers, suppliers, and the wider community.

Moral minimum p. 143   A corporate ethical philosophy in which a company strives to act as ethically as possible as long as a reasonable profit is made. Ethics and corporate social responsibility are priorities.

Maximizing profits p. 143   A corporate ethical philosophy in which a company strives to make as much money as possible with an emphasis on not breaking the law. Ethics and corporate social responsibility are often secondary concerns.

Morals p. 145   Generally accepted standards of right and wrong in a given society or community.

Ethics p. 145 A conscious system used for deciding moral dilemmas.

Utilitarian p. 146 Model of moral philosophy that holds that an action is ethically sound if it produces positive results for the most people.

Values management p. 148 Managerial system that emphasizes prioritizing moral values for the organization and ensuring that behaviors are aligned with those values.

CHAPTER REVIEW QUESTIONS

1. A(n) _____ system of morals holds that an action is ethical if it promotes good outcomes overall.
   a. Ethical-based
   b. Principles-based
   c. Contract-based
   d. Rastafarian-based
   e. Consequences-based

2. Which of the following statements is most consistent with a Kantian or duty-based system of ethics?
   a. Like cases should not be treated alike because people are different.
   b. "Do not do unto others as you would have them do unto you."
   c. One must abide by the same rules that one would apply to others.
   d. One should strive to promote the greatest good for the greatest number.
   e. One should imagine what rules people would agree to in the Original Position.

3. Which of the following statements regarding business ethics is generally true?
   a. Law and ethics are always synonymous.
   b. One should weigh the interests of all stakeholders equally.
   c. The moral minimum theory creates a moral ceiling, not a moral floor.
   d. Stakeholders include a company's owners, investors, employees, customers, suppliers, and the wider community.
   e. Stockholders are secondary stakeholders compared to the wider community.

4. The main difference between the moral minimum view of business ethics and the maximizing profits model is _____.
   I. The moral minimum theory requires business to take active steps to avoid harm, even at the expense of some additional profits.
   II. The moral minimum theory encourages business to take active steps to avoid harm as long as profits are not negatively affected.
   III. The maximizing profits model encourages companies to make as much money as possible as long as no laws are broken.
   a. I only
   b. II only
   c. III only
   d. I and II
   e. I and III

5. Which of the following statements is most consistent with the broad view of corporate social responsibility (CSR)?
   a. A company's primary responsibility is to serve the public good and promote the triple bottom line.
   b. A company's primary responsibility is to maximize wealth.
   c. A company's primary responsibility is to comply with the law.
   d. A company's primary responsibility is to its stockholders and investors.
   e. A company's primary responsibility is to protect the environment.

Answers and explanations are provided at the end of this chapter.

THEORY TO PRACTICE

Java Road (Java) is a corporation that retails high-quality coffee products through coffee carts in conveniently placed locations, such as malls and office complexes. Java owns 10 such carts and employs a workforce of 20 to maintain its business operations. The owner, Miguel, founded the company 10 years ago with the idea that a high-quality coffee product could be sold at a profit by limiting overhead to the product, employee compensation, and the carts. Although he has always stressed honesty with his employees, he has never developed a written code of ethics.

1. Suppose that Jacob, an employee who works at one of the most profitable carts, has one or two cups of free coffee a day. He bases his justification for doing so on the fact that the cart is so profitable that no one will notice. Given the lack of a written code of ethics, is it okay for Jacob to drink a free cup of coffee from the cart?
2. Suppose that one customer consistently buys coffee from Jacob and leaves a small tip. In an effort to increase the size of the tip, Jacob gives the customer a free coffee every Friday. Is it ethical for Jacob to do this? Is it ethical for the customer to take the free coffee?
3. What theories of moral philosophy helped your decision making in answering Questions 1 and 2?
4. Suppose that Miguel's general manager suggests that he develop a code of ethics for Java Road. Miguel bristles at the idea and replies that business ethics "cannot be managed—people are either ethical or not." What responses could the general manager use to persuade Miguel to employ a values management system?
5. Assume that Miguel finds a vendor that will sell him coffee beans at a discounted price. However, Miguel reads an article about the fact that the vendor uses child labor in Asia to produce the product. The vendor argues that the beans are high quality and that its practice of employing child labor is perfectly legal in Asia. Which view of corporate social responsibility (CSR) would result in Miguel's refusal to buy the beans? What is the vendor's view of CSR?

LEGAL STRATEGY 101

Strategic Ethics?

For many Fortune 500 corporations, ethics has become a big business. Combined, such companies now spend billions of dollars doing good deeds and self-promoting those myriad efforts to the public. The expectation, of course, is that ethically minded consumers will prefer the products and services of these companies.[15]

But is it ethical for such companies to use ethics so strategically? Should business and ethics mix in this way?

Many companies now claim that their products are made with high ethical standards or eco-friendly production methods. Starbucks, for instance, recently declared it has invested over $70 million to promote sustainable coffee harvesting and that 99 percent of the

Starbucks logo. mangpor2004/Shutterstock

---
[15]Remi Trudel & June Cotte, *Does Being Ethical Pay?*, Wall St. J., May 12, 2008.

coffee beans in its beverages are "ethically sourced."[16] Meanwhile, other companies are starting to tout their living wage and health care policies. At Whole Foods, for example, the average hourly wage was $18.89 in 2013. As John Mackey, the company's co-founder and co-CEO, likes to say, "There's no inherent reason why business cannot be ethical, socially responsible, and profitable."[17]

But even if a company can be ethical and profitable at the same time, are Starbucks, Whole Foods, and other such ethically minded companies really any more virtuous than their competitors?

Consider Starbucks's highly touted *ethical-sourcing* program. Although Starbucks has invested significant resources ($70 million) in this campaign, it's not clear how much of this money has been devoted to advertising. Also, for what it's worth, Starbucks generated well over $16 *billion* in revenue in 2014, the year before it announced it reached its 99 percent ethical-sourcing plateau. A cynic could argue that Starbucks has invested a mere 0.0003 percent of its annual revenue to do what it should be doing anyway.

For its part, Whole Foods claims, "Buying organic supports the small, family farmers that make up a large percentage of organic food producers." But this claim is misleading at best. In reality, although there are a lot of small, family-run organic farmers, their share of the organic crop—and their share of the produce sold at Whole Foods—is minuscule.[18] Whole Foods, of course, knows this, so its claim about the "small family farmers that make up a large percentage of organic food producers" is dubious, if not downright fraudulent.

CRITICAL THINKING QUESTIONS

1. So, what does it mean to act "ethically"?
2. In your opinion, is it ethical to use ethics *strategically*, to promote a company's "ethical brand" or attract new customers?

---

[16]Bruce Horovitz, *Starbucks: 99% Ethically Sourced Java*, USA Today, Apr. 10, 2015.

[17]Field Maloney, *Is Whole Foods Wholesome?*, Slate, Mar. 17, 2006.

[18]*See* Whole Foods Notice of Annual Meeting of Shareholders.

MANAGER'S CHALLENGE

Assume that you are Miguel's general manager in this chapter's Theory to Practice problem. In groups (or individually), draft a one- to two-page code of ethics that would be appropriate for Java Road. Refer to the Strategic Legal Solutions—Developing Codes of Ethics and Conduct feature earlier in this chapter for guidance.

See Connect for Manager's Challenge sample answers.

CASE SUMMARY 5.1 Goswami v. American Collections Enterprise, Inc., 377 F.3d 488 (5th Cir. 2004)

ETHICS IN DEBT COLLECTION

American Collections Enterprise, Inc. (ACEI), is a debt collection company that contracted with Capital One bank to provide debt collection services. Under the terms of the collection agreement, Capital One assigned delinquent accounts to ACEI for collection, and ACEI collected these debts on a contingent fee basis. Under the collection agreement, Capital One gave ACEI the authority to settle any of its accounts at a discount according to a set formula. Pooja Goswami owed approximately $900 on her Capital One credit card and failed to make her payment. Capital One then referred her debt to ACEI for collection on March 20, 2001, and ACEI pursued Goswami's delinquent account. The debt collection letter offered to settle the outstanding balance due with a 30 percent discount off the balance owed and stated that no other offers would be forthcoming. Unbeknownst to Goswami, ACEI actually had authority to settle for up to a 50 percent discount under the terms of ACEI's agreement with Capital One. The Fair Debt Collection Act prohibits misleading statements by debt collectors.

CASE QUESTIONS

1. Is the letter misleading?
2. Is it unethical to tell a partial truth as ACEI did here?
3. Is failure to disclose a fact the same as telling a lie?

CASE SUMMARY 5.2 Greenen v. Washington State Board of Accountancy, 110 P.3d 224 (Wash. App. 2005)

PROFESSIONAL ETHICS

Marilyn Greenen was a certified public accountant (CPA) licensed by the state of Washington. During the course of her employment as a CPA, Greenen failed to inform her employer's health care plan administrator that she and her spouse had divorced. The effect of her failure to disclose the divorce was that Greenen's ex-husband continued to receive health care benefits even though he was no longer eligible under the rules of the plan. After her employer discovered the discrepancy, Greenen was charged by the State Board of Accountancy with a breach of the CPA's ethical code for professional misrepresentation. Greenen countered that the CPA ethical code governed accounting-related transactions and practices only and that she should not be subject to sanction for failing to disclose her divorce.

CASE QUESTIONS

1. Should ethical codes apply to employees outside their scope of employment?
2. If Greenen were accused of shoplifting at a store, would she have been charged by the State Board of Accountancy for an ethical violation?
3. What is the purpose of mandatory ethical codes for professionals such as CPAs or attorneys?

CASE SUMMARY 5.3 Luther v. Countrywide Home Loans Servicing, 533 F.3d 1031 (9th Cir. 2008)

CORPORATE SOCIAL RESPONSIBILITY

In 2007, Countrywide was the largest provider of home mortgage loans in the world. Countrywide specialized in so-called subprime mortgage loans that allowed homebuyers with relatively low credit scores the opportunity to qualify for a mortgage by paying a higher interest rate along with a monthly premium to insure the loan in case of a default. One of Countrywide's mortgages featured "teaser rates" that made initial payments artificially low. Nearly 50 percent of Countrywide's customers ended up defaulting within one year of when the teaser rate adjusted upward. Several customers filed complaints with regulatory authorities contending that Countrywide never disclosed that the payments would increase so dramatically and applicants relied on Countrywide's judgment that they could afford the loan.

CASE QUESTIONS

1. Does Countrywide have an ethical obligation to not make risky loans?
2. Does Countrywide have an ethical obligation to verify the income of its loan applicants?
3. What ethical duties do applicants have when applying for a loan?

CASE SUMMARY 5.4 *In re Exxon Valdez*, 296 F. Supp. 2d 1071 (D.C. Alaska 2004)

LITIGATION ETHICS

Fishermen who were injured by the sinking of the oil tanker *Exxon Valdez* in 1989 brought suit against Exxon alleging, among other things, that Exxon was negligent for allowing the oil tanker to be captained by an employee who had a known history of alcohol abuse. The captain was, in fact, intoxicated at the time of the crash that spilled 11 million gallons of crude oil in Prince William Sound, Alaska. Commercial fisheries were temporarily and permanently damaged as a result of the spill. A jury awarded $5 billion in punitive damages against Exxon. Exxon appealed the judgment on the basis that the damages were grossly excessive. The appellate court upheld the jury's finding, but reduced the punitive damage award by 50 percent.

CASE QUESTIONS

1. Is it ethical to try to bankrupt a company by means of a lawsuit?
2. Should appellate courts be able to reduce punitive damage awards?
3. Is a $5 billion punitive damage award excessive against a company as large as Exxon?

CASE SUMMARY 5.5 Dodge v. Ford Motor Co., 204 Mich. 459, 170 N.W. 668 (1919)

STAKEHOLDERS' INTERESTS AND CORPORATE SOCIAL RESPONSIBILITY

Henry Ford, majority shareholder of the Ford Motor Company, announced that rather than pay a special dividend to the company's shareholders, he was going to reinvest the accumulated earnings in order to expand the company and hire more workers. He stated, "My ambition is to employ still more men, to spread the benefits of this industrial system to the greatest possible number, to help them build up their lives and their homes. To do this we are putting the greatest share of our profits back in the business." He further indicated that he wished to lower the price of the Model T car to make it more accessible to the general public. Two minority shareholders, John and Horace Dodge, sued to require payment of the dividend. The Michigan Supreme Court upheld the management's right to make decisions for the benefit of the company (the business judgment rule, discussed in Chapter 15, "Corporations"); however, the court said, "the corporation is a business, not a charity," and found for the Dodges because Henry Ford's decision was to benefit the public instead of shareholders.

CASE QUESTIONS

1. Should a corporation act solely to maximize shareholder wealth? How should a corporation balance corporate social responsibility with shareholder interests?
2. Were the Dodge brothers primary or secondary stakeholders? Explain.
3. Which moral philosophy approach describes Henry Ford's stated actions? Explain.
4. Although not an issue at trial, the Dodge brothers used their dividends to build their own company, Dodge Brothers Company (Dodge Motors), which was later sold to, and became a part of, Chrysler Motors. Many historians speculate that Henry Ford was actually trying to slow down the formation of the Dodge brothers' new company. If Henry Ford's alleged motive was true, was he acting in an ethical manner?

Self-Check ANSWERS Principles-Based, Consequences-Based, or Contract-Based Approach

1. Principles-based approach.
2. Consequences-based approach.
3. Contract-based approach.

CHAPTER REVIEW QUESTIONS: Answers and Explanations

1. **e.** According to a consequences-based system of ethics, the correct ethical course of action is the one that promotes the greatest happiness for the greatest number of people. Answer choices (a), (b), (c), and (d) are thus incorrect because they all refer to theories of ethics that are not consequences-based.

2. **c.** Kantian theories of morality are based on the categorical imperative and thus must pass a universalization test: "What if everybody took the same action?" Answer choices (a) and (b) incorrectly state this test. Answer choice (d) refers to a consequences-based approach to ethics, while answer choice (e) refers to a contract-based approach.

3. **d.** *Stakeholders* refers to a company's owners, investors, employees, customers, suppliers, and the wider community. Answer choice (a) is incorrect, as the Rosa Parks example shows. Answer choice (b) is wrong because the interests of primary stakeholders are weighted more than those of secondary stakeholders. Answer choice (e) is wrong because stockholders are primary stakeholders, and answer choice (c) is incorrect because the moral minimum theory sets a floor, not a ceiling.

4. **e.** The main difference between the moral minimum and maximizing profits theories is that the former requires businesses to take active steps to avoid harm, even at the expense of some additional profits, while the latter theory allows companies to make as much money as possible as long as no laws are broken.

5. **a.** The broad view of CSR emphasizes that a company's primary responsibility is to serve the public good and promote the triple bottom line. Answer choice (e) reflects only one aspect of the triple bottom line and is thus incorrect. Answer choices (b) and (d) reflect the narrow view of CSR, while answer choice (c) reflects the moderate view.

UNIT TWO — Law and Commerce

CHAPTER 6 Overview and Formation of Contracts

CHAPTER 7 Contract Enforceability and Performance

CHAPTER 8 Contracts for the Sale of Goods

CHAPTER 9 Torts and Products Liability

CHAPTER 6
Overview and Formation of Contracts

©philsajonesen/Getty Images

Learning Objectives

After studying this chapter, students who have mastered the material will be able to:

6-1 Articulate the definition and purpose of a contract and its importance to business.

6-2 Identify various categories of contracts.

6-3 Apply the correct source of law to individual contracts.

6-4 Explain the concept of mutual assent and why it is important, and identify and explain the other requirements for the formation of a valid contract.

6-5 List the events that terminate the power of acceptance, and distinguish between termination through action of the parties and termination through operation of law.

6-6 Articulate the legal requirement of consideration and identify which contracts do not require consideration.

6-7 Give examples of circumstances under which the legal requirements of capacity and legality are at issue.

The law of contracts is one of the most common and important areas of the law that business owners and managers deal with on a day-to-day basis. Everyone working in a business environment will, in one form or another, encounter contracts. Employment contracts, leases, and agreements of sale for assets, land, or merchandise are just a few examples of contracts commonly used in business transactions. The simple act of purchasing office supplies from a local merchant is a form of agreement governed by contract law.

Formation and legal enforcement of agreements have been recognized since ancient times. As early as 1780 BC, contracts were being enforced by the Babylonians by virtue of the authority of the Code of Hammurabi. During much of the rule of the Roman Empire, the Justinian Code included the rule *pacta sunt servanda* ("Agreements shall be kept").

Today, contract law is either created by statute or derived from the common law. Because business owners and managers are often involved in the day-to-day oversight of various agreements and transactions, understanding contract law reduces risk by limiting liability through the recognition of potential legal issues, the crafting of appropriate responses, and the implementation of systems to ensure compliance. Contract law is also essential to structuring business transactions in strategic ways to achieve business objectives without excessive risk.

In this chapter, students will learn

- Definitions and categories of various contracts.
- How the categories of contracts are interpreted and applied.
- The sources of law that apply to contemporary contracts.

DEFINITION OF A CONTRACT

A contract is more than an agreement between two or more parties. Contracts are *enforceable* agreements between parties. One generally accepted definition of a contract is a *promise or a set of promises enforceable by law.*[1] Put another way, a contract is simply an **agreement** that a court of law will recognize and enforce. Contract law also defines certain circumstances that excuse one or both parties from performing their obligation or enforcing the agreement's promise.

To take a simple example, suppose that Baker hires Downing to paint her apartment. The two agree on price, timing, and paint color. Downing begins to paint the apartment, and while on his lunch break, a pipe breaks and floods the apartment and he is unable to complete the work. Several contract issues are at work in this scenario. First, a court must determine whether Baker and Downing have met all of the elements of a contract (formation). If so, is Downing excused from finishing the job (performance)? Finally, is either party entitled to recover any money from the other (breach and damages)? Issues related to formation are covered in this chapter. Issues related to performance and breach are covered in Chapter 7, "Contract Enforceability and Performance."

Contracts are prevalent in business transactions that range from the sale of a cup of coffee at a diner to the acquisition of the stock of a multinational corporation. Contracts are used to carry out day-to-day business operations in manufacturing, buying, and selling products and services.

LO 6-1

Articulate the definition and purpose of a contract and its importance to business.

CONCEPT SUMMARY *Definition of a Contract*

- A contract is an *enforceable agreement* that obligates the parties to perform, as compared to a mere agreement with no enforceability.

CATEGORIES OF CONTRACTS

Because the subject of contracts is so vast, it is useful to categorize the different types of contracts in order to understand various forms of promises and agreements. This is *not* to say that these categories are mutually exclusive. In fact, all contracts may be classified in several ways.

LO 6-2

Identify various categories of contracts.

Written versus Oral Contracts

While the word *contract* is often used to describe a written document, many contracts are not in writing and yet are enforceable. Any agreement, oral or written, may result in a binding contract so long as it meets certain requirements. Some contracts, however, are *required* to be in writing in order to be enforceable. These contracts are defined by the statute of frauds, which is covered in Chapter 7, "Contract Enforceability and Performance."

Bilateral versus Unilateral Contracts

A **bilateral contract** involves two promises and two performances. *Most* contracts are bilateral contracts. To take a simple example, suppose Holmes says to Andrews: "I offer to pay you $5,000 for your delivery van." Andrews responds, "I accept." On the following day, Holmes shows up with a check for $5,000. Andrews signs over title to the delivery

---

[1] For exact wording of the definition, see Restatement (Second) of Contracts § 2.

van to Holmes. The first promise is Holmes's promise to pay $5,000 for the delivery van. The second promise is Andrews's promise to sell the delivery van for $5,000. The first performance takes place when Holmes pays the $5,000. The second performance takes place when Andrews signs over title of the delivery van to Holmes.

A **unilateral contract** involves one promise, followed by one performance, which then triggers a *second* performance from the offeror (the party making the offer). A second promise is not made, and the contract only becomes enforceable if the action specified in the original promise is performed. Perhaps the best example of a unilateral contract occurs when the offer is in the form of a reward. For example, if Jonah places several reward posters in his neighborhood and offers to pay $500 to anyone who finds his missing dog, this is an example of a unilateral offer. Jonah has made one promise, but there has been no second promise made by any of the neighbors. Therefore, the only way that a neighbor may accept the offer made by Jonah is to *perform* by finding the dog and delivering him to Jonah as specified in the promise (via the reward posters). Once a neighbor has performed, Jonah will be obligated to perform his promise (to pay a $500 reward). Of course, if no one performs, Jonah may not sue his neighbors for recovery because no return promise was ever made.

In Case 6.1, a New York court analyzes unilateral contracts in the context of a reward claim filed against a famous recording artist.

CASE 6.1 Augstein v. Leslie & NextSelection, Inc., 11 Civ. 7512 (HB), 2012 U.S. Dist. LEXIS 149517 (S.D.N.Y. Oct. 17, 2012)

FACT SUMMARY Ryan Leslie (Leslie) is an American recording artist and NextSelection is a company that owns the trademark to Leslie's name and performances. While on tour in Germany, Leslie's laptop computer, external hard drive, and certain other belongings were stolen. The laptop contained valuable and confidential intellectual property, including music and videos related to Leslie's records and performances. In videos, news articles, and online postings, Leslie stated that he would pay a reward to anyone who returned his property. Specifically, Leslie mentioned a $20,000 reward for the return of his property in a YouTube video, saying, "I am offering a reward of $20,000." On November 6, 2010, a video was posted increasing the reward to $1,000,000. At the end of the video, a message reads

> In the interest of retrieving the invaluable intellectual property contained on his laptop & hard drive, Mr. Leslie has increased the reward offer from $20,000 to $1,000,000 USD.

The increase of the reward was publicized on Leslie's Facebook and Twitter accounts, including a post on Twitter that read, "I'm absolutely continuing my Euro tour + I raised the reward for my intellectual property to $1mm," and that included a link to the video on YouTube. News organizations also published reports on Leslie's reward offer, both in print and online. Finally, Leslie was interviewed on MTV in November 2010, at which time he reiterated the $1,000,000 reward, saying, "I got a million dollar reward for anybody that can return all my intellectual property to me."

Approximately one month later, Armin Augstein (Augstein) found the laptop in a plastic garbage bag while walking his dog in a German city. He returned the laptop and hard drive to the local police and eventually the laptop was returned to Leslie in New York. When Augstein contacted Leslie, however, Leslie refused to pay the reward. Leslie alleged that the intellectual property for which he valued the laptop was not present on the hard drive when it was returned. Augstein filed suit and asked the court to grant summary judgment on whether Leslie's various promises constituted a unilateral offer of a reward for the return of his property—an offer that Augstein accepted and fully performed when he

(continued)

presented the property to the police in Germany. Leslie responded that no offer existed because a reasonable person would not have understood the mention of the reward to be an offer of a unilateral contract, but instead would have understood it to be an invitation to negotiate. Moreover, Leslie argued, even assuming that it was an offer, Augstein did not perform because he did not return the intellectual property, only the physical property.

SYNOPSIS OF DECISION AND OPINION The U.S. District Court for the Southern District of New York ruled in favor of Augstein, holding that Leslie's various reward videos and statements constituted a unilateral offer to contract. The court reasoned that Leslie's attempts to publicize the reward through social and public media were sufficiently detailed to create an objective belief that anyone who performed by returning the laptop would be paid the promised reward money. The court rejected Leslie's contention that the videos were merely an advertisement because Leslie was not seeking a promise from an individual who would return his belongings. Rather he was seeking performance—the actual return of his property. In addition, the court pointed out that his videos and other commentary cannot be reasonably understood as an invitation to negotiate because, similarly, Leslie was not soliciting help in finding his property, but the actual return itself.

WORDS OF THE COURT: Unilateral Offer to Contract "Leslie's videos and other activities together are best characterized as an offer for a reward. Leslie 'sought to induce performance, unlike an invitation to negotiate [often an advertisement], which seeks a reciprocal promise.' . . . A reasonable person viewing the video would understand that Leslie was seeking the return of his property and that by returning it, the bargain would be concluded. The increase of the reward from $20,000 to $1,000,000, the value of the property lost (in particular the unreleased album) and the news reports regarding the reward offer would lead a reasonable person to believe that Leslie was making an offer. As such, the video constitutes a valid offer and summary judgment is granted as to that issue. '[I]f a person chooses to make extravagant promises . . . he probably does so because it pays him to make them, and, if he has made them, the extravagance of the promises is no reason in law why he should not be bound by them.'"

Case Questions

1. Why isn't the relationship between Leslie and Augstein considered a bilateral contract?
2. What was Leslie's defense to the allegation that he had made a unilateral contract offer? Why did the court reject it? Do you agree?
3. *Focus on Critical Thinking:* What could Leslie have done to prevent his YouTube video from forming a unilateral offer? Would some type of disclaimer have worked? If there was evidence that Augstein had stolen the laptop instead of found it, would he still have been able to collect the reward money? Why or why not?

Aftermath: The case went to trial in January 2013 and the jury awarded Augstein $1 million plus interest. Leslie did not appeal.

Express versus Implied versus Quasi-Contracts

An **express contract** is created when the parties have knowingly and intentionally agreed on the promises and performances. An **implied contract** is one in which the agreement is reached by the parties' *actions* rather than their words. For example, when you order food at a restaurant, the server, after taking your order, does not ask if you promise to pay for the food at the end of the meal. Your act of ordering food and consuming it will create an obligation to pay. The contract is formed as an implied contract *in fact*.

In some cases where no express or implied contract exists, a party may still be able to recover losses based on a **quasi-contract**. The law permits quasi-contracts to be enforceable when one party suffers losses as a result of another party's unjust enrichment. This theory of contract is based on an implied-in-law recovery, whereby one party does not actually request a certain service but still benefits from the services rendered. Suppose that an unconscious patient is brought into a hospital, the hospital administers aid, and the patient survives. The hospital will be able to recover the reasonable costs of its services even though the patient never agreed or never performed an act agreeing to the hospital's assistance. If the patient were able to avoid payment, then he would be receiving a benefit without payment and thereby be unjustly enriched.

Other Categories

Contracts may also be classified in other ways. Keep these definitions in mind as you continue your study of contract law. Each is explained in more detail later in this chapter.

- *Valid:* When a contract has the required elements, it is called a **valid** contract.
- *Void:* When an agreement lacks one of the required elements or has not been formed in conformance of the law from the outset, the contract is considered to be **void** (sometimes called void *per se*).
- *Voidable:* A contract is **voidable** when the law gives one or more parties the right to cancel an otherwise valid contract under the circumstances.
- *Unenforceable:* Although a contract may have met the required elements and be considered valid, it still may be **unenforceable** because one party asserts a legal defense to performing the contract.

 Self-Check Categories of Contracts

Choose the category that applies to each contract.

1. Gates purchases a laptop computer from a local office supply store. (Express/Implied/Quasi)
2. In his neighborhood, Brown distributes flyers that read: "Reward: Lost Beagle. If found return to me for $500 reward." (Offer of a bilateral/unilateral contract)
3. Andrews is going out of town until Sunday and tells Cardozo that if he mows her lawn, she'll pay him $50. Cardozo agrees to cut the lawn before Sunday. (Offer of a bilateral contract/unilateral contract)
4. Webster calls Daniel's Catering and orders 100 deviled eggs to be delivered for an office party. (Express/Implied/Quasi)

Answers to this Self-Check are provided at the end of the chapter.

CONCEPT SUMMARY Categories and Types of Contracts

- Contracts may be *written* or *oral*. Oral contracts, while harder to prove, are valid and legal unless required to be in writing by statute.
- Contracts may be *bilateral* (formed by an exchange of promises) or *unilateral* (when a promise requires acceptance by a required performance).
- Contracts are *express* when the parties knowingly and intentionally come to an agreement. *Implied* contracts arise from the party's conduct, and *quasi*-contracts are imposed by the law in the absence of an express or implied agreement in order to remedy a party's losses due to one party's unjust enrichment at the other's expense.

- A contract may be *valid*—a fully enforceable contract; *void*—a contract missing a required element; *voidable*—a seemingly valid contract that one party has the right to cancel; or *unenforceable*—a valid contract that is subject to a defense.

SOURCES OF CONTRACT LAW

In general, contracts for *services* (e.g., legal, accounting, or engineering) or *real estate* (such as an agreement of sale for an office building or a lease for a commercial retail space) are governed by **state common law**. Contracts for *goods* or *products* (defined as items that are movable at the time of identification in the contract) are governed by **state statutory law** based on the Uniform Commercial Code (UCC).[2] The UCC also covers transactions related to leasing of equipment. Note that the UCC provisions for sales and leases are covered extensively in Chapter 8, "Contracts for the Sale of Goods."

Some contracts involve terms for both goods *and* services. These are known as **hybrid contracts**. In a hybrid contract, the source of law is established by determining the *predominant thrust* of the contract subject matter. If the contract is predominantly for services, and the goods are incidental, then the contract is governed by the common law. If, on the other hand, goods are the main feature of the contract and the services come incidentally, then the contract is governed by statutory law. For example, Huxley is a manager charged with the task of hiring an artist to paint a portrait of the company's founder, which will be displayed in the lobby. Huxley hires Pablo, and Pablo paints the portrait. This is a hybrid contract because it involves services (of the artist) and goods (Huxley gets the canvas, paint, etc., at the conclusion of the services). However, in this case the goods are *incidental* to the services; thus, it is primarily a contract for services and therefore governed by the common law. In determining the source of law governing a hybrid contract, courts will examine (1) *allocation of price* in the contract (value of goods versus value of services) and (2) *uniqueness* of the services (do they require special talent, as in the case of the portrait artist?). The more unique the service, the more likely it is that the contract is covered by the common law.

LO 6-3

Apply the correct source of law to individual contracts.

> **KEY POINT**
>
> Contracts for services or real estate are governed by state common law. Contracts for goods or products are governed by state statutes. Contracts for goods and services are called hybrid contracts and the source of law is established by determining the *predominant thrust* of the contract subject matter.

LEGAL IMPLICATIONS IN CYBERSPACE

The Uniform Electronic Transactions Act (UETA) is best thought of as a procedural model law that applies to transactions as long as the parties to a contract agree to use electronic commerce for the transaction. This means that the UETA does not create substantive rights or protections (such as providing consumers with a right to sue) but rather gives legal recognition to certain electronic media. Whether the parties have agreed to conduct a transaction by electronic means is determined from the context and surrounding circumstances, including the parties' conduct. The UETA essentially elevates

(continued)

---

[2]Recall from Chapter 1, "Legal Foundations," that the UCC is a "model" statute drafted by the National Conference of Commissioners of Uniform State Laws (NCCUSL). Each state legislature makes its own decision about whether to adopt the UCC in total, in part, or not at all. Louisiana is the only state to have rejected the UCC in its entirety.

electronic signatures and records to the same legal status as that accorded to traditional signatures and paper records, memorandums, notices, and so forth. The law covers both e-commerce sale-of-goods transactions and the use of electronic communication alongside paper contracts.

The UETA gives formal legal recognition of electronic records, signatures, and contracts by providing that (1) a record or signature may not be denied legal effect or enforceability solely because it is in electronic form; (2) a contract may not be denied legal effect or enforceability solely because an electronic record was used in its information; (3) if a law requires a record to be in writing, an electronic record satisfies the law; and (4) if a law requires a signature, an electronic signature satisfies the law. Currently, 47 states along with the District of Columbia, Puerto Rico, and the U.S. Virgin Islands have adopted the UETA in some form.

 Self-Check Source of Law

Which source of law governs each contract?

1. A contract for the sale of an office building from Abel to NewCo.
2. A contract providing for installation of networking cable in an office facility where the materials are $5,000 and the labor is $20,000.
3. A consulting contract between a management consulting firm and a software development company.
4. The sale of several completed sculptures from an artist to a retail art dealer for a total of $10,000.
5. A contract between the owner of a building and a painting company to paint the building's lobby over a holiday weekend for $5,000. The owner agrees to supply all of the paint.

Answers to this Self-Check are provided at the end of the chapter.

CONCEPT SUMMARY Sources of Law

- Contracts for services or real estate are governed by state common law, while contracts for goods are governed by state statutory law based on the Uniform Commercial Code.
- For contracts involving a combination of goods and services (hybrid contracts), the source of law is established by determining the predominant thrust of the contract subject matter.

CONTRACT TRANSACTIONS

Before learning the individual components required to form a contract and the rules that govern the parties, it is helpful to consider a typical contract transaction from a macro perspective. First, a contract is formed when two or more parties agree to a particular set of terms. One party typically agrees to provide services, real estate, or goods in exchange for something of value (usually money). An agreement is recognized as legally binding so long as it meets certain *formation* requirements. Second, after the formation requirements

TABLE 6.1	Overview of a Contract Transaction		
Formation		**Enforceability**	**Performance**
Parties reach mutual agreement on terms. All formation elements are met.		Contract meets legal requirements necessary to enforce terms.	Contract governs parties' performance (or nonperformance) of the terms of the agreement and provides compensation if one party fails to perform.

are met, the contract is governed by laws that set out requirements for *enforceability* of the agreement. Finally, assuming that the contract was properly formed and is legally enforceable, the law sets out rules and consequences related to how the parties will fulfill their obligations to one another. This is known as *performance* (or *nonperformance*) of the agreement. Table 6.1 provides an overview of these three elements of a contract transaction.

For example, suppose that Ahab agrees to provide ship repair services to White Whale Industries. Using e-mail exchanges, the parties negotiate a monthly fee and specify that Ahab is to repair and maintain White Whale's fleet of ships as necessary for two years. At this point, a contract is likely to have been *formed,* assuming that all of the necessary elements for mutual assent have been met. However, suppose that one month into the agreement Ahab notifies White Whale that he has a better-paying opportunity in another city and cannot perform the services in the agreement as planned. White Whale counters that the e-mail exchanges were sufficient to meet the legal requirements. The resolution of this issue depends on the *enforceability* of the contract. Alternatively, assume that the parties have a written contract. White Whale notifies Ahab that it will be reducing the monthly fee for the remainder of the agreement by 30 percent. Can Ahab sue White Whale immediately? Does White Whale have any defense? What can Ahab expect to recover to compensate for losses? These are issues of *performance*. Formation is covered in this chapter. Enforceability and performance are covered in Chapter 7, "Contract Enforceability and Performance."

Understanding contract law helps business owners limit their company's liability and manage risk.
Thinkstock/Getty Images (left); Photodisc/Getty Images (right)

LO 6-4

Explain the concept of mutual assent and why it is important, and identify and explain the other requirements for the formation of a valid contract.

CONTRACT FORMATION

A valid contract is formed when four elements are met: mutual assent (offer and acceptance), consideration, capacity, and legality. The broad underlying requirement of an enforceable contract is the notion of **mutual assent** (also referred to simply as *assent* or *agreement*). Typically, the parties reach mutual assent using a combination of **offer** and **acceptance**. In most cases, the *offeror* makes a valid offer to the *offeree,* who in turn must accept the offer in order for the parties to be bound by the agreement's terms. This is known as a *meeting of the minds* because the parties have agreed to certain promises and obligations.

Offer

An offer is a promise or commitment to do (or refrain from doing) a specified activity such as selling a good at a certain price or offering to provide services at a given rate. An offer also is the expression of a willingness to enter into a contract by the offeror's promising an offeree that she will perform certain obligations in exchange for the offeree's counterpromise to perform. To take a simple example, suppose that Lewis offers to sell Williams a rare book for $1,000. In this case, Lewis is the *offeror* and is promising to perform through a transfer of ownership rights to the book so long as Williams, as the *offeree,* counterpromises to perform by paying $1,000.

Offers must meet three criteria to be valid: They must be (1) clear, (2) serious, and (3) communicated. *Clear* means that the language of the offer must be such that the offeree knows what is being offered. *Seriousness* of an offer requires that the offeror have an **objective intent** to contract when making the offer. Generally, the offeror must have a *serious intention* to become bound by the offer, and the terms of the offer must be *reasonably certain*. Finally, courts look at how an offer is *communicated*. That is, they examine the *language* of the offer and the *actions* of the parties to determine how a reasonable person would interpret that language. Does the language indicate a *serious intent to form* a contract? Or perhaps the language indicates intent to negotiate rather than agree. Or is the language so innocuous that a reasonable person would conclude that there was no intent at all (for example, an offer made in jest)? Note that it does not matter what the offeror *actually* intended. Rather, the objective test is what a reasonable person would ordinarily believe the language and conduct (collectively referred to as *manifestations* of intent) mean in those circumstances. Otherwise, the offer is considered simply an offer to discuss or negotiate the terms of an agreement. For example, an e-mail from the owner of a computer retail store to a computer hardware wholesaler may contain the following language: "I am interested in purchasing 10 new personal computers. Please contact me about the price and delivery terms regarding the computers." This message does not express an immediate objective intention to contract. Rather, a reasonable person would look at this language as an invitation to *negotiate.*

Under modern case law, the importance of the parties' intention, or lack of intention, to form a contract depends largely upon the context of the agreement. When an agreement is in the context of a business transaction, there is a strong presumption that the parties intended the agreement to be legally enforceable.

In Landmark Case 6.2, one of the most famous in American contract law, a state supreme court considers the circumstances of a transaction and the language of the parties in determining whether an offer involved an objective intent to contract.

Legal Speak >))

Assent

A conscious approval or confirmation of facts. In contract law, assent is the knowing, voluntary, and mutual approval of the terms of a contract by each party.

KEY POINT

The elements of a contract are (1) mutual assent (offer and acceptance), (2) consideration, (3) capacity, and (4) legality.

LANDMARK CASE 6.2 Lucy v. Zehmer, 84 S.E.2d 516 (Va. 1954)

FACT SUMMARY W.O. Lucy (Lucy) was a farmer who knew A.H. Zehmer (Zehmer) for a period of 15 to 20 years. At one point during their relationship, Lucy offered to buy Zehmer's farm for $20,000, but Zehmer rejected the offer outright. Seven years later, Lucy met Zehmer at a restaurant and had a conversation over a period of hours while the two drank whiskey together. During this conversation, Lucy again offered to purchase Zehmer's farm. According to the testimony at trial, the following exchange of words took place:

Lucy: I bet you wouldn't take $50,000 for that farm.

Zehmer: You haven't got $50,000 cash.

Lucy: I can get it.

Zehmer: But you haven't got $50,000 cash to pay me tonight.

Eventually, Lucy persuaded Zehmer to put in writing that he would sell Lucy the farm for $50,000. Zehmer handwrote the following on the back of the pad: "I agree to sell the Ferguson Place [Zehmer's farm property] to W. O. Lucy for $50,000 cash." (See Figure 6.1.) The parties then modified this writing several times and discussed terms over a period of 30 to 40 minutes. At the end of the evening, each party had signed the modified document that agreed to a sale of Zehmer's farm to Lucy for $50,000. The next day, Lucy believed that the contract was valid and proceeded to act accordingly by seeking financing for the purchase and checking title. However, Zehmer notified Lucy that he would not transfer title because no contract was formed. Rather, Zehmer had understood the whole transaction as a joke. At trial Zehmer testified that he "was high as a Georgia pine" while modifying and discussing the contract and that he was just "needling" Lucy because he believed Lucy could never come up with the money. Zehmer claimed that before he left the restaurant that night, he told Lucy that it was all a big joke, that the negotiations were just the "liquor talking." Zehmer claimed that he had not actually intended to sell the property; thus, the contract lacked serious intent and was void.

FIGURE 6.1 Check from Ye Olde Virginnie Restaurant at Issue in *Lucy v. Zehmer*

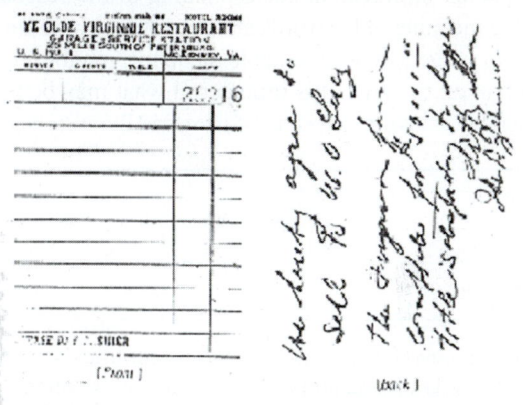

"We agree to sell to W.O. Lucy the Ferguson farm complete for $50,000, title satisfactory to buyer." Signatures of the parties.

SYNOPSIS OF DECISION AND OPINION The court ruled that Zehmer was bound by the contract even if he had no *actual* (subjective) intent to sell the farm and may have been joking. The court used the objective standard in determining that a reasonable person would have construed Zehmer's actions and words as a serious intent to contract. The court held that evidence from the trial indicated that Zehmer took the transaction seriously, and that Lucy was not unreasonable in believing that a contract was formed under the circumstances. The court made clear that actual mental intent is not required for formation of a contract.

WORDS OF THE COURT: Manifestation of Intent to Contract "The appearance of a contract; the fact that it was under discussion for forty minutes

(continued)

or more before it was signed; Lucy's objection to the first draft; . . . [and] the discussion of what was to be included in the sale . . . are facts which furnish persuasive evidence that the execution of the contract was a serious business transaction rather than a casual, jesting matter as the defendant now contends.

"An agreement or mutual assent is of course essential to a valid contract but the law imputes to a person an intention corresponding to the reasonable meaning of his words and acts. If his words and acts, judged by a reasonable standard, manifest an intention to agree, it is immaterial what may be the real but unexpressed state of his mind."

Case Questions

1. What factors does the court focus on when deciding whether Lucy's understanding of the contract formation was reasonable?

2. What facts could you change in this case that would result in the court determining that no contract existed?

3. *Focus on Critical Thinking:* Did a meeting of the minds actually occur here? Should words written on the back of a restaurant check be enough evidence to indicate objective intent? Why or why not?

KEY POINT

The objective test for intent to form a contract is: Given the language and circumstances of the offer, would a reasonable person in the position of the offeree conclude that the offer was an objective manifestation of serious intent to contract?

Advertisements as an Offer Most advertisements appearing in the mass media, in store windows, or in display cases are *not* offers. Rather, the law recognizes mass advertisements as an invitation for the consumer to make an offer to the seller to purchase the goods at a specified price. Frequently, these advertisements do not constitute an offer because they do not contain a specific commitment to sell. For example, suppose Big Time Appliance runs an advertisement in a local paper that misprints the ad as "Giant plasma screen TV for $10" instead of "$1,000." Ernest shows up at Big Time Appliance with a $10 bill and excitedly hands over the bill to a cashier, saying, "I accept your offer to sell me this television for $10." Big Time Appliance is not obligated to perform (i.e., sell the television for $10).[3] The law recognizes Ernest's actions not as an acceptance of Big Time's offer but rather as an offer by Ernest to buy the television—which Big Time may accept or reject. Even a price tag on a product in the store is an invitation for the customer to make an offer and not an offer to sell at that price by the business.

The primary exception to this rule occurs when the advertisement is *specific* enough to constitute a unilateral contract. Advertisements that offer to sell a particular number of certain products at a certain price may constitute an offer. In the previous example, if the advertisement offered giant plasma televisions for $10 to the first 50 buyers on Friday, then the advertisement would be specific enough to constitute a valid offer requiring Big Time Appliance to sell as promised. Or if the advertisement invites the other party to accept in a *particular manner,* courts will treat this type of advertisement as a valid offer for a unilateral contract. For example, Anti-Flu Inc. sells an herbal inhaler device that it claims will work to prevent the flu as effectively as any flu shot vaccine. The company advertises, "We will pay $1,000 to anyone who uses the Anti-Flu herbal inhaler for two consecutive weeks and still contracts the flu." Pauline uses the device for two weeks (thereby accepting Anti-Flu's

---

[3]Restatement (Second) of Contracts§ 26 cmt. b. Also note that this example is a contracts analysis. In the case of advertising, certain state consumer laws may apply to protect buyers against merchants acting in bad faith by using advertising as a "bait-and-switch" method (discussed in Chapter 21, "Warranties and Consumer Protection Law").

offer) and contracts the flu one day later. In this case, Anti-Flu would be obligated to perform its promise by paying the $1,000 sum because Anti-Flu's advertisement invited any party to accept the company's offer in a particular manner (by using the device).[4]

In Case 6.3, an appellate court considers whether a claim made by a famous company created an offer through a television advertisement.

CASE 6.3 Leonard v. PepsiCo, Inc., 210 F.3d 88 (2d Cir. 2000) [affirming lower court decision and reasoning in 88 F. Supp. 2d 116 (S.D.N.Y. 1999)]

FACT SUMMARY Pepsi ran an advertisement on national television promoting its Pepsi Points program, whereby consumers could obtain points by purchasing Pepsi products and then redeem the points for certain apparel and other items. An alternate way to accumulate points was to purchase them for a certain dollar figure. The Pepsi advertisement opened with the morning routine of a high school student. The commercial was based on a *Top Gun* movie theme and depicted the student wearing apparel such as a leather bomber jacket, a Pepsi T-shirt, and aviator sunglasses. For each item, the advertisement would flash the corresponding number of Pepsi points required to obtain the item. For example, when showing the actor with the aviator sunglasses, the advertisement featured the subtitle "Shades 175 Pepsi Points." The advertisement then showed a view of the cover of a Pepsi Stuff Catalog with a narration of "Introducing the new Pepsi Stuff Catalog" and the subtitle "See details on specially marked packages." Finally, the advertisement showed the student arriving at his high school in a Harrier fighter jet to the amazement of his friends and teachers. The student hops out of the jet and says, "Sure beats the bus." At this point, the subtitle flashed, "Harrier jet 7,000,000 Pepsi points."

Leonard filled out the Pepsi Stuff order form (located in the catalog produced by Pepsi), but since there was no mention of the Harrier jet, Leonard simply wrote in the item on the order form and sent the order to Pepsi with a check for $700,000, the amount necessary to purchase the requisite points as stated in the advertisement. Pepsi refused to transfer title on the basis that no contract existed. The trial court ruled in favor of Pepsi. Leonard appealed, among other reasons, on the basis that the Pepsi advertisement was specific enough to constitute a valid offer of a unilateral contract through its advertisement.

SYNOPSIS OF DECISION AND OPINION The court ruled against Leonard. While acknowledging that certain advertisements could be an offer if the promise is clear, definite, and explicit, such was not the case here. The advertisement was not sufficiently definite because it reserved the details of the offer to a separate writing (the catalog).[5]

WORDS OF THE COURT: Requirements for Advertisements as a Unilateral Offer "In the present case, the Harrier Jet commercial did not direct that anyone who appeared at Pepsi headquarters with 7,000,000 Pepsi Points on the Fourth of July would receive the Harrier Jet. Instead, the commercial urged consumers to accumulate Pepsi Points and refer to the catalog to determine how they could receive their Pepsi Points. The commercial sought a reciprocal promise, expressed through the acceptance of, and in compliance with, the terms of the Order Form. . . . [T]he catalog contains no mention of the Harrier Jet."

(continued)

---

[4]Based on the landmark case *Carlill v. Carbolic Smoke Ball Co.* [1893] EWCA (Civ) 1,1 Q.B. 256 (Eng.).

[5]The court also rejected Leonard's other primary argument that the advertisement constituted an objective intent by Pepsi to sell a $23 million Harrier jet for $700,000. The court ruled, "In light of the obvious absurdity of the commercial, the court rejects plaintiff's argument that the commercial was not clearly in jest."

Case Questions

1. What facts would support Leonard's primary argument as to why this commercial was a unilateral offer to contract?
2. If the wording on the catalog order form had allowed a consumer to write in the item (rather than check a box next to the item), would that change the outcome of this case?
3. Should a reasonable person seeing the television commercial reasonably believe that Pepsi would sell a $23 million Harrier jet for only $700,000?

Acceptance

A valid offer creates the power of *acceptance* for the offeree. An acceptance is the offeree's expression of agreement to the terms of the offer. An offeree typically communicates the acceptance in writing or orally but, in some cases, may accept via some action or conduct (as in a unilateral contract). So long as the offer is still in force (has not yet been terminated), the offeree may accept the terms of the offer, thereby forming an agreement. Only the party or parties to whom the offer is intended has the power of acceptance and may accept. Suppose that during class, a professor says to a particular student, "I'll sell you my briefcase for $100." Only that student may accept, and no other student present in class has the power of acceptance. If instead the professor says, "I'll sell my briefcase for $100 to the first student in this class who accepts," then the power of acceptance is extended to the entire class, but not to the professor's students in other classes. In order for agreement to exist though, the offer has to be *properly* accepted by the offeree.[6] Note that the offeror is considered the "master" of the offer and, therefore, has the power to terminate, modify its terms, or prescribe the method of acceptance of the offer *up and until the offer has been accepted* by the offeree. Once the offer has been terminated, the offeree has lost the power to accept and form an agreement.

LO 6-5

List the events that terminate the power of acceptance, and distinguish between termination through action of the parties and termination through operation of law.

Termination of an Offer The power of acceptance is terminated when the offer is terminated either through *actions of the parties* or by *operation of law*. In both cases, the opportunity for the offeree to accept ends at the same time that the offer is terminated.

An offer may be terminated by action of the parties in one of three ways: (1) **revocation**, where the offeror revokes (withdraws) the offer prior to acceptance; (2) **rejection**, where the offeree rejects the offer; and (3) **counteroffer**, where the offeree rejects the original offer and proposes a new offer with different terms. Offers may also be terminated by **operation of law**.

Revocation When the offeror decides to revoke (withdraw) the offer by expressly communicating the revocation to the offeree prior to acceptance, the offer is terminated by revocation. Revocation is consummated through an express repudiation of the offer (e.g., "I revoke my offer of May 1 to paint your office building for $1,000") or by some *inconsistent act* that would give reasonable notice from the offeror to the offeree that the offer no longer exists. For example, on Monday, Owner offers WidgetCo the nonexclusive opportunity to purchase a parcel of land for $100,000 with a deadline of Friday

---

[6]Restatement (Second) of Contracts§§ 29, 50, 54.

for responding. On Wednesday, WidgetCo learns that Owner has entered into a contract with ServiceCo for the land. On Thursday, WidgetCo calls Owner with an acceptance. No contract exists between Owner and WidgetCo because Owner's inconsistent acts were sufficient to give WidgetCo notice of the transaction.[7]

One important issue with revocation is the timing of the revocation. Most states follow the rule that revocation is effective only *upon receipt* by the offeree or the offeree's agent.[8] For example, on Monday, Adams sends, via same-day courier, a letter of revocation to Bell's office. Bell's administrative assistant receives the revocation on that same day, but Bell is traveling in Japan and never actually sees the letter. On Wednesday, from his hotel room in Tokyo, Bell calls Adams and accepts Adams's initial offer. No contract exists because the revocation would be deemed effective upon receipt by Bell's administrative assistant. At that point, even though Bell had no *actual* knowledge of the revocation by Adams, the offer is revoked and Bell may no longer accept the offer.

Note that some offers are **irrevocable**: (1) offers in the form of an option contract, (2) offers that the offeree partly performed or detrimentally relied on, and (3) so-called firm offers by a merchant under the UCC (firm offers under the UCC are discussed in Chapter 8, "Contracts for the Sale of Goods").

Option contracts are sometimes used to provide flexibility in commercial real estate transactions.
Creatas Images/PictureQuest

Option Contracts One way to make an offer irrevocable is for the offeror to grant the offeree an *option* to enter a contract. Typically, the offeror agrees to hold an offer open (not enter into a contract with another party) for a certain period of time in exchange for something of value (known as *consideration,* discussed later in this chapter). In the example discussed above, WidgetCo could have protected itself and enforced the "until Friday" deadline by entering into an *option* with Owner. If WidgetCo had paid Owner $1,000 to keep the offer to purchase the land open until Friday, Owner would now be obligated to keep the offer open and not entertain offers by third parties. However, if, at the end of Friday, WidgetCo hadn't communicated an acceptance of the offer to sell, Owner would keep the $1,000 and now be permitted to sell the property to another party.

Partial Performance and Detrimental Reliance There are certain offers whereby the offeree may, prior to actual formation of the contract, take some action that *relies* on the offer; for example, the offeree begins to perform based on a unilateral offer. Recall that a unilateral offer is one in which the offer makes clear that acceptance can occur only through performance and not through a promise. This is known as *partial performance* and can render an offer temporarily irrevocable. For example, Burns offers

---

[7]Based on Restatement (Second) of Contracts § 42, illus. 1.

[8]Note that a few states, notably California, do not follow the "receipt" rule, opting instead to make revocation effective upon dispatch of the revocation notice.

Realtor a commission of 10 percent of the sales price if Realtor can find a buyer for the Burns Building for $500,000. Realtor spends funds to research and obtain potential buyer contact information and locates Walters, who is willing to accept the $500,000 offer to sell from Burns. Before any transaction takes place, Burns revokes his offer to Realtor and refuses to sell the property to Walters. Burns's revocation is *not effective*. Burns's promise to pay for a particular performance (a unilateral contract) was rendered irrevocable once Realtor performed by finding a buyer for the building.[9] Also, an offer may be rendered irrevocable if the offeree makes preparations prior to acceptance based on a reasonable reliance on the offer. This is known as **detrimental reliance**. For example, SubCo is a subcontractor for GeneralCo. GeneralCo relies on SubCo's bid in preparing to make an offer to renovate a commercial office complex. After GeneralCo is awarded the renovation contract, SubCo notifies GeneralCo that its bid was too low due to the poor business forecasting of one of SubCo's partners. Because it is no longer interested in the job, SubCo attempts to revoke its offer/bid. In this case, SubCo is *still required to perform* even at a loss. GeneralCo reasonably relied on SubCo's bid and would suffer a significant detriment based on this reliance. SubCo's offer became irrevocable once GeneralCo exercised reasonable reliance on the offer.[10]

Rejection and Counteroffer   An offer is also terminated once the offeree either rejects the offer outright or makes a counteroffer by rejecting the original offer and making a new offer. Under the common law,[11] the offeree's response operates as an acceptance only if it is the *precise mirror image* of the offer. If the response conflicts with the original offer even slightly, the original offer is terminated and the new offer is substituted. This principle is called the **mirror image rule**. Once the offeree has rejected the offer or made a counteroffer, her power of acceptance is terminated. For example, apply the mirror image rule to the following conversation:

Franz: I will pay you $1,000 to paint the interior of our office building.

Josef: I've seen your office; it is going to cost you more than that.

Franz: How much more?

Josef: I'll do it for $2,000.

Franz: Ah, yes. Well, let's split it down the middle. I'll pay you $1,500.

Josef: OK. I agree to do it for $1,500, but you must also supply the paint, brushes, ladder, tarps, cleaner, and other equipment I need.

Does a contract exist between Josef and Franz? Carefully examine the language of the parties. Josef made an outright rejection of Franz's first offer to paint the office for $1,000. Then Josef made an offer to paint the office for $2,000. Franz then rejected the offer via *counteroffer* and now has made a new offer for Josef to accept or reject his offer to pay $1,500 for the services. Although Josef starts out his response with "OK," he adds additional terms (Franz must supply the paint, etc.). Therefore, Josef has rejected the offer because his acceptance was *not the mirror image* of Franz's offer. Despite the "OK" language, the law treats Josef's response as a counteroffer (and therefore a rejection).

---

[9]Based on Restatement (Second) of Contracts§ 45, illus. 5.

[10]Based on Restatement (Second) of Contracts§ 87(2), illus. 6 [*Drennan v. Star Paving*, 51 Cal. 2d 409 (1958)].

[11]Note that the UCC rules are different regarding counteroffers. The UCC rules for counteroffers are discussed in Chapter 8, "Contracts for the Sale of Goods."

Franz's offer is now terminated, and *no* contract exists at this point. Of course, Franz is now free to accept or reject Josef's counteroffer.

Termination by Operation of Law
An offer may also be terminated by certain happenings or events covered by operation of law. Generally, these include (1) lapse of time, (2) death or incapacity of the offeror or offeree, (3) destruction of the subject matter of the contract before acceptance, and (4) supervening illegality.

> **KEY POINT**
>
> The mirror image rule, which applies to common law contracts (not UCC contracts), requires that any acceptance by the offeree must be the mirror image of the original offer. Any deviation from the original offer is a rejection and counteroffer.

Lapse of Time Following the "offeror is the master of his offer" rule, the offeror will frequently attach some time limit on the offeree's power of acceptance. Once the time limit has expired, the offer is considered to have terminated via **lapse of time**. If, however, the offeror has not set a time limit, the offer will still expire after a *reasonable time*. Courts determine the "reasonable time period" for an acceptance by analyzing the circumstances that existed when the offer and attempted acceptance were made. When the offer involves a speculative transaction in which the subject matter is subject to sharp fluctuations in value, a reasonable time period will be considerably shorter. For example, Milton sends Dryden an e-mail: "I offer to sell you my private stock in Local Oil Company for $500 per share." Dryden waits one week, and the price of oil skyrockets in the week, making stock in Local Oil rise to $700 per share. He responds to Milton's e-mail: "I accept your offer of last week." In this case, Dryden would likely not be obligated to perform because the subject matter of the offer was so speculative that it dictated a short time period for expiration. On the other hand, if Milton wishes to sell Dryden a used lawn mower for $100, waiting one week would still be well within a reasonable time period for acceptance of the offer.

Death, Incapacity, Destruction, or Supervening Illegality In the event that the offeror or the offeree either dies or becomes incapacitated before acceptance, the offer automatically terminates. Similarly, if the subject matter of the contract is destroyed before acceptance, the offer is considered terminated by operation of law. A supervening illegality occurs when changes in the law make a previously legal offer illegal. For example, suppose NewCo offers to sell 100 UltraWidgets to a vendor in the fictional country of Freedonia. Before the vendor accepts, Congress passes a law prohibiting the sale of U.S. goods to Freedonia. NewCo's offer is terminated via supervening illegality. Death, incapacity, destruction, and supervening illegality are all examples of what many courts refer to as *impossibility*.

When Acceptance Is Effective: The Mailbox Rule
The **mailbox rule** governs common law contracts and is a rule that determines when a contract is considered to be deemed accepted by the offeree, thus depriving the offeror of the right to revoke the offer. In essence, the mailbox rule provides that the acceptance of an offer is generally effective upon dispatch of the acceptance when sent in a commercially reasonable manner (e.g., when the offeree places the acceptance in the mailbox, sends it by overnight mail, or faxes it) and not when the acceptance is received by the offeror. The time of acceptance depends on whether the offeror has specified a method of acceptance or not. Table 6.2 provides an illustration that summarizes the rules governing when acceptance is effective.

TABLE 6.2 When Is Acceptance Effective?

Method Offeror Used to Make Offer	Method Used to Accept by Offeree	Rule
Specified in offer *(e.g., "you must accept this offer via overnight mail")*.	Used method specified by offeror, or a commercially reasonable substitute *(e.g., same-day courier)*.	*Mailbox rule:* Acceptance effective upon dispatch by offeree.
Specified in offer.	Used slower method *(e.g., regular U.S. mail)*.	Offer considered *rejected* and considered a counteroffer back to the original offeror.
Not specified in the offer *(e.g., I offer to paint your office for $1,000)*.	Used the same/faster method to accept than the offeror used to make the offer, or used a commercially reasonable method.	*Mailbox rule:* Acceptance effective upon dispatch by offeree.
Not specified in the offer.	Used a slower method than the offeror used to make the offer.	Acceptance effective upon *receipt* of acceptance by offeror.

 Self-Check Mailbox Rule

For each transaction, does a contract exist? If yes, why, and what is the date of the contract? If no, why not?

PROBLEM 1

Day 1: Conley sent a fax to Raleigh's office: "We offer to provide you with widget-covering services for $1,000 per month for six months starting January 1."

Day 2: Raleigh sends a letter via U.S. mail to Conley: "I accept your offer of Day 1."

Day 3: Conley telephones Raleigh and tells him: "I revoke my widget-covering offer of Day 1." Upon hearing this, Raleigh states, "Too late, I already put my acceptance in the mailbox!"

Day 4: Conley receives Raleigh's letter of acceptance on Thursday.

PROBLEM 2

Day 1: BookCo's manager e-mails an offer to sell a rare first edition of *For Whom the Bell Tolls,* signed by Hemingway, for $50,000 to Rare Book Retailer (RBR).

Day 2: RBR receives the offer; prints out the e-mail; writes, "ACCEPTED, 1 Hemingway Book for $50,000, RBR Manager"; and faxes BookCo the acceptance.

Day 3 (9:00 a.m.): BookCo's receptionist receives RBR's fax.

Day 3 (12:00 p.m.): BookCo's manager calls RBR to revoke her offer.

Day 3 (1:30 p.m.): The RBR acceptance fax is delivered to BookCo's manager.

PROBLEM 3

Day 1: On Monday, McGlyn mails an offer to Timothy.

Day 2: On Tuesday, McGlyn changes her mind and mails a revocation of the offer to Timothy.

(continued)

Day 3: On Wednesday, while the revocation is in the mail, Timothy receives McGlyn's offer and immediately mails his acceptance.

Day 4: On Thursday, while the acceptance is in the mail, Timothy receives the revocation.

Day 5: On Friday, McGlyn receives Timothy's acceptance.

Answers to this Self-Check are provided at the end of the chapter.

CONCEPT SUMMARY Mutual Assent

- The formation of a contract requires mutual assent, whereby the parties reach an agreement and a meeting of the minds.
- An agreement results from the offeror's making a valid offer and the offeree's accepting the terms of the offer and agreeing to be bound by its terms. This meeting of the minds may come from a true understanding or may be inferred through words and actions of the parties (objective intent).
- Advertisements are generally not considered an offer. Rather, they are an invitation for the consumer to make an offer to a seller of goods or services. If an advertisement is highly specific in its terms, it may constitute a unilateral offer.
- For an offer to be valid, the parties must reach agreement on all of the essential terms of the agreement. An offer that is too vague or indefinite cannot be the basis for an agreement.
- Most offers may be terminated either by the actions of the parties or by operation of law. However, certain offers are considered irrevocable.
- The time acceptance becomes effective is governed by the mailbox rule.

Silence as an Acceptance Under most circumstances, acceptance cannot be imposed or inferred from an offeree's silence after receiving an offer. Therefore, courts will not enforce a contract in which the offer states that failure to respond will be considered an acceptance of the offer. An exception occurs if the parties had previously agreed that silence acts as an acceptance. For example, restaurants often have delivery agreements with food suppliers to accept deliveries daily. Suppose Mackey's, a restaurant, enters into an agreement with a bakery to supply 10 dozen hamburger and hot dog buns each morning at 7 a.m. The agreement may contain a provision stating that if the bakery does not receive a cancellation of the delivery by 4 p.m., the next morning's delivery will be made and accepted. Mackey's failure to cancel by 4 p.m. on Tuesday, therefore, represents an acceptance of delivery on Wednesday, and so on.

Insufficient Agreement

In some cases the parties may actually have satisfied the elements of offer and acceptance, but the agreement still lacks *mutual assent* and the agreement is insufficient to constitute a properly formed contract. Some common circumstances where parties lack mutual assent are in cases when the agreement's terms are too indefinite or when one or both parties are mistaken about an important term.

Indefinite Terms   For an offer to be valid, the parties must reach mutual assent on all of the *essential terms* of the agreement. Even though two parties who are negotiating with each other may have an objective intent to contract, there is no valid contract if the terms are too vague to be performed. Typically, these terms must either be expressly agreed upon or capable of being reasonably inferred. These essential terms are (1) parties to the contract, (2) subject matter of the contract, (3) time for performance or delivery, and (4) price or other consideration to be exchanged.

Note, however, that courts have become increasingly tolerant of uncertainty in terms before allowing a contract to be voided for indefiniteness. The *Restatement* test requires a court to examine the terms of the agreement to determine whether "they provide a basis for determining the existence of a breach and for giving an appropriate remedy."[12] Thus, even though an agreement does not contain all of the required terms, courts have held that missing terms may be supplied by the court when the term may be implied as "reasonable" or by the course of past dealing. So long as the agreement is definite enough to allow the court to determine whether one party failed to fulfill the obligations of the agreement and to award some kind of reasonable damages to the wronged party, the contract is not void for indefiniteness. For example, suppose that LeisureTeesCo has been ordering 50 dozen baby-blue T-shirts from ShirtCo for the past 13 years. Each April an order is placed for baby-blue T-shirts, and each May ShirtCo delivers 600 baby-blue T-shirts to LeisureTeesCo. A new manager has put in this year's order and lists the color on the contract simply as blue. If ShirtCo delivers 600 navy blue tees and LeisureTeesCo rejects them, the court will likely find for LeisureTeesCo and require ShirtCo to provide baby-blue tees. Because the word *blue* is ambiguous, the court will look to the past dealing of the companies and see that, despite the indefiniteness and seeming confusion, the extrinsic evidence mandates an interpretation of baby blue.

Agreements to Agree   In certain circumstances in the business environment, the parties enter into an agreement with an essential term unfilled, intending to agree upon the term in the future. Although historically courts were reluctant to enforce such agreements, the modern trend is to allow such agreements to be enforced with the court supplying the missing term according to industry standards and market values. So long as the court determines that the parties themselves intended to make a binding contract, the agreement is enforceable and a court may supply the missing term. For example, suppose that Ernest offers to purchase an office building from Whitehead for $100,000 in 30 days. At the time of the agreement, Ernest is unsure of the method that he will use to pay the purchase price, so the parties leave that term unfilled. On the day of the purchase, Ernest pays Whitehead $10 in cash and signs a promissory note for $99,990. Whitehead refuses to complete the transaction and demands a check or cash for the full $100,000. In this case, a court would likely hold that (1) the agreement to agree on the payment terms was enforceable because it is clear the parties intended to enter into a contractual relationship and (2) the court can supply the missing term with a degree of reasonableness based on the pattern of past practices and/or industry standards (e.g., requiring that Ernest obtain a mortgage or pay in cash for the property).

Mistake   Over the course of a business life cycle, it is inevitable that a manager involved in a contract will make a **mistake** (or contract with a mistaken party). The law recognizes certain mistakes and provides a remedy intended to make the parties whole again. One famous legal commentator wrote that "mistake is one of the most difficult

---

[12] Restatement (Second) of Contracts§ 33(2).

[doctrines] in the law, because so many men make so many mistakes, of so many different kinds, with so many varying effects."[13]

Generally, a mistake is defined in contract law as a *belief that is not in accord with the facts*.[14] It is important to note that not *all* erroneous beliefs are classified as a mistake. A mistake is an erroneous belief about an *existing* fact, not an erroneous belief as to what will happen in the future. Erroneous beliefs about the future are covered by doctrines of impossibility and impracticability, which are discussed in the next chapter. Mistakes are classified as either *mutual* (both parties) or *unilateral* (one party).

A **mutual mistake**, in which both parties hold an erroneous belief, may be the basis for *canceling* a contract (also called *avoiding* the contract). For the adversely affected party to cancel the contract, the mistake must concern a *basic assumption* on which the contract was made. For example, in *Raffles v. Wichelhaus*,[15] a landmark case on the doctrine of mistake, a court ruled in favor of a buyer of goods who mistakenly accepted goods not intended for him from a freight ship. The court held that the contract delivery terms (in particular, the name of the freighter ship) were ambiguous and the mutual misunderstanding resulted in a lack of mutual assent.

Other examples of mutual mistakes include mistakes as to the existence of the subject matter (e.g., parties agree to the sale of goods, but the goods were already destroyed by fire at the time of the contract) and the quality of the subject matter (e.g., parties agree to the sale of a rare first-edition book that turns out to be a second edition and not nearly as valuable). Courts will *not* generally consider market conditions (such as the fair market value of a piece of real estate) or financial ability (such as relying on one party's representation that she can receive adequate credit to purchase the real estate) as a mistake that allows a contract to be avoided.

In a **unilateral mistake**, only one party has an erroneous belief about a basic assumption in the terms of the agreement. Courts are much less willing to allow a mistaken party to cancel a contract for a unilateral mistake than they are in the case of a mutual mistake. In fact, the general rule is that a unilateral mistake is not a valid reason to avoid a contract. However, if the nonmistaken party had reason to *know* of the mistake or his actions *caused* the mistake, a court will allow the mistaken party to avoid the contract. For example, General Contractor solicits bids from Cement Inc. in order to calculate a bid for a new construction project. Cement Inc. sends a letter offer with a clerical error that promises to provide $20,000 worth of cement for $2,000. General Contractor sends an e-mail accepting the $2,000 bid. A court would likely allow Cement Inc. to cancel the cement contract based on unilateral mistake.[16] Note that courts are much less willing to allow a party to cancel a contract if the unilateral mistake is essentially an error in business judgment rather than a clerical error.

Consideration

For a binding contract to exist, not only must there be agreement (i.e., offer and acceptance), but the agreement must be supported by **consideration**. Consideration is defined as the mutual exchange of benefits and detriments. In plain terms, this means that each party receives something of value from the other and each party gives up something of value, called *legal detriment,* to the other. This results in a bargained-for exchange. The benefits and detriments may take the form of (1) money, (2) goods, (3) services, or (4) the giving up of a legal right. When someone goes to a store to purchase a sweater, the exchange of goods (the sweater) and cash paid is the contract consideration. When a homeowner hires

LO 6-6
Articulate the legal requirement of consideration and identify which contracts do not require consideration.

---

[13]Arthur Linton Corbin, *Corbin on Contracts*§ 103 (1963).
[14]Restatement (Second) of Contracts§ 151.
[15][1864] 159 Eng. Rep. 375 (Eng.).
[16]Based on Restatement (Second) of Contracts§ 154 illus. 6.

someone to mow her lawn, the exchange of the cash paid and the service rendered (mowing the lawn) is the contract consideration. Suppose that a neighbor's teen throws a ball through your front window. You and your neighbor agree that if he pays for the cost of replacement, you'll promise not to sue him. Your promise is called **forbearance** and is valuable consideration. However, giving something up does not always create legal forbearance. What is forfeited must be a legal right. For example, suppose that nervous parents tell their 19-year-old daughter, a freshman college student leaving home for the first time, that if she refrains from drinking alcohol for the entire year, they will give her $1,000. Even if she does forgo alcohol for the year, because a 19-year-old is not legally allowed to drink alcohol, she has not given up a legal right and thus has not provided valuable consideration.

Legal Speak >))

Forbearance
The giving up of a right that you *legally* possess. This can be used as consideration in a contract.

Legal Detriment   Proper consideration requires that the parties suffer some type of detriment that the law recognizes as adequate. This is satisfied if the party promises to perform something that the party is not legally obligated to do (such as promising to sell your car for $5,000) or to refrain from doing something that the party had a right to do (such as waiving your rights to pursue a lawsuit when you have been injured). In one famous decision from 1891, an appellate court in New York held that one party's promise to abstain from the then-legal practices of drinking, smoking, and gambling until age 21, in exchange for a promise by his uncle to pay him $5,000,[17] was sufficient legal detriment for both parties and thus was an enforceable contract.[18] The nephew had given up a legal right that was sufficient to satisfy the legal detriment required (forbearance).

Amount and Type of Consideration   Consideration exchanged does not need to be of equal value. Ordinarily, in deciding the validity of consideration, courts will not look to the *amount* or *type* of consideration or the relative bargaining power of the parties (except in the rare case of a contract so burdensome on one party as to indicate unconscionability, discussed later). So long as some bargained-for exchange is contemplated, the contract will be deemed enforceable. For example, Sheila purchases a pair of designer shoes for $1,300. When her husband finds out, he is irate and demands that she return them. When she goes to the showroom to do so, the store will not accept them because she has worn them outside, walking on a sidewalk. If she files a lawsuit claiming that the value she paid was in excess of the cost of the shoes, the court won't care about the cost of the leather or the company's manufacturing costs; it will simply want to know whether Sheila voluntarily entered into the contract and understood that she was paying $1,300 for a pair of shoes.

Contracts may be based on **nominal consideration** (i.e., consideration that is stated in a written contract even though it is not actually exchanged). Most courts have held that the consideration requirement is still met even if the nominal amount is never actually paid so long as the amount is truly nominal (such as $1). In *Bennett v. American Electric Power Services Corp.*,[19] a state appellate court ruled against an employee who had signed an employment agreement that assigned all of his rights for any invention made in the scope of employment to his employer "in consideration of the sum of One Dollar" even though the actual dollar was never paid. The court reasoned that the offer of employment to the employee in the contract was a sufficient bargained-for exchange.[20]

---

[17]Using the consumer price index rate to calculate the time value of money, this sum would be approximately $104,000 in today's dollars.

[18]*Hammer v. Sidway*, 124 N.Y. 538 (1891).

[19]2001 WL 1136150 (Ohio Ct. App. Sept. 27, 2001).

[20]In its opinion, the court wrote, "Although ancient, the best authorities on the issue hold that nonpayment of such nominal consideration will not constitute breach, at least in instances where the actual value of the subject of the contract does not, in fact, correspond to the nominal consideration."

Preexisting Duty Rule   If a party does or promises to do what she is already legally obligated to do, the law generally does *not* recognize this as a legal detriment and, thus, the contract is unenforceable. The classic example is that a police officer cannot collect the reward for arresting a fugitive because the officer has a **preexisting duty** to find and arrest fugitives. More often, however, the preexisting duty rule applies in circumstances where one party claims he wishes to modify an existing contract because of unforeseen difficulties in performing his obligations. For example, Helsel contracts with Mullen to renovate Helsel's office building. During the renovation, Mullen discovers the costs of renovation will be more than he anticipated. Mullen threatens to walk off the job unless Helsel agrees to pay an amount higher than stated in the contract. Because Helsel's choices would be limited to either agreeing or hiring a new contractor and then suing Mullen, he consents to the price increase. Most courts would *not* enforce Helsel's promise to pay the additional amount because Mullen already had a preexisting contractual duty to perform for the original price.

The modern trend in the law recognizes a number of exceptions to the preexisting duty rule.[21] For example, if a party who promises to do what she is already bound to do assumes additional duties, her undertaking of these duties is considered sufficient legal detriment.[22] Also, courts may allow an exception in a case where certain circumstances were not reasonably *anticipated* by either party when the original contract was formed. For example, Waste Disposal Company (WDC) contracts with ManufacturerCo to collect garbage from ManufacturerCo's warehouse for one year. Six months into the agreement, WDC requests an additional $5,000 per month to provide this service because the ManfacturerCo warehouse is now unexpectedly producing some hazardous material waste that must be removed by specifically designed equipment. The parties then execute a modification to the contract, agreeing to the increase. One month later, ManufacturerCo changes managers, and the new manager refuses to pay the additional sum, citing the preexisting duty rule. In this case, most courts would *enforce* the modification as an exception to the preexisting duty rule.[23]

Bargained-for Exchange   Even if a legal detriment is suffered by one party, that alone does not satisfy the consideration requirement. The **bargained-for exchange** aspect of consideration primarily distinguishes contracts from **illusory promises**. Some promises do not support a bargained-for exchange and will not support contractual consideration. Such promises are called *illusory promises*. Examples of illusory promises are (1) deathbed promises, in which you make a promise to a friend or loved one just prior to her death to comfort her; (2) promises of a gift, in which a promise is made but no reciprocal promise is exchanged; (3) promises of love and friendship; and (4) promises that by their terms are not binding. For example, a manager announces to his employees that each may have three personal days in December if he can get it approved by senior management. This is an illusory promise because neither the manager nor the company is bound by his statement. Because gift promises are not enforceable and contract promises are, it is important to understand the precise difference. A performance or return promise is "bargained for" only if it was exchanged for another promise.

Past Consideration   Another type of consideration that is not considered to meet the bargained-for exchange requirement is a promise made in return for a detriment previously made by the promisee. This is known as **past consideration**, and it is not sufficient

---

[21]In fact, some states (such as New York) have repudiated the preexisting duty rule altogether and allow a good faith modification made in writing to be enforceable.
[22]Restatement (Second) of Contracts§ 73.
[23]Based on *Angel v. Murray*, 332 A.2d 630 (R.I. 1974).

> **KEY POINT**
>
> Consideration must be performed or exchanged after the mutual assent. Any agreements made after the consideration is performed or exchanged will not support a valid contract.

to meet the consideration requirement. Suppose that O'Connor has been working at her job for 40 years and is retiring. Her boss approaches her a week before her last scheduled day and tells her that because she has been such a faithful and effective employee for the last 40 years, on Friday, her last day, there will be a party and she will be presented with a gold watch. She gratefully thanks him and accepts the offer of a party and watch. On Thursday she is disappointed when informed that there will be no party and she will not receive a gold watch. Although the party and watch contract includes both an offer and an acceptance, it is *unenforceable* because it lacks consideration. O'Connor's contention that her 40 years of dedicated service are sufficient consideration is false because it is past consideration, performed prior to the current agreement. Thus, the offer of a party and watch is an offer of a gift and is not enforceable as a contract. Now suppose the company's employment manual, in force since she started work, states that employees receive a gold watch after 25 years of employment. In this case, O'Connor is entitled to the watch because she acted based on a promise made before she began performing.

Promissory Estoppel If one party justifiably relies on the promise of another to her detriment, under certain circumstances the relying party may recover costs of the reliance from the promisor even though the original promise agreement lacked consideration. Under the theory of **promissory estoppel**, a relying party may recover damages if (1) the promisor makes a promise that is *reasonable;* (2) the promisee *actually* relied on the promise (the promise must have induced the act) and suffered an injury; (3) the promisee's reliance was *reasonably foreseeable* to the promisor (what an objectively reasonable person would have foreseen under the same circumstances); and (4) principles of *equity and justice* (did each party act in good faith and fair dealing?) are served by providing compensation to the reliant party.

One particularly important domain of promissory estoppel for managers is the promise of employment. Most commonly, this arises in a situation where an employer makes a promise of employment to an at-will[24] employee candidate and then revokes the promise before the employee's start date (or soon thereafter). Typically, the employee would have left her previous position and potentially incurred moving expenses. In those cases, courts have held that the revocation of the employment-at-will promise before any consideration was exchanged triggers the doctrine of promissory estoppel, whereby the innocent party is entitled to damages. In promissory estoppel cases, courts frequently award damages equal to the out-of-pocket costs plus what the employee lost in quitting her job and declining employment elsewhere.[25] For example, suppose that Donatello is given a written offer of employment to go to work for Renaissance Architect Firm (RAF) for an annual salary of $50,000 to begin in 30 days. Donatello gives his current employer notice of his resignation and then moves his home 100 miles in order to be closer to RAF's headquarters. The day before Donatello shows up for work, RAF informs him that due to financial difficulties, it can no longer honor its offer of employment. When Donatello attempts to regain his old employment, he is told that his position was filled and there is no chance of rehiring him. Donatello cannot prevail on a breach of contract claim because no consideration

---

[24]At-will employees are those who may be fired with or without cause because they are not covered by a contract or any other promises of continued employment. Employees at-will are discussed in detail in Chapter 10, "Agency."

[25]Note that generally courts do *not* measure damages by looking at what the employee would have earned from the defendant in a certain time period.

was actually ever exchanged and, therefore, the promise is not supported by consideration and not enforceable as a contract. However, a court would likely award Donatello damages based on promissory estoppel. RAF may be liable for damages related to Donatello's actions in reliance on RAF's promise, such as the moving expenses and compensation in connection with Donatello's resignation from his previous employer.[26]

Capacity

In addition to having to meet the requirements for agreement and consideration, contracts will be enforced by the courts only if each party has the legal **capacity** to enter into a contract. Certain classes of persons have only limited power to contract: **minors** and those with **mental incapacity**. These parties may seek to *avoid* (cancel) the contract immediately, or they may enforce the contract with the option of avoiding it at any time up until the time they regain capacity. Once the party has regained capacity, the contract becomes binding on both parties.

LO 6-7

Give examples of circumstances under which the legal requirements of capacity and legality are at issue.

Minors Until a person reaches her majority age, any contract that she may enter into is *voidable* at the minor's option. Minors (referred to as *infants* in legal terminology) are defined by most states as those who are younger than 18. For example, Junior is 17 and enters into an agreement to purchase a pickup truck from Roscoe's Dealership. Junior later changes his mind and decides not to go through with the transaction. Roscoe may not enforce the agreement against Junior. However, Junior may still enforce the contract against Roscoe if he so desires.[27]

A minor may avoid a contract even before she reaches the age of majority.[28] It is important to remember that a contract made by a minor is not *automatically* void. Rather, the minor either avoids the contract or may enforce the contract. While a minor may avoid a contract up until the age of majority, the minor may also *ratify* the contract upon reaching the age of 18. Note that a minor is assumed to have ratified the contract upon reaching the age of 18 if she fails to *disaffirm* (avoid) the contract in a reasonable time period.[29] In the case where the minor has disaffirmed and avoided the contract, the other party may be entitled to an economic adjustment if the minor received some economic benefit from the contract. Generally, this means that the minor will have to return any goods or make restitution for any damages that affected the value of the good or service. In the example discussed above, suppose that Junior goes through with the truck purchase and avoids the contract on his 18th birthday. Roscoe is entitled to claim the truck back and may be entitled to compensation for the loss of the truck's market value from the previous year.

Virtually all jurisdictions recognize an *exception* to the minor-capacity rule for necessities such as food, clothing, and shelter. Thus, a 16-year-old customer at a restaurant may not disaffirm a contract to purchase french fries when presented with the bill.

Mental Incompetents Like minors, mental incompetents are treated as having limited capacity to contract. This category covers not just obvious cases (such as mental disorders or dementia) but also temporary incompetence such as people who are highly

---

[26] Based on *Grouse v. Group Health Plan, Inc.*, 306 N.W.2d 114 (Minn. 1981).

[27] In cases where the minor misrepresents her age, courts differ in their treatment of the transactions. In some cases, courts place a greater burden of restitution for any misrepresentations. In other cases, courts have allowed either party to avoid the contract.

[28] Michigan is the only state with an exception to this rule.

[29] There is no definitive test for determining what is a "reasonable time" because the time period may be case-specific depending on individual industry standards and practices.

intoxicated, people severely depressed, or people under severe or traumatic pressure. The question is whether the person was **lucid** at the time he entered into the contract. Although there is no universally accepted definition, courts have held that a party who is lucid is one who is not suffering from delusion or confusion.

In general, a person lacks capacity because of mental illness or defect if he or she is either (1) *unable to understand* the nature and consequences of the contract or (2) *unable to act in a reasonable manner* in relation to the transaction and the other party has *reason to know* of that person's condition.[30] For example, Oliver has Alzheimer's disease and enters into a contract with Wendell to sell 100 widgets for $1 per widget (the widget's fair market value). Oliver may avoid the contract even though the contract terms were fair and Wendell had no notice of Oliver's condition. This is true because Oliver has met the "unable to understand" criteria. Intoxication, whether it be through drugs or alcohol, can also affect capacity. Suppose that Oliver and Wendell were at a bar drinking heavily. Wendell writes on a cocktail napkin: "Because you bought me so many pints of beer, I will sell you 100 widgets for only five cents per widget." The next day Wendell sobers up and realizes what he did. Wendell may avoid the contract because he was so intoxicated that he was unable to act in a reasonable manner *and* because Oliver had *reason to know* of Wendell's condition. On the other hand, if Oliver and Wendell were drinking but neither was obviously impaired, their intoxication would likely have no effect on the validity of the contract. Remember that in *Lucy v. Zehmer* (Landmark Case 6.2, earlier in this chapter) even though the parties had been drinking, the contract to sell Zehmer's farm was upheld.

In a majority of states, contracts made by an incompetent are *voidable,* not void. If the incompetent party regains her mental capacity, or has a guardian appointed, she may ratify the contract. Note that the other party does *not* have the power to avoid the contract. However, many states classify a contract as *void per se* (not valid from the outset) if one party has been legally declared to be incompetent prior to entering into the contract. In Case 6.4, a state's highest court considers a claim that a contract is void because one party does not have sufficient mental capacity.

Legal Speak >))

Lucid
Being able to think clearly and rationally.

CASE 6.4 Sparrow v. Demonico, 461 Mass. 322 (2012)

FACT SUMMARY A family dispute over ownership of what had been the family home in Woburn, Massachusetts, prompted Frances M. Sparrow (Sparrow) to file a complaint in a state trial court against her sister, Susan Demonico, and Susan's husband, David D. Demonico (Demonicos). Prior to trial, the parties resolved their differences by entering into a settlement agreement reached during voluntary mediation. However, when Sparrow attempted to obtain a court order to enforce the agreement, the Demonicos argued that the contract was void because Susan Demonico lacked the capacity to enter into the agreement. A trial court agreed with the Demonicos, ruling that the contract was void because it may have been the product of an emotionally overwrought state of mind and Susan was not able to understand in a reasonable manner the nature and consequences of her actions. The appellate court reversed the trial court's decision and issued an order enforcing the settlement agreement.

The Demonicos appealed again and argued that Susan's withdrawal symptoms from the antidepressant drug Zoloft rendered her unable to act reasonably at the time of the agreement. They cited her behavior, such as the slurring of words, crying,

(continued)

---

[30]Restatement (Second) of Contracts§ 15(2).

and having to leave the room, as evidence that she was suffering from a mental breakdown on the day of the mediation. Sparrow countered that however upset Susan was during the mediation, it didn't rise to the level of incapacitation required under the law and that the Demonicos had produced no medical evidence or experts to support their claim about the Zoloft.

SYNOPSIS OF DECISION AND OPINION The Supreme Judicial Court of Massachusetts ruled in favor of Sparrow. Although the court ruled that a party *could* establish incapacity to contract without proof of a mental condition that is permanent, degenerative, progressive, or long standing, they also held that any finding of incapacity must still be supported by medical evidence. According to the court, the proper inquiry as to the capacity to contract focuses on a party's understanding or conduct only at the time of the disputed transaction. In this case, the Demonicos failed to present medical evidence regarding a diagnosis that would have required her to take Zoloft, or the effect, if any, that ceasing to take the medication would have had on her medical or mental condition.

WORDS OF THE COURT: Evidence of Incapacity "We conclude that our evolving standard of contractual incapacity does not in all cases require proof that a party's claimed mental illness or defect was of some significant duration or that it is permanent, progressive, or degenerative; but, without medical evidence or expert testimony that the mental condition interfered with the party's understanding of the transaction, or her ability to act reasonably in relation to it, the evidence will not be sufficient to support a conclusion of incapacity . . . [T]here was no expert or medical testimony to explain the effect of Susan's experiences or behavior on her ability to understand the agreement, to appreciate what was happening, or to comprehend the reasonableness of the settlement terms or the consequences to her of authorizing the settlement. Without such medical evidence, there was no basis to conclude that Susan lacked the capacity to contract."

Case Questions

1. What does the court say was missing from the Demonicos' argument about capacity?
2. What factors went into the trial court's decision to void the settlement agreement?
3. *Focus on Critical Thinking:* Under the court's decision, are there any circumstances when medical evidence would not be necessary? If one party was acting in a bizarre manner, such as talking to oneself or making irrational statements, would that be sufficient to void a contract based on capacity? Does public policy require that medical evidence support all claims of incapacity?

Legality

For a contract to be enforceable, it must meet the requirement of **legality**; that is, both the subject matter and performance of the contract must be legal. Depending on the state, some contracts are specifically barred by statute (e.g., a contract related to illegal gambling such as betting on sports events[31] or a contract for the sale of goods that is banned by a trade embargo), while other contracts are illegal because the terms violate some **public policy** objective (such as an overly broad restriction on employment possibilities, known as a *restrictive covenant*). As a general rule, an illegal contract is *void automatically,* and neither party may enforce it against the other. This is true even when only one party's performance is illegal. For example, if Holmes promises to paint Cardozo's home in exchange for Cardozo's promise to smuggle 500 Cuban cigars into the United States in violation of federal law, then neither Holmes nor Cardozo may enforce the contract.

---

[31]Many states do allow "small games of chance" such as church-sponsored bingo or an office football pool.

CONCEPT SUMMARY Contract Formation

Mutual Assent	Consideration	Capacity	Legality
The offer must represent a serious, objective intent to contract; proper acceptance of the offer must occur prior to termination by the parties or operation of law.	There must be the possibility of legal detriment to the promisee and a bargained-for exchange on the part of the promisor.	If one of the parties is a minor, the contract is voidable by the minor or the minor's guardian. If one of the parties is mentally incapacitated and the other party has reason to know of the incapacity, the contract may be avoided.	The subject matter of the contract and the transaction must be legal.

KEY TERMS

Agreement p. 171   Any meeting of the minds resulting in mutual assent to do or refrain from doing something.

Bilateral contract p. 171   A contract involving two promises and two performances.

Unilateral contract p. 172   A contract involving one promise followed by one performance, which then triggers a second performance from the offeror.

Express contract p. 173   A contract that is created when the parties have knowingly and intentionally agreed on the promises and performances.

Implied contract p. 173   A contract in which the agreement is reached by the parties' actions rather than their words.

Quasi-contract p. 173   A classification that permits a contract to be enforceable in cases where no express or implied contract exists and one party suffers losses as a result of another party's unjust enrichment.

Valid contract p. 174   A contract that has the necessary elements and, thus, can be enforceable.

Void contract p. 174   A contract that lacks one or more of the basic required elements of a contract or that has not been formed in conformance with the law from the outset of the agreement and, thus, cannot be enforced by either party.

Voidable contract p. 174   A contract that one party may, at its option, either disaffirm or enforce.

Unenforceable contract p. 174   A contract that meets the elements required by law for an otherwise binding agreement but is subject to a legal defense.

State common law p. 175   The body of law governing contracts for services or real estate.

State statutory law p. 175   The body of law governing contracts for goods or products; based on the Uniform Commercial Code.

Hybrid contract p. 175   A contract that involves terms for both goods and services; the source of law is established by determining the predominant thrust of the subject matter.

Mutual assent p. 178   For the formation of a valid contract, the broad underlying requirement that the parties must reach an agreement using a combination of offer and acceptance and that the assent must be genuine.

Offer p. 178   A promise or commitment to do (or refrain from doing) a specified activity. In contract law, the expression of a willingness to enter into a contract by the offeror's promising an offeree that she will perform certain obligations in exchange for the offeree's counterpromise to perform.

Acceptance p. 178   The offeree's expression of agreement to the terms of the offer. The power of acceptance is created by a valid offer.

Objective intent p. 178   For an offer to have legal effect, the requirement that, generally, the offeror must have a serious intention to become bound by the offer and that the terms of the offer must be reasonably certain.

Revocation p. 182   An action terminating an offer whereby the offeror decides to withdraw the offer by expressly communicating the revocation to the offeree prior to acceptance.

Rejection p. 182 An action terminating an offer whereby the offeree rejects the offer outright prior to acceptance.

Counteroffer p. 182 An action terminating an offer whereby the offeree rejects the original offer and proposes a new offer with different terms.

Operation of law (contracts) p. 182 Termination of an offer by the occurrence of certain happenings or events, which generally include lapse of time, death or incapacity of the offeror or offeree, destruction of the subject matter of the contract prior to acceptance, and supervening illegality.

Irrevocable offers p. 183 Offers that cannot be withdrawn by the offeror; include offers in the form of an option contract, offers that the offeree partly performed or detrimentally relied on, and firm offers by a merchant under the Uniform Commercial Code.

Detrimental reliance p. 184 Situation in which the offeree acts, based on a reasonable promise made by the offeror, and would be injured if the offeror's promise is not enforced.

Mirror image rule p. 184 Principle stating that the offeree's response operates as an acceptance only if it is the precise mirror image of the offer.

Lapse of time p. 185 An event covered under operation of law in which a contract may be terminated once either the offeror's expressed time limit has expired or a reasonable time has passed.

Mailbox rule p. 185 Principle stating that the acceptance of an offer is effective upon dispatch of the acceptance via a commercially reasonable means and not when the acceptance is received by the offeree; governs common law contracts.

Mistake p. 188 In contract law, an erroneous belief that is not in accord with the existing facts.

Mutual mistake p. 189 An erroneous belief held by both parties that concerns a basic assumption on which a contract was made.

Unilateral mistake p. 189 An erroneous belief held by only one party about a basic assumption in the terms of an agreement.

Consideration p. 189 The mutual exchange of benefits and detriments; for the formation of a valid contract, the requirement that each party receives something of value (the benefit) from the other and that each party gives up something of value (the legal detriment) to the other, resulting in a bargained-for exchange.

Forbearance p. 190 The giving up of a legal right as consideration in a contract.

Nominal consideration p. 190 Consideration that is stated in a written contract even though it is not actually exchanged.

Preexisting duty p. 191 A duty that one is already legally obligated to perform and, thus, that is generally not recognized as a legal detriment.

Bargained-for exchange p. 191 The aspect of consideration that differentiates contracts from illusory promises by holding that a performance or return promise is bargained for only if it was exchanged for another promise.

Illusory promise p. 191 A promise that courts will not enforce because the offeror is not truly bound by his vague promise or because a party cannot be bound by his promise due to the lack of a bargained-for exchange. Promises of gifts and deathbed promises are two examples.

Past consideration p. 191 A promise made in return for a detriment previously made by the promisee; does not meet the bargained-for exchange requirement.

Promissory estoppel p. 192 Theory allowing for the recovery of damages by the relying party if the promisee actually relied on the promise and the promisee's reliance was reasonably foreseeable to the promisor.

Capacity p. 193 For the formation of a valid contract, the requirement that both parties have the power to contract. Certain classes of persons have only limited powers to contract, including minors and those with mental incapacity.

Minors p. 193 Category of individuals who have limited capacity to enter into a contract; includes those younger than the majority age of 18. Until a person reaches her majority age, any contract that she may enter into is voidable at the minor's option.

Mental incapacity p. 193 Category of individuals who have limited capacity to enter into a contract; includes anyone who is unable to understand the nature and consequences of the contract and anyone who is unable to act in a reasonable manner in relation to the transaction when the other party has reason to know of that person's condition.

Lucid p. 194 Sane and thinking clearly.

Legality p. 195 For the formation of a valid contract, the requirement that both the subject matter and performance of the contract must be legal.

Public policy p. 195 Part of the legality requirement for a valid contract; necessitates that the terms be consistent with public policy objectives.

CHAPTER REVIEW QUESTIONS

1. In a contract to install network cable in a new office building, the parties allocate the price as follows: 75 percent for the installation and 25 percent for materials. What source of law governs the contract?

    a. Common law
    b. Statutory law
    c. Hybrid law
    d. Regulatory law

2. Ginsberg signs an agreement with Roberts to lease a 1,000-square-foot warehouse for one year. Which of the following categories does this contract fall into?

    a. Express and unilateral
    b. Implied and written
    c. Bilateral and implied
    d. Express and bilateral

3. The night before his commencement ceremony, Leland's uncle promises to buy him a new car after he actually sees Leland receive his diploma. Leland gladly accepts. After the ceremony, Leland's uncle says, "Just kidding, no car!" Leland cannot prevail in a breach of contract claim because the agreement lacks _____.

    a. Offer
    b. Acceptance
    c. Consideration
    d. Legality

4. Which of the following does *not* result in the termination of an offer?

    a. Revocation
    b. Renunciation
    c. Rejection
    d. Death of the offeror

5. Junior is 17 years old and has entered into an agreement to purchase a vintage Ford Mustang from his neighbor. Which of the following is true about the transaction?

    a. The contract is automatically void.
    b. Junior has the right to void the contract until he turns 18.
    c. The contract lacks consideration.
    d. No contract exists because there was no mutual assent.

Answers and explanations are provided at the end of this chapter.

THEORY TO PRACTICE

On Monday, the owner of Quick Oil Change (Quick) has a breakfast meeting with the owner of Digital Solutions (DS) to discuss DS's proposal to provide digital consulting services for Quick over a period of two years. The parties discuss price, services to be provided, hardware and software to be purchased, and the timeline to implement the services. When Quick asks DS to lower the price, DS takes out an index card and writes down the following:

- 5 tablet computers (inc. software): $1,500
- 2 years of Gold Package of Services: $5,000 (10% discount)

Quick reads the card and says, "Great. I like this price much better. Let's get started." The two shake hands and leave the meeting. On Tuesday, Quick receives the following e-mail from the owner of DS:

> Due to our commitment to a larger customer, I must revoke my offer of yesterday.

1. Did DS make a valid offer on Monday? Why or why not? Name a case to support your answer.
2. Were the terms definite enough to constitute an offer? If not, what term was missing?

3. Was DS's revocation on Tuesday an effective termination of its Monday offer? Explain your answer.
4. Assume that a contract exists between the parties. What source of law governs the contract? Why?
5. Assume that a contract exists between the parties but that the owner of Quick was under the influence of a mind-altering prescription drug at the Monday meeting, although she was acting and speaking in an ordinary manner. Will the owner of Quick be successful in a claim that the contract is void due to her incapacity? Name a case to support your answer.

LEGAL STRATEGY 101

Ticketmaster's Strategic Contracts

Ticketmaster is the leading live entertainment electronic ticketing service with billions in annual revenues. To achieve this competitive position in the marketplace, Ticketmaster designed and implemented unique contracts that make it extremely difficult for competitors to compete with Ticketmaster in this industry.

To understand how Ticketmaster strategically uses and leverages contract law, it is necessary to first understand how the live entertainment industry operates and how Ticketmaster departed from the industry's traditional business model and contracting practices. First, it is important to assess the various players in the live entertainment industry, as depicted in the following industry value chain.

The model before Ticketmaster was for the ticketing companies to charge the venues an inside charge for each ticket sold to the fan. This was normally limited by contract to $1 per ticket. The convenience charges assessed against the fans were likewise kept at a minimum and retained by the ticketing company. These two relatively modest fees were the primary revenue sources for ticketing companies before Ticketmaster's arrival. Ticketmaster's pioneering model, however, challenged these practices and used contracts to preserve its competitive advantage.

First, Ticketmaster did away with the inside charge so that the venues would never have to pay to use Ticketmaster's service and technology. To earn profits, Ticketmaster negotiated with each venue the contractual right to obtain the complete and exclusive inventory of ticketing for all the venue's live entertainment events for three to five years. In exchange for this major concession, Ticketmaster promised to assess convenience and order processing fees against the fans that would then be shared with the venue at a guaranteed percentage reflected in the written contract between Ticketmaster and each venue. The ticket receipt below demonstrates the two charges assessed by Ticketmaster against a ticket purchaser: the convenience charge and the order processing fee.

The following contract term, standard among Ticketmaster's contracts, was negotiated between Ticketmaster and a county-owned venue in Florida:

Principal [the venue] shall be entitled to receive Ticket sales royalties from Ticketmaster with respect to each Convenience Charge and Processing Fee; all to the extent received (and not refunded) by Ticketmaster. The amount of the Royalties are as set forth below:

Type of Royalty	Amount of Royalty
Convenience Charge	35% of the Convenience Charge
Processing Fee	35% of the Processing Fee

This unique rebate model allowed Ticketmaster to contractually lock in all the major venues across the nation. Eventually, Ticketmaster signed similar rebate contracts with all the major promoters who represent the most popular artists. This locked in all the key industry players and prevented the venues from negotiating directly with the promoters.

CRITICAL THINKING QUESTIONS

1. If you had a superior electronic ticketing technology, how might you compete against Ticketmaster?
2. Is it fair for companies to be able to use contracts such as these to preserve their market leadership position?
3. Can you think of other businesses that employ the "rebate model" that Ticketmaster used in the electronic ticketing industry? What role do contracts have in these industries?

MANAGER'S CHALLENGE

Managers are frequently on the front lines when ambiguous preliminary agreements are involved and therefore must have a relatively sophisticated knowledge of what constitutes a contract and what rules govern contracts. In this chapter's Theory to Practice problem, the parties did not communicate their intent very clearly and certain important terms were missing.

Prepare a two-page written offer on behalf of your company to engage a web design and maintenance firm. Research data such as price, description of services, guarantees, and so on by searching the websites of various providers such as Parker Web (parkerweb.com) or Iceberg Web Design (icebergwebdesign.com). Be sure to reread sections of the chapter for guidance on essential terms. The offer should not create any ambiguity and should fit the standards for objective intent to contract discussed in this chapter.

See Connect for Manager's Challenge sample answers.

CASE SUMMARY 6.1 Chambers v. Travelers Companies, 668 F.3d 559 (8th Cir. 2012)

UNILATERAL CONTRACT

Chambers worked for Travelers as a managing director. Questions arose regarding her management style and effectiveness, and she was fired. Among her claims against Travelers, she claimed that she was due a bonus earned. In February 2007, Travelers provided Chambers a Total Compensation Summary for the year that included a bonus of $30,000. The summary clearly stated that bonuses were at the discretion of Travelers. In September 2007, her boss provided Chambers a written performance review, giving her positive ratings in every performance category. The next month, in response to employee complaints, a climate survey was administered to the employees whom she supervised and it came back extremely negative. She was also found to have irregularities in various expense reports, and in January 2008, she was terminated. Chambers alleged that Travelers's failure to pay a $30,000 bonus for her work during 2007 breached a unilateral employment contract that she accepted by her performance.

CASE QUESTIONS

1. Suppose Chambers performed her job well, the climate survey came back positive, and no irregularities occurred in her expense reports. If she was still terminated due to cutbacks, could she have compelled Travelers to pay her the bonus?
2. Was Travelers's bonus statement in the compensation summary a unilateral offer that could be accepted by performance?

CASE SUMMARY 6.2 Rochon Corp. v. City of Saint Paul, 814 N.W.2d 365 (Minn. Ct. App. 2012)

VOID CONTRACT

Rochon Corporation lost the municipal general-contract bidding contest to construct the Lofts at Farmer's Market for the city of St. Paul to Shaw-Lundquist Associates. When the city opened the sealed bids, Shaw-Lundquist appeared to be the clear winner. But Shaw-Lundquist discovered that it had bid $619,200 lower than it had intended due to a clerical error. Bidding instructions included the following: "A bid may not be modified, withdrawn, or canceled by the Bidder for a period of sixty (60) days following the time and date designated for the receipt of bids, and each Bidder so agrees in submitting a bid." Nevertheless, the city allowed Shaw-Lundquist to change its bid, raising it to cover not only the $619,200 error but adding $89,211 more. Still, Shaw-Lundquist's raised bid was lower than Rochon's bid, and the city awarded Shaw-Lundquist the contract for $8,041,411. State common law long held that a contract entered into in violation of competitive bidding laws is void. The state supreme court had previously stated that a competitive bidding contract is void even "without any showing of actual fraud or an intent to commit fraud, if a procedure has been followed which emasculates the safeguards of competitive bidding."

CASE QUESTIONS

1. The city claimed that it benefited the public by allowing the bid change because it resulted in monetary savings for the city. Does this explanation justify the city's disregard of established precedent? Can the court of appeals disregard established state precedent?
2. Shaw-Lundquist was able to prove that its original bid was wrong due to a legitimate clerical error. Should this have mattered?
3. Why is it good policy to not permit amendments of bids in competitive bidding situations?

CASE SUMMARY 6.3 Forest Park Pictures v. Universal Television Network, Inc., 683 F.3d 424 (2d Cir. 2012)

IMPLIED CONTRACTS

Forest Park formulated a concept for a television show called *Housecall*, in which a doctor, after being expelled from the medical community for treating patients who could not pay, moved to Malibu, California, and became a "concierge" doctor for the rich and famous. Forest Park created a written series treatment for the idea, including character biographies, themes, and story lines. It mailed this written material to Alex Sepiol, who worked for USA Network. A meeting was then held at which Forest Park explained its concept. It was common practice in the industry for writers and creators to pitch creative ideas to prospective purchasers with the object of selling those ideas for compensation. Sepiol admitted that before hearing the idea for *Housecall*, he had never heard of "concierge" doctors, or doctors who make house calls for wealthy patients, and "thought it was a fascinating concept for a television show." The parties communicated for a week, and then no further contact occurred. A little less than four years later, USA Network produced and aired a television show called *Royal Pains*, in which a doctor, after being expelled from the medical community for treating patients who could not pay, became a concierge doctor for the rich and famous in the Hamptons, an extremely affluent community on Long Island in New York. Forest Park had no prior knowledge of *Royal Pains*, did not consent to its production, and received no compensation from USA Network for the use of its idea for the show. Forest Park sued, claiming breach of contract.

CASE QUESTIONS

1. Who wins and why?
2. What allows Forest Park to argue that this is an implied contract?

CASE SUMMARY 6.4 Morrow v. Hallmark Cards, Inc., 273 S.W.3d 15 (2008)

UNENFORCEABLE CONTRACTS

Mary Kay Morrow was hired by Hallmark in 1982. At the start of 2002, while Morrow was working as an associate product manager, Hallmark adopted, effective January 5, 2002, a policy applicable to its employees called the Hallmark Dispute Resolution Program. This policy provided that if an employee continued to work for Hallmark after the policy became effective, the employee would thereby be deemed to have agreed to submit to the company's procedures for resolving claims against the company, which included binding arbitration in lieu of litigation. Hallmark reserved the right to unilaterally make changes and retained the right to select the arbitrator. Morrow received a copy of the policy, and she continued working for Hallmark through and after the effective date of January 5, 2002. On April 8, 2003, Hallmark terminated Morrow's employment. Morrow claimed that Hallmark discriminated against her because of her age and retaliated against her for complaining about Hallmark policies. Hallmark's position was that Morrow was terminated for poor work performance after failed attempts to improve her performance through coaching and a performance improvement plan. Hallmark sought to enforce the binding arbitration provision, and Morrow contended that arbitration should not be compelled in this case.

CASE QUESTIONS

1. Employment agreements for binding arbitration are valid only if agreed to. Should Morrow's continued employment be considered an agreement to the Hallmark Dispute Resolution Program terms?
2. Should the binding arbitration provision of the Hallmark Dispute Resolution Program be found enforceable or unenforceable? Why or why not?

CASE SUMMARY 6.5 Arizona Cartridge Remanufacturers Association v. Lexmark, 421 F.3d 981 (9th Cir. 2005)

MUTUAL ASSENT/ACCEPTANCE

Lexmark is a manufacturer and distributor of ink cartridges for computer printers. It introduced a rebate plan called Return Program Cartridges whereby a consumer could receive a "prebate" (i.e., a discount upon purchase) on ink cartridges. This price discount was given in exchange for an agreement by the consumer not to tamper with the cartridge. The consumer simply had to agree to return the empty cartridge to Lexmark. The agreement was printed on the ink cartridge box, and Lexmark claimed that by opening the box the consumer agreed to the terms of the Return Program Cartridges program. A consumer group challenged Lexmark's program, contending, among other things, that Lexmark could not enforce an agreement on the box because the consumer had never formally accepted the terms of Lexmark's offer.

CASE QUESTION

1. Can one party be deemed to accept an offer simply by opening a product box even if there is no evidence that the party *actually* read the terms?

CASE SUMMARY 6.6 Biomedical Systems Corp. v. GE Marquette Medical Systems, Inc., 287 F.3d 707 (8th Cir. 2002)

LEGALITY

GE Marquette Medical Systems (GE) contracted with Biomedical Systems Corp. to manufacture a new medical instrument based on technology owned by Biomedical. The contract required GE to obtain clearance from the Food and Drug Administration (the federal regulatory agency that covers such medical devices) within 90 days in order to move ahead on the project. After this contract was signed, GE determined that obtaining this clearance was not a prudent path to reach its ultimate objective of having the product approved for selling to the public. Rather than seek the clearance required by the Biomedical contract, GE decided to pursue a different strategy with the FDA that took several years to complete. When Biomedical sued GE for breach of contract, GE defended on the basis that the clearance provision in the contract was a violation of FDA procedure and, thus, the term was illegal and the contract was void.

CASE QUESTIONS

1. Can a party make a unilateral judgment as to illegality on a term of the contract when there is no affirmative finding from a regulatory authority?
2. If GE had gone ahead with the clearance process and the FDA had told GE that it was not the proper procedure, would the contract be void for illegality?

CASE SUMMARY 6.7 Reed's Photo Mart, Inc. v. Monarch, 475 S.W.2d 356 (Tex. Civ. App. 1971)

MISTAKE

Reed owned a small photography store and purchased his price label products from Monarch. Over a period of years, Reed ordered no more than 4,000 labels at a time from Monarch. While preparing a new order form for labels, Reed was interrupted by a customer and wrote "4MM" on the order form instead of "4M." In the industry, *4M* means 4,000 labels, while *4MM* means 4 million labels. Reed sent the mistaken order to Monarch. Despite the course of past dealings and the fact that the maximum order that Monarch had ever received from a single customer was 1 million labels, Monarch proceeded to produce and deliver 4 million labels to Reed. Reed refused delivery and defended on the basis of mistake.

CASE QUESTIONS

1. Who prevails and why?
2. Is this a unilateral or mutual mistake? What's the difference?

 Self-Check ANSWERS Categories of Contracts

1. Express.
2. Offer of a unilateral contract (reward).
3. Bilateral (promise with a return promise).
4. Implied. Price is set by the caterer.

Source of Law

1. Common law (real estate).
2. Hybrid contract governed by common law based on (1) price allocation weighted to services and (2) uniqueness of services.
3. Common law (services).
4. Statutory law (sale of goods).
4. Common law (services) because no goods are sold (the owner supplies the paint).

Mailbox Rule

PROBLEM 1

No contract. Conley still had the power to revoke the offer on Day 3 because Raleigh used a slower method (U.S. mail) to accept than Conley used to make the offer (fax). Therefore, Raleigh's acceptance could take effect only upon receipt of the acceptance by Conley. Because Conley did not receive the acceptance until Day 4, his revocation of Day 3 is effective and no contract exists.

PROBLEM 2

Contract exists on Day 2 upon dispatch (mailbox rule) because RBR used a reasonable method to accept (using fax to accept an e-mail offer is reasonable because both methods are similar in that they are relatively instantaneous when sending). When the offeror actually received the acceptance is irrelevant.

PROBLEM 3

Contract exists on Day 3 upon dispatch (mailbox rule) because Timothy used the same method to accept that was used to convey the offer. It is irrelevant that the revocation was already in the mail and equally irrelevant that the acceptance was received by McGlyn after Timothy had received the revocation.

CHAPTER REVIEW QUESTIONS: Answers and Explanations

1. **a.** Although this is a hybrid contract, the allocation of price indicates that it is primarily a contract for services covered under the common law. Answer choice (b) is wrong because statutory law applies to contracts primarily for goods. Answer choices (c) and (d) are wrong because they are nonsensical.

2. **d.** The contract is two promises and two performances, so it is bilateral. The contract is intentional between the parties, so it is express. All others are wrong because they include a category that doesn't apply.

3. **c.** This is an illusory gift promise that may be revoked even after acceptance. Leland suffered no burden, so the contract lacks consideration. (a), (b), and (d) are wrong because a legal offer was made and accepted, but no contract was formed.

4. **b.** Renunciation is not a term used in contract law (however, it is a term used in agency law). All other answers result in the termination of an offer.

5. **b.** Contracts involving minors are voidable by the minor (or guardian) due to capacity until the age of majority. Answer choice (a) is wrong because the contract is voidable at the minor's option, not automatically. Answer choice (c) is wrong because there was a bargained-for exchange. Answer choice (d) is wrong because the parties had mutual assent.

CHAPTER 7
Contract Enforceability and Performance

©philsajonesen/Getty Images

Learning Objectives

After studying this chapter, students who have mastered the material will be able to:

7-1	Identify and explain what makes a contract enforceable.
7-2	Define what a condition is used for in a contract and distinguish conditions precedent from conditions subsequent.
7-3	Apply the doctrines related to good faith performance, discharge of a contract, and substantial performance.
7-4	Identify the ethical dilemmas that a manager faces in the context of good faith performance.
7-5	Articulate circumstances that give rise to events of discharge via mutual consent and operation of law.
7-6	Recognize events that result in breach of contract and explain anticipatory repudiation.
7-7	Identify the appropriate remedy available to nonbreaching parties.
7-8	Explain the responsibilities of an injured party to mitigate damages, comply with the clean hands doctrine, and tender performance.
7-9	Describe the rights of third parties in a contract assignment, in a delegation, or as a third-party beneficiary.

Once it has been established that a valid contract has been formed, the next step in the analysis is determining whether the contract is enforceable. So long as a contract is both valid and enforceable, the law imposes certain duties and obligations in performing the contract. In this chapter, we discuss enforceability (genuine assent and the statute of frauds) and issues related to performance and nonperformance (known as *breach*) of a contract.

ENFORCEABILITY

If the parties have formed a valid contract, the analysis turns to **enforceability**. A contract is of little use if it is not enforceable in a court of law, and business owners and managers can reduce risk and the likelihood of exposing their company to unnecessary liability by ensuring that contracts are not only properly formed but legally enforceable. Even if the elements of a contract are met, the contract still must (1) be the product of genuine assent and (2) be in writing under certain circumstances.

Genuineness of Assent

Recall from the discussion in the previous chapter that an agreement must reflect mutual assent (sufficiently definite terms, lack of mistake, etc.) in order to legally form a contract. For a contract to be enforceable, the contract must *also* be the result of **genuine assent**. This means that for a contract to be valid and enforceable, the law requires the parties to have given genuine assent on the terms of the contract. A lack of genuine assent occurs in cases of (1) misrepresentation and fraudulent misrepresentation, (2) duress, (3) undue influence, and (4) unconscionability.

LO 7-1
Identify and explain what makes a contract enforceable.

Misrepresentation When one party to an agreement makes a promise or representation about a material fact that is not true, the other party may avoid the contract on the basis of **misrepresentation**. This is true even if the misrepresenting party doesn't actually know that the promise or representation is false. Consequently, the defense is sometimes called *innocent misrepresentation,* which distinguishes it from *fraudulent misrepresentation* (discussed later). For one party to avoid the contract on the basis of misrepresentation, she must prove (1) the misrepresented fact was *material* (i.e., it concerns a basic assumption in the agreement, or the false representation somehow changes the value of the contract), (2) she *justifiably relied* on the misstatement when forming an agreement (such as determining the price to be paid for a commercial office building), and (3) the misrepresentation was one of *fact* and not just someone's opinion or mere puffing (e.g., "This building's roof is only five years old" is a verifiable fact, whereas "The roof is in great shape" is puffing).

Sometimes it is difficult to distinguish between fact and opinion. In one famous case, a dance student sued her dancing school on the basis of misrepresentations by her instructor who had frequently assured her that she had "excellent potential" for dance so long as she kept purchasing pricey lessons from the dancing school. Eventually, the student sought another teacher, who informed her that she had minimal dance aptitude and could barely detect a musical beat. The dance school argued that the advice was merely opinion and, therefore, could not be the basis for a misrepresentation claim. Nonetheless, the court ruled in favor of the student and reasoned that because the dancing school had "superior knowledge" on the subject, it had a duty to act in good faith in its contract transactions.[1]

Fraudulent Misrepresentation When one party has engaged in conduct that meets the standards for misrepresentation, but that party has actual *knowledge* that the representation is not true, this is known as **fraudulent misrepresentation** (sometimes referred to simply as *fraud*). That is, misrepresentation plus knowledge (also known as *guilty knowledge*[2]) equals fraudulent misrepresentation. The primary difference between misrepresentation and fraudulent misrepresentation, from a manager's perspective, is

> **KEY POINT**
>
> The elements of misrepresentation (materiality, justifiable reliance, and fact) *plus* the element of actual knowledge of the misrepresented fact is considered *fraudulent misrepresentation,* and the innocent party may be entitled to additional recovery.

the relief available to the innocent party. In both cases, the innocent party may *avoid* the contract and be released from any obligations. In cases of misrepresentation, the innocent party has only limited relief in terms of money damages because recovery in many states is limited to any actual out-of-pocket damages. In cases of fraudulent misrepresentation, most states classify the contract as void and the innocent party is generally entitled to recover money damages for any losses incurred plus more for speculative damages such as loss of future profits. Some states go so far as to allow an award of **treble damages**, which are three times the actual damages.

To better understand the difference between innocent misrepresentation and fraudulent misrepresentation, suppose Marshall negotiated to purchase Nino's office building.

---

[1] *Vokes v. Arthur Murray, Inc.*, 212 So. 2d 906 (Fla. Dist. Ct. App. 1968).
[2] The legal term for this type of guilty knowledge is *scienter.*

During the negotiations, Marshall asked Nino if the building had any radon[3] in the underground storage basements. Nino replied that he had owned the building for 10 years and there was no radon. Marshall then agreed to buy the property for $100,000, but before the closing date he found out that radon was present in the basements and that it would cost $15,000 for a radon evacuation system to be installed. In this case, the radon was a material fact (it changed the value of the contract by $15,000), Marshall relied on that fact in calculating the price, and Nino's representation was of a fact that turned out to be false. Marshall may, therefore, avoid the contract based on *innocent misrepresentation*.

However, suppose that after Marshall cancels the contract, Nino finds another party to buy the building (New Buyer). When New Buyer asks Nino about the radon, Nino gets nervous about the sale falling through and lies, saying, "As far as I know, there is no radon." New Buyer may avoid the contract on the basis of fraudulent misrepresentation because Nino's statement fits the requirements for misrepresentation and, unlike in the earlier case, he now has knowledge that his statement is false. Thus, New Buyer will also be entitled to additional money damages from Nino for any losses that New Buyer suffers as a result of the *fraudulent misrepresentation*.

In Case 7.1, a court analyzes a fraudulent misrepresentation claim in the context of promises made by a landlord to a lessee regarding the condition of a building being rented for use as a restaurant.

CASE 7.1 Italian Cowboy Partners, Ltd. v. The Prudential Insurance Company of America, 341 S.W.3d 323 (Tex. 2011)

FACT SUMMARY Jane and Francesco Secchi negotiated a lease for space for purposes of opening the Italian Cowboy restaurant. The negotiations took place through the property manager, Powell, who gave the Secchis various assurances that the leased space was practically new, was in perfect condition, and had no defects. Based on these representations, the Secchis entered into a lease agreement with Prudential (the landlord) for the space and commenced renovations. During this initial period, the Secchis learned that the previous tenant in the space had complained to Powell about a noxious odor that made the space unfit for use. When confronted with the information, Powell denied that the previous tenant had complained and gave further assurances to the Secchis that there had never been a problem with the property. Eventually the odor became sufficiently offensive that the Secchis employed a variety of plumbers and workers to eliminate it, but these attempts were unsuccessful and their restaurant customer base dwindled.

After they confirmed that the former tenant had, in fact, complained about the odor directly to Powell, the Secchis terminated the lease and sued their landlord and property manager for fraudulent misrepresentation. Prudential argued that Powell's representations were puffery and could not be the basis for a material misrepresentation. The trial court ruled in favor of the Secchis, but the court of appeals reversed.

SYNOPSIS OF DECISION AND OPINION The Texas Supreme Court found in favor of the Secchis based on fraud. The fact that Powell had been on the premises and had experienced the odor problems firsthand showed that her statements were made with an intention to hide the truth. The court also ruled that the statements were beyond mere puffery and were in fact material to the contract.

WORDS OF THE COURT: Material Fact "Initially, it defies common sense and any plausible meaning of the word 'problem' to infer from the first two representations that in Prudential's 'opinion,' the sewer gas odor was not a problem for [the previous tenant]. A foul odor is obviously problematic to a restaurant. Testimony indicated

(continued)

---

[3]Radon is an invisible, naturally occurring gas that the EPA has determined to be a risk factor for cancer.

that Powell herself personally experienced the odor and described it as 'almost unbearable' and 'ungodly.' According to its regional manager, [the previous tenant] had even indicated to Powell that it was late in making rent payments because of the odor. In light of the circumstances, we conclude that the statements concealing the odor 'problem' are more properly statements of fact, not pure expressions of opinion. . . . We conclude that as a matter of law, Powell's representations were actionable, and legally sufficient evidence existed to demonstrate that they were known to be false when made."

Case Questions

1. Why did the court determine that the statements made by Powell were material?
3. Should the Secchis have contacted the prior tenant to verify Powell's statements?
3. Because the court found that fraud existed, what remedies and damages are the Secchis entitled to?
4. *Focus on Critical Thinking:* If the Secchis had contacted the prior tenant and found out that a prior problem existed, would that have affected the outcome of this case? Why or why not?

Concealment of Material Fact Although many fraudulent misrepresentations stem from affirmative promises (such as the age of a roof), sometimes a fraudulent misrepresentation occurs when one party *conceals* a material fact. While parties do *not* have a general duty to disclose all information to each other, courts have allowed the use of

---

 Self-Check Fraud and Misrepresentation

For each transaction, does either fraud or misrepresentation exist?

1. Brittany buys a horse from Tex. She buys the horse because Tex tells her that the horse "runs like the wind." In fact, the horse can't run more than 50 yards without stopping to rest.
2. Hawkins is interested in buying Joan's home. He asks her if the roof leaks, and she truthfully answers that she's lived in the home for 13 years and the roof has never leaked. Three days later, it rains and the roof leaks. Hawkins returns a week later, Joan says nothing, and Hawkins purchases the home.
3. Paul bought a used car from John. John had turned back the odometer and changed public records to hide the fact that the car had been in three accidents. One year later, Paul sold the car to George. George bought the car because it had low mileage and public records showed no accidents.
4. Tony is selling his golf clubs. After Mel comes to look at them, he agrees to buy them and leaves for the bank to get cash. When he returns, he pays Tony and puts the golf clubs in his car. Tony and Mel shake hands, and Tony says, "You got a really good deal—these clubs once belonged to Tiger Woods." A week later, Mel discovers that Tiger Woods never owned or used the clubs.
5. Flo is selling her car. The car has an oil leak, so there is oil evident to anyone who looks at the engine. Just before Tom comes over to look at the car, Flo has the engine steam-cleaned. When Tom looks at the engine, it is spotless and he does not ask if it leaks oil.
6. Lisa needs a new battery for her car. The salesperson tells her that the Try-Hard battery is the best battery that money can buy. She always likes things that are the best, so she buys the battery. A week later she discovers that the Try-Hard battery is inferior and is not very well regarded by those who know car batteries.

Answers to this Self-Check are provided at the end of the chapter.

misrepresentation in cases where a party has asserted a half-truth that leads to an overall misrepresentation, where one party takes affirmative action to conceal truth from the other, and where one party fails to correct a past statement that the other party subsequently discovers is untrue.

Duress If one party to a contract uses any form of unfair coercion to induce another party to enter into or modify a contract, the coerced party may avoid the contract on the basis of **duress**. Generally, the law recognizes three categories of duress: (1) violence or threats of a violent act,[4] (2) economic threats such as wrongful termination or threats to breach a contract, and (3) threats of extortion or other threats whereby the other party has no meaningful choice. One important point to consider is that if one party threatens another with a certain act, whether he would ordinarily have the legal right to perform that act is *irrelevant*. This becomes a central principle in a case where some economic duress is at issue. For example, Bloom works for Joyce as an employee-at-will (that is, either party may terminate the employment with or without cause).[5] Joyce threatens to fire Bloom unless he agrees to sell his stock to Joyce for $5 per share. Bloom has no choice, so he sells the stock. A court will allow Bloom to avoid the contract based on this threat even though Joyce has a legitimate right to fire Bloom with or without just cause.

Undue Influence The defense of **undue influence** gives legal relief to a party who has been induced to enter into a contract through the improper pressure of a trusted relationship. Undue influence allows the influenced party to avoid a contract when the court determines that the terms of the contract are *unfair* and the parties had some type of relationship that involved a *fiduciary duty* or some duty to *care* for the influenced party. For example, Edna is a caregiver for June, a wealthy widow who is confined to a wheelchair. Edna informs June that she can no longer be her caregiver unless June signs a contract to assign to Edna $50,000 worth of Microsoft stock. June cannot imagine the thought of being alone or finding another caregiver, so she goes ahead with the contract. In this case, a court would likely allow June to avoid the contract based on the undue influence that Edna had asserted over her.

Unconscionability When an agreement is reached between two parties that have met the required elements and are not subject to the defenses discussed previously, the contract may still potentially be avoided on the grounds that one party suffered a grossly unfair burden that shocks the objective conscience. Recall from our discussion of consideration (in Chapter 6, "Overview and Formation of Contracts") that courts will generally not be inclined to weigh the amount and type of consideration to determine whether the exchange is objectively fair. While this doctrine remains true, the defense of **unconscionability** gives the court the tools to refuse to enforce a contract where the consideration is grossly unequal. For example, in *Waters v. Min Ltd.*,[6] an appellate court allowed one party to avoid a contract in which she signed over an annuity insurance contract with an immediate value in excess of $150,000 in exchange for a check for $50,000. The fully annuitized value of the contract would have been over $530,000. The court ruled that although there was a written contract that met the elements required under the law, the disparity of value in

---

[4]Note that duress is one of the few areas of contract law based on the subjective belief of one of the parties in the agreement. That is, regardless of the form and content of the threats, if the coerced party shows that he was, for example, unusually timid or in an unusually vulnerable state of mind, he may use the duress defense even if an ordinarily reasonable person would not have been intimidated by such threats. *See, generally,* J.D. Calamari, J.M. Perillo & H.H. Bender, *Cases and Problems on Contracts* 309 (4th ed. West/Thomson 2004).

[5]Employment-at-will is discussed in detail in Chapter 11, "Employment Relationships and Labor Law."

[6]587 N.E.2d 231 (Mass. 1992).

the exchange, along with other circumstances such as drug dependency and lack of legal advice, was "too hard of a bargain for a court [to enforce]." While courts apply this defense *very* narrowly, it remains a viable defense when one party has been induced to enter the contract through oppressive terms and no bargaining is possible. Thus, high-pressure sales tactics that mislead illiterate consumers may be one case in which a court would likely allow a party to avoid the contract.[7] Courts have also been suspicious of standardized preprinted contracts, known as *adhesion contracts,* because there is an assumption that the nondrafter has not genuinely bargained for the terms of the agreement. For example, in *Henningsen v. Bloomfield Motors, Inc.,*[8] an appellate court held that a disclaimer of a warranty that was buried in small print in a preprinted agreement to purchase a used car was *void* because the drafter had "gross inequity of bargaining position" and an ordinary person would not be able to fully comprehend what legal rights he was giving up. Therefore, the court held that enforcement of the disclaimer was against public policy. In some cases, courts have held that arbitration clauses contained in contracts are unconscionable.[9] The enforceability of arbitration clauses in contracts is discussed in detail in Chapter 4, "Resolving Disputes: Litigation and Alternative Dispute Resolution."

Statute of Frauds

The **statute of frauds** is the law governing which contracts must be *in writing* in order to be enforceable. As its title suggests, the statute's purpose is to prevent fraud by requiring that certain contracts have written evidence of their existence and terms in order to be enforceable. This is not to say, however, that the statute requires all contracts to be in writing. Nor does it require that the contract writing be in a prescribed format. For example, in one case, courts held that an agreement on a brown piece of wrapping paper written in crayon between an art buyer and an artist was acceptable as an enforceable writing because it contained a signature, noted the quantity, and was supported by circumstances that indicated a contract with the artist for the sale of paintings.[10] The one element that is uniformly required is a *signature of the party* against whom enforcement of the contract is sought.

The statute of frauds primarily applies to five types of contracts:[11]

- Contracts that involve the sale of *interest in land.*
- Contracts that cannot be (i.e., are *not able* to be, by their terms) performed in *under one year.*
- Contracts to pay the *debt of another* (e.g., a loan surety).
- Contracts made in consideration of *marriage* (e.g., a prenuptial agreement).
- Contracts for the *sale of goods for $500 or more* and lease transactions for goods amounting to $1,000 or more (UCC contracts).

> **KEY POINT**
>
> The statute of frauds governs which contracts must be in writing to be enforceable. Although it does not prescribe a particular format, the writing must be signed by the party against whom enforcement is sought.

Case 7.2 is a cautionary tale involving a party's use of the statute of frauds as an affirmative defense to a breach of contract claim.

---

[7] In the landmark case *Frostifresh Corp. v. Reynoso,* 274 N.Y.S.2d 757 (1966), the court held that a contract in which one party sold a freezer to another party who spoke very little English was unconscionable because of unethical sales practices, an oppressive credit installment agreement, and little benefit to the buyer.

[8] 161 A.2d 69 (N.J. 1960).

[9] *Brower v. Gateway 2000, Inc.*, 246 A.D.2d 246 (N.Y. App. Div. 1998).

[10] *Rosenfeld v. Basquit,* 78 F.3d 184 (2d Cir. 1996).

[11] A sixth application (involving executors) exists, but it does not have any implications for business owners or managers.

> ✓ **Self-Check** Statute of Frauds
>
> Which of the following contracts would need to be in writing to be enforceable?
>
> 1. A contract whereby the president of NewCo gives a personal guarantee (i.e., uses personal assets as collateral) for a $150,000 revolving line of credit loan to NewCo from First National Bank.
> 2. An agreement of sale for a piece of real estate for a corporation to build a new warehouse for $500,000.
> 3. A contract for consulting services for $10,000 over the next 90 days.
> 4. A two-year advertising contract between a retail store and a local newspaper.
> 5. Phillip purchases a small piece of land for $499.
>
> *Answers to this Self-Check are provided at the end of the chapter.*

CASE 7.2 Holloway v. Dekkers & Twin Lakes Golf Course, 380 S.W.3d 315 (Tex. Ct. App. 2012)

FACT SUMMARY Twin Lakes is a Texas corporation that operates a golf course located in Canton, Texas; Dekkers is an officer of the corporation. Holloway, a PGA professional, met with Dekkers and others in mid-July 2008 about becoming the head golf professional at Twin Lakes. Dekkers offered Holloway the job, and Holloway agreed to start work as soon as he could move to Texas from Illinois. At the July 2008 meeting, the parties discussed the duration of Holloway's contract, salary, and benefits. The parties then communicated via e-mail throughout the month of July and ultimately agreed to pay and benefit terms. With respect to the duration of the contract, they agreed that Holloway would work for a one-year term with the understanding that prior to the expiration of that period, they would renegotiate the contract for an additional three-year period if Holloway fulfilled Dekkers's performance expectations.

Holloway started work at Twin Lakes on August 5, 2008. Within a week of that date, Holloway was given a one-page employment agreement, dated July 23, 2008, that outlined the salary, benefits, and a bonus structure. The document also listed the services Holloway was to provide. As to term, the document provided for a "[y]early contract that will be up for renewal after annual performance evaluation." It also contained a statement that the contract was agreed upon by both Dekkers and Holloway and "verified by their signatures." Holloway signed the two originals of the document. The signature line for Dekkers as owner of Twin Lakes remained blank. Holloway made a copy of the document, but he never presented it to Dekkers to sign.

Approximately eight weeks later, Holloway was terminated from his employment at Twin Lakes. As a result, he filed suit against both Dekkers and Twin Lakes for breach of contract. The trial court dismissed Holloway's lawsuit on summary judgment, ruling that the employment agreement was unenforceable under the statute of frauds. Holloway appealed, arguing that the statute of frauds did not apply to this agreement because it was for less than one year. He contended the contract's language indicated that Holloway would be employed for 364 days before his performance review, and therefore that it fell outside the statute of frauds.

SYNOPSIS OF DECISION AND OPINION The Court of Appeals of Texas ruled in favor of Dekkers/Twin Lakes. The court rejected Holloway's argument that the agreement was for one day less than a year. In determining whether an agreement is capable of being performed within one year, courts use two points of reference: (1) the time of making the

(continued)

contract and (2) the time when performance is to be completed. In this case, the court pointed out that the agreement exceeded one year no matter whether the starting point was calculated as the date on the employment document or the date Holloway actually began his employment. Because the document did not have the signature of Dekkers, the statute of frauds rendered the contract unenforceable.

WORDS OF THE COURT: One-Year Calculation

"Although Holloway argues on appeal that the agreement was 'clearly intended' to be for a period of 364 days or 'less than a year,' he specifically testified to a one-year agreement that was made in mid-to-late July 2008 and began on August 5, 2008. If Holloway had worked for Twin Lakes for the one-year term as contemplated by the July 23 document, he would have worked through August 4, 2009, one year later. If you counted the days from the July 23 date reflected on the document Holloway signed to the date he completed his performance on August 4, 2009, the term plainly exceeded one year. Thus, to the extent Holloway alleges Dekkers and Twin Lakes breached an agreement based on the July 23 document, that agreement is within the statute of frauds. As a result, the agreement is unenforceable because it is not signed by [Dekkers/Twin Lakes]."

Case Questions

1. Could the combination of e-mails and the unsigned agreement be the basis for satisfying the signature requirement of the statute of frauds? Why or why not?
2. Did the court calculate the date correctly? Couldn't Holloway's performance review/renewal have taken place well before the end of one year? If so, doesn't that mean the contract falls outside of the statute of frauds?
3. *Focus on Critical Thinking:* Is the court allowing Dekkers to use the statute of frauds as a shield to defend a legitimate claim by Holloway? Is that fair? If Dekkers was the one who prepared the document, isn't it reasonable to assume that he agreed to it? Shouldn't it be enforceable? Why or why not?

LEGAL IMPLICATIONS IN CYBERSPACE

E-Mail and the Statute of Frauds

One question that continues to work its way through various state courts and legislatures is to what extent e-mail transmissions can be used to satisfy the statute of frauds. Although states vary in handling this issue, most states do allow e-mails to satisfy the statute of frauds under certain conditions.

For example, Arizona statutes allow an e-mail to satisfy the writing requirement "only to transactions between parties each of which has agreed to conduct transactions by electronic means." Under the Arizona statute, "[w]hether the parties agree to conduct a transaction by electronic means is determined from the context and surrounding circumstances, including the parties' conduct."[12]

In New York, an appellate court ruled that the statute of frauds was satisfied via e-mail for a real estate contract:

> [G]iven the vast growth in the last decade and a half of the number of people and entities regularly using e-mail, we would conclude that the terms "writing" and "subscribed" in [the statute of frauds] should now be construed to include, respectively, records of electronic communications and electronic signatures . . .[13]

---

[12] A.R.S. 44-7005 and 44-7007

[13] *Noldi v. Grunberg*, 2010 NY Slip Op. 07079, at p.2 (decided on October 5, 2010).

Interpretation Rules for Written Contracts In adjudicating disputes concerning the contents of a contract, courts use interpretation rules to guide their analysis. Before signing a written agreement, the parties typically engage in preliminary negotiations that involve discussions and perhaps documents, such as letters or memos, that are intended to help the parties come to an agreement. The **parol evidence rule** provides that any writing intended by the parties to be the *final* expression of their agreement may not be *contradicted* by any oral or written agreements made prior to the writing. Note that the parol evidence rule does not bar admission of the preliminary documents when they are being used to determine the meaning that the parties intended concerning a particular term in the contract.

> **KEY POINT**
>
> Contracts that include restrictive covenants must protect a legitimate business interest of an employer and be reasonable in terms of scope and duration.

STRATEGIC LEGAL SOLUTIONS

Enforcing Covenants Not to Compete

PROBLEM: *How do you protect the company's interests from employees who depart the company in order to directly compete with their ex-employer?*

STRATEGIC SOLUTION: *Use a* **covenant not to compete** *(also called a restrictive covenant) as part of an employment agreement. In such contracts, one party agrees not to compete with another party for a specified period of time. Courts have historically subjected these contracts to close judicial scrutiny. This is not to say that covenants not to compete are unenforceable; rather, courts use a "reasonableness" approach in determining the extent to which the covenant is enforceable. Even if a court finds that the terms of the covenant were unreasonable, most courts will opt to enforce the covenant to the extent required to protect the legitimate interests of the business. For example, Jordan signs a noncompete agreement with Robert, her employer, whereby Jordan agrees not to contact any of Robert's clients anywhere in the United States for two years after she has left Robert's company. After Jordan quits and starts her own firm, Robert finds out that Jordan has been contacting Robert's clients. Robert sues to enforce the covenant. If a court finds the covenant to be too broad, the covenant may be pared back by the court to, say, one year and a more limited geographic region. This is an alternative to striking down the covenant completely.*[14]

Be sure that your company's restrictive covenant agreements are narrowly tailored, keeping the following requirements and standards in mind:

- ***Source:*** Covenants not to compete most often arise out of either (1) the sale of a business, whereby the buyer is purchasing business assets, goodwill, and promises by the seller's principals not to compete with the buyer, or (2) part of an employment contract.

- ***Sale of a business:*** In the context of a sale of a business, courts are willing to enforce such covenants, but they are often focused on the geographic area involved. If the covenant restriction is substantially broader than the area in which the buyer and seller are currently doing business, courts are unwilling to enforce such an overly broad restriction.

- ***Employment agreements:*** Covenants that are part of an employment contract (or an employment relationship) are subjected to a higher degree of scrutiny. Courts will generally permit the employment covenant to stand so long as it is designed to cover a recognized legitimate interest of the employer. Courts recognize an employer's interest in guarding *trade secrets* from being disclosed or used by an ex-employee.[15] Employers also

(continued)

---

[14]Based on Restatement (Second) of Contracts § 184(2) cmt. b, illus. 2.

[15]Generally, a trade secret is a process, a system, or data (e.g., customer lists, formulas) that give a company a competitive edge over another. Trade secrets are covered in depth in Chapter 24, "Intellectual Property."

have a legitimate interest in ensuring that former employees do not act in a way that could *damage relationships* with their existing customers. Therefore, courts have permitted contracts that prevent ex-employees from soliciting (or even contacting) customers of the ex-employer for a certain period of time. However, these types of covenants must be *reasonable* in duration, subject-matter scope, and geographic scope. Although these standards vary from industry to industry, some general guidance regarding reasonableness is helpful.

- **Duration:** The higher the position of the employee, the longer the employer can restrict the employee. A sales staffer who quits after only one year will likely not be bound any more than one or two years. The CEO of a corporation may be bound in the range of five years or more. In any case, the duration must be no greater than is required for the protection of the employer while still considering the potential for undue hardship on the employee.
- **Scope of subject matter:** The restriction must be directly tied to the employee's work responsibilities. For example, if Foley works 10 years as an insurance agent for Garvey's Insurance Agency, the restrictive covenant may cover only a competing interest of insurance sales. Thus, if Foley quits Garvey Insurance, starts a career as a golf instructor, and contacts customers he met while employed by Garvey, a court would not enforce a covenant to prevent this contact because any such restriction is too broad in terms of the scope of the subject matter.
- **Geographic scope:** Employers must limit the geographic area in which the employer conducts business, *and* the geographic region must not impose an undue hardship on the employee. While some companies may legitimately claim that they do business in all 50 states, courts are still reluctant to allow a restriction to be effective countrywide because that would require ex-employees to move abroad in order to comply with the covenant. On the other hand, a small manufacturing company in Philadelphia may wish to restrict its ex-engineering employees from competing within a radius of several miles of the city. This would likely be seen as a protection of legitimate business interests without an undue burden to the employee.

Sometimes contracts contain **ambiguous terms**. In such cases, these terms are construed by the court *against the interest* of the side that drafted the agreement. Courts may also *supply* a reasonable term in a situation where the contract is silent and has **omitted terms**.

NATURE AND EFFECT OF CONDITIONS

Parties to an agreement sometimes wish to allocate or adjust a particular risk associated with performing a contract. This risk allocation is typically accomplished by attaching some event, known as a **condition**, that must occur before a particular performance obligation is triggered. Ordinarily, the parties express such conditions using language such as "on the condition that" or "provided that" or "unless." For example, suppose that Graham hires Frost as a sales representative. The parties agree to a base salary and other basic employment terms. In addition, Graham offers to pay Frost a $1,000 bonus *provided that* Frost secures 10 new accounts during his first 30 days as an employee. Frost is able to secure only nine new accounts in that time period. Therefore, Graham has no duty to perform (pay Frost $1,000) because his duty to pay was conditional on the achievement of the 10 new accounts requirement. Because Frost did not meet the condition set in the agreement, Graham is discharged from his obligation to pay the bonus.

LO 7-2

Define what a condition is used for in a contract and distinguish conditions precedent from conditions subsequent.

Categories of Conditions

A condition is categorized as either a *condition precedent* (an event that must occur *before* performance under a contract is due, as in the Graham-Frost example discussed above) or a *condition subsequent* (an event that occurs after the performance under the contract and discharges the parties' obligations). Assume that Robert interviews with a trucking company for a position as a driver. His employment and start date are conditional upon his producing proof that he possesses a valid commercial driver's license. This requirement is a condition precedent. The requirement that his continued employment is contingent upon retaining his commercial driver's license is a condition subsequent.

Typical conditions precedent in a business context include the delivery, inspection, and approval of merchandise prior to payment being due and the securing of financing prior to the closing of a real estate transaction. Conditions subsequent include passing the bar exam or CPA exam or meeting some other licensing requirement within one year of beginning employment with a company or the ability to secure a zoning permit for a particular business use within 60 days of the date of a contract.

Frequently, a condition subsequent is found in insurance contracts. For example, NewCo enters into a fire insurance contract with Big Carrier Inc. that provides

> No lawsuit for recovery under this contract shall be valid unless the lawsuit is commenced within 12 months of the fire.

A fire destroys NewCo's office, and the company files an immediate claim; however, Big Carrier refuses to pay based on an exclusion in the policy. NewCo takes no further action until 14 months after the fire and then files a lawsuit to recover damages under the policy. A court will dismiss NewCo's claim because Big Carrier is discharged from its obligation to pay (or even to litigate the dispute) by virtue of the time-period condition in the policy.[16] The parties may also agree to *concurrent conditions* whereby each party is required to render performance simultaneously. If Abel contracts with Baker to paint Abel's portrait, the parties may agree that Abel will pay the full price of the contract at the same time as Baker delivers the portrait painting to him. If Baker fails to perform, Abel is no longer obligated to meet his obligation, and he may seek legal redress for any losses suffered as a result.

Modern contract law does not recognize any substantive difference between these categories of conditions.[17] In fact, today most courts do not make any distinction between them. Rather, the law defines a condition as "an event, not certain to occur, which must occur, . . . before the performance under a contract becomes due."[18] Generally, courts do enforce a strict compliance standard for conditions. In *Luttinger v. Rosen*,[19] an appellate court ruled that a condition—namely, that a real estate buyer be able to obtain financing at a certain rate before going through with the purchase—must be strictly applied.

CONCEPT SUMMARY Conditions

- A condition is an event that triggers a particular performance in order to allocate the risk that some part of a contract may not be completed.
- Conditions are normally signaled by phrases such as "only if," "unless," or "provided that."
- A condition is categorized as a condition precedent (an event must occur *before* performance is due), a condition subsequent (an event must occur *after* performance of one party), or a concurrent condition (simultaneous performance).

---

[16]Based on *Abolin v. Farmers American Mutual Life Insurance*, 100 Pa. Super. 433 (1931).

[17]Note, however, that the two differ *procedurally* with respect to who bears the burden of proof.

[18]Restatement (Second) of Contracts § 230.

[19]316 A.2d 757 (Conn. 1972). The contract in question was conditional upon the buyer obtaining a mortgage at a rate not to exceed 8.5 percent. The only lending institutions in the area that would lend to the buyer charged 8.75 percent. Even after the seller offered to subsidize the loan so that the effective rate was 8.5 percent for the buyer, the court held that the buyer's duty to perform was discharged by failure of a condition.

GOOD FAITH PERFORMANCE AND DISCHARGE

If the promises to perform in an agreement are not conditional, the duty to perform is absolute. Most commonly, the parties agree on terms and the parties perform the contractual obligations in **good faith** in order to complete the contract. This completion is known as **discharge** because both parties have now "discharged" their obligation to the other by performing the agreed-upon duties. Performance may also be accomplished by delivering products to an agreed-upon location (such as a warehouse). This is known as *tendering goods* (discussed in detail in Chapter 8, "Contracts for the Sale of Goods"). The law also imposes an affirmative duty of good faith in performing obligations. In every contract, the parties have the duty of good faith and fair dealing in performance and enforcement.[20] Although the good faith requirement is ordinarily met by the parties' simply performing their obligations completely—a situation known as *perfect performance*—the law recognizes that there are some cases in which one party does *not* perform completely yet has still acted in good faith and is entitled to enforce the remaining obligations in the contract against the other party.

LO 7-3

Apply the doctrines related to good faith performance, discharge of a contract, and substantial performance.

LO 7-4

Identify the ethical dilemmas that a manager faces in the context of good faith performance.

BUSINESS ETHICS PERSPECTIVE

Good Faith and the Nuclear Condition Option

Note that while the law imposes a good faith requirement on all contracting parties, as a practical matter the law may also protect those who are ostensibly acting in good faith but may have unethical motives. In some contracts, the parties agree to a conditional clause sometimes known as a *nuclear condition,* that is, a clause whereby one party may cancel the contract completely if a condition is not met to that party's subjective satisfaction. Consider the case in which the president of WidgetCo assigns Manager to purchase a piece of real estate. Manager enters into a contract with Owner for the sale of a piece of commercial real estate. Manager insists that the contract contain an "acceptable financing" clause as follows: "As a specific condition precedent to WidgetCo's obligation to close, the parties agree that WidgetCo must obtain financing for the transaction on terms and conditions acceptable to WidgetCo in WidgetCo's sole discretion."

After entering into the agreement with Owner, the president notifies Manager that WidgetCo is no longer interested in the property and that Manager is to use all "legal means" necessary to break the contract with Owner. Assume that Manager also learns that WidgetCo is able to obtain financing on extremely favorable terms according to industry standards.

1. Given that the contract requires that any financing terms must be acceptable to WidgetCo, what are Manager's legal obligations to go through with the transaction? Does this differ from Manager's ethical obligations?

2. Is it possible for Manager to comply with the good faith requirement and still avoid the contract with Owner?

3. Recall the discussion of ethical decision-making models in Chapter 5, "Business Ethics, Corporate Social Responsibility, and Law." How could these models help guide Manager's course of action?

4. Assume that the president orders Manager to lie on the loan application, thereby ensuring that any financial institution will reject the loan application. Note that lying on a bank loan application is a crime. What are Manager's options at that point?

5. Is this a case where using the nuclear option is simply a good, hard-nosed business practice? Are there any circumstances you could articulate under which Manager has no legal obligation but does have an ethical obligation to Owner?

---

[20]Restatement (Second) of Contracts § 205.

Substantial Performance

In some situations, the parties agree to terms of a contract and pursue good faith performance, but one party cannot give perfect performance. The law recognizes a party's good faith effort to *substantially perform* her obligations by allowing the **substantial performance** to satisfy the requirements of the agreement and trigger the other party's obligation to perform. In order to prevail in a substantial performance case, the party trying to enforce the contract must show that she acted in good faith and that any deviation from the required performance was not **material**. In this context, *material* refers to some deviation from the contract that results in a substantial change in the value of the contract or that changes a fundamental basis of the agreement. Suppose that a retailer has contracted to purchase 500 pairs of jeans and 500 T-shirts from a clothing manufacturer. Despite a good faith effort, only the jeans and 400 T-shirts can be delivered. Because the delivered jeans and T-shirts can be sold without the missing 100 T-shirts, the missing T-shirts will not be material to the overall contract and the contract will be considered substantially performed.

Note that although the doctrine of substantial performance allows a party to meet her obligations in a contract through less-than-perfect performance, the innocent party is still entitled to collect *damages* to compensate for the imperfect performance. Generally, courts allow the substantially performing party to be paid the full amount of the contract price (or other performance due) *less* any costs suffered. Therefore, in the example discussed above, the clothing manufacturer will be paid only for the jeans and 400 T-shirts. Landmark Case 7.3, known as the *Reading Pipe* case, has been used for decades as a guidepost for applying the doctrine of substantial performance.

 Self-Check Substantial Performance

Which of the following constitute substantial performance?

1. Wholesaler contracts with Delicatessen to deliver 50 cases of bottled beverages each week in exchange for a $3,000 monthly payment. Due to heavy holiday volume, the December shipment contains only 45 cases.
2. The Yellow Pages agrees to publish a half-page advertisement for Local Dry Cleaner in exchange for $2,000. The advertisement is published, but one digit in the telephone number is incorrect.
3. A vegetable cannery contracts with Farmer to buy 54 units of "fancy-grade" spinach, defined as "dark green in color, firm in texture, and with a leaf/stem ratio of less than 15 percent stem." Farmer delivers spinach with a leaf/stem ratio of 25 percent stem.
4. Widower contracts with Artist to paint a portrait of his late wife. The portrait is done on time and professionally, but the likeness, while resembling her, does not look exactly like the woman.
5. Book publisher agrees to sell and deliver certain named textbooks to a college bookstore with delivery on July 1, eight weeks before classes are to begin. Delivery occurs on July 5.

Answers to this Self-Check are provided at the end of the chapter.

LANDMARK CASE 7.3 Jacob & Youngs v. Kent, 129 N.E. 889 (N.Y. 1921)

FACT SUMMARY Kent contracted with Jacob and Youngs (JY) for the construction of Kent's vacation home in upstate New York. The contract required JY to use "standard pipe of Reading manufacture." During the construction, one of the JY subcontractors mistakenly used some pipe made by other manufacturers. Just before the construction was complete, Kent's architect discovered the mistake and directed JY to remove the non-Reading pipe. However, the pipe was already sealed off and encased within the walls, and, thus, costly demolition would have been necessary to repair the mistake. JY claimed that the substitute pipe was the same in terms of quality, appearance, market value, and cost as the Reading pipe. Thus, JY completed construction but refused to fix the pipe mistake. Kent refused to pay the remaining balance on the contract, and JY sued to recover the amount due.

SYNOPSIS OF DECISION AND OPINION The court ruled in favor of JY under the doctrine of substantial performance. In its opinion, the court focused on practical application to obtain fairness rather than a strict application of performance requirements and pointed out that trivial and innocent omissions may not always be a breach of a condition. Although there are limits to the substantial performance doctrine, in this case the omission of the Reading pipe was not the result of fraud or willfulness. Moreover, there was no evidence of substantial change in the value of the contract.

WORDS OF THE COURT: Applying Substantial Performance "Where the line is to be drawn between important and trivial cannot be settled by formula.... Nowhere will change be tolerated, however, if it is so dominant or pervasive as in any real or substantial measure to frustrate the purpose of the contract.... We must weigh the purpose to be served, the desire to be gratified, and the excuse for the deviation by the letter, and the cruelty of enforced adherence."

Case Questions

1. A dissenting opinion in this case pointed out that JY's failing to use the correct pipe was grossly negligent and, thus, JY should bear the costs of reinstalling the Reading pipe. Does that strike you as convincing? Why or why not?
2. *Focus on Critical Thinking:* If Kent had a vested interest in the use of Reading pipe (suppose Kent was the heir to the Reading pipe fortune), what condition could he have inserted in the agreement that would have ensured the use of Reading-brand pipe?

In the *Jacob & Youngs v. Kent* case, the court ruled that a contractor's substitution of non-Reading-brand pipe during construction of a home constituted substantial performance.
Brand X/Fotosearch

LO 7-5

Articulate circumstances that give rise to events of discharge via mutual consent and operation of law.

OTHER EVENTS OF DISCHARGE

As discussed earlier in this chapter, in a contract, the most common way for the parties to discharge their obligations is by good faith performance. However, there are other circumstances under which the parties may be discharged from obligations. Parties may be discharged via **mutual consent** or **operation of law**.

Mutual Consent

If neither party has fully performed, the parties may agree to cancel the contract. This cancellation is known as a **rescission**, and each party gives up rights under the contract in exchange for the release by the other party from performing their obligations. For example, Earl hires Peter to paint his office lobby for $1,000. The fee is to be paid in a lump sum upon Peter completing the entire lobby. After beginning work and painting one wall, Peter realizes that he vastly underestimated the time and supplies necessary to make the job profitable and he now has another customer across town where he could make a profit. So long as Peter offers to rescind the contract and Earl accepts, the contract is canceled and Peter no longer has to perform. At the same time, despite the fact that Earl's lobby has been partially painted, Earl does not have to pay any sums due under the original contract.[21] It is important to note that rescission occurs only if both parties agree to rescind. A unilateral rescission, by only one party, is not permitted.

In some cases, the parties to a contract agree to accept performance that is different from the originally promised performance. Under the doctrine of **accord and satisfaction**, one party agrees to render a *substitute performance* in the future (known as *accord*), and the other party promises to accept that substitute performance in discharge of the existing performance obligation. Once the substitute performance has been rendered, this acts as a *satisfaction* of the obligation. Note that discharge of the obligation occurs only when the terms of the accord are actually performed. If the accord performance is *not* rendered, the other party has the option to recover damages either under the original contract or under the accord contract. For example, in the Earl-Peter painting contract, suppose that Peter finishes the job but Earl does not have the $1,000 fee to pay Peter in one lump sum. Therefore, Earl offers to pay Peter $1,100 in 60 days and Peter accepts. The new agreement on payment terms is an *accord*. Once Earl has paid the $1,100 in 60 days, his accord will be *satisfied* and Peter will not be able to sue for any damages that he may have suffered as a result of Earl's failing to pay as originally agreed in the contract.[22]

The parties to a contract may also discharge their obligations by replacing the original contract with a **substitute agreement**, also known as a **modification**. The substitute agreement is generally used to compromise when two parties have a dispute as to performance of the contract and wish to amend its terms. The substituted agreement, unlike the accord agreement discussed above, *immediately* discharges any obligations under the original contract. For example, in the Earl–Peter painting contract, suppose that Earl and Peter enter into a substitute agreement whereby Earl agrees to pay $1,100 in 60 days so long as Peter agrees to extinguish the $1,000 debt immediately. If Earl does not perform (by paying), then Peter now has only one option: to recover for damages under the *substitute agreement*. He cannot recover damages under the original agreement. Earl's obligation to pay the $1,000 sum at conclusion of the work was immediately discharged by the substitute agreement.

---

[21]Based on Restatement (Second) of Contracts § 283, illus. 1.

[22]Because an accord does not discharge the previous contractual duty as soon as the accord is made, if Earl does not perform the accord agreement, Peter may recover damages from Earl under either the original contract obligation ($1,000 lump sum due upon completion) or the accord agreement ($1,100 in 60 days from completion).

When the parties agree to substitute a third party for one of the original parties to the contract, the agreement may be discharged through **novation**. Essentially, a novation is a kind of substitute agreement that involves a substitute third *party* rather than a substitute promise. A novation revokes and *discharges* all of the replaced party's obligations under the old contract. For example, in the Earl-Peter painting contract, suppose that Peter starts work and the next day he receives an offer from another customer for a major painting job. Peter proposes to Earl that Pablo (another painter who Peter knows does excellent work) complete the painting work under the original contract. If Earl then agrees to allow Peter to substitute Pablo for the performance of the lobby-painting duties articulated in the original Earl-Peter contract, then a novation has occurred and Peter is now discharged from his obligation to perform the Earl-Peter contract. Earl is bound only by the new novation terms with Pablo.

STRATEGIC LEGAL SOLUTIONS

Understanding Check Deposits as Accord and Satisfaction

PROBLEM: *In some cases, a business may inadvertently agree to an accord by simply depositing a check.*

Managers must have a fundamental understanding of this concept and businesses should have mechanisms in place to avoid an accidental accord and satisfaction claim. For example, General Contractor Inc. (GCI) contracts with Windows R Us (WRU) to install specially designed windows in a new office building, constructed by GCI, for a total of $100,000 to be paid after services are completed. After WRU installs the windows, GCI notifies the contractor that it is dissatisfied with the installation work. WRU claims that the windows were installed to industry standards and demands payment. GCI then sends a check for $50,000 (half of what is owed to WRU under the contract) to WRU's office. The check contains the indorsement "Payment in Full for Installation Services at the Office Center Site."

STRATEGIC SOLUTION: *Consider WRU's options and the consequences of each option.*

- *Deposit the check as is.* In most states, this option would result in an accord and satisfaction. When GCI sent the check with a restrictive indorsement, in effect it offered to render a substitute performance in the future (pay $50,000 instead of $100,000) as an accord agreement. Most courts view depositing a check as an affirmative acceptance of that accord offer; thus, when the check has cleared the bank's processing, it is considered a satisfaction of the accord agreement and WRU cannot sue for damages.

- *Write "Under Protest" under the check and deposit it.* In most states, this option would result in an accord and satisfaction. Just as in the previous option, when GCI sends the check with a restrictive indorsement, in effect it has offered to render a substitute performance in the future (pay $50,000 instead of $100,000) as an accord agreement. Most courts view depositing a check as an affirmative acceptance of an accord offer regardless of any attempt by the receiving party to unilaterally alter the check. Thus, writing the words "in protest" ordinarily has no effect. When the check has cleared the bank's process, it is considered a satisfaction of the accord agreement and WRU cannot sue for damages.

- *Strike out the "payment in full" language with a black marker and then deposit the check.* The result of this option is the same as above. Unilateral attempts by the offeree to alter the substitute-offer check will not bar GCI's discharge through accord and satisfaction.

- *Return the check to GCI with a letter stating that the offer is rejected and demanding full payment.* This is the only method that will fully protect WRU from accepting the accord via satisfaction. By returning the check with an affirmative statement that the substitute accord has been rejected, WRU makes it clear that no satisfaction has occurred. It may now sue for damages if appropriate.

Operation of Law

Contract obligations also may be discharged through *operation of law*. Despite the fact that the parties have fulfilled the requirements to form a valid contract, the law provides a discharge under certain circumstances where fairness demands it.

In some cases, after the parties have formed a contract, unexpected events occur that affect the probability of one party's ability to perform. In such cases, the law allows the parties to be excused from performance under the contract. Courts analyze these special circumstances according to three separate doctrines: **impossibility**, **impracticability**, and **frustration of purpose**.

Impossibility

After the parties have entered an agreement, the contemplated performance of the obligations may become impossible and, therefore, may be subject to discharge. When encountering a situation in which one party is claiming impossibility, it is important for managers to understand that the impossibility must be *objective* (a reasonable person would consider the obligation impossible to perform) rather than *subjective* (one party decides unilaterally that performance is impossible) in order for the obligation to be discharged.[23] This can sometimes be a tricky distinction, and the modern trend of courts is against allowing impossibility as a defense unless it fits into one of four intervening events:

1. *Destruction* of the subject matter: A promises to sell B 1,000 widgets to be delivered on Tuesday. On Monday, a fire destroys the widgets. A is discharged from her obligation to provide the widgets.
2. *Death or incapacitation* of one of the parties to the contract:[24] A promises to paint B's portrait. Prior to the sitting date for the portrait, A becomes incapacitated. A is discharged from his obligation to paint the portrait.
3. The *means of performance* contemplated in the contract cannot be performed: W, a wholesaler, agrees to sell R, a retailer, 5,000 widgets. Prior to the W-R contract, W contracted with M, a manufacturer, to supply him with 10,000 widgets. M halts production and cannot produce the widgets for W. W may be discharged from performance (unless the parties agreed otherwise about risk allocation).
4. Performance of the obligation has become *illegal* subsequent to the contract but prior to performance: Importer promises to buy 1,000 cigars from Producer, a manufacturer in the Dominican Republic. Subsequent to the agreement, but before Producer ships the cigars, Congress passes a federal statute imposing a complete trade embargo on the Dominican Republic. Importer and Producer are discharged from performance based on impossibility.

Legal Speak >))

Supervening Illegality
A supervening illegality occurs when the performance of a contract becomes illegal subsequent to the contract formation but prior to performance.

Sometimes performance is *temporarily impossible* for one or both parties. The illness of a party who is to perform unique personal services may prevent her from performing on a timeline contemplated by the parties. However, in most cases, an illness will not prevent the performance forever. The doctrine of impossibility operates to *suspend* (not discharge) the obligation to perform until the impossibility ceases. Note that an exception to this general rule occurs when, after the temporary impossibility ends, the performance is considerably more burdensome than it would have been if the parties had performed on time (i.e., the lapse of time affected the parties' abilities to perform). Courts then will allow the obligation of the burdened party to be discharged.

---

[23] Restatement (Second) of Contracts § 261 cmt. c. Comment c distinguishes between the two standards by giving an example of objective impossibility ("the thing cannot be done") versus subjective impossibility ("I cannot do it").

[24] Note that unless a contract for services calls for *unique personal* services, it cannot be discharged via impossibility. The law contemplates that nonunique personal services should simply be delegated to another appropriate substitute party.

Impracticability There are certain agreements under which, although performance is not objectively impossible (as defined above), performance becomes extremely burdensome due to some unforeseen circumstance occurring between the time of agreement and the time of performance. If the burden is both *unforeseeable and extreme,* courts may allow the burdened parties' obligations to be discharged before performance. Suppose that Ace Pools contracts with Homeowner to install an in-ground pool on her property. Ace is a small company but is profitable because it can complete two pools a week during the spring, summer, and fall seasons. It has installed numerous pools in the neighborhood without any complications. Prior to signing the contract, Ace does a preliminary test dig and finds no impediments to excavation. Once it begins actual excavation, however, Ace discovers that 80 percent of Homeowner's property is solid rock beginning three feet below the surface. In order to successfully install the pool, explosives must be used, requiring a series of permits and the hiring of demolition experts. This will triple the contract cost and tie up Ace Pools for 30 days at the job site. If Homeowner does not want to pay the additional cost and Ace does not want to lose business by being at one site for 30 days, Homeowner and Ace may mutually agree to rescind the contract and end both of their obligations under the contract. But what if Homeowner decides that he wants the pool installed despite the increased time and cost? Can Ace be required to complete the contract? Ace will be able to claim that the impracticality of losing approximately eight jobs in order to complete this single job is too burdensome and will harm the company. Ace's past experience in the neighborhood and its preliminary experimental dig will be evidence that the burden caused by the rock was both unforeseen and extreme, excusing Ace from performance due to impracticability.

In Case 7.4, a state appellate court discussed the doctrine of impossibility in a construction case in which the parties dispute the impact of a *force majeure* clause.

Legal Speak >))

Force Majeure
A term recognized in modern law that derives from French law meaning an event or act that is impossible to anticipate or control (e.g., severe weather or civil conflicts).

CASE 7.4 Holder Construction Group v. Georgia Tech Facilities, Inc., 282 Ga. App. 796 (2006)

FACT SUMMARY Holder Construction Group, LLC (Holder), entered into a contract with Georgia Tech Facilities (GTF) for the construction of the Georgia Tech Family Apartments project. Under this contract, Holder assumed the obligation to construct the project for a guaranteed maximum price. This is known as a construction-manager-at-risk contract, under which Holder bears the risk for performance deficiencies, construction delays, and cost overruns. The parties also negotiated a clause in the contract concerning any delay of performance by including the following *force majeure* clause:

> *If Construction Manager* [Holder] *shall be unable to perform or shall be delayed in the performance of any of the terms and provisions of this Agreement as a result of (i) governmental preemption of materials in connection with a national emergency declared by the President of the United States; (ii) riot,* insurrection, or other civil disorder affecting performance of the Work; or (iii) unusual and extreme weather conditions constituting Acts of God, then, and in any such event, such inability or delay shall be excused, and the time for completing the affected portions of the Project shall be extended.

After construction on the project had begun, Holder experienced difficulties due to an increase in steel prices and the late delivery of steel materials. Because of these problems, Holder requested a 67-day time extension. GTF denied the request. Holder then filed a declaratory judgment action, arguing that it was entitled to an adjustment of more than $1 million in the contract price due to cost overruns and a time extension of no less than 63 days for completing the project.

The trial court granted summary judgment in favor of GTF, and Holder appealed the decision.

(continued)

SYNOPSIS OF DECISION AND OPINION The Georgia appellate court affirmed the decision of the trial court and allocated the risk of steel price increases and shipment delays to Holder. The court analyzed the *force majeure* provision in the context of delays and found that the sudden price increase fell outside of the *force majeure* clause. The court held that price increases are purely economic and cannot be classified as unforeseeable under the doctrine of impossibility. Absent a price escalation plan in the contract, the risk falls on Holder.

WORDS OF THE COURT: Risk for Delay "It is undisputed that the late delivery of the steel was not the result of any of the causes stated in the 'Force Majeure' clause.

"The contract goes on to state that late deliveries of materials, for reasons other than those set out in the 'Force Majeure' clause, 'do not constitute reason for extending the Date for Final Completion' and it is the construction manager's responsibility to make adequate provision for this when scheduling the work. . . . Accordingly, under the contract, Holder bore the risk of the late delivery of the steel because it was not due to any of the reasons set out in the 'Force Majeure' clause. . . .

"Likewise, GTF was entitled to summary judgment on Holder's claim for damages due to the rise in steel prices. As the trial court held, the contract did not contain [a price] escalation clause, and Holder had already been paid from the construction contingency fund for this claim."

Case Questions

1. How might have Holder avoided the risk of bearing the unforeseen and significant increase in steel prices?
2. If you are Holder, how would you rewrite this contract to avoid liability in the future?
3. *Focus on Critical Thinking:* If the parties had left out the *force majeure* clause, how would the case have been decided?

KEY POINT

For a contract to be discharged under impracticability, the burden must be *unforeseeable* and *extreme* in terms of cost.

Frustration of Purpose In some cases, events may occur that destroy a party's *purpose* in entering into the contract even though performance of the contract itself is not objectively impossible. When one party's purpose is completely or almost completely frustrated by such supervening events, courts will discharge that party from performance.[25] Frustration of purpose may be used to discharge an obligation if, after the parties enter into an agreement, (1) a party's *principal purpose* is substantially frustrated without her fault; (2) some event occurs, when the *nonoccurrence* of the event was a central assumption of both parties when entering into the contract; and (3) the parties have not otherwise agreed on who bears the risk of such an occurrence. Just as with impracticability, frustration of purpose requires the burdened party to show that the event was unforeseeable and extreme. For example, Padraig contracts with White Hall Inn to rent a room that faces Main Street for a period of two days. Padraig's intent is to have a balcony view of the street to see the St. Patrick's Day parade. One week before the parade is scheduled, White Hall sends Padraig a confirmation of the agreement:

> Confirmed: Balcony Room at White Hall Inn (Guaranteed view of Main Street) for Padraig. $200 per night (St. Patrick's Day Parade Special). Two days. $100 deposit due in 5 days—Balance due upon checkout.

Padraig signs the letter and sends it back with a $100 bill. Much to Padraig's dismay, the St. Patrick's Day Committee cancels the parade due to a last-minute regulatory problem

---

[25]Restatement (Second) of Contracts § 265.

in obtaining a permit. Padraig cancels his reservation. If Padraig sues for his $100 to be refunded (contending that his obligation has been discharged by virtue of frustration of purpose) and White Hall countersues for the $300 balance owed (contending that Padraig can still use the room even if there is no parade), who will prevail? It is likely that Padraig will prevail because the letter sent by White Hall *acknowledges* that the primary purpose of the contract is to have the balcony view of the parade. Assuming a court finds that the parade cancellation was reasonably unforeseeable, was not the fault of Padraig, and was a basic assumption of the agreement, Padraig would prevail due to frustration of purpose.[26]

Consider, alternatively, that the parties had agreed on risk allocation through the use of language in the letter such as, "In the event that the St. Patrick's Day parade does not take place for any reason, the parties agree that Padraig will pay only 50 percent of the full price for the room whether he uses the room or not. Such amount shall be due on the checkout date." In that event, a court will very likely consider the parties to have bargained away any notion of frustration (or impossibility for that matter) as an event of discharge and, thus, enforce the agreed-upon terms.

The parties may also be discharged through operation of law when (1) a contract is **unilaterally altered** by a party (the other party is discharged from performing); (2) a contract is subject to relief of the **Bankruptcy** Code (the debtor is entitled to complete discharge from any contract once the bankruptcy filing has been approved by a court); or (3) the **statute of limitations** (also known as the *statute of repose* in certain states), where state law imposes a time limit on enforcement of contract obligations, has expired.

CONCEPT SUMMARY Performance and Discharge

- If two parties to a contract complete their performances in a manner that is faithful to the mutual goals of the contract, and in good faith, perfect performance has occurred and it will result in a discharge for both parties.
- If a party substantially performs only essential duties of the contract, a court will enforce the agreement; however, the party remains liable for anything left undone.
- A party may be discharged from the original terms of the contract by a mutual consent to rescission, a substitute performance, or a modification to the original agreement.
- A party may be discharged from the original terms of the contract by the operation of law if the contract has become impossible (no one can do it) or impracticable (I can't do it) or if its purpose has been frustrated (why would I want to do it now?).

BREACH OF CONTRACT AND ANTICIPATORY REPUDIATION

LO 7-6

Recognize events that result in breach of contract and explain anticipatory repudiation.

When a party to an agreement owes a duty to perform and fails to fulfill her obligation, she is said to have **breached** the contract. In cases where the breach is material (i.e., relates to a fundamental term of the contract or has an effect on the value of the contract), it is

---

[26]Based on the landmark case *Krell v. Henry* [1903] 2 KB 740 (Eng.). This is commonly known as the *coronation case* because it involved room reservations to view a parade in connection with the coronation of the king of England. When the king fell ill, Henry refused to use the premises or make payment. When the landlord, Krell, sued, the court ruled in favor of Henry, and the doctrine of frustration of purpose had its modern-day launch.

called a *total breach* and the nonbreaching party is entitled to either suspend performance or be discharged from his obligations completely. The party that suffered the breach is also entitled to sue the breaching party in an attempt to recover *money damages*. Money damage awards are one of the ways in which the law provides a method to compensate the nonbreaching party for losses suffered. These methods are known as **remedies**. Remedies are discussed later in this chapter.

There are some cases in which the breach is not material; this is sometimes referred to as a *partial breach*.[27] In such cases, the nonbreaching party may not be relieved from performing; however, the nonbreaching party may still recover damages related to the breach from the breaching party. Recall the *Jacob & Youngs v. Kent* (*Reading Pipe*) case earlier in the chapter. In that case, the court decided that because the deviation from expected performance was not material, it was only a partial breach. Because the breach was partial, the court awarded the nonbreaching party damages equal to the difference in price between the Reading-brand pipe and the pipe actually used.

Anticipatory Repudiation

After the parties have entered into an agreement but before performance has occurred, it sometimes becomes apparent that one party does not intend to perform as agreed. This may be apparent through the party's words or conduct. Under certain circumstances, the law provides an avenue of recovery for the nonbreaching party even *before* the nonperforming party actually breaches the contract or even before the performance is due. For example, on December 15, Manager enters into an agreement with Consultant to provide operation-consulting services for a period of six months to commence January 2. On December 20, Manager is told to cut costs, so Manager contacts Consultant in an e-mail: "Dear Consultant: We don't require your services. Sorry. —Manager." At this point, Manager has not technically breached the contract because performance is not due until January 2. However, Consultant would still be entitled to sue immediately for damages (or other remedies if appropriate) under the doctrine of **anticipatory repudiation**, without waiting for the actual breach to occur on January 2.

When one party uses unequivocal language (such as in the Manager-Consultant contract in the preceding paragraph) to repudiate, there is no question that the other may file suit immediately. Any threatened breach must be a material, or a total, breach (discussed earlier) for the nonbreaching party to exercise its right to claim an anticipatory repudiation.

In cases where the language is more ambiguous or when conduct is the basis for determining the repudiation, the analysis is more complex. Modern courts have held that repudiation occurs in one of three ways:

- A *statement* by one party of her intent not to perform. Note that the statement must be such that a reasonable person would have believed that the promisor is *quite unlikely* to perform. Vague doubts about the statements are insufficient.[28]
- An *action* by the promisor that renders her performance impossible. For example, A agrees to sell an office building to B with conveyance in 30 days. Several days later B learns that A subsequently sold and conveyed the building to C. B may sue immediately for A's breach and need not wait the full 30-day period in the contract.
- Knowledge by the parties that one party may be *unable* to perform despite both parties' best efforts.

Enforcing rights under anticipatory repudiation can be crucial to some businesses, particularly if the business depends on products needed as components in its own manufacturing

Legal Speak >))

Anticipatory Breach
An *anticipatory repudiation* is also commonly referred to as an *anticipatory breach*. The two terms are synonymous.

---

[27] Arthur Linton Corbin, *Corbin on Contracts* § 1374 (1963).

[28] Note that under a UCC sales contract, a potentially aggrieved party may ask for "assurances" of performance even for doubts. A right to assurances is covered in Chapter 8, "Contracts for the Sale of Goods."

process. Suppose that a doll manufacturer has contracted with a company to produce and deliver 100,000 plastic eyes to be installed on its product. Delivery is scheduled for September 1, which will allow the doll company to install the eyes and ship the finished dolls to retailers in time for the holiday sales season, the company's primary source of profit. On August 1, the doll company discovers that the eye manufacturer has sold its entire stock of plastic eyes to another doll company for a higher profit and will not be able to complete its contract. By claiming an anticipatory repudiation, the doll company will not have to wait until September 1 before the actual breach occurs. It will be able to find another company to supply the needed plastic eyes, salvaging its top selling season. If the second company sells the plastic eyes at a higher price than the first, the doll company will be able to sue the original manufacturer for the difference.

In Case 7.5, a state supreme court analyzes whether one party is entitled to damages after claiming anticipatory repudiation by another party.

CASE 7.5 Thomas v. Montelucia Villas, LLC, 302 P.3d 617 (Ariz. 2013)

FACT SUMMARY In 2006, Ralph and Carolee Thomas (Thomas) signed a contract with Montelucia Villas, LLC (Montelucia), for the construction of a custom villa for $3,295,000. As part of the purchase agreement, Thomas made three installment deposits totaling $659,000, representing 20% of the villa's purchase price. The remainder of the purchase price was due when Thomas took title to the completed villa. The contract characterized the payments as "earnest money deposits." The contract also provided that Montelucia could retain the payments as damages if Thomas breached the construction agreement.

On April 25, 2008, Montelucia notified Thomas by letter that it had set the closing date of May 16 to transfer title to the villa in exchange for payment of the remainder of the purchase price from Thomas. When the letter was sent, Montelucia did not have a certificate of occupancy for the property, which the contract required as a condition for closing. Thomas responded on May 6 with a letter stating that they would not close on May 16 and they were terminating the purchase contract alleging that Montelucia had not performed its obligations and had violated Arizona statutes governing the sale of subdivided land. The Thomas letter asked Montelucia to return the $659,000 in deposits. Montelucia did not respond to the letter or refund the deposits. Instead, it unsuccessfully attempted to obtain a certificate of occupancy for the property on May 8 and May 14.

Montelucia ultimately obtained the certificate on August 27.

In February 2009, Thomas sued to recover the deposits. Montelucia counterclaimed for breach of contract. Although the trial court ruled in favor of Thomas, the court of appeals reversed and ruled that Thomas had anticipatorily repudiated the contract by sending the May 6 letter. Thomas appealed.

SYNOPSIS OF DECISION AND OPINION The Arizona Supreme Court reversed the decision of the court of appeals and remanded the case to a lower court. The court ruled that although the doctrine of anticipatory breach could be applied in this case, damages for the nonbreaching party turned on whether Montelucia was ready, willing, and able to perform its obligations. Because there was a factual dispute as to whether Montelucia would have been able to perform, the court ordered the trial court to determine whether Montelucia was able to close in accordance with the contract. If it was ultimately determined that Montelucia was ready, willing, and able to perform as required by the contract, the court could then determine the appropriate remedy available to Montelucia under the contract.

WORDS OF THE COURT: Ready and willing to perform "An anticipatory repudiation is a breach of contract giving rise to a claim for damages and also excusing the necessity for the non-breaching

(continued)

party to tender performance. Yet, an anticipatory breach, by itself, does not entitle the injured party to damages. To recover damages, '[i]n addition to proving repudiation, the non-breaching party need only show that he would have been ready and willing to have performed the contract, if the repudiation had not occurred.' Thus, '[a] party's duty to pay damages for total breach by repudiation is discharged if it appears after the breach that there would have been a total failure by the injured party to perform his return promise.'"

Case Questions
1. Why did Montelucia claim that the May 6 letter was an anticipatory repudiation of the contract?
2. Is the fact that Montelucia ultimately obtained a certificate of occupancy important? Why or why not?
3. *Focus on Critical Thinking:* Ultimately, the villa was completed and Thomas refused to pay. Is Thomas trying to use a technicality in the law as a shield from contractual obligations?

CONCEPT SUMMARY Breach of Contract

- Total breach occurs when one party fails to perform its duties under the contract; partial breach is a failure to perform that is not substantial enough to discharge the nonbreaching party.
- Repudiation occurs by a statement that, reasonably interpreted, communicates nonperformance; an action that makes performance impossible; or knowledge by the parties that one party will be unable to perform.
- The doctrine of anticipatory repudiation allows a nonbreaching party to suspend performance and recover damages before performance is due if the other party has made an unequivocal statement or action suggesting that performance will not occur.

REMEDIES AT LAW

LO 7-7

Identify the appropriate remedy available to nonbreaching parties.

The law provides certain relief for aggrieved parties that suffer losses as a result of another party's breach of contract. These relief mechanisms are collectively referred to as *remedies*. Recall the distinction discussed in Chapter 1, "Legal Foundations," between *remedies at law* and *remedies in equity*. For most contracts, the remedy at law will be **money damages** awarded by the court to the nonbreaching party. This is simply a legal mechanism for compelling the breaching party to compensate the innocent party for losses related to the breach. In a contract claim, money damages are primarily limited to (1) *compensatory* (also called *direct* or *actual*) *damages*, (2) *consequential damages*, (3) *restitution*, and (4) *liquidated damages*.[29]

Compensatory Damages

Compensatory damages cover a broad spectrum of losses for recovery of *actual damages* suffered by the nonbreaching party. These damages are an attempt to put the nonbreaching party in the same position she would have been in if the other party had performed as

---

[29]Two other forms of civil damages recognized as a remedy at law are punitive damages (intended to deter conduct and/or punish a wrongdoer) and nominal damages (a breach exists, but no actual damages have been suffered). However, these forms of damages are rare in contract cases.

agreed. This includes such sums as out-of-pocket damages and even potential profits that would have been earned if performance had occurred. For example, BigCo hires LowPrice to prepare BigCo's tax returns and financial statements in time for BigCo's shareholders meeting on March 1 for a fee of $5,000. On February 15, the principal of LowPrice notifies BigCo that she cannot prepare the returns because she has decided to switch careers and shut down the tax practice. BigCo must then hire HighPrice to prepare the documents. Because of the short timeline, HighPrice charges a fee of $12,000. BigCo is entitled to recover the difference between the price actually paid ($12,000) and the price that would have been paid if LowPrice had performed as originally agreed ($5,000). Thus, BigCo is entitled to $7,000 as compensatory damages (plus any additional out-of-pocket costs related to locating and hiring a new accounting firm).

Consider again the doll company example earlier in this chapter. If the original contract is for 10 cents per plastic eye, for a total contract cost of $10,000, and the second firm charges 15 cents per eye, the doll company will suffer $5,000 in compensatory damages. What if the doll company, after a good faith effort, cannot find replacement eyes and is unable to sell its product? Could the breaching plastic-eye manufacturer have reasonably foreseen that, without eyes, the dolls couldn't be sold? Such a conclusion seems likely. If the profits lost amount to $40 per doll and the doll company cannot sell the 50,000 dolls for which it has orders, then the consequential damages could add up to $2 million.

Consequential Damages

Consequential damages compensate the nonbreaching party for *foreseeable indirect* losses not covered by compensatory damages. An aggrieved party is entitled to recover consequential damages if the damages are caused by unique and foreseeable circumstances beyond the contract itself. In order to recover consequential damages, the damages must flow from the breach (i.e., the damages were a consequence of the breach). For example, in the BigCo-LowPrice case discussed above, suppose that LowPrice had breached on the day before the tax returns were due and that BigCo needed the tax returns as documentation for a bank loan on that day. Because the tax returns were not ready until one month after the due date, the bank charged BankCo a delay fee and then raised the interest rate on the loan. These costs to BankCo are related to the unique circumstances (the tax returns were needed on a certain date) and were foreseeable (assuming LowPrice had reason to know of the bank loan).

The rules that limit damages for which a nonbreaching party may recover were set out in *Hadley v. Baxendale*,[30] a landmark case on consequential damages that has been followed almost universally by U.S. courts. The case involved Hadley, a 19th-century mill owner, who was forced to cease operations due to a broken crankshaft. The mill owner sent the shaft out for repairs by hiring Baxendale to deliver the shaft to a repair shop in another city. Baxendale had no reason to know that the mill was shut down, and, in fact, it was common practice in the industry for mill owners to have a backup shaft for just such an occasion. Baxendale delayed delivery of the shaft, and this resulted in additional days of shutdown for the mill and, thus, lost profits for Hadley. Hadley sued Baxendale for the lost profits as consequential damages. The court ruled in favor of Baxendale because Hadley had not shown that a reasonable person could have *foreseen* Hadley's ongoing damages. Because Hadley had not actually communicated the unique circumstances, Baxendale was not liable for the damages related to the delay.

Restitution

Restitution is a remedy designed to prevent *unjust enrichment* of one party in an agreement. In the event that one party is in the process of performing the contract and the other

---

[30] [1854] 156 Eng. Rep. 145 (Eng.).

party commits a material breach, the nonbreaching party is entitled to rescind (cancel) the contract and receive fair market value for any services rendered. For example, BuildCo contracts with WidgetCo to build a new warehouse for WidgetCo's inventory. One-third through the construction, WidgetCo fails to make its payments on time and, therefore, materially breaches the contract. BuildCo rescinds the contract and, in a lawsuit against WidgetCo, BuildCo may recover restitution equal to the fair market value of the work performed.

Liquidated Damages

Liquidated damages are damages that the parties agree to ahead of time. In some cases it may be very difficult to determine actual damages, so parties may agree at the time of the contract that a breach would result in a fixed damage amount. Liquidated damage provisions are commonly used in license agreements (such as a software user's license), whereby the parties agree, for example, that a breaching party will pay $10,000 in the event of a breach caused by one party making unauthorized copies of the software. In order for such provisions to be enforceable, courts have held that liquidated damage clauses must be directly related to the breach and a reasonable estimate of the actual damages incurred (i.e., damages cannot be excessive so as to penalize the breaching party).

EQUITABLE REMEDIES

Although the usual remedy for a breach of contract is money damages, there are some instances when money damages are insufficient to compensate the nonbreaching party or when one party was unjustly enriched at the other party's expense. In these cases, a court may grant **equitable relief**. This relief comes primarily in the form of (1) *specific performance,* (2) *injunctive relief,* or (3) *reformation.*

Specific Performance

Specific performance is an equitable remedy whereby a court orders the breaching party to render the promised performance by ordering the party to take a specific action. This remedy is available only when the subject matter of the contract is sufficiently *unique* so that money damages are inadequate.[31] Therefore, specific performance is rarely available in a sale of goods case unless the goods are rare (such as a coin collection) or distinctive (such as a sculpture) so the buyer cannot reasonably be expected to locate the goods anywhere else.

One of the most common circumstances in which specific performance is awarded is real estate contracts. Most courts consider each parcel of land to be sufficiently unique to trigger specific performance as a remedy. For example, Andrews agrees to sell Baker an office building in 30 days. At the closing where conveyance of the title is to take place, Andrews breaches the agreement by refusing to sell the building. In this case, Baker cannot be completely compensated for the breach because Baker chose that building for its location, convenience, accessibility, appearance, and other important factors. Baker contracted for a unique parcel of real estate and is entitled to the benefit of the agreement for the same parcel. The court will require Andrews to *perform as promised* by conveying the property to Baker. If, however, Andrews has already sold the property to a good faith buyer, then Baker may be awarded only money damages as a remedy.

Specific performance is also an appropriate remedy in a narrow category of personal-service contracts in which the parties agree that a *specific individual* will perform the services and the individual possesses a *unique quality* or expertise central to the contract. For example, if Marcel contracts with Constantine to paint Marcel's office lobby in whitewash

---

[31]Restatement (Second) of Contracts § 359.

and Constantine breaches, a court would not consider specific performance as an option because the work is not specialized enough. On the other hand, if the Marcel-Constantine contract requires that Constantine paint a special mural on the wall, that would be sufficiently unique to qualify for specific performance.

Injunctive Relief

A court order to refrain from performing a particular act is known as **injunctive relief**.[32] In the Andrews-Baker office building contract, suppose that Andrews promises to sell the building to Baker in 30 days. Baker learns that Andrews is intending to breach the contract and sell the building to Dominguez for a higher price. In this case, both money damages and specific performance are inadequate because Baker still wants the building instead of compensation for the breach. Baker will ask the court to issue an injunction that would prevent the sale of the building to Dominguez as an equitable remedy consistent with the notion of putting the aggrieved party in the same position as he would have been if the other party had performed as agreed.

Reformation

When the parties have imperfectly expressed their agreement and this imperfection results in a dispute, a court may change the contract by rewriting it to conform to the parties' actual intentions. This contract modification is called **reformation**. For example, in the Andrews-Baker building contract, suppose Andrews's real estate broker accidentally deletes a decimal in the price, making it $10,000 instead of the parties' agreed-upon price of $100,000. At the closing, Baker gives Andrews the check for $10,000 and refuses to pay any more, citing the price in the contract. So long as there was a sufficient basis for believing the parties intended the price to be $100,000, a court may simply reform the contract. Andrews may then show that Baker breached the contract and request specific performance as an additional remedy.

AVOIDANCE AND MITIGATION OF DAMAGES

The law imposes an obligation on the parties in a contract to take appropriate steps to avoid incurring damages and losses. So long as a party can avoid the damages with reasonable effort, without undue risk or expense, she may be barred from recovery through a lawsuit. The rule preventing recovery for reasonably avoidable damages is often called the *duty to mitigate*.[33] For example, Leonardo contracts with NewCo to design a new office building for NewCo. Midway through the design planning process, NewCo changes its management, notifies Leonardo that it believes that the design contract is invalid, and orders him to stop work. Despite this, Leonardo continues the design process, submits the final work product to NewCo, and demands payment in full. In this case, it is likely that a court will not allow Leonardo to recover for any damages occurring after the NewCo stop order. Once Leonardo learned of NewCo's claim, he had an obligation to avoid the further damages incurred by his failure to stop the work even if NewCo's stop order breached the contract.

Managers may encounter a mitigation of damages issue when dealing with employees who claim that their employer breached an employment contract. If an employee has been wrongfully terminated, for example, that employee has a duty to seek new employment (of similar type and rank) if available in order to avoid damages resulting from the alleged breach by the employer.

LO 7-8

Explain the responsibilities of an injured party to mitigate damages, comply with the clean hands doctrine, and tender performance.

---

[32]The concept of injunctive relief is covered in more detail in Chapter 4, "Resolving Disputes: Litigation and Alternative Dispute Resolution."

[33]Restatement (Second) of Contracts § 350.

Clean Hands and Tender of Performance

Along with the duty to mitigate damages, a party suing another for breach of contract must do so with **"clean hands."** *Clean hands* (an equitable maxim discussed in Chapter 1, "Legal Foundations"), as applied to contract enforcement, requires that the party show that it had no fault in the breaching of the contract and that it was ready, willing, and able to perform its required obligations under the contract. This readiness to perform is called **tender of performance**. Suppose that Company A has agreed to sell a property and attached building to Company B. On the day of settlement, representatives of Company A arrive with all of the paperwork and keys necessary to transfer ownership of the property, but no one from Company B shows up. When Company A sues for breach of contract, it will be able to show that it was without fault and had tendered performance. If, however, neither party shows up at settlement, Company A will not be successful in a breach of contract action because it will have failed to meet its clean-hands burden.

CONCEPT SUMMARY *Remedies and Damages*

- For a breach of contract, courts will award monetary damages to the nonbreaching party to remedy the loss suffered by nonperformance.
- Monetary damages can be (1) *compensatory*—direct losses from nonperformance, (2) *consequential*—indirect but foreseeable losses from nonperformance, (3) *restitution*—losses equal to the amount that the breaching party has been unjustly enriched by the nonbreaching party, or (4) *liquidated*—losses of a predetermined value according to the contract.
- Equitable relief is given when the monetary damages are insufficient; it takes the form of (1) injunctive relief, (2) specific performance, or (3) reformation.
- The duty to mitigate is the nonbreaching party's obligation to avoid excessive or unnecessary damages through reasonable efforts or else be barred from recovery for those avoidable costs of nonperformance.

LO 7-9

Describe the rights of third parties in a contract assignment, in a delegation, or as a third-party beneficiary.

CONTRACTS INVOLVING RIGHTS OF A THIRD PARTY

In some cases, a party to an existing contract wishes to substitute another party in her place. Because the contract involves more than two parties, the law recognizes a special set of rules to govern such a substitution. One party may wish to do this by transferring to a third party her own rights in the contract (a transfer known as an *assignment*) or by appointing another to perform her duties (a transfer known as a *delegation*). Another form of contract that involves the rights of a third party occurs when a person who is not a party to the contract at the time of formation becomes a *third-party beneficiary* because the parties to the contract intended to confer a benefit on that person.

Assignment

An **assignment** is a transfer of current rights (not future rights) under a contract by one party in a contract to a third party. The party making the assignment is known as the *assignor,* and the third party receiving the rights is the *assignee*. Once a valid assignment occurs, the assignor's rights under the contract are extinguished and the rights may be exercised only by the assignee. The assignee then has the right to demand performance from the other party and to legally enforce the obligations. For example, Abel contracts to sell Baker 10,000 gallons of gasoline at $3 per gallon for Baker's fleet of delivery vehicles. Cain's research reveals that the price of gasoline may jump as high as $10 per gallon over the next year, so Cain contracts to pay Baker $70,000 for an assignment of Baker's rights under the Abel-Baker contract. Baker's rights (the assignor) are now extinguished, and Abel is compelled to perform his obligations by providing the gasoline to Cain (the assignee) at $3 per gallon. If Abel refuses to perform, Cain (but not Baker) may enforce the contract against Abel.

Generally, all rights in a contract are assignable at the sole discretion of the assigning party. Mutual consent is not required. However, in some instances, an assignment would be unfair to the nonassigning party. Therefore, some rights are not assignable:[34]

- Assignment is not permitted when the parties have included an *antiassignment clause,* using such language as "No rights under this contract may be assigned."
- Assignments are invalid when the assignment *materially alters the duty* of the other party by increasing a *burden or risk.* For example, an insurance contract that insures risk of one building against a flood may not be assigned to another building owner who owns a property in a flood plain. The obligor's (insurance company's) risk for the premium paid is materially altered. Thus, this assignment is prohibited.
- Some states have added additional assignment prohibition statutes related to general *public policy* matters (e.g., some states prohibit assignment of alimony payments before they become due).[35]

Delegation

Parties to a contract may also substitute another party to perform any *duties* owed under the agreement. A **delegation** is a transfer of current duties owed by one party under a contract to a third party. The party making the delegation is known as the *delegator,* and the third party receiving the rights is the *delegatee.* One major difference between assignment and delegation is that when a party delegates duty, the delegator remains liable for the obligation. Thus, if the delegatee fails to perform, the delegator must either perform or suffer liability for the breach of contract.

Although duties generally may be delegated without mutual consent of the parties, in some circumstances duties are nondelegable:

- When the duties involve *special personal skills,* such as those of an attorney, physician, portrait artist, or actor.
- When a contract contains an *antidelegation clause.*
- When the delegatee is a *competitor* of the obligee (the nondelegating party).[36]

Third-Party Beneficiaries   In an assignment or delegation, the third party's rights occur *after* the formation of the contract. However, sometimes a party may form a contract to benefit not herself, but a third person. In this case, that person, called the **third-party beneficiary**, becomes a party to the contract and certain rights arise to protect the third party. The key to understanding whether these rights arise or not is to examine whether the parties *intended to confer a benefit* on the third party. Such a third party is known as the **intended beneficiary** and has rights to enforce the contract as appropriate. For example, suppose Ernest borrows money from Scott to pay his living expenses while Ernest writes

---

[34]Restatement (Second) of Contracts § 322.
[35]J.D. Calamari, J.M. Perillo & H.H. Bender, *Cases and Problems on Contracts* 683–84 (4th ed. West/Thomson 2004).
[36]*See Sally Beauty Company v. Nexxus Products Co.*, 801 F.2d 1001 (7th Cir. 1986).

a novel. In negotiating a contract for his novel with Scribner's Publishing, Ernest asks that 50 percent of the royalties be paid to Scott in payment of the debt Ernest owes him. Because Scott is an intended beneficiary of this contract, he may sue Scribner's if it fails to perform by not paying the royalties as agreed.

In contrast, third parties who are not contemplated as beneficiaries by the original contracting parties are known as **incidental beneficiaries**. Incidental beneficiaries may not sue to enforce contractual rights. For example, Perkins owns a retail bookstore in the Main Street Mall (MSM). MSM contracts with Big Buy Appliances for the space next to Perkins's bookstore. Perkins is ecstatic upon learning of this because Big Buy is a major retail chain with high customer drawing power. After the lease is signed, Big Buy backs out. Although Perkins did benefit from the MSM–Big Buy contract, he cannot sue any of the parties in that contract because he is an incidental beneficiary.[37]

CONCEPT SUMMARY   Third-Party Rights

- Assignment is the unilateral shifting of rights under a contract from one party to a third party and is permitted only in the absence of an antiassignment clause, material change to the burden, or legal prohibition.
- Delegation is the transfer of contractual duties to a third party when the original party still remains liable for nonperformance, and it is permitted except in cases involving special personal skills or a nondelegation clause, or when the delegatee is a competitor of the nondelegating party.
- A third party who benefits from a contractual promise between two other parties may seek damages only if she is an intended beneficiary as opposed to an incidental beneficiary.

In Case 7.6, a state appellate court must determine whether a homeowner is an intended or incidental beneficiary of a contract between a general contractor hired by the homeowner and a subcontractor hired by the general contractor.

CASE 7.6 Emmelyn Logan-Baldwin v. L.S.M. General Contractors, Inc., 942 N.Y.S.2d 718, 94 A.D.3d 1466 (N.Y. 2012)

FACT SUMMARY Logan-Baldwin and other owners (collectively Logan-Baldwin) contracted with L.S.M. General Contractors (LSM) to renovate a historic residence. LSM subcontracted to Henry Isaacs Home Remodeling (Isaacs) to perform roofing work as part of the renovations. Isaacs then contracted with Brewster to install a new roof on the residence. Soon after the roof was completed, it showed signs of leaking, and it became clear that the roof was not installed correctly. LSM and Isaacs attempted to fix the problems, but they were unsuccessful and subsequently abandoned the project. Logan-Baldwin hired other contractors to fix the problems and sued LSM, Isaacs, and Brewster for breach of contract. Isaacs defended that it did not directly contract with Logan-Baldwin and therefore could not be sued for breach of contract. Logan-Baldwin argued that they had contract rights over

(continued)

---

[37]Based on Restatement (Second) of Contracts § 302, illus. 16.

Isaacs because they were an intended third-party beneficiary. The trial court ruled in favor of Isaacs, and Logan-Baldwin appealed.

SYNOPSIS OF DECISION AND OPINION The N.Y. Supreme Court Appellate Division reversed the trial court and held for Logan-Baldwin. The court reasoned that a nonbreaching party is entitled to damages as long as the underlying contract is entered into for the benefit of a third party. In this case, because Logan-Baldwin, as the owners of the house, were logically the intended beneficiary of the home renovations, they had rights as a third-party beneficiary. Because they were the intended third-party beneficiary, the court ruled that Logan-Baldwin had the right to maintain a breach of contract claim against Isaacs.

WORDS OF THE COURT: Third-Party Beneficiaries "Parties such as the plaintiffs herein who are 'asserting third-party beneficiary rights under a contract must establish (1) the existence of a valid and binding contract between other parties, (2) that the contract was intended for [their] benefit and (3) that the benefit to [them] is sufficiently immediate, rather than incidental, to indicate the assumption by the contracting parties of a duty to compensate [them] if the benefit is lost.' . . . Indeed, '[i]t is almost inconceivable that those who render their services in connection with a major construction project would not contemplate that the performance of their contractual obligations would ultimately benefit the owner. . . . It is obviously inferable that they knew, or should have known, that someone owned the [property], and that such person or entity was to be the ultimate beneficiary of their services.' . . . To the extent that the [trial] court interpreted our decision in . . . as holding that an express contractual provision was required [for an intended beneficiary to exist], the court erred. An express contractual provision concerning third-party beneficiaries 'is but an alternative factor upon which a court might base a finding that a certain party is, in fact, a third-party beneficiary.'"

Case Questions

1. Does an intended beneficiary have to be named in a contract to have rights to enforce the contract? Explain.
2. Why did the court rule that Logan-Baldwin had a right to sue for breach of contract?
3. *Focus on Critical Thinking:* Suppose that the plaintiff's historical residence was typically open to the public for tours on weekends. Philip, a history buff, plans a trip to tour the home, but upon his arrival he finds it closed because the shoddy roofing work made the premises unsafe for the public. Does Philip have a cause of action against any of the defendants? Why or why not?

KEY TERMS

Enforceability p. 206 The ability of a properly formed contract to be enforceable in a court of law; determined by examining whether the contract is a product of genuine assent and is in writing (under certain circumstances).

Genuine assent p. 207 The knowing, voluntary, and mutual approval of the terms of a contract by each party; required for a contract to be enforceable.

Misrepresentation p. 207 Situation in which one party to an agreement makes a promise or representation about a material fact that is not true; basis for avoiding a contract.

Fraudulent misrepresentation p. 207 Situation in which one party has engaged in conduct that meets the standards for misrepresentation and that party has actual knowledge that the representation is not true; basis for avoiding a contract.

Treble damages p. 207 Triple damages; often awarded in fraud cases.

Duress p. 210 The use of any form of unfair coercion by one party to induce another party to enter into or modify a contract; basis for avoiding a contract.

Undue influence p. 210   A defense that gives legal relief to a party who was induced to enter into a contract through the improper pressure of a trusted relationship.

Unconscionability p. 210   A defense that may allow a party to potentially avoid a contract on the grounds that she suffered a grossly unfair burden that shocks the objective conscience.

Statute of frauds p. 211   The law governing which contracts must be in writing in order to be enforceable.

Parol evidence rule p. 214   Interpretation rule stating that any writing intended by the parties to be the final expression of their agreement may not be contradicted by any oral or written agreements made prior to the writing.

Covenant not to compete p. 214   Type of contract in which one party agrees not to compete with another party for a specified period of time.

Ambiguous terms p. 215   Contract terms that are vague and indefinite. In contract law, these terms are construed by the court against the interest of the side that drafted the agreement.

Omitted terms p. 215   Contract terms that are left out or absent. In contract law, courts may supply a reasonable term in a situation where the contract is silent.

Condition p. 215   An event that must occur before a contract obligation is triggered.

Good faith p. 217   In contract law, the duty to honestly adhere to the contract's common purpose. Under this obligation neither party can do anything to prevent the other party from enjoying the "fruits of the contract." Instead, both must try to make the deal work as written.

Discharge p. 217   In contract law, the removal of all legal obligations under the agreement.

Substantial performance p. 218   Performance of the essential terms of the contract such that performance can be considered complete less damages for anything still unperformed.

Material p. 218   Something that is important to the contract by being necessary and generally indispensable to the contract.

Mutual consent p. 220   Circumstance under which contracting parties may be discharged from their obligation although neither party has fully performed because they agree to cancel the contract.

Operation of law (contracts) p. 220   Termination of an offer by the occurrence of certain happenings or events, which generally include lapse of time, death or incapacity of the offeror or offeree, destruction of the subject matter of the contract prior to acceptance, and supervening illegality.

Rescission p. 220   Cancellation of a contract that occurs when both parties agree to discharge each other from all duties under the contract and end the agreement, no matter what has been done or left undone.

Accord and satisfaction p. 220   A doctrine that allows one party to create an agreement, or accord, with the other party to accept a substitute performance in order to satisfy the original performance; the completion of the new duty discharges the old one.

Substitute agreement (modification) p. 220   An agreement that replaces the original contract when the two parties agree to different duties. The new duties then replace and dissolve the obligations of the original contract.

Novation p. 221   A type of substitute agreement in which the duties of the contract remain the same but a new, third party assumes the duties of an original party, discharging the original party from further obligations. (*Note:* Many courts use novation for new parties and new terms or substitute agreements.)

Impossibility p. 222   Doctrine that excuses performance when an essential part of the contract has become impossible because a crucial, irreplaceable thing has been destroyed; a crucial person has died; a crucial means of performance no longer exists; or a crucial action has become illegal.

Impracticability p. 222   Doctrine that excuses performance when an extreme circumstance occurs or reveals itself that destroys the value of the performance to the party and that circumstance was not the fault of either party and was not reasonably foreseeable.

Frustration of purpose p. 222   Doctrine that excuses a party from performance if, before a breach, a state of things that was the basis for forming the contract no longer exists, by no fault of either party.

Unilaterally altered p. 225   Term pertaining to a contract in which one party changes a term of the offer or acceptance after the contract was made and without the consent of the other party, who is then discharged from performing.

Bankruptcy p. 225   A procedure by which a debtor's assets are reorganized and liquidated by a court order to pay off creditors and free the debtor from obligations under existing contracts.

Statute of limitations p. 225   The time limit within which a lawsuit must be filed or the lawsuit will be barred forever (*ch. 4*). State law that places a time limit on the enforcement of certain contracts in order to ensure diligent enforcement (*ch. 7*).

Breach p. 225   Condition that exists when one party has failed to perform her obligation under the contract. If the breach is material, the nonbreaching party is excused from his performance and can recover monetary damages.

Remedies p. 226   Judicial actions, which can be monetary or equitable, taken by courts that are intended to compensate an injured party in a civil lawsuit.

Anticipatory repudiation p. 226   Doctrine under which, when one party makes clear that he has no intention to perform as agreed, the nonbreaching party is entitled to recover damages in anticipation of the breach rather than waiting until performance is due. Also called *anticipatory breach*.

Money damages p. 228   Sums levied on the breaching party and awarded to the nonbreaching party to remedy a loss from breach of contract.

Compensatory damages p. 228   Damages that are meant to make the injured party whole again. In contract law, they are an attempt to place the nonbreaching party in the position he would have been in had the contract been executed as agreed. Also called *direct* or *actual damages*.

Consequential damages p. 229   Damages that repay the injured party for any foreseeable but indirect losses that flow from the breach of contract.

Restitution p. 229   A remedy that restores to the plaintiff the value of the performance that he has already rendered to the breaching party and by which the breaching party has been unjustly enriched.

Liquidated damages p. 230   Reasonable estimates of the actual damages that will result if the contract is breached; agreed to by the parties ahead of time.

Equitable relief p. 230   Relief granted in the form of either specific performance ("do it") or an injunction ("stop doing it") when monetary damages are insufficient due to the unique or irreversible consequence of the breach.

Specific performance p. 230   An equitable remedy whereby a court orders the breaching party to render the promised performance by ordering the party to take a specific action.

Injunctive relief p. 231   A court order to refrain from performing a particular act.

Reformation p. 231   Contract modification in which the court rewrites the contract to conform to the parties' actual intentions when the parties have imperfectly expressed their agreement and the imperfection results in a dispute.

Clean hands p. 232   An equitable doctrine whereby a party seeking to enforce a breach of contract against the opposing party must prove that he has no fault in causing the breach. Clean hands are shown by proving that you are prepared to tender performance.

Tender of performance p. 232   An offer or attempt to perform what is required under a contract.

Assignment p. 232   The transfer of one party's current rights under a contract to a third party, thereby extinguishing the original party's rights.

Delegation p. 233   The transfer of one party's current duties under a contract to a third party to perform, with the original party remaining liable for any breach.

Third-party beneficiary p. 233   Someone who, while not a party to a contract, stands to benefit from the existence of the contract. (See *Incidental beneficiary* and *Intended beneficiary* in this glossary.)

Intended beneficiary p. 233   Someone who, while not a party to the contract, stands to benefit from the contract because the contracting parties intended that he receive a benefit. He has enforceable rights under the contract.

Incidental beneficiary p. 234   Someone who, while not a party to the contract, stands to benefit from the contract simply because she may be in the right place at the right time. The contract was not entered into to benefit her specifically and she has no enforceable rights under the contract.

CHAPTER REVIEW QUESTIONS

1. The key difference between misrepresentation and fraud is:
   a. Material fact
   b. Guilty knowledge
   c. Reliance
   d. Puffing

2. Which of the following does *not* fall within the statute of frauds?
   a. Contract for a new car worth $25,000.
   b. Agreement to provide office cleaning services for a period of six months.
   c. Co-signer agreeing to guarantee a bank loan for her sister.
   d. Agreement to purchase a warehouse.

3. Jackson agrees to provide consulting services to Frankfurter Industries for a period of two years. Before he begins his services, Jackson finds out he has won the lottery and decides he no longer wants to work for Frankfurter. Frankfurter agrees. The parties have discharged their obligations through
   a. Modification
   b. Substitute agreement
   c. Impossibility
   d. Rescission

4. In order to claim discharge through substantial performance, the deviation cannot be _____.
   a. Minor
   b. Substantial
   c. More than $500
   d. Material

5. Which remedy compensates a nonbreaching party for foreseeable indirect losses?
   a. Consequential damages
   b. Specific performance
   c. Liquidated damages
   d. Compensatory damages

Answers and explanations are provided at the end of this chapter.

THEORY TO PRACTICE

After a 30-year career as a shipping logistics executive, Ishmael retired and began to offer his services as a logistics consultant. Ishmael entered into a consulting contract with the general manager at Export Co to provide logistical advice to the company for 12 months. The parties agreed in the contract that Export will pay Ishmael $5,000 per month on the last day of each month. Ishmael promised to devote "100 percent of his professional time" to Export for a period of at least eight consecutive weeks.

1. After one week on the worksite, Ishmael finds that he is devoting more time to Export than he initially believed was necessary, so he attempts to convince Export to pay him $6,000 per month for his consulting services. Export does not agree to any change, so Ishmael begins to cut down his hours so that he is spending only 80 percent of his professional time at Export. If Export sues Ishmael for breach of contract, are there any circumstances under which Ishmael may use the doctrine of substantial performance to complete his performance obligation? Why or why not?

2. Two months after the Ishmael-Export contract, Export loses a large client. The company sends Ishmael a letter explaining that the financial emergency has caused it to consider rescinding Ishmael's contract under the theory that Export is discharged from the remaining months of the contract based on the doctrine of impracticability. Will a court support Export's theory?

3. In Question 2, if a manager from Export notifies Ishmael on March 1 that the company does not intend to pay him for the month of March, must Ishmael wait to sue Export until the date performance is actually due (recall that he is paid his fee on the last day of each month)? What doctrine may help Ishmael recover compensation without incurring further damages by waiting until performance is due?

4. What type of remedies would be most appropriate for Ishmael if a court were to find that Export breached the contract as described in Question 2? Would specific performance be appropriate? Why or why not?

5. Suppose that Ishmael meets with another potential client and the needs of the client are such that Ishmael's immediate services are required and he cannot complete the work for Export. Because there is no antiassignment clause in the contract, he assigns the contract to his brother, who is also familiar with importing logistics. Export objects. Must Ishmael perform, or must Export accept Ishmael's brother in his place? What legal doctrines apply?

LEGAL STRATEGY 101

Turtle versus Saigon

There are no lawyers or dramatic courtroom scenes in HBO's hit show *Entourage,* but nevertheless, this TV series offers many real-world lessons about legal strategy in the entertainment industry. If you haven't seen the show, *Entourage* revolves around the fictional Hollywood movie star Vincent Chase (played by Adrian Grenier) and his "entourage" of childhood friends, including his manager Eric Murphy (played by Kevin Connolly), who everyone refers to as "E"; Vincent's older half-brother Johnny "Drama" (played by Kevin Dillon); and Turtle (played by Jerry Ferrara).

In one episode, Turtle accidentally finds a "mixtape," a homemade music CD produced by an unknown hip-hop artist.[38] Turtle loves the music on the mixtape, and he eventually tracks down the musician, whose stage name is "Saigon." Turtle then signs the up-and-coming hip-hop artist to a management deal. As Saigon's new manager, Turtle promises to get Saigon a record deal with a major label.

Turtle keeps his end of the bargain and gets Saigon a major record deal, but when the day comes for Saigon to sign with the record label, he is nowhere to be found.[39] Along with his friend Johnny "Drama," Turtle drives all over Los Angeles trying to find Saigon, and after a bit of detective work, they finally locate him partying in a swank hotel suite . . . along with Saigon's other manager! Saigon forgot to tell Turtle that he was already contractually obligated to another manager before signing with Turtle and that they had just signed a better deal with a hip-hop music label.

To make things right, Saigon asks his new (old) manager to buy Turtle out for $40,000, the same

Cast of *Entourage.*
AF archive/Alamy

amount of money Turtle would have made if Saigon had signed with Turtle's record label. Should Turtle accept Saigon's offer?

CRITICAL THINKING QUESTIONS

1. Assume that Turtle's commission from his record deal—if Saigon had showed up to sign with Turtle's record label—would have been $40,000. Is this monetary amount equivalent to compensatory damages, consequential damages, liquidated damages, or restitution?

2. If you were Turtle, would you prefer to sue Saigon in court, or would you rather settle out of court by accepting Saigon's offer of $40,000? Likewise, if you were Saigon, would you offer to settle with Turtle out of court for $40,000, or would you make Turtle take you to court?

---

[38]Synopsis: *Entourage: Good Morning Saigon* (season 2, episode 12) (HBO, not dated), https://www.hbo.com/entourage/season-02/12-good-morning-saigon/synopsis.

[39]Synopsis: *Entourage:I Wanna Be Sedated* (season 3A, episode 10) (HBO, not dated), https://www.hbo.com/entourage/season-03a/10-i-wanna-be-sedated/synopsis.

MANAGER'S CHALLENGE

Although at the beginning of a contract the parties may have a certain understanding, managers are sometimes in a position where a change in the agreement becomes necessary. In this chapter's Theory to Practice problem, it is clear that the parties need to retool their agreement to reflect (1) Ishmael's concern that the assignment is more work than originally anticipated, (2) Export's weakened financial position, and (3) Ishmael's desire to substitute his brother to complete the assignment. Draft a memorandum to your senior manager outlining specific options and consequences for altering these agreements through rescission, accord and satisfaction, substitute agreement, and/or novation.

See Connect for Manager's Challenge sample answers.

CASE SUMMARY 7.1 MediaNews Group v. McCarthey, 494 F.3d 1254 (10th Cir. 2007)

STATUTE OF FRAUDS

McCarthey sold controlling stock interests of his newspaper publishing company to TCI in 1997. During that sale transaction (which involved a detailed contract covering all aspects of the sale), McCarthey allegedly articulated a "side agreement" with TCI that provided McCarthey with the right to repurchase the stock from TCI on the five-year anniversary of the sale (in 2002). The side agreement was never memorialized. Before the five-year anniversary, TCI sold its interest in the newspaper to MediaNews. When McCarthey sued for breach of the oral agreement, TCI asserted that the statute of frauds barred his claim.

CASE QUESTIONS

1. Is the oral agreement enforceable? Why or why not?
2. Could the parol evidence rule apply here?

CASE SUMMARY 7.2 Harley-Davidson Motor Co. v. PowerSports, Inc., 319 F.3d 973 (7th Cir. 2003)

FRAUD

PowerSports applied for a franchise license from Harley-Davidson (Harley) to sell Harley products in Seminole County, Florida. During Harley's interview of PowerSports, officers of PowerSports made certain representations and promises about PowerSports's business practices and procedures. This was an important part of the negotiations because Harley had strict standards of quality and customer service with which all of its dealers had to comply. Based on these representations, Harley granted the franchise license, and PowerSports became an authorized dealer. Just days after it signed the franchise agreement, Harley became aware that PowerSports had taken significant steps toward plans to take the company public (sell company stock on the public market). This was inconsistent with Harley's requirements and conditions for owning a franchise. Harley alleged that the representations made by PowerSports were false, and it sued PowerSports for fraudulent misrepresentation, demanding a rescission of the contract plus additional damages.

CASE QUESTIONS

1. Were PowerSports's misrepresentations "material"? Why or why not?
2. Suppose PowerSports went public two years after the awarding of the franchise agreement. Could Harley still sue for rescission? How about 10 years?

CASE SUMMARY 7.3 Tafel v. Lion Antique Investments & Consulting Services, 2011 U.S. Dist. LEXIS 96445, (N.D. Ga. Aug. 26, 2011)

UNENFORCEABILITY

Tafel Racing Team, Inc. (Tafel Racing), and Lion Antique Investments & Consulting Services, Inc. (Lion), entered into an agreement to purchase two Ferrari race cars. Pursuant to the agreement, Lion agreed to loan the race cars to Tafel Racing for use in the 2008 American Le Mans Series. Tafel Racing was obligated to purchase or sell the race cars 90 days after the conclusion of the 2008 American Le Mans Series. The plaintiff, James Tafel Jr. (Tafel), is the former CEO of Tafel Racing. East Coast Jewelry (East Coast) agreed to purchase one of the Ferrari race cars for $700,000. Vladislav Yampolsky is a partial owner of East Coast. Although East Coast paid Tafel Racing $700,000, Tafel Racing did not deliver the car or refund East Coast's money. Tafel Racing filed a Voluntary Petition for Bankruptcy and listed Yampolsky as one of Tafel Racing's creditors holding unsecured nonpriority claims in the amount of $600,000. Tafel Racing also identified Tafel as a codebtor for each of Tafel Racing's creditors. At Yampolsky's request, Tafel executed a nonnegotiable promissory note in the principal amount of $600,000, plus $22,454.14 in interest, payable to Yampolsky. Tafel also executed a Deed to Secure Debt granting Yampolsky a security interest in Tafel's residence in Georgia. The note stated that it was "executed and delivered . . . in consideration of advances by Yampolsky to Tafel." Tafel, however, made no payments on the note. Yampolsky assigned his rights and interest in the note to Lion. Tafel claimed that the note was invalid and unenforceable. (*Hint:* Be sure to make a distinction between *Tafel Racing* and *Tafel*.)

CASE QUESTIONS

1. What defense can Tafel assert that would make the note unenforceable?
2. What must the note contain to make the note enforceable? Give an example.

CASE SUMMARY 7.4 Dalton v. Educational Testing Service, 87 N.Y.2d 384 (1995)

GOOD FAITH AND SPECIFIC PERFORMANCE

Dalton took the SAT exam in May 1991. He retook the exam in November 1992 and scored 410 points higher. The Educational Testing Service (ETS), which administers the exam, has a policy of flagging score differentials greater than 350 points. After analyzing handwriting on the two tests, ETS concluded that someone else may have taken the exam for Dalton. Before the exam, Dalton signed a contract with ETS stating that if he was flagged for cheating, he had five options: Cancel the score, have a third party review it, go to an arbitrator, retake the test, or send in information relevant to whether or not he had cheated. Dalton sent in information showing that he had mononucleosis during the first test and that he had taken a prep course, and he provided affidavits from people who saw him at the test site. Testimony from the ETS showed that officials were convinced that the handwriting issue meant that Dalton had only the option to retake the test and, thus, they failed to consider the information he sent to them unless it dealt directly with the handwriting analysis.

Dalton sued for specific performance to have the scores reported as official by ETS. He argued that by giving him the contractual option of sending in information relevant to the cheating accusation, the ETS had a good faith obligation under the contract to examine and fully consider what he had sent in.

CASE QUESTIONS

1. Who prevails and why?
2. Why is specific performance an option here as a remedy?

CASE SUMMARY 7.5 Pepsi-Cola Co. v. Steak 'n Shake, Inc., 981 F. Supp. 1149 (S.D. Ind. 1997)

REMEDIES

The Steak 'n Shake restaurant chain entered a contract with Pepsi to replace King Cola with Pepsi in all its stores. Several issues surrounding the contract's execution strained the agreement, and Steak 'n Shake canceled the contract and refused to perform. Pepsi sued, and in court Steak 'n Shake insisted that Pepsi had no "legally cognizable" damages because all potential profits were purely speculative. Pepsi argued that it stood to gain from the contract and should be compensated for the breach even though damages could not be calculated exactly. The damages could be equal to what it reasonably stood to gain from the contract if not for Steak 'n Shake's breach.

CASE QUESTIONS

1. Will a court award damages to Pepsi even though the company admitted the damages could not be calculated exactly?
2. What other types of damages or relief could Pepsi seek?

CASE SUMMARY 7.6 DiFolco v. MSNBC, 622 F.3d 104 (2d Cir. 2010)

ANTICIPATORY REPUDIATION

DiFolco and MSNBC entered into a two-year employment agreement for DiFolco to work as a television commentator covering the entertainment industry. MSNBC had the right to terminate the agreement after the first year by giving DiFolco 60 days' advance notice. DiFolco's first eight months of employment were tumultuous, and she had several disputes with her supervisors over her assignments and working conditions. Through a series of e-mails, DiFolco complained to her supervisors about being forced off the air through MSNBC's change in schedule and coverage. One of these e-mails indicated that she wished to have a meeting to discuss her exit from the shows and to give MSNBC ample time to replace her. In that same e-mail, though, DiFolco also wrote that she wanted to be part of the MSNBC team "for a long time to come." Nonetheless, MSNBC took these e-mails to mean that DiFolco intended to repudiate her contract and sent her a proposed separation agreement claiming that she had resigned. DiFolco filed a breach of contract action against MSNBC. The trial court dismissed DiFolco's claim and ruled that the e-mail constituted DiFolco's anticipatory repudiation of her contract with MSNBC.

CASE QUESTIONS

1. Who prevails and why? What standard should the court apply?
2. If you received an e-mail from an employee that concerned her "exit," would you believe she was quitting? Is the situation with DiFolco any different?

CASE SUMMARY 7.7 Taylor v. Palmer, 31 Cal. 240 (1966)

ASSIGNMENT TO A THIRD PARTY

The city of San Francisco contracted with a builder to do several tasks associated with roadwork and refurbishment. The contractor assigned the work to another contractor. The city sought breach of contract for, among other things, inappropriate assignment in that the service was of a personal nature, which under common law cannot be unilaterally assigned to a third party. The contractor argued that the roadwork in the contract was not of a personal nature and thus could lawfully be assigned by the original contractor to the third-party contractor.

CASE QUESTIONS

1. Who prevails and why?
2. Is the task specialized?

Self-Check ANSWERS Fraud and Misrepresentation

1. No fraud or misrepresentation exists. This was sales talk (puffing), so Brittany has no course of action.
2. This is a fraud. Even though Joan initially told the truth, the facts changed and her nondisclosure makes her liable for fraud.
3. John has committed a fraud against Paul by changing the mileage and accident records, two material facts in car negotiations. Paul committed a misrepresentation when he sold the car to George because, even though he had no knowledge of the true facts and did not intentionally conceal anything, the mileage and accident records were nevertheless false representations of material facts.
4. Tony's statement came after the contract had been executed, so Mel did not rely on Tony's statement when making the deal. (If the statement had been made during negotiations and Mel was a huge Tiger Woods fan, it could be argued that the statement was an intentional falsehood of a material fact and therefore a fraud.)
5. Flo is guilty of fraud because she has concealed a material fact, the fact that the engine leaks oil.
6. No fraud or misrepresentation exists. This was sales talk (puffing), so Lisa has no course of action.

Statute of Frauds

1. Writing required. Promise to pay the debt of another.
2. Writing required. Real estate/land.
3. Careful! No writing required. Despite the high fee, the services can be performed in less than one year; thus, the contract is not subject to the statute of frauds requirements.
4. Writing required. A two-year contract for services that cannot be performed in less than one year.
5. Writing required. Even though the price is below $500, it is for the purchase of an interest in land.

Substantial Performance

1. Wholesaler has substantially performed, but Delicatessen is entitled to a reduction in price.
2. No substantial performance. The most important term in the contract (the phone number) was not met by Yellow Pages, and the value of the contract to Dry Cleaner is now zero. Based on *Georges v. Pacific Telephone & Telegraph Co.*, 184 F. Supp. 571 (D.C. Or. 1960).
3. No substantial performance. The industry standard is such that a 15 percent leaf/stem ratio is substantially more valuable than the 25 percent leaf/stem ratio. See *Del Monte Corp. v. Martin*, 574 S.W.2d 597 (Tex. Civ. App. 1978).
4. Substantial performance or perfect performance, depending on whether the portrait objectively meets the criteria for a professional painting of that type.
5. Publisher has substantially performed because the delay likely causes no harm to the bookstore with so much time before classes begin.

CHAPTER REVIEW QUESTIONS: Answers and Explanations

1. **b.** Guilty knowledge means that the misrepresentation was intentional and constitutes fraud. Answer choices (a) and (c) are incorrect because they are common elements. Answer choice (d) is incorrect because it is not related to determining fraud.

2. **b.** This contract is to be performed in less than one year, so it does not fall within the statute of frauds. Answer choices (a), (c), and (d) involve a contract for the sale of goods over $500, the promise to pay the debt of another, and an agreement for real estate, respectively. Therefore, they all fall within the statute of frauds.

3. **d.** If neither party has performed, the parties may agree to cancel the contract through rescission. Answer choices (a) and (b) are incorrect because there is no substitute agreement. Answer choice (c) is incorrect because performance is still possible.

4. **d.** Substantial performance results in discharge only if the deviation is not material (a significant change in the contract's value or the parties' obligations). All other answers are incorrect because they are nonsensical.

5. **a.** Consequential damages allow recovery for damages that are unique and foreseeable beyond the contract itself. Answer choice (b) is incorrect because it is an equitable remedy. Answer choice (c) is incorrect because liquidated damages are agreed to ahead of time. Answer choice (d) is incorrect because compensatory damages are for actual losses suffered.

CHAPTER 8

Contracts for the Sale of Goods

©philsajonesen/Getty Images

Learning Objectives

After studying this chapter, students who have mastered the material will be able to:

8-1   Articulate the fundamental purpose and role of the UCC in commercial transactions and explain why it is important to business owners and managers.

8-2   Identify which contracts are governed by UCC Article 2.

8-3   Discuss the requirements for agreement in a sale of goods contract and identify what terms the UCC provides in a sales agreement with open or missing terms.

8-4   Classify which contracts must be in writing and understand what the writing must contain to be enforceable under the statute of frauds.

8-5   Express how risk of loss is allocated among the parties in a sales contract and identify steps managers take to limit risks and ensure performance.

8-6   Recognize the UCC rights and obligations of buyers and sellers and the consequences of breaching a contract.

8-7   Identify appropriate remedies and damages available to buyers and sellers.

8-8   Explain the risks involved in sales transactions with foreign companies and know how to mitigate those risks by understanding international commercial laws.

This chapter continues the coverage of the challenges that managers face in the formation and performance of contracts, but it focuses on the role of Article 2 of the Uniform Commercial Code (UCC).[1] Article 2 sets out the rules that govern contracts involving the sale of goods. Because UCC transactions typically include shipping, risk of loss, inspection, cure, and other issues unique to goods, it is important for business owners and managers to understand how UCC rules are applied. In this chapter, we discuss

- The scope of Article 2 coverage.
- The formation of agreements for the sale of goods recognized under the UCC and how contracts governed by the UCC differ from those governed by the common law.
- Legal rules regarding passing of ownership and allocation of risk for goods in a commercial transaction.
- UCC provisions governing the obligations of the parties in a sales agreement as well as UCC protections for innocent parties on occasions when the other party violates the agreement.
- How sellers can mitigate or eliminate damages when they initially fail to perform properly.
- The international commercial law principles governing sale of goods contracts with a company in a foreign nation.

---

[1]Note that the UCC also contains other articles pertaining to different aspects of commercial law. For example, Article 2A covers the *leasing* of goods. Leasing of goods is discussed in Chapter 23, "Personal Property, Real Property, and Land Use Law." This chapter focuses exclusively on Article 2: Sales of Goods.

INTRODUCTION TO ARTICLE 2 OF THE UCC

Recall from the previous chapters that contracts for the *sale of goods* are governed by statutory law in the form of the Uniform Commercial Code (UCC, or sometimes referred to simply as the *Code*). The UCC is a model statute published by the National Conference of Commissioners of Uniform State Laws (NCCUSL).[2] Every state except Louisiana has adopted all (or substantially all) of Article 2 of the UCC. In 2003, the NCCUSL came out with a revised Code; however, the revisions were substantial and met opposition in state legislatures. To date, no state has adopted the revised Code.[3] As a result of the opposition by the states, in May 2011, the American Law Institute voted to withdraw the 2003 amendments.

UCC Coverage and Definitions

The UCC applies only to **sales contracts** that are agreements for the *sale of goods*. The UCC defines **goods**[4] as property that is (1) tangible (i.e., has a physical existence, as does a laptop computer) and (2) movable from place to place. Therefore, real estate contracts or employment contracts are *not* covered by the UCC. While many sales contracts involve the sale of goods to a consumer, Article 2 also contains special provisions that apply only in transactions between *merchants*. A **merchant** is one that is *regularly engaged* in the sale of a particular good. The UCC imputes a certain level of knowledge and awareness to merchants and allows their transactions to proceed in an expedited manner without the necessity for safeguards intended for average consumers. For example, suppose that Caesar's Equipment Co sells a lawn tractor to Sanjay for $600. This sales agreement is subject to Article 2, but because Sanjay is not a merchant, certain UCC requirements exist primarily to protect Sanjay's interests in the sale. However, if Caesar's is a wholesaler and Sanjay is the owner of a retail store, this is a *merchant* transaction and triggers special business standards that are intended to allow the parties to transact business unimpeded by any consumer protections.

Recall from Chapter 6, "Overview and Formation of Contracts," that it is important to distinguish between contracts governed by the UCC and those governed by the common law and to understand how to determine the source of law for hybrid contracts. This is critical knowledge for business owners and managers because the parties' rights and obligations under the common law differ from those under the UCC.

Function of the UCC

The underlying policy of the UCC is to promote commercial efficiency by providing standardized procedures that merchants and consumers may rely upon. The provisions of the UCC were drafted with the goal of promoting the *completion* of a business transaction. Article 2 is intended to modify some of the stricter common law requirements and facilitate business transactions by providing merchants and consumers with a standard set of rules for the sale of goods.

In the context of sales contracts, the UCC should be thought of primarily as a *gap filler* in cases where the parties have not agreed otherwise. Typically, two parties will enter into a sales contract after negotiating certain terms. Terms of such a sales contract, assuming that they do not conflict with a UCC prohibition, are fully enforceable. The UCC principally comes into play when the parties to a sales transaction have *not* expressly agreed on certain terms. For example, suppose that on Monday, Hadley and Martha enter into an agreement for the sale of 1,000 Brand-A watches at $1 per Brand-A watch to be delivered

---

LO 8-1

Articulate the fundamental purpose and role of the UCC in commercial transactions and explain why it is important to business owners and managers.

LO 8-2

Identify which contracts are governed by UCC Article 2.

Legal Speak >))

Goods

Tangible personal property that is movable at the time of identification to a contract of sale. Future goods—especially manufactured goods, the unborn young of animals, growing crops, and identified things attached to realty—are included. Money and information are not considered goods under the UCC.

---

[2]The NCCUSL and other similar organizations are discussed in more detail in Chapter 1, "Legal Foundations."
[3]Only Kansas, Nevada, and Oklahoma considered adopting the 2003 amendments. The Kansas and Nevada bills never came to a vote, and Oklahoma voted to adopt only a revised definition of goods that excluded information.
[4]UCC § 2-103.

Contracts for the sale of goods are covered under Article 2 of the Uniform Commercial Code. Getty Images

> **KEY POINT**
>
> Article 2 of the UCC acts to fill in only missing or open terms (when the parties have not expressly agreed otherwise) in a contract for the sale of goods between merchants.

to Martha's warehouse on Friday. However, the parties do not bother to negotiate any terms other than price and delivery date. Suppose that Hadley runs out of Brand-A watches and ships 1,000 Brand-B watches instead. Must Martha accept the watches? What are her options under the law? Suppose that the watches are damaged in transit before they are delivered to Martha's warehouse. What are the parties' rights and responsibilities regarding the sale? Who will bear the risk of the loss? Because the parties have not specifically agreed on this contingency, they must turn to the UCC for the answers regarding those missing terms.

LO 8-3

Discuss the requirements for agreement in a sale of goods contract and identify what terms the UCC provides in a sales agreement with open or missing terms.

AGREEMENT IN A SALES CONTRACT: OFFER

Recall that the UCC generally aims to *promote* a sales transaction to be completed rather than shelter a party who doesn't complete the transaction. The formation elements for a sales contract, for example, are easier to meet and do not require the level of intent required for common law contracts. Article 2 lowers the bar for formation by allowing an enforceable contract to arise "in any manner sufficient to show agreement" between the parties.[5] Therefore, the UCC allows a contract to be enforced based on a larger picture that consists of (1) past commercial conduct, (2) correspondence or verbal exchanges between the parties, and (3) industry

---

[5] UCC § 2-204(1).

standards and norms. In fact, the parties need not even have a definite time of formation, so long as the conduct of the parties indicates some basis for a reasonable person to believe a sales contract *exists*. For example, Wholesaler delivers 1,000 digital music players to Retailer on the 15th of each month. Over a period of six months, Wholesaler has delivered the players on or about the 15th of the month and Retailer has sent Wholesaler a check within 10 days. Assume that in the digital music player industry, payment is generally made within 10 days after delivery. In month seven, Wholesaler delivers the product on the 15th, but Retailer never pays. Most courts would hold that the seventh month was an enforceable contract even if Retailer did not subjectively *intend* to have the music player contract linger into seven months. Under the UCC, the larger picture was that the parties' *conduct* indicated that they had an ongoing series of contracts with certain terms. Retailer must exercise some conduct to indicate that the contract is at an end (a simple e-mail would suffice) before the delivery date in the seventh month in order for the contract to be considered at an end.

Offers with Open Terms

Sometimes merchants wish to engage in a sales transaction, but the parties overlook or are unsure about some key element of the contract, such as quantity, delivery, payment terms, or even the price of the goods. The missing provisions, known as **open terms**, are entirely acceptable under the UCC so long as there is evidence that the parties *intended* to enter into a contract and the other terms are sufficiently articulated to provide a basis for some appropriate *remedy* in case of breach. This is where the UCC provides gap filling. The UCC provides a variety of answers based on what terms are missing.

Quantity While quantity is generally a *required* term necessary to create an enforceable contract, two important exceptions exist to this general rule. First, quantity *may* be an open term if the buyer agrees to purchase *all* of the goods that a seller produces (known as an **output contract**). In this case, the seller has given up the right to sell the goods elsewhere. Second, when the buyer agrees to purchase all or up to an agreed amount of what the buyer needs for a given period (known as a **requirements contract**), a court will generally enforce that agreement despite the missing quantity. For example, suppose that Builder wishes to purchase small pine trees from Grower for use at one of Builder's commercial office complex sites. If Builder agrees to purchase all of the pine trees grown by Grower over the period of one growing season, this is an output contract. If, on the other hand, Builder agrees with Grower to purchase all of the trees that are needed for this site only, the parties have agreed to a requirements contract. In both cases, an enforceable contract exists despite the missing quantity.[6]

Other Open Terms When a sales contract is missing other terms and the parties have not had an established course of past conduct, the UCC provides the gap fillers as follows:[7]

- *Delivery:* Buyer takes delivery at the *seller's* place of business (i.e., seller is not responsible for delivery). If no time of delivery is specified, the UCC provides for a reasonable time under the circumstances.
- *Payment:* Payment is due at the time and place where the seller is to make delivery and may be made in any commercially reasonable form (such as a business check).
- *Price:* The UCC requires the court to determine a reasonable price at the time of delivery. This is based on industry customs and market value.

---

[6]UCC § 2-306(1).

[7]Delivery: UCC § 2-308(a); payment: UCC § 2-310; price: UCC § 2-305(1).

Firm Offers by Merchants

Recall from Chapter 6, "Overview and Formation of Contracts," that the *offeror* has the right to revoke or modify an offer at any time prior to acceptance by the *offeree* (i.e., "offeror is the master of the offer"). There are certain exceptions to that principle under the common law, such as an option contract. The UCC creates its own brand of irrevocable offer known as a **merchant's firm offer** that applies only to transactions in which the offeror is a *merchant*. A firm offer is created when a merchant offers to buy or sell goods with an explicit promise, in writing, that the offer will be held open for a certain time period. In general, the UCC provides that the offer can be irrevocable for a maximum period of three months. This obligation is binding on the offeror even though the offeree has paid no consideration. Note that if the offeree has paid consideration tied to the offer, this constitutes an option contract and not a firm offer.

AGREEMENT IN SALES CONTRACTS: ACCEPTANCE

The rules provided by Article 2 for accepting an offer in a sales contract are not as rigid as the common law rules. If the offeror does not clearly provide for a method of acceptance, the UCC allows the offeree to accept the offer in any "reasonable manner."[8] One important difference between acceptance standards in the UCC and the common law is that acceptance may still be effective even if the acceptance does *not* match the offer exactly (recall the common law mirror image rule from Chapter 6, "Overview and Formation of Contracts"). Not only does the UCC recognize that a contract may in some cases be created in which the acceptance does not match the offer, but it also fills in gaps to create certainty for the parties to the transaction.

Battle of the Forms

As a practical matter, businesses frequently use preprinted forms to initiate or respond to an offer to sell a good. These forms usually have some blanks for the particular negotiated terms unique to the transaction. Normally, the offer takes the form of a **purchase order** from the buyer that contains preprinted clauses (that typically favor the buyer) and blanks that a purchase manager fills in with terms such as shipment date, product information, quantity, and so forth. The seller's firm will then typically issue an **acknowledgment form**, also called an *invoice,* which also has preprinted provisions (typically favoring the seller) and blanks to accommodate the specifics of that transaction.[9] The UCC provides guidelines on how to resolve a dispute when the terms in these forms conflict. This dilemma is known as the **battle of the forms**.

In a battle of the forms case, the UCC provides that (1) a document may constitute acceptance even though it states terms that are additional to or different from those offered by the offeror and (2) in certain transactions the additional terms proposed in the acceptance may become part of the contract.

Figure 8.1 is a purchase order issued by the hypothetical company Blue Jay Industries.

Nonmerchant Transactions If one of the parties in a sales contract is *not* a merchant, the contract is formed as *originally* offered. That is, the contract is considered accepted, but the additional terms are *not* part of the contract.

---

[8] UCC § 2-206.
[9] UCC § 2-207.

FIGURE 8.1 Purchase Order

Blue Jay Industries

PURCHASE ORDER
Vendor's Name and Address
Roberts' Robes, Inc.
1 First St NE
Washington, DC 20543

SHIP TO:
Blue Jay Industries
100 Alpha Drive
Carltown, PA 17022
Attn: Warehouse Manager

P.O. Date	P.O. Number	Shipping Terms/F.O.B.	Terms
27 August 2020	18-4401	Carrier/Jobsite	30 days from delivery
Buyer Contact	Freight	Date of Delivery	Remarks
Ed Chung	N/A	15 September 2020	Time is of the essence

Quantity Required	Units	Item #/ Description	Unit Cost	Extended Cost
1,000	Clothing piece	White, terry cloth bathrobes (Large) Catalog Item # A5400	$20	$20,000
500	Clothing piece	White, terry cloth bathrobes (Medium) Catalog Item # B5400	$20	$10,000
1,500	Accessory	Specialty bathrobe tote bags	$5	$7,500
		TOTAL		$37,500

Authorized by: *Edwin Chung* Title: Purchase Manager Date: 8/27/2020

Terms and Conditions
1. This Purchase Order is Blue Jay Industries' (BJI) offer to the vendor named above and acceptance is expressly limited to its terms.
2. Please send an invoice/acknowledgment/confirmation to BJI's shipping address.
3. Vendor shall notify BJI as soon as possible if it is unable to fulfill this order on the terms and conditions in this Purchase Order.
4. Delivery beyond the date stated in this Purchase Order shall be subject to cancellation without penalty.

Merchant Transactions If both parties are merchants, the rules for additional terms are more complicated. In a sales contract acceptance between merchants, additional terms *automatically* become part of the enforceable contract unless one of the following conditions exists:

- The offeror has expressly and clearly limited acceptance to the original terms through language such as "The terms of this Purchase Order may not be altered or changed and any alteration of the original terms are expressly rejected" (this is common language on a purchase order);
- The additional term is a *material* change that diverges significantly from those contained in the offer (i.e., one that changes the value of the contract or affects the parties' obligation to perform in a significant way);[10]
- The offeror raises an objection to the additional terms within a reasonable time period according to industry standards.

---

[10]For example, some courts have held that the insertion of an arbitration clause materially alters an offer. *See Dorton v. Collins & Aikman Corp.*, 453 F.2d 1161 (6th Cir. 1972).

In some cases, one merchant proposes a certain term in the offering document (e.g., the purchase order), but the other merchant's acceptance (e.g., the acknowledgment form) states a term that is *different* from the offer. In such a case, the majority of states use the **knockout rule**. Under this rule, the conflicting clauses knock each other out and neither clause becomes part of the contract. Instead, the parties look to the UCC's gap-filler provisions to supply the term.

In Case 8.1, a state appellate court considers the impact of an additional term in an invoice in a merchant transaction.

CASE 8.1 Hebberd-Kulow Enterprises v. Kelomar, No. D066505, 2016 Cal. App. Unpub. LEXIS 696 (Jan. 27, 2016)

FACT SUMMARY Hebberd-Kulow Enterprises (HKE) sold agricultural supplies to Kelomar over a period of approximately 20 years between 1987 and 2007. During that time period, Kelomar would routinely order products over the phone. In these phone calls, the parties' representatives would discuss and agree to the type of item, its quantity, and its price. Kelomar would provide HKE with a purchase order number for the requested items, but it never sent a formal purchase order document. After delivery of the items to Kelomar, HKE would send Kelomar an invoice that corresponded to the applicable purchase order number. In 2003, HKE began to include a provision for late payments on its invoices: "Unpaid invoices beyond terms will be assessed a monthly service charge of 1-1/2%." According to HKE, the late penalty interest rate was standard in the industry. Although Kelomar often paid late, HKE never charged Kelomar interest on the late payments because of their long-term business relationship. HKE never informed Kelomar of the new provision and Kelomar never objected to it.

A dispute between the parties arose after HKE delivered approximately $250,000 worth of goods in 2007. These goods were shipped separately with corresponding invoices. Kelomar refused to pay the invoices because it claimed to have incurred damages in a *different* set of contractual transactions with HKE that were unrelated to the $250,000 shipment. HKE sued for the price of the goods and also for late payment interest on the amount due based on the late payment provision included on the invoices. A jury awarded HKE damages for the unpaid 2007 invoices and awarded HKE the late payment interest included on the invoices. Kelomar appealed, arguing, among other things, that the penalty interest was not part of the agreement under the UCC's battle of the forms provision and that failing to enforce the late payment penalty in the past barred HKE from recovering it in this case.

SYNOPSIS OF DECISION AND OPINION The California Court of Appeals affirmed the jury's award in favor of HKE. The court concluded that the jury had properly applied the battle of the forms standards in finding that the late payment penalty was part of the contract in the 2012 invoices. The court rejected Kelomar's argument that the interest language on the invoices, even if known to it, contained an additional term that would never be enforced because of their course of past dealing. The court pointed out that HKE established that Kelomar did not raise objections to the interest provision and that this was a standard provision in the industry that was not unexpected between merchants.

WORDS OF THE COURT: Battle of the Forms "In this [review of the evidence], we are satisfied that the jury verdict awarding interest pursuant to the [2012] invoices, on the basis of supplemental contractual terms known to and agreed to by the parties, is well supported by the testimony [at trial], which showed the general course of dealing in the industry and the specific transactions between these parties occurring within that framework. After the interest provision was added to the invoices and made known to Kelomar, the parties continued to close their deals over time, and [the UCC] required the jury to take into account what really happened between the parties. This included consideration

(continued)

of Kelomar's refusal to pay and HKE's reasonable expectations that this changed the nature of their contractual arrangements and made a known term, previously held in abeyance, become enforceable."

Case Questions

1. Why didn't HKE ever charge Kelomar the late interest charge until this dispute?
2. Why did the court reject Kelomar's argument that it was reasonable to think that HKE had waived the late interest charge and was barred from recovering it? Should HKE be able to choose when it does and when it doesn't enforce the clause?
3. *Focus on Critical Thinking:* What should HKE do in the future to avoid any such argument that it has waived the right to enforce the late payment term? What could Kelomar do in order to be sure that any future invoice from any future seller does not result in additional terms being added?

 Self-Check Existence of a Sales Contract

Does a sales contract exist? If so, what are the terms of the contract?

1. Boston Hardware Co agrees to buy all the snow shovels it needs from New England Shovel Co. In past years, this has been around 5,000 shovels per year. The mild winter in 2009 causes Boston Hardware to require only 250 shovels, leaving New England Shovel Co with over 4,000 unpurchased shovels.
2. New York High School agrees to purchase 200 desks for $100 each from Big Apple School Supply Inc. The desks are to be ready for September 1, 2008, but there are no delivery terms in the contract.
3. A patient has a dentist install porcelain overlays meant to improve the appearance of her teeth. This was not an emergency or even a necessary procedure. The installation of the overlays was incidental to the purchase of the overlays.
4. L.A. Outfitters offers to sell West Coast Burrito Co 1,100 uniforms by sending West Coast Burrito a letter with price, quantity, and delivery terms and an offer to keep the offer open for seven months. Six months later, West Coast Burrito responds with a standard acknowledgment and acceptance form. The standard form includes an agreement to arbitrate.
5. Chicago Toy Depot Inc. sends a purchase order to Midwest Dolls Inc. for 10,000 "Fancy Nancy" dolls by November 1, 2010, in time for the holiday season. Midwest Dolls returns an acknowledgment letter guaranteeing the dolls for January 1, 2011.

Answers to this Self-Check are provided at the end of the chapter.

Consideration

Recall from the coverage in Chapter 6, "Overview and Formation of Contracts," that most contracts must be supported by consideration. Remember also that most cases involving a nongoods agreement (i.e., those governed by the common law) cannot be *modified* without some additional consideration. While the UCC follows a similar rule that consideration must support sales contracts, a major difference is that the UCC allows contracts to be modified even *without* any additional consideration. The UCC recognizes that market conditions are not static and that the parties may have good faith reasons for modifying a contract without having some additional burden to continue its enforceability. For example, suppose that Wargrave sells 2,000 golf balls to Owen on credit. Owen agrees to pay Wargrave $1,000 plus 6 percent interest on the principal still owed per month for a period

Legal Speak >))

Sales Contract
A sales contract under the UCC is a transfer of title (ownership) to goods for consideration.

of 24 months. After two months, Owen's cash flow is impaired by an unexpected downturn in Owen's business. Owen and Wargrave agree to modify the contract so that it will allow Owen to pay a smaller monthly payment ($500 per month) but at the same interest rate until the balance is paid off in full. Later, Wargrave runs into his own cash flow problems and demands that Owen honor the original Wargrave-Owen credit contract terms. Despite the fact that no additional consideration was given for the modification, the *modified* Wargrave-Owen contract is fully enforceable and the original contract is canceled.

STATUTE OF FRAUDS

LO 8-4

Classify which contracts must be in writing and understand what the writing must contain to be enforceable under the statute of frauds.

The statute of frauds is a legal requirement that certain contracts be in writing in order to be enforceable. The UCC contains a specific section detailing the writing requirements for sales transactions. Any sales contract for goods with a total value of *$500 or more* must be in writing.[11]

While common law contracts require several *specific* terms of a contract to be in writing, the UCC has a much more liberal rule concerning what must be in writing. The UCC's statute of frauds provision is satisfied so long as the writing contains (1) quantity, (2) the signature of the party against whom enforcement is sought, and (3) language that would allow a reasonable person to conclude that the parties intended to form a contract. All other terms and conditions may be proved via testimony concerning oral agreements, past practices, and industry standards. For example, in *Rosenfeld v. Basquiat,* a federal appellate court held that a brown piece of wrapping paper that had quantity, price, a deposit amount, the name of the goods, and the signature of both parties in crayon was more than sufficient to satisfy the UCC's statute of frauds. The case involved the famous artist Jean-Michel Basquiat, who sold several paintings to Michele Rosenfeld, an art dealer. Rosenfeld requested a receipt for a deposit, and Basquiat, a known eccentric, found a brown piece of wrapping paper and, with a crayon in hand, wrote the names of the paintings, the amount paid, and the names of the parties and then signed the paper. Basquiat died soon after the sale of the paintings but before the art dealer could take delivery. Basquiat's estate refused to honor the contract on the basis that the writing was not a formal enough contract because it never specified delivery terms. Rosenfeld sued and won damages. Basquiat's estate appealed, and the U.S. Court of Appeals for the 2nd Circuit affirmed the trial court's decision on the statute of frauds, holding that delivery terms were not required to satisfy the statute of frauds under UCC Article 2.

> Because the writing, allegedly scrawled in crayon by Jean-Michel Basquiat on a large piece of paper, easily satisfied the requirements of § 2-201 of the U.C.C., the estate is not entitled to judgment as a matter of law. It is of no real significance that the jury found Rosenfeld and Basquiat settled on a particular time for delivery and did not commit it to writing. . . .[12]

KEY POINT

The UCC statute of frauds is satisfied if a writing contains the quantity of goods, the signature of the party against whom enforcement is sought, and language that indicates an objective intent to contract.

The statute of frauds section of the UCC also provides a relatively lenient rule for sales contracts between two merchants. A merchant who receives a signed **confirmation memorandum** from the other merchant will be bound by the memorandum just as if she had signed it, unless she promptly objects. Thus, if Abel telephones Cain to order 1,000 golf balls and then Cain sends a written confirmation of the agreement with the correct quantity and price, Abel will be bound by the contract and the statute of frauds is satisfied.

---

[11] UCC § 2-201(1).
[12] *Rosenfeld v. Basquiat,* 78 F.3d 84 (2d Cir. 1996).

It is important to note that the UCC recognizes electronic records and signatures in a sales transaction as valid. This means that the hard copies of documents with original signatures are not always necessary. Although the UCC does not require electronic transactions, it makes clear that a sales contract cannot be held unenforceable simply because it is in electronic form.[13]

CONCEPT SUMMARY *Formation under the UCC*

- In order to encourage the formation and execution of sales contracts, the UCC offers more lenient rules regarding offer, acceptance, consideration, breach, and the statute of frauds.
- An agreement is still valid despite the fact that delivery, pricing, or payment terms are left *open;* the UCC provides standards to fill in the gaps left by the missing terms.
- A written offer by a merchant includes an implied promise to keep the offer open for a stated or unstated amount of time even absent consideration for the option.
- When two merchants submit standardized offer and acceptance forms with conflicting terms, the UCC will still consider the contract accepted unless (1) the offer states explicitly the terms of acceptance, (2) the conflicting terms substantially change the duties of the contract or its value to one party, or (3) the new terms are rejected in a timely manner by the offeror.
- A sales contract can be modified without additional consideration.
- The UCC statute of frauds requires that contracts for the sale of goods valued at more than $500 must be written; however, it requires only that the document contain (1) quantity, (2) the signature of the party against whom enforcement is sought, and (3) language that reasonably shows the parties intended to form a contract.

LEGAL/ETHICAL REFLECTION AND DISCUSSION

The UCC sets out different rules regarding contract formation when a sales contract involves two nonmerchants, a merchant and a nonmerchant, or two merchants.

1. Two nonmerchants may strike a $1,000 deal for the sale of a used television, while two merchants may contract to buy 1,000 new televisions for $1 million. Why are the rules of contract formation stricter for the two nonmerchants than they are for the two merchants?
2. Are different rules necessary? Why or why not?
3. Would UCC gap-fillers work for nonmerchant contracts? Why or why not?
4. If company A sends a purchase order to company B and company B returns an acknowledgment of the order with additional or modified terms, courts may determine that those additional or modified terms become part of the final contract. Is it ethical to force company A to adhere to the additional or modified terms without an express agreement to those terms by company A? Is company B acting unethically by adding or modifying the terms of company A's purchase order?

---

[13]UCC § 2-211.

TITLE AND ALLOCATION OF RISK

LO 8-5

Express how risk of loss is allocated among the parties in a sales contract and identify steps managers take to limit risks and ensure performance.

Business owners and managers must have a working knowledge of the UCC provisions regarding title and risk allocation because these rules play an important part in determining commercial risks at various stages of a business transaction. Once an agreement has been made between the parties, there is likely to be a lapse of time before the buyer actually comes into physical possession of the goods. For example, assume ManufactureCo agrees to sell a new printing press to CopyCo for $100,000 to be delivered within 30 calendar days. What happens if, during the delivery process, the press is damaged in a trucking accident? Or suppose that the press is delivered to a port to be picked up by CopyCo, but a warehouse fire destroys the press before the buyer picks it up. Who bears the burden of the loss? In both cases, CopyCo still needs a press, while ManufacturerCo made good faith efforts to deliver the merchandise as agreed upon. The UCC provides answers to these types of questions in its provisions governing **risk of loss**.[14] Of course, as with other provisions of the UCC, the risk of loss rules apply *only* when the parties have not specifically agreed to risk allocation. If the buyer and seller negotiate and agree to provisions relating to the risk of loss and/or the time that the ownership of goods actually passes, the UCC provisions are not applicable.

Title

Title is the legal term for the right of ownership in a good. Thus, the UCC refers to *passing of title* to indicate the point in time when actual ownership of the good is transferred from seller to buyer. A party holds title to a good when (1) the good is actually in *existence* in tangible form and (2) the good is *identified* in the contract.[15] Identification takes place when the seller has marked or designated the good in some fashion (such as by serial number or lot designation). Once the requirements for title have been met, the UCC provides that title passes to the buyer at the time and place that the seller *completes performance* by making a physical delivery of the goods.

Risk of Loss

The UCC provides a delineation as to when the title actually passes between the seller and the buyer, and it allocates *risk of loss* based on whether the agreement is categorized as either a **shipment contract** or a **destination contract**.

- *Shipment contracts* require the seller to use a carrier (such as a delivery company) to deliver the goods. As a general rule, all contracts for goods are considered shipment contracts *unless* the parties have agreed otherwise. Thus, the seller needs only to deliver the goods to the "hands" of the carrier to achieve complete performance. Once the seller has accomplished this, title is deemed to have passed to the buyer.[16] Normally, the *risk of loss* is allocated to the seller until such time as the seller has delivered the goods to the carrier. If the goods are destroyed after that point, the loss is ordinarily borne by the buyer. Note that the buyer may have recourse against the *carrier* but not against the seller. For example, Schubert agrees to sell Beatrice a specially designed grand piano for $50,000. Beatrice instructs Schubert to deliver the piano from his factory via a specific carrier, Piano Delivery

> **KEY POINT**
>
> Determining the title holder is important because it allows that owner to assert an insurable interest in the goods and obtain protection from possible loss.

---

[14] UCC § 2-401.
[15] UCC § 2-401(1).
[16] UCC § 2-401(1)(a).

Services (PDS), within 10 business days. On day 1, Schubert delivers the piano to PDS in good condition. On day 2, the PDS truck catches on fire and the piano is destroyed. Because the title and risk of loss passed to Beatrice at the point when Schubert delivered the good (piano) to the carrier (PDS), Beatrice has no course of action against Schubert. However, she may have a claim against the carrier (PDS).

- *Destination contracts* require the seller to deliver the goods to a *specified* destination. Typically, the destination is the buyer's place of business or home, but it also can be a third-party destination that the buyer designates. The UCC provides that complete performance occurs when the goods have been **tendered** at the specified destination. Tendering is the legal term for delivery of the *conforming* goods (i.e., the seller delivered what the buyer actually ordered) to the destination that allows the buyer to take delivery.[17] Normally, so long as the goods were properly tendered as agreed, the risk of loss is allocated to the buyer at the time of tender. For example, in the Schubert-Beatrice contract discussed above, suppose that the parties specifically designate their agreement as a *destination contract* and agree that Schubert must deliver the piano to Beatrice's studio in New York City. Schubert selects his own carrier, Cheapo Trucks, and the truck catches on fire in transit. In this case, the loss must be borne by the seller (Schubert) because the piano is destroyed before it arrives at its New York City destination.[18]

Contracts involving shipping generally include the term *FOB* ("free on board"). In the United States, the **FOB point** generally requires the shipper to get the goods to the named location and put the goods in possession of the common carrier. It is at the named FOB point that title and risk of loss pass from seller to buyer. Once the goods are in the hands of the common carrier, the seller's responsibility ends and the buyer's responsibility begins. Therefore, a contract that says, "FOB Buyer's Warehouse, Miami, FL," will require the seller to get the goods to the designated location in Miami. If the seller is in San Francisco, it will be responsible for the goods until they have crossed the entire country. If the contract reads, "FOB Seller's Manufacturing Plant, San Francisco, CA," the buyer will take possession in San Francisco and be responsible for the goods from that point on. When FOB is used in international contracts, it applies only to shipping via freighter ship. This is discussed later in this chapter.

Goods Picked Up by the Buyer

In some cases, the goods are to be picked up by the buyer rather than delivered by the seller. In that case, the risk of loss generally depends on whether or not the seller is a *merchant*. Recall from our earlier discussion that a merchant is one who is regularly engaged in the sale of a particular good. If the seller is a merchant, the risk of loss to goods held by the seller passes to the buyer only when the buyer takes physical possession of the goods. If the seller is not a merchant, the risk of loss to goods held by the seller passes to the buyer on tender of the goods.[19] For example, suppose that on Monday, Gates agrees to purchase 20 computers from CompCo, a computer retail outlet. Gates tells CompCo that he will pick up the computers on Friday. CompCo marks each of the 20 computers with a tag "Sold to Gates." However, Gates cannot make it to CompCo's warehouse on Friday. On Saturday, a thief steals all 20 computers. In this case, CompCo bears the loss because CompCo is a merchant and Gates has not yet taken physical possession of the goods. On the other hand, let's suppose Gates agrees to buy 20 used computers from Local College (a nonmerchant) on Monday. Gates tells Local College he will pick them up on Friday. On Thursday, Local

---

[17] UCC § 2-503(2)(b).

[18] Note that, depending on the circumstances, Schubert may recover his losses from Cheapo Trucks.

[19] UCC § 2-509(3).

College tenders the goods by calling Gates and notifying him that they are ready to be picked up in the lobby of the college's Alpha Hall on Friday anytime between the hours of 8 a.m. and 5 p.m. Gates fails to show up on Friday. During the weekend, a thief breaks into the building and steals the computers. In this case, Gates bears the burden of the loss because Local College is not a merchant under the UCC and Local College tendered the computers by giving Gates proper notice regarding when pickup could occur and where the goods were located.

✓ Self-Check Risk of Loss

Who bears the risk of loss?

1. Marshall Clothing entered a shipment contract with Chase Department Stores to send Chase 3,000 black robes via Mercury Shipping Co. The robes were irreparably damaged in Mercury's warehouse by moths.
2. Taney's Treats purchased 450 gallons of ice cream from Harlan Dairy Co. The contract states that payment is due upon receipt of the ice cream at Taney's store. All 450 gallons melt in transit on a broken truck owned by Hermes Food Delivery Service.
3. Holmes Hats enters a destination contract to deliver 1,000 top hats to Cardozo Men's Stores. The courier delivers 1,000 bowler hats to Cardozo. Before Cardozo can return the incorrect hats, a flood ruins the entire delivery.
4. Smooth Lager is a brewery located in Montana. It enters into a contract to brew 500 kegs of its beer for shipment to a distributor in Alabama. The contract says, "FOB Distributor's Warehouse, Mobile, AL." Smooth Lager delivers the 500 kegs to the common carrier, but the kegs are destroyed when the truck carrying the beer has an accident while driving through Nebraska.
5. White purchases a car from Brennan Motors. The contract states specifically that title is not transferred prior to the title document being signed by both parties. The clerk is out sick, so the title papers cannot be produced that day. White drives the car home with the contract signed only by him and crashes the car.

Answers to this Self-Check are provided at the end of the chapter.

CONCEPT SUMMARY Title and Allocation of Risk

- Risk allocation provisions in the UCC do not apply if the contract specifically lays out terms for risk allocation or title transfer.
- Neither the seller nor the buyer can hold title to goods until the goods are in physical existence and have been identified.
- The risk of loss is borne by the party who has title to the goods.
- Tender of goods occurs when the seller produces conforming goods and provides adequate notice of their delivery to the buyer.
- In a shipping contract, title is transferred from seller to buyer when the goods are given to the courier; in a destination contract, title passes to the buyer when the goods are tendered to the buyer.

PERFORMANCE OF SALES CONTRACTS

Once the parties to a sales contract have agreed on its terms, the law imposes certain other duties and obligations in performing the contract. In addition to the express terms by the parties, the UCC imposes a requirement of *good faith* and spells out the standards for place, time, and acceptance of delivery. Additionally, courts may also look to the customary standards in the particular industry and the course of past dealing between the parties in interpreting the parties' duties and obligations. Of course, the parties may always expressly agree to unique delivery, risk allocation, or payment terms. But if the terms are not expressed, the UCC helps to fill in any gaps and the parties are bound by the UCC terms.

LO 8-6

Recognize the UCC rights and obligations of buyers and sellers and the consequences of breaching a contract.

Obligations of All Parties

The UCC has a *good faith* provision (similar to the duty of good faith in a common law contract) that imposes a duty of good faith and commercial reasonableness as the bedrock of any sales contract.[20] Good faith is defined in the UCC as "honesty in fact in the conduct or transaction concerned."[21] Additionally, merchants also have the duty to act in a *commercially reasonable* manner. Generally, this means that merchants (merchants only) must observe industry standards and practices that may be unique to a particular industry or field.

For example, in *Sons of Thunder v. Borden,* the New Jersey Supreme Court held that a buyer breached the duty of good faith by willfully trying to circumvent its contractual obligations to a seller that made a significant investment to carry out its obligations. The case involved a contract between a food company and a supplier of clams to purchase a certain number of clams per month. The seller purchased two specialty boats to fulfill the contract and took out a significant loan to finance the purchase. Soon thereafter, the buyer's company changed management and concluded that the contract was not profitable. As a result, the buyer began to buy only a fraction of its clams from the seller's boats, and this significantly reduced the revenue produced by the boats. When the seller sued for breach of contract, the jury awarded damages to the seller, including damages for breach of good faith. The court ruled

> The obligation to perform in good faith exists in every contract, including those contracts that contain express and unambiguous provisions permitting either party to terminate the contract without cause. . . . Accepting those facts and the reasonable inferences therefrom offered as true, we determine that the jury had sufficient evidence to find that [the buyer] was not "honest in fact" as required by the UCC.[22]

Seller's Obligations and Rights

Fundamentally, the seller's primary obligation is to transfer and deliver conforming goods to the buyer. *Conforming goods* simply means that the goods must conform exactly to the agreed-upon description of the goods. Under the doctrine referred to as **tender of delivery**, the UCC obligates the seller to have or tender the goods, give the buyer appropriate notice of the tender, and take any actions necessary to allow the buyer to take delivery.[23] Absent any specific agreement between the parties to the contrary, the UCC uses a general *reasonableness requirement* to govern the delivery process. That is, the goods must be delivered

---

[20] UCC § 1-203.
[21] UCC § 1-201(19).
[22] *Sons of Thunder v. Borden,* 148 N.J. 396 (1997).
[23] UCC § 2-503(1).

at a reasonable hour, in a reasonable manner, and in one shipment. In the case of goods that are to be picked up, the goods must be made available at a reasonable time to allow the buyer to take possession.

Perfect Tender Under the UCC, the seller's obligation actually goes beyond just delivering conforming goods. The seller must tender the goods in a manner that matches the contract terms in every respect. This is known as the **perfect tender rule**.[24] If the seller fails to achieve perfect tender, the buyer has three options: (1) Reject the entire shipment of goods within a reasonable time, (2) accept the shipment of goods as is, or (3) accept any number of commercial units and reject the rest of the goods in a reasonable time (e.g., accepting 100 nonconforming computer chips from a delivery of 500 nonconforming computer chips).

Although the perfect tender rule may sound oppressive, the UCC also gives the seller certain rights intended to promote the completion of the original contract.

Legal Speak >))

Seasonable Notice
Notification to the other party within either an agreed-upon time or a reasonable amount of time given the nature and goals of the contract.

Cure If the seller has delivered goods and the buyer rejects them under the perfect tender rule, the seller has the right to repair or replace the rejected goods *so long as the time period for performance has not expired*. Once the time contemplated for performance has expired, the seller's right to **cure** also expires. If, however, the time for the seller's performance has not expired, the seller may cure by (1) giving notice of her intent to cure and (2) tendering conforming goods in replacement of the rejected goods.[25] For example, on April 1, Lewis contracts with Clarke to provide Clarke with 100 Type-A compasses at $10 per unit to be delivered no later than May 1. Lewis delivers 100 Type-B compasses on April 15, and Clarke rejects the goods as nonconforming. At this point, Lewis has the option to cure because the date for performance is still two weeks away. So, if Lewis notifies Clarke that he intends to cure and then ships 100 Type-A compasses to Clarke on April 30, he has completed performance consistent with the UCC requirements and, assuming the new shipment of goods conforms, Clarke must accept the goods.

In some instances, the right to cure may exist even *after* the time period for performance has come due. The UCC provides that if the seller reasonably believes that the nonconforming goods will be acceptable to the buyer (perhaps because the seller has shipped a more expensive product or because of a course of past dealing between the buyer and seller) with or without a money allowance, then the seller gets additional time to cure after the time under the contract has passed. The seller must seasonably notify the buyer of her intent to cure.[26]

In the Lewis-Clarke contract discussed above, suppose that Lewis discovers that the Type-A compasses are out of stock, so he instead ships Clarke Type-A1A compasses (a more expensive and newer model) on the last day for performance. If Lewis rejects the goods, most courts would allow Clarke, so long as he has given Lewis seasonable notice, to cure even though the time period for performance has passed. This is because Clarke has been reasonable in his assumption that a newer and more expensive model would be an acceptable substitute for the ordered model.[27]

Figure 8.2 illustrates the two alternatives for cure in the Lewis-Clarke contract.

---

[24]UCC § 2-601.
[25]UCC § 2-508(1), (2).
[26]UCC § 2-508(2).
[27]Based on *Bartus v. Riccardi*, 284 N.Y.S.2d 222 (1967).

FIGURE 8.2 Two Ways to Cure the Lewis-Clarke Agreement

Number 1 Cure (Conforming Goods)

| April 1 Lewis-Clarke Agreement 100 Type-A compasses (value = $10/ea) Due May 1 | → | April 15 Lewis ships 100 Type-B compasses Clarke rejects goods | → | Before May 1, Lewis ships 100 Type-A compasses |

Number 2 Cure (Substitute Goods)

| April 1 Lewis-Clarke Agreement 100 Type-A compasses (value = $10/ea) Due May 1 | → | May 1 Lewis ships 100 Type A-1-A compasses (value = $20/ea) | → | May 1 If Clarke accepts nonconforming goods, no need to cure | → | May 1 If Clarke rejects goods, Lewis may notify Clarke that he intends to cure in a reasonable time |

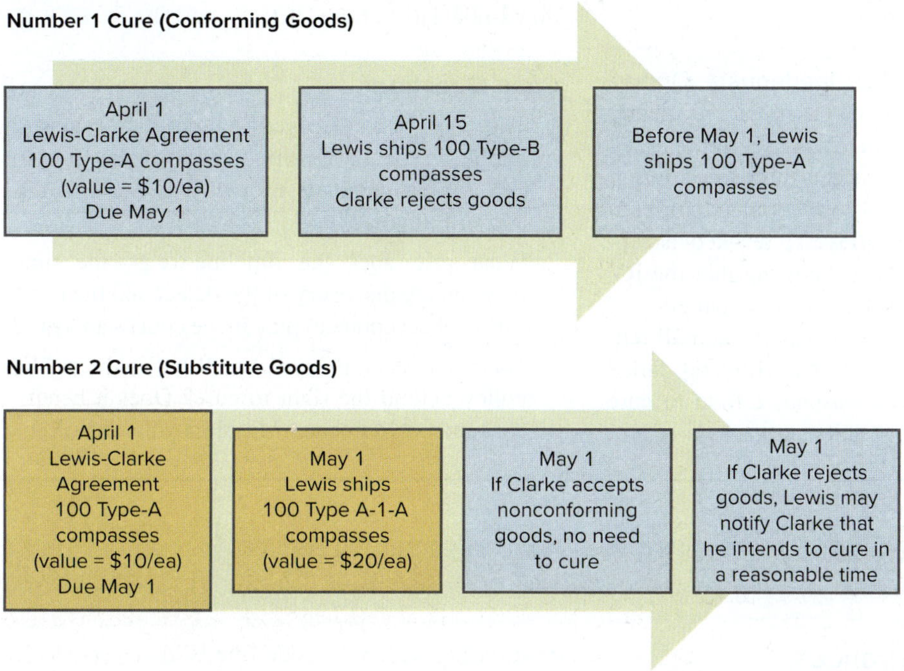

In Case 8.2, a state appellate court analyzes a revocation and a seller's right to cure.

CASE 8.2 Accettura & Wozniak v. Vacationland, Inc., 2018 IL App (2d) 170972 (Sept. 28, 2018)

FACT SUMMARY In April 2014, Accettura and Wozniak (Buyers) bought a new recreational vehicle (RV) from Vacationland, Inc. In July 2014, Buyers discovered a leak in the RV that allowed water from a rainstorm to leak into the dinette area, resulting in water and electrical damage to the RV. Buyers brought the RV to Vacationland for repair on July 14, but representatives at Vacationland determined that the RV needed to be sent to the manufacturer for repair and informed the Buyers that they could not estimate how long the manufacturer would take to repair the RV. On August 2, Buyers verbally revoked acceptance of the RV. The manufacturer had the RV in repair from approximately August 4 through September 23, 2014. On September 28, the Buyers' attorney sent Vacationland a letter revoking acceptance of the RV and demanding a refund of the full purchase price. Vacationland refused and the Buyers filed suit for breach of contract under a variety of theories. The trial court awarded summary judgment to Vacationland and the Buyers appealed, arguing, among other things, that Vacationland did not adequately cure the defects in the RV; thus, Buyers had the right to cancel the contract.

SYNOPSIS OF DECISION AND OPINION The Appellate Court of Illinois affirmed the judgment of the trial court in favor of Vactionland. The court reasoned that the trial court's conclusion that the Buyers did not give the seller the opportunity to cure under section 2-608(1) of the state commercial code (UCC) was properly determined. They found that the UCC requires that the buyer give the seller a reasonable amount of time to cure a defect. Although the UCC does not define "reasonable," the court explained that the Buyer's revocation of

(continued)

acceptance was not valid because the seller here (Vacationland) offered a proper cure (i.e., sending the RV to the manufacturer).

WORDS OF THE COURT: Inadequate Opportunity to Cure "In this case, the record clearly establishes that on July 14, 2014, [Buyers] asked [Vacationland] to cure the defects discovered during their trip to Michigan and [Vacationland] offered [Buyers] a proper cure. [Buyers] revoked acceptance about two weeks later, knowing that the RV was going to the manufacturer to be repaired. . . . Thus, the material facts are undisputed and all reasonable minds would agree that [Buyers] failed to allow [Vacationland] a reasonable time to cure before their purported revocation, as a matter of law.

Accordingly, the trial court properly determined that [Buyers'] revocation was improper under section 2-608(1)(b) of the UCC."

Case Questions

1. The court acknowledged that the UCC doesn't define reasonable in the context of the time to cure. What standard of reasonableness did it apply? Explain.
2. What role does the timeline (e.g., the time between the discovery of the defect and the revocation of acceptance) play in the court's analysis?
3. *Focus on Critical Thinking:* What is the public policy behind the right to cure? Does it benefit consumers? Merchants? Explain your answer.

STRATEGIC LEGAL SOLUTIONS

Performance Assurances

PROBLEM: *In ongoing relationships with vendors, there may be a time when a manager becomes wary about a provider's ability to sell or a buyer's ability to continue making regular payments.*

Perhaps this skepticism is based on conduct of certain parties or on conversations with the vendor. What legal methods will help reduce the risk that the company won't be left fighting other creditors in bankruptcy or suffer any further losses? For example, suppose two companies enter into an agreement for the sale of electronic components. Whiteside agrees to purchase 50 lots of components per month, from January through June, from Greenside and to pay Greenside $7,500 per lot *within 10 days* after the lots are delivered. On January 2, Greenside tenders a conforming delivery, and Whiteside pays by check on January 6. In February, Greenside delivers a second lot, but Whiteside fails to make the payment as agreed. As the end of February approaches with Whiteside's monthly invoice still unpaid, Greenside's manager faces a dilemma. While she wishes to preserve the potentially lucrative contractual relationship with Whiteside, she is also responsible for protecting Greenside's interests and inventory.

STRATEGIC SOLUTION: *Greenside's manager should seek UCC assurances about the past-due and future payments.*

The UCC provides both parties the right to demand **assurances** from each other concerning performance. The UCC provides that when one party has *reasonable grounds* to believe that the other will not perform, she has the right to demand that the other party give her written assurance that performance will take place as agreed.[28] If that party does not provide adequate assurance of performance within 30 days, the demanding party may then suspend performance until she receives the requested assurance. In the Whiteside-Greenside contract, suppose that one week prior to the date when the March delivery is scheduled, Greenside's manager requests that Whiteside provide her with *written assurances* that (1) Whiteside will pay the amount due immediately and (2) Whiteside will continue to pay Greenside within the 10-day period as stated in the original contract. If Whiteside

(continued)

---

[28]UCC § 2-609(1).

ignores the request or does not provide the requested assurances, Greenside's manager then has the right to suspend performance and has no duty to deliver another lot until she receives assurances from Whiteside. By using this UCC protection, Greenside's manager minimizes losses without breaching the original agreement. She preserves the contractual relationship until such time as the payment problems may be worked out to Greenside's satisfaction.

At that point, delivery may resume and continue in accordance with the original contract. If, however, conditions are sufficient to allow Greenside to reasonably believe that Whiteside intends to *renege* on its obligations in the contract, Greenside may cancel the contract and pursue legal remedies (such as a lawsuit to recover money damages) under the UCC provisions governing *anticipatory repudiation* (discussed in the next section).

Commercial Impracticability   Recall from the previous chapter that the common law excuses performance when a contract becomes **commercially impracticable**. The UCC applies a commercial impracticability rule when a delay in delivery or nondelivery has been made impracticable by the occurrence of an unanticipated event, so long as the event directly affects a basic assumption of the contract. Commercial impracticability is a *narrow doctrine*. For example, most courts will not allow a commercial impracticability defense for an unexpected increase in prices of materials or labor because a reasonable businessperson should have been aware that the economic conditions could affect the price of the contract.

In Case 8.3, a federal appellate court considers whether shifting market prices can be the basis for commercial impracticability.

CASE 8.3 Hemlock Semiconductor Operations v. SolarWorld Industries Sachsen, 867 F.3d 692 (6th Cir. 2017)

FACT SUMMARY Hemlock Semiconductor Operations (Hemlock) and SolarWorld Industries Sachsen (Sachsen) are both involved in manufacturing components of solar-powered products. They entered into a series of long-term supply agreements (LTAs), by which Hemlock in Michigan would supply Sachsen in Germany with set quantities of polysilicon (Silicon) at fixed prices between the years 2006 and 2019. The market price of the Silicon was above the LTA price in the initial year of the agreement. However, the market price of Silicon plummeted several years later after the Chinese government began subsidizing its national production of polysilicon materials. As a result, Hemlock and Sachsen reached a temporary agreement to lower the LTA price in 2011. When that agreement expired in 2012, however, the price reverted to the original amount. Hemlock then demanded that Sachsen pay the original LTA price for the specified quantity of Silicon for the 2012-billing year. Sachsen refused, and Hemlock sued Sachsen for breach of contract. The trial court granted Hemlock's motion for a summary judgment and awarded it $800 million in damages. Sachsen appealed based on, among other theories, commercial impracticability due to the Chinese government's unforeseeable and extreme actions.

SYNOPSIS OF DECISION AND OPINION The U.S. Court of Appeals for the Sixth Circuit affirmed the trial court's judgment in favor of Hemlock. The court ruled that the impracticability defense applies only if an unanticipated circumstance has made performance of the promise vitally different from what should reasonably have been within the contemplation of both parties when they entered into the contract. In other words, the defense is viable only if an unforeseen event occurs and the nonoccurrence of that event was a basic assumption on which both

(continued)

parties made the contract. Because a shift in market prices for goods and supplies is a basic fact of doing business, it cannot be the basis of a commercial impracticability defense.

WORDS OF THE COURT: Shifts in Market Prices "The expectation that current market conditions will continue for the life of the contract is not a basic assumption; [thus,] shifts in market prices ordinarily do not constitute impracticability. Likewise, the simple fact that a contract has become unprofitable for one of the parties is generally insufficient to establish impracticability. This is especially true when the parties have entered into a contract for the sale of goods at fixed prices because such contracts are made for the very purpose of establishing a stable price despite a fluctuating market.... 'Neither is a rise or a collapse in the market itself a justification [for asserting the impracticability defense], for that is exactly the type of business risk which business contracts made at fixed prices are intended to cover.' . . . Even relatively drastic changes in the market have been held insufficient to trigger the impracticability defense."

Case Questions

1. The court ruled that the Chinese government's subsidization of polysilicon was not the basis for a commercial impracticability defense. Is the economic turbulence caused by one of the world's largest economies an "unforeseen event"? Why or why not?

2. What does the court suggest in offering, "such contracts are made for the very purpose of establishing a stable price despite a fluctuating market"?

3. *Focus on Critical Thinking:* Is there any way of drafting a sales contract that *does* consider market conditions? Try using a sliding-scale type of price agreement to adjust the contract in this case. Would it work or not? Why?

Buyers have a reasonable time to inspect the goods to be sure that they conform to the contract.

Thomas_EyeDesign/Getty Images

Buyer's Rights and Obligations

The buyer's primary obligation is triggered when the seller tenders delivery. Once the buyer has accepted the goods, the buyer must pay for them in accordance with the contract. Payments may come in a variety of forms, and frequently the parties have negotiated and agreed on the details of payments (cash versus credit, terms of payment, etc.). In the absence of agreement, the UCC provides that the buyer must make full payment at the time and place that she has received the goods.[29] When the parties have agreed on credit for payment, the amount owed is paid out over a period of time at a certain rate of interest. Typically, interest begins accruing 30 days after shipment.[30]

Buyer's Right of Inspection: Acceptance or Rejection Unless the parties agree otherwise, the buyer has a reasonable time period to inspect the goods to be sure they conform to the contract. After inspection, the buyer may (1) communicate to the seller that she has accepted the goods; (2) do nothing, and thus be presumed to have accepted the

---

[29] UCC § 2-310(a).

[30] UCC § 2-310(d) provides that the credit period begins on the date of shipment from the seller—not on the date of receipt.

goods unless she gives prompt notice of a rejection (or partial rejection); or (3) notify the seller that she is rejecting the goods[31] (or part of the goods). If the buyer properly rejects the goods, the buyer may also cancel the balance of the contract and pursue any appropriate legal remedies against the seller (breach and remedies for sales contracts are discussed in the next section). The buyer has an obligation to affirmatively notify the seller of the rejection in a timely manner so that the seller still has some opportunity to cure or a reasonable amount of time to recover the goods.

If the seller has shipped conforming goods as agreed, the buyer has the *duty to accept* them and become the owner of the goods in accordance with concepts of title.[32] If the seller has shipped nonconforming goods, but the buyer is still willing to accept them, the UCC provides the buyer with the opportunity to later revoke acceptance *only* if the nonconformity substantially impairs the value of the goods. The acceptance of nonconforming goods by the buyer triggers the buyer's obligation to pay consistent with the terms of the agreement.

 Self-Check Buyer's Rights and Obligations

Does the grocer have an obligation to pay? Why or why not?

1. Grocer orders 100 Grade-A eggs from Farmer per month at market price for a period of three years. Farmer delivers Grade-A eggs every month for one year, but Grocer then begins rejecting the eggs, claiming that the market price for eggs is too high and the egg contract is commercially impracticable.
2. Grocer receives 40 bushels of corn rather than the tomatoes he ordered, but he signs a receipt for the corn anyway. The next day Grocer changes his mind and sends back the rejected corn.
3. Grocer orders 50 gallons of whole milk from Dairy to be delivered December 23. On December 20 he receives 60 gallons of skim milk. He rejects the order but does not inform Dairy of his rejection. On January 2, Dairy demands full payment.
4. Two days before Thanksgiving, Grocer orders 100 turkeys, but the next morning he receives a delivery of 200 chickens. Afraid of losing all his customers the day before Thanksgiving, Grocer accepts 100 chickens and notifies the seller that he is rejecting part of the delivery.

Answers to this Self-Check are provided at the end of the chapter.

Special Rules for Installment Contracts

Cash flow or other business reasons sometimes require delivery and billing in two or more separate lots. The UCC provides for such circumstances through use of an **installment contract**. In an installment contract, each lot must be accepted and paid for separately. This means that a buyer can accept one installment without giving up the right to reject any additional installments that are nonconforming. This is essentially an exception to the perfect tender rule because the standard for rejection is more restrictive and, thus, provides additional tender protection to the seller. In an installment contract, the buyer

---

[31]Recall the good faith requirement of the UCC. Note that the parties do not have an absolute right to reject the goods. The buyer must have a good faith and lawfully recognized reason to reject (such as when the seller has shipped nonconforming goods). UCC §§2-601 and 2-602 allow for a rejection of goods on reasonable grounds only.
[32]UCC §§2-606, 2-607.

may reject an installment only if the nonconformity *substantially* impairs the value of that installment *and* the nonconformity cannot be cured. If a buyer subsequently accepts a nonconforming installment of the goods and does not notify the seller that she is canceling the contract, the UCC provides that the seller may assume the contract to be reinstated.

CONCEPT SUMMARY Performance of Sales Contracts

- Under the UCC, parties to a sales contract have an implied good faith obligation to be "honest in fact in the conduct of the transaction concerned."
- Except in the case of commercial impracticability, the seller must fulfill an obligation to perfectly tender goods in accordance with the contract or the buyer may reject the goods.
- When nonconforming goods have been delivered and time exists that will allow conforming goods to be delivered before performance is due, the seller may cure by delivering the conforming goods.
- When nonconforming goods equal to or superior to the contracted-for goods have been delivered in good faith, the seller has the right to cure even if the time for performance has expired, as long as the buyer is not injured by the delay.
- The buyer can accept the goods or reject them with seasonable notice, but if he accepts, his obligation to pay is then triggered.
- An installment contract permits delivery of goods in separate lots and payment at separate times, with the new right to accept or reject each time.

LO 8-7

Identify appropriate remedies and damages available to buyers and sellers.

BREACH AND REMEDIES IN SALES AGREEMENTS

Although the UCC is grounded in the principle that the law should encourage the consummation of business transactions, it also defines what constitutes nonperformance, known as **breach**, and provides relief for parties that have acted in good faith and sustained damages through no fault of their own. These relief mechanisms are called **remedies**[33] in the UCC and are based on the goal of placing the innocent (nonbreaching) party back in the same position he would have been in if the contract *had been performed* by the parties as originally contemplated in the agreement.

Anticipatory Repudiation in the UCC

Recall that, under the common law, contracting parties have a right to cancel the contract even before any performance is due if it becomes clear that one party does not intend to perform as agreed. The UCC embraces that same right by recognizing that if one party communicates in a way that is inconsistent with performance—whether in writing, orally, or by some action—this is a *repudiation* of the agreement. The UCC treats this as a breach even if performance was *not yet due*. The nonbreaching party may then either (1) suspend her own performance, treating the breach as final, and pursue any remedies available (remedies are discussed in the next section) or (2) suspend her own performance, wait for a period of time for the breaching party to *retract* the repudiation, and promise to perform.

---

[33] UCC § 2-701 et seq.

Remedies Available to the Seller

A buyer breaches a sales contract when she does any one of the following: (1) rejects the goods despite the fact that the goods conformed to the contract specifications, (2) wrongfully revokes an acceptance, (3) fails to pay the seller in accordance with the contract, or (4) fails to meet her obligations under the contract. In the event of one or more of those instances, the UCC allows the seller to pursue certain remedies against the buyer to recover any losses and prevent future losses. Note that the UCC allows the seller more than one remedy as long as each remedy is *necessary* to help the nonbreaching party recover damages. The choice of remedies depends on *when* the breach occurs relative to whether the goods have been delivered.

Goods in Hands of Seller
When the breach has occurred before the goods were actually received by the buyer, the seller may

1. Cancel the contract outright or discontinue his own performance (such as withholding or stopping delivery).
2. Resell the goods at fair market value to another party or dispose of the goods for recycling in accordance with reasonable commercial standards of the industry. Commercial standards vary depending on the nature of the goods and are subject to state law. If goods are nonperishable, commercial standards and state law may require a public auction advertised over a period of time. Perishable goods are excluded from typical advertising requirements in an effort to mitigate damages.
3. Recover any incidental damages related to the exercise of the reselling remedy, such as hard costs of resale (e.g., broker's commission, auction fees), and any difference in value between the original contract price and the resale price.[34]
4. If unable to sell the goods at fair market value, recover the full value of the contract from the buyer. If the seller exercises this remedy, he may no longer resell the goods even if a new buyer is found.

Legal Speak >))

Incidental Damages under the UCC Any commercially reasonable charges, expenses, or commissions incurred in stopping delivery or in transportation, care, and custody of goods after a buyer's breach.

Goods in Hands of Buyer
In the case of nonpayment after the buyer has accepted (or such time has passed that the buyer is assumed to have accepted) the goods, the seller may recover the *entire* contract price plus incidental damages. This is also true if the goods are damaged or destroyed, assuming the risk of loss has been passed to the buyer via contract terms or by virtue of the UCC.

In the case of wrongful rejection (rejecting conforming goods) or wrongful revocation of acceptance, the seller may *reclaim* the goods and exercise the remedies provided for in the UCC when the goods are in the hands of the seller, including the recovery of costs related to the reclamation.

Remedies Available to the Buyer

The primary way that a seller breaches a contract is by delivering *nonconforming* goods to the buyer or by failing to make timely delivery of all or part of the lot. A seller who has repudiated the contract prior to delivery of the goods (recall the doctrine of *anticipatory repudiation,* discussed earlier in this chapter) is also deemed to have breached the contract, and the buyer is entitled to pursue remedies. The UCC provides remedies to protect the buyer from further damages and to compensate her for any losses suffered due to the breach.

---

[34]UCC § 2-207(1).

Remedies Following Rejection of Goods The UCC provides buyers with the immediate remedy of **rightful rejection** of all or part of the lot when the seller delivers nonconforming goods. In the case of rejection due to nonconformity, the buyer must give the seller *seasonable notification* of the rejection. By exercising the right of rejection, the buyer has canceled the contract and is thus discharged from performing (paying) under the agreement and may recover any money already paid (such as a deposit). Rejection also enables the buyer to pursue additional remedies to prevent any further losses and/or recover losses incurred as a result of the breach.

Cover Consider the dilemma of the buyer when the seller has not made a timely delivery or has delivered defective goods. No matter what the legal impact of the seller's actions, the buyer who requires the goods in order to conduct business operations must act immediately to prevent her own losses. The UCC provides the buyer with an option to take immediate steps by canceling the contract and purchasing *substitute* goods from another vendor (a right known as **cover**) in order to continue business operations. The UCC requires the covering party to purchase the goods in good faith and without unreasonable delay.[35] The right of cover also allows the covering party to bring a lawsuit to recover from the seller the difference between the *cost of cover* and the *original* contract costs. Covering parties may also recover incidental or consequential damages. However, if the buyer actually saved expenses because of the breach by the seller, those costs are deducted.

For example, suppose that on June 1, PartCo agrees to sell ToyCo goods based on the following memorandum drafted by ToyCo's manager:

1. *Item and Quantity:* 1,000 Type-A toy parts.
2. *Price:* $5 per toy part.
3. *Delivery:* On or before June 30 by Swift Trucking Company to ToyCo warehouse. Delivery charge of $500 to be paid by buyer.

On July 1, the parts have not arrived, but ToyCo has invested substantial sums in preparing its manufacturing operations to be ready in anticipation of the June 30 shipment date. Thus, ToyCo's manager opts to cancel the contract and contacts a local company, NewCo, to order the substitute goods (toy parts). NewCo's price per part is $7. However, because NewCo is a local company, the delivery charge will be only $100. The damages calculation is

Cover damages:
$7 (reasonable price of substitute goods) less $5 (contract price) = $2 per part for 1,000 parts
Plus:
Incidental and consequential damages (if applicable)
Minus:
Costs saved by virtue of the seller's breach ($400 reduction on delivery charges)

Lawsuit for Money Damages There may be certain instances in which the buyer properly rejects the goods but does not think it prudent or necessary to use the right to cover. In this case, the UCC gives the buyer the right to sue the breaching party for damages sustained due to the breach. If the buyer chooses this option (not to cover), the measure of damages is different from the covering damage measure. The major difference

---

Legal Speak >))

Consequential Damages under the UCC
Such damage, loss, or injury as does not flow directly and immediately from the act of the party, but only from some consequences or results of such act.[36]

---

[35]UCC § 2-712(1).
[36]UCC § 2-715(1).

is the *point in time* used to calculate any losses. In a no-cover case, the recovery is derived by taking the difference between the contract price and the market price at the *time that the buyer learned* of the breach.

Specific Performance Sometimes it is simply not feasible for the buyer to use cover or a suit for money damages as a remedy. This occurs, for example, when the goods in question are *unique* and cannot be obtained elsewhere in the market, as in the case of a sales contract for a rare book, a particular work of art, or a unique coin collection. In these circumstances, the UCC provides the buyer with a remedy of **specific performance**, which allows the buyer to obtain a court order that compels the breaching party to perform his obligation under the contract.

Remedies Following Acceptance of Nonconforming Goods

Commercial conditions or special circumstances may sometimes make the buyer accept (knowingly or unknowingly) nonconforming goods. The UCC recognizes certain situations in which, even though the buyer has accepted the goods, there still may be a need to protect the buyer's rights by providing remedies for relief.

Revocation of Acceptance Sometimes a buyer may not realize that the goods are *nonconforming*, and after a cursory inspection the buyer may *unknowingly* accept the goods. The UCC provides protection for such buyers, so long as they act within a reasonable time after discovery of the nonconformance. Buyers who have accepted the goods that turn out to be defective or nonconforming may still recover for any losses by **revoking acceptance**. For a buyer to effectively revoke acceptance, the UCC requires that the nonconformance must *substantially* impair the value of the goods and the buyer must notify the seller within a reasonable time after he discovers (or should have discovered) the breach.[37] Once a reasonable time (generally in accordance with industry standards) has passed after acceptance, the buyer is then barred from pursuing a remedy.

Lawsuit for Money Damages The buyer may wish to accept the nonconforming goods with full knowledge that the tender of delivery was less than perfect. In this case, the UCC gives protection to the buyer by making it clear that the buyer does *not* give up the right to sue the seller for the buyer's damages resulting from the seller's delivery of nonconforming goods.[38] Just as in a revocation of acceptance (discussed earlier), in order to preserve the right to sue for damages, the buyer must *notify* the seller within a *reasonable time* after the defect was or should have been discovered.

Risk of Loss

An important UCC provision that protects the buyer when a seller has shipped nonconforming goods relates to the risk of loss. The UCC protects a buyer when delivery of nonconforming goods creates a right of rejection. It provides that the risk of loss *remains on the seller until cure or acceptance*. This protection also exists where the buyer rightfully revokes acceptance. The idea is that the law does not allow a seller to shift the risk of loss to the buyer unless the contract conforms with all the agreed-upon conditions. In Case 8.4, a state appellate court reviews a trial court's risk of loss analysis in the context of rejected goods.

---

[37] UCC § 2-607(3)(a).
[38] UCC § 2-714(1).

CASE 8.4 3L Communications v. Merola d/b/a NY Telecom Supply, No. M2012-02163-COA-R3-CV, 2013 Tenn. App. LEXIS 589 (Sept. 6, 2013)

FACT SUMMARY 3L Communications (3L) is a merchant that sells high-end optical telecommunications equipment. Merola does business as NY Telecom Supply (Merola) and is a wholesaler in the telecommunications equipment business. 3L entered into an agreement with Merola for 3L to purchase five optical circuit boards. In accordance with the agreement, Merola shipped the circuit boards via Federal Express, with the balance of $35,090 due on delivery in the form of a cashier's check. The circuit boards arrived at 3L's office and were paid for as agreed. However, upon inspection of the circuit boards, 3L discovered that the boards were damaged and were not as Merola had described. 3L immediately contacted Merola and notified her that the boards were unusable and that 3L was returning them. In response, Merola provided shipping instructions and an account number to be used for returning the goods. 3L followed the shipping instructions and the boards were returned to Merola's address. Two weeks later, 3L sent an e-mail message to Merola regarding the refund for the boards. Merola responded that she had not received the returned boards. 3L then supplied Merola with tracking information from the carrier that indicated that the boards had been delivered two weeks earlier. Despite Merola's insistence that she had not received the boards, detailed records from the carrier indicated that the goods were, in fact, delivered. After Merola stopped responding to 3L inquiries, 3L filed suit to recover its $35,090 payment. Merola filed a counterclaim, arguing that 3L had the risk of loss for the returned boards. The trial court held in favor of 3L, finding that risk remained with Merola. She appealed.

SYNOPSIS OF DECISION AND OPINION The Court of Appeals of Tennessee affirmed the trial court's decision on the issue of risk of loss. The court ruled in favor of 3L, reasoning that the evidence indicated that 3L discovered certain problems and seasonably notified Merola of the problems and ultimately rejected all of the boards as nonconforming with the parties' agreement. Because 3L could not resell the boards, the only alternative was to return the goods and demand a refund. The court rejected Merola's claim that the risk passed to 3L on the original delivery. It was clear that the goods were nonconforming and, according to the state's UCC provisions, the risk stays with the seller in the case of proper rejection of nonconforming goods.

WORDS OF THE COURT: Risk of Loss "[I]t is undisputed that the boards at issue here did not conform to [Merola's] representation that they had been tested and were in good condition. Rather, [3L] discovered that the boards had been repaired with 'jumper repairs,' and that at least one of the boards did not have a serial number. It is undisputed that [3L] was unable to sell the product to its customer. From the record, we cannot conclude that the boards conformed to the agreement between the parties. . . . Based upon the facts of this case, we [affirm] the trial court's determination that the [UCC] applies to this transaction [and] that the risk of loss remained with Ms. Merola."

Case Questions

1. 3L had the option of obtaining cover as a remedy. Why did 3L pursue money damages instead?
2. Suppose that instead of shipping the faulty boards to 3L, Merola shipped a more expensive brand than 3L ordered. How would that impact 3L's rights as a buyer?
3. *Focus on Critical Thinking:* In this case, Merola also argued that she was not a "merchant" for purposes of the UCC because she operated as a sole proprietor out of her home. The court ruled against her. What is the definition of a merchant? Should someone who has minimal business experience or education be held to the standard of a merchant? Why or why not?

CONCEPT SUMMARY Breach and Remedies in Sales Agreements

- The UCC seeks to remedy breach by placing the nonbreaching party in the same situation she would have been in had the contract been executed as written.
- Faced with anticipatory repudiation by the other party, a party under the UCC can either withdraw and sue for damages or halt performance until the repudiation is retracted.
- If a buyer breaches before delivery by rejection of or nonpayment for conforming goods, then the seller may stop further performance, resell the goods, or, if unable to resell, seek damages. If the buyer's breach occurs after delivery, the seller may sue for the full contract price or reclaim the goods and collect incidental damages.
- If a seller breaches by delivering nonconforming goods, the buyer may reject the goods, seek cover and sue for damages incurred by the new purchase, not seek cover and sue for damages for the difference between the contract and market prices at the time of breach, or ask for specific performance. If the buyer accepts the nonconforming goods out of ignorance or necessity, he still retains the right to sue for damages incurred by the nonconformance.

CONTRACTS FOR INTERNATIONAL SALES OF GOODS

More than ever before in the history of commerce, business managers and owners are engaged in commercial transactions that reach beyond the borders of their own nation. Extraordinary advances over the last two decades in technology, shipping methods, and logistics control have lowered the global barrier to entry for many businesses. In this section we focus on international transactions for the sale of goods by examining the international counterparts to the UCC: the U.N. Convention on Contracts for the International Sale of Goods (CISG) and the International Chamber of Commerce (INCO) terms. In Chapter 25, "International Law and Global Commerce," international law is covered in broad strokes to facilitate an understanding of the sources of international law, foreign legal systems, trade protections, and the public policy objectives of trading partners.

LO 8-8

Explain the risks involved in sales transactions with foreign companies and know how to mitigate those risks by understanding international commercial laws.

U.N. Convention on Contracts for the International Sale of Goods

In 1988, the United States became a signatory nation to a U.N. treaty that attempts to establish an international commercial code. The **U.N. Convention on Contracts for the International Sale of Goods (CISG)** governs sale of goods transactions between businesses in any of its 90 member countries.[39] Much like the UCC, the CISG exists to fill in the missing terms of a sale of goods contract when the parties haven't otherwise agreed on terms. Parties are free to negotiate the allocation of risk, insurance requirements, delivery, payment terms, choice of law, and the like to displace the CISG principles. It is particularly important for managers to understand *choice of law and forum* principles in international contracts because risk and expense of enforcement become increasingly important factors that should be considered in arriving at appropriate pricing, delivery proposals, and insurance needs.

Legal Speak >))

Choice of Law and Forum Clauses
Terms of a contract that predetermine which nation's laws and court system will be used in a potential lawsuit under that contract.

---

[39] In April 2019, the Democratic People's Republic of Korea (North Korea) became the 90th country to adopt the CISG. It will enter into force for North Korea April 1, 2020. See http://www.uncitral.org/.

If one party will have to travel significant distances or hire special counsel to enforce an agreement or recover for damages suffered, adjusting the price or delivery terms accordingly may sometimes help to reduce risk.

Coverage and Major Provisions of CISG

The CISG operates on the same fundamental principle as many commercial codes around the world (including the UCC) in that the law favors the completion of a transaction as agreed upon but also provides relief when one party has breached. The CISG covers parties that maintain a place of business in one of the signatory countries. Note that citizenship of shareholders, directors, or officers is not a factor under the CISG. The CISG covers contracts for the sale of goods between *merchants*. This is perhaps the biggest difference between the UCC and the CISG. The CISG provisions do *not* apply to transactions in which one party is a nonmerchant. Other major provisions of importance are discussed below.

No Writing Required The CISG has no formal writing requirement (such as the UCC's statute of frauds) and specifically provides that contracts are not subject to requirements as to format. A totality of the circumstances, such as course of past dealing, evidence of oral or written negotiations between the parties, and industry practice, may be sufficient to prove that an enforceable contract exists.

Offer and Acceptance A contract for the sale of goods between businesses located in different CISG signatory countries begins with offer and acceptance. As with the UCC, the offer need not have complete terms in order to be valid. The offer requires only (1) a brief description of the goods, (2) quantity, and (3) price. Beyond those three terms, so long as there is some evidence that the parties intended to form a contract, nothing more is needed for a valid offer. Acceptance may be made within a reasonable time and is effective only when it is received by the offeror (thus, the offer may be withdrawn at any point prior to that time).

Remedies The CISG provides for a party that has delivered nonconforming goods to be given an adequate opportunity to cure the problem. In general, the CISG gives sellers an absolute right and obligation to cure, and buyers must allow the seller the opportunity to cure even if the time for performance is past due. Of course, a buyer must give notice of the nonconformance in a timely manner in order to trigger the seller's cure obligations. If the seller does not cure, the CISG provides a right for the buyer to pursue remedies.

Many international sales transactions are governed by the U.N. Convention on Contracts for the International Sale of Goods. Glowimages/Getty Images

INCO: International Chamber of Commerce Terms

With respect to title, risk of loss, and delivery terms, sometimes the language barrier in international sales can lead to confusion among the parties and disputes regarding a loss. The International Chamber of Commerce provides international abbreviations, known as **INCO terms**, to designate many of the responsibilities. INCO terms are generally used in conjunction with the CISG and are used in domestic shipping contracts as well. For example, in the absence of any agreement between the parties, the CISG provides that risk passes at the point at which the seller has delivered the goods to a carrier. If the goods are not to be delivered, the risk of loss passes in accordance with the INCO term *EXW* (ex works). The INCO term EXW has the universal meaning that the parties understand the goods will not be delivered or transported by the seller. Rather, the seller need only make the goods available to the buyer at the seller's place of business and provide the buyer with appropriate documentation of title. There are 11 INCO terms in all. The most common ones are

- *FCA ("free carrier")*: This term means that the seller provides transportation at the seller's expense only to the carrier named by the buyer.
- *FOB ("free on board")*: This term is always accompanied by the name of a port (e.g., FOB New York) and applies only when transportation is via freighter ship. It means that the seller's expense and risk of loss *end* when the seller delivers goods "over the ship's rail" to the freighter ship. The buyer is responsible for the freighter delivery charge and any losses occurring en route to delivery.

CONCEPT SUMMARY Contracts for International Sales of Goods

- The CISG, the international counterpart to the UCC, is a U.N. treaty that governs sales contracts between businesses located in signatory countries.
- Four major differences between the CISG and the UCC are (1) it does not apply to nonmerchants, (2) it has no statute of frauds, (3) offers can be withdrawn at any point prior to the offeror's receiving the acceptance, and (4) the right to cure exists even after the performance period is over.
- INCO terms are standardized contractual terms and designations used in international sales contracts to avoid confusion due to language barriers and differing legal systems.
- Some INCO terms are also used in domestic transactions and can have different applications. For example, FOB is used both domestically and internationally and sometimes indicates dissimilar buyer and seller rights and obligations.

KEY TERMS

Sales contracts p. 247   Agreements to transfer title to real property or tangible assets at a given price.

Goods p. 247   Tangible personal property that is movable at the time of identification to a contract of sale.

Merchant p. 247   One that is regularly engaged in the sale of a particular good.

Open terms p. 249   Unspecified terms in a sales contract that do not detract from the validity of the contract so long as the parties intended to make the contract and other specified terms give a basis for remedy in case of breach.

Output contract p. 249   A contract in which the buyer agrees to buy all the goods that the seller produces for a set time and at a set price and the seller may sell only to that one buyer. The quantity for the contract is the seller's output.

Requirements contract p. 249   A contract in which the buyer agrees to buy whatever he needs from the seller during a set period and the buyer may buy only from that one seller. The quantity for the contract is what the buyer requires.

Merchant's firm offer p. 250   An offer in writing between merchants to buy or sell goods along with a promise without consideration to keep that offer for a stated amount of time or, if unstated, no longer than three months.

Purchase order p. 250   A form commonly used in sales contracts as an offer from the buyer; contains preprinted clauses along with blanks to accommodate the specifics of the transaction.

Acknowledgment form p. 250   A form commonly used in sales contracts as an acceptance from the seller in response to a purchase order; contains preprinted provisions and has blanks to accommodate the specifics of the transaction. Also referred to as an *invoice*.

Battle of the forms p. 250   The conflict between the terms written into standardized purchase (offer) and acknowledgment (acceptance) forms that differ in that one form favors the buyer and the other the seller. The UCC attempts to broker a truce in this battle while keeping the contract of sale intact.

Knockout rule p. 252   As applied in many states, the view that when a buyer and seller engage in a battle of the forms and different terms are exchanged, both the seller's and buyer's differing terms drop out and substitute UCC gap fillers complete the contract.

Confirmation memorandum p. 254   A written verification of an agreement. Under the statute of frauds section of the UCC, a merchant who receives a signed confirmation memorandum from another merchant will be bound by the memorandum just as if she had signed it, unless she promptly objects.

Risk of loss p. 256   The risk of one party's having to bear the loss due to damage, destruction, or loss of goods bargained for under a sales contract.

Title p. 256   The legal right to ownership in a good and to all the privileges and responsibilities that ownership entails.

Shipment contract p. 256   A contract in which the seller is required to send the goods to the buyer via a carrier. When the carrier receives the goods, the seller has fulfilled his duty and the buyer assumes title and bears the risk of loss.

Destination contract p. 256   A contract in which the seller is required to deliver the goods to a chosen destination and not just to the carrier. When the goods have been tendered at the destination, the seller has fulfilled his duty and the buyer takes title and risk of loss.

Tender p. 257   An unconditional performance of the seller by delivering the purchased goods or otherwise making them available to the buyer.

FOB point p. 257   *Domestic:* A shipping term that indicates the place to which the seller must deliver goods. In the absence of a contract provision to the contrary, title and risk of loss pass to the buyer at this point. *International:* An INCO term indicating that goods are to be shipped via freighter ship and that title and risk of loss transfer to the buyer when the goods are delivered to the named ship.

Tender of delivery p. 259   Seller's obligation under which, for delivery of goods, tender occurs when the seller produces goods conforming to the contract and provides adequate notice of their delivery to the buyer.

Perfect tender rule p. 260   Rule that requires the seller to deliver her goods exactly as the contract requires in quantity, quality, and all other respects or risk the buyer's lawful rejection of the goods.

Cure p. 260   The right of a seller to replace nonconforming goods before final contract performance is due. If nonconforming goods were delivered in good faith and were considered equal to or superior to what was ordered, the seller may cure after final contract performance is due if the buyer will not suffer injury.

Assurance p. 262   A pledge or guarantee that gives confidence to one party that the other party is able to complete performance under a contract.

Commercially impracticable p. 263   Rule applied by the UCC when a delay in delivery or nondelivery has been made impracticable by the occurrence of an unanticipated event so long as the event directly affected a basic assumption of the contract.

Installment contract p. 265   A contract allowing delivery of goods and payments for goods at separate times, with the goods being accepted or rejected separately.

Breach p. 266   The failure to meet a contractual obligation.

Remedies p. 266   Judicial actions, which can be monetary or equitable, taken by courts that are intended to compensate an injured party in a civil lawsuit.

Rightful rejection p. 268   The justified refusal to accept nonconforming goods under a sales contract.

Cover p. 268   A nonbreaching buyer's right to purchase substitute goods on the open market after a delivery of nonconforming goods from the original seller and to sue for the difference.

Specific performance p. 269   A court order compelling the breaching party to perform as the contract states when monetary damages would be an insufficient remedy.

Revoking acceptance p. 269   Remedy whereby the buyer, even after accepting the goods, can still revoke acceptance if the goods are nonconforming in a way that substantially affects their value and he notifies the seller of the revocation in a timely fashion.

U.N. Convention on Contracts for the International Sale of Goods (CISG) p. 271   Treaty that governs international sales contracts among businesses located in U.N.-member countries that have ratified it.

INCO terms p. 272   Standardized contractual terms and designations used in international and some domestic sales contracts to avoid confusion due to language barriers and differing legal systems.

CHAPTER REVIEW QUESTIONS

1. If the parties have not agreed otherwise, what are the delivery terms in a contract for sale of goods?
   a. Buyer takes delivery at seller's place of business.
   b. Seller delivers to carrier.
   c. Seller delivers to buyer's place of business.
   d. Buyer takes delivery at the closest port.

2. When one merchant sends another merchant a preprinted purchase order and the receiving merchant then issues a preprinted invoice that has additional terms, this is known as
   a. A nonmerchant transaction.
   b. An open terms form.
   c. Battle of the forms.
   d. An output contract.

3. In a shipping contract, the risk of loss shifts to the buyer when
   a. The seller delivers to the buyer's warehouse.
   b. The seller delivers to the hands of the carrier.
   c. The buyer accepts delivery at the buyer's place of business.
   d. The buyer accepts delivery from a common carrier.

4. The UCC requires the seller to tender the goods in a manner that matches the contract terms in every respect. This requirement is called
   a. Consideration.
   b. Perfect tender rule.
   c. Every respect doctrine.
   d. Mirror image rule.

5. Ultrawidgets agrees to purchase 1,000 Grade-B widgets from SupplyCo for $10 per part to be delivered by December 1. On November 30, SupplyCo realizes it has only 800 Grade-B widgets. SupplyCo gives Ultrawidgets seasonable notice and ships 800 Grade-B and 200 Grade-A widgets as substitute goods. Grade-A widgets are worth 20 percent more than Grade-B widgets. Ultrawidgets rejects the Grade-A widgets on December 1 and sues. Who prevails?
   a. SupplyCo because the cure period is extended past the date of performance.
   b. Ultrawidgets because of the perfect tender rule.
   c. SupplyCo because it substantially performed.
   d. Ultrawidgets because the time for performance has passed.

Answers and explanations are provided at the end of this chapter.

THEORY TO PRACTICE

Bentley is a manager at a high-end printing company called Graphic Communications Inc. (GCI). GCI designs and produces posters and other materials for advertising purposes for a variety of clients, including a local symphony orchestra and Main Street University. After GCI received a large order from the university that required a special press, Bentley was assigned to locate a suitable press, negotiate the purchase terms, and arrange for delivery no later than July 1. Bentley negotiated a price with Armstrong Press Manufacturing for the Armstrong model 2000 printing press. The press was sufficiently large as to require that it be delivered in three separate pieces and then assembled on-site. One factor in choosing Armstrong as a vendor was that GCI had used Armstrong before for purchases of smaller presses and had been satisfied with its products and services. In those previous transactions, GCI had used its own standard preprinted purchase order, and no disputes developed.

Once the parties agreed on price, Bentley issued a preprinted purchase order. The purchase order was one page long and had very few terms. It contained only the price, description of the press, the date of the purchase order, a provision that agreed that all three pieces of the press would be delivered and operational by July 1, and Bentley's signature. After Armstrong received the purchase order, Armstrong's manager handwrote this phrase in the delivery section of the purchase order: "Acknowledged as a destination contract. To be delivered and assembled in three installments to GCI over the month of May." Armstrong's manager then signed the purchase order, faxed the purchase order back to Bentley, and began to process the order. Armstrong shipped the first part of the press using its own delivery service. Before delivery, the truck was involved in an accident, and the first part of the press was destroyed.

1. Is Armstrong's addition of the delivery term binding on GCI? Explain the UCC analysis governing the additional terms added by Armstrong.
2. Does the fact that the parties had a history of past dealings with each other impact your analysis in Question 1? Why or why not?
3. When does title to the goods pass in this contract? Who has the risk of loss? How is your answer related to your analysis of Question 1?
4. Is the purchase order sufficient to satisfy the statute of frauds? Why or why not?
5. Assume that Armstrong ships the first two parts of the press with no problem but anticipates a significant delay for the third part. Knowing that GCI requires the press to be ready on July 1, Armstrong substitutes a newer and more expensive version of the final piece of the press by June 15. Has Armstrong breached the contract? When it is delivered, must GCI accept the final piece because it is newer and more expensive than the goods it had bargained for?
6. In Question 5, if GCI accepts the replaced good but one week later discovers that the new press component is incompatible with the first two components, may GCI still reject the goods despite the fact that it has accepted them and one week's time has passed? What UCC provision covers this situation?
7. If GCI rejects the final shipment of goods, what are GCI's options in terms of a remedy?

LEGAL STRATEGY 101

The Battle of the Forms

Recall our discussion about a typical merchant-to-merchant transaction for the sale of goods. Imagine two commercial parties: Buyer and Seller. The Buyer sends the Seller a purchase order manifesting his intent to buy some goods, and the Seller then ships the goods, along with an acknowledgment form/invoice to the Buyer for the purchase price. Typically, the Buyer's purchase order will contain some contract terms; at the same time, the Seller's invoice will also contain some contractual language.

In other words, both the Buyer and the Seller have issued different standard contract forms for the same transaction, with the Buyer's contract terms being pro-buyer and the Seller's contractual language being pro-seller. As a result, this strategic situation poses two difficult legal questions:

- Is there a binding contract?
- If so, whose contract terms govern—those of the Buyer or those of the Seller?

From a business perspective, the battle of the forms can produce delays, disruption, and disorder. In the worst-case scenario, the parties might end up in court—leading to costly and protracted litigation. Litigation is a worst-case scenario because the parties could end up spending hundreds of hours of their own time as well as tens of thousands of dollars on attorneys' fees and then wait several years for the opportunity to have the court tell them whether or not a contract exists.

Valentine cartoon.

Mark Anderson, www.andertoons.com. All rights reserved. Used with permission.

Worse yet, if the court determines that a contract *does* exist, it is the court—and not the parties involved—who will decide what the terms are. In other words, the parties are letting the court decide what their contract is because the court might end up writing the contract.

If you are a business owner or manager, how can you avoid the battle of the forms? According to one expert on commercial sales, it depends on whether you are the buyer or the seller in the transaction:

> . . . if you are the Seller of goods or services and you want the contractual terms in your form to control the entire sales process, your liability or any other specific business concerns you may have, your form should have a provision in it which makes acceptance by the Buyer "expressly conditional on the Buyer's assent to only the terms set forth in the Seller's contract." If, on the other hand, you are the Buyer, and you want your terms to control the purchase, your liability or any other specific business concerns you may have, you must state in your . . . purchase order that your acceptance is expressly conditional on the Seller's agreement to the additional or different forms set forth in [your] form.[40]

In sum, if you have any questions regarding the terms in your business's standard-form contracts, you should consult with your counsel. You can't completely eliminate the risk of the battle of the forms, but if you think strategically, you can take steps to minimize that risk as much as possible.

CRITICAL THINKING QUESTION

Do some research on the Internet and look up a hypothetical or real-world example of the battle of the forms. Then draft your own version of a Buyer's Purchase Order and a Seller's Acknowledgment that might be strategically favorable to either Buyer or Seller.

---

[40]See blog post, "Battle of the Forms: Will You Win, Lose, or Draw?" by the law firm of Bingham, Greenebaum, Doll (Feb 1, 2009), available at https://www.bgdlegal.com/blog/battle-of-the-forms-will-you-win-lose-or-draw

MANAGER'S CHALLENGE

Managers have a responsibility to protect their company from legal liability or disputes as much as possible through the use of various prevention measures. In this chapter's Theory to Practice, the crux of the potential dispute depends on the comprehensiveness of the purchase order. Even if ultimately the press is delivered, GCI could have avoided a number of potential liabilities through the inclusion of basic language of agreement in the purchase order. Assume that Bentley is required to submit a memorandum to her senior manager describing how the purchase order could be revised to provide protection for GCI by ensuring that any future purchases anticipate potential problems with the vendor. Be sure to provide a potential solution for each problem posed in the Theory to Practice problem.

See Connect for Manager's Challenge sample answers.

CASE SUMMARY 8.1 Fisherman Surgical Instruments, LLC v. Tri-anim Health Services, Inc., 502 F. Supp. 2d 1170 (Kan. 2007)

REQUIREMENTS CONTRACTS AND GOOD FAITH

Fisherman makes high-end surgical instruments for use by medical professionals. Not long after the company opened, it contracted with a medical supply dealer, Tri-anim, to sell its instruments to doctors. The contract did not include quantity but did state that Tri-anim would buy from Fisherman based on "mutually agreed upon sales goals." The parties also agreed that Tri-anim would not sell products that competed with Fisherman's instruments. Shortly after Tri-anim began selling the products, surgeons complained that the quality of Fisherman's instruments was substandard. Tri-anim then began selling a competitor's products. It also canceled the contract with Fisherman, saying it was void under the UCC because the agreement did not specify the quantity of goods.

CASE QUESTIONS

1. Who prevails and why?
2. Is this a requirements contract or output contract?
3. If Tri-anim did not cancel the contract but instead bought nothing and sold nothing, would Fisherman have any cause of action against Tri-anim? If so, what would be the appropriate remedy?

CASE SUMMARY 8.2 General Motors Corp. v. Acme Refining Co., 513 F. Supp. 2d 906 (E.D. Mich. 2007)

RIGHT OF REJECTION

Acme Refining collects, melts down, and resells scrap metal. In producing its cars, General Motors (GM) creates a massive amount of scrap metal that must be removed. Acme contracted to purchase and pick up scrap metal from GM's plant. The contract provided that the metal was to be taken "as-is, where-is." After removing 850,000 tons of metal from the GM plant, Acme realized the metal was corrupted by nonmetal products and waste oils, making smelting much more costly. Instead of rejecting the metal, Acme e-mailed GM over several weeks in an attempt to negotiate a lower price. Unable to bring down the price, Acme then rejected all the scrap metal.

CASE QUESTIONS

1. Was Acme's rejection lawful?
2. Did Acme give seasonable notification of rejection?

CASE SUMMARY 8.3 Glenn Distributors Corp. v. Carlisle Plastics, Inc., 297 F.3d 294 (3d Cir. 2002)

COVER

Glenn Distributors sells closeout merchandise to discount stores. The merchandise consists of goods that have been changed or discontinued, so large quantities can be bought at bargain prices. Carlisle Plastics makes "Ruffies" name-brand trash bags. Glenn contracted to buy $990,000 worth of Ruffies bags from Carlisle, but Carlisle shipped Glenn only $736,000 worth of the bags and sold the others to a different buyer. Glenn claimed it was unable to cover because the only name-brand bag for that price was Ruffies and only Carlisle made Ruffies. Unable to cover, Glenn sued for $230,000 in lost profits.

CASE QUESTIONS

1. Did Glenn make reasonable efforts to cover?
2. Should Glenn have to cover the lost profits by buying products other than trash bags? Why or why not?

CASE SUMMARY 8.4 S.W.B. New England, Inc. v. R.A.B. Food Group, LLC, 2008 WL 540091 (S.D.N.Y. 2008)

SPECIFIC PERFORMANCE

SWB is a distributor of kosher food products in New England. SWB's only substantial competitor is Millbrook. SWB entered a contract to buy kosher products from Rokeach. Rokeach is the dominant kosher food supplier in the region and has established a trusted brand name in New England for kosher products. After the SWB-Rokeach contract was in place, RAB Food Group (Food Group) purchased Rokeach. Food Group refused to honor the SWB-Rokeach contract and began to sell only to Millbrook. SWB brought suit, asking for specific performance from Food Group and Rokeach.

CASE QUESTIONS

1. What are the specific requirements for a court to grant specific performance to SWB?
2. Do these requirements fit this case?

CASE SUMMARY 8.5 Movado Group, Inc. v. Mozaffarian et al., 938 N.Y.S.2d 27, 92 A.D.3d 431 (2012)

BATTLE OF THE FORMS

Mozaffarian and his wife, each suing individually and as d/b/a (doing business as) three companies they owned, signed a credit agreement in which they expressly acknowledged receipt of, and agreed to be bound by, terms and conditions contained in an extrinsic (external) document, which they neither read nor requested a copy of to read. The credit agreement identified the terms and conditions as those contained on each invoice. After the credit application was approved, they then saw, for the first time, the terms and conditions, which contained a New York forum selection clause. Movado proved by a preponderance of the evidence that the terms and conditions of the extrinsic document were incorporated into the credit agreement and that the defendants acknowledged receipt and agreed to be bound by the same. The credit agreement, which identified the terms and conditions as those contained on each invoice, was sufficient to put the defendants on notice that there was an additional document of legal import to the contract they were executing.

CASE QUESTIONS

1. Was the forum selection clause an additional term, a different term, a confirmatory writing, or a term incorporated into the document? Explain.
2. Does the fact that Mozaffarian et al. never requested to see the extrinsic document have any bearing on the case? Why or why not?

CASE SUMMARY 8.6 Ner Tamid Congregation of North Town v. Krivoruchko, 638 F. Supp. 2d 913 (N.D. Ill. 2009)

COMMERCIAL IMPRACTICABILITY

In 2007, real estate developer Igor Krivoruchko contracted with Ner Tamid Congregation of North Town, an Illinois not-for-profit corporation, to purchase property Ner Tamid owned on Rosemont Avenue in Chicago. After postponing the closing once, Krivoruchko refused to go forward with the deal because he said he could not obtain the kind of financing he hoped to get. The purchase contract contained no financing contingency clause because, believing he was "creditworthy" and had not had problems in the past with the lender with which he was dealing, Krivoruchko did not desire one. Ner Tamid sued for breach of contract, and Krivoruchko defended, in part claiming commercial impracticability because he could not obtain the financing he wanted due to an "unanticipated" and "unforeseeable" downturn in the economy.

CASE QUESTIONS

1. In its decision, the district court cited newspaper articles that discussed the volatility of the economy and specifically the real estate market. Do these articles act in any way to support or defeat Krivoruchko's claim?
2. Should a defense of commercial impracticability be effective under circumstances in which prices are affected by changes in the local or national economy? Explain.
3. How might Krivoruchko have protected himself under this contract?
4. How might Ner Tamid Congregation of North Town have protected itself under this contract?

✓ Self-Check ANSWERS Existence of a Sales Contract

1. Yes. This is a requirements contract, so Boston Hardware is obligated to purchase only what it requires (250 shovels).
2. Yes. The delivery terms would be supplied by the UCC because they are missing from the contract. Therefore, New York High School takes delivery at Big Apple's place of business. Big Apple needs only to have the desks available by September 1 for pickup by New York High School.
3. Yes. But for the patient's acquisition of the overlays, the dentist's services would have been unnecessary. This contract is predominantly one for goods.
4. No contract. Careful! While this is a merchant's firm offer for seven months, the UCC restricts a merchant's firm offer to no more than *three months* (see UCC § 2-205). Therefore, L.A.'s offer is no longer valid.
5. No contract. Midwest's return of the acknowledgment with the change in date of delivery would be considered a material change because the delivery date was such an important condition of the contract (holiday season).

Risk of Loss

1. Chase. In a shipment contract, the seller (Marshall) needs only to deliver the goods to the hands of the carrier. In this case, title passed to Chase when Marshall placed them in Mercury's hands. (*Note:* Of course, Chase may be able to sue Mercury for any losses, but Marshall is entitled to payment for the goods from Chase.)
2. Harlan Dairy Co. The fact that parties agreed to delivery and payment to be made at a specific destination indicates that this is a destination contract. In a destination contract, risk of loss is borne by the seller (Harlan) until the goods are tendered.
3. Holmes. Careful! Although this is a destination contract, Holmes delivered *nonconforming goods* (bowler hats instead of top hats). Therefore, Holmes did not complete performance, and the risk of loss never passed to Cardozo.
4. Smooth Lager. "FOB Distributor's Warehouse, Mobile, AL" indicates that the title and risk of loss will transfer when the goods are satisfactorily delivered to the buyer at the buyer's warehouse in Mobile, Alabama. Smooth Lager retains ownership and risk of loss until delivery occurs.
5. White. The buyer, White, took physical possession of the good, and, according to the UCC, risk of loss passes at that point so long as the seller is a merchant.

Buyer's Rights and Obligations

1. Grocer is obligated to buy eggs at market price from Farmer for the duration of the contract. Commercial impracticability is a narrow doctrine and generally does not apply in cases where changing economic conditions impact the contract.
2. Grocer is obligated to pay for the corn. Grocer's knowing acceptance of the nonconforming goods has triggered his obligation to pay.
3. Grocer is obligated to pay for the skim milk because he failed to affirmatively notify the seller of his rejection in a timely manner.
4. Grocer is obligated to pay the fair market value for 100 chickens (not turkeys). Because the seller didn't deliver a perfect tender, Grocer could have (1) rejected the entire shipment, (2) accepted the entire shipment, or (3) accepted part of the shipment and rejected the rest. He opted for the last choice and, thus, is obligated only for the goods he accepted.

CHAPTER REVIEW QUESTIONS: Answers and Explanations

1. **a.** The UCC supplies missing terms when the parties have not agreed. UCC § 2-308 requires the buyer to take delivery at the seller's place of business. Answer choices (b), (c), and (d) are incorrect as they are inconsistent with the UCC provision governing delivery terms.

2. **c.** *Battle of the forms* is the terminology used to describe the process of determining which additional terms become part of a contract and which do not. Answer choice (a) is incorrect because both parties are merchants. Choice (b) is nonsensical. Choice (d) is incorrect because it does not refer to conflicting terms.

3. **b.** UCC § 2-401 prescribes that the risk of loss in a shipping contract passes when the seller delivers the goods into the hands of a *carrier*. Answer choice (a) is incorrect for a shipping contract. Answer choices (c) and (d) are incorrect because a risk of loss analysis focuses on the seller's obligations.

4. **b.** The perfect tender rule requires a seller to go beyond a delivery of conforming goods so that the tender matches the contract in every respect. Answer choice (a) is incorrect as consideration is unrelated to tender. Choice (c) is nonsensical. Choice (d) is incorrect because the mirror image rule does not apply in UCC transactions.

5. **a.** SupplyCo's right to cure is extended because it shipped more expensive substitute goods. Answer choices (b) and (d) are incorrect because cure is an exception to the perfect tender rule. Choice (c) is incorrect because substantial performance does not apply under the UCC.

CHAPTER 9
Torts and Products Liability

©philsajonesen/Getty Images

Learning Objectives

After studying this chapter, students who have mastered the material will be able to:

- **9-1** Articulate a basic definition of a tort and identify the source of law governing various types of torts.
- **9-2** Determine the classification of tort based on the conduct of the wrongdoer.
- **9-3** Give specific examples of how tort law applies in the business environment.
- **9-4** Apply the elements and defenses of the torts of defamation, trade libel, and product disparagement and discuss the applicability of each in the business environment.
- **9-5** Identify the differences in terms of liability for traditional print defamation and defamation in cyberspace.
- **9-6** Distinguish business competition torts from other intentional torts and understand their applicability in commercial relationships.
- **9-7** Recognize conduct that is classified as negligent and identify any potential defenses.
- **9-8** Provide alternate theories of liability and defense that can be applied when a product is the cause of an injury.
- **9-9** Articulate what must be proved in negligence and strict liability cases and appreciate how the levels of proof differ.

Learning to recognize situations in which a business venture may have potential liability to another party is an important part of limiting risk in business operations. Tort law and products liability law set out certain conduct and standards of reasonableness and provide legal recourse when a violation of those standards results in an injury causing losses. Because business owners are ordinarily responsible for the intentional or accidental conduct of their employees who cause another party harm, it is essential for managers to understand ways in which to control risk and reduce liability. In this chapter, we discuss

- The fundamental principles of tort law, types of torts, and how each applies in a business context.
- Rules governing intentional and business competition torts.
- How liability arises for negligent acts and the defenses to liability.
- Special rules governing strict liability and products liability.

OVERVIEW OF TORT LAW

A **tort**[1] is a civil wrong where one party has acted, or in some cases failed to act, and that action or inaction causes a loss to be suffered by another party. The law provides a remedy for one who has suffered an injury by compelling the wrongdoer to pay compensation to the injured party. Tort law is best understood as law that is intended to compensate injured parties for losses resulting in harm from some unreasonable conduct by another.[2] One who commits a tort is known as the **tortfeasor**. The tortfeasor's wrongful conduct is described as **tortious conduct**. Recall from Chapter 1, "Legal Foundations," that an individual may commit a criminal offense and a civil wrong in the very *same* act. While criminal statutes are intended to punish and deter the wrongdoer, the common law of torts is primarily intended to provide *compensation* for the victim. In some cases, tort law also may be used to deter wrongful conduct in the future.

LO 9-1

Articulate a basic definition of a tort and identify the source of law governing various types of torts.

SOURCES OF LAW

For the most part, tort law is governed by state common law principles. Recall from Chapter 1, "Legal Foundations," that courts look to rules articulated by the American Law Institute (ALI) for guidance on applying common law legal principles. For tort law, these rules are known as the **Restatement of Torts**. The ALI has amended the Restatements twice, and, therefore, these sources of law are called the *Restatement (Second) of Torts* and the *Restatement (Third) of Torts*. Remember that courts are not bound by any of the Restatements, but they do recognize them as widely applied principles of law. The Second Restatements have the benefit of volumes of case law and wide acceptance, and therefore references to the Restatements in this chapter refer to the Second Restatements unless otherwise noted.

Laws that cover individuals who are injured by a product, known as *products liability laws,* may take the form of state common law or state statutes that expressly impose liability for injuries that result from products. These statutes are based primarily on the Restatements and are relatively uniform from state to state.

LO 9-2

Determine the classification of tort based on the conduct of the wrongdoer.

CATEGORIES OF TORTS

Torts fall into one of three general categories: *intentional torts, negligence,* and *strict liability.* An **intentional tort** is one in which the tortfeasor is *willful* in bringing about a particular event that causes harm to another party. **Negligence** is an accidental (without willful intent) event that causes harm to another party. The difference between the two is the mind-set and intent of the tortfeasor. For example, suppose that Pangloss is the delivery van driver for Cultivate Your Garden Flowers Inc. One day while on a delivery he spots his archenemy crossing the street, so he accelerates his truck and hits him. In this case, Pangloss has committed an intentional tort (battery). If, on the other hand, Pangloss is late for his delivery, carelessly speeds around a turn, and accidentally hits a pedestrian crossing the street, he has committed the tort of negligence.

Strict liability torts, in which a tortfeasor may be held liable for an act regardless of intent or willfulness, applies primarily in cases of defective products and abnormally

LO 9-3

Give specific examples of how tort law applies in the business environment.

Legal Speak >))

Willful Conduct Intentional behavior directed by the "will."

---

[1] The term *tort* originally derives from the Latin root *tortus,* meaning "twisted" or "wrested aside." As with many legal terms, Latin words were given a French twist in English common law via the Norman kings. Thus, the shortened term *tort* is a French root meaning "wrong."

[2] *Black's Law Dictionary* (10th ed. 2014).

dangerous activities (such as major construction demolition). Owning a wild animal or even some breeds of dogs can result in strict liability should the animal harm an individual, regardless of the precautions taken by the animal's owner.[3]

INTENTIONAL BUSINESS-RELATED TORTS

LO 9-4

Apply the elements and defenses of the torts of defamation, trade libel, and product disparagement and discuss the applicability of each in the business environment.

While the law provides relief for injured parties in a variety of circumstances, there are some intentional torts that are more important to business owners and managers because they have the potential to impact business relationships and operations.

Defamation

The law recognizes an individual's or a company's reputation as a valuable asset by imposing liability on any party that makes false and defamatory statements affecting another party's reputation. In this context, the term *party* means an individual, business, or product. Just as in all civil lawsuits, the *untrue statements* must have caused the victim to suffer *damages*. Generally, we think of written defamation as **libel** and oral (spoken) defamation as **slander**. In order to recover for a defamation action, the plaintiff must prove four elements:

- *Defamatory statement:* A *false* statement concerning a party's reputation or honesty or a statement that subjects a party to hate, contempt, or ridicule. In order to qualify as defamatory, the statement must have a tendency to harm the reputation of the plaintiff.[4] Because many statements can be interpreted in more than one way, the law provides that the statement is defamatory so long as a defamatory interpretation is an objectively reasonable one and the plaintiff shows that at least one of the recipients did in fact make that interpretation. Note that the statement must be false, not merely unkind. Moreover, if a statement was *pure opinion*, that statement is not defamatory. That is, a defamatory statement is one that must be *provable as false*.

- *Dissemination to a third party:* In the Restatements, this requirement is referred to as *publication*, but in this context it does not literally require the statement to be published. Rather, this element requires that the statement must somehow reach the ears or eyes of someone other than the tortfeasor and the victim. For example, suppose a manager telephones one of his employees and says, "You are the one who stole $100 in petty cash, so you're fired." Even if the accusatory statement is false, the manager has not defamed the employee based on that action alone. No third party heard the statement, and, thus, the dissemination element is missing.

- *Specificity:* The statement must be about a particular party, business, or product. Thus, any general statement about a profession as a whole cannot constitute defamation, but a false statement about a specific company can be the basis of a reputation claim.

- *Damages:* In a business context, the aggrieved party must be able to prove that he or she suffered some *pecuniary* harm. Examples of damages in a defamation suit include situations in which the victim has lost a valuable client due to the tortfeasor's defamatory comment or the victim is unable to secure employment because of a tortfeasor's defamatory comment during a reference check.

Legal Speak >))

Pecuniary Harm
Lost revenue or profits, both actual and potential.

Legal Speak >))

Malice
The intent, without justification or excuse, to commit a wrongful act or inflict harm.

Public Figure Standard
If the victim is a public figure, such as a candidate for political office or a celebrity, the defamation must have been committed with *malice* or

---

[3]Numerous cities and municipalities have declared certain breeds of dogs such as pit bulls, rottweilers, and mastiffs to be dangerous animals, and many have even banned the ownership of such animals. *See, e.g., Tracy v. Solesky*, 25 A.3d 1025, 421 Md. 192 (2011).

[4]Restatement (Second) of Torts § 559.

reckless disregard for the truth. This "public figure" rule is based on the U.S. Supreme Court's landmark ruling in *New York Times v. Sullivan*.[5] The case involved a public official, the police commissioner of New York City, who sued *The New York Times* for defamation based on allegations printed in the newspaper that accused him of complicity in criminal activity. In announcing the public figure standard, the Court ruled that, in order for a public figure to prevail in a defamation case, the plaintiff must provide evidence that the defamer either had "actual knowledge" that the statement was false or made the defamatory statement with a "reckless disregard for the truth."

In Case 9.1, a federal court of appeals considers whether a professional football coach is a public figure in a defamation context.

CASE 9.1 Turner v. Wells, 879 F.3d 1254 (11th Cir. 2018)

FACT SUMMARY The National Football League hired the law firm of Paul, Weiss, Rifkind, Wharton & Garrison LLP and one of its partners, Theodore Wells (collectively Wells), to investigate allegations of bullying within the Miami Dolphins organization. The investigation centered on the bullying of a football player, Jonathan Martin, who abruptly left the Dolphins team midway through the 2013 season. At the time, Martin was an offensive lineman in his second year with the Dolphins. After leaving a Dolphins facility on October 28, 2013, Martin checked himself into a hospital for psychological treatment. Later, Martin explained that he left the team because of persistent taunting from other Dolphins players.

After several months of investigation, Wells published a 144-page report (the Report) that concluded that bullying by other Dolphins players contributed to Martin's decision to leave the team. The Report also included several references to their offensive line coach, James Turner (Turner), and opined that Turner's unprofessional conduct played a role in Martin's struggles. The Report noted that Dolphins coaches and players created a culture that enabled the bullying by discouraging players from snitching on other players, known in the organization as "the Judas Code." It concluded that the treatment of Martin and others in the Miami Dolphins organization at times was "offensive and unacceptable in any environment."

After receiving the Report in February 2014, the Dolphins fired Turner, who in turn filed a defamation lawsuit against Wells and his law firm. The trial court found in favor of Wells because (1) the Report consisted of opinions and therefore was not actionable in a defamation suit and (2) Turner was a public figure and failed to adequately plead actual malice in his complaint. Turner appealed.

SYNOPSIS OF DECISION AND OPINION The U.S. Court of Appeals for the eleventh Circuit affirmed the decision of the trial court in favor of Wells. The court held (1) the Report was a product of a careful balance in the investigation and that the statements were opinion-based and could not be categorized as false or misleading and (2) Turner was a public figure and therefore had an even higher hurdle to clear, malice, but that there was no evidence of malice during the investigation or upon publication of the subsequent report.

WORDS OF THE COURT: Fact versus Opinion "Notably too, the Report included several cautionary statements that inform a reasonable reader that the conclusions contained therein are opinions. For example, the Report stated several times that it sets forth the Defendants' opinions, based on a lengthy investigation: '[t]he opinions set forth in the findings and conclusions below and elsewhere in this Report are our own'; '[i]n our opinion, the factual record supports the following findings' . . . Further, it is well settled in Florida that commentary or opinion based on accurate facts set forth in an

(continued)

---

[5]376 U.S. 254 (1964).

article 'are not the stuff of libel.' That is precisely the case here."

WORDS OF THE COURT: Public Figure "'[S]ports figures are generally considered public figures because of their position as athletes or coaches.' . . . Here, Coach Turner chose to put himself in the public arena. As the Report noted, Turner was the focus of the 2012 season of Hard Knocks, an HBO television program that 'showcase[ed] Turner's coaching style and featur[ed] interviews and footage of him on the field and in the locker room.' During his coaching career, Turner was the subject of several articles discussing his career and coaching philosophy. Turner was a prominent person on the closely followed Dolphins professional sports team. . . . [Turner] has failed to provide any evidence of malice in this case."

Case Questions

1. Why is it important that the court concluded that the Report was largely the opinions of Wells and his colleagues?
2. Why is malice an important factor in analyzing this case?
3. *Focus on Critical Thinking:* Why is there a special standard for public figures? Is that good public policy or does it prevent public figures from pursuing legitimate claims?

Defenses to Defamation

The second phase of a defamation analysis is an inquiry into whether the defendant may avail him- or herself of a statutory or judicially recognized defense.

Truth Truth is an absolute defense to a charge of defamation. If the statement made is truthful, no defamation has occurred. To assert truth as a defense, the defendant must prove that the statement was either literally true or substantially true.

Privilege Defenses If the injured party meets all of the requirements of a defamation claim, the defendant may still avoid liability if the defamatory statement falls into the category of *privileged statements*. Privilege is a defense that recognizes either a legal or public policy–based immunity from a defamation claim. It is divided into two subcategories: **absolute privilege**, whereby the defendant need not offer any further evidence to assert the defense, and **qualified privilege**, whereby the defendant must offer evidence of good faith and be absent of malice to be shielded from liability.

Absolute Privilege Courts generally recognize three types of absolute privilege:

- *Government officials:* The framers of the Constitution recognized the need for free debate among members of Congress and gave immunity in the Constitution via the Speech and Debate Clause, which shields members of Congress from liability for any statement made during a congressional debate, hearing, and so on, while in office. The U.S. Supreme Court later extended that protection to all federal officials.[6]
- *Judicial officers/proceedings:* All states now recognize some protection of participants of a judicial proceeding for statements made during the proceeding. This includes judges, lawyers, and, in some cases, witnesses.
- *State legislators:* Similar immunity has been extended by the states to protect state legislators for statements made in the course of carrying out their duties.

---

[6]*Barr v. Matteo*, 360 U.S. 564 (1959).

Qualified Privilege Courts also recognize certain qualified privileges that are grounded in public policy:

- *Media:* Employees of media organizations (e.g., television, radio, periodicals) are afforded a qualified protection from defamation liability. So long as the media have acted in good faith, *absent of malice,* and without a reckless disregard for the truth, the media are protected from liability through privilege as a defense for unintentional mistakes of fact in their reporting.

- *Fair report privilege:* If one relies on an official public document or a statement made by a public official and cites the document or public statement when making an allegedly defamatory statement, no cause of action for defamation occurs unless the speaker knows the statement is false.

- *Employers:* An increasing number of states have extended some liability protection for employers who are providing a reference for an ex-employee. In most cases, employers do not have liability if the employee's defamation claim is connected to a reference check. However, an employer may lose this privilege if it provides false information or acted with malice.

Some states provide statutory or common law immunity from defamation claims for employers providing references for ex-employees, so long as the information is factual.
Flying Colours Ltd/Getty Images

In Case 9.2, a state appellate court considers an employer reference privilege as a defense to defamation.

CASE 9.2 Nelson v. Tradewind Aviation, 111 A.3d 887 (Conn. App. Ct. 2015)

FACT SUMMARY Tradewind Aviation (TA) employed Nelson as a pilot for a small commercial airline that primarily flew from New York and New Jersey to Martha's Vineyard and Nantucket. Over the course of the summer of 2007, Nelson copiloted 137 flights without incident or complaint from passengers. Nelson was never removed from flying status for a performance-based reason or disciplinary reason. Although some senior pilots did complain about Nelson, he was never given a written warning, disciplined, or suspended. As the summer ended, TA announced that some pilots would be laid off due to a decrease in demand during the off-season. Nelson committed to working during the first part of the off-season; however, TA informed Nelson it would be unable to continue his employment. TA's human resources office completed necessary paperwork indicating that Nelson was laid off due to "lack of work."

In December 2007, Nelson was offered a job by Republic Airways (Republic). As part of his initial interview, Nelson signed authorizations that gave TA permission to verify his employment with TA and to release all of his employment records to Republic. This authorization also required TA to send copies of these records to Nelson so that he had an opportunity to submit written comments to correct any inaccuracies. TA completed the reference forms and indicated that (1) Nelson had been involuntarily terminated from TA and (2) Nelson had been involuntarily removed from flying status based on poor performance. Responding to Republic's request for more details, TA faxed Republic a letter stating that Nelson was terminated "after he failed to perform to company standards. Prior to that date, he was given several opportunities to discuss the need for improvement as well as additional training to help him perform at the levels we needed." TA never

(continued)

sent the records or letter to Nelson. Republic subsequently revoked its job offer. Nelson sued TA for, among other claims, defamation. The jury awarded the plaintiff a total of $307,332.94 in damages. TA appealed, asserting the employer reference privilege.

SYNOPSIS OF DECISION AND OPINION The court affirmed the jury's verdict in favor of Nelson. The court reasoned that it was well settled that defamation is actionable if it charges improper conduct or lack of skill or integrity in one's profession or business and is of such a nature that it is calculated to cause injury to one in his profession or business. The court rejected TA's argument that Nelson had not proven that TA's statements rose to the level of being malicious. The court held that a qualified privilege in a defamation case may be defeated if it can be established that the holder of the privilege acted with malice in publishing the defamatory material. Based on the facts in this case, the jury's conclusion that the statements were made with malice was reasonable.

WORDS OF THE COURT: Improper Motive "A review of the evidence reveals that the jury reasonably could have concluded that the defendant's defamatory statements were made with knowledge that they were false and with an improper motive. The jury reasonably could have found that [Nelson] was laid off due to lack of work, that [TA supervisors] never removed the plaintiff from a flight for performance or professional competency reasons, that [Nelson] was never offered or sent for any additional training. . . . Additionally, the jury reasonably could have found that the statements were made with an improper motive in light of the timing and manner in which the statements were made."

Case Questions

1. What statements by TA, specifically, do you consider to be malicious? Why?
2. How could TA's management have prevented the defamation from occurring?
3. *Focus on Critical Thinking:* What is the public policy behind the employer reference privilege? Is it fair to the employee who may have a different perspective on the circumstances of his or her termination? Have you ever heard an employer defaming an ex-employee?

Trade Libel and Product Disparagement Laws

In cases where a competitor has made a false statement that disparages a competing product, an injured party may sue for **trade libel**. This tort requires that the statement (1) be a clear and *specific* reference to the disparaged party or product (e.g., using the actual brand name of the product), (2) be made with either knowledge that the statement is false or reckless disregard for the truth, and (3) be communicated to a third party (similar to defamation).

Some states have passed **product disparagement statutes** intended to protect the interest of a state's major industries, such as agriculture, dairy, or beef.[7] In perhaps the most famous product disparagement case, the Texas Cattle Ranchers Association sued Oprah Winfrey under a Texas law allowing recovery for any rancher who suffers damages as a result of false disparagement. On her television show, Winfrey agreed with statements made by one of her guests that alleged certain U.S. market hamburger meat could cause mad cow disease, which is fatal to humans. At the end of the segment, Winfrey took the position that she would cease eating any hamburgers. The ranchers showed evidence that beef sales dropped precipitously immediately after the broadcast and alleged that Winfrey's statements were false and caused the ranchers lost revenue. The jury rejected the cattle ranchers' claim as too broad and without sufficient evidence that the remarks alone were the cause of the losses.[8]

---

[7] For example, disparagement of Idaho potatoes is covered in Idaho Code § 6-2003. For a list of many such laws, see *Of Banana Bills and Veggie Hate Crimes: The Constitutionality of Agricultural Disparagement Statutes*, 34 Harv. J. Legis. 135 (1997).

[8] *Texas Beef Group v. Winfrey*, 201 F.3d 680 (5th Cir. 2000).

Fraudulent Misrepresentation

Recall the discussion of misrepresentation and fraudulent misrepresentation in Chapter 7, "Contract Enforceability and Performance." It is important to note that there are some important overlapping legal principles of tort and contract law. For example, in some cases contract law allows a contract to be canceled if one party has made false representations concerning a *material fact*. This means that the misrepresented fact must involve an important aspect of the basis of the contract, such as a change in the value of the contract or an increase in one party's risk. Fraudulent misrepresentation (sometimes referred to simply as *fraud*) is *also* recognized as a tort in cases where the law provides a remedy to recover damages when the innocent party suffers a pecuniary loss as a result of the false representation. In cases of fraudulent misrepresentation, the law allows the innocent party to recover if (1) the misrepresentation was a material fact known to be false by the tortfeasor (or was a reckless disregard for the truth); (2) the tortfeasor intended to persuade the innocent party to rely on the statement, and the innocent party did, in fact, rely on it; and (3) damages were suffered by the innocent party. For example, Buyer asks Seller whether Seller's property is properly zoned for a manufacturing facility. In an effort to induce Buyer to purchase the property, Seller misrepresents that the property is zoned for manufacturing. Buyer then enters into a purchase agreement for the property with a 10 percent down payment, balance due in 30 days. Buyer then proceeds to spend money by hiring an architect to visit the site and draw plans for the new facility. The day after the agreement is signed, Seller applies to the zoning board for a change in zoning, hoping that it will be changed before Buyer completes the agreement by paying the balance owed. The zoning board does not change the status. In a case against Seller for fraud, Buyer would be entitled to cancel the contract *and* recover any losses in tort suffered as a result of Seller's fraudulent misrepresentation (such as the money spent on hiring the architect).

> **KEY POINT**
>
> Fraudulent misrepresentation (in both contracts and torts) must center on a *material fact*; that is, a fact that is significant or would impact the parties' rights or obligations in a transaction as opposed to a minor and inconsequential detail.

LO 9-5

Identify the differences in terms of liability for traditional print defamation and defamation in cyberspace.

LEGAL IMPLICATIONS IN CYBERSPACE

Protections for Online Content Providers

Along with holding the actual tortfeasor liable in a defamation case, the law imposes certain liability upon the publisher of libelous statements as well. However, the law does not impose liability on the *distributor* of the publication (such as a bookstore or newsstand). For example, suppose a famous movie star is the subject of a gossip feature in a hypothetical tabloid called the *American Tattler*. The feature implies that the movie star was seen at a local restaurant and was so intoxicated that she could not control her conduct. In a lawsuit for defamation, the movie star proves that the story was false and that it led to her being fired by her movie studio. In terms of liability, both the author of the defamatory feature and the publication (*American Tattler*) may be liable for damages.

However, the rules pertaining to publishers of online content in cyberspace are different. In our movie-star example, suppose that instead of the *American Tattler* publishing the defamatory feature, a gossip columnist hired by America Online (AOL) wrote the article for an AOL entertainment news board. There would be no doubt of the liability of the author, but would AOL be liable as the "publisher"?

(continued)

CHAPTER NINE | Torts and Products Liability

As Internet accessibility increases rapidly, courts have struggled with this question. In the 1991 case *Cubby Inc. v. CompuServe, Inc.*,[9] the plaintiffs filed a defamation action against CompuServe as a "publisher" of defamatory materials contained in an online publication called *Rumorville, USA*. *Rumorville* was composed, written, and edited by a third party who was not employed by CompuServe. The federal trial court in the southern district of New York held that CompuServe was *not* a publisher in the context of defamation law but rather was more akin to a bookstore, and, thus, Internet service providers (ISPs) such as CompuServe were to be treated as "distributors." Consequently, CompuServe was not subject to liability for any defamatory statements so long as it did not "edit, review or reformulate" the publication.

However, not all courts have taken that view. A few years later, as the number of ISPs grew, a New York state trial court issued a very different ruling. In *Stratton Oakmont v. Prodigy Services Company*, decided in 1995,[10] the court ruled that an ISP could be held liable as a publisher of defamatory material. The case involved a Prodigy-maintained electronic bulletin board, available to its subscribers, called "Money Talk." Although Prodigy did not formally edit the postings, it had a policy that reserved the right to eliminate postings if they were objectionable. The plaintiff filed suit against Prodigy as a publisher of material that was allegedly libelous. In stark contrast to the *Cubby* court, a state trial court in New York ruled that Prodigy was a publisher in the context of a defamation claim and, therefore, could be liable for damages resulting from defamatory comments in its electronic bulletin board.

The court held that Prodigy's "conscious effort to maintain editorial control" over the content was sufficient to qualify it as a *publisher* as that term is understood in defamation law.

In an apparent effort to address the pleas of ISPs for a uniform standard, Congress enacted the **Communications Decency Act (CDA) of 1996**.[11] This law extended immunity to the ISPs by protecting them from any defamation liability as a "publisher or speaker of any information provided by another information content provider." In effect, Congress made the policy choice that ISPs were to be treated as newsstand-like distributors.

One of the first cases to interpret this law was *Blumenthal v. Drudge and America Online, Inc.*[12] Although the case was decided by a trial court, the reasoning is often cited by appellate courts when applying the ISP safe harbor. The case involved a defamation lawsuit filed by a high-profile White House adviser (Blumenthal) against a controversial political journalist (Drudge) and America Online (AOL) because of spousal abuse and cover-up allegations in a column written by Drudge. The column was posted on an AOL news board as part of an agreement between Drudge and America Online. After Drudge posted a retraction and acknowledged that the allegations were false, Blumenthal sued Drudge and AOL for defamation. The trial court dismissed the case against AOL, citing the Communications Decency Act's safe-harbor provisions for ISPs. The court noted that even if AOL could conceivably be categorized as a *publisher* of defamatory material under previous cases, Congress specifically exempted ISPs such as AOL from civil suits for defamation.

Every state has enacted a consumer fraud protection act. These acts severely punish those who commit fraud and, in many instances, allow victims of fraud to sue and collect treble damages.

Courts will also allow recovery for misrepresentations that are not intentional but are *negligent* misrepresentations. In most cases, the parties have to have some type of business relationship for the innocent party to recover. Any statement made by a party that turns out

---

[9]776 F. Supp. 135 (S.D.N.Y. 1991).

[10]1995 N.Y. Misc. LEXIS 229.

[11]18 U.S.C.A. § 1462. Note that some portions of the CDA, namely Congress's attempt to regulate Internet pornography, were struck down as unconstitutional by various federal courts. However, this section survived judicial scrutiny.

[12]992 F. Supp. 44 (D.D.C. 1998).

to be inaccurate may still allow the innocent party to recover if the tortfeasor's statement was negligent. In the Buyer-Seller case discussed earlier, suppose that Seller had no actual knowledge of the zoning status for the property but made a statement that it was zoned for manufacturing. Buyer would still be able to recover despite the fact that Seller did not know that the statement was false. Seller is still liable because he was negligent in his duty to know such an important fact (negligence is discussed in detail later in this chapter).

Legal Speak >))

Treble Damages Treble damages are a remedy in fraud cases whereby the victim of fraud can collect triple the amount of actual damages.

False Imprisonment

The tort of false imprisonment is defined by the Restatements as the "intentional infliction of a confinement upon another party." In the business context, a merchant most commonly encounters these circumstances in cases of suspected retail theft. While the merchant has the right to briefly detain a suspected shoplifter, she must be cautious about giving rise to a false-imprisonment claim when detaining an individual or attempting to recover the merchandise. The Restatements provide for a **merchant's privilege**[13] to shield a merchant from liability for temporarily detaining a party who is *reasonably* suspected of stealing merchandise. This privilege, however, is very narrow. In order to gain protection under the privilege, the merchant must follow certain guidelines:

- *Limited detention:* The privilege applies only for a short period of time under the circumstances. Some courts have limited this time period to as few as 15 minutes. However, most courts follow a case-by-case analysis with the general framework that the detention may last the time duration necessary to confront the accused party, recover any goods stolen, and wait for the authorities to arrive (if necessary).
- *Limited to premises:* Generally, the privilege applies only if the suspected party is confronted on the merchant's premises or an immediately adjacent area (such as a parking lot).
- *Seizure of property:* The merchant or merchant's agent may seize alleged stolen property in plain view but may not search the accused shoplifter.
- *Coercion:* The merchant or merchant's agent (such as a store security guard) may not attempt to coerce payment, purport to officially arrest the detained party, or attempt to obtain a confession.

Table 9.1 provides an overview of other types of intentional torts and examples of each.

Business Competition Torts

Tort law also provides for the promotion of fairness in business dealings and for the reimbursement of a party that has suffered some damages as a result of a competitor's tortious acts. These common law torts arise when a tortfeasor (typically a competitor to the harmed party) interferes with an existing contract or hinders a prospective contract between two parties.

LO 9-6
Distinguish business competition torts from other intentional torts and understand their applicability in commercial relationships.

Tortious Interference with Existing Contractual Relationship When one party *induces* another party to break an existing contract with a third party, the inducing party may be liable for any damages suffered by the innocent party as a result of breaking the contract. For the injured party to recover damages, the tortfeasor must have (1) had *specific knowledge* of the contract, (2) actively *interfered* with the contract, and (3) caused some *identifiable* damages (losses) to the injured party. Business owners and managers may encounter contract interference torts in the context of employment contract restrictions against working for competitors (known as a *restrictive covenant*[14]) or

---

[13] Also known as *shopkeeper's privilege*. *See* Restatement (Second) of Torts § 120A.

[14] Restrictive covenants are covered in detail in Chapter 7, "Contract Enforceability and Performance."

TABLE 9.1 — Other Intentional Torts

Tort	Definition	Example
Battery	Intentional touching of another person, without that person's consent, in a harmful or offensive manner.	An employee touches another employee, without consent, causing embarrassment, a feeling of harassment, or physical injury.
Intentional infliction of emotional distress	Extreme, outrageous, or reckless conduct that is intended to inflict emotional or mental distress (physical harm is not necessary).	A bill collector contacts a debtor's mother and threatens to physically harm and imprison the debtor son and to put a lien on the mother's house. The mother suffers two heart attacks after the threats persist.*
Trespass (land)	The act of entering another's land or causing another person or object to enter land owned by a private party without the owner's consent.	A survey crew mistakenly surveys the wrong property. While working, the crew damages landscaping. The landowner is entitled to compensation as a result of the crew's trespass.
Trespass (chattel†)	The act of interfering with another's use or possession of chattel (such as personal property).	An employee takes home his employer's drill for personal use without the employer's permission and with the intent to return it the next morning. The drill is broken while under the employee's control. The employee is liable for costs of repair/replacement and any lost profits resulting from the downtime.
Conversion	The civil counterpart to theft; intended to reimburse a party who suffers damages as a result of theft or any other substantial interference with the party's ownership, where fairness requires that the tortfeasor reimburse the injured party for the full value of the property.	The controller of a corporation embezzles corporate funds and covers up discrepancies on the financial statements. In addition to the controller's facing criminal charges, the controller's employer may sue her for conversion in an attempt to recover the embezzled funds.
Civil assault	The act of putting someone in fear and apprehension of immediate harmful or offensive contact (battery). No actual contact is required.	A worker yells at a customer and starts moving toward the customer in a hostile manner. If the customer reasonably believes that she is about to be struck, she has been civilly assaulted even if she runs away without being touched.

*Based on *George v. Jordan Marsh Co.*, 268 N.E.2d 915 (Mass. 1971).

in defending an allegation of interference in the process of hiring a new employee away from a competitor. For example, Lee is a talented software programmer and signs a contract with Computer Researchers Inc. (CRI) for three years. The contract stipulates that Lee will not work for any of CRI's competitors during that time even if he is terminated or voluntarily resigns from CRI. After one year, one of CRI's competitors, MultiCom, contacts Lee and attempts to convince him to leave CRI and work for MultiCom. During the negotiations, Lee shows MultiCom his contract with CRI, and MultiCom's manager then offers a higher salary and a $1,000 signing bonus to Lee. Lee resigns from CRI with two years left on his contract and goes to work for MultiCom. CRI must then spend several thousand dollars recruiting and training a new programmer to finish Lee's projects. In this case, many courts would consider holding MultiCom liable for CRI's damages because CRI was injured as a result of MultiCom's tortious interference with the CRI-Lee contract. Of course, CRI would also be entitled to recover damages from Lee for breaking the contract.

Note that interference does not occur when a competitor merely offers a better price to a competitor's customer. For example, suppose that Chung is the owner of several self-service car washes and signs a two-year agreement with Mega Distributor for the supplying of snack vending machines in the lobby of each of Chung's car washes. Under the contract, Chung will receive 30 percent of the sales from the machines. Shortly thereafter, Chung is contacted by a sales rep from Start-Up Snacks and offered the same terms as the Mega contract except that Chung will receive 60 percent of the sales from the machines. Chung crunches the numbers and concludes that the increase in revenue will more than make up for any penalties incurred for breaching the Chung-Mega contract, so he breaks his contract with Mega and enters into a new contract with Start-Up. Despite the fact that Start-Up knew of the Mega contract, the level of interference is *not* sufficient to constitute a tort. In this case, Chung decided on his own to break the contract with Mega and was not *induced* to do so by Start-Up. It is important to note, however, that Mega could still sue Chung for failing to perform his obligations as agreed in the contract.[15]

> **Legal Speak >))**
>
> **Induce**
> To bring about or give rise to. In the context of tortious interference, liability is triggered if interference causes the harm.

Tortious Interference with Prospective Advantage In addition to providing protection against interference from third parties in existing contracts, the law also protects interference with *potential* contract (prospects) or other business relationships. The protections and definition of interference are similar to the existing contractual interference rules discussed earlier. However, because no contract actually exists, courts allow recovery for this tort only under limited circumstances in which the tortfeasor's conduct was highly anticompetitive. For example, assume that OldCo intends to sabotage NewCo's efforts to obtain a new customer through a competitive bidding process. An OldCo employee hacks into NewCo's computer and destroys the proposal forms. NewCo cannot submit the bid before the deadline and, thus, doesn't get the contract. Assuming that NewCo can prove it suffered damages, OldCo could be held liable for interference with prospective advantage.

✓ **Self-Check** Intentional Torts

Which tort, if any, fits each of the following facts?

1. Jason and Elaine are both being considered for a promotion to VP of Sales. Jason starts a false rumor that Elaine doctored the books to make her accounts look better than they actually are. Because of the investigation and the need to fill the position, Elaine is dropped from consideration and Jason gets the promotion.

2. MOT Corporation does all of its banking with Second National Bank. MOT receives a 1 percent interest rate on its savings account and pays a fee of $.02 per check written. A representative of Third National Bank visits MOT's offices and tells the company that Third National pays 1.25 percent interest and has free corporate checking. MOT closes its accounts with Second National and moves all its banking business to Third National.

3. Wayne gets into his car after work, but it won't start. He returns to his office, and everyone has gone home. He takes the keys to a company vehicle and drives home, intending to drive it back to the office in the morning. That night, a violent storm causes a tree branch to fall on the car, causing extensive damage.

4. Nancy has triplets attending eighth grade. Every once in a while she takes small quantities of paper, pens, paper clips, and other stationery supplies home from work and gives them to her kids for school use.

(continued)

---

[15]Based on Restatement (Second) of Torts § 766, illus. 3.

5. Frank is a used-car salesman. He is working with a customer who decides to buy a car. The price is agreed to, and the customer tells Frank that he will go to the bank to get a certified check. They shake hands. Frank then says, "You should know that this car used to be owned by Bill Gates!" The customer returns with the certified check, all paperwork is signed, and the customer drives the car home. The next day, the customer discovers that Bill Gates never owned the car.

Answers to this Self-Check are provided at the end of the chapter.

CONCEPT SUMMARY Business-Related Intentional and Competition Torts

- A tort is a civil wrong and can be classified as intentional, negligent, or strict liability.
- Defamation is a false statement that specifically concerns an individual, company, or product; is communicated to a third party; and results in pecuniary harm to the victim.
- A victim of fraud must show intentional misrepresentation by the tortfeasor of a material fact, reliance on that fact, and damages resulting from that reliance.
- False imprisonment is an intentional tort unless the tortfeasor is a merchant who temporarily and reasonably detains a suspected thief.
- When a business competitor's actions exceed standard competitive practices, that company may be liable for intentional interference with a contract by a third party if the company has specific knowledge of a contract and intentionally disrupts its proper execution.

NEGLIGENCE

LO 9-7

Recognize conduct that is classified as negligent and identify any potential defenses.

Tort law also applies when one party fails to act reasonably and harm occurs, even though that party did not intend to cause harm. The negligent party is liable for any injuries or damages suffered by another party as a result of his unreasonable conduct. This category of tort is called *negligence*. Recall from the first section of this chapter that the primary difference between intentional torts and negligence is the mind-set of the tortfeasor. When a tortfeasor causes harm to an injured party by creating an *unreasonable risk of harm*, the law provides the injured party a remedy regardless of the tortfeasor's intent. The Restatements also recognize certain defenses that may be asserted in a negligence case.

Elements of Negligence

The law requires that specific elements be proved in order to recover in a lawsuit against a tortfeasor for negligence. The injured party must prove five fundamental elements by answering certain questions about the conduct in question:

- *Duty:* Did the tortfeasor owe a duty of care to the injured party?
- *Breach of duty:* Did the tortfeasor fail to exercise reasonable care?
- *Cause in fact:* Except for the breach of duty by the tortfeasor, would the injured party have suffered damages?

- *Proximate (legal) cause:* Was there a legally recognized and close-in-proximity link between the breach of duty and the damages suffered by the injured party?
- *Actual damages:* Did the injured party suffer some physical harm that resulted in identifiable losses?

Duty   The initial consideration in a negligence analysis is whether or not the tortfeasor owed the injured party a *legal* **duty**. The law imposes a general duty on all parties to act reasonably and not to impart unreasonable risk to others. In addition to having this general duty, some parties owe a special (heightened) duty of conduct to avoid liability for negligence.

General Duty of Reasonable Conduct

The law imposes a general duty on every party to act as a *reasonably prudent person* would under the circumstances. That is, everyone owes a duty to everyone else to act in a manner that does not impose unreasonable risk. The reasonably prudent person standard emphasizes that the conduct must be *objectively* reasonable. This means that at trial a fact finder (such as the jury) could conclude that a reasonably prudent person in the same circumstances should have realized that certain conduct would be risky or harmful to another person. In general, the scope of that duty is defined by *foreseeability*. In tort law, the term *person* in the reasonably prudent person standard is meant to be a generic term. The scope of duty is frequently defined by a particular industry or occupation. For example, the level of duty for a physician is defined by what a reasonably prudent *physician* would have done under the circumstances. It is important to understand that duty is an element that *expands* and *contracts* based upon whether or not it was foreseeable that the conduct in question would cause an unreasonable risk of harm. For example, Cain is a guest on a shock-host television show. The owners of the show arrange to have Abel surprise Cain on the show with an embarrassing secret. Cain is embarrassed and runs off the stage, and no further incident ensues. Three days later, Abel persists in calling Cain and harassing him about this secret. Cain then shoots and kills Abel later that afternoon. Cain is sentenced to a life term, so Abel's heirs sue the owners of the shock-host television show for negligence, claiming they owed Abel a duty to protect him from Cain. In this case, a court will likely rule that due to the time period between the show and the shooting (three days) and the fact that no incident occurred on the show or immediately thereafter, the duty owed to Abel ended when the show ended and did not extend to the time of the incident. This is primarily because it was not reasonably foreseeable under the factual circumstances of this case that Cain would act in such a rash manner then or thereafter.[16]

No General Duty to Act

The duty of care, discussed above, does *not* include a general duty to act or to rescue another. Tort law allocates liability based on a fundamental difference between some *act* by one party that harms or endangers another party, known as **misfeasance**, and the failure to act or intervene in a certain situation, known as **nonfeasance**. While injured parties may generally recover for misfeasance, injured parties may not hold a defendant liable for failing to act *unless* the parties had a **special relationship** to each other. Special relationships that are set out in the Restatements include those of a common carrier (such as a bus company) to its passengers, innkeepers to guests, employers to employees, a school to students, and a landlord to tenants.[17] One important special relationship of interest to business owners and managers is a business's duty to *warn* and *assist* any business visitors or patrons in regard to potential danger or harm (such as a slippery floor) on business

---
[16] Based on *Graves v. Warner Brothers,* 656 N.W.2d 195 (Mich. App. 2002).
[17] Restatement (Second) of Torts § 314A.

premises. Therefore, businesses have a special relationship with their visitors and patrons that would allow recovery even in a case of nonfeasance.

Landowners Landowners owe a general duty to parties off the land from any unreasonable risks to them caused by something on the land. Courts use a reasonableness standard to determine the point at which the landowner should have acted. For example, the owner of GreenAcre plants several trees on the edge of his property, which is adjacent to a busy suburban street. One month later, one tree is dead, with no green vegetation and evidence of decaying bark and cracks in the roots. Eventually, the tree falls onto the road and injures a passerby. In this instance, a court may find that the landowner had a duty to inspect and remove the tree because it was foreseeable that the dead tree would be a risk to passersby if it fell.[18]

Landowners also owe a special duty to certain parties based on categories spelled out in the Restatements. It is important to understand that in a situation where a tenant is in possession of *leased space,* the tenant has the same special duties and level of liability that is imposed on landowners. Once a landlord/owner has given possession of the property to the tenant, the landlord is generally *not held liable* except for certain common areas (e.g., common stairwells, restrooms, or lobby).[19] The expected level of care varies by category. Table 9.2 sets out the categories of special relationship duties owed by landowners to licensees, invitees, and trespassers.

Assumption of Duty Another exception to the no general duty to act/rescue is when one party voluntarily begins to render assistance even when there is no legal obligation to

TABLE 9.2 Special Relationship Duties Owed by Landowners

Special Relationship to	Definition	Example	Duties Owed
Licensee	Party has owner's consent to be on property for a nonbusiness purpose.	Social guest	Warn licensee of any known dangerous conditions on or about the premises. *No* duty owed to licensee to inspect for hidden dangers.
Invitee	Party is invited onto property by owner for business purposes or because landowner holds the premises open to the public.	Customer in a retail store	Warn invitee of any known dangerous conditions on or about the premises. Duty to inspect the premises for hidden dangers and take reasonable efforts to fix any defects.
Trespasser	Party enters premises without owner's consent.	Landscaping crew that accidentally mows wrong property	No duty to warn, inspect, or repair. Exception is a general duty of care when (1) owner has reason to know of regular trespass (such as a worn pathway) or (2) owner has reason to anticipate that young children might trespass on the property.

---

[18] It should be noted that the Restatements do except "natural" conditions from the general duty. However, if a landowner planted shrubs or excavated land, this falls under the category of *artificial* and is not an exception to the landowner's general duty to persons off the property.

[19] There are exceptions to this rule, such as a situation in which the landlord transferred possession knowing of a certain defect but failed to warn the tenant about it.

do so. This is known as *assumption of duty* and it requires that the party rendering assistance must proceed with reasonable care. This includes the duty to continue rendering aid and to take care not to leave the injured party in a worse position.[20] For example, suppose that Davis, a delivery truck driver, hears a call for help during one of his deliveries. He discovers that the call is coming from a nearby apartment that is on fire. Davis enters the building and rescues the caller. Although Davis has no legal duty to rescue, he undertakes the rescue and therefore assumes the duty to keep the caller safe. For example, if the caller is unconscious, Davis must use reasonable care to secure medical help and cannot abandon the caller.

In Case 9.3, a state appellate court considers a claim by a college student, injured as part of a fraternity prank that went awry, that he was owed a duty under both a landowner theory and an assumption of duty theory.

CASE 9.3 Yost v. Wabash College, Phi Kappa Psi Fraternity, 3 N.E.3d 509 (Ind. 2014)

FACT SUMMARY Brian Yost (Yost) was an 18-year-old first-year student at Wabash College (Wabash) and a pledge at the local Phi Kappa Psi fraternity (Local Fraternity). Part of the Local Fraternity's traditions involve "creeking," meaning that a fraternity brother is thrown into a nearby creek. In September 2007, Yost and his pledge brothers confronted some of the Local Fraternity's member brothers in an attempt to toss one of these members, Yost's Pledge Father, into a nearby creek. Later that night, several Local Fraternity brothers retaliated by attempting to forcibly place Yost in the shower. This action was also a tradition of the Local Fraternity, and one in which Yost and his pledge brothers had previously participated two other times the evening of his injury. During this attempt, several Local Fraternity member brothers were carrying Yost to the shower when one of the fraternity members put him into a headlock that rendered Yost unconscious. The other member brothers panicked and dropped Yost to the ground.

Yost suffered significant physical and psychological injuries from the incident that caused him to withdraw from college. Yost filed suit alleging his injuries were a result of negligence and seeking damages from, among others: (1) Wabash College (the owner and landlord of the fraternity house), contending that a special relationship existed, and (2) the Local Fraternity on an assumption of duty theory. The trial court granted summary judgment to both Wabash and the Local Fraternity and Yost appealed.

SYNOPSIS OF DECISION AND OPINION The Indiana Supreme Court affirmed the summary judgment for Wabash but reversed the summary judgment for the Local Fraternity. In the case of Wabash, the court reasoned that a landlord has no liability to tenants or others for injuries on the property when the tenant is in full control of the leased premises. In the case of the Local Fraternity, the court held that there was sufficient evidence to reasonably conclude that Yost may be able to show that the Local Fraternity assumed a duty and that the actions of its members increased the risk of harm to him. This was especially true as the activity which led to the incident was a fraternity tradition.

WORDS OF THE COURT: Wabash College's Duty as Property Owner "Within the contours of this duty, we have held that landowners have a duty to take reasonable precautions to prevent foreseeable criminal acts against invitees. However, when the landowner is a lessor and the lessee is in operational control of the premises, such duty rarely exists. . . . In the absence of statute, covenant, fraud or concealment, a landlord who gives a tenant full control and possession of the leased property will not be liable for personal injuries sustained by the tenant or other persons lawfully upon the leased property."

WORDS OF THE COURT: Local Fraternity's Assumed Duty "Here, Yost's argument is not

(continued)

---

[20]Restatement (Third) of Torts §43.

that a conventionally recognized duty (such as a landowner's duty to an invitee or common carrier's duty to a passenger) existed, but rather that the local fraternity assumed a duty requiring the local fraternity to act with reasonable care. As the above facts show, Yost was living at the local fraternity, subject to the mentorship of a Pledge Father from the local fraternity, participating in traditions maintained at the local fraternity, was involved in the pledgeship program being run by local fraternity members, and, therefore, at least partially under the control and direction of the local fraternity. . . . The undisputed designated evidence does not preclude the possibility that Yost may show at trial that the local fraternity undertook to render supervisory services intended to reduce the risk of harm to members like Yost, that upon which supervision Yost relied, and further that by failing to exercise reasonable care the local fraternity increased the risk of harm to Yost."

Case Questions

1. What factors did the court use to determine that the Local Fraternity may have assumed a duty here? Do you agree? Why or why not?
2. Why did the court find that Wabash College had no liability for this incident?
3. *Focus on Critical Thinking:* One of Yost's unsuccessful arguments against Wabash centered on a doctrine called *in loco parentis* (i.e., in place of the parent). The doctrine has largely disappeared from higher education since 1961. Yost claimed that the college had a duty to protect him and should have had a system in place to prevent fraternity pranks from becoming dangerous. Do you agree? Should an 18-year-old college student have full responsibility for his own safety while in a college-owned facility? Should colleges and universities have *in loco parentis* liability?

Breach of Duty Once it has been established that one party owes another a general or special duty, the next factor in the analysis is whether or not the party has fulfilled her obligations. Failing to meet these obligations is known as a **breach of duty**. As discussed earlier, duties include (1) general obligations to act in a reasonable manner so as not to put another in harm's way; (2) special duties to certain parties, including the duty to inspect or the duty to warn of defects; and (3) assumption of duty. While the Restatements don't actually list events of breach, courts have traditionally looked to certain guideposts for determining whether a breach of duty has occurred.

Violation of Safety Statute If the legislature has passed a statute intended to promote safety and one party violates the statute, there is a strong presumption that the party violating the statute has also breached her general duty to those who are protected by the law. Violations of safety statutes are sometimes referred to as *negligence per se*. For example, suppose the state legislature passes a law requiring that construction companies provide hard hats for all workers and visitors on a construction site. One day a prospective tenant visits an office building construction site to check on its progress, but there are not a sufficient number of hard hats available. The site manager allows the visitor on the site without a hard hat. The visitor is then injured by falling debris. In this case, the construction company has violated the state safety statute, and a court may find a breach of duty occurred without delving into a reasonably prudent person analysis.

States also pass statutes intended to establish specific liability standards in certain circumstances. For example, *dram shop laws,* enacted in most but not all states, impose liability on the owners and employees of a public establishment where alcohol is being served. These laws allow a third party who has been injured or harmed by an intoxicated tortfeasor to recover damages against the owner or employee who served the obviously intoxicated patron.[21]

---

[21]Note that an increasing number of state legislatures have also imposed similar liability for all social hosts, including the serving of alcohol in a private home.

Common Law Standards of Behavior   When the state legislature has been silent, appellate courts in each individual state have usually developed a fairly extensive body of cases in their common law so that certain standards of behavior may be used in judging whether or not a breach occurred. Standards related to maintenance of property (such as clearing ice from sidewalks) and safety measures (such as keeping one's car in good repair if driving on public roads) are examples of nonstatutory standards for reasonable behavior.

Res Ipsa Loquitur   The doctrine of *res ipsa loquitur* (a Latin phrase meaning "the thing or matter speaks for itself") is deep-seated in American tort law. This doctrine allows an injured party to create a presumption that the tortfeasor was negligent by pointing to certain facts that infer negligent conduct without showing exactly how the tortfeasor behaved.[22] An English judge first used this Latin phrase over a century ago in a case involving a pedestrian who was struck by a flour barrel that fell from a warehouse owned by the defendant. Although the injured party could not actually show how or why the barrel fell, the court held that the facts themselves were sufficient to impute a presumption of negligence.[23]

Assume that Ginsberg notices smoke coming out from under the hood of her car. She has the car towed to a mechanic, who determines that a valve cover gasket is leaking. She instructs him to make the necessary repairs. When she picks up the car, she pays the bill and drives off. One mile later, while stopped at a light, Ginsberg sees smoke coming from the hood again and gets out of the car just before it catches fire. The fire consumes the car, causing the engine to melt, and thus no specific cause for the fire can be determined. Ginsberg cannot prove exactly what the mechanic did wrong, but the car shouldn't have caught fire if the mechanic had repaired the car properly. She can use *res ipsa loquitur* to infer negligence.

Cause in Fact   After establishing that a breach of duty has occurred, the injured party must also prove that the tortfeasor's conduct was the **cause in fact** of the damages suffered by the injured party. In other words, there must be a *link* between breach of duty and damages. The overwhelming majority of courts use a simple test, known as the *but-for test,* to establish a link. Thus, the question that must be answered is this: "But for (except for) the breach of duty by the tortfeasor, would the injured party have suffered damages?" If the answer is no, then there is a link between the tortfeasor's conduct and the harm suffered by the injured party. The question can also be asked this way: "If the tortfeasor had complied with her legal duty, would the injured party have suffered damages?" Again, a no answer indicates a link and, thus, cause in fact. For example, suppose that Donald checks into Hotel's 20th-floor luxury suite. He watches a beautiful sunset while leaning on the balcony railing, but the railing snaps and Donald falls 20 stories. In a negligence analysis, one can reasonably conclude that Hotel owes Donald both a general duty and a special duty (innkeeper) and that the duty was breached because the rail was presumably defective in some way. To establish cause in fact, one would ask: But for the breach of duty by Hotel, would Donald have suffered damages? The answer is clearly no because if Hotel hadn't breached its duty (e.g., had inspected and kept the railing in good repair), Donald would not have suffered damages. Thus, the breach of duty by Hotel was the *cause in fact* of Donald's injuries.

Scope of But-For Test   One problem in applying the but-for test is its overreaching broadness. Its application may result in holding a tortfeasor liable for injuries that occurred

---
[22]Restatement (Second) of Torts § 328(D).
[23]*Byrne v. Boadle* [1863]159 Eng. Rep. 299 (Eng.). The court wrote, "[A] barrel could not roll out of a warehouse without some negligence, and to say the plaintiff who is injured by it must call witnesses . . . is preposterous."

well beyond the foreseeable scope of the wrongdoing. For example, in the Donald-Hotel case, suppose that after Donald's balcony rail snaps, Donald falls, but the broken balcony rail also falls and penetrates the windshield of a car on the street below, injuring the driver. The injury causes the driver of the car to swerve, hit a pedestrian, and crash into an adjacent canal. A witness to the accident then attempts to rescue the driver of the car from the canal but drowns doing so. Five blocks away, a shopkeeper is so startled by the noise from the accident that she drops a priceless vase on her foot. In this set of accidental chain reactions, using the but-for test would impose liability on Hotel for each injury and damage, including those sustained by Donald, the driver of the car, the struck pedestrian, the drowned rescuer, and the shopkeeper who suffered foot injuries resulting from the destroyed vase. Nevertheless, a sense of fairness demands that the law cannot reasonably impose *all* of this liability on Hotel. At what point, if any, is the tortfeasor relieved from liability? The broad sweep of the but-for test requires a further step to establish liability. This step, known as **proximate (legal) cause**, is discussed next.

Proximate (Legal) Cause

In addition to showing that the tortfeasor's breach of duty was the cause in fact of the damages, the injured party must also prove that (1) the tortfeasor's conduct was also the closest-in-proximity cause of the damages and (2) the tortfeasor's liability wasn't canceled due to a superseding cause. These *proximate cause* concepts protect tortfeasors from liability for far-reaching and out-of-the-ordinary injuries resulting in damages from the tortious act.

Closest-in-Proximity

The majority of courts favor using *foreseeability* to define the scope of the risk. In the Donald-Hotel example discussed above, the jury would be charged with determining the scope of Hotel's liability. Liability would hinge on whether or not it was foreseeable that a faulty balcony railing would result in damages to be suffered by Donald (probable liability), the driver of the car (possible liability), the pedestrian (possible liability), the drowned rescuer (improbable liability), and the owner of the vase (very improbable liability). The Restatements define proximate cause as that which helps draw the line that determines when a tortfeasor is "not liable for harm different from harms whose risk made the [tortfeasor's] conduct tortious."

The proximate cause concept was first enunciated in Landmark Case 9.4, which is perhaps the most famous case in American tort law.

LANDMARK CASE 9.4 Palsgraf v. Long Island Railroad Co., 162 N.E. 99 (N.Y. Ct. App. 1928)

FACT SUMMARY Palsgraf bought a railroad ticket for Rockaway Beach, New York, and was waiting on the platform for her train. A different train arrived on a platform 100 yards away, allowed passengers to board, and began to depart from the station. Running to catch the departing train, two commuters grabbed onto the side and tried to hoist themselves up and into the moving car. To aid one of the men, the conductor on the train pulled him onto the train but dislodged a package covered in newspaper that the passenger was carrying. The package, which turned out to be fireworks, fell to the platform and exploded. The blast shook the station with sufficient force that large iron scales (used to weigh freight on various trains) hanging over Palsgraf fell on her, resulting in a severe injury. Palsgraf sued the Long Island Railroad for the conductor's negligent conduct of pulling the commuter onto the train, which eventually caused the explosion and her injury from the falling scales.

(continued)

SYNOPSIS OF DECISION AND OPINION In a famous opinion written by Judge Benjamin Cardozo (who would later serve on the U.S. Supreme Court), the New York Court of Appeals ruled in favor of the Long Island Railroad. Cardozo reasoned that because the conductor *could not have known* that the man he was helping onto the train had a box full of fireworks, the action of the conductor was not a proximate-enough cause to incur liability for Palsgraf's injuries.

WORDS OF THE COURT: Proximate Cause
"[T]he orbit of the danger as disclosed to the eye of reasonable vigilance would be the orbit of the duty. One who jostles one's neighbor in a crowd does not invade the rights of others standing at the outer fringe when the unintended contact casts a bomb upon the ground. The wrongdoer as to them is the man who carries the bomb, not the one who explodes it without suspicion of the danger. Life will have to be made over, and human nature transformed, before prevision so extravagant can be accepted as the norm of conduct, the customary standard to which behavior must conform.... The risk reasonably to be perceived defines the duty to be obeyed, and risk imports relation; it is risk to another or to others within the range of apprehension."

Case Questions
1. Are all the other elements of a negligence tort satisfied in this case?
2. Who else might Palsgraf have sued? For what?
3. *Focus on Critical Thinking:* Context is always important. This case was decided before any federal or state benefits for health care or lost time from work. The dissenting opinion in this case argued that public policy demanded that the Railroad pay for the injury because they were in the best position to pay and that some correlation existed between conduct and injury. In the 1928 context, does that strike you as a convincing argument? Why or why not?

Superseding Cause Sometimes an *intervening* event takes place after the tortfeasor's negligent act. The intervening act may also contribute to the negligence by producing additional damages to the injured party. Some (but not all) intervening acts may be the basis for limiting a tortfeasor's liability. These acts are called *superseding causes* (i.e., they supersede the tortfeasor's liability) and they are also defined by *foreseeability*. For example, in the Donald-Hotel case, suppose that Donald falls only one story and sustains a broken wrist. While being driven to the hospital, a freak tornado hits the car that Donald is in and the wrist injury is made worse. In a case for damages related to the injury, even though the but-for test would impose liability on Hotel even for the aggravated broken wrist, Hotel's liability is discontinued (though not eliminated for the original injury) once the tornado hits the car. The tornado is a superseding cause and thus Hotel is not liable for the aggravated injury. This limit applies because it was not reasonably foreseeable by Hotel that Donald would be injured by a tornado en route to the hospital.

 Self-Check Proximate Cause

Is proximate cause met in these situations?

1. A truck driver crashes into a guardrail. During the accident, a defective steering wheel rapidly spins around, breaking the driver's arm. The driver sues the maker of the steering mechanism.
2. A tenant hurts herself falling down defective steps. The tenant sues the landlord's insurance company, alleging that it knew the steps were defective but insured him anyway, thus discouraging him from fixing them.

(continued)

3. An employer burns down his warehouse for the insurance money. An employee is arrested and falsely imprisoned by the police for the crime. The employee sues the employer for negligence.

4. A passenger is injured in an automobile accident. The passenger sues the liquor store that sold alcohol to the driver of the car, who was already visibly intoxicated.

Answers to this Self-Check are provided at the end of the chapter.

Legal Speak >))

Estate
In addition to land, assets, and personal property, a person's *estate* also consists of legal rights and entitlements after death, including the right to sue for the tortious conduct that caused the death.

Actual Damages In order to recover in a negligence case, the tortfeasor must have caused another party **actual damages**. This means that the party alleging injury must prove that she has suffered some type of physical harm derived from an injury caused by the tortfeasor. An injured party may not prevail if the injuries are limited to mental and/or emotional harm alone. However, once a party has proved some *physical* harm, she is eligible for a variety of other types of damages, including out-of-pocket economic losses (such as medical bills), pain and suffering, lost time from employment, and similar categories. Punitive damages may be awarded but are rare because they can be awarded only when the tortfeasor's conduct has been extremely reckless or willful and wanton.[24]

Many states allow a spouse or children of an injured party to recover damages related to the negligence. This includes loss of companionship or marital relations (known as *loss of consortium*). Moreover, if the injured party dies, his *estate* may sue for the damages that the injured party would have recovered if he had survived. Spouses and children may also recover damages for losses sustained by virtue of the death of an injured party.

Figure 9.1 provides an illustration of a negligence analysis.

Defenses to Negligence Claims

Once the elements of negligence are met, the analysis then shifts to potential defenses available to the tortfeasor. The two primary defenses to claims of negligence are **comparative negligence** and **assumption of the risk**.

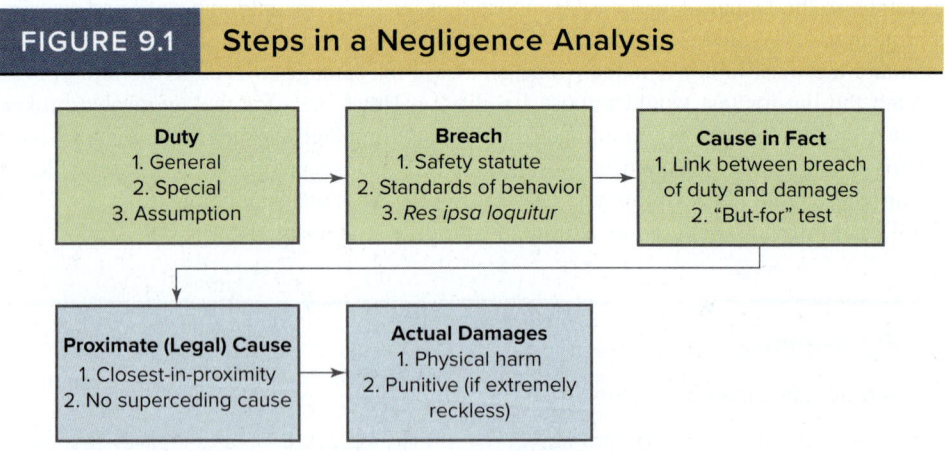

FIGURE 9.1 Steps in a Negligence Analysis

---

[24]Punitive damages were sought in 12 percent of the estimated 25,000 tort and contract trials concluded in state courts in 2005. Punitive damages were awarded in 700 (5 percent) of the 14,359 trials in which the plaintiff prevailed. Among the trials in which punitive damages were requested by plaintiff winners, 30 percent received these damages. The median punitive-damage award among the 700 trials that resulted in punitive damages was $64,000 in 2005, and 13 percent of these cases had punitive awards of $1 million or more. Office of Justice Programs, U.S. Dep't of Justice, *Special Report, Punitive Damage Awards in State Courts, 2005* (2011).

TABLE 9.3 Comparative Negligence Formula

Suppose Abel is injured by Baker's conduct and suffers damages totaling $100,000. A jury finds that Baker was 80 percent responsible for the injury but that Abel also contributed to his own injury and was 20 percent responsible for the harm. How much does Abel ultimately recover?

Damages suffered × Percentage of Baker's negligence = Recovery amount
$100,000 × 80% = $80,000

Comparative Negligence In cases where the injured party's conduct has played a factor in the harm suffered, the Restatements allow the tortfeasor to assert the defense of *comparative negligence*. This defense requires a jury to allocate the proportion of negligence committed by each party in terms of percentage (see Table 9.3). Ultimately, successfully asserting comparative negligence reduces (but does not eliminate) the final award to the plaintiff.

Note that comparative negligence is a cousin to the common law doctrine of *contributory negligence*, whereby even 1 percent of negligence on the part of the plaintiff is a complete bar to any plaintiff recovery. The overwhelming majority of states do not follow this standard because of its harshness on the injured party. Four states—Alabama, Maryland, North Carolina, and Virginia—along with the District of Columbia continue to recognize the contributory negligence defense. Indiana follows the contributory negligence rule in medical malpractice cases only.

Assumption of the Risk When the injured party knows that a substantial and apparent risk is associated with certain conduct and the party goes ahead with the dangerous activity anyway, the Restatements allow the tortfeasor to assert the defense of *assumption of the risk* so long as (1) the injured party/plaintiff knows or should know (by virtue of the circumstances, warning signs, etc.) that a risk of harm is inherent in the activity and (2) the injured party/plaintiff voluntarily participates in the activity. Certain activities are considered to be "inherently dangerous" (such as bungee jumping or parachuting), and companies that are providers of these activities may have limited protection from liability if they act reasonably in minimizing the dangers and make full disclosures of the risks to participants.

In Case 9.5, a state appellate court considers the assumption-of-the-risk defense in the context of leisure sports.

Legal Speak >))

Punitive Damages Monetary damages, generally a multiple of the actual damages, that are awarded partly to punish the tortfeasor and partly to deter others from acting in a similar manner.

CASE 9.5 Zeidman v. Fisher, 980 A.2d 637 (Pa. Super. Ct. 2009)

FACT SUMMARY Zeidman and Fisher were participants in a golf foursome at a charity tournament. On one hole where the view of the fairway was partially blocked, the foursome became concerned that they might inadvertently hit any players hidden by the blind spots on the fairway ahead of them. The group agreed that Zeidman would take a golf cart and ride ahead to see whether the course was clear for the group to hit. Zeidman made his observation and returned to his foursome in the cart. Because he intended on returning to his foursome to report that the group ahead was out of harm's way and because he never signaled to his group that it was safe to hit, Zeidman never entertained the possibility that one of his group would hit a shot. Before Zeidman returned, Fisher, becoming impatient, hit his shot

(continued)

while Zeidman was driving his cart back to the foursome. Fisher's shot was errant, and the ball struck Zeidman in the face, causing serious and permanent injuries. The trial court dismissed Zeidman's negligence lawsuit against Fisher on summary judgment, ruling that Zeidman had assumed the risk of participating in the golf match and this assumption of risk barred any recovery. Zeidman appealed.

SYNOPSIS OF DECISION AND OPINION The Pennsylvania Superior Court reversed the trial court's decision and ruled in favor of Zeidman. The court reasoned that the assumption-of-the-risk doctrine requires that the evidence show that the injured party (1) fully understood the specific risk, (2) voluntarily chose to encounter it, and (3) manifested a willingness to accept the known risk. In this case, an objectively reasonable person may have assumed that no risk existed because Zeidman's agreed-upon task was to check whether the fairway was clear and then report to his own foursome if it was safe to hit. Because he had not yet completed this task, Zeidman did not manifest a willingness to accept a known risk.

WORDS OF THE COURT: Assumption-of-the-Risk Doctrine "In the circumstances of the present case, it is obvious that Zeidman, on returning from his forward observer mission, did not consciously assume the risk of friendly fire when, to the contrary, he had every right to anticipate none of his playing partners would attempt a tee shot until his return to the tee box. To grant summary judgment on the basis of assumption of the risk it must first be concluded, as a matter of law, that the party consciously appreciated the risk that attended a certain endeavor. . . . Accordingly, whether Zeidman is able to convince a jury that his version of events is true remains to be seen, he, in any event is entitled to his day in court."

Case Questions

1. If Zeidman had signaled to his partners that all was clear from the fairway and was then hit while returning in the cart, would Fisher be entitled to a summary judgment based on assumption of the risk?
2. What duty did Fisher owe Zeidman in the first place? Was it a special-relationship duty?
3. *Focus on Critical Thinking:* What other leisure sports or activities might be covered under the assumption-of-the-risk doctrine? Is it good public policy to shield negligent parties with the doctrine?

CONCEPT SUMMARY Negligence Analysis

- *Duty:* Did the tortfeasor owe a duty to the injured party?
- *Breach:* Did the tortfeasor breach the reasonably prudent person standard?
- *Causation:* Except for the tortfeasor's breach of duty, would the plaintiff have suffered the injury?
- *Proximate (legal) cause:* Was the breach the closest in proximity? Were there any superseding causes? Was the harm foreseeable?
- *Damages:* Did the injury to person or property result in losses?
- *Defenses:* Did the injured party contribute to the injury (comparative negligence)? Did the injured party know of the risk but go ahead anyway (assumption of the risk)?

STRICT LIABILITY TORTS

The tort liability theories covered so far in this chapter are based on either intent or negligence. The Restatements also provide for liability in certain cases where neither intent nor negligence need be proved. This category of tort is known as *strict liability* and is recognized in the Restatements primarily for abnormally dangerous activities and for defective products (discussed in the next section).[25] Strict liability is a concept rooted in the notion that the general public benefits when liability is imposed on those who engage in certain activities that result in harm to another party, even if the activities are undertaken in the most careful manner possible (without negligence).

Abnormally Dangerous Activities

The Restatements set out a six-factor test to determine whether abnormally dangerous activities trigger strict liability for any harm caused by the activity:

- Does the activity involve a high degree of risk of some harm?
- Is there a likelihood that the harm that results will be great?
- Is it possible to eliminate the risk by exercising reasonable care?
- Is the activity relatively common?
- Is the location of the activity appropriate to the risk?
- Is there any community value that outweighs the dangerous attributes?

For example, suppose that ChemicalCo produces 100 pounds of plastic explosives for use in the demolition of a building. It leases a railroad car and ships the explosives to its storage warehouse until the buyer can pick them up. Before the buyer picks them up, thieves break in and inadvertently ignite the explosives. The explosion causes damage to several buildings and an injury to a party standing in the surrounding area. Using the

Strict liability is imposed on businesses engaged in abnormally dangerous operations such as the use of explosives in building demolition. ImageSource/Corbis

---

[25]Strict liability is also imposed under the common law for the keepers of wild or dangerous animals.

six-factor test, a court will likely impose strict liability on ChemicalCo due to the nature of the abnormally dangerous activity of storing explosives. Other strict liability cases have involved the storage and use of toxic flammable liquids, nuclear power, and blasting for demolition or construction.

PRODUCTS LIABILITY

LO 9-8
Provide alternate theories of liability and defense that can be applied when a product is the cause of an injury.

Products liability refers to the liability of any seller (including the manufacturer, retailer, and any intermediary seller such as a wholesaler) of a product that, because of a defect, causes harm to a consumer. Note that modern products liability law protects not only the actual purchaser but also any ultimate users who are harmed by the product's defect. In a products liability case, the injured party may pursue a legal remedy against the seller under one of three theories: (1) negligence, (2) warranty, or (3) strict liability.

Negligence

The negligence analysis covered earlier in this chapter may also be applied to the seller of a product. Although historically negligence was severely limited as a remedy because the law protected only the actual purchaser, a revised rule announced in the landmark case of *MacPherson v. Buick*[26] has been adopted in every state. Under the *MacPherson* rule, one who negligently manufactures a product is liable for *any injuries to persons* (and, in some limited cases, property) proximately caused by the negligence. For example, suppose that Holmes purchases a motorcycle from a dealer and gives it to his son Wendell. Wendell is injured on the motorcycle and sues the manufacturer for negligence. So long as Wendell can prove negligence, the manufacturer will be liable for Wendell's injuries despite the fact that Wendell was not the one who entered into the purchase agreement with the dealer or the manufacturer.

Courts have found that manufacturers have the duty of care regarding proper design, manufacturing, testing, inspection, and shipping. Retailers do not have as comprehensive a duty as the manufacturer but still have a duty to warn consumers of any product they know or suspect to be unreasonably dangerous.

Warranty

Historically, warranty laws have been an important protection for purchasers because they impose liability even in the absence of negligence. When the seller makes a representation of fact about a product, this is known as an *express* warranty. If the seller has not made a specific representation about the product, the buyer may still be protected by a Uniform Commercial Code–imposed *implied* warranty. Warranties are set out in Article 2 (Sales) of the UCC and are discussed in detail in Chapter 21, "Warranties and Consumer Protection Law."

LO 9-9
Articulate what must be proved in negligence and strict liability cases and appreciate how the levels of proof differ.

Strict Liability

The most appealing option for pursuing a products liability case is the doctrine of strict liability because the injured party need not prove the elements of negligence. In *Greenman v. Yuba Power Products, Inc.*,[27] the California Supreme Court decided a groundbreaking case that paved the way for adoption of a strict liability standard for product defects by ruling that "a manufacturer is strictly liable in tort when an article he places on the market,

---

[26]111 N.E. 1050 (N.Y. 1916). The historical requirement that negligence suits could only be brought by the direct purchaser was known as *privity of contract.*

[27]377 P.2d 897 (Cal. 1963).

knowing that it is to be used without inspection for defects, proves to have a defect which causes injury to a human being." Two years after the *Greenman* case was decided, a similar doctrine of strict liability tort for the sellers of products was included in the *Restatement (Second) of Torts* in § 402A. The Restatements specifically indicate that liability still exists even if the seller has used all possible care. Note that the term *seller* means not only the product's manufacturer but also all business parties through the chain of commerce, including the retailer.

Section 402A is a bedrock for strict products liability because a substantial majority of states have adopted the section that imposes special liability on the seller of a product that could harm the user. Specifically, § 402A imposes strict liability on the seller so long as the injured party can show that the product was in a *defective* condition and that the defect rendered the product *unreasonably dangerous*. Liability under § 402A is triggered only when

- The seller is engaged in the business of selling such a product, and
- The product is expected to and does reach the user or consumer without a substantial change in the condition in which it is sold.

Section 402A's strict liability is imposed on the seller even though

- The seller has exercised all possible care in preparation and sale of the product, and
- The user or consumer has not bought the product from or entered into any contractual relationship with the seller (i.e., no *privity of contract* is required).

Defining "Defect" For a party to recover for an injury caused by a product, the product must have been defective and must have created a danger that is outside the reasonable consumer's expectations. Courts have recognized several theories of unreasonably dangerous defects.

Design or Manufacturing Defect A product may become dangerous if it is *designed* improperly in that foreseeable risks of harm posed by the product could have been reduced or avoided by some *alternative* design. Even products that are designed properly may still be rendered dangerously defective by some mistake made during the *manufacturing* process. For example, suppose CarCo designs a new car intended to have higher-than-average gas mileage. It achieves this by moving the gas tank to a different position on the car. The design, however, results in the gas tank rupturing during a rear-end crash. This is a classic *design* defect.[28] On the other hand, suppose CarCo designs the new car properly, but one of the factory workers improperly installs the brakes and this eventually results in an injury. In this case, the product has been rendered unreasonably dangerous via a *manufacturing* defect.

Inadequate Warning Products that are ostensibly safe may carry risks unknown to a reasonable consumer. In such cases, the law requires the product to carry sufficient warnings and instructions. Failure to warn may render the product unreasonably dangerous even absent any manufacturing or design defect. One common category of inadequate-warning cases involves prescription drugs, but the theory of unreasonable danger applies to all products that carry some danger in use (such as a lawn mower or snow thrower).

In Case 9.6, an appellate court in California considers an inadequate-warning claim against the manufacturer of an above-ground pool.

---

[28]See Landmark Case 5.3 in Chapter 5, "Business Ethics, Corporate Social Responsibility, and Law," for a case involving a design defect in an automobile that caused rear-end explosions.

CASE 9.6 Bunch v. Hoffinger Industries, 123 Cal. App. 4th 1278, 20 Cal. Rptr. 3d 780 (2004)

FACT SUMMARY Bunch, an 11-year-old girl, dove into an above-ground pool that was only four feet deep. As a result, Bunch suffered a severe injury to her spine that rendered her quadriplegic. Bunch filed suit against Hoffinger as the manufacturer of the pool alleging, among other theories, that Hoffinger was liable for failing to provide adequate warnings that could have prevented the tragedy. Hoffinger argued that it did not owe any duty to warn consumers because the danger was "open and obvious." At trial, Bunch testified that she saw only a sticker that depicted a man doing a *pike* dive (knees straight and body bent at the waist) with the word "caution" and she thought that the caution referred only to pike diving. Bunch also called expert witnesses to testify that warnings to children between the ages of 7 and 12 must be concrete and spell out any consequences of diving into shallow water. Another of Bunch's experts testified that the risk of spinal paraplegia was not readily apparent to an 11-year-old and that it was difficult for someone in that age group to judge the depth of a pool. Hoffinger countered that (1) warning labels on pools were not feasible before it left the factory because the label would become distorted by the stretching of the liner and (2) Bunch had assumed the risk because she had swum in that same pool prior to that occasion and ignored an adult present at the pool who warned against diving. The jury returned a verdict in Bunch's favor and awarded her $16,112,306. Hoffinger appealed.

SYNOPSIS OF DECISION AND OPINION The California Court of Appeals affirmed the judgment and verdict in favor of Bunch. The court rejected Hoffinger's contention that it owed no duty to warn Bunch of possible head injury from the open and obvious danger of diving headfirst into a shallow above-ground pool. Although the court acknowledged that some previous cases have held that no recovery was available for those who made a shallow dive into an above-ground pool because the danger was obvious, they distinguished those cases from the facts in this case because Bunch was only 11 years old. Age was one of the important factors in determining an awareness of open or obvious danger. It also rejected Hoffinger's assumption of the risk argument and ruled that any assumed risk by an injured party does not insulate equipment suppliers from liability for injury from providing defective equipment.

With respect to the failure-to-warn issue, the court held that the jury's conclusions were sound and in accord with expert testimony that pool industry standards require manufacturers to prominently display permanent warnings on their pools and that Hoffinger's sticker was below industry standards. Thus, the court concluded that the record supported the jury's determination that Hoffinger's warnings were inadequate.

WORDS OF THE COURT: Lack of Effective Warning "Given the testimony of Bunch and her two expert witnesses, we find sufficient evidence to support the conclusion that the lack of adequate warning label was neither a negligible nor theoretical contribution to Bunch's injury. The evidence presented at trial revealed that the lack for persuasive label outlining the consequences of diving into the pool was a substantial factor in causing the injury. As the [California] Supreme Court points out 'a very minor force that does cause harm is a substantial factor.' Here, at the very least, the lack of an effective warning was a minor force in bringing about the fateful dive."

Case Questions

1. Why is the injured party's age one of the most important factors in considering a failure-to-warn claim?
2. Do you agree with Hoffinger's contention that the injured party assumed the risk? Why or why not?
3. *Focus on Critical Thinking:* What other products can you think of that may require a more effective warning given the age of the average user? Should bicycles, skateboards, and snowboards fall into the same category? Why or why not?

Improper Packaging A product can be rendered unreasonably dangerous by a defect in the packaging. Cases that have recognized this theory of defect are primarily asserted against manufacturers of products that require safety-proof containers as well as food or beverage packages that clearly indicate whether the product is sealed or whether there is evidence of tampering (e.g., a seal on a bottle of juice). Perhaps the most famous case related to improper packaging involved the well-publicized Tylenol scare in 1986. In *Elsroth v. Johnson & Johnson*,[29] a federal court in New York held that Johnson & Johnson, the manufacturer of Tylenol, was not liable for the death of a consumer who was the victim of tampering by an unknown third party. The estate of the consumer brought suit, claiming that improper packaging had led to the tampering when an unknown third party removed a package of Tylenol from a supermarket shelf, laced it with cyanide, and then somehow resealed the container and box so the tampering was not readily detectable. However, the court pointed to the fact that the Tylenol bottle featured a foil seal glued to the mouth of the container, a shrink-wrap seal around the neck and cap of the bottle, and a box sealed with glue in which the bottle was placed. Because Johnson & Johnson went above and beyond existing standards by using three different methods to prevent consumption of a tampered product, the company could not be held liable under § 402A.

A court found that Tylenol's packaging was not defective and thus the company was not liable for any injuries resulting from third-party tampering.

Roberts Publishing Services/Joshua Roberts. All rights reserved.

Unavoidably Unsafe Some products are inherently dangerous. That is, some products are designed and manufactured correctly, and adequate warning has been given, but the product is still dangerous (such as a handgun). Courts have struggled to adjudicate strict liability standards in cases relating to prescription drugs, cigarettes, and guns. In each case, the product was properly manufactured and designed. The evolving view of products liability theories for cigarettes and guns is explored in more detail in *Legal/Ethical Reflection and Discussion*.

LEGAL/ETHICAL REFLECTION AND DISCUSSION

Products Liability and Guns

The prevalence of gun violence in America has led some victims to use products liability theories in an attempt to halt sales of certain guns used in mass shootings and hold gun manufacturers liable for damages suffered by the victims. The families of the victims in the 2012 Sandy Hook Elementary School massacre in Newtown, Connecticut, filed a products liability lawsuit against Remington Firearms International for, among other claims, wrongful death and pain and suffering. Remington is the parent company that manufactures and markets the Bushmaster XM15, a version of the notorious AR-15 semiautomatic rifle. The AR-15 has a bloody pedigree. In addition to the Sandy Hook murders, killers used an AR-15 style rifle in mass shootings at a high school in Parkland, Florida (2018); a nightclub in Orlando, Florida (2016); a workplace in San Bernardino, California (2015);

(continued)

---

[29]700 F. Supp. 151 (S.D.N.Y. 1988).

community college campuses in Roseburg, Oregon (2015), and Santa Monica, California (2013); and a movie theater in Aurora, Colorado (2012).

The Sandy Hook lawsuit is a products liability claim based on both negligence and strict liability for unsafe products. The suit alleged that the AR-15 is the "weapon of choice for shooters looking to inflict maximum casualties," and "American schools are on the forefront of such violence." The Sandy Hook plaintiffs drew on similar legal strategies used in the past to hold cigarette manufacturers liable for smoking-related deaths. As more than 40 states brought lawsuits against the tobacco industry by 1998, manufacturers agreed to an array of marketing and product use restrictions such as a ban on billboards, transit advertisements, and tobacco brand logos on clothing and merchandise. The tobacco settlement also required cigarette makers to pay $1.45 billion to finance advertisements deterring underage tobacco use. Despite the settlement, tobacco companies still faced increasingly successful lawsuits from individuals and were stung recently by a $51 million award of a California jury to a heavy smoker with inoperable lung cancer. The jury rejected big tobacco's standard defense, assumption of the risk, after finding substantial evidence that tobacco's manufacturers conspired to cover up the known dangers and addictions of cigarette smoking for decades. Tobacco companies are continuing to suffer heavy losses in courtrooms across America.

However, the Sandy Hook plaintiffs had to overcome a significant barrier that tobacco plaintiffs did not. The Protection of Lawful Commerce in Arms Act (PLCAA)[30] exempts gun manufacturers from products liability lawsuits brought by parties suffering damages as a result of a third party's criminal act. The law was a response to a wave of products liability lawsuits filed against gun manufacturers starting in 2002. Nonetheless, the law does contain important exceptions related to negligent entrustment and improper marketing. Therefore, the Sandy Hook plaintiffs strategically decided to focus primarily on Remington's marketing and sales strategies as reckless:

> Remington knowingly sold the AR-15 with no conceivable use . . . other than the mass killing of other human beings and unscrupulously marketed and promoted the assaultive qualities and military uses of AR-15s to a demographic of young civilians. . . . Invoking the unparalleled destructive power of the weapon, [Remington's] advertising copy read: "Forces of opposition, bow down. You are single-handedly outnumbered."
>
> *Soto v. Bushmaster Firearms*, Conn. Superior Ct., Plaintiff's First Am. Compl. 72–74, (Oct. 29, 2015)

Remington filed a motion to dismiss the lawsuit asserting immunity under the PLCAA. The trial court refused to dismiss the claims ruling that the Sandy Hook plaintiffs had asserted a legally cognizable theory that Remington's conduct fell into a PLCAA exception. The court ruled that the issue of whether the PLCAA exception applied was one for a jury and therefore the lawsuit could not be dismissed.[31]

Discussion Questions

1. Should gun manufacturers be held strictly liable for harm caused by their products? Why or why not? Is it good public policy?

2. Compare and contrast the theories used by tobacco plaintiffs versus gun manufacturing plaintiffs. How are they similar and how are they distinguishable?

3. Why did Congress opt to pass legislation to protect gun manufacturers when no other industry has similar protection? Was it pure politics or is there a policy justification? Was it ethical?

4. *The Wall Street Journal* reported that the sale of guns increased after the Sandy Hook and Orlando massacres. How do you account for that phenomenon?

5. According to CNBC, over 5 million Americans own an AR-15 style weapon.[32] As a practical

(continued)

---

[30] 15 U.S.C. §§ 7901–7903.

[31] *Soto v. Bushmaster Firearms*, Docket No. FBT-CV-15-6048103-S, Memorandum of Decision (Conn. Super. Ct. Apr. 14, 2016).

[32] John W. Schoen, *Owned by 5 Million Americans, AR-15 Under Renewed Fire After Orlando Massacre*, CNBC (June 13, 2016), www.cnbc.com/2016/06/13/owned-by-5-million-americans-ar-15-under-renewed-fire-after-orlando-massacre.html.

matter, would an outright ban on the weapon be effective? What would be the commercial, social, and political impacts of a government-imposed ban on semiautomatic rifles?

6. Use your favorite search engine to find "Sandy Hook Hoax," which will reveal a dark side of social media. Should the First Amendment cover such speech? What remedies are available to the families of the victims against the hoax theorists? Is the theory of Sandy Hook as a hoax proper subject matter to debate? Should Facebook or other social media sites take action against the hoax theorists?

Causation and Damages Once it has been established that the product is unreasonably dangerous, the injured party must prove only that the defective product was the cause of the injuries and that the product caused an actual injury that resulted in damages.

Seller's Defenses Although strict liability imposes a relatively onerous burden on the seller, the law recognizes several defenses for a seller even if the injured party has established all of the required elements for liability.

Substantial Change The Restatements draw a line of liability based on the condition of the product at the time it leaves the seller's control. For strict liability to apply, the product must reach the end user without substantial change. Thus, if a product leaves the manufacturing plant in a reasonable condition (not dangerous) and then is contaminated or damaged in the next stage of the commercial chain of delivery, any resulting harm is outside the strict liability model. Depending on the circumstances, of course, the manufacturer may still be liable for negligence but not under strict liability.

Assumption of the Risk Although courts apply this defense narrowly,[33] it is still recognized as a defense for sellers in a strict product liability case. An injured party has assumed the risk if the party knows or should have known about the risk and disregards this risk by continuing with the activity at issue for her own benefit. For example, suppose that WidgetCo owns a high-speed machine for producing widgets and a foreign object lodges in the machine while it is operating. The instructions warn to shut down the machine before removing the object, but the plant manager decides against a shutdown, fearing it will cost money from lost production time. If the plant manager is injured while removing the object from the operating machinery and sues the machine's manufacturer under a strict product liability theory, the manufacturer may successfully assert the assumption-of-the-risk defense.[34]

Sometimes a large quantity of goods are sold to the public before a dangerous defect in the product is discovered. That product may then be recalled. If a consumer is made fully aware of a product recall due to a design or manufacturing defect but continues to use the product, assumption of risk may be asserted if injury and a lawsuit result.

Misuse of Product In a case where the injured party may not know of a certain risk and yet fails to use the product in a manner in which an ordinarily prudent person would, the seller may use product misuse as a defense. Courts have been reluctant to allow this defense unless the particular use of the product is so far from its ordinary use that it is not reasonably foreseeable by the seller.

Figure 9.2 provides an analysis of how liability is determined to apply or not apply under *Restatement (Second) of Torts* § 402A.

---

[33]*See Assumption of Risk and Strict Products Liability*, 95 Harv. L. Rev. 872 (1982).

[34]Based on *Micallef v. Miehle Co.*, 348 N.E.2d 571 (N.Y. Ct. App. 1976).

| FIGURE 9.2 | Section 402A Liability |

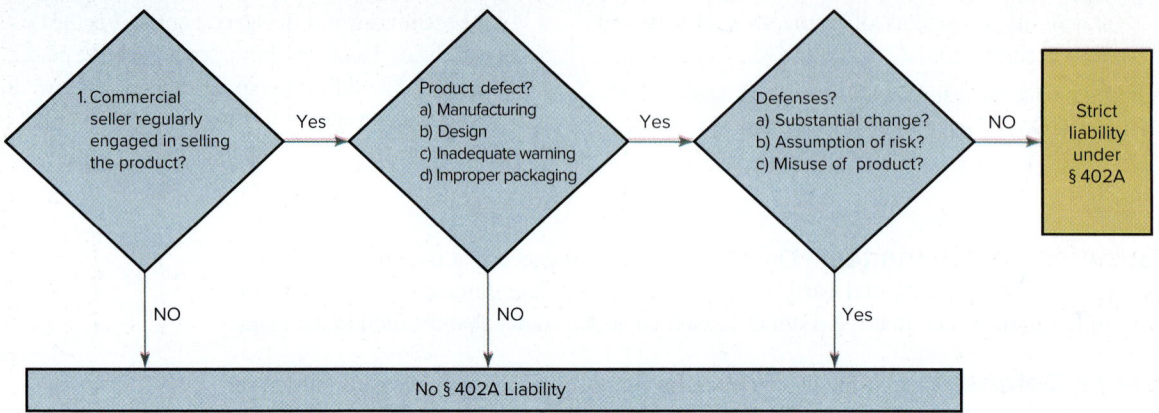

CONCEPT SUMMARY Strict Liability and Products Liability

Strict liability
- Applies to abnormally dangerous activities.
- Applies in the absence of negligence.
- Applies regardless of the care exercised by the tortfeasor.

Products liability
- Makes a company liable for design or manufacturing defects that cause harm.
- Applies in the absence of proof of negligent design or manufacture.
- Requires that injured parties prove only the defect and injuries; causation is not required.
- Can apply if a warning of a known danger or defect is not issued.

KEY TERMS

Tort p. 283 A civil wrong in which one party's action or inaction causes a loss to be suffered by another party.

Tortfeasor p. 283 One who commits a civil wrong against another that results in injury to person or property.

Tortious conduct p. 283 The wrongful action or inaction of a tortfeasor.

Restatement of Torts p. 283 An influential document issued by the American Law Institute that summarizes the general principles of U.S. tort law and is recognized by the courts as a source of widely applied principles of law. ALI has amended the Restatements twice, resulting in the *Restatement (Second) of Torts* and the *Restatement (Third) of Torts*.

Intentional torts p. 283 A category of torts in which the tortfeasor was willful in bringing about a particular event that caused harm to another party.

Negligence p. 283 A category of torts in which the tortfeasor was without willful intent in bringing about a particular event that caused harm to another party.

Strict liability p. 283 A category of torts in which a tortfeasor may be held liable for an act regardless of intent or willfulness; applies primarily to cases of defective products and abnormally dangerous activities.

Libel p. 284   Written defamation, in which someone publishes in print (words or pictures), writes, or broadcasts through radio, television, or film an untruth about another that will do harm to that person's reputation or honesty or subject a party to hate, contempt, or ridicule.

Slander p. 284   Oral defamation, in which someone tells one or more persons an untruth about another that will harm the reputation or honesty of the person defamed or subject a party to hate, contempt, or ridicule.

Absolute privilege p. 286   A defense to a defamation claim whereby the defendant need not proffer any further evidence to assert the defense; provided to government officials, judicial officers and proceedings, and state legislatures.

Qualified privilege p. 286   A defense to a defamation claim whereby the defendant must offer evidence of good faith and be absent of malice to be shielded from liability; provided for the media and employers.

Trade libel p. 288   A tort in which a competitor has made a false statement that disparaged a competing product.

Product disparagement statutes p. 288   Statutes intended to protect the interest of a state's major industries, such as agriculture, dairy, or beef.

Communications Decency Act (CDA) of 1996 p. 290   Federal legislation that extends immunity to Internet service providers (ISPs) by protecting them from any defamation liability as a "publisher or speaker of any information provided by another information content provider."

Merchant's privilege p. 291   A narrow privilege, provided for in the Restatements, that shields a merchant from liability for temporarily detaining a party who is reasonably suspected of stealing merchandise.

Duty p. 295   A fundamental element that must be proved to recover in a negligence lawsuit against a tortfeasor: The injured party must prove that the tortfeasor owed him a duty of care.

Misfeasance p. 295   An act by one party that harms or endangers another party.

Nonfeasance p. 295   The failure to act or intervene in a certain situation.

Special relationship p. 295   In tort law, a heightened duty created between certain parties, such as that of a common carrier to its passengers, innkeepers to guests, employers to employees, businesses to patrons, a school to students, and a landlord to tenants and landowners.

Breach of duty p. 298   A fundamental element that must be proved to recover in a negligence lawsuit against a tortfeasor: The injured party must prove that the tortfeasor failed to exercise reasonable care in fulfilling her obligations.

Cause in fact p. 299   A fundamental element that must be proved to recover in a negligence lawsuit against a tortfeasor: The injured party must prove that, except for the breach of duty by the tortfeasor, he would not have suffered damages.

Proximate (legal) cause p. 300   A fundamental element that must be proved to recover in a negligence lawsuit against a tortfeasor: The injured party must prove a legally recognized and close-in-proximity link between the breach of duty and the damages suffered.

Actual damages p. 302   A fundamental element that must be proved to recover in a negligence lawsuit against a tortfeasor: The injured party must prove that she suffered some physical harm that resulted in identifiable losses.

Comparative negligence p. 302   A defense to claims of negligence in which the injured party's conduct has played a factor in the harm suffered and, thus, the proportion of negligence should be divided.

Assumption of the risk p. 302   A defense to claims of negligence in which the injured party knew that a substantial and apparent risk was associated with certain conduct and the party went ahead with the dangerous activity anyway.

CHAPTER REVIEW QUESTIONS

1. Which of the following is *not* an element of defamation?
   a. Specificity
   b. Damages
   c. Dissemination to a third party
   d. Malice

2. A breach of duty may be established by showing
   a. Violation of a safety statute.
   b. Breach of common law standards of behavior.
   c. *Res ipsa loquiter* ("the thing/matter speaks for itself").
   d. All of the above.

3. Ginger uses the wrong type of cleaner fluid to clean out the deep fryer in her café and causes an explosion. The explosion causes the café's front window to shatter and injures a pedestrian walking on the public sidewalk in front of the café at the time of the explosion. In a suit against Ginger for negligence

   a. Ginger wins because she owed no duty to the pedestrian.
   b. Ginger wins because there is not sufficient proximate cause.
   c. Pedestrian wins because Ginger owes him a special duty.
   d. Pedestrian wins because Ginger's actions were the cause and proximate cause of the injury.

4. Stuart attends a baseball game and, on his way to his seat, he is struck by a foul ball. He sues the stadium owner for negligence. What will be the owner's best defense?

   a. Contributory negligence
   b. Comparative negligence
   c. Assumption of the risk
   d. Products liability

5. A product may be unreasonably dangerous due to a _____ or _____ defect.

   a. Risk, reward
   b. Risk, design
   c. Design, manufacturing
   d. Manufacturing, assumption

Answers and explanations are provided at the end of this chapter.

THEORY TO PRACTICE

Computer Installers (CI) Inc. is a company that sells, installs, and maintains computer networks for organizations that have large numbers of users. CI entered into a contract with Big Time Firm (BTF) to replace the firm's computer network. CI's contract included routine installation tasks such as laying network cable and wiring in the various offices to facilitate numerous network users simultaneously, installing new PCs in one-third of the network user stations, and setting up an appropriate network server with sufficient backup capability. CI arrived on March 1 and began work on rewiring BTF's office to facilitate the new computer system. In the process of installing the new cabling for the network, a CI technician accidentally rewired the system that controlled the fire sprinklers and rendered the sprinklers inoperable.

Office Cleaners (OC) Inc. was cleaning BTF's offices at night on March 2. One of OC's employees left a lit cigarette in one of BTF's restrooms. That night, as a result of the lit cigarette, a small fire began in the restroom. Because the sprinklers were inoperable, the fire spread and caused damage to the entire office and equipment in the amount of $50,000.

1. What level of duty does CI owe to BTF, and has CI breached that duty?
2. To what extent is the concept of cause in fact versus proximate cause important in regard to CI's liability?
3. At what point, if any, is CI's liability cut off? Does OC assume full liability for the fire?
4. Assume that BTF had fired its night security guard on February 1 and never refilled the position. Thus, no guard was present when the fire started. Articulate a possible defense for CI and OC based on this fact.
5. Suppose that after the incident the sales manager of Data Management Inc., one of CI's competitors, is having lunch with Sheldon, the chief information officer of City Hospital. City Hospital has an existing contract with CI to maintain City Hospital's network. During lunch, Data Management's sales manager tells Sheldon about the fire incident and also states that, based on his personal knowledge, CI is a shoddy outfit that has a poor reputation in the industry. The sales manager then proposes a new Data Management information system for City Hospital at a lower price than CI's. When Sheldon is reluctant to consider the offer, Data Management's sales manager offers to pay any penalty that City Hospital suffers as a result of canceling the CI contract. Sheldon cancels the contract with CI, citing customer service problems. What possible torts have been committed? What are the requirements for CI to recover damages?

LEGAL STRATEGY 101

Disclaimers

An essential legal strategy in the world of business is *legal risk management* or *prevention*. In brief, business firms work in tandem with their attorneys in order to anticipate legal problems before they occur and to take effective steps ahead of time to minimize such legal risks and potential civil liability exposure. This legal strategy identifies and minimizes future legal risks to the business.

A common method for minimizing legal risks in tort cases, for instance, is the use of disclaimers or "limitation of liability" clauses in business contracts. Although disclaimers are generally legally enforceable, courts may or may not enforce a particular disclaimer, depending on the facts of each case and the wording of the disclaimer. From a strategic perspective, however, disclaimers are designed to protect business firms from potential civil liability for negligence and other harms under tort law.

Thus, a well-drafted disclaimer is a strategic or defensive measure, one that anticipates and attempts to reduce the risk of tort liability in certain situations. By way of example, consider the "terms and conditions" that computer users must agree to when installing a software update or when signing up for a free Internet service like Gmail or Facebook. Among the many provisions in the terms and conditions, there may be a disclaimer, and by clicking "I Agree" in the dialogue box, users are agreeing to the disclaimer as a matter of contract.

To illustrate, let's take a look at an actual disclaimer. Apple operates a *cloud computing* or data-storage service called iCloud. This service provides iCloud users the ability to save and store their personal data on remote servers, including such electronic data as photos, documents, and music files. After the iCloud accounts of many celebrities (e.g., Jennifer Lawrence, pictured) were hacked, Apple inserted (in ALL CAPS

Jennifer Lawrence. Gabe Ginsberg/WireImage/Getty Images

and underlined) the following disclaimer language in its iCloud Terms and Conditions:

> APPLE DOES NOT REPRESENT OR GUARANTEE THAT [iCLOUD] WILL BE FREE FROM LOSS, CORRUPTION, ATTACK, VIRUSES, INTERFERENCE, HACKING, OR OTHER SECURITY INTRUSION, AND APPLE DISCLAIMS ANY LIABILITY RELATING THERETO.[*]

CRITICAL THINKING QUESTIONS

1. Based on what you have studied in this chapter, was Apple negligent for not taking stronger measures to protect the iCloud accounts of its users from third-party hackers?
2. What legal or nonlegal strategies could iCloud users employ against Apple to defeat or circumvent Apple's disclaimer?

*iCloud terms and conditions: http://www.apple.com/legal/internet-services/icloud/en/terms.html.

MANAGER'S CHALLENGE

Another context in which managers encounter tort law is the area of employment checks and references. Suppose that the technician installer employed by CI in the Theory to Practice problem was suspended for incompetence. The installer was so enraged that he threatened his fellow employees with bodily harm and was subsequently fired. The installer sought new employment and listed several CI managers as references on his application to a prospective employer. Consider the conundrum of the manager asked for a reference. How would you address the question? On the one hand, CI may be liable for any defamatory statements made by its managers in this situation. On the other hand, if CI simply refuses to say anything in a reference and it turns out that the installer is dangerous and assaults a colleague at his new workplace, an injured party could possibly claim that CI was negligent in not providing the new employer with important information about the ex-employee installer's potential for danger.

In groups or individually, develop a policy for CI managers on giving references for ex-employees that balances the concern of defamation with that of negligence in failing to inform a prospective employer about a potentially dangerous employee. Assume that your state has the same laws as those applied in the *Nelson v. Tradewind Aviation* case, Case 9.2, found earlier in this chapter to help develop a legally sound policy. A more comprehensive briefing of the case is available on this textbook's website in Connect. Be sure to address (1) a brief overview of the background and a summary of the legal ramifications of not having a sound reference defamation policy and (2) how your policy fits into the privilege defense in the law.

See Connect for Manager's Challenge sample answers.

CASE SUMMARY 9.1 Maher v. Best Western Inn, 717 So. 2d 97 (Fla. App. 5th Dist. 1998)

SPECIAL RELATIONSHIPS

Maher is a blind woman who checked into a Best Western that welcomed pets like her seeing eye dog, Ina. Shortly after Maher checked in with her parents, another motel patron walked by with two unleashed dogs—one German shepherd and one pit bull. The two unleashed dogs attacked Ina, Maher, and her parents. Maher sued Best Western for negligence.

CASE QUESTIONS

1. What duty did Best Western owe Maher?
2. Was it *reasonable* for Best Western to do more to prevent the attack?
3. Would a bystander have had a duty to prevent the attack if it occurred on the street?

CASE SUMMARY 9.2 Wurtzel v. Starbucks Coffee Co., 257 F. Supp. 2d 520 (E.D.N.Y. 2003)

RES IPSA LOQUITUR

Wurtzel bought a cup of coffee in her local Starbucks and placed it in her car's cup holder. Shortly after leaving the store, she was making a turn when the lid came off the coffee and the liquid spilled over Wurtzel's right leg, burning her severely. Wurtzel never looked to see if the lid was on correctly and did not see the coffee spill or the clerk secure the lid to the cup. She sued Starbucks for negligence, invoking the doctrine of *res ipsa loquitur*.

CASE QUESTIONS

1. Was Starbucks clearly negligent without any need for witnesses?
2. Who else may have been negligent?

CASE SUMMARY 9.3 Coker v. Wal-Mart Stores, Inc., 642 So. 2d 774 (Fla. App. 1st Dist. 1994)

NEGLIGENCE PER SE

Bonifay and Fordham bought a box of .32-caliber bullets from a Walmart in Florida. Four hours later, the two men robbed an auto-parts store and killed Coker with those bullets. When they bought the ammunition, both Bonifay and Fordham were under 21 years of age.

The federal Gun Control Act makes it illegal to sell ammunition to anyone under the age of 21. Coker's wife sued Walmart for the wrongful death of her husband.

CASE QUESTIONS

1. Is Walmart liable?
2. What if it was reasonable to assume that the two men were over the age of 21?
3. Could Walmart have foreseen the robbery any more than the train conductor could have foreseen the bag full of fireworks in *Palsgraf*?

CASE SUMMARY 9.4 Gorran v. Atkins Nutritionals, Inc., 464 F. Supp. 2d 315 (S.D.N.Y. 2006)

STRICT PRODUCTS LIABILITY

Gorran suffered a heart attack after following the diet plan of *Dr. Atkins' New Diet Revolution*. Gorran claimed the heart attack was a result of the high-fat, high-protein diet advocated by Dr. Atkins. He sued the publisher for selling a defective product—a diet plan that causes a heart attack.

CASE QUESTIONS

1. Can a diet plan be considered a "product"?
2. Why would Gorran want to sue under products liability theory rather than just negligence?

CASE SUMMARY 9.5 Aaris v. Las Virgenes Unified School District, 64 Cal. App. 4th 1112 (1998)

ASSUMPTION OF RISK

In 1994, Aaris injured her right knee practicing a gymnastic stunt called the "cradle." The stunt requires that two cheerleaders face each other to form a "base" and launch a third cheerleader, the "flyer," into the air. After the flyer pikes, she descends toward the ground where the base cheerleaders are supposed to catch her. A fourth cheerleader acts as a spotter to assist in the catch. As the team practiced, the flyer kept landing awkwardly, even scratching the faces of the base cheerleaders. Aaris told her coach that they were having problems cradling the flyer, but the coach attributed their problems to "bad technique" and told them that they "need to keep on trying it over and over again." Aaris felt uncomfortable performing the stunt and asked: "Do we have to do this stunt?" Her coach responded: "You should be doing it every single time." Finally, while trying to do the stunt, the flyer wobbled and fell on Aaris, injuring Aaris's leg. In 1993, Aaris had received stunt training while she was on the freshman high school cheerleading squad. She had then participated in tryouts and made the junior varsity cheerleader team. Aaris received formal instruction in stunt technique and safety, and she knew that the stunts were dangerous. As a freshman, she injured her left knee performing a toe-touch stunt. Evidence showed that the flyer and the other base cheerleader had also received formal stunt technique and safety training. Aaris sued the coach and school for negligence. The coach and school district asserted the defense of assumption of risk.

CASE QUESTIONS

1. What must Aaris prove in order to hold her coach and the school district liable for her injuries?
2. For a defense of assumption of risk to be successful, what must the coach and school district prove?

CASE SUMMARY 9.6 Burton v. MDC PGA Plaza Corp., 78 So. 3d 732 (Fla. App. 4th Dist. 2012)

DANGEROUS CONDITION AND COMPARATIVE NEGLIGENCE

Burton worked for a marketing and merchandising company that helped new retail businesses prepare for openings. She was brought in to work at a new CVS Pharmacy getting ready for its grand opening. While unloading trucks, Burton noticed a pothole about 10 or 15 feet from the store's back door. The pothole was approximately 1 foot wide and 2 inches deep. Burton informed her co-workers and CVS's management of the pothole and urged everyone to exercise caution. One week later, Burton was seriously injured when, while loading a vehicle, she stepped into the pothole, tripped, and fell to the ground. Burton filed suit against both CVS and its landlord, MDC.

CASE QUESTIONS

1. Can a property owner be liable for injuries when a dangerous condition is open and obvious? Does the owner have a duty to warn when the dangerous condition is open and obvious?
2. Can a property owner be liable for injuries when a dangerous condition is open and obvious and the injured party was well aware of the dangerous condition?
3. Does Burton's knowledge of the dangerous condition merely raise an issue of fact as to her own comparative negligence?

✓ Self-Check ANSWERS Intentional Torts

1. Defamation. Specifically, it is slander because the statements Jason made were oral.
2. No tort has been committed. This is not a tortious interference with a contract because Third Bank merely offered a better price for its services and MOT made the decision to switch.
3. Trespass to chattel. Wayne has interfered with his company's ability to use the car and will be responsible for the repairs and any damages suffered by the company because the car is unavailable.
4. Conversion. Nancy is stealing the stationery supplies and civilly is responsible for paying the company back for the full value of the supplies she has taken.
5. No tort has been committed. This is not a fraud because the deal had already been agreed to and the intentionally false statement was not material to the deal.

Proximate Cause

1. Yes. The injury (broken arm) was sufficiently proximate to the negligence (defective steering column). *McCown v. International Harvester Co.*, 342 A.2d 381.
2. No. Too many acts of intervening negligence on the part of the landlord. *Matthias v. United Pacific Ins. Co.*, 67 Cal. Rptr. 511, 514.
3. Yes. It was reasonably foreseeable that the employee would have been falsely arrested for the fire. The jury found that the employer had framed the employee. *Seidel v. Greenberg*, 260 A.2d 863, 871.
4. Yes. It was reasonably foreseeable that the intoxicated driver would have an accident, and the liquor store also violated state dram shop laws. *Gonzales v. Krueger*, 799 P.2d 1318, 1321.

CHAPTER REVIEW QUESTIONS: Answers and Explanations

1. **d.** Malice is only required when the defamed party is a public figure or to disqualify a qualified privilege (e.g., media). Answer choices (a), (b), and (c) are incorrect because they are all elements of a defamation claim.

2. **d.** Each of the listed responses in (a), (b), and (c) is a breach of duty.

3. **d.** Ginger owes a general duty not to cause harm to the pedestrian. This duty was breached (*res ipsa*) and the explosion was the cause and proximate cause of the injuries. Answer choice (a) is incorrect because she owes him a general duty. Answer choice (b) is nonsensical. Answer choice (c) is incorrect because there is no special duty owed, only a general duty.

4. **c.** The fan knew of the risk, understood the risk, and went ahead with the activity. Answer choices (a) and (b) are incorrect because the fan did not contribute to his own injury. Answer choice (d) is unrelated to a negligence analysis.

5. **c.** Products can be made unreasonably dangerous by either a design (improperly engineered) or a manufacturing (improperly made) defect. Answer choices (a), (b), and (c) are wrong because each contains a term unrelated to products liability.

BUSINESS LAW SIMULATION EXERCISE 1

©philsajonesen/Getty Images

Restrictive Covenants in Contracts: Neurology Associates, LLP v. Elizabeth Blackwell, M.D.

Learning Objectives

After studying this simulation, students who have mastered the material will be able to:

1. Explain the legal doctrines that govern the use of restrictive covenants.
2. Interpret and apply the rules set forth in current case law.
3. Articulate a cogent argument for each party/side in the dispute.
4. Negotiate a tenable solution as an alternative to a judicial forum.

Chapters 6 and 7 provided you with a variety of legal doctrines and rules governing contract formation and performance and then illustrated how these doctrines and rules apply in the corporate sector context. This simulation is designed to help you understand how the various topics covered in the contract law chapters connect. By focusing on a simulated legal dispute, you will replicate a real-world experience by applying legal doctrines and using analytical and critical-thinking skills. This simulation is a sequential decision-making exercise structured around a model in which the participants assume a role in managing tasks and work toward a tenable solution.

The simulation is structured in three parts:

- Part 1 is a hypothetical fact pattern describing events leading up to a legal dispute in the hypothetical U.S. state of Longville.
- Part 2 is a set of two hypothetical case summaries from Longville appellate courts that provide a brief set of facts, several legal points, and short excerpts from the opinion itself. While these cases are hypothetical, they are based on actual cases from appellate courts in various states and represent the view of the majority of state courts in the United States.
- Part 3 is an assignment sheet that will be provided to you by your instructor to be used in conjunction with this simulation.

Part 1: Stipulated Facts

1. In May 2015, Dr. Elizabeth Blackwell (Blackwell) had earned her medical doctor degree and completed all necessary requirements to receive a license to practice medicine in the state of Longville. She specialized in neurological medicine. Although she was offered professional opportunities in several large hospitals, she pursued an employment offer with Neurological Associates, LLC (NA). NA is a two-physician practice located in a small town in the southwestern area of the state of Longville and 20 miles north of Galway, the largest city in Longville. Although the pay was lower than that in the larger hospitals, Blackwell wanted to be close to her family and did not wish to engage in a practice that required the strenuous schedules associated with larger medical providers.

2. NA was managed by two partners, Dr. Richard Cohn (Cohn) and Dr. Jean Valjean (Valjean). While negotiating Blackwell's employment agreement,

In this simulation exercise, a physician in a health care practice becomes involved in a dispute over a provision in her contract that restricted future employment.
Jetta Productions/Getty Images

Cohn was the primary contact and the parties agreed to compensation terms, vacation, on-call duties (after hours), and a fringe benefit package. The employment agreement included an arbitration clause requiring that the parties agree to nonbinding arbitration in the event of a dispute arising from the agreement. It also provided for Blackwell to have paid time off to study for and take the examinations required to become board-certified in neurology. NA agreed to a $1,000 payment to be used for a course intended to help prepare candidates for the test. Blackwell began her employment with NA on June 1, 2015.

3. Immediately after hiring Blackwell, NA paid for Blackwell to accompany the partners to a medical conference at which they were scheduled to speak. At the conference, Cohn and Valjean introduced her to a number of physicians in hopes of building the referral base for the practice.

4. In July 2015, Cohn approached Blackwell and told her that he needed her to sign an additional document that was supposed to be part of her contract but that he had neglected to mention during negotiations. He explained that the document was standard procedure in medical practices and that he had been so busy during the negotiation period that he had forgotten to mention it to Blackwell. He went on to explain that Blackwell should sign the document by the end of the workday and that this would "make the lawyers happy."

5. The document was titled "Addendum to Contract—Restrictive Covenant and Noncompete Clause" and read in pertinent part

Section 1: The parties hereby agree, in consideration of the exchange of good, valuable, and sufficient consideration, to be bound by the following provision:

For a period of three years after the date of her separation from NA, Blackwell agrees that she will not contract with any provider of neurological services, nor compete in any way with NA, within a radius of 50 miles of NA's practice location. It is acknowledged that this restriction covers the entirety of the southwestern region of Longville.

6. Blackwell felt that she should have a lawyer review the document, but Cohn insisted the addendum was normal procedure and she needed to sign it quickly to make things "legal." He emphasized that he would have to have the signed document by the end of the day or, as it was a condition of her employment, Blackwell's payroll check could not be processed until the document was signed. Blackwell reluctantly signed the document and submitted it to Cohn.

7. In August 2015, Blackwell began to have conflicts with Cohn and, to a lesser extent, Valjean. While Cohn and Valjean took frequent vacations during the summer, Blackwell was left to staff the practice alone. She felt overwhelmed and met with Cohn to discuss a more equitable work schedule. Cohn refused any negotiation, explaining that Blackwell was hired as a "workhorse" and that her salary was fair given the size of the practice and market. Cohn urged Blackwell to continue her hard work and not to complain about her work schedule. Eventually, explained Cohn, Blackwell would become a partner in the practice and would enjoy the fruits of her labor.

8. In September 2015, Blackwell continued to handle a very heavy caseload, seeing almost twice as many patients as Cohn or Valjean. In response to Blackwell's plea for additional staff, NA hired a new physician to help manage the caseload. Although Blackwell was initially relieved, the situation at work continued to deteriorate. The workload was such that Cohn kept denying Blackwell's request for time off to prepare for the upcoming board certification exam, advising her to put it off until the caseload lightened up a bit.

9. Blackwell began to receive phone calls from recruiters trying to lure her away from the practice to work at a new neurology clinic in Galway Hospital (located in the city of Galway). The recruiters offered a significant amount of money because there was a substantial shortage of neurologists in the southwest region of Longville. However, Blackwell never pursued these opportunities because she believed the restrictive covenant prevented her from working in Galway.

10. In January 2016, Blackwell was granted her paid leave to prepare for her board certification, and she took the exam in February 2016. However, after she returned to the practice, she began to feel even more isolated from the other physicians.

11. On March 1, 2016, Blackwell, fed up with NA, announced that she was giving NA 60 days' notice that she was leaving the practice to join Galway Hospital and that her resignation would be effective on May 1, 2016. She anticipated starting at Galway on June 1, 2016. Galway was forming a new neurology practice group, and it had offered to employ Blackwell as one of the founding physicians in the group.

12. Cohn immediately sent Blackwell a letter informing her that he accepted her resignation but that she had responsibilities under her contract that prevented her from accepting a new position with a competitor.

Part 2: State of Longville Case Law

Wellspan Hospital and Medical Group v. Phillip Bayliss, M.D.

Supreme Court of the State of Longville (2005)

Facts

- This is the leading case on restrictive covenants/noncompete agreements in the context of medical practices in the state of Longville. It has not been modified or reversed since it was decided.
- Wellspan is a not-for-profit health care system located in Columbus County in the southeastern portion of the state of Longville. Bayliss is a physician specializing in OB/GYN services.
- Wellspan hired Bayliss as its medical director in 2000, at which time Bayliss signed an employment agreement that included a restrictive covenant under which Bayliss agreed not to engage in medical practice in Columbus County and five other contiguous counties (this covered the entire southeastern region of Longville) for a period of two years after the separation of employment between Wellspan and Bayliss.
- Wellspan invested over $1 million in equipping Bayliss's practice, hiring additional physicians, and undertaking promotional strategies intended on marketing the practice and increasing the number of referrals.
- Relations between Wellspan and Bayliss deteriorated when they disagreed over Wellspan's expansion strategy. In February 2004, Bayliss resigned his position at Wellspan and established his OB/GYN practice only five miles from the Wellspan practice. This was within the area covered under the restrictive covenant.
- The state's highest court considered the enforceability of Wellspan's restrictive covenant against Bayliss.

POINTS OF LAW AND OPINION EXCERPTS

Point (a)
The Longville state courts will enforce a restrictive covenant *only* if it is *reasonably necessary* to protect the legitimate interests of the employer, and courts either may strike down a covenant altogether or may reform (known as *bluelining*) a covenant if it is overbroad in some way.

Excerpt (a)

"Courts in the State of Longville have historically been reluctant to enforce contracts that place restraints on trade or on the ability of an individual to earn a living; however, postemployment noncompetition covenants are *not* per se unreasonable or unenforceable."

Point (b)

The threshold requirement for enforceability of a covenant is that the employer must be protecting a *legitimate business interest*. The primary legitimate business interests that Longville courts have held to be protectable in a covenant are (1) trade secrets or confidential business information, (2) customer goodwill, and (3) investments in the employee.

> *Legal Speak >))*
>
> **Threshold Requirement**
> A requirement that must be met by the plaintiff prior to the court engaging in further legal analysis to determine the rights of the parties.

Excerpt (b1)

"A *trade secret* is a legitimate business interest because it may include a compilation of information which is used in one's business that gives one an opportunity to obtain an advantage over competitors. A trade secret does not include an employee's aptitude, skill, dexterity, manual and mental ability, or other subjective knowledge. In addition, if a competitor could obtain the information by legitimate means, it will not be given protection as a trade secret."

Excerpt (b2)

"The interest protected under the umbrella of *goodwill* is a business's positive reputation. Goodwill represents a preexisting relationship arising from a continuous course of business which is expected to continue indefinitely. A business's goodwill is considered a protectible interest even when the goodwill has been acquired through the efforts of an employee. The concept of customer goodwill as a protectible interest has been applied to patient relationships when the noncompetition covenant at issue involves a health care professional. This court has cited the erosion of the ex-employer's patient relationships as one factor in the decision to enforce a restrictive covenant."

Excerpt (b3)

"A third protectible interest recognized by Longville courts is the *efforts and financial resources invested by an employer* to provide to its employees specialized training in the methods of the employer's business. In a past case, the defendant was a salesman of securities who had received extensive and continuous training from his employer, particularly with respect to methods and problems in the sale of mutual fund shares. He then voluntarily left his position with his employer and started his own business selling mutual fund shares. The court enforced the noncompetition covenant at issue, enjoining the defendant from engaging in the business of selling mutual fund shares in Pennsylvania. The court found merit in the argument that it would be inequitable for the defendant to start a new business in direct competition with his ex-employer after having received extensive, specialized training in the methods and problems of the business directly from his ex-employer."

Point (c)

A medical practice's patient referral base is a legitimate protectable business interest when a medical practice can demonstrate that it has invested in the production and generation of such a base.

Excerpt (c)

"A patient referral base is a protected interest, [and] protecting the investments required to develop such a base is consistent with our holding in other employer–employee situations outside the health care field. In the context of a noncompetition covenant, we think that the referral bases of a specialized medical care institution are analogous to a physician's patient relationships or an employer's customer relationships. Viewed in such light, recognition of a patient referral base as a protected interest fits squarely within Longville case law."

Point (d)

If the threshold requirement of protectable interest is met, the next step in the analysis is to apply two *balancing tests:* (1) the employer's protectable interest balanced against the employee's interest in earning a living and (2) the employee and employer interests with the interests of the public.

Excerpt (d1)

"In weighing the competing interests of employer and employee, the court must engage in an analysis of *reasonableness.* First, the covenant must be reasonably necessary for the protection of the employer. In addition, the temporal and geographical restrictions imposed on the ex-employee must be reasonably limited."

Excerpt (d2)

"Regarding the second balancing test, in the context of noncompete agreements among physicians, the *interests of the public* are defined as a function of the availability of appropriate medical services to the community. Since there is no evidence of a lack of availability of OB/GYN physicians within the restricted area, the interests of the public are served and, thus, enforcement of the covenant against Bayliss does not result in public harm."

Held

Because Wellspan had shown that it had a legitimate business interest in protecting its patient referral base and because the court had determined that the restriction was tailored to those interests and that no public harm would be suffered by enforcement of the restriction, the court found *in favor of Wellspan.*

Legal Speak >))

Declaratory Judgment
A remedy used to determine the rights of the parties in a set of circumstances (such as the enforceability of a contract) that is binding on the litigants even though no damages were awarded.

Regional General Hospital v. Anesthesiology Associates, Inc.
Appellate Court of the State of Longville (2007)

Facts

- Anesthesiology Associates, Inc. (AAI), is a medical practice that employs physicians and certified registered nurse anesthetists (employees). In January 2002, AAI entered into a contract with Regional General Hospital (Regional) to provide mutually agreed-upon services to Regional's patients.
- The employment agreements that AAI has with its employees contained a postemployment restrictive covenant wherein employees agreed to the following restrictions: (1) that for a period of two years from separation from AAI, ex-employees would not contract with or compete against AAI at any facility where AAI was currently the provider of anesthesiology services and (2) that for a period of one year from separation, ex-employees agreed not to contract or compete against AAI at any facility where AAI

has provided services for the last 12 months ending on the period of the employee's departure date. Because AAI provided services to more than 35 hospitals in five different states, the geographic restrictions effectively covered a five-state region.
- Regional let the agreement with AAI expire and offered direct employment to several AAI employees. Fearing that employees of AAI would not accept these employment offers for fear of a lawsuit by AAI based on breach of the restrictive covenant, Regional filed suit against AAI seeking a declaratory judgment that the covenant was unenforceable because it was overly broad in scope and duration and unduly restricted AAI employees from accepting employment with Regional.

POINTS OF LAW AND OPINION EXCERPTS

Point (a)

In accordance with the Longville Supreme Court's decision in *Wellspan v. Bayliss,* the court will enforce a restrictive covenant *only* if it is *reasonably necessary* to protect the legitimate interests of the employer.

Point (b)

In addition to serving a legitimate business interest, the restriction must be tailored narrowly enough so that it is reasonably necessary to protect the interest of the employer. If an employer does not compete in a particular geographic area, enforcement of a covenant in that area is not reasonably necessary for the employer's protection. Any restriction that is *overly broad in geographic scope and duration* renders it unenforceable, and courts have the authority to either pare back the restriction or set it aside entirely.

Excerpt (b1)

"In determining reasonableness of scope and duration, we must balance the interest the employer seeks to protect against the important interest of the employee in being able to earn a living in her chosen profession. The court finds that neither the time limitations, nor the territorial scope of the agreement are overly broad or unreasonable. Furthermore, although the noncompete clause covers five states in scope, such restriction is reasonable given the *regional nature* of their current hospital clientele. In this case, the restrictions are narrowly tailored to be limited only to certain providers within that region."

Held

In favor of AAI. AAI's restrictive covenants in its employment agreements were reasonably related to AAI's business interests and were not overly broad.

UNIT THREE — Regulation in the Workplace

CHAPTER 10   Agency

CHAPTER 11   Employment Relationships and Labor Law

CHAPTER 12   Employment Discrimination

CHAPTER 10

Agency

©philsajonesen/Getty Images

Learning Objectives

After studying this chapter, students who have mastered the material will be able to:

10-1 Recognize, define, and give examples of an agency relationship.

10-2 Classify agents as either employees or independent contractors by applying the direction and control tests.

10-3 Explain the process for creating an agency relationship and the impact of that relationship on the liability of the principal.

10-4 List the sources of an agent's authority to bind the principal in contract and give examples of each source.

10-5 Apply the doctrine of respondeat superior and identify its impact and limits.

10-6 Define the duties that collectively comprise a fiduciary obligation owed by the agent to the principal.

10-7 Articulate the duties owed by a principal to the agent and to third parties.

10-8 List the two primary methods used to terminate agency relationships and give examples of each method.

10-9 Recognize the dangers of the principal's failing to notify third parties of an agent's termination.

Agency relationships are fundamental to the business environment because they set out rules and standards for situations in which one party hires another party to act on the hiring party's behalf. Business owners and managers who understand the obligations and liabilities of such a relationship are in a favorable position to limit their company's liability to both the hired party and third parties. Understanding **agency law** is also a crucial first step to understanding laws that govern rights, duties, and obligations between employers and employees.

In this chapter, we discuss

- The definitions, categories, and sources of law that govern agency relationships.

- Liabilities, duties, and obligations that are created by an agency relationship.

DEFINITIONS AND SOURCES OF AGENCY LAW

Agency is a legal relationship in which the parties agree, in some form, that one party will act as an **agent** for another party, called the **principal**, subject to the control of the principal. Agency relationships are common and essential in the business environment and exist in a variety of forms. A common form of agency arises in an employer-employee relationship, but there are other important forms of agency as well.

In all agency relationships, the principal authorizes the agent to provide services or accomplish some task on behalf of the principal and under the principal's charge. Understanding agency law requires awareness of (1) legal requirements for *creating* an agency, (2) *liability* of a principal for the agent's conduct, and (3) *duties* and obligations of the parties. The principal and agent may be either individuals or entities (such as a corporation). Agency law generally exists on the state statutory level and is based on the **Restatement (Third) of Agency**. Some states have also retained some common law doctrines of agency that operate in tandem with the statutes.

CLASSIFICATION OF AGENTS

Agents are classified into one of three broad categories: (1) *employee agents,* (2) *independent contractor agents,* and (3) *gratuitous agents.* Understanding these categories is important for business owners and managers primarily because the liability of the principal for acts of the agent depends on the agency relationship between the principal, the agent, and any relevant third parties.

Employee Agents

Individual employees who are authorized to transact business on behalf of the employer principal are called **employee agents**. Principals are liable for the actions or omissions (such as negligence) of employee agents. However, it is important to understand that not every employee is an agent. In order to be classified as an employee agent, the employee must have some source of authority to represent the employer. The nonagent employee relationship is sometimes referred to as the *master-servant relationship* to distinguish it from an employer-employee agent relationship. For example, at the local branch of Mega Bank, the teller is an employee agent of Mega Bank who is authorized to conduct certain limited transactions (such as cashing a check) on Mega Bank's behalf. The branch manager at Mega Bank is also an employee agent, and her agency is likely wider in scope to include approval of small business loans and similar transactions. The security guard at the local branch is also an employee but is not an employee agent because the guard does not have authority to transact business on Mega Bank's behalf. Therefore, the guard could be characterized as the servant in a master-servant relationship.

By contrast, an **independent contractor agent** (usually referred to simply as an "independent contractor") is not considered an employee and has no legal protections of employees such as minimum-wage and overtime-compensation laws. An equally important factor is that the principal generally has no liability for actions and omissions of an independent contractor agent. In the business environment, professional service providers such as attorneys, outside accountants, and architects are all examples of independent contractors.

Agents who act on behalf of a principal without receiving any compensation are called **gratuitous agents**. To take a simple example, if you ask your roommate to pick up your laundry on your behalf as a favor, he is your gratuitous agent. In most respects, the rights and duties of gratuitous agents are the same as those of paid agents except that the duty of care applicable to the gratuitous agent is not as great (an agent's duty of care is discussed later in this chapter).

LO 10-1

Recognize, define, and give examples of an agency relationship.

LO 10-2

Classify agents as either employees or independent contractors by applying the direction and control tests.

> **KEY POINT**
>
> Agents are classified as either employee agents, independent contractors, or gratuitous agents. The classification is important in determining potential liability of a principal.

Employee Agents versus Independent Contractors: Direction and Control

Although the parties themselves may agree to a certain classification, the status of an agent is not based on what the parties agreed to but is instead determined by the *actual*

Business owners and managers depend on their agents to help carry out business operations.
courtneyk/Getty Images

> ### KEY POINT
>
> The agent is classified based on the amount of *direction and control* that the principal has over the agent in terms of setting a work schedule, pay rate, and day-to-day supervision requirements.

working relationship between principal and agent. Courts apply the *substance-over-form*[1] analysis to determine the classification of an agent. Fundamentally, the agent is classified based on the amount of *direction and control* that the principal has over the agent in terms of setting the agent's work schedule and pay rate and determining the level of day-to-day supervision required. In an employer-employee agent relationship, the employer principal typically sets work hours, decides what salary to pay, and exercises control over the employee agent's working conditions and responsibilities. Independent contractors usually work based on a deadline but typically choose their own schedule to accomplish that deadline. In terms of payment, independent contractors usually send an invoice on a monthly basis (sometimes longer) for services rendered rather than drawing a weekly or biweekly paycheck. Courts also use other criteria for determining the status of an agent that focus on the nature of the agent's duties. For example, an *independent occupation or profession* in which the agent has more than one customer or client (as in the case of accountants, attorneys, architects) indicates an independent contractor. On the other hand, if the principal provides tools or heavy equipment to the agent at the workplace, this generally indicates that the agent is an employee.

State Law Courts look to state common law and statutes for guidance in determining independent contractor status. Many states have adopted the **ABC test** in their agency statutes as a standard for determining agency status.[2] Statutes that set out the ABC factors typically create a presumption that the agent is an employee unless three tests are

---

[1] Recall that the substance-over-form standard is the equitable maxim discussed in Chapter 1, "Legal Foundations," whereby courts look to the intent of the parties involved and adhere to a standard of good faith and fair play instead of applying a technical and superficial standard or the parties' subjective intent.

[2] *See, e.g.*, Mass. Gen. Laws Ann. ch. 149, § 148B(a)(1)–(3).

satisfied: (A) the individual is free from direction and control, applicable both under contract for the performance of service and in fact; (B) the service is performed outside the usual course of business of the employer; and (C) the individual is customarily engaged in an independently established trade, occupation, profession, or business of the same nature as that involved in the service performed. In Case 10.1, a state appellate court analyzes the agency status of a sales representative.

CASE 10.1 Avanti Press v. Employment Department Tax Section, 274 P.3d 190 (Or. Ct. App. 2012)

FACT SUMMARY Waiau was an employee of One Coast, a company that represented various businesses, including Avanti. In early 2009, One Coast dissolved. Waiau, who had nearly 30 years of experience as a product sales representative in the greeting card and gift industries, then entered into a written Service Agreement (Agreement) with Avanti to sell the company's greeting cards, journals, and calendars. The Agreement provided, among other things, that

- Waiau would be Avanti's exclusive sales representative for retail outlets in southwestern Oregon and would personally visit Avanti customers at their retail outlets at least once every 12 weeks for purposes of soliciting orders in accordance with the services Agreement and Avanti's policies, catalogs, supplements, and price information furnished to Waiau by Avanti.
- Waiau had no authority to bind Avanti to any sales and had no authority to accept orders or receive payments on Avanti's behalf.
- Avanti reserved the right to establish and change prices, products, ways, methods, or terms of payment or shipment and any other conditions or terms of sale.
- Waiau had the authority to hire, fire, and train her own sales associates. Waiau would pay all employee taxes and all her own expenses.

In exchange for her services, Avanti would pay Waiau a commission based on a percentage of the product invoice price less cash discounts, taxes, shipping, insurance, and other deductions. The Agreement would automatically renew for one-year terms, unless earlier terminated by 30 days' written notice from either party.

During the relevant time, Waiau maintained a home office with a desk, chair, fax machine, scanner, printer, telephone, computer, travel case, and sample bags. She used the office equipment almost exclusively for business and deducted home office expenses on her personal income tax return. She also used her personal vehicle for business travel. Avanti did not reimburse Waiau for postage, travel, meals, or lodging expenses. Waiau set her own work schedule and decided how frequently to visit customers. Her commissions were based entirely on her sales, and not on the number of hours that she worked.

However, Waiau did not register a business name, nor did she carry liability insurance or performance bonds, and she did not advertise or market her services as a product sales representative. During that period, she passed out business cards that stated, "Andrea Waiau, Avanti Greeting Cards."

After Waiau sought unemployment insurance benefits claiming that she was an employee rather than an independent contractor, the state's labor agency determined that Waiau was, in fact, an employee of Avanti, thereby making Avanti liable for unemployment taxes. An administrative law judge (ALJ) ruled that Waiau was an employee, and Avanti appealed.

SYNOPSIS OF DECISION AND OPINION The Oregon Court of Appeals reversed the findings of the ALJ and ruled in favor of Avanti. The court reasoned that Avanti did not have a sufficient amount of direction and control over Waiau and that she should be classified as an independent contractor. The court concluded that Waiau controlled when and how often she worked. Specifically, the court pointed to the fact that Waiau set her own schedule and that Waiau could decide how frequently to visit customers. The court also found that Waiau worked

(continued)

strictly as a commissioned salesperson and worked as frequently or infrequently as she liked and that a commission sales representative who works on a part-time basis, selling only at her convenience or when the opportunity presents itself, is typically an independent contractor. They rejected the assertion that managerial control existed because the company expected her to make a certain amount of sales per month because such an expectation has to do solely with end results rather than with method.

WORDS OF THE COURT: Direction and Control
"Waiau had her own home office and vehicle; set her own hours and visited customers as frequently or infrequently as she desired; was compensated solely based on commission; communicated with Avanti concerning only the results of her efforts; and could simultaneously perform the same services for other greeting card companies. Those facts, too, must be considered in the context of the agreement itself. As noted, Waiau had been performing the same services for Avanti while she was employed by another company, One Coast; after One Coast dissolved, Waiau and Avanti entered into an agreement by which she agreed to provide the same services directly to Avanti as an independent contractor. The terms of that agreement and the parties' conduct are consistent with their express understanding that Waiau would be working as an independent contractor, not an employee subject to the company's direction and control."

Case Questions
1. If Waiau had been paid a salary *in addition* to her commission, how might that impact the court's analysis?
2. Although the Agreement did not prohibit Waiau from working for another company, as a practical matter she was working full time for Avanti. Shouldn't that be a factor in the court's analysis? Why or why not?
3. *Focus on Critical Thinking:* Is there a danger that employers will opt to create independent contractor positions rather than employee positions in order to avoid liability and taxes? Is it ethical to generate revenue based on the efforts of a sales representative, but not provide them with benefits available to employees such as managers and clerical workers?

Legal Speak >))

Codified
A legislative body adopting principles from a court decision by incorporating into their statutory code.

California's Independent Contractor Law California has been an epicenter of the independent contractor classification battles since 2013 when its state labor board began to classify gig-economy workers as employees rather than independent contractors. Most famously, Uber resisted employee-classification efforts, arguing that its drivers have so much flexibility that they are not under any direction or control as in a traditional employer-employee relationship. In 2018, the California Supreme Court decided *Dynamex Operations West, Inc. v. Superior Court*,[3] which discarded a previously used multifactor test and adopted the ABC test for determining an agent's category. The practical impact was that agents were to be classified as employees by default unless the employer established each of the three prongs of the test. The court decision not only expanded the definition of employee under the California labor law, it also imposed an affirmative burden on businesses to prove that independent contractors are being properly classified.

Although the court's adoption of the ABC test was clear, other issues of jurisdiction and coverage were left unanswered until 2019 when the California state legislature stepped in by passing Assembly Bill 5 which codified and expanded the *Dynamex* decision by amending the California labor code. Beginning in January 2020, workers classified under the new state law will be eligible for wage and overtime protections, workers' compensation coverage, unemployment insurance, various benefits, paid sick

---
[3] 4 Cal.5th 903 (2018).

days, and state family leave. They will also be protected by state anti-discrimination laws and have the right to unionize. The new law does limit the protections via *exempting* certain workers from the ABC test:

- doctors, dentists, and veterinarians;
- lawyers, architects, engineers, private investigators, and accountants;
- securities broker-dealers and investment advisers;
- travel agents;
- marketers, graphic designers, grant writers, fine artists, certain photographers or photo-journalists, and certain freelance writers and editors.

IRS's Three-Prong Test Because so many questions regarding agency status occur in an employment tax context (e.g., is the employer liable to pay legally mandated employment taxes on a certain worker?), the Internal Revenue Service (IRS) has devised a three-prong test to determine an agent's status. While this test is not binding on courts, some appellate courts cite it as a useful tool in determining an agent's classification.[4] The IRS considers

- *Behavioral* aspects of the agency. (Does the company control what the worker does and how the worker does the job assigned?)
- The *financial arrangements* between principal and agent. (Are the business aspects of the worker's job controlled by the payer?)
- The type of *working relationship* the parties have in terms of benefits and promises of continuing employment.

Liability for Misclassification The consequences of a business owner's or manager's misclassifying an employee can be severe. Both federal and state labor and tax authorities have taken an increasingly aggressive approach to enforcing their agency classification laws. In addition to the employer's obligation to pay back taxes or benefits owed, some states impose civil penalties on a principal who misclassifies an agent especially if there is any evidence that the classification was intentional. A minority of states also impose criminal liability and, in some states, repeat offenders are subject to felony charges.

To take a simple example of the potential impact of misclassification, suppose that Computer Warehouse Corporation (CWC) classifies five computer programmers as independent contractors even though CWC sets their schedule, supervises their work, and pays them every two weeks based on a set hourly rate. This practice continues for one year until the state Department of Revenue audits CWC and determines that the programmers were actually employees. In addition to assessing CWC back taxes, penalties, and interest, CWC may also be assessed a civil penalty or be subject to a criminal complaint depending on state law. This would also be followed by a similar investigation by the state's Department of Labor to determine whether CWC owes any unpaid state-mandated employee benefits. Because state tax agencies typically communicate with federal tax authorities on matters of unpaid taxes, the state tax assessment is likely to trigger an audit by the U.S. Internal Revenue Service and, depending on the size of the employer, the Department of Labor. Depending on the pay rate and the length of time the employees were misclassified, the amount due could exceed several hundred thousand dollars of unplanned liability.

---

[4]This three-prong approach replaced the IRS's notorious 20-point test in 1997. The IRS specifically disclaims the 20-point test and takes the position that there is "no magic or set number of factors that makes the worker an employee or an independent contractor."

 Self-Check Agency Classification

What is More's agency classification?

1. More, an author, is hired by Henry VIII Publications to write a book tentatively titled *Utopia*. The parties agree that More will be paid a lump sum of $50,000 when the book is complete and that the manuscript will be due in six months.

2. More is hired by Henry to work as a computer consultant. The parties agree that More will be on-site at Henry's office on Mondays from 9 a.m. to 5 p.m. for eight consecutive weeks and will be paid each week upon receipt of an invoice by Henry's bookkeeper. More has eight other clients.

3. More is hired by Henry to work as a sales associate for his retail clothing store. The parties agree that More will work at the store Monday through Friday from 10 a.m. to 6 p.m. at a rate of $9 per hour plus a 15 percent commission on merchandise sold by More.

4. More is Henry's neighbor and agrees to do him a favor by transporting Henry's valuable rare coin collection to a local trade show.

5. More is hired by Henry to make telemarketing calls for Henry's media company. The parties enter into a written agreement titled "Independent Contractor Agreement" in which both parties agree that More will be an independent agent. Henry sets More's schedule and pays him $1,000 every other week plus a $500 bonus every year during the holiday season. More uses equipment owned by the media company.

6. More, a professional athlete, is hired by Henry, the owner of a major-league baseball franchise, to play baseball at an annual salary of $1 million. More's contract requires that he show up for all off-season camps, practices, and games for the entire length of the event. If he fails to show up, he agrees to a reduction in pay via a fine. More is paid every other week, and Henry pays for More's health and retirement benefits.

Answers to this Self-Check are provided at the end of the chapter.

STRATEGIC LEGAL SOLUTIONS

Limiting Liability for Misclassification

PROBLEM: *While some agent classifications are clear, as the global economy evolves and new positions and types of occupations are created, managers may face the difficult choice of classification. Misclassification can result in significant tax, benefit, and tort liability.*

STRATEGIC SOLUTION: *Limit liability through (1) screening, (2) agreements, (3) operational controls, and/or (4) verification.*

Screening

A strategic step in limiting liability for misclassification is to only hire independent contractors who have incorporated their own businesses, rather than those who operate as sole proprietors or partners in a partnership. When a principal hires an incorporated independent contractor, the law treats that transaction as a contract between the principal and the corporation instead of an arrangement between the principal and the individual independent contractor. The principal pays the worker's corporation,

(continued)

which pays the worker, who is an employee of the corporation. The corporation is a legal "person" that stands between the principal and the independent contractor. Therefore, the corporation is responsible for state and federal payroll taxes, benefits, and workers' compensation insurance.

Managers should also consider hiring an employee leasing company (sometimes called a temp agency) because employee leasing provides many of the benefits of hiring ICs directly. The benefit of leasing workers is that the leased workers are the leasing firm's employees, not yours. The leasing company pays all wages, taxes, and benefits required by law.

Agreement

Although written agreements with an independent contractor are not required for classification purposes, it can be a helpful way to document the working relationship. The agreement need not be lengthy or complicated, but it should be clear that no employment relationship exists and should describe the work assignment or project the independent contractor is to perform. After the original assignment is complete, any new work assignments should be articulated in a new agreement. The agreement should also detail the terms of payment and require the independent contractor to submit monthly invoices that are to be paid at the same time as other outside vendors. Independent contractors should not be paid on a weekly or bi-weekly basis, or be given benefits or bonuses, because these are indicators of an employer-employee relationship.

The agreement should also make clear that independent contractors are not required to work set days or hours and that any deadlines for work assignments are met through the independent contractor's judgment as to when, how, and where the work is completed.

Operations

Even when independent contractors are incorporated or are provided by employee leasing companies, it is important to continue to limit liability through operational methods related to direction and control. Most importantly, don't supervise the independent or his or her assistants. The independent contractor should perform services without direction of the principal. In order to monitor quality control, ask the independent contractor to submit progress reports as part of the monthly invoices. Other operational methods to consider are

- If possible, don't let the independent contractor work at the business's offices or locations unless the nature of the services absolutely requires it.
- Don't give the independent contractor employee handbooks or company policy manuals.
- Avoid any ongoing instructions or training.
- Be sure independent contractors use their own equipment or materials if possible.
- Restrict any use of company business cards or stationery by an independent contractor.
- Don't give an independent contractor a title or any supervisory authority.
- Don't invite an independent contractor to employee meetings or functions.

Verification

Form SS-8 was created by the IRS to assist business owners and managers in complying with tax regulations regarding independent contractor status. Filing the form gives the principal/employer assurances that either (1) the classification by the employer is correct or (2) the classification needs to be changed and similar positions in the future should be classified in the same way. The other benefit to filing the form is that it may be evidence of good faith efforts to comply with the tax law. If the IRS determines that the principal/employer made a good faith mistake in classifying the agent, no penalty is imposed. If the IRS regards the principal/employer's classification as reckless or made without requisite good faith compliance efforts, penalties and interest are added to the assessment of back taxes.

LO 10-3

Explain the process for creating an agency relationship and the impact of that relationship on the liability of the principal.

OVERVIEW OF AN AGENCY TRANSACTION

Fundamentally, an agency transaction involves one party hiring another party to transact business on behalf of (or perform a task for) the hiring party. In a business context, this relationship is crucial because business owners and managers depend on agents to carry out the daily operations of the business.

Business owners and managers use agents to enter into contracts, perform necessary services, and advance their objectives in various ways. First, an agency relationship is typically created expressly by the parties with the duties of the agent being set out by the principal. Second, the parties perform their respective duties in accordance with their agreement and agency law. Finally, an agency transaction is ended by the termination of the agency by the parties. In some cases, the agency is terminated by operation of law (e.g., the principal hires the agent to paint a building, but the building is destroyed by fire before the agent begins to paint). Table 10.1 provides an overview of an agency transaction.

Creation of an Agency Relationship

The Restatements define the creation of an agency relationship in terms of *consent* and *control*. Specifically, agency is described as a *fiduciary* relationship that results from manifestations of consent by the principal to the agent to act on the principal's behalf subject to her control. The agent must also give consent to perform the act.

Manifestations and Consent The first step in creating an agency relationship is for the principal to **manifest** some offer to form an agency. **Consent** occurs when an agent agrees to act for the principal. In order to determine whether the parties have in fact manifested an offer of agency and acceptance by the agent, courts apply an objective standard. That is, given the parties' outward expressions, actions, and words, would a reasonable person believe that the principal intended that an agency be created and that the agent did in fact consent to the agency relationship? Courts do not look to the subjective intent of the parties as definitive. Rather, courts use the *objective* standard of what a reasonable person would have concluded about the manifestations and consent in the context of the relationship between the parties.

Legal Speak >))

Fiduciary Relationship A broad term embracing the notion that two parties may agree that one will act for the other party's benefit with a high level of integrity and good faith in carrying out the best interests of the represented party.

Control In addition to giving consent, the parties must have an understanding that the principal is in control of the agency relationship. The control need not be total or continuous and need not extend to the way the agent performs, but there must be some sense that the principal is defining the tasks and objectives of the agency relationship.

Formalities The law does not require any formal expression of an agency relationship between the parties. Most states do not require that the parties consent to the agency

TABLE 10.1 Agency Transaction Overview

Creation of Agency	Performance of Obligations and Duties	Termination of Agency
Principal wishes to form agency and agent consents.	Agent performs as agreed and in accordance with fiduciary obligations. Principal's primary obligation is payment of the agent.	Express act of parties or operation of law.

in writing. In fact, conduct alone can be the sufficient basis for formation of the agency relationship and can create rights and obligations of the principal and agent. However, a minority of states have a statutory equal dignity rule that specifies the formalities for certain principal-agent transactions.

In Case 10.2, an appellate court considers whether the conduct of the parties gave rise to an agency relationship.

CASE 10.2 Bosse v. Brinker Restaurant Corp. d/b/a Chili's Grill and Bar, 2005 Mass. Super. LEXIS 372 (Aug. 1, 2005)

FACT SUMMARY Bosse was part of a group of four teenagers ordering and eating a meal at the Chili's restaurant in Dedham, Massachusetts. The tab for the meal came to $56, but the group fled from the restaurant without paying and drove off. A regular patron of the restaurant saw them leave without paying and followed them in his own car. The teenagers saw the patron following them, so they stopped their car and confronted him in a parking lot at a nearby retail center. The pursuing patron yelled that he had seen them skip out on their bill at Chili's and that they would not get away with it. The patron's car was unmarked; it bore no Chili's insignia. He wore civilian clothing and no uniform or other insignia of employment at Chili's.

The teenagers then fled the lot, and a high-speed chase ensued through residential side streets. During the chase, the patron used his cell phone to call a Chili's employee and provided him with a description of the teenagers' car and the path of the chase. The Chili's employee then related this information to a 911 dispatcher. In the course of the high-speed chase, the teenagers collided with a cement wall and were injured. The pursuing patron left the crash scene area and was never identified.

Bosse sued the restaurant owner, Brinker Restaurant Corp. doing business as Chili's Grill and Bar, for damages related to the crash. Bosse argued that the actions of the parties resulted in the Chili's patron being converted to an agent of Chili's, that he conducted his chase as an agent of the restaurant, and that the restaurant should be liable for the consequences of his negligent or reckless pursuit. Brinker filed a motion for summary judgment on the grounds that no genuine issue of fact existed regarding the lack of an agency relationship through express acts or implication.

SYNOPSIS OF DECISION AND OPINION The Massachusetts Superior Court granted Brinker's motion for a summary judgment. The court held that an agency relationship requires three elements: (1) consent, (2) right of control, and (3) agent's conduct that benefits the principal in some way. In this case, the court ruled that the evidence was insufficient to create a genuine issue whether Chili's authorized the patron to act as a posse to conduct a chase. No information indicates any preliminary communication between the patron and restaurant employees. The events were spontaneous and fast-breaking. No member of Chili's house staff joined in the pursuit, and, in fact, Chili's had an unwritten but express policy forbidding staff to pursue a tab-dodger out of the building. The court concluded that Chili's had no chance or desire to control the patron and that any benefit Chili's received was minimal at best.

WORDS OF THE COURT: Elements of an Agency Relationship "For these reasons no genuine issue of material fact emerges upon a claim of an agency relationship. The information generated by discovery does not permit an inference that Chili's consented to such a relationship; that it had the right of control necessary for such a relationship; or that it possessed a genuine interest or benefit in such a relationship. The burden of the plaintiffs is to establish at least a genuine question of the presence of all three elements. If the evidence had failed to materialize upon any one of those elements, the deficiency would be fatal to the lawsuit.

(continued)

The evidence appears to have failed to materialize upon all three of the elements. Consequently, the plaintiffs enjoy no reasonable expectation of proving an agency relationship. Full summary judgment is appropriate."

Case Questions

1. If the pursuing patron were actually an off-duty employee of Chili's, how would that impact your agency analysis?
2. When the pursuing patron called the Chili's employee with a description of the pursuit and that employee in turn called the police, wasn't that an act of consent by Chili's?
3. *Focus on Critical Thinking:* What facts could you change in this case that would change the result?

Overlay of Agency Law with Other Areas of Law

Note that the law of agency often overlays and interacts with other areas of the law, especially contracts and torts. It is important to understand that several areas of law may all be operating in tandem during a given transaction but that each area regulates a different aspect of the transaction. For example, although agency itself is not a contractual relationship, the parties to an agency often enter into contracts to accomplish a particular objective. While the contract governs the *terms* of performance for the parties, agency law governs the agent's authority to *bind* the principal to a third party. Contract law does not displace agency law. Rather, the two areas of the law operate together. This is also true concerning torts such as negligence. While negligence law guides us in defining what constitutes an act of negligence and provides defenses, agency law governs whether or not the *principal* is liable for any alleged negligence of the agent.

CONCEPT SUMMARY Overview of Agency Law

- Agency is a legal relationship in which the parties agree, in some form, that one party will act as an agent for another party, called the principal, subject to the control of the principal.
- Agency law generally exists on the state statutory level and is based on the *Restatement (Third) of Agency*.
- The agent is classified, applying a substance-over-form analysis, as either an employee or an independent contractor based on the amount of direction and control that the principal has over the agent in terms of work schedule, pay rate, and day-to-day supervision.
- Liability of a principal for any acts or omissions of the agent and regulation by federal and state labor laws are related to the relationship between the principal, the agent, and any relevant third party.
- The law of agency operates in tandem with other areas of the law, especially contracts and torts.

LIABILITY OF THE PRINCIPAL FOR ACTS OF THE AGENT

One of the most important aspects of agency law involves understanding the ways in which actions of an agent result in liability for the principal. For agency purposes, liability can arise either through a contract obligation or through vicarious liability (liability for another) in tort. Therefore, when a third party claims that the principal is liable for an agent's act, he is asserting that the principal is responsible for any legal consequences of that act (such as damages or losses suffered by the third party).

LO 10-4
List the sources of an agent's authority to bind the principal in contract and give examples of each source.

Authority

Creation of an agency relationship typically involves the agent's power to bind the principal to third parties (and third parties to the principal) in an agreement of some type. The power to bind the principal in a certain transaction is derived from the agent's *authority*. This authority arises primarily through one of three ways. The primary sources of an agent's power are (1) *actual authority*, (2) *apparent authority*, and (3) *ratification*.

Actual Authority   Typically, an agent's power to bind is through **actual authority**, which arises either when the parties expressly agree to create an agency relationship or when the authority is *implied* based on custom or the course of past dealings. For example, the president of a corporation is thought of as having implied powers to bind the corporation to virtually all contracts that she determines are in the best interest of the corporation. The president need not obtain express approval from the board of directors for day-to-day transactions (although the president may be required by statute or by virtue of the organization's bylaws to obtain approval from the board prior to entering into certain contracts, such as a contract to sell all or most of the company's assets, and making other major decisions).[5]

Apparent Authority   An agent may also gain power to bind the principal from the *appearance* of legitimate authority to a third party. This is known as **apparent authority**. Determining whether an agent has apparent authority can be difficult because it is a source of power that is not expressly authorized by the principal. The key to understanding this power is to determine whether a third party was objectively *reasonable* in his belief that the apparent agent is in fact authorized to act for the principal.[6] Apparent authority arises from the actions of a principal that lead a third party to believe that an agent has the authority to act on the principal's behalf. In Case 10.3, a state appellate court analyzes the doctrine of apparent authority in the context of a wrongful death lawsuit.

CASE 10.3 GGNSC Batesville, LLC d/b/a Golden Living Center v. Johnson, 109 So. 3d 562 (Miss. 2013)

FACT SUMMARY   Johnson was the court-appointed representative of her brother's estate and filed a wrongful death lawsuit against GGNSC Batesville, LLC d/b/a Golden Living Center (Golden Living) alleging that Golden Living's negligence caused the death of her brother, Mose Cooper, who was a former resident of the Golden Living nursing home. Golden Living moved to compel arbitration based on

(continued)

---

[5] The authority of officers to bind a corporation is discussed in detail in Chapter 15, "Corporations."
[6] Restatement (Third) of Agency § 27.

an arbitration clause in its standard admission agreement. The trial court denied the motion and ruled that no valid contract existed because Johnson, not Cooper, signed the agreement during the nursing home's admissions process and Johnson had no legal authority to act as Cooper's agent.

SYNOPSIS OF DECISION AND OPINION The Mississippi Supreme Court affirmed the decision of the trial court and ruled in favor of Johnson. The court held that Golden Living had failed to provide any evidence that Johnson had any actual authority for health care or other decisions on Cooper's behalf. The court rejected Golden Living's argument that the relationship between Johnson and Cooper coupled with Johnson's presence during the admissions process was sufficient to establish apparent authority.

WORDS OF THE COURT: Apparent Authority
"To prove that Johnson had apparent authority over Cooper, Golden Living must put forth sufficient evidence of (1) acts or conduct of the principal indicating the agent's authority, (2) reasonable reliance upon those acts by a third party, and (3) a detrimental change in position by the third person as a result of that reliance. The record is utterly devoid of any acts or conduct of Cooper indicating that Johnson was his agent for the purpose of making health care decisions. Because Golden Living failed to put forth sufficient evidence, or indeed any evidence at all, of prong one, we need not address prongs two and three. Thus, Johnson did not have the apparent authority to bind Cooper to the contract, and consequently, a valid contract does not exist."

Case Questions

1. As a practical matter, what was the impact of the court's ruling on Johnson and Golden Living?
2. Was it reasonable for Golden Living to assume that Johnson had authority for Cooper's health care decisions? Why or why not? Could Cooper's conversation with the nursing home staff during admissions be sufficient to satisfy the first prong of the test? What words would indicate authority?
3. *Focus on Critical Thinking:* What other areas of the law are important to this analysis? Is it consistent with good public policy for courts to invalidate an agreement even when there was no question that party (e.g., Cooper) gained a benefit as a result of the agreement?

Ratification An agent can also have retroactive (after-the-fact) power to bind through **ratification**. Ratification occurs when the principal affirms a previously unauthorized act. That is, even though the agent did not have the authority to bind the principal initially, the principal may subsequently give after-the-fact authority by either (1) expressly ratifying the transaction or (2) not repudiating the act (i.e., retaining the benefits while knowing that they resulted from an unauthorized act by the agent). For example, suppose that Manager is the general manager of an apartment complex and is the agent of Owner. After a series of burglaries, Manager hires InstallCo to install an expensive burglar alarm system in the complex. InstallCo has never done business with Manager previously but allowed him to sign an alarm service contract as Owner's agent. During the weeklong installation, Owner notices the workers on the site and asks Manager to fill him in on the details. It is at this point that the authority is either ratified or disclaimed. Owner never expressly gave Manager authority to contract with InstallCo, and given the expense, nature of the contract, and lack of past dealing, it is unlikely that any implied or apparent authority exists. Nonetheless, Owner may be pleased with Manager's decision and ratify (affirm) the transaction. Owner also ratifies the transaction if he does nothing to disaffirm the transaction (such as stopping InstallCo from continuing work) because Owner is still reaping the benefits of what he knows to have been an unauthorized transaction. Thus, if Owner learns of the transaction, says nothing, and receives the benefits, he may not now refuse to honor the contract on the basis that Manager lacked the agency power to bind Owner to a contract with InstallCo.

Agent's Contract Liability to Third Parties

An authorized agent who enters into a contract with a third party binds the principal to perform certain obligations, and the third party may legally enforce the contract against the principal. However, there are circumstances in which the agent may also be held liable to perform the contract in the event that the principal refuses to perform. An agent's liability to third parties in a contract hinges on whether the agency relationship is *fully disclosed, partially disclosed,* or *undisclosed.*

Fully Disclosed Agency   When the third party entering into the contract is aware of the identity of the principal and knows that the agent is acting on behalf of the principal in the transaction, then the agency relationship is a **fully disclosed agency**. In a fully disclosed agency relationship, only the principal is contractually obligated to the third party. Because the agent has no liability, third parties have no legal recourse against the agent if the principal fails to meet her obligations under the contract. For example, suppose that Abel is hired by Peters to locate and purchase a suitable piece of real estate for Peters's new warehouse. Abel locates the property and enters into a contract to purchase the property from Thompson. Abel signs the contract "Abel, as agent for Peters." In this case, if Peters changes his mind and decides not to complete the transaction, Abel has no liability because his agency was fully disclosed. Thompson's sole remedy is to pursue a breach of contract lawsuit against Peters.

Partially Disclosed Agency   If the third party knows that the agent is representing a principal but does not know the *actual identity* of the principal, the agency relationship is a **partially disclosed agency**. In some cases, the agent may identify the principal only as an "interested real estate buyer" or by some other generic terminology. In a partially disclosed agency relationship, both the principal and the agent may be liable for the obligations under the contract.[7] Because the principal is not identified, the third party must rely on the agent's good faith dealings and credit. Therefore, the law imposes liability on the agent in the event that the principal does not perform her contractual obligations. For example, in the Abel-Peters-Thompson transaction, suppose that Peters is a high-profile real estate developer and he hires Abel to purchase Thompson's land on Peters's behalf. Peters believes that Thompson may hold out for a higher price if he knows that the buyer is a wealthy land developer, so he instructs Abel not to make his identity known when entering into the real estate purchase contract with Thompson. Although Thompson is aware that Abel is an agent, he is not aware of the principal's identity. Abel signs the contract without any indication that Peters is the principal. If Peters later changes his mind and refuses to perform under the contract, Thompson may pursue remedies against Abel and/or Peters. If Thompson is successful in his case against Abel, Abel has the right of indemnification from Peters.

---

[7]Restatement (Third) of Agency § 321.

Legal Speak >))

Indemnification
Right of reimbursement from another for a loss suffered due to a third party's act or default.

Undisclosed Agency When a third party is completely unaware that an agency relationship exists and believes that the agent is acting on her own behalf in entering a contract, this is called an **undisclosed agency**. In an undisclosed agency relationship, the agent is fully liable to perform the contract. Because the third party has no reason to know that an agency exists, he relies on the agent's good faith dealings and credit. Therefore, the law imposes liability on the agent in the event that the principal does not perform the contractual obligations. For example, in the Abel-Peters-Thompson transaction, suppose that Peters is a high-profile real estate developer and he hires Abel to purchase Thompson's land on Peters's behalf. Peters believes that Thompson may hold out for a higher price if he knows that the buyer is a wealthy land developer. Moreover, Peters is sufficiently confident in his belief that his identity will drive up the price that he takes extraordinary efforts to keep his interest in the property confidential. He instructs Abel not to inform Thompson of his status as an agent and to enter into the real estate purchase contract with Thompson in Abel's individual name. Because Thompson is not aware that Abel is an agent, nor is he aware of the principal's identity, this is an undisclosed agency relationship. Therefore, if Peters later changes his mind and refuses to perform under the contract, Thompson may pursue remedies against Abel. In some states, if Thompson subsequently finds out that Peters is the actual principal, he may pursue legal remedies against Peters as well. In any case, if Abel is made to pay, Abel has the right to indemnification from Peters.

In Case 10.4, a state appellate court considers the liability of an undisclosed agent.

CASE 10.4 Carroll Management Group, LLC v. A Carpet & Paint, LLC, 779 S.E.2d 26 (Ga. Ct. App. 2015)

FACT SUMMARY Hidden Village Associates, LLC (Hidden Village) used Carroll Management Group (Carroll) to manage and maintain a residential complex owned by Hidden Village. Carroll's on-site manager, Herbert Shaw, hired A Carpet & Paint (A Carpet) to perform carpet and cleaning work at the Highland Village complex but did not inform A Carpet's owner that he was merely acting as an agent. After its invoices for work at Highland went unpaid, A Carpet filed suit against Shaw, Carroll, and Hidden Village. A Carpet moved for summary judgment against Carroll, contending that Carroll never disclosed its agency relationship with Hidden Village and, therefore, was liable for the full amount of the unpaid invoices as an undisclosed agent. The trial court agreed and ruled in favor of A Carpet. Carroll appealed on the basis that A Carpet should have exercised reasonable diligence and investigated the possibility of an agency relationship when entering the contract.

SYNOPSIS OF DECISION AND OPINION The Georgia Court of Appeals affirmed the decision of the trial court in favor of A Carpet. The court rejected Carroll's argument that A Carpet had a duty to inquire and investigate whether Carroll's employee was an agent of the principal or the actual principal. The court held that it was well settled in agency law that if an agent fails to disclose the principal, the contracting party may settle with either the agent or the principal.

WORDS OF THE COURT: Liability of Undisclosed Agent "'An agent who makes a contract without identifying his principal becomes personally liable on the contract. If the agent wishes to avoid personal liability, *the duty is on him to disclose his agency,* and not on the party with whom he deals to discover it.' . . . These facts show, at most, that A Carpet could have determined whether Carroll is the owner of the property. A Carpet, however, did not have an affirmative

(continued)

duty to investigate the possibility of Carroll being an agent."

Case Questions

1. Why do you think that Carroll's employee (Shaw) never disclosed that Carroll Management was an agent of the principal?

2. How could Carroll avoid liability in similar situations in the future?

3. *Focus on Critical Thinking:* Is the nondisclosed agent rule outdated? Isn't it relatively easy for a party entering into a contract to check whether he is dealing with a principal or an agent? If so, should the burden remain on the agent in every case?

Tort Liability to Third Parties

In some cases, a principal may be held liable for an agent's tort, most commonly the tort of negligence, even though the principal has not engaged in any wrongful conduct. This is particularly true when the agent is an employee. For example, suppose Pep's Pizza Parlor employs a driver to deliver its products. On the way to a delivery, the driver is negligent and injures a pedestrian. Pep's is held liable for damages suffered by the pedestrian even though it exercised all due care (checking the driver's record before hiring him, etc.). Liability for principals of agents who are classified as employees is derived from the doctrine of **respondeat superior**.[8] Note that respondeat superior also holds employers liable for negligent acts of both employee agents and nonagent employees. This is a form of *vicarious liability* because it involves one party's liability for the act of another party. However, principals are generally *not* liable for negligent acts of agents that are independent contractors. This question of liability is yet another reason why correct classification of agents by business owners and managers is crucial to controlling risk.

Physical Injury Requirement You may recall from Chapter 9, "Torts and Products Liability," that parties who suffer purely economic losses as a result of a tortfeasor's negligence may only recover if those losses were a result of injury to person or property. This is also important in the context of respondeat superior. As a general rule, if the employee's misconduct causes physical harm to a third party's person or property, the employer is liable for both the injury and any related economic losses. However, if the employee's misconduct results in harm only to emotional state or reputation, or a purely economic loss, respondeat superior does not apply.

Scope of Employment The doctrine of respondeat superior is also limited by a requirement that in order for a principal (employer) to be liable for the employee's tort, the act must have occurred within the employee's *scope of employment*. Respondeat superior is a powerful tool for an injured third party because it allows the party to recover damages from the employer under the assumption that the employer's resources and insurance coverage are more abundant than those of the employee agent who committed the negligence. The scope of employment rule is an attempt to place some limitations on the principal's liability. Thus, for the principal to be liable, the agent's tortious conduct must have (1) been related to her duties as an employee of the

LO 10-5

Apply the doctrine of respondeat superior and identify its impact and limits.

Legal Speak >))

Vicarious Liability Liability that a supervisory party (typically an employer) bears for the actionable conduct of a subordinate or associate (such as an employee).

---

[8]Literal Latin translation: "let the master answer"; *Collins Latin* (2008).

> **KEY POINT**
>
> The doctrine of respondeat superior stands for the proposition that a principal (employer) is liable for the servant's or agent's (employee's) tort when that act resulted in physical harm or injury and occurred within the employee's scope of employment.

principal, (2) occurred substantially within the reasonable time and space limits, and (3) been motivated, in part, by a purpose to serve the principal.

Frolics and Detours The other exception to the respondeat superior doctrine occurs when an agent, during a normal workday, does something purely for her own reasons that are unrelated to employment. During this time, the employee's conduct is thought of as being outside the zone that is governed by respondeat superior. The law recognizes this activity, called a **frolic**, as a protection for the principal against any harm suffered as a result of an agent's negligence while on the frolic. The frolic exception is sometimes thorny to apply because determining the precise times that the frolic began and that it ended can be difficult. Moreover, if the conduct is a small-scale deviation that is normally expected in the workday, it is not considered a frolic but rather a simple **detour**. Detours are still within the ambit of respondeat superior. Courts use a case-by-case approach in applying the frolic doctrine because the conduct is judged based on the degree to which it is or is not within the scope of employment.

To understand the difference between frolic and detour, consider the following two hypothetical cases. Flash is employed by Apollo Messenger Service as the driver of its delivery van. During his workday, he is speeding in the delivery van and negligently injures a pedestrian. Suppose that at the time of the accident Flash is on his lunch break and driving the van to the local stadium to purchase tickets for his family to a ball game to be played that night. In this case, a court will likely rule that Apollo is not liable under respondeat superior because of the frolic exception. Alternatively, suppose that Flash was on his way to pick up a cup of coffee at the local coffee shop and he struck the pedestrian in the parking lot. The coffee stop would likely be considered a detour. Although he was not acting for the employer, the negligence would likely be imputed to Apollo because Flash made only a short stop that constituted a small-scale deviation from his employment duties. Because it can reasonably be expected that delivery van drivers will take short breaks during the workday, a court may find that Apollo is liable for Flash's conduct under respondeat superior.

Traveling to and from Work One case that arises in the context of liability under respondeat superior is when an employee causes an injury while traveling to or from the workplace. Many courts have adopted the **going-and-coming rule** whereby employers are generally not liable for tortious acts committed by employees while on their way to and from work. The law shields the employer from liability because employees are said to be outside of the course and scope of employment during their daily commute. Rather, the employment relationship is said to be suspended from the time the employee leaves the workplace until she returns or that in commuting she is not rendering service to the employer.

An important exception to the going-and-coming rule is when the employee's use of her own car gives some incidental benefit to the employer. This is known as the *required-vehicle exception* and it applies if the use of a personally owned vehicle is either an express or an implied condition of employment. It also applies if the employee has agreed, expressly or implicitly, to make the vehicle available as an accommodation to the employer.

In Case 10.5, a state appeals court analyzes the going-and-coming rule and its exceptions.

CASE 10.5 Moradi v. Marsh USA, Inc., 219 Cal. App. 4th 886 (2013)

FACT SUMMARY Bamberger was employed by Marsh as a salesperson, which required her to provide educational seminars, make presentations, and become involved with civic organizations such as the chamber of commerce and the Rotary Club. She met with prospective clients, typically at their location and convenience, and meetings could occur before, during, and after regular work hours. To reach these various destinations, Marsh required Bamberger to use her personal vehicle. Two to five times a week, Bamberger used her personal vehicle to attend off-site appointments and meetings. She also used her personal vehicle to transport Marsh executives, clients, and co-employees to offsite meetings, appointments, and seminars.

At the end of the workday on April 15, 2010, Bamberger planned to stop on the way home for some frozen yogurt and, thereafter, to attend a 6:00 p.m. yoga class. While still at work, she changed clothes from business attire to activewear. She also packed her laptop and other sales materials in a briefcase and took them with her in her car. On her way to a frozen yogurt shop, she was involved in an accident with Moradi, who was riding a motorcycle. Moradi filed a negligence suit against Bamberger and against Marsh as Bamberger's principal/employer under a theory of respondeat superior. Marsh defended on the basis that it was not liable for Bamberger's negligence because, at the time of the collision, Bamberger was neither at work, nor working, nor pursuing any task on behalf of her employer but was pursuing personal interests, namely, going to yoga class and stopping for yogurt on the way.

SYNOPSIS OF DECISION AND OPINION The Court of Appeals of California ruled in favor of Moradi because it determined that Bamberger's trip from the office to her home fell into the exception to the general going-and-coming rule. The court pointed out that the rule generally exempted an employer from respondeat superior liability for any tortious acts committed by employees while on their way to and from work because employees are said to be outside the scope of employment during their daily commute. However, an exception to this rule exists when the employee's use of her own car gives some *incidental benefit* to the employer. The court ruled that Marsh's conditions of employment required regular use of her personal car for company business. Among other factors, the court cited Bamberger's regular use of the car to visit clients, other sales-related uses, and her plans to use the car the next day to drive directly to a client appointment as evidence that Marsh gained an incidental benefit from use of the car. The court also ruled that Bamberger's route home via the yogurt shop and yoga class was a minor deviation and did not relieve Marsh of respondeat superior liability.

WORDS OF THE COURT: Exception to the Going-and-Coming Rule "A well-known exception to the going-and-coming rule arises where the [employee's] use of [his or her own] car gives some *incidental benefit* to the employer. . . . The exception can apply if the use of a personally owned vehicle is either an express or implied condition of employment . . . , or if the employee has agreed, expressly or implicitly, to make the vehicle available as an accommodation to the employer and the employer has 'reasonably come to rely upon its use and [to] expect the employee to make the vehicle available on a regular basis while still not requiring it as a condition of employment.'"

WORDS OF THE COURT: Minor Deviation "In addition, Bamberger's planned deviation was necessary for her comfort, convenience, health, and welfare. [W]e can think of no conduct more predictable than an employee's stopping [for something to eat or taking an exercise class] . . . on the way home. Where, as here, the trip home is made for the benefit of the employer, . . . accidents occurring during such minor and foreseeable deviations become part of the 'inevitable toll of a lawful enterprise.' It would have been unreasonable and inconvenient for Bamberger to drive all the way home, stop momentarily, turn around, and drive back to the yogurt shop and the yoga studio."

(continued)

> **Case Questions**
>
> 1. What was Marsh's theory of the case as to why they shouldn't be liable for Bamberger's negligence? Do you agree or disagree?
> 2. Where should the law draw the line between a "minor" deviation and one that takes the employee out of her scope of employment?
> 3. *Focus on Critical Thinking:* What kind of public policy reasons support (1) the general going-and-coming rule and (2) the incidental benefit exception? Should employers have to pay for the negligent acts of employees even where employers have taken all reasonable care to prevent any accident? Should the relative resources (i.e., deep pockets) of the potential defendant matter in this case (Marsh's assets versus Bamberger's personal assets)?

Intentional Torts Generally, intentional torts by an agent (such as committing an assault in the workplace) are thought to be outside the scope of employment, and, therefore, employers are not liable for such conduct unless the assault has a close connection to serving the principal. In a well-known decision on this topic, a state supreme court ruled that a sales associate employed by Nabisco who had assaulted the manager of a store in his territory was acting within his scope of employment because the original dispute involved shelf space at the store where the assault took place. The court held that because the agent employee was in the store on Nabisco business and the assault stemmed from his job as a sales associate, even an intentional tort such as battery could be covered by respondeat superior.[9] Thus, even unauthorized acts by an agent do not necessarily exempt the conduct from liability for the principal.

Negligent Hiring Doctrine

A majority of states recognize a tort-based theory of liability for employers for negligent or intentional torts of employees when the employer had *reason to know* that the employee may cause harm within his scope of employment. This liability theory is called the **negligent hiring doctrine**, and it requires employers to take reasonable steps (such as criminal background investigation and reference checks) to protect third parties, particularly customers and other employees, from harm at the hands of an employee. Courts are especially inclined to hold employers liable under this doctrine in cases where (1) the employees are required to have a high level of public contact, as occurs with service and maintenance personnel, real estate agents, or delivery persons, or (2) the employees are entrusted with caring for the sick, elderly, or other particularly vulnerable populations.

Negligent hiring occurs when, prior to the time the employee is actually hired, the employer knew or should have known of the employee's unfitness.[10] Liability generally focuses on the employer's methods of determining suitability for the position. For example, in *Abbot v. Payne*,[11] a state appellate court in Florida held the owners of a pest control company liable for negligent hiring when the company's management failed to

---

[9]*Lange v. National Biscuit Company*, 211 N.W.2d 783 (Minn. 1973).
[10]Restatement (Third) of Agency §§ 401–411.
[11]457 So. 2d 435 (Fla. App. 1984).

run a criminal background check on an employee who subsequently sexually assaulted a customer during a home service call. The employee had a record of multiple arrests for sexually related crimes, and the court found that the employer had a duty to screen the employee for any information that indicated that the employee should not have been placed in a position of trust with regular access to customer information and regular contact with the public on the employer's behalf. The doctrine also includes *negligent retention* if circumstances arose *after* the hiring process that should have given notice to the employer of a potential for an employee to cause harm.

Independent Contractors   Recall from earlier in this chapter that, as a general rule, principals are not liable for the negligent acts or omissions of an independent contractor agent. One important exception to this rule occurs when the principal has been negligent in hiring, and it is based on the *peculiar risk doctrine* that is rooted in the Restatements. The doctrine requires a principal to take reasonable steps to determine the fitness of an independent contractor agent to perform an inherently dangerous task. For example, a land developer that hires a demolition company to take down a large old building with dynamite has a legal obligation to ensure that the demolition company has reasonable safety measures in place, experienced personnel, proper safety licensing and permitting, and so on.

CONCEPT SUMMARY   Principal and Agent Liability to Third Parties

Contracts

Agency Relationship	Liability of Principal to Third Party	Liability of Agent to Third Party
Fully disclosed (Third party knew of agency relationship and the identity of the principal.)	Full liability to perform contract obligations.	None (so long as agent did not exceed scope of authority).
Partially disclosed (Third party knew of agency relationship but not the identity of the principal.)	Full liability to perform contract obligations.	Full liability to perform contract obligations if the principal fails to meet contractual obligations. If agent is made to pay, she is entitled to reimbursement (indemnification) from the principal.
Undisclosed (Third party had no reason to know that any agency relationship existed.)	Full liability to perform contract obligations.	Full liability to perform contract obligations if the principal fails to meet contractual obligations. In some states, if the third party finds out the identity of the principal, she may pursue the principal for remedies. In any case, if agent is made to pay, she is entitled to reimbursement (indemnification) from the principal.

(continued)

Torts

Type of Tort	Liability of Principal to Third Party	Liability of Agent to Third Party
Intentional torts of employees	No liability unless the act was directly tied to the employee's responsibilities.	Fully liable to third party for damages or losses.
Intentional torts of independent contractor	No liability.	Fully liable to third party for damages or losses.
Negligence of employees	Vicariously liable under doctrine of respondeat superior for acts of all employees (including employee agents and employee servants) that resulted in injury to persons or property and were within the employee's scope of employment.	Fully liable to third party for damages or losses.
Negligence of independent contractors	No liability (except in cases of negligent hiring; see below).	Fully liable to third party for damages or losses.
Negligent hiring of employees	Vicariously liable for damages or losses if employer could have foreseen possible harm by the employee through a determination of fitness for the position.	N/A
Negligent hiring of independent contractors	None except in cases where the principal hires a contractor for an inherently dangerous job that poses a peculiar risk.	N/A

DUTIES, OBLIGATIONS, AND REMEDIES OF THE PRINCIPAL AND AGENT

LO 10-6

Define the duties that collectively comprise a fiduciary obligation owed by the agent to the principal.

LO 10-7

Articulate the duties owed by a principal to the agent and to third parties.

Inherent in an agency relationship are certain duties and obligations of the parties. Agents owe duties to principals, and principals owe duties to agents. If either party fails to fulfill his duties and obligations, the law provides a remedy for the party suffering an injury or loss.

Agent's Duties to the Principal

The very essence of an agency relationship involves the creation of duties for the agent to act in good faith and in the principal's best interest at all times. These duties are automatic and need not be specifically agreed upon by the parties. The duties that define an agency relationship are collectively called a *fiduciary* duty, which requires the agent to act according to higher standards than nonfiduciaries in a transaction. Fiduciary duty consists of five subduties: *loyalty, obedience, care, disclosure,* and *accounting*.

Loyalty The duty of loyalty is the centerpiece of fiduciary obligation. The law requires that the agent hold the principal's objectives paramount. Unless the principal has knowingly agreed to the contrary or extraordinary circumstances exist, the agent is obliged to advance the principal's interest over her own interests. The Restatements require the agent to act *solely* for the benefit of the principal in all matters connected with the agency. This includes obligations of the agent to refrain from *self-dealing*, or engaging in any competition or other conflicts of interest, and to keep information about the principal and transaction *confidential*. For example, suppose that Jingle, a real estate agent, is hired by Landis to market and sell a parcel of land. Landis expects to sell the land for $100,000, but Jingle knows the property's value to be higher. Unknown to Landis, Jingle forms a partnership with two friends and buys the land at the discounted price. Jingle has breached his duty of loyalty to Landis by engaging in self-dealing (benefiting from the undervalued property) and a conflict of interest. Jingle cannot represent both sides (taking a commission from both buyer and seller) without express permission from Landis.

The duty of loyalty applies universally to all agents irrespective of the scope of the agency. Therefore, all employees owe a duty of loyalty to their employers, but the specific implications of the duty vary with the position the employee occupies. If a clerk at a chain of retail stores mentions to a customer that "business is slow," it is unlikely that the employee violated the duty of loyalty, which includes keeping business information confidential. However, if the company's chief financial officer mentions to a friend at a neighborhood block party that "the company's revenues are dropping like a stone," this may constitute a breach of loyalty through discussion of confidential business information. In Case 10.6, a state appellate court considers whether an employee violated the duty of loyalty.

CASE 10.6 SP Midtown, Ltd. v. Urban Storage, LP, Tex. App. LEXIS 3364 (May 8, 2008)

FACT SUMMARY Getz was the co-owner of a self-storage facility called Space Place. In April 2005, Getz hired Stacy Welch as a property manager for its Houston facility. Part of Welch's employment agreement required her to maintain strict confidentiality of Space Place's business and customer information. In November of the same year, Welch accepted employment with Midtown, one of Space Place's competitors, but continued to work for Space Place for the rest of the month. Getz was unaware of Welch's employment with Midtown but became suspicious when sales at the Houston facility dropped precipitously. An internal investigation revealed that Welch had used a variety of techniques to divert customers from Space Place to Midtown's facility. This included falsely telling inquirers that Space Place had limited availability and that Midtown's storage rates were lower. The investigation also revealed that Welch received bonuses from Midtown based on the amount of clients she referred to them.

Space Place sued Welch and Midtown. Space Place's claims against Welch included an allegation that she breached her fiduciary duty of loyalty owed as an agent of Space Place. Welch filed a motion for summary judgment on this claim and others, but the trial court denied the motion. Welch appealed.

SYNOPSIS OF DECISION AND OPINION The Texas Court of Appeals ruled in favor of Space Place and held that sufficient evidence of a breach of fiduciary duty existed for the case to proceed to trial. The court ruled that certain employees owe a fiduciary duty to their employers under an agent/principal theory. Because Welch was an employee who occupied a position of confidence at Space Place, the relationship created a fiduciary relationship. Given Welch's responsibilities and authority to transact business such as financial transactions, she is considered an employee agent and subject to fiduciary duties including the duty of loyalty. The court reasoned that Welch owed Space Place the duties associated with an agency including the duty not to act as, or on behalf of, an adverse party without the principal's consent.

WORDS OF THE COURT: Fiduciary Duties "When a fiduciary relationship of agency exists between employee and employer, the employee has a duty to act primarily for the benefit of the employer in matters connected with his agency. Among the agent's fiduciary duties to the principal is to account for profits arising out of employment, the duty not to act as, or on account of, an adverse party without the principal's consent, the duty not to compete with the

(continued)

principal on his own account or for another in matters relating to the subject matter of the agency, and the duty to deal fairly with the principal in all transactions between them. If an agent, while employed by his principal, uses his position to gain a business opportunity belonging to his employer, such conduct constitutes an actionable wrong."

Case Questions

1. One of Welch's issues on appeal was that she was not an employee that had agency authority. Why did the court decide that Welch had an agency relationship rather than a master-servant relationship? Do you agree?
2. What impact does the confidentiality clause in Welch's employment agreement have on your analysis as to whether a breach of fiduciary duty occurred?
3. *Focus on Critical Thinking:* What other areas of law might impact this case? Could the lawsuit have been brought on any other legal theory rather than breach of fiduciary duty?

KEY POINT

The duty of loyalty is the centerpiece of fiduciary obligation: The agent is obliged to advance the principal's interest over her own interests.

Obedience An agent also has the duty to obey *lawful instructions* from the principal and cannot substitute her own judgment for the judgment of the principal (unless specifically authorized). Instructions from the principal are considered to be manifestations of the principal's objectives. Note that agents who are instructed to conduct unlawful activities do not breach the duty of obedience by refusing to perform the illegal conduct.

Care An agent has the duty to act with **due care** when conducting business on behalf of the principal. This requires the agent to act in the same careful manner when conducting the principal's affairs as a reasonable person would in conducting her own personal affairs. The duty of care standard is similar to the standard discussed in Chapter 9, "Torts and Products Liability," in the context of negligence; that is, the duty expands and contracts based on the circumstances of the case and the position of the parties. Agents with specialized knowledge are held to a higher standard of care than are nonspecialists.

Gratuitous Agents Recall from earlier in this chapter that gratuitous agents are agents that are not compensated for their work. A gratuitous agent is held to a lower duty of care than is a paid agent. For a gratuitous agent to breach his duty of care to the principal, he must have acted so recklessly that a reasonable person would regard the conduct as *grossly* negligent.

Disclosure Agents have an ongoing duty to keep the principal informed and disclose any and all relevant facts to the principal. This duty is based on the notion that because agents may bind principals, it is essential that the agent provide as much information as possible to the principal. This includes all aspects of the relationship, such as keeping the principal informed during negotiations of a transaction. The duty also includes the obligation to disclose any pertinent negatives. This means that if the agent has a lack of information about an important fact, he must disclose that lack. For example, suppose that Buyer is interested in purchasing the assets of BigCo and hires Agent to investigate the possibility of an acquisition and to determine the value of the company. Agent has an obligation to inform Buyer of any contact and information he may have about the transaction. Agent must also disclose the fact that he cannot verify the actual value of the assets and that his

An agent owes the principal a duty to account for any money spent or received on behalf of the principal.
Stockbyte/Getty Images

estimates are best guesses. The fact that Agent cannot verify actual value is a pertinent negative and must be disclosed.

Accounting Unless the parties agree otherwise, the agent must keep appropriate written records for any money that the agent spends or receives in the course of the agent's representation. Known as the duty to **account**, this includes keeping records on data such as reimbursable expenses, checks or cash received on behalf of the principal, and any liabilities incurred in the course of the agent's conduct. The duty to account includes a prohibition against intermingling the principal's funds (or property) with the agent's own funds or possessions. For example, suppose that Penelope gives her agent, Julia, a check for $100,000 and instructs her to use it for a deposit on a warehouse that Penelope wishes to purchase for her business. Julia has a large personal tax bill that must be paid that same day, so she deposits the $100,000 in her personal account and writes a personal check to pay her tax bill using Penelope's money. She knows that her employment check will be arriving the next day, so she is confident that she will be able to pay the money back without Penelope's knowledge. Julia has breached her fiduciary duty by failing to keep a proper accounting through commingling the funds.[12]

Principal's Remedies for Breach

If an agent's breach of duty to the principal causes damages to the principal, the principal may recover those damages by suing the agent for the breach. If an agent's breach of duty resulted in the principal's becoming liable to a third party, then the agent must indemnify and hold harmless the principal from any losses as a result of the liability.

---

[12]Julia has also committed the criminal offense of embezzlement, which is discussed in detail in Chapter 22, "Criminal Law and Procedure in Business."

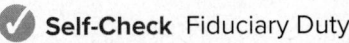 **Self-Check** Fiduciary Duty

Which fiduciary duty, if any, was breached?

1. Dorian is an employee of Gray Industries. His roommate works for a competitor to Gray. Dorian photocopies Gray's customer list and information and gives it to his roommate.
2. Dorian is a stockbroker for the Gray Family Trust with express authority to buy and sell stocks for the trust. Dorian knows that stock in High Flyers Inc. is overpriced and does not promise solid returns. However, he buys the stock in High Flyers because his commission will be higher than that for other stocks.
3. Gray hires Dorian to represent his interests as his agent in a business transaction and expressly instructs him not to sign any contracts with Grendel. Dorian attends a meeting and decides that a contract with Grendel would be a good deal for Gray. Dorian signs the contract on Gray's behalf.
4. Gray hires Dorian to sell widgets on Gray's behalf. Dorian accepts cash payments from Gray's customers but places the cash in his personal bank account for safekeeping and forgets to keep a record of the payments.

Answers to this Self-Check are provided at the end of the chapter.

Rescission and Disgorgement If the agent breaches the duty of loyalty, the principal's remedies also include the ability to *rescind* any transaction between the principal and agent. A court may also order the agent to return any funds earned as a result of the breaching conduct (this is known as *disgorgement*). For example, suppose that Coleridge hires Wordsworth as an employee in Coleridge's investment banking firm. Unknown to Coleridge, Wordsworth launches a competing firm and uses Coleridge's client lists to develop business for his own firm. In fact, in its first year, Wordsworth's new firm collected $100,000 in fees generated from client lists belonging to Coleridge. Because Wordsworth breached his duty of loyalty, not only is Coleridge entitled to out-of-pocket losses and damages, but a court will also order disgorgement of Wordsworth's profits by ordering him to pay Coleridge $100,000 in addition to any other damages suffered by Coleridge as a result of Wordsworth's breach.

Unauthorized Acts of Agents A principal is responsible for the acts of an authorized agent even if particular acts were unauthorized. The risk of loss from the unauthorized acts of a dishonest agent falls on the principal that selected the agent. Agency law presumes liability of a principal even when the agent acts less than admirably, exhibits poor business judgment, or commits fraud. In Case 10.7, a state appellate court analyzes the liability of principals for embezzlement by an authorized agent.

CASE 10.7 Romanelli v. Citibank, 60 A.D.3d 428 (N.Y. App. Div. 2009)

FACT SUMMARY Romanelli hired Schor as an accountant and financial adviser for his business and personal matters. Schor suggested opening new accounts at Citibank in order to obtain a lower interest rate on a line of credit. Romanelli, as principal of Romanelli, Inc., signed a business account

(continued)

application, corporate resolution, and signature card and gave it to Schor. Eventually, Romanelli changed his mind and instructed Schor not to open the account. However, unbeknownst to Romanelli, Schor added his signature to the Romanelli signature card and opened an account in the name of Romanelli, Inc. Over the next four years, Schor used this account to embezzle several hundred thousand dollars from Romanelli. Romanelli sued Citibank and others that participated in the transactions under the theory that Schor was not authorized to conduct business on Romanelli's behalf and that the banks were negligent in allowing him to do so. The trial court ruled in favor of Citibank and Romanelli appealed.

SYNOPSIS OF DECISION AND OPINION
The New York appellate court affirmed the lower court's decision in favor of Citibank. The court ruled that laws of agency that made principals liable for authorized acts of agents also made the principals liable for *unauthorized* acts. The court reasoned that the common law has traditionally placed the risk on the principal because the principal is generally better-suited than a third party to control the agent's conduct.

WORDS OF THE COURT: Acts of Dishonest Agents
"The risk of loss from the unauthorized acts of a dishonest agent falls on the principal that selected the agent. Plaintiffs' principal testified that he hired the accountant to act as a financial adviser for plaintiffs and gave him the checks to pay plaintiffs' taxes. The accountant, therefore, was plaintiffs' agent and was authorized to endorse the checks payable to plaintiffs and issue checks payable to the taxing authorities. The bank properly cashed the checks since the endorsement by the accountant was authorized by the principal."

Case Questions
1. Romanelli argued that Schor was acting outside his scope of authority and thus no liability for the principals exists. Does that strike you as convincing?
2. What remedy does Romanelli have against Schor?
3. *Focus on Critical Thinking:* Shouldn't the bank have been more careful in preventing fraud? What systems could be put into place to prevent any similar fraud from occurring in the future?

Duties and Obligations of the Principal to the Agent

When an agent acts on behalf of its principal, the agent may incur expenses, make payments, suffer an injury, or cause damages to third parties. In such cases, the principal has a duty to *reimburse and indemnify* its agents. This duty applies in the following cases:

- Payments made or expenses incurred within the agent's *actual authority.*
- Payments made by the agent for the principal's benefit but done *without authority,* so long as the agent acted under a mistaken good faith belief that he had the authority to act.
- Claims made by third parties on contracts entered into by an authorized agent and on the principal's behalf.
- Claims made by third parties for torts allegedly committed by the agent if the agent's conduct was within the agent's actual authority or the agent was unaware that the conduct was tortious.

The principal must provide the costs of a legal defense including attorney fees and any resulting liability settlement payment. In order to obtain the principal's protection, the agent must give the principal reasonable notice of the claim and cooperate with the principal in managing the defense (e.g., by appearing as a witness).

However, a principal does *not* have a duty to reimburse or indemnify the agent if the payments made or expenses incurred were (1) outside the agent's actual authority, (2) from losses resulting from the agent's negligence, or (3) from losses resulting from the agent's intentional tort or an illegal act.

Agent's Remedies for Breach

When a principal breaches a duty owed to an agent, the agent generally has the right to recover damages in court. The most common breach occurs when the principal refuses to reimburse or indemnify the agent. Assuming that the principal's obligation to do so is triggered by law, but she still refuses to properly compensate the agent, the agent's sole remedy is to file suit in order to collect any money owed to the agent and to be reimbursed for out-of-pocket and incidental costs. As a practical matter, the principal and agent may have entered into some type of express agreement that spells out specific remedies the parties may exercise in the event of a breach. For example, suppose that Cardozo hires Holmes Inspection Company to perform an engineering inspection on a building Cardozo is considering buying. Cardozo agrees to pay Holmes $1,000 for services rendered, plus any out-of-pocket expenses, within 10 days of the inspection services. Although Holmes performs the services, Cardozo loses interest in the transaction and fails to pay Holmes the fee. Cardozo has breached his duty as a principal by failing to pay Holmes. Holmes may sue for damages and is entitled to the agreed-upon fee and reimbursement of the out-of-pocket expenses. However, suppose that Cardozo and Holmes signed a written agreement that included a *penalty clause* whereby Cardozo agreed to pay a late fee and 10 percent interest per month for every month the invoice was outstanding. In this case, Holmes not only may recover the fee and expenses by virtue of Cardozo's breach of his duty as a principal but may also recover the late fees and interest by virtue of their contractual agreement.

TERMINATION OF THE AGENCY RELATIONSHIP

LO 10-8

List the two primary methods used to terminate agency relationships and give examples of each method.

LO 10-9

Recognize the dangers of the principal's failing to notify third parties of an agent's termination.

An agency relationship may be terminated in a variety of ways. Termination is an important issue for business owners and managers because termination of the agency relationship also terminates the principal's duties and obligations to the agent and to third parties. It is equally important to understand the circumstances under which a third party must be notified of the termination in order to cut off the liability of the principal at a definite point. Failing to properly notify appropriate parties may result in *continued liability* of the principal for acts of the agent despite the termination. In general, an agency relationship is terminated either through **express acts** or through **operation of law**.

Express Acts

In a typical agency relationship, both the principal and the agent have the power to dissolve the agency at any time. Either party may end the agency through **termination** by simply communicating the desire to terminate the relationship. Termination by the principal is known as *revocation*. When the agent initiates the termination, it is known as *renunciation*. It is important to understand that the legal *power* of termination is not synonymous with the legal *right* of termination. Therefore, the principal may terminate the agreement (thereby revoking her authority for the agent to act in her place), but the termination may still be unlawful because the law did not give the principal the right to end the agreement before mutual performance. Thus, the agent may be entitled to damages as a result of the principal's conduct of wrongful termination. For example, suppose that Foley hires Paul to paint the lobby of Foley's office building. The parties agree that Paul will paint the lobby over a period of two weeks and that Foley will pay him $1,000 upon completion. Halfway through the work, Foley learns that a major tenant has filed for bankruptcy, so he calls Paul and tells him to stop work because he can no longer afford the costs of painting. In this case, Foley, as the principal, has the power to terminate the agency relationship by revocation. However, because Foley's actions are a breach of the Foley-Paul contract,[13] Foley's termination is unlawful and Paul may recover any damages that he suffered as a result of the breach of contract.

---

[13] Recall from Chapter 7, "Contract Enforceability and Performance," that economic factors may generally not be used to excuse performance of a contract obligation (such as Foley's obligation to pay).

STRATEGIC LEGAL SOLUTIONS

Eliminating Lingering Liability

PROBLEM: The effect of termination of an agency relationship is that the agent no longer has actual authority. However, agency law recognizes that in a case where a principal has terminated an agency by an express act, the agent may still have apparent authority to bind the principal to a contract with a third party. When the principal has acted in a way that would give a third party the belief that his agent has actual authority but then revokes the actual authority of the agent, the agent may still have lingering authority from the third party's perspective.

For example, suppose that Sergio is employed as a buyer for High End Furniture Manufacturing Company (High End). One of Sergio's responsibilities is to order appropriate amounts of materials from Lumber Depot. Sergio would place the order by telephone with Lumber Depot and then he would pick up the materials in a rented truck for delivery to High End's workshop. Lumber Depot would issue an invoice and High End would pay within 30 days. This same transaction occurred approximately 10 times in six months. Assume that Sergio is terminated, but the next day he calls in an order to Lumber Depot from his home telephone. He then picks up the materials and absconds with them. This is a situation in which High End may still have liability to pay Lumber Depot based on Sergio's apparent authority. In order to terminate liability to a third party for the acts of Sergio, High End must notify the third party of the termination. This is especially true in cases where, as in the High End case, the pattern of repeated conduct (Sergio would order and pick up materials, Lumber Depot would issue an invoice, and then High End would pay) creates a reasonable belief that Sergio's authority was express and ongoing.

SOLUTION: Implement a third-party notification system to eliminate lingering authority and prevent liability based on apparent authority. Whenever an agency relationship has been terminated by an express act, the principal must notify any third parties (such as vendors or suppliers) who may be affected by the termination. Without a systematic approach in place, an employer may still be liable for the acts of the former agent even without the agent's having actual authority. Therefore, as part of its human resource management system, companies may put into place a third-party notification system whenever an agent employee has been terminated.

In the High End–Sergio case, High End could avoid liability by making third-party notifications part of its procedure when terminating an employee (or any agent). While typical employee termination checklists focus on return of company property, final paycheck, and other administrative tasks, a solution to lingering authority may be as simple as adding notification to the list. If High End had sent an e-mail to the manager of Lumber Depot notifying her of Sergio's status, that would eliminate any liability for High End for apparent authority actions of Sergio. The e-mail need not be lengthy or detailed[14] but should be specific:

> Dear Lumber Depot Manager: Please note that, effective immediately, Sergio is no longer employed by High End. Any purchases made on High End's behalf must be accompanied by a purchase order signed by me until further notice. Sincerely, Vice President of High End.

This type of notice satisfies the termination notice required under agency law and, thus, eliminates any potential apparent authority claims by third parties based on Sergio's conduct.

More often than not, the parties in an agency relationship will have agreed to a fixed term for the representation. In that case, the agency relationship may be terminated by **expiration**. The expiration may be tied to a *time period* (principal hires agent for a one-year period) or an *event* (principal hires agent as a substitute worker only until an injured

---

[14] In order to avoid any potential liability for defamation, caution should be exercised in not giving any information about *why* the termination took place.

worker returns). Instead of setting a fixed time or event, the parties may agree to end the agency once the agency's *purpose* has been accomplished. For example, in the Foley-Paul agency relationship, discussed earlier, suppose that Foley did not attempt to terminate the agency but instead the painting services were finished on time. In this case, the agency ends automatically because the purpose of the agency, as originally contemplated by the parties, has been accomplished.

Operation of Law

Agency may also be terminated as provided for by statute or through certain common law doctrines. First, an agency relationship is terminated by the *destruction* of essential subject matter of the relationship. So long as the agent's role is predicated on some particular property being at the disposal of the principal and the property is no longer practically or legally available, agency is automatically terminated. For example, Foley hires Paul to paint the lobby of Foley's office building. The day after the two agree, Foley's building burns down. The Foley-Paul agency relationship is thus terminated.

An agency relationship is also terminated automatically if either the principal or the agent *dies,* files for *bankruptcy,* or does not have the requisite *mental capacity* to continue the relationship. However, it is important to note that exceptions exist to these common law doctrines. Increasingly, various jurisdictions have prescribed statutory exceptions to certain events of termination. For example, in the case of the death of a principal, some state statutes permit the agent to continue to have actual authority until the agent learns of the death. Therefore, so long as the agent is acting in good faith, the agent may continue his duties until he actually receives notice of the death of the principal.

CONCEPT SUMMARY Duties, Obligations, and Remedies of the Parties

- Agents owe a fiduciary duty to principals. This duty requires the agent to act according to higher standards than nonfiduciaries in a transaction, including the duties of loyalty, obedience, care, disclosure, and accounting.
- The duty of loyalty is the centerpiece of fiduciary obligation because the agent is obliged to advance the principal's interest over her own interest.
- If an agent's breach of duty to the principal causes damages to the principal, the principal may recover those damages from the agent.
- If an agent's breach of duty resulted in the principal's becoming liable to a third party, then the agent must indemnify and hold harmless the principal from any losses as a result of the liability.
- If an agent breaches the duty of loyalty, the principal may rescind any agreement between principal and agent and the agent may be liable to return profits earned as a result of the breach.
- Principals have a duty to reimburse and indemnify agents for expenses incurred, injuries suffered, or damages caused to third parties when the agent acted within actual authority or in good faith on behalf of the principal.
- A principal owes independent duties to third parties to use reasonable care in screening, hiring, informing, training, and supervising its agents.
- An agency relationship is terminated either through express acts (termination or expiration) or through operation of law (destruction of subject matter, death, bankruptcy, or mental capacity).

KEY TERMS

Agency law p. 328 The body of laws that govern the relationships created when one party hires another party to act on the hiring party's behalf.

Agent p. 328 One who agrees to act and is authorized to act on behalf of another, a principal, to legally bind the principal in particular business transactions with third parties pursuant to an agency relationship.

Principal p. 328 An agent's master; the person from whom an agent has received instruction and authorization and to whose benefit the agent is expected to perform and make decisions pursuant to an agency relationship.

Restatement (Third) of Agency p. 328 A set of principles, issued by the American Law Institute, intended to clarify the prevailing opinion of how the law of agency stands.

Employee agents p. 329 One of three broad categories of agents; includes, generally, anyone who performs services for a principal who can control what will be done and how it will be done.

Independent contractor agents p. 329 One of three broad categories of agents; includes, generally, anyone who performs services for a principal who has the right to control or direct only the result of the work and not the means and methods of accomplishing the result.

Gratuitous agents p. 329 One of three broad categories of agents; includes, generally, anyone who acts on behalf of a principal without receiving any compensation.

ABC test p. 330 Statutory standard used by many states to determine agency status.

Manifest p. 336 Apparent and evident to the senses. In the context of agency law, courts apply an objective standard to determine whether the principal intended that an agency be created.

Consent p. 336 An agent's agreeing to act for the principal. In the context of agency law, courts apply an objective standard to determine whether the agent did in fact agree to the agency relationship.

Actual authority p. 339 A source of the agent's authority that occurs either when the parties expressly agree to create an agency relationship or when the authority is implied based on custom or the course of past dealings.

Apparent authority p. 339 A source of the agent's authority that occurs when there is an appearance of legitimate authority to a third party rather than express authorization by the principal.

Ratification p. 340 A retroactive source of the agent's authority that occurs when the principal affirms a previously unauthorized act by either (1) expressly ratifying the transaction or (2) not repudiating the act (i.e., the principal retains the benefits while knowing that they resulted from an unauthorized act by the agent).

Fully disclosed agency p. 341 A type of agency relationship in which the third party entering into the contract is aware of the identity of the principal and knows that the agent is acting on behalf of the principal in the transaction.

Partially disclosed agency p. 341 A type of agency relationship in which the third party knows that the agent is representing a principal but does not know the actual identity of the principal.

Undisclosed agency p. 342 A type of agency relationship in which a third party is completely unaware that an agency relationship exists and believes that the agent is acting on her own behalf in entering a contract.

Respondeat superior p. 343 (Latin for "let the master answer") A common law doctrine under which a principal (employer) is liable for the tortious action of the servant or agent (employee) when that act resulted in physical harm or injury and occurred within the agent's scope of employment.

Frolic p. 344 An exception to the respondeat superior doctrine that occurs when an agent, during a normal workday, does something purely for her own reasons that are unrelated to her employment.

Detour p. 344 Conduct classified as a small-scale deviation that is normally expected in the workday and, therefore, is within the ambit of respondeat superior.

Going-and-coming rule p. 344 Rule whereby employers are generally not liable for tortious acts committed by employees while on their way to and from work.

Negligent hiring doctrine p. 346 A tort-based theory of liability for employers for negligent or intentional torts of employees when the employer had reason to know that the employee may cause harm within his scope of employment.

Due care p. 350 A subduty of fiduciary duty that requires that the agent act in the same careful manner when conducting the principal's affairs as a reasonable person would in conducting her own personal affairs.

Account p. 351 A subduty of fiduciary duty that requires that the agent keep records such as a written list of transactions, noting money owed and money paid, and other detailed statements of mutual demands.

Express acts p. 354 Acts by which an agency relationship is terminated; can be either simple communication of the desire to terminate the relationship, the expiration of a fixed term, or satisfaction of purpose.

Operation of law p. 354   Method whereby an agency relationship is terminated as provided for in a statute or through certain common law doctrines covering the destruction of essential subject matter, death, bankruptcy, or lack of requisite mental capacity.

Termination p. 354   Method of ending an agency relationship whereby either the principal (revocation) or the agent (renunciation) simply communicate the desire to dissolve the relationship.

Expiration p. 355   Method of ending an agency relationship whereby the parties agree to a fixed term for the relationship.

CHAPTER REVIEW QUESTIONS

1. A principal and agent relationship requires a/an
   a. Formal written agreement
   b. Definite time period
   c. Express oral agreement
   d. Agreement of consent and control
   e. Attorney

2. Manager hires Ernest to supervise all shipments made from the company's central delivery center. Ernest's workweek is set by Manager and he is paid a salary and gets benefits. What is Ernest's agency classification?
   a. Employee agent
   b. Independent contractor agent
   c. Nonagent employee (master/servant)
   d. Gratuitous agent
   e. Supervisory agent

3. Dorian enters into a supply contract with BigCo on behalf of Gray Industries. Dorian is a manager for Gray Industries but is not authorized to enter into supply contracts. Which of the following statement(s) is/are true?
   I. Gray Industries may still ratify the supply contract.
   II. Dorian had actual authority to enter into the contract.
   III. Gray Industries must honor the contract under any circumstances.
   a. I only
   b. II only
   c. I, II, and III
   d. I and II
   e. II and III

4. NewCo hires Troy as a consultant to assist the company with improving its technical efficiency. Which of the following is *not* true?
   a. Troy owes a fiduciary duty to NewCo.
   b. If Troy breaches his fiduciary duty, NewCo is entitled to rescission as a remedy.
   c. NewCo owes Troy the duty of loyalty.
   d. Troy cannot engage in any activity that is a conflict of interest with NewCo's interests.
   e. If Troy dies, the agency is terminated through operation of law.

5. The duty of _____ is an agent's fiduciary duty to act in the same careful manner when conducting the principal's affairs as a reasonable person would use in conducting his own personal transactions.
   a. Care
   b. Loyalty
   c. Accounting
   d. Cooperation
   e. Obedience

Answers and explanations are provided at the end of this chapter.

THEORY TO PRACTICE

Cold Case Trucking (CCT) specializes in transportation of products that require refrigeration or freezing while being transported from the product's manufacturer to a wholesaler's warehouse. In an effort to improve its shipping logistics operations, CCT hired Crusoe, who had experience in operations logistics, as a consultant. CCT and Crusoe agreed that Crusoe would study CCT's operations by conducting interviews with employees and customers and then would design a new logistics plan and oversee its implementation. The parties agreed that Crusoe would give regular updates on his progress by attending weekly CCT management meetings. Because the CCT project was so time-intensive, Crusoe devoted 100 percent of his work time to CCT. The company also agreed to pay Crusoe $200 per documented hour for work on the project upon receiving an invoice from Crusoe and to make office space available at CCT's headquarters for Crusoe's exclusive use.

1. What is Crusoe's agent classification? What factors should CCT analyze in making this determination?
2. What is the source of Crusoe's authority to act as CCT's agent?
3. Assume that Crusoe is driving to interview one of CCT's customers for his study of CCT's logistical operations. While en route, he negligently hits a pedestrian. Is CCT liable for injuries to the pedestrian caused by its agent (Crusoe) under the doctrine of respondeat superior? Explain your analysis.
4. Suppose that Crusoe learns several important CCT trade secrets in the course of his agency and sells the information to a CCT competitor for $500,000. Which fiduciary duty has Crusoe breached? Explain your analysis. What are CCT's potential remedies against Crusoe?
5. Assume that part of Crusoe's agreement with CCT allowed Crusoe to use CCT's account at a local office supply store. Over a period of three months, Crusoe ordered any office machinery or supplies he needed for his work directly from the store. The store billed CCT directly and was paid (along with any other charges by authorized CCT employees) within 30 days of CCT's receipt of the bill. Suppose that a dispute arises between CCT and Crusoe about the quality of Crusoe's work and CCT terminates the consulting agreement. The next day Crusoe picks up a new computer from the office supply store, charges it to CCT's account, and absconds with it. Is CCT liable for payment to the office supply store for the computer? Explain your analysis.
6. What steps should CCT have taken to prevent possible liability in Question 5?

LEGAL STRATEGY 101

LeBron James's Agent

Thus far, this chapter has explored the nuts and bolts of various aspects of agency law, including an agent's express and implied authority to negotiate legally binding contracts on behalf of a principal. Agency law may sound very technical, so here we will take a quick *time out* to see how the law of agency can be used strategically to create value, even in difficult and delicate circumstances.

To see the possible value-creating side of agency law, imagine two potential business partners who for whatever reason don't trust each other. Maybe they dislike each other for purely personal reasons. Perhaps they had a misunderstanding in the past. If the parties could somehow put aside their differences, however, they could negotiate a mutually beneficial agreement, one in which both sides would be better off.

Specifically, let's consider the case of NBA All-Star LeBron James and Dan Gilbert, the owner of the Cleveland Cavaliers pro-basketball franchise. LeBron began

LeBron James. Jason Miller/Stringer/Getty Images

his pro-basketball career with the Cavs, but when he became a free agent in July of 2010, he decided on live TV to "take my talents to South Beach" by joining the Miami Heat. "The Decision," as it became known, upset many Cleveland fans, who felt betrayed by their hometown hero. The owner of the Cavs, Dan Gilbert, even wrote an open letter publicly criticizing James's decision to leave Cleveland.[15] Among other things, Gilbert described the decision as a "shameful display of selfishness and betrayal by one of our very own" and a "shocking act of disloyalty from our home grown 'chosen one.'"

Now, fast forward to the summer of 2014. LeBron James's contract with the Miami Heat is about to expire. At this stage in his career, LeBron James is seriously considering the possibility of returning to Cleveland, and Dan Gilbert would probably like to have his franchise player back in order to win a championship—but in real life, how will James and Gilbert be able to put aside their past personal differences in order to make a new deal? Agency law, that's how!

Simply put, instead of negotiating directly with the owner of the Cavs, LeBron could ask his sports agent Rich Paul to negotiate a new deal with Dan Gilbert on his (LeBron's) behalf.[16] After all, an agent has the authority to enter into legally binding contracts on behalf of a principal. As a result, the Cavs's owner has the legal assurance that whatever agreement he is able to negotiate with Rich Paul will be binding on LeBron James himself. The rest, as they say, is history.

CRITICAL THINKING QUESTIONS

1. In real life, LeBron James's agent Rich Paul negotiated a new deal on LeBron's behalf with the owner of the Cavs in July 2014. But what if a day later LeBron had a change of heart and decided to retire instead of honoring his new contract with the Cavaliers?

2. Given the scenario described in Question 1, what legal remedies would Dan Gilbert have against LeBron James? Would Rich Paul (LeBron's agent) also be legally liable on the contract?

---

[15] You can read the full text of Dan Gilbert's 2010 open letter criticizing LeBron James's decision here: http://espn.go.com/nba/news/story?id=5365704.

[16] To learn more about Rich Paul, see Chris Littmann, *Who Is Rich Paul? Eight Things to Know About LeBron's Agent,* Sporting News, July 7, 2014.

MANAGER'S CHALLENGE

Legally astute managers are able to limit their company's risk by recognizing potential liability during business planning. Spotting potential legal issues and understanding when to contact counsel are important management skills. Suppose that in the Theory to Practice problem you are a CCT manager and that Crusoe presents his logistics and operations improvement plan at a management meeting. Part of Crusoe's plan involves converting the delivery truck drivers from employees to independent contractors. Crusoe claims that this will save employment taxes and limit CCT's liability for driver negligence. Crusoe recommends having the drivers sign independent contractor agreements and paying them based on a monthly fee rather than as hourly employees. After the meeting, you receive the following e-mail from the vice president of operations:

> To: All managers
> Fr: VP/Operations
> Re: Crusoe's plan

Please give me any feedback or concerns you have about Crusoe's recommendations presented at today's management meeting. I will be drafting a summary memorandum for top-level management next week, and we will be moving to implementation of some or all of Crusoe's recommendations shortly.

Draft a three- to five-paragraph e-mail to your vice president concerning the proposal to convert drivers to independent contractors. Using your knowledge of agency law, be sure to raise any pertinent legal issues and discuss potential liability in explaining your concerns. Conclude the e-mail with a brief recommendation on how best to proceed.

See Connect for Manager's Challenge sample answers.

CASE SUMMARY 10.1 Hannington v. University of Pennsylvania, 809 A.2d 406 (Pa. Super. 2002)

APPARENT AUTHORITY

Hannington, a graduate student at the University of Pennsylvania (Penn), brought suit against the university for breach of contract. Attorneys for both sides appeared to have reached a settlement when, just prior to trial, Hannington's attorney notified the court that a settlement had been reached and sent Penn a final draft of the settlement agreement. Penn agreed to the settlement terms and sent the settlement agreement back to Hannington's attorney with Penn's authorized signatures. However, Hannington refused to sign the settlement agreement, hired a new attorney, and opted to proceed to trial. The trial court refused to allow Hannington's case to go forward and held that Hannington's attorney had apparent authority to settle the case and Penn had reasonably relied on Hannington's attorney as being an agent authorized to settle the case.

CASE QUESTIONS

1. Who prevails and why? Did Hannington's attorney have apparent authority? What is the standard?
2. Because Hannington never actually signed the agreement, was it reasonable for Penn to assume that Hannington's attorney had obtained his express consent to the terms? Has the court effectively deprived Hannington of his right to proceed to trial?
3. Suppose that in the middle of settlement negotiations, Hannington becomes frustrated with the impasse. He hires his neighbor, another attorney not yet involved in the case, to draft a settlement agreement and sends it to Penn. Is apparent authority created in this circumstance? Explain.

CASE SUMMARY 10.2 Bishop v. Texas A&M University, 105 S.W.3d 646 (2002)

VICARIOUS LIABILITY

A drama club at Texas A&M University (TAMU) performed *Dracula,* which was directed and supervised by a faculty adviser employed by TAMU. Bishop, a student at TAMU, was playing Vlad the Impaler in the performance when, during the final scene, a fellow student missed the stab pad attached to Bishop's chest and stabbed him with a bowie knife. Bishop suffered a collapsed lung and brought suit against TAMU, alleging that, under the doctrine of respondeat superior, TAMU was liable for the injuries he sustained as a result of the negligence of its faculty adviser employee. TAMU prohibited deadly weapons campuswide, and Bishop argued that the employee was negligent in using a real knife and in not ensuring that TAMU policies were being enforced.

CASE QUESTIONS

1. Do you believe TAMU should be held vicariously liable under the doctrine of respondeat superior in this case? Why or why not?
2. Assume that the directors were independent contractors rather than university-employed faculty. How does that affect your analysis? Explain.

CASE SUMMARY 10.3 Toms v. Links Sports Management Group, L.P., U.S. Dist. LEXIS 114677 (W.D. La. Aug. 14, 2006)

FIDUCIARY DUTY

Parker, a sports agent, represented David Toms, a professional golfer. Parker also represented Shaun Micheel and other professional golfers. Parker received a 20 percent commission on any endorsement contracts signed by Toms and a 25 percent commission on endorsement contracts signed by Micheel. In 2003, Parker was in the middle of negotiations with Cleveland Golf on Toms's behalf. After Micheel was the surprise winner at the PGA Championship, Parker convinced Toms that he should hold out for a more lucrative endorsement deal than was being offered by Cleveland, and he subsequently signed Micheel, instead of Toms, to the Cleveland Golf deal.

CASE QUESTIONS

1. What agency relationship exists between Toms and Parker?
2. If an agency relationship exists, when was a fiduciary duty created and what subduties apply to this case? Explain.
3. Is Parker's employer also liable for the actions of Parker? Why or why not?

CASE SUMMARY 10.4 Estrada v. FedEx Ground Package System, Inc., 64 Cal. Rptr. 3d 327 (2007)

INDEPENDENT CONTRACTOR STATUS

All employees who were hired by Federal Express (FedEx) as long-haul delivery drivers were required to sign an operating agreement that identified the driver as an independent contractor. Under the terms of the agreement, the driver would provide his own truck, mark the truck with the FedEx logo, pay all costs of operating and maintaining the truck, and use the truck exclusively in the service of FedEx, along with other specific obligations. The drivers brought a class action suit contending that for the purpose of their entitlement to reimbursement for work-related expenses, they were employees, not independent contractors.

CASE QUESTIONS

1. Should the drivers be classified as independent contractors?
2. What tests should the court apply to determine the status of the drivers?

CASE SUMMARY 10.5 Edgewater Motels, Inc. v. A. J. Gatzke & Walgreen Co., 277 N.W.2d 11 (Minn. 1979)

SCOPE OF EMPLOYMENT

Gatzke was employed as a district manager for Walgreen Company (Walgreen), which owned a chain of restaurants. He was assigned to supervise the opening and preliminary operations of a new Walgreen-owned restaurant in Duluth, Minnesota. This assignment required Walgreen to pay for Gatzke's temporary housing at the Edgewater Motel, which was located near the Duluth site, for several weeks. He used his motel room as a makeshift office and would use the desk in the room for routine paperwork, including expense reports. Gatzke was a management-level, salaried employee and, therefore, had no set work hours. On one workday, Gatzke and several employees had spent the entire day on-site at the new restaurant and then had a business dinner and after-dinner drinks until approximately midnight. Gatzke then returned to his motel room and was filling out his expense report when he accidentally dropped a lit cigarette in the trash can next to the desk in his room. A fire started, and although Gatzke escaped unharmed, the motel was severely damaged. Among other defendants, Edgewater sued Walgreen claiming that it was vicariously liable for the acts of Gatzke as its employee agent.

CASE QUESTIONS

1. Was Gatzke's negligent smoking outside the scope of his employment? Why or why not?
2. If the evidence showed that Gatzke had intentionally tried to commit arson, how would that impact the court's analysis?
3. Suppose that Gatzke had been writing out personal postcards and not been filling out an expense report when he started the fire. Would Walgreen be liable?

Self-Check ANSWERS Agency Classification

1. Independent contractor. Factors: (a) A publisher has very little direction and control of an author in terms of time and schedule; (b) lump-sum payment; and (c) no ongoing relationship.
2. Independent contractor. While More may appear at first glance to be an employee due to the schedule, consider that (a) More has eight such clients (he doesn't work exclusively for Henry), (b) More is paid through invoice, and (c) a short-term agreement exists with no promise of continuing employment.
3. Employee. Factors: (a) full direction and control over More's schedule and (b) hourly wages (in addition to the commission).
4. Gratuitous agent.
5. Employee. While this may appear at first glance to be an independent contractor relationship because of the agreement, remember that courts apply a substance-over-form analysis in determining agency status. Consider that (a) More's schedule is set by Henry, (b) More is paid the same amount on a biweekly basis, (c) the annual holiday bonus may be evidence of continuing employment, and (d) More uses Henry's equipment to do his job.
6. Employee. Level of salary is not determinative in an agency classification analysis. More's schedule is set, Henry provides his pay and benefits, and More predominantly uses Henry's equipment to perform his work.

Fiduciary Duty

1. Loyalty. Dorian's actions were a conflict of interest and violated a duty to keep business information confidential.
2. Loyalty. Dorian's actions constitute self-dealing because he put his interest ahead of Gray's interests.
3. Obedience. Gray's instructions were clear and lawful, and Dorian violated his obligation to follow the instructions of the principal.
4. Accounting. Dorian's commingling of the cash he accepted on Gray's behalf with his own cash violated his fiduciary duty.

CHAPTER REVIEW QUESTIONS: Answers and Explanations

1. **d.** An agency is fundamentally about the elements of consent (by words or actions) and control of the agent by the principal. (a) and (b) are wrong because no formal agreement is required and no definite time period need exist. (c) is wrong because parties may form an agency relationship not only expressly but also impliedly. (e) is wrong because an agency relationship does not require an attorney.

2. **a.** Manager sets Ernest's workweek (direction and control) and he is paid a regular salary and benefits rather than being paid upon invoice. Thus, he must be an employee agent and thus (a) is correct and (b) and (d) are wrong. (c) is wrong because Ernest was hired to "supervise." (e) is wrong because no such agency classifications exist.

3. **a.** Under the rules of ratification, the principal (Gray Industries) may still ratify the contract even if its agent (Dorian) was not authorized to do so at the time. (b), (c), (d), and (e) are wrong because (1) Dorian's authority was clearly not "actual" and (2) Gray may still disavow the contract because there was not actual or apparent authority.

4. **c.** The principal's duty to the agent is typically limited to payment and reimbursement. The duty of loyalty is owed by agents, but not by principals. (a), (b), (d), and (e) are all correct statements of law regarding the agency relationship.

5. **a.** The duty of care requires the highest level of conduct in the handling of the agent's affairs. (b), (c), and (e) are all fiduciary duties that are not related to the duty of care. (d) is an incorrect legal term.

CHAPTER 11

Employment Relationships and Labor Law

©philsajonesen/Getty Images

Learning Objectives

After studying this chapter, students who have mastered the material will be able to:

11-1 Assess the origins and impact of the labor movement on modern labor law.

11-2 Explain the fundamentals and impact of the employment-at-will doctrine.

11-3 Describe the main statutory protections for workers and regulations for employers in the areas of wages and hours, retirement, health care, sudden job loss, work-related injuries, and workplace safety.

11-4 List the benefits provided by federal law for workers who are in need of a leave for medical purposes or to care for an ill family member.

11-5 Identify federal statutes that impact labor-management relations and give examples of specific protections for workers that are set out in each law.

11-6 Explain the process for forming a certified labor union.

11-7 Describe the rights of and limits on workers in regard to engaging in collective bargaining and strikes and analyze the potential impact of a work stoppage.

11-8 Differentiate between an economic strike and an unfair labor practices strike.

11-9 Provide examples of illegal work stoppages.

The nature and character of the relationship between employer and employee is continually evolving. Modern-day employees enjoy protection via federal, state, and municipal laws and administrative regulations that are intended to guard against abusive or oppressive actions or policies of employers. This chapter covers laws related to the *well-being* of employees, and it examines *labor law,* which governs the rights of workers to organize and operate labor unions. A working knowledge of employment regulation and labor law is fundamental for business owners and managers for reducing the risk of liability in hiring and managing their workforce. Note that employment discrimination law is covered in the next chapter. In this chapter, students will learn about

- Federal and state laws related to employee wages and hours, retirement, health care, unemployment, and workplace injuries and safety and special laws and protections for employees who are minors.
- Laws that guarantee workers the right to unionize and those that protect workers from being required to join a union.
- Regulations that govern labor union practices and employer conduct in regard to dealing with proposed and established labor unions.

364 UNIT THREE | Regulation in the Workplace

ORIGINS OF EMPLOYMENT REGULATION AND LABOR LAW

As the American economy boomed with the dawn of the industrial age, employment opportunities shifted away from agriculture and toward industrial production beginning in the mid-1880s. The Industrial Revolution was fueled in part by the availability of an abundant workforce consisting of immigrants and displaced farmers willing to work long hours for low wages. Conditions in the industrial plants were brutal and dangerous, and exploitation of unskilled labor was common and of little concern to most politicians of that era. Workers who were injured on the job were terminated and given no compensation for medical care. In the absence of any compulsory education laws or financial alternatives, industrial labor families sent young children to work, including work in coal mines and slaughterhouses. Attempts by workers to organize or to bargain were met by industrialists with physical intimidation, assault, and job loss.

However, in the early 1900s, a growing labor movement, inspired by the increased political power of immigrant groups and a growing intolerance of the public for corporate abuses,[1] forced the federal government to legislate federal protections for employees regarding working conditions, unionization, and child labor laws. Eventually, additional worker protections related to wages and hours, injuries on the job, workplace safety, and layoffs were added to the federal labor statutes.

LO 11-2

Explain the fundamentals and impact of the employment-at-will doctrine.

EMPLOYMENT-AT-WILL DOCTRINE

The **employment-at-will** doctrine is a deep-seated common law rule that exists in some form in every U.S. jurisdiction.[2] Fundamentally, the doctrine permits employers to terminate an **at-will employee** with or without advance notice and with or without just cause, subject to certain exceptions. So long as the termination does not fall under one of the exceptions, the employer is insulated from a wrongful-termination lawsuit. The employment-at-will doctrine reflects the principal's wide latitude in decision making when exercising the power and right to terminate an employee. However, several important exceptions limit the applicability of the rule. The employment-at-will doctrine does not apply in cases where (1) the employee has an express or implied contract, (2) courts have fashioned a common law exception, or (3) there is some specific statutory protection against job termination (such as antidiscrimination laws).

LO 11-1

Assess the origins and impact of the labor movement on modern labor law.

Express Contracts

One major exception to the employment-at-will rule occurs when an employee has an express contractual relationship with the employer that is intended to displace the employment-at-will rule. When the parties enter into a contract, the rights of the **contractual employee** in the case of termination are spelled out in the contract. Typically, an employment contract will provide that employers may terminate the employee only for "good cause," such as a violation of a workplace rule or commission of a criminal act in the course of his employment. The contract ordinarily lists the events that cause termination, and the parties agree on any posttermination obligations. The parties may also formally agree to some type of severance pay in the event that the employer terminates the employee for any other reason than the causes listed in the contract.

---

[1]Upton Sinclair's classic novel *The Jungle,* which detailed employee abuses and described unthinkable sanitary conditions in turn-of-the-century Chicago meat factories, is cited in the legislative history for many worker protection statutes as a basis for the need for regulation. It is an example of how literature can influence the law.

[2]One state, Montana, does not use the term *employment-at-will,* but a common law doctrine insulating employers from wrongful-termination claims under certain circumstances does exist.

CHAPTER ELEVEN | Employment Relationships and Labor Law

Labor Contracts While some employment agreements are contracts between managers and a business entity, some contracts give rights to nonmanagement employees as well. These contracts, called *collective bargaining agreements (CBAs),* are negotiated by a labor union on behalf of a group of employees. CBAs often provide protection by prescribing a process that must be used by the employer before terminating an employee. The process is designed to ensure that treatment of employees is consistent with the standards in the CBA. CBAs and labor unions are covered in detail later in this chapter.

Common Law Exceptions

The employment-at-will rule is decidedly tilted towards protecting the interests of the employer, and courts have recognized that a strict application of the rule sometimes results in unjust treatment of the employee and a detriment to the public at large. Courts have fashioned several common law exceptions that help to limit the harshness of the rule on employees. They are (1) protection via an *implied contract* and (2) *the public policy exception,* also called *the covenant of good faith and fair dealing exception* in some states. It is important to note that not every state recognizes every exception, and some states, such as Georgia, Florida, and Rhode Island, do not recognize any common law exceptions to the rule. Figure 11.1 shows the employment-at-will exceptions by state.

Implied Contracts An employment-at-will relationship may be converted to a contract relationship if the employer acts in a manner that would lead a reasonable person to believe that the employer intended to offer the employee protection from termination without cause. This protection, called an *implied contract,* may arise in two circumstances. First, a manual or bulletin (such as an employee handbook) that is drafted and distributed

FIGURE 11.1 Employment-at-Will Exceptions by State

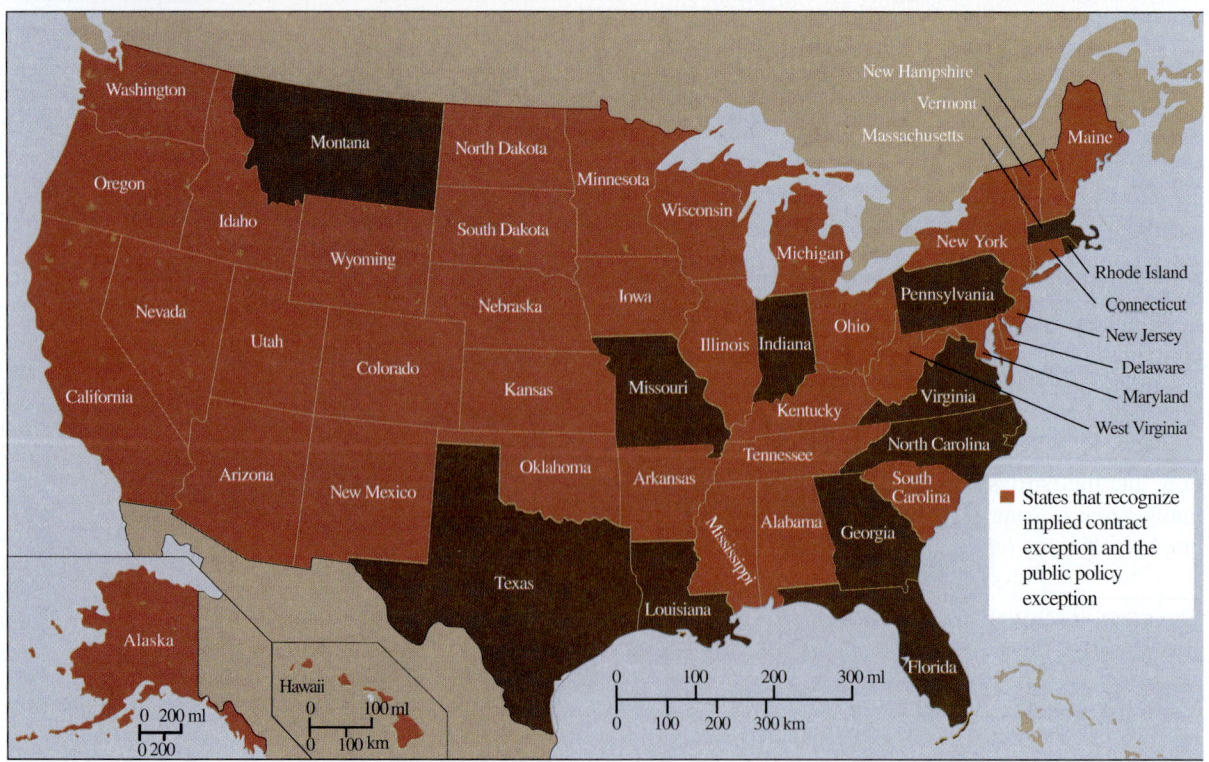

by the employer may give rise to an implied contract theory if the manual extends some protections or process to the employee that she would not have under the employment-at-will doctrine. If the employee shows that she would reasonably conclude that the employer was presenting the manual as a statement of the conditions under which employment could continue, an implied contract may exist. This may be true even where the employer has inserted disclaimer language (e.g., "This handbook is not a contract") so long as it was reasonable for an employee to assume that he was entitled to a benefit by virtue of the handbook's provisions.

In Case 11.1, a state appellate court reviews a jury's conclusion that an employer's use of a progressive discipline system in its employee handbook created an implied contract.

CASE 11.1 Buttrick v. Intercity Alarms, 2009 Mass. App. Div. 97 (2009)

FACT SUMMARY From the late 1980s through 2004, Intercity Alarms employed Buttrick during three nonconsecutive periods of years. During that time, it issued at least three versions of its Employee Reference Manual (Manual). At the start of this second period of employment, the operations manager reviewed the Manual with Buttrick and insisted that it was "very necessary" to sign the acknowledgment form. Buttrick subsequently left Intercity Alarms on good terms. In February 2002, Intercity Alarms recruited Buttrick back to the company to fill the position of senior service technician. Before he returned for his third stint, Buttrick was given the Manual, which contained day-to-day employment policies such as attire as well as a system of progressive discipline. The section entitled "Disciplinary Policy" stated: "It is the policy of Intercity Alarms that no disciplinary action taken against any employee will be arbitrary, capricious, unreasonable or discriminatory."

The next paragraph provided, "No company likes to discipline or separate its employees from employment, however, disciplinary action will be taken whenever an employee violates any rule of the company, fails to adhere to any policies and procedures, or fails to uphold the spirit of our corporate objectives. . . . [T]he severity of the action taken will be in accordance with the following: Verbal Counseling . . . Written Counseling . . . Suspension."

There was no provision for termination in that section. The Manual also stated that the employer may unilaterally modify the Manual's terms, and that the Manual serves only as a guide, not an employment contract.

On May 4, 2004, a dispute developed regarding Buttrick's handling of a potential sales lead. The general manager fired Buttrick without any warning or counseling. Buttrick sued Intercity for wrongful termination, arguing that the Manual was an implied contract and that Intercity had breached the contract because it failed to adhere to its own system of progressive discipline. A jury found in favor of Buttrick and awarded him $41,800 in damages. Intercity appealed.

SYNOPSIS OF DECISION AND OPINION The Appeals Court of Massachusetts upheld the jury's verdict in favor of Buttrick. While the court conceded that a number of factors weighed against the finding of an implied contract, a number of factors were present that supported its existence. The court reasoned that when Buttrick began his second and third stints at Intercity Alarms, he signed for a Manual and gave his consent to the terms as a condition of his employment. His employer called special attention to the Manual by not only distributing copies on four occasions, but also by at least on one occasion reviewing its terms personally with Buttrick and requiring him to sign for it because of the importance of the noncompetition clause. Therefore, the court concluded that the terms of the Manual, including progressive discipline, were part of an implied employment contract.

WORDS OF THE COURT: Reliance Requirement "Intercity Alarms failed to show that Buttrick's reliance upon the manual as creating binding employer obligations was unreasonable as a matter of law. [T]he context of the preparation and distribution of

(continued)

the policies is . . . the most persuasive proof that it would be almost inevitable for an employee to regard it as a binding commitment, legally enforceable, concerning the terms and conditions of employment. In light of the special attention paid to the manual here, as well as the mandatory language, specificity, and detail, Buttrick reasonably could have expected that his employer had committed to abiding by the terms therein. Neither the standard disclaimer nor the reservation of the right to make unilateral modifications precluded the formation of an enforceable contract. The modern trend in the law undermined the employer's position here."

Case Questions

1. Why did the court overlook the "disclaimer language" in the Manual? Shouldn't that have influenced its analysis?
2. What procedures should have Intercity followed to avoid liability in this situation?
3. *Focus on Critical Thinking:* Should the appellate court allow the jury's verdict to stand from a public policy perspective? If there is no statute to follow, isn't the court filling in the gaps and inserting its own view of how employees should be treated rather than leaving it to the legislature?

The second way in which an implied contract may be created involves an oral promise made by an employer and that a reasonable person would believe extends protection against termination without cause. Suppose, for example, that Rousseau has worked for 20 years at World Industries. At a luncheon honoring Rousseau, the president of World Industries says, "In honor of your excellent service, you have a job at this company until you wish to retire!" The next week, Rousseau is terminated. If a court determines that the language used by the president would lead a reasonable person to believe that Rousseau was more than just an employee-at-will, World Industries may be liable for a wrongful-termination claim. Of course, any contract theory, express or implied, must be based on the standards in contract law for formation and performance of a contract, which were covered in Unit Two.

> **KEY POINT**
>
> Courts apply exceptions very narrowly. An employee-at-will must clearly fit into one of the categories of exceptions in order to be protected.

Public Policy Exception One important exception that displaces the employment-at-will rule recognizes that allowing employers to terminate an employee for certain reasons may contradict *public policy* (welfare of the general public). The public policy exception is a narrowly applied common law rule that places the public welfare ahead of the rights of an employer. This provision is best thought of as a backstop provision for situations in which no specific statute is applicable, but the termination was inconsistent with the general public's well-being.

However, it should be stressed that courts have been *reluctant* to expand the narrow public policy exception. In *Bammert v. Don's Super-Valu, Inc.,*[3] the Wisconsin Supreme Court refused to apply the public policy exception when the wife of a police officer alleged that she was fired in retaliation for her husband's arresting her employer's wife. The court held that the public policy exception was too narrow to include specific retaliatory conduct when there was a dubious connection to any public policy objectives.

The *Bammert* decision illustrates an important point in understanding the public policy exception to the employment-at-will doctrine: It is limited in scope. Absent a specific statutory protection (such as a whistleblower law), the threshold for relief using a public policy justification is very high. Some examples include refusal to commit an illegal act (such as filing a false tax return), exercising a legal right (such as refusal to take a polygraph test),

---

[3] 646 N.W.2d 365 (Wis. 2002).

or performing an important act (such as the prevention of a violent crime). For example, in *Gardner v. Loomis Armored Inc.*,[4] the Washington Supreme Court ruled that an armored car guard who was fired after he violated company rules by leaving his armored car was entitled to be reinstated in his job. Gardner had left his truck to save a bank manager who was running from the bank and being chased by a knife-wielding bank robber. After locking the truck, he ran to her rescue and prevented harm to her. The court explained that there was no specific legal duty for Gardner to act; however, public policy and societal values encourage heroic conduct and assistance for those whose life is in danger.

Statutory Exceptions

Certain federal and state statutes also displace common law employment-at-will rules. Perhaps the best examples are the antidiscrimination laws that prohibit termination (and many other workplace actions) based on certain discriminatory motivations such as race or gender.[5] Other statutes prevent employers from terminating employees for specific reasons such as being absent due to jury duty[6] or attempting to form a union.

State Whistleblower Statutes Important statutory prohibitions for business owners and managers are derived from federal and state statutory protections of **whistleblowers**. *Whistleblower* is a colloquial term used in reference to an employee or agent who reports unlawful conduct or a statutory violation by his employer to the authorities. In general, employers may not terminate an employee for making a report to the authorities (i.e., "blowing the whistle") about the employer's conduct. Each state follows its own whistleblowing statute, but, most commonly, whistleblowers are protected when they report the violation of a law or standard by their employer to the authorities. Some states cover whistleblowing only by government employees or employees of government contractors. Although certain jurisdictions limit whistleblower protection to employees whose disclosures involve conduct that could result in some harm to the employees or the public at large, a minority of states have extended that protection to employees whose disclosures involve *any* illegal or improper conduct.

Most states also require that the whistleblower must suffer an adverse employment action to be covered under the statute. Therefore, prospective employees and job applicants are typically not covered. For example, in *Wurtz v. Beecher Metro District,*[7] the Michigan Supreme Court held that a city administrator whose contract was not renewed by the municipal board could not maintain a whistleblower suit because he was not an "employee" as defined by the state whistleblower protection law. The court pointed out that the the city administrator would have been covered during the duration of his contract, but once the contract expired, he was no longer protected.

Separate and Independent Defense Employers may terminate employees who are whistleblowers if they can show that they terminated the employee for reasons that are *separate* and *independent* of any whistleblowing. For example, suppose that Padraig is an employee of Celtic Crystal Company (CCC). Over the past year, Padraig has been suspended twice for poor work and lateness. His manager warned him that any more instances of lateness would result in termination. On Monday, Padraig discovers that CCC has failed

---

[4]913 P.2d 377 (Wash. 1996).

[5]Employment discrimination is covered in detail in Chapter 12, "Employment Discrimination."

[6]For example, a statute in Pennsylvania prohibits employers from terminating, demoting, or depriving employees of seniority or other benefits because they have responded to a jury summons or have served as a juror. See 42 Pa. Cons. Stat. § 4563.

[7]848 N.W.2d 121 (Mich. 2014).

to take appropriate measures to remove a hazardous substance from the CCC warehouse. Padraig notifies the authorities that CCC is out of compliance. CCC learns of the complaint and its source on Tuesday. On Friday, Padraig is late for work and is terminated. Padraig is clearly protected as a whistleblower in most jurisdictions. However, if CCC provides evidence that it intended to terminate Padraig prior to the whistleblowing or that the decision, in light of Padraig's disciplinary record at CCC, was made independent of the whistleblowing, CCC will most likely avoid liability for wrongful termination in violation of the whistleblower statute.

In Case 11.2, a state court analyzed whether an employer's reasons for termination of an employee were sufficiently separate and independent to avoid liability under a state whistleblower law.

CASE 11.2 McQueary v. The Pennsylvania State University, No. 2012-1804 (Pa. Ct. Com. Pl. Nov. 30, 2016)

FACT SUMMARY After the results of a grand jury investigation related to the sexual abuse of children by a Pennsylvania State University (Penn State) employee and a subsequent cover-up by Penn State administrators were released in November 2011, Penn State's interim athletic director summoned Mike McQueary, an assistant football coach at Penn State, to a meeting. At the meeting, the interim athletic director read a script that had been prepared by a Penn State attorney that informed McQueary that he was being placed on administrative leave and banned him from all Penn State facilities and activities including his own office. He was also required to turn in his keys, cell phone, and any university-owned property. Subsequently, McQueary learned during a July 2012 press conference called by Penn State administrators that he had been officially terminated.

McQueary filed a claim under the Pennsylvania Whistleblower Act alleging that Penn State had fired him when they discovered that McQueary had provided testimony to the grand jury about McQueary witnessing the sexual abuse of a minor by Penn State football coach Jerry Sandusky in a Penn State locker room in 2001. McQueary testified that he told head football coach Paterno, Penn State athletic director Curley, and vice president for administration Shultz about the incident. Based on McQueary's and other witnesses' testimony, the grand jury charged Sandusky, Curley, and Shultz with various criminal offenses related to sexual abuse of minors and failing to report the abuse to authorities. Penn State defended the whistleblower claim by asserting that McQueary was an employee-at-will whose appointment was not renewed after the new incoming head football coach determined there was no room for McQueary to continue as part of the team's new coaching staff.

SYNOPSIS OF DECISION AND OPINION The court ruled in favor of McQueary and awarded him $5 million in damages under the Whistleblower Act plus $1.7 million in legal fees. The court held that McQueary's good faith reporting of the sexual abuse to his supervisors qualified under the statute as a protected act of whistleblowing. Under the state Whistleblower Act, the burden shifts from McQueary to Penn State to prove that the termination was for "separate and legitimate reasons" from any whistleblowing activity. The court rejected Penn State's contention that McQueary's termination was unrelated to his grand jury testimony and was the result of routine personnel changes and a new incoming head coach. The court pointed to evidence that the new head coach had never interviewed McQueary and had never looked at his personnel file and that the decision to fire McQueary was contemporaneous with the administrators finding out about his grand jury testimony.

WORDS OF THE COURT: Separate and Legitimate Reason "Penn State's asserted defenses must be analyzed in the context of its conduct both pre and post Grand Jury Presentment as this is a case where actions speak louder than words. . . . But for the Grand Jury presentment, no Penn State

(continued)

coach would have lost their job and [the new head coach] would not have been hired. Accordingly, [the new head coach's] decision not to interview or hire Mr. McQueary does not constitute a separate and legitimate reason for the termination of Mr. McQueary."

Case Questions

1. What does the court mean when it calls this "a case where actions speak louder than words"?
2. If the new head football coach had interviewed McQueary, reviewed his personnel file, and then concluded that he was not qualified for the job, would that have affected McQueary's whistleblower claim? Why or why not?
3. *Focus on Critical Thinking:* In addition to his whistleblower claim, McQueary also filed suit against Penn State for intentional torts. What other claims might McQueary have against Penn State? McQueary reported the sexual abuse to his supervisors but not to any law enforcement agency. Did he have an ethical obligation beyond reporting it to Penn State administrators? Should he have reported it directly to law enforcement authorities? Should he have intervened when he witnessed the abuse? Explain.

Federal Whistleblower Statutes Federal employees are protected from retaliation for whistleblowing by the Whistleblower Protection Act of 1989.[8] The law also covers employees of companies that contract with the government to provide goods or services (e.g., a construction company building a federal highway). Additionally, some federal statutes give specific antiretaliation protections for employees who disclose conduct that violates the particular statute. For example, the False Claims Act protects employees who disclose that their firm has committed fraud in dealing with contracts with the federal government. Similarly, both the federal Fair Labor Standards Act and the Sarbanes-Oxley Act (related to the regulation of corporations) provide whistleblowers with specific statutory protections for reporting or testifying against their employer in an investigation, hearing, or trial.

CONCEPT SUMMARY *Employment Relationships*

- The employment-at-will doctrine holds that employers have the right to terminate an employee with or without advance notice and with or without just cause, subject to certain exceptions.
- An important exception to the employment-at-will rule occurs when an employee has an express contractual relationship with the employer.
- An employment-at-will relationship may be converted into an implied contract relationship if the employer has acted in a manner that would lead a reasonable person to believe that the employer intended to offer the employee protection from termination without cause; the employer's action could be either a statement in a manual or bulletin or an oral promise.
- Certain federal and state statutes also displace common law employment-at-will rules, including statutes providing protection for whistleblowers.
- The public policy exception is a narrow common law rule that places the public welfare ahead of the rights of an employer and prohibits employers from terminating an employee for certain reasons that contradict public policy.

---

[8] 5 U.S.C. § 1201.

LO 11-3

Describe the main statutory protections for workers and regulations for employers in the areas of wages and hours, retirement, health care, sudden job loss, work-related injuries, and workplace safety.

EMPLOYMENT REGULATION

Congress and state legislatures have passed laws intended to protect employees from oppressive or unfair practices in the workplace.[9] These employment protection laws are intended to safeguard the welfare of individual workers who have little or no bargaining power in the employer-employee relationship. Federal law often works in tandem with state law in regulating employers with respect to minimum wages, overtime pay, use of child labor, sudden job loss, workplace injuries, workplace safety, and medical leaves.

Wages and Hours

The centerpiece of wage and hour law protections is the **Fair Labor Standards Act (FLSA)**[10] passed in 1938 and intended to cover all employers engaged in interstate commerce.[11] Although the statute is expansive, its primary provisions mandate (1) payment of a minimum wage,[12] (2) a maximum 40-hour workweek, (3) overtime pay, and (4) restrictions on children working in certain occupations and during certain hours. The FLSA and its regulations are administered and enforced by the U.S. Department of Labor.

Minimum Wage, Maximum Hours, and Overtime

The FLSA establishes a minimum wage to be paid to every employee covered under the act. Over the years, Congress has raised the minimum wage to its current level of $7.25.[13] However, states are permitted to set a higher minimum wage level for employees working within a state's jurisdictional boundaries. Many legal issues that surround the wage and hour provisions of the FLSA involve whether employees are entitled to be paid for time in the workplace that is not directly related to the employee's job duties. Congress provided clarification by amending the FLSA with the **Portal-to-Portal Act**[14] to provide guidelines for what constitutes compensable work. The Portal-to-Portal Act provides two broad exceptions to FLSA wage and hour requirements. Unless the activity is integral and indispensable to their principal job, employees are not entitled to compensation for (1) time spent by an employee traveling to and from the actual place of the employee's job and (2) time spent by an employee on activities performed before or after the principal activities in a workday.

Courts have interpreted principal activity to include all activities that are an integral and indispensable part of the principal activity. For example, the U.S. Supreme Court ruled that the time battery-plant employees spent showering and changing clothes because the chemicals in the plant are toxic to human beings was compensable.[15] The Court also held that the time meatpacker employees spent sharpening their knives was compensable because dull knives would slow down production on the assembly line and affect the appearance of the meat, cause waste, and lead to accidents.[16] In contrast, courts rejected a claim by poultry-plant employees that time spent waiting to don protective gear was compensable because such waiting was two steps removed from the production activity on the assembly line.[17]

In Case 11.3, the U.S. Supreme Court considered whether employees' time spent undergoing routine security screenings is compensable under the Fair Labor Standards Act.

---

[9]Note that although some municipalities have also passed worker protections that supplement the federal and state protections, the employer-employee relationship is typically considered the province of state and federal lawmakers.
[10]29 U.S.C. § 201.
[11]Given the interpretation by modern courts, the statute covers virtually all employers.
[12]The FLSA is sometimes called the *minimum wage law* but actually includes substantially more protections.
[13]For an update on the federal minimum wage, see Connect.
[14]29 U.S.C. § 251.
[15]*Steiner v. Mitchell*, 350 U.S. 247 (1956).
[16]*Mitchell v. King Packing Co.*, 350 U.S. 260 (1956).
[17]*IBP, Inc. v. Alvarez*, 546 U.S. 21 (2005).

CASE 11.3 Integrity Staffing Solutions v. Busk, 574 U.S. 27 (2014)

FACT SUMMARY Integrity Staffing Solutions, Inc. (Integrity), provides warehouse staffing to Amazon throughout the United States. Jesse Busk (Busk) worked as an hourly employee of Integrity at warehouses in Nevada. As a warehouse employee, Busk retrieved products from the shelves and packaged those products for delivery to Amazon customers. Integrity required its employees to undergo a security screening before leaving the warehouse at the end of each day. During this screening, employees removed items such as wallets, keys, and belts from their persons and passed through metal detectors.

In 2010, Busk and another employee filed suit against Integrity for alleged violations of the FLSA and Nevada labor laws, alleging that they were entitled to compensation under the FLSA for time spent waiting to undergo and actually undergoing the security screenings. They alleged that such time amounted to roughly 25 minutes each day and the screenings were conducted to prevent employee theft and thus occurred solely for the benefit of the employers and their customers. The trial court ruled in favor of Integrity, but the court of appeals reversed. The court of appeals held that the screenings were compensable as they were required by the employer, necessary to the employees' primary work as warehouse employees, and done for Integrity's benefit. Integrity appealed.

SYNOPSIS OF DECISION AND OPINION The U.S. Supreme Court reversed the court of appeals's decision and found in favor of Integrity. The Court ruled that the lower court erred in focusing on whether the activity was required by the employer. Instead, the appropriate test was based on whether or not the activities were the principal activity or activities that the employee was employed to perform. Because Integrity did not employ its workers to undergo security screenings, but to retrieve products from warehouse shelves and package those products for shipment to Amazon customers, the activities did not qualify as compensable under the FLSA. Moreover, the activity did not meet the "integral and indispensable" standard.

WORDS OF THE COURT: Intrinsic Element Requirement "The security screenings also were not 'integral and indispensable' to the employees' duties as warehouse workers. [A]n activity is not integral and indispensable to an employee's principal activities unless it is an intrinsic element of those activities and one with which the employee cannot dispense if he is to perform those activities. The screenings were not an intrinsic element of retrieving products from warehouse shelves or packaging them for shipment. And Integrity Staffing could have eliminated the screenings altogether without impairing the employees' ability to complete their work."

Case Questions

1. The employees in this case pointed to the fact that Integrity could have greatly reduced the amount of time for screening to just a few minutes by employing more personnel and metal detectors. Should the Court have given more weight to that fact? Why or why not?
2. What did the Court identify as the error made by the court of appeals? Why was it important?
3. *Focus on Critical Thinking:* Is this decision consistent with the objectives of the FLSA? Does it protect workers from unfair and harsh treatment by an employer? Should Congress or the Department of Labor define work hours more carefully? How would you craft a definition?

40-Hour Workweek In addition to setting the minimum wage, the FLSA sets a standard workweek at 40 hours in a seven-day period. Any hours worked by an employee over the standard workweek are entitled to **overtime compensation**. Overtime compensation is calculated by multiplying the hourly base rate of the employee times one and one-half. Thus, an employee making $10 per hour in her normal base pay is entitled to $15 per hour for overtime compensation. Note that all wage and hour laws under the FLSA assume a base unit of time of one week. For example, suppose that Mikhail has morning child care responsibilities and requests a schedule for seven hours a day on Monday through Friday and five hours on Saturday. Although Mikhail works six days per week, he is not entitled to overtime pay under the FLSA because his total hours did not exceed 40 in a one-week period. Employees are not entitled to overtime pay based on an eight-hour workday. If Mikhail were to work four days a week for 10 hours a day, no overtime would be earned.

Some workers receive a set weekly salary for a 37.5-hour workweek. Suppose that Kim works as a shipping clerk from 8 a.m. until 4:30 p.m., with a 60-minute lunch, on Monday through Friday. One day, her boss asks her to stay late to finish preparing a shipment, and she stays until 6:30 p.m. Kim is not entitled to overtime pay because she has worked only 39.5 hours in that week.

Exempt Employees

Perhaps the most important concept that business owners and managers should understand about the FLSA is that the act does not cover all employees. Employers are not bound by the FLSA for employees classified as **exempt employees**. The underlying concept behind the FLSA is to level the playing field for employees who are in an untenable bargaining position with employers. Consistent with that concept, the law imputes a certain level of bargaining power for professional and management-level employees and, therefore, exempts them from FLSA protections. When the FLSA was first enacted, the division between management and labor was relatively clear and classification was based on salary thresholds. However, as the lines between labor and management blurred during the rise of the information age and the general rise in the skill, education, and wages of workers, classification became increasingly problematic. In 2016, the U.S. Department of Labor issued a rule that updated the annual salary threshold below which workers qualify for FLSA protection (including overtime pay). To be considered exempt, an employee must make a minimum annual salary of $47,476 per year, or $913 per week. Those earning more than $134,004 are classified as highly compensated employees and are always presumed to be exempt. The rule also included a new system of automatic updates of the annual salary threshold beginning in 2020 that ensures the threshold amount is raised to the 40th percentile of full-time salaried workers in the "lowest-wage Census region."[18]

Typically, workers paid by the hour are not considered exempt. However, being paid a salary does not automatically make an employee exempt. Exempt duties can be classified as either executive, administrative, or professional. Note that although the term *white-collar employees* is somewhat outdated, in the context of FLSA law, white-collar employees typically engage in employment that does not require physical labor or involve repetitive tasks, and they are typically paid an annual salary rather than on an hourly basis. In classifying an employee as covered or exempt, employers must take into account multiple factors that are known as the *duties* test:

- Education or skill level or certifications required for the position, salary level, and compensation method (i.e., commission versus hourly).
- Amount of physical labor required.
- Amount of repetitive tasks (e.g., performing an unskilled task over and over again, as does a clerk in a company mailroom).
- Degree of supervision required by the employer.

---

[18] 29 C.F.R. pt. 541.

Examples of employees who are *not* covered by the FLSA include (1) professionals who require specialized study and certifications, such as attorneys, physicians, teachers, and accountants; (2) management or supervisory employees; (3) computer programmers and engineers; and (4) employees subject to certain certification and regulatory requirements, such as insurance adjusters or dental hygienists.

In Case 11.4, a federal appeals court analyzes the FLSA's executive exemption.

> **KEY POINT**
>
> Employees are covered under the FLSA if (1) they earn below the minimum salary threshold established by the Department of Labor or (2) the duties test indicates that an employee's job requirements qualify him for coverage. Highly compensated employees are always considered exempt.

CASE 11.4 Madden v. Lumber One Home Center, 745 F.3d 899 (8th Cir. 2014)

FACT SUMMARY Madden, O'Bar, and Wortman were hired by Lumber One Home Center (Lumber One) to serve as supervisors and managers in a newly established Lumber One store. The employees were salaried, labeled as executives, and classified by Lumber One as exempt from overtime pay under the FLSA provision that exempted "any employee employed in a bona fide executive, administrative, or professional capacity" from overtime pay requirements.

In anticipation of the new store opening, Madden and O'Bar assembled shelves and received merchandise. Once the store opened, Madden and O'Bar completed data entry tasks and helped out in the lumberyard by assisting customers, unloading trucks, and collecting trash when needed. Wortman worked in the lumberyard and waited on customers, helped load trucks, and on occasion would direct the truck drivers regarding where to make deliveries. The parties agreed that the plaintiffs worked overtime throughout their employment at Lumber One. However, because Lumber One classified Madden, O'Bar, and Wortman as executives, the employees were not paid overtime.

Madden, O'Bar, and Wortman filed suit against Lumber One claiming they were improperly classified as executives rather than as employees and therefore were entitled to overtime pay under the FLSA. The jury found in favor of Lumber One, but the trial court overturned the jury's verdict and ruled in favor of the employees. Lumber One appealed the court's ruling.

SYNOPSIS OF DECISION AND OPINION The U.S. Court of Appeals for the Eighth Circuit ruled in favor of Madden and O'Bar but reversed the trial court's ruling relating to Wortman. The court reasoned that in order to qualify for an executive exemption, Lumber One must show, among other things, that the exempt employees had the authority to hire or fire employees, or that their recommendations regarding personnel decisions were given particular weight by the decision maker. Because Lumber One's owner made all of the hiring and firing decisions at the store and did not consult Madden or O'Bar, the court reasoned that Lumber One did not satisfy the "authority" test or the "particular weight" required to exempt an employee from FLSA coverage. The court rejected Lumber One's argument that the owner's informal solicitation of input from existing employees about an applicant was sufficient to meet the exemption requirements.

In the case of Wortman, the court ruled that Lumber One had made a sufficient showing that Wortman had been involved in recommending at least one driver to Lumber One's owner. Therefore, the court held that Wortman could reasonably be classified as a supervisor who is exempt from overtime under the FLSA.

WORDS OF THE COURT: Personnel Decisions Requirement "[Lumber One's owner] testified that none of the plaintiffs hired or fired other employees. Therefore, in order to satisfy the fourth element, Lumber One needed to present evidence at

(continued)

trial that the plaintiffs were consulted about personnel decisions and that [the owner] gave each of their opinions particular weight regarding specific hiring decisions. Prior to hiring a new employee, [the owner] generally asked all of the [store] employees if they knew the applicant and could provide information about that person, and Lumber One believes this is sufficient to support the jury's verdict.

"At trial, [the owner] generically described how he elicited input from employees about applicants and how he used the information he received. For example, when asked if the plaintiffs were ever consulted during the screening process for new applicants, [he] responded: '[W]e would always ask all of our people if they knew someone before we hired them. When we would be interviewing them, we would ask for input from them because these guys were from the local area and we'd always ask if they knew the people or could recommend or knew anything at all about them.' [The owner] also said he took this information seriously, adding that 'it was good information. We're hiring blind here, so any input we could have or reference, it was used in making that determination.' Lumber One did not present any evidence that the plaintiffs were involved in, for instance, screening applicants, conducting interviews, checking references, or anything else related to its hiring process. . . .

"The material point, however, is that in order to meet the fourth element of the executive exemption, Lumber One must present some proof that the purported executives' input into personnel decisions was given particular weight. For example, one way they could have done this is to show that the purported executives' input had more influence than hourly employees' input. This is especially true if that recommendation is the only evidence relied on for the exemption, which is what happened in this case."

Case Questions

1. What was Lumber One's primary argument as to why these employees were exempt from FLSA protection?
2. What distinction did the court make between Madden's and O'Bar's roles at Lumber One versus Wortman's role?
3. *Focus on Critical Thinking:* Recall from Chapter 4 that a court can sometimes disregard a jury's verdict and substitute its own ruling. That's what happened in this case. Is that fair? A jury of the employees' peers found that the employees were exempt under the FLSA, but a single judge disagreed. Should a judge have that power? What impact does such a ruling have on the community's confidence in the justice system?

KEY POINT

Coverage by the FLSA is not determined by job title. Some employees have job titles that include the word *executive*, but they still qualify for FLSA coverage (e.g., executive secretary).

Misclassification The consequences of misclassification may be severe. Unless an employee is clearly exempt from the FLSA coverage, she should be classified as a **covered (nonexempt) employee** under the FLSA provisions until such time as the employer has legal assurances that the employee is exempt. To understand the dilemma faced by employers over misclassification, suppose that Standish hires Alden as a customer service agent to handle complaints over the phone. Alden has a significant amount of practical experience and a diploma from a technical school. Standish agrees to pay Alden an annual base salary of $26,000. Because the work does not involve physical labor, Standish classifies Alden as exempt from the FLSA. Over the course of the next six months, due to an increase in customer complaints, Alden works an average of 50 hours per week on the phones trying to resolve complaints. Because Standish classified Alden as an employee with an annual salary and exempt from the FLSA, he does not pay Alden any overtime compensation.

Assume that the Department of Labor audits Standish and reclassifies Alden as being covered by the FLSA because of his relatively low salary level, the minimal educational

FIGURE 11.2 FLSA Liability

1. Calculate Alden's approximate hourly base rate:
   $26,000/52\ \text{weeks} = \$500\ \text{per week}$
   $\$500/40\ \text{hours} = \$12.50\ \text{per hour}$

2. Calculate Alden's overtime rate:
   $\$12.50 \times 1.5 = \$18.75$

3. Calculate overtime pay owed:
   $10\ \text{hr/wk} \times 24\ \text{wk (6 mo)} = 240\ \text{hr}$
   $\$18.75 \times 240 = \$4,500$

Because of the misclassification over six months, Standish owes Alden $4,500 in back pay, plus interest, as set out by the FLSA regulations.

---

requirements for the position, and the repetitive task of answering customer calls. In addition to any fine levied against Standish for violating the FLSA, the Department of Labor will order Standish to pay Alden back pay for any time worked by Alden over the 40-hour workweek. Figure 11.2 represents a sample calculation of Standish's potential liability.

 Self-Check Exempt versus Covered (Nonexempt) Employees

Which employees are exempt from the FLSA protections?

1. A chief information officer at a manufacturing company who earns an annual salary of $150,000.
2. An architect hired to work for a design-build construction company at a rate of $85,000 per year.
3. A cashier at a supermarket who is paid $10 per hour.
4. An assistant store manager whose duties also include routine work such as stocking shelves during busy seasons.
5. A secretary who is paid a salary of $500 per week and has set hours of employment.
6. An employee hired to sell life insurance for an insurance company who is paid a base salary of $15,000 plus a 10 percent commission on all insurance sold.

Answers to this Self-Check are provided at the end of the chapter.

Child Labor Laws

The FLSA outlaws the once common practice of sending school-age children to work instead of to school by imposing restrictions on hiring workers under 18 years old. Table 11.1 sets out restrictions for the age requirements that have been issued by the Department of Labor pursuant to its FLSA authority. It is important to note that children in family agricultural jobs and child actors are not subject to the FLSA restrictions, but state statutes often require appropriate educational standards to be met through the use of tutors and home schooling.

Every state has passed a child labor statute to supplement the federal law. For example, while the FLSA sets no limits on the hours a 16- or 17-year-old may work, most states have implemented their own hour limits for this age group. The FLSA is silent regarding employment certificates, commonly called *working papers,* yet most states have mandated some sort of documentation policy. It is imperative that a manager be aware of both federal and state law requirements.

TABLE 11.1 Child Labor Restrictions

Age	Restriction
Under 14	No employment except newspaper sale and delivery
14–15	Limited hours during school days in nonhazardous jobs (such as a busboy or dishwasher in a restaurant)
16–17	No limits on hours, but cannot work in dangerous jobs such as mining or heavy industry and other hazardous jobs as defined in FLSA regulations

State Wage and Hour Laws

In addition to federal statutes that protect the interest of workers, some states have adopted additional employee protections. These protections fit into one of four general categories:[19]

- **Minimum paid rest periods.** Some states require a minimum rest period for workers that is typically based on the ratio of rest period versus hours worked. For example, in Kentucky, employers are required to provide a 10-minute break for every four hours worked. These rest periods must be in addition to the regularly scheduled meal break.
- **Minimum paid meal periods.** Twenty-one states require employers to provide a certain period of time, typically 30 minutes, for a meal break during a normal workday. For example, in Nebraska, employers are required to pay employees for a 30-minute meal break for each eight-hour shift.
- **Payday requirements.** Many states regulate the frequency of paydays for employees. For example, in Maine, employers are required to pay employees twice per month with no more than a 16-day interval between pay periods.
- **Prevailing wages requirements.** The majority of states require that whenever taxpayer money is in a construction project above a certain threshold, the contractor must pay the prevailing wage. The prevailing wage refers to the hourly wage, usual benefits, and overtime paid in the largest city in each county to the majority of workers, laborers, and mechanics. For example, in Montana, prevailing wages must be paid for any publicly funded construction project costing in excess of $25,000.

Retirement

Employers are not required to establish retirement plans for their employees, although as a competitive matter many often do so to attract and retain high-quality employees. If an employer does offer retirement benefits, they are typically offered in the form of a **pension** or through a **tax-deferred retirement savings account** such as a 401(k)[20] plan. In a pension plan, the employer promises to pay a monthly sum to employees who retire from the company after a certain number of years of service. The amount is ordinarily based on the length of service and the employee's final salary rate as of the date of retirement. In a retirement savings account, the employee commits to saving a certain percentage of base pay in an account that is controlled directly by the employee and not the employer. The employee then has the ability to allocate her savings via various investment vehicles that range from very safe to high risk. Some employers match the employee's contribution by paying an extra amount into the account based on a certain percentage of the employee's base salary.

---

[19] *See State Labor Laws,* Wage & Hour Div., U.S. Dep't of Labor.

[20] The term *401(k)* is a shorthand reference to the Internal Revenue Code regulation that regulates tax-deferred savings plans.

The major benefit for the employee is that retirement savings grow without triggering any tax liability until the employee is ready to make retirement withdrawals from the account.

Regulation of Pensions and Retirement Accounts If employers establish either a pension fund or a retirement savings plan, the employer is subject to the requirements of a federal statute called the **Employee Retirement Income Security Act (ERISA)**[21] of 1974. The ERISA is a comprehensive set of laws and regulations that requires employers to make certain disclosures related to investment risk and provides transparency for plan beneficiaries. The ERISA establishes rules for conflict of interest (such as how much of a company's own stock can be held in a pension plan) and imposes certain fiduciary standards for investing and managing pension plans or administering retirement savings plans. Employers must adhere to record-keeping regulations and must treat all employees in accordance with a set of standardized vesting rules. The ERISA authorizes the Department of Labor to monitor pension and retirement savings plan administration. The department oversees the Labor Management Services Administration, in part to implement, administer, and enforce the ERISA.

Social Security

In addition to any pension or retirement plans offered by employers, workers are entitled to a retirement income from the federal government by virtue of the **Social Security Act (SSA) of 1935**. The SSA provides a broad set of benefits for workers that are funded by mandatory employment taxes paid by both employer and employee into a trust fund administered by the federal government. These employment taxes are mandated by the Federal Insurance Contributions Act (FICA).[22] Employees are entitled to retirement benefits based on how many credits they have earned during their working life. Credits are accrued as a worker progresses through his career no matter how many different employers the worker has over a lifetime. The SSA also provides for payments to be made when a worker becomes disabled, and it provides survivor benefits for spouses and children upon the death of a worker.

Health Care

The Patient Protection and Affordable Care Act,[23] discussed in Chapter 2, "Business and the Constitution," and below, mandates that all U.S. citizens be covered by a health care insurance plan. The law primarily relies on a combination of employer plans and government managed health care exchanges. While the public policy goal is that businesses will provide their employees with health care coverage, a business may choose not to provide coverage and instead pay a penalty fee to the U.S. government. As a competitive matter, many companies do provide employees with a health care plan option whereby the employer and employee share the costs of the insurance plan. If the employer does provide a health care plan, two federal statutes regulate certain aspects of administering the plan. First, the Health Insurance Portability and Accountability Act (HIPAA) sets administrative rules and standards designed to protect employee medical information and records from disclosure to a third party. Second, the Consolidated Omnibus Budget Reconciliation Act (COBRA)[24] mandates that employers provide continuous coverage to any employee who has been terminated even if the worker was terminated for cause.[25] COBRA requires that

Legal Speak >))

Vesting
An ERISA (Employee Retirement Income Security Act) guideline stipulating that employees are entitled to their benefits from various employer-contributed benefit plans within a certain period of time, even if they no longer work for the employer.

---

[21] 29 U.S.C. § 1001 et seq.
[22] 26 U.S.C. § 3101 et seq.
[23] 26 U.S.C. § 5000A.
[24] 29 U.S.C. § 1161.
[25] In egregious cases, such as that of an employee who is terminated for theft from the company, COBRA benefits may not apply.

the employer provide the exact same health coverage for up to 18 months. It is important to note that COBRA does not require employers to *pay* for the health plan premiums of a former employee. The employee has full responsibility for payment of all insurance premiums and administrative fees.

Patient Protection and Affordable Care Act of 2010 and Health Care and Education Reconciliation Act of 2010 On March 23, 2010, the Patient Protection and Affordable Care Act (PPACA) was signed into law. One week later, on March 30, 2010, the Health Care and Education Reconciliation Act (HCERA) of 2010 was enacted, adding to and amending parts of the PPACA. Together they have overhauled the U.S. health care system. The legislation was the subject of intense debate and extended media coverage, but from a business manager's perspective, much of the law's mandate was triggered in 2015. The law requires employers with 50 or more full-time employees to purchase health care insurance for their employees or face a penalty. It also offers small business owners (those employing fewer than 25 full-time workers) immediate tax incentives if they offer health care coverage to their employees and pay at least 50 percent of the total costs for their employees' coverage. Individuals not covered through their employer's policy are legally required to purchase health care insurance from a health care exchange that is set up by individual states (or groups of states). In 2018, employers that offer high-end health care plans (plans that cost more than $27,500 per year) to their employees are required to pay an additional tax based on the total cost of the plan.

Sudden Job Loss

After the Great Depression sent unemployment rates soaring to 20 percent and higher, Congress responded with the **Federal Unemployment Tax Act (FUTA)**[26] of 1935, which provided limited payments to workers who had been temporarily or permanently terminated from employment through no fault of their own. FUTA established a state-administered fund to provide payments to workers who have suffered sudden job loss. Only the employer pays FUTA taxes. In order to obtain unemployment benefits, the worker must actively seek new employment and, if necessary, retraining in a different field. Unemployment compensation is intended to cover workers who lose their jobs because of economic difficulties; it is not intended to reward an employee who was terminated for cause. However, because states set their own standards and procedures, the exact eligibility requirements and the amount available vary among different jurisdictions. The amount paid to those who qualify for assistance is generally nowhere near the gross or even net salary the displaced worker was earning.

Workplace Injuries

While historically tort law was the only mechanism for compensating an employee who suffered an injury on the job or a job-related illness, all states now have **workers' compensation** statutes. These statutes establish a structure for an injured employee to be compensated through a statutorily mandated insurance program as the *exclusive* remedy for workplace injuries or illnesses. Employees with job-related injuries or illnesses are paid based on a percentage of the employee's salary at the time of the occurrence. Workers' compensation statutes typically require the establishment of a system for processing claims through the state workers' compensation board (or a similarly named agency), and the compensation is funded through employer-paid insurance policies. Companies may also be self-insured if they meet their individual state's requirements for establishing a

---

[26] 26 U.S.C. § 3301 et seq.

fund that is sufficient to make payments to injured employees. The most important aspect of the workers' compensation system is that the employee is generally paid *regardless* of any issues related to fault or negligence of the employee, the employer, or any third party; however, certain defenses to a workers' compensation claim may be asserted by the employer. This plan ensures an injured worker a continuous income for an injury that requires her to stop working. In exchange for this compensation, the employee is barred from pursuing a negligence lawsuit related to the injury against the employer. The state statutes are often broad in terms of coverage, but most states exempt domestic workers and temporary or seasonal employees from protection.

Defenses to Workers' Compensation Claims   In many states, an injured worker is not entitled to workers' compensation if the injury is intentionally self-inflicted or was the result of a knowing violation of safety rules by the employee, the employee's willful misconduct or horseplay not condoned by the employer, or the employee's intoxication or illegal drug use. Should the employee fail to give the employer timely notice of the injury as determined by state statute, the claim is lost, and a failure to bring a claim within the state's statute of limitations can bar a claim.

Intentional Actions or Recklessness of the Employer   Two important exceptions to the workers' compensation laws are cases in which (1) an employer has engaged in actions that intentionally create conditions that result in harm or (2) an employer acts with a reckless disregard for the safety of its employees. In these cases, the injured or ill party may bypass the workers' compensation system and sue the employer for a full recovery including punitive damages. As a practical matter, however, although an injured employee may recover a higher amount through litigation, the prospect of immediate compensation and the uncertainties and delays inherent in litigation mean that many people will opt to file a workers' compensation claim rather than pursue litigation. In any case, once the injured party files a workers' compensation claim, he is barred from suing his employer in any suit related to the injury.

Course of Employment   In order to trigger protection under workers' compensation laws, the injury must meet two main criteria: (1) The injury was accidental and (2) the injury occurred within the course of employment. Accidental injuries are injuries that occur without any intent to cause harm or injure. The course of employment requirement varies by jurisdiction, but most state courts have interpreted the scope of employment requirement broadly and in favor of coverage of the injured worker. While cases where the employee is injured on the job at the worksite during regular business hours are clearly covered, off-premises activity is also covered so long as it is sufficiently related to the worker's employment. Even when the injury is indirectly related to the employee's job responsibilities, courts have been willing to extend workers' compensation coverage to the injured employee.

Regulation of Workplace Safety

While workers' compensation laws are designed to protect workers who are injured, the federal statute intended to *prevent* workplace injuries is the **Occupational Safety and Health Act (OSHA)**,[27] passed in 1970. The objective of OSHA statutes and regulation

---
[27] 29 U.S.C. § 651 et seq.

The OSHA statute was passed to prevent employee injuries in the workplace. Thurtell/Getty Images

is to make the workplace as safe as possible for workers engaged in business operations through (1) setting national safety standards, (2) mandating information disclosure and warnings of hazardous working areas and assignments, (3) establishing record-keeping and reporting requirements, and (4) imposing a general duty upon employers to keep a workplace reasonably safe. The OSHA law has broad coverage encompassing virtually every private employer. Federal, state, and local government units are exempt.

Occupational Safety and Health Administration The OSHA statute created the Occupational Safety and Health Administration, under the jurisdiction of the Department of Labor, to administer and enforce the statute. The administration has expansive enforcement authority, including routine or unscheduled worksite inspections, in carrying out the provisions of the law. Industries that are ultrahazardous (such as mining) are highly regulated by OSHA administrative rules. The administration also investigates complaints made by employees alleging that an employer violated safety standards. Employees making a complaint to the administration are protected from retaliation by the employer via the OSHA's whistleblowing provisions.[28]

OSHA Provisions The OSHA regulations have evolved into a complex and lengthy set of rules and standards because so many of the regulations are industry-specific. However, there are some provisions that apply to all employers. For example, employers with 11 or more employees are required to maintain records about the company's safety records and to document the investigation of any accidents. These reports must be kept current and prepared for inspection by the administration without any subpoena or advance notice required. If an employee is killed in a work-related accident or if three or more employees are hospitalized in one event, the employer is required to notify the administration as soon as possible and no later than eight business hours after the accident. Once notification is made, the administration dispatches an inspector to investigate the accident. If the employer is found to have been in violation of a specific or general safety standard, then the administration takes appropriate enforcement action, including levying fines, issuing cease-and-desist orders, and, in egregious cases, pursuing criminal charges against the company and its officers. In the event of a workplace death, the administration cooperates with local authorities that may also have jurisdiction, especially in criminal cases.

Under the OSHA rules, employees have a limited right to walk off the job when faced with a hazardous workplace condition. In *Whirlpool v. Marshall*,[29] the U.S. Supreme Court held that, despite the lack of any specific language in the OSHA statute that allows employees to walk off the job, the law permitted employees this right under the narrow circumstances in which (1) the employee faces a condition that he reasonably believes will result in serious injury or death and (2) the context makes it impractical for the employee to contact administration inspectors.

---

[28]Whistleblowing protections were discussed in detail earlier in this chapter.
[29]445 U.S. 1 (1980).

Family and Medical Leave Act

As American society has changed since the Industrial Revolution, so has society's need to provide for employees who are faced with choosing between caring for a loved one and losing a job, seniority, or a promotion. In response to pressures on the workforce to care for a family member, in 1993 Congress passed the **Family and Medical Leave Act (FMLA)**,[30] which sets out the basic protections for workers who need a brief leave from work to care for themselves or an immediate family member. Some states have similar leave statutes that allow for additional time periods or provide additional medical leave protections to employees within the state's jurisdiction.

LO 11-4

List the benefits provided by federal law for workers who are in need of a leave for medical purposes or to care for an ill family member.

FMLA Scope and Coverage The FMLA is administered by the Department of Labor and applies to employers that have 50 or more employees within 75 miles. For example, if BrewCorp operates three coffeehouses in Kansas City with 20 employees at each location, the company would be considered to have 60 employees within a 75-mile radius. An employee, to be eligible for benefits, must have worked for the company for at least 12 months and have worked 1,250 hours during the past 12 months. The law mandates that the employers provide up to 12 weeks of unpaid leave to employees for purposes related to family medical matters during any 12-month period. An eligible employee may take an FMLA leave when the employee needs to care for a newborn or newly adopted baby or when a *serious health condition* affects the employee or the employee's spouse, child, or parent. For an employee to be eligible for an FMLA leave, the serious health condition must require continued treatments by a health care provider and must be of such severity as to render the person unable to care for herself for three consecutive days. The employee must give 30 days' notice of his intent to take a leave unless an emergency arises, which allows reduced notice. All conditions that are covered under the FMLA must be properly documented by a physician and are subject to periodic reevaluation at the employer's request.

Some states have enacted laws reducing the size of the companies covered and some have expanded coverage to include organ donations and bone marrow transplants. Certain states have also extended coverage to include the care of grandparents, domestic partners, and others.

FMLA Protections Although the FMLA does not require employers to pay employees on leave, it does require that the employer maintain the employee's health care benefits uninterrupted throughout the leave period. The FMLA also affords employees certain protections related to job security: (1) Employers are restricted from taking or threatening any adverse job action against the employee because of an FMLA leave; (2) upon returning from the leave, employees are guaranteed employment in the same or a similar job at the same rate of pay; and (3) employers must reinstate an FMLA-leave employee immediately upon the employee's notification that the leave is over. The FMLA does *not* require, however, that returning employees be credited with seniority that was accrued while on leave.

There are two distinct theories of recovery under the FMLA. First is the interference/entitlement theory, in which the employee alleges that the employer denied the employee the right to use the FMLA provisions. Second, if the employee alleges that the employer took an adverse employment action against him (e.g., termination) that was connected to an FMLA claim made by the employee, the retaliation/discrimination theory applies. An employee may use either or both theories in pursuing an FMLA claim.[31]

In Case 11.5, a federal appeals court considers an FMLA retaliation claim.

---

[30] 29 U.S.C. § 2601 et seq.

[31] *Seeger v. Cincinnati Bell Tel. Co., LLC*, 681 F.3d 274, 281 (6th Cir. 2012).

CASE 11.5 Jaszczyszyn v. Advantage Health Physician Network, 504 F. App'x 440, 2012 WL 5416616 (6th Cir. Nov. 7, 2012)

FACT SUMMARY In 2008, Advantage hired Jaszczyszyn as a part-time employee, and she was eventually promoted to a full-time position in Advantage's billing department. After a period of time in which Jaszczyszyn failed to report for work due to back pain, Advantage's human resources department informed Jaszczyszyn that she did not have enough paid time off to cover her absences and recommended that she submit FMLA forms to formalize the request. One necessary form was a Certification of Health Care Provider (Certification) to show that she suffered from a serious medical condition. Although the Certification submitted to Advantage reflected a need for intermittent FMLA leave (to be taken whenever she was having a back pain flare up), Jaszczyszyn treated the leave as continuous, open-ended, and effective immediately. Consequently, she never returned (or attempted to return) to work.

One month after submitting the Certification, Jaszczyszyn attended Pulaski Days, a local Polish heritage festival. Over a period of at least eight hours, she visited three Polish Halls with a group of her friends. One friend shared approximately 127 pictures from that day with Jaszczyszyn, who then posted the pictures of her dancing and laughing on Facebook. Because Jaszczyszyn was Facebook friends with several of her co-workers, the pictures were visible to them. One of those co-workers, upset about Jaszczyszyn's behavior, brought the photographs to the attention of Advantage's management. At a meeting between Jaszczyszyn and Advantage management, she could not explain the discrepancy between her claim of complete incapacitation and her activity in the photos. Advantage gave Jaszczyszyn her notice of termination at the conclusion of the meeting.

Jaszczyszyn sued Advantage, alleging that she was terminated in retaliation for exercising her rights pursuant to the FMLA. The trial court granted Advantage's Motion for Summary Judgment and Jaszczyszyn appealed.

SYNOPSIS OF DECISION AND OPINION The U.S. Court of Appeals for the Sixth Circuit affirmed the trial court's decision in favor of Advantage. The court held that for a retaliation claim, a plaintiff must establish that (1) she was engaged in an activity protected by the FMLA; (2) the employer knew that she was exercising her rights under the FMLA; (3) after learning of the employee's exercise of FMLA rights, the employer took an employment action adverse to her; and (4) there was a causal connection between the protected FMLA activity and the adverse employment action. In this case, the court ruled that Jaszczyszyn failed to prove any causal connection. The evidence of fraud, in and of itself, was sufficient justification for the termination and was not related to her legitimate rights under the FMLA.

WORDS OF THE COURT: Retaliation and Fraud "As in [precedent cases], Advantage 'rightfully considered workplace [FMLA] fraud to be a serious issue,' and its termination of Jaszczyszyn because of her alleged dishonesty constituted a non-retaliatory basis for her discharge. While Jaszczyszyn relies heavily upon a significant amount of after-the-fact medical evidence (such as the deposition of her treating physician) in trying to cast Advantage's justification as [not the actual reason for the termination], Advantage's investigation was adequate and turned in large part on Jaszczyszyn's own behavior at the termination interview, which she does not address at all. She did not refute Advantage's honest belief that her behavior in the photos was inconsistent with her claims of total disability. Thus, as a result of her fraudulent behavior, her claim of FMLA retaliation fails. We therefore conclude that the district court did not err in granting summary judgment to Advantage."

Case Questions

1. If the Facebook photos were not posted, would Advantage still have been justified in terminating her? Why or why not?
2. What steps should Advantage take to be sure this doesn't happen again?
3. *Focus on Critical Thinking:* What type of employee privacy issues may be involved in this case? Is it ethical for employers to monitor social media to police their employees? Should employers be permitted to monitor all of the nonwork activities of their employees?

Key Employees If an employee's salary range is in the top 10 percent of all salaries in the company, the FMLA classifies him as a *key employee*. Although key employees are entitled to the FMLA protections, employers have a right not to reinstate the employee if reinstatement would cause a "substantial and grievous economic injury." However, courts apply this exception narrowly, and employers must comply with required notifications and procedures set out by the statute, including the duty to notify an employee who is taking the leave of her key-employee status and the limits of the FMLA protections.

> **KEY POINT**
>
> The FMLA requires that an employee returning from a medical leave be reinstated at the same rate of pay.

CONCEPT SUMMARY Employment Regulation Laws

Federal Statute	General Provisions	Coverage
Fair Labor Standards Act (FLSA)	Wages and hours; child labor	Mandates (1) payment of minimum wage, (2) maximum 40-hour workweek, (3) overtime pay rate, and (4) restriction on children working in certain occupations and during certain hours.
Employee Retirement Income Security Act (ERISA)	Pensions and retirement funds	Subjects employers that establish retirement benefits to the requirements of ERISA laws and regulations, which primarily require employers to (1) make certain disclosures related to investment risk and (2) provide transparency to plan beneficiaries.
Social Security Act	Retirement income	Provides a broad set of benefits for workers, including a retirement income from the federal government; funded by mandatory employment taxes paid into a trust fund by both employer and employee and administered by the federal government.
Federal Unemployment Tax Act (FUTA)	Temporary and permanent unemployment	Provides limited payments to workers who have been temporarily or permanently terminated from employment through no fault of their own; funded by the employer only.
Workers' compensation statutes (state level)	Workplace injuries	Serves as a mandatory alternative to negligence lawsuits by offering compensation to an employee who suffers an accidental injury (in the course of employment) as the exclusive remedy for the injury; funded through employer-paid insurance policies.
Occupational Safety and Health Act (OSHA)	Workplace safety	Sets workplace rules and regulations, administered and enforced by the Occupational Safety and Health Administration, to promote the safety of workers and prevent workplace injuries.
Family and Medical Leave Act (FMLA)	Medical leaves	Requires that an employee returning from a medical leave, whether taken to care for himself or an immediate family member, be reinstated at the same rate of pay.

EMPLOYEE PRIVACY

The privacy of employees while they are at the workplace or are off-site performing work-related tasks is an issue of growing concern because many employers regularly monitor employee behavior in some form. In a study coauthored by the American Management Association and the ePolicy Institute, 73 percent of employers reported that they monitored employee e-mail messages and 48 percent regularly employed video surveillance. Ten percent even monitored social-networking sites.[32] Other issues related to employee privacy include telephone and voice-mail monitoring and drug and alcohol testing in various employment contexts. As a general matter, an employee's right to privacy in the workplace is very limited. However, employees may have some limited rights that are typically afforded by a statute.

Monitoring of E-Mail and Internet Usage

An employee's activities while using an employer's computer system are not protected by any privacy laws. All computer use is ordinarily subject to employer monitoring, including the right to

- Track websites visited by employees.
- Count keystrokes and mouse clicks.
- Block employees from visiting specific Internet sites.
- Limit the amount of time an employee may spend at a specific website.

A company's information technology services may use filters, keystroke-recording software, and other detection devices for determining whether the use of e-mail is inconsistent with company policy. At large companies, part of the management team may include compliance officers assigned to coordinate monitoring and ensure that employees are following all company e-mail and Internet policies.

Employer Liability Employers are increasingly employing elaborate employee monitoring measures primarily to limit their risk of vicarious liability (liability for the act of an employee) in areas such as defamation and employment discrimination. For example, in the AMA/ePolicy survey cited earlier, 15 percent of the companies surveyed had faced a lawsuit triggered by employee e-mail. Companies typically adopt specific guidelines and policies for e-mail and Internet use and inform employees that all Internet and e-mail usage is subject to monitoring.

Telephone and Voice Mail

While the right of an employer to monitor e-mail and Internet usage of workplace computers for business reasons is very expansive, employees are afforded certain protections for telephone calls and voice mail by the **Electronic Communications Privacy Act (ECPA)**.[33] The ECPA updated existing wiretap laws and restricts an employer from monitoring an employee's personal calls (even those from the workplace) without the employee's consent. Employers may monitor business calls but must disconnect the moment they recognize that a call is personal. Employers are also restricted from accessing an employee's office voice mail without the employee's consent. However, the ECPA has two exceptions that severely limit its protections for employees. First, the business-extension exception permits an employer to monitor employee electronic communications on company-owned

---

[32]*See* American Management Association & ePolicy Institute, *The 2007 Electronic Monitoring & Surveillance Survey* (2007).

devices so long as this is done in the ordinary course of business. Second, the ECPA allows an employer to avoid liability if the employee consents to the monitoring. Some employers now routinely require employees to consent to monitoring as a condition of employment.

Drug and Alcohol Testing

Employee privacy protection from use of regular or random drug or alcohol tests in the workplace is governed primarily by state statutes, and these laws vary considerably. Some states permit employee testing so long as the employer follows certain procedural safeguards intended to ensure confidentiality, safety, and accuracy. Other states permit testing only when the employee's job carries a great deal of risk to the employee or the public or when a worker has been involved in a work-related accident in which drug use is suspected.

Americans with Disabilities Act Considerations One important issue that arises with drug and alcohol testing is the rights of an employee under the Americans with Disabilities Act (ADA). The ADA, which is discussed in detail in Chapter 12, "Employment Discrimination," prohibits discrimination on the basis of a physical disability. If the testing uncovers a former drug addiction (or current alcoholism), under certain circumstances the employee is protected from discipline or termination under the ADA.

The ADA also places restrictions on medical examinations and tests. Employers may require a medical examination only after a job offer has been made. The job offer may be made contingent upon passing the medical test, so the test must be administered after all other hiring information is obtained and found satisfactory. If an employer requires medical testing, the tests must be administered to all prospective employees and may not be used to target those with disabilities or to determine whether women are pregnant. Data obtained through medical testing must be kept in a separate file and be available only to those with a demonstrable "need to know."

In Case 11.6, a company requires a medical test too soon and is sued by two prospective employees.

CASE 11.6 Leonel v. American Airlines, Inc., 400 F.3d 702 (9th Cir. 2005)

FACT SUMMARY Leonel and two other applicants were given conditional offers of employment by American Airlines. The offers of employment were contingent upon passing background checks and medical examinations. Prior to the background checks being completed, American sent Leonel and the other applicants to its on-site facility for the required medical exams, and each applicant filled out a medical questionnaire. Although Leonel and the other applicants were HIV-positive, they did not disclose their condition or related medications on the questionnaire. After blood tests revealed that the applicants were HIV-positive, American rescinded the employment offers, citing each applicant's failure to disclose relevant information on the medical questionnaires. Leonel and the other applicants filed suit under the Americans with Disabilities Act (and similar state statutes), arguing that the medical exams were premature. The trial court ruled in favor of American Airlines.

SYNOPSIS OF DECISION AND OPINION The Court of Appeals for the Ninth Circuit reversed the trial court and ruled in favor of Leonel and the other two applicants. The court held that the ADA and California state statutes prohibit the use of medical testing prior to such time as the application process has been completed. The court rejected American's argument that the expedited medical examinations were necessary to remain competitive for the best candidates.

(continued)

---

[33]18 U.S.C. § 2510 et seq.

> **WORDS OF THE COURT: Premature Medical Testing** "Here, it is undisputed that American's offers were subject to both medical and non-medical conditions when they were made to the appellants and the appellants were required to undergo immediate medical examinations. Thus the offers were not real, the medical examination process was premature and American cannot penalize the appellants for failing to disclose their HIV-positive status—unless the company can establish that it could not reasonably have completed the background checks before subjecting the appellants to medical examinations and questioning. It has not done so.
>
> "As justification for accelerating the medical examinations, American's Manager of Flight Service Procedures, . . . explained that the company found it important to minimize the length of time that elapsed during the hiring process in order to compete for applicants. But competition in hiring is not in itself a reason to contravene the ADA's and FEHA's [California's Fair Employment and Housing Act] mandates to defer the medical component of the hiring process until the non-medical component is completed."
>
> **Case Questions**
> 1. Why should medical tests be given only after all nonmedical tests are completed satisfactorily?
> 2. Why did the court determine that American had not truly tendered a conditional offer of employment?
> 3. *Focus on Critical Thinking:* At what point would a true conditional offer of employment have been appropriate?

Polygraph Testing

In 1988, Congress passed the **Employee Polygraph Protection Act**,[34] which prohibits most private sector employers from requiring a polygraph (lie detector) test as a condition of employment. Additionally, employers are prohibited from taking or threatening action against current employees who refuse to take the test. However, the act permits employers to use polygraph tests when investigating losses attributable to theft or other economic loss or when the employee is in the security or pharmaceutical industry. The law does not apply if the employer is a federal, state, or local government entity. Note that some state statutes give employees added protections related to the use of polygraph tests such as limiting their use to preemployment screening only.

LABOR UNIONS AND COLLECTIVE BARGAINING

LO 11-5

Identify federal statutes that impact labor-management relations and give examples of specific protections for workers that are set out in each law.

Another source of legal protections for workers is labor unions. Union membership peaked in the early 1950s, when nearly one-third of American workers were unionized. By 2012 the percentage of wage and salary workers who were members of a union was 11.3 percent, down from 11.8 percent in 2011.[35] Today most labor unions in America are members of one of the two larger umbrella organizations: the American Federation of Labor–Congress of Industrial Organizations (AFL-CIO) and the Changes to Win Federation, which split from the AFL-CIO in 2005.

Labor Law

The **National Labor Relations Act (NLRA)**,[36] originally passed in 1935, is the centerpiece of labor-management regulation statutes. It provides general protections for the

---
[34]29 U.S.C. § 2001 et seq.

[35]News Release, Bureau of Labor Statistics, U.S. Department of Labor, Union Members Summary (Jan. 23, 2013).

[36]29 U.S.C. § 151 et seq. This law is also called the *Wagner Act,* and it displaced an earlier attempt at labor regulation, the Norris-LaGuardia Act, which proved ineffective.

rights of workers to organize, engage in **collective bargaining**, and use economic weapons (such as a strike) in the collective bargaining process. Collective bargaining is the process of negotiating an agreement on behalf of an entire workforce, as opposed to individuals negotiating privately on their own behalf (or not negotiating at all). The statute also contained an enabling provision that formed the **National Labor Relations Board (NLRB)** to administer, implement, and enforce the law's wide-sweeping provisions. In addition to the traditional administrative agency duties of implementation and enforcement, the NLRB monitors union elections for fraud and sets guidelines for employers and unions in regard to fair labor practices.

In general, the NLRA covers all employers whose business activity involves some aspect of interstate commerce. As a practical matter, under modern interpretation by the courts, this means that the NLRA coverage is practically universal. Some workers are specifically exempted by statute, including railroad and airline employees.[37] To be eligible for protection under the NLRA, the worker must be a *current* employee (not an applicant or retiree).

Labor-Management Relations

Through amendments to the NLRA since its enactment, Congress clarified and reformed the legal standards applicable to employers and unions to ensure fairness to both labor and management in resolving differences. These laws deemed certain labor practices illegal, thus making them *unfair* labor practices under the NLRA.

> **KEY POINT**
>
> The NLRA provides general protections for the rights of workers to organize and engage in collective bargaining.

Labor Management Relations Act Passage of the NLRA brought about a wave of industrial strikes that impacted daily commercial activity across the United States. This created a backlash sufficient to cause Congress to limit certain union practices and rights by amending the NLRA with the **Labor Management Relations Act**[38] in 1947. The amendment prohibited employers and employees from agreeing that union membership is *required* as a condition for employment. The law also authorizes states to enact **right-to-work laws**, which make it illegal for employers to agree with unions that union membership be required for *continuing* employment. In sum, this permitted states to outlaw what had become a common part of labor-management agreements: forcing employees to join or continue membership in a union as a condition of employment. The law also made clear that employers had the right to voice their reasons for opposition to formation of a union and gave a specific authorization for the president of the United States to suspend a strike for up to 80 days in times of national emergency.[39]

Labor-Management Reporting and Disclosure Act In response to increasing allegations of corruption in major trade unions, Congress enacted the **Labor-Management Reporting and Disclosure Act** in 1959,[40] which established a system of reporting and checks intended to uncover and prevent fraud and corruption among union officials.

---

[37] Separate statutes govern railroad and airline labor-management regulations.

[38] 29 U.S.C. § 141 (also known as the *Taft-Hartley Act*).

[39] Labor unions waged an extensive lobbying campaign to oppose the bill, but the provision related to the right to suspend a strike in the event of national emergency was popular with the citizenry—many of whom still had vivid memories of World War II. President Truman vetoed the law, but Congress overrode the veto.

[40] 29 U.S.C. § 1154 (also known as the *Landrum-Griffin Act*).

> **KEY POINT**
>
> Right-to-work laws do not guarantee employment. They address only the right not to join or be forced to contribute to a union.

The law (1) regulates the internal operating procedures of a union, including election processes, procedures, and rights of members at membership and officer meetings; (2) requires extensive financial disclosures by unions; and (3) gives the NLRB additional oversight jurisdiction for internal union governance.

LO 11-6

Explain the process for forming a certified labor union.

Union Formation

While major labor unions such as the AFL-CIO are a well-known part of the American landscape, regional unions or even unions that have only one employer are recognized by the NLRA as well. If an employer has not already recognized a union, and a group of employees decides that it wants to form a **collective bargaining unit** to deal with labor-management matters such as negotiating a contract, the NLRA sets out a procedure for forming a union.

Authorization Cards Typically, a group of employees organizes an effort to have other workers sign **authorization cards** indicating that they wish to form a local union and/or join an existing union. At least 30 percent of the authorization cards must be signed by employees in a certain bargaining unit. Employees may bargain collectively only if they have a mutuality of interests (similar nonmanagement jobs, worksites, and conditions). Bargaining units may be recognized as employees of a single employer or those of an entire region or industry.

Election Once the union organizers obtain authorization cards from at least 30 percent of the members of a bargaining unit, the authorization cards are filed with the NLRB. The formal union certification process begins when the NLRB sets a date for an **election** (a vote to elect or reject unionization) by the entire bargaining unit. During the period of time prior to the election, union organizers are permitted to *campaign,* for example, by distributing flyers and leaflets to employees. However, employers still have a right to *limit* any union campaign activities that take place on the employer's property and/or during the regular workday so long as they can justify the limits as being based on business reasons (such as safety or interference with business operations) and not simply an effort to stop unionization. One appellate court has held, for example, that employer restrictions on distribution of pro-union literature during an unpaid lunch hour in an employee cafeteria were overly restrictive and not sufficiently related to legitimate business objectives.[41] Although employers may not impose overly burdensome restrictions on employees engaging in pro-union campaigns, employees cannot use threats or coercion in their efforts to convince other bargaining-unit employees to unionize. In a 1992 case, the Supreme Court ruled that nonemployee union organizers may *not* distribute pro-union flyers in a company-owned parking lot without permission of the company.[42] Misconduct during a campaign constitutes an unfair labor practice and results in the NLRB or a court setting aside any election results as well as taking other enforcement action (and sometimes criminal charges).[43] Employers also have a right to campaign *against* unionization, but they are subject to regulatory restrictions designed to prevent employers from using economic pressure to influence employee voting. The NLRA regulations prohibit employers from using threats of termination or demotions or incentives (such as a bonus or additional vacation time) in exchange for a nonunion vote.

---

[41] *International Transportation Service v. NLRB*, 449 F.3d 160 (D.C. Cir. 2006).
[42] *Lechmere, Inc. v. NLRB*, 502 U.S. 527 (1992).
[43] *Associated Rubber Co. v. NLRB*, 296 F.3d 1055 (11th Cir. 2002).

TABLE 11.2 Forming a Union

Authorization Cards	Filing with NLRB	Campaign	Election	Certification or Rejection
A group of employees, with a mutuality of interests, organizes an effort to have other workers sign authorization cards; 30 percent of the collective bargaining unit must sign in order to proceed to the next step.	Authorization cards are filed with the NLRB, and a formal union certification process begins when the NLRB sets a date for an election.	Union organizers campaign according to fair labor practices. Management is also permitted to engage in certain practices to campaign against unionization.	Entire bargaining unit votes to either elect or reject unionization. A simple majority is required to certify the union.	If a simple majority voted *for* unionization, the union is certified. The employer must recognize the union as the exclusive bargaining representative of the workers and is required to bargain in good faith with the union thereafter. If a simple majority voted *against* unionization, the union is rejected.

Certification After a legally sound election is held, a simple majority of pro-union votes is required for the NLRB to **certify** the collective bargaining unit as a union. The employer must then recognize the union as the exclusive bargaining representative of the workers and is required to bargain in good faith with the union thereafter. Table 11.2 summarizes the union formation process.

Reform Efforts Beginning in 2007, several efforts have been made to amend the NLRA with the Employee Free Choice Act (sometimes referred to by the media as the *Card Check Act*), which would provide workers an option of procedures for having a union certified as the legal representative of the bargaining unit. The most controversial provision of the law would authorize the NLRB to certify unions either when an NLRB-supervised election results in a majority of pro-union votes or when the bargaining unit can show that over 50 percent of the employees in the bargaining unit have signed an authorization card. The proposed law is supported by labor unions on the basis that it protects the unionization process from employers that are resistant to collective bargaining. Employers are generally against the law on the basis that it puts undue pressure on employees to sign authorization cards and the employees' cards would not be secret. The proposed law has not yet received sufficient support for congressional passage. In 2009, the Secret Ballot Protection Act[44] was introduced in the House of Representatives, but it has not yet garnered enough congressional support to become law. A direct response to the *card-check* process, the proposed law would preserve a worker's right to cast private votes.[45] For an update on any amendments to the NLRA, see Connect.

LO 11-7

Describe the rights of and limits on workers in regard to engaging in collective bargaining and strikes and analyze the potential impact of a work stoppage.

Collective Bargaining

Collective bargaining is the process of negotiating terms and conditions of employment for employees in the collective bargaining unit. These terms are typically negotiated and,

---
[44]H.R. 1176, 111th Cong. (2009–2010).

[45]In response to the Employee Free Choice Act's pending status, four states—Arizona, South Carolina, South Dakota, and Utah—have amended their state constitutions to guarantee their workers the right to secret ballots when voting for or against union representation.

if a collective bargaining agreement is reached, the parties enter into a binding contract. The NLRA regulations set out certain guidelines regarding which terms must be negotiated and which terms are not subject to the bargaining requirements. Union contracts typically include terms related to wages, benefits (such as health care insurance and pension accounts), work hours, overtime procedures, and promotion systems, as well as procedures for handling disciplinary violations, suspensions, terminations, and layoffs.

Good Faith Bargaining Requirements The NLRA requires that both parties engage in good faith negotiations. This is not a requirement that one side or the other concede a particular term. Rather, the parties are obligated to demonstrate that they are engaged in moving toward an agreement. Tactics by either side that are intended to delay, stall, or hinder the process or to undermine the union through economic pressure on workers constitute unfair labor practices, and the NLRB may opt to intervene and conduct labor negotiations or pursue enforcement action for unfair labor practices if appropriate.

Grievances Union contracts normally specify the means of arbitrating union **grievances** against an employer action or practice. Enforcement is initiated when an affected union member files an employee grievance. The union is given the exclusive authority to invoke the arbitration provisions of the agreement, and it conducts the proceedings before the arbitrator on behalf of the employee. The arbitrator's decision is always subject to review by courts that are applying federal standards related to fairness and good faith. However, a court will not set aside an arbitrator's decision simply because the court disagrees with it. Courts give great deference to arbitrators and will intervene only in cases of fundamental unfairness in some procedural or substantive way.

If the union chooses not to bring a grievance to arbitration, the individual union member is normally *not* authorized to pursue a lawsuit against the employer to enforce contract provisions. The union has broad discretion in deciding when to seek arbitration on the basis of a union member grievance.

LO 11-8

Differentiate between an economic strike and an unfair labor practices strike.

Strikes and Other Work Stoppages

The NLRA specifically provides that union employees can commence a **strike** in order to induce the employer to concede certain contract terms during collective bargaining. Certain occupations, though, may be restricted from striking via statute if allowing a strike would significantly jeopardize public health or safety (such as air traffic controllers, law enforcement, or emergency services). Although the right to strike is protected, the NLRA also provides guidelines on when, where, and how a strike may be carried out. Most strikes are commenced when the employer-union negotiations have reached an impasse and the union membership has determined that extreme action is necessary to continue the bargaining process. During an impasse, the union leadership will call for the members to vote for "strike authorization" to be given to leadership if the employer refuses to continue the bargaining process. Although most strikes occur in a collective bargaining context, unions may also commence a strike against an employer that is engaging in unfair labor practices.

Poststrike Rehiring While a strike is a potent economic weapon of a union, its impact on striking union members can be harsh. Workers are cut off from any pay, medical benefits, and other compensation until the strike is over. Moreover, employers have no *legal* obligation to rehire striking workers or provide retroactive pay in cases of a strike for economic reasons. Although, as a practical matter, the rehiring of striking workers and partial or full retroactive pay are frequently guaranteed by the poststrike contract agreement, it is still a risk for some workers. However, if a strike is commenced due to an *unfair labor practice* rather than for *economic* reasons, the striking employees are entitled to immediate reinstatement with back pay once they unconditionally return to work. Economic strikes typically arise in the context of union members' failing to agree with the employer on wages or benefits. In Case 11.7, a federal appeals court distinguishes between economic strikes and unfair labor practice strikes.

CASE 11.7 NLRB v. Midwestern Personnel Services, Inc., 322 F.3d 969 (7th Cir. 2003)

FACT SUMMARY Midwestern Personnel Services (MPS) provided cement and transport truck drivers to River City Holdings (River City), a construction materials company that serviced a variety of locations in different states. MPS contracted to supply drivers to River City for a project at a union job site. The contract for the project guaranteed that MPS would supply River City with unionized drivers. MPS obtained driver-employee signatures on union authorization cards by advising drivers that membership in an out-of-state union, which MPS had selected, was required to keep their jobs at MPS. Eventually, the drivers became dissatisfied with the out-of-state union and formed a local union for collective bargaining purposes. When MPS refused to recognize the local union on the basis that the agreement with the out-of-state union remained in effect, the drivers went on strike. MPS subsequently refused the employees' unconditional offer to return to work and hired replacement workers. The National Labor Relations Board (NLRB) concluded that the employees' strike at MPS was based on MPS's unfair labor practices, rather than an economic dispute, and ordered the drivers reinstated with back pay. MPS appealed.

SYNOPSIS OF DECISION AND OPINION The U.S. Court of Appeals for the Seventh Circuit ruled in favor of the employees and affirmed the NLRB's findings. The court held that the strike was clearly based on MPS's unfair labor practices and, thus, the employees were entitled to reinstatement with back pay. The court noted that MPS unlawfully assisted the out-of-state union by negotiating with and recognizing it without any indication of uncoerced majority support by the employees. Further, the union authorization cards were unlawfully obtained by threats of termination, and the refusal to reinstate the employees was itself an unfair labor practice.

WORDS OF THE COURT: Unfair Labor Practice Strikes "Under [the NLRA], unfair labor practices strikers are entitled to immediate reinstatement with back pay once they unconditionally offer to return to work, whereas economic strikers may be permanently replaced. An unfair labor practices strike does not lose its character as such if economic motives contribute to its cause, however; it remains an unfair labor practices strike so long as the employees are motivated in part by unfair labor practices. . . . In determining whether management–labor cooperation has crossed over from permissible cooperation to unlawful coercion, courts consider a confluence of factors, with no one factor being dispositive. This nonexclusive list of factors includes whether the employer solicited contact with the union; the rank and position of the company's solicitor; whether the employer silently acquiesced in the union's drive for membership; whether the employer shepherded its employees to meetings with a prospective union; whether management was present at meetings between its employees and a prospective union; whether the signing of union authorization cards was coerced; and whether the employer quickly recognized the assisted union after the employees signed authorization cards yet exhibited prejudice against another union selected by the employees. . . . Normally a court defers to the credibility determinations of the NLRB unless there is some extraordinary reason why the court should ignore them, for instance if those findings are inherently incredible or patently unreasonable. . . . We conclude that substantial evidence in the record as a whole supports the Board's conclusions that the strike was an unfair labor practices strike."

(continued)

Case Questions

1. Why does the court criticize MPS for recognizing the out-of-state union as the exclusive bargaining representative of the workers?
2. Suppose that MPS did recognize the local union and, subsequently, MPS and the local union negotiations reached an impasse over wages. Does MPS have any legal obligations to rehire the striking workers? Explain.
3. *Focus on Critical Thinking:* What are the public policy justifications for differentiating the type of strike (unfair labor practice versus economic)? Isn't an economic issue strike a legitimate reason for a work stoppage? Why or why not?

From the perspective of the union, however, a strike also has the potential to result in significant economic harm for the employer company. Because the NLRA also gives other employees the right to refuse to cross a picket line, a strike can be devastating to the revenue of the employer if the strike requires a full or partial shutdown of business operations.

Strikers have the right to engage in **picketing** at the employer's facilities, although there is no right to picket at the actual property site owned by the company. Picketing must be peaceful and not interfere with the operations of the employer. Picketing cannot be used to prevent or harass customers or nonstriking employees.

Unions may also call for union member and public boycotts of the employer's product or services as a method of pressuring management to engage in negotiations or concede a disputed point in a collective bargaining contract. If other unions recognize the boycotts, the economic impact on the employer may be significant.

The NLRA provides unionized workers with the right to strike and picket in a peaceful manner in front of the employer's facilities. McGraw-Hill Education/Christopher Kerrigan, photographer

Illegal Work Stoppages and Boycotts

> **LO 11-9**
>
> Provide examples of illegal work stoppages.

The term *strike* implies a statutorily authorized work stoppage under the NLRA. Other types of work stoppages (or slowdowns) are illegal, and employers may terminate employees, unionized or not, for engaging in illegal work stoppages. Most importantly, if peaceful picketing turns violent or union members threaten management, then the strike becomes an illegal work stoppage and union members engaged in that conduct are not protected under the NLRA. Other illegal work stoppages include

- *Wildcat strikes:* When individual union members or small groups of union members go on strike for short bursts of time without union authorization, this is called a *wildcat strike*. Wildcat strikes are illegal, but sometimes the form of a wildcat strike can be subtle, as when several employees simultaneously use sick time to perpetrate a work stoppage or slowdown.
- *Sit-in strikes:* Any occupation of an employer's facility for the purpose of a work stoppage is illegal.
- *Strikes during a cooling-off period:* The NLRA allows a federal court to enforce a strike prohibition for a period of 80 days if a strike threatens national public health or security. During this cooling-off period, the government facilitates negotiations between the parties, and any strike during this time is illegal.
- *Secondary boycotts:* Efforts to increase the pressure on an employer involved in collective bargaining by directing a strike against a third party (such as a supplier or customer of the employer) is illegal. For example, suppose that Trade Union (TU) is at an impasse with BigCo. In addition to striking against BigCo, TU organizes a picket line in front of the headquarters of one of BigCo's main customers, SellerCo, with signs stating "Boycott SellerCo! They Support Unfair Labor Practices!" TU's action toward SellerCo is a secondary boycott and constitutes an unfair labor practice.

Lockouts and Replacement Workers

Employers who are faced with the prospect of a strike have several options under the law. First, any employer that reasonably anticipates a strike by a group of employees may employ a **lockout** by shutting down the business and preventing employees from working, thus depriving them of their employment and putting economic pressure on the union's members before the union can do the same to the employer through a strike. For example, in the BigCo-TU negotiations discussed earlier, suppose the parties reach an impasse in contract negotiations in October. BigCo is concerned that TU may be waiting until BigCo's busy holiday season in December before commencing a strike in order to exert maximum economic pressure on BigCo.[46] Under these circumstances, BigCo is permitted to shut down its plant immediately, locking out union members, in hopes of driving the union to the bargaining table in an effort to reach an agreement well ahead of the company's busy season. Some lockouts are not permitted under the NLRA. Any time an employer lacks a *legitimate business reason* for employing a lockout, it may be an unfair labor practice. Additionally, any time a lockout is used for undermining the collective bargaining process or disrupting union organizing efforts, the practice is illegal.

A second option for employers who are subject to a strike is to hire nonunion **replacement workers** in order to continue operations during the strike. When the strike is over, employers may either retain the replacement workers or discharge them (without liability) in favor of returning workers.

> **KEY POINT**
>
> Lockouts are a permissible labor practice so long as a legitimate business reason underlies the lockout.

---

[46]Based on the Supreme Court's decision in *American Shipbuilding Company v. NLRB*, 380 U.S. 300 (1965).

✓ Self-Check Unfair Labor Practices

Which of these actions may constitute an unfair labor practice under the NLRA?

1. Management refuses to recognize a certified union on the basis that several employees in the union have presented a petition that indicates that 40 percent of the employees in the proposed bargaining unit oppose unionization.
2. During a union-vote campaign, management throws an anti-union dinner banquet party and invites all employees and their families to attend. During the banquet, management gives speeches and points out the benefits of working in a non-unionized workplace.
3. During a union-vote campaign, pro-union employees distribute leaflets to fellow employees in the employee locker room as they leave the plant at the end of their shift.
4. Management at a school supplies manufacturing company is at an impasse with a certified union over contract terms. Because the managers fear that the union will call a strike just before the company's fall busy season, they shut down the plant and lock out employees.
5. Workers strike in a right-to-work state over stalled salary negotiations during collective bargaining. After the strike is settled, management refuses to rehire some of the striking employees. They assert that they must be rehired due to the state's right-to-work statute.
6. A certified union strikes over management's refusal to abide by the terms of an existing collective bargaining agreement. Once the dispute is resolved in arbitration, management refuses to rehire half of the striking workers.

Answers to this Self-Check are provided at the end of the chapter.

KEY TERMS

Employment-at-will p. 365   Deep-seated common law principle that employers have the right to terminate an employee with or without advance notice and with or without just cause, subject to certain exceptions.

At-will employee p. 365   Any employee who is not a contractual employee; may be terminated at any time and for any reason except in cases where public policy is violated or the termination is illegally discriminatory or is prohibited by statutory or common law exceptions.

Contractual employee p. 365   An employee who works under an agreement that defines when the employee begins employment and when the employment ends.

Whistleblower p. 369   An employee or agent who reports illegal misconduct or a statutory violation by his or her employer to the authorities.

Fair Labor Standards Act (FLSA) p. 372   A federal law enacted in 1938 and intended to cover all employers engaged in interstate commerce; mandates payment of a minimum wage, a maximum 40-hour workweek, overtime pay, and restrictions on children working in certain occupations and during certain hours.

Portal-to-Portal Act p. 372   Provides guidelines for what constitutes compensable work under the FLSA's wage and hour requirements.

Overtime compensation p. 373   A higher rate of pay for the hours that nonexempt employees work in excess of 40 hours in one seven-day workweek; calculated at one and one-half times the employee's hourly base rate.

Exempt employees p. 374   Classification of employees who are not covered by FLSA protections; generally consists of employees whose responsibilities are primarily executive, administrative, or professional.

Covered (nonexempt) employees p. 376   Employees who are protected by the FLSA and other statutes.

Pension p. 378   A retirement benefit in which the employer promises to pay a monthly sum to employees who retire from the company after a certain number of years of service. The amount is ordinarily based on the length of service and the employee's final salary rate.

Tax-deferred retirement savings account p. 378
A retirement savings plan in which the employee commits to saving a certain percentage of base pay in an account that is controlled directly by the employee. The funds grow tax-free until they are withdrawn.

Employee Retirement Income Security Act (ERISA) p. 379   A federal law enacted in 1974 consisting of a comprehensive set of laws and regulations that requires employers to make certain disclosures related to investment risk, thus providing transparency for plan beneficiaries.

Social Security Act (SSA) of 1935 p. 379   A federal law providing a broad set of benefits for workers, including a retirement income; funded by mandatory employment taxes paid into a trust fund by both employer and employee and administered by the federal government.

Federal Unemployment Tax Act (FUTA) p. 380
A federal law enacted in 1935 that established a state-administered fund to provide payments to workers who have suffered sudden job loss; funded through employment taxes shared by employer and employee.

Workers' compensation p. 380   State statutes that provide an employee who is injured in the course of employment with a partial payment in exchange for mandatory relinquishment of the employee's right to sue the employer for the tort of negligence; funded through employer-paid insurance policies.

Occupational Safety and Health Act (OSHA) p. 381
A federal law enacted in 1970 that sets forth workplace rules and regulations to promote the safety of workers and prevent workplace injuries.

Family and Medical Leave Act (FMLA) p. 383   A federal law enacted in 1993 that requires certain employers to give time off to employees to take care of their own or a family member's illness or to care for a newborn or adopted child.

Electronic Communications Privacy Act (ECPA) p. 386
A federal law enacted in 1986 that extends legal protection against wiretapping and other forms of unauthorized interception and explicitly allows employers to monitor employee communications on company equipment as long as this is done in the ordinary course of business or the employee consents to the monitoring.

Employee Polygraph Protection Act p. 388   A federal law that prohibits most private sector employers from requiring a polygraph test as a condition of employment.

National Labor Relations Act (NLRA) p. 388   A federal law enacted in 1935 that provides general protections for the rights of workers to organize, engage in collective bargaining, and take part in strikes and other forms of concerted activity in support of their demands. Also known as the *Wagner Act*.

Collective bargaining p. 389   The process of negotiating terms and conditions of employment for employees in the collective bargaining unit.

National Labor Relations Board (NLRB) p. 389   An independent federal agency created by the NLRA and charged with administering, implementing, and enforcing NLRA provisions, as well as monitoring union elections for fraud and setting guidelines for employers and unions in regard to fair labor practices.

Labor Management Relations Act p. 389   A federal law, enacted in 1947 as an amendment to the NLRA, that prohibits requiring employees to join or continue membership in a union as a condition of employment. Also known as the *Taft-Hartley Act*.

Right-to-work law p. 389   A state law prohibiting employers from requiring that employees join a union to continue working and that nonunion employees contribute to certain union costs such as the cost related to collective bargaining.

Labor-Management Reporting and Disclosure Act p. 389   A federal law enacted in 1959 that established a system of reporting and checks intended to uncover and prevent fraud and corruption among union officials by regulating internal operating procedures and union matters. Also known as the *Landrum-Griffin Act*.

Collective bargaining unit p. 390   An employee group that, on the basis of a mutuality of interests, is an appropriate unit for collective bargaining.

Authorization cards p. 390   Signed statements by employees indicating that they wish to unionize and/or are electing to be represented by an existing union.

Election p. 390   A vote to elect or reject unionization by the entire bargaining unit.

Certify p. 391   In labor law, to recognize a collective bargaining unit as a union. The NLRB's certification process occurs when a legally sound election reveals a simple majority of pro-union votes.

Grievance p. 392   In labor law, a complaint filed with or by a union to challenge an employer's treatment of one or more union members.

Strike p. 392   A concerted and sustained refusal by workers to perform some or all of the services for which they were hired in order to induce the employer to concede certain contract terms during collective bargaining or to engage in fair labor practices.

Picketing p. 394   A union's patrolling alongside the premises of a business to organize the workers, to gain

Lockout p. 395   The shutdown of a business by the employer to prevent employees from working, thus depriving them of their employment and putting economic pressure on the union's members before the union can do the same to the employer through a strike.

Replacement workers p. 395   Nonunion employees hired by a company in order to continue its operations during a strike.

CHAPTER REVIEW QUESTIONS

1. **The employment-at-will rule does not apply when**
   a. An employee has an express contract.
   b. An employee is covered by a collective bargaining agreement (CBA).
   c. The employee has worked over one year for an employer.
   d. a and b.
   e. a, b, and c.

2. **The Fair Labor Standards Act (FLSA) does not include**
   a. Setting the minimum wage.
   b. Restrictions on child labor.
   c. Workplace safety standards.
   d. Standard pay rate for overtime.
   e. Setting a maximum 40-hour workweek.

3. **In the hypothetical state of Carltown, the legislature passes a statute that prohibits an employer from retaliating against an employee on the basis that the employee notified authorities of employer actions that may harm the public. The Carltown law is an example of what exception to the employee-at-will rule?**
   a. Public policy
   b. Whistleblower statute
   c. Federal antidiscrimination
   d. Implied contract
   e. Fair dealing and good faith

4. **Ahab is covered by the FLSA and works four consecutive weeks as follows: Week 1: 45 hours; Week 2: 41 hours; Week 3: 38 hours; Week 4: 36 hours. How many hours of overtime must Ahab's employer pay for this time period?**
   a. 0
   b. 6
   c. 8
   d. 16
   e. 24

5. **The Family Medical Leave Act (FMLA) provides for**
   a. Paid leave for caring for a sick spouse or child; unpaid leave for all other relatives.
   b. Paid leave for childbirth; unpaid leave to care for family members.
   c. Unpaid leave for nonkey employees; paid leave for key employees.
   d. Unpaid leave to care for a newborn baby.
   e. Unpaid leave to attend parenting and childbirth classes.

Answers and explanations are provided at the end of this chapter.

THEORY TO PRACTICE

Collegiate Banner Company (CBC) is a manufacturer and distributor of flags and banners bearing the names, logos, mottos, and mascots of American colleges and universities. Its products are purchased for retail sale by college bookstores as well as large-scale retail outlet sports equipment chains. CBC's administrative headquarters and sole manufacturing facility are located in different buildings on the same site. Its total workforce is 121 employees, with 76 employees located in the plant and the remaining 45 employees working in the office. CBC classifies its employees into two broad categories: administrative employees and trade employees. The breakdown is illustrated in the table below.

1. Name the FLSA classification (covered or exempt) for each position in the table below, and give your analysis for each classification.
2. Suppose that Falstaff is a plant manager and exercises his right to take a leave under the FMLA. When Falstaff returns, he is told that the replacement plant manager has increased efficiency in the plant by 30 percent and that he is being reassigned as a skilled tradesperson because no other jobs are available. Has CBC violated the FMLA? Could CBC limit its liability by informing Falstaff that he is a key employee? What is the impact of key-employee classification in this case?

Administrative Employees

Position	Primary Duty	Pay Range	Location	Number of Employees
Executive manager	Business planning and operations	$150,000 and above	Office	5
General manager	Hiring, supervision, and evaluation of professional staff	$75,000–$100,000	Office	10
Professional staff	Operational functions such as accounting, customer service, marketing, logistics, and human resources	$50,000–$100,000	Office	15
Support staff	Support managers and professional staff with administrative tasks such as scheduling, preparing documents and reports, answering calls, and keeping track of expenses	$20,000 (entry level) to $75,000 (president's administrative assistant)	Office	15

Trade Employees

Position	Primary Duty	Pay Range	Location	Number of Employees
Plant supervisor	Day-to-day supervision of line managers and employees in the manufacturing facility	$30/hour	75% plant 25% office	1
Line manager	Supervision of line workers in various sections of the plant; responsible for evaluation, efficiency reports, and ensuring quality control	$25–$30/hour	90% plant 10% office	10
Skilled tradesperson	Work involving the use of specialized equipment for product designs and layouts	$20–$25/hour	Plant	20
Tradesperson	Line work involving repetitive tasks required to manufacture the product	$12–$20/hour	Plant	30
Delivery truck driver	Loading and delivering products to retailers or wholesalers	$12–$25/hour	Plant	15

3. Assume that CBC management is concerned about productivity and hires a consultant to restrict its company computers from accessing certain websites in the month of March during the national college basketball playoffs. Has CBC violated the employees' rights to privacy?

4. Suppose that several employees are interested in forming a union. Which groups of people have sufficient mutuality of interests to form a collective bargaining unit under the NLRA? Can any administrative employees be recognized as a collective bargaining unit? Why or why not?

5. Assume that workers employed as tradespersons obtain sufficient authorization cards and the NLRB schedules an election. One of the organizers of the union effort passes out union fliers in the plant cafeteria during an unpaid lunch hour. The plant manager halts the practice on the basis that no union solicitation is permitted on CBC's property. Has CBC committed an unfair labor practice by prohibiting the distribution of the fliers? Suppose that the pro-union organizer distributed the fliers while the tradespersons were on the line working. Could CBC ban that practice? Why or why not?

6. Assume a union for skilled tradespersons is certified, but CBC refuses to recognize the union. The union workers strike and picket outside of CBC's headquarters. They also organize a picket line in front of several Sports Outlet stores because Sports Outlet is a major retail store customer of CBC. Are these two pickets (in front of CBC and in front of Sports Outlet) permitted under the NLRA? Why are they different? If the union workers cease the strike and offer unconditionally to come back to work, must CBC reinstate them? Is this an economic strike? Why or why not?

LEGAL STRATEGY 101

Strikes and Lockouts

When a labor union and an employer are engaged in contract talks, each side to the negotiations has a potential legal weapon at its disposal: strikes and lockouts. In brief, the National Labor Relations Act (NLRA) protects a union's right to strike, and courts have ruled that employers may lock out their employees at any time there is no contract in effect.

More importantly, a labor union's decision to call a strike—like an employer's decision to lock out its workers—is a strategic one: A labor union can threaten to go on strike if its demands are not met, while an employer can threaten to lock out its workers if its demands are not met. As a result, workers in a labor union are more likely to go on strike when they think striking will put pressure on their employer to agree to their labor contract demands, such as higher pay, greater fringe benefits, or better working conditions. By the same token, employers may consider locking out their workers in order to pressure them to accept contract terms the employer wants, like lower pay, lower benefits, and so on.

To illustrate the strategic nature of strikes and lockouts, consider the world of pro sports. The National Football League (NFL) is a professional sports league consisting of 32 teams. The National Football League Players Association (NFLPA) is a labor union consisting of hundreds of pro-football players. When the previous contract between the players' union and the team owners expired in March 2011, after the regular season and playoffs had ended, the NFL called an indefinite lockout.

NFL Players Association press conference.
Doug Benc/Getty Images

In response to the NFL's lockout, the players made a surprising strategic move of their own: They voted to disband their own union!

This strategic move allowed individual players to challenge the legality of the NFL's lockout in federal court. Among other players, superstar quarterback Tom Brady of the New England Patriots brought a lawsuit against the NFL in the federal district court in Minnesota, and the court initially ruled for the players, declaring the lockout illegal because the players were no longer members of a union. When this legal decision was later overturned on appeal, the players voted to reestablish their union and agreed to a new 10-year deal with the NFL in August 2011.

CRITICAL THINKING QUESTION

The current NFL season starts in August with preseason exhibition games and ends in late January or early February with the Super Bowl. The existing deal between the players and the team owners is set to expire in March of 2020. (Section 1 of Article 69 of the current NFL Collective Bargaining Agreement states, "This Agreement shall be effective from August 4, 2011, until the last day of the 2020 League Year," and Article 1 of the agreement defines the start and end of the "League Year" to occur in March.) In your opinion, do these provisions make a strike or a lockout more likely to occur?

MANAGER'S CHALLENGE

Companies that have a unionized workforce must incorporate union considerations into their business planning. Managers may be faced with difficult choices if union members are threatening to strike. Assume that you are employed as a general manager at CBC in the Theory to Practice problem and that the delivery truck drivers are unionized. You receive a voicemail from an executive manager informing you that negotiations over a union contract for the delivery truck drivers have stalled and that the union has threatened to hold a strike vote. She requests that you (individually or in small groups) compose a two- to three-page memorandum that describes the advantages and disadvantages from CBC's perspective of (1) a lockout; (2) a strike, with CBC hiring replacement workers; or (3) further negotiations. Be sure to address legal, ethical, economic, and employee-relations implications.

See Connect for Manager's Challenge sample answers.

CASE SUMMARY 11.1 Jasper v. H. Nizam, Inc., 764 N.W.2d 751 (Iowa 2009)

PUBLIC POLICY EXCEPTION

Jasper was hired as the director of Kid University (KU), a child care facility in Johnston, Iowa. She was paid an hourly wage, and there were no specific terms of employment. A short time after Jasper started her employment, the husband and wife owners of KU announced that the facility would need to cut staff in order to reduce overhead. Jasper complained that any staff cuts would place KU in jeopardy of violating state administrative regulations related to the minimum ratios between staff and children. The issue of the staff-children ratio was the source of considerable tension between Jasper and KU's owners. The owners insisted that Jasper find a way to cut staff expenses, and Jasper continued to assert that the current staffing was necessary for compliance with state regulations. The owners eventually proposed that Jasper and her assistant director begin to work in the classroom to help reduce staffing costs. However, Jasper protested any job responsibility change and asserted that the staffing ratio would still not be compliant with state regulations. Soon thereafter, KU terminated Jasper from her employment at the facility.

Jasper brought a wrongful-discharge suit against KU and its owners, claiming that her firing was based on her refusal to violate the staff-children ratio and that such a termination was a violation of public policy. The trial court found in favor of KU because Jasper was an employee-at-will and had not demonstrated that KU violated "well-recognized and clearly defined public policy."

CASE QUESTIONS

1. Who prevails and why?
2. KU pointed out that there was no evidence that it actually violated the regulation during Jasper's period of employment. Shouldn't an employer have to "act" before any public policy concerns justify an exception to the employment-at-will rule?
3. Does the court's ruling mean that all state administrative regulations are now the source of public policy considerations?

CASE SUMMARY 11.2 Bonilla v. Baker Concrete Construction, 487 F.3d 1340 (11th Cir. 2007)

COMPENSATION FOR COMMUTING

Bonillo was one of several workers hired by Baker Concrete to work on construction at the Miami airport. During construction, airport security required the workers to pass through a security gate and ride in an airport-authorized bus to the site. Baker Concrete paid the workers for being at the site from 7:30 a.m. until 4 p.m. Because of the security requirements, the workers had to arrive at the airport an hour early in order to get to the site on time, and their commute home was extended 15 additional minutes. The workers sued, contending that under the Fair Labor Standards Act they should have been compensated for time spent being transported to and from the employee parking area to the construction site.

CASE QUESTIONS

1. Who prevails and why?
2. Explain your analysis and construct a hypothetical situation in which the losing party may have prevailed.

CASE SUMMARY 11.3 Sisco v. Quicker Recovery, Inc., 180 P.3d 46 (Or. Ct. App. 2008)

WORKERS' COMPENSATION

Sisco worked as a tow truck driver for Quicker Recovery, a towing company in Oregon that had a contract to provide towing services for a municipal police department. The contract required Quicker to provide a tow truck within 30 minutes of receiving the request for services. Sisco was dispatched to tow an impounded truck and was en route to the location when the police stopped him for speeding in the tow truck. Sisco refused to produce his driver's license or any other identification for the police and was arrested pursuant to a state statute allowing the police to arrest any traffic violator who cannot be identified sufficiently for purposes of issuing a citation. Sisco physically resisted arrest, but he was eventually subdued by officers who used an electronic stun gun to take him into custody. The day after the arrest, Sisco complained of neck pain and recurring spasms caused by the altercation with the officers. He claimed that the pain prevented him from carrying out his job responsibilities as a tow truck driver and submitted a workers' compensation claim.

CASE QUESTIONS

1. Suppose Sisco's altercation occurred while he was en route to his house during an unpaid one-hour lunch break. Would Sisco still be eligible for compensation? Why or why not?
2. Would Sisco have been better served trying to articulate a negligence claim? Explain.
3. Doesn't public policy prevent a worker from claiming compensation for an incident involving a criminal act? Should the court take public policy considerations into account?

CASE SUMMARY 11.4 Waremart Foods v. NLRB, 354 F.3d 870 (9th Cir. 2004)

UNFAIR LABOR PRACTICES

WinCo operates a grocery store in California on a 10-acre lot. In accordance with company policy, WinCo allows no solicitors on its premises except for allowing scouts to sell cookies. When a local union was campaigning for the upcoming election, nonemployee union representatives came on the premises and passed out pro-union literature in the company parking lot and in the employee cafeteria during an unpaid lunch hour. WinCo forced the organizers to vacate the premises, and the union complained.

CASE QUESTIONS

1. Does WinCo have the right to limit the local union's campaign activities on its property? What would WinCo have to prove in order to do so? Cite an example.
2. Would the union's actions have any impact on the upcoming election? Explain.

CASE SUMMARY 11.5 Casserly v. State, 844 P.2d 1275 (Colo. Ct. App. 3d Div. 1992)

COMPENSATION FOR ON-CALL TIME

Casserly and the other plaintiffs were employed as physician assistants at the State Correctional Facility at Canon City, Colorado. Each was assigned to a single facility for full-time duties requiring not less than 40 hours per week. In addition, on a rotating basis, each plaintiff was required to provide emergency medical services to inmates after regular working hours. During on-call periods, the plaintiffs were required to respond to any of seven facilities covering an eight-mile radius within 20 minutes of receiving a call. The number and frequency of calls received during any on-call shift were not predictable. The need to respond immediately to medical calls required the plaintiffs to maintain a constant state of readiness. They did not engage in recreational activities during these hours, nor did they use this time for their own personal purposes. The plaintiffs testified that they did not shower, walk for recreation, cook meals, eat in restaurants, entertain guests, perform yard work, or attend sporting events during their on-call hours. They could not be alone with their children. Some even rented motel rooms in Canon. Casserly and the other physician assistants were paid $1.75 per hour for their on-call time but were paid at one and one-half their regular rate of pay for the hours they were physically present at a facility responding to a call.

CASE QUESTIONS

1. Because the on-call employees had to remain in a constant state of readiness, was their time for their benefit or for the employer's benefit?
2. Are the on-call physician assistants justly compensated by the $1.75 per hour, or are they entitled to one and one-half times regular pay under the FLSA? In other words, should they be paid at the one-and-one-half rate even when sitting at home?

CASE SUMMARY 11.6 Sullivan v. U.S. Postal Service, No. 2011-3220, 464 F. App'x 895 (Fed. Cir. 2012)

FAMILY AND MEDICAL LEAVE ACT

Sullivan was employed by the USPS. In January 2009, he requested leave under the Family and Medical Leave Act (FMLA). In support of his request, he submitted a physician's certification that he suffered from frequent and painful attacks of gout in his feet and ankles that would require his absence from work for 5 to 10 days every month in 2009. A USPS committee, including the FMLA coordinator, reviewed the certification and decided to exercise the agency's right to obtain a second medical opinion. Sullivan was sent a letter notifying him that he was required to obtain the second medical evaluation. He was told when and where to report for the examination and advised that failure to appear could result in the denial of his FMLA request. Sullivan did not report for the examination. USPS informed Sullivan that his failure to appear was considered a failure to act in good faith but gave him an opportunity to explain his absence. He claimed that he didn't receive the notification letter. This reason was deemed not credible because the FMLA director had confirmed delivery of the letter. He was told that his application was denied and no leave would be approved in 2009. Sullivan still submitted 6 to 7 additional FMLA-leave requests in 2009 and approximately 14 FMLA-leave requests in 2010. All were denied for failure to show entitlement. He was disciplined twice for noncompliance with rules, and after 45 unscheduled absences for which he did not follow agency leave-requesting procedures, he was terminated for failure to comply with the agency's leave regulations.

CASE QUESTIONS

1. Even though Sullivan supplied a physician's certification, did the agency have the right to require a second medical evaluation?
2. How could Sullivan have avoided the conflict and qualified for leave?

CASE SUMMARY 11.7 Haynes v. Zoological Society of Cincinnati, 652 N.E.2d 948 (Ohio Ct. App. 1995)

WHISTLEBLOWER PROTECTION

Haynes, an animal keeper at the Zoological Society of Cincinnati (Zoo), was assigned to the bear and walrus areas and was responsible for feeding and taking general care of the animals. Haynes lodged several complaints with her supervisors about the unsafe conditions in her assigned areas, but Zoo failed to address her concerns. One afternoon, a co-worker, Stober, stopped in front of the den of a male polar bear and offered the bear a grape through the bars of the bear's cage. The bear pulled Stober's hand through the bars and bit off a portion of her arm. Haynes, who was with Stober when the attack occurred, gave a statement to authorities about the incident and blamed lack of personnel training and poor conditions inside the bear den as factors contributing to Stober's injuries. The next day, Haynes was demoted to an entry-level position at the birdhouse and then, a few days later, was suspended without pay for insubordination. Haynes sued Zoo, asserting that Zoo had demoted and suspended her in retaliation for reporting alleged unsafe working conditions to authorities. Zoo countered that Haynes was a member of a union and therefore could not avail herself of whistleblower protections that were afforded to other employees.

CASE QUESTIONS

1. Should Haynes be prevented from asserting a whistleblower claim because she is a member of a union?
2. Could Haynes claim the public policy exception in regard to this termination? Why or why not?

 Self-Check ANSWERS Exempt versus Covered (Nonexempt) Employees

1. Exempt. The salary level indicates a highly compensated employee.
2. Exempt. Professional with advanced study and certification.
3. Covered. Hourly wage earner under the salary threshold with repetitive work tasks.
4. Covered. Routine physical tasks typically trigger coverage regardless of job title.
5. Covered. Nonprofessional with no advanced study or certification requirements.
6. Exempt. White-collar employees are likely to be regulated by state insurance laws.

Unfair Labor Practices

1. Unfair labor practice. Once an election has taken place, if a simple majority (51 percent) of the bargaining unit votes to unionize, the union is certified and must be recognized even if 40 percent oppose unionization.
2. Probably not an unfair labor practice. Management is permitted to campaign against unionization in such a way—so long as there are no financial incentives (such as bonuses) offered. Management may not threaten employees with pay cuts, demotions, or the like during the campaign.
3. Given that the workers are leaving at the end of the shift and that the fliers are distributed in the employee locker room, this is likely a permissible labor practice even though it takes place on the employer's premises.
4. This is a lockout. So long as there is a legitimate business reason, lockouts are permitted by the NLRA.
5. Right-to-work statutes protect workers only from (1) having to join a union to guarantee continued employment and (2) having to share certain union costs. Right-to-work statutes do not guarantee anyone the right to a job.
6. Refusal to rehire is an unfair labor practice because the workers were striking over an unfair labor practice (refusing to abide by an existing collective bargaining contract) rather than for economic reasons. See *NLRB v. Midwestern Personnel Services, Inc.*, in Case 11.7.

CHAPTER REVIEW QUESTIONS: Answers and Explanations

1. **d.** Express contracts between the parties, including collective bargaining agreements (labor contracts), are out of the realm of the employment-at-will doctrine because it is assumed that the terms of employment were negotiated and not at-will. (c) is incorrect because the length of employment is not related to the scope of the employment-at-will doctrine.

2. **c.** Workplace safety standards are set out in laws such as the Occupational Safety and Health Act and are not part of the FLSA. All other answers are provisions of the FLSA.

3. **b.** A whistleblower statute is one where the legislature carves out an exception to the at-will rule in cases where the employee has reported illegal or improper conduct by his employer. (a), (d), and (e) are wrong because they are common law exceptions and are not applicable when a statute exists. (c) is wrong because no elements of antidiscrimination statutes are in question.

4. **b.** Employees covered under the FLSA have a maximum 40-hour workweek as calculated weekly. Anything over 40 hours in any one workweek must be paid at an overtime rate. In Week 1, Ahab worked five extra hours. In Week 2, he worked one extra hour. It is not relevant that he did not work 40 hours in Week 3 and Week 4.

5. **d.** The FMLA allows employees to take an unpaid leave of absence for family-related care (such as a newborn baby). (a), (b), and (c) are all incorrect because the FMLA has no paid leave provisions. (e) is incorrect because the law only covers care giving.

CHAPTER 12
Employment Discrimination

©philsajonesen/Getty Images

Learning Objectives

After studying this chapter, students who have mastered the material will be able to:

12-1 Define the term *employment discrimination,* articulate the origins of antidiscrimination law, and explain the role of the Equal Employment Opportunity Commission (EEOC).

12-2 List and describe the protections afforded under the major federal antidiscrimination statutes and identify the protected classes and theories of discrimination under Title VII.

12-3 Apply the two standards used in a sexual harassment claim and articulate ways to reduce liability for harassment.

12-4 Describe the provisions of the Age Discrimination in Employment Act (ADEA) and the Americans with Disabilities Act (ADA) and their impact on business operations.

12-5 Describe the procedures for asserting a discrimination claim.

12-6 List and apply the major defenses available to employers.

12-7 Explain the role of state law in employment discrimination cases.

One of the most frequent legal challenges encountered by business owners and managers involves laws that prohibit *discrimination* in the workplace. Lawsuits related to employment discrimination have increased substantially in recent decades, and managers frequently find themselves involved in employment discrimination claims as a witness, supervisor, defendant, or plaintiff/victim. Discrimination can be intentional or unintentional, and even a policy that applies to everyone equally can result in some form of discrimination. This area of law has developed very rapidly over the last 50 years, and the numerous statutes, along with standards and tests developed by courts to apply the rules, combine to form a relatively complex body of law from a variety of sources. In this chapter, students will learn

- The definition, source, and statutory framework of discrimination law.
- Theories of discrimination and employer defenses.
- The role of affirmative action in the workplace.
- Additional workplace antidiscrimination laws imposed by the states.

DEFINITION, SOURCE OF LAW, AND STATUTORY ORIGINS

Recall from previous chapters that one of the major exceptions to the employment-at-will doctrine (i.e., employers may discharge employees with or without cause without triggering liability) occurs when a statute prohibits the employer's action. The largest category of statutes that prohibit employers from terminating employees is antidiscrimination statutes that bar any job action, such as hiring or termination, based on certain discriminatory motives. The term

employment discrimination has a broad-based definition encompassing workplace-related discrimination that includes (1) the hiring process; (2) the treatment of employees in terms of promotions and demotions, work schedules, working conditions, and assignments; and (3) disciplinary action such as reprimands, suspension, or termination. Historically, U.S. common law had recognized virtually no protections for employees from discrimination based on race, color, gender, religion, national origin, age, disabilities, and other characteristics. For example, until the Equal Pay Act of 1963, employers could arbitrarily pay men and women, doing the same work, at different levels with no consequences. One year later, Congress passed the most sweeping antidiscrimination protections for workers in U.S. history as part of the Civil Rights Act of 1964. In addition to federal statutes, legislation enacted in some states provides additional antidiscrimination protections in the workplace.

LO 12-1
Define the term *employment discrimination*, articulate the origins of antidiscrimination law, and explain the role of the Equal Employment Opportunity Commission (EEOC).

Equal Employment Opportunity Commission (EEOC)

An important part of the Civil Rights Act of 1964 was the creation of an agency to monitor employer compliance with the statute. The administrative agency[1] charged with carrying out federal workplace antidiscrimination laws is the **Equal Employment Opportunity Commission (EEOC)**. The EEOC is a five-member commission whose members are appointed by the president with approval of the Senate. As an administrative agency, the EEOC uses its rulemaking authority, investigatory powers, and enforcement action as necessary to administer the statutory mandates established by Congress. The EEOC plays two important roles in ensuring discrimination victims' protection under various statutes. First, filing a complaint with the EEOC is the first step for a party claiming unlawful employment discrimination (procedures for asserting a discrimination claim are discussed later in this chapter). Second, in certain cases the EEOC will sue on *behalf* of an aggrieved employee. This is a powerful method of enforcing antidiscrimination laws because it gives aggrieved employees the full resources of the federal government, which can be particularly crucial when bringing an individual claim of employment discrimination against a large employer.

However, as a practical matter, the EEOC can pursue only a fraction of the claims that are made by employees. In 2012, 99,412 charges were filed; in 2013, 93,727 charges were filed; in 2014, 88,778 charges were filed; and in 2018, 76,418 charges were filed with the agency.[2] Because of the large volume of complaints filed, the EEOC typically focuses on cases that have some important legal significance or that involve employer conduct that was particularly egregious or was in bad faith (e.g., attempting to prevent an employee's EEOC claim with a threat of termination or demotion).

FEDERAL WORKPLACE ANTIDISCRIMINATION STATUTES

The primary federal antidiscrimination statutes are (1) **Title VII** of the Civil Rights Act of 1964[3] and its subsequent amendments, especially the Civil Rights Act of 1991;[4] (2) the **Age Discrimination in Employment Act (ADEA) of 1967**;[5] and (3) the **Americans with Disabilities Act (ADA) of 1990**,[6] which was last amended in 2009.

LO 12-2
List and describe the protections afforded under the major federal antidiscrimination statutes and identify the protected classes and theories of discrimination under Title VII.

---

[1]An administrative agency is a statutorily created body with responsibilities related to the formation, implementation, and enforcement of regulations intended to administer a federal law. Administrative agencies and law are covered in detail in Chapter 17, "Administrative Law."

[2]*Charge Statistics (Charges filed with EEOC) FY 1997 Through FY 2017*, U.S. Equal Employment Opportunity Commission, www.eeoc.gov/eeoc/statistics/enforcement/charges.cfm.

[3]42 U.S.C. § 2000e et seq.

[4]42 U.S.C. § 1981a et seq.

[5]29 U.S.C. § 621 et seq.

[6]42 U.S.C. § 12101 et seq.

The **Equal Pay Act of 1963** is actually part of the Fair Labor Standards Act but contains some antidiscrimination provisions as well.

These statutes may be categorized into two classes that are helpful in understanding their purpose: (1) laws that require the person in the protected class to receive *equal treatment* to that of nonclass members and (2) laws that require the person in the protected class to receive *special treatment*. For example, Title VII of the Civil Rights Act of 1964 requires women to be treated equally with men. In contrast, the Americans with Disabilities Act (discussed later in this chapter) requires that persons with certain disabilities be given special treatment via reasonable accommodations by their employer, when possible.

To illustrate the contours of the federal antidiscrimination statutes, suppose that Prescott is seeking employment as an internal accountant and provides a résumé and supporting application materials to WidgetCo, a manufacturing firm with 50 employees. This hypothetical example is used throughout the chapter to discuss possible scenarios involving various employment discrimination theories and defenses.

TITLE VII

Title VII of the Civil Rights Act of 1964 and its amendments make up the centerpiece of antidiscrimination statutes. Even when interpreting antidiscrimination statutes that are not part of Title VII, courts often apply the antidiscrimination law using the Title VII statutory model and application procedures. Title VII applies to any private sector employer with 15 or more full-time employees, as well as to labor unions, employment agencies, state and local governments, and most federal government employees. The law covers a comprehensive set of job-related transactions including hiring and firing, promotion and demotion, disciplinary actions, work schedule, pay rate, job assignment, and other employer actions. Referred to simply as *Title VII,* the law prohibits discrimination in the workplace on the basis of an employee's race, color, national origin, gender, or religion. These classifications are known as **protected classes**. In 1978, Congress amended Title VII to specifically add pregnancy as a protected class as well.[7]

Protected Classes

It is important to understand that one fundamental tenet of federal antidiscrimination laws is that not all discrimination is illegal. Under Title VII or any other antidiscrimination laws, statutory protection is extended only to those who have been discriminated against based on their membership in a protected class. For example, in our Prescott hypothetical, discussed earlier, suppose that Prescott has been hired by WidgetCo as an accountant. Prescott shows up on the first day wearing a T-shirt and blue jeans. His manager points out that his attire is not consistent with company dress policy and requests that he leave and return in more formal business attire. Prescott refuses to comply with his manager's request, so he is terminated. For purposes of understanding employment discrimination statutes, there are two important questions. First, was Prescott discriminated against? The answer is clearly yes. Prescott was terminated not for his poor performance but for wearing certain attire. Thus, it can be said that Prescott was the victim of anti-blue-jeans discrimination. However, the second question is more important: Was Prescott discriminated against based on

---

[7]Pregnancy Discrimination Act of 1978, 42 U.S.C. § 2000e(k).

his membership in a *protected class*? In other words, did WidgetCo terminate Prescott based on his color, race, national origin, religion, or gender? The answer is clearly no. Because this particular type of discrimination was not based on Prescott's association with a protected class, WidgetCo's discriminatory action (his termination) is not prohibited by Title VII.

It is also important to note that the plaintiff need not be in a *minority* within the protected classes in order to be covered by Title VII. While the majority of discrimination cases filed are based on discrimination related to a minority within a protected class, the statute protects against any discrimination based on association with a protected class and does not require that the plaintiff be a member of a certain ethnic category. For example, in *McDonald v. Santa Fe Train*,[8] the U.S. Supreme Court held that racial discrimination against white employees violates Title VII if the employer was motivated by race. However, there are certain instances in which an employer's preference for certain minority class members in an employment decision is *permitted* by an affirmative action plan (discussed later in this chapter).

Sexual Orientation as a Protected Class

The issue of whether sexual orientation is covered as a protected class is an excellent example of how the law, even interpretation of statutory law, can evolve over time. Proponents of the theory of recognizing

Antidiscrimination laws cover job-related transactions such as the hiring process. Ryan McVay/Getty Images

sexual orientation as a protected class argue that if an employer discriminates against an employee based on sexual orientation, it amounts to discrimination based on sex and is thus illegal under federal discrimination statutes. Up until recently, no court of authority has ruled that sexual orientation is covered under Title VII. However, in 2015, the EEOC issued a ruling that recognized discrimination based on sexual orientation as a form of sex discrimination. The EEOC reasoned that sexual orientation is inherently a sex-based consideration and, accordingly, an allegation of discrimination based on sexual orientation is necessarily an allegation of sex discrimination under Title VII. Although the rulings in federal courts have been mixed since the EEOC's ruling, both the U.S. Court of Appeals for the Seventh Circuit and the U.S. Court of Appeals for the First Circuit recently ruled that Title VII *does* cover sexual orientation claims. Most recently, another federal appellate court reversed its previous position on the issue of sexual orientation in the context of Title VII.

In Case 12.1 the court explains the reasoning behind its reversal of its previous interpretations of whether sexual orientation is a protected class.

---

[8]427 U.S. 273 (1976). The case involved a lawsuit brought by a white employee who was terminated for allegedly stealing from the company. The same incident involved a black employee who was also alleged to have stolen from the company but was given only a reprimand.

CASE 12.1 Zarda v. Altitude Express, 883 F.3d 100 (2d Cir. 2018)

FACT SUMMARY In 2010, Donald Zarda, a gay man, worked as a sky-diving instructor at Altitude Express. As part of his job, he regularly participated in tandem skydives, strapped hip-to-hip and shoulder-to-shoulder with customers. In an environment where close physical proximity was common, Zarda's coworkers routinely referenced sexual orientation and Zarda sometimes told female customers about his sexual orientation to alleviate any concern they might have about being strapped to a man for a tandem skydive. During preparation for one jump with a female customer, Zarda told a female client with whom he was preparing for a tandem skydive that he was gay "and ha[d] an ex-husband to prove it." According to Zarda, this disclosure was intended simply to preempt any discomfort the client may have felt in being strapped to the body of an unfamiliar man. However, the customer alleged that Zarda inappropriately touched her and disclosed his sexual orientation to excuse his behavior. After the customer complained to Altitude management, Zarda was fired. Zarda denied inappropriately touching the client and insisted he was fired solely because of his reference to his sexual orientation.

Zarda filed a discrimination charge with the EEOC concerning his termination and later brought a lawsuit against Altitude claiming that in addition to being discriminated against because of his sexual orientation, he was also discriminated against because of his gender. The trial court dismissed Zarda's complaint ruling that Zarda had failed to establish a gender discrimination case because previous case law had never recognized sexual orientation as a protected class.

SYNOPSIS OF DECISION AND OPINION The U.S. Court of Appeals for the Second Circuit reversed the trial court's decision and ruled in favor of Zarda. The court considered the EEOC's position on the matter of sexual orientation being a protected class under Title VII and agreed that there was an inescapable link between allegations of sexual orientation discrimination and sex discrimination. The court reasoned that if sexual orientation is a function of sex and sex discrimination is prohibited under Title VII, then sexual orientation must also violate Title VII. The court pointed out that the *Zarda* case was an example of associational discrimination because an employee alleging discrimination on the basis of sexual orientation is alleging that his or her employer took his or her sex into account by treating him or her differently for associating with a person of the same sex

WORDS OF THE COURT: Sex as a Motivating Factor "Title VII's prohibition on sex discrimination applies to any practice in which sex is a motivating factor. . . . [S]exual orientation discrimination is a subset of sex discrimination because sexual orientation is defined by one's sex in relation to the sex of those to whom one is attracted, making it impossible for an employer to discriminate on the basis of sexual orientation without taking sex into account. Sexual orientation discrimination is also based on assumptions of stereotypes about how members of a particular gender should be, including to whom they should be attracted. Finally, sexual orientation discrimination is associational discrimination because an adverse employment action that is motivated by the employer's opposition to association between members of particular sexes discriminates against an employee on the basis of sex."

Case Questions

1. Why was Zarda's case an example of "associational discrimination"?
2. Should the fact that a customer complained about Zarda impact a Title VII analysis? Why or why not?
3. *Focus on Critical Thinking:* The dissent in this case pointed out that Congress had ample opportunity to add sexual orientation into the statute, but did not. The dissent accused the majority of filling in a portion of Title VII that the court found lacking, but the legislature has not changed the law in decades. Is that a compelling argument? Why or why not? Did the court "legislate from the bench"?

Theories of Discrimination

For several years following the passage of the Civil Rights Act of 1964, courts struggled with having to apply such a massive statutory scheme in the workplace with virtually no comparable protections in the history of labor law to use as precedent. The result was that federal courts applied the statutes unevenly and variously, which resulted in overly broad or overly narrow interpretations of the law. Beginning in 1971, the Supreme Court began to develop guidance for the courts on how to apply Title VII. In a number of landmark cases, the Court developed several theories of discrimination that plaintiffs may pursue based on the type of discrimination alleged. These cases also provided the lower courts with a system of tests that are used to apply the various theories of discrimination. Thus, the three most common theories and attendant tests are sometimes referred to by their case names. The theories are (1) **disparate treatment** (*McDonnell Douglas*[9] standard); (2) **mixed motives** (*Hopkins*[10] standard); and (3) **disparate impact** (*Griggs*[11] standard). Note that subsequent amendments to Title VII have added statutory language consistent with the case law on disparate treatment and disparate impact. Nonetheless, the theories are still commonly referred to by their case names.

> **KEY POINT**
>
> For an employee to be protected under Title VII, the employer's discriminatory decision must have been based on the employee's membership in a *protected class*.

Disparate Treatment Disparate treatment is overt and intentional discrimination. Simply put, when an employer treats an employee (or potential employee) differently based on her membership in a protected class, this constitutes discrimination under Title VII. Specially, the statute makes it unlawful for an employer

> (1) to fail or refuse to hire or to discharge any individual, or to otherwise discriminate against any individual with respect to his compensation, terms, conditions, or privileges of employment, because of such individual's race, color, religion, sex, or national origin; or
>
> (2) to limit, segregate, or classify employees or applicants for employment in any way which would deprive or tend to deprive any individual of employment opportunities or otherwise adversely affect his status as an employee, because of such individual's race, color, religion, sex, or national origin.
>
> 42 U.S.C. 2000e–2(a).

This theory of discrimination may be proved through the use of either *direct* or *indirect* evidence. Direct evidence is evidence that proves a fact without any further inference or presumption. For example, suppose in our working hypothetical that Prescott is a woman who has applied for the position at WidgetCo. After the interview, the manager informs her that she will not get the position and states: "I think you are the most qualified applicant, but we prefer a man in that role because this job may involve night work and I would be concerned about a woman's safety." Here, WidgetCo is treating Prescott differently based on a protected class—gender. Even though the manager's decision seems to be based on a true concern for Prescott's well-being, the fact that Prescott is being deprived of an employment opportunity solely because she is a woman violates Title VII.

Overt and intentional discrimination does not have to be with discriminatory intent in order to trigger liability for the employer.[12] In fact, in some cases the employee does not need to prove that his employer had actual knowledge that the employee required a Title VII accommodation that was in conflict with the employer's policy. In Case 12.2, the U.S. Supreme Court analyzes Title VII's provisions relating to religious discrimination.

---

[9]*McDonnell Douglas Corp. v. Green*, 411 U.S. 792 (1973).
[10]*PriceWaterhouse v. Hopkins*, 490 U.S. 228 (1989).
[11]*Griggs v. Duke Power Co.*, 401 U.S. 424 (1971).
[12]*Vaughn v. Edel*, 918 F.2d 517 (5th Cir. 1990).

CASE 12.2 U.S. Equal Employment Opportunity Commission v. Abercrombie & Fitch Stores, Inc., 135 S. Ct. 2028 (2015)

FACT SUMMARY Abercrombie & Fitch Stores, Inc. (Abercrombie), operates several lines of clothing stores and maintains policies consistent with the image Abercrombie seeks to project. One such policy, known as the Look Policy, governs its employees' dress. The policy prohibits "caps" as too informal for Abercrombie's desired image. Samantha Elauf (Elauf) is a practicing Muslim who, consistent with her understanding of her religion's requirements, wears a headscarf. She applied for a position in an Abercrombie store, and using Abercrombie's ordinary system for evaluating applicants, the interviewer gave Elauf a rating that qualified her to be hired. However, the interviewer was concerned that Elauf's headscarf, known as a hijab, would conflict with the store's Look Policy and consulted Abercrombie's district manager. The manager concluded that the headscarf would violate the Look Policy, as would all other headwear, religious or otherwise, and Elauf was not hired. The EEOC sued Abercrombie on Elauf's behalf, claiming that its refusal to hire Elauf violated Title VII. The trial court granted EEOC summary judgment on the issue of liability and awarded $20,000 in damages. The U.S. Court of Appeals for the Tenth Circuit reversed and awarded Abercrombie summary judgment based on its conclusion that ordinarily an employer cannot be liable under Title VII for failing to accommodate a religious practice until the applicant (or employee) provides the employer with *actual* knowledge of his need for an accommodation. The EEOC appealed to the U.S. Supreme Court.

SYNOPSIS OF DECISION AND OPINION The U.S. Supreme Court reversed the decision of the lower court and ruled in favor of the EEOC. The Court focused on the text of Title VII that gives religion favored status and provided a straightforward rule for disparate-treatment claims based on a failure to accommodate a religious practice: An employer may not make an applicant's religious practice, confirmed or otherwise, a factor in employment decisions. The Court rejected Abercrombie's argument that the employer must have actual knowledge of the employee's need for religious accommodation because there was no language in the statute that required such knowledge in order to trigger liability. Instead, an applicant need only show that her need for an accommodation was a motivating factor in the employer's decision.

WORDS OF THE COURT: Actual Knowledge Not Required "Abercrombie urges this Court to adopt the Tenth Circuit's rule 'allocat[ing] the burden of raising a religious conflict.' This would require the employer to have actual knowledge of a conflict between an applicant's religious practice and a work rule. The problem with this approach is the one that [results] in most incorrect interpretations of statutes: It asks us to add words to the law to produce what is thought to be a desirable result. That is Congress's province. We construe Title VII's silence as exactly that: silence."

WORDS OF THE COURT: Religious Accommodation "A request for accommodation, or the employer's certainty that the practice exists, may make it easier to infer motive, but is not a necessary condition of liability. . . .

"Nor does the statute limit disparate-treatment claims to only those employer policies that treat religious practices less favorably than similar secular practices. Abercrombie's argument that a neutral policy cannot constitute 'intentional discrimination' may make sense in other contexts. But Title VII does not demand mere neutrality with regard to religious practices . . . Rather, it gives them favored treatment, affirmatively obligating employers not 'to fail or refuse to hire or discharge any individual . . . because of such individual's religious observance and practice.' An employer is surely entitled to have, for example, a no headwear policy as an ordinary matter. But when an applicant requires an accommodation as an 'aspec[t] of religious . . . practice,' it is no response that the subsequent failure to hire was due to an otherwise neutral policy. Title VII requires otherwise-neutral policies to give way to the need for an accommodation."

Case Questions

1. Why does the Court conclude that "actual knowledge" is not necessary?

(continued)

2. What strategies should employers deploy in order to reduce their liability for violating the religious accommodations requirement in Title VII?
3. *Focus on Critical Thinking:* Just before the decision in this case was announced, Abercrombie changed its policies relating to how employees look and dress. This was a significant change to its business model. To what extent should business owners and managers consider legal doctrines when designing or redesigning their business model? Are there any other areas of law that should be taken into consideration by businesses when designing policies related to their business model?

Employers should also be aware of a federal appellate court ruling in which special efforts made by an employer to avoid a discrimination charge resulted in a Title VII violation. The case involved an African American woman who, despite low productivity, was given satisfactory work ratings from her supervisor. The supervisor testified that he had intentionally overstated his satisfaction with the employee's performance on her annual evaluation because a top-level manager was concerned about a possible discrimination claim. Eventually, the company undertook a cost-cutting study that revealed the employee's poor performance, and she was terminated as a result of the study. The court held in favor of the employee and ruled that the employer's decision not to apply the usual evaluation procedures was a racial decision and violated Title VII.

In *McDonnell Douglas Corp. v. Green,* the U.S. Supreme Court crafted a template for disparate treatment proof that plaintiffs could use to obtain relief under Title VII. This method of proof is usually referred to as the *McDonnell Douglas* standard, and it contemplates a burden-shifting analysis (explained below).

The *McDonnell Douglas* standard has three stages. In the first stage, the plaintiff must establish a prima facie[13] case of discrimination.

To establish a claim of discrimination that satisfies the prima facie requirement under the *McDonnell Douglas* standard, the Supreme Court created a four-prong disparate treatment test that lower courts adapt to fit the type of discrimination at issue. The plaintiff must establish that

1. She is a member of a protected class.
2. She applied for and was qualified for the job (or promotion, etc., depending on the factual circumstances of the controversy) and met the employer's legitimate expectations.
3. She was rejected by the employer.
4. The employer continued to seek applicants or filled the position with a person outside the protected class.

In cases involving types of discriminatory action unrelated to hiring or promotion, the appropriate prong is adjusted accordingly. For example, in a wrongful-termination claim, the plaintiff would have to satisfy prongs 2 and 3 (candidate was qualified and rejected despite the qualification) by proving that she was terminated by her employer despite qualifications and performance and that, following the discharge, she was replaced by someone with comparable qualifications who was not in the same protected class.

Once the plaintiff makes out a prima facie case, the second stage of the *McDonnell Douglas* standard requires the **burden of proof** to *shift* to the employer, who then must articulate a *legitimate, nondiscriminatory* reason for the discriminatory action. If the

Legal Speak >))

Prima Facie Case Establishing certain evidence that is sufficient to prevail in a discrimination claim without proving additional facts, unless disproved or rebutted by the opposing party.

---

[13] A Latin phrase meaning "at a first view," which, according to the authoritative *Collins Latin Gem,* is sometimes mistakenly translated as "on its face."

employer does provide a legitimate, nondiscriminatory reason for firing the plaintiff, the third stage of the standard contemplates that the burden then *shifts back* to the employee to show that the reason given by the employer is not the actual reason for the employment action. A false reason under these circumstances is called a **pretext**. It should be noted that issues related to proving discrimination and pretext are *fact* questions for the jury to decide. In a disparate treatment case, the plaintiff is alleging intentional discrimination and the employer is asserting a legitimate reason for its action. It is up to the jury as the finder of fact to decide which version of facts is more compelling and believable.

Suppose that in our hypothetical case Prescott was African American and was hired by WidgetCo as a junior accountant. After three years, she was promoted to senior accountant and given a pay raise. When a manager's position was posted a year later, Prescott applied and was hopeful that with her four years of experience and other qualifications she would get the promotion. However, she was passed over for this position and for several subsequent openings for management positions. Eventually, she learned that two managers who had been promoted ahead of her each had only one year of experience and that all of the managers promoted ahead of her were either white or male. Prescott's disparate treatment claim under the *McDonnell Douglas* standard's four-prong test would likely be sufficient to establish a prima facie case because (1) Prescott was in a protected class, (2) she had applied for and was qualified for the promotion, (3) she was not promoted, and (4) WidgetCo promoted less experienced individuals. At this point, the burden of proof *shifts* to WidgetCo to provide a legitimate, nondiscriminatory reason for not promoting Prescott. Suppose that WidgetCo submits employee records that indicate that Prescott was late for work three times in the last two years and the company cites that as its legitimate reason. The burden of proof then *shifts back* to the employee/plaintiff to provide evidence that WidgetCo's reason is merely a pretext for discriminatory action. For example, Prescott could provide evidence of pretext by citing attendance records of others in the company to prove that a record of only three incidents of lateness did not disqualify other employees from being promoted.

> ### KEY POINT
>
> As in all civil cases, the initial burden of proof in a Title VII action rests upon the plaintiff to prove her case. Once the plaintiff establishes a prima facie case, a presumption is created that the employer discriminated against the employee. However, this presumption is rebuttable (refutable) because the burden of proof then shifts to the employer to provide a nondiscriminatory reason for the decision. If the nondiscriminatory reason is plausible and supported by the evidence, this creates a presumption that the employer is not liable for discrimination. The burden then shifts once again back to the employee, who then has the opportunity to offer evidence that tends to prove that the reason offered by the employer is a pretext.

Mixed Motives Although the U.S. Supreme Court made it easier for plaintiffs to assert their Title VII rights under a disparate treatment theory, employers were being consistently insulated from liability from Title VII by asserting legitimate, subjective-based reasons (such as inability to work as a member of a team) to defeat a Title VII claim. Even when these cases involved unlawful discriminatory reasons for the employment action, so long as the employer could cite even one legitimate reason, the employee could *not* recover under a disparate treatment theory. To alleviate this problem, the U.S. Supreme Court articulated an alternative theory of protection under Title VII when the cause of the employment action is motivated by both legitimate *and* discriminatory motives. The mixed motives theory was articulated in *PriceWaterhouse v. Hopkins*.[14]

The case involved Hopkins, a woman employed as an associate at the global accounting and consulting firm of PriceWaterhouse (now PricewaterhouseCoopers). Like many professional service firms, associates are eventually proposed for partnership in the firm after a certain length of time. Hopkins was proposed for partnership, and as part of the process,

Legal Speak >))

Pretext
A false excuse that is intended to cover up a discriminatory motive or action.

---

[14]490 U.S. 228 (1989).

the firm's partners were asked to write evaluations of Hopkins and make a recommendation as to whether the firm should offer her partnership. In general, associates who are not voted in as partners are either terminated or held over for reconsideration in the next year. Hopkins's evaluations were mostly positive, with partners praising her role in securing a large government client. They also evaluated her as extremely competent, bright, and hardworking. However, a significant number of partners were concerned about her interpersonal skills. She was abrasive, shouted at the staff, and used foul language in public. Several partners, though, went further and criticized her using gender-stereotypical, demeaning comments, such as advising Hopkins to "act more like a lady" or "take a course in charm school." One partner even made a suggestion that Hopkins should "walk more femininely, talk more femininely, dress more femininely, and wear makeup" if she wanted to improve her chances for partnership. As a result of these negative comments, the firm initially opted to hold Hopkins over for one more year but eventually notified her that she would not be placed for a partnership vote again. Hopkins sued under Title VII using a theory of disparate treatment, but the firm pointed to the documented legitimate reasons relating to Hopkins's inability to work as a team member. In essence, the case involved both legitimate reasons for the job action that were mixed with illegitimate discriminatory motives as evidenced by the evaluations written by the partners.

Ultimately, the Supreme Court adopted a new theory and framework for certain intentional discrimination: *mixed motives*. Under this theory, an employee is protected under Title VII in a case where legitimate motives are mixed with illegitimate motives if the employee proves the protected-class membership was a *substantial factor in the decision-making process*. Once established, the burden then shifts to the employer to offer evidence that it would have made the same employment decision regardless of the protected characteristics. In the *Hopkins* case, the Court held that Hopkins had met her burden of proving that gender was a substantial factor in the firm's decision-making process because the language of the evaluations was so closely tied to gender discrimination.[15] The Court also held that the employer's burden need only be proved by a preponderance of the evidence.

Legal Speak >))

Preponderance of the Evidence More likely than not. A lower standard of proof as compared to "clear and convincing evidence."

Disparate Impact Even when an employer is not motivated by discriminatory intent, Title VII prohibits an employer from using a facially neutral practice (i.e., one that applies to all employees regardless of class membership) that has an unlawful *adverse impact* on members of a protected class. When it first announced this theory in *Griggs v. Duke Power Co.*,[16] the Supreme Court recognized that *intent* was *not* always a necessary element to prove discrimination and that certain evaluation techniques for employee selection, promotion, and assignment—such as written tests, height and weight requirements, educational requirements, and oral candidate interviews—could be administered uniformly to all candidates yet still impact certain protected-class members adversely. The Court ruled that some testing mechanisms operate as "built-in headwinds" for minority groups and are unrelated to measuring job capability.

The disparate impact framework is similar to that of intentional discrimination cases in that the plaintiff must first prove a prima facie case by showing that certain methods resulted in statistically significant differences that adversely impacted members of a protected class. To satisfy this requirement, the plaintiff frequently provides statistical data related to a testing measure. The EEOC's *Uniform Guidelines on Employee Selection Criteria* defines adverse impact as occurring when members of a protected class are

---

[15]In the majority opinion, Justice Brennan opined that "if an employee's flawed 'interpersonal skills' can be corrected by a soft-hued suit or a new shade of lipstick, perhaps it is the employee's sex and not her interpersonal skills that has drawn the criticism."

[16]401 U.S. 424 (1971).

selected at a rate less than 80 percent of that of the highest-scoring group.[17] For example, suppose that Prescott's mother is Cuban and, therefore, Prescott can be considered Latino in the national-origin class under Title VII. He was required to take a test for the accounting position at WidgetCo. Of all candidates taking the exam, Asian candidates faired best, with 10 of 20 candidates passing the test. Among Latino candidates as a group, only 3 out of 20 candidates passed. Because the number of Latino candidates who passed was less than 80 percent of the number who passed among the highest-scoring group (Asians), this would be important evidence in Prescott's disparate impact claim of discrimination. Once the prima facie elements are established, the burden of proof then shifts to the employer to provide evidence that the challenged practice is *job-related* for the position in question and is a *business necessity*. However, even if the employer shows a valid business necessity, the plaintiff may still prevail if he proves that the employer refused to adopt an alternative practice that would satisfy the employer's interests without having the adverse impact.

Despite the EEOC guidelines and federal court decisions, disparate impact is still a very thorny area of discrimination law.

In *Ricci v. DeStefano,* the U.S. Supreme Court ruled that the City of New Haven's decision to discard results of a promotional exam for firefighters was a violation of Title VII even if the discriminatory treatment was based on the employer's concern that promotion examination results would possibly lead to a disparate impact lawsuit. The Court ruled

> [Employers] may not take the . . . step of discarding the test altogether to achieve a more desirable racial distribution of promotion-eligible candidates—absent a strong basis in evidence that the test was deficient and that discarding the results is necessary to avoid violating the disparate impact provision.[18]

> **KEY POINT**
>
> Discarding results of a race-neutral employment or promotion test, even if done to avoid disparate impact liability, may give rise to a disparate treatment claim by affected employees or promotion candidates.

LO 12-3

Apply the two standards used in a sexual harassment claim and articulate ways to reduce liability for harassment.

SEXUAL HARASSMENT

Because Title VII includes gender as a protected class, federal law extends protection to employees who are being sexually harassed. Unwelcome sexual advances, requests for sexual favors, and other verbal or physical conduct of a sexual nature are considered violations of Title VII if the conduct (1) occurs in the context of explicit or implicit conditions of an individual's employment or as a basis for any employment decisions or (2) unreasonably interferes with an individual's work performance or creates an offensive work environment. Generally, a victim of sexual harassment alleges one of two theories. In the *quid pro quo* theory (derived from the Latin phrase meaning "something for something else"), for example, the harasser demands sexual favors as a condition of continued employment or a prerequisite for a promotion or pay raise. More commonly, sexual harassment takes the form of a **hostile work environment**. Under this theory, a violation of Title VII occurs when the conduct of the harasser (or group of harassers) is of such a severe and crude nature, or is so pervasive in the workplace, that it interferes with the victim's ability to perform her job responsibilities. It is important to understand, however, that the standards for proving hostile work environment are relatively burdensome and require a discriminatory activity that is beyond teasing, offhand comments, or isolated

---

[17]29 C.F.R. § 1607.4(D).
[18]557 U.S. 557 (2009).

incidents. In *Faragher v. City of Boca Raton,* the U.S. Supreme Court gave guidance on the hostile work environment theory:

> Workplaces are not always harmonious locales, and even incidents that would objectively give rise to bruised or wounded feelings will not on that account satisfy the severe or pervasive standard. Some rolling with the punches is a fact of workplace life.[19]

However, if the behavior is sufficiently abusive and the abuse led the employee to quit, the employee is still permitted to file a complaint.[20] This rule is different from a typical discrimination case in which the employer must have actually taken some adverse action for a violation to occur. While there is no formula for determining a hostile work environment, courts have deemed certain behaviors as a violation of Title VII. These include (1) initiating a discussion of sexual acts, activities, or physical attributes in workplace areas (such as the employee cafeteria); (2) engaging in unnecessary or excessive physical contact; (3) using crude, demeaning, or vulgar language; and (4) displaying pornographic pictures or movies. In determining whether a hostile work environment has been created, courts will generally require that the harassment be severe and pervasive. This means that if an inappropriate incident occurred but was not subsequently repeated, that one-time incident will likely not support a claim for harassment.

In Case 12.3, a federal appellate court applies the severe or pervasive standard to a hospital workplace.

CASE 12.3 Morris v. City of Colorado Springs d/b/a Memorial Health System, 666 F.3d 654 (10th Cir. 2012)

FACT SUMMARY Morris was a registered nurse at Memorial Health System (Memorial) and was assigned to the Heart Team that performed all heart surgeries done at the hospital. Dr. Bryan Mahan (Mahan) is a surgeon on Memorial's Heart Team. During the time Morris was on the Heart Team with Mahan, she contends that he harassed her on multiple occasions. Specifically, she alleges that he made a number of demeaning comments to her and treated her differently than male employees.

In one incident, after Mahan surgically removed heart tissue from the patient on the operating table, he threw it in Morris's direction. Although Mahan claimed that he intended only to throw the tissue on the floor behind him, the tissue hit Morris's leg and Mahan joked about it afterwards. Morris reported the incident to (1) her supervisor, (2) Memorial's director of surgery, and (3) Memorial's director of human resources. In response, Memorial's Chief of Staff temporarily suspended Mahan from the operating room and required members of the Heart Team to attend a team-building exercise. Both Morris and Mahan attended the training and worked together for three months afterwards.

Still, Morris filed a Notice of [Discrimination] Claim alleging that she had suffered damages as a result of the heart tissue incident and stated she would pursue claims against Memorial and Mahan. Memorial's Human Resources office sent Morris an acknowledgment of the Claim and notified her that she would be removed from the Heart Team and assigned to the main operating room because of Memorial's obligation to place her in a work environment that was comfortable.

In 2009, Morris filed suit against Memorial in federal district court alleging discrimination. Among other claims, Morris asserted a claim under Title VII alleging that Mahan engaged in unlawful gender-based harassment and created an abusive and hostile working environment. The trial court

(continued)

---

[19] 524 U.S. 775, 778 (1998).
[20] *Harris v. Forklift Systems, Inc.*, 510 U.S. 17 (1993).

dismissed the case on summary judgment, ruling that Morris could not establish that the alleged harassment was based on her gender or that it was sufficiently "severe" or "pervasive" to affect her working environment. Morris appealed.

SYNOPSIS OF DECISION AND OPINION The Court of Appeals for the Tenth Circuit ruled in favor of Memorial and affirmed the trial court's dismissal of the case. The court held that Mahan's conduct did not rise to the level of a hostile work environment. The court explained that the comments made by Mahan to Morris and the tissue-throwing incident were not sufficient to meet the "severe or pervasive" standard. The court pointed to past cases that were based upon sexual discrimination where there was evidence that the plaintiffs had been subjected to both a number of gender-based incidents occurring over a long period of time, including sexual propositions, and multiple incidents of hostile and physically threatening conduct. Because Mahan's conduct did not rise to that legal standard, the court concluded that summary judgment by the trial court level was appropriate.

WORDS OF THE COURT: Severe or Pervasive Standard "Title VII does not establish a general civility code for the workplace. Accordingly, the run-of-the-mill boorish, juvenile, or annoying behavior that is not uncommon in American workplaces is not the stuff of a Title VII hostile work environment claim. . . . Not all offensive conduct is actionable as harassment; trivial offenses do not suffice. An employer creates a hostile work environment when the workplace is permeated with discriminatory intimidation, ridicule, and insult that is sufficiently severe or pervasive to alter the conditions of the victim's employment and create an abusive working environment. . . .

"While Dr. Mahan's conduct (construing the facts in the light most favorable to Ms. Morris) was unquestionably juvenile, unprofessional, and perhaps independently tortious, viewed in context, we cannot conclude from this record that it objectively altered the terms and conditions of Ms. Morris's employment."

Case Questions

1. Why does the court find that Mahan's conduct did not rise to the level necessary to create a hostile work environment? Do you agree?
2. What type of conduct is required for harassment to be considered severe or pervasive? Give an example of hypothetical conduct by Mahan that may have led the court to believe that Morris had met her burden of proof.
3. *Focus on Critical Thinking:* Could Morris pursue other legal avenues against Mahan for his conduct? Is there any civil liability in tort? Could Morris pursue a breach of contract claim against the hospital for reassigning her from the Heart Team?

Same Sex Harassment

In *Oncale v. Sundowner Offshore Services, Inc.,*[21] the U.S. Supreme Court held that an employee on an oil rig who was subject to homosexual advances by his co-workers was protected under Title VII. The Court made clear that Title VII was gender-neutral and recognized sexual harassment as a form of discrimination regardless of the gender of the victim or the harasser.

Vicarious Liability of Employers

Recall from Chapter 10, "Agency," that employers are typically liable for the tortious actions of their employees when they are acting within their scope of employment. In 1998, the U.S. Supreme Court decided two companion cases that extended vicarious liability to employers for sexual harassment under certain circumstances. The Court held in the *Faragher*[22] and *Ellerth*[23] cases that an employer could be held vicariously liable for sexual harassment by an employee when a nonsupervisory co-worker is the harasser if the

---

[21] 523 U.S. 75 (1998).
[22] *Faragher v. City of Boca Raton*, 524 U.S. 775 (1998).
[23] *Ellerth v. Burlington Industries*, 524 U.S. 951 (1998).

employee can prove that the employer was negligent in either (1) discovering the conduct or (2) failing to respond to a sexual harassment complaint made to a supervisor.

Strict Liability for Harassment by Supervisor

If the harassing employee is a supervisor, then the employer is strictly liable for any sexual harassment claim if the harassment culminates in a tangible employment action such as termination or transfer to a less desirable job. If the harassment does not result in a tangible employment action (e.g., demotion), employers may avoid liability via the *Faragher/Ellerth* defense by proving that a system was in place that was intended to deter, prevent, report, and correct any harassment. The employer must also prove that the employee failed to take advantage of the preventative or corrective opportunities that the employer provided.

One important issue in a vicarious liability case centers on the definition of a supervisor. In *Vance v. Ball State University*,[24] the U.S. Supreme Court clarified the definition of a supervisor for purposes of liability for harassment by co-workers. In that case, Vance was employed as a catering assistant at Ball State University (BSU) and was allegedly subject to harassment primarily by a BSU employee whose job title was "Catering Specialist." Although the alleged harasser was responsible for oversight of catering occasions where Vance was working, the alleged harasser did not have the power to hire, fire, demote, promote, transfer, or discipline Vance. The Court ruled that the alleged harasser did *not* qualify as a supervisor and thus BSU could not be held vicariously liable unless Vance could prove that BSU was negligent in either discovering the conduct or in failing to respond to a harassment complaint made to a supervisor.

Impact of the #MeToo Movement

In response to high-profile celebrities who began to accuse Hollywood mogul Harvey Weinstein of covering up a long pattern of sexual assault and sexual harassment, the #MeToo movement used social media to bring to the forefront of the world's consciousness the magnitude and severity of sexual harassment in all aspects of society. The hashtag went viral after actress Alyssa Milano tweeted: "If all the women who have been sexually harassed or assaulted wrote 'Me too' as a status, we might give people a sense of the magnitude of the problem."

Although the #MeToo movement broadly encompasses sexual assault and harassment, it has helped to educate society on the hurdles that litigants face when accusing employers of sexual harassment in the workplace. Moreover, because sexual harassment can be the result of one party feeling that he or she has the power to abuse a subordinate without consequences, this type of social movement helps to curb abuses before they begin.

STRATEGIC LEGAL SOLUTIONS

Proactive Harassment Prevention Framework

PROBLEM: Sexual harassment in the workplace creates a toxic environment for employees that results in low morale, severe stress, illness, and high turnover among the workforce, translating into significant lost revenue for both the business and employee.[25] Vicarious liability for the harassment may result in multimillion-dollar jury verdicts against the business. According to Business Insider, juries have awarded the following for sexual harassment

(continued)

---

[24] 570 U.S. 421 (2013).

[25] L. Fitzgerald & S. Schulman, *Sexual Harassment: A Research Analysis and Agenda*, 42 J. Vocational Behav. 5 (2003).

claims: $10.6 million to a UBS sales assistant (2011); $11.6 million to an executive of the New York Knicks (2007); $30 million to clerks of Ralph's Fresh Fare grocery chain (2002); $95 million to a salesperson at Aaron's Rent-to-Own (2011); $168 million to a physician's assistant at Mercy General Hospital (2012); and $250 million to female staffers at Novartis (2010).

SOLUTION: *Create a Harassment Prevention Framework that is intended to prevent, investigate, and remediate harassment in the employer's workplace. By incorporating elements of the Faragher/Ellerth defense into the framework, the employer also limits vicarious liability for harassment.*

Step 1. Prevention: Define, Distribute, and Deter

The primary goal of the Harassment Prevention Framework is to *prevent* incidents of sexual harassment. The strongest deterrent to harassment is the knowledge by employees as to what constitutes sexual harassment, how to report it, assurances that reports will be investigated thoroughly, and a commitment to discipline those found responsible.

- Review all job descriptions and revise them if necessary to be sure they clearly identify which employees are considered supervisors (i.e., authority to hire, fire, demote, promote, transfer, or discipline a subordinate).
- Work with counsel to develop a specific anti-harassment policy that addresses sexual harassment as well as other forms of workplace harassment (e.g., racial). The policy should define harassment, provide specific examples, and set out sanctions for violators. Employers should also consider incorporating an anti-bullying policy into their Harassment Prevention Framework.
- Incorporate the anti-harassment policy into all Employee Handbooks within the organization and distribute the policy as a separate document to all employees. Place "Anti-Harassment Policy" posters that summarize the policy in all employee common areas such as cafeterias, locker rooms, lounges, etc.
- The chief executive officer or another high-profile leader should personally speak to groups of employees about the policy and explain how the policy aligns with the company's values and ethics.
- Dedicate in-service training periods to the subject of sexual harassment in order to have a frank discussion of specific examples of inappropriate behavior that constitute sexual harassment and provide a legal primer on personal and vicarious liability under Title VII. If possible, have an outside expert conduct a seminar on recognizing and preventing sexual harassment. For new employees, ensure that the anti-harassment policy is distributed and discussed during their orientation. Supervisors should have special training in detecting, identifying, and reporting harassment.

Step 2. Reporting and Investigation

A crucial part of your anti-harassment policy should be the reporting procedure and a defined investigative path. The policy cannot be effective if employees are not assured a safe, confidential method for reporting harassment and are not given a degree of assurance that their claims will be taken seriously.

- Designate multiple "intake supervisors" from various departments throughout the business who are trained to take detailed information for use in a harassment investigation. These supervisors should be identified as intake supervisors in company publications, on websites, and at in-service training.
- Create alternatives for employees to report harassment such as a designated voicemail box. Consider establishing a link on the company website that helps employees find more information about the anti-harassment policy and provides a mechanism for reporting violations of the policy.
- Appoint one senior corporate official (typically from executive management) to investigate all claims received by intake supervisors and the website. This includes the investigation of anonymous complaints. This official must have sufficient training, authority, and experience to investigate and properly document the review, investigation, and conclusions related to the complaint.
- Begin the investigation of the complaint no later than one business day if possible. Conclude the investigation as soon as possible without sacrificing thoroughness or accuracy. Counsel may be

(continued)

alerted at this stage, but it is typically not necessary to hire counsel to conduct the investigation.
- Ensure that confidentiality and fairness are the two guiding principles of the investigation and that reporting employees are informed about the progress of the investigation and protected from retaliation.

Step 3. Enforcement and Remediation

If the investigation reveals that an employee was subject to harassment, employers are required to take immediate disciplinary and remedial action in order to avoid liability through the *Faragher/Ellerth* defense. It is also important to realize that employers should also examine potential changes to operational practices and workplace rules that may have contributed to the harassment.

- Discipline any employee who has violated the anti-harassment policy by applying sanctions as set out in the policy (or that may be set out in other parts of the Employee Handbook). Many companies have adopted a zero tolerance policy for harassment that includes termination of harassers.
- Incidents that do not rise to the level of harassment should still be considered serious and appropriate sanctions should be applied.
- As in any employee-related discipline matter, documentation is pivotal to reducing the liability of the employer and establishing a record that will be helpful if litigation or other legal proceedings become necessary.
- Remediate any workplace condition, operation, policy, or procedure that may have contributed to the harassment.

 Self-Check Theories of Discrimination

What is the best potential theory of discrimination for the plaintiff to pursue?

1. Lian, an American of Chinese descent, is employed as an architect in a large regional firm. His evaluations by his superiors have been mostly positive for two years, apart from the consistent exception that he arrived late for client meetings on a frequent basis. On one evaluation, his superior wrote, "I thought Asians were supposed to be efficient. What happened here?" One month later, Lian is denied a promotion based on his record of "tardiness and other general considerations."
2. The city of Oz advertises for police officers. It requires that applicants be a minimum of 6 feet tall and weigh a minimum of 180 pounds.
3. Dothard applies for a position as a firefighter. She is excluded because she cannot lift the free-weight requirement mandated in the job description. Over the past five years, men have passed the test 50 percent of the time and women have passed 20 percent of the time.
4. Pettigrew, a woman, was an insurance adjuster at a company that had a rule that no adjusters were allowed to enroll in law school because the employer perceived doing so as a conflict of interest. The company was aware of several adjusters who were in fact enrolled in law school, but it did not act against them. Pettigrew enrolled in law school, and when the company found out about it, she was terminated. The other adjusters were all male.
5. Bronte was employed as a bookkeeper at the nation's largest toy store, where she worked with Barnes. Barnes had a reputation as the office comedian and, over the course of several months, had made various jokes related to Bronte's figure and recommended that she come on casual day dressed in sexy lingerie. Bronte tried to laugh at the jokes but was in fact very upset about the remarks. When she confronted Barnes about the behavior, he advised her to "lighten up" and told her that he was equally sarcastic toward male employees. Bronte quit one day later.

Answers to this Self-Check are provided at the end of the chapter.

Figure 12.1 illustrates the steps in a Title VII analysis.

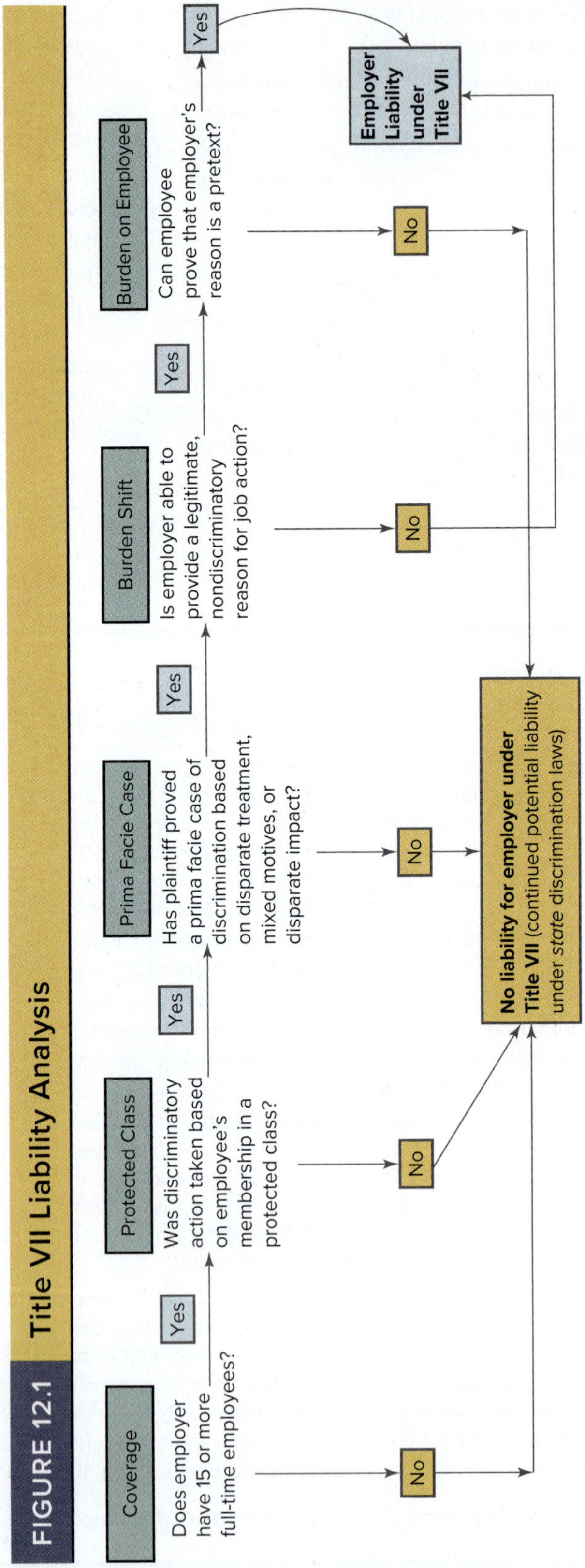

FIGURE 12.1 Title VII Liability Analysis

Coverage: Does employer have 15 or more full-time employees? — Yes →

Protected Class: Was discriminatory action taken based on employee's membership in a protected class? — Yes →

Prima Facie Case: Has plaintiff proved a prima facie case of discrimination based on disparate treatment, mixed motives, or disparate impact? — Yes →

Burden Shift: Is employer able to provide a legitimate, nondiscriminatory reason for job action? — Yes →

Burden on Employee: Can employee prove that employer's reason is a pretext? — Yes → **Employer Liability under Title VII**

No answers at Coverage, Protected Class, and Prima Facie Case lead to: **No liability for employer under Title VII** (continued potential liability under *state* discrimination laws)

No answers at Burden Shift and Burden on Employee lead to: **Employer Liability under Title VII**

Remedies

Title VII provides aggrieved employees with a broad range of remedies to compensate for unlawful discrimination. These remedies include an injunction (a court order to cease from engaging in a particular unlawful practice or an order compelling a party to act), reinstatement, compensatory damages in the form of back pay, retroactive promotions, and requirements that the employer take certain actions in order to remedy patterns or practices resulting in discrimination. Punitive damages (intended to deter future conduct of employers) are available only when a plaintiff proves that a private employer acted with malice, in retaliation, or with reckless disregard to the employment discrimination laws.

CONCEPT SUMMARY Title VII

- Title VII of the Civil Rights Act of 1964 applies to any private sector employer with 15 or more full-time employees, as well as to labor unions, employment agencies, state and local governments, and most to federal government employees.
- Title VII prohibits discrimination in the workplace on the basis of membership in a protected class. The protected classes are race, color, national origin, gender, pregnancy, and religion.
- There are three basic theories of discrimination: (1) disparate treatment (the *McDonnell Douglas* standard), (2) mixed motives (the *Hopkins* standard), and (3) disparate impact (the *Griggs* standard).
- Disparate treatment is overt and intentional discrimination and occurs when an employer treats an employee differently based on membership in a protected class.
- Under the *McDonnell Douglas* test, a plaintiff must make a prima facie case showing that (1) the plaintiff is a member of a protected class, (2) the plaintiff was qualified for and applied for a job, (3) the plaintiff was rejected, and (4) the position was filled by a nonclass member. Then the burden shifts to the employer to show a legitimate nondiscriminatory reason for the action. Finally, the burden shifts back to the individual to show that the reason given by the employer was not the actual reason for its action.
- The mixed motives theory articulated in *Hopkins* protects employees when legitimate motives are mixed with illegitimate motives and an employee is discriminated against. Under this theory, the employee must prove that membership in a protected class was a substantial factor in the decision-making process. The burden then shifts to the employer to offer evidence that it would have made the same employment decision regardless of membership in a protected class.
- The disparate impact test articulated in *Griggs* prohibits an employer from using a facially neutral practice that has an adverse impact on members of a protected class.
- Under the disparate impact theory, a plaintiff must prove that the evaluation methods resulted in statistically significant differences that adversely impacted members of a protected class.
- An employer can be held vicariously liable for sexual harassment by an employee when a nonsupervisory co-worker is the harasser if the employee can prove that

(continued)

- the employer was negligent in either (1) discovering the conduct or (2) failing to respond to a sexual harassment complaint made to a supervisor.
- If the harassing employee is a supervisor, then the employer is strictly liable for any sexual harassment claim if the harassment culminates in a tangible employment action such as termination or transfer to a less desirable job.
- Title VII provides for various remedies, including injunctions, reinstatement, compensatory damages, retroactive promotions, and remedial actions by the employer.

AGE DISCRIMINATION IN EMPLOYMENT ACT

LO 12-4

Describe the provisions of the Age Discrimination in Employment Act (ADEA) and the Americans with Disabilities Act (ADA) and their impact on business operations.

Among the fastest-growing varieties of employment discrimination claims are those based on age. Under the Age Discrimination in Employment Act (ADEA), employers that have 20 or more employees are prohibited from discriminating against employees on the basis of their age once employees have reached age 40. The ADEA is similar to Title VII in that the protected employees are not entitled to special treatment but are included as members of a protected class when employers discriminate against them in favor of a *substantially younger* employee. Courts use a Title VII–based analysis for evaluating age claims. For example, *disparate treatment* under the ADEA requires that the employer's intentional discrimination against the employee based on the employee's age be proved using a modified *McDonnell Douglas* standard for establishing a prima facie case. Therefore, plaintiffs may make ADEA claims based on only (1) protected-class membership (40 or over), (2) satisfactory job performance (based on employer's legitimate expectations), (3) adverse job action such as termination or demotion, (4) replacement with someone substantially younger (or more favorable treatment toward someone substantially younger), or (5) other evidence that indicates that it is *more likely than not* that the employee's age was the reason for the adverse employment action.[26]

If the employee makes a prima facie case, then the employer must present a nondiscriminatory reason for the adverse employment action. Once the employer presents the nondiscriminatory reason, then it is up to the employee to convince the fact finder that the reason the employer gave is false (pretextual) and the real reason is age discrimination.

The ADEA also acts to prohibit mandatory retirement policies. Exceptions are made for certain executives and those with high policymaking positions,[27] federal law enforcement officers, pilots, air traffic controllers, and firefighters.[28] States are also permitted to set defensible police and firefighter retirement ages.[29] If an employer can prove a bona fide occupational qualification (BFOQ), discussed later in this chapter, age may be taken into consideration regarding mandatory retirement.[30]

Substantially Younger Requirement

If a plaintiff is attempting to prove age discrimination based upon the fact that younger employees are treated more favorably, then the plaintiff must prove that the younger employees are *substantially younger*. The federal courts vary in their interpretation of what constitutes substantially younger, but many courts follow the general rule that the age difference must be at least 10 years in order to qualify as substantially younger.[31]

---

[26]*Robin v. Espo Engineering Corp.*, 210 F.3d 1081 (7th Cir. 2000).

[27]29 U.S.C. § 631(c)(1).

[28]5 U.S.C. § 8335.

[29]29 U.S.C. § 623(j).

[30]29 U.S.C. § 623(f)(1).

[31]*Pitasi v. Gartner Group, Inc.*, 184 F.3d 709 (7th Cir. 1999).

One important distinction of an ADEA claim is that it is irrelevant whether the younger employee is a member of the protected class or not. For example, let's assume Prescott is hired at WidgetCo and is 50 years old. He is terminated and replaced by another employee who is 40 years old. Both employees are members of the protected class (40 years old and older), but because someone substantially younger has replaced Prescott, he may still pursue his claim by proving that the reason he was replaced was based on age discrimination. Suppose, however, that Prescott is a 69-year-old employee and is replaced by a 67-year-old employee. That age difference is not sufficient to make a claim of age discrimination.

The ADEA protects only older employees. In fact, the U.S. Supreme Court has said that the ADEA does not prohibit employers from discriminating against employees under 40 years old in favor of those in the intended protected class.[32]

Disparate impact claims under the ADEA, which do not require proof of an intent to discriminate, are rare, but disparate impact (similar to a *Griggs*-type standard based on statistical evidence of exclusion) was specifically recognized as an ADEA discrimination theory by the U.S. Supreme Court in *Smith v. City of Jackson, Miss.*[33] In that case, the Court held that the ADEA authorizes disparate impact claims but that the employer's burden to show the reasonableness of the business practice at issue is *minimal.* That is, the employer does *not* have to meet the higher standard of proof required in Title VII disparate impact cases: that the practice at issue was a *business necessity.* Thus, it is easier for employers to prevail in an ADEA disparate impact action than in a disparate impact action alleging (for example) race discrimination under Title VII.

AMERICANS WITH DISABILITIES ACT

One of the most significant federal antidiscrimination laws that impacts business owners and managers is the Americans with Disabilities Act (ADA).[34] The ADA was originally passed in 1990, but it was amended in 2008 to settle some of the more controversial court interpretations related to the *definition* of disability. Fundamentally, the ADA seeks to eliminate discriminatory employment practices by employers with 15 or more employees against persons with disabilities that would prevent otherwise-qualified individuals from obtaining or continuing employment, being promoted, or obtaining benefits available to nondisabled employees. To establish a prima facie case of disability discrimination, a plaintiff must show that he (1) is disabled, (2) is a qualified individual, and (3) was subjected to unlawful discrimination because of his disability. The ADA also requires employers to make **reasonable accommodations** for a disabled employee in the workplace so long as the accommodations do not cause the employer to suffer an undue hardship.

Documented-Disability Requirement

In order to qualify for an accommodation, the employee must have a documented **disability**. The ADA defines *disability* as a *physical* or *mental* impairment that substantially limits a person's ability to participate in *major life activities.* Courts have ruled that certain disabilities such as blindness, cancer, heart disease, paraplegia, and acquired immune deficiency syndrome (AIDS) all fit squarely into the disability category. However, the definition and interpretation of the disability requirement have been the subject of considerable uncertainty since the passage of the original version of the ADA. Because Congress did not specify examples of major life activities in the original ADA statute, courts and the EEOC have struggled to establish appropriate limits.

---

[32]*General Dynamics Land Systems v. Cline*, 540 U.S. 581 (2004).
[33]544 U.S. 228 (2005).
[34]42 U.S.C. § 12101 et seq.

In a series of cases beginning in 1999, the Supreme Court narrowed the definition of what disabilities were covered under the ADA and ruled that any condition that could be corrected, such as severe myopia causing poor vision,[35] was not a disability covered by the act. In subsequent years, the Court ruled that carpal tunnel syndrome was also not covered because it could not be considered so debilitating as to interfere with any major life activity.[36]

ADA Amendments Act of 2008

As the narrow interpretation of ADA solidified in federal courts, Congress passed an amendment to the ADA that effectively reversed the Supreme Court's efforts to read the disabilities category as a narrow class of ailments. The ADA Amendments Act of 2008 (ADAAA) became effective for any ADA discrimination occurring on or after January 1, 2009. The ADAAA expanded the definition of disability with specific statutory definitions intended to urge courts to interpret the definition of disability "in favor of broad coverage of individuals under this Act, to the maximum extent permitted by terms of this Act."[37]

Although the basic definition of disability under the original ADA was left in place, the ADAAA expanded the statutory protections to specifically cover disabilities that had been excluded from coverage by virtue of the Supreme Court's ADA case law. The ADAAA includes a requirement that courts make a determination of one's disability without regard for the ability to correct the condition with "medication, artificial aids," and other "assistive technology." However, for an individual to be protected under the ADAAA, the plaintiff must still have a physical or mental impairment that substantially limits one or more major life activities.[38]

"Regarded-as" Test

Even if an individual does not meet the definitional requirements of disability under the ADA, employees may still be protected by the ADA under an alternative theory of the act known as the *regarded-as* test. Like the definitional scope of the disability requirement in the ADAAA, the regarded-as standard has been substantially broadened by Congress as well. The standard applies when an employee is *regarded as having an impairment* by her employer (even if the impairment is not *actually* a disability). For example, Babak is diagnosed with a chronic medical condition, but the condition doesn't require any accommodation in the workplace. Babak applies for a promotion to supervisor but is denied because his manager is fearful that Babak's condition will limit his energy level and impact his ability to fulfill his role. Under the ADAAA, Babak would be protected by the statute even though his condition is not a disability as defined in the ADA. This is true because Babak's employer *regarded him as* disabled by virtue of his condition.[39]

---

[35]*Sutton v. United Airlines*, 527 U.S. 471 (1999).

[36]*Toyota Motor Manufacturing v. Williams*, 534 U.S. 185 (2002).

[37]ADA Amendments Act of 2008, Pub. L. No. 110-325, § 4, 122 Stat. 3553, 3555 (codified at 42 U.S.C. § 12102(4)(A)).

[38]The statute also requires that there be "a record of" the disability. As one commentator has pointed out, this requirement is nearly obsolete and unaffected by the ADAAA. See A. Long, *Introducing the New and Improved Americans with Disabilities Act: Assessing the ADA Amendments Act of 2008,* 103 Nw. U. L. Rev. Colloquy 106 (2008).

[39]There is an ongoing debate as to the coverage of the regarded-as test in light of the passage of the ADAAA. This explanation and example are based on EEOC guidance and public information contained on the website.

Qualified Individual

The ADA defines *qualified individual* as someone who, with or without reasonable accommodation, can perform the "essential functions" of the employment position that such individual holds or desires.[40] Essential functions are the fundamental job duties of the employment position, but they do not include the marginal functions of the position.[41] In Case 12.4, a federal appellate court interprets the essential functions requirement.

CASE 12.4 Samson v. Federal Express Corporation, 746 F.3d 1196 (11th Cir. 2014)

FACT SUMMARY In 2009, Richard Samson (Samson) applied for a position as a technician with Federal Express (FedEx) at its facility in Fort Myers, Florida. According to FedEx's online job description, a successful candidate would provide timely, quality maintenance for FedEx vehicle fleet and ground support equipment, including preventative maintenance, troubleshooting, repairs, modifications, and documentation. After an interview, FedEx sent Samson, who it acknowledged was the best candidate to apply, a letter offering him the position. The letter stated that the job offer was contingent upon successful completion of a DOT medical examination because technicians were occasionally required to test drive FedEx fleet vehicles. During the medical examination, Samson disclosed to the medical examiner that he is a Type-1 insulin-dependent diabetic. Because insulin-dependent diabetics are automatically disqualified from being medically certified as physically qualified to operate a commercial motor vehicle in interstate commerce, absent an exemption, Samson failed his medical examination. Two days later, FedEx sent Samson a letter withdrawing his job offer solely because he had failed his DOT medical examination. Samson filed suit alleging a violation of the ADA by failing to hire him due to his diabetes. He argued that test-driving was not an essential function of the technician position and cited evidence of another technician who had test-driven FedEx trucks only three times in three years and never across state lines. The trial court granted Federal Express's motion for summary judgment, ruling that the job description and FedEx safety policies both satisfied the requirement that test-driving was an essential element of the job.

SYNOPSIS OF DECISION AND OPINION The Court of Appeals for the Sixth Circuit reversed the trial court's ruling and held in favor of Samson. The court reasoned that there was a genuine issue of fact as to whether the test-driving requirement was truly "essential" to the job. The court considered several factors that could lead a reasonable jury to differ on whether test-driving FedEx trucks is an essential function of the technician position. The court cited evidence from other FedEx technicians that the amount of time test-driving FedEx vehicles was insignificant.

WORDS OF THE COURT: Essential Function "[Many] factors, however, weigh in favor of finding that test-driving is not an essential function of the [technician] position. First, although FedEx employs only one [technician] at its airport facility in Fort Myers, there are nine other licensed truck drivers at that facility among whom the test-driving could be distributed. In fact, Rotundo—the technician hired instead of Samson—testified that, at least on one occasion, another employee test-drove while he sat in the passenger seat diagnosing the reported mechanical problem. Second, the amount of time that the incumbent [technician] at the Fort Myers facility actually spends test-driving is miniscule. Indeed, Rotundo further testified that in the approximately three years

(continued)

---

[40] 42 U.S.C. § 12111(8).
[41] 29 C.F.R. § 1630.2(n)(1).

he has been on the job, he has only test-driven FedEx trucks three times. If test-driving were such an essential function, as FedEx contends, one would expect it to be performed with regularity. Third, with respect to the current work experience of employees in similar jobs, the record shows that other FedEx [technicians] throughout Florida generally test-drive an average of about 3.71 hours per year—an insignificant portion of their total time on the job. . . . This issue, therefore, should not have been taken away from the jury and resolved as a matter of law."

Case Questions

1. Is it reasonable to conclude that the online job description implies that test-driving is part of the job? Why or why not?
2. What steps could FedEx take to avoid liability for a similar incident in the future?
3. *Focus on Critical Thinking:* Is the court interfering with FedEx's legitimate safety concerns in its own business operations? Is this a concern of public safety? Why or why not?

Reasonable Accommodations

Once an employee has established that she has a covered disability, the ADA requires an employer to make *reasonable accommodations* that allow the employee to perform essential job functions. The ADA states that reasonable accommodations may include (1) existing facilities made readily available to individuals with disabilities and (2) job restructuring, part-time or modified work schedules, reassignment to vacant positions, and provision of readers or interpreters. Courts have held that accommodations such as installing wheelchair ramps, making training manuals or other materials available in oral form, modifying work assignments or a work schedule, and providing sound amplification are all reasonable.

However, the statute does not require the employer to provide accommodations that constitute an *undue hardship* on the employer. The statute defines an undue hardship as one that would result in significant difficulty or expense in the context of the overall resources of the employer, the number of persons employed, the effect on expenses or resources, or the impact of the accommodation upon the operation of the facility. For example, Gant is disabled and unable to walk stairs. He is employed as an accountant in a local real estate firm that occupies a converted Victorian house as its headquarters. Gant informs his employer that an elevator will need to be installed in the Victorian house because he occasionally needs to visit the upstairs to collect documents necessary to perform his job. It is likely that Gant's employer could demonstrate an undue hardship for Gant's elevator request. However, if Gant requests that his employer assign an employee to regularly bring documents from the upper floors to Gant's desk, this would likely be a reasonable accommodation.

The fact that an employer is required to provide reasonable accommodations does not mean that the employer must provide a specific accommodation demanded by the employee. If any of multiple accommodations would work appropriately, the employer is free to choose among them, taking into account cost and convenience.[42]

EQUAL PAY ACT

In 1963, President Kennedy signed the Equal Pay Act (EPA) into law, making it illegal for employers to pay unequal wages to men and women who perform substantially equal work. Technically, the EPA is an amendment to the Fair Labor Standards Act[43] and is therefore

---

[42]*Stewart v. Happy Herman's Cheshire Bridge, Inc.*, 117 F.3d 1278 (11th Cir. 1997).
[43]29 U.S.C. § 206(d).

not always categorized as an antidiscrimination statute. Nonetheless, the EPA does prevent discrimination by requiring an employer to provide equal pay for men and women who perform equal work unless the difference is based on a factor other than gender.[44]

To establish a prima facie case, a plaintiff must demonstrate that (1) the employer pays different wages to employees of the opposite sex; (2) the employees perform equal work on jobs requiring equal skill, effort, and responsibility; and (3) the jobs are performed under similar working conditions.[45] If a prima facie case is established, the burden shifts to the employer to prove that the wage differential is justified by a preponderance of the evidence under one of four affirmative defenses: (1) a seniority system, (2) a merit system, (3) a system pegging earnings to quality or quantity of production, or (4) any factor other than sex. Equal Pay Act claims are often combined with Title VII claims of sex discrimination in compensation. Courts, however, have found separate essential elements and standards of proof for the two statutory claims.

Lilly Ledbetter Fair Pay Act of 2009

The Lilly Ledbetter Fair Pay Act (Ledbetter Act) effectively reversed the U.S. Supreme Court's decision in *Ledbetter v. Goodyear Tire & Rubber Co.*[46] In the *Ledbetter* case, a 19-year veteran of Goodyear Tire & Rubber Co. sued the company when she learned that for much of her career, male counterparts had been paid more for doing the same work that she did. Although the Supreme Court did not deny that Ledbetter had been discriminated against, it ruled that she should have filed suit within 180 days of *receiving* her first unfair paycheck, not 180 days from the time she *learned* of the difference in pay. The ruling upended the long-standing practice in courts across the country that had held that the 180-day-period begins when an employee becomes *aware* of his or her plight. Under the Supreme Court's framework, any employer that could hide pay discrimination for six months could effectively avoid liability under the law and leave workers with no recourse. Because pay information is often confidential, pay discrimination is difficult to detect. Thus, if employers are insulated from liability after 180 days, they have little incentive to correct pay discrimination. The Ledbetter Act declared that each discriminatory paycheck, not simply the employee's first check, resets the period of time during which a worker may file a pay discrimination claim. The Ledbetter Act therefore ensures that employees subject to wage discrimination on the basis of race, color, national origin, gender, religion, age, or disability have the opportunity to challenge *every* discriminatory paycheck that they receive.

CONCEPT SUMMARY *Other Federal Employment Discrimination Statutes*

- The Age Discrimination in Employment Act (ADEA) prohibits employers from discriminating against employees on the basis of their age if (1) the employee is 40 years old or over, (2) the employee's job performance is satisfactory, (3) the employee is adversely affected by the job action, and (4) better treatment is given to someone substantially younger.

(continued)

---

[44] At the time of the EPA's passage in 1963, women earned only 59 cents for every dollar earned by men. Although enforcement of the EPA as well as other civil rights laws has helped to narrow the wage gap, disparities remain.

[45] *Corning Glass Works v. Brennan*, 417 U.S. 188 (1974).

[46] 550 U.S. 618 (2007).

- The Americans with Disabilities Act (ADA) seeks to eliminate discriminatory employment practices against disabled persons by requiring that employers with 15 or more employees make reasonable accommodations to allow the disabled employee to perform essential job functions, so long as the accommodations do not cause the employer to suffer an undue hardship.
- The Equal Pay Act (EPA) makes it illegal for employers to pay unequal wages to men and women who perform substantially equal work unless the difference is based on a factor other than sex.

PROCEDURES FOR ASSERTING A CLAIM

LO 12-5
Describe the procedures for asserting a discrimination claim.

Federal antidiscrimination statutes prescribe a specific procedure for employees alleging employment discrimination. First, an aggrieved employee must file a **complaint (discrimination)** against the employer with the local office of the EEOC (generally within 180 days of the adverse job action). The EEOC then notifies the employer and commences a preliminary investigation. As an administrative agency, the EEOC may use its authority to obtain documents, statements from witnesses, and other evidence that will aid in the investigation. Courts have granted the EEOC wide latitude in investigating discrimination claims, including the authority to have access to confidential employer files.

During and immediately after the investigation, the EEOC is required by statute to engage in **conciliation negotiations**. This means that the EEOC has an affirmative statutory duty to make good faith efforts in favor of settlement of the case instead of filing a lawsuit.

If efforts at conciliation fail, the EEOC may choose to file suit against the employer on the employee's behalf or may decide not to take any action at all. After 180 days have passed from the time of the complaint, the employee may demand that the EEOC issue a *right-to-sue letter*. This letter entitles the employee to file a lawsuit in a federal court. Note that even though all employment discrimination claims must begin with the EEOC,

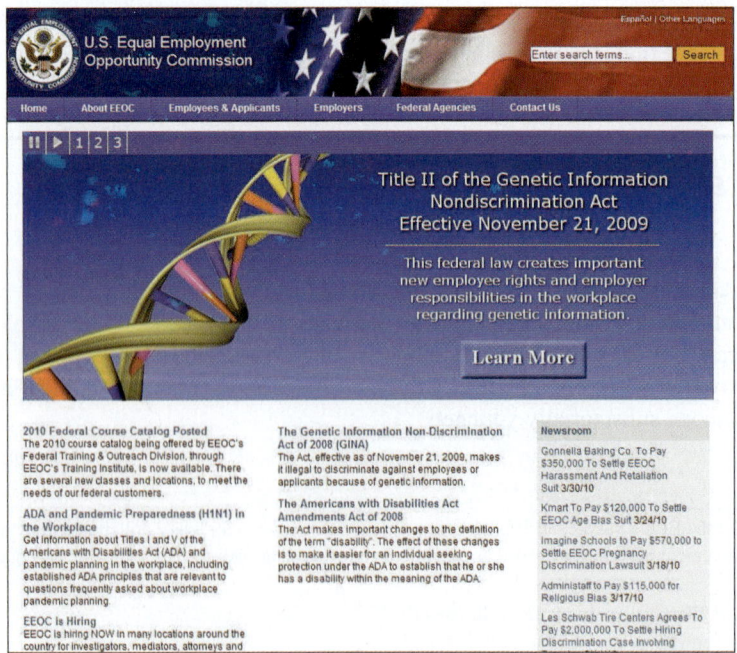

Employees alleging discrimination by their employer must first file a complaint with the EEOC, which then notifies the employer of the allegations and begins a preliminary investigation.

Source: www.eeoc.gov

ultimately the employee will have an opportunity to present his case in court. This is true even if the EEOC decides that the case has no merit and declines to investigate.

EMPLOYER DEFENSES

Earlier in the chapter, we saw that the burden-shifting scheme in a discrimination case is subject to the employer either offering a nondiscriminatory motive for the action in question or asserting a legally recognized *defense*. Each antidiscrimination statute has its own set of defenses, but there is some level of commonality among employer defenses.

> **LO 12-6**
> List and apply the major defenses available to employers.

Business Necessity

Perhaps the broadest defense to employment discrimination is when a business can justify discrimination on the basis that it is *legitimately necessary* to the business operations of the company. The **business necessity test** is a defense used to rebut a *disparate impact* claim when a certain practice or procedure has impacted a particular protected class. For example, suppose MovingCo requires all of its workers to be able to lift 100 pounds. During the application process, the applicants are required to pick up a 100-pound piece of furniture. After one year, the test has resulted in more women than men being eliminated from job consideration. If sued under a disparate impact theory, MovingCo has a strong business necessity defense so long as the standard has been applied neutrally to all candidates. Another common business necessity is a particular level of education, such as a requirement by an accounting firm that all of its professionals have at least a bachelor of science degree in accounting.

Faragher/Ellerth Defense

The *Faragher/Ellerth* defense is a judicially created affirmative defense whereby an employer may avoid vicarious liability by proving that a system was in place that was intended to deter, prevent, report, and correct any harassment. The employer must also prove that the employee failed to take advantage of the preventative or corrective opportunities that the employer provided. Although the defense was initially created in the context of sexual harassment claims, courts have allowed employers to use the defense in other types of cases such as racial harassment.[47] Use of the *Faragher/Ellerth* defense is discussed in detail earlier in this chapter in *Strategic Legal Solutions: Proactive Harassment Prevention Framework*.

Bona Fide Occupational Qualification

Federal antidiscrimination statutes allow employers to hire and employ on the basis of religion, gender, or national origin in certain instances when the classification is a **bona fide occupational qualification (BFOQ)** that is reasonably necessary to the normal operation of the particular business or enterprise.[48] Note that the statutes do not allow race to be used as a BFOQ. The ADEA has a similar BFOQ defense. Although the ADA does not have an express BFOQ provision, the statutory scheme allows exclusion of persons with disabilities if the person, with or without reasonable accommodation, cannot perform essential job functions (a concept similar to BFOQ).

Classic examples of BFOQ classifications are religion for the employment of clergy and the use of gender to hire a movie actor. In cases that are not as clear, the employer must prove that members of the excluded class cannot safely and effectively perform *essential*

---

[47]*Vance v. Ball State University*, 570 U.S. 421 (2013).
[48]42 U.S.C. § 2000e-2(e).

job duties. Courts have held that BFOQ cannot be based on paternalism (protecting women from work in potentially dangerous positions such as mining, construction, or law enforcement). In the landmark case of *Diaz v. Pan Am World Airways, Inc.*,[49] a U.S. court of appeals made clear that customer preference could not be used as a BFOQ, rejecting the airline's justification for employing only women as flight attendants based on passenger surveys. Similarly, when an oil company refused to promote a woman because many foreign companies will not do business with women, a federal appellate court ruled, "No foreign nation can compel the non-enforcement of Title VII here."[50]

This rule is subject to qualification. When a business is protecting the modesty of its employees or customers, as in female locker rooms, or when the privacy of medical patients is involved, gender may be a valid BFOQ.

Seniority

Federal antidiscrimination statutes also provide a defense for employers using a seniority system as the basis for certain job decisions. For an employer to assert this defense, the seniority system must be based on objective elements of seniority (actual number of years on the job) and the employment decisions must have been made in good faith and pursuant to that established objective system. The employee/plaintiff has the burden of proving improper motivation behind the employer's adoption or use of the system.

Employee Misconduct

Employers are not required to overlook misconduct when complying with antidiscrimination statutes. When an employee commits an act of misconduct, so long as that act has been identified to the employee as misconduct, employers may discipline the employee in accordance with the company's general practices without liability for discrimination. If the employer's practices and procedures are set forth in a workplace publication (usually in the employee handbook or a similar company document), misconduct is a powerful defense.

The U.S. Supreme Court has even extended that protection to employers when the employer discovered the misconduct *after* the adverse employment action.[51] So long as the employer shows that the misconduct was sufficiently grave as to warrant the adverse employment action (such as termination for theft of a petty cash account), an employer may use evidence of misconduct acquired post-complaint in its defense.

> **KEY POINT**
>
> Managers must be very careful to apply discipline evenly. Treating two employees differently for similar infractions can lead to a disparate treatment discrimination charge.[52]

AFFIRMATIVE ACTION PROGRAMS

Affirmative action as it is understood today includes, but goes beyond, outreach attempts to recruit minority applicants, special training programs, and the reevaluation of the effect of selection criteria. Affirmative action in employment began during World War II when President Franklin D. Roosevelt issued an executive order banning racial, religious, and gender discrimination in the defense industry. Executive Order 11246,[53] issued by President Lyndon B. Johnson in 1965, extended affirmative action's reach by requiring that

---

[49]442 F.2d 385 (5th Cir. 1971).
[50]*Fernandez v. Wynn Oil Co.*, 653 F.2d 1273 (9th Cir. 1981).
[51]*McKennon v. Nashville Banner Publishing Co.*, 513 U.S. 352 (1995).
[52]*Coleman v. Donahoe*, 667 F.3d 835 (7th Cir. 2012).
[53]30 Fed. Reg. 12319 (Sept. 28, 1965); 41 C.F.R. pts 60-1, 60-2.

employers who have a contract with the federal government for services and supplies initiate good faith efforts to implement an affirmative action plan in their companies. Although most employers are not subject to the executive order, social pressures and/or threat of litigation has induced many employers to adopt voluntary affirmative action plans. Affirmative action may also be imposed on an employer by courts as a judicial remedy when they find that the employer acted in a pattern of egregious discrimination against employees.

Legality

Although federal antidiscrimination statutes do not require employers to give preferential treatment to minority employees, the Supreme Court has upheld the constitutionality of Executive Order 11246 and has allowed certain affirmative action plans to apply to private employers as a condition to a contract with the federal government. State and local governments soon followed suit with affirmative action plans aimed at addressing inequalities in the workplace and in education.[54] Affirmative action does not require absolute equality. Companies must work to ensure that their employee workforce reflects the available qualified workforce with respect to race and gender. Therefore, a local company in a city whose population is 75 percent white and 25 percent black (assuming all are qualified) may have an employee workforce that is 75 percent white and 25 percent black. As long as the company advertises openings properly and conducts legal and appropriate hiring policies, the company is in compliance. Should a discrepancy exist, a company may be approved, through a plan, to allow preferences in hiring until the proper goal is met. In *Adarand Constructors, Inc. v. Pena*,[55] the Supreme Court ruled that state and local government affirmative action plans in race-based or gender-based preferences for hiring contractors would be subject to the *strict scrutiny* standard. Recall from Chapter 2, "Business and the Constitution," that the strict scrutiny standard is the highest level of scrutiny and more often than not results in a finding of unconstitutionality. However, the Court's ruling made clear that a state and local government affirmative action program is constitutional so long as it (1) attempts to remedy an actual past practice of discrimination and (2) does not employ a system of quotas (e.g., hiring according to a mathematical formula based on race). One of the most misunderstood issues under affirmative action involves quotas. Many businesses and organizations wrongly adopted mathematical quotas as a simplistic means of compliance; however, the Supreme Court has ruled that the strict use of quotas not only is prohibited under affirmative action but is unconstitutional.[56]

STATE ANTIDISCRIMINATION STATUTES

In addition to complying with federal antidiscrimination statutes, certain employers are also subject to regulation under a state antidiscrimination statutory scheme. Each state has its own statutes that are often modeled after the federal statutes (although they have different titles, such as the Human Relations Act). In addition, states also have their own administrative agencies (modeled after the EEOC) charged with enforcing and adjudicating discrimination cases.

LO 12-7

Explain the role of state law in employment discrimination cases.

---

[54]The Supreme Court decided several cases specifically related to admissions by state-sponsored universities beginning in 1978. Most recently, in *Gruttinger v. Bollinger*, 539 U.S. 306 (2003), the Court held that affirmative action in admissions is constitutional so long as the minority status of the applicant is used as a plus factor and not in accordance with a rigid formula reserving certain seats for minority applicants.

[55]515 U.S. 200 (1995).

[56]*Wygant v. Jackson Board of Education*, 476 U.S. 267 (1986) (laying off white employees to hire minorities to achieve the goal violates the Equal Protection Clause); *Regents of the University of California v. Bakke*, 438 U.S. 265 (1978) (a medical school's strict racial admission quota violated the Fourteenth Amendment).

State antidiscrimination statutes sometimes differ substantially from federal laws in two ways that impact business owners and managers. First, state statutes tend to cover more employers, with some states imposing antidiscrimination statutes on small businesses with just *one* employee. Many federal statutes cover only employers (unions, etc.) with 15 or more employees. Second, while federal statutes are relatively conservative in exactly what constitutes a protected class, some states have expanded protected-class membership, most notably to discrimination based on sexual orientation or gender transformation. In Case 12.5, a state appellate court compares New Jersey's state statutory antidiscrimination protections with the protections under Title VII.

CASE 12.5 Enriquez v. West Jersey Health Systems, 777 A.2d 365 (N.J. Super. Ct. App. Div. 2001)

FACT SUMMARY Enriquez, a biological male, was hired as a medical director for an outpatient treatment center operated by West Jersey Health Systems. Soon after his employment began, Enriquez began an external transformation from male to female. This transformation was a result of Enriquez's gender identity disorder. During the transformation, Enriquez was approached by co-workers and managers who voiced discomfort with her transformation. A Health Systems manager, citing Enriquez's obligation to contribute to a productive work atmosphere, requested that Enriquez halt the transformation process and go back to her prior appearance. When her contract came up for renewal, Enriquez was told that her contract would not be renewed unless she ceased the transformation. After Enriquez refused, her contract was not renewed and she was informed that the termination was permanent. After the termination, Enriquez completed the surgical portion of her transformation.

SYNOPSIS OF DECISION AND OPINION The New Jersey Superior Court found for Enriquez. The court held that while Title VII does not bar discrimination based on sexual orientation or gender identity disorders, New Jersey's Law Against Discrimination (LAD) does. The court reasoned that because the LAD makes it unlawful to discriminate against someone based upon sex and affectional or sexual orientation, individuals who were transsexual or affected by a gender identity disorder were also considered to be members of a protected class and were protected from discrimination.

WORDS OF THE COURT: Coverage under LAD "Title VII of the Civil Rights Act of 1964 does not contain language barring discrimination based on one's affectional or sexual orientation. Moreover, the federal courts construing Title VII have unanimously concluded that discrimination on the basis of gender dysphoria is not sex discrimination. Basically, the federal courts conclude that discrimination on the basis of sex outlaws discrimination against women because they are women, and against men because they are men. . . . We disagree with [this] rationale. . . . A person who is discriminated against because he changes his gender from male to female is being discriminated against because he or she is a member of a very small minority whose condition remains incomprehensible to most individuals. . . . It is incomprehensible to us that our Legislature would ban discrimination against heterosexual men and women; against homosexual men and women; against bisexual men and women; against men and women who are perceived, presumed or identified by others as not conforming to the stereotypical notions of how men and women behave, but would condone discrimination against men or women who seek to change their anatomical sex because they suffer from a gender identity disorder. We conclude that sex discrimination under the LAD includes gender discrimination so as to protect plaintiff from gender

(continued)

stereotyping and discrimination for transforming herself from a man to a woman."

Case Questions

1. Why couldn't this case have been covered by Title VII on the basis of gender?
2. If Enriquez's employment with Health Systems were not terminated, would she still have a claim for discrimination? Would the conduct of her co-workers and managers have been sufficient to prevail on a discrimination suit? Why or why not?
3. *Focus on Critical Thinking:* The court acknowledges that transgendered employees are not specifically named in the state discrimination statute, but still rules that the statute prohibits discrimination by an employer. Is this a case of judges "legislating from the bench" or is it a logical interpretation of the existing statute?

KEY TERMS

Employment discrimination p. 407   Workplace-related discrimination in the hiring process and treatment of employees; encompasses everything from promotions and demotions to work schedules, working conditions, and disciplinary measures.

Equal Employment Opportunity Commission (EEOC) p. 407   A five-member federal administrative agency that administers congressional mandates that ensure adequate protection for victims of discrimination; accepts and investigates worker complaints and, in certain cases, will sue on behalf of employees.

Title VII p. 407   The section of the Civil Rights Act of 1964 that serves as the centerpiece of antidiscrimination law; covers a comprehensive set of job-related transactions and prohibits discrimination in the workplace on the basis of an employee's race, color, national origin, gender, religion, or pregancy. The law applies to any private sector employer with 15 or more full-time employees and to unions, employment agencies, state and local governments, and most of the federal government.

Age Discrimination in Employment Act (ADEA) of 1967 p. 407   A federal statute that prohibits employers from discriminating against employees on the basis of their age once employees have reached age 40.

Americans with Disabilities Act (ADA) of 1990 p. 407   A federal statute that seeks to eliminate discriminatory employment practices against persons with disabilities; requires that employers with 15 or more employees make reasonable accommodations for an employee with disabilities in the workplace as long as the accommodations do not cause the employer to suffer an undue hardship.

Equal Pay Act of 1963 p. 408   A federal statute that makes it illegal for employers to pay unequal wages to men and women who perform substantially equal work.

Protected classes p. 408   The classifications of individuals that are specified in Title VII, including color, race, national origin, religion, gender, and pregnancy.

Disparate treatment p. 411   Theory of employment discrimination predicated on overt and intentional discrimination; includes being treated differently because of one's membership in a protected class.

Mixed motives p. 411   Theory of employment discrimination in which the cause of the adverse employment action was motivated by both legitimate and discriminatory motives.

Disparate impact p. 411   Theory of employment discrimination in which employee evaluation techniques that are not themselves discriminatory have a different and adverse impact on members of a protected class.

Burden of proof p. 413   The responsibility of producing sufficient evidence in support of a fact or issue and favorably convincing the fact finder of that fact or issue.

Pretext p. 414   A false reason offered to justify an action.

Hostile work environment p. 416   Theory of liability under Title VII for sexual harassment that is of such a severe and crude nature or is so pervasive in the workplace that it interferes with the victim's ability to do the job.

Reasonable accommodations p. 425   Accommodations, required under the Americans with Disabilities Act, that allow disabled individuals to adequately perform essential job functions.

Disability p. 425 A physical or mental impairment that substantially limits a person's ability to participate in major life activities.

Complaint (discrimination) p. 430 A form that an aggrieved employee files against his employer with the EEOC that details how the employee was discriminated against.

Conciliation negotiations p. 430 The required attempts by the EEOC to settle a discrimination case instead of filing a lawsuit.

Business necessity test p. 431 A defense used to rebut disparate impact claims when a business can prove that a certain skill, ability, or procedure is absolutely necessary to the operation of the business. Discrimination is permitted even if a protected class is adversely affected.

Bona fide occupational qualification (BFOQ) p. 431 A provision in certain federal antidiscrimination statutes that allows discrimination based on religion, gender, or national origin when it can be shown that such discrimination is reasonably necessary to the business operation.

Affirmative action p. 432 An action plan designed to maintain equal employment opportunities and to remedy past employment discrimination of women, persons of color, persons with disabilities, and other underutilized protected classes.

CHAPTER REVIEW QUESTIONS

1. Reilly is a waiter at an exclusive hotel that requires male waiters to have short hair. After he refuses to cut his hair in accordance with the standards, he is fired. Which of the following is true?
   a. Reilly has a claim under Title VII based on disparate impact.
   b. Reilly has a claim under the Age Discrimination in Employment Act if the employer replaces him with someone younger.
   c. Reilly has no claim under Title VII because of the protected class requirement.
   d. Reilly has no claim under Title VII because he is an exempt employee.
   e. Reilly has a claim unless the employer has a legitimate seniority system.

2. Which theory of discrimination is typically based on statistical data that show that some method or measure resulted in discrimination?
   a. Disparate impact
   b. Disparate treatment
   c. Mixed motives
   d. Disparate motives
   e. Statistical systems

3. Dawson is a 50-year-old sales representative who was terminated by High Flyer Corporation due to poor performance. Dawson finds out that he was replaced by a 41-year-old employee, so he files suit under the Age Discrimination in Employment Act. Dawson will
   a. Prevail because he was replaced by a younger employee.
   b. Prevail under the mixed motives theory.
   c. Prevail only if High Flyer's reason is pretextual.
   d. Not prevail because the replacement employee is not substantially younger than Dawson.
   e. Not prevail, so long as High Flyer had a legitimate seniority system.

4. The Americans with Disabilities Act (ADA) requires
   a. Employers to accommodate disabled employees regardless of costs.
   b. An employee to have a documented disability in order to trigger coverage.
   c. Employers who "regard employees as" having disabilities to reasonably accommodate them.
   d. b and c.
   e. a and b.

5. Blackwell works in Shipping Supplies, Inc.'s warehouse. Although no employees have ever made sex-based comments, the male employees regularly watch pornographic videos in the company cafeteria during their lunch hour and pass around publications with lewd sexual content among employees. If Blackwell brings a claim for sexual harassment, what is her likely theory of the case?
   a. Disparate impact
   b. Quid pro quo
   c. Hostile work environment
   d. Protected class membership
   e. Bona fide occupational qualification

Answers and explanations are provided at the end of this chapter.

THEORY TO PRACTICE

Hudson runs a successful business operation called Cleaning Inc. and employs a workforce of over 100 people in various positions. The company has contracts with several companies to provide office-cleaning services. One employee, Curt, had been with the company for almost two years when he applied for a supervisory position. The position involved higher pay and better benefits. Although he was qualified to be a site supervisor, Curt was not promoted. Cleaning Inc. explained that *only* a woman could be hired because the position involved regular searches of the women employees' locker room to look for any items reported stolen from cleaning sites.

1. If Curt files suit against Cleaning Inc. for discrimination, what statute will he be relying on and what is his probable theory of discrimination?
2. What would Curt need to prove in order to shift the burden to Cleaning Inc.?
3. What is the company's best defense to a charge of discrimination?
4. In order to file the complaint against Cleaning Inc., what procedures must Curt follow? May he file a lawsuit immediately?
5. Assume that Curt was not promoted because he was undergoing a series of sex change procedures and that other employees were uncomfortable with him. Is Curt protected under federal antidiscrimination statutes? Why or why not?
6. Applying the same facts as in Question 5, now assume Curt filed suit in a state that had a statute similar to New Jersey's antidiscrimination law (as seen in Case 12.5, *Enriquez v. West Jersey Health Systems*). Would Curt be covered under the state law? Why or why not?

LEGAL STRATEGY 101

The Wage Gap

The Equal Pay Act of 1963 requires equal pay for equal work, yet by all accounts a significant wage gap based on gender exists in both the private and public sectors.[57] By way of example, when the Equal Pay Act was enacted into law in the 1960s, women earned about 60 percent of the wages men earned on average; today, women earn about 80 percent of men's wages on average.[58] Why is this? Might some employers be exploiting legal loopholes in order to avoid complying with the law?

In fact, a wide variety of factors might contribute to the overall gender wage gap. Historically, for example, women have worked in lower-paying fields than men. Also, in some industries women might work fewer

Demonstrating for equal pay. In the foreground are former U.S. senators Barbara Boxer (left) and Barbara Mikulski. Tom Williams/CQ Roll Call/Getty Images

---

[57] *See generally* Danielle Kurtzleben, *Everything You Need to Know About the Gender Wage Gap, Vox,* Oct. 1, 2014.

[58] *See, e.g.,* Borgna Brunner & Beth Rowen, *The Equal Pay Act: A History of Pay Inequity in the U.S.,* Infoplease, https://www.infoplease.com/equal-pay-act.

hours on average than men. But an additional factor contributing to unequal pay might involve strategic behavior by business firms and government agencies, including such strategies as avoidance or even outright noncompliance. By way of example, soon after the enactment of the Equal Pay Act, some employers acted strategically to exploit loopholes in the law—for instance, by changing the job titles of women workers in order to pay them less than men.

Another strategic factor relevant to the gender gap is the informal employer policy of "pay secrecy."[59] In summary, some employers might discourage or even prohibit their employees from discussing their salaries with their fellow workers. Pay secrecy might then contribute to unequal pay because it's easier for differentials in wages to remain in place when workers don't know whether such discrepancies exist in the first place.

Let's conclude this strategic section on a positive note. In the words of President John F. Kennedy, who signed the historic Equal Pay Act into law in 1963, the legal principle of equal pay for equal work "affirms our determination that when women enter the labor force they will find equality in their pay envelope."[60] Today, women under age 25 working full time earn over 93 percent of men's salaries on average.[61]

CRITICAL THINKING QUESTIONS

1. Should Congress enact a law affirmatively requiring private employers to publicly post or disclose information regarding the actual salaries paid to their employees?
2. Does Congress have the power under Article I of the U.S. Constitution to enact such a law?

---

[59]See, e.g., Tom Dreisbach, *"Pay Secrecy" Policies at Work*, National Public Radio, Apr. 13, 2014.

[60]The White House, *Remarks of the President at Signing of the Equal Pay Act of 1963 in the President's Office*, John F. Kennedy Presidential Library and Museum, June 10, 1963.

[61]Brunner & Rowen, *The Equal Pay Act*.

MANAGER'S CHALLENGE

Recall that employers may be liable for sexual harassment under the *Faragher* case when the employer has not taken affirmative steps to deter harassment or has failed to have a structure in place to enforce sexual harassment policies, such as a system for deterring and reporting sexual harassment. Assume you are a manager at Cleaning Inc. (as in the Theory to Practice problem) and you receive the following e-mail from the company's vice president of operations:

> I just read an article about a company that was sued under the sexual harassment laws. I know we have a good policy, but we need a system in place for claims and compliance. Please draft a two- to three-page memorandum that outlines how to implement a system that will (1) help deter sexual harassment, (2) ensure that our policy is well known by the employees, and (3) provide a procedure for initiating and investigating complaints.

See Connect for Manager's Challenge sample answers.

CASE SUMMARY 12.1 Dumas v. Union Pacific Railroad Co., 294 F. App'x 822 (5th Cir. 2008)

MISCONDUCT

Dumas was an African American employee of UPRC, which employed him as a regional manager. UPRC, a rail freight company, was named in a discrimination claim by a co-worker of Dumas. During the EEOC investigation, Dumas supported his co-worker's claims by offering statements verifying discriminatory practices at UPRC. After the co-worker's claim was settled, UPRC conducted a routine audit that found that Dumas had falsified his track inspection records over a period of time in the past. UPRC immediately terminated Dumas.

CASE QUESTIONS

1. Does Dumas have a valid employment discrimination claim?
2. If so, what theories would be best advanced by Dumas?

CASE SUMMARY 12.2 PGA Tour, Inc. v. Martin, 532 U.S. 661 (2001)

REASONABLE ACCOMMODATIONS

Martin is a professional golfer who is afflicted with a degenerative circulatory disorder recognized as a disability under the Americans with Disabilities Act (ADA). The disorder causes Martin severe pain due to an obstruction of blood flow between his legs and his heart. The Professional Golf Association (PGA) Tour rules require that players in tournaments walk the course. However, because walking caused Martin pain and anxiety, and generally worsened his condition, he could not walk the course. Although PGA Tour rules prohibit players from using golf carts on the final two stages of the qualifying tournaments, Martin petitioned for a waiver on the basis that he was covered by the ADA. The PGA rejected his request on the grounds that it was not a reasonable accommodation. The PGA asserted that walking was a fundamental part of golf and waiving it for any reason would fundamentally alter the nature of the competition. They argued that the fatigue from walking is a critical factor in the outcome of tournaments. Martin countered by noting that even with the use of a cart he would be required to walk one mile during each round of golf and, because his disability causes him pain and fatigue, the use of the cart would not allow him an advantage over other players.

CASE QUESTIONS

1. Who prevails and why?
2. Why was the PGA so reluctant to allow Martin to use a golf cart, especially considering carts are allowed in other tournaments? Do you agree with the Court's reasoning that allowing Martin to use a golf cart during tournaments does not give him an advantage? Why or why not?
3. Are there any scenarios in which use of a cart might provide an advantage and, as a result, alter the fundamental nature of the game? Given the Court's reasoning, would a request to double the size of the hole so that a partially blind competitor could see it when putting fundamentally alter the game?

CASE SUMMARY 12.3 U.S. Airways, Inc. v. Barnett, 535 U.S. 391 (2002)

ADA

Barnett, a baggage loader for U.S. Airways (USA), injured his back while loading an inordinately heavy suitcase. His doctor diagnosed him with a permanently slipped disk and recurring back spasms. Barnett's condition is permanent, and he is considered to be disabled under the ADA. Upon returning to work, USA offered to reassign him from baggage loader to luggage deliverer, a job in which he would drive the baggage carts from plane to plane. However, Barnett wanted a position in the mailroom sorting mail. USA denied Barnett's request because it operated on a strict seniority system for filling vacancies.

CASE QUESTIONS

1. Does Barnett have a cause of action under the ADA? Why or why not?
2. Has USA fulfilled its duty of reasonable accommodation?

CASE SUMMARY 12.4 Hope v. California Youth Authority, 134 Cal. App. 4th 577 (2005)

STATE ANTIDISCRIMINATION PROTECTION

Hope, a gay man infected with HIV, was hired as a cook in a youth correctional facility in California. While there, he was continually the subject of derogatory comments made by male guards and a supervising cook because of his sexual orientation. These comments were numerous and spoken in front of co-workers. Moreover, while other cooks received assistance in cleaning their stations, Hope received no such help and often his co-workers would throw their trash in his station. During his first five years of employment, Hope's medical condition never affected him. However, he eventually started to miss work because of the side effects of his medication, combined with the stress from the harassment he was subjected to. After informing his supervisors of his condition, he was put on administrative leave and later terminated for abusing sick leave policy.

CASE QUESTIONS

1. Is Hope a member of a protected class under Title VII?
2. Can he bring a federal claim for employment discrimination?
3. Suppose California has a state antidiscrimination statute that protects sexual orientation. Would Hope have a state claim for discrimination? Why or why not?
4. Had Hope not been terminated, would he have had a claim? Why or why not?

CASE SUMMARY 12.5 Aquino v. Honda of America, Inc., 158 F. App'x 667 (6th Cir. 2005)

PRETEXT

Aquino, a man of Chinese-Filipino origin, worked on a Honda assembly line. His time at Honda was tumultuous, and he had been suspended on numerous occasions for disciplinary violations. Upon returning from a suspension in 2001, Aquino was assigned to an engine installation station. Concurrent with Aquino's assignment, Honda experienced a number of cases of vehicle tampering and vandalism. A Honda manager conducted an investigation and concluded that Aquino was the only person with access to the tools necessary to conduct the vandalism. Upon Honda's complaint, Aquino was arrested, but the charges were eventually dropped due to insufficient evidence. Nonetheless, Honda terminated Aquino's employment after an internal investigation confirmed its initial conclusions on the matter. Aquino filed suit, claiming his termination was based on the fact that he was the only nonwhite employee assigned to the unit. At trial, Honda asserted that its investigation and conclusion that Aquino had committed the vandalism were legitimate reasons for firing Aquino. When the burden shifted back to Aquino, he asserted, but did not provide any evidence, that Honda manipulated the evidence of the incidents.

CASE QUESTIONS

1. Who prevails and why?
2. Why did Aquino have the burden of proving that Honda's reason for discharging him was a pretext? Didn't he already prove a prima facie case?
3. Considering the criminal charges against him were dropped, what would Aquino need to have shown in order to meet his burden of proof that Honda's reasons for dismissing him were pretextual?

CASE SUMMARY 12.6 Bradley v. Pizzaco of Nebraska, Inc., 7 F.3d 795 (8th Cir. 1993)

RACE DISCRIMINATION

Bradley was an African American man who worked as a delivery man for Pizzaco, doing business as Domino's. He was fired for noncompliance with Domino's no-beard policy. The no-beard policy was established nationwide by Pizzaco's franchisor, Domino's Pizza, Inc. Bradley alleged that he suffered from psuedo-folliculitis barbae (PFB), a skin condition affecting approximately 50 percent of African American males and causing half of those affected to be unable to shave at all. Bradley claimed that the no-beard policy deprived him and other African American males suffering from PFB of equal employment opportunities in violation of Title VII. Domino's defended the policy, saying that it was common sense that the better its people looked, the better its sales would be. Domino's also stated that any exceptions would make the policy too difficult to enforce. A survey was introduced showing that 20 percent of those surveyed would react negatively to a delivery man with a beard. The EEOC contended that Domino's failed to show business justification for its inflexible no-beard policy, and the commission sought injunctive relief to enjoin Domino's ongoing policy. (Bradley was shown to have only a mild case of PFB and could have been cleanshaven, so he was found not to be entitled to relief and was not part of this suit.)

CASE QUESTIONS

1. Is customer preference a persuasive argument for this policy? Why or why not?
2. Is this a disparate treatment or disparate impact case?
3. What would Domino's have to prove to successfully support a business necessity claim?
4. How could a manager allow an exception for an employee claiming PFB yet maintain the no-beard policy for other employees?

✓ Self-Check ANSWERS Theories of Discrimination

1. Mixed motives. This is similar to the *PriceWaterhouse* case. There are legitimate reasons for the denial of promotion (tardiness) mixed with potentially illegitimate reasons (based on national origin stereotyping).
2. Disparate impact. This facially neutral policy will have an unfair impact on women because the majority of women will not meet the height and weight requirements.
3. Disparate impact. Based on the EEOC guidelines, a disparate impact claim could be made because women are impacted in a disparate manner. The fire department must show that the free-weight requirement is a business necessity in order for it to be valid.
4. Disparate treatment. A neutral workplace rule (prohibition) was applied (or not applied) differently to men than to women. The *McDonnell Douglas* framework applies here.
5. Sexual harassment via hostile work environment theory. This theory applies as long as there is evidence that the behavior was so crude as to interfere with the plaintiff's job function and that it led her to resign.

CHAPTER REVIEW QUESTIONS: Answers and Explanations

1. **c.** Any Title VII claim must be based on discrimination because of an employee's membership in a protected class. Hair length is not a protected class, so he is not eligible to bring a claim and therefore (a) and (b) are wrong. (d) and (e) are wrong because they are incorrect statements of law.

2. **a.** Whenever the plaintiff in a Title VII claim is alleging discrimination based on statistical data, the theory is disparate impact. (b) and (c) are theories of discrimination but do not involve statistical data. (d) and (e) are incorrect statements of law.

3. **d.** In order to bring a claim under the ADEA, the plaintiff must demonstrate that the replacement employee was substantially younger (10 years or more age difference), thus (a) is wrong. (b), (c), and (e) are incorrect statements of law.

4. **d.** The ADA requires that an employee have a documented disability to be covered under the Act. Also covered are employees who the employer believes are not able to work because of a disability ("regarded as"). (a) and (e) are wrong because employers are not required to make accommodations regardless of costs.

5. **c.** Hostile work environments are created when employees engage in behavior that is of such a severe and crude nature that it interferes with the victim's ability to perform the job (e.g., displaying pornographic movies or photographs in the workplace). (b) is wrong because a quid pro quo theory requires a promise in exchange for sexual favors. (a), (d), and (e) are incorrect statements of law.

©philsajonesen/Getty Images

BUSINESS LAW SIMULATION EXERCISE 2

Employment Discrimination: John Falstaff v. Paul Revere Furniture Company

Learning Objectives

After studying this simulation, students who have mastered the material will be able to:

1. Explain the legal doctrines that govern employers in the context of antidiscrimination statutes.
2. Interpret and apply the rules set forth in current case law.
3. Articulate a cogent argument for each party/side in the dispute.
4. Negotiate a tenable solution as an alternative to a judicial forum.

The chapters in this unit covered a variety of legal doctrines and rules governing labor and employment discrimination law as well as examples of how these doctrines and rules apply in the workplace. This simulation is designed to help you understand how the various topics covered in the employment discrimination chapter connect. By focusing on a simulated legal dispute, you will gain virtually real-world experience in applying legal doctrines and using analytical and critical-thinking skills. This simulation is a sequential decision-making exercise structured around a model in which the participants assume a role in managing tasks and work toward a tenable solution.

The simulation is structured in three parts:

- Part 1 is a hypothetical fact pattern describing events leading up to a legal dispute in the hypothetical U.S. state of Longville, which is located in the jurisdiction of the fictitious U.S. Court of Appeals for the 14th Circuit.
- Part 2 contains (1) a statutory excerpt from the actual Americans with Disabilities Act Amendments Act (ADAAA) and (2) two case summaries from hypothetical appellate courts, each of which provides a brief set of facts, several legal points, and short excerpts from the opinion itself. While these cases are hypothetical, they are based on actual cases from federal appellate courts and represent the view of the majority of federal courts.
- Part 3 is an assignment sheet handout that will be provided to you by your instructor.

Part 1: Stipulated Facts

1. Paul Revere Furniture Company (Revere) is a manufacturer and retailer of high-end furniture based in Longville. Revere sells its products at its retail outlets across the United States and employs a workforce of approximately 800 employees in 30 states. Its largest retail outlet is adjacent to its headquarters in Longville.

2. On July 1, 2015, John Falstaff (Falstaff) applied for a position at Revere as a floor manager in Revere's Longville store. Falstaff applied for the position after finding out about the opportunity on Revere's website. The position description is shown in Exhibit A.

> **EXHIBIT A:** Job Posting on Revere's Website
>
> **Paul Revere Furniture Company—Employment Opportunity**
>
> **Position:** Store floor manager (Longville)
>
> **Pay Scale:** Based upon experience
>
> **General Description:** Floor managers are responsible for ensuring overall productive and efficient operations of a retail store location. This includes supervising a sales force of 4–6 people, keeping appropriate corporate records, resolving customer complaints, joining the sales team on the showroom floor during busy holiday seasons, tracking inventory, setting up "Manager's Special" displays, and doing occasional physical work related to tracking and placing merchandise in showrooms in a fashion conducive to maximizing sales.
>
> **Physical Requirements:** Applicants must be in good overall health sufficient to meet physical requirements of (1) long periods of standing without a break (1–2 hours) and (2) when necessary, occasional climbing, kneeling, bending, stooping, balancing, reaching, and lifting of items (such as furniture) in excess of 50 pounds.
>
> **Qualifications:**
> - High school diploma or G.E.D. required.
> - Two years of experience working as a supervisor in a large retail setting is preferred.
> - Ability to fulfill physical requirements.
> - No convictions for felonies or any theft-related offenses.
> - Reliable transportation to work.
>
> **Applications:** Applications are available on our website at www.revere.com/employment.

3. After an interview with Constance Howe (Howe), Revere's regional vice president who supervised all floor managers in the retail stores in the Longville region, Falstaff was hired for the position on July 5, 2015. At the time of hire, Falstaff filled out a personnel form on which he reported that he was in good general health with no injuries or conditions that would prevent him from performing his job, including the physical tasks, and that his weight was approximately 215 pounds and his height was approximately 6 feet.

4. From his start date through May 2016, Falstaff received favorable reviews for his performance as floor manager, and no policy violations were noted in the file. In late June 2016, Falstaff called in sick for three consecutive days, complaining of a back injury. Revere's standard operating procedure required the regional vice president to contact any manager who called in sick more than two consecutive days. Howe telephoned Falstaff, who explained that he had strained his back and was having severe back pain that prevented him from being able to stand or sit comfortably for more than one hour. Falstaff also acknowledged that the pain was subsiding and that he anticipated being able to return to work after one more day of rest. Howe wished Falstaff the best and advised him that he had only two more sick days left. Howe also informed Falstaff that he should consider filing a claim for disability insurance if his condition did not improve soon.

In this simulation exercise, an employee of a furniture company claims that he was terminated due to a disability. Marc Leon/Getty Images

5. Despite his assurances, Falstaff did not return to work as promised and called in sick for a sixth day. Howe then contacted Falstaff and directed him to see a company-hired physician for a determination as to whether Falstaff could return to work or whether he should be certified as disabled for purposes of filing a claim of disability with Revere's insurance carrier.

6. On July 1, Falstaff was examined by Dr. William Jefferson, a physician hired by the company. Dr. Jefferson concluded that Falstaff was not disabled and had suffered a mild sprain in his lower back region. Dr. Jefferson prescribed ice, over-the-counter pain relief, and a period of two weeks of light duty, during which Falstaff would not be required to lift anything over 10 pounds. After that, Dr. Jefferson advised that Falstaff would be ready to return to his regular duties as floor manager.

7. On July 2, Falstaff returned to work on light-duty status. Howe assigned Falstaff to desk duties only and instructed other floor managers that Falstaff was not to engage in any lifting of objects that weighed 10 or more pounds.

8. During the next three months, Falstaff's attendance at work was spotty. Although he never called in sick to work, he arrived late six times, took an extended lunch hour three times, and left work early nine times. On each occasion, Falstaff would explain his absence using the excuse that his back was causing him too much pain to sit up and that even the light lifting required on the floor was difficult for him. When Falstaff was at work, he would complain loudly to subordinates and customers that the company was making him work and that working was making his condition worse.

9. Falstaff's absences and workplace complaints also began to affect his performance. His monthly reports to Howe had been chronically late, as were his payroll records. This resulted in several complaints by sales employees about Falstaff's performance. On September 1, 2016, Howe issued Falstaff a "Corrective Action" letter advising that Falstaff's performance was not satisfactory and outlining the specific violations, including the late reports, his attendance problems, and his inappropriate workplace comments. The letter also warned Falstaff that failure to take corrective action to improve would result in termination.

10. After receiving the letter, Falstaff sent an e-mail to Howe claiming that the poor performance was due to "increasing back pain" and that he had developed "shortness of breath" when exerting any physical labor such as moving the furniture displays as required.

11. During this same period of time (June–September), Falstaff's weight increased significantly, from 215 pounds to 320 pounds. As Falstaff's weight increased, he was increasingly reluctant to perform any physical tasks and would order subordinates to move furniture, arrange "Manager's Special" displays, and do other physical activities. During his shift, Falstaff would frequently stay in the manager's office, never coming out to the showroom.

12. In October 2016, Falstaff sought help from his own physician. Falstaff's physician, Dr. Amanda King, examined Falstaff and diagnosed him with a strained lower back. However, in her report, she also made note that "the most significant factor in patient's health is his obesity. His weight increases the strain on his lower back, limits his range of motion, and leaves him short of breath after just a few steps. His weight severely impacts or eliminates his ability to stand for significant periods of time and to pick up anything over 5 lbs." Falstaff sent Dr. King's report to Howe.

13. In two phone conversations with Falstaff over several days after Dr. King's report, Howe indicated that she was concerned that Falstaff may not be able to fully perform the duties required. Falstaff indicated that he could still effectively manage the store so long as other employees were assigned to do any heavy lifting in Falstaff's store.
14. In December 2016, Revere terminated Falstaff. Revere cited lower-than-expected revenue for the previous fiscal year as the primary reason for cutting back its workforce. On his discharge slip, Howe wrote that the reasons for Falstaff's termination were strategic need to cut costs and poor job performance.
15. Falstaff alleges that his termination violated the ADAAA.

Part 2: Statutory and Case Law

Statute: United States Code

Excerpt from Americans with Disabilities Act Amendments Act (ADAAA)

§ 1 This Act shall become effective January 1, 2009

§ 2 Definition of disability

As used in this Act:

(1) **Disability:** The term "disability" means, with respect to an individual—
   (a) A physical or mental impairment that substantially limits one or more major life activities of such individual;
   (b) A record of such an impairment; or
   (c) Being regarded as having such an impairment on major life activities.

(2) **Major life activities:** In general, for purposes of paragraph (1), major life activities include, but are not limited to, caring for oneself, performing manual tasks, seeing, hearing, eating, sleeping, walking, standing, lifting, bending, speaking, breathing, learning, reading, concentrating, thinking, communicating, and working.

(3) **Major bodily functions:** For purposes of paragraph (1), a major life activity also includes the operation of a major bodily function such as brain, respiratory, circulatory, and endocrine.

(4) **Regarded as having such an impairment:** For purposes of paragraph (1)(c), an individual meets the requirement of "being regarded as having such an impairment" if the individual establishes that he or she has been subjected to an action prohibited under this Act because of an actual or perceived physical or mental impairment whether or not the impairment limits or is perceived to limit a major life activity.

(5) **Exclusions:** Paragraph (1)(c) shall not apply to impairments that are transitory and minor. A transitory impairment is an impairment with an actual or expected duration of six months or less.

(6) **Rules of construction regarding the definition of disability:** The definition of "disability" in paragraph (1) shall be construed in favor of broad coverage of individuals under this Act, to the maximum extent permitted by the terms of this Act.

Case Law

Grindle v. Watkins Motor Lines

14th Circuit Court of Appeals (2012)

Facts

- Grindle was hired as a dockworker by Watkins Motor Lines in 2010. The job description provided that applicants must be able to lift packages over 50 pounds on a repetitive basis and that the job involved daily loading and unloading of heavy freight, standing for eight hours at a time, and tolerance for outdoor weather on the loading dock. At the time of hire, Grindle weighed 345 pounds, and he reported on his application that he had no medical conditions that he was aware of.

- Over a period of one year, a supervisor at Watkins disciplined Grindle several times for failing to load his freight in a timely manner. Grindle had several written reprimands for this violation in his file and was placed on probation. Under the Watkins employee handbook, Grindle faced termination if his performance did not improve.

- Grindle complained to his manager that Watkins's loading-time goals were impossible to meet as Grindle was not physically able to perform the tasks in the time given. After a third letter of reprimand in April 2011, Grindle asked his manager for a different set of time goals, but Watkins's management refused this option.
- The day after his request for a time schedule adjustment was denied, Grindle saw a physician because he was unable to sleep due to the fear that he would lose his job. During the visit, Grindle's physician reported that Grindle's weight, which was now at 450 pounds, was classified as obese and that extended lifting and standing caused potential injury. The physician advised Grindle not to engage in these strenuous work activities until he had lost at least 75 pounds.
- When Grindle returned to work, he again requested a time schedule adjustment, citing his physician's report and recommendation. Again, Watkins refused any adjustment.
- Shortly thereafter, Grindle was terminated due to his inability to perform the job duties for his position. After receiving a right-to-sue letter from the EEOC, Grindle filed suit against Watkins, claiming that the company was required under the ADA to accommodate his obesity as a disability.

POINTS OF LAW AND OPINION EXCERPTS

Point (a)

A claim of disparate treatment under the ADA will be analyzed under the *McDonnell Douglas* standard.

Excerpt (a)

"We have held that claims under the ADA are analyzed under the framework set forth in *McDonnell Douglas v. Green*. In order to establish a prima facie case under the ADA, the plaintiff must prove that (1) the defendants are subject to the ADA; (2) the plaintiff is disabled within the meaning of the Act; (3) the plaintiff could have performed the job if accommodations had been provided; (4) the plaintiff was subject to an adverse employment action because of the disability."

Point (b)

The threshold requirement to qualify as an ADA-covered disability is that the disability must be physical or mental impairment that substantially limits one or more of the major life activities of the individual.

Excerpt (b1)

"An impairment, for purposes of the ADA, is any 'physiological disorder, or condition, cosmetic disfigurement, or anatomical loss affecting one or more of [various] body systems such as: musculoskeletal; special sense organs; respiratory, including speech organs; cardiovascular; reproductive, digestive, genito-urinary; hemic and lymphatic; skin; and endocrine.'"

Excerpt (b2)

"Examples of normal life activities in past cases in this circuit include seeing, walking, lifting a child, communicating with co-workers and sleeping."

Point (c)

Abnormal physical characteristics in height or weight that have no physiological cause are not considered disabilities under the ADA.

Excerpt (c1)

"We observed in previous cases that physical characteristics that are not the result of a physiological disorder are not considered impairments for the purposes of determining either actual or perceived disability."

Excerpt (c2)

"For example, in one previous case, we held that a plaintiff-firefighter's claim that he was disciplined because his weight did not meet a union standard failed because 'obesity, except in special cases where the obesity relates to a physiological disorder, is not a physical impairment within the meaning of the statutes.'"

Point (d)

This circuit declines to follow a minority of courts' rulings that adopts a medical-based formula (such as body mass index) to determine whether certain levels of obesity rise to the level of disability. Without any physiological cause, obesity is not covered as a disability.

Excerpt (d)

"We specifically decline to follow some trial courts' application of a body mass index or other height-weight calibrations because such calculations belie our previous holding in which we repeatedly emphasized that a physical characteristic must relate to a physiological disorder in order to qualify as an ADA impairment."

Held

Because Grindle had not shown that his obesity was a result of some physiological condition or that it prevented him from engaging in normal life activities as required in the ADA, the court found in favor of Watkins.

Adams v. Salt River Master Carvers
2d Circuit Court of Appeals (2014)

Facts

- Adams was employed as a welding technician by Salt River Master Carvers, an employer covered by the ADA. His position required strenuous physical activity.
- Approximately one year after his employment began, Adams was diagnosed by his family doctor as an insulin-dependent type 2 diabetic. His doctor prescribed medication and a strict eating regimen requiring daily insulin injections and certain types of food at certain times of the day related to the time of the insulin injection.
- In January 2012, Adams informed his supervisor of his condition, submitted the doctor's report and recommendations, and requested that his schedule be adjusted to accommodate four to six breaks per day from his eight-hour work shift. He said this

was necessary or else he would become too dizzy and lightheaded and could pose a safety risk.
- Salt River then required Adams to see a company-hired physician. The company physician agreed with the diabetes diagnosis but recommended that Adams have only one insulin injection per day and that he be given two breaks for eating to balance the insulin. The doctor also recommended that Adams not be assigned any more than an 8-hour shift in any 24-hour period.
- A Salt River manager then met with Adams and told him that he was "concerned with Adams's ability to get the job done" and that diabetes had "slowed him down considerably." Salt River then implemented the company physician recommendations regarding Adams's work assignment.
- In March 2012, amid economic turbulence in the industry, Salt River announced that workforce reduction terminations were necessary. Adams, despite having more seniority than most of his co-workers, was terminated on March 31, 2012, with Salt River citing the work reduction plan as the reason.

POINTS OF LAW AND OPINION EXCERPTS

Point (a)

Because the alleged discrimination took place after January 1, 2009, the provisions of the ADA Amendments Act (ADAAA) of 2008 apply to this case.

Point (b)

The ADAAA significantly broadened the definition of disability necessary for protection under the ADA. Specifically, under the ADAAA, a disability is any impairment that substantially limits a major life activity. That statute specifically adds several activities that have yet to be formally recognized. They include eating, sleeping, standing, lifting, bending, and reading.

Excerpt (b1)

"Under both the ADA and the ADAAA, our analysis of whether the impairment is substantially limiting is based on the nature and severity of the impairment, the duration or expected duration of the impairment, as well as the permanent or long-term impact of the impairment."

Excerpt (b2)

"We conclude that Adams's diabetes substantially limits his life activity of eating. The record is replete with statements, by both Adams and his doctors, that to manage his disease Adams is required to strictly monitor what, and when, he eats. Adams stated that these restrictions constrain him every day, 'whether it's a workday, a weekend or a holiday.' He cannot eat large meals or skip meals, and must eat a snack every few hours. He must schedule each day's blood tests, medications, and food intake. He 'sometimes become[s] weak and dizzy without warning,' and only when he eats something do these sensations quickly subside. If he fails to follow his diet regimen for more than a meal or two, his blood sugar rises to a level that aggravates his disease. Adams's doctor testified that controlling diabetes is like being on a chemical roller coaster."

Point (c)

Even if the physical impairment was not actually a disability, Salt River's conduct indicates that the company regarded Adams as disabled. The regarded-as standard was also expanded under the ADAAA and would be applicable to this case.

Excerpt (c1)

"This court has held that an individual need not actually have a physical impairment to state a claim under the ADA . . . as long as that individual is 'regarded as having such an impairment.' To be 'regarded as' having a disability, a plaintiff must prove he is regarded as having an impairment that substantially limits one or more major life activities. A plaintiff must allege that the employer perceived that the employee suffered from an impairment that would be covered under the statute."

Excerpt (c2)

"Evidence in this case shows that Salt River management was 'concerned with Adams's ability to get the job done' and that they had concluded that the diabetes had 'slowed him down considerably.'"

Point (d)

The correlation of the discrimination and the termination may, coupled with other factors, constitute a pretextual reason for the discharge.

Excerpt (d)

"When an employer offers inconsistent explanations for an adverse employment decision a genuine issue of material fact is raised with regard to the veracity of the nondiscriminatory reason. Here, the defendants have offered various explanations for Adams's termination including financial reasons, poor performance, and inappropriate conduct. The allegations regarding Adams's poor performance and inappropriate conduct are questionable in light of their failure to raise these issues prior to the proceedings in the trial court."

Held

The court found in favor of Adams. The ADAAA covers Adams's disability under both the disparate treatment discrimination theory and the regarded-as theory.

UNIT FOUR: Business Entities, Securities Regulation, and Corporate Governance

CHAPTER 13   Choice of Business Entity, Sole Proprietorships, and Partnerships

CHAPTER 14   Limited Liability Companies and Limited Liability Partnerships

CHAPTER 15   Corporations

CHAPTER 16   Regulation of Securities, Corporate Governance, and Financial Markets

CHAPTER 13
Choice of Business Entity, Sole Proprietorships, and Partnerships

©philsajonesen/Getty Images

Learning Objectives

After studying this chapter, students who have mastered the material will be able to:

13-1 Articulate the factors that business owners should consider when selecting a business entity.

13-2 Identify methods through which sole proprietorships and partnerships may be capitalized (funded).

13-3 List the elements required to form a general partnership and the statutory requirements for forming a limited partnership.

13-4 Recognize the effect and role of the RUPA for general partnerships and the RULPA for limited partnerships.

13-5 Distinguish between personal and tax liability for general partners and limited partners.

13-6 Differentiate the consequences of partner separation versus dissolution.

13-7 Recognize the role of franchises in business.

All business ventures operate as a legally recognized form of business entity.[1] Business owners and managers who have a fundamental knowledge of the structure, advantages, and risks associated with each form of business entity are more effective at focusing on business opportunities while limiting potential liability. Most states recognize at least six forms of business entities. In addition to providing an overview of the forms of business entities and factors used to determine the best choice of entity for a given business, this chapter focuses on the law governing two basic forms of entity: sole proprietorships and partnerships. Other forms of entities are covered in the next two chapters. In this chapter, we discuss

- The factors to be considered in determining what business form fits which business type.
- Fundamental principles of the law governing sole proprietorships.
- Legal regulation for formation and governance of partnerships, including the personal liability of partners for business debts and other liabilities.
- Rules governing the separation of partners from the partnership and procedures for dissolving a partnership.

---
[1] Business entities are sometimes referred to as *business organizations*.

CHOOSING A BUSINESS ENTITY

The best choice of business entity is primarily driven by the risk, tax, and operational objectives of the owner(s) and the type of business operations contemplated. Choosing a business entity is an important part of business planning for both start-up entrepreneurs and the managers of a business supervising the launch of an additional venture that supplements the existing business. Each form of entity has its attendant advantages and drawbacks and a variety of legal consequences for the *owners,* known as **principals**, of the business. In choosing a business entity, principals should consider at least the following factors:

- *Formation:* How easy is the entity to form and maintain? Must there be more than one principal? What annual filings or fees are required, and what formalities need to be followed?
- *Liability:* To what extent are the principals *personally* liable for debts and other contract or tort liabilities of the business entity itself? To take a simple example, suppose Gardner owns a consulting business and rents office space from Landlord under a five-year lease agreement. After one year, Gardner loses a large client and can no longer afford the office space. He cancels his lease and moves his office to the basement of his home. If the assets of the consulting business are insufficient to pay a court judgment in favor of the damaged party (Landlord), does Landlord, as the injured party, have a claim for the balance against Gardner's personal assets (such as a personal bank account or stock portfolio)?
- *Capitalization:* How will the business entity fund its operations? May the principal(s) sell ownership rights in the business to raise capital?
- *Taxation of income:* How will tax authorities treat the entity? Will the entity itself pay taxes, or are the taxes passed through to the principals?
- *Management and operation:* How, and by whom, will the business venture be operated? Will the principals be involved in the day-to-day operations of the business? What duties do the principals owe to the business and to each other? How will the profits and losses be split? If a principal decides to leave the business entity, may the remaining principals continue to operate?

Table 13.1 sets out the most common forms of business entities.

> **LO 13-1**
>
> Articulate the factors that business owners should consider when selecting a business entity.

TABLE 13.1 Common Forms of Business Entities

Name of Entity	Brief Description	Coverage in Text
Sole proprietorship	One-person entity in which the debts and liabilities of the business are also personal debts and liabilities of the principal.	Chapter 13
Partnerships: General Limited	Two or more principals that agree to share profits and losses in an ongoing business venture. Debts and liabilities of the business are also personal debts and liabilities of the general partners. Limited partners have limited liability.	Chapter 13
Limited liability partnership	Two or more principals that agree to share profits and losses in an ongoing business venture. The principals have heightened liability protection from debts and liabilities of the partnership.	Chapter 14
Limited liability company	Two or more principals in an ongoing business venture with potentially favorable tax treatment and limited liability for the principals.	Chapter 14
Corporation	One or more principals that invest money in exchange for ownership (stock). The principals generally have no personal liability for debts and liabilities of the business.	Chapter 15

LO 13-2

Identify methods through which sole proprietorships and partnerships may be capitalized (funded).

Legal Speak >))

Execute the Judgment

If a winning plaintiff has obtained a court order for the defendant to pay the amount of the judgment, the plaintiff may take certain steps to collect the money owed from the defendant. In extreme cases, this may take the form of seizing the defendant's personal property for sale by the sheriff or garnishing the wages of the defendant.[3]

Sole Proprietorships

The easiest single-person ownership entity to form and maintain is a **sole proprietorship**. A sole proprietorship requires only a minimal fee, involves a straightforward filing requirement with the appropriate state government authority, and typically requires no annual filings. Its ease of formation and maintenance makes this entity a top choice for start-up businesses with relatively low annual revenues and expenses. An individual planning to conduct a sole proprietorship business under a trade name, rather than her individual name (e.g., "Gates IT Consulting" rather than "Joan Gates") will also file a "doing business as," or DBA, certificate (a DBA name is sometimes known as a *fictitious name*) with a local or state office. There may be additional licenses required by the state and city where the business operates (sales tax licenses, etc.). These requirements vary by jurisdiction.

Sole proprietorships are limited in their options for raising money and are typically capitalized through a proprietor's personal resources or a private or commercial loan that is secured by the proprietor's personal assets.[2] A sole proprietorship business is not subject to corporate income taxation, and no tax return is filed on behalf of the business. Rather, the principal reports business income and expenses on her own individual tax return and pays taxes on business income (or deducts business losses) based on her own individual tax rate. It is important to note that although most sole proprietorships are relatively small in terms of assets and revenues, sole proprietorships are not restricted in terms of the number of employees and can operate in as many locations as the principal desires.

The chief drawback to this form of entity is a complete *lack of protection* of the principal's personal assets for unpaid debts and liabilities of the business. All debts and liabilities

Principals in start-up business ventures have several alternatives when selecting a business entity. Fuse/Getty Images

---

[2]A secured loan is one in which the borrower grants the lender legal rights to something of value until the loan is paid back in full (e.g., a car secures a car loan).

[3]Note that all states prohibit certain assets from being seized to satisfy a judgment, such as the principal's home residence. Some states also exempt retirement portfolios as well.

of the business are also *personal debts and liabilities* of the principal. For example, suppose Redfern is the principal of Redfern Catering, a sole proprietorship. Redfern Catering has approximately $5,000 in assets. One of Redfern's employees negligently uses spoiled ingredients in a soup that is served to customers. Marshall is a customer who develops food poisoning and obtains a court judgment against Redfern Catering to compensate him for damages that resulted from medical bills in the amount of $50,000. Assuming that Redfern Catering had no insurance coverage for this event, Marshall would have $45,000 of judgment unpaid after exhausting the business of its assets ($50,000 judgment minus $5,000 assets). Thus, Redfern would be *personally* liable to Marshall for the remaining unpaid judgment. This means that Marshall could execute the judgment against Redfern by using a judicially sanctioned process for seizing funds from Redfern's personal bank account, stock portfolio, and other assets. As a result of this lack of protection, sole proprietors often purchase comprehensive liability insurance for the business in amounts sufficient to cover potential tort liabilities such as the one described in the Redfern-Marshall example.

Termination A sole proprietorship is terminated either by an express act of the principal or by operation of law in the case of the death or personal bankruptcy of the proprietor. Although a sole proprietor may sell the assets of her business to another party, the proprietor's *ownership* interest in a sole proprietorship cannot pass to her heirs through a gift or an estate. In Case 13.1, an appellate court analyzes the termination of a sole proprietorship in the context of successor liability.

CASE 13.1 Biller v. Snug Harbor Jazz Bistro of Louisiana, L.L.C., 99 So. 3d 730 (4th Cir. 2012)

FACT SUMMARY Brumat was the sole proprietor of Snug Harbor Jazz Bistro of New Orleans (Snug Harbor), a restaurant, bar, and music club. Brumat had leased a building on Frenchmen Street in New Orleans. In July 2007, Brumat died, and pursuant to his last will and testament, all of his property, except a piano, was left to his niece, Luana Brumat (Luana). In September 2007, Luana and Schmidt, Brumat's former bookkeeper, properly registered Snug Harbor, L.L.C., as a Louisiana limited liability company. The registration listed Luana and Schmidt as the L.L.C.'s officers and used the Frenchmen Street address as its domicile and mailing address.

In 2009, Biller obtained an $80,000 judgment against Snug Harbor as a result of an accident that occurred at the Snug Harbor restaurant in April 2007. Seeking to enforce the judgment, Biller filed a petition alleging that the business entity Snug Harbor has operated continuously before and after the death of Brumat and that Snug Harbor, L.L.C., was a successor in interest to the Brumat sole proprietorship. On that basis, Biller argued that the LLC was liable for Brumat's debts in connection with the operation of the Snug Harbor restaurant.

Snug Harbor, L.L.C., denied liability for the judgment, arguing that Snug Harbor was a sole proprietorship that terminated upon the death of Brumat, and Snug Harbor, L.L.C., was a limited liability company that was formed after Biller's injury and after Brumat's death and was a separate and distinct entity. The trial court ruled that Snug Harbor, L.L.C., was a not a successor in interest to Snug Harbor because at the time of the accident, Brumat owned and operated Snug Harbor as a sole proprietorship. Biller appealed.

SYNOPSIS OF DECISION AND OPINION The Court of Appeals for the Fourth Circuit affirmed the trial court's decision in favor of Snug Harbor, L.L.C. The court rejected Biller's argument that Snug Harbor, L.L.C., continued operating Snug Harbor as usual following Brumat's death because Snug Harbor's former bookkeeper was engaging in the same business at the same address. The court

(continued)

ruled that the business entity owned by Brumat terminated upon his death because it was a sole proprietorship. The parties (an heir and a former employee of Brumat) then properly and promptly formed a new entity that was a separate and distinct business entity (an LLC) from the sole proprietorship. The court pointed to the fact that the new entity entered into a new commercial lease agreement for the Frenchmen Street building and other necessary contracts as evidence that a new entity was formed after Brumat's death.

WORDS OF THE COURT: No Successor Liability "After reviewing the record, we find no error in the trial court's conclusion that Snug Harbor, L.L.C., is a separate, distinct entity from the late Mr. Brumat and his estate, and therefore, not liable for the debts of the succession. The evidence supports the trial court's finding that Snug Harbor, L.L.C., did not exist at the time of Mr. Biller's accident and was formed after Mr. Brumat's death. . . .

We also note that [Biller] neither asserted nor offered evidence that Ms. Brumat and Mr. Schmidt formed Snug Harbor, L.L.C., with the intent to defraud any creditor(s) of the succession. Absent any evidence of fraud and considering the evidence before us, we find the trial court properly dismissed plaintiffs' claims against Snug Harbor, L.L.C."

Case Questions
1. What evidence did Biller claim indicates that the LLC was a continuing entity and not a separate entity? Why did the court reject his theory?
2. The court pointed out that there was no evidence of fraud in the formation of the new entity. Why is that important? What kind of fraud could be committed in this context?
3. *Focus on Critical Thinking:* Is this a case of business owners using the law as a shield against a legitimate claim? Is this fair to Biller? What are the public policy implications of this decision?

LO 13-3

List the elements required to form a general partnership and the statutory requirements for forming a limited partnership.

LO 13-4

Recognize the effect and role of the RUPA for general partnerships and the RULPA for limited partnerships.

Partnerships

An entity with *more* than one principal has a number of additional choices. The simplest multiple-person business entity is a **partnership**. There are two traditional subcategories of partnerships: general partnerships and limited partnerships. Most partnerships are **express partnerships**, in which the principals agree to some ongoing business relationship. In some cases, however, even though the parties did not intend on being partners, the law recognizes the relationship as a partnership and imposes the same liability on the principals as would be imposed if the parties had formed an express partnership. Two other related types of partnerships are limited liability partnerships (LLPs) and limited liability limited partnerships (LLLPs). These are hybrid forms of partnership (having characteristics common to several different entities) and are covered in detail in Chapter 14, "Limited Liability Companies and Limited Liability Partnerships."

General Partnerships Unlike most business entities, general partnerships are not created by filing a form with a government agency. Instead, the law recognizes two or more principals as being a general partnership if they have *demonstrated* an intent to carry on as co-owners of a business for profit. While some general partnerships have extensive written agreements detailing the internal operations of the business and the rights and responsibilities of the principals, others operate without any written agreement at all. In the absence of an agreement, the Revised Uniform Partnership Act (RUPA) governs a general partnership. Just like the Uniform Commercial Code, the RUPA is a *model statute* drafted and occasionally revised by the National Conference of Commissioners on Uniform State Laws. To date, approximately 40 states have adopted all or substantial portions of the RUPA. States that have not yet adopted the RUPA operate under the RUPA's predecessor, the Uniform

Partnership Act (UPA).[4] The RUPA should be thought of as a default set of laws that apply only when the principals have not expressly agreed otherwise (similar to the UCC's gap-filler function). The RUPA also contains certain agency principles, including fiduciary duties of partners to each other and to the partnership. In addition to the RUPA, the common law plays a role in general partnership law in certain cases where principles of general fairness must be applied and the RUPA doesn't contemplate that particular situation.[5]

Formation No formal document or government filing is necessary to form a general partnership. In fact, it is important to note that the parties may not actually *intend* to be partners, but the law still recognizes their relationship as an **implied partnership**. For example, suppose that Carl and Jan are neighbors and during a block party Carl mentions that his family's secret salad dressing was popular with the neighbors and friends. Jan loves the dressing and offers to help Carl sell the dressing at local gourmet stores in exchange for 50 percent of the profits. Carl agrees so long as he is responsible for making the dressing and Jan is responsible for providing bottles and labels, transporting, and selling. Here, despite the fact that the parties may have intended to have an informal arrangement, legally they have created a general partnership. This is important because this arrangement gives rise to potential liability for both Carl and Jan even though they never intended to assume such risks. In Case 13.2, a state appellate court analyzes whether a romantic relationship created an implied partnership in business.

CASE 13.2 Waddell v. Rustin, 2011 Tenn. App. LEXIS 377 (2011)

FACT SUMMARY Waddell and Rustin entered into a romantic relationship soon after meeting in 1999. Waddell maintained that their association started as personal and also grew into a business partnership. Rustin denied that they were ever express or implied business partners. At the time the two met, Rustin and his brother owned and operated a store called "Lots of Christmas," and Waddell began working at the store in 2000. One year later, Rustin started a construction and excavation business. Both at the Lots of Christmas store and at the construction company, Waddell claimed that she had management and oversight over business projects, had access to the company checkbook, paid company bills, helped Rustin choose construction projects, and even changed the store's name from "Lots of Christmas" to "Aluminum Decor and More" to improve sales. Waddell testified that she did not receive any paychecks for her work, but that the couple ran the businesses as partners. When the personal relationship ended, Waddell brought suit claiming that she was entitled to a percentage of the profits because the relationship had been an implied partnership. The trial court ruled that no implied partnership was created.

SYNOPSIS OF DECISION AND OPINION The Court of Appeals of Tennessee affirmed the trial court and held in favor of Rustin. The court ruled that because there was no written partnership agreement between Waddell and Rustin, Waddell bore the burden of proving the existence of a partnership by clear and convincing evidence. Given that Waddell had no experience in construction or excavation when they met and that Rustin had engaged in construction work for years, it was clear that his efforts had made the business viable. Waddell did not contribute equipment, experience, or capital. Therefore,

(continued)

---

[4]Louisiana is the only state not to adopt the UPA or the RUPA.

[5]RUPA § 104(a) refers to this, stating, "Unless displaced by particular provisions of this [act], the principles of law and equity supplement this act."

the court held that one cannot reasonably conclude that Waddell's relationship with Rustin rose to the level of an implied partnership.

WORDS OF THE COURT: Implied Partnership "Rustin acknowledges, as do we, that Waddell performed certain work related to Rustin's business enterprises. However, it cannot be said of this case that the parties' prosperity was due in equal part to Waddell's efforts. Rustin and his brother ran the store prior to Waddell's relationship with Rustin. Waddell's work at the Store is better characterized as helping out rather than the contribution of an equal partner. Notwithstanding Waddell's activities related to certain houses or cabins, the record shows that Rustin, with his experience in construction and excavation, clearly was the primary driver of the construction enterprise. Waddell testified that she contributed no real property; personal property; money; formal training in interior design; excavation experience; or construction experience to any partnership."

Case Questions

1. What was Waddell's theory of the case as to why an implied partnership existed?
2. Could a personal relationship ever be considered a partnership? At what point does a personal relationship create an implied partnership?
3. *Focus on Critical Thinking:* Given the court's ruling, what could Waddell have done differently to ensure that she would have had partner status?

Fundamentally, a general partnership is thought of as (1) an association of two or more people or entities (2) who are co-owners and co-managers of the business and (3) who share in the profits of an ongoing business operation. General partnerships typically use the designation *GP* at the end of their business name to signify the general partnership as their form of entity. Ideally, the partners set a specific future date or event for when the partnership will be dissolved (of course, the partners may agree to extend this date as necessary). However, partnerships where the partners have not agreed to remain partners until the expiration of a definite term or event are known as **partnerships at will**.[6]

Sometimes, the parties wish to have only a limited-in-time relationship instead of an ongoing business entity. This relationship is generally referred to as a **joint venture** and is governed by the same legal principles as a general partnership.

Liability of the Principals

Much like sole proprietors, general partners have no protection of their personal assets for unpaid debts and liabilities of the partnership. However, the RUPA imposes *additional* liability on general partners by making all general partners **jointly and severally liable** for unpaid debts and liabilities of the partnership. This means that general partners' personal assets are at risk both together (jointly) and separately (severally) for all debts and liabilities of the partnership, regardless of the source of the debt or liability. For example, in the Redfern Catering example discussed earlier, suppose that Redfern and Colgate formed a general partnership to operate the catering business as Redfern-Colgate Catering, GP. Marshall obtains a judgment against the business for medical damages related to food poisoning. Marshall must first exhaust all of the assets of the partnership. If the assets are not enough to satisfy the judgment, Marshall may then attempt to collect the unpaid portion of the judgment from the personal assets of Redfern and Colgate together or separately because Redfern and Colgate are jointly and severally liable for the entire debt. Thus, Marshall may choose to collect 50 percent from Redfern and 50 percent from Colgate or any combination thereof (60/40, 70/30, etc.). Suppose that Redfern has no assets and moves to Key West to become a shrimper. In this case, Marshall may choose to collect the *entire* unpaid judgment from Colgate.

---

[6]RUPA § 101(10).

An express partnership is created when two or more principals agree to share profits in an ongoing business relationship.
Stockbyte/Getty Images

However, because generally the partners share in losses as well as profits, Colgate could try to pursue Redfern through a civil suit for 50 percent of the loss he suffered in paying out the judgment to Marshall. This joint and several liability rule may *not* be altered by the parties' agreement, nor may the principals limit their liability based on the principals' agreement to split profits and losses on a percentage basis. So, in the Redfern-Colgate example, now suppose that when they formed their partnership they agreed that Colgate would receive 30 percent of the profits. Regardless of this agreement, Colgate may *not* assert that his liability to Marshall is limited to 30 percent of the total unpaid judgment.

Capitalization General partnerships are generally funded either through debt (i.e., borrowing money from the principals, a commercial lender, or a private individual third party) or through a sale of equity (selling a percentage of ownership rights in the partnership and any future profits of the business). Partnerships may not, however, sell ownership rights through the public markets such as the New York Stock Exchange. Sometimes general partners hedge their financial investment through a combination of debt and equity. The concepts of debt and equity are discussed in detail in Chapter 16, "Regulation of Securities, Corporate Governance, and Financial Markets."

> **KEY POINT**
>
> General partners' personal assets are at risk for the full amount of the debts and liabilities of the partnership jointly (all partners together) and severally (each and every partner separately), regardless of their percentage of ownership interest in the partnership.

Taxation of Partnership and Principals Just as in the case of a sole proprietorship, a partnership is a **pass-through entity**. This means that the partnership entity pays no level of corporate tax. Rather, profits are taxed *after* they pass through the business and are distributed to the individual partners. The income is reported on the individual general partner's *personal tax return* (the familiar tax form 1040) and taxed based on the individual rate of the general partner. In fact, the partnership entity itself does not file a tax return, but it does file an *information return* for purposes of providing the government with

The principals in the hypothetical Redfern-Colgate Catering, GP, have joint and several liability for all debts and liabilities of the partnership.

Klaus Vedfelt/Getty Images

documentation regarding how much, when, and to whom profits were paid. Of course, partners also report business partnership losses on their individual tax returns and are permitted to deduct those losses to offset certain types of income.

Management and Operation of the Partnership   Absent an agreement by the parties, the RUPA also governs certain internal operations of the general partnership. For example, unless the parties agree otherwise, each partner receives an equal share of the partnership profit payments regardless of the partner's involvement in the success of the business. The same rule applies to losses. Absent an agreement to the contrary, general partners have the general power to *bind* the partnership to a contractual obligation (e.g., a lease for office space) even if the other general partners have no knowledge of the transaction.

Note that partners who provide labor to the partnership are not entitled to any compensation (other than a share of profits) for this work unless the principals have agreed ahead of time to certain compensation terms. For example, assume that in the Redfern-Colgate general partnership, Redfern works in the kitchen 80 hours per week while Colgate spends no time working on behalf of the partnership. Absent any advance agreement between the partners, Redfern is not entitled to any compensation for the kitchen work.

Fiduciary Obligations   General partners have a set of duties that ensure they are acting in the best interest of the partnership. These duties are known as **fiduciary duties**.[7] They are very similar to the duties owed by an agent to a principal that were discussed in Chapter 10, "Agency." Fundamentally, the RUPA sets out these duties as threefold: (1) loyalty, (2) care, and (3) good faith. The loyalty standard prohibits a general partner from engaging in competition with the interests of the partnership and also prohibits other conflicts of interest with the partnership such as using the partnership property for personal gain at the expense of the interests of the entity. Partners must also exercise due care in handling the affairs of the partnership and treat business affairs with the same diligence

---

[7]RUPA § 404.

as they would apply in treating their own personal business affairs. The good faith standard requires that partners exercise appropriate discretion in dealing with other partners and third parties concerning the partnership's business enterprise operations.

Limited Partnerships A limited partnership is an entity that exists by virtue of a *state statute* that recognizes one or more principals as managing the business enterprise while other principals participate only in terms of contributing capital or property. A limited partnership has at least one general partner (managing principal) and at least one limited partner (investing principal). In the absence of an agreement, the Revised Uniform Limited Partnership Act (RULPA) governs a limited partnership. However, the RULPA actually works in tandem with the RUPA. That is, when an issue of liability or operation arises, the written partnership agreement governs. If there is no agreement or the agreement is silent on this issue, then the RULPA resolves the issue. If the RULPA does not provide rules on a particular issue, courts may sometimes look to the RUPA for guidance.

> **LO 13-5**
> Distinguish between personal and tax liability for general partners and limited partners.

Formation To form a limited partnership, the general partner files a **certificate of limited partnership** with the state government authority[8] (usually in the secretary of state's office). Generally, the certificate is not overly complex. It requires routine information, such as the name, address, and capital contribution of each partner. Although the RULPA does not formally require a partnership agreement, the vast majority of limited partnerships have one. The agreement details the rights, obligations, and relationships between partners. These partnerships typically use the designation *LP* at the end of their business name to signify the limited partnership as their form of entity. Figure 13.1 presents a sample certificate of limited partnership.

Personal Liability of Principals Each general partner in a limited partnership is *personally liable* for all of the partnership's debts and liabilities, just as if the general partners were in a general partnership. However, limited partners do *not* have the same automatic personal liability of a general partner.[9] Rather, the limited partner's liability is limited to whatever the limited partner *contributed* to the partnership. For example, suppose that Redfern initially operates Redfern Catering as a sole proprietor but decides to expand his business operations. He decides to raise capital through the selling of some ownership interest in his business. Redfern convinces Alexandra Macduff to invest $20,000 in Redfern Catering. However, Macduff has substantial personal assets she wishes to protect and no interest in running the day-to-day operations of the business. The two form Redfern Catering, LP, with Redfern as the general partner and Macduff as the limited partner. In an effort to cut costs, Redfern negligently uses spoiled ingredients, and a customer, Marshall, is sickened. Marshall obtains a judgment against Redfern Catering, LP, but after the assets of the partnership are exhausted, Marshall is still owed a balance from the judgment. Because Redfern is a general partner, Marshall may recover the balance from Redfern's personal assets, but *not* from Macduff as a limited partner. There are some exceptions to the liability rule spelled out in the RULPA. The primary exception occurs when a limited partner acts *illegally* or *negligently* within the scope of partnership duties. When a limited partner engages in wrongful conduct on behalf of the limited partnership and causes an injury resulting in damages, the limited partner is personally liable to pay damages to the injured party.

In Case 13.3, the Texas Supreme Court considers the impact of a partnership structure in the context of a medical malpractice claim.

---

[8] RULPA § 201.
[9] RULPA § 403(b).

FIGURE 13.1 Sample Certificate of Limited Partnership for Redfern Catering, LP

D

The Commonwealth of Massachusetts
William Francis Galvin
Secretary of the Commonwealth
One Ashburton Place - Room 1717, Boston, Massachusetts 02108-1512

Limited Partnership Certificate
(General Laws Chapter 109, Section 8)

(1) The exact name of the limited partnership:

Redfern Catering, LP

(2) The general character of the business of the limited partnership:

Catering services

(3) The street address of the limited partnership in the commonwealth at which its records will be maintained:

1000 Restaurant Avenue
Boston, MA 02108

> Basic information including name, purpose, and address of the partnership. Note that Redfern Catering is using the LP (limited partnership) designation.

(4) The name and street address of the resident agent:

Francis Redfern   1000 Restaurant Avenue
                         Boston, MA 02108

(5) The name and business address of each general partner:

Francis Redfern
1000 Restaurant Avenue
Boston, MA 02108

> State statutes require that all business entities have a physical address within the state jurisdiction. Out-of-state entities use a resident agent to satisfy this requirement. Some commercial services offer resident agent services for a fee. Attorneys sometimes serve as resident agents for their business clients. A resident agent typically provides services such as accepting legal documents (such as a complaint in a lawsuit) for the partnership. In-state partnerships simply use a partner as their resident agent (as in the case of Redfern Catering, LP).

(6) The latest date on which the limited partnership is to dissolve: October 10, 2030

(7) Additional matters:

Alexandra Macduff

> Most states require the partners to select an ending date for the partnership but allow the partners to continue the partnership after the ending date by simply filing an additional form extending the date.

Signed *(by all general partners)*: *Francis Redfern*

Consent of resident agent:

I Francis Redfern, resident agent of the above limited partnership, consent to my appointment as resident agent pursuant to G.L. c109 Section 8 (a) (3)*

*or attach registered agents consent hereto.

> The resident agent consents to serve in compliance with responsibilities set out by the state statute.

Source: The Commonwealth of Massachusetts

CASE 13.3 Doctors Hospital at Renaissance v. Andrade, 493 S.W.3d 545 (Tex. 2016)

FACT SUMMARY Dr. Rodolfo Lozano (Lozano) was sued for negligence by Jesus and Jessica Andrade (Andrades), who were the parents of a baby delivered by Lozano at Women's Hospital at Renaissance (Hospital). The Andrades alleged that Lozano's negligence in delivering their daughter resulted in her permanent injury, including nerve damage and permanent paralysis of one arm. Eventually, Doctors Hospital at Renaissance, Ltd. (Renaissance), and RGV Med, LLC, were also added as defendants under the theory that these entities were vicariously liable for Dr. Lozano's negligence. Renaissance was a limited partnership that owned and operated the Hospital, and RGV Med was Renaissance's general partner. Lozano, an independent contractor physician with admitting privileges at the Hospital, was a limited partner in Renaissance. Renaissance and RGV Med moved for summary judgment, arguing that they were not liable for Lozano's conduct under the applicable partnership statute because he was not acting within the scope of the partnership or with partnership authority when providing medical care to his patients. The trial court and appellate court ruled against Renaissance and RGV Med, holding that an issue of fact existed as to whether Lozano was acting within the scope of the partnership or with the partnership's authority when delivering the baby. In the interim, Lozano settled his claim with the Andrades, but Renaissance and RGV Med appealed the decision of the lower courts.

SYNOPSIS OF DECISION AND OPINION The Texas Supreme Court reversed the decision of the lower courts and ruled in favor of Renaissance and RGV Med. The court held that the applicable partnership statute renders Renaissance liable for the conduct of a limited partner only if he was acting in the ordinary course of the partnership's business or with partnership authority. The court pointed to the partnership agreement and the daily operation of the entities as evidence that Lozano was *not* acting pursuant to the partnership agreement and that providing medical care was not part of the partnership's ordinary course of business.

WORDS OF THE COURT: Ordinary Course of Business "The record conclusively demonstrates that the ordinary course of Renaissance's business does not include the provision of medical care. . . . Here, the partnership agreement states that the purposes of the limited partnership are:

> (i) to develop, construct and operate such Health Care Facilities as the General Partner may deem appropriate from time to time; (ii) [rights of first refusal for real estate ownership]; (iii) to own, develop, operate and engage in such other business activities as the General Partner may deem appropriate from time to time; and (iv) to enter into, make and perform all such agreements and undertakings, and to engage in all such activities and transactions, as the General Partner may deem necessary or appropriate for or incidental to the carrying out of the foregoing objects and purposes."

WORDS OF THE COURT: No Authority "Here, the partnership agreement provides that limited partners may not perform any act on behalf of the partnership unless specifically authorized under the agreement. The partnership agreement does not give the limited partners, some of whom are not physicians, any authority to provide medical care at partnership-owned facilities. In fact, the partnership agreement does not give the limited partners any specific authority to act on the partnership's behalf at all. Consistent with its organization as a limited partnership instead of a general partnership, the limited partnership agreement expressly authorizes the general partner to act on behalf of the entity, but not the limited partners."

Case Questions

1. Why does the court find that Lozano was not acting within the scope of the partnership?
2. Why was the partnership agreement so crucial to deciding this case?
3. *Focus on Critical Thinking:* Does it defy common sense to rule that a doctor who is providing medical care is acting outside the scope of a partnership composed solely of physicians? Should the partnership be able to escape all liability? Explain.

Capitalization Limited partnerships are generally funded either through debt (i.e., borrowing money from the principals, a commercial lender, or private individual third parties) or through a sale of equity (selling a percentage of ownership rights in the partnership and any future profits of the business). Limited partnerships may not, however, sell ownership rights through the public markets such as the New York Stock Exchange (NYSE). Although not considered publicly traded equity, when limited partnership interests are sold to the public (usually through a broker-dealer with contacts in the investment community), they are subject to strict federal securities laws and state securities laws. Securities law is discussed extensively in Chapter 16, "Regulation of Securities, Corporate Governance, and Financial Markets."

Taxation of Partners and Partnership Limited partnerships are pass-through entities just like general partnerships. The same rules apply for taxation as in a general partnership. That is, profits or losses are reported in the principal's personal tax return, and tax is paid in accordance with the individual partner's individual tax rate. The general partner is responsible for filing an *information return* with taxing authorities, but limited partnerships do not pay corporate taxes. As in the case of general partnerships, this information return informs tax authorities of profits or losses of the partnership entity.

Management and Operation of the Partnership One of the primary differences between general partners and limited partners is the extent to which they are permitted to be involved in day-to-day operations of the business. General partners manage the business and are permitted to bind the partnership. Limited partners may *not* participate in daily management of the business, do not have authority to bind the partnership, and remain primarily investors. Limited partners who do engage in daily management and operations *jeopardize* their limited partnership status. Under the RULPA, limited partners may engage in consulting and contribute expertise but may not engage in management activities such as supervision of employees.[10]

> **KEY POINT**
>
> Limited partners may *not* participate in daily management of the business, do not have authority to bind the partnership, and remain primarily as investors.

Although sometimes limited partners are referred to colloquially as *silent partners,* limited partners have the right to access partnership information (such as inspection of financial records) about the business and general information about the partnership's operations (such as contracts the partnership has executed). The partnership agreement may expand the limited partner's role in management (though not to the point where the limited partner's role constitutes day-to-day involvement in running the business) and may also expand her rights and prerogatives, such as the right to remove a general partner or the right to block admission of new partners. These provisions in a partnership agreement are relatively common because they allow the limited partner to better protect her investment.

Limited partnerships also differ from general partnerships in terms of the default rule for sharing profits and losses. Recall from our earlier discussion that the RUPA contemplates that partners, absent agreement to the contrary, share equally in profits and losses. However, in a limited partnership, the partners share in profits and losses in proportion to "the value of contributions made by each partner to the extent they have been received by the partnership and have not been returned."[11] For example, suppose Pablo, Vincent, and

---

[10] RULPA § 303(b), (c).
[11] RULPA § 403(c).

Frida form a limited partnership for the purpose of starting an art auction house. The partnership is initially structured as follows:

Partner	Initial Capital Contribution	Role
Pablo	$20,000	General partner; salaried employee
Vincent	45,000	Limited partner
Frida	45,000	Limited partner

The partnership agreement provides for a salary for Pablo but is silent on distribution of profits and losses. Frida has an immediate need for cash, so the parties agree to return $10,000 of her investment. Under the RULPA, profits and losses are now allocated with 20 percent to Pablo, 35 percent to Frida, and 45 percent to Vincent.

In some cases, the principals in a partnership make specific agreements and label themselves as limited partners. This labeling is not sufficient to maintain a limited partner status (and, thus, protection from certain liabilities). The focus of the inquiry is the principals' *conduct*. The question is not how they *labeled* themselves or how they signed certain documents or what they called themselves. Rather, the question is this: Did the principals *operate* as a limited partnership?

Family Limited Partnerships Another type of partnership is a family limited partnership. A family limited partnership is simply a limited partnership that is used for estate planning for families of considerable wealth. The actual process and legal procedures governing family limited partnership transactions are a very complex area of tax and estate law. The fundamental purpose of a family limited partnership is to enable wealthy members of one generation to distribute assets (in the form of an IRS-recognized gift) to heirs using a method that allows the distributing generation to claim a much lower market value than the actual market value of the gift. It also allows the distributing generation to transfer assets out of their large estate into the smaller estates of their heirs and avoid estate taxes upon their death. Some states have amended their RULPA statutes to accommodate the special circumstances of a family limited partnership with respect to partner dissociation (discussed next).

CONCEPT SUMMARY Sole Proprietorships versus Partnerships

	Sole Proprietorships	Partnerships, LP and GP
Formation	Low start-up costs and minimal filing. One-person entity.	Minimal filing requirements. Partnership agreement may result in some legal fees. GP has two or more partners. LP must have at least one general partner and one or more limited partners.
Liability of principal(s)	All debts and liabilities of the business are the personal liabilities of the sole proprietor. All of the proprietor's assets are at risk to satisfy business debts and liabilities.	GP: Each general partner is jointly and severally liable for debts and liabilities of the partnership. All personal assets of a general partner are at risk. LP: Personal assets of the limited partners are not at risk for debts and liabilities of the entity.

	Sole Proprietorships	Partnerships, LP and GP
Capital	Proprietor uses personal assets or bank loan secured by personal assets.	Each partner contributes capital as needed. The partnership agreement governs how and when additional calls for partners' contributions are made. Bank loans secured by partnership assets and/or personal guarantees.
Taxes	All income taxes of the business are paid at the proprietor's individual tax rate and reported on the proprietor's individual income tax return. Miscellaneous state and local taxes to operate business.	No taxation at the partnership entity level. All income tax of the business passes through the partnership, is distributed to the partners, and is paid at the individual tax rate of the receiving partner. Partnership files information return to inform IRS of profits or losses. Miscellaneous state and local taxes to operate business.
Management and control	One-person entity.	Management and control as outlined in partnership agreements or under RUPA/UPA if not agreed upon. Limited partner cannot have day-to-day involvement. Fiduciary duties are owed by partners.
Designation	John Doe d/b/a Doe Consulting Services	Doe Partners, GP Doe Partners, LP

LO 13-6

Differentiate the consequences of partner separation versus dissolution.

Partner Dissociation and Dissolution of the Partnership

When a partner no longer wishes to be a principal in the partnership, she may choose to leave the partnership. The RUPA[12] uses the term **dissociation** to describe this act of separation, while the RULPA uses the term **withdrawal**. Both the RUPA and RULPA give the partners substantial rights that govern withdrawal under the partnership agreement, but they differ significantly if the partners have not agreed to displace the RUPA and RULPA provisions.

Dissociation under the RUPA

The RUPA lists 10 specific events that are events of dissociation, but the majority of dissociations are the result of one of the following three events: (1) voluntary separation from the partnership, whereby one partner gives specific notice to withdraw from the partnership; (2) expulsion by the *unanimous* vote of the other partners; or (3) the partner's inability to carry out her duties to the partnership (as in the case of incapacity or death) or inability to have an economic stake in the business (as in the case of an individual partner filing for bankruptcy protection). The RUPA makes a distinction between *rightful* and *wrongful* dissociation. When a partner exercises a rightful dissociation, she is no longer liable for the debts and liabilities incurred by the partnership. Although the partner is still liable for predissociation liability, she no longer owes any fiduciary duty to the partnership or the remaining principals. A wrongful

---

[12]The rules governing dissociation and dissolution are perhaps the biggest difference between the UPA and RUPA. Under the UPA, such events cause an automatic dissolution of the partnership. The RUPA allows the partnership to continue under certain circumstances.

dissociation occurs if a partner's withdrawal violates the partnership agreement or if a partner withdraws from a partnership before the expiration of a previously agreed-upon time has elapsed. In the event of a wrongful dissociation, the wrongfully dissociated partner "is liable to the partnership and to the other partners for damages caused by the dissociation."[13] For example, suppose that Abel, Baker, and Cain are general partners in ABC Landscape Design and have a written agreement about the partnership that sets the initial expiration at five years. Abel is knowledgeable in the operation of specific equipment crucial to the success of the business. ABC enters into a contract to provide services to several large office centers. After a few months, Abel withdraws from the partnership to pursue another career. As a result, the partnership cannot perform the services on time and breaches several agreements while attempting to locate a replacement to operate the equipment. In this case, Abel would be liable for damages suffered by the partnership.

In Case 13.4, a federal trial court considers one partner's allegation that another partner wrongfully dissociated.

CASE 13.4 Robertson v. Mauro, LEXIS 91610 (D. Idaho, 2013)

FACT SUMMARY Mauro operates a business conducting seminars to teach people how to trade in foreign currency. Robertson became acquainted with Mauro after attending a seminar Mauro taught in October of 2009. Robertson alleges that in January of 2010, he and Mauro orally agreed to form a partnership, which included an agreement to evenly divide profits among the partners. The purpose of the partnership was to facilitate Robertson's business plan to establish a series of seminars, taught by Mauro, that would instruct students on foreign currency trading. Robertson was to manage all financial and operating aspects of the partnership, which included promoting the seminars, as well as other duties. Robertson began to schedule seminars in various locations, which Mauro taught. Robertson collected the fees for the seminars and distributed the profits according to the parties' agreement. This arrangement continued throughout the remainder of 2010, into the first quarter of 2011.

In early 2011, Mauro allegedly stated to Robertson that he "needed a break" temporarily from teaching the seminars but would resume the partnership later that year. Robertson alleges this statement was false, and that instead of taking a break, Mauro continued with the business without him. Robertson filed suit against Mauro for, among other things, wrongful dissociation because neither party expressed the intent to dissolve or wind up the partnership, yet Mauro's actions essentially accomplished a disintegration of the partnership without Robertson's consent.

SYNOPSIS OF DECISION AND OPINION The U.S. District Court in Idaho ruled in favor of Mauro on the dissociation claim. The court held that in order for a partner to wrongfully dissociate, they must fit into one of the categories listed in the state statues based on the RUPA. The court ruled that because there was no partnership agreement and the entity was an at-will (implied) partnership, Mauro's action could not constitute a wrongful dissociation.

WORDS OF THE COURT: Standard for Wrongful Dissociation "Based upon the allegations in the Complaint and Robertson's concession that the partnership was at will, Robertson's claim that Mauro's dissociation was wrongful does not meet [the partnership statute's] requirements. First, Robertson has not alleged breach of an express provision of the partnership agreement other than that the particular undertaking for which the partnership was organized had not been completed. Robertson does not identify the 'particular undertaking' at

(continued)

---

[13]RUPA § 602(c).

issue. And Robertson's concession in his response brief that the partnership was 'at will' is at odds with that assertion. By definition, [state partnership law] does not apply to an at-will partnership. The two provisions are mutually exclusive."

Case Questions

1. What was Robertson's theory of the case?
2. Why is it important that the partnership was "at will"?
3. *Focus on Critical Thinking:* In addition to the wrongful dissociation claim, Robertson alleged Mauro committed other wrongs related to their business relationship. Can you guess what they are? What other areas of law could be implicated in this case?

When a partner dissociates herself (rightfully or wrongfully) from the partnership, the partnership does *not* automatically dissolve. In fact, the RUPA leans toward the notion that the partnership can continue.[14] If the remaining principals wish to continue operating the business partnership, they must purchase the partnership interest of the dissociating partner based on a formula contained in the RUPA. Again, it is important to note that these are RUPA default rules and that a partnership agreement often fixes the method or formula for determining the buyout price.

There may be certain cases where the remaining principals wish to dissolve the partnership after dissociation. The dissolution does not actually end the partnership but rather triggers the process of **winding up**. Only after windup is complete is the partnership officially considered terminated. Windup is the period of time necessary to settle the affairs of the partnership and includes activities such as discharging the partnership's liabilities, settling and closing the partnership's business, marshaling the assets of the partnership, and distributing any net proceeds to the partners.

Withdrawal under the RULPA

Because the overwhelming majority of limited partnerships operate under a partnership agreement that spells out detailed rules for withdrawal of a general or limited partner, the RULPA does not play as significant a role as does the RUPA for general partnerships. However, the RULPA does set down default rules for withdrawal of partners in the event that the written agreement does not cover withdrawal or its consequences sufficiently. A *general partner* may withdraw at any time without causing dissolution of the partnership. The withdrawal does not result in automatic dissolution provided that (1) the partnership still has at least one remaining *general partner* and (2) all of the partners (both general and limited) agree in writing to continue the partnership.

If the partner's withdrawal does not result in dissolution of the partnership, the partnership must pay the departing partner the fair market value of her interest in the limited partnership within a reasonable time after withdrawal.[15]

In contrast, *limited* partners are subject to restrictions on withdrawal. Absent an agreement in writing to the contrary, the general rule is that limited partners may *not* withdraw from a partnership before the partnership termination time agreed on by the partners. If the limited partnership agreement does not provide for a certain time before termination, limited partners must give at least six months' prior written notice to

> **KEY POINT**
>
> The dissociation (under the RUPA in a general partnership) or withdrawal (under the RULPA in a limited partnership) does not result in automatic dissolution so long as the remaining partners wish to continue.

---

[14]RUPA § 606(a).
[15]RULPA § 604.

the other partners before withdrawing. Some states have passed additional restrictions, including an absolute prohibition of withdrawal, intended to address special circumstances in family limited partnerships.

 Self-Check Rules for Dissociation/Withdrawal

Is there a basis for rightful dissociation/withdrawal?

1. Under RUPA, a general partnership that owns a diner has 10 partners. One partner never works, only shows up to eat, and harasses servers. Seven partners vote to throw him out.
2. Under RUPA, a tax lawyer who is a partner in a small law firm wants to start a new career at the IRS. She informs her colleagues of her departure at the end of the year, just before the busy tax season.
3. Under RULPA, a limited partner in a partnership that owns a baseball team decides he no longer wants to be part of the steroid scandals, so he withdraws.
4. Under RULPA, a limited partner in a juice company wants to leave and get into the wind-powered energy business. The partnership agreement allows limited partners to leave so long as they do not invest in another beverage company for three years.

Answers to this Self-Check are provided at the end of the chapter.

Other Events of Dissolution Dissociation is not the only way that a partnership may be dissolved. A partnership may also be dissolved when the partnership has reached its agreed-upon term (a certain date set out in the filings and/or partnership agreement) or when dissolution is mandated by court order or, in the case of a general partnership, agreed to by unanimous consent of the partners. Note that dissolving a limited partnership does not require unanimous consent of all partners. Rather, unanimous consent of each general partner and consent of any limited partner that owns a majority of the rights to receive a distribution as a limited partner is sufficient to dissolve the partnership.

CONCEPT SUMMARY *Partner Dissociation or Withdrawal and Dissolution of the Partnership*

	GP (RUPA/Dissociation)	**LP (RULPA/Withdrawal)**
Result for departing principal	Rightful → Personal liability and fiduciary duties cease. Wrongful → Liable for damages to partnership.	GP: Rightful → Personal liability and fiduciary duties cease. Wrongful → Liable for damages to partnership. LP: Restricted from withdrawal → RULPA requires 6 months' notice.
Result for entity	Continue → Principals **unanimously** agree Dissolve → Begin wind-up by paying creditors, etc.	Continue → Principals **unanimously** agree Dissolve → Begin wind-up by paying creditors, etc.

CHAPTER THIRTEEN | Choice of Business Entity, Sole Proprietorships, and Partnerships

LO 13-7

Recognize the role of franchises in business.

Franchises: A Method Rather Than an Entity

An existing entity that wishes to distribute its products to a broader market without the overhead costs of retail space, equipment, and employees can do so through the use of a **franchise**. A franchise should be thought of as a *method* of conducting business that centers on a contractual relationship rather than as a business entity. Federal statutes define a franchise as an arrangement of a continuing commercial relationship for the right to operate a business pursuant to the franchisor's trade name or to sell the seller's branded goods. A franchise involves the **franchisor**, a business entity that has a proven track record of success, selling to a **franchisee** the right to operate the business and use the business's trade secrets, trademarks, products, and so on. The franchisor assists the franchisee with financing, supplies, training, and other aspects of running a successful operation.

Franchise Agreements The parties are typically bound to each other via a franchise agreement. The franchise agreement covers some of the following terms that govern the relationship between franchisee and franchisor: (1) the term (time limit) of the agreement; (2) franchise fees, payment terms, and ongoing investment or buying requirements; (3) territory rights that usually provide the franchisee with an exclusive geographic area; (4) commitments from the franchisor for training, ongoing management support, and advertising; (5) commitments from the franchisee to follow operating protocol; (6) royalties and other fees that the franchisee must pay; and (7) franchisee termination and/or cancellation policies.

FTC Regulation The Federal Trade Commission (FTC) is the federal regulatory authority that oversees the regulation of franchisors. The FTC regulations are primarily designed to ensure full disclosure of all information relating to a franchise company prior to a franchisee investment. The FTC regulations are very detailed, but almost all focus on mandatory disclosures about the financial condition of the franchise, success rates, and other important information used by potential franchisees faced with making the decision

McDonald's worldwide market success was accomplished through franchising.

John Flournoy/McGraw-Hill Education

to invest in the franchise. The disclosure process is lengthy and complex and almost always requires the counsel of an attorney skilled in franchise law.

State Regulation Most states have implemented their own individual franchise rules and minimum disclosure requirements to supplement the federal legislation. These additional requirements usually entail filing a registration statement with a state regulatory agency (the state-level equivalent of the FTC). The registration statements are public documents and often require detailed disclosures and biographical information on the principals of the franchise.

KEY TERMS

Principals p. 453   Owners of a business entity.

Sole proprietorship p. 454   One-person business entity with minimal filing requirements.

Partnership p. 456   Multiple-person business entity in which the partners conduct an ongoing business relationship and share profits and losses.

Express partnership p. 456   Partnership formed when the parties have agreed to conduct a partnership on certain terms and conditions.

Implied partnership p. 457   Partnership formed when the parties have acted like general partners even though the parties did not agree or intend to form a partnership.

Partnership at will p. 458   A partnership in which the partners have not agreed to remain partners until the expiration of a definite term or the completion of a particular undertaking.

Joint venture p. 458   Business relationship between two or more parties for a limited-in-time venture.

Jointly and severally liable p. 458   Legal principle that imposes liability on general partners both together (jointly) and separately (severally) for debts and liabilities of the partnership.

Pass-through entity p. 459   A business entity that does not pay corporate taxes, such as a partnership. Rather, any profits are taxed at individual rates after they pass through the business and are distributed to the partners.

Fiduciary duties p. 460   Under the Revised Uniform Partnership Act, general partners' duties of loyalty, care, and good faith; intended to ensure that the partners are acting in the best interest of the partnership.

Certificate of limited partnership p. 461   The document filed with the state government authority by the general partner to form a limited partnership; requires routine information such as the name, address, and capital contribution of each partner.

Dissociation p. 466   Term used in the RUPA to describe the act of separation of a partner from the partnership. Also, the process in which an individual member of an LLC exercises the right to withdraw from the partnership.

Withdrawal p. 466   Term used by the RULPA to describe the act of separation of one partner from the partnership.

Winding up p. 468   After dissolution, the process of paying the debts of the partnership and liquidating and/or distributing the remaining assets.

Franchise p. 470   A business arrangement (not a form of business entity) of continuing commercial relationship for the right to operate a business pursuant to the franchisor's trade name or to sell the seller's branded goods.

Franchisor p. 470   A business entity that has a proven track record of success and ability to franchise its products.

Franchisee p. 470   Individual or business with the legal right to operate a franchised business and use the business's trademarks and trade secrets.

CHAPTER REVIEW QUESTIONS

1. Which of the following factors in choosing an entity refers to the business's option for funding its operations?
   a. Personal liability
   b. Capitalization
   c. Management
   d. Taxation
   e. Formation

2. All of the following are true about a sole proprietorship entity <u>except</u>
   a. It does not protect the personal assets of the principal.
   b. It is formed by filing a set of forms with the federal and state governments.
   c. It provides pass-through taxation for the principal.
   d. It is a single-person entity.
   e. It may be capitalized through a loan.

3. Abel and Baker formed AB Partners, L.P. Abel contributed $1,000 and became the managing general partner and Baker contributed $50,000 as a limited partner. AB Partners, L.P., was successfully sued for an injury it caused to a third party. What is the potential personal liability for Abel and Baker respectively?
   a. $1,000/$50,000
   b. Unlimited/$50,000
   c. $0/$50,000
   d. $0/$0
   e. Unlimited/$0

4. Which of the following are methods used by partnerships to raise capital?
   I. Borrow money from a bank.
   II. Sell equity to private investors/partners.
   III. Borrow money from partners.
   IV. Sell equity through public markets such as the NYSE.
   a. I and II
   b. II and III
   c. II and IV
   d. I, III, and IV
   e. I, II, and III

5. Whiteside is a partner in High Flyer Partners, a general partnership. The partnership agreement for High Flyer restricts the parties from leaving the partnership for one full year. Six months after Whiteside signs the agreement, he notifies his partners that he is dissociating. Under the RUPA, what is the impact of Whiteside's dissociation on High Flyer Partners?
   a. The partnership is dissolved via operation of law.
   b. The partnership may be dissolved by express agreement of the remaining partners.
   c. There is no impact on continuation of the partnership.
   d. The remaining partners are now jointly and severally liable.
   e. Whiteside is now classified as a limited partner.

Answers and explanations are provided at the end of this chapter.

THEORY TO PRACTICE

Demuth is a sole proprietor of a business that specializes in designing and manufacturing custom-made medical instruments for health care professionals. Several hospitals and physician practice groups have approached Demuth and asked him to design and produce a highly specialized surgical instrument that is currently unavailable in the market from larger manufacturers. Demuth, unable to finance the research and development costs, has convinced Warren, a private investor, to fund the project. Demuth also has recruited Oakley, a physician, to lend her medical expertise. Demuth has drafted a letter to Warren and Oakley thanking them for their confidence in the project and setting out certain terms for the venture. The letter is very brief and states that the parties will be equal participants in the business venture intended to develop and manufacture a certain surgical instrument. Demuth will contribute his expertise, laboratory workspace, and manufacturing facilities to the project. Warren will contribute $100,000 as a capital contribution, and Oakley will contribute medical expertise, research knowledge, and $10,000 in capital. The letter ends with a statement that the business venture will last for five years unless the parties mutually agree on extending the term. Profits or losses will be calculated annually, and each party will be paid in equal shares for any profits or bear equal losses. Warren and Oakley each write "Agreed" and sign and date the letter on the bottom. Demuth then goes on to hire a top engineer and purchases equipment to work on the Demuth-Warren-Oakley project.

After a year of slow progress on the project, Demuth is concerned that the initial capital contribution is not going to be sufficient to carry the venture into its second year. Demuth approaches Warren for an additional $100,000. Warren, who is disgruntled about the slow progress, refuses. Demuth, anxious about keeping the venture afloat, negotiates a *loan* on behalf of the business with Strand, another private investor. Without the knowledge of the other principals, Demuth signs the promissory note "Demuth-Oakley-Warren Partnership, by Demuth, Partner."

1. What form of entity have Demuth, Warren, and Oakley formed? What law governs the operation of the partnership and the rights of the partners?

2. If the venture becomes insolvent (runs out of money to pay its regular monthly bills), will Demuth, Warren, and/or Oakley be liable for any, some, or all of the debt owed to Strand? If, just after the venture becomes insolvent, Demuth files for personal bankruptcy, will Warren and Oakley now be liable 100 percent for the debt owed to Strand?

3. Assume that when Oakley finds out about the loan to Strand, she is so angered that she gives notice to Demuth that she is withdrawing from the partnership before the agreed-upon five-year period. What is the legal impact of Oakley's dissociation on the partnership? Is the partnership automatically dissolved? Is Oakley still liable for the Strand debt and to any creditors to which the partnership owes money?

4. In Question 3 above, suppose that Demuth and Warren decide they cannot continue without Oakley's expertise and they dissolve the partnership. In the process, they are forced to breach several contracts with their vendors. What is Oakley's postdissociation liability to Demuth and Warren for any damages suffered by breaching the vendor contracts?

5. Suppose that, instead of the conflict that developed, the parties end up being profitable on the venture and are eager to continue the business. What are the factors that the parties should consider in choosing a business entity that will suit the company's needs now and in the future?

LEGAL STRATEGY 101

Should Friends Be Business Partners?

Should friends ever go into business together? Some of the most successful business ventures in history were founded by friends. Google, for example was founded by friends Larry Page and Sergey Brin when they were students at Stanford. At the same time, however, starting a business with a friend can pose legal risks down the road.

Consider the founding of Facebook as depicted in the movie *The Social Network*. This movie retells a remarkable story of genius and betrayal: how two close friends, college students Mark Zuckerberg and Eduardo Saverin, became informal business partners when Zuckerberg launched "The Facebook" from his dorm room in early 2004, and how their friendship ended after they had a falling out.

In real life, Zuckerberg and Saverin eventually became involved in a costly and protracted legal battle, and although the two former friends were able to settle their dispute out of court, the litigation posed a significant risk to Facebook's future.

Accordingly, one of the lessons of the founding of Facebook is that you should always think carefully before you start a business with your best friend. Moreover, a good legal strategy may help potential partners to anticipate legal problems before they occur. Here is some sound strategic advice:

Mark Zuckerberg. Kristoffer Tripplaar/Alamy

> First and foremost, before investing any time, money, or other resources into a business partnership, you and your partner should have a signed agreement that clearly specifies your company's vision, your roles in the business, your compensation amounts and ownership breakdown, your investment amounts, a conflict resolution protocol (like arbitration), and a succession plan, among other things.[16]

> Secondly and just as important, you and your partner should never mix your personal finances together when starting a business partnership; instead, you should put into place from day one a set of agreed financial best practices in order to reduce the risk of mismanagement of company funds.[17]

We close with the wise words of John D. Rockefeller: "Friendships based on business are much better than businesses founded on friendships."[18]

CRITICAL THINKING QUESTIONS

1. Why is having a signed document in writing a good legal strategy when friends go into business together?
2. What should be in the document?

---

[16]*See, e.g.*, Ryan Robinson, *Should You Start a Business with Your Best Friend?* ryrob.com (Sept. 29, 2015).

[17]Source: Robinson, Ryan. "Should You Start a Business With Your Best Friend?" ryrob.com (Sept 29, 2015).

[18]Eve Tahmincioglu, *Friends Don't Always Make Good Business Partners,* N.Y. Times (Sept. 7, 2006).

MANAGER'S CHALLENGE

A basic understanding of business entities is important when individuals are considering a start-up venture, such as the one contemplated in the Theory to Practice problem, or when a company wishes to start a new business, joint venture, or partnership with another company or individual that leverages its existing business. Suppose you are a manager of Network Associates Corp., a company that retails, installs, and maintains computer networks for business clients. You receive the following e-mail from your senior manager:

> Our company has been approached by NewComp Inc. to form a business relationship that will involve our company being the exclusive supplier of NewComp computer networking products for the northeast and mid-Atlantic regions of the United States.

This could be a lucrative opportunity for us. To avoid any liability problems for Network Associates, we are considering a new entity, separate and apart from the corporation. I will be consulting our counsel and analyzing whether the return will be worth the liability and investment risk. To assist me in my analysis, please write a two- to three-page memorandum that gives me some basic information on (1) what factors we should consider when selecting an entity and (2) whether, if we just begin doing business jointly without any formal agreement, we are exposing ourselves to liability unnecessarily.

See Connect for Manager's Challenge sample answers.

CASE SUMMARY 13.1 Conklin v. Holland, 138 S.W.3d 215 (Tenn. Ct. App. 2003)

PARTNERSHIP LIABILITY

Lewis and Holland bought a run-down home in Memphis, Tennessee, to renovate and then sell for a profit. The two agreed that Lewis would live in the house during the renovations. In this time period, 20-year-old Amanda Conklin visited the house, where Lewis provided her with alcohol and illicit drugs. As a result of the use of this combination, Conklin died. Lewis attempted to conceal the death by placing her in the car in the garage of the home under construction. Police discovered Conklin's body a month and a half later and arrested Lewis. Conklin's estate sued Holland for civil damages related to Conklin's death under the theory that Holland and Lewis were partners in the co-ownership of the property and, as Lewis's partner, Holland was liable for whatever Lewis did upon the land they co-owned as general partners.

CASE QUESTIONS

1. Was there a partnership?
2. What was the partnership formed to do?
3. As a practical matter, why would Conklin's estate sue Holland instead of Lewis for partnership liability?

CASE SUMMARY 13.2 Vernon v. Schuster, 688 N.E.2d 1172 (Ill. 1997)

TERMINATION OF SOLE PROPRIETORSHIP

James Schuster was a sole proprietor doing business as Diversey Heating and Plumbing and contracted with Vernon to install and maintain a boiler in his building. Schuster also promised Vernon a 10-year warranty, and the parties agreed to a long-term service agreement whereby Schuster was to perform an annual prewinter inspection of the boiler and render any service needed for upkeep. Schuster performed the services for a period of three years, but he died in October 1993 before performing the prewinter inspection on Vernon's boiler. After Schuster died, his son Jerry Schuster began to operate Diversey and serve Diversey customers. In February 1994, Vernon discovered that the boiler was broken beyond repair and needed to be replaced. Vernon brought a breach-of-warranty lawsuit against Jerry Schuster on the basis that he had continued the sole proprietorship that his father had started and therefore Jerry Schuster should honor the warranty given by James Schuster. Jerry Schuster maintained that he had no responsibility to honor a warranty provided by a predecessor business. The trial court dismissed most of the lawsuit, holding that Jerry Schuster could not be held liable for the obligations of his father's sole proprietorship interest.

CASE QUESTIONS

1. Who prevails and why? Name a case from this chapter that supports your answer.
2. If Jerry Schuster changed the name of the business but still used the tools he inherited, how would that impact your analysis?

CASE SUMMARY 13.3 Meinhard v. Salmon, 249 N.Y. 458 (1928)

FIDUCIARY DUTY

Salmon and Meinhard were partners who entered into a 20-year leasing agreement to operate Hotel Bristol in midtown Manhattan. In exchange for his capital contribution, Meinhard would receive 40 percent of the profits for the first five years and 50 percent every year after until the 20th year, when the lease ended. All losses would be born equally. Salmon alone would "manage, lease, underlet and operate" the hotel. At first, the two lost money, but after 20 years the hotel was very profitable. Just before the lease was about to end, the owner of the hotel (who also owned the five lots surrounding the hotel) approached Salmon and encouraged him to lease the whole city block, including the hotel, for a term of 80 years. Salmon agreed to the expansion plan and drafted the agreements so that the new arrangement began the day after the Meinhard-Salmon lease ended. Under the new arrangement, Salmon had sole control of the hotel and the rest of the block. Meinhard sued Salmon for breach of fiduciary duty. Salmon asserted that their original partnership had ended when the 20-year lease expired and that he owed Meinhard no duty because they were not partners in the new venture. In its opinion, the court wrote: "Many forms of conduct permissible in a workaday world for those acting at arm's length, are forbidden to those bound by fiduciary ties. A trustee is held to something stricter than the morals of the market place. Not honesty alone, but the punctilio of an honor the most sensitive, is then the standard of behavior."

CASE QUESTIONS

1. Whom did the court side with?
2. What duty did Meinhard claim was breached?
3. Does fiduciary duty end when the partnership expires?

CASE SUMMARY 13.4 Rahemtulla v. Hassam, 539 F. Supp. 2d 755 (M.D. Pa. 2008)

GOOD FAITH

Rahemtulla met Hassam at his religious congregation. Hassam visited Rahemtulla and his wife many times at their home before he pitched his idea to open a steak house restaurant in the Howard Johnson's Inn. Hassam owned the inn along with several other partners. Hassam told the Rahemtullas that revenues from the steak house could be over $2 million a year. Hassam knew that Rahemtulla had absolutely no experience in the food and beverage industry but offered to help him. Rahemtulla quit his job in the corporate sector and borrowed $100,000 using his house as collateral. The $100,000 was Rahemtulla's capital contribution in the partnership. The two entered into a partnership and signed a lease with the Howard Johnson's Inn partnership for the restaurant space. The restaurant opened and Rahemtulla began to co-operate it with Hassam. From the beginning, the restaurant was losing money, and Hassam began to make unilateral decisions that would help cut expenses. The restaurant was dealt a serious financial setback when authorities refused to approve a liquor license for the restaurant, thus lowering revenue potential. After several months, Rahemtulla complained that he had been cheated by Hassam, whose financial reward came from the lease without any concern about the restaurant operations. Hassam blamed Rahemtulla for incompetence in managing the venture. Rahemtulla sued Hassam for breach of fiduciary duty and dealing in bad faith.

CASE QUESTIONS

1. What duties did Hassam owe Rahemtulla?
2. Does it matter that Rahemtulla made foolish decisions when he trusted his friend?
3. What potential conflict arises when Hassam creates a partnership to lease from another partnership he is part of?

CASE SUMMARY 13.5 *In re* Spree.com Corp., 2001 WL 1518242 (Bankr. E.D. Pa. 2001)

DUTY OF LOYALTY

Technology Crosser Ventures (TCV), LP, is a venture capital fund that invests as a limited partner in technology companies that require an infusion of capital. Among the partners are Testler, Hoag, and Kimball. One of the companies they invested in was Spree.com. The partnership was structured to allow Spree, a corporation, to be the general partner with TCV as the limited partner. As part of the partnership agreement, Testler would represent TCV as a member of the board of directors of Spree.com. On August 24, 2000, *The Wall Street Journal* reported a story about TCV and its partners that depicted Testler, Hoag, and Kimball discussing their investments at Testler's office. The paper quoted Testler saying, "What do we want to do with this puppy? The cash runs out soon." Hoag then asked, "They're going to be looking at us for more capital, aren't they?" Kimball added, "I don't want to be supporting them until who knows when." The three men were talking about Spree.com. Spree became insolvent (unable to pay bills as they became due) not long after the article appeared. Spree sued TCV, arguing that the article made it impossible for the company to get more investors. Spree sued Testler for breach of loyalty and due care.

CASE QUESTIONS

1. Who prevails and why?
2. Does this case show potential problems with venture capital firms as limited partners?
3. Was TCV in "control" of Spree.com because it held the purse strings?

CASE SUMMARY 13.6 Clancy v. King, 936 A.2d 852 (Md. 2008)

FIDUCIARY DUTY

In February 1992, author Thomas Clancy formed Jack Ryan Limited Partnership (JRLP), named after Clancy's fictional hero. Clancy's only partner in the venture was his wife, King. JRLP's purpose was to generate revenue related to the writing, publishing, and sale of certain novels. Each partner owned a half interest in JRLP. The partnership agreement had standard provisions imposing the duty of diligence but also contained a specific provision that allowed each partner to compete freely on an individual basis with the interests of JRLP. Specifically, each partner gave up the right to claim that the other partner breached the duty of care by participating in a competing venture. Clancy had the absolute right to withdraw the use of his name for the series of novels at any time. By 1996 Clancy and King were divorced but remained partners in the highly profitable JRLP entity. In 2001, Clancy announced that he was exercising his right to withdraw the right to use his name for the series starting in 2004. When Clancy did finally withdraw the right to use his name, King filed suit against him, alleging that Clancy's withdrawal of the right to use his name was a breach of fiduciary duty that he owed to King and was done out of ill will toward her stemming from the divorce. Clancy countered that he had the right to conduct the partnership as he thought best and pointed to the partnership agreement's provision on insulation from liability for due care.

CASE QUESTIONS

1. Are there any circumstances under which there could be a *good faith* reason for Clancy to withdraw the right to use his name?
2. Why didn't the provision effectively waiving a breach-of-duty-of-care lawsuit by one partner against another govern this dispute?

✓ Self-Check ANSWERS Rules for Dissociation/Withdrawal

1. No. In order to expel a partner, assuming the absence of a partnership agreement, the RUPA requires *all* of the other partners to vote to expel.
2. Probably not. Her departure at the end of the year just before the busy tax season may result in the partnership's being unable to perform the services on time and possibly breaching agreements while attempting to locate a replacement. Under the RUPA, the departing lawyer may be liable for damages suffered by the partnership.
3. No. Under the RULPA, *limited* partners are subject to restrictions on withdrawal. Absent an agreement in writing to the contrary, the general rule is that limited partners may *not* withdraw from a partnership before the partnership termination time agreed on by the partners. If the limited partnership agreement does *not* provide for a certain time of termination, limited partners may withdraw after providing at least six months' prior written notice to the other partners. Some states have passed additional restrictions, including an absolute prohibition of withdrawal intended to address special circumstances in family limited partnerships.
4. Yes, so long as the partner acts in good faith. Partnership agreements always displace any RUPA or RULPA rules.

CHAPTER REVIEW QUESTIONS: Answers and Explanations

1. **b.** Capitalization is the factor that is used to consider options for the best way to fund a business's start-up and/or operations. All other answers are factors in the choice of entity but are unrelated to funding.

2. **b.** In many states, no formal filing is required to launch a sole proprietorship unless the principal is using a fictitious name. In any case, no federal filing is necessary because business formation is typically a state statutory matter.

3. **e.** Abel, as a general partner, has unlimited personal liability for tort liabilities of the partnership. Baker is a limited partner so his personal assets are not at risk if the business has no assets.

4. **e.** Partnerships use debt (private loans and bank loans) and/or limited equity offerings (sale of ownership interests) to raise capital. The other answers are incorrect because partnerships may not sell equity through public exchanges (such as the NYSE).

5. **b.** Under the RUPA, the partners may choose to continue the venture or dissolve the partnership. (a) is incorrect because the RUPA does not require the partnership to dissolve upon a disassociating partner's exit. (c) is incorrect because the partners must now decide to continue or dissolve. (d) and (e) are incorrect statements of law.

CHAPTER 14

Limited Liability Companies and Limited Liability Partnerships

©philsajonesen/Getty Images

Learning Objectives

After studying this chapter, students who have mastered the material will be able to:

14-1 Identify the sources and level of laws that govern LLC and LLP entities.

14-2 Explain the function of an operating agreement and the fundamental structure of an LLC.

14-3 Distinguish between the formation and management of an LLC and the formation and management of an LLP.

14-4 Determine the rights of principals upon withdrawal from an LLC.

14-5 Articulate the legal protections from personal liability afforded to the principals in an LLC and LLP.

14-6 Identify the tax treatment schemes of an LLC and LLP.

14-7 Provide the primary methods for capitalizing limited liability entities.

This chapter continues the discussion of forms of business entities and laws that govern business organizations by focusing on limited liability companies (LLCs) and limited liability partnerships (LLPs). The use of these entities has grown rapidly since states first began to recognize them in the late 1970s. They have become a common part of the modern business environment because they offer flexibility advantages for certain business ventures. In this chapter, we discuss

- The background and laws related to the operation of a limited liability company (LLC) and a limited liability partnership (LLP).
- The legal liability of principals in an LLC and LLP.

OVERVIEW OF LLCS AND LLPS

Prior to the development of LLCs and LLPs, principals who wished to avoid the double taxation of a corporation but still desired liability protection for their personal assets had few choices. In 1977, the Wyoming legislature gave businesses the choice of new hybrid entities that were designed to have characteristics of a partnership while providing full protections afforded to the principals of a corporation. The first hybrid entity was known as a **limited liability company (LLC)**. After the Internal Revenue Service (IRS) began to classify the LLC as a partnership for tax purposes in 1988, many states followed suit and passed their own limited liability statutes primarily modeled on Wyoming's statute. The Uniform Limited Liability Company Act (ULLCA) is the model statute used by the vast majority of state legislatures. A subsequent IRS ruling in 1997 made the selection of the LLC even more attractive because the IRS eliminated strict operating requirements that previously had to be met for an entity to qualify as a partnership for tax purposes.[1] Now all states recognize and provide both procedural (formation) and internal default rules (in the event the parties do not agree otherwise) for the LLC. However, LLC statutes can vary considerably from state to state. Most recently, states began to adopt statutes based on the Revised Uniform Limited Liability Company Act (RULLCA), which was published in an amended form in 2013 by the Uniform Law Commission. The revised version modifies the original act in the areas of formation, organizational matters, and the operating agreement and otherwise attempts to clarify some of the more technical aspects of LLC governance, such as the handling of deadlocks and the rights of members who depart the LLC. As of 2016, 14 states and the District of Columbia had adopted a version of the RULLCA. In areas where the RULLCA differs substantially from the original ULLCA, this chapter covers both acts.

The growth in popularity of limited liability companies led state legislatures to consider the liability dilemma of general partners, and they consequently expanded liability protection for general partners in a partnership. In 1991, Texas enacted the first **limited liability partnership (LLP)** statute, which provided limited protection to general partners. By 1996, many states had adopted a more extensive shield from liability for LLP debts and other liabilities for general partners. Now, about half of all states provide the same level of liability protection to a general partner in an LLP as is provided to a limited partner in a limited partnership entity.

LO 14-1

Identify the sources and level of laws that govern LLC and LLP entities.

Beginning in 1977, state legislatures began to authorize hybrid forms of business entities that afforded favorable tax treatment and limited liability for principals. Nati Harnik/AP Images

---

[1] Note that a minority of states do not permit partnership taxation at the *state* level.

> **KEY POINT**
>
> States vary considerably in terms of how LLCs are taxed and operated.

While LLCs and LLPs are similar in many ways to corporations and partnerships, the legal terminology for describing the procedural and governance aspects of these entities is different. It is important to understand the differences to avoid any confusion about the form of entity.

Limited Liability Companies (LLCs)

A limited liability company is an entity whose primary characteristics are that it offers its principals the same amount of liability protection afforded to principals of a corporate form of entity and it offers pass-through tax treatment for its principals without the restrictions on ownership and scope required for other pass-through entities (such as an S corporation, discussed in detail in the next chapter). For example, suppose that Developer Inc. wants to start a land use project to build a commercial office building. It wishes to partner with Garrett, the owner of several pieces of property in the area under consideration. Both the principals of Developer Inc. and Garrett wish to have pass-through tax treatment but also wish to have as much protection as possible from liability of personal assets. Because Developer Inc. is a corporate principal, the parties cannot choose a pass-through corporate entity. They can, however, achieve these objectives by forming an LLC. In an LLC, owners are known as *members*.

Formation An LLC is formed by filing **articles of organization** (also called **certificate of organization**) with the state public filing official in the secretary of state's corporation bureau. Although historically LLCs were required to file fairly extensive articles, modern-day trends require the same type of information as included on a corporation's articles of incorporation. Most states require only basic information such as the name of the entity, the location of its principal place of business, and the names of its members. A number of states also require a contemporaneous filing with tax authorities to notify them of the existence of the LLC. A sample certificate of organization for an LLC is presented in Figure 14.1.

Most importantly, LLCs are frequently governed by agreement of the parties in the form of an **operating agreement**.[2] If the parties do not execute an operating agreement, the state LLC statute sets out default rules. Operating agreements, similar to partnership agreements, cover many of the internal rules for the actual operation of the entity. One of the primary benefits of an LLC is that it affords its members a great deal of flexibility in terms of the rights and responsibilities of each member. This flexibility includes

- *Structure of governance and responsibility of members:* The agreement will typically set forth a structure for managing the entity through a single member or a board of "managing members" (akin to a board of directors), and the agreement will define their responsibilities in terms of the day-to-day operations of the entity. This provision will also spell out voting rights of members, procedures for voting, transactions that require a vote of the general members (such as the sale of the LLC assets to another company), and procedures for the admission of any new members.
- *Death, incapacity, and dissolution:* Members often agree to a series of "what ifs" of managing an LLC through their operating agreement. If a member can no longer perform the duties required by the agreement, this section details a procedure for handling the circumstance of a member's death or incapacity. The procedure is typically different for managing members and members, but in most cases the operating agreement allows

---
[2] Some states call this document an "LLC agreement" or other similar names.

FIGURE 14.1 Sample LLC Certificate of Organization

PENNSYLVANIA DEPARTMENT OF STATE
CORPORATION BUREAU

Certificate of Organization
Domestic Limited Liability Company
(15 Pa.C.S. § 8913)

Name: Daniel J. Webster, Esquire
Address: 1000 Professional Avenue, Suite 120
City, State, Zip Code: Philadelphia, PA 19130

Document will be returned to the name and address you enter to the left.

Typically, a business attorney will prepare this document for the LLC and assist the principals with administrative start-up.

Fee: $125

In compliance with the requirements of 15 Pa.C.S. § 8913 (relating to certificate of organization), the undersigned, desiring to organize a limited liability company, hereby certifies that:

1. The name of the limited liability company (*designator is required, i.e., "company", "limited" or "limited liability company" or abbreviation*):
   Redfern Catering, LLC

2. The (a) address of the limited liability company's initial registered office in this Commonwealth or (b) name of its commercial registered office provider and the county of venue is:

   (a) Number and Street: One Alpha Drive, City: Elizabethtown, State: PA, Zip: 17022, County: Lancaster
   (b) Name of Commercial Registered Office Provider: c/o: None, County:

Basic information about the LLC and its registered location. Note that an LLC may opt to use a commercial registered office provider (similar to resident agent services) for a fee. The provider typically provides services such as accepting legal documents (e.g., a complaint in a lawsuit) for the LLC.

3. The name and address, including street and number, if any, of each organizer is (*all Organizers must sign on page 2*):

Name	Address
Francis Redfern	One Alpha Drive, Elizabethtown, PA 17022
Alexander Colgate	10 Flamingo Drive, Dania Beach, FL 33004

Organizers are those who start up the LLC initially. Once the LLC is formed, they become members.

(continued)

FIGURE 14.1 Sample LLC Certificate of Organization

DSCB:15-8913-2

4. *Strike out if inapplicable term*
   A member's interest in the company is to be evidenced by a certificate of membership interest.

   > These provisions allow the LLC's organizers to choose (1) whether the LLC actually has to issue a certificate to evidence a member's interest and (2) whether the LLC is to be manager-managed or member-managed.

5. *Strike out if inapplicable:*
   Management of the company is vested in a manager or managers.

6. The specified effective date, if any, is: **October 10, 2020**
   month   date   year   hour, if any

7. *Strike out if inapplicable:* The company is a restricted professional company organized to render the following restricted professional service(s):
   Not applicable

   > LLCs are sometimes used by professional service firms (such as a law firm or a group of architects). If the LLC wishes to restrict the business to members with professional licenses in a certain field, the profession is inserted here.

8. For additional provisions of the certificate, if any, attach an 8½ × 11 sheet.

   > The organizers may add additional provisions of LLC management unique to the company by attaching a sheet to the certificate of organization.

IN TESTIMONY WHERE OF, the organizer(s) has (have) signed this Certificate of Organization this _____ day of _____, _____.

Francis Redfern
Signature

Alexander Colgate
Signature

_____
Signature

> Signature of all organizers.

Source: Pennsylvania Department of State Corporation Bureau.

the venture's remaining members to choose whether or not to continue. In the event the members choose not to continue, the procedure for dissolution (including preferences of members in terms of who gets paid first after liquidation) is typically outlined in the agreement.

- *RULLCA:* The revised LLC statute addresses several issues related to the operating agreement. First, it establishes the primacy of the operating agreement in evidencing the relationship among the limited liability company and its members, the rights and duties of any managers, and the activities and affairs of the company. Second, it lists those matters that are not subject to change by the operating agreement by setting forth 17 nonwaivable statutory provisions related to liability of the entity and its members. These are discussed in more detail later in this chapter. Third, it confirms that an operating agreement may include specific penalties or other consequences if a member fails to comply with its terms or upon certain events specified in the operating agreement.

Liability Another important feature of an LLC is the limited liability of its members. LLC members are insulated from personal liability for any business debt or liability (contract or tort) if the venture fails. For example, suppose that Phillips is the managing member of Active Wear LLC and signs a five-year lease agreement with Landlord on behalf of Active Wear. One year into the lease, Active Wear has a downturn in business, is forced to breach the lease, and moves out hoping to convert to an online business model. Landlord's rights are against the LLC entity only. Landlord may not obtain a judgment against Phillips or collect back rent or other damages from Phillips's personal assets.

However, two important factors moderate this limited liability. First, landlords and other creditors will often require a **personal guarantee** from the members whereby the members pledge personal assets to guarantee payment obligations of the business venture.[3] Second, a court may discard the protection in a case where the court finds that fairness demands that the LLC members should compensate any damaged party when the entity is without resources to cover the full amount owed (e.g., in a case where the members engaged in fraud). Also note that the RULLCA imposes personal liability in cases where authorized members consent to an improper distribution. An *improper distribution* is defined as any distribution of money made when the LLC is insolvent.

> **KEY POINT**
>
> Although LLC members are insulated from personal liability for any business debt or liability, creditors often require LLC members to sign personal guarantees and, in cases of fundamental unfairness, a court may disregard the LLC protections.

Taxation Another attractive advantage of an LLC is the various tax treatment alternatives. Although many LLCs are typically treated as pass-through entities, the LLC's members may also elect to be taxed as a corporation if they consider the corporate tax structure to be more favorable. Recall from the discussion in previous chapters of pass-through entities that their advantages are primarily (1) the ability to flow through to the investors the tax deductions and losses that are typically generated by an emerging company or a company with significant up-front debt and (2) the ability to distribute earnings without incurring double-level taxation (i.e., without having a tax imposed on both the entity and the member).

Capitalization LLCs are capitalized primarily through debt via private lenders or commercial lenders or through a sale of equity ownership in the LLC itself. The operating agreement of the LLC often controls the amount and methods of capitalizing the business.

Legal Speak >))

Insolvent
Under the RULLCA, an LLC is insolvent if (1) the LLC "would not be able to pay its debts as they become due in the ordinary course of the company's activities and affairs; or (2) the company's total assets are less than the sum of its total liabilities."

---

[3]Personal guarantees are discussed in more detail in the next chapter.

LO 14-2

Explain the function of an operating agreement and the fundamental structure of an LLC.

LO 14-3

Distinguish between the formation and management of an LLC and the formation and management of an LLP.

Management and Operation LLC statutes typically assume that the members will agree on the specifics of managing the venture through a *management agreement,* sometimes called an *operating agreement.* Some states require the entire agreement to be in writing, some require only certain parts of the agreement to be in writing, and other states have no writing requirement at all. Most states distinguish between a **member-managed LLC** and a **manager-managed LLC**. In a member-managed LLC, the management structure of the entity is similar to that of a general partnership, with all the members having the authority to bind the business. In a manager-managed LLC, a named manager (or managers) generally has the day-to-day operational responsibilities, while the nonmanaging members are typically investors with little input on the course of business taken by the entity except for major decisions (such as a merger). In a manager-managed LLC, nonmanaging members generally do not have the authority to act on behalf of the business venture. The choice of manager-managed or member-managed is generally made on the public filing of the articles of organization and is available to third parties for purposes of checking the authority of an individual to bind the LLC. While the new RULLCA eliminates the term "managing member" in favor of "authorized representative," the revised act still requires an LLC to choose between being member-managed or manager-managed.

As in many business relationships, the managers of an LLC owe the *fiduciary duties* of care and loyalty to the LLC's other members. Controlling members (those with veto power or the ownership stake to block decisions by other members) also owe a duty of loyalty to the other members. LLC statutes regarding fiduciary duties vary by state and can be strengthened or pared back by the operating agreement. In fact, the modern trend is to specifically eliminate any liability for a breach of the duty of care through the operating agreement. This has been a source of controversy, and courts have been strict about requiring unambiguous language in the operating agreement that limits any fiduciary duty. In any case, managers and controlling members (i.e., members with ownership sufficient to decide or veto internal operational matters) must adhere to the duty of loyalty, are prohibited from self-dealing, and must act in good faith when dealing with the LLC's business matters. In response to the controversy, the RULLCA does not allow any manager or member to avoid personal liability under any circumstances in which the liability was the result of a member's bad faith or willful misconduct.

> **KEY POINT**
>
> Managing members and controlling members owe a fiduciary duty to other members.

In Case 14.1, an appellate court in Delaware addresses the issue of limiting fiduciary liability through the operating agreement under the ULLCA.

CASE 14.1 AK-Feel, LLC v. NHAOCG, LLC, 62 A.3d 649 (Del. Ch. 2012)

FACT SUMMARY Feeley was the managing member of AK-Feel, LLC (AK-Feel), and formed a new entity with several investors who were organized as a separate entity called NHAOCG, LLC (NHA). After a series of business discussions among the parties, the principals of the two LLCs formed a new entity, called Oculus, for the purpose of finding and developing real estate parcels and profiting from their sale. AK-Feel and NHA each held a 50 percent member interest in Oculus, but AK-Feel served as the managing member. Because Feeley served as the managing member of AK-Feel, he also controlled the activities of Oculus.

Approximately one year later, the parties' relationship soured. NHA accused Feeley of gross negligence in the handling of several real estate deals. In

(continued)

one case, NHA alleged that Feeley's incompetence resulted in a significant loss in an aborted real estate transaction. Dissatisfied with Feeley, the principals of NHA decided to end their business relationship with Feeley and attempted to take over Oculus. Feeley and AK-Feel filed suit in which they sought to block NHA's attempt and establish their continuing control. NHA filed a countersuit for, among other things, breach of fiduciary duty and sought damages that it suffered as a result of Feeley's gross negligence. The parties resolved the control issue, but NHA did not drop its countersuit. Feeley and AK-Feel filed a Motion to Dismiss NHA's countersuit, arguing that any fiduciary duty was limited or eliminated through the Operating Agreement.

SYNOPSIS OF DECISION AND OPINION On the claim of breach of fiduciary duty, the Chancery Court of Delaware ruled in favor of NHA and denied AK-Feel's motion to dismiss. The court ruled that the Operating Agreement did not unambiguously limit any fiduciary duties of the managing member. The court pointed to a section of the Operating Agreement that specifically recognizes certain fiduciary duties. While some of NHA's claims were dismissed, the breach of fiduciary duty claim survived the Motion to Dismiss.

WORDS OF THE COURT: Limiting Fiduciary Duties "Drafters of an LLC agreement must make their intent to eliminate fiduciary duties plain and unambiguous. . . . The plain language of this portion of [the Operating Agreement] eliminates monetary liability unless, among other things, 'the act or omission is attributed to gross negligence [or] willful misconduct or fraud. . . .' [This] [s]ection . . . does not limit or eliminate fiduciary duties. . . . Rather than eliminating fiduciary duties, the [Operating Agreement's] language recognizes their continuing existence. . . . If [the Operating Agreement] had eliminated fiduciary duties, as AK-Feel argues, then it would be counter-intuitive for the same provision to recognize exceptions [for] gross negligence and willful misconduct and to authorize the managing member to obtain insurance against actual or alleged breaches of fiduciary duty and require Oculus to pay the premiums."

Case Questions

1. Why does the court state that the language in the Operating Agreement actually recognizes the "continued existence" of the fiduciary duties?

2. Should NHA have agreed to the structure of the Oculus entity? How could it have been more proactive during the structuring of the entity?

3. *Focus on Critical Thinking:* As explained in the text, the RULLCA limits the right of managing members to eliminate their fiduciary duty to the other members. Which approach do you agree with and why? Is the Operating Agreement a contract or a set or rules? If it's a contract, shouldn't the parties be able to negotiate whatever risks they wish?

Dissolution, Dissociation, and Expulsion of Members

LLC laws define **dissolution** of an LLC as a liquidation process[4] triggered by an event that is specified in the operating agreement (such as the death of a key member) or by the decision of the majority of membership interests (or the percentage called for in the operating agreement) to dissolve the company. The members of an LLC may have also agreed to a maximum term for conducting business in the operating agreement. If the term expires, but the members want the LLC to continue, they must have a unanimous vote to fix an additional term *or* the majority of LLC member interests may vote to continue the LLC at will (with no fixed term and subject to dissolution at any time). **Dissociation** occurs when an individual member decides to exercise the right to withdraw from the partnership. Generally, upon a dissociation the remaining members may either continue the LLC or decide

LO 14-4

Determine the rights of principals upon withdrawal from an LLC.

---

[4]Liquidation includes preserving the assets of a business, paying creditors, and then distributing any remaining profits to the individual members.

to trigger dissolution. Of course, the parties may agree to their own unique set of rules through the operating agreement. Members may also agree to standards and procedures for expulsion (involuntary separation) of a member by a majority vote of other members. Many state LLC statutes also provide for judicial expulsion if one or more members of the LLC demonstrate to a court that a member has (1) engaged in wrongful conduct that has adversely and materially affected the LLC, (2) willfully committed a material breach of the operating agreement, or (3) engaged in conduct relating to the company's activities that make it not reasonably practicable to carry on the activities with the member.[5] Agreeing ahead of time on what will happen if one member decides to withdraw or if expulsion becomes necessary and reducing the agreement to writing is a strategic way to avoid future disputes. In Case 14.2, a federal trial court considers whether actions of an LLC member are sufficient for a judicial expulsion.

CASE 14.2 Headfirst Baseball LLC v. Elwood, 239 F. Supp. 3d 7 (D.D.C. 2017)

FACT SUMMARY Elwood and Sullivan were each members and managers of a variety of LLCs related to amateur baseball training camps including Headfirst Baseball, LLC (collectively "Headfirst"). In 2012, Elwood made several loans to himself totaling $600,000 from Headfirst, although Sullivan had authorized only a single $200,000 loan. Sullivan first learned about Elwood's unauthorized loans in late 2012 based on a conversation with the company's bookkeeper. Sullivan confronted Elwood about the unauthorized loans, and further investigation uncovered unauthorized credit card purchases made by Elwood in the LLC's name. After receiving an unsatisfactory response from Elwood about his expenditures, Sullivan terminated Elwood's management position at Headfirst. Sullivan conceded, however, that the Operating Agreement did not authorize him to terminate Elwood's membership status in the LLC. Soon after his termination, Elwood began a campaign of retaliation. For example, (1) Elwood caused Headfirst's website registration to be suspended, resulting in its website being shut down for several days; (2) Elwood provided false information to Bank of America that resulted in a two-month freeze of Headfirst's bank account, which at the time contained $600,000; and (3) Elwood deprived Headfirst of its access to its Google AdWords account, an advertising tool Headfirst used to recruit potential customers. Elwood denied that his actions were retaliatory, explaining instead that he was exercising his rights as a member of the LLC. On behalf of the LLC, Sullivan filed suit against Elwood asking the court to issue an order to expel Elwood pursuant to the District of Columbia's LLC statute.

SYNOPSIS OF DECISION AND OPINION The federal District Court for the District of Columbia ruled in favor of Headfirst. The court held that although the LLC Operating Agreement was silent on expulsion of members, Elwood's conduct was sufficient to justify a judicial expulsion. The court reasoned that the Elwood materially breached the LLC Operating Agreement in a way that triggered the right to expel him.

WORDS OF THE COURT: Material Breach of the Operating Agreement "'A breach is material only if it relates to a matter of vital importance or if it goes to the essence [of the contract] and frustrates substantially the purpose for which the contract was agreed to by the injured party.' The evidence adduced at trial showed that [Elwood's conduct] constituted a breach of the implied covenant of good faith and fair dealing contained in [Headfirst's Operating Agreement]. Given the

(continued)

---

[5] *See, e.g.,* D.C. Code § 29-806.02(5).

circumstances of this case, in which the operation of the several Headfirst entities was closely managed by both Elwood and Sullivan, the Court finds that Elwood's [unauthorized use] of [Headfirst's] funds—companies Elwood managed in conjunction with Sullivan—and his acts of 'sabotage' in 2013 with respect to [Headfirst]—a company Elwood co-owned with Sullivan—relate to a matter of vital importance to the agreement between them, i.e., Sullivan's ability to rely on Elwood to act in good faith as a business associate. The Court therefore finds that Elwood's conduct warrants his expulsion as a member of [Headfirst] pursuant to [D.C.'s LLC statute]."

Case Questions

1. What does the court mean when it cites a "breach of the implied covenant of good faith"? What specific acts constituted bad faith?
2. Because the Operating Agreement did not address whether Sullivan could terminate Elwood's membership in the LLC, didn't Elwood have the right to continue to act on behalf of the LLC? Explain.
3. *Focus on Critical Thinking:* What kind of language and procedure could have been included in the Operating Agreement that may have prevented the LLC from having to seek a judicial expulsion of one of its members?

Limited Liability Partnerships (LLPs)

Most states recognize limited liability partnerships through their partnership statutes. Recall that the chief danger of being a general partner is the amount of potential liability for acts of other general partners or the debts and liabilities of the partnership itself. LLP statutes provide general partnerships with the right to convert their entity and gain the protective shield ordinarily afforded only to limited partners or corporate shareholders. Although the origins of LLP laws are rooted in the protection of professional service firm partnerships (law, accounting, etc.), the use of LLPs is much more widespread now as some family businesses have also used the LLP form as a way to handle issues unique to the transition from one generation to another.

Members of an LLC can prevent disputes from occurring by planning for events, such as death or dissociation of a member, in their operating agreement. 10'000 Hours/Getty Images

Formation Limited liability partnerships are formed when a general partnership files a **statement of qualification** with the appropriate public official. The conversion of the partnership must be approved by a majority of the ownership. The statement includes the name and street address, an affirmative statement electing to become an LLP, an effective date, and the signatures of at least two of the partners. Some states also require a filing to inform tax authorities of the existence of the entity. Once approved, the filing becomes part of the public record.

LO 14-5

Articulate the legal protections from personal liability afforded to the principals in an LLC and LLP.

Liability Of all of the business entities that we have discussed thus far, the LLP has the greatest variance of liability protection under state law. While the general idea behind being an LLP is that all partners have liability protection for debts and liabilities of the partnership, some states impose conditions on these limits. In cases where a partner has

LO 14-6

Identify the tax treatment schemes of an LLC and LLP.

LO 14-7

Provide the primary methods for capitalizing limited liability entities.

engaged in some misconduct or tortious conduct (such as negligence), the LLP acts to shield only the personal assets of *other* partners—never the partner who committed the misconduct or negligence.

In Case 14.3, a federal appeals court analyzes the potential personal liability of partners after an LLP has been dissolved.

CASE 14.3 Dillard Department Stores, Inc. v. Chargois & Ernster, 602 F.3d 610 (5th Cir. 2010)[7]

FACT SUMMARY Chargois and Ernster (C&E) were individuals who formed and registered a limited liability partnership to operate their law practice in 2002. In an attempt to solicit business, C&E developed a website in June 2003 that included a link using Dillard Department Stores' corporate name and trademarked logo. C&E had represented several Dillard customers, and the website gave potential clients access to content created by C&E that allegedly documented acts of illegal profiling by Dillard. Dillard sued C&E for trademark infringement, cyber piracy, and various business torts.

In 2004, while the litigation continued, Chargois and Ernster executed a separation agreement that provided for dissolution of the partnership. C&E's registration as an LLP was not renewed with state authorities, and the registration expired later that same year. However, the defunct LLP entity remained a party to the Dillard litigation, and no party was substituted on its behalf. On November 2, 2004, the court entered a final judgment ordering "Chargois & Ernster, L.L.P." to pay Dillard $143,500.

Dillard could not collect on the judgment because the entity had been dissolved and had no assets. Dillard sought a declaration that the two principals were personally liable, jointly and severally, for the 2004 final judgment entered against C&E. Chargois and Ernster argued that they were shielded from any partnership liability or debt by the state LLP statute. The trial court granted judgment for Dillard in the amount of $143,500 against Chargois and Ernster, jointly and severally, and each appealed.

SYNOPSIS OF DECISION AND OPINION The U.S. Court of Appeals for the Fifth Circuit ruled in favor of Dillard and held Chargois and Ernster personally liable for the judgment owed to Dillard. The court rejected arguments that the partners were insulated from liability because C&E's debt was incurred when the infringing website was created in June 2003, at which time C&E was still a registered limited liability partnership. Instead, the court found that the debt was incurred when the judgment was entered on November 2, 2004, at which time the LLP had lost its liability-limiting attributes and no longer protected Chargois and Ernster.

WORDS OF THE COURT: Timing of a Liability "Although the terms 'debt' and 'incurred' are not defined by the [statute], a plain reading of the statute's text supports Dillard's proffered interpretation. Neither partner was necessarily aware in June 2003 that displaying the Dillard's mark on the law firm website would ultimately lead to a partnership debt. The underlying conduct gave rise to the possibility of a future debt, but to say that a debt was 'incurred' at that time unrealistically distorts the meaning of the word. After all, [C&E's] conduct may have gone undetected, it may have been adjudged perfectly innocent, or Dillard's may have opted not to sue. Under any of those scenarios, no debt would ever have been incurred, let alone incurred in June 2003. It was only when the district court entered judgment against [C&E] in November 2004 that a payable debt came into existence. It was then that [C&E] incurred the debt within the meaning of the provision."

(continued)

---

[7]The reported citation of this case includes Evanston Insurance Company as a party for procedural reasons. For the sake of clarity, the case citation has been abbreviated.

> **Case Questions**
> 1. Why did the court rule that the two partners were personally liable for the debt?
> 2. Could it be argued that the debt actually was incurred once C&E had notice that it had infringed on Dillard's trademark? Why or why not?
> 3. *Focus on Critical Thinking:* Is it sound public policy to require that two partners who have agreed to separate be forced to continue the LLP's existence for a certain period of time? Is it necessary to protect creditors? Is there any other way to accomplish that goal?

Some states provide liability shields for LLP partners *only* when the liability arises from some *negligence* by another partner but not for other types of liabilities, such as those resulting from a breach of contract. For example, suppose that the LLP state statutes of New Chipperville provide for liability protection for partners when one partner acts negligently. Two accountants, Milton and Cowley, form a limited liability partnership called MC Tax Services LLP in New Chipperville. On behalf of the LLP, the partners sign a lease for space with Landlord and invest several thousand dollars from their own assets for start-up capital. One year later, Milton commits a serious error on a client's tax return, and the client sues the firm for malpractice and obtains a $50,000 judgment against the LLP. Because of the negative attention of this case, MC Tax Services loses several large clients and can no longer make its lease payments to Landlord, and the partnership dissolves. Assume that the judgment is not covered by insurance and exceeds the assets of the LLP. Under the law of New Chipperville, the client may pursue Milton's individual assets to pay the $50,000 judgment but not Cowley's. The liability shield protects Cowley for any acts of his partner when the liability results from a *tort* (in this case professional malpractice, a form of negligence). However, Cowley is still liable to Landlord for defaulting on the lease because the liability resulted from a *contractual* obligation.

Consider the plight of someone who has suffered damages due to another's negligence but cannot recover compensation because of the protection of an LLP. In the Milton-Cowley example, suppose that the client who was damaged by Milton's error cannot actually recover the judgment awarded to him because Milton is without assets. Because Cowley is not liable, the client is left with a court order that is worthless. In order to be sure that parties have at least some ability to recover, an increasing number of states require that the LLP and individual partners carry and maintain a certain amount of *liability insurance* as a condition of LLP formation.

Taxation   LLPs are treated as pass-through entities. They are not subject to tax; any income is taxed only when it is distributed to its partners. Because it is not a taxable entity, an LLP files an information return that informs federal and state tax authorities of the profits and losses of the LLP. All income or losses are reported on the partners' individual tax returns. Any losses are deductible and may sometimes help to reduce taxes on other sources of revenue in the individual's tax return.

Capitalization   LLPs are capitalized in the same way as a partnership: through debt via private or commercial lenders or by a sale of partnership equity for ownership in the LLP itself. The partnership agreement of the LLP often controls the amount and methods of capitalizing the business and the procedures for collecting additional contributions from partners as necessary (a process known as a *capital call*). Additional capital contribution requirements are frequently the subject of a partnership agreement. There are some cases in which the partnership has the right to "call" for more money contributions from each partner in order to keep the partnership afloat. Although terms vary, partners that are not in a position to make a call contribution may be forced to sell their interest in the partnership.

Management and Operation   Although not required by statute, limited liability partnerships will frequently have a partnership agreement that sets out the management and operational structure. LLPs are sometimes governed by one or more managing partners and/or some type of executive committee elected by the other partners. The day-to-day operations and powers of the partners and board of partners are spelled out in the partnership agreement as well. The election procedures, qualifications, compensation, meeting times, and other organizational matters are typically addressed in the partnership agreement. In most states, the default agreement is the governing RUPA or UPA provision.

CONCEPT SUMMARY LLCs and LLPs

	Limited Liability Company (LLC)	Limited Liability Partnership (LLP)
Personal liability of principals	LLC members and managers are not personally liable for any debts or liabilities of the LLC so long as state law conditions are met.	LLP partners are generally not liable for the debts of the partnership or the liabilities of the other partners. Partners are personally liable for their own negligence.
Organization/start-up expenses	Articles of organization. Legal fees are usually based on number of members and complexity of organization.	Statement of qualification. Legal fees are usually based on number of members and complexity of organization.
Management and control	Managed through managing member(s) (no officers, directors, or shareholders). Members abide by operating agreement for management and control issues.	Managed through managing partner(s) and/or executive committee (no officers, directors, or shareholders). Members abide by partnership agreement for management and control issues.
Capital	Typically sells shares of financial interest in the LLC and/or secures private or commercial loans.	Private or commercial loans. Personal financial contributions of partners may be required in partnership agreement.
Taxes	Option of being treated as a corporation or as a pass-through entity. May also have to pay miscellaneous state and local taxes to operate business.	Pass-through taxation treatment (no tax is paid on income to the entity, but when the entity distributes dividends, tax is paid at the individual partner's individual tax rate). May also have to pay miscellaneous state and local taxes to operate business.
Designation	Doe Group, LLC	Doe and Associates, LLP

KEY TERMS

Limited liability company (LLC) p. 480   A multiperson form of business entity that offers liability protection for its principals along with various tax options.

Limited liability partnership (LLP) p. 481   Form of business entity that provides the same level of liability protection to a general partner in an LLP as is provided to a limited partner in a limited partnership form of entity.

Articles of organization p. 482   Document filed to create an LLC; in most states, requires only basic information such as the name of the entity, the location of its principal place of business, and the names of its members. Also called *certificate of organization*.

Operating agreement p. 482   Document that governs an LLC; sets out the structure and internal rules for operation of the entity.

Personal guarantee p. 485   Pledge from LLC members of personal assets to guarantee payment obligations of the business venture.

Member-managed LLC p. 486   LLC management structure similar to that of a general partnership, with all the members having the authority to bind the business.

Manager-managed LLC p. 486   LLC management structure in which the members name a manager (or managers) who generally has the day-to-day operational responsibilities, while the nonmanaging members are typically investors with little input on the course of business taken by the entity except for major decisions.

Dissolution p. 487   In the context of an LLC, a liquidation process triggered by an event that is specified in the operating agreement (such as the death of a key member) or by the decision of the majority of membership interests (or the percentage called for in the operating agreement) to dissolve the company.

Dissociation p. 487   Term used in the RUPA to describe the act of separation of a partner from the partnership. Also, the process in which an individual member of an LLC exercises the right to withdraw from the partnership.

Statement of qualification p. 489   Document filed to form a limited liability partnership by converting a general partnership.

CHAPTER REVIEW QUESTIONS

1. Under the ULLCA, which of the following is true about limited liability companies (LLCs)?
   a. Its principals are called members.
   b. Principals do not have personal liability for liabilities of the LLC.
   c. Principals have joint and several liability for debts resulting from an LLC contract.
   d. Both A and B are true.

2. Which of the following is typically found in an LLC operating agreement?
   a. Procedure in the event of the death of a key member
   b. Business advertising materials
   c. Financial statements
   d. Disclosures of risk

3. Principals who manage an LLC owe its members a _____ duty.
   a. Joint and several
   b. Liability
   c. Manager's
   d. Fiduciary

4. Julian, Curt, and Drew were all principals in JCD Associates, LLC. In the operating agreement they agree that any principal is permitted to bind the LLC. JCD Associates is
   a. Member-managed.
   b. Manager-managed.
   c. Principal-managed.
   d. President-managed.

5. Which of the following is not true about a limited liability partnership (LLP) entity?
   a. Partners are entitled to pass-through taxation.
   b. There is no personal liability for negligent acts of other partners.
   c. Partners are authorized to bind the partnership in contract.
   d. There is no personal liability for that partner's own negligence.

Answers and explanations are provided at the end of this chapter.

THEORY TO PRACTICE

Beverly Hills Autos (BHA) LLC is a retail car dealership organized as a limited liability company and engaged in the business of selling various brands of luxury automobiles and SUVs in several dealership locations. The LLC was structured as a manager-managed LLC with two managing members and six other members who were primarily investors. The parties had an operating agreement that provided the structure and authority of managing members, included a provision eliminating liability for a breach of the duty of care, and stated that the members agreed to abide by the default LLC statute in their state based on the Uniform Limited Liability Company Act (ULLCA) for terms not in the agreement. One of the nonmanaging members, Luciano, began a conversation with the owner of another car dealership and eventually negotiated a merger agreement. However, the managing members were out of town, and Luciano signed the agreement on behalf of the partnership without the managers' knowledge. When the managing members learned of the merger, they immediately attempted to cancel the contract on behalf of BHA.

1. Will a court support BHA's attempt to cancel the contract? What will be BHA's likely theory of the case?
2. Assume that the managing members agreed with the transaction and signed on in agreement. Given BHA's choice of business entity, what are the options for financing this transaction?
3. Would an LLP be a better form than an LLC for BHA? Why or why not?
4. Assume that Luciano didn't bring the opportunity to the LLC members but rather purchased the competing dealership with another partner outside the LLC. Subsequently, Luciano offers to sell the dealership to BHA at a premium over what he paid for it. Has Luciano breached his fiduciary duty? If so, which one?
5. If Luciano decides to exercise his dissociation rights, what is the impact on the remaining members of the LLC? Is dissolution of the LLC triggered by Luciano's dissociation?

LEGAL STRATEGY 101

"thefacebook LLC"

When an entrepreneur launches a new venture—like Harvard sophomore Mark Zuckerberg did when he invented "thefacebook" during the 2003–2004 academic year—he must also figure out what type of legal structure the business will have. Specifically, will the new business be run as a sole proprietorship, a general or limited partnership, a limited liability company, or a corporation?

As it happens, Facebook's early company history, which is dramatically depicted in the Academy Award–winning movie *The Social Network,* provides a memorable illustration of many of these various legal structures. Today, Facebook is a publicly held corporation, with its shares listed and traded on the NASDAQ stock exchange. However, years before Facebook became a major corporation, it started as a sole proprietorship in Mark Zuckerberg's college dorm room.

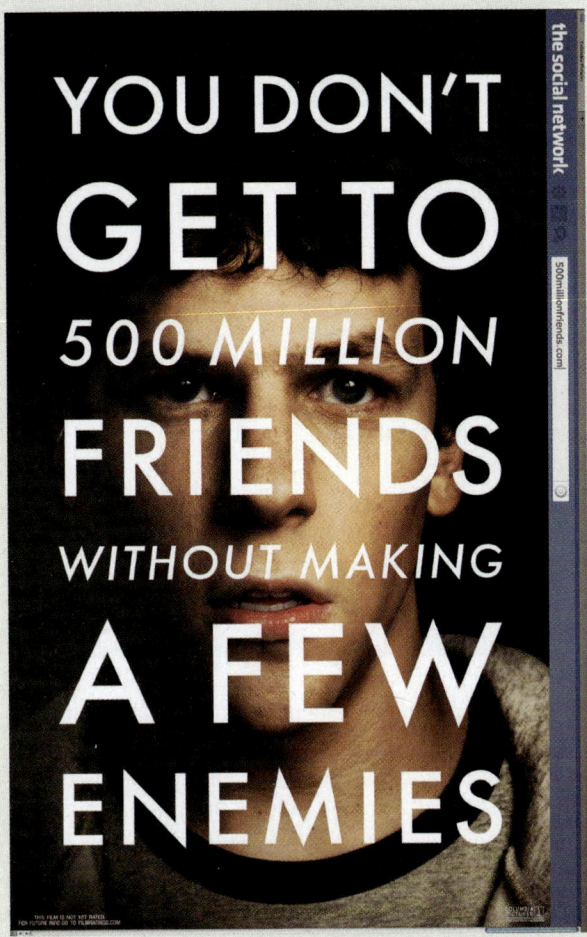

Movie: *The Social Network.* AF archive/Alamy

Mark Zuckerberg wasn't the only founder of Facebook, however. Early in the company's history, Zuckerberg decided to team up with his best friend, Harvard junior Eduardo Saverin. Facebook then evolved into a general partnership when Zuckerberg and Saverin became business partners. In exchange for Saverin's financial support, the two partners agreed to split their respective ownership interests 70-30—with Zuckerberg obtaining a 70 percent stake in the new company and Saverin receiving a 30 percent interest.[8]

Zuckerberg then launched The Facebook (as it was then called) from his dorm room on February 4, 2004, and his website became an instant success.[9] Facebook soon spread to other campuses: Columbia (February 25), Stanford (February 26), and Yale (February 29).[10] By April 2004, Zuckerberg and Saverin—and a third founder, Dustin Moskovitz, who grew up in Ocala, Florida, before going to Harvard—decided to formally register Facebook as a "limited liability company" in the state of Florida. The rest, as they say, is history. . . .

CRITICAL THINKING QUESTION

Facebook was launched in February 2004. From a legal perspective, the company first began as a sole proprietorship and then morphed into a general partnership before becoming a limited liability company in April 2004. Why do you think the founders of Facebook decided to structure their company as an LLC so early in the company's history?

---

[8]See Ben Mezrich, *The Accidental Billionaires: The Founding of Facebook: A Tale of Sex, Money, Genius, and Betrayal* (Anchor 2010).

[9]Alan J. Tabak, *Hundreds Register for New Facebook Website,* Harv. Crimson, Feb. 9, 2004.

[10]See David Kirkpatrick, *The Facebook Effect: The Inside Story of the Company That Is Connecting the World* (Simon & Schuster 2011).

MANAGER'S CHALLENGE

Members in an LLC typically begin negotiating an operating agreement by meeting and developing a list of concerns and objectives that are addressed in an LLC operating agreement. Assume that you are a founding principal in Beverly Hills Auto (BHA) in the Theory to Practice problem. Individually or in groups, develop a one-page bullet-point memorandum that outlines concerns that the BHA members may have. Be sure to address issues related to profit and loss split; managing members; insurance; day-to-day operations; meetings; voting rights; procedures for death, disability, or bankruptcy of a member or managing member; and a procedure in case of deadlock.

See Connect for Manager's Challenge sample answers.

CASE SUMMARY 14.1 Kaycee Land & Livestock v. Flahive, 46 P.3d 323 (Wyo. 2002)

LIABILITY OF LLC MEMBER

Flahive is the managing member of Flahive Oil and Gas, LLC. The LLC entered into an agreement with Kaycee to mine oil and gas from Kaycee's property. During the mining, Kaycee alleged that Flahive's process was flawed and resulted in contamination of Kaycee's property. After discovering that the LLC was without assets, Kaycee sued Flahive individually. Flahive defended on the basis that the contract was between the LLC and Kaycee and that he has no personal liability.

CASE QUESTIONS

1. Can the court disregard the LLC entity in this situation?
2. Does fairness demand that Flahive be personally responsible for the LLC's negligence?

CASE SUMMARY 14.2 Emprise v. Rumisek, 2009 WL 2633649 (Kan. Ct. App. 2009)

PERSONAL GUARANTEES OF LLC MEMBERS

Four physicians formed an LLC to operate a medical practice. They capitalized the venture with a bank loan to the LLC. Each physician signed a personal guarantee to secure a proportionate part of the loan (25 percent each). A dispute developed that led two of the physicians to depart and move to another practice. The bank became concerned that the loan was in jeopardy, so it brought suit against the remaining physicians in the practice to recover the amount due under the loan from them. While the bank sued the remaining physicians, the departing physicians were engaged in litigation with the remaining physicians over mismanagement of their former practice. The remaining physicians contended that the bank could not enforce the personal guarantees until disputes among the physicians were resolved because the LLC may still have assets if the litigation is successful.

CASE QUESTIONS

1. Does the bank have to wait until the litigation is complete to enforce the personal guarantees against the physicians? Why or why not?
2. What is the impact of the departing physicians' dissociation from the LLC?

CASE SUMMARY 14.3 Lamprecht v. Jordan, LLC, 75 P.3d 743 (Idaho 2003)

INVOLUNTARY WITHDRAWAL

Lamprecht was a founding member of an accounting firm, Jordan & Company. He and other members of his firm formed an LLC for purposes of acquiring and maintaining real estate for the firm's offices. The LLC members signed an operating agreement that required withdrawal from the LLC upon termination from Jordan & Company and specified that the ex-member would be entitled to only the balance in his or her capital account. In November 2000, Lamprecht assaulted a colleague in the office and was eventually charged with battery. Jordan & Company terminated Lamprecht and offered approximately $3,000 as payment for his capital account. Lamprecht refused to accept the payment and disputed that he was required to withdraw, claiming that the operating agreement covered only voluntary cessation of employment. Lamprecht also claimed that the agreement to pay the capital account balance was unfair and that any payment should be based on market value.

CASE QUESTIONS

1. May the LLC members force Lamprecht to withdraw?
2. Is it fair to base the payment on the capital account balance (typically very small) rather than fair market value (typically a larger amount) when the withdrawal is forced?

CASE SUMMARY 14.4 First American Title v. Lawson, 827 A.2d 230 (N.J. 2003)

LLP INNOCENT PARTNERS

Wheeler, Lawson, and Snyder formed an LLP for their law practice. Wheeler was the managing partner for the LLP and oversaw the firm's business affairs, including malpractice insurance coverage. When applying to First American Title for the firm's malpractice insurance, Wheeler made a material misrepresentation on the insurance application. Both Wheeler and Lawson engaged in unethical and illegal conduct by failing to properly administer client trust funds and using the funds for their own benefit. Snyder was located at a separate office and had little contact with his partners and no knowledge of their misrepresentations or illegal conduct. Eventually, the firm was sued for malpractice and damages by various clients. First American Title paid out several claims and then sought recovery from each of the partners and canceled their policy based on the misrepresentation by Wheeler. Snyder argued that he should not be liable for the negligent or intentional acts of his partners.

CASE QUESTIONS

1. Does the LLP shield protect Snyder's personal assets from negligence committed by other partners?
2. Should Snyder have been more active in regard to being aware of his partners' deeds? Did he have a duty to inquire?

CASE SUMMARY 14.5 Lieberman v. Wyoming.com LLC, 82 P.3d 274 (Wyo. 2004)

MEMBER WITHDRAWAL

Lieberman was a member and vice president of Wyoming.com LLC (Wyoming), with a $20,000 ownership stake in the LLC at the time of formation in 1994. After a dispute between the parties in 1998, Lieberman was terminated as vice president by the other LLC members. Lieberman served Wyoming with a "notice of withdrawal" and demanded that Wyoming pay for Lieberman's "share of the company" in the amount of $400,000. Wyoming held a meeting of remaining members and voted to accept Lieberman's withdrawal and continue operating the LLC. Wyoming then notified Lieberman that it accepted his withdrawal but offered him only $20,000 because that was his initial ownership stake. Lieberman rejected the $20,000 offer. Because the operating agreement was silent on the issue of dissociation, Wyoming filed suit asking for a declaratory judgment of its rights against Lieberman.

CASE QUESTIONS

1. Who prevails and why? Explain.
2. If the court determines that Lieberman's withdrawal constituted dissociation, what is the legal impact of that decision?

CHAPTER REVIEW QUESTIONS: Answers and Explanations

1. **d.** An LLC's principals, called members, are shielded from liabilities of the LLC's business operations. (c) is incorrect because the whole point of an LLC is to avoid the joint and several liability associated with other entities such as a partnership.

2. **a.** Operating agreements typically cover events such as death, disability, or bankruptcy of a key principal. Advertisements, financial statements, and disclosures are not part of an operating agreement.

3. **d.** Fiduciary duties are owed by managers to members to act in the best interest of the LLC and to prohibit them from self-dealing. The remaining answers are incorrect statements of law.

4. **a.** If all members may bind the LLC, this is member-managed. (b) is incorrect because if one or more members are designated to manage the LLC, the entity is considered manager-managed. (c) and (d) are incorrect statements of law.

5. **d.** In an LLP, partners cannot escape liability for their own negligence. The remaining answers are all true statements about LLPs.

CHAPTER 15
Corporations

©philsajonesen/Getty Images

Learning Objectives

After studying this chapter, students who have mastered the material will be able to:

15-1 Identify the sources and level of law governing the formation and internal matters of corporations.

15-2 Recognize the liability associated with improper formation by a promoter.

15-3 Explain the primary methods for capitalizing a corporation.

15-4 Categorize corporate entities on the basis of how their income is taxed and understand the concept of flow-through taxation.

15-5 Describe the fundamental structure and roles of officers, directors, and shareholders in the corporate form of entity, and understand the functions of each role and how the structure is governed.

15-6 Identify the major fiduciary duties owed by insiders of a corporation to its shareholders and give examples of each duty.

15-7 Apply the business judgment rule to an alleged breach of fiduciary duty by an insider.

15-8 Distinguish between a shareholder derivative suit and a direct action suit.

15-9 Identify circumstances under which a court will pierce the veil and explain the impact on the principals.

This chapter continues the discussion of business entities that provide liability protection for principals. The principals of some business ventures form a *corporation* to achieve their objectives and gain flexibility not found in other entities. Although the corporate form is sometimes associated with large multinational corporations, in fact many corporations are relatively small, with a limited number of principals (sometimes just a single owner). In this chapter, students will learn about

- The governing source of law and categories of corporations.
- Rules governing the formation of a corporation.
- The personal liability of the principals for corporate liabilities and debts.
- How corporations are capitalized, taxed, and structured.
- The duties of corporate managers, such as officers and directors, to the owners of the corporation.

CORPORATE ENTITIES

A **corporation** is a fictitious legal entity that exists as an independent "person" separate from its principals. Although this corporate "person" is a legally created fiction, it is a well-established and deeply seated principle of American law. Recall from Chapter 2, "Business and the Constitution," that the U.S. Supreme Court has ruled that corporations are entitled to full First Amendment protection for political speech. In a business context it is also important to note that a corporation, like an individual person, may file suit or be sued and may form a contract or breach a contract. In contrast to sole proprietorships and partnerships, the obligations of corporations are separate and distinct from the personal obligations of their principals.

Corporations are created through a state law filing, and their formation is governed through *state statutes*. State statutes vary in their corporate formation and governance rules, but each state has a specific law, often called the **business corporation law** or something similar, that covers such matters as the structure of the corporation, oversight of the activity of the corporation's managers, rights of the principals in the case of the sale of assets or ownership interests, annual reporting requirements, and other issues that affect the internal rules of the business venture. Over half of the states have adopted all or substantial portions of a model act known as the **Revised Model Business Corporation Act (RMBCA)**,[1] drafted by the American Law Institute. While state statutes regulate the internal governance of a corporation, federal laws regulate the offering or trading of ownership interests to the public and set certain standards for internal governance for some companies.[2]

LO 15-1
Identify the sources and level of law governing the formation and internal matters of corporations.

LO 15-2
Recognize the liability associated with improper formation by a promoter.

Categories of Corporations

Corporations may be classified into one or more categories that reflect their overall purpose, capitalization (how they are funded), location, and structure. The two major categories are *privately held corporations,* which are owned exclusively by a group of private individuals, and *publicly held corporations,* which sell their ownership interests via public stock exchanges.

Privately Held versus Publicly Held The most common category is a **privately held corporation**. Privately held corporations are those that do not sell ownership interests through sales via a broker to the general public or to financial institutions or public investors. Privately held corporations have substantial flexibility in terms of their internal operating procedures and do not generally have to comply with rigorous corporate structures or formalities. For example, in lieu of an actual meeting, privately held corporations often use a single document signed by each principal to dispose of necessary tasks such as electing directors or issuing stock. This document is known as a *unanimous consent resolution.* Many states give privately held corporations the option of electing to become a *closely held* or *family-held* entity. This option further restricts the number or type of owners that a corporation may have, but it provides even more flexibility in regard to how the business venture may be organized and managed.

Note that even though many privately held corporations have a relatively small number of shareholders, there is no limit in terms of revenue. It is not uncommon for corporations with revenues in the eight-figure range to be privately held. Often, the flexibility of a privately held corporation outweighs any desire of the principals to capitalize the business through a sale to the general public.

---

[1] The American Law Institute also issued *Principles of Corporate Governance* in 1994.
[2] Federal securities law is discussed in detail in Chapter 16, "Regulation of Securities, Corporate Governance, and Financial Markets."

When a privately held corporation wishes to fund capitalization through the sale of ownership interests to the general public and commercial investors, the principals pursue an initial public offering (IPO) and then continue their corporate existence as a publicly held corporation. After the IPO, the corporation trades (buys and sells) stocks through a public stock exchange (the New York Stock Exchange, or NYSE, is perhaps the most famous and influential, but many more exist). A publicly held corporation is subject to a substantial amount of federal and state regulation, primarily through securities laws and corporate governance statutes such as the Sarbanes-Oxley Act. A publicly held corporation is subject to close scrutiny by a variety of regulatory agencies because investors across the globe depend on regulation to ensure integrity among the insiders managing the corporation. Regulation of publicly held corporations is discussed extensively in Chapter 16, "Regulation of Securities, Corporate Governance, and Financial Markets."

Other Categories Besides being classified as publicly held or privately held, corporations may fall into one of the following categories:

- *Domestic:* In the state of its incorporation, a corporation is referred to as a *domestic* corporation.
- *Foreign:* A corporation that transacts business in a state other than its state of incorporation is known as a *foreign* corporation in the other state. For example, WidgetCo is incorporated in Florida and sells its widgets in Florida and Georgia. In Florida, WidgetCo is referred to as a domestic corporation. In Georgia, it is referred to as a foreign corporation.
- *Alien:* A corporation formed outside the United States that transacts business in the United States is referred to as an *alien* corporation.
- *Nonprofit: Nonprofit* corporations are those that do not have profit-seeking owners but rather exist to perform some service to the public at large. (Examples include charities, educational institutions, and certain hospitals.)
- *Benefit:* These corporations exist with the dual purpose of providing a benefit to society while seeking profits for its owners. They differ from nonprofits because benefit corporations are actually owned by its principals.
- *Public: Public* corporations are those formed by a government body to serve the public at large, such as public mass transit companies. A public corporation has a similar structure to a private corporation but has no owners. Be sure not to confuse *publicly held* corporations (discussed earlier) with *public* corporations.
- *Professional: Professional* corporations are those in which the ownership is restricted to a particular profession licensed in a certain field. These corporations have a corporate structure but are open only to members who are in good standing in a particular profession. For example, law firms that are organized as a professional corporation may be owned only by attorneys admitted to the practice of law who are currently active and in good standing.

Formation

Compared to other entities, a corporation has perhaps the most formal filing and reporting requirements. Principals who wish to form a corporation do so by filing a document with a state authority, usually the corporation bureau of the secretary of state's office, which sets out the corporation's name and purpose, the number of shares issued, and the address of the corporation's headquarters. This document, known as the **articles of incorporation**,[3] sets in motion the incorporation process. In addition to requiring the articles of incorporation, state statutes often require filings with tax authorities to notify them of a corporation's existence.

---

[3] In a minority of states, this is known as the *corporate charter*.

State authorities then review the articles, and if they are in satisfactory form, the authorities register the document in public archives and the venture is considered formed. In most states, the date of incorporation is actually made retroactive to the date of filing with the state authorities.

Preincorporation Activity: Liability of Promoters

In most cases, an individual or group of individuals begin to carry out a business venture's activity before actually filing the articles of incorporation. These activities may include arranging for necessary capital through a loan, recruiting personnel, leasing property, and arranging to have the business incorporated. The individual who performs these activities is known as a *promoter*. If the promoter makes a contract on behalf of a not-yet-formed corporation, she may have some degree of *personal liability* to perform under the contract. Generally, the promoter is personally liable when she knows (and the other party has *no reason* to know) that the corporation is not in existence on the day of the signing. The RMBCA provides that anyone purporting to act on behalf of a corporation, knowing incorporation has not yet occurred, is jointly and severally liable for all liabilities created by the acts. For example, Edgar anticipates opening a private detective agency and enters into a one-year lease agreement for office space with Landlord, signing on behalf of the yet-to-be-formed Edgar Detective Agency Inc. One month later, Edgar's financing falls through, and he abandons the idea. Edgar would be a promoter and personally liable for the lease payments (or any penalty for breaching the lease contract) to Landlord.

However, a promoter's personal liability *ceases* at the moment that the corporation is formed and has adopted the contract. In the Edgar-Landlord contract, suppose that Edgar signs on behalf of the corporation, incorporates the business venture the next day, and opens up a bank account. For the first month's rent, Edgar pays the rent via company check. Because the corporation has been formed and, by virtue of accepting a company check, Landlord has adopted the contract, Edgar's personal liability has been extinguished. If Edgar abandons the business after six months, his personal assets are not subject to the Landlord's reach.

Case 15.1 illustrates the risks of preincorporation activity by promoters.

CASE 15.1 Branch v. Mullineaux, 2010 NY Slip Op 31850(U) (N.Y. Sup. Ct. July 15, 2010)

FACT SUMMARY Branch agreed to provide $75,000 in short-term financing to three individuals, Mullineaux, Gefter, and Satsky (MGS), for purposes of starting up a venture called "Stereo House" in which the principals would profit by arranging parties in a luxury beach house in the Hamptons (Long Island, New York) and charging guests to attend these events. Branch entered into an agreement with MGS whereby they agreed that the yet-to-be-formed venture would pay back the money to Branch at an interest rate of 10 percent over four months. After Branch provided the funding and entered into the agreement, MGS allegedly formed the Stereo House entity but did not open a bank account, did not execute the proper legal documents, and did not ratify any of the Branch transactions. The venture was ultimately unsuccessful, and Stereo House was unable to pay back the majority of the loan. Branch sued MGS as individuals under a theory of promoter liability. MGS defended by claiming that the $75,000 was an investment and therefore the entire amount was at risk without any liability on MGS's part.

(continued)

SYNOPSIS OF DECISION AND OPINION The New York court held in favor of Branch. The court ruled that because the agreement was executed prior to formation of the entity, MGS created individual liability to Branch. MGS were liable as individuals because promoters who execute preincorporation contracts in the name of a proposed corporation are personally liable on the contract unless the parties have agreed otherwise. In this case, it was undisputed that the corporate entity did not exist at the time that the agreement was entered into. Thus, as preincorporation promoters, MGS were personally liable for the agreement executed prior to the incorporation of an entity, even if the entity would otherwise be considered the contracting party.

WORDS OF THE COURT: Liability of Promoters
"Indeed, a corporation which did not exist at the time the contract was entered into, cannot be bound by the terms thereof unless the obligation is assumed in some manner by the corporation after it comes into existence by adopting, ratifying, or accepting it. [W]hen a promoter executes a contract on behalf of a nonexistent corporation, the promoter is presumed to be personally liable under that contract absent proof of the parties' contrary intent or until there has been a novation between the corporation and the other contracting party. Here, defendants have proffered no evidence that the Stereo House entity adopted, ratified or accepted the agreement they made with plaintiff. Thus, there is no basis for the court to overcome this presumption and shift the individual [MGS's] liability for repayment to [the Stereo House entity]."

Case Questions
1. What steps should MGS have taken to help limit their promoter liability?
2. What steps could Branch have taken to limit his losses?
3. *Focus on Critical Thinking:* Isn't Branch's loss a risk of doing business? Why should MGS be individually liable?

Choice of State of Incorporation

One of the first considerations for principals forming a corporation is choosing in what state to incorporate the business venture. Most corporations with a relatively small number of principals choose to incorporate in the state in which they will locate their principal office and operate the business venture. Some corporations choose the state of Delaware as the state of incorporation because of the advantages of that state's permissive rules on the flexibility of how a corporation's managers (in the form of officers and directors, discussed later) operate the business. For the most part, publicly held corporations decide that incorporation in Delaware is a wise choice because the Delaware statutes give officers and directors of those corporations wide latitude in decision making that does not require shareholder consent. Delaware has also adopted statutes that offer officers and directors strong protections from shareholder lawsuits that allege managerial negligence has resulted in damages to shareholder interest. This protection, known as the **business judgment rule**, is discussed in more detail later in this chapter. Moreover, Delaware has a well-established body of case law that allows more reliability in corporate planning. Note that despite some myths to the contrary, Delaware's tax structure is *not* favorable to out-of-state corporations that incorporate in Delaware. Although Delaware has no sales tax on retail merchandise, this rule applies to in-state sales only. Thus, an out-of-state business that uses Delaware to incorporate but does not sell any products or services in Delaware has no tax advantage at all. In fact, in the big picture, corporations with a relatively small number of principals will end up paying more in taxes, considering the assessment of business franchise taxes or fees in both Delaware and the state in which most of the business venture's activity takes place.

> **KEY POINT**
>
> Despite some significant advantages that large publicly held corporations gain by incorporating in Delaware, most corporations are better served by incorporating in the state in which they are headquartered.

Capitalization

Corporations have perhaps the widest range of options when considering how to finance their operations. They may be funded through debt or through equity (ownership interests) in a variety of forms.

LO 15-3

Explain the primary methods for capitalizing a corporation.

Debt Corporations often borrow money from either commercial lenders (such as banks) or private investors to fund day-to-day operations, and this is usually evidenced by a loan agreement and a promissory note. For larger projects, corporations may also use more sophisticated forms of debt such as issues of bonds or debentures. Bonds are debt money issued by a corporation to the general public with promises to pay the bondholders back at a specified rate of interest for a specified length of time and to repay the entire loan upon the expiration of the bond (known as the *maturity date*). Note that bondholders are not shareholders but, rather, become creditors of the corporation.

Equity Corporations also sell equity to capitalize their operations. For modest amounts of funding, corporations may turn to private investors or groups of investors. Sometimes a corporation will hire a registered broker–dealer that drafts a document describing the company and the intended use of the funds and distributes it to qualified individuals who are seeking investment opportunities with relatively high risk, in hopes of higher returns. This process constitutes the issuance of a security and, thus, is highly regulated. Securities law is discussed extensively in Chapter 16, "Regulation of Securities, Corporate Governance, and Financial Markets."

Venture Capital Firms When a corporation seeks a more significant amount of capital, the corporation may turn to a *venture capital* firm. Venture capital is funding provided by a group of professional investors for use in a developing business. These firms are frequently focused on one industry (e.g., health care or the technology sector). The major advantage of venture capital is that these firms often have substantial resources and are also a source of expertise in operations and expansion of the corporation. However, in exchange for this, principals usually insist on substantial control over the corporation via its board of directors and even its officers. Venture capitalists are not thought of as long-term investors. They will usually require an "exit strategy" whereby the venture capital firm exits the corporation with a substantial return. This exit strategy may be to take the company public through an initial public offering or to get the company to grow to a point at which a competitor would be willing to pay a substantial premium to purchase the corporation.

Public Offerings Privately held corporations may find that their expansion plans require even more capital than can be raised using private investors. In that case, some companies opt to proceed through a very complex and time-consuming process of converting the corporation from privately held to publicly held by engaging in an initial public offering (IPO). At that point, the corporation may raise equity by selling its shares to the general public and to financial institutions.

Initial Organizational Meeting

After filing the articles of incorporation, the principals typically hold an organizational meeting. This allows the principals to resolve any pending issues and to amend the articles of incorporation to reflect any changes in the principals' strategy since the time of formation. Specifically, the principals will address such issues as

- *Bylaws:* Although state statutes govern some of the internal rules of a corporation, there are still some issues left to the principals. These rules are generally articulated in the corporation's bylaws. The bylaws typically specify the date, time, and place for the annual shareholders' meetings; the number of officers and directors of the corporation; and the process for electing the board of directors. The bylaws also provide a listing of each officer, along with a description of that officer's duties (the responsibilities and liability of officers and directors are discussed later in this chapter). Note that the bylaws are not filed with the state filing official, and thus are not public, but are kept in the corporate records.

- *Board of directors and officers:* In some cases, the members of the board of directors are reported in the articles of incorporation. If they are, the principals may make changes at this organizational meeting by holding another election for the board by the owners of the corporation. Officers are also identified at this meeting, and depending on the bylaws, the officers are appointed by the board or, in some special cases, elected by the board.

- *Issuance of shares:* The organizational meeting also often involves the official issuance of ownership interests consistent with the articles of incorporation filing. The ownership interests are referred to as *shares* and are evidenced by a stock certificate that indicates the owner's name and the number of shares issued. Therefore, owners of a corporation are referred to as **shareholders**. The issuance of shares is usually recorded in a stock register, which is kept by the secretary of the corporation along with other corporate records of the business (such as meeting minutes, resolutions, etc.). In a privately held corporation, the stock certificates and register are not public documents and are kept with the corporate records in the corporation's registered place of business.

Commencement of Business and Corporate Formalities

Once the corporation has been properly formed and postformation organizational matters have been attended to, the corporation's officers commence business operations. As a practical matter, the business entity may have already commenced operations under the promoter, and thus the business operations are simply continued by the newly formed corporate entity. Even after commencement of business operations, officers and directors have a responsibility to comply with state statutory requirements regarding shareholders' and directors' meetings, filing of annual reports, and disclosures to shareholders, and they must use their best efforts to keep corporate records and bylaws up to date. These responsibilities are examples of corporate formalities. Failing to attend to corporate formalities may subject the principals to personal liability (discussed in detail later in this chapter).

Liability Perhaps the most attractive feature of a corporation is its limited liability for the personal assets of its owners and, with certain exceptions, for its officers and directors. In general, shareholders, directors, and officers of a corporation are insulated from personal liability in the event that the corporation runs up large debts or suffers some liability. This liability protection is often referred to as the **corporate veil**. For example, Roscoe and Pound are shareholders of Roscoe Corporation, and they obtain a credit card from Express Credit. They use it in good faith to make purchases to operate the business. For several years, Roscoe Corporation conducts business and pays its debts regularly. However, industry conditions worsen for Roscoe Corporation, and it defaults on its payments to Express Credit. Assuming that Roscoe Corporation has no assets, any attempt to collect the credit card debt from Roscoe or Pound individually will be thwarted by the protection of the corporate veil.

While this appears to be a boon for shareholders, officers, and directors at first glance, there are two important factors that temper the liability issue. First, most lenders, such as banks, will require a *personal guarantee* from the principals to back any loan given to a corporation with personal assets. Second, in some cases courts will discard the corporate veil and allow parties to reach through the corporation to access the personal assets of one or more shareholders. This is known as **piercing the corporate veil**. Piercing the corporate veil is covered later in this chapter.

Personal Guarantees As one would imagine, banks, landlords, and other creditors are fully aware of the limited liability provided by the corporate veil. Thus, if a corporation is a start-up or has limited assets, these creditors will almost always require that the shareholders provide a personal guarantee. A personal guarantee allows the creditor to obtain a judgment against the personal assets of one or more shareholders in the event of a default by the corporation. Personal guarantees are frequently *in addition to* any collateral that is pledged by shareholders or the corporation itself. For example, suppose that Chef Perrier wishes to start his own restaurant and forms Le Chef Inc. as the sole shareholder. For Le Chef Inc. to obtain a lease, the landlord will require a contract with Le Chef Inc. and *also* with Perrier personally. For the company to obtain a loan from the local bank to purchase equipment, inventory, and furniture, the bank will require that (1) Le Chef Inc. agree to a loan repayment schedule; (2) Le Chef Inc. give the bank a right to claim the equipment and inventory as collateral; and (3) Chef Perrier provide a personal guarantee of the loan.

CONCEPT SUMMARY Corporate Formation

Preformation	Legal Formation	Postformation	Start of Business Operations	Corporate Formalities
1. Principals* decide that the corporate entity is advantageous to business objectives. 2. Promoter drafts articles of incorporation according to the principals' needs. 3. Promoter is personally liable for any preformation debts or activities on behalf of the future corporation.	1. Promoter files articles of incorporation with state agency. 2. Upon approval by state agency, the corporation is legally recognized as a business entity. 3. Promoter is no longer personally liable for debts or actions on behalf of the corporation.	1. Principals hold initial organizational meeting to approve bylaws, elect directors, and appoint officers. 2. Officers and directors formally issue stock certificates as evidence of shares in the corporation. 3. Shareholders typically sign a shareholders' agreement in which the parties agree to certain procedures for selling or transferring stock, etc.	Officers and directors oversee the start of business operations.	1. Officers and directors are responsible for complying with annual meeting, reporting, and filing requirements. 2. Bylaws and shareholders' agreement are subject to ongoing review and adjustment when necessary.

*While *principals* is used here, this summary applies equally to corporations that have only a single principal.

Taxation

For multiperson ventures, it is not uncommon for the tax-related needs of the individuals to differ. For example, Abel, Baker, and Cain wish to form NewCo.com. The corporate form may favor Abel, while the interests of Baker may be better served by a partnership. Before selecting an appropriate form of entity, the parties try to anticipate the best way to minimize taxes while maintaining an appropriate degree of liability protection.

LO 15-4

Categorize corporate entities on the basis of how their income is taxed and understand the concept of flow-through taxation.

FIGURE 15.1 Taxation of C Corporations and S Corporations

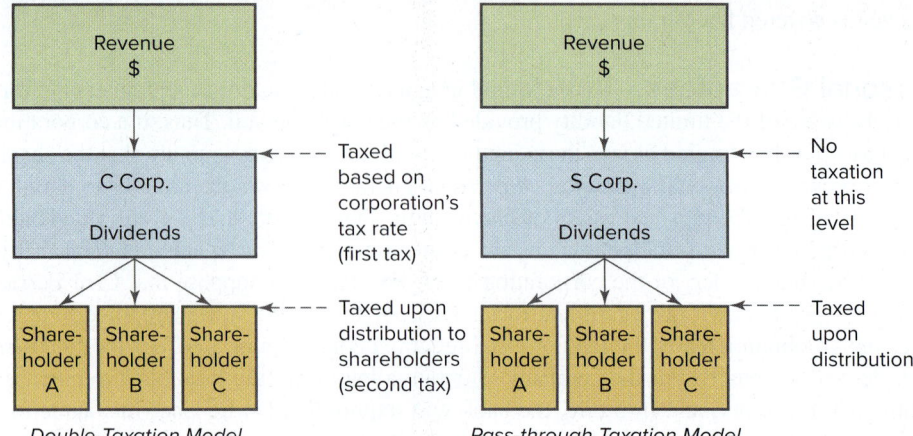

Double-Taxation Model   Pass-through Taxation Model

C Corporations Every C corporation is considered a legal, taxable entity that is separate from the owners for income tax purposes. Therefore, corporations pay tax on their earnings, and then shareholders pay tax on any corporate earnings distributed to them in the form of dividends. This system is known as *double taxation:* The taxation occurs at both (1) the corporate level, when income is earned by the corporation, and (2) the individual level, when it is distributed as a dividend (profit) to the shareholder.

S Corporations Corporations that qualify for and elect *Subchapter S* treatment receive flow-through (also known as *pass-through*) tax treatment. The term *Subchapter S* is simply a designation named after the section of the Internal Revenue Code that details requirements to qualify for flow-through tax treatment as a corporation. Subject to certain exceptions under the tax laws, Subchapter S corporations are not subject to tax at the entity level.

Figure 15.1 provides a comparison of the tax implications of C corporations and S corporations.

CONCEPT SUMMARY Corporate Form of Entity

Personal liability of principals	Corporations exist as a separate legal "person."
	Officers, directors, and shareholders are not personally liable for any debts or liabilities of the corporation (absent fraud).
	Corporate veil protection.
Organization and start-up expenses	Formation procedures are relatively easy if the entity is privately held and has limited shareholders.
	Bylaws, shareholders' agreement, and resolutions are drafted by an attorney, resulting in higher costs.
	Publicly held companies or "private offerings" involve extensive legal documentation and higher fees.
Management and control	Shareholders elect directors. Directors appoint officers.
	Officers have day-to-day control over management with directors' oversight.
	Shareholders must vote on significant corporate decisions (merger, sale of significant assets, or stock issuance).
	Bylaws are the internal operating rules of the entity.

(continued)

Capital	Capital may be raised by the sale of shares (equity) or through loans. Some corporations may also raise money by issuing bonds and other debt instruments.
Taxes	A C corporation pays taxes at the corporate rate on all income of the entity. When the entity distributes profits to shareholders *(dividends)*, the income is taxed again at the shareholder's individual rate. This is known as *double taxation*. An S corporation has *pass-through* taxation treatment. No tax is paid on income to the entity, but when the entity distributes dividends, tax is paid at the individual shareholder's rate.
Designations	Doe, Inc. Doe Corporation Doe Company

STRUCTURE, MANAGEMENT, AND OPERATION

Fundamentally, corporations are structured around an allocation of power based on three categories: *shareholders, directors,* and *officers*. Shareholders are the owners of the corporation and act principally through electing and removing directors and approving or withholding approval of major corporate decisions. **Directors** are responsible for oversight and management of the corporation's course of direction. **Officers** carry out the directors' set course of direction through management of the day-to-day operations of the business. Although this allocation of power is based on the RMBCA, many states allow a corporation to alter the structure as necessary to meet the needs of the entity. Very large corporations and very small corporations often manage their operations using a modified form of this structure. For example, in some cases, a corporation has only one or two shareholders, each of whom acts as a director and an officer. This structure is essentially useless, so they may opt to adopt a slightly different structure through the bylaws and/or an agreement among the shareholders as to the rights and responsibilities of each shareholder.

Shareholders

Shareholders are the owners of the corporation. While shareholders do not directly manage the corporation, most states give shareholders certain rights to protect their ownership interests. Most importantly, shareholders, assuming a majority of the ownership consent, have the power to elect and remove directors at the annual shareholders' meetings. State statutes also give rights to shareholders to veto any fundamental changes to the corporation that are proposed by the directors and officers. Examples of fundamental changes are selling substantial assets, engaging in a merger, issuing more capital stock, pursuing venture capital financing, and issuing a bond. Shareholders also must approve any changes in the structure of the corporation through amending the articles of incorporation or bylaws. For example, Widget Manufacturing Inc. is structured as follows:

Name	Percentage of Total Stock Owned	Role
Abel	10	Officer, director, shareholder
Baker	10	Officer, director, shareholder
Cain	20	Director, shareholder
David	20	Shareholder
Elias	40	Shareholder

LO 15-5

Describe the fundamental structure and roles of officers, directors, and shareholders in the corporate form of entity, and understand the functions of each role and how the structure is governed.

LO 15-6

Identify the major fiduciary duties owed by insiders of a corporation to its shareholders and give examples of each duty.

Suppose that Abel and Baker locate what they believe to be an excellent opportunity to merge with a larger competitor. They will need to convince either Cain and David or Elias to approve the transaction in order to move ahead. If they are able to convince only Cain or David and Elias resists the transaction, Elias and the remaining shareholder would have the ability to block the merger from taking place. Note also that some corporations, particularly closely held corporations, issue *voting stock* to some shareholders and *nonvoting stock* to other shareholders. This is done to ensure that a certain shareholder or group of shareholders can control the corporation, but it still allows other shareholders the ability to receive payments from the corporation's profit (called *dividends*) and other benefits of ownership. For example, in the Widget Manufacturing Inc. example above, suppose that Elias was the father of Abel, Baker, Cain, and David. He wishes to be sure that his heirs receive dividends in certain proportions but does not yet wish to cede control of the corporation to them. Elias could issue nonvoting stock to Abel, Baker, Cain, and David but still retain the power to elect and remove them as directors or to void any transaction. However, it is important to note that shareholders cannot bind the corporation, nor can shareholders demand that the directors take a certain action or adopt a certain policy.

Board of Directors

While shareholders have the power to veto transactions, it is the board of directors that actually sets the strategy and policies of the corporation. The board of directors also has an important oversight function, and state statutes contemplate that the body be *independent* from the shareholders and officers. Most planning initiatives that result in a change to the corporation, such as an acquisition of another corporation's assets or stock, are overseen by the board prior to submitting the plan to shareholders for approval.

Election of Directors
Shareholders elect directors. In most corporations, directors hold office for one year, but the bylaws can set any term. The bylaws also set the

The board of directors typically makes use of committees to carry out its work and oversight responsibilities. Hero Images/Getty Images

procedures and requirements for an election in terms of time and date, notification to shareholders, and the number of shareholders who must be present to hold a vote (known as the *quorum requirement*). Some states require at least three directors, except in the case of a closely held corporation, where the number of directors is equal to the number of shareholders. Therefore, a one-person corporation requires only one director. Other states (such as Delaware) have abolished any minimum number of directors. The number of directors is typically set out in the corporation's bylaws.

Removal of Directors Directors may be removed by a shareholder vote or, less frequently, by a court order. Absent a contrary provision in the articles of incorporation, shareholders may remove a director with or without cause.[4] The removal process is usually set out in the bylaws, but in almost all cases the shareholder vote must take place at a properly called shareholders' meeting. Most states also allow a *court* to order a director to be removed, but only for *cause* (such as fraud). This is a rare event but would be necessary if the director at issue is also a shareholder with sufficient voting power to defeat removal votes by minority shareholders.

Meetings Acts of the board of directors take place only at official meetings that occur at a regular annual or semiannual time as specified in the corporation's bylaws or by a statute. Special meetings to handle pressing matters may also be called so long as a notification procedure is followed in accordance with the bylaws. The votes of a majority of the directors who are present at a meeting are required to take action. Most states allow board action to take place without a meeting if the directors act through unanimous written consent (all directors agree in writing to the action) or the directors agree to meet via a communication means through which all directors can hear and speak with one another at the same time (such as through videoconferencing or webcam). For routine matters such as approving the choice of the corporation's auditing firm or legal counsel, corporations often choose these alternate routes to board action.

Committees Much of the board's work is done through its committees. Each committee consists of a small group of board members who are charged with overseeing or performing a given task and making recommendations to the full board. Examples of such committees are a compensation committee (investigates appropriate compensation for its officers, etc., and makes a recommendation), an audit committee (oversees the proper reporting of earnings and other audit functions), and an election committee (supervises the procedures for director elections).

Officers

The corporation's officers are appointed by, and may be removed by, the board of directors. The officers carry out the day-to-day operations of the corporation and execute the strategy and mandates set out by the board of directors. As a practical matter, officers work closely with the directors in setting the course of a corporation's path, but major changes in the corporation may not be taken through officer action alone. Although some states still require the traditional officer roles to be filled (president, vice president, secretary, and treasurer), the current trend is to allow the titles and responsibilities of the officers to be set by the bylaws or the board of directors.[5] Officers have both express and implied authority. Express authority comes from the bylaws or through a board of directors' resolution

---

[4]RMBCA § 8.08(a).

[5]*See* Del. Code Ann. tit. 8, § 142(a) (General Corporation Law).

Tim Cook, CEO of Apple, follows in Steve Jobs's shoes by using annual shareholders' meetings as an event to launch products. Paul Sakuma/ASSOCIATED PRESS

that gives specific authority to a particular officer. For example, the board of directors may pass a resolution authorizing the treasurer of a corporation to open a bank account or to start a money market account for surplus cash on hand. Officers may also have inherent authority, based on their position, to act on behalf of the corporation. Recall from Chapter 10, "Agency," that certain corporate officers have *implied authority* to be an agent of the corporation. This is an important concept in corporate law because it helps define the powers of corporate officers.

President Traditionally, the president has the implied power to bind the corporation in ordinary business operation transactions and to oversee nonofficer employees. Therefore, the president of a manufacturing corporation has the authority to enter into a distribution contract with wholesalers or to hire and fire employees.

Vice President Depending on the size and scope of the corporation, the vice president may have some limited implied authority. For example, a vice president for marketing would likely have implied authority to bind the corporation to a vendor of advertising. The implied authority of a vice president may also include additional powers to bind the corporation in ordinary business transactions if such authority is a routine practice in a certain industry.

Treasurer Aside from the routine tasks of collecting the accounts receivable and paying the accounts payable, the treasurer has little or no other implied authority.

Secretary The secretary has the implied authority to certify the records and resolutions of the company. When the board of directors passes a resolution, it is the secretary who affixes his signature to it, which confirms that the document is genuine. Third parties in a particular transaction may rely on this certification. For example, suppose that

Antonin, the secretary of MusicCo, delivers a forged resolution to a bank that authorizes MusicCo to borrow $50,000. The resolution has Antonin's signature affixed to it with a statement that the resolution was duly passed at a board of directors' meeting. The bank loans the money to MusicCo based on the resolution. MusicCo then becomes financially insolvent and attempts to avoid repaying the loan on the basis that MusicCo's directors did not in fact authorize the loan. The bank would prevail because, by virtue of Antonin's implied authority, it had the right to rely on Antonin's certification as secretary.[6]

Fiduciary Duties of Officers and Directors

Officers, directors, and controlling shareholders of a corporation (known as *insiders*) are in a unique position of trust to guide the corporation in a certain direction. Officers and directors owe the corporation's shareholders several well-defined fiduciary duties: the **duty of care** and the **duty of loyalty**. Breaching these duties may result in *personal liability* for the officer or director. Officers and directors must act carefully when they act on behalf of the corporation and must also not put their *own* interests ahead of the corporation's interests. The duty of loyalty also applies to *controlling shareholders* in relation to other shareholders. The duty of care is tempered by a protection for officers and directors when they act in good faith and yet make an unwise decision that results in some loss to the corporation. This protection is known as the *business judgment rule*.

Duty of Care Fundamentally, officers and directors must exercise the degree of skill, diligence, and care that a reasonably prudent person would exercise under the same circumstances. Most states define the duty of care through a three-part test. First, the officers and directors must always act in good faith. Second, they must also act with the care that an objectively prudent person in a like position would exercise under similar circumstances. Third, they must carry out their duties in a manner that is reasonably calculated to advance the best interests of the corporation. This duty applies to all directors and officers regardless of whether the corporation is large or small or whether the directors are paid or unpaid. Courts have held that a director breaches her duty of care when she fails to fulfill her role in oversight. This may occur in several ways:

- *Negligence:* When a director doesn't read reports, financial records, or other information provided by the corporation or doesn't attend meetings, this weighs heavily in favor of a finding of a breach of duty.
- *Failure to act with diligence:* Directors have the obligation to question any suspicious activity by the corporation or its officers. If the issue is outside their field, they must investigate it by consulting outside experts (such as a CPA or an attorney). They must attempt to have more than just a cursory understanding of the inner workings of the corporation and must monitor the corporation and the business practices of its officers.
- *Rubber stamp:* Directors have the duty to be sure that any transaction proposed by the officers (or by other directors) is, from the *best information* available to them at the time, in the best interest of the corporation and is not imprudent. They have a duty to determine whether the proposed action will impact the corporation in a negative way, and thus they cannot act as a "rubber stamp." If they disagree with a decision being made by other directors, they must register their dissent in the record of the meeting.

This is not to say that directors cannot rely on the expertise and assurances of others. Under the RMBCA, directors still fulfill their duty of care even when they do not personally verify the records or other information provided to them by officers or outside experts. A director may rely on opinions, reports, statements, and financial records if they

---

[6]Based on *In re Drive-In Development Corporation*, 371 F.2d 217 (7th Cir. 1966).

are presented by the officers of a corporation whom the director "reasonably believes . . . to be reliable and competent in these matters."[7] Directors may also rely on professionals such as attorneys and auditors or on board committees so long as that reliance is reasonable in terms of the directors' belief in the source's competence.

Business Judgment Rule

LO 15-7
Apply the business judgment rule to an alleged breach of fiduciary duty by an insider.

At first glance, the duty of care looks onerous. When a corporation engages in a certain transaction or in a certain course of conduct that generates losses, some shareholders may inevitably believe it was the fault of the directors' lack of care. The business judgment rule protects officers and directors from liability for decisions that may have been unwise but did not breach the duty of care. This rule insulates directors and officers from liability when, despite being based on reasonable information at the time, a transaction or course of action turns out badly from the standpoint of the corporation. Directors and officers often seek protection of this rule when an individual shareholder or group of shareholders files a lawsuit against them.

Although the RMBCA does not include a business judgment rule, every state has adopted the rule (by either including it in their statutes or recognizing its applicability in common law) as a defense to a breach-of-the-duty-of-care claim against a director. Fundamentally, directors must have acted in *good faith* to insulate themselves from liability for breach of care. Most courts define good faith by requiring directors and officers to clear three hurdles in order to obtain the protection of the business judgment rule:

- *No private interest:* In order to claim protection under the business judgment rule, the director must have had no financial self-interest in the disputed transaction or decision. Being a shareholder of a merging company or a supplier to a corporation may be dangerous territory for a director because a transaction with the merger partner or supplier may have some degree of self-dealing contamination that will deprive the director of any business judgment rule protection.

- *Best information:* An important prerequisite to protection by the business judgment rule is the requirement that directors be active in keeping themselves informed on all material aspects of the decision or transaction at issue. Directors and officers have a duty to be diligent in investigating any proposal, decision, or transaction, and this includes, when appropriate, consulting outside experts.

- *Rational belief:* The third requirement that directors and officers must meet in order to be protected under the rule is that the decision or approval of the transaction must have been the product of some reasoned decision making based on rational beliefs. This rational-belief requirement means that courts focus on the process of the decision making. Directors' and officers' decision-making procedures must be set up in a way that allows careful decisions to be made regarding the best interests of the corporation. Boards will often form committees to carry out their work, and often this committee structure itself is a significant step in establishing a procedure that helps preserve the business judgment rule protection.

> **KEY POINT**
>
> To have protection under the business judgment rule, directors and officers must exercise good faith, have no private financial self-interest, and use diligence to acquire the best material information related to a proposed decision.

Despite the fact that Delaware is generally thought of as a state that has fairly broad business judgment rule protection, Landmark Case 15.2, which sent shockwaves through corporate boardrooms nationwide, illustrates the importance of the duty to investigate all *material* facts of a proposed transaction before approving it.

---

[7]RMBCA § 8.30(b).

Self-Check Business Judgment Rule

Will these directors be protected by the business judgment rule?

1. Directors of a bank consult with legal, banking, and industry experts concerning a proposed merger. They set up a directors' subcommittee to investigate the merger and ultimately approve moving ahead after two months of deliberation. The day after the merger, a substantial drop in the stock price of the bank takes place and shareholders lose nearly 30 percent of the value of their investment.
2. The company president recommends to the board that NewCo hire Dewey, Cheatham, and Howe as its auditing firm. In the same meeting as the recommendation, the directors approve the firm. One year later, it is revealed that the audits were fraudulent and that the president has been looting the company, resulting in several millions of dollars in losses.
3. Shareholders of a major-league baseball franchise corporation sue the directors because the team refuses to schedule night games. The shareholders argue that the revenue lost from night games is responsible for the poor financial performance of the company. The directors refuse to schedule night games because they believe it would have a deteriorating effect on the neighborhood.
4. The company vice president recommends that the directors of the corporation purchase a parcel of prime real estate on which to build a new office building for the company. Four of the six directors are members of a real estate partnership that owns that property. Without any disclosures, the directors vote unanimously to approve the purchase, and the decision is made the same day as the vice president's recommendation. One month later, it is revealed that the price paid by the corporation was 20 percent above fair market value for the property.

Answers to this Self-Check are provided at the end of the chapter.

LANDMARK CASE 15.2 Smith v. Van Gorkom, 488 A.2d 858 (Del. 1985)

FACT SUMMARY Van Gorkom was an officer, director, and shareholder of Trans Union Corporation. Trans Union's stock was traded on the New York Stock Exchange (NYSE) and had never sold for higher than $39 per share. Prior to announcing his retirement, Van Gorkom sought to sell his shares to Pritzker, an individual investor, for $55 per share. Because Van Gorkhom's holdings in Trans Union were substantial, he was required to get the approval of Trans Union's board of directors for the sale to Pritzker. Van Gorkom proposed the sale to the board in an oral presentation. Most of the other officers opposed the sale on the basis that the price was too low given the value of the company. Indeed, the chief financial officer advised the directors that the price was in the "low range." The directors did not review the terms of the Van Gorkom–Pritzker agreement, did not perform any valuation analysis on the company, and did not consult any of the company's investment bankers. After Van Gorkom pressured the directors by informing them that Pritzker would withdraw the offer within three days, the board deliberated for several hours and approved the transaction. A group of shareholders brought a lawsuit against the directors of Trans Union based on a breach of the duty of care that resulted in the stock being sold at a value well under its actual worth. The directors sought protection under the business judgment rule, claiming they relied on Van Gorkom's representations and the NYSE stock price.

SYNOPSIS OF DECISION AND OPINION The Delaware Supreme Court ruled *against* the directors, holding that they could not be afforded the protection of the business judgment rule. The court's

(continued)

decision was primarily based on the conclusion that the directors had failed to obtain all material information and had not conducted any investigation about the transaction. The court pointed to the fact that the board never even reviewed the Van Gorkom–Pritzker agreement, nor had the board undertaken anything more than a cursory inquiry into the actual value of the corporation.

WORDS OF THE COURT: Duty to Be Informed

"We do not say that the Board of Directors was not entitled to give some credence to Van Gorkom's representation that $55 was an adequate or fair price. [T]he directors were entitled to rely upon their chairman's opinion of value and adequacy, provided that such opinion was reached on a sound basis. Here, the issue is whether the directors informed themselves as to all information that was reasonably available to them. Had they done so, they would have learned of the source and derivation of the $55 price and could not reasonably have relied thereupon in good faith.

"None of the directors, management or outside, were investment bankers or financial analysts. Yet the Board did not consider recessing the meeting until a later hour that day (or requesting an extension of Pritzker's deadline) to give it time to elicit more information as to the sufficiency of the offer, either from inside management or from Trans Union's own investment banker, Salomon Brothers, whose Chicago specialist in merger and acquisitions was known to the Board and familiar with Trans Union's affairs. Thus, the record compels the conclusion that the Board lacked valuation information adequate to reach an informed business judgment as to the fairness of $55 per share for sale of the Company."

Case Questions

1. Assume that the directors were highly sophisticated business executives. Should they have to consult others on issues about which they already have sufficient knowledge (such as the company's valuation)?
2. The court ruled that the directors were liable because they did not obtain "material" information. Give some examples of what may constitute material information.
3. *Focus on Critical Thinking:* In response to Van Gorkom, many states (including Delaware) passed statutes that extended the scope of the business judgment defense. Should the business judgment rule protect directors even when they fail to verify the statements of internal management concerning a corporate transaction that is being touted to officers as advantageous to the corporation?

Duty of Loyalty

An additional fiduciary duty owed to shareholders by officers, directors, and controlling shareholders is the *duty of loyalty*. Shareholders that have some degree of control over corporate decisions also owe this duty, and it is principally a duty intended to prevent oppression of minority shareholders. The duty of loyalty is primarily focused on providing protection to shareholders when a transaction occurs in which the possibility of self-dealing is present.

Prohibition against Certain Self-Dealing

Self-dealing in this context occurs when an officer, director, or controlling shareholder has a personal financial stake in a transaction that the corporation is engaged in and that individual helps to influence the advancement of the transaction. For example, recall our working hypothetical structure for Widget Manufacturing Inc.:

Name	Percentage of Total Stock Owned	Role
Abel	10	Officer, director, shareholder
Baker	10	Officer, director, shareholder
Cain	20	Director, shareholder
David	20	Shareholder
Elias	40	Shareholder

Suppose that Cain owns port properties and leases warehouse space to industries using the port. Abel, as president of the corporation, searches for a warehouse for Widget Manufacturing's storage needs, and he identifies several potential properties. Abel writes a report for the board of directors describing the advantages and disadvantages of each property. Because Cain is an officer and director, this transaction has at least the *potential* to conflict with the best financial interests of the corporation. This potential for conflict, however, is not a breach of the duty of loyalty automatically. The RMBCA provides that a self-dealing transaction is not a breach of the duty of loyalty so long as a majority of disinterested parties (those with no self-interest conflicts) approve it after *disclosure* of the conflict.[8] In the Widget Manufacturing example, Cain would simply need to disclose his interest in the property and abstain from influencing other directors about the vote. After disclosure, the vote of Abel and Baker to approve the transaction insulates Cain from a charge of breaching his duty of loyalty to Widget's other shareholders.

Even if the transaction was not formally approved as provided in the RMBCA, the modern trend has been for courts to allow such transactions so long as they are, under the circumstances, fair to the corporation and performed in good faith.

Corporate Opportunity Doctrine The duty of loyalty also requires disclosure and good faith when an insider (i.e., director, officer, or controlling shareholder) learns of a potentially lucrative business opportunity that could enrich her individually but is related to the corporation's business. That is, an insider may not *usurp* for herself a business opportunity that belongs to the corporation or would benefit the corporation in some direct way.

To determine when an opportunity belongs to a corporation and is therefore off-limits to insiders who are officers, directors, or controlling shareholders (unless they have followed specific disclosure steps), courts use several questions: (1) Can the corporation realistically expect to seize and develop the opportunity? (This is sometimes called the "reasonable expectations" test.) (2) Is it fair to the corporation's shareholders to allow another to usurp a certain interest? (3) Is the opportunity closely related to the corporation's existing or prospective business activities? In answering these questions, courts will take into consideration whether the officer, director, or controlling shareholder learned of the opportunity because of his role in the corporation and whether a party used corporate resources to take advantage of the opportunity. In Case 15.3, a state appellate court analyzes a corporate opportunity claim.

Legal Speak >))

Usurp
In the context of the corporate opportunity doctrine, to *usurp* is to seize a particular opportunity for oneself when the opportunity rightfully belongs to the corporation.

CASE 15.3 Ebenezer United Methodist Church v. Riverwalk Development Phase II, 45 A.3d 883 (Md. Ct. Spec. App. 2012)

FACT SUMMARY Green was a real estate developer who was president and part-owner of a Synvest Real Estate Trust (Synvest). Synvest's practice was to hold undeveloped property in its own name while it arranged construction financing, then transfer the property to a newly created entity once the funds had been secured and development could begin. In the course of this business, Synvest came to own certain properties that it prepared for construction and conveyed to a new entity known as River Walk Development (Riverwalk I). In 2002, Ebenezer United Methodist Church (EUMC) purchased a 50 percent interest in Riverwalk I for $250,000, and construction commenced soon afterwards.

(continued)

---

[8]RMBCA § 8.60.

At some point in time before EUMC completed its investment in Riverwalk I, it learned that Synvest had come to own a new 32-acre parcel now at the center of this dispute and six additional lots in the same county as Riverwalk I. In 2003, Synvest formed River Walk Development Phase Two (Riverwalk II), which purchased the 32-acre parcel later that month. In 2004, Green caused Riverwalk I, Riverwalk II, and a third entity to enter into a line-of-credit agreement for $2.1 million for the three entities, collectively.

Riverwalk I developed and sold several units and conveyed the proceeds to EUMC. Eventually Synvest repurchased EUMC's interest, which yielded EUMC a profit of $30,000 on its $250,000 investment. Only after this business had concluded did EUMC learn of the line-of-credit agreement that had been tied to the Riverwalk I assets. EUMC filed suit against Green, Synvest, and Riverwalk II, alleging that they violated the corporate opportunity doctrine by failing to disclose the additional real estate transaction involving a new, 32-acre parcel, transferring it secretly to Riverwalk II, a new entity solely owned by Green. EUMC claimed that it should share in any profits of Riverwalk II. The trial court ruled in favor of Green/Riverwalk II and EUMC appealed.

SYNOPSIS OF DECISION AND OPINION The Maryland Court of Special Appeals upheld the trial court's judgment in favor of Green/Riverwalk II. While the court acknowledged that Green owed fiduciary duties to Riverwalk I and the other members, including the duty not to exclude principals from corporate opportunities, the court used the reasonable expectations test to determine if the corporate opportunity was usurped. It held that a reasonable expectation or interest in a corporate opportunity requires something more than mere proximity of geography, management, or finance.

WORDS OF THE COURT: Reasonable Expectations Test "This test focuses on whether the corporation could realistically expect to seize and develop the opportunity. If so, the director or officer may not appropriate it and thereby frustrate the corporate purpose. If the opportunity is a corporate one, then the director or officer to whom it is presented or who becomes aware of it must first present it to the corporation, before pursuing it himself. Only if the corporation rejects the opportunity may a director or officer exploit it for his own benefit. . . . [P]rojects related by management are not automatic mutual corporate opportunities. Joint financial risk is simply too common to give rise to any particularized interest or expectancy."

Case Questions

1. Why did EUMC believe that it was entitled to become a partner in Riverwalk II?
2. EUMC reaped a substantial profit from its Riverwalk I investment. Should that be a factor in the court's analysis? Why or why not?
3. *Focus on Critical Thinking:* What other fiduciary duties may Green have breached given these facts? Explain. Could Green assert the business judgment rule as a defense?

Officers, directors, and controlling shareholders who become aware of a business opportunity belonging to the corporation must disclose the opportunity to the corporation in total. That is, all plans and relevant information on the opportunity must be presented to the board of directors. If the board, for whatever reasons, rejects the opportunity, the insider is then free to pursue the opportunity with no fear of liability.

For example, in our Widget Manufacturing Inc. example, suppose that the directors all discuss the need for a new warehouse facility and they authorize Abel to find a suitable lot on which to build. While Abel pursues this objective, Cain's neighbor makes him aware of a parcel of land that would fit Widget's needs in terms of space, zoning, workforce population, access, and price. Cain purchases the property for himself at a price of $100,000. He then tells a commercial real estate broker to contact Abel and advise him that the property is on the market for $200,000. In this case, because Cain was an insider who knew of a business opportunity that would benefit Widget Manufacturing and knew that the corporation was in the market for a parcel of land, he had an obligation to disclose the opportunity to the corporation first rather than buying it.

However, suppose that, instead of buying the lot, Cain discloses the opportunity to the corporation's board of directors. If the directors reject that opportunity to purchase, then Cain is free to make the purchase and even to sell it or lease it to Widget Manufacturing at a profit. Failing to follow the disclosure rules is a breach of the duty of loyalty.

CONCEPT SUMMARY Fiduciary Duties of Officers, Directors, and Controlling Shareholders

- Officers, directors, and controlling shareholders (sometimes called *insiders*) owe corporate shareholders the fiduciary duties of care (use of skill, diligence, and care to advance the best interests of the corporation) and loyalty (prohibition against self-dealing or conflicts of interest).
- The business judgment rule protects insiders from liability for breach of the duty of care so long as the insider acted in good faith, was diligent about making a well-informed decision, and had no financial self-interest in the decision.

Breach-of-Fiduciary-Duty Lawsuits by Shareholders

LO 15-8

Distinguish between a shareholder derivative suit and a direct action suit.

One objective of this chapter is to focus on the rights of shareholders and the standards for fiduciary duties owed to shareholders by insiders such as officers, directors, and controlling shareholders. But how do shareholders actually enforce their rights in a corporation? Shareholders enforce their rights and fiduciary duties through the use of a lawsuit in the form of a shareholder's *derivative action* or a shareholder's *direct action*.

In a derivative suit, an individual shareholder (or a group of shareholders) brings a lawsuit against an insider in the name of the corporation itself. Most derivative lawsuits are brought because the shareholder alleges a breach of fiduciary duty of care or loyalty by an insider. There are several special procedural requirements for a derivative action, but the most important of them is that the shareholders must first make a formal demand on the board of directors to take corrective action and must allow sufficient time for correction. Only if the board refuses to act may the shareholder commence a derivative suit.

Shareholders may also file a direct action (where the shareholder is bringing suit on her own behalf) in cases where the shareholder alleges oppression of minority shareholders or where a question of voting rights or shareholder inspection rights arises.

Limiting Director Liability
In response to a growing number of director liability lawsuits for breach of the duty of care, some states have enacted statutory protections. States have taken a variety of approaches including: (1) allowing shareholders to use the corporate charter to eliminate or reduce directors' personal liability so long as the the director acted in good faith;[9] (2) lowering the requirements of the standard of care so that only *egregious* conduct triggers personal liability;[10] and (3) placing a monetary limit on damages that may be recovered against a director or officer.[11]

---

[9] See, for example, Delaware GCL Section 102(b)(7).
[10] Ohio Code Section 1701.59.
[11] Va. Code Section 13.1-692.1.

LO 15-9

Identify circumstances under which a court will pierce the veil and explain the impact on the principals.

Piercing the Corporate Veil

A court will sometimes discard the corporate veil when it believes that fairness demands doing so. Although there is no single rule on when the corporate entity may be disregarded, courts typically examine the entire spectrum of facts to determine whether the corporate form has been abused. However, four factors in particular have been adopted by many courts as guideposts for determining whether to pierce the corporate veil.

- *Inadequate capitalization:* One important factor courts examine in deciding whether to pierce the veil is whether or not a corporation has been adequately capitalized. When a corporation is merely a shell with nothing invested, courts are inclined to pierce the corporate veil as a matter of fairness. Similarly, if the corporation had initial capitalization, but the shareholders siphoned the profits and assets, a court will view it as an inadequately capitalized corporation.

- *Nature of the claim:* When the claim involves a voluntary creditor, such as a trade creditor who provides a corporation with inventory based on credit, courts are generally not inclined to pierce the corporate veil because the creditor had an opportunity to mitigate the risk of loss (e.g., by requiring a personal guarantee). On the other hand, courts are more likely to pierce the corporate veil when the claim involves some sort of tort, such as negligence by the corporation's employees or even the principals themselves. This is essentially because the victims of negligence (such as a pedestrian struck by a delivery truck operated by a corporate employee) have become *involuntary* creditors and have never had the opportunity to mitigate the risk of loss.

- *Evidence of fraud or wrongdoing:* If the shareholders, officers, or directors have committed fraud or have engaged in some type of serious and willful wrongdoing, this is an important factor in a court's decision to pierce the corporate veil. Misrepresentations to creditors regarding important facts about the financial condition of the company or lying to investors about potential liabilities of the corporation are examples of fraud that could lead to a piercing of the veil.

- *Failure to follow corporate formalities:* Another important factor used by the courts in deciding whether piercing the veil is appropriate is the corporation's adherence to the statutes, rules, and practices governing a corporation. For example, corporations that file articles of incorporation but never bother to follow up with required or standard practices are in danger of losing their corporate veil protection. Specifically, courts may look at whether there is a proper separation between the corporation and the individual shareholder(s), whether stock certificates were ever issued, whether shareholders' meetings were ever held, and whether proper corporate records (such as minutes of the meetings, resolutions, and a stock register) were maintained. For example, suppose that two brothers, Abel and Cain, form AC Inc. by filing articles of incorporation. Because they are brothers, they decide to split the profits 50-50 and, wishing to save the expense of hiring an attorney, they fail to keep up with corporate formalities after the articles have been filed. In the event that a claim is made against AC Inc., Abel and Cain have potentially exposed their personal assets to claimants if AC Inc. does not have sufficient assets to pay the claim.

> **KEY POINT**
>
> The corporate veil that shields the personal assets of principals from corporate debts and liabilities may be pierced in certain cases of inadequate capitalization, fraud, or failure to follow corporate formalities.

In Case 15.4, an appellate court analyzes a claim in which one party has asked the court to pierce the corporate veil.

CASE 15.4 Florence Cement Co. v. Vittraino, 292 Mich. App. 461 (2011)

FACT SUMMARY Shelby Property Investors (Shelby) was a company engaged in developing and selling residential real estate that was chiefly managed by Essad, one of three principals in the entity. Florence Cement Company (Florence) contracted with Shelby to perform concrete and asphalt work at one of Shelby's properties. Ultimately, Shelby's real estate venture did not yield a profit, but Shelby was able to pay all subcontractors on the job except one—Florence. When Florence sued to recover $114,557 it was owed, Shelby was without assets. Florence sought to pierce Shelby's corporate veil and hold the principals personally liable. Florence argued that the evidence suggested that Shelby (1) was not an authentic business entity because of the principals' mixing of personal and business transactions and (2) had engaged in fraud by misrepresenting facts to its bank concerning a loan used to pay subcontractors. The trial court ruled that piercing the corporate veil was not warranted.

SYNOPSIS OF DECISION AND OPINION The Court of Appeals of Michigan reversed the trial court's decision and ruled in favor of Florence on the issue of piercing the corporate veil. The court pointed to Shelby's company history, which indicated that the principals treated their own liabilities as Shelby's liabilities and vice versa and intentionally undercapitalized Shelby, causing Shelby to be continuously insolvent, including at the time it contracted with Florence. Essad also falsified the sworn statement in the final loan draw request to the bank, and this constituted use of Shelby for fraudulent purposes. Therefore, Florence satisfied the elements for piercing the corporate veil.

WORDS OF THE COURT: Factors Favoring Corporate Veil Piercing "Shelby was defendants' alter ego. [The principals] made no distinction between their own debts and Shelby's debts. [The principals] did not treat Shelby as a separate entity. Such a failure is a hallmark of a claim for piercing the corporate veil. Essentially, where members do not treat an artificial entity as separate from themselves, neither will this Court.

"The facts of this case further show that defendants used Shelby to commit a wrong or fraud. Essad falsified the sworn statement that he submitted to [the bank] for the final draw of the remaining loan proceeds. It is undisputed that the request for the draw stated that Shelby "OWES NO MONEY FOR THE IMPROVEMENT OTHER THAN AS SET FORTH ABOVE." However, Essad knew that Shelby owed Florence more than the $142,000 indicated on this request for the draw because Essad had signed the contract with Florence on behalf of Shelby. Thus, the evidence overwhelmingly shows that Essad knowingly falsified the request for the draw, which amounted to fraud. And, as such, Essad clearly used Shelby to commit a wrong or fraud."

Case Questions

1. What did the court mean when it ruled that Shelby was the defendants' "alter ego"? How did that determination impact the court's decision?
2. If Essad had not committed the fraudulent bank transaction, would the court have allowed the veil to be pierced? Why or why not?
3. *Focus on Critical Thinking:* What steps could Shelby's principals have taken to help prevent any piercing of their corporate veil?

KEY TERMS

Corporation p. 501   A fictitious legal entity that exists as an independent "person" separate from its principals.

Business corporation law p. 501   Often the title for a specific state law that covers such matters as the structure of the corporation, oversight of the activity of the corporation's managers, rights of the principals in the case of the sale of assets or ownership interests, annual reporting requirements, and other issues that affect the internal rules of the business venture.

Revised Model Business Corporation Act (RMBCA) p. 501   Model act drafted by the American Law Institute and adopted by over half of the states as a template for compiling their own statutes governing corporations.

Privately held corporation p. 501 A corporation that does not sell ownership interests through sales via a broker to the general public or to financial institutions or investors.

Articles of incorporation p. 502 The document filed with a state authority that sets in motion the incorporation process; includes the corporation's name and purpose, the number of shares issued, and the address of the corporation's headquarters.

Business judgment rule p. 504 A principle that protects corporate officers and directors from liability when they have made an unwise decision that results in a loss to the corporation, but they have acted in good faith, had no private financial self-interest, and used diligence to acquire the best information related to the decision.

Shareholders p. 506 The owners of a corporation; act principally through electing and removing directors and approving or withholding approval of major corporate decisions.

Corporate veil p. 506 The liability protection afforded to shareholders, directors, and officers of a corporation whereby they are insulated from personal liability in the event that the corporation runs up large debts or suffers some liability.

Piercing the corporate veil p. 507 Action in which a court discards the corporate veil and holds some or all of the shareholders personally liable because fairness demands doing so in certain cases of inadequate capitalization, fraud, and failure to follow corporate formalities.

Directors p. 509 Individuals responsible for oversight and management of the corporation's course of direction.

Officers p. 509 Individuals appointed by the board of directors to carry out the directors' set course of direction through management of the day-to-day operations of the business.

Duty of care p. 513 A fiduciary duty owed to shareholders by officers and directors; requires that the fiduciaries exercise the degree of skill, diligence, and care that a reasonably prudent person would exercise under the same circumstances, acting in good faith and in a manner that is reasonably calculated to advance the best interests of the corporation.

Duty of loyalty p. 513 A fiduciary duty owed to shareholders by officers, directors, and controlling shareholders; requires that the fiduciaries put the corporation's interests ahead of their own and do not engage in self-dealing or conflicts of interest.

CHAPTER REVIEW QUESTIONS

1. The formation of a corporation is governed by _____.
    a. Federal statutes
    b. State statutes
    c. Federal regulations
    d. State common law

2. Fresh Farm Corporation (FFC) operates 50 produce stands across Georgia and 100 stands in its home state of Florida. It is incorporated in Florida. In Florida, what category of corporation does FFC fall into?
    a. Domestic
    b. Foreign
    c. Off-shore
    d. Nonprofit

3. Corporations that do not sell ownership interests through a broker to the general public or financial institutions are categorized as _____.
    a. Privately held
    b. Publicly held
    c. Public interest
    d. Equity firms

4. Which of the following are typically handled at the initial organizational meeting?
    I. Officers and directors are appointed/elected.
    II. Shares of stock are issued.
    III. Personal guarantees are made for all corporate debt.
    IV. Articles of incorporation are filed.
    a. I and II
    b. I, II, and III
    c. II, III, and IV
    d. I, III, and IV

5. Which of the following is <u>not</u> considered a factor by a court when judging whether fairness demands that the corporate veil should be pierced?
    a. Inadequate capitalization
    b. Fraudulent transactions by the principals
    c. The personal wealth of the principals
    d. Failure to follow corporate formalities

Answers and explanations are provided at the end of this chapter.

THEORY TO PRACTICE

Adams and Barker were two individual scientists engaged in research related to inventing a patentable pharmaceutical product. Once they had gained critical mass for the project, they convinced Barker's old college roommate, Cornelius, to invest $100,000 in exchange for an ownership share in a newly formed company called Pharma Corporation (Pharma). The parties agreed that Adams and Barker would continue product development until the company was ready to apply for a patent and then Cornelius would use his contacts to find a manufacturer to produce and market the patented drug. Pharma was structured as follows:

Name	Stock Owned (%)	Role
Adams	35	President, director
Barker	35	Vice president and secretary, director
Cornelius	30	Shareholder

The parties hired counsel to incorporate Pharma, issue stock certificates, and draft bylaws. The corporate records were then turned over to Barker, and she filed them in her desk drawer. No additional formalities were followed, and the records were not maintained, nor were any directors' or shareholders' meetings held.

In year 2, Pharma's application for a patent was rejected. The rejection required Adams and Barker to hire an additional expert to help with research and put the project behind by approximately 16 months. Adams hired Elliot, a well-known scientist, to help with the project. At this point, though, Pharma's financial resources were drying up. Trying to keep the company afloat, Adams began to pay certain Pharma bills with his personal credit card, and Barker sometimes wrote personal checks for lab equipment.

1. What category of corporation is Pharma, and what are the options in terms of structure and raising capital?
2. Is Pharma eligible for S corporation status? If one of the shareholders objected, could the other two vote to become an S corporation without the third?
3. Did Adams have the right to hire Elliot without the others' consent? Suppose that Cornelius believes that Elliot is not a good hire for Pharma. Can he fire Elliot?

In year 3, the financial condition of Pharma continued to worsen. A representative of the dominant pharmaceutical company in the market, Multi-Drug (MD), approached Adams and Barker with an acquisition offer. MD offered to pay $50,000 to buy all of Pharma's assets and offered a five-year employment agreement with MD to both Adams and Barker. On the same day as the offer, Adams and Barker sent a one-page e-mail to Cornelius, informing him that they had voted to approve the sale of assets of Pharma to MD and the transaction would take place in one business day.

4. Suppose Cornelius is unhappy with the transaction. Does he have any say in the matter? Does he have the power to stop the sale?
5. Have Adams and Barker breached their fiduciary duties to Cornelius? If so, which duties, specifically, and how were they breached?
6. Are Adams and Barker protected by the business judgment rule? Why or why not?
7. What type of lawsuit, derivative or direct, would be filed by Cornelius to
    a. Force Adams and Barker to have a shareholders' meeting and formal vote?
    b. Recover against Adams and Barker for damages Cornelius suffered as a result of an alleged breach of duty?

LEGAL STRATEGY 101

Facebook, Inc.

The movie *The Social Network* depicts the series of events leading up to the founding of Facebook, including the moment Facebook decided to become a Delaware corporation . . .

In brief, Harvard sophomore Mark Zuckerberg launched "The Facebook" in February 2004.[12] A few months later, Zuckerberg moved to Palo Alto, California, in order to devote his efforts full time to his new venture. By the middle of the summer of 2004—just a few months after launching the website from his dorm room—angel

Facebook logo.   Sean Gallup/Getty Images

investor Peter Thiel of Clarium Capital agreed to invest $500,000 in Zuckerberg's start-up business.

Here is how the movie reenacts this pivotal event (Peter Thiel's angel investment) in the founding of Facebook:[13]

PETER
"We took a look at everything and congratulations. We're gonna start you off with a $500,000 investment. Maurice is gonna talk to you about some corporate restructuring."

MAURICE
"We'll file as a corporation in Delaware and come up with a stock structure that allows for new investors."

At the time Peter Thiel made his angel investment, Facebook was a limited liability company registered in the state of Florida. So, why did Peter Thiel want to restructure Facebook as a Delaware corporation as a condition of his investment?

One reason is Delaware's modern and flexible General Corporation Law. Delaware was one of the first legal jurisdictions in the world to enact streamlined incorporation procedures, allowing anyone to create a corporation simply by raising money and filing the necessary articles of incorporation with the state's Secretary of State.

Another reason is Delaware's Court of Chancery, a 220-year-old business court that has decided most of the leading cases in modern U.S. corporation case law. Moreover, the Court of Chancery is a "court of equity," not a "court of law." As a result, business cases are decided by judges, called chancellors, and not by juries.

Today, more than 50 percent of publicly traded corporations in the United States (like Facebook, which is listed on NASDAQ)—and more than 60 percent of all Fortune 500 companies worldwide—are incorporated in Delaware.[14]

CRITICAL THINKING QUESTION

Do some independent research on the Internet. What are some of the most important corporation law cases that have been decided by the Delaware Court of Chancery? Should *all* businesses incorporate in Delaware? Why or why not?

---

[12] Alan J. Tabak, *Hundreds Register for New Facebook Website,* Harv. Crimson, Feb. 9, 2004.

[13] *The Social Network* (screenplay by Aaron Sorkin, not dated), p. 138.

[14] *About Agency,* State of Del.: Dep't of State: Div. of Corps. (not dated), corp.delaware.gov.

MANAGER'S CHALLENGE

In the Theory to Practice problem, the principals have made a series of errors that could result in the piercing of the corporate veil. Corporations of all sizes can make similar mistakes if they are not diligent. Suppose that you receive an e-mail from a senior manager who has just read a newspaper article about the liability of one company's principals in a case in which the court decided to pierce the corporate veil. She asks you to draft a two-page memorandum that recommends a standard operating procedure and policy aimed at preserving your company's corporate veil. Use the mistakes made by Pharma as one guide for avoiding potential liability.

See Connect for Manager's Challenge sample answers.

CASE SUMMARY 15.1 Miner v. Fashion Enterprises, Inc., 794 N.E.2d 902 (2003)

PIERCING THE CORPORATE VEIL

Karen Lynn, Inc. (Lynn Corporation), was a wholly owned subsidiary of Fashion Enterprises, Inc. This meant that the sole shareholder of Lynn Corporation was the corporate entity of Fashion Enterprises, Inc. Lynn Corporation entered into a 10-year lease for retail space in Chicago with Miner, providing neither personal guarantees nor any guarantee by Fashion Enterprises. The company defaulted on the lease by not making rental payments, and Miner obtained a court judgment against Lynn Corporation. The corporation was without assets, and Miner asked the court to pierce the corporate veil and allow the judgment to be enforced against its sole shareholder, Fashion Enterprises, Inc. The trial court dismissed the suit, holding that Miner was entitled to only the assets of Lynn Corporation. Miner appealed.

CASE QUESTIONS

1. Who prevails and why?
2. What factors would the court weigh in deciding whether to pierce the veil?

CASE SUMMARY 15.2 Goldman v. Chapman & Region Associates, 44 A.3d 938 (N.Y. 2007)

CORPORATE VEIL PROTECTION

Chapman was the sole shareholder, officer, and director of Region Associates (Region). In 2001, Goldman obtained a judgment against Region in the amount of $209,320 as a result of Goldman's lawsuit against Region (but not Chapman individually). Goldman attempted to collect the judgment from Region but was unsuccessful because Region was without any substantial assets. After exhausting all efforts to collect the judgment from Region, Goldman filed suit asking the court to allow him to pierce Region's corporate veil and collect the judgment from Chapman's personal assets.

CASE QUESTIONS

1. Who prevails and why?
2. Did Chapman use the law to perpetrate an injustice?
3. Is it fair that Goldman is stuck with a worthless judgment and that Chapman may simply start a new company?

CASE SUMMARY 15.3 Morrison v. Gugle, 142 Ohio App. 3d 244 (2001)

SHAREHOLDER RIGHTS

Morrison and Gugle incorporated a company, opened a retail store together, and agreed to a half ownership each. Each shareholder was an officer (Gugle as president, Morrison as secretary and treasurer), and each was a director. Additionally, each was an active employee of the business. Gugle and Morrison had a variety of business disputes, and eventually Gugle, as president, fired Morrison. After the termination, Morrison demanded the right to inspect corporate records and financial documents, but Gugle refused to provide any information or access to the records, citing her authority to do so as president of the corporation. Morrison sued Gugle for, among other counts, breach of fiduciary duty.

CASE QUESTIONS

1. Who prevails and why?
2. Does the president have the power to fire a fellow officer and director who is also half owner of the corporation?
3. What fiduciary duty, if any, was breached here?

CASE SUMMARY 15.4 Grobow v. Perot, 539 A.2d 180 (Del. 1988)

BUSINESS JUDGMENT RULE

H. Ross Perot became the single largest shareholder and a director of General Motors as a result of GM's acquisition of Perot's highly successful company Electronic Data Systems (EDS). A rift grew between Perot and GM's other directors, and after appointing a subcommittee of directors to study possible alternatives, GM's directors offered to purchase back Perot's stock at a significant premium over market value. In exchange for the payment, Perot agreed to leave his director's seat, not compete with any GM subsidiary (particularly EDS), and cease any criticism of GM's directors. A group of GM shareholders sued the directors under the theory that the directors had breached their fiduciary duty by wasting corporate assets in buying Perot's silence. The directors asserted the business judgment rule as a defense.

CASE QUESTIONS

1. Who prevails and why?
2. What fiduciary duty is at issue?

CASE SUMMARY 15.5 Burdick v. Koerner, 988 F. Supp. 1206 (E.D. Wis. 1998)

LIABILITY OF DIRECTORS

Koerner, Inc., was found to have violated a copyright owned by Burdick. Burdick brought suit against each of Koerner's directors on the basis that the directors had financially benefited from the copyright infringement and, therefore, were liable for the copyright infringement damages by virtue of their membership on the board of directors. The directors argued that there was no evidence of day-to-day involvement, intent, or any specific knowledge of the infringement by the directors and, thus, they were not personally liable.

CASE QUESTIONS

1. Who prevails and why?
2. Does the corporate veil protect directors in these circumstances?

 Self-Check ANSWERS Business Judgment Rule

1. Yes. The directors fulfilled their duties by consulting outside experts and appointing an oversight subcommittee. They acted in good faith and had a rational belief that the merger was in the interests of the company.
2. No. The directors have the obligation to investigate the auditing firm and not to rubber-stamp the decision of the president. This is either gross negligence or willful ignorance. Either way, the directors violated their duty of care and were not acting with the best information and, thus, cannot be shielded by the business judgment rule.
3. Yes. Even if the directors' explanation is a result of poor business judgment, it is not an act of bad faith and is done with a rational belief. Thus, the directors are protected by the business judgment rule.
4. No. The four directors violated the corporate opportunity doctrine by failing to disclose their financial interest in the real estate. This is an act of bad faith, and, therefore, those four directors are not shielded by the business judgment rule.

CHAPTER REVIEW QUESTIONS: Answers and Explanations

1. **b.** The formation of a corporation is exclusively a matter of state statutory law. While other aspects of corporation law may involve federal statutes, formation (such as filing the Articles of Incorporation) is accomplished at the state level. Therefore (a), (c), and (d) are incorrect.

2. **a.** The category of this corporation in its state of incorporation is domestic. (b) is wrong because foreign refers to an out-of-state business. (c) and (d) are not indicated in the question.

3. **a.** Privately held corporations, those that do not sell ownership interests through sales via a broker to the general public and financial institutions, are the most common category of corporation. (b) is wrong because it refers to publicly issued stock. (c) and (d) are wrong because they are not categories of corporations.

4. **a.** Elections and issuance of stock certificates are typically handled at the initial organizational meeting. (b), (c), and (d) are wrong because articles are filed before the initial meeting and personal guarantees are not an initial organizational matter.

5. **c.** When considering whether or not to pierce the corporate veil, courts do *not* consider the personal wealth or business judgment of the principals. (a), (b), and (d) are all factors used by courts, so they are incorrect.

CHAPTER 16

Regulation of Securities, Corporate Governance, and Financial Markets

©philsajonesen/Getty Images

Learning Objectives

After studying this chapter, students who have mastered the material will be able to:

16-1 Articulate the factors that differentiate the primary and secondary securities markets and list the laws that regulate them.

16-2 Apply the legal test for what constitutes a security.

16-3 Distinguish between classifications of equity and debt instruments and give an example of each.

16-4 Recognize the fundamental reason behind securities regulation and have a working knowledge of the legal process leading to issuance of original securities.

16-5 Describe the role of the Securities and Exchange Commission (SEC) in securities law compliance and enforcement.

16-6 List the major categories of securities offerings and identify transactions that are exempt from registration requirements.

16-7 Articulate the ethical and legal duties of corporate insiders.

16-8 Identify any defenses that may be asserted in a securities fraud suit against directors and officers and articulate the impact of the Private Securities Litigation Reform Act.

16-9 Explain the role of state blue-sky laws in securities regulation.

16-10 Demonstrate an awareness of the impact of the Sarbanes-Oxley Act on a corporation's officers and directors and its corporate governance.

16-11 Articulate key protections afforded by regulation of the financial markets.

The options that various business entities have for funding operations were covered in the previous chapters in this unit. This chapter focuses on the entities that sell ownership of a venture, known as *equity*, to investors who are interested in receiving a return on their investment based on the success of the business. Other entities find it advantageous to raise money by issuing *debt* instruments to public investors who wish to receive a fixed rate of return regardless of the profitability of the business entity. The issuance and trading of equity and debt instruments to public investors is highly regulated by federal and state *securities law*. In addition to securities regulation, federal laws impose mandates on corporate governance procedures in certain corporations and regulate broad financial markets.

The actions of business owners and managers who are engaged in raising capital or operate in the financial markets, as well as the corporate governance of publicly held entities, are subject to the scrutiny of regulatory authorities, and the consequences of noncompliance can be severe.

In this chapter, we discuss

- The background and scope of the primary and secondary securities markets and the role of regulatory agencies in enforcement.
- Classifications of securities and the rules that regulate their issuance, sale, and trading and, for qualified ventures, provide exemptions from certain securities laws.
- Legal mandates associated with corporate governance and regulation of the broader financial market.

FUNDAMENTALS OF THE SECURITIES MARKET

Securities transactions occur in two settings: (1) the *primary market*, in which businesses sell original issues and reissues of securities to raise capital, and (2) the *secondary market*, in which investors buy and sell issued securities among themselves. Both of these markets are governed by federal and state **securities law**, and various securities regulations require registration and disclosures and prescribe certain procedures intended to give investors confidence in the value of a particular security.

In the primary market, issuers raise capital by selling securities in public markets (to the general investment community) or in private placements (to limited groups of investors, such as venture capitalists or institutional investors). Issuing securities to the public markets for the first time is known as an *initial public offering (IPO)*. A company is said to "go public" when it decides to sell its voting common shares for the first time to outside investors through public markets such as the New York Stock Exchange (NYSE). The sale is made through the use of a mandatory registration statement that discloses important facts about the offering to potential investors.

In the secondary market, the trading of already-issued securities does not raise capital for the issuing business. Rather, investors sell to other investors in hopes of making a profit or preventing a loss. Once a company has sold shares to the public, it becomes subject to extensive reporting requirements to federal regulators. In theory, this secondary market provides cash flow for investors to continue their investments in primary markets.

Not all securities offerings and transactions are subject to the full burden of the federal and state regulatory schemes. Some securities transactions are exempt from full registration, and the law allows a fast-track system for securities that fall into the category of relatively small offerings or private placements. These exemptions are not automatic. The issuer or trader of a security must craft the security transaction to conform to the exemption requirements according to federal and state laws.

LO 16-1

Articulate the factors that differentiate the primary and secondary securities markets and list the laws that regulate them.

Defining a Security

Given the regulatory requirements that are triggered by a securities transaction, business owners and managers need a working knowledge of the instruments and transactions that federal and state laws define as securities and securities offerings. The regulations include registration and disclosure requirements, specific requirements to exempt a securities offering from the federal securities scheme, liability for misrepresentation or omissions in the offering materials, anti-fraud protections for buyers of securities, and criminal sanctions under certain circumstances for those engaged in fraud while selling or trading securities.

Federal Securities Law Stocks and bonds are perhaps the most well-known types of securities that are regulated by federal and state law. In addition, partnership interests, stock options, warrants, agreements to invest, participation in a pool of assets, use of crowdfunding resources, certain types of promissory notes, and many other arrangements that might commonly be considered investments are also regulated by securities laws.

Federal securities statutes define securities very broadly using a two-prong approach. First, the law recognizes specific forms of securities, such as notes, stocks, treasury stocks, transferable shares, bonds, and debentures. Second, securities statutes use a catchall definition of other investment transactions in a more generic sense, including participation in profit-sharing agreements; collateral trust certificates; preorganization certificates or subscriptions; investment contracts; and a fractional, undivided interest in gas, oil, or other mineral rights. In some cases, even a business plan, depending on the language and circumstances, may constitute a securities offering. Note that certain types of debt instruments, such as a promissory note secured by a home mortgage or by accounts receivable or other business assets, are *not* securities.

Companies may raise money through issuing securities to investors via a public exchange such as the New York Stock Exchange (NYSE). The NYSE is the world's largest stock exchange, with over $19 trillion in market capitalization. Gerald Holubowicz/Alamy

LO 16-2

Apply the legal test for what constitutes a security.

Based on these definitions, the general standard for determining whether an arrangement or offering is defined as a security is quite broad: A security is any *investment* that involves a person giving something with an *expectation of profit* through the efforts of a *third party*.

The U.S. Supreme Court articulated a four-part test that helped to give lower courts a framework for defining a security and securities offering in the landmark case of *SEC v. W. J. Howey Co.*[1]

In *Howey,* the defendant offered investment opportunities in its citrus operations through a contractual arrangement that combined a real estate purchase with an option to share in the profits from citrus grown on that parcel of land. The SEC alleged that these opportunities constituted a securities offering. The Court agreed:

---
[1]328 U.S. 293 (1946).

[A]n investment contract for purposes of the Securities Act means a contract, transaction or scheme whereby a person invests his money in a common enterprise and is led to expect profits solely from the efforts of the promoter of a third party, it being immaterial whether the shares in the enterprise are evidenced by formal certificates or by nominal interests in the physical assets employed in that enterprise.

The Court's opinion is the basis for what is now called the *Howey* test. Although the *Howey* test remains largely intact, federal courts have added further clarification that has expanded the definition of what constitutes a securities offering. Courts now apply an even more sweeping standard that includes the investment itself, commonality, profit expectations, and the efforts of others.

Modern Application of the *Howey* Test

Fundamentally, the *Howey* test requires a comprehensive, case-by-case analysis of an opportunity to determine whether or not it meets the definition of a security. Each part of the test must be met.

- **Investment:** The investment may be a cash or a noncash instrument for which the investing party receives only the speculative promise of a return and not any tangible commodity or assets.
- **Commonality:** Courts have ruled that an investment scheme may satisfy this requirement either through *horizontal commonality* (multiple investors have a common expectation of profit in the investment) or via *vertical commonality* (a single investor has a common expectation of profit with the *promoter* of her investment).
- **Profit Expectations:** The expectation of a return on investment (profitability) must be the primary reason for the investment.
- **Efforts of Others:** The efforts of the promoter(s) or the agents of the promoter(s) must be the primary sources of revenue that results in profits. Note that *Howey* actually required that the investor not be involved in any way with generating the profits. However, the modern trend is for courts to allow some *limited passive involvement* by the investor so long as the promoter/agent has been the primary source of the efforts.

CONCEPT SUMMARY Modern *Howey* Test

Investment	Commonality	Promoter
Cash or noncash instrument Investor's primary motive is expectation of profit	Multiple investors in single transaction (horizontal) Single investor in single transaction (vertical)	Uses investor money to generate profits primarily by promoter's efforts *Modern rule:* Limited passive action by investor OK

 Self-Check The *Howey* Test

Do the following opportunities constitute a securities offering under the *Howey* test?

1. Smith offers to sell earthworms to third-party investors. The investors enter into a contract whereby, after the purchase, Smith will raise the worms in such a way as to promote massive reproduction, and he guarantees to repurchase the worms from the investors at a certain rate based on the actual sale price to third-party farmers. Thus, an investor can purchase a certain dollar amount of worms, have

(continued)

Smith raise the worms and locate a farmer buyer, and then have Smith repurchase the worms from the investor at a higher price than the investor's original price based on the sale price to the farmer.

2. Utley offered to sell one-half-acre beachfront lots to the public at $50,000 per lot. After the completion of a sale, Utley offered to perform services as a general contractor for purposes of building a shore house on the lot. Among the buyers of the lots, 20 percent of the owners hired Utley to build the houses, but the other 80 percent either hired their own contractors or left the land undeveloped. Once the houses were built, Utley offered to find a buyer for a 10 percent commission on a complete sale.

3. Alliance was a leasing company that devised an opportunity for third-party investors in which the investors paid money to Alliance for the purchase of commercial or kitchen equipment. Alliance then acted as an agent to arrange an equipment lease with the business lessee who needed the equipment. Alliance entered into a joint venture agreement with the investors to sell them the equipment and to broker a lease between the investor and a lessee. The lease agreement provided for lease payments to be paid by the lessees directly to the investor on a monthly basis over a two-year period, at the end of which a balloon payment (the entire principal) would be due. Alliance represented that the investors would earn a 14 percent rate of return on their investment and that risk was low.

Answers to this Self-Check are provided at the end of the chapter.

Stock Market Games Potential investors who are interested in learning more about the market or wish to try a particular trading strategy without risking their money have several Internet-based stock market simulators at their disposal. These simulators, often referred to as stock market games, virtual stock exchanges, or investment games, are programs/applications that reproduce some features of a live stock market so that a player can simulate a particular strategy or method and compare the performance of several different models. Participation in stock market games has increased markedly since major financial firms began to develop their own versions for their clients and potential clients. The transactions in a stock market game are similar to the fantasy sports model in that the buying and selling are imaginary. However, government regulators have kept a close eye on websites that blur the line between simulation and reality by offering some type of reward or prize for successful trading. For example, in *SEC v. SG, Ltd.*,[2] the government alleged that a company that operated a stock market gaming website called "StockGeneration" was violating securities laws. SG offered users the opportunity to purchase shares in fantasy companies listed on the website's virtual stock exchange. Although the website was clearly marked as a game, the court ruled against the company because SG had gone beyond personal entertainment in representing that investors could expect a 10 percent profit monthly.

Crowdfunding The media attention generated by crowdfunding investments has made it a permanent part of fundraising lexicon. One industry analyst quoted in *Inc.* magazine estimated that more than 1 million campaigns globally have raised more than $5 billion in one year.[3] Fundamentally, crowdfunding is asking a crowd of people to invest or donate a defined amount of money for a specific cause. From an entrepreneurial

---

[2] 265 F.3d 42 (1st Cir. 2001).
[3] L. Kim, "Top 10 Crowdfunding Platforms," *Inc.*, November 2018.

standpoint, crowdfunding is a way to raise money by asking individuals who are interested in investing to fund a certain business venture. Because the investments can be very small, it has the potential to tap into a larger investor community and generate significant sums of money for business ventures in relatively short order. This type of fundraising is done via the Internet through crowdfunding firms such as Kickstarter or RocketHub. Crowdfunding may be used to raise money either through debt or equity, and the crowdfunding firm typically charges a percentage fee for its services. Crowdfunding sites range from those that work only for charitable donations to those that focus on funding entrepreneurs and innovation. Although the SEC has struggled with applying an appropriate amount of regulation, it has recently settled on rules to govern crowdfunding. We discuss these regulations in more detail later in this chapter.

Parties in the Securities Market

The securities market functions through the interaction of three parties: investors, issuers, and intermediaries. *Investors* are seeking a return from their investment based on the value of the security. They include individual investors, who hold securities directly or through a brokerage firm, and institutional investors, such as pension funds and mutual funds. *Issuers* are those institutions and entities that sell securities to investors. They include business corporations, state and local governments, and other entities that are seeking to raise capital through investors. *Intermediaries* are financial institutions that provide services for investors and issuers related to securities transactions. Most commonly, intermediaries are brokerage firms (referred to as broker-dealers) that buy and sell securities on behalf of a client. Intermediaries also include mutual funds, investment banks, and some commercial banks. For example, suppose Williams calls her stockbroker at Mega Brokers and finds out that NewCo. is raising capital by selling its stock to the public. She believes the stock is priced low and that she will make a profit in the future, so she orders her broker to purchase 1,000 shares. In that case, Williams is the investor, NewCo. is the issuer, and Mega Brokers is the intermediary.

CATEGORIES OF SECURITIES

Securities fall into one of two general categories: **equity** or **debt**. Each category includes an inventory of *instruments* that are tangible representations of the security and that define the rights of the owner of the security. Some securities have restrictions on the ownership rights (such as the right to sell the security to another party).

LO 16-3

Distinguish between classifications of equity and debt instruments and give an example of each.

Equity Instruments

Equity instruments represent an investor's ownership interests in a venture, in which the financial return on the investment is based primarily on the performance of the venture that issued the securities. However, equity holders have no specific right or guarantee on the investment. Therefore, investors with equity interests may profit considerably from a company that is consistently profitable. However, if the company fails, the equity interest becomes worthless and the investor is without any legal recourse (assuming that no fraud or malfeasance occurred that led to the company's demise) to recover her original investment. Two prevalent forms of equity instruments issued by corporations are *common stock* and *preferred stock*.

Common Stock The most frequently used form of equity instrument is **common stock** (also called **common shares**), which entitles the equity owner to payments based on the current profitability of the company. The payments are known as *dividends*, and the decision on whether to pay dividends to equity owners, as well as how much

Legal Speak >))

Subordinate

In the context of stock ownership rights, a *subordinate* position is a lower or secondary position in terms of being entitled to profits or assets. For example, common stockholders are subordinate to preferred stockholders.

Legal Speak >))

Senior in Priority

When a business must liquidate assets because it fails and either dissolves or files for bankruptcy protection, payments to creditors and shareholders are made according to priority. Thus, those that are "senior" in priority get paid first.

to pay, rests with the company's board of directors. Common stock owners also have the right to payment in the event that the corporation is sold for a profit or the company is dissolved (assuming any value is left in the company). In certain companies, common stock may be *voting* or *nonvoting*. A nonvoting common stockholder is entitled to all benefits of ownership except the right to vote for directors or on major corporate decisions. However, most common stockholders are typically entitled to full voting rights. Rights and duties of shareholders, directors, and officers are discussed in detail in Chapter 15, "Corporations." While common stockholders share in the profits, they also bear the greatest risk of loss because they are typically *subordinate* to all creditors and preferred stockholders if the corporation files for bankruptcy protection or simply dissolves with limited assets.

Preferred Stock Preferred stock is an alternative form of equity that has less risk than common stock because it has certain quasi-debt features. Perhaps the biggest advantage of preferred stock is that preferred stockholders have preference rights over common stockholders in receiving dividends from the corporation. In the event that the corporation fails or files for bankruptcy, preferred stockholders are ahead of common stockholders when trying to recover their losses from the liquidation proceeds. Like common stock, preferred stock may be voting or nonvoting.

Debt Instruments

Debt is another common tool for raising capital. Holders of debt instruments, which include promissory notes, bonds, and debentures, are generally entitled to receive payments that are *senior in priority* to those of preferred or common stockholders. *Promissory notes* are the most commonly used debt instrument. The note simply represents a promise to pay back a certain sum of money (principal) plus accrued interest over an agreed-upon time period. The lender is paid back with principal and interest payments, typically monthly, in accordance with the terms of the note. *Bonds* are debt instruments that are issued by a corporation and are secured by certain assets of the company. *Debentures* are unsecured debt instruments that are issued by a corporation and are backed by the pledge of the corporation's general credit. Investors holding debt instruments are primarily interested in a fixed rate of return regardless of the profitability of the corporation and expect repayment of the debt after a certain period of years.

Use of Bonds and Debentures Bonds and debentures represent the borrowing of money from investors to raise capital for the corporate issuer of the debt instrument. Larger corporations prefer bonds as a method of splitting up their long-term debt, and they blend the use of bonds with conventional borrower-lender (bank) loans for short-term debt. Because bonds are debt instruments, investors expect fixed payments at regular intervals until the bond *matures*, at which time the principal amount of the bond, known as its *face amount*, is paid to the investor.

Although bonds are thought of as capital-raising tools of major corporations, some newer bond issues, known as *micro bonds*, streamline paperwork, reduce fees, and are appealing to smaller business ventures that wish to take advantage of bond financing in the $500,000 to $1,000,000 range.

Peer-to-Peer Lending One impact of the global recession that began in 2008 was the extreme tightening of capital and credit available to businesses. This was especially true for entrepreneurs, who typically lack the traditional track record of success that is important to lenders. FinTech, a term coined by the financial media to describe a new financial sector model, became an increasingly popular alternative to traditional lending. FinTech firms leverage innovative technology in order to lower overhead costs and provide higher levels of service to their users. One of the most successful FinTech models centers on peer-to-peer lending (abbreviated as P2PL), in which a firm offers a web-based platform to match borrowers with investors. Most of these loans are fundamentally unsecured personal loans from an investor to one or more principals of a business venture. While interest rates are set based on the borrower's creditworthiness, these rates and fees are often lower than those of traditional lenders. Prosper and Lending Club, early pioneers in peer-to-peer lending, have collectively serviced over 180,000 borrowers with over $2 billion in loans. Loans by peer-to-peer lenders are considered by regulatory authorities to be securities offerings and therefore must comply with all securities laws and regulations. Market conditions have also been a significant challenge to the FinTech industry.

CONCEPT SUMMARY Categories of Securities

- Securities fall into one of two categories: equity (selling ownership) or debt (fixed rate of return for investor).
- Equity is commonly offered as common stock or preferred stock.
- Debt may be offered in various forms such as promissory notes or bonds.
- Peer-to-peer lending is treated by the SEC as a securities offering.

SECURITIES REGULATION

Fundamentally, all securities regulation has the same rationale: To protect investors and ensure public confidence in the integrity of the securities market. Note that securities laws are not meant to provide insurance for losses or to punish a venture's principals simply because the business does not earn a profit. The underlying premise of all securities regulation is **disclosure**. Much of the regulation concerning fraud or securities sales boils down to whether the seller or issuer has made truthful and sufficiently full disclosures about the security itself. Securities law is primarily a matter of federal statutes and regulations, but all states have similar disclosure and fraud laws within state borders.

Securities and Exchange Commission

The **Securities and Exchange Commission (SEC)** is the federal administrative agency charged with rulemaking, enforcement, and adjudication of federal securities laws. Unlike many administrative agencies, the SEC is an *independent agency* that does not have a seat in the president's cabinet and is not subject to direct control by the president. Five commissioners, appointed by the president and subject to advice-and-consent approval by the Senate, compose the SEC. Commissioners may be removed for misconduct, but no commissioner has been removed since the SEC was formed by Congress in 1934. In addition to being a source of expert information on securities laws, the SEC has wide-ranging executive, legislative, and judicial powers.

The SEC's executive powers include the power to investigate potential violations of securities laws and regulations. The SEC also has a variety of administrative enforcement mechanisms,

LO 16-4
Recognize the fundamental reason behind securities regulation and have a working knowledge of the legal process leading to issuance of original securities.

LO 16-5
Describe the role of the Securities and Exchange Commission (SEC) in securities law compliance and enforcement.

The Securities and Exchange Commission (SEC) is an independent federal administrative agency that is charged with regulating the issuing and trading of securities.
ASSOCIATED PRESS

such as issuing a cease and desist order.[4] In egregious cases, the SEC initiates criminal charges against an individual and/or company that has allegedly violated securities law. The SEC's legislative authority is granted by Congress and allows the SEC to draft and publish securities regulations and interpretations of statutes, rules, and court decisions. Pursuant to its legislative powers, the SEC also issues interpretative letters and no-action letters to advise the securities investment and trading community on how the SEC will treat a proposed transaction. These letters are not binding on the SEC, but they do carry significant weight with courts and are crucial to the day-to-day operations of publicly held companies. The SEC's judicial powers are primarily rooted in its role as a hearing tribunal for enforcing certain securities violations, including alleged indiscretions of brokers in their business dealings. The SEC has the power to suspend or revoke the professional licenses of brokers and others regulated by securities laws.

Though it is the primary regulatory authority of the securities markets, the SEC works closely with many other institutions, including Congress, other federal agencies, self-regulatory organizations (such as stock exchanges), state securities regulators, and various private sector organizations. The chair of the SEC is one of four members[5] of the President's Working Group on Financial Markets.

The SEC is composed of several divisions and departments. The highest-profile divisions are Enforcement and Corporation Finance because they are primarily responsible for investigating and enforcing any action against violators. Much of the SEC's

> **KEY POINT**
>
> The SEC is an independent regulatory agency with broad executive, legislative, and judicial authority over securities issuance, transactions, investors, and brokers.

---

[4] An administrative order requiring a certain party to halt unlawful activity.

[5] The other members are the chair of the Federal Reserve, the chair of the Commodities Futures Trading Commission, and the secretary of the Treasury.

day-to-day work is done through its 11 regional offices, which are spread throughout the United States.

Figure 16.1 shows the SEC's organizational structure.

EDGAR An important function of the SEC is to maintain a national clearinghouse for public corporation disclosures and filings required by federal securities laws. This clearinghouse is made available to the public through the SEC's computer database known as EDGAR (Electronic Data Gathering, Analysis, and Retrieval). In addition to providing access to EDGAR, the SEC's website serves as a source of information to educate investors on risks and SEC procedures.

The Securities Act of 1933

The primary scope of the **Securities Act of 1933**[6] (the '33 Act) is the regulation of original issuance (and reissuance) of securities to investors by business venture issuers. The '33 Act mandates (1) a registration filing for any venture selling securities to the public, (2) certain disclosures concerning the issuer's governance and financial condition, and (3) SEC oversight over the registration and issuance of securities. The system is designed to give potential investors a transparent view of the financial information, potential liabilities, management practices, and other pertinent information that a business venture is required to disclose in its registration materials. The '33 Act also provides defrauded investors with remedies against issuers that violate the statutory requirements. Congress has provided *special exemptions* for issuance of securities to relatively small groups of qualified investors.

> **LO 16-6**
> List the major categories of securities offerings and identify transactions that are exempt from registration requirements.

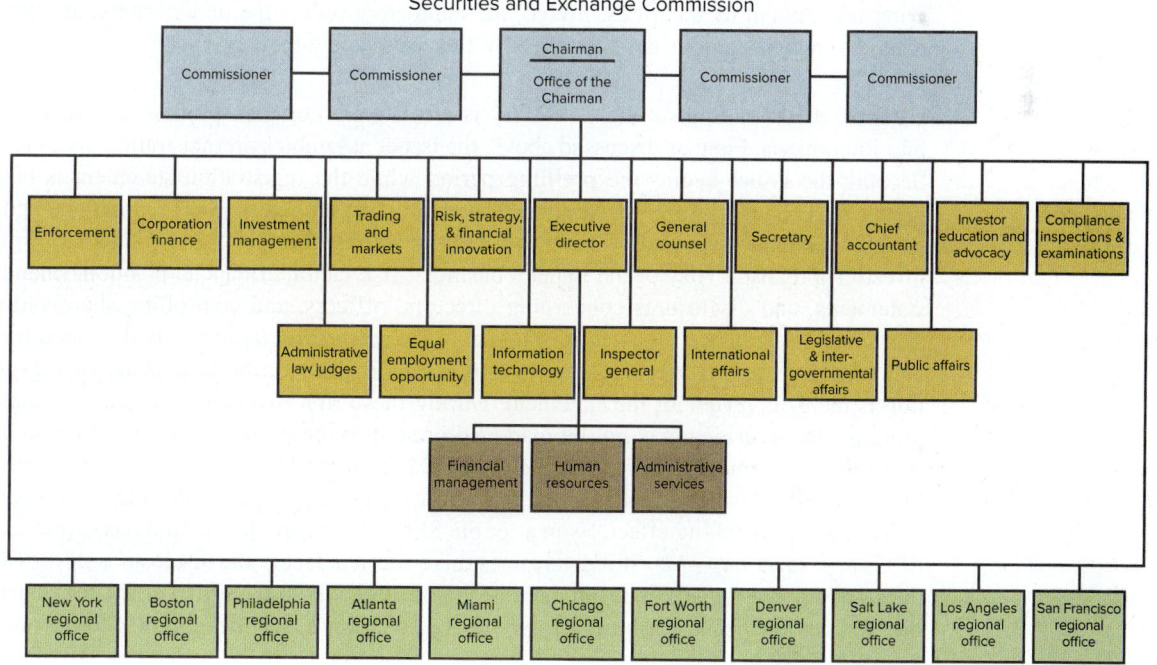

FIGURE 16.1 Structure of the Securities and Exchange Commission

---

[6]15 U.S.C. § 77a et seq.

The Process of a Public Offering

The centerpiece of the '33 Act is Section 5, which makes it illegal to sell any security by use of mail or facilities of interstate commerce unless the security has been registered or unless the security fits into one of the statutory *exemptions*. Section 5 also requires that the registration statement must become "effective" prior to the actual sale of the security. What is commonly referred to as a public offering is actually a process of registration and disclosure mandated by the '33 Act. Section 5 separates the registration process into the following three stages related to the issuance of a security, each of which entails its own statutory requirements: (1) the prefiling period, (2) the waiting period, and (3) the posteffective period. In addition to mandates set out in the '33 Act, the SEC has added significant regulatory requirements pursuant to its authority as an independent regulatory agency. It is also important to understand that, as a practical matter, the '33 Act requirements for registration only apply to a limited number of issuers. This is because the law exempts a significant number of nonpublic offerings. These exempt offerings are discussed in more detail later in this chapter.

> **KEY POINT**
>
> The Securities Act of 1933 covers the processes of issuing and reissuing securities to the public. The law requires registration and certain disclosures and authorizes the SEC to oversee the transactions.

Preregistration Documentation The '33 Act and the SEC regulations require extensive documentation even before the registration statement is filed. This documentation requires the expertise of a variety of professionals, but ultimately it consists of legal documents that are drafted by highly specialized attorneys skilled in securities law. Required documentation before registration includes a *letter of intent* (issuer indicates management and board approval of the issuing of shares); *comfort letters* (including an opinion letter from the issuer's corporate counsel, verifying the business venture's adherence to corporate formalities, and a letter of compliance and opinion from the business venture's accounting firm, verifying the accuracy of the business's financial records); and an *underwriting agreement,* in which the issuer enters into an agreement with a syndicate of underwriters[7] specifying the amount of securities offered, the compensation for the underwriters, and terms related to representations and warranties of the issuer and underwriters.

Registration Registering a security is a relatively complex process that is divided into four phases. First, as discussed above, the issuer assembles preregistration documents. Second, the issuer begins the prefiling period while the registration statement is being prepared. The form of the registration statement is prescribed by SEC regulations and is broken down into two parts. The first part is the **prospectus**, which is intended to give investors a realistic view of the issuer's business, risk factors, financial position, financial statements, and disclosures concerning directors, officers, and controlling shareholders. The second part of the registration statement is *supplemental information* that documents and supports the prospectus. Once the prospectus is drafted, the next phase of registration is the *SEC review* of the statement. During these first two phases of the registration process, the securities may not be marketed or sold to the public. In the third phase, the registration statement is submitted and the SEC has 10 days to review it for incomplete or misleading disclosures. In phase four, the SEC may issue a *refusal order* that prevents the registration from taking effect. Even after the SEC's 10-day review period has expired, the SEC can issue a *stop order* if it determines there was a defect in the disclosures. If the SEC does not act, the registration statement becomes effective 20 days after it is filed. During the SEC review phase, the security may not be sold, but it may be *marketed* to the public

---

[7]In this context, an underwriter is a professional in the securities market that agrees to facilitate the sale of stock to the public for a fee.

subject to strict SEC regulations. Once the registration statement has become effective, the securities are permitted to be sold to the public. After the offering's contemplated registration statement expires, securities may still be sold and marketed to investors, but investors must receive a prospectus and the marketing materials are still subject to the SEC's oversight. Table 16.1 illustrates the phases of securities registration under the '33 Act.

Exemptions from Registration

While the SEC regulations pertaining to registering securities are intended to protect investors, the process itself is extremely onerous and expensive for issuers who are engaged in a relatively small offering. In order to assist business ventures seeking smaller amounts of capital from the public investment community, the securities laws allow a number of **exemptions** from registration for smaller issuers. For a number of economic, legal, and other practical reasons, *most businesses offer their securities on an exempt basis*. From a federal standpoint, the most common exemption is one for *nonpublic* offerings to a limited number of sophisticated investors who have prior business relationships with the issuer or who privately negotiate their securities purchases. Another common exemption, known as a regulatory *safe harbor*, involves offerings with specified dollar limitations and/or limitations on the number of *nonaccredited investors*. While the security may be exempt from the burdensome regulations of the '33 Act, a seller of securities is still required to make available or prepare and deliver *certain disclosures* to prospective investors. The breadth and content of these disclosures vary depending upon the particular requirements for registration or exemption imposed by law. The following securities are common examples of securities that are exempt from full registration requirements:

- Commercial paper (such as promissory notes that are purchased by sophisticated investors and investment banks) with a maturity date of less than nine months.
- Securities of charitable organizations.
- Annuities and other issues of insurance companies.
- Government-issued securities such as municipal bonds.
- Securities issued by banks and other institutions subject to government supervision.
- In certain cases under Regulation D, Regulation A, and Regulation Crowdfunding (explained next).

> **KEY POINT**
>
> Most businesses offer their securities to investors on an exempt basis in order to reduce costs and simplify the process of compliance with the '33 Act.

TABLE 16.1 Phases of Securities Registration

Phase 1 Pre-registration	Phase 2 Registration Statement	Phase 3 SEC Review	Phase 4 SEC Response
Proposed issuer assembles preregistration documents such as letters of intent, comfort letters, and an underwriting agreement.	Proposed issuer drafts prospectus with disclosures and financial information and submits the statement to the SEC.	The SEC reviews the registration statement over a period of 10 days.	The SEC may either: (1) Issue a refusal order during the 10-day review period or issue a stop order after the review period. Proposed issuer must revise and resubmit. (2) Take no action, in which case the registration becomes effective 20 days after the original SEC filing. The security may now be sold to the public.

Regulation D: Private and Small Transactions

In addition to the exemption for some *types* of securities, the securities laws also exempt certain *transactions* that an issuer may use to sell the security. Some of the more common transaction exemptions fall under the securities law provision **Regulation D**. Regulation D exemptions are for limited offers of a relatively small amount of money or offers made in a limited manner. The exemption is grounded in an assumption that certain investors are sophisticated enough that they do not need the level of protection afforded by the '33 Act's full disclosure requirements. This allows issuers to keep transaction costs significantly lower than required for nonexempt offerings. Offerings under Regulation D are often called *private placements*.[8]

Accredited Investors   A crucial component of the exemption rules depends on categorizing investors as *accredited* versus *nonaccredited*. Rule 501 of the Regulation D sets out various ways in which investors may be categorized as accredited. Institutional investors (e.g., banks, mutual funds), corporations with assets exceeding $5 million, venture capital firms, and key insiders of the issuers (e.g., officers, directors, partners) are automatically considered accredited investors. In order for individual investors to be accredited, they must have (1) a net worth of over $1 million or (2) income in excess of $200,000 (or joint income with a spouse of $300,000) in each of the two most recent years and a reasonable expectation of reaching the same income level in the current year to meet the accredited investor criteria.[9]

Rule 504: Smaller Offerings   Rule 504 exemptions are for relatively small offerings through which privately held, noninvestment companies seek to raise capital for a specific purpose. The exemption covers offerings up to $5 million in any 12-month period. There are no disclosure requirements, the prospectus is not required to be registered, there is no limit on the number of investors, and there is no requirement that the investor be accredited. However, most issuers will nonetheless include important disclosures in their offering materials because it helps the issuer defend against later allegations that the issuer violated anti-fraud laws. As a general matter, the offering cannot be publicly advertised or accomplished through widespread solicitation. The issuer is required to take steps to be sure that there are no resales of the securities to the public.

Rule 506: Larger Private Placements   Regulation D provides an important exemption for a larger offering through Rule 506 that is typically referred to as a **private placement**. Rule 506 exempts private, noninvestment company offerings in unlimited amounts that are not generally advertised or available to the general public. However, Rule 506 offers two alternatives for private placement based on restrictions in terms of the type and sophistication of investors who may purchase the securities. Rule 506(b) placements may be offered to an unlimited number of investors who qualify as accredited under SEC rules. Rule 506(b) offerings may *also* have up to 35 nonaccredited investors who qualify as "sophisticated." This means that the issuers must reasonably believe that the investors have sufficient experience, business savvy, and knowledge of the market that the law imputes a certain cognizance of investment risk and the ability to protect their own interests. Additionally, Rule 506(b) requires issuers to give any nonaccredited investors disclosure documents that generally contain the same type of information that is provided in a registered

---

[8]Strictly speaking, *private placement* refers only to Rule 506 offerings. However, many investor publications refer to any Regulation D offering as a private placement.
[9]Rule 501 also includes sophisticated trusts and accredited-owned entities as accredited investors.

offering. Rule 506(c) provides issuers with the right to broad general solicitation and advertisement of a security to an unlimited number of *accredited investors only*. The SEC requires the issuer to take reasonable steps in order to ensure that investors are accredited. Note that while the offering amount is limited by the rule, issuers may (and often do[10]) use Rule 506 for smaller offerings. For example, if an issuer plans on a $5 million offering, it may choose its exemption category from either Rule 504 or Rule 506.

Regulation A: Large Exempt Offerings

Regulation A allows large offerings to be exempt from registration, although these offerings are more closely regulated than either Rule 504 or Rule 506 exemptions. Regulation A is split into two tiers: Tier 1, for securities offerings of up to $20 million in a 12-month period; and Tier 2, for securities offerings of up to $50 million in a 12-month period. Regulation A sets out special requirements for issuer eligibility, offering circular contents, advertising, disclosures, and disqualification for some individuals. Tier 2 issuers are required to include audited financial statements in their offering documents and to file annual, semiannual, and current reports with the SEC on an ongoing basis. Securities offered under Tier 1 have no qualifications regarding who may invest, whereas purchasers of Tier 2 offerings must either be accredited investors or be subject to certain limitations on their investment.

Disclosures Required

It is important to emphasize that exempt private placement offers under Rules 504 and 506 are still required to make important anti-fraud-related disclosures to potential investors about the business and its principals. These disclosures are made through a *private placement memorandum*.

CONCEPT SUMMARY Exemptions from Registration

- For a number of economic, legal, and other practical reasons, most businesses offer their securities on an exempt basis.
- Exemption from registration does not exempt issuers from anti-fraud laws, disclosures to nonaccredited investors, and financial transparency for all investors.

	Rule 504	Rule 506(b)	Rule 506(c)	Regulation A
Maximum issue in 12 months	$5 million	Unlimited	Unlimited	*Tier 1:* $20 million *Tier 2:* $50 million
Investor requirements	Unlimited investors (no accreditation requirements)	Thirty-five sophisticated/nonaccredited; unlimited accredited	Unlimited; all investors must be accredited	*Tier 1:* None *Tier 2:* Unlimited accredited; nonaccredited subject to investment limits
Solicitation regulations	Limited solicitation	No requirements	General solicitation permitted	General solicitation permitted

---

[10]See Rutherford B. Campbell, Jr., "The Wreck of Regulation D," *The Business Lawyer* 66, no. 4 (August 2011), pp. 919, 928.

> **KEY POINT**
>
> Exemption from registration does not exempt issuers from appropriate disclosures to investors and financial transparency.

Crowdfunding Crowdfunding gained a significant boost after the passage of the Jumpstart Our Business Startups (JOBS) Act of 2012. The law required the SEC to carve out a niche in securities laws that permitted crowdfunding as a fundraising tool for small business. In 2013, the SEC adopted rules that attempt to balance concerns about protecting relatively unsophisticated investors from fraud with helping to grow the economy by making more capital available from the investing public. The rule restricts companies from raising more than $1 million per year through crowdfunding sources. Investors also have similar caps based on their own resources. Table 16.2 sets out investor limits in a crowdfunding context.

Issuers using crowdfunding are now subject to certain disclosure requirements about the principals, the use of funds, and financial conditions. The SEC also created a new registered intermediary category called a "funding portal" (similar to a broker-dealer registrant). These rules include limits on the amounts raised by a business venture and restrictions on the amount invested by individual investors (discussed earlier). The SEC rules also impose disclosure requirements on companies that engage in fundraising through crowdfunding. These disclosures include:

- Biographical information on directors, officers, and shareholders owning 20 percent or more of the company.
- Specific description of how the company intends to spend the proceeds.
- Description of the financial condition of the company.
- In larger campaigns, the company must provide financial statements of the company accompanied by a copy of the company's tax returns.
- Background checks on all principals with 10 percent or greater ownership and the disclosure of pertinent details revealed through the background check.

TABLE 16.2 Crowdfunding Investor Qualifications and Limits

Investor Annual Income	Investor Net Worth	Calculation	Investment Limit
$30,000	$105,000	Greater of $2,200 or 5% of $30,000 ($1,500)	$2,200
$150,000	$80,000	Greater of $2,200 or 5% of $80,000 ($4,000)	$4,000
$150,000	$107,000	10% of $107,000 ($10,700)	$10,700
$200,000	$900,000	10% of $200,000 ($20,000)	$20,000
$1,200,000	$2,000,000	10% of $1,200,000 ($120,000), subject to $107,000 cap	$107,000

Source: Composed by the authors based on SEC's "Regulation Crowdfunding: A Small Entity Compliance Guide for Issuers."

Liability for Violations The '33 Act and its subsequent amendments impose both civil and criminal penalties on offerors and sellers of securities who violate the Act's provisions. The penalties include (1) rescission of the investment by the investor, (2) civil penalties and fines, and (3) incarceration for egregious cases. The SEC has broad authority to pursue civil and criminal sanctions when an offering is accomplished by false or misleading means. Table 16.3 provides specific remedies and penalties for noncompliance with securities issuance regulations.

TABLE 16.3	'33 Act Liabilities and Penalties
Violation	**Remedy/Penalty**
Noncompliance with registration requirements	Investors who purchased unregistered securities are entitled to rescind the investment and to be paid back in full.
Fraud in registration statement or offering	Investors may recover damages from the issuer if they relied on the statements in considering the purchase.
Fraud in any transaction or offering	The issuer is subject to criminal penalties, including substantial fines and incarceration.

Defenses and Safe Harbors

Businesses issuing stock in a public or private sale (both exempt and nonexempt) that are alleged to have violated the anti-fraud provisions of the '33 Act have two categories of defenses at their disposal. First, the issuer may avoid liability or penalties by successfully asserting that both the transaction and the issuer are immune from liability through a *statutory safe harbor*. Second, the issuer may avoid liability through common law defenses of *materiality* or the *bespeaks caution doctrine*. If the violator is not actually the issuer of the stock but a third party involved in the transaction (such as an underwriter), that party may avoid liability by proving he acted with due diligence in verifying the veracity and completeness of the required disclosures.

Safe Harbors: The Private Securities Litigation Reform Act of 1995

In the early 1990s, the securities regulation community and publicly held companies became concerned about what they believed to be an increasingly unwarranted number of lawsuits that they characterized as abusive or frivolous. Indeed, a number of law firms specialized in the initiation of class action litigation on behalf of allegedly defrauded shareholders. In many class action cases, the shareholders recovered minimal amounts, but sizable legal fees were awarded to law firms. The lawsuits were frequently based on optimistic predictions of future growth and other such public comments by company executives. Congress, in an attempt to curtail this type of litigation, passed the **Private Securities Litigation Reform Act of 1995 (PSLRA)**.[11] The PSLRA imposes significant procedural rules and substantive standards that make it more difficult to pursue litigation under the securities laws based solely on written or oral statements by the company's officers and directors. The PSLRA defines suits as frivolous if the "shareholder derivative actions [are] begun with [the] hope of winning large attorney fees or private settlements, and not with intention of benefiting [the] corporation on behalf of which [the] suit is theoretically brought."

The centerpiece of the PSLRA is the *safe-harbor* provision that shields the issuer from liability based on statements and forecasts contained in the prospectus or made by executive management and authorized spokespersons of the issuer. The law provides the issuer with an automatic defense to any private lawsuit arising out of federal securities laws. In the context of the '33 Act, the safe harbor is typically used to halt a claim of misrepresentation. The PSLRA also covers the anti-fraud provisions of the Securities Exchange Act of 1934, discussed in the next section.

The PSLRA safe harbor offers substantial protection for issuers because there is no "state of mind" requirement in order for the company to be insulated from liability for violations of the '33 Act. The safe harbor protects issuers from private investor lawsuits by

---

[11] 15 U.S.C. § 78u.

shielding the issuer from liability related to forward-looking statements made in its prospectus or orally by officers/directors. The law defines forward-looking statements broadly and includes

- Projection of total revenues, income, or income losses; and
- Projections of earnings/losses per share, capital expenditures, or capital structure; and
- Statements of the plans or objectives of management for future operations.

The safe harbor is most easily understood as a two-pronged liability protection shield for forward-looking statements. First, the statements must be identified as "looking-ahead" and must be accompanied by *meaningful cautionary language* identifying important factors that could cause actual results to be materially different from those predicted by statement. Second, if the investor's claim does not establish that the statement was made with actual knowledge that the statement was false or misleading, the statement falls into the safe harbor protection.

Materiality The definition of *materiality* is significant because the import and truthfulness of information presented in a prospectus is at the very heart of statutory disclosure requirements. Courts use a *total-mix* test to determine whether or not an omission or representation is material. That is, even when the most important information is omitted from the prospectus, an omission cannot be considered material if the total mix of information was already reasonably available to the investing public. Thus, if an investor should have known about a particular fact that was available in the total mix of information, she cannot later claim that the undisclosed fact was a material omission.

Bespeaks Caution Doctrine One of the most powerful defenses for an issuer is the judicially created *bespeaks caution doctrine*. This defense allows an issuer who included specific and narrowly tailored cautionary disclosures in the prospectus to negate any allegedly misleading or overly optimistic prediction. However, an issuer cannot be protected through the bespeaks caution doctrine if the cautionary statements were overly broad or too general. Rather, courts require that the cautionary language be specifically tailored to the prediction.

In Case 16.1, an appellate court considers the bespeaks caution doctrine in the context of an investment in the Trump Taj Mahal Casino Hotel in Atlantic City.

CASE 16.1 Kaufman v. Trump's Castle Funding, 7 F.3d 357 (3d Cir. 1993)

FACT SUMMARY Trump and his codefendants offered securities to the public in order to finance the purchase, construction, and operation of the Trump Taj Mahal, which was billed as the most lavish casino resort in Atlantic City. The prospectus accompanying the bonds estimated the costs for completion and disclosed the plan for securing the entire financing package, which included bond proceeds, capital from Trump, and various loans and lines of credit. The prospectus stated: "The Partnership believes that the funds generated from the operation of the Taj Mahal will be sufficient to cover all of its debt service (interest and principal)." The prospectus also contained numerous cautionary statements on factors including the intense competition in the casino industry, the absence of an operating history for the Taj Mahal, and the possibility that the enterprise may become unable to repay the interest on the bonds in the event of a mortgage default and subsequent liquidation of the Taj Mahal. When Kaufman and other investors discovered that Trump and his codefendants planned to file for reorganization under Chapter 11 of the bankruptcy code, they filed a suit alleging that the

(continued)

Taj Mahal offering's prospectus contained material misstatements and omissions and constituted fraud. The trial court ruled in favor of Trump and held that the cautionary statements that surrounded each representation barred any misrepresentation claim. Kaufman appealed.

SYNOPSIS OF DECISION AND OPINION The U.S. Court of Appeals for the Third Circuit affirmed the trial court's ruling in favor of Trump. The court applied the bespeaks caution doctrine, whereby cautionary language in a prospectus negates the materiality of an alleged misrepresentation. The court held that the defendants had included substantive statements that were tailored to address specific future projections and estimates or opinions in the prospectus. The bespeaks caution doctrine means that cautionary statements included in a prospectus may render the challenged predictive statements or opinions immaterial as a matter of law.

WORDS OF THE COURT: Bespeaks Caution Doctrine "Because of the abundant and meaningful cautionary language contained in the prospectus, we hold that [Kaufman has] failed to state an actionable claim regarding the statements that the Partnership believed it could repay the bonds. We can say that the prospectus here truly bespeaks caution because, not only does the prospectus generally convey the riskiness of the investment, but its warning and cautionary language directly address the substance of the statement of [Kaufman's] challenge. That is to say, the cautionary statements were tailored precisely to address the uncertainty concerning the partnership's ability to repay the bondholders."

Case Questions

1. Kaufman claimed that the prospectus failed to disclose the fact that the average casino "win" would have to top $1.3 billion per day in order to pay the debt back. Should the partnership have disclosed that fact?
2. Do issuers have a legal duty to disclose negative information in the prospectus? Do they have an ethical duty? Why or why not?
3. *Focus on Critical Thinking:* Is the bespeaks caution doctrine consistent with the '33 Act's public policy goal of transparency and disclosure in a securities issuance? Why or why not? How could the doctrine be modified to be more favorable to the public investor community?

The Securities Exchange Act of 1934

While the '33 Act regulates the *issuance* of securities to the public by a corporation, the **Securities Exchange Act of 1934**[12] (the '34 Act) regulates the sale of securities between investors *after* an investor has purchased them from a business entity issuer. Therefore, the '34 Act's authority is over brokers, dealers, securities associations, brokerage firms, and other business entities that are engaged in the sale of securities between investors. Similar to the '33 Act, this statute requires registration with the SEC for issuers who wish to have their securities offered on a *national exchange,* such as the New York Stock Exchange, and compels all sellers of securities to fully disclose all pertinent details to potential investors. The '34 Act also regulates the relationship between existing stockholders and the corporation by requiring disclosure of information concerning (1) the financial performance of the company, (2) corporate governance procedures, and (3) any changes that increase or decrease risk that have occurred since the last report (such as the company being named as a defendant in a lawsuit).

Section 10b Section 10b of the '34 Act is the primary *anti-fraud* provision covering the trading of securities. The section makes it a criminal offense to engage in any fraud, directly or indirectly, in connection with the purchase and sale of any security. Its scope is very broad, and the SEC strictly enforces this section, often referred to as *rule 10b-5.* Although the term *10b-5* is perhaps best known for its use by the SEC in

---
[12]15 U.S.C. § 78a et seq.

prosecuting insider-trading cases, in reality this section is a very expansive anti-fraud provision intended to cover all actions, conspiracies, or schemes that could potentially result in an investor's being defrauded, damaged, or misled.

LO 16-7

Articulate the ethical and legal duties of corporate insiders.

Insider Trading The SEC has continued to be aggressive in enforcing rule 10b-5 with respect to **insider trading**. Essentially, when a corporate insider has access to certain information not available to the general investor public, the insider may not trade in the company's stock. In 1988, Congress passed the **Insider Trading and Securities Fraud Enforcement Act**, which raised the criminal and civil penalties for insider trading, increased the liability of brokerage firms for wrongful acts of their employees, and gave the SEC more power to pursue violations of rule 10b-5.

In order to trigger liability under rule 10b-5 for insider trading, the investor must have (1) bought or sold stock in a publicly traded company, (2) possessed nonpublic information that was material and that was significant to the decision of the investor, and (3) had a special relationship with the source of information as an insider or as a "tippee" if he received information from an insider. Insiders include executives, managers, corporate or outside counsel, consultants, managers, brokers, internal or external accountants, vendors, partners, and even majority shareholders. Moreover, even lower-level employees such as secretaries who learn inside information as part of their employment are considered insiders. The U.S. Supreme Court has recognized two complementary theories of insider trading:

- *Traditional insider trading* (sometimes called the "classic" insider-trading theory) occurs when the insider trades in securities based on material, nonpublic information learned as an insider who owes a duty either to abstain from trading or to disclose the inside information.

- *Misappropriation* is a violation of rule 10b-5 even when the investor acting on the nonpublic information is not an insider. Rather, it occurs when a person misappropriates confidential information for securities trading purposes, uses the information for trading, and breaches a duty to disclose that is owed to the *source* of the information. Such conduct violates rule 10b-5 because the misappropriator engages in deception by pretending loyalty to the principal while secretly converting the principal's information for personal gain. For example, suppose that O'Hagan is an attorney who buys stock in Tectonic Corporation after learning that Mega Inc., a client of O'Hagan's law firm, was planning a takeover of Tectonic. Because O'Hagan is an outsider to Tectonic, he cannot be held liable under a traditional insider-trading theory. However, O'Hagan still violated rule 10b-5 under the misappropriation theory because he violated a duty to disclose the source of his information to Mega and to his law firm.[13]

It is also important to note that courts do not require that the breach of duty required to trigger liability be a breach of *fiduciary* duty. In Case 16.2, a federal appeals court analyzes whether the misappropriation theory applies absent any fiduciary duty owed to the source.

CASE 16.2 United States v. McGee, 763 F.3d 304 (3d Cir. 2014)

FACT SUMMARY Timothy McGee, a financial advisor with more than 20 years of experience, first met Christopher Maguire while attending Alcoholics Anonymous (AA) meetings. As a newcomer to AA, Maguire sought support from McGee, who shared similar interests and had successfully

(continued)

---

[13]*United States v. O'Hagan*, 521 U.S. 642 (1997).

achieved sobriety for many years. For the better part of a decade, McGee informally mentored Maguire in AA. They shared intimate details about their lives to alleviate stress and prevent relapses. Given the sensitive nature of their communications, McGee assured Maguire that their conversations would remain private. Likewise, Maguire never repeated information that McGee entrusted to him. This comported to the general practice in AA, where a "newcomer can turn . . . with the assurance that no newfound friends will violate confidences relating to his or her drinking problem."

During this same time, Maguire was a member of executive management at Philadelphia Consolidated Holding Corporation (PHLY), a publicly traded company. In early 2008, Maguire was closely involved in negotiations to sell PHLY and experienced sporadic alcohol relapses. During a conversation in which McGee was trying to convince Maguire to return to AA, Maguire blurted out the inside information about PHLY's imminent sale, telling McGee that he was under extraordinary pressure and that "we're selling the company . . . for three times book [value]." McGee agreed that he would keep the information that Maguire had told him confidential as he had in all previous conversations.

After this conversation, McGee purchased a substantial amount of PHLY stock on borrowed funds without disclosing to Maguire his intent to use the inside information. Before the conversation, PHLY stock represented one-tenth of McGee's stock portfolio. Less than a month later, it constituted 60 percent of his holdings. Before this information became public, McGee borrowed approximately $226,000 to help finance the purchase of PHLY shares. Shortly after the public announcement of PHLY's sale, McGee sold his shares, resulting in a $292,128 profit.

On November 15, 2012, a jury found McGee guilty of violating the insider-trading laws under rule 10b-5. McGee appealed, arguing that he could not be liable under the misappropriation theory absent a *fiduciary* relationship between a misappropriator (McGee) and his source (Maguire).

SYNOPSIS OF DECISION AND OPINION The U.S. Court of Appeals for the Third Circuit ruled against McGee and upheld his conviction for insider trading. The court rejected McGee's defense that the misappropriation theory required a fiduciary duty between McGee and Maguire in order to trigger insider-trading liability. The court held that the U.S. Supreme Court's precedent cases did not define the relationship so narrowly. Rather, any duty of loyalty, confidentiality, trust, or confidence would suffice for "recognized duties" to establish misappropriation liability.

WORDS OF THE COURT: Broad Meaning of Duty "Contrary to McGee's contention, Supreme Court precedent does not unequivocally require a fiduciary duty for all § 10(b) nondisclosure liability. . . . [T]he Court stressed that misappropriation liability extends to those who breach a recognized duty. . . . The Court painted with a broader brush, referring to the requisite relationship as a fiduciary or other similar relationship, an 'agency or other fiduciary relationship,' a 'duty of loyalty and confidentiality,' and a 'duty of trust and confidence.' We will not assign a meaning to 'recognized dut[ies]' that the Court did not acknowledge.

"The Supreme Court's traditional insider trading precedent does not change this result. [Previous cases] call for a 'specific relationship between two parties.' Although these cases often referred to fiduciaries, they spoke also in broader terms. [For example], for traditional insider trading, there is no duty to disclose if the trader is not an agent, a fiduciary, or 'a person in whom the sellers [of the securities] had placed their trust and confidence'. . . ."

Case Questions

1. Why was this case considered a misappropriation theory case rather than a traditional insider-trading case?

2. If McGee had disclosed his trading to Maguire, would that have relieved him from liability? Why or why not?

3. *Focus on Critical Thinking:* Was McGee's conduct what Congress intended to prohibit or has rule 10b-5 been applied too broadly? Isn't the underpinning of the Act's Section 10b to prevent insiders from using confidential information to profit? Why should that apply to outsiders such as McGee? If McGee had overheard the information while Maguire told someone else, would that change your analysis? Was McGee's conduct ethical? Why or why not?

Tipper-Tippee Liability Insider trading liability is not confined to insiders or misappropriators who trade for their own account. Rule 10b-5 also extends specifically to outside parties who learn of the insider information and trade stock on the basis of the information. This is known as *tipper-tippee liability* (and can even be extended to other parties whom the tippee told about the internal information) and is a criminal offense under the '34 Act. Rule 10b-5 is violated if (1) the information released by the tipper constituted a breach of the tipper's *fiduciary duty* to the company, (2) the tipper obtained some personal *benefit* by giving the tip, (3) the tippee knew or should have known that the information was *wrongfully disclosed,* and (4) the tippee *benefited* from the information. For example, suppose that Charles, the executive assistant to the chief financial officer at a public company, discovers information that is likely to adversely impact the price of the stock of the company. Because Charles owns no stock in the company, there is no possibility of direct rule 10b-5 liability for insider trading. However, suppose that Charles knows that his *neighbor* owns stock in the company and offers his neighbor the information in exchange for a fee. When the neighbor hears the insider information, he sells all of his stock in the company. The next day, the stock price falls by 50 percent. Both Charles (as tipper) and the neighbor (as tippee) are liable for violating rule 10b-5 under the tipper-tippee theory. Charles benefited by earning the fee, and the neighbor benefited by selling the stock on the basis of the inside information.

Personal Benefit Test Courts define "personal benefit" to the tipper to include not only financial gain (e.g., a cut of the profits or payment of a fee by the tippee), but also a nonfinancial benefit obtained from making the tip a gift or favor to a relative or friend who trades based on the tip. However, the burden is on the government to show that potential gain is an objective benefit. Federal courts require the government to satisfy the personal benefits test in one of two ways: (1) if the tipper and tippee share a "close personal relationship," such as being siblings,[14] or (2) if the tipper simply intended to benefit the tippee in an objective, consequential way.[15]

Table 16.4 summarizes the primary insider-trading theories applied by courts.

> **KEY POINT**
>
> Investors violate insider trading laws through either traditional insider trading, misappropriation, or tipper/tippee liability.

TABLE 16.4 Insider-Trading Theories

Theory of Insider Trading	Basic Requirements
Traditional (Classic)	Insider obtains confidential information and trades based on the information.
Misappropriation	Outsider obtains confidential information from an insider and trades without disclosure to the source of information.
Tipper-Tippee	Insider (tipper) obtains confidential information, breaches fiduciary duty by recklessly revealing the information to an outsider (tippee), and both benefit from the tippee's trade.

---

[14] *United States v. Newman,* 773 F.3d 438 (2d Cir. 2014).

[15] *United States v. Martoma,* 894 F.3d 64 (2d Cir. 2017), *amended* June 25, 2018, *corrected* July 3, 2018.

Section 16 While rule 10b-5 prohibits insider trading using information based on insider or tipper-tippee knowledge, **Section 16** of the '34 Act imposes restrictions and reporting requirements on ownership positions and stock trades made by certain corporate insiders named in the statute. It was most recently amended in 1991 to clarify certain provisions and extend its reporting requirements, but fundamentally Section 16 mandates transparency of all stock trades by insiders and prohibits insiders from earning short-swing profits.

Section 16a classifies any person who is an executive officer, a director, or a shareholder owning 10 percent or more of a company's total stock as an *insider* and requires such insiders to file regular reports with the SEC disclosing their stock ownership and any trading of their company's stock. This reporting requirement allows the SEC and the investment community to monitor unusual stock activity, such as whether a company's chief executive officer sells substantial portions of his stock in the company during a short time frame. Although an insider's stock sale could be the result of outside influences unrelated to the company, many investors would see it as a sign of trouble. The SEC regularly investigates such activity as it may be indicative of stock manipulation.

Section 16b includes a clawback provision that allows a corporation to recapture any profits earned by an insider on a purchase or sale of the company's stock that occurred within a six-month period. These earnings are called *short-swing profits*, and the prohibition against them is intended to deter insiders from profiting by manipulating the stock's short-term performance. Section 16b is a strict liability statute because it applies even if the insider did not use any insider information or intend any stock manipulation in realizing a short-swing profit.

Rule 10b-5 and Section 16 in Tandem

To understand how the two primary regulations of insiders work in tandem, consider the following example: Suppose that RocketCo is a publicly held corporation subject to the provisions of the '34 Act. Armstrong is the company's chief financial officer, and Shepard is on the board of directors. The company has invested several million dollars on a 10-year research project to produce an alternate fuel product that will result in substantially lower pollution. As of the end of last year, Armstrong and Shepard each owned 10,000 shares of RocketCo's stock. This year, they traded as follows:

January 1	Armstrong purchases 1,000 shares at $10/share.
	Shepard purchases 5,000 shares at $10/share.
March 1	Shepard purchases 5,000 additional shares at $10/share.
May 1	Shepard purchases 1,000 additional shares at $20/share.
	Armstrong sells 1,000 shares at $20/share.
November 1	Shepard sells all of his shares of RocketCo at $25/share.
December 1	RocketCo stock drops to $2/share.

Assume further that on October 30, both Armstrong and Shepard learned in advance of public knowledge that the Environmental Protection Agency (EPA) failed to give regulatory approval to RocketCo's new alternative fuel and that improvements to the formula would likely take many more years of research and testing. On November 30, after the EPA publicly disclosed its adverse decision, RocketCo's stock price dropped precipitously.

- *Rule 10b-5 liability:* Because Armstrong and Shepard are both unquestionably insiders, the information about the EPA's adverse decision cannot be used as the basis for selling RocketCo stock. The timing of Shepard's sale of a substantial portion of RocketCo's stock gives rise to an inference that the insider information precipitated the sale of the stock. If he engaged in insider trading, Shepard faces potential civil liability to injured shareholders as well as possible criminal liability and SEC enforcement action under the '34 Act. Because there is no indication that Armstrong's May sale of the stock was related to the EPA's adverse decision, she does not face rule 10b-5 liability.

- *Section 16a coverage:* Armstrong and Shepard are both statutory insiders of RocketCo and, therefore, are required to report each and every trade to the SEC. Indeed, Section 16a is designed to alert investors and the SEC to potential wrongdoing when an insider takes abrupt action in trading, as in the case of Shepard's sale of all of his stock.

- *Section 16b liability:* Because Shepard did not profit from a short swing (his last purchase was in May and he did not sell until November), he does not have Section 16b liability. Armstrong's sale of 1,000 shares in May would trigger liability under Section 16b because she reaped profits of $10 per share when selling within six months of her purchase. Therefore, the corporation would be entitled to recapture the $10,000 profit realized by Armstrong's short swing. Note that it is irrelevant that Armstrong did not use insider information to make the profit. Section 16b short-swing liability is a *strict liability* provision.

Self-Check Insider Trading

Which theory of insider trading is at issue?

1. Aaron is a psychologist who overhears his patient discussing a confidential corporate acquisition with a business associate on his smartphone while in the waiting room. Aaron knows that the patient is the CEO of publicly held Moors, Inc., so he acquires 50,000 shares of Moors the next day. One week later, Moors announces the acquisition and Aaron nets a $100,000 profit.

2. Edmund works in the mailroom at publicly held Gloucester Company. While he is delivering mail, he notices a document marked "Confidential" to be delivered to the company CFO. Before delivering it, Edmund ducks into a breakroom and reads the document. Based on that information, Edmund sells all of his stock in Gloucester. The next day, a federal regulatory agency reveals that Gloucester is being investigated for fraud. Gloucester's stock price drops 20 percent.

3. Cornwall is an internal accountant at publicly held Lear Corp. After discovering that Lear Corp. has just landed a multimillion-dollar contract with a new client, he conspires with his sister, Regan, to purchase 50,000 shares of Lear stock in Regan's name. The next week, Lear announces the new deal and its stock price rises by 25 percent. Cornwall and Regan split the profits.

Answers to this Self-Check are provided at the end of the chapter.

LO 16-8

Identify any defenses that may be asserted in a securities fraud suit against directors and officers and articulate the impact of the Private Securities Litigation Reform Act.

Defenses

Recall our discussion earlier in this chapter related to the statutory safe harbors afforded to issuers under the Private Securities Litigation Reform Act (PSLRA). The PSLRA safe harbors also protect those alleged to have misrepresented material facts to investors in a securities trading context (purchase or sale) that results in a private action brought by investors under Section 10(b) and rule 10b-5. However, under the Securities Exchange Act, investors face an additional hurdle of proving scienter as an essential element of a fraud case. The element of **scienter** in the context of a securities fraud case means that the seller of securities either knew or believed the represented facts to be untrue. Scienter may also be established if the seller lacked a reasonable basis for the representation.

Based on the scienter requirement, courts require investor plaintiffs to itemize particular facts that give rise to a strong inference that the defendant acted with the required deceptive state of mind.

Securities Litigation Uniform Standards Act of 1998

After the passage of the PSLRA, corporate concerns about shareholder litigation continued because shareholders could still engage in litigation by suing corporations in state courts, under *state* securities statutes, for inadequate or overly optimistic statements. Congress responded by enacting the **Securities Litigation Uniform Standards Act of 1998**.[16] The law, which took the form of an amendment to the '34 Act, is intended to prevent private parties from instituting certain lawsuits in federal *or* state court that are based on the statutory or common law of any state that punishes "a misrepresentation or omission of a material fact" or the use of "any manipulative device or contrivance" concerning the purchase or sale of a covered security.

In the landmark case of *Tellabs v. Makor Issues and Rights, Ltd.,*[17] the U.S. Supreme Court made clear that shareholders faced a substantial hurdle in proving scienter.

> To determine whether the plaintiff has alleged facts that give rise to the requisite "strong inference" of scienter, a court must consider plausible, nonculpable explanations for the defendant's conduct, as well as inferences favoring the plaintiff. The inference that the defendant acted with scienter need not be irrefutable, *i.e.,* of the "smoking-gun" genre, or even the "most plausible of competing inferences,".... Yet the inference of scienter must be more than merely "reasonable" or "permissible"—it must be cogent and compelling, thus strong in light of other explanations. A complaint will survive, we hold, only if a reasonable person would deem the inference of scienter cogent and at least as compelling as any opposing inference one could draw from the facts alleged.

Securities Regulation by States: Blue-Sky Laws

State securities laws are commonly known as **blue-sky laws**, named after the original state statutory protection of investors from unsavory issuers selling nothing more than "blue sky." Blue-sky laws are frequently constructed to match federal securities statutes. In theory, these state statutes are intended to cover purely intrastate securities offerings (those in which the issuers and all potential investors are within one state's borders), but, as a practical matter, state securities regulations are an additional safeguard for investors when the federal government declines to exercise its jurisdiction over a particular securities offering. A majority of states have adopted all or substantially all of the Uniform Securities Act. Typical provisions include prohibition against fraud in the sale of securities, registration requirements for brokers and dealers, exemptions, civil liability for issuers failing to comply, and state court remedies for defrauded investors.

REGULATION OF CORPORATE GOVERNANCE AND FINANCIAL MARKETS

In addition to regulating the issuing and trading of securities, federal and state statutes also regulate certain internal governance procedures of publicly held corporations. **Corporate governance** is the process used by the officers and directors to establish lines of responsibility, approval, and oversight among key stakeholders and set out rules for making corporate decisions. While corporations have traditionally resisted any form of direct government regulation of internal corporate decision making, public scandals have caused

---

[16] 15 U.S.C. § 77z et seq.
[17] 551 U.S. 308 (2007).

Legal Speak >))

Scienter
In the context of securities litigation, scienter means specific intent to deceive, manipulate, or defraud.

LO 16-9
Explain the role of state blue-sky laws in securities regulation.

LO 16-10
Demonstrate an awareness of the impact of the Sarbanes-Oxley Act on a corporation's officers and directors and its corporate governance.

LO 16-11
Articulate key protections afforded by regulation of the financial markets.

Congress to impose certain mandates meant to ensure public confidence in the publicly traded markets and to protect investors. Professionals from outside firms that conduct services for publicly held corporations, notably accounting firms, are also subject to certain regulatory requirements when they conduct audits of public corporations. The financial crisis that was part of the global recession of 2008 spurred regulatory reforms via Congress and through administrative agencies in the area of corporate governance, specifically for firms and institutions involved in the financial markets.

STRATEGIC LEGAL SOLUTIONS

Cybersecurity and Disclosures

PROBLEM: *According to research by the Ponemon Institute,[18] the global average cost of a data breach is $3.62 million. The average cost for each lost or stolen record containing sensitive and confidential information is $141. Although most boards have robust processes for addressing their most pressing responsibilities, such as financial planning and compliance, processes related to cybersecurity issues, such as regular discussions about cyber risks, were lacking or nonexistent. In a study published in Harvard Business Review, researchers found that only 24% of directors at public companies rated cybersecurity as above average or excellent.[19]*

STRATEGIC SOLUTIONS: *Plan and Disclose* Corporate governance experts suggest a two-prong approach. First, the board of directors should take specific planning steps to examine and plan for risk in the same way that they plan for other risks—through a specialized subcommittee. Second, the board should closely examine the SEC's recent Interpretation Action[20] for guidance on preparing disclosures about cybersecurity risks and incidents.

Board Planning

- Prioritize cybersecurity issues by forming a subcommittee (similar to an audit committee) to ask questions and determine whether appropriate processes are in place.

- Boards must also hold executive management accountable for evaluating cybersecurity risks and maintaining prevention and response plans.

- Cybersecurity debriefings should be a regular agenda item at full board meetings. The subcommittee may report on (1) authorizing investments in data security and infrastructure and (2) consulting with external experts on prevention and response plans.

- Use a risk calculator to assess the potential cost of a cyberattack: One may be found at https://databreachcalculator.mybluemix.net/.

Disclosures

- Public companies should disclose the role of boards of directors in cyber risk management, at least where cyber risks are material to a company's business.

- Companies should have identifiable controls that ensure important cyber risk and incident information is a significant factor in the disclosure decisions.

- Cyber risks and incidents may constitute material nonpublic information implicating insider-trading laws. This means that the SEC expects companies to examine their controls and procedures, with not only their securities law disclosure obligations in mind, but also reputational considerations around sales of securities by executives.

- The SEC also advises companies to carefully consider how disclosures of cyber incidents to affected individuals or transaction partners as part of due diligence align with disclosures made publicly to investors.

---

[18]Ponemon Institute, *12th Annual Cost of Data Breach Study*, IBM, https://www.ibm.com/security/data-breach.

[19]J.Cheng & B. Groysberg, *Why Boards Aren't Dealing with Cyberthreats*, Harv. Bus. Rev., Feb. 22, 2017.

[20]Sec. Exchange Comm'n, Release Nos. 33-10459 & 34-82746, *Commission Statement on Public Company Cybersecurity Disclosures* (2018).

The Sarbanes-Oxley (SOX) Act of 2002

In the wake of the infamous corporate fraud and malfeasance scandals beginning in 2000—most memorably Enron, MCI WorldCom, Global Crossing, HealthSouth, and Tyco—a public outcry and a growing lack of investor confidence in corporate financial disclosures caused Congress to overhaul the entire corporate governance regulatory structure by passing the **Sarbanes-Oxley (SOX) Act of 2002**.[21] Most commentators agree that the SOX Act provided the most sweeping and comprehensive amendments to the '33 and '34 Acts in securities law history. While substantial portions of SOX are aimed at solving specific mechanism failures in auditing and other accounting procedures, the law also imposes higher levels of fiduciary responsibilities on those involved in corporate governance. It was widely believed that a lack of oversight by gatekeepers, such as auditors and federal regulators, was a leading factor in the fraud and malfeasance that caused the high-profile demise of these large, publicly held corporations.

> **KEY POINT**
>
> The Sarbanes-Oxley (SOX) Act of 2002 was passed in response to revelations of corporate fraud and malfeasance in publicly held companies. The law aims to solve specific mechanism failures in accounting methods and requires higher levels of fiduciary responsibilities for those involved in corporate governance.

The SOX Act was intended to impose stricter regulation and controls on how corporations do business through regulation of three broad areas: *auditing, financial reporting,* and internal *corporate governance*. The SOX Act also provided for an additional enforcement apparatus and increased penalties for violation of existing securities laws.

Reforms in the Accounting Industry As various corporate fraud and mismanagement scandals came to the public's attention, incidents of public corporations misreporting important financial information spiked[22] and Congress replaced the accounting industry's self-regulation of auditing with a new federal agency called the Public Company Accounting Oversight Board (PCAOB). The PCAOB implements, administers, and enforces the SOX Act mandates. Accounting firms that audit public companies accessing U.S. capital markets are required to register with the PCAOB and are subject to its oversight and enforcement authority. The PCAOB also establishes regulations that standardize certain auditing procedures and ethical parameters.

One major contributing factor in the collapse of several large companies was the questionable independence of the auditors from large accounting firms. The SOX Act seeks to increase auditor independence through setting mandatory rotation of auditing partners, banning accounting firms from providing nonauditing consulting services for public companies for which they provide auditing, and restricting accounting firm employees involved in auditing from leaving the auditing firm to go to work for an audit client.

Financial Reporting The SOX Act makes key corporate officers more accountable for financial reporting by requiring that chief executive officers and chief financial officers personally certify the accuracy of all required SEC filings. These two corporate officers must also ensure that the certification is based on reliable and accurate information through the maintenance of internal financial fraud detection controls that are subject to review by outside auditors. The SOX Act regulations set standardized financial reporting formats and restrict certain types of accounting methods that are not transparent to auditors, such as using special offshore tax entities to hold corporate assets.

---

[21] 15 U.S.C. § 7241.

[22] From 1990 to 1997, the number of publicly held corporations that misreported their revenue and had to restate earnings averaged 49 per year. In 2002, 330 corporations restated earnings.

Martin Shkreli, the 32-year-old hedge-fund manager turned pharmaceutical-company C.E.O., was convicted for securities fraud in 2017. Bloomberg/Getty Images

> **KEY POINT**
>
> The SOX Act imposes stricter regulation and controls on how corporations do business by regulating three broad areas: *auditing, financial reporting,* and internal *corporate governance.*

Corporate Governance The SOX Act requires that publicly held companies maintain audit committees composed entirely of independent directors and specifies that the committee must contain at least one director with sufficient financial acumen to probe audits in depth. Audit committees have substantial regulatory obligations under the SOX Act. These obligations include (1) using their authority to engage, monitor, and terminate the company's outside auditing firm; (2) implementing a system of controls that involves a comprehensive examination of the audit reports and methods used by the company and outside auditors to properly report information that truly reflects the financial condition of the company; and (3) establishing a structure that facilitates direct communication between the audit committee and the auditors (not using corporate officers as go-betweens).

The SOX Act also requires publicly held companies to establish a code of ethics and conduct for their top financial officers, and it prohibits certain practices such as a public corporation's lending money to its officers and directors (with some narrow exceptions). In addition, officers and directors are obligated to disclose their own buying and selling of company stock within a certain time frame. To prevent the secret looting of a company by its officers, the act includes what is known as a *clawback provision;* under this provision, executive performance bonuses must be retroactively forfeited back to the company if the bonuses are tied to any financial reports that are later deemed false or if they have been issued without appropriate controls.

Enforcement under SOX

The SOX Act also greatly expanded the scope and methods of enforcing securities law. The SEC's jurisdiction, enforcement alternatives, and enforcement budget were substantially increased by the SOX Act.

Emergency Escrow Recognizing that many of the remedies in the SOX Act are largely useless if the corporation's assets have been looted by insiders engaged in fraud, the law specifically gives the SEC the authority to intervene in any extraordinary payments made by a company that may be the subject of an SEC investigation. Upon approval by a federal court, the SOX Act allows the SEC to force any extraordinary corporate payouts into a government-controlled emergency escrow fund, where they are held pending further investigation by authorities. This is a powerful weapon in the SEC's enforcement arsenal because the SOX Act does not require any formal allegation of wrongdoing as a prerequisite for intervening in an extraordinary payment. For example, in a 2005 case, *SEC v. Gemstar-TV Guide International, Inc.,*[23] a federal appeals court held that the SEC was reasonable in intervening when a corporation's board of directors authorized multibillion-dollar payments to its executives who were resigning under fire after the company had to revise its past earnings

---

[23] 401 F.3d 1031 (9th Cir. 2005).

statements sharply downward. The court held that the payments to two executives, totaling $37 million, constituted an extraordinary payment and triggered the SEC's right to intervene and the court's right to approve the SEC's request for an emergency escrow. The court pointed out that although the SEC had not launched a formal investigation, the substantial revision of earnings statements coupled with the fact that insiders were departing the company in the wake of the scandal was sufficient to give the SEC intervention rights under the SOX Act.

Substantial Penalties   Violators of the SOX Act are subject to both civil penalties and criminal prosecution. For example, officers who certify a required financial report filing knowing that the report either is inaccurate or was not subject to required controls before the certification are subject to criminal penalties of up to $1 million in fines and 10 years of incarceration. For cases in which the certification was used as part of a larger fraudulent scheme, the penalties increase to $5 million in fines and 20 years of incarceration. The SOX Act also specifically directs the U.S. Sentencing Commission to amend sentencing guidelines to provide for harsher penalties for those convicted of securities fraud statutes.

Whistleblowers   Parties that communicate information relating to any illegal conduct in financial reporting or corporate governance are protected against any retaliation by the company. Audit committees must have a structure in place to process and investigate any whistleblower[24] complaints, and any party that engages in retaliation is subject to civil action and federal criminal prosecution.

The Dodd-Frank Act (discussed in more detail below) also created a $300 billion fund to reward whistleblowers who provide significant information about securities fraud to regulatory authorities. Employees of publicly held entities may collect a bounty of 10 to 30 percent of the monetary sanctions collected in the action if the information they provide to government agencies results in a penalty exceeding $1 million. The SEC has the discretion to base the amount of the whistleblower award on the significance of the information provided, the level of assistance provided by the whistleblower, and the government's interest in deterring securities fraud.

Document Destruction Rules   The SOX Act created new provisions for punishing individuals who destroy the evidence that might be relevant to the investigation of any violation of federal securities laws. Anyone who alters, destroys, or conceals relevant documents is subject to up to 20 years of incarceration. The law applies universally to any party who has control over the documents and covers any actions performed either before, during, or after any formal investigation is commenced.

Conspiracy to Commit Fraud   The definition of *securities fraud* was expanded by the SOX Act, and the creation of a new federal criminal law outlawing *conspiracy* to commit fraud has made pursuing criminal fraud charges against officers and directors substantially easier for government prosecutors. The law also extended the statute of limitations for civil lawsuits filed by defrauded investors attempting to recover lost money.

CONCEPT SUMMARY Sarbanes-Oxley (SOX) Act of 2002

- The SOX Act imposes regulations on publicly held corporations in three broad areas: auditing, financial reporting, and corporate governance.
- The PCAOB is the body created by the SOX Act as an oversight board for firms performing audits of public companies and for SEC-registered brokers and dealers.

(continued)

---

[24]*Whistleblower*, a term used to describe an employee or agent who reports some legal misconduct or statutory violation to the authorities, is discussed in detail in Chapter 11, "Employment Relationships and Labor Law."

- Certain corporate officers are responsible for certifying the accuracy and completeness of financial reports and disclosures.
- The SOX Act requires a publicly held corporation to form an audit committee, prescribes the composition of the committee, and imposes substantial responsibility on the committee to prevent and detect fraud.
- Enforcement provisions of the SOX Act include (1) authorization of the SEC to intervene in any extraordinary payments made by a company and to hold the payments in an emergency escrow fund until further investigation is conducted; (2) enhanced criminal penalties for violations, especially for destruction of documents; (3) protection of whistleblowers; and (4) expansion of the definition of securities fraud by outlawing any conspiracy to commit fraud.

Congressional Response to the Financial Crisis

As the financial crisis that began in 2008 unfolded, increasing fears of a disastrous global financial meltdown and substantial public pressure caused Congress to act on two fronts. First, the government would prevent massive business failures by providing loans to key industries to help them through the crisis. Second, Congress imposed tighter restrictions on financial markets and the extent to which firms could engage in risky investment transactions.

Troubled Assets Relief Program (TARP)

Once it was apparent that several key industries were in financial jeopardy, Congress authorized direct government loans to corporations that were most acutely impacted by the crisis. These loans were intended primarily for large corporations in the financial services and insurance sectors (such as Citigroup and AIG), but federal loans were also extended to companies in other troubled industries, such as auto manufacturers. However, as a condition of the loan, recipients were required to abide by corporate governance and executive compensation mandates. The loan program and its mandates were created in the **American Recovery and Reinvestment Act of 2009**,[25] which established the Troubled Assets Relief Program (TARP) to administer the loans. In general, TARP loan recipients agreed to (1) impose restrictions on compensation (including bonuses) of officers, (2) form an independent compensation committee, and (3) give shareholders more say on compensation of officers and directors. The TARP provisions empower the Department of the Treasury to recover any bonuses paid that are inconsistent with the law's requirements.

A key provision of TARP is the recipient's agreement to abide by certain rules and practices until all TARP money has been paid back. This restriction led several recipients to repay the funds relatively soon. TARP recipients are required to apply for release from the program after showing that their financial condition is sufficiently stable. Within a year of passage of TARP, more than 50 banks were approved to pay back TARP funds, including a $25 billion payment from JPMorgan Chase and a $3.6 billion payment from Capital One Financial.

Financial Market Regulation

Companies that do business in the financial markets are regulated by a complex structure of federal regulatory schemes that are enforced through a variety of administrative agencies and regulatory bodies. The Securities and Exchange Commission, the Federal Reserve, the Office of the Comptroller of the Currency, and the Federal Trade Commission all have some degree of jurisdiction over various aspects of transactions in the global financial markets. The regulated financial transactions include commercial and consumer loans, investments, credit, insurance, and commodities exchange.

---

[25]Pub. L. No. 111-5, 123 Stat. 115 (2009).

Dodd-Frank Act of 2010

In 2010, at the urging of the Obama administration and chief government regulators, Congress passed a new law with sweeping reforms of the financial regulatory system. The law was designed to address the systemic failure of previous regulatory systems and agencies to detect the financial crisis that began in 2008 and sent global financial markets reeling, in an effort to prevent a recurrence of such a crisis. The law, which is commonly referred to as Dodd-Frank, is officially titled the **Dodd-Frank Wall Street Reform and Consumer Protection Act of 2010**.[26] It significantly overhauled the regulation of U.S. financial services and markets.

Financial Stability Oversight Council

The Dodd-Frank law created the Financial Stability Oversight Council (FSOC) as a new independent body with a board of regulators to address dangerous risks to the global financial markets posed by risky investments or the actions of large financial institutions. The FSOC is chaired by the Secretary of Treasury and consists of 10 voting members who are the heads of various agencies involved in the financial system (e.g., the Federal Reserve) and one independent member who is appointed by the president, subject to Senate confirmation. The FSOC also has five nonvoting members representing the FSOC's research arm and state-level financial and insurance regulators.

The FSOC exercises its oversight function in three ways:

- *Risk Analysis:* The FSOC assesses and reduces risk through a systematic and independent analysis of potential emerging threats in the global financial markets and reports to Congress annually.
- *Early Warning:* The FSOC promotes discipline in the financial markets and reduces expectations of a TARP-like bailout plan and responds to any emerging threats.
- *Identifying Financial Risk in Firms:* The FSOC is charged with identifying nonbanking financial institutions that pose a risk to the stability of the U.S. economy and designating them as "systemically risky financial institutions," or SIFIs. To date, the FSOC has designated MetLife, American International Group (AIG), GE Capital Corporation, and Prudential Financial as SIFIs. Being designated as a SIFI subjects the institution to heightened scrutiny by the Federal Reserve and other regulators. The FSOC also has a significant role in identifying financial firms that pose a grave threat to financial stability and determining what action should be taken to break up such firms. These institutions have been dubbed by commentators as "too big to fail" and were a central issue in the financial crisis of 2008.

Once the FSOC has designated a nonbank financial institution as a SIFI, Dodd-Frank empowers the Federal Reserve to assume oversight and impose heightened prudential standards. Banks with over $50 billion in assets are subject to the Federal Reserve's tougher capital requirements and must undergo annual *stress tests* that are designed to test the bank's ability to withstand financial market volatility. Dodd-Frank requires that all financial institutions follow certain prudent practices that discourage speculative investing practices and encourage sufficient reserves to protect consumers.

Consumer Financial Protection Bureau

The law also created a federal administrative agency called the Consumer Financial Protection Bureau (CFPB) that has direct oversight of companies providing mortgages, credit cards, savings accounts, and annuities. The CFPB also has the authority to write new regulations that add additional layers of protection for consumers regarding disclosures, fees, and restrictions on certain lending practices. The CFPB is discussed in detail in Chapter 21, "Warranties and Consumer Protection Law."

---

[26]15 U.S.C. § 78(o).

Expanded SEC Jurisdiction and Enforcement Dodd-Frank expanded the SEC's jurisdiction and provided it with more money and mechanisms for investigation and enforcement of securities law violations. This includes

- *Investigations*. The SEC is not required to disclose records or information related to its investigations or inquiries. This includes surveillance, risk assessments, or other regulatory and oversight activities (except for judicial or congressional inquiry). The effective result of this change is that the federal Freedom of Information Act no longer applies to the SEC; the SEC can refuse to supply documents it deems as being part of its regulatory and oversight activities.
- *Fiduciary Duty of Broker-Dealers*. The law authorized the SEC to establish a fiduciary duty for brokers and dealers when providing personalized investment advice to retail customers—the fiduciary duty is the same standard applicable to investment advisers.
- *Hedge Funds*. Advisers to hedge funds and private equity funds must register with the SEC as investment advisers and provide information about their trades and portfolios necessary to assess systemic risk.

Whistleblower Provisions An important part of the new financial regulatory scheme is the protection of whistleblowers who report illegal conduct committed by employees, directors, and executives of the company. The structure of the Dodd-Frank whistleblower provision is a bounty plan. That is, money is awarded to individuals who provide information that leads to an SEC enforcement action in which certain sanctions are levied. Whistleblower rewards range from 10 to 30 percent of the recovery.

The law also has a strong anti-retaliation provision that protects the job status for SEC whistleblowers and promises confidentiality for them. In the event they are terminated for Dodd-Frank whistleblowing, the anti-retaliation provision allows the whistleblower to collect double her back pay.

One significant legal controversy surrounding the whistleblower provision was created when the SEC issued regulations that qualified a whistleblower as anyone who reports the illegal conduct to the SEC, another federal agency, or the company's internal management.

In Case 16.3, the U.S. Supreme Court analyzes the statutory definition of the Dodd-Frank whistleblower provision.

CASE 16.3 Digital Realty Trust v. Somers, 138 S. Ct. 767 (2018)

FACT SUMMARY Somers worked as vice president of Digital Realty Trust (Digital Realty) from 2010 to 2014. In the course of his duties, Somers discovered possible violations of securities laws by Digital Realty, which caused him to file several reports to senior management. Soon after these reports were filed, he was terminated by Digital Realty's executive management. Somers did not report his concerns to the Securities and Exchange Commission (SEC) before he was terminated. Somers then sued Digital Realty, alleging violations of state and federal laws, including the anti-retaliation protections created by the Dodd-Frank Act. Digital Realty argued that because Somers did not actually report the possible violations to the SEC, he was not a "whistleblower" as defined in the Act and thus not entitled to protection under its provisions. Somers argued that the SEC was entitled to enforce its interpretation of the statute and that SEC's interpretation was more consistent with Dodd-Frank's intent and purpose. The trial court ruled in favor of Somers, ruling that the provision extends to all those who make disclosures of suspected violations, regardless of whether the disclosures are made internally or to the SEC. The court of appeals upheld the trial court's decision, and Digital Realty appealed to the U.S. Supreme Court.

(continued)

SYNOPSIS OF DECISION AND OPINION The U.S. Supreme Court reversed the lower court's decision and ruled in favor of Digital Realty. The Court held that the anti-retaliation provision for "whistleblowers" in the Dodd-Frank Act protects only individuals who report alleged misconduct to the SEC. The Court reasoned that the Act explicitly defines *whistleblower* as any individual who provides information on possible securities violations to the Commission, and this definition is corroborated by Dodd-Frank's purpose to aid the SEC's enforcement efforts by incentivizing people to tell the SEC about violations. Whistleblowers who report violations to other federal agencies or an internal supervisor are not within the scope of this express definition of whistleblower in the Dodd-Frank Act. Because the language of the statute is clear, the SEC is not permitted its own interpretation.

WORDS OF THE COURT: Statutory Interpretation "'When a statute includes an explicit definition, we must follow that definition,' even if it varies from a term's ordinary meaning. . . . Our charge in this review proceeding is to determine the meaning of 'whistleblower' in . . . Dodd-Frank's anti-retaliation provision. The definition section of the statute supplies an unequivocal answer: A 'whistleblower' is 'any individual who provides . . . information relating to a violation of the securities laws *to the Commission*.' (emphasis added). Leaving no doubt as to the definition's reach, the statute instructs that the 'definitio[n] shall apply in this section,' that is, throughout [the Dodd-Frank statute]."

WORDS OF THE COURT: Statute's Design and Purpose "Dodd-Frank's purpose and design corroborate our comprehension of [the] reporting requirement. [According to its legislative history, the] 'core objective' of Dodd-Frank's robust whistleblower program, as Somers acknowledges, is 'to motivate people who know of securities law violations to *tell the SEC*' (emphasis added). By enlisting whistleblowers to 'assist the Government [in] identify[ing] and prosecut[ing] persons who have violated securities laws,' Congress undertook to improve SEC enforcement and facilitate the Commission's 'recover[y] [of] money for victims of financial fraud.' To that end, [the statute] provides substantial monetary rewards to whistleblowers who furnish actionable information to the SEC."

Case Questions

1. Why didn't the Court defer to the SEC's interpretation?
2. Why does the Court examine Dodd-Frank's "core objectives"?
3. *Focus on Critical Thinking:* Is statutory protection for whistleblowers good public policy? Does it encourage managers to be more vigilant about compliance with legal and ethical codes? Why or why not? What specific incentives result from those provisions for the employer and employee? Are these incentives consistent with good public policy?

KEY TERMS

Securities law p. 529 The body of federal and state laws governing the issuance and trading of equity and debt instruments to public investors.

Equity p. 533 Ownership interest in a corporation whereby financial return on the investment is based primarily on the performance of the venture.

Debt p. 533 A common tool for raising capital; includes promissory notes, bonds, and debentures that offer investors a fixed rate of return, regardless of the profitability of the corporation, and repayment after a certain period of years. Debt is senior in priority to equity instruments.

Common stock (common shares) p. 533 A form of equity instrument that entitles the equity owner to payments based on the current profitability of the company.

Preferred stock p. 534 A form of equity instrument that has less risk than common stock because it has certain quasi-debt features. Preferred stockholders have preference rights over common stockholders in receiving dividends from the corporation.

Disclosure p. 535 The process in which companies are to release all information, positive or negative, that might bear on an investment decision; serves as the underlying premise of all securities regulation and is required by the Securities and Exchange Commission to protect investors and ensure public confidence in the integrity of the securities market.

Securities and Exchange Commission (SEC) p. 535 The independent federal administrative agency charged with rulemaking, enforcement, and adjudication of federal securities laws.

Securities Act of 1933 p. 537 Federal legislation that covers the processes of issuing and reissuing securities to the public; requires registration and certain disclosures and authorizes the Securities and Exchange Commission to oversee the transactions.

Prospectus p. 538 The first part of the security registration statement prescribed by Securities and Exchange Commission regulations; intended to give investors a realistic view of the issuer's business, risk factors, financial position, financial statements, and disclosures concerning directors, officers, and controlling shareholders.

Exemptions p. 539 For smaller issuers of securities, types of offerings or transactions in selling a security that are not subject to certain Securities and Exchange Commission regulations on registration; intended to assist business ventures seeking smaller amounts of capital from the public investment community.

Regulation D p. 540 A securities law provision that exempts an issuer from registration on the basis of certain transactions; applies to limited offers that involve a relatively small amount of money or offers that are made in a limited manner.

Private placement p. 540 A securities law provision that exempts an issuer from registration when the issuer accepts investments only from those who meet the standards for accredited investors.

Private Securities Litigation Reform Act of 1995 (PSLRA) p. 543 Federal legislation making it more difficult to pursue litigation under the securities laws that is based solely on commentary by company executives; intended to protect publicly held companies from frivolous litigation.

Securities Exchange Act of 1934 p. 545 Federal legislation that regulates the sale of securities between investors after an investor has purchased them from a business entity issuer.

Insider trading p. 546 Illegal securities trading in which a corporate insider uses information not available to the general investor public as the basis for trades in the company's stock.

Insider Trading and Securities Fraud Enforcement Act p. 546 Federal legislation passed in 1988 that raised the criminal and civil penalties for insider trading, increased the liability of brokerage firms for wrongful acts of their employees, and gave the Securities and Exchange Commission more power to pursue violations of insider trading.

Section 16 p. 549 Provision of the Securities Exchange Act of 1934 that imposes restrictions and reporting requirements on ownership positions and stock trades made by certain corporate insiders named in the statute.

Scienter p. 550 Specific intent to deceive, manipulate, or defraud.

Securities Litigation Uniform Standards Act of 1998 p. 551 An amendment to the Securities Exchange Act of 1934 that prevents private parties from instituting certain lawsuits in federal or state court that are based on the statutory or common law of any state that punishes "a misrepresentation or omission of a material fact" or the use of "any manipulative device or contrivance" concerning the purchase or sale of a covered security.

Blue-sky laws p. 551 State securities laws intended to cover purely intrastate securities offerings.

Corporate governance p. 551 The process used by corporate officers and directors to establish lines of responsibility, approval, and oversight among key stakeholders and set out rules for making corporate decisions.

Sarbanes-Oxley (SOX) Act of 2002 p. 553 Amendments to the 1933 and 1934 Securities Acts that impose stricter regulation and controls on how corporations do business, through regulation of auditing, financial reporting, and internal corporate governance.

American Recovery and Reinvestment Act of 2009 p. 556 Federal legislation that created a loan program and underlying mandates for corporations most acutely impacted by the financial crisis that began in 2008; also established the Troubled Assets Relief Program (TARP) to administer the loans.

Dodd-Frank Wall Street Reform and Consumer Protection Act of 2010 p. 557 Federal legislation designed to overhaul the regulation of U.S. financial services and markets.

CHAPTER REVIEW QUESTIONS

1. In the _____ _____, issuers raise capital by selling securities in the public markets or in private placements.
   a. Stock exchange
   b. Primary market
   c. Secondary market
   d. Debt exchange

Facts for Questions 2 and 3: NewCo is planning to expand its global operations and is considering financing the operations as follows:

   I. Issuance of $500,000 of securities in a 12-month period to 145 investors.
   II. Borrowing of $1,000,000 from a bank through a promissory note.
   III. Issuance of $2,000,000 of securities over three years to 10 investors.

2. Which transaction(s) would require registration under the '33 Act?
   a. I and II
   b. II and III
   c. I only
   d. III only

3. Which transaction(s) would be exempt from registration under Regulation D?
   a. I and II
   b. II and III
   c. I only
   d. III only

4. Carla is an accountant for WidgetCo. In the course of her employment, she discovers that WidgetCo's application for a patent has been approved. Before the news is announced publicly, she calls her neighbor Sam and tells him about the patent. She also tells him to buy as much WidgetCo stock as possible. The two agree to split any profit. After the patent news is announced, WidgetCo's stock price doubles. Which of the following is true?
   a. Carla's tip violated rule 10b-5, but Sam has no liability.
   b. Sam is not liable because he did not benefit from the tip.
   c. Carla and Sam both violated rule 10b-5.
   d. Sam violated Section 16 because of a short swing.

5. High Flyer Inc., a publicly held company, made an extraordinary corporate payout of a bonus to its CEO while it was under investigation by the SEC for fraud. Under SOX, the SEC may
   a. Claw back the bonus into an emergency escrow fund.
   b. Require High Flyer to register the payment.
   c. Terminate the auditing company.
   d. Assess civil penalties against the directors who authorized the bonus.

Answers and explanations are provided at the end of this chapter.

THEORY TO PRACTICE

Four individuals are the collective owners, directors, and shareholders ("principals") of Cool Runnings Manufacturing Company (CRMC), which designs and manufactures snow sports equipment such as snowboards, racing skis, and related products. The principals built the company over a 10-year period from start-up to over $20 million in annual revenue. Six months ago, the principals met and decided to embark on an aggressive expansion plan with the objective of doubling CRMC's production capacity in five years.

This plan required approximately $50 million to fund the purchase of real estate, equipment, expanded payroll, additional taxes, and marketing expenses. One reason for this expansion plan was to develop a new snowboard product, the Tectonic Board, which early marketing research indicated would become one of CRMC's best-selling products. The principals were under pressure to develop this new product because of an overall slump in sales. However, given CRMC's current facilities and budget, the product was currently only halfway through the design phase and not expected to be on the market for at least three more years. The demand for CRMC's existing brands of snowboards was slowly, but steadily, declining. In fact, the company's profits had been so stagnant that it could not reasonably afford to borrow the entire amount of the expansion cost given its recently diminishing cash flow. However, because of the development of the Tectonic Board, the principals are hopeful that they can attract capital by selling stock to investors.

1. What are the alternatives for financing this expansion plan? Should CRMC consider a bond? Why or why not? Would selling equity be more or less advantageous than issuing a bond?
2. Assume that the principals decide to issue stock to the public in order to raise money. They know of five investors that may be interested in this opportunity, so they send each a copy of the business plan for CRMC's expansion along with a cover letter explaining the price of the stock and giving instructions on how to buy the stock. Has CRMC committed a violation of securities laws by sending out the business plan and cover letter? Could that constitute the sale of a security?
3. Suppose that, instead of sending the business plan (as in Question 2 above), the principals consult counsel and inform her that they wish to develop a prospectus and distribute it to a limited number of high-net-worth investors. Must the securities be registered before marketing or selling them? If not, what exemption(s) could they fall into?

Assume that the principals proceed as in Question 3 and send the plan to 15 high-net-worth potential investors. During face-to-face and videoconference meetings with the investors, the CEO makes the following statements in response to investor questions:

Question: Is CRMC's financial position currently sound, or are there threats to your financial well-being?

CEO: CRMC's cash flow is expected to increase steadily because the Tectonic Board is the board for a new generation of boarders. Our research shows that it has potential to bring us a sizable return on our investment.

Question: What stage of development is the Tectonic Board in?

CEO: If all goes well, it will be on store shelves in less than one year.

Question: Is there a current demand for your existing snowboard products?

CEO: We have had very strong sales. However, like every product, they have their ups and downs. They're likely to be on the upside shortly.

4. Based on the CEO's statements, one investor purchases a substantial amount of stock. If the business venture fails before the Tectonic Board is released, will the investor have any recourse against CRMC and its CEO based on the statements made by the CEO? Why or why not?
5. If an investor files a fraud suit against CRMC and its CEO, will his statements alone be sufficient to pass the PSLRA standards for scienter?
6. Do any of the statements themselves constitute the required elements under PSLRA? What type of conduct, if coupled with the statements, could meet the scienter standard?

LEGAL STRATEGY 101

"Mr. Ponzi"

We have thus far shown you a wide variety of legal and business strategies in the "Legal Strategy 101" sections of this textbook. Yet there is one particular legal strategy we have barely mentioned: *noncompliance*.

Simply put, we can't always assume that people and firms will comply with the law because noncompliance is always an option. One of the most egregious examples of the legal noncompliance strategy is Wall Street investor Bernie Madoff's massive, multibillion-dollar fraudulent investment scheme.

Before his ultimate downfall, Madoff was a respected member of the Wall Street elite and the founder and chairman of a successful investment firm, Bernard L. Madoff Securities LLC. But unbeknownst to his unsuspecting and innocent investors, Madoff was actually operating one of the most elaborate and enormous fraudulent investment firms in the history of Wall Street!

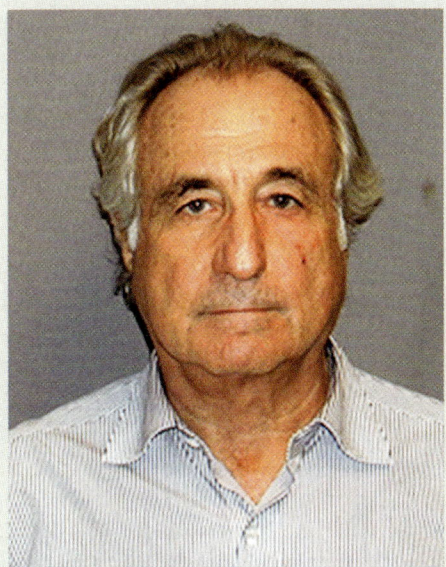
Bernie Madoff. Mug Shot/Alamy Stock Photo

The essence of Madoff's fraudulent operation was a so-called Ponzi scheme. In brief, a Ponzi scheme is a fraudulent investment operation in which the operator pays returns to his or her initial investors from funds paid to the operator by subsequent investors, rather than from profits earned by the operator.[27] In other words, instead of investing his clients' monies in legitimate investments and generating steady returns as his clients had believed, Madoff would simply deposit his clients' money into his own bank account. When clients wanted their money, Madoff "used the money in the Chase Manhattan bank account that belonged to them or other clients to pay the requested funds."[28]

Noncompliance on such a massive scale is no doubt a dangerous and reckless strategy with catastrophic legal consequences. In the case of Bernie Madoff, for example, after he confessed to operating the largest private Ponzi scheme in history and pled guilty to 11 federal crimes, the financier was sentenced to 150 years in prison and ordered to pay restitution of $170 billion to his victims.

CRITICAL THINKING QUESTIONS

In response to cases of severe domestic loss, Congress and other parties have created special victim compensation funds (e.g., 9/11 attacks, BP-*Deepwater Horizon* oil spill). Should a special fund be set up for victims of Madoff's financial crimes? Why or why not?

---

[27] See generally Ponzi Schemes—Frequently Asked Questions, U.S. Securities & Exchange Commission.

[28] Jonathan Stempel, *Madoff Trustee Sues JP Morgan for $6.4 Billion*, Reuters, Dec. 2, 2010.

MANAGER'S CHALLENGE

From the facts in the Theory to Practice problem, one can see the potential complications and hazards of selling equity as a form of raising capital. Assume that the principals approach you as their senior manager and ask that you devise a potential plan to raise money without actually issuing securities. Individually, or in a small group, draft an "Opportunity Plan" that describes a process by which CRMC could raise money without being subject to securities laws. The effectiveness of your Opportunity Plan will depend on your knowledge of the *Howey* test to be sure that the opportunity does not qualify as a security that is subject to registration.

See Connect for Manager's Challenge sample answers.

CASE SUMMARY 16.1 United States v. Bhagat, 436 F.3d 1140 (9th Cir. 2006)

TRADITIONAL INSIDER TRADING

Bhagat was employed as an engineer by NVIDIA, a publicly held corporation located in Silicon Valley that manufactured graphics processors and media communication devices. On Sunday, March 5, 2000, the chief executive officer of NVIDIA sent an e-mail to all company employees announcing that NVIDIA had entered into a contract with Microsoft to develop and manufacture 3-D graphics for Microsoft's Xbox. The e-mail contained a prediction that the deal would result in nearly $2 billion in revenue over the next five years. On Monday, March 6, NVIDIA's management sent out several follow-up e-mails, including one from the vice president of marketing that was entitled "Xbox shhhh" and gave specific instructions to keep the information confidential. NVIDIA's management imposed an employee trading blackout (i.e., employees were not permitted to purchase or sell any NVIDIA stock) for several days. Employees were also required to cancel any open or outstanding orders for NVIDIA stock.

Bhagat arrived at his office on that same Monday morning, and approximately 20 minutes after the trading-blackout e-mail was sent, he purchased a large quantity of NVIDIA stock—his largest purchase in three years. After the news about NVIDIA's contract with Microsoft was released, NVIDIA's stock rose sharply and Bhagat reaped a substantial profit. On the same day that he purchased his stock, Bhagat contacted two friends, who also purchased unusually large quantities of NVIDIA. The Securities and Exchange Commission (SEC) investigated the trade, and Bhagat claimed that he had read his e-mail only after he had bought the stock and that, by the time he tried to cancel the transaction, he was told it was too late to do so. Bhagat was convicted by a jury of insider trading, securities tipping, and lying to the SEC investigators. Bhagat appealed on the grounds that the government presented no direct evidence that Bhagat had read his e-mail prior to executing the trade.

CASE QUESTIONS

1. Is Bhagat liable as an insider even though he was just an employee? Why?
2. What role did Bhagat's credibility play in this case?
3. Given that NVIDIA had access to this confidential information, should it have taken more precautions than simply to send out an e-mail and impose a trading blackout on employees? Is it possible that Bhagat did not know at the time that his conduct was illegal? Does that matter? Were his actions ethical? Why or why not?

CASE SUMMARY 16.2 Nursing Home Pension Fund v. Oracle Corp., 380 F.3d 1226 (9th Cir. 2004)

SCIENTER

Software giant Oracle released its newest product, the 11i Suite, in 2000. The company issued press releases and disseminated other information to the public that touted the software as a significant achievement that would enhance its revenue. Over the next 12 months, executive management continued making overly optimistic forecasts about the software and earnings. During that same period, Oracle's CEO, Larry Ellison, sold nearly $1 billion worth of his personal stock in Oracle.

Shortly after Ellison's sale was completed, Oracle released negative news about earnings and it became obvious that the 11i Suite sales were substantially below expectations. The stock price dropped sharply.

CASE QUESTIONS

1. Does the timing of the insider sale and the release of the negative earnings statement constitute sufficient scienter to clear the PSLRA's scienter hurdle?
2. Who prevails and why?

CASE SUMMARY 16.3 In re Vantive Corporation Securities Litigation, 110 F. Supp. 2d 1209 (N.D. Cal. 2000)

MATERIAL MISSTATEMENTS

Vantive is a manufacturer of client management software designed for use by sales representatives from various industries. Vantive is also a retailer and provides support services for the software. After a successful public offering in 1995, the company's stock sold for $6 per share and soon rose to as high as $35 per share. When the tech sector slumped in 1998, the stock dropped to less than $15 per share over an eight-month period. During this eight-month period, management forecast strong gains in income by using a model that recognized millions of dollars in revenue based on software licenses that would not actually be realized unless the licensees were successful in selling *sublicenses* for the software. A group of shareholders brought suit under rule 10b-5.

CASE QUESTIONS

1. Were the forecasts sufficient to constitute a material misstatement of fact and an omission that violated securities laws? Explain.
2. Is Vantive protected by the PSLRA?

CASE SUMMARY 16.4 Mark v. FSC Securities Corporation, 870 F.2d 331 (6th Cir. 1989)

EXEMPT SECURITIES

FSC was a securities brokerage firm that sold limited partnership interests to Mark and 27 other investors. All investors executed a *subscription agreement* in which each investor revealed his or her income and represented that he or she had the opportunity to review relevant information, including risk factors, and was sufficiently knowledgeable and savvy to understand the implications of the investment. However, FSC managers never actually reviewed the completed subscription agreements, and all who applied to be investors were admitted. When the interests dropped in value, Mark sued to rescind the contract on the basis that the securities were not registered and that he was not a qualified investor. FSC defended that the offering qualified under the '33 Act safe-harbor provision of Regulation D.

CASE QUESTIONS

1. Should Mark prevail?
2. Is it relevant that FSC never reviewed the subscription agreement?

CASE SUMMARY 16.5 City of Philadelphia v. Fleming Companies, Inc., 264 F.3d 1245 (10th Cir. 2001)

GOOD FAITH IN PSLRA

Fleming is a publicly held company involved in litigation with another company over a trade dispute. During the litigation, the officers of Fleming disclosed the litigation and the relevant factual basis for the litigation in its SEC-required disclosure materials. The litigation resulted in a $200 million jury verdict against Fleming, causing Fleming's stock to drop precipitously. After an appellate court reversed part of the verdict and Fleming settled the case for $20 million, the stock regained some of its previous value but never returned to its prelitigation levels. A group of shareholders sued Fleming's officers and directors, claiming that the disclosure of litigation was not detailed enough, did not disclose the potential downside risks of a losing jury verdict, and thus constituted a misleading statement and omissions in violation of the 1934 Securities Exchange Act. Fleming's officers defended that they disclosed all known facts of the litigation and were protected by the Private Securities Litigation Reform Act's safe-harbor provisions because they acted in good faith and disclosed all the facts they were privy to at the time.

CASE QUESTIONS

1. Who prevails and why?
2. Should Fleming's officers be protected by the PSLRA?

CASE SUMMARY 16.6 Leon v. IDX Systems Corporation, 464 F.3d 951 (9th Cir. 2006)

WHISTLEBLOWER PROTECTION

Leon was the director of medical information at IDX Systems. After IDX began an investigation of Leon's activities, it required him to turn over his company-issued laptop computer. When he refused, IDX terminated Leon and required him to return his laptop computer. After initial resistance, Leon turned over his laptop. A forensic examination of the laptop showed that files were deleted and that a user had deployed special software in an attempt to "write over" and hide documents. Leon eventually filed suit claiming that IDX terminated him in violation of the whistleblower provision of the SOX Act and that his termination was based on the fact he had evidence on his laptop about IDX improprieties.

CASE QUESTIONS

1. Is Leon protected under the SOX Act even if there is no evidence that he actually had information about unlawful IDX activities?
2. Could Leon be in violation of the SOX Act document-destruction rules for deleting files?

✓ Self Check ANSWERS The *Howey* Test

1. This question is based on *Smith v. Gross,* 604 F.2d 639 (9th Cir. 1979), in which the court decided that the earthworm scheme did constitute a securities offering. It fit all elements of the *Howey* test and had vertical commonality because the investor profited from the work of the promoter.

2. Careful! This question first appears to be a replica of the *Howey* case's facts, but there are substantial differences in the investment opportunities. Utley's plan would likely *not* constitute offering a security. He was offering developing and real estate services, but they were not a requirement for purchasing the property. Owners of the property may simply have purchased it for their own vacation use and not as an investment with expectations of return. Utley's services did not have the required commonality, nor did investors necessarily benefit from Utley's efforts.

3. This question is based on *SEC v. Alliance Leasing Corp.,* Litigation Release No. 16488, 2000 LEXIS 5227 (S.D. Cal. 2000), in which the court held that Alliance's leasing plan was a securities offering under the *Howey* standards. The investment opportunity had both vertical and horizontal commonality, and the investors profited primarily due to the efforts of Alliance in arranging the leases.

Insider Trading

1. Misappropriation. Aaron is an outsider, but he learned of nonpublic, material information from an insider. He breached his duty of confidentiality with his patient and never disclosed the transaction to the source of information while he traded based on the information.

2. Traditional insider trading. Edmund, despite his position, is considered an insider. He used nonpublic, material information to avoid losses in connection with Gloucester's stock price.

3. Tipper-tippee liability. Cornwall was the insider who gave Regan nonpublic, material information that Regan acted on. Both profited.

CHAPTER REVIEW QUESTIONS: Answers and Explanations

1. **b.** *Primary market* is the term used to refer to the original issuance (or reissuance) by a business entity that sells its securities to the public markets (the general investment community) or in private placements (limited groups of investors). (c) is wrong because the secondary market involves the trading of already-issued securities, which does not raise capital for the issuing business.

2. **d.** Because the offer is over a period of three years, it does not qualify for exemption. (a), (b), and (c) are incorrect because the $500,000 offering is exempt under rule 504 and a bank's promissory note is not considered a security under the '33 Act.

3. **c.** The amount of the offering and the limited time period bring this transaction squarely under the exemption in rule 504 under Regulation D. (a), (b), and (d) are incorrect because the $2,000,000 offering is not exempt due to the three-year time period and a bank's promissory note is not considered a security (and therefore does not require an exemption) under the '33 Act.

4. **c.** Carla has liability as a tipper (an insider who breaches a duty by revealing inside information to a third party) and Sam has liability as a tippee (someone who benefits from an insider's tip and knows the information is not public); both have liability under rule 10b-5. (d) is incorrect as Sam is not an insider and cannot have Section 16 liability.

5. **a.** The SOX Act gives the SEC the power to preserve corporate assets and prevent looting of the corporation by creating an emergency escrow fund for "extraordinary" payments such as a bonus. The other answers are incorrect because the SEC does not have authority to terminate or assess penalties in this situation.

UNIT FIVE Regulatory Environment of Business

CHAPTER 17 Administrative Law

CHAPTER 18 Environmental Law

CHAPTER 19 Antitrust and Regulation of Competition

CHAPTER 20 Creditors' Rights and Bankruptcy

CHAPTER 21 Warranties and Consumer Protection Law

CHAPTER 22 Criminal Law and Procedure in Business

CHAPTER 23 Personal Property, Real Property, and Land Use Law

CHAPTER 24 Intellectual Property

CHAPTER 25 International Law and Global Commerce

CHAPTER 17
Administrative Law

©philsajonesen/Getty Images

Learning Objectives

After studying this chapter, students who have mastered the material will be able to:

17-1   Explain the purpose of administrative law.
17-2   List and articulate the primary functions of an administrative agency.
17-3   Give examples of several administrative agencies that regulate business.
17-4   Identify the primary sources of law that provide authority and set limits for administrative agencies.
17-5   Discuss how the Administrative Procedures Act (APA) and enabling statutes interrelate to provide an agency with its jurisdiction and scope of authority.
17-6   Identify and explain the steps used in administrative rulemaking.
17-7   Define the powers of administrative agencies in the areas of licensing, inspection, and adjudication.
17-8   Describe the limits on agency powers imposed by the legislative, executive, and judicial branches of the government.
17-9   Name two federal public disclosure statutes and describe how these statutes make administrative agencies more accountable to the public.

Much of the law's reach over business occurs through federal and state agencies that create regulations based on legislatively set policy objectives and then administer the policies through monitoring and enforcement actions. The various laws that prescribe or regulate this process are known as *administrative laws*. The regulations are created and carried out by *administrative agencies,* and business owners and managers encounter these agencies at various levels. Although these agencies have broad powers, they are still limited by the Constitution, statutes, and judicial review. In this chapter, students will learn

- The definition and role of administrative law in the U.S. legal system.
- The functions and scope of administrative agencies and the limits on these agencies' powers.
- Ways in which administrative agencies are accountable to the public.
- The role of state administrative law.

DEFINITION, FUNCTION, AND SOURCES OF ADMINISTRATIVE LAW

Administrative law is the body of law, drawn from various sources, that defines and regulates federal regulatory agencies and limits the exercise of authority by these agencies. Federal regulatory agencies include bodies that function within a particular executive branch *department* (such as the Internal Revenue Service functioning within the Department of the Treasury) as well as *nondepartment* agencies (such as the Environmental Protection Agency). The federal government also has *independent agencies* (such as the Securities and Exchange Commission) that have been designated by Congress as independent of the executive branch and do not exist by virtue of the authority of the president or a department. Departments are headed by a *cabinet secretary* who reports directly to the president. Department agencies, nondepartment agencies, and independent agencies are either headed by *administrators* or composed of *commissioners* and headed by the commission chair. These department, nondepartment, and independent agencies are collectively referred to as **administrative agencies**.

Primary Functions of Administrative Agencies

Administrative agencies have a wide range of functions related to the formation, implementation, and enforcement of regulations intended to administer a federal law. Although the agencies are primarily thought of as part of the executive branch and, therefore, exercise *executive powers* to enforce federal laws related to a particular agency's jurisdictional expertise, they also exercise important *legislative* and *judicial* functions as well.

Policymaking One of the most important functions of an administrative agency is its responsibility of making policy that is consistent with the implementation of federal law. When Congress passes a piece of legislation, it is often crafted in broad strokes that may include findings of fact and/or objectives of the law. However, the practical aspects of implementing the laws often require more complex and detailed policies. Administrative agencies are frequently charged by Congress to study potential solutions to a problem and then to exercise a legislative function by creating legally enforceable rules, known as *administrative regulations,* that purport to satisfy Congress's will by filling in the details of the statute. This policymaking function is known as **rulemaking**.

Administrative agencies also use a system of adjudicatory bodies established within the administrative agency to decide cases that involve an alleged violation of the agency's rules. These adjudicatory bodies are staffed with administrative law judges who are actually employees of the particular regulatory body. This judicial function is known as **adjudication**.

These rulemaking and adjudication powers and processes are discussed in more detail later in the chapter.

Investigation and Enforcement Many administrative agencies also have an agency enforcement division devoted to investigating alleged violations of the agency's administrative regulations and recommending enforcement actions such as fines and other sanctions. Agencies have a wide range of discretion as to when and how they enforce regulations against a violator. Administrative agencies also monitor compliance with regulatory requirements through inspection of the facilities and grounds of business sites under their jurisdiction.

LO 17-1
Explain the purpose of administrative law.

LO 17-2
List and articulate the primary functions of an administrative agency.

LO 17-3
Give examples of several administrative agencies that regulate business.

Licensing and Permitting Some administrative agencies also are responsible for licensing and permitting in a wide variety of areas, including licenses for professionals and industries. For example, the Securities and Exchange Commission issues licenses to certain individuals involved in the public trading of stocks, and the Federal Communications Commission licenses television and radio stations. Agencies also issue permits, such as those issued by the Environmental Protection Agency to control air and water pollution.

Distribution of Federal Statutory Benefits to the Public When Congress confers a benefit to the citizenry at large, administrative agencies are the portal used by the law to actually distribute those benefits. Agencies are involved in the application process and distribute benefits according to law. These benefits include loan guarantees for students, medical care for the poor and elderly, compensation for workers laid off by their employers, and many other federal programs. For example, the Social Security Administration is responsible for distributing retirement and medical benefits to eligible citizens.

Figure 17.1 is an organizational chart that shows the major federal administrative agencies.

Sources of Administrative Law

LO 17-4

Identify the primary sources of law that provide authority and set limits for administrative agencies.

Administrative law is not thought of as a *separate* body of statutes that govern administrative agencies. Rather, administrative law is a combination of four distinct sources of law that operate in tandem: the U.S. Constitution; the Administrative Procedures Act (APA); enabling statutes; and common law.

U.S. Constitution The U.S. Constitution places limits on the type of powers that agencies may exercise and also places limits on the methods that agencies may employ in carrying out their duties. Examples of provisions of the Constitution that limit agency powers include the Due Process Clause; doctrines derived from the principle of separation of powers, including the nondelegation doctrine; and the Fourth Amendment protections against certain warrantless searches by agency personnel.

Administrative Procedures Act (APA) The Administrative Procedures Act (APA)[1] of 1946 is a federal statute that imposes specific procedural structures and due process requirements on administrative agencies' duties of rulemaking, adjudication, and other agency functions. The APA also provides for the judicial review of agency actions and determinations.

Enabling Statutes Congress will sometimes choose to create a new administrative agency to carry out the details of macro objectives set by the law. When Congress wishes to establish an administrative agency, it passes a federal law called an **enabling statute**. Enabling statutes are important because they are the source of an agency's authority and establish the agency's scope and jurisdiction over certain matters. For example, in 1970 Congress passed the Occupational Safety and Health Act,[2] which established the Occupational Safety and Health Administration (OSHA) and set this agency's mission as the *prevention* of workplace injuries and the assurance of safe working conditions for employees. The enabling act portion of the law placed OSHA under the authority of the Department of Labor and provided for the jurisdiction necessary to study and develop workplace

---

[1] 5 U.S.C. §§ 551–559.
[2] 29 U.S.C. §§ 651–678.

FIGURE 17.1 — Administrative Agencies in the Context of the U.S. Government Organizational Chart

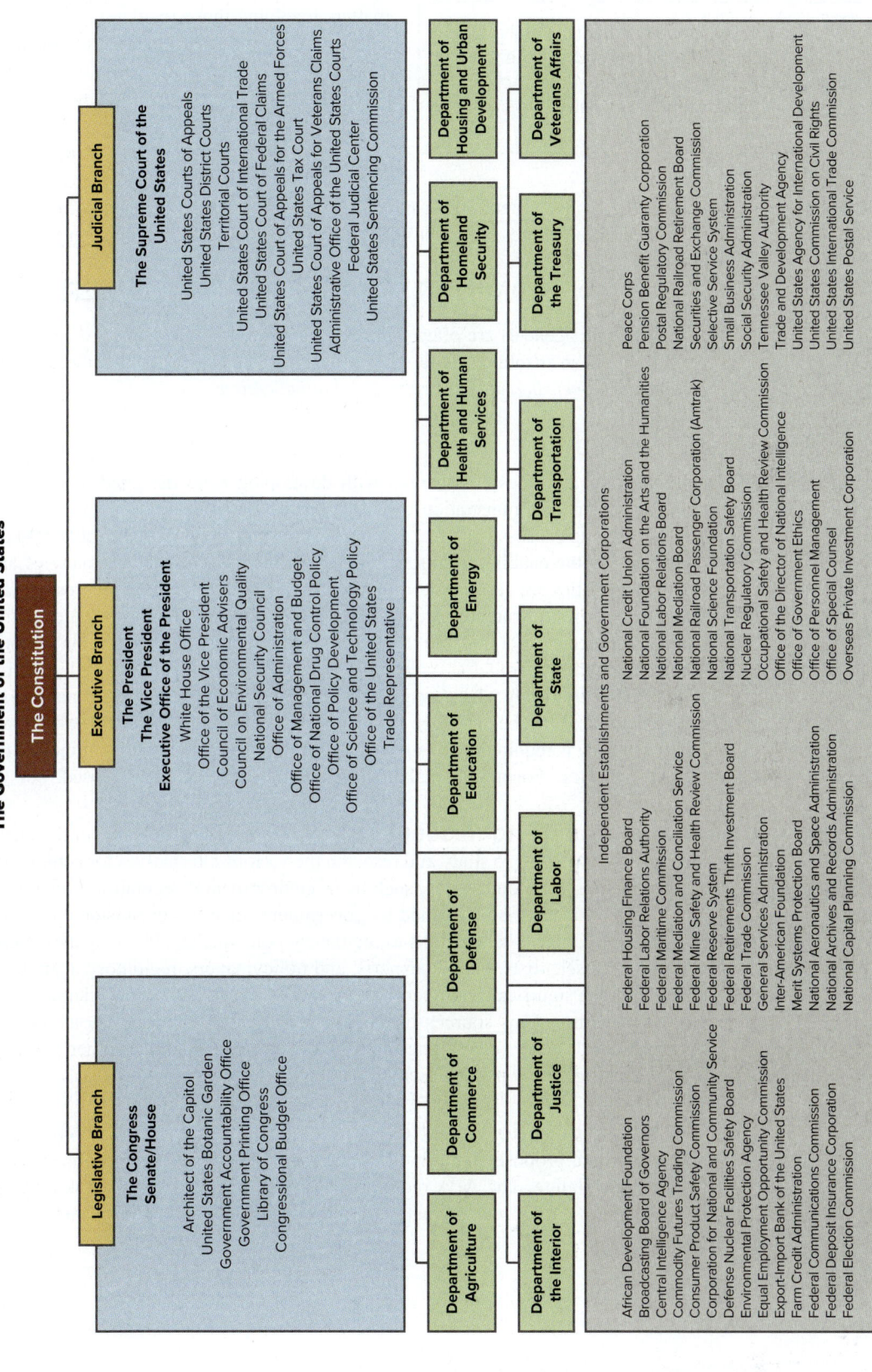

Source: https://www.gpo.gov/fdsys/pkg/GOVMAN-2015-07-01/pdf/GOVMAN-2015-07-01-Government-of-the-United-States-4.pdf.

> **KEY POINT**
>
> *Administrative law* is a combination of several different sources of law. The primary sources are the Constitution, the Administrative Procedures Act (APA), and enabling statutes. Common law also plays a minor role.

safety regulations, in addition to establishing the agency's authority to investigate, enforce, and adjudicate matters involving those regulations. Enabling acts are also used by Congress to *charge* an agency with certain additional responsibilities or to provide additional authority for the agency in a particular area of need.

Common Law Prior to the establishment of the APA, a body of common law that regulated administrative agencies existed. While much of the common law has been codified through the APA, courts sometimes still refer to the common law in applying or interpreting the APA.

SCOPE OF ADMINISTRATIVE AGENCY POWER

Administrative agencies are often granted broad powers by Congress to accomplish objectives set out in an enabling statute. These powers include policymaking through *rulemaking; enforcement, licensing, and inspection;* and *adjudication.*

Rulemaking

Administrative agencies are charged with developing *rules* designed to facilitate the federal government's administration of the law and programs as set down in federal statutes. The rulemaking process is set out in the Administrative Procedures Act (APA) and is supplemented by the enabling statutes passed by Congress. In practice, many of an agency's rulemaking duties are carried out through *informal* rulemaking procedures that are permitted under the basic structure of the APA.[3] Despite its name, informal rulemaking actually involves a procedure set down in the APA that is centered on the concepts of notice, public comment, publication of a final rule, and the opportunity to challenge a rule in court. *Formal* rulemaking is used only when Congress has specifically indicated in the enabling statute that the agency rules must be made "on the record after a hearing." In the case of formal rulemaking, the agency is required to engage in an extensive hearing process outlined in the APA to develop the rules.[4] Formal rulemaking is very cumbersome and rarely used.

Agency Study and Research Depending on the mandates in the enabling statute, the agency begins to study and research the various alternatives for achieving the goals set by Congress. In some cases, such as in environmental regulation, much of the study and research function is performed by government scientists or outside contractor experts who provide data and conclusions to regulatory policymakers in the agency. In addition to working with scientists, outside experts, and policymakers, regulatory agencies also typically employ a significant number of attorneys who ensure that the rulemaking process is compliant with various sources of administrative law. Agencies may also have separate divisions unrelated to rulemaking for enforcement, licensing, and other functions. These nonrulemaking functions are described later in this chapter.

Notice: Publication of the Proposed Rule After research and study, the agency drafts a proposed rule that purports to achieve one or more objectives set out in the enabling statute. The APA requires that notice of proposed rulemaking be published in the *Federal Register* and that the notice must include "actual terms, substance and

---

LO 17-5
Discuss how the Administrative Procedures Act (APA) and enabling statutes interrelate to provide an agency with its jurisdiction and scope of authority.

LO 17-6
Identify and explain the steps used in administrative rulemaking.

---

[3] APA § 553.
[4] APA §§ 556, 557.

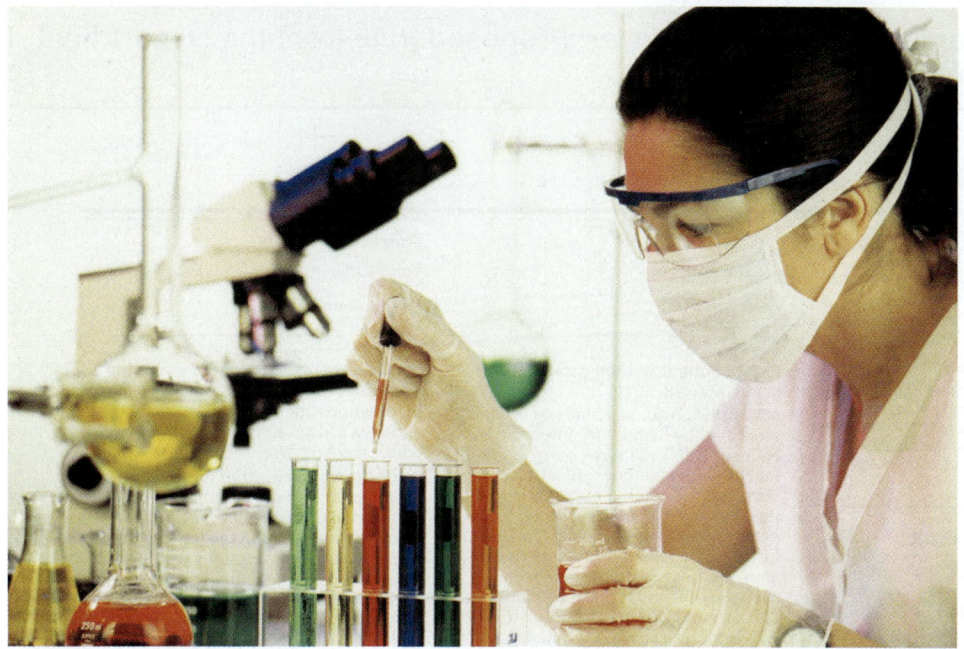

Many administrative agencies employ scientists to conduct research and provide data and conclusions to policymakers. Comstock/Getty Images

description" of the proposed rule.[5] In theory, this requirement puts parties that have some stake in the rule on notice that the rule will become law unless the regulatory agency is persuaded otherwise or a court challenge is brought.

Agencies are also required to publicly disclose any studies, reports, data, or other pertinent material that the agency relied upon in creating the proposed rule. Figure 17.2 is an excerpt from the *Federal Register*. It sets out part of a proposed rule by the Department of Labor under the authority of the Fair Labor Standards Act.

Public Comment Once the proposed rule has been published in the *Federal Register,* the agency must then give time for the public to comment. In fact, the APA requires that the affected parties be allowed to participate in the rulemaking through submission of their own research and findings and that the agency make a good faith effort to study anything submitted and to consider the arguments made in the comment period. In cases that impact a particular region of the country, agencies sometimes choose to meet public comment requirements by holding public hearings at strategic times and locations during the comment period. In practice, many of the comments and much of the evidence submitted on proposed rules are generally delivered by representatives from, among others, (1) various factions from business and industry (such as the National Manufacturers Association), (2) professional associations that represent large blocks of constituents (such as the National Association of Realtors), and (3) public advocacy groups (such as the Natural Resources Defense Council). For example, suppose the Securities and Exchange Commission proposes new rules relating to corporate reporting disclosure requirements for publicly held companies.[6] The SEC would likely expect various groups representing publicly

Legal Speak >))

Federal Register
A daily publication distributed by the federal government (found in major libraries) primarily used to communicate proposed agency rules, final agency regulations, and other administrative agency or executive branch announcements, such as executive orders.

---

[5]APA § 553.

[6]A publicly held company's stock is sold to the general public via a public exchange such as the New York Stock Exchange. Such companies are regulated by a variety of federal agencies and are discussed in detail in Chapter 16, "Regulation of Securities, Corporate Governance, and Financial Markets."

FIGURE 17.2 Sample of *Federal Register:* Proposed Rule from the Department of Labor

11888

Proposed Rules

Federal Register

Vol. 84, No. 61

Friday, March 29, 2019

This section of the FEDERAL REGISTER contains notices to the public of the proposed issuance of rules and regulations. The purpose of these notices is to give interested persons an opportunity to participate in the rule making prior to the adoption of the final rules.

DEPARTMENT OF LABOR

Wage and Hour Division

29 CFR Parts 548 and 778

RIN 1235–AA24

Regular Rate Under the Fair Labor Standards Act

AGENCY: Wage and Hour Division, Department of Labor.

ACTION: Notice of proposed rulemaking and request for comments.

SUMMARY: The Fair Labor Standards Act (FLSA or Act) generally requires that covered, nonexempt employees receive overtime pay of at least one and one-half times their regular rate of pay for time worked in excess of 40 hours per workweek. The regular rate includes all remuneration for employment, subject to the exclusions outlined in section 7(e) of the FLSA. Part 778 of Title 29, Code of Federal Regulations (CFR), contains the Department of Labor's (Department) official interpretation of the overtime compensation requirements in section 7 of the FLSA, including requirements for calculating the regular rate. Part 548 of Title 29 implements section 7(g)(3) of the FLSA, which permits employers, under specific circumstances, to use a basic rate to compute overtime compensation rather than a regular rate. The Department has not updated many of these regulations, however, in more than half a century—even though compensation practices have evolved significantly. In this Notice of Proposed Rulemaking (NPRM), the Department proposes updates to a number of regulations both to provide clarity and better reflect the 21st-century workplace. These proposed changes would promote compliance with the FLSA; provide appropriate and updated guidance in an area of evolving law and practice; and encourage employers to provide additional and innovative benefits to workers without fear of costly litigation.

DATES: Submit written comments on or before May 28, 2019.

ADDRESSES: You may submit comments, identified by Regulatory Information Number (RIN) 1235–AA24, by either of the following methods: *Electronic Comments:* Submit comments through the Federal eRulemaking Portal at *http://www.regulations.gov.* Follow the instructions for submitting comments. *Mail:* Address written submissions to Division of Regulations, Legislation, and Interpretation, Wage and Hour Division, U.S. Department of Labor, Room S–3502, 200 Constitution Avenue NW, Washington, DC 20210. *Instructions:* Please submit only one copy of your comments by only one method. All submissions must include the agency name and RIN, identified above, for this rulemaking. Please be advised that comments received will become a matter of public record and will be posted without change to *http://www.regulations.gov,* including any personal information provided. All comments must be received by 11:59 p.m. on the date indicated for consideration in this rulemaking. Commenters should transmit comments early to ensure timely receipt prior to the close of the comment period, as the Department continues to experience delays in the receipt of mail. Submit only one copy of your comments by only one method. *Docket:* For access to the docket to read background documents or comments, go to the Federal eRulemaking Portal at *http://www.regulations.gov.*

FOR FURTHER INFORMATION CONTACT: Melissa Smith, Director of the Division of Regulations, Legislation, and Interpretation, Wage and Hour Division, U.S. Department of Labor, Room S–3502, 200 Constitution Avenue NW, Washington, DC 20210; telephone: (202) 693–0406 (this is not a toll-free number). Copies of this NPRM may be obtained in alternative formats (Large Print, Braille, Audio Tape or Disc), upon request, by calling (202) 693–0675 (this is not a toll-free number). TTY/TDD callers may dial toll-free 1–877–889–5627 to obtain information or request materials in alternative formats. Questions of interpretation and/or enforcement of the agency's regulations may be directed to the nearest WHD district office. Locate the nearest office by calling WHD's toll-free help line at (866) 4US–WAGE ((866) 487–9243) between 8 a.m. and 5 p.m. in your local time zone, or log onto WHD's website for a nationwide listing of WHD district and area offices at *http://www.dol.gov/whd/america2.htm.*

Electronic Access and Filing Comments: This proposed rule and supporting documents are available through the **Federal Register** and the *http://www.regulations.gov* website. You may also access this document via WHD's website at *http://www.dol.gov/whd/.* To comment electronically on Federal rulemakings, go to the Federal eRulemaking Portal at *http://www.regulations.gov,* which will allow you to find, review, and submit comments on Federal documents that are open for comment and published in the **Federal Register**. You must identify all comments submitted by including "RIN 1235–AA24" in your submission. Commenters should transmit comments early to ensure timely receipt prior to the close of the comment period (11:59 p.m. on the date identified above in the **DATES** section); comments received after the comment period closes will not be considered. Submit only one copy of your comments by only one method. Please be advised that all comments received will be posted without change to *http://www.regulations.gov,* including any personal information provided.

SUPPLEMENTARY INFORMATION:

I. Executive Summary

The FLSA generally requires covered employers to pay nonexempt employees overtime pay of at least one and one-half times their regular rate for hours worked in excess of 40 per workweek. The FLSA defines the regular rate as "all remuneration for employment paid to, or on behalf of, the employee"—subject to eight exclusions established in section 7(e).[1] Parts 548 and 778 of CFR Title 29 contain the regulations addressing the overtime compensation requirements in section 7 of the FLSA, including requirements for calculating the regular rate of pay.

The Department promulgated the majority of part 778 more than 60 years ago, when typical compensation often consisted predominantly of traditional wages; paid time off for holidays and vacations; and contributions to basic medical, life insurance, and disability

---

[1] *See* 29 U.S.C. 207(e).

Source: https://www.govinfo.gov/content/pkg/FR-2019-03-29/pdf/2019-05687.pdf.

held companies, as well as the executives of the affected companies, to comment urging the SEC to not make the requirements too burdensome. On the other hand, the SEC is also likely to receive comments from consumer advocacy and shareholder watchdog groups urging the agency to adopt even stricter disclosure requirements.

Protection of Small Business Owners The Regulatory Flexibility Act (RFA) of 1980, as amended by the Small Business Regulatory Enforcement Fairness Act (SBREFA) of 1996, requires agencies to ask for and consider regulatory proposals that address the size of the businesses or other organizations subject to regulation. When a proposed regulation will have a significant economic impact on a substantial number of small businesses, the RFA requires, among other things, that agencies analyze and take into consideration small business concerns. Under the RFA, when an agency issues a rule that will have a significant economic impact on a substantial number of small entities, the agency must provide small businesses the opportunity to participate in the rulemaking. Providing the opportunity to participate may include soliciting and receiving comments from small businesses. The participation of small businesses helps agencies fulfill their statutory objectives while reducing, as much as possible, the burden on small businesses.

Revision or Final Publication After the comment period has ended, the agency may either revise the rule or simply publish the final rule in the *Federal Register*. If the agency revises the rule between the time that it was originally proposed and the time that it is published as final, there is generally *no* legal obligation to provide an additional comment period. As a practical matter, agencies publishing controversial proposed rules may opt for a second comment period, but there is no legal mandate to do so. One exception to this rule occurs when the agency's revised rule is a *substantial* or *material alteration* of the originally proposed rule. Courts have given agencies broad latitude in publishing a revised final rule *without* an additional comment period so long as the revisions are a *logical outgrowth* of the originally proposed rule. Revisions that stay within the original scope of the proposed rule do not trigger the requirement of a second comment period. In Case 17.1, a federal court of appeals applied the logical-outgrowth test of the APA to the U.S. Department of Education's decision to revise a proposed rule and publish it as final.

CASE 17.1 Association of Private Sector Colleges and Universities v. Duncan and the U.S. Department of Education, 681 F.3d 427 (D.C. Cir. 2012)

FACT SUMMARY Congress passed the Higher Education Act (HEA) to foster access to higher education and provide more than $150 billion in new federal aid to approximately 14 million postsecondary students and their families. Students receiving this aid attend private for-profit institutions, public institutions, and private nonprofit institutions. The U.S. Department of Education (Department) is charged with the oversight and administration of the HEA. After several investigations into for-profit universities (such as the University of Phoenix) revealed systematic attempts to mislead and engage in fraud, the Department promulgated a set of new rules because it determined that the existing regulations were too lax. The proposed rules impacted institutions of higher education in several operational ways and were intended to deter fraud and improve accountability. After a public comment period, the Department published the final rules as originally proposed, but it also included an

(continued)

additional final rule with new regulatory requirements for colleges offering distance learning.

The final rules were challenged by the Association of Private Sector Colleges and Universities (APSCU), which represents for-profit institutions of higher education. APSCU alleged a violation of the APA on the basis that the Department had failed to provide adequate notice of the distance learning rule to regulated parties. The trial court agreed and ruled in favor of APSCU on the issue of the distance learning rule. The Department appealed, arguing that the new distance learning rule was simply a logical outgrowth of the existing rule and that the other proposed regulations gave fair notice that the Department was considering changing the rule related to distance education programs.

SYNOPSIS OF DECISION AND OPINION The Court of Appeals for the D.C. Circuit upheld the trial court's ruling on the distance learning regulations in favor of APSCU. The court ruled that the Department had not provided interested parties with a sufficient opportunity to comment on the proposed rule and therefore violated the APA. The court rejected the Department's argument that the new rule was a logical outgrowth of the original rule because the new rule was a significant regulatory shift for providers of distance education programs. As such, the Department was required to publish the proposed rule and provide interested parties with an opportunity to comment.

WORDS OF THE COURT: Logical Outgrowth "[The proposed rule] and the final rule need not be identical: '[a]n agency's final rule need only be a logical outgrowth of its notice.' A final rule qualifies as a logical outgrowth 'if interested parties should have anticipated that the change was possible, and thus reasonably should have filed their comments on the subject during the notice-and-comment period.' By contrast, a final rule fails the logical outgrowth test and thus violates the APA's notice requirement where 'interested parties would have had to divine [the agency's] unspoken thoughts, because the final rule was surprisingly distant from the proposed rule' [quoting from *CSX Transportation, Inc. v. Surface Transportation Board*].

"The Department does not point to anything in its Notice of Proposed Rulemaking that specifically addressed distance education. Nor did the Department solicit comments about the adoption of such a rule. These failures cut against the Department's claim that the distance education regulation is a logical outgrowth of the proposed rules. More importantly, we find the Department's claims that parties should have anticipated the regulation [without merit]."

Case Questions

1. How could the Department of Education have avoided a successful challenge to the distance education rule?
2. What does the court mean when it explains that a previously unpublished rule violates the APA if "interested parties would have had to divine [the agency's] unspoken thoughts"?
3. *Focus on Critical Thinking:* What are the contrasting arguments for the APA's extensive publication, comment, and revision process? Does it prevent government regulators from responding effectively to public policy problems such as fraud by for-profit universities? Does the rulemaking process protect the public?

If the agency's view has not been swayed during the comment period, the agency will publish the proposed rule in the *Federal Register* as final.[7] When publishing the final rule, the agency is required by the APA to include "a concise general statement of basis and purpose." This statement is used to meet the legal requirement that the decision be based on *reasoned decision making* and not made arbitrarily or capriciously. The agency must also state its conclusions on major issues of fact or policy that were used in its decision making when issuing the final rule. Agencies also typically include an effective date in the final

---

[7] APA § 552(a)(1)(D).

The Association of Private Sector Colleges and Universities (APSCU), which represents for-profit institutions of higher education, challenged a rule by the U.S. Department of Education. Kristoffer Tripplaar/Alamy

rule as well. Once it is in effect, the rule is called a **regulation** and is published in the Code of Federal Regulations (CFR).

In 1990, Congress passed the Negotiated Rulemaking Act,[8] which provides an alternative to normal rulemaking policies in cases where it is possible that various cooperating parties could ultimately reach an *agreement* on the negotiated proposed rule. The law provides guidelines for administrative agencies to engage in a formal negotiation procedure intended to draft rules that have the support of affected parties even prior to publication. The negotiations are conducted through committees composed of representatives from the agency and parties that have an interest in the rule. However, the act does not relieve the agency of the responsibility to properly publish and establish a comment period for the negotiated proposed rule. Nor does the act require that the agency end up actually publishing the negotiated rule instead of an agency-made rule.

Judicial Challenges After the final rule is published, the APA allows adversely affected parties to challenge the final rule in court.[9] Courts apply the *arbitrary and capricious* standard when reviewing a final rule. That is, for the rule to pass judicial muster, the evidence must show that the agency made its final decision based on a consideration of relevant factors without any clear errors of judgment and that its process was consistent with the APA procedural requirements. The right to judicial review of final rules is a relatively narrow one, and courts give great deference to agency authority in the area of rulemaking. Judicial review as a limit on nonrulemaking agency action and authority is discussed in the next section.

Legal Speak >))

Arbitrary and Capricious
Failure to exercise honest judgment instead of reasoned consideration of all relevant factors.

---

[8] 5 U.S.C. §§ 561–570a.
[9] APA §§ 701–706.

CONCEPT SUMMARY *Steps in the Rulemaking Process*

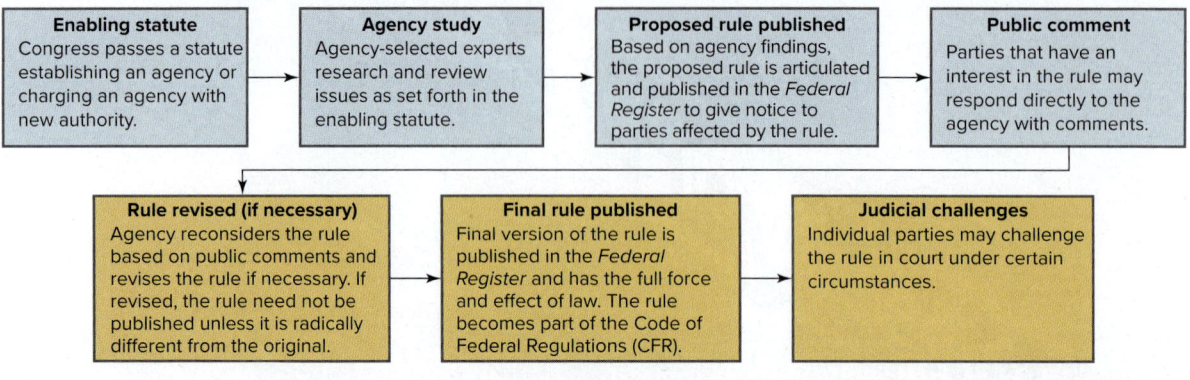

LO 17-7

Define the powers of administrative agencies in the areas of licensing, inspection, and adjudication.

Enforcement, Licensing, and Inspection

In terms of **enforcement**, the U.S. Supreme Court has ruled that agencies have broad discretion as to *when* and *whom* to regulate. This authority, known as the agency's *prosecutorial discretion*, has been held as practically unreviewable by the judiciary. While enabling statutes can sometimes narrow the agency's authority, courts are still highly deferential to an agency's decision on when and how to enforce its regulations. Absent a showing that the agency engaged in a patent abuse of discretion in enforcement, parties challenging administrative agency actions have a substantial obstacle to overcome in order to justify judicial interference. Agencies have a separate division (apart from rulemaking) that carries out enforcement responsibilities through the use of investigators and the agency's Office of General Counsel.

Administrative agencies also regulate and administer laws through **licensing**. Agencies are frequently delegated the statutory power to issue, renew, suspend, or revoke a license to conduct a certain business. Once a company is licensed, the agency may impose fines or restrictions upon the *licensee* for any violation of agency regulations. One of the more high-profile examples of an agency that regulates through licensing is the Federal Communications Commission (FCC), which issues licenses for use of broadcast frequencies. Administrative agencies at the state level often issue *occupational licenses* and regulate professionals such as attorneys and physicians, as well as occupations such as those of hairstylists and contractors. State administrative agencies are discussed in more detail later in this section.

Some agencies also monitor compliance with administrative regulations by conducting **inspections** of businesses and individuals within their jurisdiction. Recall from Chapter 2, "Business and the Constitution," that government agents are restricted from engaging in unreasonable searches without a search warrant. Administrative agencies are, of course, covered by the same restriction, and ordinarily an agency must secure an *administrative warrant* before government agents may enter and inspect a business to monitor compliance with an administrative regulation. However, certain businesses are classified as *pervasively regulated,* and, therefore, the Supreme Court has fashioned an exception to the warrant requirement that covers situations in which the agency conducts regularly scheduled inspections pursuant to a rule. For example, suppose MillCo operates several mills that are subject to a hypothetical enabling statute called the Mill Control Act (MCA). The MCA provides that all mills must be maintained in a certain way and that the administrative agency with jurisdiction over the MCA should promulgate rules that include monthly inspections to ensure compliance. Any inspections of MillCo's facilities pursuant to the rule would generally not require a warrant because MillCo qualifies as a pervasively regulated business as defined in the MCA.

Even in cases where courts have held that administrative agencies are required to obtain an administrative warrant to conduct an inspection of a business, the Supreme Court has held that agencies are subject to a lower standard of probable cause in obtaining a warrant than the standard that must be met by the government in obtaining a criminal warrant. In Case 17.2, a federal appeals court considers the difference between an administrative warrant and a criminal warrant.

> **KEY POINT**
>
> Courts are highly deferential to agency decisions involving how and when an agency enforces a regulation.

CASE 17.2 Trinity Marine Products v. Secretary of Labor Elaine Chao, 512 F.3d 198 (5th Cir. 2007)

FACT SUMMARY Compliance officers from the Occupational Safety and Health Administration (OSHA)[10] arrived at the facilities of Trinity Marine Products to conduct an inspection pursuant to their authority under the Occupational Safety and Health Act. Trinity's managers turned the OSHA inspectors away, so OSHA obtained an administrative warrant and returned with federal marshals. After the threat of arrest by the marshals, Trinity officials allowed the search under protest. Trinity later brought an action against OSHA, contending that the warrant had been issued without probable cause and that administrative warrants could not be legally executed by using force against nonconsenting parties. Trinity argued that refusal by a party to honor an administrative warrant should trigger a contempt-of-court proceeding to determine the validity of the warrant and that the government may not use force or arrest to enforce an administrative warrant.

SYNOPSIS OF DECISION AND OPINION The Fifth Circuit Court of Appeals ruled in favor of OSHA, reasoning that the standards for probable cause were lower for administrative warrants than for criminal warrants and that federal statutes and case law allowed administrative warrants to be executed using a reasonable degree of force. In this case, the government had shown that it had sufficient information to justify an inspection and, because Trinity would not honor the warrant, that use of the marshals to gain entry was appropriate and consistent with the statutory intent that allows OSHA to "investigate and inspect without delay."

WORDS OF THE COURT: Probable Cause for Administrative Warrants "[A]dministrative warrants are distinguishable from traditional criminal warrants in a number of ways. They have, for instance, a different—linguistically idiosyncratic—'probable' cause standard: Probable cause may be based either on specific evidence of an existing violation, as in the traditional criminal context, or on a lesser showing that 'reasonable legislative or administrative standards for conducting an inspection are satisfied with respect to a particular establishment.'"

Case Questions

1. Would Trinity's case against OSHA have been stronger if the inspectors showed up with the marshals and forcibly searched the premises without first attempting to inspect without a warrant? Why or why not?
2. What are some examples of situations in which the probable cause standard for administrative warrants would not be met?
3. *Focus on Critical Thinking:* Should the standards for warrants be different for different companies? Does that raise any constitutional concerns?

---

[10]OSHA is an administrative agency under the auspices of the Department of Labor.

Also within the agencies' enforcement powers is the right to require businesses subject to the agency's jurisdiction to (1) keep certain records for inspection, (2) turn over relevant documents that may be useful in determining compliance with a particular rule, and (3) request statements or other information from the business's principals or managers.

Adjudication

Many (but not all) administrative agencies have authority to *adjudicate* matters under their jurisdiction. Adjudication is a hearing in which the government and the private party each presents evidence in a quasi-judicial setting. In most agencies, the presiding officer is an **administrative law judge (ALJ)** who is typically an attorney employed by the agency to adjudicate disputes.

Recall from Chapter 2, "Business and the Constitution," that federal adjudicatory powers are constitutionally vested exclusively in federal courts. However, federal courts have permitted agency adjudication when it occurs in the context of public rights disputes (a private party dispute with an agency over the agency's action or inaction) or when two private parties are disputing rights that arise within an area of the agency's jurisdiction.[11]

Appeals The losing party in an ALJ case generally has an automatic appeal to the administrative head of the agency, who may overturn or affirm the ALJ's ruling. An adverse decision from the agency may also be challenged in a federal trial court. Court challenges are discussed in detail in the next section of this chapter.

CONCEPT SUMMARY Scope of Administrative Agency Power

- Administrative agencies have broad powers, including rulemaking, enforcement, licensing, and adjudication.
- Agencies develop rules to be used in facilitating the government's administration of the law.
- The rulemaking process involves agency research, publication of a proposed rule in the *Federal Register,* a period for public comment on the proposed rule, and either revising the rule for additional comment or publishing a finalized rule.
- Agencies must use a reasoned decision-making process that is not arbitrary or capricious.
- After a final rule is published, the APA allows adversely affected parties to challenge the rule in court. However, courts give great deference to the agency's decisions.
- Agencies have prosecutorial discretion in deciding when and whom to regulate.
- Administrative agencies also regulate and administer laws through the licensing process, in which they issue, renew, suspend, or revoke a license to conduct certain types of business.

(continued)

---

[11] Some agencies use their adjudication power to actually set policy as an alternative method to their traditional rulemaking authority when they wish to take a particular course of action in a given case. This is a controversial method of making policy, but the U.S. Supreme Court has allowed agencies to use adjudication instead of rulemaking in instances where the adjudication promotes a fundamental fairness. However, the Court made clear that this was a relatively narrow power that may be exercised only when fundamental fairness to the parties requires it.

- Some agencies also monitor compliance with regulation by conducting inspections of businesses and individuals within their jurisdiction.
- Administrative agencies have the authority to adjudicate matters under their jurisdiction by holding a hearing between the government and private parties in front of an administrative law judge.

LIMITS ON ADMINISTRATIVE AGENCIES

Although the powers delegated to administrative agencies are broad, it is important to remember that all administrative agencies, including independent agencies, are limited in their authority by the three-part system of the federal government. The legislative, executive, and judicial branches all have various means of power that limit the authority of administrative agencies.

LO 17-8

Describe the limits on agency powers imposed by the legislative, executive, and judicial branches of the government.

Executive Branch

From a structural perspective, administrative agencies are extensions of the executive branch's authority to carry out the legislative mandates, and the Supreme Court has acknowledged that the president of the United States has some inherent general right to exercise power over administrative agencies in a variety of ways. Although this inherent power is notoriously vague, from an administrative law perspective, the president's power is derived from the Appointments Clause[12] and from direct power through executive orders and, to a lesser degree, through budgetary control.

Appointments Clause The Constitution gives the president the power to appoint "officers of the United States" consistent with the Appointments Clause in Article II. Although subject to confirmation by the Senate, the president has the exclusive right to nominate principal officers such as *cabinet members* or *commissioners* of independent agencies that report directly to the president. Although not specifically articulated in the Constitution, the Supreme Court has held that the president also has the power to remove any principal officers at any time with or without cause and without any congressional approval. However, Congress sometimes passes an enablement act with a *restriction* on the president's power to remove a particular officer of the government. Federal courts have held that this limiting type of statutory restriction is constitutional so long as the restrictions do not impair the president's ability to carry out his constitutional duty.[13] In fact, Congress has designated certain agencies, such as the Securities and Exchange Commission (SEC) and the Federal Trade Commission (FTC), as *independent* of the president's direct powers, and the heads and commissioners of independent agencies may be removed only for good cause (such as corruption) and not for mere differences in policy views between the agency and the president.

Direct Power For the last several decades, presidents have exercised *direct power* over administrative agencies to accomplish the president's public policy objectives. For example, in 1982, in response to what President Reagan perceived as a regulatory system that was so burdensome on certain industries that it impacted the industrial output of the country, he issued an executive order requiring that all federal administrative agencies

---

[12]U.S. Const. art. II, § 2, cl. 2.
[13]U.S. Const. art. II, § 2, cl. 2.

submit to cost-benefit analysis along with any proposed regulation as part of a mandatory review process by the Office of Management and Budget (OMB). OMB was assigned to encourage agencies to be as cost-conscious as possible when imposing regulatory schemes on certain industries. This executive order is thought of as direct power over the agencies because the OMB reports directly to the president.

Congress

Although the U.S. Supreme Court narrowed congressional review of agency actions in the famous 1983 case of *INS v. Chadha*,[14] Congress still retains significant power to influence, amend, or void actions of an administrative agency. For example, Congress may exercise its constitutionally granted *power of the purse* over government funding of particular agencies, or it may simply enact legislation that restricts an agency's authority or pass a new law to overrule an administrative regulation. In 1996, Congress amended the APA[15] to restore its own authority to cancel an agency's final rule if (1) both houses agree, (2) they pass a resolution to overrule within 60 days, and (3) the overruling resolution is presented to the president.

Congress also has oversight over administrative agencies by virtue of the Senate's power of *advice and consent*[16] in the appointment of certain high-ranking agency officers. Although Congress may not appoint administrative officials,[17] as a practical matter it still wields broad influence over appointments by virtue of the political realities involved in agency-head selection. Ultimately, Congress has the power to remove an administrative agency head via impeachment by the House of Representatives and removal by the Senate.

Figure 17.3 provides an example of how an administrative agency is organized.

Judicial Review

The APA sets various standards of review for cases where administrative agency actions are challenged in a federal court.[18] Of course, courts will set aside any agency action that is inconsistent with the Constitution. But the APA also authorizes courts to void agency actions if the agency has exceeded its *statutory authority* or if agency actions have been taken without adhering to the statutorily established *procedure*.

Statutory Interpretation by Agencies   Because Congress uses very broad objectives when it passes an enabling act and other laws, administrative agencies must sometimes interpret an ambiguous statute in order to carry out their duties or take administrative action. In 1984, the Supreme Court adopted the *Chevron* test[19] as the framework to analyze the validity of administrative agency statutory interpretation and action. First, courts look to the language of the statutory authority given to the agency by Congress. If the agency's interpretations or actions conflict with the plain-language meaning of the statute, then a court may hold that the agency's interpretation or actions were unlawful.

---

[14]462 U.S. 919 (1983). The Court held that a decades-old congressional procedure for overruling agency regulations, known as a *legislative veto*, violated the bicameralism and presentment requirements of the U.S. Constitution.

[15]The APA was amended by the Contract with America Advancement Act in 1996, which provides for congressional authority to review administrative regulations. See 5 U.S.C.§§ 801–808. The amendment was intended to reestablish congressional power to nullify agency regulations by addressing the constitutional problems with the legislative veto as outlined in *INS v. Chadha,* 462 U.S. 919 (1983).

[16]U.S. Const. art. II, § 2, cl. 2 (the Appointments Clause).

[17]*Buckley v. Valeo*, 424 U.S. 1 (1976).

[18]APA § 706 et seq.

[19]*Chevron USA, Inc. v. NRDC*, 104 S. Ct. 2778 (1984).

FIGURE 17.3 Typical Organizational Structure of an Administrative Agency: Food and Drug Administration (FDA)

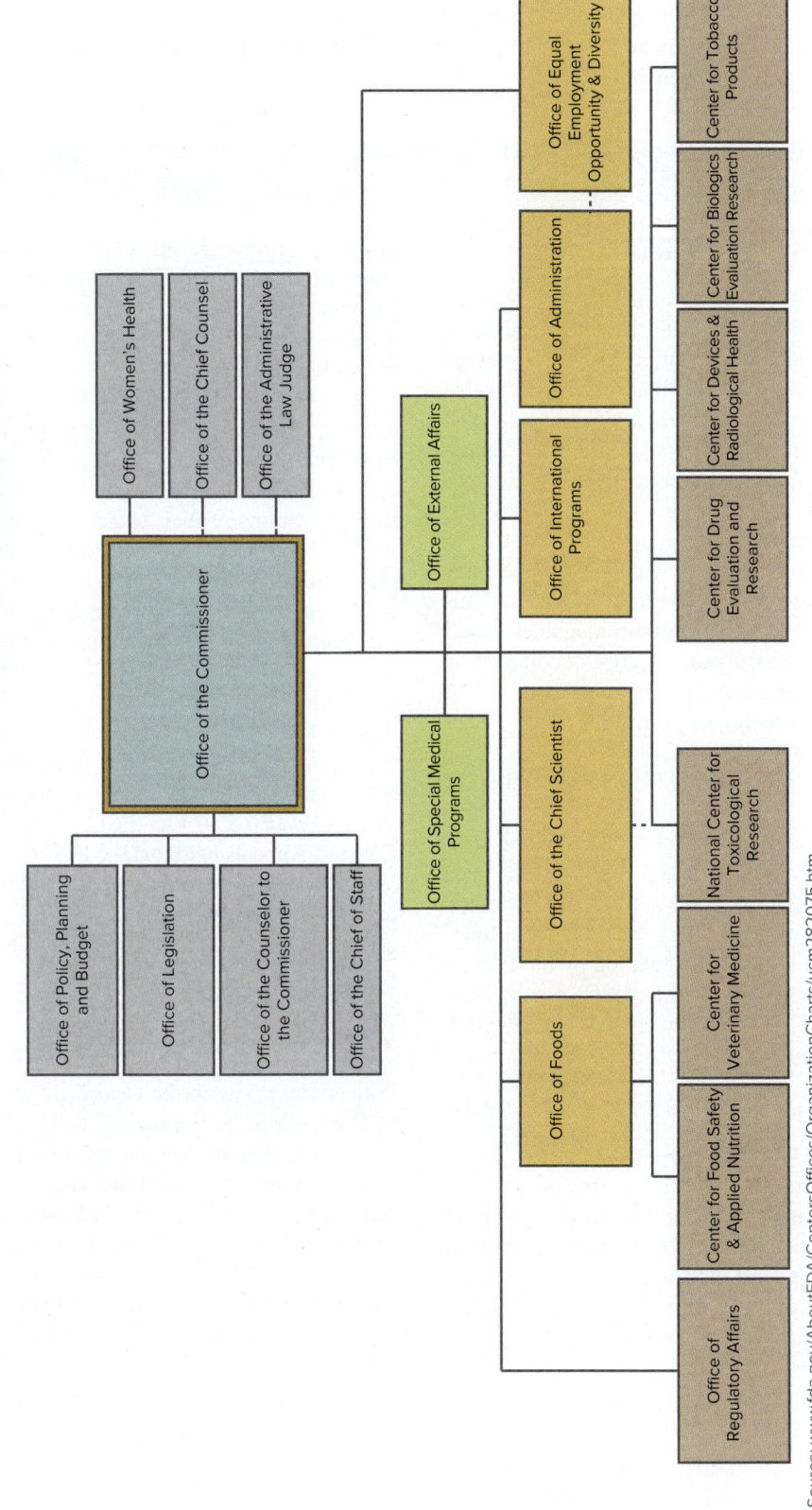

Source: www.fda.gov/AboutFDA/CentersOffices/OrganizationCharts/ucm282075.htm.

If, however, the statute is silent or ambiguous on the agency's authority, the court applies the **arbitrary and capricious standard** to determine whether the agency's actions were lawful. A heightened standard, known as the *substantial evidence test,* applies only in a relatively small number of cases where the formal rulemaking process has been required by the enabling act.

LEGAL IMPLICATIONS IN CYBERSPACE

The Battle over Net Neutrality

Net neutrality is the principle that all movement and content on the Internet should receive equal treatment. Proponents of net neutrality—typically users, content providers, and online businesses—argue that a *neutral* Internet encourages innovation and that telecommunications providers' restriction of bandwidth for certain Internet services stifles advances by entrepreneurs. They oppose broadband providers blocking Internet content and applications of competitors on the basis that users paying for the same level of service should receive the same level of service. The net-neutrality argument is another aspect of the larger question about the scope of competition regulation in cyberlaw in the modern age.

Opponents to the concept of complete net neutrality argue that some regulation is necessary. Some Internet service providers (ISPs), other members of the telecommunications industries (especially cable companies such as Comcast and Verizon), and large hardware companies have argued that some data discrimination, such as packet filtering of viruses, is positive and even necessary to a functional Internet. They insist that more regulation by the Federal Communications Commission (FCC) would actually discourage innovation by preventing ISPs from charging higher fees for tiered services.

Initial FCC Regulation and the Comcast Case

The Federal Communications Commission (FCC) is the primary regulator to issue rules on net neutrality because its jurisdiction includes oversight of broadband providers. In 2005, the FCC adopted its first Policy Statement with regard to the neutrality of the Internet. The FCC's purpose was to ensure that broadband networks are widely deployed, open, affordable, and accessible to all consumers. In 2007, some of the subscribers to Comcast's high-speed Internet service found out that Comcast was interfering with their use of applications for peer-to-peer networking. These peer-to-peer programs, which allow users to directly share large files with one another, consume large amounts of bandwidth. The FCC ruled that Comcast had significantly impeded consumers' ability to access the content and use the applications of their choice, and that Comcast's method of bandwidth management contravened federal policy because there were other options it could use to manage network traffic without discriminating against peer-to-peer communications. On appeal, Comcast challenged the FCC's authority to impose net neutrality obligations on broadband providers such as Comcast. Comcast contended that the FCC was trying to officially set net neutrality regulations but that it did not have the jurisdiction to do so.

In *Comcast Corp v. FCC*,[20] the D.C. Circuit Court of Appeals held that the FCC did not have the legal authority to regulate the way ISPs manage user traffic. Therefore, the FCC did not have the authority to enforce net neutrality in accordance with its 2005 policy.

FCC's Open Internet Order

Prior to the ruling in the *Comcast* case in 2010, the FCC revamped its approach but still rejected reclassifying broadband Internet services as telecommunications services. Instead, it sought comments on a proposed rule that eventually became the Open Internet Order.[21] The Order required broadband providers to (1) publicly disclose accurate information regarding their network management systems, (2) adhere to antiblocking requirements and refrain from blocking

(continued)

---

[20] 600 F.3d 642 (D.C. Cir. 2010).

[21] 25 F.C.C. Rcd. 17905, 17907 (2010).

consumers from accessing a particular edge provider such as Netflix, and (3) adhere to an antidiscrimination rule in which all network is treated as neutral. However, in *Verizon v. FCC*,[22] a federal appeals court invalidated the antiblocking and antidiscrimination provisions of the Open Internet Order.

FCC's Regulation of the Internet as a Public Utility

Soon after the *Verizon* case was decided, political and industry leaders called on the FCC to take aggressive action by promulgating regulations that would regulate the Internet as a public utility. Initially, the FCC favored a "hybrid approach" that would place certain controls on the commercial relationship between Internet service providers and content companies. In 2015, the FCC announced that high-speed Internet service was to be regulated as a public utility pursuant to its authority under Title II of the Communications Act[23] that governs common utility carriers (such as landline phone systems). Although the FCC did not prohibit the use of paid-peering agreements between broadband providers and large content providers (e.g., Netflix) and network intermediaries (e.g., Level 3 Communications), the agency had authority to police such agreements and prevent any deals that were not in the public interest.

FCC's Reversal of Course

After the 2016 election, the composition of the FCC changed and so did its view on net neutrality. In 2017, the FCC voted to move ahead with a Notice of Proposed Rulemaking titled *In the Matter of Restoring Internet Freedom*[24] that justifies the reversal on the basis that the regulation of broadband providers saddles providers with outdated regulations and creates regulatory uncertainty that stifles innovation. Almost immediately, attorney generals from 19 states challenged the FCC's decision, and some states have passed their own version of net neutrality. The issue is still making its way through the courts.

The FCC's net neutrality rules have been controversial.

Chris Kleponis/Bloomberg/Getty Images

---

[22]740 F.3d 623 (D.C. Cir. 2014).

[23]47 U.S.C. § 151.

[24]Federal Communications Commission, Restoring Internet Freedom, WC Docket No. 17-108, FCC 17-60, 82 Fed. Reg. 25568 (June 2, 2017) (adopted May 18, 2017).

CHAPTER SEVENTEEN | Administrative Law 585

Applying the Arbitrary and Capricious Standard In order to meet the judicial review requirements, agencies must provide evidence that a *reasoned decision-making* process was used rather than an action that was *arbitrary and capricious*. This standard applies to all agency actions, including rulemaking, adjudication, enforcement, inspection, and licensing. Arbitrariness and capriciousness are found when the agency has taken action that is not based on a consideration of relevant factors, including viable alternatives available to the regulatory agency, or is a result of a clear error of judgment by the agency. The APA specifically requires that courts review only the information that the agency had available to it at the time it took the action in question.

Although the power of courts to set aside an administrative agency's action is clear, courts have traditionally been sparing in the use of this power. The U.S. Supreme Court has consistently held that judicial deference to administrative agencies is an important part of administrative law and that a court should not substitute its judgment for that of the agency.[25]

The Court provided guidance for lower courts in applying the arbitrary and capricious standard in *Motor Vehicle Manufacturing Association v. State Farm Mutual Automobile Association*.[26] In that case, the Court ruled that agency action was arbitrary and capricious if the agency (1) relied on factors that Congress had not intended it to consider, (2) failed to consider an important aspect of the problem, (3) offered an explanation for its decision that ran counter to the evidence before the agency, or (4) offered an explanation that was so implausible that it could not be ascribed to a difference in view or the product of agency expertise.

The arbitrary and capricious standard received significant media attention when it was the central issue in a case challenging the Department of Interior's six-month ban on deepwater drilling in the wake of the *Deepwater Horizon* (BP) oil spill disaster. The government's drilling moratorium suspended drilling on 33 exploratory wells and halted the issuing of any new permits. In a June 2010 ruling by the U.S. District Court in Louisiana, the government's drilling moratorium was found to be arbitrary and capricious, and the court issued an injunction against the government's action. Judge Martin Feldman wrote, "[t]he court is unable to divine or fathom a relationship between the findings [of the government agency] and the immense scope of the moratorium." The court invalidated the agency's actions based on its conclusion that the government failed to "cogently reflect the decision to issue a blanket, generic, indeed punitive, moratorium."[27] Ultimately, the Secretary of the Interior withdrew the moratorium. Note that the legal aspects of the *Deepwater Horizon* oil spill are covered in more detail in Chapter 18, "Environmental Law."

In Case 17.3, a federal appellate court applies the *Motor Vehicle Manufacturing Association* reasoning to a decision by the Federal Elections Commission.

CASE 17.3 Van Hollen v. Federal Elections Commission, 811 F.3d 486 (D.C. Cir. 2016)

FACT SUMMARY In 2002, Congress passed the Bipartisan Campaign Reform Act (BCRA) to regulate electioneering communications, which the law defines as communications that refer to a clearly identified candidate made within 60 days of a general election or 30 days of a primary election. Among other provisions, the BCRA banned corporations and unions from using their general treasuries to fund electioneering communications. In BCRA's wake, the Federal Elections Commission

(continued)

---

[25] *Citizens to Preserve Overton Park, Inc. v. Volpe*, 401 U.S. 402 (1971).
[26] 463 U.S. 29 (1983).
[27] *Hornbeck Offshore Services LLC v. Salazar*, 696 F. Supp. 2d 627 (E.D. La. 2010).

(FEC) promulgated several rules to enforce the various statutory reforms. Christopher Van Hollen Jr. (Van Hollen), a member of the U.S. House of Representatives, challenged this rule as arbitrary and capricious. The trial court ruled in favor of Van Hollen that the new rules represented an arbitrary and capricious use of the FEC's regulatory authority.

SYNOPSIS OF DECISION AND OPINION The Court of Appeals for the D.C. Circuit reversed the trial court's decision and ruled in favor of the FEC. The court rejected Van Hollen's argument that the FEC failed to adequately explain its decision to adopt the new rules. The court held that, while an agency is required to adequately explain its decision, this does not mean that its explanation must be a model of analytical precision. Rather, so long as the reviewing court can reasonably discern the agency's analytical path, that is sufficient to satisfy the reasoned decision-making standard. The court concluded that the FEC cleared that low hurdle because it examined the relevant data and articulated a satisfactory explanation for its action, including a rational connection between the facts found and the choice made.

WORDS OF THE COURT: Arbitrary and Capricious Standard "Here, we acknowledge the FEC's explanation was not one of 'ideal clarity,' but, again, ideal clarity is not the standard. The FEC advanced three explanations for its [rule], which we refer to as the 'support,' 'burden,' and 'privacy' rationales. Because we can reasonably discern the FEC's analytical path from these three rationales, we uphold its purpose requirement against Van Hollen's challenge. . . . Granted, as Van Hollen is quick to point out, the FEC's assertions here were not corroborated with any hard evidence [to support its decision]. But these assertions are, 'at the very least, speculation based firmly in common sense and economic reality.'"

Case Questions

1. The court ruled that the FEC's rationale was not of "ideal clarity." Shouldn't an agency have to at least be clear about its rationale to avoid a finding of arbitrariness?

2. Why do you think Van Hollen objected to these rules?

3. *Focus on Critical Thinking:* Recall the discussion of First Amendment rights for political speech of corporations from Chapter 2, "Business and the Constitution." Does the BCRA violate the rights of corporations and unions by banning electioneering completely? Why or why not?

 Self-Check Arbitrary and Capricious

Is the agency's action arbitrary and capricious?

1. After a series of deadly vehicle accidents on the nation's highways that were caused by underinflated tires, the National Highway Traffic Safety Administration (NHTSA)—the administrative agency charged with regulating the nation's highways to make them safer—proposed a rule requiring automobile manufacturers to include tire pressure monitoring systems (TPMSs) as standard equipment on all new cars. These systems warn drivers when they have underinflated tires. The rule states that manufacturers must provide a TPMS that warns drivers when one tire is 30 percent or more underinflated. Despite the fact that a 20 percent standard proved to be more reliable and safer, the NHTSA settled on the 30 percent standard because of its slightly lower cost. A safety advocacy group challenged the rulemaking decision to adopt the 30 percent standard.

2. Pursuant to a congressionally set objective of improving and maintaining the quality of public bodies of water, the Clean Water Act (CWA) authorizes the Environmental Protection Agency (EPA) to issue permits to and regulate any facility discharging pollutants into waters of the United States. OilCo is a company

(continued)

specializing in refining pure Alaskan crude oil, which is found only in the town of Barren Ground, Alaska. Barren Ground is one of the few places in the United States that has perfect, pollutant-free water due to the town's remote location. OilCo wishes to build three new refining plants in Barren Ground that each uses a state-of-the-art refining system. However, the system requires cooling via a saline-based solution. OilCo applied for a permit to discharge its used coolant into Barren Ground Bay, but the EPA granted OilCo a discharge permit with a maximum pollution level of 0. This means OilCo cannot discharge any of its coolant without first treating it to the point at which it is no longer a pollutant but rather pure water. This process will be very expensive to implement, so OilCo has challenged the EPA ruling on the permit.

3. The Federal Energy Regulatory Commission (FERC) is an administrative agency responsible for permitting new power plants. Under the Save the Waters Act, the FERC is responsible for establishing a permitting process and issuing permits to individuals and companies wishing to construct hydroelectric power plants. Under the established process, a company must obtain a permit in order to gather information, conduct feasibility studies, and create architectural plans. The information gathered can be used for subsequent applications for licenses to construct and operate the plants. Clean Green Electric Co. (CGEC) wants to build two hydroelectric power plants on the Raging Waters River in Colorado in an area outside Small Town. CGEC applied for a permit to begin gathering information about the feasibility of locating the power plants outside Small Town. However, the FERC denied the company's permit application based in part on information from two prior permits CGEC had obtained for construction of the same power plants at the same site. CGEC challenged the ruling, arguing that the FERC should consider only the information in the most recent permit application.

Answers to this Self-Check are provided at the end of the chapter.

PUBLIC ACCOUNTABILITY

LO 17-9

Name two federal public disclosure statutes and describe how these statutes make administrative agencies more accountable to the public.

Because administrative agencies are granted broad powers and discretion, Congress has developed several safeguards to make agencies accountable to the public and to make their work as transparent as possible. This is accomplished through statutorily authorized citizen suits as well as mandatory-disclosure and open-meeting laws.

Private Citizen Suits

In addition to limits imposed on federal administrative agencies by the executive, legislative, and judicial branches, many enabling statutes contain provisions authorizing any member of the public at large who is directly affected by a particular agency action (or inaction) to bring a lawsuit against violators of a particular regulation and/or the administrative agency itself for failing to fulfill a duty imposed by statute. These suits are called **citizen suits** and are particularly prevalent in statutes related to protection of the environment.[28] Asbestos is a human-made material that was commonly used to make ceiling and floor tiles until the 1980s, when governmental health agencies determined that asbestos dust was linked to cancer. As a practical matter, organized activist groups such as the Sierra Club or the Natural Resources Defense Council (NRDC), in the case of environmental regulation, often file citizen suits.

---

[28]*See, e.g., Bennett v. Spear*, 520 U.S. 154 (1997) (interpreting the citizen suit provisions of the Endangered Species Act, 16 U.S.C. § 1540).

In terms of suits against the government, it is important to realize that citizen suits cannot be used to attack the *substance* of a regulation that has been properly promulgated. Citizen suit provisions may be used only to compel the agency to act in a manner consistent with the enabling act or another federal statute. For example, suppose that Congress passed an enabling statute that required the Occupational Safety and Health Administration (OSHA) to promulgate regulations that provide a safe procedure for the removal of asbestos-laden ceiling tiles within one year of the date of the law's passage. The OSHA properly promulgates a regulation pursuant to the statute, but an activist group, Friends of Workers (FOW), believes that the regulations do not do enough to protect employees in workplaces with asbestos. If FOW files a citizen suit against OSHA claiming that OSHA failed to carry out the enabling act's objectives, most courts would dismiss the suit because FOW is challenging the substance of the regulation. However, suppose that OSHA fails to provide any regulations within the statutorily prescribed one-year period. In that case, FOW would be able to bring a citizen suit against OSHA to compel it to promulgate the regulation.

> **KEY POINT**
>
> *Citizen suits* may be brought against a private party (as a violator) or against the administrative agency for failing to act in a manner consistent with the enabling statute's requirements.

Federal Disclosure Statutes

One way that administrative agencies are accountable to the public is through transparency, which requires public access to informational records held by the government and disclosures concerning open hearings and other business conducted by federal agencies. Congress provides two primary mechanisms to achieve these transparency objectives: the *Freedom of Information Act (FOIA)*, which gives the public the right to examine a great many government documents, and the *Government in the Sunshine Act,* which requires that certain agency meetings be open to the public.

Freedom of Information Act (FOIA)

The Freedom of Information Act (FOIA—frequently pronounced "foy-a") was passed by Congress in 1966 (and expanded by amendments in 1974)[29] to open up certain agency records for public inspection. Fundamentally, the FOIA requires agencies to publish certain matters and, upon the request of an individual or agency (such as a media outlet), to allow public inspection of all other records created or obtained by the agency in the course of doing its work. In order to ensure agency cooperation in complying with the FOIA, the law allows private parties to sue the agency if the records are wrongfully withheld.

However, the FOIA also contains nine separate categories of exceptions designed to protect legitimate interests. The most commonly excluded records are documents that contain (1) sensitive national defense or foreign policy information; (2) agency personnel matters or agency policies on purely administrative issues, such as schedules, performance reviews, records related to personnel, medical files, and other private matters; and (3) trade secrets and privileged commercial information, such as a secret process or device submitted by a business to the agency. For example, assume that ProductCo applies to the Environmental Protection Agency for a permit to discharge waste products into a stream after they are treated for pollution by a secret cleaning process designed by ProductCo's scientists. This process would likely need to be identified in ProductCo's permit application and, thus, would be within the ambit of the FOIA.

---

[29] 5 U.S.C. § 552.

However, it would fall into the trade secret exception and would be protected from disclosure to the public at large.

In Case 17.4, an appellate court considers whether daily calendars of government officials that contain personal entries are records subject to FOIA disclosure.

CASE 17.4 Consumer Federation of America v. Department of Agriculture, 455 F.3d 283 (D.C. Cir. 2006)

FACT SUMMARY In February 2001, the U.S. Department of Agriculture (USDA) published notice of a proposed rule regulating exposure to *Listeria*, a dangerous, food-borne bacterium that can be found in ready-to-eat meat and poultry. The USDA later issued an interim final rule that Consumer Federation of America (CFA) regarded as significantly weaker than the originally proposed rule. CFA suspected that the interim final rule was the result of pressure applied by industry representatives during lobbying meetings with agency officials.

Seeking to learn whether USDA officials had met exclusively, or nearly exclusively, with industry representatives who favored the weakening of the original proposed rule, CFA filed a Freedom of Information Act (FOIA) request for access to the public calendars of five senior USDA officials and one USDA administrative assistant. When the USDA failed to provide a substantive response within the statutory time period, CFA filed suit in district court to compel production of the calendars.

Ultimately the USDA took the position that the calendars were not "agency records" as defined in the FOIA and therefore that CFA had no right to access. The trial court agreed and ruled that the officials' appointment calendars were not agency records. CFA appealed.

SYNOPSIS OF DECISION AND OPINION The D.C. Circuit Court of Appeals ruled in favor of CFA and held that the calendars were agency records under the FOIA and were subject to public access. The court ruled that because the USDA calendars were continually updated, distributed to employees, and used to conduct agency business, the calendars were included under the FOIA. The court pointed out that unlike a personal diary containing an individual's private reflections on his or her work—but that the individual does not rely upon to perform his or her duties—the USDA calendars were in fact relied upon by both their authors and their authors' colleagues to facilitate the day-to-day operations of the department's work. The court also ruled that the administrative assistant's calendar was *not* an agency record covered by the FOIA because it was not distributed among senior officials and was more of a personal time schedule.

WORDS OF THE COURT: Personal Information and Agency Records "USDA protests that, because the calendars contain personal as well as business entries, they cannot be considered 'agency records.' There is no doubt that 'the presence of such information may be relevant in determining' the use of a document. But as we said in [previous cases], the 'inclusion of personal information does not, by itself, take material outside the ambit of FOIA.' Were that not true, an official could avoid disclosure of the only documentation of a meeting held with industry officials during the pendency of a rulemaking—the very information that CFA seeks in this case—simply by adorning the document with personal entries. In [a previous case], we held that [a government official's] daily agendas were 'agency records,' notwithstanding that the 'personal information contained in the agendas [was] identical to that found in [his] appointment calendars,' which we found to be personal records. The distinguishing factor was that the agendas were 'distributed to staff' for their 'use in determining [his] availability for meetings.'"

Case Questions

1. What did CFA expect to uncover through the use of the FOIA?
2. What were the key factors in the court's determination that calendars fell under FOIA?
3. *Focus on Critical Thinking:* If government officials know that they will have to reveal their personal calendars, won't that potentially chill necessary debate within or outside the agency?

Government in the Sunshine Act The Government in the Sunshine Act requires that agencies announce their meetings at least one week in advance and open the meetings to the public unless a meeting falls within one of the Sunshine Act exceptions. However, the law does not apply to meetings that are purely consultative in character or that concern investigatory or adjudication matters.

ADMINISTRATIVE LAW AT THE STATE LEVEL

In addition to federal agencies, business owners and managers should also expect to encounter state administrative agencies. Although our discussion has focused primarily on federal administrative law, state agencies also have broad executive, legislative, and adjudication discretion in matters of state administrative law. Indeed, many state agencies exist to accomplish substantially the same objectives as those of federal agencies, but they operate at a comparatively micro level, with state administrative law more tailored to the needs of the particular state. California, for example, supplements existing federal air pollution regulations with additional state regulations designed to reduce smog problems in its major cities.

States often have their own versions of federal agencies. For example, all states have a department of revenue (or some similarly named agency) that is the state's version of the Internal Revenue Service. States frequently have agencies devoted to the regulation of parties within the state's borders in regard to the sale of securities (selling a business entity's stock to the public), protection of the environment, regulation of banking and insurance companies, workplace safety, consumer protection, and labor and employee antidiscrimination regulations. Federal and state agencies also share information and work together on joint operations. State administrative law is very similar to the federal scheme in terms of how regulations are developed, implemented, and enforced.

KEY TERMS

Administrative law p. 569   Refers to both the law made by administrative agencies and the laws and regulations that govern the creation, organization, and operation of administrative agencies.

Administrative agencies p. 569   Governmental bodies, including department, nondepartment, and independent agencies, that have the authority to implement and administer particular regulations.

Rulemaking p. 569   The legislative function of administrative agencies, whereby they create legally enforceable rules in order to fill in the details of a statute.

Adjudication (administrative) p. 569   The judicial function of administrative agencies, whereby the agencies make policy. Administrative law judges hear cases brought before the specific agency.

Enabling statute p. 570   A law passed by Congress when it is establishing an administrative agency; serves as the source of the agency's authority and describes the agency's scope and jurisdiction over certain matters.

Regulation p. 577   A rule that is in effect, is published in the Code of Federal Regulations, and has the force of a law.

Enforcement p. 578   The function of administrative agencies whereby they investigate alleged violations of their administrative regulations and recommend enforcement actions; generally carried out through an agency's Office of General Counsel. In deciding when and whom to regulate, the agencies have prosecutorial discretion that is practically unreviewable by the judiciary.

Licensing p. 578   The task of issuing a license authorizing a business or industry to do something.

Inspection p. 578   The act of monitoring a business's compliance with administrative regulations. An administrative agency ordinarily secures a warrant and then enters and inspects the business's premises.

Administrative law judge (ALJ) p. 580 An individual, typically an attorney, who is employed by an agency to adjudicate disputes.

Arbitrary and capricious standard p. 584 The broad judicial benchmark used to determine whether an agency's actions were a result of a reasoned decision-making process.

Net neutrality p. 584 The principle that all movement and content on the Internet should receive equal treatment.

Citizen suits p. 588 Lawsuits initiated by members of the public who are directly affected by an agency action and brought against violators of the regulation and/or the administrative agency itself for failing to fulfill a duty imposed upon it.

CHAPTER REVIEW QUESTIONS

1. An administrative agency's policymaking function is known as _____.
   a. Publication
   b. Investigation
   c. Rulemaking
   d. Licensing

2. Which of the following is *not* a source of administrative law?
   a. Rulemaking Control Act
   b. U.S. Constitution
   c. Enabling statutes
   d. Administrative Procedures Act

3. Both the proposed rule and the final rule are published in the _____.
   a. *National Notice*
   b. *Administrative Times*
   c. *Federal Register*
   d. *Rulemaking Register*

4. Many agencies have the authority to adjudicate matters. Which of the following carry out the adjudication function?
   a. Common pleas judges
   b. Administrative law judges
   c. Board of appeals
   d. Departmental judges

5. Challenging a rule through judicial review on the basis of *Motor Vehicle Manufacturing Association v. State Farm* requires evidence that agency actions were _____ and _____.
   a. Arbitrary and unwise
   b. Arbitrary and confused
   c. Unfounded and capricious
   d. Arbitrary and capricious

Answers and explanations are provided at the end of this chapter.

THEORY TO PRACTICE

Main Line Restaurant Group (MLRG) is a company that owns and operates a national chain of Italian-themed restaurants. Each of its restaurants is equipped with a series of hoods that ventilate smoke from a wood-burning pizza oven to the outside via a roof vent.

Last year, as part of a broader air pollution control law, Congress passed a statute that authorized the appropriate administrative agency to implement rules intended to decrease the amount of pollution caused by debris in the air from commercial use of wood-burning ovens.

1. What administrative agency would likely have jurisdiction under this statute?

2. When Congress passes a law such as the one described above, what is this type of statute called?

Assume that the appropriate administrative agency studies the issues presented in the pollution control law and proposes a rule that all wood-burning ovens used in a commercial establishment must be either replaced by gas ovens or retrofitted with a certain pollution control device that will cost $15,200 per hood. Although a similar, lower-cost device is available, the agency does not view cost as a barrier to implementation when proposing the rule. The proposed rule also requires the hoods to be installed within five years.

3. What options does MLRG have for effecting a change in the proposed rule so that it includes the lower-cost device as an option?

Assume that the agency publishes a revised final rule that includes an amendment allowing the use of the lower-cost device but also includes an added provision that shortens the implementation deadline from the original five years to one year.

4. Is the administrative agency required to publish the amended rule again and allow a second comment period before it finalizes the rule? What rule would govern this analysis?

5. Assume that the administrative agency is *not* required to republish and allow an additional comment period. What are MLRG's options for challenging the rule at this point?

6. What standards will a court use to judge the validity of the final rule?

LEGAL STRATEGY 101

The Audit Lottery

The Internal Revenue Service (IRS) is the U.S. government agency in charge of federal tax collection and tax law enforcement. Like most government agencies, however, the IRS has limited resources. Simply put, the IRS doesn't have enough time, people, or money to individually review and audit every single tax return.

This legal reality—the fact that the IRS has limited resources for enforcement—has given rise to a form of strategic behavior among some taxpayers known as the "audit lottery."[30] In brief, the audit lottery is a gambit in which taxpayers claim tax benefits to which they are not entitled in the hope that the IRS will never audit their returns or, if audited, the improper benefits will not be discovered. The audit lottery is thus a strategy that attempts to exploit the IRS's limited resources.

The IRS, though, is aware of this potential for strategic behavior. As a result, its audit selection procedures are not entirely random. Instead of random selection of tax returns, the IRS employs sophisticated statistical models that measure the "risk of tax avoidance" to decide which tax returns to audit.[31]

Specifically, the IRS assigns a risk score to every tax return using two statistical systems: the Discriminant Function System (DIF) and the Unreported Income DIF (UIDIF).[32] The DIF computer program,

Internal Revenue Service Building. Andrew Harrer/Bloomberg/Getty Images

by way of example, measures 66 different risk categories, such as the number of deductions and total income—though some of the categories are kept secret—in order to determine which tax returns have the most audit potential. The higher the risk score assigned to a tax return, the more likely a tax return will be selected for auditing.

In short, the audit lottery is one lottery you don't want to win.

CRITICAL THINKING QUESTION

The DIF is a computer program the IRS uses to decide which tax returns to audit. Would it be legal to create and market a "counter-DIF" computer program to taxpayers to help them minimize their chances of being audited?

---

[30] *See, e.g.,* Theo Francis, *How Google, GE and U.S. Firms Play the Tax "Audit Lottery,"* Wall St. J., Dec. 17, 2014.

[31] *See* Press Release, Internal Revenue Service, Prepared Remarks of IRS Commissioner Doug Shulman at the National Press Club (Apr. 6, 2011).

[32] *See* Internal Revenue Service, *The Examination (Audit) Process,* FS-2006-10 (Jan. 2006).

MANAGER'S CHALLENGE

The following guide is excerpted from a federal administrative agency publication that sets out guidance for submitting public comments. Based on this guide, and referring to the facts in this chapter's Theory to Practice problem, draft a two-page letter to the appropriate administrative agency on MLRG's behalf, explaining why you would urge the agency to change the proposed rule concerning wood-burning ovens.

SUGGESTIONS FOR SUBMITTING COMMENTS

There are four general areas that you may wish to comment on concerning regulations:

1. *The need for the rule.*
2. *Other options.* If the agency has proposed or discussed requirements, you may be able to think of other things the agency could do that would solve the problem in a less costly way for your firm or industry. One option that has often been suggested is for the agency to give small firms more time to comply with a regulation, such as a change to a food label. Another option may be for the agency to identify a goal companies must meet, but to allow each firm to achieve the stated goal in its own way. Another option may be to request an exemption for certain types of businesses for which the requirements are not applicable. Because the quality and persuasiveness of your comment affects the agency's decision, including data, logical reasoning, and other information to support your comment always helps.
3. *Benefits of the rule.* You may want to explain (in detail if possible) whether you think a specific requirement would achieve the intended results. For example, you may want to provide detailed information documenting whether your industry has a particular problem. Furthermore, you may want to comment on the degree to which a proposed requirement is already common practice, and how much a federal rule would change practices in your industry.
4. *Costs of the rule.* In many cases, the regulatory options and costs of the rule will be the areas that you will know most about and may want to include in your submission. The following chart gives examples of costs that your company or industry may experience as a result of a regulation.

COST FACTOR CHART

The factors outlined below can be used for commenting on each proposed requirement in the codified section. This chart is only a suggestion for submitting comments. You are free to comment in any manner you wish or not at all. You may also, for example, respond by plant, firm, industry group, or in any other manner.

See Connect for Manager's Challenge sample answers.

Category	Explanation	Examples
1. What new capital equipment or materials will you have to buy to comply with the regulation?	Estimate the actual cost of new capital equipment or materials that you will have to purchase (one time or annually) and any loss of equipment that can no longer be used.	Chemicals for new tests will cost $40 per test for each of the 4 tests per week. The depreciated value of an extruder that will no longer be able to be used is $7,500.
2. What is the size of your firm?	Estimate the size of your firm either by number of employees or by annual sales. A range may be given.	Our firm has 200 full-time employees and 20 part-time employees. Annual sales are between $10 and $50 million.
3. What products do you make?	Describe the type of products that your firm makes that are covered by the potential regulation.	Our firm makes 2 varieties of herbal supplements in 3 sizes each. We make 4 flavors of Larry's Ice Cream in 2 sizes each.
4. What are your average annual profits?	Again, *do not report sensitive information*, but you may wish to provide an approximate annual amount that you can use to finance new requirements.	My firm makes between $20,000 and $50,000 per year.
5. Who owns your firm? How many plants do you have?	Explain whether or not you are a subsidiary of a larger firm.	We are a solely owned firm with 2 plants.

Source: www.regulations.gov.

CASE SUMMARY 17.1 Int'l Union, United Mine Workers of America v. Mine Safety & Health Admin., 407 F.3d 1250 (D.C. Cir. 2005)

LOGICAL-OUTGROWTH TEST

The secretary of the Mine Safety and Health Administration proposed a new rule intended to increase the safety of workers by ensuring proper ventilation in mines. The proposed rule required a minimum velocity of 300 feet per minute (fpm) to be kept through the ventilation regulator to ensure adequate mine ventilation. During the comment period, empirical data were submitted that suggested that requiring *minimum flow* was the safest alternative and, thus, the agency would not set a *maximum flow*. However, when the final rule was published, it provided for a maximum airflow of 500 fpm. A mining company challenged the final rule because there was no comment period to discuss maximum airflows.

CASE QUESTIONS

1. Is the maximum-airflow rule a logical outgrowth of the proposed rule? Why or why not?
2. Is the agency required to republish the rule?

CASE SUMMARY 17.2 American Medical Association v. U.S. Internal Revenue Service, 887 F.2d 760 (7th Cir. 1989)

RULEMAKING UNDER THE APA

The Internal Revenue Service (IRS) proposed a rule concerning the allocation of membership dues paid to nonprofit organizations under which certain nondues revenue was to be treated as taxable revenue. According to the proposed rule, the IRS intended to determine tax liability from this revenue using a seven-factor test. After the comment period, the IRS replaced the seven-factor test with a new allocation method that the IRS considered to be more fair and consistent. The new method carved down the factors used in the original rule, and a new *three-factor test* was published as a final rule without any additional comment period.

The American Medical Association (AMA) is a nonprofit corporation that charges its members dues that cover a variety of services. The AMA also publishes several journals from which the AMA derives revenue. Under the IRS's three-factor test for allocation, the AMA's tax liability increased significantly. After the IRS assessed the AMA's tax liability under the three-factor test, the AMA brought a lawsuit claiming that the new three-factor allocation regulation was invalid because the IRS had never given the proper public notice required by the APA when the agency departed from its original seven-factor test.

CASE QUESTIONS

1. Is the new test a logical outgrowth of the original test? Why or why not?
2. How could the IRS have avoided a successful challenge to this new rule?

CASE SUMMARY 17.3 Federal Express Corporation v. Holowecki, 552 U.S. 389 (2008)

JUDICIAL REVIEW

Paul Holowecki was employed by Federal Express Corporation (FedEx) when FedEx implemented two new performance programs that tie employee compensation and continued employment to certain performance measures. Holowecki, along with other FedEx employees over the age of 40, claimed that the incentive programs unlawfully discriminated against older employees. Under the Age Discrimination in

Employment Act (ADEA), claimants must file a *charge* with the Equal Employment Opportunity Commission (EEOC) and then wait a statutorily defined period of time before filing suit in federal court. However, the ADEA does not define what constitutes a charge. The EEOC, using its authority to implement procedures necessary to carry out its objectives, promulgated a rule that states a "charge shall mean a statement filed with the Commission by or on behalf of an aggrieved person which alleges that the named prospective defendant has engaged in or is about to engage in actions in violation of the Act." Before filing suit, Holowecki submitted an intake questionnaire with the EEOC and filed a six-page affidavit. FedEx claimed that the questionnaire and affidavit did not constitute a formal charge against the company because they were only one step in a formal complaint procedure. FedEx argued that the EEOC's interpretation of the definition of "charge" was outside the agency's statutory authority.

CASE QUESTIONS

1. Who prevails and why?
2. Will the court defer to the EEOC's interpretation?
3. What is the standard used by the courts in cases such as this one?

CASE SUMMARY 17.4 Ranchers Cattlemen Action Legal Fund United Stockgrowers of America v. U.S. Department of Agriculture, 499 F.3d 1108 (9th Cir. 2007)

ARBITARY AND CAPRICIOUS

In response to outbreaks of mad cow disease, the Food and Drug Administration and the U.S. Department of Agriculture (USDA) implemented a number of regulations to protect American consumers and cattle herds. Chief among them was a regulation banning cattle imports from countries in which mad cow disease was known to exist. Shortly after the ban went into effect, the USDA partially reversed course and published a proposed rule allowing certain low-risk products into the United States. During the comment period, some groups objected to the proposed rule due to evidence of potential contamination even in low-risk products. The agency then published its final rule, which modified existing regulations to allow the import of low-risk products. The Ranchers Cattlemen Action Legal Fund United Stockgrowers of America challenged the agency's decision to allow low-risk products as arbitrary and capricious even though the agency had held several comment periods.

CASE QUESTIONS

1. Is the decision arbitrary and capricious? Why or why not?
2. Does the fact that the agency held several comment periods impact your analysis?

CASE SUMMARY 17.5 Gardner v. U.S. Bureau of Land Management, 638 F.3d 1217 (9th Cir. 2011)

CITIZEN SUITS

Little Canyon Mountain had been an "open-use" park adjacent to private properties since 1985. In 2003, a federal agency's environmental assessment resulted in a plan for limited off-road-vehicle access in a certain area of the park. This plan was called the *fuels-reduction project*. The U.S. Bureau of Land Management (BLM) has regulatory authority to change off-road-vehicle use designations when these vehicles are "causing or will cause considerable adverse effects upon soil, vegetation, wildlife, wildlife habitat, cultural resources, historical resources, threatened or endangered species, wilderness suitability, other authorized uses, or other resources." After this plan was implemented, the BLM received numerous complaints from adjacent landowners regarding off-road-vehicle use in that area of the park. Gardner and Concerned Citizens for Little Canyon Mountain sued the BLM and argued that the 2003 environmental assessment for the fuels-reduction project by a BLM specialist was reason to require action by the BLM to close Little Canyon Mountain to off-road vehicles.

CASE QUESTIONS

1. Is Gardner challenging the substance of a regulation or how a regulation was promulgated?
2. What is Gardner's main concern, and what is he asking the court to do?

 Self-Check ANSWERS Arbitrary and Capricious

1. The agency's decision is likely to be considered arbitrary and capricious. The NHTSA is charged with making the nation's highways safer, and by ignoring the fact that a four-tire, 20 percent TPMS is safer and more reliable and choosing a slightly cheaper, less safe alternative, the agency is not making a reasoned decision. See *Public Citizen, Inc. v. Mineta*, 340 F.3d 39 (2d Cir. 2003).

2. The EPA's decision is *not* arbitrary and capricious because the EPA is tasked with improving or maintaining the nation's water quality under the CWA. Therefore, its decision to issue OilCo a permit with an effluent limitation of 0 is perfectly reasonable because that is the level necessary to maintain water quality in that region. See *Texas Oil & Gas Ass'n v. United States EPA*, 161 F.3d 923 (5th Cir. 1998).

3. The FERC's decision is *not* arbitrary and capricious because there were no changed circumstances. The same power plants and the same sites were involved; therefore, the FERC could rely on the prior permits and information from its review to determine whether or not to issue another permit for this site. See *Symbiotics, L.L.C. v. FERC*, 110 F. App'x 76 (10th Cir. 2004).

CHAPTER REVIEW QUESTIONS: Answers and Explanations

1. **c.** Administrative agencies form policy through rulemaking. (a), (b), and (d) are all functions of an agency, but they are not related to policymaking.

2. **a.** (a) is correct because no such law exists. (b), (c), and (d) are incorrect because they represent either constitutional or statutory sources of administrative law.

3. **c.** The *Federal Register* is the exclusive publication used by administrative agencies for rulemaking. (a), (b), and (d) are not actual publications.

4. **b.** Administrative law judges carry out adjudication functions of an agency. (a), (c), and (d) are incorrect because they either are state courts or don't exist.

5. **d.** Arbitrary and capricious is the standard used by courts. (a), (b), and (c) are incorrect because they use incorrect terminology.

CHAPTER 18
Environmental Law

©philsajonesen/Getty Images

Learning Objectives

After studying this chapter, students who have mastered the material will be able to:

18-1 Explain the impact of environmental regulation on business.

18-2 Identify the origins and sources of environmental law.

18-3 Describe the role of the Environmental Protection Agency and state agencies in the implementation and enforcement of environmental laws.

18-4 Explain the role of citizen suits in enforcing environmental regulations.

18-5 Describe the primary objectives and provisions of major federal statutes that protect the environment.

18-6 Provide examples of various industries regulated by air and water pollution laws related to the disposal of waste and hazardous materials.

18-7 Articulate the potential liability of various parties under the federal environmental cleanup statutes.

18-8 Distinguish between removal and remedial cleanup efforts in the context of environmental regulation.

Environmental law is a collection of federal, state, and local laws that protect natural resources and promote a healthier environment for the public at large. Whether it concerns the federal regulation of industrial plants or a city ordinance prohibiting the use of certain pesticides by landscapers within municipal limits, business owners and managers from across the spectrum of commercial sectors encounter environmental law and regulation in their daily operations and in their business planning. In this chapter, students will learn

- Environmental law's origins, sources, and enforcement mechanisms.
- Major federal environmental statutes that apply to business operations.
- Laws that impose liability on private individuals and businesses for environmental cleanup costs.

IMPACT OF ENVIRONMENTAL LAW ON BUSINESS

Business owners and managers all too often assume that environmental law and regulation is a concern only for owners of large industrial plants that produce smokestack pollution or dump waste into rivers. Yet it is clear that environmental laws must be thought of as having broad coverage and that an understanding of environmental law is important in limiting a company's liability and ensuring regulatory compliance. Any assumption that environmental laws are not pertinent to a particular business's operation may be costly in terms of liability and may result in missed opportunities for proactive business planning and risk control.

As the American public becomes increasingly concerned over threats to the environment and related issues such as oil spills and greenhouse gases, governments at the federal, state, and local levels have broadened environmental regulation and liability for environmental cleanups. Local businesses such as dry cleaners, bakeries, mechanic shops, gas stations, landscaping firms, contracting firms, and a host of others are now subject to various environmental laws.

Liability for environmental cleanup is another concern for business owners and managers if their business operations involve the ownership of land. Certain federal statutes (discussed in detail later in this chapter) create liability for owners of property that is contaminated even if the owner has not contributed to the contamination. This strict liability concept is an important factor when planning a land purchase.

LO 18-1

Explain the impact of environmental regulation on business.

ORIGINS AND SOURCES OF ENVIRONMENTAL LAW

The origins of environmental protections are primarily based on the common law doctrine of **nuisance**. In a suit for nuisance, an aggrieved party sues to compel a polluter to cease polluting based on the aggrieved party's right to enjoy her property without interference from a third party. Local zoning ordinances are generally designed to prevent nuisance by segmenting a municipality into zones—industrial, residential, and so forth. However, this common law doctrine is a protection of a party's *individual property rights*. Historically, the federal government has left regulation of the environment to state and local authorities. This has resulted in a patchwork of standards, with some areas of the country allowing heavy industrial pollution while other areas regulate or ban such pollution. Because pollution does not respect state boundaries, federal statutes have become necessary to achieve meaningful environmental protections.

Modern environmental protection statutes at both the federal and state levels have largely supplanted any common law protections. In addition, local municipalities often have environmental ordinance standards related to safety and local public policy (such as proper disposal of engine oil or other hazardous waste by a local mechanic). Environmental protection statutes are wide-ranging, but federal and state statutes that impact businesses are primarily designed to (1) ensure that government agency decisions have the least possible impact on the environment, (2) promote clean air and water through regulation and permits, (3) regulate the use and disposal of solid and hazardous waste, (4) clean up property or waterways that are contaminated with hazardous waste, and (5) protect wildlife and endangered species.

LO 18-2

Identify the origins and sources of environmental law.

GOVERNMENT ENFORCEMENT

Federal environmental laws are primarily administered, implemented, and enforced by the U.S. Environmental Protection Agency (EPA). The EPA, created in 1970, works in tandem with other administrative agencies in handling a broad range of environmental concerns at the federal level. For example, the U.S. Fish and Wildlife Service primarily enforces

LO 18-3

Describe the role of the Environmental Protection Agency and state agencies in the implementation and enforcement of environmental laws.

CHAPTER EIGHTEEN | Environmental Law

statutes protecting endangered species. However, if the use of pesticides is responsible for depleting the population of certain endangered species, the EPA will work to use environmental regulation to halt the use of the pesticides. Other agencies that have certain environmental regulation jurisdiction include the Food and Drug Administration (FDA) and the Nuclear Regulatory Commission (NRC).

Like all administrative agencies, the EPA has broad powers to implement and enforce environmental laws by promulgating rules,[1] providing permits, issuing advisory opinions, and investigating potential violations of federal environmental protection statutes, as well as using traditional enforcement tools such as administrative fines and penalties, civil suits, and, in egregious cases, criminal complaints.

In addition to the EPA and other federal agencies, each state has its own environmental agency to implement and enforce state environmental statutes. In certain municipalities, a local environmental agency may exist to enforce local ordinances such as illegal dumping. The name of the agency varies among jurisdictions, but titles such as Department of Environmental Protection or Department of Natural Resources, or some variation of the two, are common. An important feature of many federal environmental laws is that state governments are often mandated to work in conjunction with (or under the supervision of) the EPA when implementing and enforcing federal environmental statutes such as the Clean Water Act.

Citizen Suit Provisions and Watchdog Groups

LO 18-4

Explain the role of citizen suits in enforcing environmental regulations.

Perhaps more than in any other area of the law, citizen interest organizations (also called *watchdog groups*) have contributed to the enforcement of environmental statutes and policy. These citizen interest organizations and individual citizens are statutorily authorized to file a lawsuit against either a polluter who is in violation of environmental statutes or regulations or a government agency or unit (such as the EPA or a municipality) that is not taking legally mandated steps to carry out environmental law enforcement. Individuals and groups derive this authority to file enforcement lawsuits by virtue of **citizen suit provisions** that are a part of many federal and state environmental statutes.

When an environmental statute authorizes citizen suits, it generally requires that notice of a citizen suit be given to the agency with jurisdiction over the matter. The statute also allows the agency to decide whether to initiate agency action instead of allowing the citizen suit to go forward. A private citizen or group cannot profit from an enforcement action, and frequently the initiator of the suit is simply seeking a court order that will prevent or require a certain action. Typically, citizen suit provisions in environmental law spell out a procedure that gives the appropriate government agency and the polluter specific notice of the complaint and provides a period of time (usually 60 days) for action by the agency or compliance by the violator. If the time period expires without any action, the citizen suit may be filed in court. Citizen suits may not be commenced against a polluter if the government agency is already prosecuting the same violator. Some of the more common initiators of environmental law citizen suits include the Sierra Club, the Natural Resources Defense Council, and the Environmental Defense Fund. Local environmental watchdog groups in different regions of the United States tend to focus on a particular concern unique to the region (e.g., the Spotted Owl Defense League of Oregon).

In Case 18.1, an appellate court analyzes the procedure used in a citizen suit under the Clean Water Act.

---

[1] Recall from Chapter 17, "Administrative Law," that administrative agencies are authorized by statute to implement binding legal regulations following a rulemaking process.

Citizen suit provisions in many environmental laws permit watchdog groups such as the Sierra Club to file suit against alleged polluters or the government to enforce the statute.
Rick Bowmer/AP Images

CASE 18.1 Friends of the Earth v. Gaston Copper Recycling Corp., 629 F.3d 387 (4th Cir. 2011)

FACT SUMMARY Gaston owned a metals smelting facility in South Carolina and operated it until 1995. After 1995, Gaston continued to treat contaminated storm water at the facility and to release this treated water into a lake on Gaston's property. However, the lake's water overflow discharged into other waterways and spread pollutants that resulted from the contact of rainwater with scrap metal stored by Gaston on its property. Friends of the Earth is an environmental citizen action group whose members include owners of property affected by the Gaston pollutants. Although Gaston attempted to solve the problem, the company continued to miss compliance deadlines for reducing the pollutants being discharged into the waterways. Friends sent Gaston a notice letter that alleged its noncompliance with the statute and named over 300 specific violations committed by Gaston. The Clean Water Act required that this statutory notice be sent prior to bringing a citizen suit. Ultimately, Friends brought a citizen suit, and the trial court imposed a $2.3 million fine on Gaston based on the violations alleged by Friends in the required prelawsuit notice and additional violations that were uncovered during the discovery phase of the litigation. Gaston appealed the trial court's decision, arguing that the imposition of the citizen suit fine was not authorized by the statute because much of the penalty was related to pollutants that were not identified in the original notice letter.

SYNOPSIS OF DECISION AND OPINION The Fourth Circuit Court of Appeals reversed the civil fines imposed by the trial court on Gaston for all violations except the ones that were articulated in Friends' citizen suit notice. The court held that the notice letter provision in the statute has the legislative objective of bringing a polluter into regulatory compliance by means of citizen suit provisions. That objective would be frustrated if courts were to impose civil fines on a polluter based on violations that were unknown to the violator at the time of the notice letter. However, the court upheld several fines that were related to the allegations contained in the notice letter from Friends.

WORDS OF THE COURT: Purpose of the Notice Letter Requirement "This regulation provides, in relevant part, that the notice shall include sufficient information to permit the recipient to identify

(continued)

the specific standard, limitation, or order alleged to have been violated. Notice given by a citizen plaintiff under the Clean Water Act thus must provide the alleged violator with enough information to attempt to correct the violation and avert the citizen suit. . . .

"Our conclusion is not altered by the fact that when the plaintiffs sent their notice letter, they did not have access to information that they later acquired in discovery in this case. The plaintiffs' lack of information before their suit was filed cannot excuse the deficiencies in the notice letter, because those deficiencies prevented attainment of the legislative objectives of encouraging pre-suit governmental involvement and securing violator compliance."

Case Questions

1. Did Gaston escape a substantial civil fine based on a statutory technicality?
2. What could Friends have included in the notice letter that might help it prevail in a future case where the true extent of the violation is unknown?
3. *Focus on Critical Thinking:* Are citizen suit provisions an effective way to achieve environmental objectives? Do citizens have the expertise necessary to make legal or scientific determinations that are inherent in environmental regulation? Should enforcement be left to the government? Why or why not?

NATIONAL ENVIRONMENTAL POLICY ACT

LO 18-5

Describe the primary objectives and provisions of major federal statutes that protect the environment.

One of the first attempts at comprehensive legislation to address environmental regulation was the **National Environmental Policy Act (NEPA)**,[2] enacted in 1969. The law was intended to serve as a national charter for environmental regulation, but its focus is one of planning and prevention rather than achieving a certain result (such as cleaner water) according to scientific standards. The NEPA established a process that must be followed by federal agencies in making decisions that have the potential to have a significant impact on the environment. The NEPA also created the Council on Environmental Quality to oversee the NEPA procedures and to make periodic progress reports to Congress and the president.

NEPA Coverage and Procedures

The NEPA procedures are triggered when a federal agency takes any action that may be reasonably considered as having an impact on the environment. This action may be in the form of an agency's issuing a permit or license or engaging in rulemaking. The NEPA is also activated when Congress passes a law that requires federal funding (such as federal highway or bridge construction). Note that actions by private individuals, businesses, and state and local governments are not regulated by the NEPA. However, all states have enacted parallel statutes (laws similar to the NEPA statute but covering a wider range of parties) to cover state and local government actions as well.

Procedural Steps

Federal agencies are required to incorporate the NEPA procedural steps into their decision-making process at the earliest possible opportunity by identifying the purpose of and need for a promised project, possible alternatives, and the environmental impact of certain actions. Once this step has been accomplished, the agency must categorize the action into one of three classifications based on its level of environmental impact:

- *Categorical exclusion (CE):* The CE category is used for those actions that have little or no potential for significant environmental impact. A CE classification also may be

---
[2]42 U.S.C. § 4321 et seq.

mandated by a particular statute, thereby having the effect of exempting certain actions from any further environmental assessment.

- *Environmental assessment (EA):* Projects and actions in which the environmental impact is unknown are classified in the EA category. Actions classified as EA require the agency to produce a public document setting forth the need for the proposed action, alternatives, the environmental impact of the proposed action and its alternatives, and a list of agencies and persons consulted. The EA is used to determine whether the action requires preparation of a more extensive report called an *environmental impact statement*. If, however, based on the EA, the agency makes a finding of no significant impact, the agency may proceed with the proposed action.

- *Environmental impact statement (EIS):* The EIS category is used for actions classified as having the potential for *significant impact* on the environment. If an EA provides evidence that some significant environmental impact is at issue, the agency must prepare a draft of an EIS and publish it for public comment. The EIS is an expanded form of an EA that includes (1) a description of the proposed action, (2) a statement of significant issues and specific forecasting of what environmental risks are involved with the proposed action, (3) alternatives to the actions and an assessment of the environmental risk of the alternatives, (4) financial assessments of the promised actions and alternatives, and (5) plans for reducing or preventing environmental harm. Once the public and interested constituencies have commented on the EIS, the agency revises the EIS as necessary and issues a final EIS. The final EIS also sets out the agency decision on environmental impact and its chosen alternative for pursuing the agency action.

As a practical matter, the NEPA process gives public notice and affords consumer interest groups, businesses, and private citizens a chance to influence the agency's decision. The NEPA also contains a citizen suit provision whereby private individuals and organizations may sue a federal agency directly to force compliance with the NEPA procedures.

CONCEPT SUMMARY National Environmental Policy Act

- The National Environmental Policy Act (NEPA) of 1969 established a process that must be followed by federal agencies when they are making decisions that may reasonably impact the environment or when Congress passes a law that requires federal funding.

- Federal agencies are required to incorporate NEPA procedural steps into their decision-making process by identifying the purpose of and need for a promised project, possible alternatives, and the environmental impact.

- Once the procedural steps are accomplished, the agency must categorize the action into one of three classifications based on its level of environmental impact: (1) categorical exclusion (little or no potential impact), (2) environmental assessment (unknown impact), or (3) environmental impact statement (potentially significant impact).

- The NEPA process gives public notice and affords consumer interest groups, businesses, and private citizens a chance to influence the agency's decision or directly force compliance via citizen suit provisions.

LO 18-6

Provide examples of various industries regulated by air and water pollution laws related to the disposal of waste and hazardous materials.

THE CLEAN AIR ACT

Enacted in 1963, the **Clean Air Act (CAA)**[3] is a considerably complex statute aimed at improving outdoor air quality in the United States. The CAA replaced earlier legislation that had proved ineffective. The law has been amended several times since its original passage, most recently in 1997 to expand its coverage and provide a system of market-based incentives and enforcement options intended to encourage voluntary compliance with clean air standards. As its starting point, the CAA authorized the EPA to establish the National Ambient Air Quality Standards (NAAQS), which set permissible levels of certain air pollutants such as carbon monoxide, lead, and particulate matter (microscopic ash and dirt that are the ingredients for smog). Although the statute itself is multifaceted, its basic structure focuses on **stationary sources of air pollution** (such as an industrial manufacturing plant) and **mobile sources of air pollution** (such as motor vehicles).

Stationary Sources of Air Pollution

An important feature of the CAA is that *state legislatures* are required to determine the best way to achieve the NAAQS. State governments have a uniquely local understanding of state industries, geography, and demographics and are usually in the best position to decide on a solution. Each state is required to develop a collection of regulations that will help it achieve a reduction in each pollutant to below the maximum level set in the NAAQS. This plan takes the form of a mandated **State Implementation Plan (SIP)**, and the SIP must be submitted to the EPA within certain time frames set out in the statute. If the SIP is not acceptable, the EPA may either impose sanctions on the state (such as withholding certain federal funding) or step in to implement its own plan.

SIPs also feature a program for issuing **operating permits** to existing stationary sources that emit pollutants at special levels. Operating permits include information on which pollutants are being released, how much is being released, and steps the source is taking to reduce pollution, including technological requirements and methods to monitor the pollution. SIPs also include the requirements for obtaining a *preoperating permit* for any new source of pollutants being planned. Preoperating permits require the applicant to show that the construction of a stationary source has incorporated state-of-the-art technology to control the NAAQS pollutants. The CAA regulations also require a new source permit when a plant owner makes substantial modifications to an existing stationary source. Sometimes an issue arises as to what constitutes modification. This is an important factor in business planning because certain modifications may trigger additional regulatory measures and permit requirements.

Market-Based Approaches

One relatively controversial part of the CAA is the law's **market-based approach**. This approach was implemented by the 1990 amendments to the CAA and is accomplished through (1) *emission trading* via the permitting process and (2) a *cap and trade* plan intended to achieve lower levels of pollutants that contribute to acid rain.[4] Although the plans have separate procedural systems, they are both considered market-based approaches. Under these approaches, businesses have certain choices as to how they may reach their pollution reduction goals, including pollution allowances that can be traded, bought, and sold. In that same vein, a business may be allowed to expand its pollution output in one

---

[3]42 U.S.C. §§ 7401–7671.

[4]*Acid rain* is a broad term referring to a mixture of wet and dry components from the atmosphere that contains significant amounts of nitric and sulfuric acids. Governmental agencies have concluded that acid rain poses significant threats to the environment and specific ecosystems.

area if it is able to offset the increase by reducing another pollutant in greater measure than the one being expanded.

Economic Incentive Theory

The emission-trading scheme embraces the economic incentive theory that overall pollution reduction will result if businesses have an economic and competitive incentive, rather than a mandate, to invest in modern equipment and plants. Proponents argue that this approach will result in businesses investing in more efficient plants that yield clean air units that can then be sold or traded to out-of-compliance buyers. As emitting pollution (and being out of compliance) becomes more expensive, every company will be forced to modernize to stay competitive in the market. For example, suppose that Citadel Manufacturing Company and Guardian Operations Inc. operate manufacturing plants that emit pollutants regulated by the CAA. Each company obtains a permit to emit 50 units of pollutant X and 50 units of pollutant Y per year. Citadel decides to modernize its plant at a cost of $1 million. The modernization results in a significant reduction in pollutant X, so now Citadel emits only 10 units per year. Guardian, on the other hand, claims it does not have the resources to modernize and its current plant will emit 80 units of pollutant X. In a market-based approach, Guardian may choose to comply by either purchasing 30 units of pollutant X emission credit from Citadel or reducing its use of pollutant Y to offset the additional units of pollutant X. If it chooses to use the offset method, Guardian will have to reduce its use of pollutant Y at least 31 units (an amount greater than the exceeding pollutant). In this example, proponents of the market-based approach would point out that (1) this approach does not force burdensome mandates that may bankrupt a company, such as requirements to purchase expensive equipment; (2) eventually Guardian is likely to begin to consider investing in new technology so as not to be dependent on sellers of pollution units; and (3) the overall pollution reduction is the same under this approach as it would be under a mandate approach.

> **KEY POINT**
>
> A market-based approach was instituted by the 1990 CAA amendments to give businesses alternative methods of complying with pollution standards.

Critics of this approach argue that it results in clean air being treated as a commodity rather than a natural resource. Opponents of market-based solutions argue that the government could achieve greater reductions in pollution through the use of gradual statutory mandates to improve pollution control and government-backed loans to help companies purchase equipment.

Figure 18.1 summarizes the pros and cons of a market-based approach to implementing the Clean Air Act.

FIGURE 18.1 Pros and Cons of Market-Based Approach and the Clean Air Act

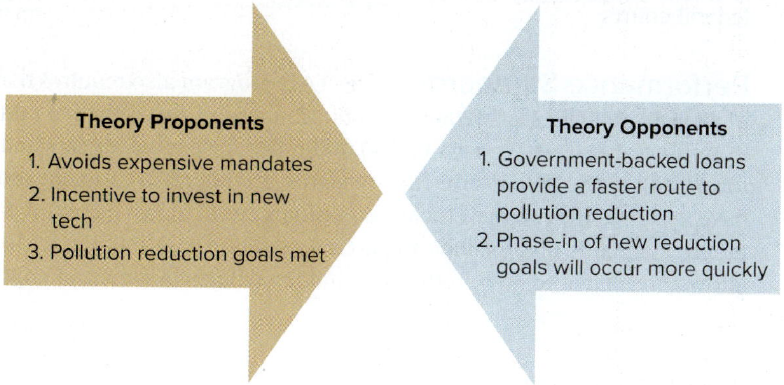

Theory Proponents
1. Avoids expensive mandates
2. Incentive to invest in new tech
3. Pollution reduction goals met

Theory Opponents
1. Government-backed loans provide a faster route to pollution reduction
2. Phase-in of new reduction goals will occur more quickly

Mobile Sources of Air Pollution

While substantial gains have been made in reducing pollution from motor vehicles over the past few decades, the internal combustion engine remains a significant source of hazardous pollutants. The EPA has issued standards intended to limit motor vehicle emissions through its Transport and Air Quality (TAQ) program. The TAQ program regulates (1) tailpipe emissions, (2) fuel economy, (3) performance standards, and (4) the composition and distribution of fuels, particularly gasoline, used in motor vehicles.

Tailpipe Emissions The CAA initially set the first federal tailpipe emission standards, but it granted California the authority to set even tighter emission standards due to the state's higher-than-average levels of air pollution. The 1990 amendments gave states the choice of either adopting the federal standards or using the California standards, but states may not adopt their own standards. Both the federal and California standards require an inspection and maintenance program to ensure that car manufacturers limit the exhaust emissions of five major pollutants that emit from tailpipes, including hydrocarbons and carbon monoxide. The difference between the two sets of standards is that the California standards have stricter miles-per-gallon (mpg) requirements and lower levels of allowable pollution.

Fuel Economy Standards Fuel economy standards set average mile-per-gallon requirements for motor vehicles and are determined by the year of the motor vehicle's production and its classification (car versus light truck). These regulations are called Corporate Average Fuel Economy (CAFE) standards, and they were enacted by Congress in 1975 with the purpose of reducing energy consumption by increasing the fuel economy of cars and light trucks. Regulating the CAFE standards is the responsibility of the National Highway Traffic Safety Administration (which sets the standards) and the EPA (which specifies a required standard calculation method for average fuel economy). The CAFE standards were overhauled in 2007 by the Energy Independence and Security Act,[5] which increased the mandated average for cars from 27.5 mpg to 35.5 mpg by 2020.

However, in early August 2018, the EPA and Department of Transportation, now operating under a new administration, issued a proposed rule to roll back some of the goals set in 2012. The new rule proposed by the EPA (and the National Highway Traffic Safety Administration), known as the *Safer Affordable Fuel-Efficient (SAFE) Vehicle Rules,* are intended to replace the original CAFE standard regulations. The rule freezes the fuel economy goals to the 2021 targets, eliminates requirements on the production of hybrid and electric cars, and prohibits states from setting more stringent standards. Following publication of the proposed rule changes, state attorneys general from California and 18 other states announced they will sue the government to have the new rule repealed. The complex legal issues surrounding these standards are still working their way through federal courts.

Performance Standards The TAQ program also requires that motor vehicle manufacturers obtain a Certificate of Conformity from the EPA that certifies that a vehicle's useful life is at least 10 years or 100,000 miles for passenger cars and up to 365,000 miles for heavy trucks. The useful-life standards are intended to make sure that manufacturers have designed the motor vehicle's emission system to last a certain period of time. Performance standards also include requirements for certain in-vehicle diagnostic systems that allow a mechanic to detect otherwise hidden defects in emission control systems.

---

[5]42 U.S.C. § 17001 et seq.

Fuel Composition and Distribution   The manufacturing and transportation of gasoline, diesel fuel, and fuel additives are regulated by the EPA under authority of the CAA. The EPA uses a registration system to ensure that any fuel product is tested and certified as safe for public health and used in compliance with CAA regulations. In addition to requiring a complete ban on the use of lead-based gasoline beginning in 1995, the law also includes a requirement that gasoline components contain certain detergents to reduce emissions.

CONCEPT SUMMARY   The Clean Air Act

- The Clean Air Act (CAA) is aimed at improving outdoor air quality based on National Ambient Air Quality Standards (NAAQS) that set permissible levels of certain air pollutants.
- The basic structure of the statute focuses on pollution from either stationary sources (manufacturing plants) or mobile sources (motor vehicles).
- State legislatures are required to determine the best way to achieve the NAAQS for stationary sources in the form of a mandated State Implementation Plan (SIP) that must be submitted to the Environmental Protection Agency (EPA).
- SIPs also feature a program for issuing (1) operating permits to existing stationary sources that emit pollutants at special levels, (2) preoperating permits for any new source of pollutants being planned, and (3) new source permits for substantial modifications to an existing source.
- A market-based approach embraces an economic incentive theory and was instituted by the 1990 CAA amendments to give businesses a choice of methods for complying with pollution standards.
- The EPA has issued standards intended to limit mobile source emissions through its Transport and Air Quality (TAQ) program, which regulates (1) tailpipe emissions, (2) fuel economy standards, (3) performance standards, and (4) fuel composition and distribution.

WATER POLLUTION CONTROL

The pollution of waterways is one of the biggest challenges facing environmental policymakers. Waterways take the form of surface water (such as lakes or rivers) or groundwater (subsurface water, such as that used for wells). Because water travels through jurisdictional boundaries and may be subject to various legal property rights,[6] water pollution and conservation regulation is necessarily addressed by a combination of federal, state, and local statutes and rules.

The Clean Water Act

Water quality standards are set primarily by and regulated through the **Clean Water Act (CWA)**,[7] a federal statute that is implemented and enforced by the EPA in tandem with the U.S. Army Corps of Engineers and state agencies. Much like the CAA, the CWA has been

---

[6]The legal term for water ownership rights is *riparian rights*.
[7]33 U.S.C. § 1251 et seq.

amended in significant ways to stem pollution from industrial, municipal, and agricultural sources. The CWA also contains important enforcement provisions. Any pollution discharge that violates the CWA triggers enhanced penalties if it was a result of gross negligence or willful misconduct.

Water Quality Regulation Each state sets water quality standards, subject to EPA review, for the navigable waterways within the state's borders. State agencies set scientifically measurable standards consisting of several criteria intended to improve the quality of surface water. The standards are set according to the designated use of the water source. Sources in which the designated uses are swimming or fishing must have the quality standards set high. Once the state has set its standards, it must monitor whether its water sources are meeting those standards and disclose the results through a mandatory reporting system. If progress toward achieving the standards is too slow or nonexistent, the state must propose a new strategy to meet the quality standards. The EPA must approve any new strategies and may step in and impose its own strategy if it determines that the state is out of compliance with the CWA.

Permitting Pollution emission into the waterways from sources such as industrial plants is regulated through the EPA's National Pollution Discharge Elimination System. The system establishes permitting procedures for businesses and individuals that require discharge of some material into a water source in order to operate their facilities. A permit is required regardless

Waterways are protected by an array of environmental regulation statutes, including the Clean Water Act.
Creatas Images/Jupiterimages

of the quality of the receiving water or whether the discharge actually causes pollution. Permits are issued as either *individual* permits, which are specifically tailored to an individual facility, or *general* permits, which cover multiple facilities within a certain category. Individual permits are often issued to business facilities, while general permits are issued for all discharges in a specific geographic area (such as a city-designated development zone).

In order to obtain a permit, existing sources of pollution are required to install pollution control technology that is the best *practical* control technology. This means that the cost of implementation is given equal weight to that of the effectiveness of pollution control. New applicants for permits are required to employ the best *available* control technology, which means that the permit applicant must install the most technologically advanced control methods on the market, regardless of cost. The EPA has established timetables for existing sources to adopt best *available* control technology as well.

Liability for Oil Spills

Largely in response to a 10-million-gallon oil spill that resulted when the *Exxon Valdez* oil tanker ran aground, Congress passed the **Oil Pollution Act (OPA)**[8] in 1990. The OPA increased the EPA's authority to prevent and respond to disastrous oil spills in public water

---
[8]33 U.S.C §§ 2702–2761.

sources. The law also imposed a tax on oil freighters in order to fund the national Oil Spill Liability Trust Fund, which is available to fund up to $1 billion per spill. Energy companies are required to file environmental impact plans with the U.S. Department of Interior, which has oversight authority over all oil drilling. The OPA was intended to promote contingency planning between government and industry to prevent and respond to a spill event. The OPA also increased penalties for noncompliance and broadened the government's response and enforcement authority. The law caps the liability of responsible parties at $75 million per spill, plus removal costs. However, in cases of *gross negligence,* the cap does not apply.

Deepwater Horizon **(BP) Oil Spill**   The largest offshore oil spill in U.S. history began on April 20, 2010, after an explosion aboard the BP-controlled oil drilling platform *Deepwater Horizon.* The *Deepwater Horizon* was situated in the Gulf of Mexico approximately 40 miles southeast of the Louisiana coast. The explosion killed 11 people working on the platform and created an oil spill that the National Oceanic and Atmospheric Administration estimated was leaking almost 5,000 barrels (210,000 gallons) per day. BP tried several methods for controlling the leak, but the logistics of such a deep-sea operation resulted in a number of failed attempts.

The gusher continued for nearly three months and resulted in an estimated 4.9 million barrels spilled into the Gulf of Mexico, making it the largest aquatic oil spill in history. The Gulf's coastal communities, whose income comes primarily from fishing and tourism, were devastated. BP faced sharp criticism for its handling of the crisis, and the Justice Department launched a criminal investigation into the incident. Although BP acknowledged its liability in the accident, the company alleged that other contractors on the oil rig were also negligent in the spill.

Eleven people were killed when *Deepwater Horizon* exploded. Nearly 5 million barrels of oil were released into the Gulf of Mexico.

Source: U.S. Coast Guard

Legal Speak >))

Multidistrict Litigation
The federal rules that govern trials provide for a Judicial Panel for Multidistrict Litigation, which evaluates cases filed in federal courts throughout the United States that are substantially related. The panel has the authority to consolidate these cases into a single trial if it serves the interest of justice.

Civil Lawsuits The *Deepwater Horizon* explosion spurred approximately 3,000 lawsuits with over 100,000 named claimants asserting a wide variety of claims, from wrongful death to economic losses resulting from the spill. Most cases were consolidated into a class action lawsuit as a Multidistrict Litigation case and assigned to the U.S. District Court in the Eastern District of Louisiana. In 2012, the court approved a settlement agreement where BP agreed to pay $7.8 billion to resolve the litigation.

Civil Fines and Criminal Charges In 2013, two of BP's partners in the oil well agreed to plead guilty to violating the Clean Water Act and the Oil Pollution Act. Deepwater Horizon, Inc., the company that owned the oil-drilling platform, paid $1.4 billion in civil and criminal fines and penalties. Halliburton Co., which had contracted with BP to provide cementing services, pleaded guilty to destruction of critical evidence after the oil spill and paid $200,000 with three years' probation. The U.S. Justice Department also filed suit against various BP executives for manslaughter, obstructing justice, lying to investigators, and obstructing Congress.

The government also charged BP, Deepwater Horizon, Inc., and Halliburton Co. with violations of the CWA and the OPA. In Case 18.2, a federal court considers whether BP's actions constituted gross negligence or willful misconduct, which would result in greatly enhanced penalties.

CASE 18.2 *In re* Oil Spill by the Oil Rig "Deepwater Horizon" in the Gulf of Mexico, on April 20, 2010, MDL 2179, (E.D. La. Sept. 9, 2014)

FACT SUMMARY The *Deepwater Horizon* was a nine-year-old semi-submersible, mobile, floating, dynamically positioned drilling rig that could operate in waters up to 10,000 feet deep. The rig was owned by Transocean, Inc. and was chartered and operated by BP from March 2008 to September 2013. It was drilling a deep exploratory well roughly 41 miles off the Louisiana coast when high-pressure methane gas from the well expanded into the drilling riser and rose into the drilling rig, where it ignited and exploded, engulfing the platform with 126 crew members on board. Eleven people were killed and 17 others were injured. The *Deepwater Horizon* sank two days after the explosion.

Subsequent investigations revealed that BP managers misread pressure data, failed to administer appropriate tests for integrity of the well, and gave their approval for rig workers to replace drilling fluid in the well with seawater. However, the seawater was not heavy enough to prevent gas that had been leaking into the well from firing up the pipe to the rig and causing the explosion. While acknowledging responsibility for the accident, BP argued that the blame should be fully shared with Transocean, the owner of the *Deepwater Horizon* oil rig, and Halliburton, a contractor that oversaw a critical step in closing up the well. Transocean and Halliburton denied any liability.

The government charged BP, Transocean, and Halliburton with, among other charges, a violation of the Clean Water Act (CWA) and Oil Pollution Act (OPA). It also asked the court to impose enhanced penalties based on the "recklessness" and "willful conduct" provisions of the CWA and OPA. The impact of such a finding would result in BP being liable for four times the maximum penalties.

SYNOPSIS OF DECISION AND OPINION
Although the case dealt with dozens of legal issues, including maritime law and the common law of torts, the court's conclusion as to BP's liability for willful and reckless conduct was clear. The court ruled that BP had acted with conscious disregard of known risks. The court pointed to the actions of BP employees at the time of the incident and found that they took risks that led to the environmental disaster. In particular, the court ruled that the evidence indicated that the results of a pressure test should have

(continued)

prompted quick action to prevent an impending blowout. The court ruled that the company was reckless and determined that several crucial conversations between BP employees indicated a willful course of conduct that fit squarely into the statutory definitions of "reckless" or "willful" in the CWA and OPA. The court also found that Transocean and Halliburton's conduct was negligent, but not reckless.

WORDS OF THE COURT: Reckless Conduct

"The Court finds that a prudent well operator in BP's position, knowing what BP knew at the time, would have run a [integrity test for the cement seal], even if its decision tree concluded otherwise and its drilling and cement contractors did not tell it to do so. The fact that BP did not opt for the [test] when the necessary people and equipment were already on location leads the Court to believe BP's decision was primarily driven by a desire to save time and money, rather than ensuring that the well was secure."

Aftermath: Despite BP's initial promise to appeal, BP, the U.S. Justice Department, and five gulf coast states announced that the company agreed to pay a record settlement of $18.7 billion in 2015. To date, BP's cost for the cleanup, environmental and economic damages, and penalties has reached $54 billion.

Case Questions

1. Why did the court find BP liable for enhanced penalties under the CWA and OPA?
2. At the time of the court's decision, BP had already paid out $28 billion in cleanup costs and economic claims. Should there be any cap on BP's liability, even if it forces the company into bankruptcy?
3. *Focus on Critical Thinking:* Consider the enhanced penalty provisions in the CWA and OPA. Enhanced penalties are common in criminal statutes to punish conduct and deter behavior that the public considers particularly egregious (e.g., hate crimes). Do violations of environmental laws rise to that standard of egregiousness? Does the public actually benefit from enhanced penalties or, in regard to events such as *Deepwater Horizon,* is this more of a political reaction to media coverage?

Drinking Water

The **Safe Drinking Water Act (SDWA)**[9] is a federal statute that sets minimum quality and safety standards for every public water system and every source of drinking water in the United States. This includes rivers, lakes, reservoirs, springs, and subsurface water wells. The SDWA's standards vary based on the size and usage of the system. The statute requires the EPA to balance both *costs* and *health* benefits in setting the standards. Public water agencies are required to test and monitor water sources and systems at various points. A report of the results must be given to the state regulatory agency on a regular basis. The SDWA also requires states to oversee programs to certify that water system operators engage in safe practices and that they have the technical and financial capacity to ensure a consistent supply of safe drinking water as well as the ability to respond quickly to any defects in the water system.

CONCEPT SUMMARY Water Pollution Control

- Water pollution and conservation regulation are addressed by a combination of federal, state, and local statutes and rules.
- Water quality standards are set and regulated through the Clean Water Act (CWA).

(continued)

---

[9]42 U.S.C. § 300f *et seq.*

- Each state sets water quality standards, subject to EPA review, for the navigable waterways within the state's borders and monitors whether the standards are being met.
- Pollution emission into waterways is regulated through the EPA's National Pollution Discharge Elimination System, which establishes procedures for issuing permits (either individual permits or general permits), which are required regardless of the quality of the receiving water or actual pollution.
- Existing sources of pollution are required to install the best *practical* control technology, whereas new applicants are required to employ the best *available* technology in order to obtain a permit.
- The Safe Drinking Water Act (SDWA) is a federal statute that sets minimum quality and safety standards for every public water system and every source of drinking water in the United States.
- Congress increased the EPA's authority to prevent and respond to disastrous oil spills in water sources through the Oil Pollution Act (OPA).

REGULATION OF SOLID WASTE AND HAZARDOUS MATERIALS DISPOSAL

Although hazardous waste was historically within the jurisdiction of state legislatures, several debacles in the early 1970s in which toxic waste was discovered to have polluted community water sources resulted in congressional action in the form of a comprehensive federal statute. Although the handling, proper disposal, and liability for cleanup of abandoned solid waste and hazardous materials are regulated by federal law, states still play a crucial role in enforcement. Solid waste generally refers to garbage, refuse, sludge from a waste treatment plant, and sewage. Hazardous materials include chemical compounds and other inherently toxic substances (such as cleaning fluids and pesticides) used primarily in industry, agriculture, and research facilities.

Resource Conservation and Recovery Act

The **Resource Conservation and Recovery Act (RCRA)**[10] is intended to regulate *active and future facilities* that produce solid waste and/or hazardous materials. The RCRA created a "cradle-to-grave" procedure for handling waste from its origins to its transportation, treatment, storage, and disposal. Like many other environmental laws, the RCRA established reporting requirements and procedures and provides for civil penalties and citizen suits. In egregious cases, the RCRA also includes criminal provisions for the prosecution of intentional violations.

The RCRA bans the open dumping of solid waste and authorizes the EPA to set standards for municipal waste landfill facilities. The law specifies special procedures that must be employed for the disposal of certain types of municipal waste, such as refrigerators (which often contain potentially toxic refrigerant solution). The regulations govern the location, design, operation, and closing of a landfill site and require regular testing for groundwater contamination.

Waste that is (or becomes) hazardous is also regulated by the RCRA. The statute regulates both those who generate the pollution and those transporting the waste. A generator is defined by the law as any facility whose processes create hazardous waste. A transporter is

---

[10] 42 U.S.C. § 6901 et seq.

an entity that moves hazardous waste from one site to another via ground, water, or air transportation. These regulations include a mandatory tracking system in which the use of a standardized hazardous waste manifest form establishes a chain of custody for the waste to ensure accountability. The RCRA also imposes a permit system for facilities that treat, store, or dispose of hazardous waste.

> **KEY POINT**
>
> The Resource Conservation and Recovery Act (RCRA) is intended to regulate *active and future facilities* that produce solid waste and/or hazardous materials. It created "cradle-to-grave" procedures for handling waste from its origins to its transportation, treatment, storage, and disposal.

Universal waste (e.g., batteries, fluorescent bulbs, and mercury-containing equipment such as thermostats) is included under the RCRA, but the EPA has issued federal rules that make compliance easier for business owners who are disposing of universal waste in the ordinary course of operations. The rules allow universal waste to be transported by common carrier rather than a more expensive hazardous waste carrier certified by the EPA. Used tires and oil are also covered by the RCRA, and the EPA has established special guidelines for the disposal of motor vehicle waste products by repair and service facilities.

Toxic Substances Control Act

The **Toxic Substances Control Act (TSCA)**[11] is a federal statute that gives the EPA jurisdiction to control risks that may be posed by the manufacturing, processing, using, and disposing of chemical compounds. The TSCA's scope is very broad: It covers every chemical substance except pesticides, tobacco, nuclear material, and items already regulated under the Food, Drug, and Cosmetic Act.[12]

The TSCA has both reporting and regulatory components. Specifically, the statute provides for (1) an EPA-maintained inventory of every chemical substance that may be legally manufactured, processed, or imported into the United States; (2) EPA authority to require companies to conduct specific screening tests that may reveal risks to public welfare; (3) EPA regulation on the use, labeling, and control measures of the substance; (4) recordkeeping requirements; and (5) an obligation to report any potential adverse impact that the manufacturer, processor, or importer may become aware of in the course of operations.

CONCEPT SUMMARY *Regulation of Solid Waste and Hazardous Materials*

- The Resource Conservation and Recovery Act (RCRA) is intended to regulate active and future facilities that produce solid waste and/or hazardous materials, and it created a "cradle-to-grave" procedure for handling waste.
- The Toxic Substances Control Act (TSCA) is a federal statute that gives the EPA broad jurisdiction to control risks that may be posed by the manufacturing, processing, using, and disposing of chemical compounds.
- Federal law regulates the handling, proper disposal, and liability for cleanup of abandoned solid waste and hazardous materials; however, states play a crucial role in enforcement.

---

[11] 15 U.S.C. § 2601.

[12] The Food, Drug, and Cosmetic Act includes food, food additives, pharmaceuticals, and cosmetics. This law is discussed in detail in Chapter 21, "Warranties and Consumer Protection Law."

LO 18-7

Articulate the potential liability of various parties under the federal environmental cleanup statutes.

COMPREHENSIVE ENVIRONMENTAL RESPONSE COMPENSATION AND LIABILITY ACT

The environmental laws that we have discussed so far focus on controlling and reducing existing or new sources of pollution. These laws do nothing to address toxic waste contamination generated prior to the enactment of waste control statutes and then abandoned by the polluter. Faced with this major hurdle to achieving environmental safety for the public, Congress passed the **Comprehensive Environmental Response Compensation and Liability Act (CERCLA)**[13] in 1980.

Superfund

The CERCLA is commonly referred to as the **Superfund** because its main provisions center on the notion that cleanup operations for abandoned toxic waste sites (including both land and water sites) are to be funded by a self-sustaining quasi-escrow fund administered by the federal government. Superfund was initially funded by fees and taxes levied upon substances that contain hazardous components, primarily in the petroleum and chemical industries. However, the statutory scheme also replenishes the fund by allocating financial responsibility to parties that are statutorily responsible for all or part of the cleanup costs. Therefore, the cleanup of a particularly toxic site could be conducted, and then the EPA could sue a statutorily responsible party for the cleanup costs. Critics of the law argue that the Superfund is consistently underfunded and that taxpayers bear a disproportionate amount of the cleanup costs. Proponents argue that the Superfund model is the most effective way to halt further damage from abandoned toxic waste sites while identifying polluters and assessing financial liability.

In 1986, the CERCLA was amended by the **Superfund Amendments and Reauthorization Act (SARA)**.[14] Although SARA's provisions were primarily clarifications and technical definitional adjustments, the law contained a new requirement for states to establish emergency response commissions to draft emergency procedures for a hazardous chemical accident and implement them in the event of such an accident. All states must maintain and revise the plan as necessary, as well as fund a hazardous materials response unit. The act also requires businesses to disclose the presence of certain chemicals within a community and imposes an affirmative obligation to notify authorities of any spills or discharges of hazardous materials. For continuity, this textbook uses the term *Superfund* to refer to all of the provisions of CERCLA and SARA, combined.

LO 18-8

Distinguish between removal and remedial cleanup efforts in the context of environmental regulation.

Removal and Remedial Responses
The Superfund law established a two-front approach to handling hazardous substance cleanup: (1) **removal**, whereby authorization is given for actions to address releases or imminent releases of hazardous materials, and (2) **remedial**, whereby the EPA identifies the most hazardous waste sites and establishes a National Priorities List (NPL) for cleanup. In determining what sites are eligible, the EPA considers the overall potential harm to public health. To date, the EPA has placed over 25,000 sites around the country on the NPL. Once on the NPL, the EPA begins the remedial enforcement process by investigating the site, identifying parties that may be liable for cleanup costs, assessing the toxicity of the site, and determining the best remedial measure to accomplish cleanup. Figure 18.2 provides a map of Superfund sites on the NPL.

> **KEY POINT**
>
> The Superfund law addresses hazardous substance cleanup in two ways: (1) removal (for imminent releases) and (2) remedial (long-term cleanup projects).

---

[13] 42 U.S.C. § 9601.

[14] 42 U.S.C. § 9601 *et seq.*

FIGURE 18.2 Superfund Sites

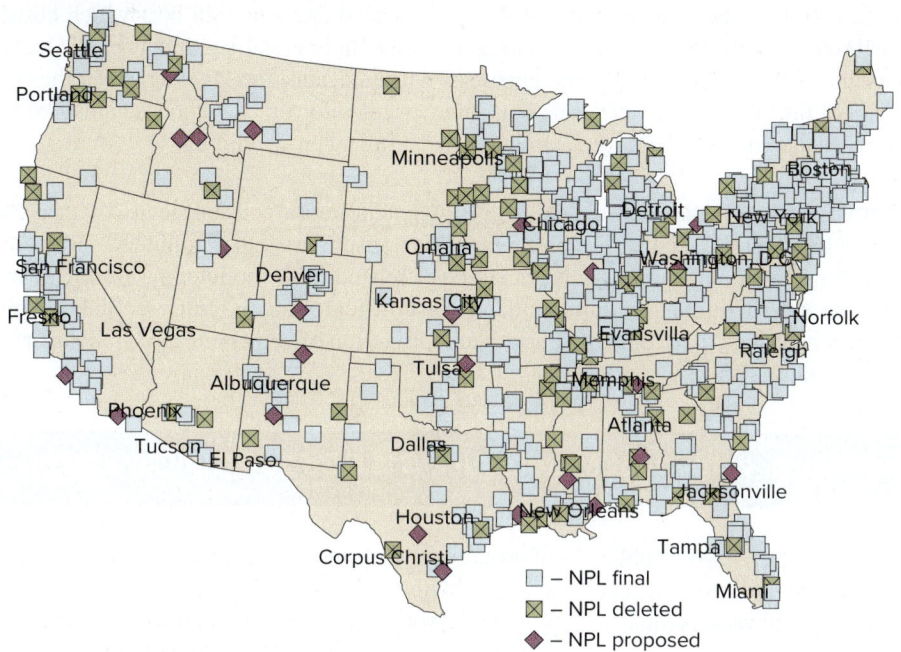

- NPL final
- NPL deleted
- NPL proposed

Source: http://toxmap.nlm.nih.gov/toxmap/superfund/mapControls.do.

Liability of Principally Responsible Parties (PRPs)
The sharpest teeth of the Superfund law are that it (1) is retroactive and, therefore, applies to any disposal made prior to its enactment in 1980 and (2) imposes broad strict liability standards for cleanup costs on certain businesses and individuals that fit the statute's definition of a *principally responsible party* (*PRP*). The Superfund also specifically imposes *joint and several liability* on PRPs. There are three classes of PRPs:

- Current owners of the site.
- Any owner or operator of the site at the time when the hazardous substances were disposed at the site.
- Any business that accepts hazardous substances for transport to the site and selected the site (such as a waste hauler).

For example, suppose that a parcel of commercial real estate is listed on the NPL because the groundwater is contaminated due to a leak in an underground storage tank. The EPA investigates the parcel and finds records of three previous owners: GasCo (which used it for a retail gasoline station), ChairCo (which used it for warehouse storage of furniture), and its current owner, DevelopCo (which is using it for real estate development and has plans to build a retail storefront). The EPA determines that hazardous materials were stored in underground tanks by GasCo. Subject to certain defenses (discussed next), both GasCo and DevelopCo have joint and several liability for the cleanup costs. Suppose further that GasCo has been dissolved or liquidated under the bankruptcy law and no longer exists as an entity. Under the Superfund law, the EPA can hold DevelopCo, the parcel's current owner as of the NPL listing, liable for the *full* amount of the cleanup costs even though DevelopCo never contributed to the contamination.

Consent Decrees
Once the EPA has contacted the PRPs, the agency begins negotiations centered on PRP liability and cleanup operations. The parties draft a series of nonbinding

Legal Speak >))

Joint and Several Liability
The legal principle that makes two or more parties liable for an entire debt either individually or jointly in any proportional combination.

agreements in order to evidence their good faith in moving ahead with the cleanup process. If negotiations result in a settlement being reached before cleanup efforts are commenced or are complete, the EPA and the PRP enter into a binding agreement, called a *consent decree*, that lays out how the cleanup plan will be implemented and who will bear which costs. If the EPA believes the PRP is not negotiating in good faith or is stalling, it may cease negotiations, implement a cleanup plan, and pursue a civil suit against the PRP to recover the entire amount of the cleanup costs. The EPA also may begin enforcement actions against the PRP that may result in civil fines or, in extreme cases, criminal prosecution.

Allocation of Liability When the EPA enters into a consent decree with a PRP, the PRP has the right to sue third parties such as transporters, other polluters, and municipalities to recover a portion of the cleanup costs related to the polluter's action. However, allocating liability among multiple polluters is a difficult process. In Case 18.3 an appellate court considers the scope of authority and discretion of courts engaged in a Superfund allocation analysis.

CASE 18.3 Goodrich Corp. v. Town of Middlebury, 311 F.3d 154 (2d Cir. 2002)

FACT SUMMARY For decades, two public landfills in Connecticut accepted industrial waste, including municipal solid waste from various municipalities. The EPA declared the landfills to be Superfund sites because they were leaking chemicals and threatening the local water supply. The EPA began the remedial enforcement process by investigating and identifying various principally responsible parties (PRPs) that contributed to the pollution, and it entered into consent decrees for them to contribute to the cost of cleanup. The PRPs, which were all corporations that had disposed of waste in the landfills, formed a coalition to represent their common interests and sued several municipalities for contribution to the cleanup costs. In a long, complicated litigation, a special master was appointed by the court to try to mediate a settlement. The special master came to certain conclusions about which parties contributed how much waste. At trial, the district court did not follow the conclusion of the special master and allocated much of the liability to the municipalities that ran the landfills. The municipalities appealed.

SYNOPSIS OF DECISION AND OPINION The U.S. Court of Appeals for the Second Circuit affirmed the district court's ruling. Appellate courts will not overturn a district court's allocation of remediation costs in Superfund cases unless there is an abuse of discretion. It was within the right of the court not to follow all of the findings of the special master and to allocate more costs to the municipalities than recommended by the master. For the court to abuse its discretion, it would have to have committed an error of law or be clearly wrong in its finding of facts.

The allocation of costs in such complicated proceedings may produce varying results; the court chose a method of allocation that was proper based on the evidence.

WORDS OF THE COURT: Court's Discretion under CERCLA "[B]ecause '[CERCLA's] expansive language . . . affords a district court *broad discretion* to balance the equities in the interests of justice[, the appellate court] will not overturn the district court's [allocation of response costs] absent an abuse of that discretion.'

"'A district court "abuses" or "exceeds" the discretion accorded to it when (1) its decision rests on an error of law (such as application of the wrong legal principle) or a clearly erroneous factual finding, or (2) its decision—though not necessarily the product of a legal error or a clearly erroneous factual finding—cannot be located within the range of permissible decisions. . . . [A] district court must give 'some deference' to a master's recommendation where the master has 'direct and extensive' knowledge about the particular circumstances of a given case. 'A district court that extends some deference to the master will consider his recommendation and the factors influencing it, but will not regard the

(continued)

recommendation as the alpha and omega of the ... analysis.' ... The Federal Rules of Civil Procedure ... expressly permit a district court to 'modify' a special master's report. ... [A] plaintiff may recover 'any ... necessary costs of response incurred ... consistent with the national contingency plan.' ... [CERCLA] 'does not limit courts to any particular list of factors.' ... 'The court may consider the state of mind of the parties, their economic status, any contracts between them bearing on the subject, *any traditional equitable defenses as mitigating factors and any other factors deemed appropriate to balance the equities in the totality of the circumstances.*'"

Case Questions

1. Suppose the coalition sues the companies that transported the waste. Are they liable as PRPs? Why or why not?
2. Why do you believe that the court rejected the special master's report? Do you agree with the court's decision?
3. *Focus on Critical Thinking:* Should courts have broad discretion when engaging in a Superfund allocation analysis? Is the public interest best served by a court deciding the allocation? Why or why not?

Defenses to Liability

As you may imagine, the Superfund law has come under fire by business advocacy groups for its potential to devastate innocent property owners and lenders. As a result, Congress carved out several defenses to liability for parties that meet certain criteria, including secured creditors, innocent landowners, and prospective purchasers.

Secured Creditors Suppose, in the DevelopCo example above, that during the EPA's investigation, DevelopCo defaults on its mortgage payments and its financial lender forecloses on the property. Because the lender is now the owner, does that subject the bank to liability under Superfund? Probably not. To protect lenders (such as banks) that have become owners of contaminated property through foreclosure, the Superfund law contains a provision that excludes any such lender from liability for cleanup costs. Lender-owners may avoid liability so long as the lender was (1) an owner by virtue of the contaminated property being used as collateral for a loan and (2) not participating in the management of the facility prior to foreclosure. The EPA has issued specific guidelines to define what activities constitute participating in management.

Innocent Landowners A current owner of a site that is listed on the NPL may avoid liability for cleanup costs so long as the owner establishes that she purchased the property without knowledge of the contamination. The owner must submit evidence that she conducted *all appropriate inquiries* into the previous ownership, using a reasonable amount of investigation to determine whether any contamination was present. So long as the owner complies with land use restrictions, takes reasonable steps to limit the impact of the hazardous substances on the general public, and cooperates with government agencies, she may avoid cleanup liability under the statute.

Prospective Purchasers In 2002, Congress enacted the Small Business Liability Relief Act,[15] which provides a defense to Superfund liability for a party that purchased the property *with knowledge* of the contamination. The statute provides for limited liability so long as the owner agrees to take reasonable steps to limit the impact of the contamination, prevent further contamination, and notify authorities of any imminent or actual pollutant release.

---

[15] 42 U.S.C. § 9607(r).

 **Self-Check** PRP Liability

Who has PRP liability? The EPA placed a parcel of land known as Noxious Flats on the NPL in 2009 due to contamination caused by chemicals from cleaning solvents and lead paint. Using the information in the following table, determine which parties have PRP liability:

Party	Relationship to Noxious Flats	Hazardous Substance Use
Richmond Industries	Owned the property from 1970 to 1979 and operated an industrial plant.	After using industrial cleaning solvents, stored the used solvents in an underground tank.
Bright Paint Company	Leased the property from Richmond from 1979 to 1985.	Dumped paint production waste into a hole in the ground and buried it.
Warehouse Storage Inc.	Purchased the property from Richmond in 1986 without any environmental investigation; installed concrete over the entire property and built warehouse spaces for lease.	No contamination by Warehouse Storage. Richmond's underground tank ruptured in 1988 and caused groundwater contamination. Warehouse Storage had no knowledge of the rupture.
The Factory Restaurant	Leased the property from Warehouse Storage from 1995 to 2008; built an upscale restaurant as part of a community revitalization project to turn blighted industrial areas into retail and restaurant zones. Lessor hired an environmental service company to survey the property before signing the lease, and no contamination was detected.	No contamination.
First Neighborhood Bank	Foreclosed on Warehouse Storage Inc., which defaulted on its loan in 2008.	None.

Answers to this Self-Check are provided at the end of the chapter.

STRATEGIC LEGAL SOLUTIONS

Avoiding Environmental Liability in Land Acquisitions

PROBLEM: *A land acquisition may result in Superfund liability for the purchasing business even if the acquirer did not contaminate the property.*

SOLUTION: *Preserve your status as an innocent landowner under CERCLA by engaging a qualified environmental screening firm.*

Step 1: Contract Contingency

When considering a property for acquisition or lease, the parties are typically under time pressure to sign an Agreement of Sale or Letter of Intent. Work with your counsel to develop a contingency clause for the contract that provides you with a period of time for environmental screening. The language "environmental contingency" is important because it helps to document your efforts to make

(continued)

appropriate inquiries into previous ownership as required for innocent landowner status.

Step 2: Transaction Screen

A simple transaction screen can be conducted to provide the buyer with more data on potential environmental problems with the property. This screen (also called an Environmental Phase I) is a minimal, relatively inexpensive assessment that typically consists of (1) record checks for ownership, code violations, or environmental agency actions; (2) an interview with the current site owner; and (3) a site visit for obvious signs of potential environmental liability (such as an aboveground port for an underground tank). If there is any evidence of contamination, advanced assessments (called Phase II and Phase III environmental assessments) that include soil and groundwater testing can be conducted. However, these advanced assessments are more expensive and could impact the cost-benefit analysis for the purchaser.

Step 3: Verify Qualifications

It is also important for business owners and managers to be sure that the firms they are hiring are *qualified* within the meaning of federal and state statutory definitions. In order to assert an innocent purchaser defense, the company must have relied on the report of a qualified environmental professional. Federal and state statutes lay out the standards for qualification. To qualify under the EPA standards, an environmental professional must (1) be certified by the federal government to perform environmental inspections, (2) be a licensed engineer or geologist, (3) have at least a bachelor's-degree level of education, and (4) have 10 years of relevant work experience.

For example, suppose that Chef Kuo is looking for a new location for expanding her restaurant operations. She locates a potential property, but when visiting the site, Kuo notices that it is adjacent to inactive railroad tracks. In the past, Kuo recalls an article in the local newspaper that reported on some railroad yards in the area that were contaminated by a toxic substance called PCB that was buried beneath the tracks when they were put down many years ago. Kuo is convinced that this property is ideal for her newest restaurant but is concerned about any potential environmental liability. Yet, at this early stage of the acquisition, she does not wish to invest in an expensive assessment. By using a transaction screen, Kuo will be in a better position to choose whether to abandon the transaction entirely and continue her search or to invest more money in further assessments. These advanced assessments are much more expensive, so Kuo will have to decide if the costs of assessment (and possible remediation) are sufficiently equal to the benefits of putting her restaurant on that site. In any case, Kuo will have accumulated documentation that she qualifies as an innocent landowner under the law.

CONCEPT SUMMARY Superfund Response

- If there is an immediate threat of hazardous materials release, the Superfund law requires immediate removal efforts. Local authorities respond pursuant to their Superfund emergency plan.
- In cases of long-term contamination of a land or water site, the Superfund law requires the EPA to determine suitability for placement on the National Priorities List (NPL).
- For sites listed on the NPL, government authorities then investigate the site's chain of ownership to determine any principally responsible parties (PRPs) and assess cleanup alternatives.
- Government officials negotiate with PRPs to determine contributions for cleanup. If an agreement is reached, the parties enter into a binding agreement called a consent decree. If the negotiations fail, the government typically files a Superfund lawsuit to collect cleanup costs from PRPs.

Table 18.1 sets out the major environmental laws discussed in this section.

TABLE 18.1 — Major Environmental Laws

Law	Description
National Environmental Policy Act (NEPA) of 1969	Establishes a process that must be followed by federal agencies when making decisions that may reasonably impact the environment or when federal funding is involved.
Clean Air Act (most recently amended in 1997)	Improves outdoor air quality based on National Ambient Air Quality Standards that set permissible levels of certain air pollutants. The law focuses on pollution from both stationary sources (manufacturing plants) and mobile sources (motor vehicles).
Clean Water Act	Sets water quality standards and regulates the disposal of pollutants into public waterways.
Resource Conservation and Recovery Act (RCRA)	Regulates active and future facilities that produce solid waste and/or hazardous materials; uses a cradle-to-grave procedure that includes regulations for handling waste from its origins to its transportation, treatment, storage, and disposal.
Comprehensive Environmental Response Compensation and Liability Act (CERCLA), commonly referred to as Superfund	Addresses hazardous substance cleanup in two ways: (1) removal (for imminent releases) and (2) remedial (for long-term cleanup projects).

WILDLIFE PROTECTION

Wildlife and aquatic life are protected by a series of specialized federal statutes, including the Marine Mammal Protection Act and the Migratory Bird Conservation Act. These laws impact industries such as fisheries or logging because they restrict certain activities even on private lands to meet the objective of protecting wildlife. Perhaps the most important wildlife protection is the **Endangered Species Act (ESA)**.[16] The ESA is administered jointly by agencies in the U.S. Department of Commerce and the U.S. Department of the Interior.

---

[16] 16 U.S.C. § 1531.

KEY TERMS

Nuisance p. 599   A common law legal action for redressing harm arising from the misuse of one's property that is based on the aggrieved party's right to enjoy his property without interference from a third party.

Citizen suit provisions p. 600   Laws that authorize private individuals or watchdog groups to file environmental enforcement lawsuits.

National Environmental Policy Act (NEPA) p. 602   Federal legislation enacted in 1969 that established a process federal agencies must follow when making decisions that have the potential to significantly impact the environment.

Clean Air Act (CAA) p. 604   Federal legislation enacted in 1963 to improve, strengthen, and accelerate programs for the prevention and abatement of air pollution; focuses on stationary and mobile sources in the United States.

Stationary sources of air pollution p. 604   Fixed-site emitters of air pollutants, including fossil-fueled power plants, petroleum refineries, petrochemical plants, food processing plants, and other industrial sources.

Mobile sources of air pollution p. 604   Nonstationary sources of air pollutants, including automobiles, buses, trucks, ships, trains, aircraft, and various other vehicles.

State Implementation Plan (SIP) p. 604   A mandated state plan for complying with the federal Clean Air Act that is submitted to the Environmental Protection Agency; consists of a collection of regulations that help to achieve a reduction in pollution.

Operating permits p. 604   Licenses issued by authorities to existing stationary sources, permitting pollution emission at certain levels.

Market-based approach p. 604   An approach to pollution control that gives businesses a choice of methods based on economic incentives for complying with pollution standards; instituted by the 1990 amendments to the Clean Air Act.

Clean Water Act (CWA) p. 607   Federal legislation that regulates water quality standards and aims to stem water pollution from industrial, municipal, and agricultural sources; implemented and enforced by the EPA.

Oil Pollution Act (OPA) p. 608   Federal legislation enacted in 1990 to streamline and strengthen the Environmental Protection Agency's ability to prevent and respond to catastrophic oil spills in water sources.

Safe Drinking Water Act (SDWA) p. 611   Federal legislation that sets minimum quality and safety standards for every public water system and every source of drinking water in the United States.

Resource Conservation and Recovery Act (RCRA) p. 612   Federal legislation enacted in 1976 to regulate active and future facilities that produce solid waste and/or hazardous materials.

Toxic Substances Control Act (TSCA) p. 613   Federal legislation that gives the Environmental Protection Agency jurisdiction to control risks that may be posed by the manufacturing, processing, using, and disposing of chemical compounds.

Comprehensive Environmental Response Compensation and Liability Act (CERCLA) p. 614   Federal legislation enacted in 1980 to create a tax on the chemical and petroleum industries and provide broad federal authority to respond directly to releases or threatened releases of hazardous substances that may endanger public health or the environment. Also called *Superfund*.

Superfund p. 614   Another name for the CERCLA, derived from that act's main provisions whereby cleanup operations for abandoned toxic waste sites are to be funded by a self-sustaining quasi-escrow fund to be administered by the federal government.

Superfund Amendments and Reauthorization Act (SARA) p. 614   A 1986 amendment to the CERCLA that requires that states establish emergency response commissions to draft emergency procedures for a hazardous chemical accident and implement them in the event of such an accident; requires that businesses disclose the presence of certain chemicals within a community; and imposes an obligation on businesses to notify authorities of any spills or discharges of hazardous materials.

Removal p. 614   Under the Superfund law, an approach to handling hazardous substance cleanup whereby authorization is given for actions to address releases or imminent releases of hazardous materials.

Remedial p. 614   Under the Superfund law, an approach to handling hazardous substance cleanup whereby the Environmental Protection Agency identifies the most hazardous waste sites and generates a National Priorities List.

Endangered Species Act (ESA) p. 620   Federal legislation enacted in 1973 that established a procedure for identifying imperiled species and preserving them from extinction.

CHAPTER REVIEW QUESTIONS

1. What agency has the authority to enforce environmental regulations?
   a. Environmental Protection Agency
   b. Food and Drug Administration
   c. Nuclear Regulatory Commission
   d. All the above

2. What category does the National Environmental Policy Act (NEPA) use for laws that have no environmental impact?
   a. Categorical exclusion
   b. Environmental assessment
   c. Environmental impact statement
   d. Nonimpact statement

3. The basic structure of the Clean Air Act (CAA) focuses on both stationary and _____ sources of air pollution.
   a. Fixed
   b. Mobile
   c. Variable
   d. Permanent

4. Cap and trade is an example of what type of approach to controlling air pollution?
   a. Regulatory
   b. Common law
   c. Permitting
   d. Market-based

5. **The federal law that provides for cleanup operations for abandoned toxic waste using funds from a self-sustaining escrow fund is known as**
   a. Cradle-to-Grave
   b. Superfund
   c. Toxic Control Act
   d. Cleanup Recovery Act

Answers and explanations are provided at the end of this chapter.

THEORY TO PRACTICE

Regional Cuisine Publications Corporation (RCPC) is the publisher of a monthly magazine that features recipes and articles on culinary traditions from various regions in the United States. RCPC began in the South and has expanded into the mid-Atlantic and New England markets in the last 10 years. As part of RCPC's business model, the actual name of the magazine distributed in a certain region takes on that region's name (*Southern Cuisine, New England Cuisine,* etc.). Although RCPC began its business by contracting with outside vendors that supplied magazine-quality paper, as it has expanded circulation, RCPC has sought to reduce its rising paper costs by producing its own paper in house. RCPC's management has located a small production facility that has been owned by Paper Production Inc. since 1950. RCPC is now considering purchasing the facility and property.

1. In investigating the purchase of the facility, what environmental laws will RCPC need to be aware of? In what way could environmental regulation affect the costs of the transaction?

2. Assume that the facility emits certain pollutants into the air. RCPC wishes to partially reconstruct the facility after its purchase for purposes of being able to run the facility for longer periods of time. Does this trigger any regulatory concerns?

3. Suppose that the facility emits more of a certain pollutant than permitted by the EPA standards. What are RCPC's options under the CAA's market-based approach?

4. Assume that the facility discharges waste from the paper production process into an adjoining river and, because Paper Production was struggling financially, the company never upgraded its technology. If RCPC purchases the facility, will it be required to upgrade the waste discharge technology under the Clean Water Act? What is the standard set by the CWA for upgrading technology?

5. What type of precautionary measures should RCPC's management take to be sure to limit potential Superfund liability prior to purchasing the site?

LEGAL STRATEGY 101

Greenwashing

The Oxford English Dictionary defines *greenwashing* as "disinformation disseminated by an organization so as to present an environmentally responsible public image,"[17] but it was a young, pony-tailed environmental activist, Jay Westerveld, who first coined this controversial term in the 1980s.[18]

During a trip to the South Pacific, Westerveld noticed a small card in his hotel room. The card was decorated with three green arrows—the universal recycling symbol—and it read as follows:

> Save Our Planet: Every day, millions of gallons of water are used to wash towels that have only been used once. You make the choice: A towel on the rack means, 'I will use again.' A towel on the floor means, 'Please replace.' Thank you for helping us conserve the Earth's vital resources.

Westerveld promptly questioned the true motives of this "Save Our Planet" policy. Specifically, was the

---

[17] *See Greenwash,* Oxford Dictionaries (not dated), available at https://www.lexico.com/en/definition/greenwash.

[18] *See* John Sullivan, *"Greenwashing" Gets His Goat: Environmental Activist Coined the Famous Term,* Times Herald-Rec. (Aug. 1, 2009).

Recycling symbol.   tang90246/123RF

"save the towel" card in his hotel room really about the hotel's commitment to protecting the environment, or was it more about the hotel wanting to save money by having to wash fewer towels?

Collectively, hotels consume massive amounts of energy and water. Take water, for example. Hotels require large amounts of water to provide amenities expected by tourists, such as swimming pools, landscaped gardens, and golf courses. The washing of towels, by contrast, uses up a small amount of water relative to these other uses—but not having to wash as many towels saves the hotel time and money. Westerveld thus coined the term "greenwashing" to describe marketing campaigns designed to manipulate consumers into believing that a company's products, aims, or policies are environmentally friendly.

Today, many major multinational firms like BP, Shell, and ExxonMobil spend millions of dollars in advertising campaigns touting their environmentally friendly policies and their commitment to the environment, but are such companies truly committed to protecting the environment beyond mere compliance with legal standards? Or are they merely "greenwashing" their corporate image in order to attract customers and increase sales?

CRITICAL THINKING QUESTIONS

1. Is "greenwashing" protected commercial speech under the First Amendment to the U.S. Constitution, or is "greenwashing" an unfair trade practice like fraud?
2. Also, in your opinion, should there be a specific law against "greenwashing" as a matter of public policy?
3. If so, who should have "standing" to enforce such a law: the Environmental Protection Agency (EPA), consumers, or rival companies?

MANAGER'S CHALLENGE

Assume that, in the Theory to Practice problem, RCPC wishes to pursue negotiations for the purchase of the facility and you are a junior manager at RCPC. You receive the following e-mail from your senior manager:

> We are pursuing the purchase of the paper facility, but we are concerned about environmental liability due to potential groundwater contamination. Please write a two- to three-page memorandum that recommends two environmental consulting firms in the area to conduct an assessment. We want to be sure that these firms are qualified as defined by the law. (1) Research what qualifications are required by our state environmental agency or the EPA, (2) determine which firms in our area are qualified, and (3) provide a brief description in your memorandum of each firm based on its website.

After rereading the Strategic Legal Solutions feature in this chapter, write a two- to three-page memorandum in response to your senior manager's request. Note that a link to EPA's standards (as well as a sample answer to this Manager's Challenge) may be found in Connect.

See Connect for Manager's Challenge sample answers.

CASE SUMMARY 18.1 Sierra Club v. El Paso Gold Mines, Inc., 421 F.3d 1133 (10th Cir. 2005)

CLEAN WATER ACT

El Paso Gold Mines owns 100 acres of land bought in 1968 near Cripple Creek, Colorado. Though El Paso did not engage in mining activity on the land, the land contained a collapsed mine shaft built in 1910. The shaft is connected to a six-mile-long drainage tunnel that is connected to other old mines draining into Cripple Creek. A citizens' watchdog group, the Sierra Club, brought suit alleging that El Paso violated the Clean Water Act by discharging pollutants (zinc and manganese) from a source, the mine shaft, into the creek without a discharge permit.

CASE QUESTIONS

1. Does the Sierra Club have an actionable claim under the Clean Water Act? Why or why not?
2. If El Paso wanted to use the land for mining activity, would the company be required to obtain a permit? If so, what would need to be done in order to obtain the permit?

CASE SUMMARY 18.2 United States v. Southeastern Pennsylvania Transportation Authority, 235 F.3d 817 (3d Cir. 2000)

SUPERFUND

The Paoli Rail Yard covers about 30 acres in Paoli, Pennsylvania, and consists of an electric train repair facility owned by Amtrak and operated by Philadelphia-based Southeastern Pennsylvania Transportation Authority (SEPTA). Prior to Amtrak's acquisition of the property, the site was owned by the Pennsylvania Railroad Company from 1939 until 1967, Penn Central Transportation until 1976, and Conrail until 1982. All previous owners are now defunct. In 1979, a toxic chemical known as PCB was discovered in the rail yard and the EPA declared the yard a Superfund site. The EPA then began the remedial enforcement process and brought an action against potentially responsible parties.

CASE QUESTIONS

1. Do any of the prior owners of the rail yard have PRP liability?
2. Could SEPTA or Amtrak have taken action to avoid liability? Explain.

CASE SUMMARY 18.3 William Paxton v. Wal-Mart Stores, Inc., 176 Ohio App. 3d 364 (2008)

RESOURCE CONSERVATION AND RECOVERY ACT

Paxton, a proprietor, intended to set up a recycling facility on one of his properties. He then contracted with Wal-Mart to recycle or dispose of various lamps and bulbs that contained spent mercury and other products that contained lead. Instead of recycling the items, Paxton crushed or shredded them and left them piled on the property. The state determined that there were hazardous waste violations, and it filed suit.

CASE QUESTIONS

1. What federal statute(s) could apply to this case? Explain.
2. Citing the RCRA "cradle-to-grave" procedure, do you think Wal-Mart was contributory in violation of the statute? Why or why not?

CASE SUMMARY 18.4 Beverly E. Black & James A. Black v. George Weston & Stroehmann Bakeries, Inc., 2008 U.S. Dist. LEXIS 92031 (W.D.N.Y. 2008)

CLEAN AIR ACT

Black, a Realtor, owned adjacent rental properties in a New York neighborhood. On the same block, Stroehmann Bakeries owned and operated a bakery. Black alleged that the bakery had emitted "noxious discharges" and that these emissions had coated his properties with mold and mold residue. As a result, Black's properties were discolored, causing a loss of rental income and resale value. An investigation was conducted, and the agency concluded that the bakery was the source of the mold growth found on Black's properties.

CASE QUESTIONS

1. What standard was used to determine whether or not the discharges constituted a violation of the Clean Air Act?
2. What common law doctrine could Black have possibly pursued in an attempt to compel Stroehmann to cease polluting?

CASE SUMMARY 18.5 No Spray Coalition, Inc. v. City of New York, 2000 WL 1401458 (S.D.N.Y. 2000)

CITIZEN SUITS

In the late 1990s, the City of New York confronted growing concerns surrounding the mosquito-borne West Nile virus by implementing an aerial and ground spraying program. The program consisted of spray planes and trucks that would douse the city with malathion, a controversial neurotoxin pesticide, in an attempt to eradicate mosquitoes carrying the potentially fatal virus. The plan was controversial because of the exposure of the general public to the potentially hazardous pesticide. The No Spray Coalition, a group of local organizations and individuals, filed suit to halt the insecticide spraying, alleging that such spraying violated the Clean Water Act.

CASE QUESTIONS

1. What would No Spray have to prove in order to have an actionable claim under the CWA?
2. Explain the significance of citizen suit provisions and watchdog groups in the context of this case.

✓ Self-Check ANSWERS PRP Liability

1. *Richmond Industries* is liable as a PRP because it owned the plant at the time of disposal of the cleaning solvents in the underground tank. Note that, under Superfund, it is irrelevant that the disposal was made prior to the Superfund law's enactment (Superfund is retroactive). It is also irrelevant that no actual contamination took place while Richmond owned the parcel.
2. *Bright Paint* is also liable as a PRP, based on the same rationale provided above.
3. *Warehouse Storage Inc.* is probably not liable as a PRP. No disposal took place under its ownership. The contamination occurred under its ownership, but Warehouse never disposed of any solid waste or hazardous materials.

(continued)

4. *The Factory Restaurant* has no liability as a disposer of materials. If the EPA placed Noxious Flats on the NPL while The Factory Restaurant was operating on the site, the business is still shielded from liability under the Superfund as an innocent lessor because it performed an environmental assessment prior to entering into the lease.

5. *First Neighborhood Bank* has no liability as a PRP. The bank is shielded because it is a secured creditor that did not actively participate in ownership or operation prior to the foreclosure.

CHAPTER REVIEW QUESTIONS: Answers and Explanations

1. **d.** All of the agencies listed have jurisdiction over different areas of federal environmental regulation. While the EPA is the primary enforcement agency, it is important to note that other agencies work in tandem with the EPA when an environmental regulation that impacts their jurisdiction is involved (e.g., NRC for nuclear waste).

2. **a.** Categorical exclusion is the NEPA category for laws that have no environmental impact. (b) and (c) are incorrect because they are categories used when environmental impact is possible or certain. (d) is incorrect because no such category exists under NEPA.

3. **b.** The CAA regulates both stationary sources (e.g., industrial plants) and mobile sources (e.g., cars). (a) and (d) are incorrect because both terms are synonyms for *stationary*. (c) is incorrect because no such source exists.

4. **d.** Cap and trade is an emissions trading scheme based on economic incentives. (a), (b), and (c) are incorrect because they are all examples of non-market-based regulation that is unrelated to cap and trade.

5. **b.** Superfund is the commonly used name for the Comprehensive Environmental Response Compensation and Liability Act (CERCLA), which is intended to be a self-sustaining fund for the cleanup of toxic waste sites. (a), (c), and (d) are incorrect because they are fictitious names.

CHAPTER 19
Antitrust and Regulation of Competition

©philsajonesen/Getty Images

Learning Objectives

After studying this chapter, students who have mastered the material will be able to:

19-1 Articulate the fundamental purpose and source of law for antitrust regulation.

19-2 Identify the main federal statutes in antitrust law.

19-3 Distinguish and explain the differences between the per se standard and the rule of reason standard.

19-4 List and articulate the primary ways that businesses use horizontal and vertical restraints of trade.

19-5 Recognize when a business has achieved a monopoly and explain the restrictions on a monopoly business under antitrust law.

19-6 Explain why the *United States v. Microsoft* case is an important part of antitrust law.

19-7 Articulate the role of more modern antitrust statutes in regulating competition.

Even in a free market economy, business owners and managers depend on certain regulation of competition in the marketplace. This regulation allows for innovation and entrepreneurial effort to thrive without the threat of being eliminated from the marketplace by larger competitors that have already established a market share. The law also promotes competition among businesses, which allows consumers to receive the benefits of competitive pricing. This chapter covers regulation of competition, which is primarily accomplished through antitrust laws enforced by the federal government. Specifically, we discuss

- The background, scope, and purpose of laws that regulate competition.
- The statutory model for antitrust laws.
- How antitrust laws are applied to various anticompetitive actions by businesses.

BACKGROUND, PURPOSE, AND SOURCE OF ANTITRUST LAW

The purpose of antitrust law is to prevent, punish, and deter certain anticompetitive conduct and unfair business practices. Original notions of antitrust law come from the shifting of the U.S. economy and its transition from predominantly family agriculture and small merchants to the Industrial Revolution era, in which the historically famous robber barons of the late 19th century accumulated and wielded such market power that other companies could not compete on a level playing field. These business entities were known as *trusts* (the most famous being Rockefeller's Standard Oil Trust) and ultimately resulted in a few companies being able to manipulate prices, thereby causing limited choices and high prices for consumers. President Theodore Roosevelt, the renowned trustbuster, led a movement that resulted, eventually, in the federal regulation of trusts that were engaged in anticompetitive behavior. Antitrust laws are exclusively federal statutes, and the agencies charged with enforcement of these laws are the Department of Justice (U.S. Attorney's Office) and the Federal Trade Commission. Violators of antitrust laws are subject to both *civil penalties* and *criminal sanctions,* including incarceration.

Modern-day antitrust enforcement is concerned primarily with protecting the *competitive process* rather than individual competitor companies. The underlying theory is that protection of this process will ultimately benefit consumers.

LO 19-1

Articulate the fundamental purpose and source of law for antitrust regulation.

FEDERAL STATUTES AND ENFORCEMENT

The statutory scheme of federal antitrust law is actually a combination of five different laws. The **Sherman Act**[1] (1890) is the centerpiece of antitrust law and prohibits contracts, combinations, and conspiracies in restraint of trade, as well as monopolization. The **Clayton Act**,[2] enacted in 1914 and significantly amended in 1936 by the **Robinson-Patman Act** and in 1950 by the **Celler-Kefauver Antimerger Act**, deals with specific types of restraints, including exclusive dealing arrangements, tie-in sales, price discrimination, mergers and acquisitions, and interlocking directorates. These restraints are covered in detail later in this chapter.

Both the U.S. Department of Justice and the Federal Trade Commission (FTC) enforce various antitrust laws. The **Federal Trade Commission Act (FTCA)**[3] of 1914, administered solely by the FTC, is a catchall enactment that has been construed as including all the prohibitions of the other antitrust laws.

In addition to providing for government enforcement of antitrust statutes, the laws also permit an aggrieved party to file a private enforcement action against an alleged antitrust violator. Some antitrust statutes allow a party that suffers damages by virtue of any antitrust violation the right to a private suit in the federal courts for *triple* the damages sustained plus reasonable attorney fees and a court order restraining future violations. These statutes are intended to provide a significant financial deterrent to antitrust infraction and to compensate parties injured through anticompetitive behavior.

LO 19-2

Identify the main federal statutes in antitrust law.

> **KEY POINT**
>
> Antitrust matters are covered by federal law, with the Sherman Act as the primary governing statute.

SHERMAN ANTITRUST ACT

Thought of as the central piece of federal antitrust law, the Sherman Act is divided into two parts. First, the act provides prohibitions against restraints of trade. The Sherman Act prohibits "[e]very contract, combination in the form of trust or otherwise, or conspiracy,

LO 19-3

Distinguish and explain the differences between the per se standard and the rule of reason standard.

---

[1] 15 U.S.C. §§ 1–7.
[2] 15 U.S.C. §§ 12–27.
[3] 15 U.S.C. §§ 41–58.

in restraint of trade or commerce."[4] The second part of the act covers monopolization. The Sherman Act provides a remedy against "[e]very person who shall monopolize, or attempt to monopolize . . . any part of the trade or commerce among the several States."[5] This prohibition does not make a monopoly illegal automatically. Only a monopoly that has been *acquired* or *maintained* through prohibited conduct is illegal. The Sherman Act has both civil and criminal penalties.

To understand the distinction between the sections, consider the difference between single-firm conduct (only one business engaged in a certain transaction or behavior) and multifirm conduct (more than one business engaged in a certain transaction or behavior). Compared to single-firm conduct, multifirm conduct tends to be seen as more likely to have an anticompetitive effect and is regulated under Section 1 of the act. Single-firm conduct is less likely to be considered as restraining trade; however, under certain circumstances (for example, using market domination to eliminate a competitor), it may be seen as having an anticompetitive effect. Single-firm conduct is covered by Section 2 of the act.

Per Se Standard versus Rule of Reason Standard

While the sweeping language of the Sherman Act, taken literally, could reasonably be read as a blanket ban on virtually every commercial agreement, the U.S. Supreme Court has long held that the statute applies only to those parties who have acted in some

The Sherman Act was created to limit the ability of corporate giants such as Standard Oil Trust, founded by John Rockefeller (left), to monopolize markets and control major industries. President Theodore Roosevelt, depicted in an editorial cartoon of the era (right), became known as the nation's trustbuster. © AP Images (left); © Corbis via Getty Images (right)

---

[4] 15 U.S.C. § 1.
[5] 15 U.S.C. § 2.

unreasonable manner that resulted in an identifiable anticompetitive behavior. The Court has developed two standards for use by federal courts in deciding whether or not a certain transaction or action violates the Sherman Act: the **per se standard** and the **rule of reason standard**. Some concerted activities are so blatantly anticompetitive that they are considered *per se* violations. Collusion among competitors to set artificially high prices—a practice known as *price-fixing*—is a clear example of a per se violation. The per se standard has been developed into a comparatively complicated body of law and tests for federal courts to apply. However, the case law still gives business owners and managers relatively clear guidance on what constitutes blatant violations of the Sherman Act that have no competitive justification. In effect, the per se rule means that if a company has committed a per se violation of the act, as articulated in the body of case law, the violator has no defense. The per se standard also promotes more consistent enforcement by regulatory authorities.

For example, suppose that SportCo operates a chain of sporting goods stores in the southeastern United States. SportCo's president contacts the owner of Main Street Athletic Gear, and the two agree not to undercut each other on the price of baseballs. They set the price at 30 percent higher than fair market value. These two have colluded against consumers by fixing an artificially high price for a product. Because the SportCo–Main Street agreement is blatantly anticompetitive, it is a per se violation of the Sherman Act.

Legal Speak >))

Per Se
A Latin term literally meaning "of, in, or by itself," that is, without any additional facts needed to prove a point.

Rule of Reason

Despite the substantial body of case law that makes up the various rules used in applying the per se standard, the economic complexities of the global business community, technology, and individual industry practices are too unique to be assessed using a strict per se standard. Recognizing the need to assess a certain transaction's impact on the broader marketplace, the Court developed a second standard known as the *rule of reason*. Even if a transaction is not considered a per se violation, the action or transaction in question must also meet the alternate standard. The rule of reason requires that a fact finder (judge or jury) embark on an examination into market complexities and industry practices in order to determine whether or not the parties' actions violate the Sherman Act. Under this standard, a business alleged to have committed a violation may offer evidence that its actions were reasonable because they were justified and necessitated by economic conditions. In essence, the rule of reason contemplates a scale in which the court weighs any anticompetitive harm suffered against the marketwide benefits of the actions. Through this examination, a court may determine whether such justification is merely a *pretext* for advancement of the violator's economic benefit or whether, in fact, the economic benefits outweigh the burdens.

For instance, in our SportCo–Main Street example discussed earlier, suppose that instead of agreeing to set a price, the president of SportCo offered to lead efforts to form Retail Business Association (RBA) with Main Street and other area retailers for the purpose of sharing ideas, information, and data. Depending on the form and content of the information sharing, the RBA may be a violation of antitrust laws. However, RBA would argue that the rule of reason (not per se) should apply, and the association would have to offer legitimate business reasons and economic justifications for its formation. If a court finds that any anticompetitive harm caused by RBA is outweighed by the marketwide *benefits* of its actions, it will conclude that RBA's formation does not violate the Sherman Act.

Two-Sided Markets Increased use of technology in the purchasing and selling of goods has created more concern by regulators over the anticompetitive effect of **two-sided markets.** Economists generally agree that a two-sided market is at work when an organization creates value primarily by enabling direct interactions between two (or more) distinct types of affiliated customers.[6] For example, suppose that MegaPlatform is a significant

---
[6]*See* Andrei Hagiu & Julian Wright, *Multi-Sided Platforms* (Harv. Bus. Sch. Working Paper No. 15-037, Oct. 2011).

FIGURE 19.1 MegaPlatform's Two-Sided Market

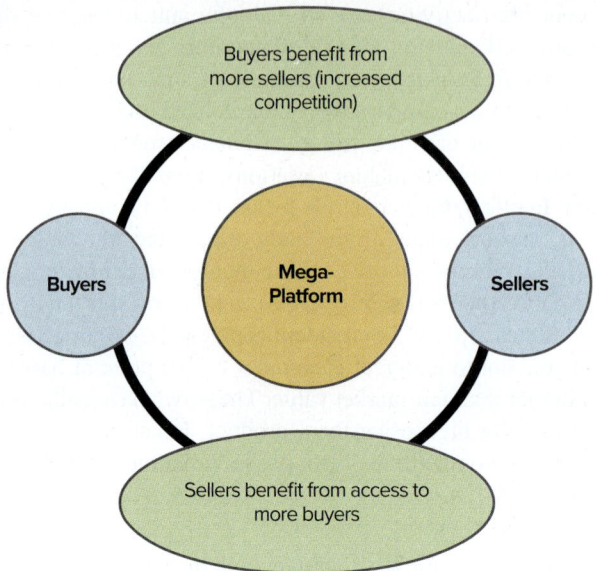

player in the online retail marketplace. MegaPlatform creates value by enabling buyers and sellers to find each other quickly. Sellers benefit from access to more buyers for their goods, and buyers benefit from access to more sellers. Figure 19.1 provides an illustration of the basics of a two-sided market.

Two-sided markets have been an important part of the economy outside of tech-based companies for many years in the form of credit cards. A credit-card transaction is two-sided in the sense that credit card companies (e.g., Visa) generate revenue by bringing together consumers and merchants. In Case 19.1, the U.S. Supreme Court uses the rule of reason to analyze two-sided market transactions in the context of antitrust law.

CASE 19.1 Ohio v. American Express Co., 138 S. Ct. 2274 (2018)

FACT SUMMARY The U.S. credit card industry is dominated by four major financial services institutions: Visa, Mastercard, American Express Co. (Amex), and Discover. The business model that these institutions use for their credit cards has been dubbed by economists as a "two-sided market." First, the financial institutions provide benefits to consumers that use credit cards by providing them with instant access to a line of credit for purchases. Second, merchants that accept the credit cards benefit because they are paid instantly for consumer purchases. The financial institutions generate revenue on each credit card transaction by deducting a transaction fee from the merchant's funds. The transaction fee is set by each individual financial institution.

In order to increase its share of the consumer credit market, Discover developed a low-transaction-fee model that provided incentives for merchants to steer consumers towards using Discover over other credit cards. In response to the low-transaction-fee model, the other financial institutions began to include "anti-steering" provisions in their agreements with merchants. These provisions prohibited merchants from, among other things, informing their customers of the different fees or offering discounts/incentives to use other credit cards.

(continued)

The Department of Justice (DOJ) and several states (including Ohio) brought a civil lawsuit against Amex, Visa, and Mastercard. While Visa and Mastercard settled the antitrust claims and agreed to remove the anti-steering language from their agreements, Amex defended its practice, arguing that there was no evidence that the anti-steering provisions would harm consumers or the overall credit card market. The trial court ruled in favor of DOJ; however, the appellate court reversed and ruled in favor of Amex. Although DOJ decided not to pursue the case any further, Ohio and other states appealed to the U.S. Supreme Court.

SYNOPSIS OF DECISION AND OPINION The U.S. Supreme Court affirmed the court of appeals' decision in favor of Amex. The Court rejected the government's argument that an increase in merchant fees on one side of the market demonstrated any anticompetitive effect. They pointed out that the government's antitrust theory wrongly focused on only one side of the two-sided credit-card platform. They ruled that evidence of a price increase on one side of a two-sided transaction platform cannot by itself demonstrate an anticompetitive exercise of market power.

WORDS OF THE COURT: Two-Sided Transactions "[T]he credit-card market must be defined to include both merchants and cardholders. Focusing on merchant fees alone misses the mark because the product that credit-card companies sell is transactions, not services to merchants, and the competitive effects of a restraint on transactions cannot be judged by looking at merchants alone. Evidence of a price increase on one side of a two-sided transaction platform cannot by itself demonstrate an anticompetitive exercise of market power. To demonstrate anticompetitive effects on the two-sided credit-card market as a whole, the [government] must prove that Amex's antisteering provisions increased the cost of credit-card transactions above a competitive level, reduced the number of credit-card transactions, or otherwise stifled competition in the credit-card market."

Case Questions

1. Why are credit card transactions considered a "two-sided market"?
2. According to the Court, what evidence would be needed to establish that anti-steering provisions violated antitrust laws?
3. *Focus on Critical Thinking:* What other types of business transactions could be considered two-sided? Are purchases from online retailers or ride-sharing companies two-sided? What is the impact of this decision on new economy companies that use technology platforms that may be considered two-sided?

Per Se Sherman Act Violations: Restraints

The U.S. Supreme Court and other federal appellate courts have developed a body of case law that deems certain actions or transactions as per se violations of the Sherman Act. Certain per se violations arise through the use of **horizontal restraints**. In a horizontal restraint of trade, one company partners with a *competing* company (i.e., one located horizontally on the chain of commercial supply, such as a competing retailer or competing manufacturer) to take action resulting in the elimination or reduction of competition from other competitors. Businesses may also commit a per se violation of the Sherman Act through use of a **vertical restraint**. In this type of restraint of trade, one company colludes with another company (other than a competitor) along the chain of commercial supply (see Figure 19.2), such as a manufacturer colluding with a retailer on the price of a product.

LO 19-4

List and articulate the primary ways that businesses use horizontal and vertical restraints of trade.

Horizontal Restraints

Although any concerted agreement among competitors to reduce competition or attempt to manipulate the competitive market is a horizontal restraint and a per se violation of antitrust law, the most common types of prohibited horizontal restraints are horizontal price-fixing, allocation of markets or customers, and boycotts.

FIGURE 19.2
Chain of Commercial Supply

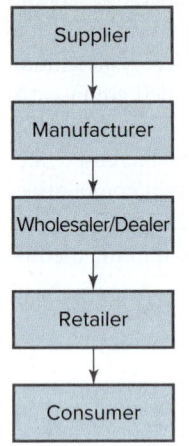

Meeting of the Minds One crucial component of a horizontal restraint is some meeting of the minds among the parties about the restraint. The statute requires the conspiring parties to *agree* to and then commit an *overt act.* As one would imagine, any illegal agreement is not likely to be explicit (or certainly not in writing), so courts have permitted proof of meeting of the minds to be satisfied through *circumstantial* evidence regarding the timing of any communication between the parties and their subsequent restraining actions.

In one of the most famous essays in the history of economic thought, *The Wealth of Nations,* Adam Smith wrote in 1766 that "people in the same trade seldom meet together even for merriment or diversity, but the conversation ends in a conspiracy against the public or in some contrivance to raise prices." This famous quote was used by prosecutors in a high-profile antitrust case against Alfred Taubman, the chairman of the well-known auction firm Sotheby's Holding, Inc., and Sir Anthony Tennant, chief executive of Christie's International. In the case, no direct evidence (such as a witness) of the agreement existed, but prosecutors used business calendars and other data to build a timeline and alleged that the two men met on 12 occasions and then engaged in an unusual course of action concerning policies on commissions that each firm followed after the last of the 12 meetings. Both executives were convicted in December 2001.

Price-Fixing Any agreement by competitors to fix the price for buying or selling a particular good or any agreement by competitors to fix the quantity of goods to be produced, offered for sale, or bought is a per se violation of the Sherman Act. For example, suppose NewCo and OldCo are competitors in the market selling computer chips. They may not agree to set the price at $250 per package of 50. Doing so would be a bare-faced attempt to increase their profits by leaving the consumer with no options. Nor may they agree to limit the production or sale of computer chips to 100,000 per month in order to manipulate the supply and demand curves that are essential to a market economy.

There are, of course, some instances in which conduct by competitors with respect to pricing policies does not constitute price-fixing. In some industries, price-leading (cutting or increasing prices based on the actions of a competitor) is commonplace. Although this may appear to be price-fixing, the element of agreement is usually not satisfied because the competitors are not taking these actions in concert. For example, suppose that Economy Jet begins to cut its airfare on the route from Boston to New York City. It is almost inevitable that all other airlines will cut their fares on that route as well. If Economy Jet cuts its price, there can be no legitimate conclusion that the parties intended to act to restrain competition.

In the past decade, the U.S. Supreme Court has narrowed the use of the per se standard and expanded the use of the rule of reason analysis in certain cases of horizontal price-fixing. In Landmark Case 19.2, the Court uses the rule of reason standard in evaluating a joint venture alleged to have engaged in price-fixing.

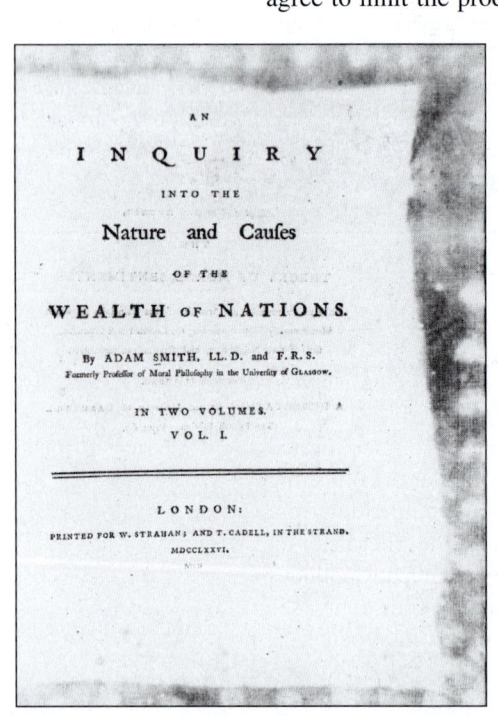

Adam Smith's *The Wealth of Nations* is often cited in support of the notion that frequent meetings and conversations by competitors are circumstantial evidence of anticompetitive collusion. Fotosearch/Getty Images

> **KEY POINT**
>
> *Horizontal restraints* are agreements between competitors. *Vertical restraints* are agreements between noncompetitors—one party acts in concert with another party on a different distributional level in the chain of commercial supply.

LANDMARK CASE 19.2 Texaco, Inc. v. Dagher, et al., 547 U.S. 1 (2006)

FACT SUMMARY Historically, Texaco and Shell Oil have competed with one another in the global markets as refiners of crude oil and suppliers of gasoline to retail service stations. In 1998, the two companies formed a joint venture, Equilon, to consolidate their operations in the western United States. Texaco and Shell agreed to share expenses and profits from the jointly controlled new entity. Although the Equilon entity engaged in the refinement of crude oil into gasoline, the actual end product was sold to retailers under the brand names of Texaco and Shell at a mutually agreed-upon price.

The retailers of Texaco and Shell products brought a class action lawsuit against Texaco and Shell, alleging that creating the joint venture was a per se violation of the Sherman Act because it ended any price competition between the two and amounted to a horizontal price-fixing scheme.

SYNOPSIS OF DECISION AND OPINION The U.S. Supreme Court ruled in favor of Texaco and Shell, holding that the rule of reason standard should apply. The Court reasoned that per se liability applies only to agreements that are so plainly anticompetitive that no study of the industry is needed to establish their illegality. In this case, the market analysis was relevant. The Court held that the joint venture agreement was *not* horizontal price-fixing because the challenged pricing policy was simply price-setting by a single entity, Equilon, and not a pricing agreement between competing entities with respect to their competing products.

WORDS OF THE COURT: Narrow Per Se Rules "'[T]his Court has long recognized that Congress intended to outlaw only *unreasonable* restraints' . . . . Instead, this Court presumptively applies rule of reason analysis, under which antitrust plaintiffs must demonstrate that a particular contract or combination is in fact unreasonable and anticompetitive before it will be found unlawful. *Per se* liability is reserved for only those agreements that are 'so plainly anticompetitive that no elaborate study of the industry is needed to establish their illegality.' Accordingly, 'we have expressed reluctance to adopt *per se* rules . . . "where the economic impact of certain practices is not immediately obvious."'"

Case Questions

1. Does this case mean that competitors may simply create a joint venture to avoid any liability for price-fixing?
2. Why did the retailers allege that forming this joint venture was anticompetitive behavior?
3. *Focus on Critical Thinking:* Is this decision consistent with protecting consumers from price-fixing?

Market Allocation Agreements among competitors that divide markets either by territory or by customer are anticompetitive and illegal per se. Such arrangements are blatantly restrictive because they leave no room for competition of any kind. Thus, competing firms may not divide among themselves the geographic areas in which they sell, nor may they distribute customers or allocate the available market. All such understandings, whether direct or indirect, are unlawful.

Boycotts In most cases, a *concerted* refusal to deal with a third party among competing firms constitutes a per se violation of the Sherman Act. Although the U.S. Supreme Court has narrowed this doctrine and has applied the rule of reason in some limited cases, a concerted agreement to boycott a supplier or consumer group is still a very risky proposition. In *United States v. Colgate*,[7] decided in 1919, the U.S. Supreme Court held that a *unilateral* boycott does not fall under the Sherman Act. However, even the so-called *Colgate* doctrine has been narrowed. In order to pass anticompetitive muster, the boycott must be truly unilateral with no other party having direct or indirect involvement.

---

[7] 250 U.S. 300 (1919).

> ✓ **Self-Check** Horizontal Restraint
>
> What type of horizontal restraint is at issue?
>
> 1. Two gasoline service stations are located on opposite sides of the same street. The two owners agree not to undercut each other on gas prices.
> 2. Two suppliers agree not to sell their product to a certain retailer because they believe that the retailer is undercutting other larger retailers in price and that this has impacted the larger retailers' purchases from the two suppliers.
> 3. Two retailers of active-wear clothing agree that one will sell only in the Miami market and the other only in the Atlanta market.
>
> *Answers to this Self-Check are provided at the end of the chapter.*

Vertical Restraints

Vertical price-fixing occurs when a seller attempts to control the resale price of a product at a lower level in the supply chain. Although concerted action or agreement between a manufacturer and a retailer to fix the price at the retail level is not considered a per se violation of the Sherman Act, courts apply a rule of reason analysis to determine whether any antitrust laws have been violated. In the 2007 case of *Leegin Creative Leather Products v. PSKS, Inc.*,[8] the U.S. Supreme Court held that all vertical price restraints were now to be judged by the rule of reason. The case involved a manufacturer of leather apparel that would not sell its products to retailers that sold its apparel at a discount. When the manufacturer discovered that a retailer was discounting the leather apparel by 20 percent, the retailer was cut off from supply. The retailer sued the manufacturer, contending that its policies amounted to a vertical restraint. The trial and appellate courts applied the traditional per se analysis, but the U.S. Supreme Court reversed the decision and instituted a rule of reason policy for vertical price restraints after being convinced that such restraints can have pro-competitive effects.

Nonprice Restraints The U.S. Supreme Court has applied the rule of reason to nonprice vertical restraints since its 1977 landmark antitrust decision in *Continental T.V. v. GTE Sylvania*.[9] Vertical restraints that do not involve price-fixing generally involve some type of restraint on the distribution of a product in the marketplace. Although business entities have always had the right to *unilaterally* assign exclusive territories to their distributors and to limit the number of distributors that are authorized to sell their product in a specific geographic area, certain agreements between sellers and distributors relating to sales of a product outside the exclusive territory may give rise to an allegation of an unlawful vertical restraint. Such restraints are frequently an attempt to control the *intrabrand competition* (i.e., the setting of different prices by different distributors for the same product) of a seller's product among various distributors, with the intent of boosting the product's *interbrand competition* (i.e., its relative competitiveness with similar products made by other sellers). For example, Raleigh is a manufacturer of expensive watches and sells its products through both Connelly and Sicius as exclusive distributors. Raleigh's interest is in making sure that Connelly and Sicius don't compete with each other in the same geographic market (intrabrand competition) because Raleigh wants to be sure that the pricing for the watches is in line with the pricing and the market share of Raleigh's competing

---

[8] 551 U.S. 877 (2007).
[9] 433 U.S. 36 (1977).

companies (interbrand competition). Therefore, Raleigh attempts to impose a restriction that limits its distributors to specific geographic territories and prohibits them from selling outside those territories. These restraints on Connelly and Sicius help ensure that Raleigh watches will continue to thrive in the marketplace. Any arrangement Raleigh makes with Connelly and Sicius is considered a vertical restraint. However, because courts use the rule of reason standard for vertical restraints, Raleigh's plan could still survive judicial scrutiny if it is justified on the grounds that it does not have a negative impact on competition in the watch-manufacturing industry.

Tying Agreements Tying agreements occur when a seller refuses to sell a certain product (the tying product) unless the buyer also purchases a different product (the tied product) from the seller. Typically, this occurs when a seller has a substantial share of the market for the tying product and is attempting to leverage the power of the tying product to gain market share for another of the seller's products. This tying arrangement model violates the Sherman Act. For example, Kahlo's firm has a substantial share of the cable modem market but has recently introduced a new brand of Ethernet cable (used to connect the cable modem to a computer). If Kahlo requires her distributors to purchase the Ethernet cable as a condition of the sale of the cable modems, she has used her market share to tie sales of the cable modems to sales of the Ethernet cable. Note also that tying arrangements may be a violation of the Clayton Act (discussed later in this chapter).

The most difficult question in analyzing a tying agreement is where to draw the line between legitimate parallel product enhancements and anticompetitive market manipulation. A producer of shoes is clearly entitled to "tie" the right shoe with the left shoe, but what about products that have separate, albeit related, functions? This problem has resulted in courts' developing a **soft per se analysis** for determining the legality of a tying arrangement. In *U.S. Steel v. Fortner Enterprises,*[10] the U.S. Supreme Court provided guidance for lower courts by setting out a four-part test. For a tying arrangement to be illegal, the government (or plaintiff) must show that (1) the agreement involves two separate and distinct items rather than integrated components of a larger product, service, or business system; (2) the tying product cannot be purchased unless the tied product is also purchased; (3) the seller has sufficient economic power in the market to appreciably restrain competition; and (4) a "not insubstantial" amount of commerce in the tied product is affected by the seller's tying agreement.

Criminal Liability

Antitrust violators are subject to criminal prosecution. The Antitrust Criminal Penalty Enhancement and Reform Act of 2004[11] enhanced penalties for violations of antitrust laws. The maximum fine for individuals was set at $1 million, and the maximum fine for corporations was raised to $100 million. The Sherman Act also provides for a prison sentence of up to 10 years for those convicted of willful antitrust violations.

CONCEPT SUMMARY Restraints of Trade

- Horizontal restraints (acting in concert with a competitor that is on the same level of distribution) include
    a. *Price-fixing:* An agreement between competitors to fix actual prices is generally illegal per se.

(continued)

---

[10] 429 U.S. 610 (1977).

[11] Pub. L. No. 108-257, 118 Stat. 661 (codified as amended in scattered sections of 15 U.S.C.).

b. *Market allocation:* An agreement between competitors to divide markets or geographic regions is illegal per se.
   c. *Boycotts:* A concerted refusal to sell or buy from an individual, firm, or group may be illegal per se or by the rule of reason, depending on the specific facts.
- Vertical restraints (acting in concert with another party on a different distributional level) include
   a. *Vertical price-fixing:* An agreement between a buyer and a seller with respect to the price of resale of the product is judged by the rule of reason standard.
   b. *Exclusive selling, territorial, and dealing agreements:* A relationship between a buyer and a seller related to an exclusive franchise and/or a specified territory is governed by the rule of reason and the Clayton Act.
   c. *Tie-ins:* A seller that ties a second product to the first product is acting illegally per se if the seller possesses sufficient market power to render the tie-in coercive.
- Antitrust laws also carry criminal penalties, including fines and incarceration.

ANTITRUST LAW AND SPORTS

A recurring debate in antitrust law centers on whether collegiate and professional sports leagues are unfairly restraining trade through league rules and policies. This includes the history of Major League Baseball's infamous exemption cases and the National Football League's attempts to offer exclusive contracts for merchandising. More recently, collegiate student-athletes have challenged the rules set out by the National Collegiate Athletic Association (NCAA) that prohibit being paid for the use of their names, images, and likenesses. In Case 19.3, a federal appellate court considers a challenge by a former college athlete that alleges a violation of the Sherman Act by the NCAA.

CASE 19.3 O'Bannon v. National Collegiate Athletic Association, 802 F.3d 1049 (9th Cir. 2015)

FACT SUMMARY For more than a century, the National Collegiate Athletic Association (NCAA) has prescribed rules governing the eligibility of athletes at its more than 1,000 member colleges and universities. Those rules prohibit student-athletes from being paid for the use of their names, images, and likenesses (NILs). Until 2014, these rules also capped the total amount of scholarship money that student-athletes could receive. In 2008, O'Bannon, a former All-American basketball player at UCLA, learned he was depicted in a college basketball video game produced by Electronic Arts (EA), a software company that produced video games based on college football and men's basketball from the late 1990s until around 2013. O'Bannon saw an avatar of himself—a virtual player who visually resembled O'Bannon, played for UCLA, and wore O'Bannon's jersey number. O'Bannon had never consented to the use of his likeness in the video game, and he had not been compensated for it.

O'Bannon sued the NCAA and the Collegiate Licensing Company (CLC), the entity that licenses the trademarks of the NCAA and a number of its member schools for commercial use, in federal court. O'Bannon argued that the NCAA's amateurism rules, insofar as they prevented student-athletes

(continued)

from being compensated for the use of their NILs, were an illegal restraint of trade under the Sherman Act. The trial court ruled that the NCAA's compensation rules were an unlawful restraint of trade. It then ordered the NCAA to cease from prohibiting its member schools from giving student-athletes scholarships up to the full cost of attendance at their respective schools and to pay up to $5,000 per year in deferred compensation, to be held in trust for student-athletes until after they leave college. The NCAA appealed on the basis that (1) the NCAA rules are not subject to antitrust laws and (2) even if they were subject to antitrust laws, their amateurism rules do not constitute unlawful restraint of trade.

SYNOPSIS OF DECISION AND OPINION The U.S. Court of Appeals for the Ninth Circuit concluded that the trial court's decision was largely correct. Although the court acknowledged that many of the NCAA's amateurism rules are likely to be procompetitive, they held that those rules are not exempt from antitrust scrutiny. Rather, they must be analyzed under the rule of reason. The court applied the rule of reason and concluded that one alternative to the current NCAA compensation rules, allowing NCAA members to give scholarships up to the full cost of attendance, was proper. However, the court reversed the trial court's remedy of allowing students to be paid cash compensation of up to $5,000 per year.

WORDS OF THE COURT: Anticompetitive Effect "The 'combination[s] condemned by the [Sherman] Act' also include 'price-fixing . . . by purchasers' even though 'the persons specially injured . . . are sellers, not customers or consumers.' At trial, [O'Bannon] demonstrated that the NCAA's compensation rules have just this kind of anticompetitive effect: they fix the price of one component of the exchange between school and recruit, thereby precluding competition among schools with respect to that component. The [trial] court found that although consumers of NCAA football and basketball may not be harmed directly by this price-fixing, the 'student-athletes themselves are harmed by the price-fixing agreement among FBS football and Division I basketball schools.' The athletes accept grants-in-aid, and no more, in exchange for their athletic performance, because the NCAA schools have agreed to value the athletes' NILs at zero, 'an anticompetitive effect.' This anticompetitive effect satisfied [O'Bannon's] initial burden under the Rule of Reason."

Case Questions

1. What is the court's reasoning for ruling that the NCAA rules have an anticompetitive effect?
2. Why does the court use a rule of reason analysis rather than a per se rule?
3. *Focus on Critical Thinking:* If college athletes were paid, how would that impact higher education generally? Should college athletes receive any other compensation from their schools? Does it strike you as fair that universities are profiting off the talent of their students? Does that occur in any case other than athletics?

Major League Baseball

The history of Major League Baseball's exemption from the Sherman Act dates back to a 1922 U.S. Supreme Court case in which the Court ruled that the business of putting on an "exhibition" of baseball did not involve interstate commerce and was therefore not subject to the provisions of the Sherman Act.[12] The Court reaffirmed the exemption in the 1952 case *Toolson v. New York Yankees*.[13] In Landmark Case 19.4, the Court reexamines its rulings on the exemption of Major League Baseball in one of the most famous cases in antitrust law.

---

[12] *Federal Baseball Club v. National League*, 259 U.S. 200 (1922).
[13] 346 U.S. 356 (1953).

LANDMARK CASE 19.4 Flood v. Kuhn, 407 U.S. 258 (1972)

FACT SUMMARY Curt Flood was a professional baseball player who was traded by the St. Louis Cardinals to the Philadelphia Phillies. For a variety of reasons, Flood was unhappy with the trade; he refused to report to his new team and was forfeiting a significant salary. Flood sent a letter to Kuhn, the commissioner of Major League Baseball, demanding free agency. Kuhn declined to grant Flood free agency on the basis of the "reserve clause" in Flood's contract. The reserve clause was a standard provision in every player's contract whereby the player agreed that upon the contract's expiration, the rights to the player were retained by the team that originally signed him. As a practical matter, the clause allowed a team to retain the rights of a player indefinitely. Therefore, the clause prevented Flood from negotiating with another team and gave St. Louis the right to trade him to a new team or renew his contract. Flood sued Major League Baseball, contending that the reserve clauses in the contracts were illegal under the Sherman Act. Flood argued that the previous cases exempting baseball from antitrust laws should be reversed because modern-day baseball is now part of interstate commerce through radio and television broadcasts.

SYNOPSIS OF DECISION AND OPINION The U.S. Supreme Court held for Kuhn and upheld the exemption primarily based on the doctrine of stare decisis. Although the Court acknowledged that it is reasonable to conclude that baseball is now engaged in interstate commerce, it did not reverse its earlier decisions because of what the Court concluded was Congress's "positive inaction" to the earlier decisions exempting Major League Baseball from the antitrust laws. The Court was unwilling to disturb 50 years of precedent when it was clear that Congress had adequate opportunity and yet did not act to introduce legislation intended to remediate the baseball exemption. The Court also made clear that no other professional sports could be considered exempt from antitrust law.

WORDS OF THE COURT: Congressional Silence "The Court has emphasized that since 1922 baseball, with full and continuing congressional awareness, has been allowed to develop and to expand unhindered by federal legislative action. Remedial legislation has been introduced repeatedly in Congress but none has ever been enacted. The Court, accordingly, has concluded that Congress as yet has had no intention to subject baseball's reserve system to the reach of the antitrust statutes. This, obviously, has been deemed to be something other than mere congressional silence and passivity."

Case Questions

1. Should stare decisis be such a powerful doctrine that it trumps modern societal realities (such as baseball's growing use of interstate commerce via radio, television, and streaming)?
2. Why were the reserve clauses important to Flood's argument?
3. *Focus on Critical Thinking:* Do you agree that, as a public policy matter, Major League Baseball should have an exemption from antitrust laws? Why or why not?

Curt Flood Act of 1998

Although Flood lost his case before the Supreme Court, it inspired other players to seek free-agency status, and the availability of free agency in general became the norm in baseball over a period of two decades. The passage of the Curt Flood Act of 1998[14] added a new provision to existing antitrust statutes that applied only to professional baseball players and eliminated the broad antitrust exemption for baseball. Still, although it permitted players to bring an antitrust action against the league, the law was full of restrictions and limitations on when and how the players could pursue an antitrust claim (e.g., the suit cannot be related to franchise expansion or relocation). Some commentators have suggested that the law generated congressional boasting but did not have any significant impact on Major League Baseball's antitrust exemption.[15]

---

[14] 15 U.S.C. § 26b (2006).

[15] For an excellent explanation and summary of commentary on the Curt Flood Act, see N. Grow, *Reevaluating the Curt Flood Act,* 87 Neb. L. Rev. 747 (2008).

National Football League

Since the first challenge in 1957,[16] the U.S. Supreme Court has declined to provide the National Football League with a baseball-type exemption. In 2010, the Supreme Court gave its latest guidance on the topic in *American Needle, Inc. v. National Football League*.[17] The case involved the NFL's licensing contract for merchandising of its teams' logos for shirts, hats, sweatshirts, and other attire and memorabilia. Although the NFL had previously extended nonexclusive merchandise rights to multiple companies, in December 2000 the NFL changed course and granted an exclusive contract to Reebok to produce and sell trademarked merchandise for *all* of the league's 32 teams. One of the companies frozen out by the new arrangement, American Needle, Inc., sued the NFL, claiming that the Reebok agreement was a result of collusion between the 32 teams that amounted to an illegal conspiracy under the Sherman Act. The NFL argued that although the teams were separately owned and operated, the league itself was a single entity for purposes of merchandising and therefore was incapable of such a conspiracy and thus effectively exempt from Sherman Act liability. Although a federal appellate court ruled in favor of the NFL, the Supreme Court unanimously reversed the appellate court's decision and held in favor of American Needle. Using a rule of reason analysis, Justice John Paul Stevens, himself a former antitrust lawyer, wrote, "When teams license such property, they are not pursuing the 'common interests of the whole' league, but, instead, the interests of each 'corporation itself.'"[18] The Court ruled that although the NFL teams did have some common objectives, they were also competitors not only on the field but as corporations. The teams compete to attract fans, increase gate receipts, and secure contracts with management and player personnel. Therefore, the Court rejected the NFL's single-entity theory and held that the league was subject to the Sherman Act.

MONOPOLIZATION

A monopoly holder has inherent power in setting prices without any chance of losing market share due to competition. Antitrust laws designed to combat this problem are known as **structural-offense laws** because the offenses generally do not involve a behavioral aspect (such as price-fixing). Section 2 of the Sherman Act was designed to prevent business monopolies, but it does not *prohibit* a business entity from becoming a monopoly. Rather, the statute outlaws *affirmative action* toward monopolizing or attempting to monopolize a part of trade or commerce. The Sherman Act also prohibits the use of *monopoly power* to create an anticompetitive market in a particular industry. In the landmark monopoly case *U.S. v. Grinnell*,[19] the U.S. Supreme Court defined monopolization as "the willful acquisition or maintenance of power in a relevant market as opposed to growth as a consequence of superior product, business acumen or historical accident." Thus, for a business entity to violate Section 2 of the Sherman Act, it must possess monopoly power and also have an overt intent to monopolize.

LO 19-5

Recognize when a business has achieved a monopoly and explain the restrictions on a monopoly business under antitrust law.

> **KEY POINT**
>
> The Sherman Act does not prohibit a business entity from becoming a monopoly, but it does outlaw affirmative action toward monopolizing or attempting to monopolize a part of trade or commerce.

Monopoly Power

A business entity that has the power to fix prices or to exclude competitors in a given market is said to have monopoly power. The focus for determining whether or not an entity has

---

[16]*Radovich v. National Football League*, 352 U.S. 445 (1957).
[17]560 U.S. 183 (2010).
[18]560 U.S. 183, 184 (2010).
[19]384 U.S. 563 (1966).

monopoly power is the entity's share of the relevant market. Although the Court has not laid down a bright-line test for what percentage of market share is required for determining that a monopoly exists, firms that have had as little as 50 percent of the market have been found to have monopoly power. In their analysis, courts may also look at other factors, such as the existence of barriers to entry of new competitors in the industry at issue.

The *United States v. Microsoft* Case

LO 19-6

Explain why the *United States v. Microsoft* case is an important part of antitrust law.

In one of the most famous monopoly cases, *United States v. Microsoft*,[20] the federal government sued Microsoft for anticompetitive behavior in the development and distribution of its Internet browser software called Explorer. The government alleged that Microsoft used its monopoly in the computer operating system market to eliminate competition from a more popular Internet browser, called Navigator, that was sold by Microsoft competitor Netscape. The trial court ruled against Microsoft and ordered the radical remedy of requiring Microsoft to reorganize its operating system entity separate and apart from its entity responsible for Explorer.

After sparring with federal and state regulators (not to mention competitors) in the courts over several years, Microsoft settled the case in 2002 by entering into a consent order. The order required Microsoft to provide competitors with the detailed technical information needed to make competing products, such as e-mail and multimedia players, work seamlessly with its Windows operating system. Microsoft also agreed to make Windows available under a standard licensing agreement (without any tying product) to computer manufacturers.

Legal Speak >))

Consent Order An agreement between the government and a party that spells out detailed conditions and compliance measures that the party agrees to take in exchange for the government's decision not to pursue a court action.

Intent to Monopolize

Once a court has determined that a particular business entity holds monopoly power, the next question centers on the entity's willful intent to acquire or maintain the monopoly. This analysis requires a court to examine whether or not the alleged monopolizer has engaged in a course of conduct that would reasonably lead one to conclude that the entity has purposefully furthered or attempted to maintain monopoly power. It is a difficult standard to spell out because each case and each industry has its own complexities. However, it is important to note that the courts have not required a showing that the entity engaged in predatory practices against a competitor (although this would clearly be a sign of intent to maintain or expand a monopoly) in order to have liability under the Sherman Act. For example, an appellate court has held that a national aluminum manufacturer and distributor violated Section 2 of the Sherman Act simply by acquiring every new opportunity relating to the production or marketing of aluminum.

Attempted Monopolization

Because actual monopoly power is relatively rare, the Sherman Act also prohibits *attempts* by a business to gain monopoly power—that is, when a business entity that does not yet have monopoly power pursues an anticompetitive course of conduct designed to achieve it. The analysis of attempted monopolization focuses on a three-part test. First, the entity must have had a demonstrable and specific intent to achieve a monopoly. Second, the entity must have acted in an anticompetitive manner designed to injure its actual or potential competition. Third, there must exist a dangerous probability that monopoly power can in fact be achieved.

CLAYTON ACT

The Clayton Act (and its amendments) curb certain anticompetitive practices that are not specifically covered by the Sherman Act. Congress clearly intended the Clayton Act to be

---

[20] 253 F.3d 34 (D.C. Cir. 2001).

a vehicle for attacking practices that monopolists had historically used to create monopoly power. As a result, the act is designed as a preventive statute. Both the Department of Justice and the Federal Trade Commission enforce the Clayton Act.

Tying Arrangements and Exclusive Dealing

One important provision of the Clayton Act prohibits tying arrangements and exclusive dealing agreements involving the sale or leasing of *commodities*. Any agreement that involves services, real estate, or intangible property must be attacked under the Sherman Act. The tying arrangement model discussed earlier in this chapter in the context of the Sherman Act is the same model that is covered by the Clayton Act. Any tying arrangement that requires a buyer to purchase one product (the tied product) as a condition of buying another product (the tying product) from the same seller is considered anticompetitive. Some courts have held that the standard for finding an antitrust violation under the Clayton Act is less rigorous than that required under the Sherman Act. These courts have held that the proof of the seller's economic power in the market, necessary to establish a Sherman Act violation, is *not* required for a Clayton Act tying violation.

Exclusive dealing agreements are also covered in Section 3 of the Clayton Act. As discussed earlier in this chapter, an exclusive dealing agreement (such as a franchise) is a form of vertical restraint. Such agreements fall under the Clayton Act because they are arrangements between buyers and sellers in which the buyer agrees to handle one seller's product exclusively or to purchase its entire product line from the same seller. Not all such arrangements violate the Clayton Act (franchise agreements, for example, are exclusive dealing arrangements that do not violate antitrust laws). Only agreements that may "substantially lessen the competition or tend to create a monopoly" violate the act.

Mergers and Acquisitions

Historically, a business entity could gain monopoly power by merging with a competitor or acquiring the competitor through a buyout. The Clayton Act was designed to prevent this monopoly strategy. The act prohibits business entities from acquiring the stock or assets of their competitors when the action will substantially lessen competition or tend to create a monopoly.

FEDERAL TRADE COMMISSION ACT

In the same year that the Clayton Act was passed, Congress also broadened antitrust coverage through the Federal Trade Commission Act (FTCA). The law is designed as a catchall statute that prohibits all unfair and deceptive methods of competition. Any anticompetitive conduct that falls outside the scope of other antitrust laws may still violate the FTCA. The law also gives broad powers to the Federal Trade Commission to investigate any complaints or instances of unfair competition. In Case 19.5, a federal appellate court analyzes allegations of FTCA violations via an exclusive dealer arrangement.

CASE 19.5 McWane, Inc. v. Federal Trade Commission, 783 F.3d 814 (11th Cir. 2015)

FACT SUMMARY McWane manufactures pipe fittings that join together pipes and help direct the flow of pressurized water in pipeline systems. McWane sells the fittings through distributors, who in turn sell them to end users such as a municipal water authority. In April 2006, McWane was the

(continued)

only U.S.-based supplier who sold the fittings. In 2009, Congress passed the American Reinvestment and Recovery Act that authorized $6 billion to fund water infrastructure projects. The law created an increased demand for the pipe fittings, and that opportunity led Star, a European-based manufacturer of pipe fittings, to enter the U.S. market and compete with McWane.

In response to Star's forthcoming entry into the U.S. market, McWane implemented its "Full Support Program" among its existing distributors. The program punished distributors who bought fittings from other companies (such as Star) by threatening to halt their rebate program and cutting off the distributor from purchasing McWane's fittings for up to three months. For example, when distributor Hajoca Corporation purchased Star fittings, McWane cut off sales of its domestic fittings to all Hajoca branches and withheld its rebates. Other distributors testified to abiding by the Full Support Program in order to avoid the devastating result of being cut off from all McWane fittings. Star was excluded by some distributors even after offering a more generous rebate than McWane. Internal documents reveal that McWane's express purpose was to raise Star's costs and impede it from becoming a viable competitor. The Federal Trade Commission charged McWane with a violation of the FTCA, and ultimately the trial court found that McWane's actions constituted an illegal exclusive dealing policy used to maintain its monopoly power in the pipe fittings market.

SYNOPSIS OF DECISION AND OPINION The U.S. Court of Appeals for the Eleventh Circuit affirmed the lower court decision in favor of the Federal Trade Commission. The court agreed that McWane's Full Support Program was an unlawful exclusive dealing arrangement that foreclosed Star's access to distributors for domestic fittings and harmed competition, thereby contributing significantly to the maintenance of McWane's monopoly power in the market. The court noted that the two largest waterworks distributors in the U.S. (with a combined 60 percent market share), prohibited their branches from purchasing domestic fittings from Star after the Full Support Program was announced. The practical effect of the program was to make it economically infeasible for distributors to drop McWane and switch to Star.

WORDS OF THE COURT: Exclusive Dealing Arrangements "As we've observed, exclusive dealing arrangements are not per se unlawful, but they can run afoul of the antitrust laws when used by a dominant firm to maintain its monopoly. Of particular relevance to this case, an exclusive dealing arrangement can be harmful when it allows a monopolist to maintain its monopoly power by raising its rivals' costs sufficiently to prevent them from growing into effective competitors. . . . Moreover, the nature of the Full Support Program arguably posed a greater threat to competition than a conventional exclusive dealing contract, as it lacked the traditional procompetitive benefits of such contracts. As we've noted, courts often take a permissive view of such contracts on the grounds that firms compete for exclusivity by offering procompetitive inducements (e.g., lower prices, better service). But not here. The Full Support Program was 'unilaterally imposed' by fiat upon all distributors, and the [trial court] found that it resulted in 'no competition to become the exclusive supplier' and no 'discount, rebate, or other consideration' offered in exchange for exclusivity."

Case Questions

1. Why is the fact that McWane had a monopoly on pipe fittings important in the analysis of this case?
2. In what way did the McWane plan make it "economically infeasible" for a distributor to purchase the fittings from a competitor?
3. *Focus on Critical Thinking:* Could McWane have avoided liability by designing the Full Support Program in a different way? The court tells us that exclusive dealing arrangements are not per se unlawful. How could this agreement be revised so it does not run afoul of antitrust laws?

Search Bias: FTC Investigates Google

Because the FTCA is so broad, the FTC often uses it when the agency is investigating a case in which the facts are not yet fully developed. The FTC recently used its powers under the FTCA to launch an investigation into Google's content practices. Competitors (including Yelp.com) complained that Google's algorithm and the design of its search engine were aimed at excluding or demoting the websites of actual or potential competitors. The FTC named this allegation "search bias" and focused on Google's alleged practice of delivering its own results in a manner that unfairly provides Google an advantage over its competitors. In January 2013, after a nearly two-year investigation, Google and the FTC agreed to a settlement in which Google agreed to provide a mechanism to ensure that competitors are not being excluded or demoted unfairly in search results. The FTC issued a statement announcing the settlement and explained that the commission would not take any further action on the issue of search bias because the evidence did not demonstrate that Google's actions had stifled competition in violation of antitrust laws. Google now faces similar antitrust claims in the European Union.

HART-SCOTT-RODINO ANTITRUST IMPROVEMENTS ACT OF 1976

The Hart-Scott-Rodino Antitrust Improvements Act of 1976[21] is a preventive statute that requires business entities that are contemplating mergers involving dollar amounts of a certain size to give advance notice to the FTC and the Department of Justice of their intention. This provides the Department of Justice with veto power on a proposed merger if the transaction would violate any of the antitrust laws (including the Sherman Act).

LO 19-7
Articulate the role of more modern antitrust statutes in regulating competition.

ROBINSON-PATMAN ACT

Although the Clayton Act covers the anticompetitive arrangement known as *price discrimination*, the Robinson-Patman Act,[22] enacted in 1936, amended the Clayton Act provisions to provide for broader regulatory authority to curb price discrimination. As a practical matter, the Robinson-Patman Act is enforced almost exclusively by the FTC.

Price Discrimination

Section 2(a) of the act makes it illegal for a business entity to discriminate in price "between different purchasers of commodities of like quality or grade." This discrimination, however, is illegal only when the discrimination results in an effect that may substantially lessen competition, tend to create a monopoly, or injure, destroy, or prevent competition with any person who either grants or knowingly receives the benefit of such discrimination.

To violate Section 2(a), a business entity must have made two or more sales to different purchasers at different prices. This means that quoting a discriminatory price or refusing to sell except at a discriminatory price is not a violation of the act.

Defenses There are essentially two defenses to a price discrimination claim, and both are centered on the fact that some price discrimination may be legitimate. First, any time a seller has different manufacturing, shipping, or operational costs that vary from buyer to buyer, no violation of antitrust laws occurs. Second, if a seller conducts a good faith campaign to meet the lower price of a competitor and this results in price discrimination between several buyers, the seller has not violated antitrust laws.

---

[21] Pub. L. No. 94-435, 90 Stat. 1383.
[22] Pub. L. No. 74-692, 49 Stat. 1526.

KEY TERMS

Sherman Act p. 629   The centerpiece of the statutory scheme of federal antitrust law; prohibits contracts, combinations, and conspiracies in restraint of trade and prohibits monopolization.

Clayton Act p. 629   A federal antitrust law enacted in 1914 as a preventive statute that deals with specific types of trade restraints, including exclusive dealing arrangements, tie-in sales, price discrimination, mergers and acquisitions, and interlocking directorates.

Robinson-Patman Act p. 629   A federal antitrust law enacted in 1936 that amends the Clayton Act provisions by providing for broader regulatory authority to curb price discrimination.

Celler-Kefauver Antimerger Act p. 629   A federal antitrust law enacted in 1950 that amends the Clayton Act provisions by severely restricting anticompetitive mergers resulting from the acquisition of assets.

Federal Trade Commission Act (FTCA) p. 629   A federal law enacted in 1914 that established the Federal Trade Commission, which administers the act; intended as a catch-all statute that has been construed as including all the prohibitions of the other antitrust laws.

Per se standard p. 631   (*per se:* Latin for "of, in, or by itself," i.e., without any additional facts needed to prove a point) A standard used by federal courts in deciding whether a certain transaction or action violates the Sherman Act; applied in cases of concerted activities that are blatantly anticompetitive.

Rule of reason standard p. 631   A second standard used by federal courts in deciding whether or not a certain transaction or action violates the Sherman Act; the rule contemplates a scale in which the court weighs any anticompetitive harm suffered against the marketwide benefit of the action.

Two-sided markets p. 631   In use when an organization creates value primarily by enabling direct interactions between two (or more) distinct types of affiliated customers.

Horizontal restraints p. 633   Per se violations of the Sherman Act in which the restraining of trade involves agreements between competitors to take action that results in the elimination or reduction of competition from other competitors.

Vertical restraints p. 633   Violations of the Sherman Act (judged by the rule of reason) in which the restraining of trade involves agreements between noncompetitors on different distributional levels in the chain of commercial supply.

Vertical price-fixing p. 636   Price-fixing in which a seller attempts to control the resale price of a product at a lower level in the supply chain.

Soft per se analysis p. 637   An approach developed by the courts for determining the legality of a tying arrangement: An arrangement in which a seller ties a second product to the first product is illegal per se if the seller possesses sufficient market power to render the tie-in coercive.

Structural-offense laws p. 641   Antitrust laws designed to combat the problem of monopolization by outlawing affirmative action toward monopolizing or attempting to monopolize a part of trade or commerce.

CHAPTER REVIEW QUESTIONS

1. When a company engages in blatantly anticompetitive behavior, which standard will a court use in a Sherman Act analysis?
   a. Per se
   b. Rule of reason
   c. Behavioral
   d. Monopoly

2. Willie's Widgets Corporation agrees with Widgets R Us, Inc., that Willie's will sell widgets only in the eastern part of the state if Widgets R Us agrees to sell widgets only in the western part of the state. Which type of horizontal restraint is this agreement?
   a. Price-fixing
   b. Market allocation
   c. Tying agreement
   d. Boycott

3. **Famous Footwear Company manufactures high-end shoes. It institutes a rule that any retailer who sells the shoes for under $500 will be cut off from any additional purchasing from Famous Footwear. Which type of vertical restraint is this agreement?**
   a. Price-fixing
   b. Market allocation
   c. Tying agreement
   d. Boycott

4. **The Sherman Act prohibits the use of _____ power to create an anticompetitive market in a particular industry.**
   a. Horizontal
   b. Vertical
   c. Structural
   d. Monopoly

5. **Thought of as a "catchall" statute designed to cover unfair methods of competition, the _____ prohibits anticompetitive conduct that may fall outside of other antitrust laws.**
   a. Federal Trade Commission Act
   b. Federal Trade Catchall Act
   c. Fair Trade Competition Act
   d. Fair Trade Collusion Act

Answers and explanations are provided at the end of this chapter.

THEORY TO PRACTICE

SurgiPro is a company engaged in the manufacture and sale of surgical instruments to physician groups and hospitals. After several decades in the market, SurgiPro has a 75 percent market share in the surgical instrument industry. SurgiPro was approached by Medical Devices Corporation (MDC), a competitor of SurgiPro with only a 5 percent market share. MDC proposed that the two companies cease undercutting each other on the retail price of scalpels. MDC also proposed that each company sell only 1,000 scalpels per month at a set price of no lower than $15 per scalpel. MDC reasoned that the sale of scalpels had such a low profit margin that the only way either SurgiPro or MDC could make a profit on the product would be through this plan. An executive at SurgiPro agreed to consider the plan.

1. Have the parties committed a violation of any antitrust laws? What laws may apply in this situation, and is the fact that SurgiPro agreed to consider the plan significant?
2. How is MDC's proposed plan best characterized in the context of antitrust law?

Assume that SurgiPro rejects MDC's proposal and instead proposes that they agree that SurgiPro will sell its products only to customers in the mid-Atlantic states and that MDC will sell its products only to customers in the southern states.

3. Which, if any, antitrust laws does SurgiPro's proposal violate?
4. If SurgiPro and MDC are sued by a competitor, should the court use the per se standard or the rule of reason? Why?

Suppose that both SurgiPro and MDC purchase raw materials for their products from SupplyCo. SurgiPro notifies SupplyCo that it will no longer purchase the supplier's raw materials unless SupplyCo ceases its sales to MDC. SupplyCo agrees because it does not want to lose the substantial revenue from SurgiPro.

5. Which, if any, antitrust laws does this action violate?
6. Assume that SurgiPro wishes to merge with MDC. What antitrust laws will need to be considered before entering into a merger agreement?

LEGAL STRATEGY 101

Is Amazon an Illegal Monopoly?

Giant retailers like Amazon and Walmart don't always offer the lowest prices, but they are among the most aggressive companies in the world in changing prices to stay ahead of their competitors.

Consider the market for e-books and e-readers like the Kindle. Amazon founder and CEO Jeff Bezos

Amazon founder and CEO Jeff Bezos. David McNew/Getty Images

(pictured) has adopted a simple pricing strategy: He wants to sell all new e-book titles for just $9.99. According to Tim Bajarin, president of the consultancy firm Creative Strategies, "Jeff's ultimate position is that instead of selling 100,000 copies at $14.95, [Amazon] would sell 200,000 copies, let's say, at $8.99 or $9.99."[23] Moreover, Amazon's Kindle device and Kindle Fire tablets are two of the most popular e-readers ever. Most of Amazon's early competitors—such as the Apple iPad, the Motorola Xoom, and the BlackBerry PlayBook—were far more expensive than the Kindle. Amazon, by contrast, chose to drive sales of the Kindle and Kindle Fire through low pricing.

In fact, Amazon typically prices its Kindle e-readers and Kindle Fire tablets at or slightly below cost.[24]

---

[23] LauraSydell, *In E-Book Price War, Amazon's Long-Term Strategy Required Short-Term Risks,* Nat'l Pub. Radio (Sept. 4, 2014).

[24] Adam Levine-Weinberg, *Amazon's Kindle Strategy Is Finally Working,* Motley Fool (Feb. 9, 2014).

Amazon's Kindle pricing strategy is simple: Amazon is willing to lose money on the sale of its devices (by selling them at or below cost) in order to lock users into the Amazon "ecosystem" by tightly integrating the Kindle and Kindle Fire with Amazon's online store. In other words, Amazon's strategy is to make money by selling lots of e-books, music, movies, and other digital content to Kindle and Kindle Fire users over the long run.

But does Amazon's pricing strategy for e-books and e-readers constitute illegal "predatory pricing" under the antitrust laws?

The business strategy of below-cost pricing may run the risk of being illegal under the Federal Trade Commission Act, which outlaws unfair methods of competition. Such a pricing strategy may also constitute an act of monopolization or an attempt to monopolize under the Sherman Act. Moreover, giant retailers like Walmart or Amazon—any business with a dominant or substantial market share—can be especially vulnerable to antitrust claims, especially if they are already under the watchful eyes of antitrust regulators.

At this point, it is still too early to tell whether Amazon's aggressive pricing strategy will expose the company to antitrust litigation. After all, competition is always just a click away via competitors such as Apple and Google, which offer their own competing e-book platforms. Perhaps Amazon is willing to run this legal risk in order to solidify its dominant position in the market for e-books.

CRITICAL THINKING QUESTION

Assume Amazon's aggressive e-book and e-reader pricing strategy works as planned and that Amazon eventually becomes the dominant seller of e-books and other digital content on the Internet. Would this outcome serve as sufficient evidence that Amazon is an illegal monopoly under the Sherman Act?

MANAGER'S CHALLENGE

Midlevel managers are sometimes required to prepare a memorandum for an executive manager to help the executive manager prepare for a meeting (a "prep memo") with another company's principals. Assume you receive the following e-mail from your executive manager:

> I will be meeting with a representative of MDC tomorrow. Please draft a two-page prep memo that provides information on entering into a joint venture with MDC for selling scalpels. We could share in expenses of manufacturing and distributing scalpels and split the profits equally. The memo should address how this venture could be structured and whether or not we could still use the brand names. I read an article in *The Wall Street Journal* about antitrust issues in a similar agreement between Texaco and Shell. Perhaps that will help you in preparing the memo.

Prepare a two-page prep memo for your executive manager.

See Connect for Manager's Challenge sample answers.

CASE SUMMARY 19.1 Covad Communications Co. v. BellSouth Corp., 299 F.3d 1272 (11th Cir. 2002)

PREDATORY PRICING

Covad is in the business of providing DSL Internet service to consumers in the southern region of the United States. BellSouth is the regional telephone company covering the area and also offers DSL Internet service. Covad and BellSouth entered into an agreement whereby Covad would lease BellSouth's phone lines used in Covad's DSL service. Covad alleged that, after the contract was executed, BellSouth engaged in predatory pricing. Covad sued BellSouth for violation of the Sherman Act, claiming that BellSouth's efforts were an attempt to further a monopoly and squeeze Covad out of the market.

CASE QUESTIONS

1. Who prevails and why?
2. What section of the Sherman Act is at issue here?
3. How should the court apply the statute to this case?

CASE SUMMARY 19.2 Data General Corporation, et al. v. Grumman Systems Support Corporation, 36 F.3d 1147 (1st Cir. 1994)

TYING

Grumman Systems accused Data General of violating the Sherman Act based on Data General's tying the sale of its copyrighted software with a requirement that the buyer enter into an agreement to purchase Data General's support services for the software. Data General defended on the basis that the support services were an integral part of its software and not a separate product.

CASE QUESTIONS

1. Is this tying arrangement a violation of antitrust laws? Explain your answer.
2. Is this an example of a horizontal or vertical restraint?

CASE SUMMARY 19.3 Greyhound v. International Business Machines Corporation, 559 F.2d 488 (9th Cir. 1977)

ANTICOMPETITIVE ACTION

IBM manufactures and sells computers and related equipment. It also has a leasing division. Greyhound was a leasing company that would purchase "second-generation" computers from IBM at up to a 75 percent discount (depending on how old the equipment was) and then lease them to its customers at a relatively inexpensive price. In fact, because Greyhound could buy at such a high discount, it was able to undercut IBM's standard lease rates. Although IBM had about 82 percent of this leasing market, IBM became concerned when its leasing market share fell. It determined that the main reason for its loss in the leasing market was that companies like Greyhound were able to offer better terms to consumers. IBM phased in reduced discount rates so that the maximum discount was 12 percent. Greyhound sued IBM, alleging monopolization in violation of the Sherman Act.

CASE QUESTIONS

1. Who prevails and why? Explain your answer.
2. Are there any similarities between this case and the *Microsoft* case?

CASE SUMMARY 19.4 Tanka v. University of Southern California, 252 F.3d 1059 (9th Cir. 2001)

HORIZONTAL RESTRAINTS

Tanka was a student athlete attending the University of Southern California (USC). When she decided to transfer to UCLA, the athletic director at USC invoked an NCAA rule that allowed USC to prevent Tanka from playing sports at UCLA for one year. The NCAA rule only applied to student-athlete transfers within a particular conference. Tanka sued USC and the NCAA, claiming that the rule amounted to a horizontal restraint violating the Sherman Act.

CASE QUESTIONS

1. Who prevails and why?
2. Should the rule of reason be used in this analysis? Explain.

CASE SUMMARY 19.5 *In re* Cardizem CD Antitrust Litigation, 332 F.3d 896 (6th Cir. 2003)

PER SE VIOLATIONS

HRM, a manufacturer of the prescription drug Cardizem CD, and Andrx, the manufacturer of a generic version of the drug, were embroiled in a patent infringement dispute in 1996. Andrx counterclaimed with allegations of unfair competition. After a year of extensive settlement negotiations, the parties entered into an agreement whereby Andrx, which had obtained FDA approval to market its generic version, agreed that it would not market the generic version in the United States for a certain period of time in exchange for payments by HRM of up to $40 million per year. Both parties agreed to drop the claims from the 1996 lawsuits against each other. The parties fulfilled the agreement faithfully, and Andrx waited until June 1999 to market its generic drug. After its release, the generic drug sold for a much lower price than Cardizem CD and captured a substantial portion of the market. A group of plaintiffs filed a class action lawsuit against HRM and Andrx, alleging that their settlement agreement was a per se violation of the Sherman Act as it was a form of horizontal price restraint.

CASE QUESTIONS

1. Who prevails and why? Explain your reasoning.
2. What type of illegal restraint is being alleged by the plaintiffs in this case?

 Self-Check ANSWERS Horizontal Restraint

1. Price-fixing.
2. Boycott.
3. Market allocation.

CHAPTER REVIEW QUESTIONS: Answers and Explanations

1. **a.** Blatant acts of anticompetitive behavior with no competitive justification are decided using the per se standard. (b) is incorrect because the rule of reason standard does not apply to blatant violations. (c) and (d) are nonsensical.

2. **b.** An agreement among competitors to divide a market by territory is a per se horizontal restraint. (a) is wrong because there was no agreement as to price. (c) is wrong because it is a vertical restraint. (d) is wrong because there was no concerted refusal to deal with a third party.

3. **a.** Vertical price-fixing occurs when a seller attempts to control the resale price of a product at a lower level in the supply chain. (b) and (d) are wrong because they are both forms of horizontal restraints. (c) is wrong because there is no second product.

4. **d.** Monopoly power is at the heart of the Sherman and Clayton Acts. (a) and (b) are wrong because the question is not related to restraints. (c) is wrong because there is no such thing as structural power (it is only used in the context of structure-offense laws).

5. **a.** The FTCA is a broad statute that is used if anticompetitive behavior does not fit squarely into the Sherman Act. (b), (c), and (d) are fictional.

CHAPTER 20

Creditors' Rights and Bankruptcy

©philsajonesen/Getty Images

Learning Objectives

After studying this chapter, students who have mastered the material will be able to:

20-1 Distinguish between unsecured and secured creditors and determine the rights of each.

20-2 Apply the framework for a secured transaction for personal property under Uniform Commercial Code (UCC) Article 9 in a business context.

20-3 Articulate the process of obtaining a secured interest in real estate.

20-4 Describe the role of sureties and guarantors in a secured loan transaction.

20-5 Explain the various options and legal ramifications for a business facing financial distress.

20-6 Determine the rights, protections, and obligations of both creditors and debtors under federal bankruptcy laws.

20-7 Distinguish between and explain the various bankruptcy options for debtors under Chapter 7, Chapter 11, and Chapter 13 of the Bankruptcy Code.

20-8 Explain the impact of the Bankruptcy Abuse Prevention and Consumer Protection Act on creditors and debtors.

The financial crisis that drove the markets sharply downward in 2008 is perhaps the most prominent confirmation of the fact that global commerce depends on credit. Creditors are one of the most important components of the global economy because they provide merchants and consumers with the opportunity to purchase goods and inventory, acquire real estate and other assets, and expand business operations without spending large sums of cash to fund current business operations. In order to encourage creditors to extend appropriate commercial credit to merchants and consumers, the law gives certain protections to creditors. At the same time, the law also provides statutory protections and other alternatives for borrowers in times of financial crisis. Business owners and managers frequently engage in extending or receiving credit, and understanding the legal ramifications in both circumstances is pivotal to protecting the interests of creditors and debtors. In this chapter, we discuss

- Laws that govern the relationship between creditors and borrowers and how they apply in a business context.
- The legal ramifications of alternatives for a business facing a financial crisis.
- The fundamental principles of the federal Bankruptcy Code and its applicability to business.

CREDITORS' RIGHTS

Although people typically think of commercial lenders and banks as being creditors, the scope of creditors is much wider, including manufacturers, suppliers, and retailers. While most creditors have little problem collecting the money owed to them, there are certain times when a creditor must take legal action to recover the debt. Laws that protect creditors' rights come primarily from common law and statutory law at the state level. Bankruptcy laws, discussed later in this chapter, are primarily federal statutes. The level of protection varies in part based on whether or not the credit was secured by some type of collateral. Credit that is not collateralized is known as **unsecured debt**. When the borrower has pledged collateral in order to obtain credit, the creditor is known as a **secured creditor**.

LO 20-1
Distinguish between unsecured and secured creditors and determine the rights of each.

Unsecured Creditors

Businesses often use unsecured debt in the form of a loan or line of credit primarily to help fund short-term operations. Examples include private loans from another party, loans from a bank or other commercial lender, and credit cards. In each of these cases, credit is extended based on the borrower's creditworthiness rather than as a result of the borrower's promise to pledge collateral. Unsecured creditors are offered very little protection if the borrower defaults on paying back the loan. Note that interest rates on unsecured loans tend to be higher than those on loans based on secured credit.

When a borrower fails to pay back the loan or make payments toward the loan as agreed, the unsecured creditor's exclusive legal remedy is to bring a lawsuit against the borrower and obtain a judgment from the court. Essentially, the basis of such a debt collection lawsuit is breach of contract in that the borrower failed to fulfill his obligations under the contract (repayment). Once the creditor has obtained a judgment, the borrower must pay the full amount of the judgment or the creditor may pursue a court order. The latter option allows the creditor to use a judicially created procedure to seize any property or assets of the borrower.[1] Certain assets, however, are exempt from seizure (such as the borrower's primary residence). Additionally, a creditor's lawsuit or execution of a judgment must be halted if the borrower files for protection under the Bankruptcy Code (discussed later). As a result, unsecured creditors have very little practical way to collect debts owed. Certain consumer loans and credit card debt are also subject to state and federal statutory regulation regarding late fees, interest rates, disclosures, and credit reporting practices. These regulations are discussed in greater detail in Chapter 21, "Warranties and Consumer Protection Law."

A credit card is the most common form of unsecured credit used in consumer transactions. Purestock/SuperStock

---

[1] In most states, the judgment is executed through use of the sheriff's department, and the seized assets are sold at auction (known as a *sheriff's sale*).

LO 20-2

Apply the framework for a secured transaction for personal property under Uniform Commercial Code (UCC) Article 9 in a business context.

Legal Speak >))

Collateral Property or land that a debtor promises to her creditor in case she fails to repay her debt.

Secured Creditors

When credit is secured by a pledge of collateral by the borrower, the creditor has more viable alternatives to collect the debt. The alternatives depend on the category of secured creditor.

SECURED TRANSACTIONS UNDER ARTICLE 9 OF THE UCC

One common way that a creditor attempts to ensure full payment by the borrower is by creating a *secured-party relationship* whereby the borrower pledges certain property of value to secure the debt owed. When personal property (e.g., goods or other assets such as cash) or fixtures to real estate (e.g., light fixtures or a built-in reception desk) are intended to serve as the collateral, Article 9 of the Uniform Commercial Code (UCC) provides a uniform set of rules to govern the transaction. With some variations, Article 9 has been adopted in all states, and it gives business owners and managers some degree of reliability in planning a loan transaction. Note that loans collateralized with real estate (also known as *real property*) are governed not by Article 9 but rather by statutes related to mortgages, discussed in the next section.

In essence, Article 9 provides a framework for secured transactions by recognizing the rights of the creditor, known as the **secured party**, against other creditors of the borrower and against the borrower himself in the event of a default in payment. In the UCC, a borrower is known as the **debtor**. Article 9 also provides a procedure for the secured party to establish priority in the collateral over other creditors; this procedure is known as **perfecting** the interest in the collateral. The rights of the secured party are known as a **security interest**. Two Article 9 requirements must be met in order for a creditor to obtain the *full* benefit of a security interest: (1) the security agreement and (2) perfection.

Security Agreement

Typically, the parties will enter into a security agreement that specifies the parties, describes the collateral, articulates the obligations of the debtor (primarily payment), and states the remedies available to the secured party in the event of default. In the event the agreement is silent on a particular matter, Article 9 acts to fill that void by providing a standard set of rules.

Perfection

Perfection of a security interest is the act of establishing the secured party's rights ahead of the rights of other creditors. Although Article 9 does not define the term *perfection*, it does describe an order of priority among creditors and the actions that a secured party must take to establish these rights. Perfection occurs at the moment of (1) taking physical possession of the collateral, (2) officially filing a statement of notice with a state and/or local government office, or (3) taking legal control of the collateral (such as establishing joint authority over a brokerage account whose funds are being used to collateralize a loan).

Secured credit transactions, such as a loan for which the debtor's inventory is used as collateral, are typically governed by a security agreement between the parties.
Andersen Ross/Getty Images

REAL ESTATE

When real estate (also called *real property*[2]) is being used to collateralize a loan, the creditor takes an interest in the collateral through use of a **mortgage**. A mortgage is a written document that specifies the parties and the real estate and is filed with a state and/or local government agency, thereby becoming a public record that others can look up. This filing is intended to give notice to the public and other creditors of the secured party's interest in the real estate collateral. The creditor is known as the **mortgagee**, and the borrower is the **mortgagor**. A mortgage is typically accompanied by a **promissory note**. The promissory note is a contract in which the borrower promises to pay back the creditor at a certain rate of interest over a specified period of years (usually 15, 20, or 30 years). State statutes primarily govern the relationship between mortgagor and mortgagee. These statutes define the procedure that the creditor must follow in order to pursue certain remedies against the debtor. In the most extreme measure, a creditor declares the loan in default and institutes a **mortgage foreclosure** in an effort to take title and possession of the real estate in hopes of selling the property to pay off the debt owed. In the wake of the mortgage foreclosure crisis that began in 2007, Congress passed the Mortgage Forgiveness Debt Relief Act.[3] The intent of this law is to assist homeowners in avoiding foreclosure by offering them certain guarantees and tax breaks from the government when they refinance a mortgage loan. Properties owned by business entities, or by individuals for business purposes (such as a vacation rental property), are not eligible for relief under this law.

> **KEY POINT**
>
> In a secured transaction, a creditor must *perfect* her security interest in the collateral in order to be fully protected under UCC Article 9.

LO 20-3

Articulate the process of obtaining a secured interest in real estate.

SURETIES AND GUARANTORS

Another common method for helping to secure a loan is to require a *third party* to back up the promises made by the debtor regarding repayment of the loan. In some cases, a creditor may be willing to extend a loan to a borrower, but the borrower's creditworthiness may be either questionable or too brief to qualify for the credit required. In such a case, the creditor will usually require a third party with sufficient creditworthiness and assets to also sign the loan agreement and become jointly liable with the debtor for his promise to repay the loan (thus the commonly used term *cosigning*). When a party agrees to be *primarily* liable to pay the loan, she is known as a **surety**. When a party agrees to be liable *only if* the debtor actually defaults, she is known as a **guarantor**. For example, in order to secure a loan for the purchase of a new car, Bank requires Cain to have a cosigner because Cain's credit is insufficient to qualify for the loan. Cain convinces Abel to be his cosigner, and Bank requires Abel to cosign as a surety. In the first year of the loan, Abel is late in making payments and eventually becomes 60 days' past due. Bank now has the option of pursuing remedies against either Cain or Abel to pay the debt. Because Abel has more assets, he is most likely the better party to pursue. However, suppose that Abel signed as a *guarantor* instead of a surety. In that case, Bank would have to pursue full remedies against Cain by obtaining a court judgment and attempting to collect as much as possible (such as repossessing the car for resale) before pursuing Abel. In the event Bank cannot recover the full amount from remedies against Cain, *only then* is Abel liable for the balance owed.

LO 20-4

Describe the role of sureties and guarantors in a secured loan transaction.

---

[2] Although some sources cite technical differences between these terms, according to *Black's Law Dictionary*, the term *real estate* is generally synonymous with *real property*.

[3] Pub L. No. 110-142, 121 Stat. 1803 (2007).

Personal Guaranties for Business Loans

Business owners and managers often encounter suretyship and guaranty concepts in the context of a **personal guaranty** of a business loan. For example, when a business borrows money to expand operations or to fund an acquisition of some type, the creditor will often require that the owners (sometimes referred to as the *principals* of a business entity) of small and midsize companies give their personal guaranty to back up the business loan. This means that in the event of a default by the business entity debtor, the principals have pledged their personal assets (such as individual bank accounts, equity in a property, or other assets) if the assets of the business are insufficient to repay the loan. Creditors realize that without this guaranty, the principals of a debtor corporation can simply walk away from the debt without any personal liability for the loan. As a result, creditors often wish to make the principals more accountable by securing a business loan with both a security interest in certain collateral *and* the personal guaranties of the principals. For example, suppose that Caulfield is the principal of Rye Inc., a manufacturing firm specializing in the production of high-quality baseball catcher's mitts, with annual revenues of $25 million. Rye has been successful over the past 10 years. Now Caulfield wishes to expand his operations and manufacture other baseball equipment and plans to fund the expansion with a loan from Big Bank. Although Rye has been profitable in the past and will likely have no problem repaying the loan from existing revenues, Big Bank not only will require a security interest in any collateral owned by Rye but also will likely require Caulfield to provide a personal guaranty as an additional measure of security. From Big Bank's perspective, the personal guaranty gives it maximum leverage over Caulfield in the event of a default by Rye.

 Self-Check Creditor Status

Determine the status of each creditor.

1. ExtremeCo, a manufacturer of a line of extreme gear such as snowboards, gives Retailer merchandise for her inventory on credit. ExtremeCo requires Retailer to sign an agreement that describes the inventory as collateral and specifies that Retailer will pay ExtremeCo monthly based on sales of ExtremeCo's product. ExtremeCo files a statement of interest in the collateral with the appropriate government agency.
2. Office Galaxy sells office supplies to a local insurance agency. Office Galaxy delivers the goods on the 1st of the month and sends an invoice on the 15th of each month to the manager of the insurance agency.
3. BigBank lends WidgetCo $100,000 to purchase land in order to build a new warehouse. WidgetCo uses the land itself as collateral.
4. BigBank lends WidgetCo $50,000 to fund the hiring of seasonal employees during the holiday rush. BigBank requires the principals of WidgetCo to sign a promissory note agreeing that they will pay the note from personal assets if WidgetCo defaults on payments.

Answers to this Self-Check are provided at the end of the chapter.

CONCEPT SUMMARY Creditors' Rights

- Unsecured creditors give loans based on creditworthiness without the security of collateral and must bring a lawsuit in the case of default.

(continued)

- A secured creditor can retain the collateral given to secure his loan; no lawsuit is necessary under the UCC if there is a security agreement and the interest has been perfected.
- A creditor uses real estate as collateral with a mortgage. In the case of default, the debtor goes into foreclosure, and the creditor sells the real estate to cover his losses.
- A debtor can obtain a loan with collateral or creditworthiness by getting a third party to pay off the loan for her (surety) or to pay off the loan if she defaults (guarantor). A business without credit can get a loan by using a creditworthy individual as a personal guaranty.

ALTERNATIVES FOR INSOLVENT BORROWERS

LO 20-5

Explain the various options and legal ramifications for a business facing financial distress.

When a business venture no longer has adequate assets to maintain its operations and can no longer pay its bills as they become due in the usual course of trade and business, it is considered **insolvent**. A company's specific response to insolvency is largely dependent on the type of financial crisis. For example, if the insolvency is a result of *temporary* poor cash flow, but the receivables will likely provide enough cash to continue operations in the future, then bankruptcy may not be the best option (or even an option at all, depending on the debt-to-assets ratio of the struggling venture). On the other hand, if the venture is cash-starved because of, for example, a particularly burdensome union contract and has no realistic way to recover from the financial crisis without some statutory protection from creditors, then the law provides the venture with the ability to hold creditors off while the business reorganizes and drafts a plan for continuing its operations in the future. This plan could include a reformation of the problematic union contract. When a business becomes insolvent, its principals have several choices in dealing with the venture's debt. Some of these options do not involve any statutory protections and, therefore, may have legal ramifications for the business and its principals.

Out of Existence

Out of existence (also known as the "lights-out option") is a nonstatutory option in which the venture simply ceases operations without paying creditors. Usually the debtor company files an out-of-existence certificate or articles of dissolution with the state corporation bureau and simply ceases doing business. However, the debts are still valid obligations of the company, and a creditor may pursue a debt collection lawsuit in an attempt to collect any available cash or assets to satisfy the debt. In fact, some states require that all creditors be notified before the business is recognized as legally dissolved. Out of existence is a particularly dangerous option if the debt has been secured through a *personal guaranty* by principals of the business (discussed earlier). However, if the debtor has no assets, no personal guaranties exist, and the debt is not substantial enough to make legal methods to collect economically viable for creditors, the lights-out option is the quickest and least expensive option.

Workouts

When the principals wish to continue the operations of a business that is underperforming and is in poor financial condition, they may hire a professional (sometimes called a *turnaround specialist*) to help revise the business model and negotiate with commercial lenders, with the objective of setting the company on sound financial footing. At the same time, in order to avoid collection lawsuits from certain suppliers and creditors, the business venture must also attempt to settle past debts. These various steps of turning around a business are often referred to by creditors as a **workout**.

Assignment for the Benefit of Creditors

Either as part of a workout plan or as a stand-alone transaction, another alternative to a bankruptcy filing is an **assignment for the benefit of creditors** (sometimes called simply an ABC). An ABC is a form of liquidation that is an alternative to bankruptcy and is provided either by state statute, state common law, or a combination of both. For example, in Delaware, state laws permit a debtor to make "a voluntary assignment of his or her estate, real or personal, or of any part thereof to any other person in trust for his or her creditors."[4]

An ABC can be an alternative in certain cases to overcome a short-term cash crunch when the business may still be viable in the long term. For example, suppose StartUpCo is a privately held venture where, after a number of rounds of investment, the investors have lost confidence in the business's ability to succeed and decide to halt their investments. StartUpCo's management is faced with a lack of cash to support its operations and has no options for commercial or private funding. It is also likely that creditors will soon demand payment. Meanwhile, StartUpCo's principals have been in discussions with a potential buyer but have not yet agreed to terms of the sale. Also, StartUpCo's commercial property lease will expire in nine months, but it's possible that the buyer might want to take over the lease. StartUpCo's options are

- *Reorganization under the bankruptcy code:* While this would hold off creditors temporarily, a bankruptcy reorganization filing is problematic because it would severely impact StartUpCo's bargaining position with a potential buyer.
- *Liquidation bankruptcy:* This would immediately scuttle any discussion between StartUpCo and the potential buyer.
- *ABC:* In many states, another option that may be available to companies in financial trouble is an assignment for the benefit of creditors that would provide more flexibility to StartUpCo's principals and allow discussion with the new buyer to continue.

Assignment Agreement Although the procedures may vary from state to state, typically the first step involves the business and the creditor (as assignee) entering into a formal assignment agreement. The company provides the assignee with a list of creditors, shareholders, and other interested parties. The assignee then gives notice to any creditors of the assignment, setting a bar date for filing claims with the assignee that is between five and six months later. As a practical matter, most businesses work with a professional liquidation firm that takes possession of the assets and arranges the sale for the largest possible amount, then pays creditors. The liquidator has a fiduciary duty to the creditors and is usually compensated based on a percentage of the sale. Recall from our earlier discussion that a fiduciary duty is the duty to carry out the best interest of another party (i.e., creditors). After the administration of assets and the expiration of the deadline to file claims, the assignee reviews the claims that are filed. If a claim is not filed before the bar date, the claim will normally be disallowed. A creditor with a lien in the assets of the business will retain the lien in the assets, even after the assignment. If a claim is in dispute, the assignee will usually file objections with the state court for a decision.

Distribution Upon resolving all claim disputes, the assignee distributes the funds first to any creditor that has a valid lien on assets, second to pay the fees and costs associated

---

[4]State of Delaware.

FIGURE 20.1　StartUpCo's ABC Process

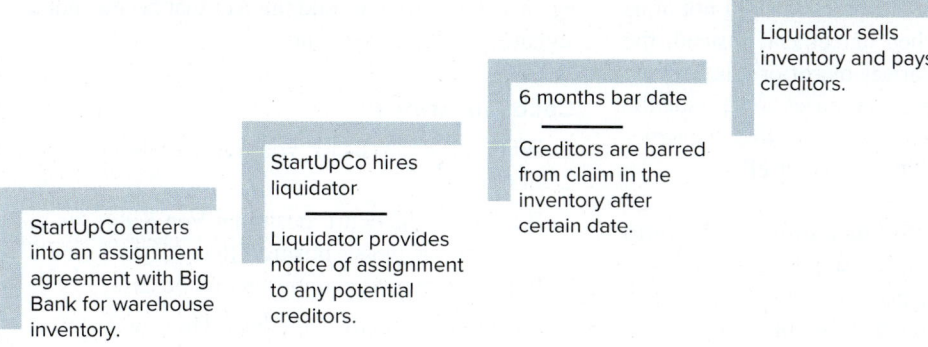

- StartUpCo enters into an assignment agreement with Big Bank for warehouse inventory.
- StartUpCo hires liquidator
- Liquidator provides notice of assignment to any potential creditors.
- 6 months bar date
- Creditors are barred from claim in the inventory after certain date.
- Liquidator sells inventory and pays creditors.

with administering the transaction, and third to pay priority unsecured creditors. Any cash remaining is distributed back to pay the owners of the business. If the funds are not sufficient to pay a particular class of creditors in full, the creditors in that class receive pro rata payments and the classes junior to that class (e.g., unsecured creditors) do not receive payment. Figure 20.1 illustrates this timeline using our StartUpCo example.

In Case 20.1, a state appellate court considers whether an assignee is bound by certain terms in an agreement between the business owners and its financial advisers.

CASE 20.1 Akin Bay Company, LLC v. Von Kahle, 180 So. 3d 1180 (Fla. Ct. App. 2015)

FACT SUMMARY In 2012 a group of Miami-based businesses (collectively ItalKitchen) hired Akin Bay Company, LLC (Akin Bay), as their financial advisor for the purposes of providing financial advice related to ItalKitchen's financial restructuring, including advice on a potential business workout and the various options such as an assignment for the benefit of creditors. ItalKitchen eventually executed an assignment for the benefit of creditors in accordance with Florida state statutes in favor of Von Kahle as assignee. Pursuant to the assignment, Von Kahle took possession of all the assets of ItalKitchen, which included all claims and demands that existed against third parties. In 2014, Von Kahle filed a lawsuit against Akin Bay alleging that it breached its fiduciary duty to Italkitchen as the assignors and that Akin Bay had been the recipient of fraudulent transfers by ItalKitchen prior to the date of the assignment. Akin Bay asked the court to dismiss the lawsuit on the grounds that the agreement by which it supplied its services to Akin Bay stipulated that any dispute between Akin Bay and ItalKitchen was to be resolved by compulsory mediation, followed, if necessary, by mandatory arbitration. Von Kahle argued that the clause is not enforceable against him in his position as assignee for the benefit of creditors because (1) he was not a party to the agreement and (2) the claims alleged in the complaint do not "arise out of or relate to" the agreement executed by Akin Bay and ItalKitchen. The trial court held in favor of Von Kahle, and Akin Bay appealed.

SYNOPSIS OF DECISION AND OPINION The Florida Court of Appeals reversed the trial court's decision and ruled in favor of Akin Bay. The court analyzed the state's Assignment for the Benefit of Creditors statute and concluded that the assignee was

(continued)

bound by any agreement between assignors and a third party such as Akin Bay. The court also rejected Von Kahle's argument that the claims did not arise from the Akin-ItalKitchen agreement. Instead, the court held that a claim arises out of or relates to an agreement if it, at a minimum, raises some issue the resolution of which requires reference to or construction of some portion of the contract itself.

WORDS OF THE COURT: Assignees Rights and Obligations "The assignee stands in the shoes of the assignor for this purpose. For this reason, with minor exceptions prescribed by the statute, the assignee cannot stand in any better position than his assignor. Under [state law] an assignee 'is subject to all the equities and burdens which attach to the property.' 'An assignee is in no better or worse position than his assignor.' While it could have done so . . ., the [Florida state] Legislature did not limit the ability of third parties to assert their contractual right to enforce arbitration clauses during the assignment for benefit of creditors' liquidation process. Accordingly, the mediation and arbitration clause in the agreement in this case is enforceable against Von Kahle despite the fact that he was not a signatory to the agreement."

Case Questions

1. What was the basis for Von Kahle's lawsuit in the first place?
2. What does the court mean that Von Kahle "is in no better or worse position than his assignor"? Explain why that is important to the case.
3. *Focus on Critical Thinking:* The court points out that the state legislature could have limited the ability of third parties to assert their contractual right to enforce arbitration clauses during the assignment for benefit of creditors' liquidation process but did not. As a matter of fairness, should the state legislature limit the rights of the parties in connection to arbitration? Should the legislature reform any other part of the ABC process? Explain.

CONCEPT SUMMARY Alternatives for Insolvent Borrowers

- Out of existence (also known as the "lights-out option") is a nonstatutory option in which the venture simply ceases operations without paying creditors.
- Workouts may be used if the principals wish to continue the operations of a business that is underperforming and is in poor financial condition, usually via a professional trained to help revise the business model and negotiate with commercial lenders.
- Assignment for the benefit of creditors (ABC) is a form of liquidation that is an alternative to bankruptcy that permits a debtor to make a voluntary assignment of his or her estate, real or personal, to any other person in trust for his or her creditors.

LO 20-6

Determine the rights, protections, and obligations of both creditors and debtors under federal bankruptcy laws.

BANKRUPTCY

Of course, there are circumstances when the debtor's best option is protection from creditors via the Bankruptcy Code. The concept of forgiveness of debt and protection of borrowers from creditors has deep historical roots that some scholars have traced back to the Old Testament. The underlying concept and public policy objectives behind bankruptcy protection are to give a debtor a "fresh start" and to prevent creditors from gaining unfair advantage over each other in being paid. In the United States, the need for bankruptcy laws is recognized in Article I of the U.S. Constitution.[5] For the most part, bankruptcy proceedings are a matter of federal law. State courts can have some limited involvement in issues that involve the borrower (usually called the *debtor* in a bankruptcy context) in one way or another, but they generally do not have any jurisdiction over bankruptcy proceedings. The law of bankruptcy is found within the federal statutes ("Bankruptcy Code"[6]). The starting place for all bankruptcy matters is the federal bankruptcy court.

The Bankruptcy Code is divided into chapters, and often the reference to someone filing for bankruptcy protection is known as "filing for Chapter 11." The most common forms of bankruptcy are Chapter 7 (liquidation of debtor's assets and discharge of debts), Chapter 11 (reorganization), and Chapter 13 (debt adjustment and repayment of consumer debt). Other chapters contain definitions, describe procedural aspects of bankruptcy, and contain special provisions for bankruptcies by municipalities, stockbrokers, and railroads. Congress amended the Bankruptcy Code in 2005 with the Bankruptcy Abuse Prevention and Consumer Protection Act, which imposed additional requirements on those seeking protection under the Bankruptcy Code. The specific provisions of the 2005 amendment are covered later in this chapter.

Automatic Stay

Filing for bankruptcy protects the debtor through an immediate **automatic stay**. The automatic stay legally prohibits creditors from either initiating or continuing any debt collection action against the debtor or her property. The stay is a powerful legal tool because it stops all collection efforts, all harassment, and all foreclosure actions. It permits the debtor to attempt a repayment or reorganization plan or simply to be relieved of the financial pressures resulting from a financial crisis. The stay also allows the bankruptcy court to deal with the debtor's assets and creditors in a single forum where the rights of all concerned may be heard at once.

> **KEY POINT**
>
> An automatic stay halts creditors, including government agencies, from all collection efforts, including litigation.

Bankruptcy Trustee

The Bankruptcy Code provides for the appointment of a **bankruptcy trustee** in certain cases. A trustee is appointed in cases where the debtor seeks liquidation and discharge of debts (Chapter 7) or in cases where the debtor is a consumer attempting to repay much of the debt over a period of time (Chapter 13). The trustee, often an attorney highly skilled in bankruptcy law, is charged with the duty of collecting the debtor's available assets, known as the **bankruptcy estate**, and reducing those assets to cash for distribution, preserving the interests of both the debtor and the creditors. Federal law gives the trustee extensive authority and power to accomplish this objective. For example, the bankruptcy trustee may void certain transfers that are considered to be an unfair advantage of one creditor over another. These are known as **voidable transfers**.

The most common voidable transfer is a *preferential transfer*. A preferential transfer occurs when the debtor makes a payment to satisfy a *prebankruptcy petition* debt to a creditor within 90 days of the petition. If the creditor receives more than it would have under the liquidation proceedings, the trustee may void the transfer. In this event, the assets are taken back from the creditor and replaced in the bankruptcy estate. The transfer is

---

[5] Article I, § 8, gives Congress the responsibility to "establish . . . uniform Laws on the subject of Bankruptcies throughout the United States."

[6] See Title 11 of the United States Code.

Insolvent business ventures have several alternatives for dealing with the business's debts, including filing for protection from creditors under the Bankruptcy Code.
Carolyn Franks/Shutterstock

not considered preferential if the debtor simply pays a bill from a creditor in the ordinary course of business. Preferential transfers to *insiders* (including relatives, partners, officers, and directors of an individual or corporate debtor) are also voidable. Under certain circumstances, any insider transfers made within one year of the petition filing can be voided and placed back into the bankruptcy estate. Additionally, a transfer is voidable as a *fraudulent transfer* if it occurs when a debtor transfers property to a third person within one year of the petition filing with intent to delay, hinder, or defraud creditors. For example, suppose that Eyre is the sole owner of Jane's Pretzel Company (JPC). After several years of reasonable success in business, JPC experiences financial difficulty and owes its creditors $100,000, with only $5,000 in assets. JPC files for Chapter 7 liquidation and discharge. After JPC files the petition, the trustee is appointed and discovers several transfers out of the ordinary course of business. First, two weeks before JPC's petition for bankruptcy, Eyre paid off the entire balance owed to an important vendor on a loan secured by Eyre's personal guaranty. If the trustee determines that the vendor obtained more than it would have from the distribution of JPC's assets under the Bankruptcy Code (which is likely in this situation, given the assets versus the debts), the payment can be voided and the money put back into the bankruptcy estate. Second, Eyre borrowed $20,000 from her brother-in-law and, despite the fact that the loan was to be paid over five years, Eyre paid back the entire amount one month before filing for bankruptcy. That transaction would be classified as an insider preferential transfer, and the trustee would void the transfer and recover the payment from Eyre's brother-in-law on behalf of the bankruptcy estate.

> **KEY POINT**
>
> The bankruptcy trustee has the legal power to void any transfer of money that the debtor made for the benefit of insiders.

DEBTOR'S OPTIONS

When filing for protection under the Bankruptcy Code, the debtor chooses one of three main options: Chapter 7, Chapter 11, or Chapter 13.

Chapter 7: Liquidation and Discharge

Chapter 7 bankruptcy is perhaps the most extreme measure a business or individual can take. In essence, the debtor agrees to have most of her property liquidated and then the cash distributed to creditors. In exchange, the bankruptcy court gives legal protection to the debtor by discharging any remaining debts. For example, suppose WidgetCo has $50,000 in debts and only $10,000 in nonexempt assets. The bankruptcy court will distribute the $10,000 to creditors, and the remaining debt ($40,000) will be discharged. WidgetCo will be out of business, but its principals will get a fresh start and will not have to pay any of the debts incurred. Chapter 7 outlines a very specific procedure for discharge of debt.

Bankruptcy Petition The proceedings are started in the bankruptcy court by the filing of a bankruptcy petition. The petition can be either *voluntary* or *involuntary*. A **voluntary bankruptcy petition** is filed by the *debtor* and includes the names of creditors; a list of debts; and a list of the debtor's assets, income, and expenses. In order to qualify for protection under Chapter 7, the debtor's income must be less than the average income in her home state (this requirement is known as the *means test*). An **involuntary bankruptcy petition** is one that is filed *against* a debtor by a group of three or more creditors with an unsecured aggregate claim of at least $15,775 who claim that the debtor is failing to pay the debt as it comes due. This is an extreme measure, and involuntary petitions are relatively rare. This option poses some risk for the creditors because the Bankruptcy Code allows a company to recover damages against creditors who attempt to drive a debtor into bankruptcy but are unsuccessful.

Automatic Stay As discussed earlier, the filing of a petition gives protection to the debtor immediately. This means that creditors must suspend all collection activity as of the day the petition is filed. Note that the suspension is temporary and designed to give the bankruptcy court the time necessary to decide the validity of the petition.

Order for Relief Once the court determines the validity of the petition, an order for relief is granted, the automatic stay effectively becomes *permanent,* and a bankruptcy estate is created consisting of all of the debtor's assets.

Appointment of Trustee Once the order of relief is granted, the court appoints an interim bankruptcy trustee to oversee the case. A permanent trustee is elected at the first meeting of creditors. Once appointed, the trustee creates a bankruptcy estate. Note that the trustee is a representative of the court and *not* a representative of either the debtor or the creditors. The trustee has the responsibility of administering the bankruptcy proceedings in accordance with the law. The trustee's primary responsibility is to preserve the bankruptcy estate and ensure that the assets are distributed in accordance with the Bankruptcy Code.

In Case 20.2, a federal court considers the motion of a bankruptcy trustee who is suing for recovery of funds used in a Ponzi scheme.

LO 20-7

Distinguish between and explain the various bankruptcy options for debtors under Chapter 7, Chapter 11, and Chapter 13 of the Bankruptcy Code.

Legal Speak >))

Exempt Assets
The Bankruptcy Code (and some state laws) allows the debtor to keep certain assets even if he has filed for bankruptcy protection. These are known as *exempt assets.* An example is the *homestead exemption,* which allows a debtor to keep all or at least part of the equity in his home.

CASE 20.2 Kelley v. Cypress Financial Trading Co., L.P., 518 B.R. 373 (N.D. Tex. 2014)

FACT SUMMARY In 2009, Thomas Petters (Petters) was convicted of operating a $3.6 billon Ponzi scheme and sentenced to 50 years in jail. Using Petters Company Inc. (PCI) as a vehicle for accepting investors' money, Petters fraudulently convinced investors that he was purchasing electronic goods and selling them to large retailers. One of those investors was Cypress Financial Trading Company, L.P. (Cypress). During the Ponzi scheme, Cypress was paid more than $11.4 million. After the Ponzi scheme was uncovered, PCI filed for bankruptcy and attorney Douglas Kelley (Kelley) was appointed as bankruptcy trustee. In his attempt to recover as much as possible for the bankruptcy estate, Kelley sued Cypress and its individual partners, alleging that the funds paid to Cypress were fraudulent transfers. Cypress then filed a petition for bankruptcy, reporting that it had no assets. In response, Kelley filed a motion to have Cypress's bankruptcy petition dismissed on the basis that it was filed as a litigation delay tactic and therefore constituted a bad faith filing. The Bankruptcy Court denied the motion and Kelley appealed.

SYNOPSIS OF DECISION AND OPINION The U.S. District Court for the Northern District of Texas reversed the Bankruptcy Court's decision and ruled in favor of Kelley. The court noted that the twin pillars of bankruptcy are (1) the discharge of the debtor and (2) the satisfaction of valid claims against the estate. Because Cypress is a corporation, it may not obtain discharge from a Chapter 7 filing. Therefore, the first pillar of bankruptcy could not be achieved through this bankruptcy filing. Additionally, because Cypress has no assets for the trustee to liquidate to pay claims, it cannot achieve the second pillar of bankruptcy. The court reasoned that because neither pillar of bankruptcy could be achieved, none of the parties to this bankruptcy proceeding will be prejudiced by dismissal.

WORDS OF THE COURT: Bad Faith "A finding of bad faith can be cause for dismissal of a Chapter 7 proceeding. '[E]very bankruptcy statute since 1898 has incorporated literally, or by judicial interpretation, a standard of good faith for the commencement, prosecution, and confirmation of bankruptcy proceedings' . . . Resort[ing] to the protection of bankruptcy laws is not proper when 'there is no going concern to preserve, there are no employees to protect, and there is no hope of rehabilitation. . . .'

". . . No legitimate end will be served by keeping this case on the docket."

Case Questions

1. Why does Kelley believe that Cypress acted in bad faith?
2. Why did Kelley sue Cypress in the first place?
3. *Focus on Critical Thinking:* Isn't Cypress a victim here? If there was no indication that Cypress knew that Petters was running a Ponzi scheme, should it be held responsible for paying back any money it received? Is it fair to the other investors who lost all of their money in the scheme if Cypress is allowed to keep the money it received?

Meeting of Creditors and Administering of the Estate Within 30 days of the order of relief, the court calls for a meeting of creditors. The debtor (usually along with an attorney) must appear and submit to questioning by the creditors regarding the debtor's assets, financial affairs, and any attempt to conceal assets or income. After the meeting of creditors and election of the trustee, the trustee takes possession of the bankruptcy estate. The estate consists of the debtor's interests in real, personal, tangible, and intangible property—no matter where that property is located at the time the petition is filed. Property acquired *after* the petition does not become part of the bankruptcy estate. The trustee's responsibility is to collect all assets that are legally required to be liquidated for the benefit of the creditors. Trustees separate exempt and nonexempt property, recover any improper transfers of funds before or during the filing of the petition, sell or otherwise dispose of the property, and finally distribute the proceeds to creditors.

In the case where the debtor is an individual, not all property is subject to liquidation. The debtor is entitled to hold on to certain assets. These assets are known as *exempt assets*. Note that in a Chapter 7 bankruptcy of a business entity, there are no exempt assets. All assets must be liquidated. For individuals, some examples of exemptions are

- Up to $23,675 in equity in the debtor's primary residence (homestead exemption).
- Interest in a motor vehicle up to $3,775.
- Interest up to $600 for a particular item, household goods, and furnishings (aggregate total limited to $12,625).
- Interest in jewelry up to $1,600.
- Right to receive Social Security and certain welfare benefits; alimony and child support; education savings accounts; and certain pension benefits.
- Right to receive certain personal injury and other awards up to $23,675.

Legal Speak >))

Ponzi scheme
A Ponzi scheme, also called a *pyramid scheme,* is a fraudulent investment arrangement whereby the wrongdoer uses proceeds from new investors to pay existing investors higher-than-market returns, thereby creating the illusion that the profits generated are through legitimate methods.

Distribution and Discharge Once the trustee has administered the bankruptcy estate, the trustee then distributes the proceeds to creditors in an order of priority set by the Bankruptcy Code. Secured creditors are paid first and in full so long as the value of the collateral equals or exceeds the amount of their security interests. Unsecured creditors are paid from the remaining proceeds of the bankruptcy estate (if any). The order of payment for unsecured debtors is specified in the Bankruptcy Code. Table 20.1 lists the order of priority for unsecured creditors. Note that some claims also have dollar amount limits and, therefore, some unsecured creditors will be only partially paid for the debt.

Note that some debts are *nondischargeable.* These include

- Claims for federal, state, and local taxes (including fines and penalties related to the taxes) within two years of the petition filing.
- Debts incurred within 90 days of the petition for luxury goods of more than $650 from a single creditor or cash advances in excess of $925 obtained by a debtor using credit cards or revolving lines of credit within 70 days of the petition.
- Alimony, maintenance, and child support.
- Debts related to willful or malicious injury to a person or property.
- Debts related to court-ordered punitive damages against the debtor.
- Student loan debts, unless the debtor can prove "undue hardship."

TABLE 20.1 Order of Priority for Unsecured Creditors

1. Administration expenses—court costs and trustee and attorney fees.
2. Involuntary bankruptcy expenses incurred from date of filing to order of relief.
3. Unpaid wages and commissions earned within 90 days.
4. Unsecured claims for contributions for employee benefits within 180 days prior to filing.
5. Claims by farmers or fishermen.
6. Consumer deposits before the petition in connection with the purchase, lease, or rental of property.
7. Paternity, alimony, maintenance, and support debts.
8. Certain taxes and penalties due to government units, such as income and property taxes.
9. Claims of general creditors.

Chapter 11: Reorganization

Although located in the Bankruptcy Code, Chapter 11 differs greatly from a liquidation bankruptcy. Chapter 11 is best thought of as temporary protection for a corporation[7] from creditors while the corporation goes through a planning process to pay creditors and continue business without the need to terminate the entity completely. Chapter 11 is an acknowledgment that, as a matter of public policy, it is better to allow a business entity the opportunity to revise its business practices without the pressure of creditors who could halt the business operations and shut down the company—actions that could result in job costs and in some creditors not getting paid anything at all.

The fundamental proceedings of a Chapter 11 case are very similar to those of a Chapter 7 case, discussed earlier. A petition is filed either voluntarily or involuntarily, the automatic stay provision is triggered, and, if the petition is proper, the order of relief then sets the reorganization process in motion. A creditor committee is appointed, and the committee can consult with the debtor and/or the trustee to formulate the repayment plan.

The major difference, however, is that unlike the case in a Chapter 7 proceeding, the debtor generally continues to *operate the business* in a Chapter 11 case. The bankruptcy court may also opt to appoint a trustee to oversee the basic management of the business entity and report back to the court. This process, known as **debtor in possession (DIP)**, gives great power to the debtor to rehabilitate the business entity.

DIP Powers In many ways, the executives in a DIP business entity have an ideal situation from a workout perspective. While the stigma of Chapter 11 may cause difficulty in raising new capital, the Bankruptcy Code gives the DIP power to void prepetition preferential payments and to cancel or assume prepetition contracts (including leases, supplier contracts, and service contracts). The so-called **strong-arm clause** of the Bankruptcy Code allows the DIP to avoid any obligation or transfer of property that the debtor would otherwise be obligated to perform.

For larger companies, a DIP's power is most important in the context of *union contracts* known as collective bargaining agreements. The Bankruptcy Code sets forth standards and procedures under which a collective bargaining contract can be rejected if the debtor has first proposed necessary contractual modifications to the union and the union has rejected them without good cause.

Reorganization Plan The centerpiece of a Chapter 11 case is the **reorganization plan**. It is a plan, generally filed by the debtor, that articulates a specific strategy and financial plan for emerging from financial distress. The DIP has the exclusive right to draft the plan within 120 days after the Chapter 11 petition. The court must approve the plan before it becomes binding on the creditors. The plan must be submitted to the creditors for a vote and generally must designate "classes" of claims and interests (such as secured versus unsecured) and provide an adequate means for partial payment to creditors. Creditors are given the opportunity to accept or reject the plan, but if they reject the plan, the Bankruptcy Code allows the debtor to request that the court force the creditors to accept the plan (the wording in the code is known as the **cram-down provision**). So long as the plan is fair, equitable, and feasible from the court's perspective, the court will require creditors to accept the plan even over their objections. The plan is binding on all parties upon its approval by the court. It is important to note that a Chapter 11 filing may be converted during any stage (even before the plan is submitted) to a Chapter 7 filing. Most financially distressed business entities will attempt a recovery using the generous provisions of

---

[7]Individual debtors are also eligible for relief under Chapter 11, but such cases are rare.

Chapter 11 before deciding to liquidate. On the other hand, some companies do, in fact, turn around and emerge very strong from a Chapter 11 filing.

Chapter 13: Repayment Plan

Also known as the "wage-earner plan," the Chapter 13 form of bankruptcy is limited to *individuals* who have a substantial debt, and it *cannot* be used to cover any business debt (even as a sole proprietor). Chapter 13 allows debtors with a regular source of income to catch up on mortgage, car, tax, and domestic support payments; repay an adjusted debt to certain creditors over time (typically five years); and still keep all of their assets. It is less expensive and less complicated than reorganization or liquidation proceedings and can be accomplished only by filing a voluntary bankruptcy petition. Payments are typically made to the bankruptcy trustee, who distributes them to creditors. Unsecured creditors frequently are paid less than they are owed, depending on the circumstances of the case.

The Fraud Exception

The Bankruptcy Code was crafted to strike a balance between providing debtors with a fresh start by discharging debts while preventing abuses of the system by debtors. To accomplish this balance, the Code exempts from discharge any money obtained through debt "for money . . . to the extent obtained by . . . false pretenses, a false representation, or actual fraud. . . ."[8]

In Case 20.3, a federal appellate court analyzes the scope of the fraud exception.

CASE 20.3 Sauer Inc. v. Lawson (*In re* Lawson), 791 F.3d 214 (1st Cir. 2015)

FACT SUMMARY Sauer, Inc. (Sauer), sued James Lawson (James) in state court to recover damages related to previous business transactions between the parties and won a judgment against James for $168,351. Just before the judgment was entered, James's daughter, Carrie Lawson (Ms. Lawson) had formed a shell entity, Commercial Construction M & C, LLC (Commercial Construction). Once the judgment was entered against James by the court, he transferred $100,150 to Commercial Construction, allegedly to impede Sauer's collection. Commercial Construction is owned by Ms. Lawson but controlled by James. Ms. Lawson then transferred $80,000 of the $100,150 from Commercial Construction to herself from February 2010 through early 2011. In March 2011, James filed for bankruptcy. In 2013, Sauer successfully sued Ms. Lawson in a state court and obtained a judgment against Commercial Construction and Ms. Lawson after the court ruled that the transfers from James and Ms. Lawson were invalid under Rhode Island's fraud recovery statute. Ms. Lawson filed a petition for bankruptcy the same month that the state court issued the judgment against her.

Sauer initiated an adversary proceeding with the bankruptcy court objecting to any discharge of the Sauer debt due to the fraud provisions of the Bankruptcy Code related to money "obtained by . . . actual fraud." The bankruptcy court dismissed Sauer's adversary proceeding, reasoning that misrepresentation is a required element of actual fraud and that there was no allegation that Ms. Lawson had made a misrepresentation in the course of the transfers. Sauer appealed, arguing that because Ms. Lawson knowingly received the fraudulent transfer and acted in a willful and malicious manner toward Sauer, her acceptance of the fraudulent conveyance constituted actual fraud.

(continued)

---

[8] 11 U.S.C. § 523(a)(2)(A).

SYNOPSIS OF DECISION AND OPINION The Court of Appeals for the First Circuit reversed the decision of the bankruptcy court and ruled in favor of Sauer. The court ruled that the bankruptcy court erred in concluding that a misrepresentation by a debtor to a creditor is an essential element of establishing a basis for the nondischarge of a debt under the fraud exception to the Bankruptcy Code. It held that fraud is not limited to misrepresentations and misleading omissions. Rather, actual fraud, by definition, consists of any deceit, artifice, trick, or design involving direct and active operation of the mind, used to circumvent and cheat another. In this case, Ms. Lawson's actions were intended to circumvent the court's judgments and cheat Sauer.

WORDS OF THE COURT: Broad Definition of Fraud "We . . . hold that 'actual fraud' under [the Bankruptcy Code] is not limited to fraud effected by misrepresentation. Rather, we hold that 'actual fraud' includes fraudulent conveyances that are 'intended . . . to hinder [the relevant] creditors.' . . . That is, the debtor-transferee must herself be 'guilty of intent to defraud' and not merely be the passive recipient of a fraudulent conveyance. Such intent may be inferred from her acceptance of a transfer that she knew was made with the purpose of hindering the transferor's creditor(s). . . . Our reading is confirmed by the structure of the text and the legislative history. [Congress amended the Bankruptcy Code so that the fraud] provision now 'explicitly lists both "actual fraud" and "false representations" as grounds for denying a discharge.'"

Case Questions

1. Why did the trial court dismiss Sauer's adversary proceeding that objected to the discharge of Ms. Lawson's debt?
2. How did the legislative history of the Bankruptcy Code affect the court's decision?
3. *Focus on Critical Thinking:* Could there be any legitimate and ethical reason for the transfers? Why or why not? If the appellate court had agreed with the trial court that fraud cannot exist with misrepresentation, what ethical considerations might be triggered?

LO 20-8

Explain the impact of the Bankruptcy Abuse Prevention and Consumer Protection Act on creditors and debtors.

BANKRUPTCY ABUSE PREVENTION AND CONSUMER PROTECTION ACT

In 2005, Congress passed legislation intended to curb perceived abuses of statutory bankruptcy protection by enacting the Bankruptcy Abuse Prevention and Consumer Protection Act (BAPCPA).[9] While the congressional sponsors of the bill touted its public policy benefits of making the consuming public more responsible with debt, the law was widely criticized by bankruptcy attorneys and judges as unnecessarily burdening the debtor, the trustee, and the court with more paperwork and expenses while not curbing abuse. The law overhauled the Bankruptcy Code for the first time since 1994 and, fundamentally, made it more difficult for debtors to seek protection under Chapter 7. The major provisions of the law are (1) a *means test* for the debtor, (2) proof of the debtor's income, (3) higher priority for alimony and support payments by the debtor, and (4) credit counseling for the debtor.

Means Test

The most important change was to increase the statutory requirements for eligibility under Chapter 7 straight liquidation by adding a "means test" that is determined by comparing the applicant's current monthly income to the median income for the applicant's state. If the applicant's income is more than the median, the applicant is not eligible for Chapter 7. Thus, a substantial number of bankruptcy applicants who previously would have been eligible for a discharge of substantially all debts must now repay them under a Chapter 13 filing.

---

[9] Pub. L. No. 109-8, 119 Stat. 23 (2005).

For example, the state of Florida's annual median family income for a family of one and a family of three is $43,136 and $57,080, respectively. Therefore, if the debtor applies for a Chapter 7 bankruptcy seeking to discharge debts, but her income is above the median, the petition will be denied and the debtor will have only Chapter 13 (debt repayment) as an option.

In Case 20.4, the U.S. Supreme Court analyzes the BAPCPA's provisions related to the means test.

CASE 20.4 Ransom v. FIA Card Services, 562 U.S. 61 (2011)

FACT SUMMARY Ransom filed for Chapter 13 bankruptcy relief in 2006. His filings included $82,500 worth of unsecured credit card debt owed to FIA Card Services. In his repayment plan, Ransom proposed repayment of 25 percent of his outstanding debt to FIA over a five-year period. Despite the fact that he owned his car outright (no debt), Ransom listed his reasonably necessary living expenses and claimed a standard amount provided for in the Bankruptcy Code for a car: $471 per month and $210.55 for maintenance costs. FIA objected to the plan based on the fact that Ransom owned his car outright and was not required to make payments. Allowing the car deduction, FIA argued, amounted to allowing Ransom to avoid paying at least $28,000 of his FIA debt. The bankruptcy court denied confirmation of Ransom's plan, and the appellate court affirmed the decision.

SYNOPSIS OF DECISION AND OPINION The U.S. Supreme Court ruled in favor of FIA and held that Ransom could not take the car-ownership deduction. The Court ruled that the Bankruptcy Abuse Prevention and Consumer Protection Act of 2005 required courts to apply a *means test* to help ensure that debtors who can pay back their creditors actually do so with the help of the Bankruptcy Code. The means test depends on accurate reporting of reasonably necessary living expenses. Because Ransom had no actual loan or lease payment due, he was not entitled to claim a car-ownership deduction. The Court rejected Ransom's argument that the language in the statute regarding applicability of the car-ownership deduction was ambiguous. The Court also explained that Ransom was entitled to "ownership costs" but that the car-ownership deduction was limited to debtors who were required to make loan or lease payments for their car.

WORDS OF THE COURT: Purpose of the Means Test "Ransom next contends that denying the ownership allowance to debtors in his position 'sends entirely the wrong message, namely, that it is advantageous to be deeply in debt on motor vehicle loans, rather than to pay them off.' But the choice here is not between thrifty savers and profligate borrowers, as Ransom would have it. Money is fungible: The $14,000 that Ransom spent to purchase his Camry outright was money he did not devote to paying down his credit card debt, and Congress did not express a preference for one use of these funds over the other. Further, Ransom's argument mistakes what the deductions in the means test are meant to accomplish. Rather than effecting any broad federal policy as to saving or borrowing, the deductions serve merely to ensure that debtors in bankruptcy can afford essential items. The car-ownership allowance thus safeguards a debtor's ability to retain a car throughout the plan period. If the debtor already owns a car outright, he has no need for this protection."

Case Questions

1. Does the Court's decision encourage responsible actions by the debtor? Does this encourage debtors to take on new debt instead of driving an old car, as Ransom suggested?
2. How did the Bankruptcy Abuse Prevention and Consumer Protection Act of 2005 affect this case?
3. *Focus on Critical Thinking:* Soon after the BAPCPA was enacted, one bankruptcy court judge wrote that "the legislation's adoption in its title of the words 'consumer protection' is the grossest of misnomers."[10] What do you suppose the judge meant by that? Does the law "protect consumers" as its name implies? Who does it protect?

---

[10]*In re* Sosa, 336 B.R. 113 (Bankr. W.D. Tex. 2005).

Proof of Income

Debtors must provide the bankruptcy trustee copies of recent tax returns and pay stubs or other income verification on a timely basis. If the debtor has failed to file a tax return for the previous year, she may be required to file a return as a condition of bankruptcy approval.

Alimony and Support

The BAPCPA gives alimony and support obligations a higher priority than certain other creditors.

Credit Counseling

Prior to filing for bankruptcy, the debtor must complete a short (approximately one-hour) credit-counseling seminar and must also complete a longer course, known as Credit Education, prior to actually receiving a discharge of debts.

Table 20.2 is a summary and comparison of various bankruptcy options.

TABLE 20.2 Bankruptcy Options

Chapter 7 (Liquidation) Individuals and Businesses	Chapter 11 (Reorganization) Individuals and Businesses	Chapter 13 (Consumer Debt Adjustment) Individuals Only
1. Petition	1. Petition	1. Petition
2. Automatic stay	2. Automatic stay	2. Automatic stay
3. Order of relief or dismissal (apply means test)	3. Debtor in possession	3. Most debts paid back over five years
4. Creditor committee	4. File plan	4. Some unsecured debts reduced; some unsecured debts discharged
5. Trustee	5. Creditors approve a "cram down"	
6. Administration of bankruptcy estate	6. Emerge from Chapter 11 or convert to Chapter 7	
7. Distribution		
8. Discharge		

CONCEPT SUMMARY *Bankruptcy and Alternatives*

- Upon a filing for bankruptcy, in most cases a trustee is appointed by the bankruptcy court to protect the remaining bankruptcy assets, known as the estate.
- The trustee has the legal power to void fraudulent or preferential transfers that the debtor made to certain creditors before filing bankruptcy.
- Once a business becomes insolvent, it can either file for bankruptcy, dissolve itself out of existence, or, if it wants to stay in business, work out terms to pay creditors.
- Either as part of a workout plan or as a stand-alone transaction, another alternative to a bankruptcy filing is an assignment for the benefit of creditors (sometimes called simply an ABC). An ABC is a form of liquidation that is an alternative to bankruptcy and is provided either by state statute, state common law, or a combination of both.

- A business debtor in a Chapter 7 bankruptcy has its assets liquidated and its debts discharged by the court.
- To avoid lost jobs and unpaid creditors, some companies enter Chapter 11, wherein a debtor in possession (DIP) tries to rehabilitate the company and partially compensate creditors under a reorganization plan.
- In a Chapter 13 bankruptcy, an individual can develop a repayment plan in order to use his income to slowly pay back debts without having to liquidate assets.

KEY TERMS

Unsecured debt p. 653   Credit that is not collateralized.

Secured creditor p. 653   A creditor that extends credit based on collateral pledged by the borrower.

Secured party p. 654   The creditor in a secured transaction.

Debtor p. 654   The borrower in a secured transaction.

Perfecting p. 654   Procedure by which the secured party establishes priority in the collateral over other creditors, as provided by Article 9 of the Uniform Commercial Code.

Security interest p. 654   The rights of the secured party in a transaction.

Mortgage p. 655   A written document that specifies the parties and the real estate being used to collateralize a loan and is filed with a state and/or local government agency.

Mortgagee p. 655   The creditor in a transaction in which real estate is being used to collateralize a loan.

Mortgagor p. 655   The borrower in a transaction in which real estate is being used to collateralize a loan.

Promissory note p. 655   A contract in which the borrower promises to pay back the creditor at a certain rate of interest over a specified period of years.

Mortgage foreclosure p. 655   A remedy against a debtor in which a creditor declares the loan in default and takes title and possession of the collateralized real estate in hopes of selling the property to pay off the debt owed.

Surety p. 655   A third party that agrees to be primarily liable to pay a loan.

Guarantor p. 655   A third party that agrees to be liable to pay a loan only if the debtor actually defaults.

Personal guaranty p. 656   In a business loan, a pledge given by the principals of a business to repay the loan with their personal assets if the assets of the business are insufficient to do so in the event of a default by the business entity debtor; serves as a safeguard for creditors.

Insolvent p. 657   Condition in which a business venture no longer has adequate assets to maintain its operations and can no longer pay its bills as they become due in the usual course of trade and business.

Workout p. 658   The process in which a debtor meets a loan commitment by satisfying altered repayment terms; intended to turn around a business when the principals wish to continue operations and the business is underperforming and is in poor financial condition.

Assignment for the benefit of creditors p. 658   A form of liquidation that is an alternative to bankruptcy and is provided either by state statute, state common law, or a combination of both.

Automatic stay p. 661   A legal prohibition whereby creditors may neither initiate nor continue any debt collection action against the debtor or her property.

Bankruptcy trustee p. 661   An individual, often an attorney highly skilled in bankruptcy law, appointed in Chapter 7 or Chapter 13 cases and charged with the duty of taking control of the bankruptcy estate and reducing it to cash for distribution, preserving the interests of both the debtor and the creditors.

Bankruptcy estate p. 661   The debtor's available assets in a bankruptcy proceeding.

Voidable transfers p. 661   In bankruptcy proceedings, certain transfers that are considered an unfair advantage of one creditor over another.

Voluntary bankruptcy petition p. 663   A petition filed in the bankruptcy court by the debtor that includes the names of creditors, a list of debts, and a list of the debtor's assets, income, and expenses.

Involuntary bankruptcy petition p. 663   A petition filed in the bankruptcy court against a debtor by a group of three or more creditors with an unsecured aggregate claim of at least $15,775 who claim that the debtor is failing to pay the debt as it comes due.

Debtor in possession (DIP) p. 666 A Chapter 11 bankruptcy process in which the debtor generally remains in control of assets and business operations in an attempt to rehabilitate the business entity.

Strong-arm clause p. 666 Provision of the Bankruptcy Code that allows the debtor in possession to avoid any obligation or transfer of property that the debtor would otherwise be obligated to perform.

Reorganization plan p. 666 A plan, generally filed by the debtor, that articulates a specific strategy and financial plan for emerging from financial distress; serves as the keystone of a Chapter 11 case.

Cram-down provision p. 666 A term used in reference to the Chapter 11 provision that allows the debtor to request that the court force the creditors to accept a plan that is fair, equitable, and feasible.

CHAPTER REVIEW QUESTIONS

1. When a borrower pledges certain properties of value as a guarantee that she will pay the debt back, the creditor is called a _____ party.
   a. Lender
   b. Secured
   c. Collateral
   d. Indebted

2. NewCo is a start-up venture applying for a bank loan. Because NewCo has no assets, the bank asks the owners of NewCo to pay back the loan from personal assets only in the event that NewCo defaults. Which of the following best describes the role of the owners in this loan?
   a. Creditors
   b. Debtors
   c. Sureties
   d. Guarantors

3. The primary protection for a debtor who files for bankruptcy, which immediately halts any collection efforts by creditors, is called _____.
   a. Assignment for benefit of creditors
   b. Workout
   c. Order for relief
   d. Automatic stay

4. Donald is the sole shareholder of Donald Corporation. The week before the corporation files for bankruptcy, Donald pays a loan back to his father that he used to help start the business last year. Although the loan was not due for another year, Donald paid off the balance entirely. Which of the following is true?
   a. Paying back the loan was a preferential transfer.
   b. Paying back the loan was a portable transfer.
   c. Paying back the loan was in the ordinary course of business.
   d. Both (a) and (b) are correct.

5. Which form of bankruptcy allows the business debtor to continue its operations as a debtor in possession?
   a. Chapter 7
   b. Chapter 11
   c. Chapter 13
   d. Chapter 15

Answers and explanations are provided at the end of this chapter.

THEORY TO PRACTICE

Yankee Export Company (YEC) is a purveyor of U.S. products for several European food market chains. YEC's annual revenue is approximately $10 million, and the company employs approximately 20 people, including YEC's only shareholders, directors, and officers: Moss and Whippany. Moss is the day-to-day manager of the venture, while Whippany is mostly an investor with no management duties other than giving consultation on business matters when asked by Moss. For several years, the venture was profitable, but due to a rapid increase in the value of the U.S. dollar against European currencies, YEC began to have cash flow problems. Its products were becoming more expensive for its European customers, and orders slowly dropped over a period of a year. When it appeared that YEC would be unable to generate enough cash to cover monthly expenses, Moss called for a meeting with Whippany and with YEC's accountants. The parties agreed that the rise of the dollar had a negative impact on all U.S. exports and that YEC was at the beginning of a financial challenge. The company's assets were approximately $200,000. The current major debts are set out in the YEC Creditor Table below.

1. Identify the probable category of each creditor. What are the rights of each creditor in the event that YEC defaults on its obligation to that particular creditor?
2. If Moss and Whippany believe the financial crisis is temporary, what are their best nonstatutory options to continue the business if it becomes insolvent? What statutory option(s) do they have?
3. If Moss and Whippany do not believe the financial crisis is recoverable, what nonstatutory and statutory options does YEC have? What are the advantages and drawbacks of each option? If the building lease were not personally guaranteed by Moss and Whippany, how would this fact change your analysis?
4. Which creditors are bound by the provisions of UCC Article 9?
5. Does the fact that YEC has 20 employees add any ethical obligations that should be considered in Moss and Whippany's decision making concerning the future of the company?
6. Suppose that the landlord begins to start eviction proceedings due to YEC's payment default. How could YEC stop the eviction?
7. If YEC files for Chapter 7, what debts are potentially dischargeable? Assuming any assets are left, in what order would the creditors be paid?

YEC Creditor Table

Creditor	Reason	Amount
IRS	Back taxes	$35,000
Ag Industries	U.S. trade creditor from which YEC buys its inventory	$20,000 balance secured with a promissory note and perfected security interest in inventory
Landlord	Five years left on the office building lease	$50,000 per year (backed by personal guaranties of Moss and Whippany)
Office Leasing Company	Two years left on equipment lease	$500 per month
Company credit card	Office supplies and miscellaneous items	$8,000 balance
Whippany	Whippany gave YEC a $15,000 personal loan evidenced only by a promissory note	$11,000 balance payable on a monthly basis for 36 more months at 8% interest

LEGAL STRATEGY 101

How Broke Is the Rapper 50 Cent?

Sometimes, debtors use bankruptcy laws strategically, a phenomenon known as "strategic bankruptcy."[11] In summary, a strategic bankruptcy occurs when an otherwise solvent company makes use of the bankruptcy laws for some specific business purpose. Consider, for example, the artist known as 50 Cent, whose legal name is Curtis James Jackson III and who filed for bankruptcy protection a few days after a jury ordered him to pay a private plaintiff $5 million in a "revenge porn" lawsuit.

In fact, 50 Cent is one of the most successful recording artists in the music industry and a successful

---
[11] *See, generally,* Kevin J. Delaney, *Strategic Bankruptcy* (University of California Press 1998).

50 Cent. Paul Archuleta/Getty Images

entrepreneur in his own right. He reportedly made as much as $100 million from his investment in Vitaminwater after it was purchased by Coca-Cola, has produced many successful music records, and has appeared in nearly two dozen films.[12] By all accounts, 50 Cent is not "broke," so why did he file for bankruptcy?

One clue is the type of bankruptcy the rapper 50 Cent filed for. Specifically, he filed for a Chapter 11 bankruptcy, a type of bankruptcy filing usually reserved for corporations that need to be restructured while they remain open for business. Firms and individuals looking to reorganize their debts might use Chapter 11 to buy more time to pay their debts and give them a chance to come up with a payment plan, an option such firms and individuals might not have without Chapter 11.

In other words, 50 Cent's Chapter 11 filing might be a strategic effort to stay in control of his assets. At the same time, 50 Cent's bankruptcy filing may make it more difficult for the plaintiff in the revenge porn lawsuit to collect the $5 million judgment against 50 Cent because the plaintiff in that lawsuit will now be one of many creditors trying to get their share of his fortune. According to Hunter Shkolnik, the plaintiff's lawyer in the revenge porn lawsuit, "We think this [50 Cent's filing for Chapter 11] is a failed attempt to avoid paying this woman who has been hurt so badly by his actions."

But filing for Chapter 11 bankruptcy also has a potential downside for 50 Cent. By filing for bankruptcy, 50 Cent will have to incur substantial additional legal fees, and he could potentially have his assets and personal finances scrutinized in court.[13] A bankruptcy judge will have the authority to review his spending, his earnings, and his estate.

Ultimately, whether these additional legal costs and public scrutiny are worth the strategic benefits is a close call. What do you think?

CRITICAL THINKING QUESTIONS

1. Is the decision to engage in a "strategic bankruptcy" an ethical one? Is it ever unethical to exercise a legal right?
2. Is there a principled way of distinguishing between strategic and nonstrategic bankruptcies?

---

[12] *See, e.g.,* Andrea Peterson, *50 Cent Filed for Bankruptcy Days after Losing a Revenge Porn Lawsuit,* Wash. Post, July 14, 2015.

[13] *See* Katy Stech, *50 Cent Bankruptcy: By the Numbers,"* Wall St. J., Aug. 4, 2015.

MANAGER'S CHALLENGE

Sometimes managers and owners are one and the same, and playing both roles can be a difficult line to walk. Relationships between parties in a business entity are governed by legal duties (these duties were discussed in Unit Four) owed to one another. Yet the manager/owner must also be sure to be attuned to the other legal requirements and the relationships between the company and third-party creditors or vendors.

Suppose that, in the Theory to Practice problem, Moss and Whippany decide to try to maintain YEC's operations for one more month and then make a final decision on whether or not to seek bankruptcy. Whippany sends an e-mail to Moss requesting that Moss authorize immediately YEC's full repayment of Whippany's personal loan. Draft a two paragraph e-mail that Moss could send to Whippany that analyzes (1) the legal risks and consequences of honoring Whippany's request, (2) the potential harm to relationships with other creditors, and (3) the ethical implications of paying back the loan early.

See Connect for Manager's Challenge sample answers.

CASE SUMMARY 20.1 *In re* Fehrs, 391 B.R. 53 (Bankr. D. Idaho, 2008)

VOIDABLE TRANSFERS

In 2002, Fehrs met and began living with her boyfriend, Murrietta. They also lived with her teenage son from a former marriage, Jae. Fehrs bought a housing lot at 464 Second Street and another at 117 Terrill Loop, both in the city of Mullan, Idaho. Fehrs and Murrietta contracted with Peter Axtman to build them a house at 464 Second Street. As construction began, problems arose. Soon Murrietta and Fehrs broke up, and Axtman filed a lawsuit against Fehrs for what he was owed for his services. Two months after the suit was filed, Fehrs transferred her property at 117 Terrill Loop to her son Jae in exchange for $1. Fehrs said she made the transfer because Jae was always drinking and partying with friends at 117 Terrill Loop and she did not want to be liable if anything should happen. Two months later Fehrs filed for bankruptcy.

CASE QUESTIONS

1. Why do you think Fehrs sold the lot to her son?
2. What can the trustee do to make sure Axtman gets all he is owed?

CASE SUMMARY 20.2 Ellison v. Comm'r of Internal Revenue Service, 385 B.R. 158 (S.D. W. Va. 2008)

AUTOMATIC STAY

Ellison ran a small company, and both he and his company filed for bankruptcy in 1994. The court issued an automatic stay to creditors. A month later, the IRS contacted Ellison about unpaid taxes from 1993. Although Ellison consented to the tax being assessed, the IRS continued to pursue payment of the back taxes even after the bankruptcy petition was filed. Ellison filed suit against the IRS for the violation of her automatic stay rights under the Bankruptcy Code.

CASE QUESTIONS

1. Will Ellison not have to pay these taxes, or can they be discharged?
2. Does the IRS have any defense to pursuing the debt during the automatic stay period?
3. If Ellison wins, what does that say about the power of an automatic stay?

CASE SUMMARY 20.3 *In re* Fedderson, 270 B.R. 733 (Bankr. N.D. Iowa 2001)

NONDISCHARGEABLE DEBTS

Fedderson ran Big Al's restaurant, which was doing poorly. In a last-ditch effort to make more money, he bought a $2,000 ice cream machine for Big Al's on his personal credit card. Sixty days later, Fedderson filed for bankruptcy. The credit card company argued that the ice cream machine debt should not be discharged because it is a luxury good that was bought too close to the bankruptcy petition.

CASE QUESTIONS

1. Should the ice cream machine debt be discharged?
2. Should it matter to the court that Fedderson should have known that he would be insolvent in two months and that trying to stop financial catastrophe with an ice cream machine was foolish?

CASE SUMMARY 20.4 *In re* Northwest Airlines Corp., 346 B.R. 333 (Bankr. S.D.N.Y. 2006)

CHAPTER 11 AND COLLECTIVE BARGAINING AGREEMENTS

In October, Northwest Airlines declared Chapter 11 bankruptcy and sought to renegotiate a collective bargaining agreement with the flight attendants' union. The contract would need to be changed for Northwest to reorganize and try to save the company. After several months of negotiations, the union finally rejected a March 1 proposal. Northwest's DIP asked the court to unilaterally enforce the terms of the rejected agreement because the union had failed to agree to reasonable terms.

CASE QUESTIONS

1. What is the name of the power that Northwest is asking the court to exercise?
2. What must the court find about the union's rejection to permit unilateral enforcement?
3. Should it matter that Northwest easily reached agreements with both the pilots' and mechanics' unions?

CASE SUMMARY 20.5 *In re* Richie, 353 B.R. 569 (Bankr. E.D. Wis. 2006)

MEANS TEST

When Charmaine Richie filed for Chapter 7 bankruptcy, she had been making a living through odd jobs over the past year yielding an income of $22,608. The median income is $37,873 for her home state of Wisconsin. Just prior to her bankruptcy petition filing, Richie completed a master's degree in outdoor therapeutic recreation administration, which qualified her to work as a therapist for those with disabilities in a camp or outdoor clinical setting. A job in this field would likely have brought Richie well above the median income and disqualified her for protection under a Chapter 7 bankruptcy. Additionally, Richie had been looking for jobs in her field but only in the Racine-Kenosha area of Wisconsin, where there were very few opportunities. She was qualified to work at many other jobs that would have brought her above the median, but she wanted employment only in her chosen field and in her home geographic area.

After her petition was filed, the bankruptcy trustee requested the court to reject the Chapter 7 petition and convert the case to a Chapter 13 petition, whereby Richie would have to pay all or much of her debt. The trustee alleged that Richie was abusing the Chapter 7 bankruptcy means test because she was *capable* of earning more money but did not. Moreover, Richie filed bankruptcy immediately after graduate school, when her future earning potential was relatively high. Richie argued that moving elsewhere to work would be a burden and having a different full-time job would hurt her future prospects for getting a job in her chosen field.

CASE QUESTIONS

1. Should Richie be forced to relocate or work in another field in order to use bankruptcy laws?
2. Richie lacks the ability to pay because she has not engaged in a broad employment search, does not wish to work outside her chosen field, and does not wish to work within her chosen field outside her geographic area. Should her creditors bear the burden of her choices?

CASE SUMMARY 20.6 *In re* Jones, 392 B.R. 116 (E.D. Pa. 2008)

UNDUE HARDSHIP

Jones earned a college degree in history with a minor in economics in the 1980s. Although Jones was supposed to enter the U.S. Army upon graduation, he gained admission to law school and earned his law degree. However, Jones could not pass the bar examination after several attempts. He spent the next 14 years in various positions including the army, substitute teaching, writing, and social work. Jones then returned to school to get a Master of Education degree in the teaching of visual arts. Jones continued his education with yet another Master's Degree in Divinity in 2005. He borrowed heavily for his education and, at the time of the bankruptcy petition, had defaulted on 18 student loans worth $140,000 of debt. Note that Jones's undergraduate and law school debts were discharged in a previous bankruptcy hearing. Jones argued that the debt was so high that to pay the debt would cause "undue hardship," and he asked the court to discharge the loan. His creditor maintained that Jones did not meet the undue hardship standard.

CASE QUESTIONS

1. Who prevails and why?
2. If Jones had been unable to work due to illness or injury, would that be sufficient to meet the undue-hardship standard set out by the court?
3. Note that one court did not find undue hardship enough to discharge student loans for a "46-year-old part-time legal secretary, raising her 14-year-old child and living with her sister, and who had psychiatric problems and had twice attempted suicide" [*In re* Brightful, 267 F.3d 324 (3d Cir. 2001)]. Why would Congress and the courts be reluctant to allow the discharge of student loans without meeting this difficult test?

 Self-Check ANSWERS Creditor Status

1. ExtremeCo has a perfected (by filing) security interest in Retailer's inventory.
2. Office Galaxy is an unsecured creditor.
3. BigBank is a secured creditor as mortgagee, with WidgetCo as mortgagor.
4. BigBank is an unsecured creditor of WidgetCo, *but* the debt is collateralized through personal guaranties in the event of default.

CHAPTER REVIEW QUESTIONS: Answers and Explanations

1. **b.** Under Article 9 of the UCC, pledging property of value creates a secured party relationship. Answer choice (a) is incorrect because not all creditors are lenders. Answer (c) is incorrect because collateral is another term for pledged assets. Answer (d) is wrong because a creditor is not the indebted party.

2. **d.** Because the owners are only secondarily liable, they are guarantors. Answer choice (c) is wrong because they are not primarily liable (this is the primary difference between guarantors and insurance). Answer choice (a) is wrong because the bank is the creditor. Answer (b) is wrong because NewCo is the debtor.

3. **d.** Filing a petition triggers an automatic stay, which gives protection to the debtor from the debt collection actions of creditors until the petition is reviewed. Answers (a) and (b) are incorrect because they are not related to a bankruptcy filing. Answer (c) is incorrect because the order for relief follows the automatic stay and is not immediate.

4. **a.** Paying the loan back is a classic preferential transfer because it occurs within 90 days before the bankruptcy filing and because the creditor (Donald's father) is an insider. Because the loan is preferential, it is also voidable. Answer choice (c) is incorrect because the payment is not in the ordinary course of business because the loan was paid back early. Answer choices (b) and (d) are incorrect because portable transfers do not exist in the Bankruptcy Code.

5. **b.** Chapter 11 allows the business to continue to operate with bankruptcy protection from creditors as the debtor reorganizes. Answer choice (a) is incorrect because Chapter 7 involves liquidation. Answer (c) is wrong because Chapter 13 is limited to individuals. Answer (d) is incorrect because Chapter 15 does not exist as a filing option in the Bankruptcy Code.

CHAPTER 21

Warranties and Consumer Protection Law

©philsajonesen/Getty Images

Learning Objectives

After studying this chapter, students who have mastered the material will be able to:

21-1 Define and give an example of a warranty.

21-2 Distinguish between express warranties and implied warranties, explain the protections afforded by each type of warranty, and articulate the standards for disclaiming a warranty.

21-3 Explain the roles of the Federal Trade Commission and the Consumer Financial Protection Bureau in terms of various statutory consumer protections.

21-4 Articulate the standards used to define false advertising and other deceptive practices and identify specific consumer protection laws applied to bulk e-mail.

21-5 Name and explain the federal statutory protections afforded to consumers for faulty or unsafe products and for food and drug safety.

21-6 Identify the parties in a credit transaction and understand the role of federal statutory laws in consumer credit transactions.

21-7 List the various components of the Truth in Lending Act and give specific examples of regulatory requirements.

21-8 Explain the protections afforded to consumers by federal statutes regulating the collection of consumer debt.

Since the height of the American industrial revolution, the body of law that protects consumers in transactions with merchants and creditors has grown dramatically. In the modern age, consumers are protected primarily through state statutes that create a **warranty** for a sale of goods transaction as well as a body of federal and state statutory law and administrative regulations commonly known as **consumer law**. These protections have become progressively more important in their impact on business owners and managers. Individuals and businesses are subject to regulation at the federal, state, and local levels in a wide variety of consumer transactions. In this chapter, we discuss how the law protects consumers in three areas

- Warranties for product quality and functionality.
- Unfair and deceptive trade practices.
- Credit transactions and consumer debt collection.

WARRANTIES

Consumers have certain statutory protections related to the quality and functionality of products sold by merchants. These protections are derived primarily from *products liability* statutes and *commercial law* statutes, which provide for *warranty* protection. Some of these statutes overlap with other consumer protection laws. Products liability statutes often operate in tandem with laws related to negligence; thus, products liability law is discussed in detail in Chapter 9, "Torts and Products Liability."

A warranty is a seller's (or lessor's) promise to a consumer concerning the quality and/or functionality of a product. Warranties are recognized as legally enforceable promises under state statutory laws that are based on Article 2 of the Uniform Commercial Code (UCC). Recall that in Chapter 8, "Contracts for the Sale of Goods," Article 2 was covered in the context of formation and performance of *sales contracts*. This chapter focuses on the *warranty provisions* of Article 2 that protect consumers. When the seller makes a representation of *fact* about a product, this is known as an **express warranty**. If the seller has not made a specific representation about the product, the buyer may still be protected by a UCC-imposed **implied warranty**.

LO 21-1
Define and give an example of a warranty.

Express Warranty

In some cases a seller expressly represents that the goods have certain *qualities* or a certain level of *efficiency*. If the goods turn out not to have these qualities, the buyer may sue for a breach of the express warranty. As a practical matter, many of these seller representations are made through advertising. In one famous case,[1] the supreme court in the state of Washington held that a car manufacturer breached an express warranty when it advertised in its brochures that the car had "shatterproof glass" that would not fly or shatter even upon the "hardest impact." After a small pebble struck the windshield and resulted in shattered glass and injuries to the driver, the court ruled in favor of the injured driver, stating that the buyer had *reasonably relied* on those representations and had no reason to suspect they were false.

Because many express warranties arise in the context of advertising, the UCC makes a distinction between factual promises and "puffery." Puffery is a *nonfactual* statement commonly used in advertising with such claims as "This car gets great gas mileage" or "Sweater made from finest wool." Of course, neither of these statements is fact-based because there is no method to verify words such as "great" or "finest." Thus, neither of these statements constitutes an express warranty. However, if the statements are changed slightly to "This car gets 35 miles per gallon when driven on the highway" or "Sweater is 100 percent Irish wool," then these statements may be considered factual promises to the buyer, thus creating an express warranty from the seller.

LO 21-2
Distinguish between express warranties and implied warranties, explain the protections afforded by each type of warranty, and articulate the standards for disclaiming a warranty.

Implied Warranties

Even in cases where the seller makes no express promise about the goods, the UCC imposes several *implied warranties*. Implied warranties apply only in specific circumstances and have certain limits as to the protections they offer buyers.

Merchantability The implied warranty of merchantability[2] applies to every sale of a product from a *merchant* to a buyer (note that the buyer may or may not be a merchant) and requires the seller to warrant that the product is fit for its ordinary use. For purposes of the

---

[1] *Baxter v. Ford Motor Co.*, 12 P.2d 409 (Wash. 1932).
[2] UCC § 2-314(2).

✓ Self-Check Express Warranty

Has an express warranty been created?

1. Randall has been the victim of several robberies in his store. He purchases a chemical weapon spray called Repel that is advertised to "instantly stop attackers" and "incapacitate groups of people instantly." Randall is robbed and attempts to use Repel to stop the crime, but the robber is not stopped. Rather, he becomes enraged and assaults Randall during the robbery.
2. Juliet sees a newspaper advertisement by a car manufacturer: "The sexiest convertible on the market."
3. Benjamin buys a watch that bears this sticker on the packaging: "100 percent waterproof."
4. Johnson watches a TV ad for running shoes that shows scenes of a jogger in a park and then switches the scene to the same runner on a snow-covered hiking trail. The catchphrase "A sneaker for all seasons" flashes on the screen. No mention is made of the shoes' suitability for use on a particular surface. Johnson purchases the shoes, and when he runs on a snowy trail, they fall apart and Johnson suffers foot injuries as a result.

Answers to this Self-Check are provided at the end of the chapter.

UCC, a merchant is one who is regularly engaged in the sale of that product. Thus, if you purchase a new or used lawn mower from your neighbor (an accountant), no implied warranty exists. Merchants must also conform to the industry safety standards in packaging and labeling the goods in order for the goods to qualify as merchantable. This UCC requirement also applies to food and drink to be consumed either on the merchant's premises or somewhere else.

Fitness for a Particular Purpose

An implied warranty also arises when a seller promises that the product is fit for a particular purpose.[3] In order for this warranty to be created, the buyer must prove that the seller knew of the buyer's desire to use the product in a specified way (not necessarily in its ordinary way) and the buyer relied on the seller's advice and recommendation. For example, suppose that Buyer consults with Salesperson and indicates that she requires a new set of boots for a hiking trip that will involve walking through small streams. Salesperson recommends that Buyer purchase brand A boots for the hiking trip. Buyer purchases the boots, but when she is hiking, it turns out the boots are not waterproof and they fall apart on the first day of hiking through a small stream. Buyer's boots are destroyed, and she suffers injuries to her feet that require medical care. Because no express promise was made concerning the boots, Buyer must turn to an implied-warranty theory. In this case, Buyer will be able to recover based on a breach of *implied* warranty of fitness for a particular use.

Warranty Disclaimers and Limitations

The UCC allows a seller to **disclaim** both implied and express warranties under certain conditions. However, in order to disclaim a warranty, the seller must do so in a conspicuous writing by using, for example, capital letters, bold print, or a larger font that stands out from the rest of the writing. Although the UCC does not require specific language to

---

[3]UCC § 2-315.

In order to disclaim express or implied warranties, a seller must conspicuously use disclaimer language such as "with all faults" or "as is." Joshua Roberts/Roberts Publishing Service

disclaim warranties, courts have held phrases such as "with all faults" or "as is" as sufficient to disclaim a warranty. However, the UCC does require that any disclaimer of the warranty of merchantability actually use the word "merchantability" in the disclaimer.

Sellers may also, under certain circumstances, *limit the remedies* of a buyer who has suffered damages because of a seller's breach of warranty. This limitation of remedies is primarily used when the only harm suffered by the buyer was the loss of the use of the product. In such cases, the seller may attempt to limit the remedy to replacement or repair of the product and cut off any consequential damages (as might arise, for example, if the buyer suffered loss of profit due to the defective product). However, the UCC makes clear that any attempt to limit damages when a *personal injury* is involved will be automatically void. It is important to note that the Magnuson-Moss Act, discussed later in this chapter, *restricts* certain disclaimers and limitations of remedies by sellers.

In Case 21.1, an appellate court considers whether alleged hearing loss from an iPod can be the basis of a breach-of-warranty claim.

CASE 21.1 Birdsong v. Apple, Inc., 590 F.3d 955 (9th Cir. 2009)

FACT SUMMARY Apple's iPod comes with a set of earbud headphones that are detachable from the iPod unit. The iPod also may be used to play music through different headphones or through various speaker systems. Apple includes the following warning with each iPod:

Avoid Hearing Damage

Warning: Permanent hearing loss may occur if earphones or headphones are used at high volume. You can adapt over time to a higher volume of sound, which may sound normal but can be

(continued)

CHAPTER TWENTY-ONE | Warranties and Consumer Protection Law 681 *damaging to your hearing. Set your iPod's volume to a safe level before that happens. If you experience ringing in your ears, reduce the volume or discontinue use of your iPod.*

Birdsong sought to bring a class action suit against Apple, alleging that the iPod is capable of producing 115 decibels, and the class members were iPod owners who had allegedly suffered hearing loss using the iPod earbuds set at the highest decibel level. Birdsong's theory of liability (among other claims) was based on Apple's breach of implied warranty of merchantability. The trial court dismissed Birdsong's suit, and he appealed.

SYNOPSIS OF DECISION AND OPINION The Court of Appeals for the Ninth Circuit upheld the decision in favor of Apple. The court rejected Birdsong's theory that the iPod was not merchantable because it comes with stock earbuds that are designed to be placed deep into the ear canal rather than over the ears, which increases the danger of hearing damage. The court pointed out that the ordinary use of the iPod was to listen to music and that the product was fit for that use. There was no allegation of malfunction, and Birdsong did not allege that the iPods failed to do anything they were designed to do, nor did he allege that he had suffered or is substantially certain to suffer inevitable hearing loss or other injury directly from iPod use.

WORDS OF THE COURT: Ordinary Purpose
"The plaintiffs admit that the iPod has an 'ordinary purpose of listening to music,' and nothing they allege suggests iPods are unsafe for that use or defective. The plaintiffs recognize that iPods play music, have an adjustable volume, and transmit sound through earbuds. The . . . complaint includes statements that (1) the iPod is capable of playing 115 decibels of sound; (2) consumers *may* listen at unsafe levels; and (3) iPod batteries can last 12 to 14 hours and are rechargeable, giving users the *opportunity* to listen for long periods of time. Taken as true, such statements suggest only that users have the option of using an iPod in a risky manner, not that the product lacks any minimum level of quality."

Case Questions

1. If the iPod is capable of playing at a certain level of sound, isn't it foreseeable that users would assume that a high level of sound was "ordinary" use?
2. If Apple did not provide the warning, how would that impact your analysis?
3. *Focus on Critical Thinking:* Do you believe that most consumers know that earbuds cause more hearing loss than earphones? Should the court have considered the knowledge of the "average" consumer?

Magnuson-Moss Warranty–Federal Trade Commission Improvement Act

Legal Speak >))

Federal Cause of Action
A statutorily created right to sue a violator in federal court. Such statutes typically give federal courts specific subject matter jurisdiction over violations of a statute.

The Magnuson-Moss Warranty–Federal Trade Commission Improvement Act,[4] generally referred to as the *Magnuson-Moss Act,* regulates warranties given by a seller or lessor to a consumer. As with other consumer protection statutes, the Magnuson-Moss Act does *not* apply to purely merchant transactions, in which the buyer and seller are regularly engaged in the sale of goods. A consumer is defined as one who purchases or leases a good with the intent of using it for *personal* reasons rather than for resale or use in a business. The Magnuson-Moss Act does *not* mandate that sellers offer a warranty to a buyer. However, if the seller or lessor does offer a **written express warranty**, the transaction is subject to the provisions of the statute. It is important to note that the Magnuson-Moss Act did not create any additional implied warranties upon which consumers can base a lawsuit; rather, it created a *federal cause of action* for the breach of consumer warranties contained in state

---
[4] 15 U.S.C.A. § 2301.

statutes. This is accomplished by permitting consumers to bring a lawsuit directly against a seller to recover damages as a result of the seller's violating the statute. However, the statute does allow the seller to resolve disputes using an alternative dispute resolution system (such as binding arbitration) so long as the seller made appropriate disclosures about the dispute resolution requirement at the time of the transaction. The Federal Trade Commission is responsible for implementing and enforcing the Magnuson-Moss Act's requirements.

Labeling Requirements   If the product being warranted costs $10 or more, the Magnuson-Moss Act requires that the warranty itself contain a label stating the conditions of the warranty. Sellers and lessors of products that carry a full-warranty label must honor a repair or replacement promise for defects. A full warranty must also include a term of duration (e.g., "full one-year warranty"). A limited-warranty label means only that the seller does not bind itself to promises of full warranty in some way (e.g., "limited warranty: engine transmission not covered by warranty").

The Magnuson-Moss Act also requires that warranties be written conspicuously and in plain and clear language. The language must be specific to the parts, products, characteristics, or functionality covered by the warranty.

Restrictions on Disclaimers and Limitations   The Magnuson-Moss Act preempts state law and imposes a restriction on disclaimers made by sellers and lessors. The statute modifies rules on disclaimers that were previously allowed by state law with respect to the implied warranty of merchantability and the implied warranty of fitness for a particular use. If the transaction is covered by the Magnuson-Moss Act (because it involves a *written, express* agreement), the seller may *not* disclaim any implied warranties. Sellers are permitted to set a time frame on the implied warranties so long as the expiration date corresponds with the expiration of any express warranties. If the seller wishes to limit certain damages, the Magnuson-Moss Act requires that such limits be conspicuously featured in the warranty. Typically, the seller complies with this conspicuous-disclosure requirement by featuring the limitation language in **bold** type or setting it apart in some other way in the document. Figure 21.1 provides an example of a warranty disclaimer and a limitation of remedies.

> **KEY POINT**
>
> The Magnuson-Moss Act does not mandate that sellers offer a warranty to a consumer-buyer, nor does it create any additional implied warranties. If the seller does offer a written warranty, the transaction is subject to the provisions of the statute.

FIGURE 21.1   Sample Disclaimer and Limitation of Remedies

Disclaimer of Warranties
The buyer agrees to take the Widget Board with **all faults** and **as is.** The seller does not make any express warranties about the Widget Board and **expressly disclaims the implied warranty of merchantability** and **disclaims** any other **implied warranty** created by law including the **implied warranty of fitness for a particular use.**

Limitation of Remedies
Seller's sole obligation and Buyer's **sole remedy** for any damages related to the failure of the Widget Board to perform are **limited to adjustment or replacement** of any part causing the failure or at the **Seller's option** to refund the purchase amount to the Buyer.

CONCEPT SUMMARY *Warranties and Product Safety*

- A warranty is a seller's legally enforceable promise to a consumer concerning the quality and/or functionality of a product.
- Express warranties are created (generally through advertising) when the seller promises that the goods have certain qualities or a certain level of efficiency.
- Puffery is a non–fact-based statement used in advertising that does not create an express warranty.
- The implied warranty of merchantability applies to every sale of a product from a merchant to a buyer and requires the seller to warrant that the product is fit for its ordinary use.
- An implied warranty is created when a seller promises that the product is fit for a particular purpose. In order for the warranty to arise, the buyer must prove (1) that the seller knew of the buyer's desire to use the product in a specified way and (2) that the buyer relied on the seller's advice and recommendation.
- In order to disclaim a warranty, the seller must do so in a conspicuous writing by using, for example, capital letters, bold print, or a larger font that stands out from the rest of the writing.
- The Magnuson-Moss Act is a federal statute that regulates warranties given by a seller or lessor to a consumer. If the seller or lessor offers a written warranty, the transaction is subject to the provisions of the statute. If an express warranty is given, the seller may not disclaim implied warranties.
- Under the Magnuson-Moss Act, if the product being warranted costs $10 or more, the act requires that warranties be written conspicuously and in plain and clear language and be specific to the parts, products, characteristics, or functionality covered by the warranty.

Consumer Product Safety Act

Congress passed the **Consumer Product Safety Act (CPSA)**[5] in response to a growing number of injuries and deaths being caused by products, particularly toys, sold to consumers.[6] The statute created the Consumer Product Safety Commission as the federal regulatory agency and as a national information clearinghouse intended to achieve the statute's objective of making consumer products safer. The commission researches, institutes, and enforces safety standards for consumer products that pose a potential risk of injury. If the commission determines that a product defect poses an ongoing threat to consumer safety, the manufacturer may be required to institute a recall. As a practical matter, manufacturers that detect a potential problem with one of their consumer products will typically issue a recall order immediately, without an order from the commission, in an effort to stem potential liability. The commission also has traditional regulatory agency authority to enforce regulations and halt any action inconsistent with the CPSA's objectives. In 2001, the commission instituted action against multinational manufacturer Cosco, Inc., a well-known maker of baby care products, when the company failed to report problems with its baby

---

[5]15 U.S.C. § 2051 et seq.

[6]Just prior to enactment of the statute, the U.S. Department of Health, Education, and Welfare reported that consumer products were causing approximately 30,000 deaths, 110,000 permanent injuries, and 20 million injuries that required medical treatment per year. Familiar toys such as Etch-a-Sketch had caused serious lacerations for dozens of children due to broken glass from the toy's screen.

strollers, car seats, and cribs. After an investigation revealed that Cosco's products had resulted in more than 300 injuries and two deaths to infants and small children, the commission levied a $1.3 million fine against Cosco—one of the largest in the agency's history. The CPSA also gives individual consumers the right to bring a lawsuit directly against a manufacturer that violates the statute.

Other CPSA Protections Subsequent amendments to the CPSA have expanded the commission's jurisdiction to include more specific categories of consumer products. The agency now administers the Flammable Fabrics Act[7] (which regulates material used in clothing, especially children's sleepwear); the Child Protection and Toy Safety Act[8] (which sets standards for components used to make toys, such as a ban on lead paint); the Poison Prevention Packaging Act[9] (which sets standards for disclosing the use of poisons in consumer products, such as detergents and cleansers); and the Refrigerator Safety Act (which was passed after several media reports of children who suffocated after climbing inside old refrigerators in refuse lots).

CONSUMER PROTECTION LAW

Until the early 20th century, the only legal protection that consumers had against unscrupulous sellers that engaged in deceit during a sale was a common lawsuit for fraud. In 1914, Congress passed the **Federal Trade Commission Act (FTCA)**,[10] one of the very first statutory protections for American consumers. The FTCA established an administrative agency called the **Federal Trade Commission (FTC)** and charged the FTC with the broad mandate of preventing unfair and deceptive acts or practices in commercial transactions. Courts have been very deferential to the FTC's wide-ranging authority over advertising, price disclosures, and representations made during the sales process of consumer goods. Under this authority, the FTC has issued regulations that define a deceptive practice as one that is likely to *mislead* a reasonably prudent consumer and that results in some sort of *detriment* to the consumer.

LO 21-3

Explain the roles of the Federal Trade Commission and the Consumer Financial Protection Bureau in terms of various statutory consumer protections.

Consumer Financial Protection Bureau

As part of its sweeping overhaul of the U.S. financial market regulatory system, Congress created the **Consumer Financial Protection Bureau (CFPB)** through the Dodd-Frank Wall Street Reform and Consumer Protection Act to consolidate positions from other agencies that had responsibilities for oversight and regulation of consumer lending. The CFPB is an independent agency housed within the Federal Reserve. Fees paid by banks fund the agency, which is charged with setting rules to curb unfair practices in regard to consumer loans and credit cards. The CFPB provides consumer protection by offering education programs and information, performing research and providing the data to lawmakers and the public, and creating policy and imposing rules intended to protect consumers from fraud or unfair practices.

The CFPB also plays a significant role in the enforcement of consumer protection laws even outside of loans and credit cards. The Dodd-Frank law gives CFPB the authority to take action against a company or individual that engages in unfair and deceptive acts or practices in the consumer financial marketplace. This includes aggressive enforcement by the CFPB against online lenders, discrimination in lending, and debt collection.

---

[7]15 U.S.C. § 1191.
[8]15 U.S.C. § 1262(e).
[9]15 U.S.C. § 2079.
[10]15 U.S.C. § 41 et seq.

Consumer Reviews

In 2016, Congress enacted the **Consumer Review Fairness Act (CRFA)**, which protects people's ability to share their honest opinions about a business's products, services, or conduct in any forum, including social media. The CRFA was passed in response to reports that some businesses try to prevent people from giving honest reviews about products or services they received. Some companies put contract provisions in place, including in their online terms and conditions, that allowed them to sue or penalize consumers for posting negative reviews. Contracts that prohibit honest reviews, or threaten legal action over them, harm people who rely on reviews when making their purchase decisions. To discourage these practices, Congress delegated enforcement authority to the Federal Trade Commission and to state attorneys general. The law specifies that a violation of the CRFA will be treated as an unfair or deceptive act or practice.

The law protects a broad variety of honest consumer assessments, including online reviews, social media posts, uploaded photos, videos, and so on. And it doesn't just cover product reviews. It also applies to consumer evaluations of a company's customer service. In summary, the Act makes it illegal for a company to use a contract provision that

- Bars or restricts the ability of a person who is a party to that contract to review a company's products, services, or conduct;
- Imposes a penalty or fee against someone who gives a review; or
- Requires people to give up their intellectual property rights in the content of their reviews.

However, the law does *not* protect reviews that

- Contain confidential or private information—for example, a person's financial, medical, or personnel file information or a company's trade secrets.
- Are libelous, harassing, abusive, obscene, vulgar, sexually explicit, or inappropriate with respect to race, gender, sexuality, ethnicity, or another intrinsic characteristic and are clearly false or misleading.

FALSE ADVERTISING

LO 21-4

Articulate the standards used to define false advertising and other deceptive practices and identify specific consumer protection laws applied to bulk e-mail.

Deceptive advertising is a significant source of consumer complaints. FTC regulations and memorandums provide several specific examples of prohibited deceptive advertising, such as making *expressly false statements* in an advertisement about a product's quality, ingredients, or effectiveness. Note that in addition to violating the FTC's regulations, expressly false advertisements also may give rise to a breach of warranty (discussed earlier in this chapter). The FTC rule also prohibits the use of fake testimonials or endorsements and the use of fake pictures of the product performing in a manner that is inaccurate.

Bait and Switch

Regulatory authorities have become increasingly aggressive in their investigation of complaints by consumers of bait-and-switch ploys. In a bait-and-switch scheme, a seller advertises an item for sale at a particularly good price (say, 30 percent off retail) or on favorable terms (zero down, zero interest), but the seller has no intention of actually selling that product at that price or on those terms. When the consumer comes to the business after seeing the advertisement, the seller discourages the purchase of the advertised item and instead tries to convince the buyer to purchase a different item for a higher price or on less favorable terms. The seller's techniques for discouraging the purchase of the product vary (e.g., telling the consumer that the product has been sold out or perhaps advertising a product that was never actually available), but the end result is the same: The buyer walks out of the store with a more expensive product than the advertised product.

The Federal Trade Commission (FTC) has broad authority to ensure that merchant advertising is not deceptive or misleading. John Flournoy/McGraw-Hill Education

For example, suppose that Widget Depot, a merchant, advertises a sale as follows: "Classic Widgets on sale: 40% off retail value! Clearance sale!" (the bait). When Copperfield shows up a day later at Widget Depot and asks for a Classic Widget, he is referred to the manager. The manager gives a false explanation to Copperfield that the Classic Widget is out of stock and more will have to be retrieved from an off-site facility. This means Copperfield will have to wait one week for a Classic Widget. However, the manager offers Copperfield an alternative: For his trouble and time, she will sell him the newly introduced Ultimate Widget, which is currently in stock at an introductory price of 5 percent off the normal retail price. The manager goes on to explain that although the Ultimate Widget is more expensive than the Classic Widget (especially given the 40 percent Classic Widget discount), the Ultimate Widget can be trusted to last longer than the Classic. Thus, the dishonest manager reasons, the Ultimate is actually a better deal than the Classic. Copperfield relies on the manager's advice and buys the Ultimate Widget. Under most state statutes, the conduct of Widget Depot's manager is unlawful and qualifies as a bait-and-switch scheme.

Pricing

Pricing is an important component of advertising and is also subject to consumer protection regulations. Some of the more common examples of deceptive advertising via pricing are

- Misrepresenting the prices of a competitor.
- Artificially inflating the original retail price of a product when featuring it as a sale item in order to make it appear that the original price was higher than it actually was.
- Using phrases such as "clearance priced" or "marked down for sale" when the items are not being sold at reduced rates.

Telemarketing

In the 1990s, public concern about deceptive telemarketing practices targeted at elderly victims resulted in Congress enacting several statutes regulating telemarketing firms and practices. The primary statutes are the **Telephone Consumer Protection Act**[11] and the **Telemarketing and Consumer Fraud and Abuse Prevention Act**.[12] These laws (1) allow consumers to *opt out* of receiving unwanted calls from telemarketers, (2) ban the use of unsolicited recorded calls and faxes, (3) regulate 900-number calls to prevent consumers from unknowingly generating charges, (4) prohibit telemarketers from making false representations, and (5) require disclosure of all the material terms of a proposed transaction. The laws prescribe *how* and *when* a telemarketer may obtain permission to obtain payment from the consumer's checking, savings, or credit accounts. It also prohibits any harassment, threats, or deceit by the telemarketer.

Do Not Call List The FTC established the Do Not Call Registry whereby consumers may sign up to be on a list that protects them from certain unsolicited calls by telemarketers. Some organizations are exempt from the Do Not Call list prohibitions. They include (1) charitable organizations, (2) certain political organizations, and (3) businesses with whom the consumer has had past commercial contacts.

Odometers

The U.S. Department of Transportation estimates that odometer rollback, the process of physically altering a vehicle's odometer in order to make it appear as if the vehicle has traveled fewer miles than it actually has, is a $3-billion-a-year enterprise.[13] Odometer fraud is perpetrated both easily and surreptitiously, and it is often impossible for a consumer to detect. The **Federal Odometer Act**[14] makes it a crime to change vehicle odometers and requires that any faulty odometer be plainly disclosed in writing to potential buyers. The law sets out regulations that (1) define and prohibit odometer tampering, (2) prohibit buying or installing any device used for tampering, (3) prescribe procedures for odometer repair, (4) require certain disclosures related to the actual mileage of the vehicle when it is sold to a new owner, (5) give jurisdiction for the implementation and enforcement of the law to the secretary of transportation, and (6) impose a record-keeping requirement on vehicle dealers and distributors.

In addition to giving the secretary of transportation the authority to enforce the statute, the law provides victims of odometer tampering with a remedy of *triple* the actual damages suffered. However, the lawsuit must take place within two years of the date of purchase.

State Statutes

In addition to federal statutes, each state has adopted consumer protections by enacting state laws aimed at preventing unfair or deceptive trade practices within state borders. The statutes often empower the state attorney general to pursue violators using enforcement mechanisms such as civil lawsuits and, in extreme cases, criminal charges. Many states have created specific task forces to police merchants' and other sellers' compliance with consumer protection statutes in regard to transactions that take place primarily within the state's borders. Enforcement powers are usually given to the state's law enforcement

---

[11] 47 U.S.C. § 227.

[12] 15 U.S.C. § 6101 et seq.

[13] *See Secretary of Transportation's Report to the Congress on the Federal Odometer Act* (2006).

[14] 49 U.S.C. § 32701 et seq.

authorities: the state attorney general and local district attorneys. State statutes often give aggrieved consumers the right to bring a lawsuit directly against any violator to recover damages. Therefore, federal agencies and state authorities are thought of as having concurrent (overlapping) jurisdiction.

Lemon Laws Lemon laws are state statutes that provide consumers a remedy in the case of a serious vehicle defect that cannot be resolved by the seller. In general, a *lemon* refers to a new or used vehicle that turns out to have hidden manufacturing defects affecting its safety, value, or utility. Although the exact criteria vary state by state, new-vehicle lemon laws require that an auto manufacturer repurchase a vehicle that has a significant defect that the manufacturer is unable to repair within a reasonable amount of time. Contrary to popular belief, it is not the dealership who has the obligation to buy back the vehicle; it is the manufacturer.

Broadly speaking, lemon laws consider the nature of the problem with the vehicle, the number of days that the vehicle is unavailable to the consumer for service of the same mechanical issue, and the number of repair attempts made. If repairs cannot be completed within the total number of days described in the state statute, the manufacturer becomes obligated to buy back the defective vehicle.

Some state lemon laws cover only certain classes of vehicles, such as vehicles purchased for individual use but not for business use or vehicles under a certain gross weight. A small number of states also have enacted lemon laws that cover used vehicles as well.

Consumer Protection Statutes State statutory protections often fill the gaps in federal protections. For example, the New Jersey Consumer Fraud Act covers certain transactions that would not be within the coverage of a federal statute. In Case 21.2, a New Jersey appellate court applies a state consumer fraud statute to a real estate transaction.

CASE 21.2 Vagias v. Woodmont Properties, 894 A.2d 68 (N.J. Super. Ct. 2006)

FACT SUMMARY Vagias hired Dingle as his Realtor and told her that he was in the market to buy a house in Montville Township, New Jersey. Vagias communicated to Dingle that he desired that particular municipality due to the favorable reputation of the township's schools. Dingle showed Vagias a house in a development called Woodmont Court at Montville, and Vagias inquired as to whether this house was actually located within the jurisdictional limits of Montville Township. Dingle and a representative of the builder, neither of whom were familiar with the township boundaries, assured Vagias that the house was in Montville Township and Vagias purchased the home for $740,000. When Vagias attempted to enroll his son in the school system, he learned that his house was actually located outside the Montville Township limits. Vagias sued to have the sale rescinded on the basis of Dingle's and the homebuilder's misrepresentation concerning location. Vagias argued that he had paid a premium for the house based on the reputation of the school system in a certain township. Woodmont argued that the misrepresentations were not intentional and that Vagias suffered no loss in the value of the home.

SYNOPSIS OF DECISION AND OPINION The Superior Court of New Jersey ruled in favor of Vagias. The court held that Vagias specified that location in Montville Township was a prerequisite to purchasing a house at Woodmont and, therefore, that location became a part of the basis of the bargain. Under the New Jersey Consumer Fraud Act, Dingle's misrepresentation need not be an intentional misrepresentation. Dingle and Woodmont knew of Vagias's concerns and made an affirmative

(continued)

misrepresentation. That is all that is necessary to prevail in a New Jersey Consumer Fraud Act case.

WORDS OF THE COURT: No Intent Required

"[W]hen [the real estate agent] told [Vagias] that the house they were looking at was in 'Montville' she made an affirmative misrepresentation. Her intent is not an issue for purposes of the Act. If she provided plaintiffs with affirmative misinformation on what she knew was a critical issue in their decision to purchase the house, she violated the Act. . . . Further, she was not an innocent bystander making a casual comment. She was assisting plaintiffs in choosing a house to buy, and she received a commission on the sale. [Thus,] Dingle's statements 'were not idle comments or mere puffery.'"

Case Questions

1. Had Dingle not known that Vagias was specifically looking for a home in Montville Township yet had still made her statements, would the outcome of the case have been different? Why or why not? Explain your answer.
2. Why did the court consider the misinformation to be a "critical issue" in Vagias's decision to buy?
3. *Focus on Critical Thinking:* Suppose Vagias paid market value for his home and was able to send his son to a highly rated elementary school. Now the only detriment imposed upon him is a lower social status due to the location of the home outside of the Montville Township. How does this affect your analysis?

LEGAL IMPLICATIONS IN CYBERSPACE

Regulation of Online Advertising

As use of the Internet by consumers increased in the late 1990s, *spam*—unsolicited e-mails advertising a product or service—became so increasingly problematic that state legislatures took the early lead in regulating spam and establishing tough criminal penalties for illegal spam suppliers. Thirty-three states passed some form of legislation that attempted to regulate unsolicited e-mails. California's law was one of the toughest because it required online marketers to obtain a consumer's permission *prior* to sending e-mail solicitations. Virginia went a step further and made sending certain unsolicited e-mails a felony and indicted two men for running a large illegal bulk e-mail operation. Some states, such as New York, passed antispam legislation as part of a larger package of identity theft laws. Then–New York Attorney General Eliot Spitzer[15] grabbed headlines by indicting a man, dubbed the "Buffalo Spammer," for sending 825 million spam messages.

However, there was no *federal* statute regulating unsolicited e-mail until Congress passed the **Controlling the Assault of Non-Solicited Pornography and Marketing Act of 2003**,[16] better known as the CAN-SPAM Act. The new law supplanted sometimes-tougher state statutes, but it still outlawed the dubious methods used by certain spam suppliers and provided for criminal sanctions in severe cases. The statute also prohibits online marketing providers from falsifying the "from" name and information in the subject line designed to fool consumers into opening an unsolicited e-mail message. It also requires the sender to provide a physical address of the producer of the e-mail and specifically label any pornographic links with adult-content warnings. The law imposes an affirmative obligation on the sender to notify the recipient of procedures to opt out of receiving any future e-mail from the sender. One controversial provision of the law required the FTC to start a "do-not-spam" list modeled on the Do Not Call list. However, the FTC resisted the notion of creating such a list based on technology and privacy grounds, and the list was never implemented.

The CAN-SPAM Act allows e-mail recipients the right to bring a lawsuit directly against the spammer as a compliance mechanism in egregious cases and in cases where the plaintiff can prove that the spam produced actual damages (such as a shutdown of a retail

(continued)

---

[15]Spitzer was later elected governor of New York but resigned in the wake of a prostitution scandal.
[16]15 U.S.C. § 7701 et seq.

store's computer server that caused loss of profits or repair charges). The FTC has been aggressively enforcing the law against the most serious offenders and pursuing criminal charges where appropriate. For example, in June 2007, two spammers were convicted under the CAN-SPAM Act for sending out millions of e-mail messages with highly offensive pornographic images. The defendants were sentenced to five years in prison and ordered to pay $1.3 million from the profits of their front company.[17] The FTC has also used its enforcement authority to file civil complaints against companies that are engaged in spamming as part of their marketing strategy. The FTC is particularly strict in its enforcement of the CAN-SPAM Act when pursuing companies whose primary market is Internet pornography.[18]

In 2005, the FTC issued a report indicating that the volume of spam had leveled off since the law had been enacted, with a marked decrease in sexually explicit e-mail, which reached fewer mailboxes. Critics of the CAN-SPAM Act contend that the decrease is due primarily to enhanced technology improvements in e-mail filtering and argue that the act is ineffective and difficult to enforce. One report featured in *PC Magazine* concluded that less than 1 percent of spam complied with the CAN-SPAM Act. Responding to some industry criticism of the effectiveness of the law, the FTC revised its regulations in 2008 to widen its jurisdiction and specifically prohibit spam distributors from charging a consumer a fee in order to process an opt-out request.

CONCEPT SUMMARY Unfair and Deceptive Trade Practices

- The Federal Trade Commission (FTC) is charged with preventing unfair and deceptive acts or practices in commercial transactions. In doing so, the FTC has wide-ranging authority over advertising, price disclosures, and representations made during the sales process of consumer goods.
- In bait-and-switch schemes, a seller advertises an item for sale at a very good price or on favorable terms but in reality has no intention of actually selling that product at that price or on those terms. Instead, when the consumer comes to the business after seeing the advertisement, the seller discourages the purchase of the advertised item and tries to convince the buyer to purchase a different item for a higher price or on less favorable terms.
- Pricing is also subject to consumer protection regulations, including a ban on misrepresenting the prices of a competitor, artificially inflating the original retail price of a product when featuring it as a sale item, and using phrases such as "clearance priced" or "marked down for sale" when the items are not being sold at reduced prices.
- The FTC established the Do Not Call Registry whereby consumers sign up to be on a list that protects them from certain unsolicited calls by telemarketers.
- The Federal Odometer Act makes it a crime to change vehicle odometers and requires that any faulty odometer be plainly disclosed in writing to potential buyers.
- The Controlling the Assault of Non-Solicited Pornography and Marketing (CAN-SPAM) Act of 2003 regulates the sending of unsolicited e-mail (spam).
- State statutes, such as lemon laws, supplement federal consumer protections.

---

[17]*United States v. Shaffer*, 472 F.3d 1219 (10th Cir. 2007). The defendants were also convicted of mail fraud and racketeering.

[18]*See* Press Release, Fed. Trade Comm'n, FTC Cracks Down on Illegal X-Rated Spam (July 20, 2005).

LO 21-5

Name and explain the federal statutory protections afforded to consumers for faulty or unsafe products and for food and drug safety.

FOOD AND DRUG SAFETY

The **Food, Drug and Cosmetic Act (FDCA)** is the federal statute that created the **Food and Drug Administration (FDA)** to regulate the testing, manufacturing, and distributing of foods, medications (including over-the-counter medications and prescription drugs), medical devices, and cosmetics. A major component of the FDCA is the requirement that makers of certain food ingredients, additives, drugs, or medical devices obtain formal FDA approval prior to selling the product to the general public. The application process is very rigorous and evaluates data supplied by the applicant as well as independent evidence from FDA scientists or government contractors. When the FDA has approved a drug for public use, any advertising for the drug is subject to FDA regulation in terms of what representations may be made and what disclosures must be included. FDA regulations also govern the *labeling* of food packages.

FDA Regulations and Enforcement: Food Safety

The FDA regulations define specific *food safety* processes, procedures, and standards, such as the requirement that employees handling food wear rubber gloves and hair netting. The statute also sets out a broader catchall standard by outlawing any generally *adulterated* food that has potential for public harm. The FDA defines adulterated food as that which contains a "filthy, putrid, or decomposed substance" or any food "unfit for consumption."

> **KEY POINT**
>
> The FDA enforces both specific and general standards for food safety. While certain regulations set out specific purity or safety standards, a catchall provision sets out a general standard banning all adulterated food.

The FDA also investigates any public outbreaks of illness related to food contamination. During its investigation of such outbreaks, the FDA uses its broad enforcement powers to detect and prevent any further contamination. These powers include seizure of contaminated products, mandatory recalls, civil enforcement lawsuits, fines, and criminal prosecution for egregious cases. One of the largest fines ever levied by the FDA was against Odwalla Juice Company in 1998. The Odwalla juice case is featured as a Capstone Case Study in the back of this textbook.

CREDIT TRANSACTIONS

LO 21-6

Identify the parties in a credit transaction and understand the role of federal statutory laws in consumer credit transactions.

Credit is one of the most important components of a stable economy.[19] The use of credit by consumers in the business environment is widespread and primarily exists in the form of loans and credit cards. A consumer credit transaction takes place between a **creditor**[20] (typically a financial institution, but any party regularly extending credit to consumers is considered a creditor) and a **borrower** (sometimes referred to as a *debtor*). Merchants are considered creditors when they regularly engage in extending credit terms to a patron. It is important for business owners and managers to be aware that establishing a credit relationship with a consumer borrower triggers protections for the borrower via federal and state statutes. There is a large body of administrative law that regulates credit transactions as well.

---

[19] A primary factor in the financial crisis that began in September 2008 was an extreme and abrupt tightening of the credit markets by financial institutions that were reeling from losses in a variety of industries but especially from increasingly high default rates on home mortgage loans. This, in turn, made consumer credit (such as a mortgage or car loan) more difficult to obtain and contributed to a slowdown in consumer spending. The inability of consumers and businesses to obtain credit is one of many factors that deepened the crisis and led to a precipitous rise in unemployment.

[20] In some contexts, the creditor is known as a *lender*.

Consumer Credit Regulation

The centerpiece of federal statutory regulation of credit transactions is the **Consumer Credit Protection Act (CCPA)**.[21] The CCPA has been amended several times and now has six components that regulate credit transactions between a creditor and a borrower. These components include consumer protections in the areas of disclosure of credit terms, credit reporting, antidiscrimination laws for credit applicants, and collection of debts from consumers. The CCPA was enhanced by the Wall Street Reform and Consumer Protection Act in 2010. Congress also centralized enforcement responsibilities of all consumer credit regulation through creation of the Consumer Financial Protection Board (CFPB).

Truth in Lending Act

The **Truth in Lending Act (TILA)**[22] is the part of the CCPA that requires lenders to disclose to borrower applicants certain information about the loan or terms of credit. It also mandates uniform methods of computation and explanation of the terms of the loan or credit arrangements. The primary objective behind the TILA is to allow consumers access to reliable information related to interest rates and other important terms and to provide a standardized reporting system for consumers to compare loan offers. The TILA's scope is limited to credit extensions made to consumers and is used primarily for personal, family, or household purposes.

> **LO 21-7**
>
> List the various components of the Truth in Lending Act and give specific examples of regulatory requirements.

The TILA covers only creditors that are *regularly* engaged in extending credit for goods and services (such as banks, department stores, suppliers, wholesalers, and retailers) plus those that are regularly engaged in *arranging* credit that is for personal, family, or household goods (such as a mortgage broker). For example, suppose Armstrong wishes to renovate the kitchen in his home and plans to finance the renovation through a loan. If Armstrong applies for a home improvement loan from his local bank, the transaction is covered under the TILA and the bank will be required to strictly comply with the act's requirements. However, suppose that, instead, Armstrong convinces his retired uncle, Rogers, to make a five-year loan. Rogers's attorney drafts a promissory note and sends it to Armstrong for signature. The Rogers-to-Armstrong loan transaction is *not* covered under the TILA, and Armstrong is without any statutory disclosure protection.

> **KEY POINT**
>
> The TILA covers only creditors that are regularly engaged in extending credit for goods and services or in arranging credit that is for personal, family, or household goods.

The TILA also authorized the Federal Reserve Board to set regulations with procedures and protections that help achieve the objectives of the act. The most important regulation for business owners and managers is **Regulation Z**, which requires that certain written disclosures be made prior to the time that a credit transaction is consummated. The two most important terms in a TILA disclosure statement are the *finance charge* and the *annual percentage rate (APR)*. These two terms are different ways of expressing the same disclosure: the total amount of interest that the consumer will pay over the life of the loan or credit extension. The finance charge must be stated in a dollar amount that represents the *sum* of interest charges that will be paid along with the required payment of principal to pay the loan back. The APR is written as a mathematical percentage that is used to determine the interest rate being paid by the consumer. Because the finance charge and APR are so important, Regulation Z requires that their disclosure

---
[21] 15 U.S.C. § 1601 et seq.
[22] 15 U.S.C. § 1605.

The Truth in Lending Act requires creditors to make certain disclosures about a loan transaction (such as fees) and allows consumers to cancel the loan contract for any reason within three business days of the transaction. Keith Brofsky/Getty Images

must be *more conspicuous* than other disclosures. The regulation also requires that fees may not be hidden within a finance charge. Therefore, transaction charges, loan origination fees,[23] and charges for required life insurance (if the borrower dies, the policy pays off the creditor) must all be disclosed, if applicable. If a creditor fails to comply with the TILA's disclosure requirements in any way, the debtor has the right to cancel any contract associated with the loan without any further obligation to the creditor. The creditor is also required to notify the debtor of her statutory right to cancel the contract for any reason within *three business days* of the transaction. Failing to provide proper notice of a cancellation right extends that right for up to three years from the date of the contract. As a practical matter, creditors can avoid liability by being sure that their notice of the right to cancel is consistent with the format prescribed by the Federal Reserve Board.

In Case 21.3, an appellate court considers a consumer's claim that the required cancellation notice was inadequate and, therefore, she was entitled to cancel the loan contract one year after signing it.

CASE 21.3 Palmer v. Champion Mortgage, 465 F.3d 24 (1st Cir. 2006)

FACT SUMMARY In March 2003, Palmer obtained a debt-consolidation loan from Champion that was secured by a second mortgage on her home. (This type of loan is also known as a *home equity loan.*) On the day the loan closing took place, she signed several loan documents as well as the required TILA disclosures. Several days later, Palmer received copies of these documents by mail along with the "notice of her right to cancel" disclosure required by the TILA. The notice of her right to cancel provided that Palmer could "cancel the transaction for any reason within three business days of (1) the date of the transaction, (2) the date she received her TILA disclosures, or (3) the date she received the notice of right to cancel." The notice also provided that if she was to cancel the transaction by mail or telegraph, the cancellation had to be postmarked no later than April 1, 2003. Palmer did not cancel the transaction within the allotted time period. However, in August 2004 she filed for cancellation of the transaction under the extended three-year statute of limitations under the TILA, claiming that Champion failed to make TILA disclosures because the time frames in the cancellation notice were too confusing.

SYNOPSIS OF DECISION AND OPINION The U.S. Court of Appeals for the First Circuit affirmed the trial court's decision and dismissed Palmer's claim. The court reasoned that the notice of right to cancel provided by Champion complied with the TILA disclosure requirements and that an objectively reasonable consumer would not find the notice confusing. Therefore, Palmer's right to rescind was not extended by a failure to follow TILA procedures.

(continued)

---

[23]Sometimes called *points,* loan origination fees are essentially prepaid interest. A loan at 7 percent with 1 point means that, upon receiving the loan, the borrower pays the creditor 1 percent (1 point) of interest based on the initial principal amount of the loan. Then the borrower repays the principal plus 7 percent in interest per year for the life of the loan.

WORDS OF THE COURT: Objectively Reasonable Notice "[I]n the TILA context . . . we, like other courts, have focused the lens of our inquiry on the text of the disclosures themselves rather than on plaintiffs' descriptions of their subjective understandings. . . . This emphasis on objective reasonableness, rather than subjective understanding, is also appropriate in light of the sound tenet that courts must evaluate the adequacy of TILA disclosures from the vantage point of a hypothetical average consumer—a consumer who is neither particularly sophisticated nor particularly dense. . . . Thus, we turn to the question of whether the average consumer, looking at the Notice objectively, would find it confusing. We conclude that she would not. . . . It clearly and conspicuously indicates that the debtor can rescind 'within three (3) business days from whichever of [three enumerated] events occurs last.' . . . We fail to see how any reasonably alert person—that is, the average consumer—reading the Notice would be drawn to the April 1 deadline without also grasping the twice-repeated alternative deadlines. . . . Because we find the Notice clear and adequate, and because the plaintiff otherwise concedes receiving all the required disclosures, her right of rescission under the TILA had long expired by the time she commenced this action."

Case Questions

1. Given the language of the time frame notice, do you agree with the court's statements that it was clear and that objectively reasonable consumers would not be confused by it? Why or why not?

2. The court says that any "reasonably alert" person is the average consumer. Do you agree that the average consumer is reasonably alert? What standard should be used to judge the "average consumer"?

3. *Focus on Critical Thinking:* Examine Figure 21.2. This is a notice that is similar to the notice Palmer received. Does it affect your analysis?

Other Federal Statutory Protections

The CCPA and the TILA have been amended several times to include additional protections for consumers related to credit discrimination, credit card issuers, and consumer leases.

Home Mortgages
In an attempt to make disclosures more transparent and understandable to home buyers, the Consumer Financial Protection Bureau (CFPB) promulgated rules that integrate existing disclosures with new requirements from the Wall Street Reform and Consumer Protection Act to improve consumer understanding of the mortgage process, aid in comparison shopping, and help to prevent surprises at the closing of the mortgage. The new rule, called the TILA-RESPA Integration Disclosure (TRID) rule, combines the TILA disclosures with disclosures required under the Real Estate Settlement Procedures Act (RESPA). It is important to note that the TRID rules do *not* apply to home equity lines of credit, reverse mortgages, mortgages secured by mobile homes or dwellings not attached to a property, or creditors that make five or fewer mortgage loans in one year.

Antidiscrimination
Denying an applicant credit on the basis of discriminatory factors relating to the applicant's race, religion, national origin, color, gender, age, or marital status is unlawful under the **Equal Credit Opportunity Act**,[24] which was passed in 1974. The statute was driven primarily by the civil rights movement of the late 1960s and early 1970s and was created to prevent what was then a relatively common practice of considering gender or race in credit decisions. The law also applies to charging higher interest rates based on discriminatory factors.

---
[24] 15 U.S.C. § 1691.

FIGURE 21.2　Sample Home Equity Loan Notice of Right to Cancel

**HOME EQUITY LINE OF CREDIT
NOTICE OF RIGHT TO CANCEL**

LENDER: Main Street Bank　　　　　　　　　　　　　DATE　10/1/2020
　　　　　　　　　　　　　　　　　　　　　　　　　LOAN NO.　5931569013
BORROWERS/OWNERS　Eva St. Clair　　　　　　　　　TYPE　Equity Line

ADDRESS　123 Stowes Lane
CITY/STATE/ZIP　New Town, MA
PROPERTY　10 Main Street, Unionville, MA

　　　We have agreed to establish an open-end credit account for you, and you have agreed to give us a mortgage/lien/security interest on your home as security for the account. You have a legal right under federal law to cancel this account, without cost, within THREE BUSINESS DAYS after the latest of the following events:

(1)　The opening date of the account, which is 10/1/2020　　; or
(2)　The date you received your Truth in Lending disclosures; or
(3)　The date you received this notice of your right to cancel the account.

　　　If you cancel the account, the mortgage/lien/security interest on your home is also cancelled. Within TWENTY CALENDAR DAYS of receiving your notice, we must take the necessary steps to reflect the fact that the mortgage/lien/security interest on your home has been cancelled. We must return to you any money or property you have given to us or to anyone else in connection with this account.

　　　You may keep any money or property we have given you until we have done the things mentioned above, but you must then offer to return the money or property. If it is impractical or unfair for you to return the property, you must offer its reasonable value. You may offer to return the property at your home or at the location of the property. Money must be returned to the address below. If we do not take possession of the money or property within TWENTY CALENDAR DAYS of your offer, you may keep it without further obligation.

HOW TO CANCEL

If you decide to cancel this account, you may do so by notifying us, in writing, at

Main Street Bank
Unionville, MA

　　　You may use any written statement that is signed and dated by you and states your intention to cancel, or you may use this notice by dating and signing below. Keep one copy of this notice no matter how you notify us because it contains important information about your rights.

　　　If you cancel by mail or telegram, you must send the notice no later than MIDNIGHT of October 5, 2020　　　　　　(or MIDNIGHT of the THIRD BUSINESS DAY following the latest of the three events listed above). If you send or deliver your written notice to cancel some other way, it must be delivered to the above address no later than that time.
I WISH TO CANCEL

_____　　　_____
CONSUMER'S SIGNATURE　　　　　　　　　　　　　　　　　DATE

The undersigned each acknowledge receipt of two copies each of NOTICE OF RIGHT TO CANCEL.

Each borrower/owner in this transaction has the right to cancel. The exercise of this right by one borrower/owner shall be effective as to all borrowers/owners.

Eva St. Clair　　　10/1/20
BORROWER/OWNER Eva St. Clair　　DATE　　BORROWER/OWNER　　　　　　　　DATE

_____　_____　_____　_____
BORROWER/OWNER　　　　　　　　　DATE　　BORROWER/OWNER　　　　　　　　DATE

Credit Cards　In May 2009, Congress overhauled the statutory scheme governing consumer credit card transactions. The **Credit Card Accountability Responsibility and Disclosure Act of 2009 (CARD Act)**[25] increases the power and oversight authority of the Federal Trade Commission over credit card issuers. The CARD Act was primarily intended

---
[25]Pub. L. No. 111-24, 123 Stat. 1734 (2009) (amending 15 U.S.C. § 1601 et seq.).

to protect consumers from unreasonable surprises when interest rates increase and credit card fees are imposed and to restrict marketing and card-issuing practices targeted to younger (18- to 21-year-old) consumers. Among other requirements, credit card issuers

- Are prohibited from issuing a credit card to any consumer under the age of 21 unless the consumer submits either (1) the signature of a cosigner over the age of 21 who has the means to repay debts incurred by the consumer or (2) financial information indicating an independent means (regular income) of repaying any debts. Special rules exist for credit cards issued to college students.
- Must comply with rules that require institutions of higher education (such as colleges and universities) to publicly disclose any contract of agreement made with a credit card issuer. Credit card issuers may not offer college students tangible items (gifts) to induce them to apply for credit cards.
- Must give 45 days' advance notice of any impending raise in rates.
- Must mail credit statements at least 21 days before the bill's due date (extended from 14 days in the previous law).

Existing Regulations under the TILA The CARD Act supplemented already existing disclosure and transaction regulations under the TILA. Those existing provisions of the TILA, which were left intact, include

- Protection of consumers when a card is used to buy what turns out to be a faulty product by requiring the card issuer to investigate and, depending on the results of the investigation, credit the consumer's account.
- A limitation of the consumer's liability for unauthorized charges of a total amount of $50. As a practical matter, consumers usually get even more favorable treatment than the law allows because many major credit card companies now have a policy of waiving any charges they determine to be fraudulent. If the card is reported stolen to the issuer *prior* to any unauthorized charge, the consumer has no liability for charges. Although credit card companies are permitted to send unsolicited cards to consumers, fraudulent or unauthorized use prior to the acceptance of the offer will not result in liability to the addressee/consumer.
- A statutory procedure for consumers who are claiming a billing error[26] or disputing a charge on their account. The procedure includes a time frame and a requirement that the credit issuer attempt to investigate the dispute and resolve it in good faith. The TILA also prohibits the credit issuer from charging the consumer interest on the charge while the dispute is being investigated.

Identity Theft In 2003, Congress gave some protections to consumers who were victims of *identity theft*. Identity theft occurs when a criminal assumes the identity of an individual for purposes of making fraudulent credit transactions in the victim's name. The **Fair and Accurate Credit Transactions (FACT) Act**[27] requires that credit bureaus stop reporting any fraudulent account information from the time a consumer alleges identity theft until the conclusion of an investigation period. The FACT Act also contains provisions that established a national fraud alert system so that consumers have a timely way to guard their credit once they suspect identity fraud has occurred.

More recently, Congress passed the Economic Growth, Regulatory Relief, and Consumer Protection Act,[28] which requires credit bureaus to provide consumers with a free

---

[26]These protections were added to the TILA by the Fair Credit Billing Act (15 U.S.C.A. § 1681 et seq.).
[27]Pub. L. No. 108-159, 117 Stat. 1952 (2003) (amending 15 U.S.C. § 1681).
[28]Pub. L. No. 115-174, S. 2155 (2018).

credit freeze service. A credit freeze (sometimes called a security freeze) restricts access to a consumer's credit file. Merchants or other creditors cannot access a consumer's credit file if the consumer has requested a freeze; this is intended to prevent identity thieves from opening new accounts in the consumer's name.

Consumer Leases In addition to its regulation of debt incurred in purchasing products or services, the TILA regulates the *leasing relationship,* whereby a creditor lessor typically gives the possession and use of equipment or a motor vehicle to a consumer debtor in exchange for monthly payments over an agreed-upon period of time. When the leasing period expires, the consumer either returns the goods or exercises an option to purchase the goods at a predetermined price. Consumer leasing is regulated by the **Consumer Leasing Act (CLA)**, which covers lessors engaged in leasing or those arranging leases for consumers in the ordinary course of business. Many of the CLA's provisions mirror the statutory protections afforded to consumer debtors in a loan transaction, such as requirements on APR disclosure and the standardization of certain information.

Credit Reports Because creditors rely so heavily on credit bureaus (private companies that compile data about a consumer's credit history as well as current liabilities), Congress gave consumers federal statutory protection in the **Fair Credit Reporting Act (FCRA)**.[29] The FCRA sets privacy rights for consumer credit reports and requires that the credit bureaus give individual consumers complete and timely access to their own credit reports. In order to ensure that the credit report is accurate, the FCRA requires each of the credit bureaus to provide individual consumers with a copy of their own credit report, free of charge, once per year. Additionally, any time the report is used in a credit-making decision (such as a loan application), the consumer has the right to obtain a free copy of the credit report used in the decision making. The FCRA also provides a dispute resolution system designed to allow consumers the right to challenge any information on their credit report if the information is incorrect. Further, the FCRA requires that credit bureaus remove any entry that is obsolete. The FCRA defines *obsolete* as any negative information (such as an account that was closed by the creditor and placed for collection) that is over seven years old and a bankruptcy filing that occurred more than 14 years prior to the date of the report.

LO 21-8

Explain the protections afforded to consumers by federal statutes regulating the collection of consumer debt.

CONSUMER DEBT COLLECTION

As discussed in the previous section, consumer credit transactions are heavily regulated in an effort to protect consumers and help level the playing field between creditors and debtor consumers. Similarly, when a creditor's agent is collecting a debt owed to the creditor by virtue of an extension of consumer credit, the collection process is subject to regulation. Agents involved in debt collection for consumer debts are directly regulated by a federal statute called the **Fair Debt Collection Practices Act (FDCPA)**.[30] The FDCPA applies only to *agents* of the debtor that are attempting to collect the debt from the consumer. These agents typically take the form of a collection agency, but others that are collecting consumer debts on behalf of the debtor (such as attorneys) may also be subject to the FDCPA under certain conditions.[31] A creditor that is attempting to collect her own debt is *not* subject to the act. However, both creditors and collection agencies are subject to additional state statutory and regulatory requirements as well.

---

[29] 15 U.S.C. § 1681 et seq.
[30] 15 U.S.C. § 1692 (now Title VII of the Consumer Credit Protection Act).
[31] *Heintz v. Jenkins*, 514 U.S. 291 (1995).

FDCPA Requirements

The FDCPA requires that the collection agency make known certain rights of the debtor in a **validation disclosure** when making the initial inquiry about the debt. This disclosure notice must inform the debtor that he has 30 days to dispute the debt. The law also requires that the collection agency investigate any disputed debt and obtain written verification of the debt from the original creditor.

In addition to requiring validation disclosure, the FDCPA prohibits certain conduct in the course of attempting to collect a debt. First, the law limits the contact that a debt collector may have with third parties such as employers. Second, certain methods are unlawful. Specifically, the FDCPA prohibits collector contact (1) at inconvenient times, such as early morning or late night calls, or at inconvenient places, such as the debtor's place of employment or sites of social events; (2) after the collector is informed that the debtor is represented by an attorney; or (3) after the debtor gives written notice that she refuses to pay the debt and requests the agent to cease contact. The FDCPA also prohibits any harassing, intimidating, or misleading tactics by collection agents, such as making threats of incarceration, posing as an attorney or law enforcement agent, or using abusive, degrading language.

Enforcement

Federal statutes that govern consumer debt collection are enforced primarily by the Consumer Financial Protection Bureau (CFPB) and the Federal Trade Commission (FTC). These agencies use a system of penalties, cease and desist orders, and civil lawsuits to enforce the FDCPA. However, the law also provides individual consumers with a statutory cause of action so that a debtor may sue a collection agent directly for any damages suffered, plus attorney fees incurred in bringing suit. On the state level, state attorneys general often have authority to prosecute collection agents engaged in abusive collection tactics within their state's jurisdiction.

In Case 21.4, the CFPB investigates the unlawful collection practices of a law firm that agrees to a consent order.

Legal Speak >))

Consent Orders
Consent orders are issued by administrative agencies and entail the violator's agreement to the imposition of civil fines and any other appropriate disciplinary sanctions. A consent order generally has the same effect as a court order.

CASE 21.4 U.S. Consumer Financial Protection Bureau v. Pressler & Pressler LLP, CFPB No. 2016-CFPB-0009 (Apr. 25, 2016)

FACT SUMMARY Pressler & Pressler, LLP (Pressler), is a law firm whose practice was entirely devoted to debt collection, primarily in New Jersey and New York. In response to numerous complaints from consumers concerning Pressler's violation of the Fair Debt Collection Practices Act (FDCPA), the Consumer Financial Protection Bureau (CFPB) investigated the practices of Pressler. The investigation revealed multiple instances of debt-collection efforts in which Pressler employees violated the "False or Unsubstantiated Representations about Owing a Debt" section of the FCRA. The CFPB found that Pressler had represented, directly or indirectly, expressly or by implication, that consumers owed debts to various clients with certain unpaid balances, interest rates, and payment due dates, which were not substantiated by documentation from creditors or were simply false. The investigation also found that from 2009 to 2014, the law firm filed more than 500,000 lawsuits against consumers on behalf of clients who sought payment for debts they purchased from various creditors. This massive litigation mill was powered through an automated claim-preparation system, and nonattorney support staff determined which consumers to sue. Actual attorneys generally spent less than a few minutes, sometimes less than 30 seconds, reviewing each case before initiating a lawsuit.

(continued)

SYNOPSIS OF DECISION AND OPINION In 2016, the CFPB announced that it had entered into a Consent Order with Pressler whereby Pressler, and its two principal partners—Sheldon Pressler and Gerard Felt—agreed to a civil fine of $1 million. The parties also agreed to halt the practice that caused the filing of inaccurate mass-produced lawsuits targeting consumers in debt in violation of both the Fair Debt Collection Practices Act and the Dodd-Frank Wall Street Reform and Consumer Protection Act, which prohibits unfair and deceptive acts or practices in the consumer financial marketplace.

WORDS OF THE CONSENT ORDER: Documentation Required "In numerous instances the representations set forth in [the CFPB Complaint] were not substantiated at the time the representations were made, including but not limited to where . . . Consumers disputed, challenged, or questioned the validity or accuracy of the debt and [Pressler] failed to obtain [documentation from the creditor] before continuing collecting on that account. [Pressler] had knowledge or reason to believe, based on its past course of dealing with its clients' accounts (including factors such as consumer disputes, inaccurate or incomplete information in the portfolio, and contractual disclaimers related to the accounts) that a specific portfolio of clients' accounts might contain unreliable data, but continued to represent that consumers owed the claimed amount on the accounts in question without reviewing [documentation]. . . . [Pressler] have unfairly collected or attempted to collect a debt by in many instances relying exclusively on summary data provided by clients without having reviewed supporting documentation underlying the facts [Pressler] asserts. . . . These practices are likely to cause substantial injury to consumers, for example, by imposing costs in defending improperly filed or outright erroneous lawsuits. These injuries are not reasonably avoidable by consumers because, among other things, when a consumer is sued, he or she must defend or otherwise respond to the lawsuit, or else face a default judgment."

Case Questions

1. Although this is an enforcement action against Pressler by the CFPB, do individuals who have been victimized by Pressler have any legal recourse?
2. Why is it relevant that actual attorneys generally spent less than a few minutes, sometimes less than 30 seconds, reviewing each case before initiating a lawsuit?
3. *Focus on Critical Thinking:* Have you, a family member, or a friend ever been contacted by a debt collector? Did the collection agent use intimidation tactics? Did it violate the FDCPA?

KEY TERMS

Warranty p. 678   A seller's (or lessor's) legally enforceable promise to a consumer concerning the quality and/or functionality of a product.

Consumer law p. 678   The statutory and administrative body of law that protects consumers engaging in transactions with merchants and creditors.

Express warranty p. 679   A warranty that arises when a seller makes a representation of fact about a product.

Implied warranty p. 679   A warranty that exists even when the seller does not make a specific representation about the product.

Disclaim p. 680   To renounce a legal right or claim.

Written express warranty p. 682   A warranty whose terms are put in writing for the consumer.

Consumer Product Safety Act (CPSA) p. 684   The federal statute that created the Consumer Product Safety Commission, with the aim of making consumer products safer.

Federal Trade Commission Act (FTCA) p. 685   A federal law enacted in 1914 that established the Federal Trade Commission, which administers the act; intended as a catch-all statute that has been construed as including all the prohibitions of the other antitrust laws.

Federal Trade Commission (FTC) p. 685 An agency charged with the broad mandate of preventing unfair and deceptive acts or practices in commercial transactions.

Consumer Financial Protection Bureau (CFPB) p. 685 Independent agency created by the Wall Street Reform and Consumer Protection Act responsible for consumer education, regulation of credit and loan companies, and enforcement of consumer protection laws.

Consumer Review Fairness Act (CRFA) p. 686 Federal legislation that protects people's ability to share their honest opinions about a business's products, services, or conduct in any forum, including social media.

Telephone Consumer Protection Act and **Telemarketing and Consumer Fraud and Abuse Prevention Act** p. 688 Two statutes that regulate telemarketing firms and practices; allow consumers to opt out of unwanted calls from telemarketers, ban the use of unsolicited recorded calls and faxes, and prohibit telemarketers from making false representations.

Federal Odometer Act p. 688 A law that makes it a crime to change vehicle odometers and requires that any faulty odometer be plainly disclosed in writing to potential buyers.

Controlling the Assault of Non-Solicited Pornography and Marketing Act of 2003 p. 690 A federal statute that regulates the sending of unsolicited e-mail (spam) by prohibiting certain practices, such as falsifying the "from" name and information in the subject line, and requiring the sender to provide a physical address of the producer of the e-mail. Also called *CAN-SPAM Act*.

Food, Drug and Cosmetic Act (FDCA) p. 692 The federal statute that created the Food and Drug Administration and that requires the makers of certain food ingredients, additives, drugs, or medical devices to obtain formal FDA approval before selling the product to the general public.

Food and Drug Administration (FDA) p. 692 The federal agency that regulates the testing, manufacturing, and distributing of foods, medications, and medical devices.

Creditor p. 692 Any party that regularly extends credit and to which a debt becomes owed.

Borrower p. 692 The party to whom credit is extended and who owes the debt.

Consumer Credit Protection Act (CCPA) p. 693 Federal legislation that regulates credit transactions between a creditor and a borrower and provides consumer protections in the areas of disclosure of credit terms, credit reporting, antidiscrimination laws, and collection of debts from consumers; serves as the centerpiece of federal statutory regulation of credit transactions.

Truth in Lending Act (TILA) p. 693 The part of the Consumer Credit Protection Act that requires lenders to disclose to borrower applicants certain information about the loan or terms of credit and mandates uniform methods of computation and explanation of the terms of the loan or credit arrangements.

Regulation Z p. 693 The part of the Truth in Lending Act requiring that certain written disclosures be made prior to the time that a credit transaction is consummated.

Equal Credit Opportunity Act p. 695 Federal legislation, passed in 1974, that prohibits discrimination of a credit applicant based on the applicant's race, religion, national origin, color, gender, age, or marital status.

Credit Card Accountability Responsibility and Disclosure Act of 2009 (CARD Act) p. 696 Federal legislation that protects consumers from unreasonable interest rate increases and credit card fees and requires card issuers to give a 45-day advance notice of any impending rate increase.

Fair and Accurate Credit Transactions (FACT) Act p. 697 Federal legislation that requires credit bureaus to stop reporting any fraudulent account information from the time a consumer alleges identity theft until the conclusion of the investigation.

Consumer Leasing Act (CLA) p. 698 Federal legislation that regulates lessors engaged in leasing or arranging leases for consumers in the ordinary course of business.

Fair Credit Reporting Act (FCRA) p. 698 Federal legislation that sets privacy rights for consumer credit reports and requires that the credit bureaus give individual consumers complete and timely access to their own credit reports.

Fair Debt Collection Practices Act (FDCPA) p. 698 A federal statute that regulates agents of the creditor involved in debt collection for consumer debts and that requires the collection agency to make known certain rights of the debtor.

Validation disclosure p. 699 A notice in which a collection agency, when making initial contact with a debtor, makes known certain rights of the debtor, including the fact that he has 30 days to dispute the debt; required under the Fair Debt Collection Practices Act.

CHAPTER REVIEW QUESTIONS

1. **Which warranty applies when a buyer relies on a seller's promises that a product can be used in a certain way that is not necessarily its ordinary use?**
   a. Express
   b. Implied—merchantability
   c. Implied—fitness for a particular purpose
   d. Implied—extraordinary use

2. **The use of the words "as is" or "with all faults" are typically sufficient to _____ express and implied warranties.**
   a. Affirm
   b. Disclaim
   c. Confer
   d. Assert

3. **Johnson helps out his neighbor Russell by lending him $1,000 to cover Russell's daughter's tuition bill. Russell fails to pay the money back and Johnson is forced to sue him to recover the costs. Russell asserts TILA as a defense because Johnson never gave him a TILA disclosure statement. Who prevails?**
   a. Johnson, because TILA doesn't apply to this transaction.
   b. Johnson, because Russell had adequate time to cancel the loan.
   c. Russell, because no TILA Notice was issued.
   d. Russell, because Johnson did not give him adequate opportunity to cancel.

4. **Which of the following is an illegal practice wherein a seller advertises a good for an artificially low price but intends on convincing buyers to buy a different good?**
   a. Discounting
   b. Bait and switch
   c. Telemarketing
   d. Breach of warranty

5. **The Fair Debt Collection Practices Act (FDCPA) prohibits agents of a creditor from which practice(s) when collecting a debt?**
   a. Contacting the debtor at inconvenient times, such as early morning.
   b. Posing as an attorney or law enforcement officer.
   c. Threatening incarceration as a method to collect the debt.
   d. All of the above.

Answers and explanations are provided at the end of this chapter.

THEORY TO PRACTICE

Outdoor World Inc. is a retailer of sporting goods gear, equipment, and accessories for use in outdoor sports and camping. Outdoor World carries two brands of tents, the Extreme Tent and the Tectonic Tent. The Extreme is more popular and less expensive, but the manufacturers of the Tectonic have promised financial incentives to Outdoor World for selling a certain amount of Tectonic Tents.

1. Suppose the manager of Outdoor World places this advertisement in the newspaper: "Extreme Tents 50% off—This week only." Willen, in the market for a tent, sees the advertisement and arrives at Outdoor World the next day. The manager explains to Willen that the Extreme is temporarily out of stock and tries to sell him the Tectonic instead. Does the manager's conduct constitute a deceptive trade practice? What law governs unfair trade practices?

2. In Question 1 above, assume that Willen informs the manager that he is moving to Iceland and will require a tent that can maintain a certain degree of warmth. The manager tells Willen that he, himself,

is an avid camper and has used the Tectonic recently. Although there is no specific reference to such a quality on the label, the manager assures Willen that the Tectonic will maintain warmth. Did the manager create a warranty? What kind of warranty?

3. In Question 2 above, assume that Willen purchases the Tectonic and that the agreement of sale for the tent contains this provision: "All implied warranties are hereby excluded." Is Willen still protected by any warranty? Which one(s)?

4. Assume that Outdoor World wishes to begin a marketing campaign by sending its existing customers e-mail advertisements of sales and new items. What kinds of requirements should Outdoor World be aware of in order to comply with the CAN-SPAM Act?

5. After a downturn in the economy and a tightening of consumer credit, Outdoor World decides to offer qualified customers credit for consumer purchases. What is the legal impact of this decision?

6. One year after Outdoor World begins offering credit accounts for its patrons (see Question 5), one customer defaults. The manager calls the customer to try to collect the debt owed. Is the manager subject to the provisions of the Fair Debt Collection Practices Act? Why or why not?

LEGAL STRATEGY 101

GMOs: To Disclose or Not to Disclose

Should Congress or the FDA require the mandatory disclosure of GMOs, or "genetically modified organisms," in food products?

According to one estimate, more than 90 percent of the corn, soybeans, and sugar beets cultivated in the United States are genetically engineered in one form or another, and GMO ingredients are now present in 75 to 80 percent of processed foods in the United States.[32] Nevertheless, in the absence of a federal law requiring GMO food labels, the FDA has taken a *laissez-faire,* or "hands off," approach and does not require GMO labeling in food products.[33]

In July of 2015, the U.S. House of Representatives passed a federal GMO labeling bill known as the "Safe and Accurate Food Labeling Act of 2015." This bill would have allowed the FDA to require GMO labeling only where there is a "material difference" between the GMO food and its conventional counterpart (in terms of functional, nutritional, compositional, allergenic, or other properties) and only where the "disclosure of

GMO foods. Onewiss/Getty Images

such material difference is necessary to protect public health and safety or to prevent the label or labeling of the food so produced from being false or misleading in any particular."[34] Although the bill was approved by the House of Representatives, it died in the Senate.

Given this inertia at the federal level, companies have filled this legislative and regulatory vacuum by following different legal and business strategies. Most companies continue to not disclose the presence of GMOs in their food and beverage products. After all, such disclosure is still not legally required at the federal level.

---

[32]*See* PR Newswire, *Studies Show GMOs in Majority of U.S. Processed Foods, 58% of Americans Unaware of Issue,* Oct. 7, 2015.

[33]*See* FDA, *Guidance for Industry: Voluntary Labeling Indicating Whether Foods Have or Have Not Been Derived from Genetically Engineered Plants* (Nov. 2015).

[34]*See* H.R. 1599, 114th Congress (2015–2016).

Some companies, however, have decided to voluntarily relabel their products to indicate that they contain no genetically engineered components. Tropicana Orange Juice containers, for example, now contain a "non-GMO" label, and General Mills has started producing non-GMO Cheerios.

A few other companies have actually chosen to voluntarily disclose the presence of GMOs in their food products! In January 2016, Campbell Soup surprised the food and beverage industry by becoming the first major company to announce that it would begin disclosing the presence of genetically engineered ingredients like corn, soy, and sugar beets in its food products.[35]

[35]Stephanie Strom, *Campbell Labels Will Disclose G.M.O. Ingredients*, N.Y. Times, Jan. 7, 2016.

CRITICAL THINKING QUESTIONS

1. If you were the CEO of a food or beverage company, which strategy would you follow?
2. Should Congress adopt a uniform, national standard regarding the labeling of GMOs in food and beverages, or should we "let the market decide" (i.e., let each company decide for itself whether to disclose or not to disclose the presence or absence of GMOs in its products)? Using the strategies you've learned in Chapter 1, "Legal Foundations," draft a one-page memorandum to your manager as to whether to disclose GMOs in your products.

MANAGER'S CHALLENGE

Managers are central in business planning discussions. Having sufficient legal acumen enables them to limit the company's liability while maximizing its opportunities. Assume that you are a manager supervising a group of midlevel managers in this chapter's Theory to Practice problem. You receive the following e-mail from the chief operating officer of Outdoor World:

> Given the decline in customers who are buying new outdoor sports accessories, senior management is considering a plan to begin selling preowned sporting equipment at discount prices. However, we want to make sure that we understand the liability exposure in tandem with the cost-benefit analysis. Lead a small group discussion among the midlevel managers about the opportunities and threats that such a plan would involve, and write a two-page summary memorandum of your conclusions.

See Connect for Manager's Challenge sample answers.

CASE SUMMARY 21.1 Barrer v. Chase Bank USA, 566 F.3d 883 (9th Cir. 2009)

TRUTH IN LENDING ACT

Barrer obtained a credit card with Chase in 2004 and accepted the cardmember agreement. In February 2005, Chase mailed a Change in Terms Notice to Barrer that notified him of an increase in the annual percentage rate from 8.99 percent to 24.24 percent in certain events, including payment default and persistently late payments. The notice provided a right for Barrer to reject these terms in writing, but he did not. In April 2005, Barrer's APR jumped to 24.24 percent.

Chase claimed that it increased the rate because of information obtained from a credit agency about Barrer's being an increased credit risk, even though that condition was not listed in the notice as an event qualifying for a rate increase.

CASE QUESTIONS

1. Do Chase's actions comply with the TILA? Why or why not?
2. Shouldn't Barrer be liable for failing to reject the new terms?

CASE SUMMARY 21.2 Myers v. LHR, Inc., 543 F. Supp. 2d 1215 (S.D. Cal. 2008)

FAIR DEBT COLLECTION PRACTICES ACT

Myers owed over $11,000 to an automobile finance company in 2001. LHR was hired to collect the debt, and an LHR agent contacted her with threats of a lawsuit and garnishment of her wages. Myers negotiated a settlement whereby LHR accepted approximately $3,000 as complete payment for the debt. Myers wire-transferred the money to LHR to satisfy the debt and later received a letter saying the debt was paid in full. However, Myers later found out that her settled debt was still reported to the credit agencies by LHR and this adversely affected her credit rating. Despite the settlement, LHR agents continued to call Myers, threatening to sue her, garnish her wages, and report her to government authorities for tax evasion.

CASE QUESTIONS

1. Were LHR's actions lawful under the FDCPA? Why or why not?
2. If LHR's actions were not lawful, what could it have done to comply with the act?

CASE SUMMARY 21.3 Phoenix of Broward, Inc. v. McDonald's Corp., 489 F.3d 1156 (11th Cir. 2007)

CONSUMER FRAUD ACT

From 1995 to 2001, McDonald's, the famous fast-food chain, sponsored promotional games including "Monopoly Games at McDonald's," "The Deluxe Monopoly Game," and "Who Wants to Be a Millionaire?" For each of these promotional games, McDonald's conducted an extensive marketing and advertising campaign through which it represented that all customers had a fair and equal chance to win and it specified the odds of winning. However, the FBI investigated McDonald's based upon claims that the game pieces required to win the high-value, "million-dollar" prizes were compromised and were being diverted to friends and family of personnel who had access to these pieces. Yet throughout this investigation, and even after individuals pleaded guilty to conspiracy charges related to the diversionary practices, McDonald's continued its advertising practices. Phoenix, a Burger King franchisee, sued under the Consumer Fraud Act (CFA), claiming that the advertisements stating everyone has a fair and equal chance to win are false and deceptive.

CASE QUESTIONS

1. Does Phoenix have a claim under the Consumer Fraud Act? Why or why not?
2. Are there any other factors affecting whether or not Phoenix has a claim?

CASE SUMMARY 21.4 American Suzuki Motor Corp. v. Carney, 37 Cal. App. 4th 1291 (1995)

IMPLIED WARRANTIES

Carney purchased a Suzuki Samurai SUV. Although Carney had never experienced any safety issues with his Suzuki, several SUV rollover incidents made him wary of continuing to drive the vehicle. Carney sued for a refund based on a theory of breach of implied warranty, citing an automotive expert who tested the Suzuki Samurai and concluded that it has a higher rollover risk because of its high center of gravity, narrow tread width, and light weight.

CASE QUESTIONS

1. Which implied warranty is Carney claiming here, and what is the legal standard for such warranties?
2. Can Suzuki disclaim this warranty? Why or why not?

CASE SUMMARY 21.5 Hauter v. Zogarts, 534 P.2d 377 (Cal. 1975)

WARRANTIES

Zogarts makes the "Golfing Gizmo" that Hauter received as a gift from his mother for his 13th birthday. The Gizmo is billed as a "completely equipped backyard driving range" and consists of a golf ball attached to a cord that causes the ball to come back to the player after it is struck. The Gizmo's box reads, "COMPLETELY SAFE BALL WILL NOT HIT PLAYER." Hauter read the safety manual and used the Gizmo a dozen times. In one hit, however, he hit too far under the ball, the cord tangled, and the ball struck Hauter in the temple. Hauter suffered severe permanent injuries. Hauter sued Zogarts for breach of express and implied warranty. Zogarts defended by pointing out that the photos of the man using the Gizmo properly were a disclaimer that it was "completely safe" only when used in that way.

CASE QUESTIONS

1. What words on the box could have created the express warranty?
2. Is the phrase "completely safe" a verifiable fact, or is it puffery?

 Self-Check ANSWERS Express Warranty

1. Express warranty created by specific advertised promises such as "instantly stops" and "incapacitates."
2. No express warranty—puffery, not promises.
3. Express warranty created by verifiable promise of fact.
4. Although advertisements can create warranties by what they show, it is unlikely that any express warranty was created here because no express promise was made about quality.

CHAPTER REVIEW QUESTIONS: Answers and Explanations

1. **c.** An implied warranty for fitness for a particular purpose arises when a buyer relies on the seller's advice that a product is fit for a certain use. Answer choices (a) and (b) are incorrect because express warranties and merchantability do not require buyer reliance on the seller's promise. Answer (d) is incorrect because no such warranty exists.

2. **b.** The UCC allows sellers to disclaim warranties through use of conspicuous language. Answer choices (a), (c), and (d) are incorrect because they are the opposite of disclaim.

3. **a.** This is a private transaction that is not subject to TILA disclosures as Johnson is not regularly engaged in the business of lending. Thus, the remaining answers are incorrect.

4. **b.** Bait and switch is an illegal practice in which a seller advertises a good for an artificially low price (the bait) but intends on convincing buyers to buy a different good (the switch). Answer choices (a) and (c) are incorrect because they are not illegal practices. Answer (d) is incorrect because it is unrelated to the price.

5. **d.** Answer choices (a), (b), and (c) are all prohibited by the FDCPA. Thus, answer (d) is correct.

CHAPTER 22
Criminal Law and Procedure in Business

©philsajonesen/Getty Images

Learning Objectives

After studying this chapter, students who have mastered the material will be able to:

22-1 Explain the origins and sources of criminal law and procedure.

22-2 Distinguish between criminal law and criminal procedure.

22-3 Compare criminal law with civil law.

22-4 Articulate the underlying tenets of criminal law and the requirements for criminal liability.

22-5 Identify circumstances in which business managers and owners may be liable for criminal violations by a corporation.

22-6 Provide specific examples of white-collar crime laws that may impact a business entity and/or its owners and managers.

22-7 Explain the steps in the criminal justice system.

22-8 Name and explain the various constitutional procedural protections afforded to those accused of a crime.

22-9 Explain the exclusionary rule and how it applies to business.

One way that the government regulates the practices and operations of business owners and managers is through **criminal law**. This chapter focuses on how criminal law, criminal procedure, and the criminal justice system impact the legal environment of business. In this chapter, we discuss

- The origins and sources of criminal law.
- Elements and examples of criminal acts.
- The steps in the criminal justice system.
- Legal protections for those accused of committing a crime.

ORIGINS AND SOURCES OF CRIMINAL LAW AND PROCEDURE

Crime in the United States is ordinarily dealt with by state authorities, predominantly under state statutory law. While each state has its own system of criminal law, there is an increasing body of federal criminal law. Thus, the federal criminal justice system exists alongside (sometimes overlapping) the state systems. Much of American criminal law is derived from English criminal law, which existed primarily as common law with some statutory mandates. However, in the 1960s, state legislatures began to assemble various statutes addressing criminal culpability and integrating state common law to form more comprehensive criminal codes.

MODERN CRIMINAL LAW: THE MODEL PENAL CODE

Nearly two-thirds of the states have enacted criminal codes based on the **Model Penal Code (MPC)** adopted by the American Law Institute (ALI) in 1962.[1] The vocabulary and formation of the MPC have been very influential in shaping criminal law notions, even in states where the MPC has not been formally adopted. However, many states have retained certain portions of their common law within their criminal codes as well.

In 1971, the congressionally appointed National Commission on Reform of Federal Criminal Laws issued a model federal criminal code that consolidated and clarified existing statutory law. However, it has long been settled that there are no federal common law crimes.[2] Although a state criminal statute and a federal criminal statute may outlaw identical or substantially identical conduct, state law and federal law may coexist unless the federal statute contains specific language that preempts state law.[3]

CRIMINAL LAW VERSUS CRIMINAL PROCEDURE

While *criminal law* defines the boundaries of behavior and prescribes sanctions for violating those boundaries, **criminal procedure** refers to the legal process and safeguards afforded to individuals (and in some cases business entities) during criminal investigations, arrests, trials, and sentencing. Criminal *law* consists of a body of law that, for the purposes of preventing harm to society, declares what conduct is criminal and prescribes the punishment to be imposed for such conduct. Criminal *procedure* sets limits on the government's authority in applying criminal law. Criminal procedure is covered in detail later in this chapter.

Criminal Law and Civil Law

Recall the distinctions between civil law and criminal law covered in Chapter 1, "Legal Foundations." Civil laws are designed to compensate parties (including businesses) for damages as a result of another's conduct. Criminal statutes are a protection of *society,* and the violation of a criminal law results in a penalty to the violator, such as a fine or imprisonment, based on the wrongdoer's level of culpability. It is important to remember that these categories are not mutually exclusive; one can violate a criminal law and commit a civil wrong in the very same act. For example, suppose that Mcduff is an accountant for Shakespeare Book Company (SBC) and steals $100,000 from the business by creating a fake employee on the company's books and secretly paying the fake employee's salary to himself. Upon discovery, SBC notifies the authorities, and Mcduff will likely be charged with various criminal offenses such as grand theft and fraud. If he is convicted, he will likely be incarcerated for an extended period of time. Although sometimes courts order restitution as part of a criminal sentence, SBC may also choose to file a civil lawsuit against Mcduff individually in order to recover the losses due to Mcduff's commission of the tort[4] of conversion (the civil counterpart of theft). SBC

LO 22-1
Explain the origins and sources of criminal law and procedure.

LO 22-2
Distinguish between criminal law and criminal procedure.

LO 22-3
Compare criminal law with civil law.

Legal Speak >))

Culpability
The quality of being blameworthy in criminal law; it is used to assess the accused's guilt and determine whether he committed the crime purposefully, knowingly, recklessly, or negligently.

> **KEY POINT**
>
> Criminal *law* defines the boundaries of behavior and prescribes sanctions for violating those boundaries; criminal *procedure* refers to legal protections provided to citizens during criminal investigations, arrests, trials, and sentencing.

---

[1] Recall from Chapter 1, "Legal Foundations," that the ALI is an organization of attorneys, judges, and law professors that produces model statutes to promote consistency in the application of the law from state to state.
[2] *United States v. Hudson & Goodwin*, 11 U.S. 32 (1812).
[3] *Goldstein v. California*, 412 U.S. 546 (1973).
[4] Torts were covered in detail in Chapter 9, "Torts and Products Liability."

may also be entitled to compensation from Mcduff for other incidental expenses it incurred as a result of the theft (such as costs of detecting the theft). If SBC is successful in obtaining a civil judgment against Mcduff, the company may then attempt to recover its losses by tapping Mcduff's personal assets.

Burden of Proof One significant difference between a criminal case and a civil case is the **burden of proof**. In a civil case, the plaintiff needs to prove only by a **preponderance of the evidence** that the defendant committed a civil wrong. This means that the fact finder need not be completely convinced that the plaintiff's arguments in the case should prevail. Rather, the fact finder need be convinced only that the defendant's liability was *more likely than not* for the plaintiff to meet her burden of proof. In criminal cases, where the stakes may involve an individual's liberty, the standard of proof is much higher. In a criminal case, the government must prove its case **beyond a reasonable doubt**. Thus, a fact finder must be convinced that the defendant's criminal liability is not in doubt to a reasonable person.

General Principles of Criminal Law

LO 22-4

Articulate the underlying tenets of criminal law and the requirements for criminal liability.

There are two important underlying tenets to criminal law: *legality* and *punishment*. The principle of **legality** is a protection of individuals from being charged with some unspecified general offense. Legality simply requires that crimes be specifically proscribed by law in advance of the conduct sought to be punished. This includes the notion that the Constitution bars both Congress and state legislatures from enacting retroactive criminal statutes (known as *ex post facto* laws). Statutes that fail to give fair warning that a particular conduct is unlawful may be struck down by the courts as too vague. The principle of **punishment** is based on the concepts that (1) criminal law acts as a *deterrent*, (2) it *removes* dangerous criminals from the population, and (3) *rehabilitation* is an important part of the criminal justice system. Punishments are applied using a sentencing system that follows a general range of years prescribed by the legislature. After conviction, a sentence is imposed by the court based on the individual trial judge's discretion and assessment of the severity of the crime and mitigating circumstances. However, starting in the 1980s, public dissatisfaction with an actual or perceived view that courts were not imposing sufficiently stiff penalties spurred federal and state legislatures to pass laws requiring courts to assess penalties based on statutorily prescribed **sentencing guidelines**. These guidelines have had the impact of severely restricting judicial discretion. This same movement is also responsible for a spate of statutes that include mandatory minimum sentences for certain offenses as well as minimum sentences for repeat offenders (for example, some states adopted a "three strikes" law, which requires a 25-year sentence for a third felony conviction). Despite criticism by many prominent judges, attorneys, and legal scholars on various fronts, state and federal legislators continue to generally support the concept of sentencing guidelines and mandatory minimums.

Legal Speak >))

Mitigating Circumstances
Facts that do not excuse a crime but may lessen the punishment. For example, mitigating circumstances that might lessen the sentence for murder from death to life imprisonment include no prior criminal history, minor participation in the killing, mental illness, or young age at the time of the killing.

Criminal Liability

From a legal perspective, a crime has two parts: (1) a physical part, in which the defendant committed an *act* or *omission,* and (2) a mental part, which involves the defendant's subjective *state of mind*. Thus, an analysis of criminal liability involves three fundamental questions: First, did the defendant actually commit the prohibited act? Second, did the defendant have a culpable state of mind? Third, does the law give the defendant a palpable defense (such as a self-defense claim to a homicide charge)?

Act Requirement The **act requirement**, also called by its Latin name, *actus reus,* requires the government to prove that a defendant's actions objectively satisfied the elements of a particular offense. The act requirement is based on the fundamental criminal law tenet that evil thoughts alone do not constitute a criminal act. Rather, there must be some overt conduct (either an act or an omission), and it must be voluntary. Courts generally follow the rule that an act is voluntary unless it is demonstrated that the defendant acted based on physical compulsion, reflex, or certain physiological or neurological diseases. An act by omission occurs when a crime is defined in terms of *failure* to act. For example, if the chief financial officer fails to disclose data required by federal securities law, she has committed an omission that satisfies the act requirement.

Mental Requirement The mental element, also called by its Latin name, *mens rea,* which translates literally into "guilty mind," requires that the defendant have a requisite degree of culpability with regard to each element of a given crime. The fundamental underpinning is that an act does not make a person guilty unless his mind is guilty.[5] The words contained in a criminal statute to express the guilty mind requirement include *intentionally, knowingly, maliciously, willfully,* and *wantonly*. However, some criminal statutes set the intent requirement at mere recklessness or negligence, rather than actual intent, in determining the level of culpability. Thus, an act or omission in which the defendant's conduct deviated from the standard of conduct so grossly that a reasonable person would judge it as criminal may also satisfy the mental element requirement.

Courts and legislatures have also established certain rules for applying the mental element requirement in cases of *mistake*. Certain statutes also impose *strict liability,* whereby the mental element is assumed by certain conduct so that the defendant's culpable state of mind need not be proved.

Figure 22.1 illustrates the typical language of the act requirement and the mental requirement, using an example from a Florida criminal statute prohibiting forgery.

Defenses Even when the requisite mental state and criminal act standards are proved, the law provides for certain defenses based on unique circumstances of the crime. **Self-defense** is an example of a defense to a criminal charge of homicide in that the law recognizes that certain cases necessitate the use of deadly force to repel an attack in which the defendant reasonably fears that death or substantial harm is about to occur either to the defendant or to a third party. The rules governing self-defense are complex and vary from state to state, especially on the question of whether the defendant is required to retreat before using deadly force. The defense afforded by the self-defense doctrine is at its height when it involves use of deadly force to repel an attack in the victim's home or place of business.

FIGURE 22.1 Excerpt from a Florida Criminal Statute: Fla. Stat. Ann. § 831.02

Uttering forged instruments

"Whoever **utters** and **publishes** as true a false, forged or altered record, deed, instrument or other writing mentioned in § 831.01 [i.e., 'letter of attorney, policy of insurance, bill of lading, bill of exchange or promissory note, or an order, acquittance, or discharge for money or other property'] **knowing** the same to be false, altered, forged or counterfeited, with **intent** to injure or defraud any person, shall be guilty of a felony of the third degree. . . ."

Excerpt from a Florida Criminal Statute: F.S.A. 831.02

---

[5]Expressed as the common law Latin maxim: *Actus reus non facit reum nisi mens sit rea* (*Collins Latin,* 2009).

The other major category of defense is **mental incapacity**. As you may imagine, this defense is very controversial and is sometimes colloquially called the *insanity defense.* That term is potentially misleading because in certain jurisdictions incapacity covers a wide variety of conditions in addition to insanity. Although mental incapacity has a variety of definitions depending on the jurisdiction, the Model Penal Code (MPC) requires the defendant's actions to be related to some type of mental disease or defect.[6] The MPC also specifically rules out any sociopathic personality disorders as the basis for a mental incapacity case.

Less frequently asserted defenses include *duress,* in which a defendant has committed a crime in response to another person's threat to inflict personal injury (threats to property or reputation are insufficient), and *intoxication,* which generally depends on whether the intoxication was voluntary or involuntary. If voluntary, the criminal act is excused only if the defendant was so intoxicated that he could not form the requisite mental intent (guilty mind) to have criminal culpability. If involuntary, the defense is broader but still requires proof that the intoxication rendered the defendant unable to understand that his conduct constituted a crime.

Types of Crimes

Crimes may be classified in several different ways. **Felonies** are crimes that generally carry *one year or more* of incarceration as the penalty. **Misdemeanors** are crimes that carry *up to one year* of incarceration as the penalty. Frequently, states also have degrees (or grades) of crimes within each of those categories that further delineate the seriousness of the crime. Thus, a premeditated murder would be referred to as a first-degree felony, whereas shoplifting a shirt may be defined as a second- (or third-) degree misdemeanor. Many states also have a classification of crimes known as *summary offenses* or *infraction offenses,* which are minor crimes that carry no threat of jail (for first offenders), such as a charge of underage alcohol use.

Crimes are also sometimes classified based on the victim or result of the crime. Crimes in which the perpetrator has used force or violence, such as murder or sexual assault, are classified as *violent crimes.* Crimes that involve offensive or disorderly conduct in public are referred to as *public order crimes.* This category also includes crimes that have no direct victim but that society has judged to be detrimental to public well-being, such as crimes related to narcotics, prostitution, or obscenity. Crimes that involve damage to or stealing of property (such as theft, vandalism, or arson) are usually referred to as *property crimes.* When crimes take place in the business environment, they are classified as *white-collar crimes.*

CRIMINAL LAW AND BUSINESS ENTITIES

LO 22-5
Identify circumstances in which business managers and owners may be liable for criminal violations by a corporation.

While any discussion of criminal law necessarily focuses on the criminal culpability of individuals, business owners and managers should have a fundamental knowledge of how criminal law may be applied to business entities. This knowledge helps business owners and managers to reduce risk and add value to the business by taking affirmative steps to limit criminal culpability for the business and its principals.

The modern trend in criminal law is to expand the scope of criminal statutes to include criminal culpability for corporations and their principals. Courts have allowed liability to exist for corporations so long as the prosecutor can prove that the corporation's agents (not just executive management) were engaged in criminal conduct on behalf of the company.

---

[6]MPC § 4.01(1).

Recall from Chapter 15, "Corporations," that courts have recognized that corporations exist as a separate legal "person." Criminal statutes have embraced the concept that a corporation may be charged with a crime along with, or apart from, its principals or agents. The Model Penal Code (MPC) provides for criminal liability for business entities if any one of the following applies:

1. The criminal act by the business's agent is within the *scope of his employment* and the statute imposes liability on the business for such an act (e.g., the agent shreds documents related to potentially unlawful conduct, creating liability under obstruction of justice).
2. The criminal omission is the failure to perform a specific duty imposed by law (e.g., the agent fails to make important disclosures in a report to investors).
3. The crime was authorized by one of the corporation's top-level managers (e.g., a chief financial officer orders an internal accountant to file a false corporate tax return).

Congress has specifically included business entities in criminal statutes in areas that impact business, including fraud, obstruction of justice, health and safety requirements, sale of ownership interests (securities law), disclosure requirements, environmental regulations, and antitrust or other anticompetition laws.

Individual Liability for Business Crimes

Congress and state legislatures have also expanded criminal culpability for individual officers and directors (and sometimes majority owners) for corporate crimes committed within the scope of their employment. These principals are often included in criminal statutes that require officers and directors to act as responsible corporate officers in complying with statutes and being diligent about adhering to standards set out in statutes and regulations. Because of the inherent difficulties in terms of proof, most statutes do not require the specific mental intent (guilty mind) that is required for other crimes. Since the mid-1970s, legislative bodies have begun to impose what amounts to strict liability statutes for corporate officers even when the officer in question did not have any actual knowledge that a crime had taken place.

Responsible Corporate Officers: The *Park* Doctrine

The *responsible corporate officer* doctrine allows the government to bring criminal charges against corporate officers who, by reason of their position in the corporation, have the responsibility and authority to take necessary measures to prevent or remedy violations of the Food, Drug and Cosmetic Act (FDCA) but fail to act. Officers may be held criminally liable as responsible corporate agents, regardless of whether they were aware of or intended to cause the violation. This doctrine was developed by the U.S. Supreme Court in a famous 1975 case, *United States v. Park,* in which the court upheld the conviction of a corporate officer for a misdemeanor crime under the FDCA after his company was held responsible for putting adulterated or contaminated food into commerce. For this reason, the responsible corporate officer doctrine is often referred to as the *Park* doctrine. The case centered on John Park, the president of a large national retail food chain with approximately 36,000 employees, 874 retail outlets, and 16 warehouses. In 1970, the Food and Drug Administration (FDA) observed and advised Park of unsanitary conditions, including rodent infestation. After the violations were not corrected, the government charged the company *and* Park with misdemeanors under the FDCA. Park argued that he could not have possibly had the requisite knowledge necessary to commit a crime, but the U.S. Supreme Court affirmed his conviction. The Court pointed out the narrowness of the decision (i.e., limited to FDCA violations), but nonetheless affirmed that corporate agents have a high level of responsibility when it comes to the well-being of the public. The Court rejected Park's argument:

> The requirements of foresight and vigilance imposed on responsible corporate agents are beyond question demanding, and perhaps onerous, but they are no more stringent than the public has a right to expect of those who voluntarily assume positions of authority in business enterprises whose services and products affect the health and well-being of the public that supports them.

U.S. v. Park, 421 U.S. 658, 672 (1975).

Case 22.1 provides an example of individual officer liability in the context of the *Park* doctrine.

CASE 22.1 United States v. DeCoster, 828 F.3d 626 (8th Cir. 2016)

FACT SUMMARY Jack DeCoster owned Quality Egg, LLC, an Iowa egg production company. Jack's son, Peter DeCoster, served as the company's chief operating officer. Quality Egg operated six farm sites with 73 barns that were filled with five million egg-laying hens. It also had 24 barns that were filled with young chickens that had not yet begun to lay eggs. Additionally, the company owned several processing plants where eggs were cleaned, packed, and shipped. Jack also owned and operated several egg production companies in Maine, and Peter worked at those facilities. In 2008, salmonella enteritidis ("salmonella") tests conducted at the Maine facilities came back positive. The DeCosters succeeded in eliminating salmonella from their Maine facilities by following the recommendations of hired consultants, including a poultry disease specialist and a rodent control expert. In its Iowa facility, however, Quality Egg did not test or divert eggs from the market despite receiving multiple positive results from hens indicating a potential for salmonella. Experts hired by Quality Egg recommended adopting the same safety measures in Iowa as had been used in Maine. Although the DeCosters claimed they adopted all of the recommendations, the precautions implemented by Quality Egg failed to eradicate salmonella.

In August 2010, federal and state officials determined that a salmonella outbreak had originated at Quality Egg's facilities, resulting in approximately 56,000 American consumers falling ill with salmonellosis. In response, Quality Egg recalled eggs that had been shipped from five of its six Iowa farm sites between May and August 2010. After a Food and Drug Administration (FDA) inspection of Quality Egg's facilities revealed dangerous conditions that could lead to contamination, the government began a criminal investigation of the company's food safety practices and ultimately filed criminal charges for failing to prevent or correct a violation of the Food, Drug and Cosmetic Act (FDCA). The DeCosters both pled guilty, as responsible corporate officers of Quality Egg, LLC, for introducing eggs that had been adulterated with salmonella into interstate commerce. The trial court sentenced Jack and Peter to three months' imprisonment. The DeCosters appeal, arguing that their prison sentences were unreasonable and disproportionate because they had no specific knowledge the eggs the company distributed had salmonella.

SYNOPSIS OF DECISION AND OPINION The U.S. Court of Appeals for the Eighth Circuit affirmed the trial court's decision to sentence the DeCosters to incarceration. The court reasoned that under the FDCA responsible corporate officer concept, individuals who by reason of their position in the corporation have the responsibility and authority to take necessary measures to prevent or remedy violations of the FDCA and fail to do so may be held criminally liable as responsible corporate agents, regardless of whether they were actually aware of or intended to cause the violation. The court agreed with the trial court's findings that

(continued)

the DeCosters knew or should have known of the risks posed by the insanitary conditions at Quality Egg in Iowa, knew or should have known that additional testing needed to be performed before the suspected shell eggs were distributed to consumers, and knew or should have known of proper remedial and preventative measures to reduce the presence of salmonella.

WORDS OF THE COURT: Prison Sentence Appropriate "On this record, the DeCosters' three month prison sentences are not grossly disproportionate to the gravity of their misdemeanor offenses. When defining the statutory penalties in the FDCA, Congress recognized the importance of placing the burden on corporate officers to protect consumers 'who are wholly helpless' from purchasing adulterated food products which could make them ill. . . . The 2010 salmonella outbreak may have affected up to 56,000 victims, some of whom were hospitalized or suffered long term injuries. For one example, a child hospitalized in an intensive care unit for eight days was saved by antibiotics which damaged his teeth, causing them to be capped in stainless steel."

Case Questions

1. Why is it important in this case that the DeCosters' conduct violated the FDCA?
2. What was the DeCosters' theory of the case on appeal?
3. *Focus on Critical Thinking:* Given what we know about the impact of the salmonella outbreak in 2010, would there be any tort claims against Quality Egg? Against the DeCosters? Explain.

CONCEPT SUMMARY Criminal Law

- Criminal law is based on state and federal laws that started as common law crimes but were codified into statutes based on the Model Penal Code (MPC).
- While some actions involve both criminal and civil liability, civil laws protect individuals by redressing injuries and criminal laws protect society as a whole by punishing wrongdoers.
- Criminal liability requires both a bad act (*actus reus*) *and* a guilty mind (*mens rea*).
- Even when a requisite mental state and bad act are proved, the accused can offer a defense such as mental incapacity, duress, or self-defense to avoid criminal liability.
- Corporations and their managers can be guilty of the crimes of their employees if the crime was committed for some corporate advantage or benefit of the company.

WHITE-COLLAR CRIME

White-collar crimes usually signify criminal violations by corporations or individuals, including fraud, bribery, theft, and conspiracy committed in the course of the offender's occupational duties. Typically, these crimes are set out in state and/or federal statutes.

Fraud

Perhaps the most common white-collar crime is fraud. *Fraud* is a broad general term used to describe a transaction in which one party makes false representations of a matter of fact (either by words or conduct) that are intended to deceive another. In certain cases,

LO 22-6

Provide specific examples of white-collar crime laws that may impact a business entity and/or its owners and managers.

active concealment of a material fact (versus an affirmative false representation) may also constitute fraud. The basic elements of criminal fraud are (1) a false representation (or concealment) concerning a material fact and (2) another party that relies on the false misrepresentation of the fact and suffers damages as a result. A material fact is one that is essential to the agreement or one that affects the value of the transaction. For example, suppose that Rasputin applies for a loan to start his business. Because his finances are in dire straits, Rasputin submits a false set of tax returns to the bank loan officer. Based on this information, the bank lends Rasputin the money. Rasputin has committed a fraud upon the bank. Bank fraud of this nature is a felony punishable under state and, depending on the bank, federal criminal statutes.

In 1990, Congress passed the **Mail Fraud Act**[7] with the intent of giving federal prosecutors significant leverage in prosecuting white-collar criminals. The statute criminalizes any fraud in which the defrauding party uses the mail or any wire, radio, or television in perpetrating the fraud. This comprehensive approach to criminalizing fraud is based on Congress's authority to regulate mail and interstate commerce. It also covers any *organization* of a scheme to defraud by false pretenses. For example, in the Rasputin example discussed earlier, suppose that Rasputin sets up an elaborate scheme to fool investors into thinking that he has invented a new product that will bring in several millions of dollars of revenue. He designs a brochure and mails it to several wealthy individuals. At this point, Rasputin has committed mail fraud even though he has not actually induced any investors. The ease of prosecution for mail fraud has made it a primary tool used by prosecutors in white-collar crime investigations.

Another form of fraud is *embezzlement*. Embezzlement is appropriately categorized as fraud (and not as theft) because it involves fraudulent concealment of financial records to perpetrate theft. Embezzlement occurs when someone in a position of trust creates fraudulent records to disguise the theft. For example, suppose that Rasputin is the controller of WidgetCo. Over the period of a month, Rasputin transfers small amounts of WidgetCo's money to his personal checking account and adjusts the monthly financial statements to indicate that the money is in WidgetCo's account. This act constitutes embezzlement because of the cover-up aspect of the scheme. If Rasputin had come into his office one morning, stolen cash from the safe, and walked out never to return, this would likely constitute theft because no scheme was involved.

Ponzi Schemes

A *Ponzi scheme* is a fraudulent investment operation that pays returns to investors from their own money or money paid by subsequent investors rather than from any actual profit earned. The scheme is named after Charles Ponzi, who became notorious for using the technique in 1903. A Ponzi scheme usually offers returns that other investments cannot match in order to entice new investors. This is generally accomplished in the form of short-term returns that are either abnormally high or unusually consistent. The perpetuation of the returns that a Ponzi scheme advertises and pays requires an ever-increasing flow of money from investors in order to keep the scheme going. The system is destined to collapse because the earnings, if any, are less than the payments. The authorities uncover some schemes before they collapse if an investor suspects that she is a victim and reports the investments to authorities. As more investors become involved, the likelihood of the scheme coming to the attention of authorities increases.

For example, suppose that High Return Investments (HRI) prints advertising brochures that promise a 30 percent return on an investment in just one month—an extraordinary return by any measure. HRI states that it uses a "complex offshore investment strategy

---

[7]10 U.S.C. § 1341.

that is the result of years of study and testing." No matter how fancy the brochures are, it is difficult to attract any large initial investments without a track record. Thus, HRI convinces a few investors to take the risk with small amounts of money. Instead of investing the money, HRI then takes out a loan and repays the initial investors with the promised 30 percent return one month later. This is where HRI sets the trap: Initial investors now invest larger sums, and new investors want a piece of the action. It is no longer necessary to take out a loan because sufficient capital from eager new investors is flowing into HRI's hands. The cascading effect then allows HRI to pay back any loans used to perpetrate the scheme and take handsome bonus fees for managing the money. HRI covers its tracks by producing false investment statements for its investors showing high returns. When one or more investors request a withdrawal, there is sufficient cash to pay out. But HRI's scheme cannot last forever. Typically, HRI's schemes will end up in one of two scenarios: (1) HRI disappears with the investment money or (2) the scheme collapses because too many investors demand their returns at the same time. The second scenario typically happens when investor confidence in the equities markets deteriorates and investors withdraw money from market-based investments in favor of cash and other safer forms. For example, when the financial crisis of 2008 began to shake investor confidence, it unraveled the largest Ponzi scheme ever operated by a single person. Federal prosecutors claim that a 20-year scheme, operated by well-known investment manager Bernard Madoff, cost his investors billions of dollars. In March 2009, Madoff pleaded guilty to 11 felonies, including fraud and perjury. He was given the maximum sentence of 150 years of incarceration. Madoff's accountant was also charged and cooperated with authorities in exchange for leniency. The Madoff case is examined in more detail in Chapter 16's "Legal Strategy 101."

Conspiracy

Conspiracy is an agreement by two or more persons to commit a criminal act. It is itself a punishable offense: All parties to the agreement are subject to prosecution. Because the crime is complete upon agreement, there is a very low threshold for satisfying the criminal act requirement. Conspiracy requires a specific *intent* to achieve the object of the conspiracy but does not require that the act actually be carried out. The Model Penal Code (MPC) contemplates conspiracy as a crime that requires two guilty minds. Therefore, both parties must actually *manifest* intent to commit the criminal act for a conspiracy to occur.

Racketeer Influenced and Corrupt Organizations Act (RICO)

The federal Racketeer Influenced and Corrupt Organizations Act[8] (RICO) was enacted in 1970 with the objective of providing the government with a powerful tool to fight the rising tide of organized crime. One purpose of the RICO law was to prevent organized crime from infiltrating legitimate business operations. The statute makes it a criminal offense for anyone associated with an enterprise to conduct or participate in its affairs through a pattern of racketeering activity. Although racketeering is generally understood to mean an organized conspiracy to commit the crimes of extortion or coercion, state and federal legislatures have added to the definition by including conduct such as engaging in illegal gambling, narcotics trafficking, and prostitution.

The modern trend is for authorities to use the RICO statute in an expansive manner, including criminal conduct that is not traditionally related to organized crime. Because RICO laws define racketeering in such broad terms, including crimes such as wire fraud, mail fraud, and securities fraud, prosecutors have been increasingly willing to bring RICO cases in white-collar crime and political corruption cases. Although the penalties under

---

[8]18 U.S.C. §§ 1961–1968.

RICO are stiff, the real teeth of the law are found in its forfeiture provisions. They allow prosecutors to seize the defendant's personal assets if the government can prove that the assets were obtained using profits from criminal activity. This is a powerful tool because it has the effect of bankrupting the racketeering enterprise while an individual convicted under the statute is incarcerated.

Insider Trading

In the wake of the financial crisis that began in 2008, the government has become increasingly aggressive about the enforcement of **insider trading laws**. These laws are federal securities statutes directed at corporate insiders who have access to certain information that is not available to the general investment public; the laws prohibit corporate insiders from trading their company's stock based on their insider knowledge. Insiders can be executives, managers, corporate counsel, consultants, certain employees, brokers, and even majority shareholders. In 1988, Congress passed the Insider Trading and Securities Fraud Enforcement Act, which raised the criminal and civil penalties for insider trading, increased the liability of brokerage houses for wrongful acts of their employees, and gave the government more authority to pursue insider trading violations. Insider trading laws and other laws regulate the issuance and trading of certain business ownership interests (such as stocks) and are discussed in detail in Chapter 16, "Regulation of Securities, Corporate Governance, and Financial Markets."

BUSINESS ETHICS PERSPECTIVE

Enforcing Insider Trading Laws

Overview

In Chapter 16, "Regulation of Securities, Corporate Governance, and Financial Markets," we discussed insider trading under rule 10b-5 of the Securities Exchange Act. That rule prohibits investors in public markets from profiting by using nonpublic information to guide their investments. However, the rule does not explicitly define insider trading and therefore courts have struggled to apply uniform standards to insider transactions. Headlines filled with stories of insider trading involving celebrities, professional athletes, and entertainers have become increasingly common. In several cases that garnered substantial media attention, appellate courts have overturned the convictions of investors who profited from insider knowledge. The lack of uniformity in enforcement and interpretation has spawned significant uncertainty in the investment community and created both legal and ethical conundrums. As you learn more about the government's efforts to enforce insider trading laws, consider the following questions. First, the murkiness that surrounds insider trading laws contradicts the very purpose of federal securities regulation: promoting investor confidence in the markets. Second, is it fair to impose substantial prison sentences on those convicted of such a vaguely defined crime? Third, if the legal rules are not clear, how can an investor understand what the ethical boundaries are? Finally, are government prosecutors that pursue questionable insider trading cases driven more by politics than public good?

The SEC Unleashed

Beginning in 2013, the SEC stepped up its enforcement activity by pursuing record numbers of insider trading cases. Consider the comments of SEC Chair Mary Jo White from a 2013 speech at the Securities Enforcement Forum where she made clear the SEC's new approach to enforcing securities laws:

> One of our goals is to see that the SEC's enforcement program is—and is perceived to be—everywhere, pursuing all types of violations of our federal securities laws, big and small . . . . I believe the SEC should strive to be that kind of cop—to be the agency that covers the entire neighborhood and pursues

(continued)

every level of violation. An agency that also makes you feel like we are everywhere. And we will do our best not to disappoint. . . . Over the last four years, we have filed an unprecedented number of insider trading actions—some 200 actions—against more than 450 individuals and firms charging illicit trading gains of nearly $1 billion. In these types of cases, one of the most challenging issues is establishing the relationship between tippee and tipper.[9]

After a number of high-profile losses, the SEC's aggressive enforcement actions became the subject of criticism by securities lawyers, commentators, and even courts. Still, the SEC continued to expand its enforcement division and set a record of 755 enforcement actions in 2014, approximately 10 percent higher than the previous year. Critics argued that the SEC had shifted its assets away from other important responsibilities to avoid political criticism that Wall Street bankers were not being held accountable for the financial crisis in 2008.

A Shift in Strategy

Despite aggressive enforcement and increased use of technology to detect insider trading, the SEC began to lose a string of enforcement actions (including insider trading cases) in federal courts. The SEC then shifted to a different tactic: It increased its use of in-house courts called administrative law courts (ALCs). As part of the Dodd-Frank Act, the SEC's enforcement powers were expanded to allow the agency to pursue securities enforcement through administrative hearings rather than in federal courts. ALCs operate much differently than federal courts. There is no independent jury, no discovery, no rules of evidence, and only limited opportunity for appeals. ALCs are staffed by administrative law judges (ALJs). ALJs are government attorneys selected, maintained, and funded by the SEC. Although they are theoretically impartial, some commentators have alleged that ALJs have a pro-SEC bias. For example, federal Judge Jed S. Rakoff warned about the loss of the securities laws' neutral character and pointed out the trend in which the SEC would essentially directly make, enforce, and adjudicate these laws. Despite these warnings, however, the SEC looks to continue its reliance on administrative proceedings unless prevented from doing so by the courts. One can understand Judge Rakoff's concern, especially in light of the statistics, which are a stunning commentary on the SEC's home-court advantage. According to a 2014 *Washington Post* article, the SEC's preference for home-court advantage in insider trading cases resulted in a 100 percent conviction rate, compared to a 66 percent conviction rate in federal courts.

Discussion Questions

1. The SEC responded to criticism of its ALCs with the rationale that ALJs are experts in securities law and therefore better at applying the law to various circumstances. It also cited the efficiency of ALCs in comparison with federal courts. Does that strike you as compelling? Why or why not? Should securities cases be decided by untrained jurors who may not fully understand the issues?

2. Does the SEC's shift toward ALCs comport with the ethical conduct that is expected of those who hold power?

3. Analyze the SEC's decision to shift toward ALCs under both a principles-based approach and a consequences-based approach to ethical decision making (see Chapter 5, "Business Ethics, Corporate Social Responsibility, and Law," for a review of the approaches). What are the results?

4. According to the SEC's website, the mission of the U.S. Securities and Exchange Commission is to "protect investors, maintain fair, orderly, and efficient markets, and facilitate capital formation." Do the actions of the SEC comport with its mission?

Cuban the Critic

One of the SEC's most vocal critics is billionaire entrepreneur Mark Cuban, who battled the SEC over a period of eight years. In 2008, the SEC alleged that Cuban violated insider trading laws by selling shares of stock in Mamma.com Inc. after learning material, nonpublic information concerning a planned private investment offering by the company. The SEC's case centered on an eight-minute telephone conversation between Mamma.com's CEO and Cuban in which the CEO reported to Cuban that an investment transaction was to take place in the near future. According to the CEO,

(continued)

---

[9]https://www.sec.gov/News/Speech/Detail/Speech/1370539872100.

Mark Cuban speaking to the press after his acquittal on insider trading charges. Mike Fuentes/Bloomberg/Getty Images

Cuban reacted angrily to the news and agreed not to disclose or trade on the information, and Cuban ended the conversation with the comment, "Now I'm screwed, I can't sell." Cuban denied that he ever agreed to keep the information confidential or that he ever agreed not to trade on that information.

Although the trial court dismissed the case against Cuban, the SEC was successful in convincing an appellate court that the case had enough to merit sending it to a jury trial. After a two-week trial in October 2013, the jury acquitted Cuban of all counts.

Discussion Questions

1. An important underlying objective of federal securities laws is to provide the public with confidence in the securities market. Did the SEC achieve that objective by bringing this case against Cuban?

2. Do the SEC and other government regulators target high-profile celebrities for enforcement under the theory that it deters lower-profile illegal activity? Does the deterrent effect work? Is it ethical? Why or why not?

3. After the trial, Cuban was highly critical of the government's conduct in the case and accused the prosecutor of lying. The government's case took five years to get to trial at an enormous cost to taxpayers. Was it worth it even if Cuban had been found guilty? Should an entire case hinge on an eight-minute telephone call?

Bribery

Bribery generally involves a scheme to pay a government official money in order to obtain favorable treatment for a personal or business transaction. Bribery is covered in both federal and state statutes. Note that bribery is an offense that requires only the *offer* of a bribe. It is not necessary that the transaction actually takes place. For example, suppose that Whitaker is the owner of a construction company and bids on a contract to build a firehouse in the city. Whitaker promises a city councilman that she will pay him 10 percent of the total profit in the contract if the councilman will vote to give Whitaker the contract. The offer itself is unlawful even if the councilman does not go along with the scheme. Of course, if the councilman does go along with the bribe (known as a *kickback* in these circumstances), he too will be culpable for bribery (and perhaps several other *public trust* laws).

Obstruction of Justice

Prosecutors have been increasingly willing to prosecute white-collar criminals under federal laws prohibiting the obstruction of justice[10] for any conduct related to attempting to cover up evidence of wrongdoing. Cover-ups take many forms, including (1) lying to investigators, (2) altering documents, (3) shredding or concealing documents or any media such as videotape, and (4) inducing other witnesses to lie or influencing witnesses to refrain from cooperating with authorities. Note that an obstruction-of-justice charge may stand *independently,* and prosecutors need not charge or convict the defendant with the underlying crime. For example, suppose that prosecutors interview Rasputin during the criminal investigation of insider trading at Rasputin's firm. Rasputin lies about his involvement in the insider trading to the authorities. When it is discovered that Rasputin has lied, prosecutors may charge Rasputin with obstruction of justice. Rasputin may be convicted of the obstruction charge even if prosecutors do not have sufficient evidence to charge Rasputin with the underlying crime (insider trading).

In one of the most famous cases of a company being charged with obstruction, federal prosecutors charged the accounting firm Arthur Andersen with obstruction, alleging that individuals within the firm shredded documents related to the collapse and fraudulent practices of the Enron Corporation. A federal grand jury also indicted individual employees of Arthur Andersen for obstruction. However, as we shall see in Case 22.2, the U.S. Supreme Court made clear that there are certain requirements of culpability in an obstruction case.

CASE 22.2 Arthur Andersen LLP v. United States, 544 U.S. 696 (2005)

FACT SUMMARY As Enron Corporation's financial difficulties became public, Arthur Andersen, Enron's auditor, instructed its employees to destroy documents pursuant to its established document retention policy. Andersen was indicted under a federal statute that makes it "a crime to 'knowingly . . . corruptly persuade another person . . . with intent to . . . cause' that person to 'withhold' documents from, or 'alter' documents for use in, an 'official proceeding.'" The jury returned a guilty verdict, and the Fifth Circuit Court of Appeals affirmed, holding that the district court's jury instructions properly conveyed the meaning of "corruptly persuades" and that the jury need not find any consciousness of wrongdoing in order to convict.

SYNOPSIS OF DECISION AND OPINION In a unanimous decision by the U.S. Supreme Court, Andersen's conviction was overturned. The Court reasoned that the instructions allowed the jury to convict Andersen without proving that the firm knew it had broken the law or that there had been a link to any official proceeding that prohibited the destruction of documents.

The Court specifically held that the jury's instructions—which stated that even if Andersen honestly and sincerely believed its conduct was lawful, the jury could still convict the firm—were improper. The statute under which Andersen was charged used the language "knowingly . . . corruptly persuade." Andersen managers did instruct their employees to delete Enron-related files, but those actions were within the firm's document retention policy. If the document retention policy was constructed to keep certain information private, even from the government, Andersen was

(continued)

---

[10]18 U.S.C. § 1001 et seq.

not corruptly persuading its employees to keep the information private.

WORDS OF THE COURT: Improper Jury Instruction "The jury instructions failed to convey properly the elements of a 'corrup[t] persuas[ion]' conviction. . . . The jury instructions failed to convey the requisite consciousness of wrongdoing. Indeed, it is striking how little culpability the instructions required. For example, the jury was told that, even if petitioner honestly and sincerely believed its conduct was lawful, the jury could convict. The instructions also diluted the meaning of 'corruptly' such that it covered innocent conduct."

Case Questions

1. What are the words from the statute that establish the act requirement and the mental requirement?
2. Why did the Court hold that the jury instructions were improper?
3. *Focus on Critical Thinking:* By the time the Court reversed Andersen's conviction, the firm had collapsed from the weight of bad publicity. The government decided not to retry the case. Was it good public policy to destroy the world's largest professional service firm for the actions of a handful of employees? Why do you suppose the government chose not to retry the case?

LEGAL IMPLICATIONS IN CYBERSPACE

Computer Fraud and Abuse Act

There are three major classes of criminal activity through use of a computer: (1) engaging in unauthorized use of a computer, which might involve stealing a user name and password or accessing the victim's computer via the Internet through a backdoor created by a Trojan horse[11] program; (2) creating or releasing a malicious computer program (e.g., computer virus, worm, Trojan horse); and (3) harassing and stalking in cyberspace.

In a 1983 incident that received substantial media attention, a group of hackers managed to access the computer system at Sloan-Kettering and alter patient files. The incident led to passage of the **Computer Fraud and Abuse Act (CFAA)**,[12] which was amended in 2001 by the USA PATRIOT Act.[13] The law prohibits unauthorized use of computers to commit seven different crimes: (1) espionage, (2) accessing unauthorized information, (3) accessing a nonpublic government computer, (4) fraud by computer, (5) damage to computer, (6) trafficking in passwords, and (7) extortionate threats to damage a computer. The CFAA has stiff criminal penalties and also allows civil actions to be brought against an offender to recover damages.

The CFAA is the primary tool used by government to prosecute individuals who hack into computer systems of government and business entities. In 2016, the CFAA was in the headlines after a federal judge sentenced a former scouting director of Major League Baseball's St. Louis Cardinals to nearly four years in prison and to pay $279,038 in restitution for his involvement in a high-tech cheating case. Christopher Correa pled guilty to violating the CFAA for hacking into the player-personnel database and e-mail systems of the Houston Astros. Prosecutors alleged that Correa gained access to the Astros's database using a password similar to that used by a former Cardinals employee who left St. Louis to become the general manager of the Astros. Correa used the password to access hundreds of pages of confidential information about player trade discussions, evaluations, and draft pick alternatives.[14]

---

[11] A Trojan horse is a virus that appears to perform one function yet actually performs another, such as the unauthorized collection, exploitation, falsification, or destruction of data.
[12] 18 U.S.C. § 1030.
[13] 18 U.S.C. § 2712.
[14] *United States v. Correa*, Case No. H-15-679, Plea Agreement (S.D. Texas Jan. 8, 2016).

Foreign Corrupt Practices Act (FCPA)

The **Foreign Corrupt Practices Act (FCPA)**[15] of 1977 is a criminal statute that was enacted principally to prevent corporate bribery of *foreign officials* in business transactions. The law prohibits a company and its officers, employees, and agents from giving, offering, or promising anything of value to any foreign (non-U.S.) official with the intent of obtaining or retaining business or any other competitive advantage. This prohibition is interpreted broadly in that companies may be held liable for violating the antibribery provisions of the FCPA whether or not they took any action within U.S. borders. Thus, a U.S. company can be liable for the conduct of its overseas employees or agents even if no money was transferred from the United States and no U.S. citizen participated in any way in the foreign bribery.

A foreign official is any officer or employee of a foreign government, regardless of rank; employees of government-owned or government-controlled businesses; foreign political parties; party officials; candidates for political office; and employees of public international organizations (such as the United Nations or the World Bank). This list can include owner-employees as well. Even if the improper payment is not accepted, just offering it violates the FCPA. Likewise, other FCPA violations include instructing, authorizing, or allowing a third party to make a prohibited payment on a company's behalf; ratifying a payment after the fact; or making a payment to a third party knowing or having reason to know that it will likely be given to a government official. Prohibited payments include not only cash and cash equivalents but also gifts, entertainment, travel, and the like. The FCPA is discussed in greater detail in Chapter 25, "International Law and Global Commerce."

 Self-Check White-Collar Crime

What white-collar crimes are at issue in the following circumstances?

1. WidgetCo applies for a permit to do business in Venezuela. The government official denies the permit, and a WidgetCo executive pays for a lavish meal at a four-star restaurant while discussing the permit application.

2. InvestCo advertises a return of 15 percent on any investments in its Super Duper Fund. Even when the market drops dramatically, Super Duper continues to perform at this level for 18 consecutive months. In its disclosures, InvestCo reports that its auditing firm is headed by an InvestCo officer's son-in-law.

3. WidgetCo and PlankCo agree to illegally fix prices so that the lack of competition drives the prices of their products artificially high. The companies begin the process to set prices but abandon the plan at the last moment.

4. Evidence exists that WidgetCo's CEO was funneling money from the corporation with the help of several other executive managers. The funds came from an investment fraud scheme in which each executive played a part to perpetrate the scheme and use WidgetCo as a front business to help bolster their scheme with investors.

Answers to this Self-Check are provided at the end of the chapter.

---

[15] 28 U.S.C. § 1602 et seq.

LO 22-7

Explain the steps in the criminal justice system.

THE CRIMINAL JUSTICE SYSTEM

The criminal justice system is best thought of as one process that operates in two phases: **investigation** and **adjudication**. This section describes the nuts and bolts of the criminal justice process. Procedural safeguards that are afforded to those suspected or accused of crimes constitute *criminal procedure* and are discussed in the next section of this chapter.

Investigation

During the investigation phase, the authorities become aware of an alleged criminal act and begin an investigation by gathering physical evidence and interviewing witnesses and potential suspects. Because most criminal acts are handled at the state level, most enforcement of criminal law is conducted by state or local police agencies. Violations of federal laws are investigated by various federal law enforcement agencies, including the Federal Bureau of Investigation (FBI). In a business context, investigators from federal regulatory agencies such as the Securities and Exchange Commission (SEC) or the Internal Revenue Service (IRS) may also undertake specialized criminal investigation. During this initial stage, investigators may also ask a court to authorize a search warrant in an effort to obtain more evidence. A warrant may be issued based only on **probable cause**. Once the authorities believe that sufficient evidence creates enough probable cause to indicate the culpability of a suspect, they will, depending on the circumstances, either obtain an *arrest warrant* or, more commonly, *arrest* the suspect by taking him into physical custody. If the criminal violation is a minor one, the authorities may simply issue a *citation*, whereby the violator may either resolve the charge by paying a fine or contest the charge in court. If an actual arrest has taken place, the authorities may continue their investigation by gathering more physical evidence, interviewing new witnesses, and attempting to further interview the suspect. The investigators then file formal criminal charges against the suspect and prepare a brief report for a local magistrate and prosecutors. The suspect, now charged, is referred to as the *defendant* and is formally read the charges by a magistrate. The magistrate then sets bail (if appropriate) and, if necessary, appoints an attorney to represent the defendant. Frequently, the prosecutor will review the investigator's report (and sometimes conduct additional investigation) and then decide whether she can prove the charges in a court of law based on available evidence. The prosecutor decides whether to (1) proceed with prosecuting the defendant on the original charge, (2) amend the charges as necessary, or (3) drop the charges altogether due to lack of evidence. The actual title of the prosecutor varies between jurisdictions, but local prosecutors are typically employed by the district attorney, state prosecutors are employed by the state's attorney general, and federal prosecutors work for the U.S. attorney general under the authority of the U.S. Department of Justice.

Legal Speak >))

Bail

The security, in the form of cash or a bond, given to the court to ensure the appearance of a defendant in court at a later date. If the defendant appears in court, the bail is returned. If he flees, the bail is forfeited.

Adjudication

If the prosecutor elects to proceed with the charges, the defendant is entitled to a **preliminary adjudication**. Some jurisdictions use the *grand jury* system, while others use a *preliminary hearing* in front of a local magistrate. In each case, the prosecutor presents evidence of the defendant's guilt, and the decision maker (either the grand jurors or the magistrate) determines whether probable cause exists to hold the defendant over for trial. If the prosecutor cannot offer sufficient evidence of probable cause, the charges are dismissed. As a practical matter, very few cases are dismissed at this stage.

The defendant is notified that he is held over for trial through either an *indictment* (in the case of a grand jury) or formal filing of an *information* (in the case of a magistrate). The defendant is then entitled to an arraignment in a state trial court, at which he is informed of the final charges and is asked to enter a *plea* of guilty, not guilty, or no contest.[16] An overwhelming majority of defendants plead not guilty at this stage, even if they intend on negotiating an eventual guilty plea with the prosecutor. Following the arraignment, the prosecutor and defense counsel will typically enter into a plea-bargaining negotiation. This involves the parties agreeing to concessions from each side that will avoid trial and result in a voluntary plea of guilty or no contest by the defendant. All states also have some type of pretrial intervention for first-time offenders of nonviolent crimes, whereby the defendant typically agrees to fulfill certain conditions (community service, drug rehabilitation, etc.) in exchange for the charges being dismissed at a later date. If a plea agreement cannot be reached, the case proceeds to trial. In a trial, the finder of fact (usually a jury in a criminal trial)[17] weighs the evidence and determines whether the prosecutor has proved the charges against the defendant beyond a reasonable doubt. If the jury finds the defendant guilty, this results in a *conviction*. If the jury finds the defendant not guilty, this results in an *acquittal* and the defendant cannot be prosecuted for the same charges again. If the jury is deadlocked (unable to reach a consensus decision), this results in a *mistrial* and the prosecutor decides whether or not to refile charges against the defendant a second time. If the defendant is convicted, he may file an *appeal* setting out the basis for having the conviction reversed.

If the defendant is convicted, the judge sets a future date for *sentencing*. In the interim, the court considers requests and reports by authorities, victims of the defendant's crime, character witnesses for the defendant, and sentencing guidelines (or statutory mandatory minimum sentences) in determining the defendant's punishment.

CONCEPT SUMMARY   The Criminal Justice Process

Investigative Phase	Adjudicative Phase
1. Investigate possible crime.	1. Preliminary adjudication (via grand jury or magistrate, depending on jurisdiction).
2. Interview witnesses.	2. File indictment (known as "information," depending on jurisdiction) *or* drop charges due to insufficient evidence.
3. Obtain search warrants if necessary.	3. Defendant enters plea and enters plea negotiations if necessary.
4. Obtain arrest warrant or take suspect into custody *or* issue a citation for minor infractions.	4. If no plea agreement is reached, defendant goes to trial.
5. Defendant is formally charged.	5. Conviction or acquittal of the defendant.
6. Local judicial authority sets bail and appoints defense counsel if necessary.	6. Sentencing (if convicted).

LO 22-8

Name and explain the various constitutional procedural protections afforded to those accused of a crime.

CRIMINAL PROCEDURE

Recall from the beginning of this chapter the differences between criminal law and criminal procedure. While criminal law defines the boundaries of behavior and prescribes sanctions for violating those boundaries, *criminal procedure* refers to legal safeguards to

---

[16]In a plea of no contest, sometimes called by its Latin form *nolo contendere*, the defendant does not admit or deny the charges but is willing to accept the sanctions as if guilty.

[17]Recall from Chapter 3, "The American Judicial System, Jurisdiction, and Venue," that the finder of fact may be either a jury *or* a judge.

Legal Speak >))

Warrant
A court order authorizing an official to do something she would otherwise be prohibited from doing. The most common are warrants for arrest, search, or seizure.

protect the rights of individuals (and in some cases business entities) during investigation by the government, arrest, trial, and sentencing. The protections are primarily provided by the U.S. Constitution's Bill of Rights. For purposes of understanding criminal procedure in a business environment, our focus is on protections found in the Fourth, Fifth, and Sixth Amendments. While the Constitution regulates many aspects of criminal procedure, as a practical matter state and federal legislatures also enact statutes and rules setting forth certain procedures that authorities must follow during investigation, arrest, criminal trial, and sentencing. State constitutions may also provide *additional* criminal procedure protections for a state's citizens. For example, one state may be more apt to require a higher level of probable cause for arrest than is prescribed by the federal rules or courts. Of course, states may not repeal the federal constitutional rights of individuals.

Searches and Arrest

Recall from Chapter 2, "Business and the Constitution," that the Fourth Amendment to the U.S. Constitution protects individuals (and sometimes businesses) from unreasonable search and seizure by government agents and permits warrants to be issued only if probable cause exists. The U.S. Supreme Court has developed a large body of law to guide courts in determining the appropriate boundaries of searches and arrests by authorities. First, the Court has held that the Fourth Amendment applies to both *searches* and *arrests*. However, a warrant is usually required before a search takes place (with certain exceptions). A warrant for arrest is generally not required in order to take a suspect into custody. Second, the Constitution requires that an impartial magistrate issue a search or arrest warrant only if probable cause has been established. Third, whether or not a search or arrest warrant exists, the action taken by authorities must always be *reasonable* and consistent with constitutional protections. Fourth, the authorities may conduct *limited,* warrantless searches in certain cases. For example, police may conduct short, pat-down searches even without probable cause when the officer has a reasonable suspicion[18] that criminal activity is taking place or when the officer's safety is an issue.

Although the Fourth Amendment requires authorities to obtain a warrant before searching a citizen, the Supreme Court has allowed the police to conduct a limited pat-down search when an officer has reasonable suspicion that criminal activity is taking place. George Doyle/Getty Images

Expectation of Privacy A fundamental part of the protections provided by the Fourth Amendment is that its protections are based on whether an individual's *reasonable expectation of privacy* has been violated by government authorities. The courts have held that individuals have the highest expectations of privacy in their own homes. However, once an individual goes into the public (such as driving a car on a public highway), the privacy expectations are diminished and Fourth Amendment protections become more limited in scope. Examples of evidence that is *not* protected under reasonable expectation of privacy include trash that has been set out on the public curb for pickup, any apparently abandoned property, and things a person says or does in public. In terms of the abandoned property example, note that if the evidence has been disposed of but is still located on the real estate (land) of the owner, then the owner may still have a reasonable expectation of privacy. For example, Scofield

---

[18]Reasonable suspicion has been described as a standard that is lower than probable cause but "more than just a hunch": *Terry v. Ohio,* 392 U.S. 1 (1968).

is being investigated for tax fraud. The authorities observe Scofield putting out large bags of paper for trash pickup. They wait until midnight and then take the bags from the curbside outside Scofield's residence. When Scofield is brought to trial, the prosecutor introduces the discarded papers as evidence of tax fraud. If Scofield claims his Fourth Amendment rights were violated, it is likely that he would lose that argument because courts have consistently held that public papers disposed of as garbage are abandoned property and not subject to reasonable expectations of privacy. Suppose, though, that the real estate at issue was a country home with a long driveway and that trash collectors actually traveled onto the property to collect the garbage. If the authorities entered the land without a warrant and confiscated the bags of discarded papers, a court may very well find the search to be illegal.

> **KEY POINT**
>
> Fourth Amendment protections apply only when an individual's reasonable expectation of privacy has been violated by government authorities (e.g., the warrantless search of a house).

Plain View Doctrine

Courts have held that authorities generally do not commit a Fourth Amendment violation when a government agent obtains evidence by virtue of seeing an object that is in his plain view and the agent has the right to be in the position to have that view. This is called the **plain view doctrine**. For example, suppose that during a routine traffic violation stop, a police officer observes an illegal handgun lying on the seat next to the driver. The officer may then arrest the driver and confiscate the weapon without a warrant because the plain view search is not prohibited by the Fourth Amendment. The plain view doctrine also allows authorities to use simple mechanical devices that are available to the general public, such as a flashlight or a camera with telephoto lenses, to enhance their view. However, courts have limited authorities' ability to obtain information by means of special high-tech devices that are not available to the general public. For example, in a 2001 case, the U.S. Supreme Court held that the use of a thermal imager (a device used to produce images of relative amounts of heat escaping from a structure) by authorities on a public sidewalk outside a residence suspected of being a marijuana growing operation was *not* covered by the plain view doctrine and constituted an illegal search. The Court reasoned that because the data could not be obtained through use of the naked eye or basic equipment available to the general public, the action constituted a search even though government authorities had not physically entered the house.[19]

The courts have adopted a similar position regarding aerial observations made by authorities. That is, so long as the plane or helicopter is in public navigable airspace, anything the police can see with the naked eye or basic equipment such as binoculars will be considered in plain view. In *Dow Chemical Co. v. United States*,[20] the Supreme Court ruled that the use of an airplane by government agents to fly over one of Dow's chemical plant complexes for purposes of taking investigative photographs with a zoom lens fit into the plain view exception and did not require a warrant because a zoom lens was readily available for purchase by the public.

Search Incident to Arrest

The search incident to arrest exception allows a law enforcement officer who has lawfully arrested a defendant to search the defendant's person without obtaining a warrant. The primary reasons that justify this exception are (1) protection of the officer/agent and others involved in the booking process and (2) prevention of the destruction of evidence by the defendant. For example, suppose that a federal law enforcement agency arrests the kingpin of a Ponzi scheme. The kingpin is handcuffed and

---

[19] *Kyllo v. United States*, 553 U.S. 27 (2001).
[20] 476 U.S. 227 (1986).

then brought to a booking facility where one of the agents discovers a small notebook with incriminating notes made by the kingpin. Despite the fact that the agent did not have a warrant, the notebook may be used as evidence against the kingpin discovered in a search incident to arrest.

Search of Electronic Devices

One increasingly important issue faced by law enforcement is the extent to which electronic devices, such as cell phones, fit into current law of unlawful search and seizure as defined by the Fourth Amendment. In Case 22.3, the U.S. Supreme Court considers whether the police need a search warrant to examine contents such as photos and videos from a suspect's cell phone.

CASE 22.3 Riley v. California, 573 U.S. 373 (2014)

FACT SUMMARY Riley was the driver of a car stopped by a San Diego, California, police officer for a traffic violation that eventually led to his arrest for concealed possession of two loaded handguns found under the seat of his car. Riley was arrested and transported to a booking facility, where police retrieved Riley's cell phone from his pocket. At the police station about two hours after the arrest, a detective specializing in criminal gangs examined the contents of Riley's cell phone. The detective found videos and photographs that connected Riley with a gang-related shooting that had occurred a few weeks earlier. Based partially on the evidence from Riley's cell phone, the state charged him with attempted murder. The prosecutor also sought an enhanced sentence based upon Riley's membership in a criminal street gang. Riley moved to suppress all evidence that the police had obtained from his cell phone, claiming a violation of the Fourth Amendment's warrant requirement. Prosecutors argued that the search of the cell phone was proper because it was incident to a lawful arrest within the guidelines of previous case law. The government argued that the cell phone search was similar to any other method used by individuals to store information (e.g., a wallet) and that cell phones fell into that same category. The trial court denied Riley's motion to suppress the evidence based on the Fourth Amendment, and Riley was convicted at trial. The state appellate court affirmed Riley's conviction and Riley appealed to the U.S. Supreme Court, arguing that the evidence obtained from his cell phone was a warrantless search that did not fall into any category of exception.

SYNOPSIS OF DECISION AND OPINION In a unanimous decision, the U.S. Supreme Court reversed the decisions of the lower courts and ruled in favor of Riley. The Court held that the digital era required a rule that individuals have a high level of expectation of privacy in their cell phones because they are capable of storing and accessing a quantity of information, some highly personal, that no person would ever have had on his person in hardcopy form. The Court also reasoned that the search incident to arrest exception to the warrant requirement had two primary purposes: officer safety and prevention of the destruction of evidence. In this case, the search of a cell phone incident to arrest could not be justified on those grounds. As a result, the Court would not extend the warrantless search exception to include cell phones confiscated from an arrested defendant.

WORDS OF THE COURT: No Danger of Harm "Digital data stored on a cell phone cannot itself be used as a weapon to harm an arresting officer or to effectuate the arrestee's escape. Law enforcement officers remain free to examine the physical aspects of a phone to ensure that it will not be used as a weapon—say, to determine whether there is a razor blade hidden between the phone and its case. Once an officer has secured a phone and eliminated any potential physical threats, however, data on the phone can endanger no one."

WORDS OF THE COURT: Importance of Warrant Requirement "Our holding, of course, is not that the information on a cell phone is immune from

(continued)

search; it is instead that a warrant is generally required before such a search, even when a cell phone is seized incident to arrest. Our cases have historically recognized that the warrant requirement is 'an important working part of our machinery of government,' not merely 'an inconvenience to be somehow "weighed" against the claims of police efficiency.' . . .

"Modern cell phones are not just another technological convenience. With all they contain and all they may reveal, they hold for many Americans 'the privacies of life.' The fact that technology now allows an individual to carry such information in his hand does not make the information any less worthy of the protection for which the Founders fought. Our answer to the question of what police must do before searching a cell phone seized incident to an arrest is accordingly simple—get a warrant."

Case Questions

1. The Court has held previously that a search incident to arrest may include the defendant's wallet/purse. Is there really a difference between a wallet and a cell phone? What if Riley's wallet had contained incriminating photographs of him? Would the police be required to get a warrant?
2. Why does the Court point out that the warrant requirement is "not merely 'an inconvenience to be somehow "weighed" against the claims of police efficiency'"? How is that related to Riley's circumstances?
3. *Focus on Critical Thinking:* In what way does this case illustrate the clash between technology and case precedent? What role does *stare decisis* ("let the decision stand") play in this case?

Searches of Business Premises Courts have been very reluctant to extend reasonable-expectation-of-privacy rights to the workplace. This is particularly true when the business is highly regulated. Recall from Chapter 17, "Administrative Law," that certain businesses are classified as *pervasively regulated* and, therefore, are not entitled to full Fourth Amendment protections. Instead, the U.S. Supreme Court has fashioned an exception to the Fourth Amendment warrant requirements that applies when an agency is conducting regularly scheduled inspections pursuant to an administrative rule. Even in cases where courts have held that administrative agencies are required to obtain an *administrative warrant* to conduct an inspection of a business, the Court has held that agencies are held to a lower standard of probable cause to obtain the warrant than would be required if the government were obtaining a criminal warrant.

Table 22.1 summarizes the application of the Fourth Amendment's warrant requirement.

Self-Incrimination

The Fifth Amendment provides that no person "shall be compelled in any criminal case to be a witness against himself." This means that individuals have the right not to offer

TABLE 22.1	Applying Fourth Amendment Warrant Requirement to Business	
Issue	**Example**	**Business Application**
No expectation of privacy	Government searches through a trashcan placed out on the public curb of a private house for pickup.	Environmental Protection Agency searches plant of a pervasively regulated business venture (government must still obtain *administrative* warrant).
Plain view	Police see a weapon laying on a car seat after a traffic stop.	Government agents use zoom lens photography to obtain information in a tax fraud investigation.
Incident to arrest	Contraband found in the pocket of an arrestee.	After the operator of a Ponzi scheme is arrested, agents find a notebook with incriminating entries in his suit coat pocket.

any information or statements that may be used against them in a criminal prosecution. If an individual believes that any statement or testimony may incriminate her in a criminal case, she may decline to testify on Fifth Amendment grounds. Note that the right against self-incrimination also protects those called as witnesses in other types of matters. For example, suppose that in the tax fraud hypothetical case discussed earlier, the government prosecutes Scofield for tax evasion. During the trial, the prosecutor issues a subpoena to Montgomery, Scofield's business partner. If Montgomery has a belief that any questions asked of him as a witness in Scofield's trial may uncover evidence of his own criminal culpability, Montgomery may refuse to testify at Scofield's trial even though he is not under investigation.

The Fifth Amendment right against self-incrimination also applies while authorities are *investigating* crimes. Generally, the context is that government authorities are interviewing an individual in the course of a criminal investigation. Although most case law surrounding this right deals with police interrogations of a suspect, in a business context business owners and managers should realize that agents of regulatory agencies, such as the Internal Revenue Service, are bound by the same guidelines as agents of police agencies are when interviewing suspects during a criminal investigation. An important element of this protection is that it is limited to *custodial* interrogations, in which the interviewee has been taken into custody or deprived of his freedom in some significant way. In this event, the authorities are required to give affirmative preinterview warnings to the suspect that he has the right not to make any statements and that any statement that is given may eventually be used as evidence against him in a criminal trial.

For example, suppose that an FBI agent telephones Barrabas and requests a meeting in Barrabas's office. The agent explains that he is investigating a fraud scheme involving government contracts. Barrabas agrees to the meeting, and during the conversation he admits to certain incriminating facts. The admission will likely be admissible as evidence despite the failure of the agent to provide the self-incrimination warning. Because the statement was made voluntarily in a noncoercive setting (Barrabas's office) and because Barrabas could have stopped the interview at any time, the interview may not be considered custodial and Barrabas's Fifth Amendment protections are not triggered. Alternatively, if the agent had arrested Barrabas and transported him to a local FBI field office, the agent would be required to give the warnings about self-incrimination.

The warning requirements are set out in one of the most famous criminal procedure cases in U.S. history: *Miranda v. Arizona*. In *Miranda,* the suspect of a violent crime was interviewed over a period of two hours and ultimately confessed to the crime. After his conviction, Miranda appealed, arguing that being interviewed in police custody is inherently coercive if the suspect is unaware of his rights. Thus, his confession was not, in fact, voluntary. The Court reasoned

> It is obvious that such an interrogation environment is created for no purpose other than to subjugate the individual to the will of his examiner. This atmosphere carries its own badge of intimidation. To be sure, this is not physical intimidation, but it is equally destructive of human dignity. . . . In order to combat these pressures and to permit a full opportunity to exercise the privilege against self-incrimination, the accused must be adequately and effectively apprised of his rights and the exercise of those rights must be fully honored.[21]

Miranda v. Arizona, 384 U.S. 436 (1966).

---

[21]What happened to Ernesto Miranda? On retrial he was found guilty based on other evidence. He spent over a decade behind bars. When he was paroled, he earned income selling police "Miranda cards" that he had autographed. In 1976, he was killed in a bar fight. *See* George C. Thomas, *Missing Miranda's story,* 2 Ohio St. J. Crim. L. 677, 683–84 (2005).

Production of Business Records

Business records such as letters, memoranda, e-mail exchanges, inventory accounts, financial documents, and the like are often at the very crux of cases where government authorities are investigating potential criminal activity in the business environment. Although the U.S. Supreme Court has held that certain business records may be classified as private papers and are protected by the Fifth Amendment, this protection has been severely narrowed over the last several decades. In 1984, the Court ruled that certain business records of a sole proprietor could be considered private papers because a sole proprietor is a form of business entity that is essentially the alter ego of the individual.[22] The Court reasoned that because there is no legal separation between the business and the sole owner (unlike a corporation, which exists as a separate legal "person"), the owner's records are considered personal and are subject to Fifth Amendment protections. However, the Court has also made clear that records of a *corporation* are not subject to Fifth Amendment safeguards because that business entity is separate and distinct from its owners and thus does not qualify for self-incrimination protections.

Trial

The Sixth Amendment provides that in all criminal prosecutions, the accused shall enjoy the right to a *speedy trial*. Although the U.S. Supreme Court has not set out specific time periods in which a trial must take place, it has given guideposts for state courts in applying the speedy trial guarantee. Courts apply a balancing test in which both the prosecutor's and the defendant's conduct is examined to determine reasons for delay. Ordinarily, a court weighs the length of the delay versus the severity of the crime. A general rule is that a delay of eight months or more is presumptively unconstitutional. The federal criminal justice system operates according to an infrastructure established by the **Speedy Trial Act**,[23] which sets out specific time periods in which an accused must be brought to trial. If the time limits are exceeded, the courts must dismiss the charges.

The Sixth Amendment also contains other important procedural rights such as a right to a jury trial for serious crimes (generally any offense that carries more than six months' incarceration as a penalty), the right to a public trial, and the right to confront witnesses through cross-examination.[24]

Double Jeopardy Although the role of the Fifth Amendment is usually thought of in the context of self-incrimination, it also protects a defendant from being subject to prosecution twice for the same offense. This guarantee is known as a prohibition of **double jeopardy**. In essence, the doctrine prevents prosecutors from retrying a defendant on the same charges after a jury has acquitted her.

Exclusionary Rule

Trial courts are required to exclude presentation of any evidence that is obtained as a result of a constitutional violation. This is known as the *exclusionary rule*. For example, if a law enforcement officer wrongfully searches a suspect's house without first obtaining a search warrant, any evidence obtained in that search may not be used against the suspect if he is arrested and brought to trial. One important exception in the business environment is

LO 22-9

Explain the exclusionary rule and how it applies to business.

---

[22]*United States v. Doe*, 465 U.S. 605 (1984).

[23]18 U.S.C. § 3161.

[24]Cross-examination and other trial terminology are discussed in detail in Chapter 3, "The American Judicial System, Jurisdiction, and Venue."

The exclusionary rule prohibits the use of evidence during a criminal trial that was obtained in violation of a defendant's constitutional rights. *wavebreakmedia/Shutterstock*

that the exclusionary rule applies only when violations of the Constitution occur and not when a government agency violates its own *internal procedures*. For example, suppose that a government agent secretly records a conversation with a suspected tax evader during a meeting in the agent's office. The suspect offers the agent a bribe. However, the agent has violated internal agency rules because he has failed to obtain a supervisor's permission to record any conversations with taxpayers. When the suspect is tried, she asserts that the recording cannot be introduced at trial because it is barred by the exclusionary rule. The U.S. Supreme Court has *rejected* such an argument and held that the exclusionary rule bars only evidence obtained in violation of a constitutional provision. In this case, an agency rule has been violated, but no constitutional violations have taken place and, thus, the exclusionary rule does not apply.[25]

Even evidence that is only indirectly obtained in violation of a defendant's rights is subject to the exclusionary rule because it is considered the *fruit of the poisonous tree*. This means that once original evidence is shown to have been unlawfully obtained, all evidence that stems from the original evidence (called *derivative evidence*) is also excluded. For example, suppose an agent of the Securities and Exchange Commission is investigating Falstaff for criminal fraud. The agent illegally searches the handbag of Falstaff's secretary and discovers evidence that Falstaff is concealing incriminating documents in his garage at home. Using the illegally obtained evidence, the agent then obtains a search warrant for Falstaff's home and discovers the incriminating documents. Because the agent's original evidence (obtained from Falstaff's secretary) was obtained in violation of the secretary's constitutional rights, a court would likely hold that the fruit of the poisonous tree doctrine renders the warrant invalid and bars use of all evidence derived from the warrant (the incriminating documents) in a criminal trial against Falstaff.[26]

The exclusionary rule itself is controversial because it tends to benefit guilty parties by excluding key evidence that would help convict them. Many legal commentators have filled volumes of journals and treatises on the topic, but ultimately the exclusionary rule is justified by its proponents on the basis that it acts as a deterrent to violations of the Constitution by government authorities. Proponents argue that the integrity of the judiciary requires that courts not be made a party to lawless invasions of constitutional rights of citizens by permitting unhindered government use of unlawfully obtained evidence. Nonetheless, the Supreme Court has fashioned several exceptions to the exclusionary rule intended to differentiate between abuse by the authorities of an individual's constitutional rights and those cases where the government has made an innocent mistake in obtaining evidence. Perhaps the most important exception to the rule occurs when the government can show that authorities were acting in *good faith* in obtaining evidence based on a search warrant issued by an authorized judge that was later found to be unsupported by an appropriate level of probable cause. In that case, even though the evidence is derived from a warrant that was granted but that was later found to have been a constitutional violation, the prosecutor may still introduce the evidence yielded from the search so long as the authorities were acting in good faith and with reasonable reliance on the search warrant.

---

[25]Based on *United States v. Caceres*, 440 U.S. 741 (1979).

[26]See *Silverthorne Lumber Company v. United States*, 251 U.S. 385 (1920).

In *Herring v. United States,* the U.S. Supreme Court considered the good faith exception in the context of a police clerical error. The case involved a defendant, Herring, who was arrested after officers were incorrectly informed that an active arrest warrant existed. In fact, no warrant existed and the incorrect information given to the arresting officer was a clerical error. After Herring was arrested, the police searched him incident to arrest and discovered illegal narcotics and a firearm. Herring sought to have the evidence excluded on the basis that it had been obtained without a warrant and only as a result of a wrongful arrest. The government cited the good faith exception because the officers were acting in objectively reasonable reliance on the subsequently invalidated warrant. The U.S. Supreme Court agreed with the government that the good faith exception applied and therefore the evidence should not be excluded. The Court wrote

> [Herring's] claim that police negligence automatically triggers suppression cannot be squared with the principles underlying the exclusionary rule, as they have been explained in our cases. In light of our repeated holdings that the deterrent effect of suppression must be substantial and outweigh any harm to the justice system, we conclude that when police mistakes are the result of negligence such as that described here, rather than systemic error or reckless disregard of constitutional requirement, any marginal deterrence does not "pay its way." In such a case, the criminal should not "go free because the constable has blundered."[27]
>
> *555 U.S. 135,146 (2009).*

LEGAL IMPLICATIONS IN CYBERSPACE

Obscenity in Cyberspace: The Communications Decency Act

The Internet has an element of entrepreneurial spirit associated with it, and many new companies and new business models were created to take advantage of the rapid growth of consumers in cyberspace. At the same time, it is clear that a significant number of business models benefiting from the boom are those associated with the distribution of pornography. In the midst of some high-profile media stories involving the ease of access to online pornography by minors, Congress attempted to curb online content with the Communications Decency Act (CDA) in 1996. The CDA was intended to ban material that was "patently offensive" or "indecent" from being online if the content providers knew that children would have access to the material.

Challenges to the CDA

Shortly after the CDA was enacted, the American Civil Liberties Union (ACLU) filed a lawsuit challenging the act as an unconstitutional infringement on free speech. The case, *ACLU v. Reno* (called *Reno I*),[28] was decided by the U.S. Supreme Court in 1997. It was the first time that the Court applied existing obscenity standards in cyberspace. One important element of the case was the Court's recognition of cyberspace as a unique medium that cannot be equated to broadcast media (such as radio or television) or any printed media (such as magazines or newspapers). This distinction was a key part of the Court's analysis that government was not entitled to as much deference in regulation of the Internet as the government is entitled to with other media. That said, the Court went on to strike

(continued)

---

[27]The Court used this famous passage from Judge Benjamin Cardozo's opinion criticizing the federal exclusionary rule, which was not then applicable to the states, from *People v. Defore,* 242 N.Y. 13 (1926). Cardozo would later become an associate justice of the U.S. Supreme Court.
[28]521 U.S. 844 (1997).

down much of the act's substance, reasoning that the CDA's prohibition against "patently offensive" material being distributed on the web is too vague to pass constitutional muster.

Congressional Response to Reno I: Child Online Protection Act of 1998

Although the Court struck down much of the CDA, the opinion did set out, for the first time, the Court's view on the government's regulation of the Internet. The Court ruled that although the government had the right to regulate Internet traffic, the means employed by Congress was too broad a sweep.

Using *Reno I* as a roadmap on constitutionality, Congress passed a similar piece of legislation the next year with the Child Online Protection Act of 1998 (COPA).

The ACLU again filed a lawsuit challenging the COPA as unconstitutional. The new case, *ACLU v. Reno (Reno II)*,[29] was decided by the U.S. Court of Appeals for the Third Circuit in 2000. The court of appeals ruled in favor of the ACLU and struck the statute down as still too overly broad. In 2002, the U.S. Supreme Court upheld the court of appeals's decision and adopted much of the court of appeals's reasoning.[30]

CONCEPT SUMMARY Criminal Procedure

- The Fourth Amendment requires authorities to obtain a warrant before searching areas where a citizen has a reasonable expectation of privacy.
- Important exceptions to the warrant requirement are plain view and search incident to arrest.
- The Fifth Amendment protects an individual from involuntary self-incrimination before, during, and after an investigation and trial, but it does not protect a person from disclosing business records made in the person's capacity as corporate agent. The Fifth Amendment does not protect corporations.
- Anything said during custodial interrogation is presumed to be involuntary unless and until the person has been read the Miranda warnings.
- The exclusionary rule bans evidence obtained in violation of the Constitution from being used at trial.

---

[29]217 F.3d 162 (3d Cir. 2000).

[30]*Ashcroft v. American Civil Liberties Union,* 535 US 564 (2002).

KEY TERMS

Criminal law p. 708 The body of law that, for the purpose of preventing harm to society, defines the boundaries of behavior and prescribes sanctions for violating those boundaries.

Model Penal Code (MPC) p. 709 A statutory text adopted by the American Law Institute in 1962 in an effort to bring greater uniformity to state criminal laws by proffering certain legal standards and reforms.

Criminal procedure p. 709 The body of constitutional protections afforded to individuals and business entities during criminal investigations, arrests, trials, and sentencing.

Burden of proof p. 710 The responsibility of producing sufficient evidence in support of a fact or issue and favorably convincing the fact finder of that fact or issue.

Preponderance of the evidence p. 710 The burden of proof used in civil cases, under which the fact finder need be convinced only that the defendant's liability was more likely than not.

Beyond a reasonable doubt p. 710 The heightened burden of proof used in criminal cases, under which a fact finder must be convinced that the defendant's criminal liability is not in doubt to a reasonable person.

Legality p. 710 A principle of criminal law that protects individuals from being charged with some unspecified general offense; requires that crimes be specifically proscribed by law in advance of the conduct sought to be punished.

Punishment p. 710 A principle of criminal law that imposes a hardship in response to misconduct; based on the concepts that criminal law acts as a deterrent, it removes dangerous criminals from the population, and rehabilitation is an important part of the criminal justice system.

Sentencing guidelines p. 710 Statutorily prescribed standards for determining the punishment that a convicted criminal should receive on the basis of the nature of the crime and the offender's criminal history.

Act requirement p. 710 For criminal liability, the requirement that the government prove that a defendant's actions objectively satisfied the elements of a particular offense. Also called *actus reus*.

Self-defense p. 711 A defense to avoid criminal liability whereby the defendant's actions are related to the necessity of using deadly force to repel an attack in which the defendant reasonably feared that death or substantial harm was about to occur either to the defendant or to a third party.

Mental incapacity (criminal) p. 712 A defense to avoid criminal liability whereby the defendant's actions are related to some type of mental disease or defect.

Felonies p. 712 Crimes that generally carry one year or more of incarceration as the penalty.

Misdemeanors p. 712 Crimes that carry up to one year of incarceration as the penalty.

Mail Fraud Act p. 716 Federal legislation enacted in 1990 as a comprehensive approach to criminalizing any fraud in which the defrauding party uses the mail or any wire, radio, or television in perpetrating the fraud.

Insider trading laws p. 718 Federal securities statutes that prohibit corporate insiders who have access to certain information that is not available to the general investment public from trading their company's stock based on the insider knowledge.

Computer Fraud and Abuse Act (CFAA) p. 722 Federal legislation that prohibits unauthorized use of computers to commit espionage, the accessing of unauthorized information or of a nonpublic government computer, fraud by computer, damage to a computer, trafficking in passwords, and extortionate threats to damage a computer.

Foreign Corrupt Practices Act (FCPA) p. 723 A federal criminal statute enacted principally to prevent corporate bribery of foreign officials in business transactions.

Investigation p. 724 The initial phase of the criminal justice process in which authorities become aware of an alleged criminal act and begin gathering physical evidence and interviewing witnesses and potential suspects.

Adjudication p. 724 A phase of the criminal justice system in which the prosecutor, after investigation, elects to proceed with the charges.

Probable cause p. 724 A reasonable amount of suspicion supported by circumstances sufficiently strong to justify a belief that a person has committed a crime.

Preliminary adjudication p. 724 A hearing at which the prosecutor presents evidence of the defendant's guilt and the decision maker (either the grand jurors or a magistrate) determines whether sufficient probable cause exists to hold the defendant over for trial.

Plain view doctrine p. 727 A doctrine stating that authorities generally do not commit a Fourth Amendment violation when a government agent obtains evidence by virtue of seeing an object that is in plain view of the agent.

Speedy Trial Act p. 731 A federal statute that sets out specific time periods in which an accused must be brought to trial.

Double jeopardy p. 731 Situation in which a defendant could be subject to prosecution twice for the same offense; prohibited by the Fifth Amendment.

CHAPTER REVIEW QUESTIONS

1. What are the general requirements for criminal liability?
   I. Preponderance
   II. Act
   III. Justice
   IV. Mental
   a. I and II
   b. II and IV
   c. II and III
   d. III and IV

2. Which doctrine was created in a case involving the conviction of an individual executive under the Food, Drug, and Cosmetic Act?
   a. *Miranda*
   b. *Park*
   c. *Riley*
   d. *Braswell*

3. The U.S. Supreme Court held that the government's use of a zoom lens in a flyover of a chemical company fell into which warrant requirement exception?
   a. Search incident to arrest
   b. Good faith
   c. Plain view
   d. Privacy

4. Greco is arrested for insider trading based on evidence obtained by the government that violates Greco's Fourth Amendment rights. The evidence cannot be used against him at trial based on the _____ _____.
   a. Rights doctrine
   b. Violation rule
   c. Exclusionary rule
   d. Wrongful statute

5. Which amendment provides the right to a speedy trial?
   a. First
   b. Second
   c. Fourth
   d. Sixth

Answers and explanations are provided at the end of this chapter.

THEORY TO PRACTICE

Dania Beach Antique Supply (DBAS) Inc. is a wholesaler of antique merchandise. DBAS employs expert buyers who purchase antiques in Europe. The company then makes any cosmetic improvements necessary (such as cleaning) and resells the merchandise to retail antique shops in the United States. Grendel is a senior-level executive at the company in charge of its primary warehouse, located in Fort Lauderdale, Florida, and a smaller facility at the Port of Miami. One of Grendel's responsibilities is to oversee worker safety in the facilities, as the processing of the antiques sometimes involves use of industrial machinery and cleaning solvents.

It was well known among DBAS employees that the Fort Lauderdale warehouse had less than ideal working conditions. The air-conditioning system was often broken, and during the summer months the indoor temperature was in excess of 100 degrees. The cleaning solvents were left unattended, and the noxious fumes made working conditions hazardous. When workers complained to Grendel, he purchased small fans to be placed in the facility but declined to overhaul the air-conditioning system, claiming that the expense was too high and that the company was struggling financially. Grendel also ordered that the cleaning solvents be properly disposed of, but the on-site manager never carried out the order. In the meantime, several employees were hospitalized for heat exhaustion during their shift, and several others were made sick by the fumes from the cleaning solvents.

1. Assume that one worker notifies the Occupational Safety and Health Administration (OSHA) and that an OSHA agent informs Grendel that an investigation will be undertaken into the allegations of workplace hazards. Grendel immediately hires an air-conditioning repair company to fix the air-conditioning system. He also tells the on-site manager to destroy any maintenance records of the warehouse air-conditioning system history of inspections and repairs. What potential criminal culpability would DBAS, Grendel, and the on-site manager have at this point? Do Grendel's preinvestigation actions constitute a criminal act? Do Grendel's actions after OSHA's notification of an investigation constitute a crime in and of themselves? Is the on-site manager criminally liable for carrying out Grendel's orders?

2. Suppose that Grendel is charged with a crime related to the workplace hazards and he defends by showing evidence that he ordered subordinates to take care of the hazards, but his directions were never carried out. Is that a valid defense? If Grendel had second thoughts about his orders to destroy maintenance records and he called the manager to reverse his previous directions, would he still have criminal liability for attempting the cover-up?

3. Assume that during the investigation, OSHA agents make a midnight visit to Grendel's residence and remove documents from Grendel's trash bin on the public curb in front of his house. The documents contain incriminating evidence. Is the OSHA search illegal? Does the exclusionary rule apply in this case?

4. Assume that OSHA has information indicating that Grendel wrote about having a guilty conscience in regard to the working conditions in the warehouse. During the criminal investigation of Grendel, OSHA issues a subpoena for Grendel's personal diary. Is Grendel's diary protected from inspection via the Fifth Amendment?

5. Is OSHA required to obtain a search warrant if OSHA investigators use cameras with telephoto lenses (that are available to the general public) to take pictures of the broken air-conditioning unit adjacent to the warehouse? Assume the investigators take pictures while standing on the public sidewalk.

LEGAL STRATEGY 101

The Original Prisoner's Dilemma

The so-called prisoner's dilemma is perhaps the most well-known and famous example of legal strategy. It's called the *prisoner's* dilemma because of the original story told to illustrate this strategic situation:

> Two suspects are taken into custody and separated. The district attorney is certain that they are guilty of a specific crime, but does not have adequate evidence to convict them at trial. He points out to each prisoner that each has two alternatives: to confess to the crime the police are sure that they have done, or not to confess. If they both do not confess, then the district attorney states he will book them on some very minor trumped-up charge such as petty larceny and illegal possession of a weapon, and they will both receive minor punishment; if they both confess they will both

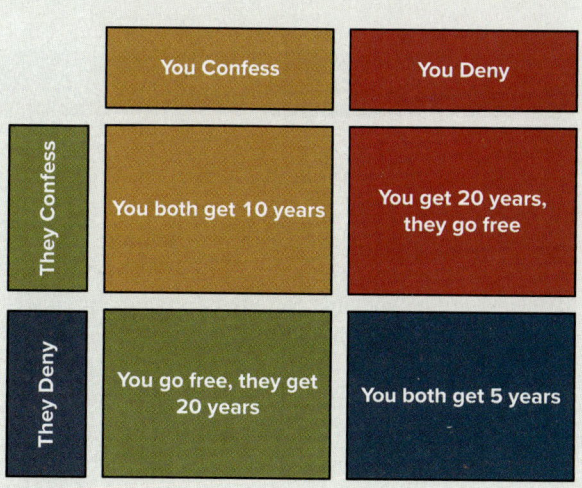

Prisoner's dilemma.

be prosecuted, but he will recommend less than the most severe sentence; but if one confesses and the other does not, then the confessor will receive lenient treatment for turning state's evidence whereas the latter will get "the book" slapped at him.[31]

The two suspects in this hypothetical will thus have a very long night ahead of them, as they separately but simultaneously mull over their options. Pop quiz: What should they do? There are three possibilities:

a. If one suspect "snitches" while the other remains silent, the "snitch" will be treated leniently (and possibly even receive immunity), while the suspect who remains silent will receive the most severe sentence.
b. If both of them snitch (i.e., turn state's evidence), they will both end up with stiff prison sentences.
c. If both suspects remain loyal to each other (i.e., refuse to snitch), both will receive light sentences.

Sounds like an easy choice, right?

It's not! The reason why the prisoner's dilemma is called a "dilemma" is because—from the strategic point of view of each suspect—no matter what the other suspect does, snitching is always the best response.[32]

To see this, let's look at the prisoners' situation from a strategic perspective. From the first suspect's point of view, if the other suspect snitches, then the first suspect should snitch as well; otherwise, he or she will receive the most severe sentence.

But here's the rub: Even if the other suspect decides not to snitch, from a strategic perspective, the first suspect should still snitch anyway. Why? Because snitching results in a lighter sentence for the first suspect when the other suspect remains silent. Because the same logic holds for the other suspect, the suspects are trapped in a true dilemma, a dilemma exploited by savvy prosecutors in many criminal cases.

CRITICAL THINKING QUESTION

Do you see any possible solution to the prisoner's dilemma? What if the suspects are not held in separate jail cells; that is, what if they are allowed to communicate with each other?

---

[31] Source: R. Duncan Luce and Howard Raiffa, *Games and Decisions: Introduction and Critical Survey*, Dover, reprint ed. (1989), p. 95.

[32] Stated formally, "snitching" in this situation is a *Nash equilibrium*. Named after the mathematician John Nash, who inspired the original version of the prisoner's dilemma, a Nash equilibrium is a combination of strategies that are mutual best responses. *See, e.g.,* Sylvia Nasar, *A Beautiful Mind: A Biography of John Forbes Nash, Jr.* 118 (Simon & Schuster reprint ed. 2011).

MANAGER'S CHALLENGE

A common element in cases where corporate executives are found guilty of criminal charges related to corporate activity is the lack of a systematic compliance procedure in the company's infrastructure. Senior managers are responsible for having systematic, internal controls in place that will help ensure compliance with federal and state statutes. Assume that you are a DBAS employee in this chapter's Theory to Practice problem and that both Grendel and the on-site warehouse manager are fired. You receive the following e-mail from the new vice president of operations:

> Congratulations! You are being promoted to on-site manager at the Fort Lauderdale warehouse.

The primary order of business is to develop a system of checks to be sure we are doing everything we can to avoid hazardous work conditions for our employees. Draft a two- to three-page memorandum that sets out a specific system for compliance. The system should address (1) how complaints from workers will be handled; (2) procedures for inspecting the facility, reporting problems, and ensuring follow-up; (3) a clear chain of command; and (4) a response plan to handle hazards that require immediate response.

See Connect for Manager's Challenge sample answers.

CASE SUMMARY 22.1 Bear Stearns & Co. v. Wyler, 182 F. Supp. 2d 679 (N.D. Ill. 2002)

PRODUCTION OF BUSINESS RECORDS

Bear Stearns had done business with Wyler, a Dutch businessman. A venture capitalist and resident of the Netherlands, Wyler kept offices in Toronto and Barbados. After the relationship soured, Bear Stearns sued Wyler for inducing one of its managing directors to make false statements and breach his fiduciary duties. In discovery, Bear Stearns requested that Wyler disclose any business records that related to that fraudulent inducement. Wyler invoked his Fifth Amendment right against self-incrimination.

CASE QUESTIONS

1. Will the court force Wyler to disclose the documents? Are they business records?
2. Does the Fifth Amendment apply in civil suits?

CASE SUMMARY 22.2 Dollar S.S. Co. v. United States, 101 F.2d 638 (9th Cir. 1939)

CRIMINAL LAW AND BUSINESS ENTITIES

A harbor patrolman was hit by a bucket of garbage "consisting of cabbage, orange peel, celery, tea leaves, and water" thrown from a steamer named the *President Coolidge* in Honolulu harbor. Unable to find the actual sailor who had dumped the trash, the government charged the ship owner under a federal law making off-loading garbage into navigable waters illegal. The ship's owner, however, had taken measures to prevent such dumping, such as issuing orders to the crew about its prohibition, hanging several warning signs in obvious places in both English and Chinese, and locking the "slop chutes" to prevent their use while in the harbor.

CASE QUESTIONS

1. Will the steamship company be criminally liable? Should it be even though it did everything to prevent the crime?
2. If the company should not be liable, what is the best way to prevent this crime?

CASE SUMMARY 22.3 United States v. Stewart, 323 F. Supp. 2d 606 (S.D.N.Y. 2004)

INSIDER TRADING

A wealthy businesswoman bought several thousand shares of a pharmaceutical company that was set to come out with a groundbreaking new cancer drug. She was a social friend of the company's CEO. On her way to vacation in Mexico, she received information from her broker that the CEO was selling all his shares. She eventually found out that the Food and Drug Administration was set to reject the cancer drug. She then sold all her shares and saved her own portfolio from devastation.

CASE QUESTIONS

1. Is the woman guilty of insider trading? Why?
2. Would you do what she did or just wait around to lose all your money?
3. Should the CEO get to sell his shares?

CASE SUMMARY 22.4 Lamb v. Philip Morris, Inc., 915 F.2d 1024 (6th Cir. 1990)

FOREIGN CORRUPT PRACTICES ACT

Philip Morris buys tobacco for its cigarettes from all around the world, including from South American growers in Venezuela. Philip Morris entered into a contract with La Fundacion del Niñó (the Children's Foundation) of Caracas, Venezuela, wherein the cigarette company would give the charity, which helped poor Venezuelan children, $12.5 million. In exchange, the Venezuelan government would put price controls on the country's tobacco crop.

CASE QUESTIONS

1. What criminal law did Philip Morris possibly violate? Why?
2. Should the criminal law have a problem with providing money to poor Venezuelan children and offering work for poor Venezuelan farmers?

CASE SUMMARY 22.5 State v. Yenzer, 195 P.3d 271 (Kan. App. 2008)

EXCLUSIONARY RULE

The police received information that Yenzer, a fugitive, would be at a local dentist's office the next day. The police arrived at the dentist's office in hopes of capturing Yenzer, but she was not there. The receptionist informed them that Yenzer's appointment had been rescheduled for the next week. The police requested the exact date and time, and the dentist's receptionist complied. The police returned to the office at the rescheduled appointment time and arrested Yenzer when she arrived. Subsequent to her arrest, the police discovered evidence of additional crimes committed by Yenzer and charged her with various felonies. The Health Insurance Portability and Accountability Act (HIPAA) of 1996 prohibits dental offices from disclosing any information (including appointment times) about patients to third parties without the patient's permission. At trial, Yenzer argued that all evidence discovered after the dentist-office arrest should be excluded because the arrest was made as a result of a HIPAA violation.

CASE QUESTIONS

1. Is Yenzer's dental appointment time protected by the Fourth Amendment? Why or why not?
2. Did the police go too far in this case by requesting confidential information from the dentist's receptionist? Isn't the exclusionary rule intended to deter unlawful conduct by authorities?

 Self-Check ANSWERS White-Collar Crime

1. FCPA. Buying a lavish meal for foreign government officials is prohibited.
2. Fraud (Ponzi scheme).
3. Conspiracy.
4. RICO.

CHAPTER REVIEW QUESTIONS: Answers and Explanations

1. **b.** Criminal liability requires both an act (or omission) and the mental element of a guilty mind. The remaining answers are incorrect because preponderance and justice are unrelated to criminal liability.

2. **b.** Created in *United States v. Park*, the doctrine is cited in the context of holding individual corporate officers liable for certain violations. The remaining answers are incorrect because they are names of cases unrelated to the *Park* doctrine.

3. **c.** In *Dow Chemical Co. v. United States*, the Court held that a zoom lens was readily available to the public and therefore could be used to enhance "plain view." Answer choice (a) is incorrect because no arrest was made. Answer choice (b) is incorrect because good faith refers to some mistake made by authorities. Answer choice (d) is not an exception to the warrant requirement.

4. **c.** The exclusionary rule requires that evidence obtained without a warrant and not falling into a warrant exception be excluded from trial. The remaining answers are fictional.

5. **d.** The Sixth Amendment provides for a speedy trial, a public trial, and the right to confront witnesses. The remaining answers are wrong because those amendments are unrelated to criminal trials.

CHAPTER 23
Personal Property, Real Property, and Land Use Law

©philsajonesen/Getty Images

Learning Objectives

After studying this chapter, students who have mastered the material will be able to:

23-1 Describe the main types of property rights and explain why such property rights are essential aspects of the legal environment of business.

23-2 Distinguish between tangible property and intellectual property.

23-3 Define and give examples of personal property used in business.

23-4 Explain the concepts of title, bundle of rights, and ownership by possession.

23-5 Identify the individual rights that landowners have in real property.

23-6 List and give examples of the major forms of real estate ownership interests most commonly held by businesses and individuals.

23-7 Give examples of two types of laws that regulate the use of real property by its owners.

23-8 Articulate the government's power of eminent domain and the main limits to this power.

Laws governing the ownership and use of property have deep historical roots and are an integral part of the American legal system. Business owners and managers regularly encounter property law issues in business planning and operations. Examples include decisions on whether to own or lease certain property, rights of property owners, landlord-tenant laws, and government restrictions on how property may be used. In this chapter, we discuss

- General categories of property rights and the concept of transaction costs.
- Specific categories of property rights that are important to conducting business operations.
- Various levels of property ownership rights, responsibilities, and restrictions.
- Specific laws governing the legal relationship between landlords and tenants.
- Methods used by the government to regulate the use of certain property.
- The government's power of eminent domain and limits to this power.

TYPES OF PROPERTY RIGHTS

When we hear the word "property," we often think of such resources as land and physical goods. In reality, however, property rights can come in many forms. By way of example, the following list describes four major types of property rights:

- *Private property,* or property that is exclusively owned by a single owner. Access, use, and management of private property are controlled by the private owner.
- *Common property,* or property that is owned by two or more individuals. Access, use, and management of common property are controlled by the joint owners.
- *Public property* (also known as state property), or property that is publicly owned by the government. Access, use, and management of public property are usually controlled by a government agency or by an organization granted such authority by the government.
- *Open-access property,* or property that is owned by no one (*res nullius*). Examples of open-access property include outer space and ocean fisheries outside of territorial borders. The government can sometimes convert open-access property into private, common, or public property through land grants or by legislating to define public/private rights previously not granted.

The legal environment of business will thus consist of some mixture of all these forms of property. Moreover, whatever form they take, property rights are an essential feature of the legal environment because they provide stability and predictability. Simply put, without some system of property rights, business firms would be unable to make plans for the future.

But property rights to a good must be defined, their use must be monitored, and possession of rights must be enforced. The costs of defining, monitoring, and enforcing property rights are often called **transaction costs**. Depending on the level of transaction costs, various forms of property and legal institutions will develop.

In this chapter, we will focus on private property rights. A private property system generally gives individuals and firms the exclusive right to use their resources as they see fit. Broadly speaking, that dominion over what is theirs leads property users to take full account of all the benefits and costs of employing those resources in a particular manner.

CATEGORIES OF PROPERTY

While the casual or ordinary (nonlegal) meaning of the word *property* is often used to refer to real estate, the Law of Property recognizes two distinct categories or private property rights: rights to tangible property (such as land or goods) and intellectual property rights (such as the rights to certain ideas created by patents). The main laws covering tangible property are discussed in this chapter, while intellectual property laws, which are also very important to business firms, are covered in the next chapter.

TANGIBLE PROPERTY

Tangible property, of course, is property that can be touched and physically possessed. The two forms of tangible property are **personal property** and **real property**.

Personal Property

Personal property is both *tangible* and *movable*. In a business context, goods, vehicles, inventory, and equipment for business operations, such as computers and desks, are all examples of personal property. Personal property may be *owned* or *leased*. Leasing, which

LO 23-1
Describe the main types of property rights and explain why such property rights are essential aspects of the legal environment of business.

LO 23-2
Distinguish between tangible property and intellectual property.

LO 23-3
Define and give examples of personal property used in business.

is governed by state statutory law modeled after the Uniform Commercial Code (UCC),[1] is discussed later in this chapter. Personal property rights of ownership, possession, and transfer are governed by a blend of state statutes and common law principles.

Personal Property: Rights of Ownership and Ownership by Possession

LO 23-4

Explain the concepts of title, bundle of rights, and ownership by possession.

The legal term for ownership rights in property is **title**. Normally, title is obtained by a grant of title by the current owner to a new owner, usually through a purchase or gift. Title generally encompasses a *bundle of rights* related to the personal property. In particular, the titleholder has the right to exclusive use of the personal property and the right to any stream of income generated by the property, as well as the rights to sell, lease, or prohibit another from using the property.

There are some instances, however, when the law allows a party to take title solely on the basis of *possession*.

> **KEY POINT**
>
> Property ownership is fundamentally a bundle of rights whereby the titleholder is granted the right to control, possess, and use the property as well as the right to sell, lease, or prohibit another from using the property.

Found Articles Under the common law, the finder's rights depend on the category of the found property. Found property is categorized in one of four ways:

- First, if the owner intentionally places the property in a certain place and later forgets about it, the property is considered *mislaid*.
- Second, if the owner unintentionally parts with the property through either carelessness or neglect, it is considered *lost*.
- Third, if the owner has thrown away or voluntarily forsaken the property, it is considered *abandoned*.
- Finally, found property is considered *treasure trove* if it is verifiably antiquated and it has been concealed for so long as to indicate that the owners are probably dead or unknown.

The finder of lost or abandoned property and treasure trove acquires the right to possess the property against the entire world *except* against the **actual owner**, regardless of the place of the finding. The finder of the mislaid property, however, must turn the property over to the premises owner to safeguard the property for the true owner. The key to determining whether the property is lost (or abandoned or considered a treasure trove) versus mislaid is the element of *involuntariness*. That is, in order to abandon personal property, one must voluntarily and intentionally give up a known right.

Suppose that the Professor finds a gold Rolex wristwatch on a public sidewalk while walking to a commuter train station. She takes the watch to Station Manager, who, after asking each passenger in the area if he or she is the owner of the watch, is unable to find the true owner. Station Manager then keeps the watch from the Professor on the basis that the Professor is not the true or original owner. Assuming the true owner is not found, a court would likely find that the Professor has title over Station Manager and everyone else, except for the original owner.[2]

The ownership rights of found property are the central issue in a surprising number of modern cases. In Case 23.1, a state appellate court analyzes a found property claim.

---

[1] Recall from Chapter 1, "Legal Foundations," that the UCC is a "model" statute drafted by a group called the National Conference of Commissioners of Uniform State Laws (NCCUSL). Each state legislature makes its own decisions about whether to adopt the UCC in total, in part, or not at all.

[2] Based on the landmark English common law case *Armory v. Delamirie,* 1 Strange 505 (K.B. 1722).

CASE 23.1 Grande, as Personal Representative of the Estate of Robert A. Spann, v. Jennings, 278 P.3d 1287 (Ariz. Ct. App. 2012)

FACT SUMMARY Robert A. Spann (Robert) lived in his Paradise Valley home until he died in 2001. His daughter, Karen Spann Grande (Karen), became the personal representative of his estate. She and her sister took charge of the house and, among other things, had some repairs made to the home. They also looked for valuables their father may have left or hidden because they knew from experience that he had hidden gold, cash, and other valuables in unusual places in his house. Over the course of seven years, they found stocks and bonds, as well as hundreds of military-style green ammunition cans hidden throughout the house, some of which contained gold or cash. In 2008, the house was sold "as is" to Sarina Jennings (Sarina). Jennings hired a contractor, Bueghly, to remodel the dilapidated home. Shortly after the work began, an employee of Bueghly's discovered two ammunition cans full of cash in the kitchen wall and found two more cash-filled ammo cans inside other walls in the house. The total amount of cash found by the employee was approximately $500,000.

After the employee reported the find to his boss, Bueghly took possession of the four ammo cans. He did not tell the new owners about the money and hid the cans in his floor safe. Sarina eventually found out from the employee about the cash and contacted the police, who then took protective custody of the cash. Sarina sued Bueghly for, among other things, a court declaration that Bueghly had no right to the money because Sarina was now the homeowner. Bueghly filed a counterclaim for a declaration that he was entitled to the found funds as a treasure trove. In the meantime, Karen (the daughter of the original owner of the house) filed suit on behalf of her father Robert's estate as the true owner. The cases were consolidated and the trial court awarded summary judgment in favor of Robert's estate. Sarina appealed this judgment.

SYNOPSIS OF DECISION AND OPINION The Arizona Court of Appeals upheld the trial court's decision in favor of Robert's estate. The court determined that the ammunition cans were mislaid property because it was undisputed that the estate's representatives did not know that the money was mislaid and did not intend to abandon the funds. Once Karen learned of the discovery, she filed a probate petition to recover the property, and this action indicates that no abandonment occurred. The court rejected Sarina's argument that a jury could have found that the money had been abandoned as a result of Karen consciously ignoring the possibility that additional large sums of money could be hidden in the home when she sold the house.

WORDS OF THE COURT: Property Not Abandoned "Arizona follows the common law. . . . 'While personal property of all kinds may be abandoned, the property must be of such a character as to make it clear that it was voluntarily abandoned by the owner. In this connection, it has been said that people do not normally abandon their money; and, accordingly, that found money will not be considered as abandoned, but as lost or mislaid property.' . . . Here, it is undisputed that [Robert] Spann placed the cash in the ammunition cans and then hid those cans in the recesses of the house. He did not, however, tell his daughters where he had hidden the cans before he passed away. His daughters looked for and found many of the ammo cans, but not the last four. In fact, it was not until the wall-mounted toaster oven and bathroom drywall were removed that [the contractor] found the remaining cash-filled cans. As a result, and as the trial court found, the funds are, as a matter of law, mislaid funds that belong to the true owner, [Robert] Spann's estate."

Case Questions

1. What was each party's—Karen (the seller), Sarina (the buyer), and Bueghly (the finder)—theory of the case as to why he or she should get the found cash?
2. Why is it important for the court to determine whether or not the property has been abandoned?
3. *Focus on Critical Thinking:* How could the facts of the case be changed to lead to a conclusion that Sarina (the buyer of the house where the cash was found) should prevail? How could the facts be changed to lead to a conclusion that Bueghly (the finder) should prevail?

Adverse Possession Every state has enacted a specific statute based on common law principles that applies to personal property held for an extended period of time by a possessor who is not the true owner. Once the statutory period has elapsed, the possessor of the goods is protected from any suit to recover the property, except by its true owner. This rule of adverse possession is also applied in a real property context and is explained in further detail later in this chapter.

Good Faith Purchasers In some cases, a buyer will purchase a good or other personal property from someone who has physical possession of the property but not the title to the property (as is the case, for example, with stolen goods). Under these circumstances, even if the buyer has no reason to know the good was stolen, the buyer does *not* acquire valid title. This situation is governed by the property law maxim that a seller cannot convey valid title unless she has valid title in the first place. Therefore, the general rule is that if a good was stolen, the actual owner may recover the property—even from a good faith buyer!

Bailments In a bailment relationship, although a possessor does not gain title via possession, the nonowner is still a rightful possessor of the goods. A bailment relationship is created when the *bailor* (the owner of the property) entrusts a *bailee* to temporarily hold the property, usually for the parties' mutual benefit. If the parties intend to create a bailment relationship, the common law imposes on the bailee a duty of *care* and a duty to act *reasonably* in protecting the property.

For example, suppose that Franz brings his gold pocket watch to Max, a jeweler, for repair. Leaving the watch with Max creates a bailment relationship. That is, Franz has entrusted Max with his watch for their mutual benefit (Franz gets his watch fixed; Max earns income). Assume that Max has to leave the store in a rush that night and accidentally leaves the door open. The store is burglarized, and Franz's watch is stolen. Max is liable for the cost of the watch due to his breach of the duty of care as bailee. On the other hand, suppose Max locks up the watch in a vault before he leaves, but a burglar with special skills breaks into the vault and takes the watch. In that case, most courts would find that Max has exercised due care and reasonableness and, therefore, is not liable for the theft.[3] Other common examples of a bailment relationship are coat-check services, dry cleaning, and valet parking.[4]

In Case 23.2 a state appellate court analyzes the limits of bailment liability.

CASE 23.2 Ziva Jewelry v. Car Wash Headquarters, 897 So.2d 1011 (Ala. 2004)

FACT SUMMARY Stewart Smith was employed by Ziva Jewelry, Inc. (Ziva), as a traveling salesman. In connection with his employment, Smith drove his own car to meet with potential customers and traveled with samples of expensive jewelry, which he typically kept locked in the trunk. In August 2000, while returning from a trade show, Smith stopped to get his car washed at a car wash owned and operated by Car Wash Headquarters (Car Wash). Smith left his keys with a Car Wash employee, watched the car as it went through the tunnel, and observed an employee driving the car a short distance to the drying area. Smith did not alert any Car Wash employee to the contents of the trunk. After the car was dried, the attendant signaled to Smith that the service was complete.

(continued)

---

[3]Based on examples in Ray A. Brown, *The Law of Personal Property* (Callaghan and Company 3d ed. 1975).

[4]Note that courts distinguish between a "self-check" parking lot (no bailment) and a valet parking lot, where an agent of the lot actually takes physical possession of the car via keys, etc. (bailment).

As Smith paid the cashier, someone jumped into Smith's vehicle and drove off. Although the police located Smith's car in just 15 minutes, jewelry valued at over $850,000 was gone from the trunk and was never recovered. Ziva sued Car Wash, alleging that Car Wash, as bailee, took possession of Smith's car and of the jewelry inside the car and that Car Wash failed to exercise due care to safeguard and return the bailed car and contents to Smith. The trial court granted Car Wash's motion for a summary judgment on the grounds that no bailment of the jewelry had been created. Ziva appealed.

SYNOPSIS OF DECISION AND OPINION The Supreme Court of Alabama affirmed the trial court's summary judgment in favor of Car Wash. The court held that Ziva could not establish that Car Wash expressly or impliedly agreed to take responsibility for the jewelry hidden inside Smith's trunk. Because Ziva acknowledged that the jewelry was not plainly visible, there was no reason for the employees to foresee that the trunk contained expensive jewelry. The court ruled that Ziva could not claim that Car Wash knew or that it should have reasonably foreseen or expected that it was taking responsibility for over $850,000 worth of jewelry when it accepted Smith's vehicle for the purpose of washing it.

WORDS OF THE COURT: Acceptance by the Bailee "Thus, there is no evidence indicating that [Car Wash] expressly or impliedly accepted responsibility for the jewelry in the trunk of Smith's vehicle. Without express or implied acceptance by the purported bailee, a bailment cannot arise."

Case Questions
1. What if Smith's car had never been recovered—would Car Wash be liable as a bailee for the car?
2. When a bailee takes a car as part of a bailment relationship, isn't the bailee also assuming liability for what is inside the car?
3. *Focus on Critical Thinking:* Is Ziva left completely without recourse, or could it advance a different legal theory? What if the theft was an "inside job" involving Smith and the employees of the Car Wash—how would that fact impact your analysis?

CONCEPT SUMMARY Personal Property

- Personal property is both tangible and movable and can be owned or leased. Examples of personal property include inventory and business systems such as telephones or computers.
- Title is the legal form of ownership of property and provides the titleholder exclusive rights to sell, lease, or prohibit others from using the property.
- Finders of lost property obtain title to the good by possession, except against the actual owner.
- Sellers cannot convey better title than what they have; therefore, if a buyer purchases stolen goods, the actual owner may still recover the property. It is irrelevant that the buyer who purchased the goods did so in good faith and did not know they were stolen.
- Bailments are created when the bailor (owner of the property) entrusts a bailee to temporarily hold the property. Common examples of bailments are coat checks, valet parking, and repair shops.

Leased Personal Property: UCC Article 2A

Businesses often choose to *lease* personal property, especially equipment, rather than purchase it outright. In an *equipment lease,* the lessor (owner of the property) gives the lessee (the party using the property) the exclusive right to possess and use the equipment for a

A bailment relationship is created when the owner of the property (bailor) temporarily entrusts it to another party (bailee) usually for their mutual benefit, as occurs when a customer gives clothes to a dry cleaner. jackf/123RF

fixed period of time. The lessee often makes a monthly payment to the lessor, but at the end of the lease term, the equipment is returned to the lessor.

As a business matter, leasing is often an attractive alternative to owning because a business firm can use the equipment on an exclusive basis for a fixed period of time without having to purchase the equipment outright. There may also be tax advantages for the lessee in some cases.

Examples of equipment that a business may lease are computers, telephones, furniture, and even heavy machinery used for manufacturing or construction. Note that leases fall into an area governed by both principles of property law and certain principles of commercial law. Lease agreements are a form of personal property contract and are governed by state statutory laws that are modeled after Article 2A of the Uniform Commercial Code (UCC). Article 2A covers many of the same subjects as the article governing the sale of goods, such as defining what constitutes a lease agreement, requiring certain lease agreements to be in writing, and allocating the risk of loss (i.e., which party will be responsible if the equipment is destroyed) to one party or the other based on the circumstances of the transaction.

REAL PROPERTY

The main source of law that governs the ownership of real property or land is primarily state statutes, although many common law principles also apply. The statutes that regulate the legal relationship between residential landlords and tenants are based primarily on a model act known as the Uniform Residential Landlord-Tenant Act (URLTA). Note that when a landlord leases real property to a business, this relationship is known as a *commercial* landlord-tenant agreement and is not governed by the URLTA.

Ownership Rights

Ownership or private property rights to a parcel (piece) of *real property,* also called *real estate,* include the land and any structures built upon it, as well as plant life and vegetation. The structures are known as the property's *improvements.* Ownership rights also extend to anything that is affixed, known as *fixtures,* to the structure, such as plumbing, heating and cooling systems, and the like. Similar to ownership rights in personal property, the ownership rights in a parcel of real property are thought of as a *bundle of rights.* This bundle includes the right to sell, gift, lease, and control the property and its improvements and fixtures. Ownership of real property is typically evidenced by a *deed.* Traditional property ownership rights are said to extend from "the soil upward into Heaven."[5] Generally, this legal principle means that certain rights are attached to the land that fit into four categories:

1. Rights related to the *use and enjoyment* of the land;
2. *Subsurface* rights;
3. *Water* rights; and
4. *Airspace* rights.

LO 23-5

Identify the individual rights that landowners have in real property.

Use and Enjoyment of the Land   Generally, landowners have the right to use and enjoy the use of their property without interference from others. This interference is known as *nuisance* and occurs when one party creates *unreasonable conditions* that affect the landowner's use or enjoyment of the property. In many nuisance cases, a residential or business property owner sues a manufacturing company for producing pollutants, making excessive noise, or emitting foul odors. Most courts apply the unreasonableness factor by examining the *nature* of the parcels of property at issue. In an area that is zoned for heavy industrial use, courts are reluctant to impose liability on a plant owner under the nuisance theory. Areas that are zoned for retail, office, or residential use are more likely to have legal protection from such nuisances.

Subsurface Rights   Landowners have rights to the soil and, most importantly, to any mineral, oil, or natural gas within the soil. These subsurface rights may be severed from the bundle of rights owned by the landowner and sold to a third party.

Water Rights   Also known as *riparian* rights, landowners have the right to reasonable use of any streams, lakes, and groundwater (water contained in soil) that are fully or partially part of their real property. *Reasonable use* means that the landowner is entitled to only as much of the water as she can put to beneficial use upon her land while balancing the rights of others who have riparian rights in the same stream or lake (such as an adjacent landowner).

Airspace Rights   The law contemplates ownership of airspace by drawing an imaginary line emanating from the borders of the property into the sky. Perhaps the most significant and pragmatic exception to this rule is that courts have held that landowners may not use this right to prevent airplane flights over their property.[6] Most airspace rights cases involving businesses arise when one property owner erects a building that somehow interferes with the air rights of another. Consider the dilemma of a resort hotel when faced with a next-door neighbor that builds a building so tall that it blocks the sun from the resort's pool. In Landmark Case 23.3, the Florida District Court of Appeal considers the question of whether a famous Miami Beach resort's airspace rights include solar rights as well.

---

[5] From English common law cases that cite the Latin phrase *cujus est solum, ejus usque ad coelum.*
[6] *United States v. Causby,* 328 U.S. 256 (1946).

LANDMARK CASE 23.3 Fontainebleau Hotel Corp. v. Forty-Five Twenty-Five, Inc., 114 So.2d 357 (Fla. Dist. Ct. App. 1959)

FACT SUMMARY The Fontainebleau Hotel was in the process of constructing a 14-story addition to its resort hotel. One of Fontainebleau's competitors, Forty-Five Twenty-Five, Inc., the owners of the Eden Roc Hotel ("Eden Roc"), an adjoining property to the Fontainebleau, filed suit asking the court to issue an order prohibiting further construction of the addition. Eden Roc alleged that in the winter months, beginning at 2 o'clock in the afternoon and continuing until sunset, the shadow caused by the new addition would extend over the Eden Roc's resort cabañas, main swimming pool, and several designated sunbathing areas. Eden Roc argued that this interference with sunlight and air violated its air rights and was causing the Eden Roc to lose profits because its resort was now less desirable for guests wishing to use the pool facilities. Eden Roc also alleged that the construction plan was based on ill will between the owners of the resorts.

SYNOPSIS OF DECISION AND OPINION The Florida District Court of Appeal ruled in favor of the Fontainebleau on the basis of the general property law rule that property owners may use their property in any reasonable and lawful manner. The court noted that landowners are not obliged to use their property in a way that would prevent injury to a neighbor. The court also pointed out that modern American courts have consistently rejected the historical English law doctrine of "ancient lights," which provides a right to the free flow of light and air from adjoining land, as unworkable in current commercial life. Therefore, the court held that there is no legal right to the flow of air or light and that there is no cause of action so long as the structure serves a legitimately useful purpose.

WORDS OF THE COURT: Air and Solar Rights "There being . . . no legal right to the free flow of light and air from the adjoining land, it is universally held that where a structure serves a useful and beneficial purpose, it does not give rise to a cause of action . . . , even though it causes injury to another by cutting off the light and air and interfering with the view that would otherwise be available over adjoining land in its natural state, regardless of the fact that the structure may have been erected partly for spite."

Case Questions
1. If the Eden Roc Hotel could prove that the addition was built completely out of spite, should this additional fact affect the court's decision?
2. Is the court correct to claim that the historical ancient lights doctrine is unworkable in modern commercial life? What about the solar energy industry?
3. *Focus on Critical Thinking:* What if the Fontainebleau were playing loud hip hop music every evening in order to attract a younger and more urban clientele? If the Eden Roc Hotel could prove that its clientele consists mostly of elderly people who prefer peace and quiet, how should the court rule?

Forms of Real Property Ownership Interests

LO 23-6
List and give examples of the major forms of real estate ownership interests most commonly held by businesses and individuals.

In most cases, real estate owners are entitled to the same general bundle of rights as those discussed in the section on personal property. However, some forms of ownership limit those general rights; therefore, it is necessary to understand the various *forms of ownership*. These are known as **ownership interests**. Although there are seven legally recognized interests in all, we will focus on the four most common ownership interests that are important to business firms: (1) fee simple, (2) life estate, (3) leasehold estate, and (4) easements.

The Florida District Court of Appeal ruled that the famous Fontainebleau Hotel in Miami Beach, seen here, had the right to construct an addition to its property despite the fact that the addition blocked the sunlight to an adjacent resort hotel. ASSOCIATED PRESS

Fee Simple The term **fee simple** actually encompasses three distinct interests,[7] all centered on the basic concept that fee simple ownership interests are the highest level of general rights associated with real estate.

Fee simple absolute means that the rights are *unrestricted* (though always subject to eminent domain and any other restrictions imposed by law, such as zoning), infinite in duration, and inheritable by the owner's heirs.

Fee simple defeasible is a fee simple right with certain restrictions. If one of these restrictions is violated, the property ownership automatically falls back *(reverts)* to the original owner. The right of reversion is why we think of the original owner as maintaining a partial ownership interest even after that owner has granted ownership interests to a third party. The restrictions primarily either limit the property to a *particular use* (e.g., it may be used only for certain charitable purposes) or entail the fulfillment of some *condition* or requirement related to the real estate (e.g., a municipality grants a contractor an interest in a 1,000-acre city-owned lot on the condition that the contractor build a landfill for public use on a 200-acre portion of the property).

Life Estate A **life estate** is simply an ownership interest that lasts for the lifetime of a particular person. The person who has a life estate interest is known as a *life tenant* because the life tenant may *not* sell, pledge, or convey the building in any way during her ownership. However, life tenants do have day-to-day ownership duties, such as paying taxes and repair/maintenance costs.

Legal Speak >))

Heirs
Individuals who are legally entitled to inherit a decedent's property.

Legal Speak >))

Defeasible
Capable of being canceled.

---

[7] A minority of states also recognize a fourth interest of *fee tail,* which ensures that certain real estate will remain within the current owner's family.

A *life estate defeasible* is a life estate with a restriction attached in some way. Life estates are sometimes used as part of a business *succession* plan designed for the transition of the ownership of a family-owned business from one generation to the next. For example, suppose that Blake Sr. has built a successful family business with assets that include a valuable piece of real estate, including a modern warehouse facility. Blake Sr. uses 75 percent of the warehouse for his business and leases the other 25 percent of the space to tenants. Blake Jr. is the sole heir and has helped run the business for many years. Blake Sr. wishes to pass the business and all of the business's property on to Blake Jr. upon his death. Blake Sr. also wishes to use the rental income from the warehouse lease to help support his spouse for as long as she lives. To achieve both objectives, Blake Sr. may use the following language as part of his estate and business succession planning documents:

> If I die before my spouse, I, Blake Sr., grant and convey my entire interest in Warehouse Real Estate to my spouse for her lifetime, on the condition that Blake Jr.'s business will pay no rent for use of the property; then to Blake Jr. in fee simple absolute.

KEY POINT

Fee simple absolute is the highest level of ownership because it allows the titleholder unrestricted ownership rights.

In analyzing this language, we can determine that Blake Sr. intends to have his widowed spouse be the sole owner of the warehouse property during her lifetime but only on the condition that Blake Jr. is not charged any rent (a *life estate defeasible*). After her death, Blake Jr. inherits the real estate with ownership rights in fee simple absolute. This condition ensures that the benefit flows to Blake Sr.'s spouse without imposing an additional burden on Blake Jr.'s ability to run the family business. Blake Sr.'s spouse cannot sell her interest in the warehouse real estate, and this condition ensures that Blake Jr. will eventually receive the property with no restrictions on use and that the continuity between generations in the business will be preserved.

Leasehold Estate A **leasehold estate** ownership interest affords the least amount of rights because it grants only a *qualified right* to use the real estate in an exclusive manner for a *limited* period of time.

The most common form of leasehold estate is the *landlord-tenant agreement,* whereby the landlord gives the tenant a qualified right to possess and use the real estate for a specified period of years that is often spelled out in a written **lease**.[8] Such an agreement creates a qualified right because the landlord retains the right to enter under certain circumstances. This leasehold estate is known as a *tenancy for years.* At the expiration of the time period, the leasehold estate expires automatically, and the tenant no longer has any ownership interests.

A landlord and tenant may also wish not to fix a specific time period but rather have a month-to-month[9] agreement that continues to renew automatically for that time period (in this case, one month) until one party or the other gives advance notice that she wishes to terminate the lease. Notice must be given at least one complete time period ahead (in this case, one month's notice would be required). This leasehold estate is known as a *periodic tenancy.* In a business context, it is not unusual for parties to use both types of leasehold estates to achieve certain business objectives.

For example, suppose that Browning is an architect with a thriving practice in commercial renovation planning. She enters into a five-year lease for office space in a small office building owned by Gilbert. Toward the end of the lease's term, Gilbert approaches

---

[8] A real estate lease is a form of contract and is, therefore, subject to the statute of frauds, which provides that certain contracts must be in writing to be enforceable. The statute of frauds is discussed in detail in Chapter 6, "Overview and Formation of Contracts."

[9] The parties will sometimes agree to even shorter time periods, such as week to week.

Browning about renewing the lease agreement for an additional five years. However, Browning informs Gilbert that she plans to expand her firm and anticipates hiring new employees over the next five years. This expansion will require Browning to move into larger office space in the future. Gilbert offers a solution by agreeing to lease on a month-to-month basis. This periodic tenancy gives Gilbert the opportunity to locate a new suitable tenant and Browning the opportunity to find a larger space without any legal commitment beyond a one-month notice period. Note that, typically, Browning would have to pay a higher monthly rental payment under the monthly agreement than she would pay if she signed another five-year lease. However, it is likely a valuable return on investment given the flexibility afforded to her in a monthly lease. Based on their business objectives, the parties shift their leasehold estate interest from a tenancy for years (the five-year lease) to a periodic tenancy (a month-to-month) lease.

Easements An **easement** is a privilege to use real estate owned by another. A common example of an easement is the grant given by property owners to utility companies for the privilege to install and maintain gas and water lines.

Easements can be created in one of three ways:

1. By an *express* grant (usually expressed in writing on the property deed);
2. By *implication* or *necessity,* in which a property is landlocked between other properties and the owner must cross through the property of another to gain access to her property; or
3. By *prescription,* in which the privilege is gained through adverse possession (discussed in the next section).

Generally, easements are transferred with the property when the real estate is sold to another party, so long as the new owner has reason to know of the easement (as is the case when the easement is expressly granted in a deed and has been publicly recorded with the appropriate government office).

By contrast, instead of granting a permanent easement, a landowner may grant a temporary *license* instead. In brief, a license is permission to use the property in a certain way but is revocable at any time at the owner's discretion. This right of revocation of the owner is the main difference between an easement and a license.

 Self-Check Ownership Interests

What is Swineburne's ownership interest?

1. Swineburne approaches Carroll with the idea of starting a charity soup kitchen. Carroll donates a parcel of real estate to Swineburne by providing this agreement: *"I convey this parcel to Swineburne in fee simple."* Swineburne uses the property to build a luxury resort hotel.
2. Swineburne approaches Carroll with the idea of starting a charity soup kitchen. Carroll donates a parcel of real estate to Swineburne by providing this agreement: *"I convey this parcel to Swineburne in fee simple provided that it be used for charitable purposes."* Swineburne uses the property to build a luxury resort hotel.
3. Swineburne approaches Carroll with the idea of starting a charity soup kitchen. Carroll agrees to rent a parcel of real estate to Swineburne for $1 a month on a month-to-month basis. The next day, Carroll gets an offer to purchase the real estate parcel for twice its market value on the condition that Carroll convey the real estate within five days. Carroll tells Swineburne to vacate the premises immediately.

(continued)

4. Swineburne approaches Carroll with the idea of starting a charity soup kitchen. Carroll donates a parcel of real estate to Swineburne by providing this agreement: *"I convey this parcel to Swineburne for his life, and then to Carroll Jr. in fee simple absolute."* Swineburne uses the property to start a soup kitchen but dies shortly thereafter. Swineburne Jr. continues the soup kitchen. Carroll Jr. then informs Swineburne Jr. that he is selling the real estate and therefore Swineburne Jr. must vacate.

5. Swineburne approaches Carroll with a request that Carroll allow Swineburne to have the use of the driveway of a commercial office building owned by Carroll, which is on a parcel of property adjacent to Swineburne's charity soup kitchen. The driveway would allow easier access for trucks delivering supplies to the soup kitchen. Carroll executes and records a new deed with the statement: *"On the parcel of my commercial office building, I convey an easement for use of the driveway to Swineburne."* Carroll subsequently sells the property to Blago. Blago informs Swineburne that he may no longer use the driveway.

Answers to this Self-Check are provided at the end of the chapter.

Adverse Possession

In some cases, a party may gain title to real estate through the doctrine of adverse possession. In order to acquire title to land through adverse possession, the acquiring party must demonstrate that she has possessed it in a certain way for a certain period of time. These requirements are often spelled out in a particular state's statutory or common law. In general, the requirements are that the party must have met a three-prong test. Obtaining title requires that the adverse possession must have been (1) open, notorious, and visible; (2) exclusive and actual; and (3) continuous.

Open, Notorious, and Visible Possession

The true holder of title cannot be relieved of that title unless she can be reasonably expected to know that another person has taken possession of the real estate and that the adverse possessor *intended* to assert a claim to its ownership. Examples of cases where courts have held that this prong was satisfied include those in which the adverse possessor had (1) demonstrated that the true owner had actual or imputed knowledge that the adverse party had taken possession of the land; (2) erected a fence or other enclosure around the property; or (3) paid taxes or other maintenance fees in connection with the land.

Exclusive and Actual Possession

The adverse possessor must also show that she was in exclusive control of the property and did not share control or possession of the property with the true owner or the public generally. This requirement means that at least a reasonable percentage of the land claimed by the adverse possessor must be in actual use.

Continuous Possession

The adverse possession of the property must be continuous for a period of time set down by state statute or common law. About two-thirds of states require 15 years or longer, but some states allow a shorter period of time if the adverse possessor pays taxes on the property. This requirement does not mean that the adverse possessor must spend every consecutive day on the property. Rather, it means that the adverse possessor cannot *abandon* the property for a period of time. If the owner retakes possession within the prescribed time period, the adverse possessor's use stops and this prong cannot be satisfied unless the true owner abandons the property again in the future.

In Case 23.4, an appellate court considers a business owner's claim of title to a parcel of property through adverse possession.

CASE 23.4 2 North Street Corp. v. Getty Saugerties Corp., 68 A.D.3d 1392 (N.Y. App. Div. 2009)

FACT SUMMARY 2 North Street is a corporation that owned a parcel of real estate used for a shopping center and a parking lot. Getty owned the adjacent lot, on which it had operated a gas station. A fence runs close to the boundary line between the properties but lies entirely on Getty's property, leaving a narrow 0.129-acre strip of land between the boundary line and the fence. 2 North maintained the strip of land from the time the company purchased the property. For a period of approximately 23 years, 2 North paid a contractor to continuously maintain the strip's grass. The contractor also planted vegetation, removed rubbish and debris, and deposited snow plowed from 2 North's parking lot upon it. Getty never questioned the activities of the contractor, nor did anyone representing Getty grant the contractor permission to perform them. In 2007, 2 North brought an action seeking a declaration that it owned the strip of land through adverse possession. Getty objected on the basis that 2 North's use of the strip was not open and notorious enough to constitute notice to others claiming an adverse and hostile interest in the land. The trial court ruled in favor of 2 North. Getty appealed.

SYNOPSIS OF DECISION AND OPINION The appellate division of the Supreme Court of New York affirmed the lower court's decision and held in favor of 2 North. The court ruled that 2 North had met its statutory burden of establishing that the character of the possession was hostile under a claim of right, actual, open and notorious, exclusive, and continuous for the statutory period of 10 years. The court was convinced that 2 North initially believed that it owned the strip and exclusively maintained it as its own, even though the strip was not included in its deed description. This evidence of 2 North's continuous use and maintenance of the strip exemplified its possession as open and notorious, constituting notice to others that it was claiming an adverse and hostile interest in it.

WORDS OF THE COURT: Improvement Requirement "[The statute also requires] usual cultivation or improvement. . . . [Evidence of] this mandate 'will vary with "the nature and situation of the property and the uses to which it can be applied" and must "consist of acts such as are usual in the ordinary cultivation and improvement of similar lands by thrifty owners."' Notwithstanding [Getty's] assertions to the contrary, [the contractor's] activities on behalf of [2 North] and its predecessor over a period of 27 years were consistent with the nature, location and potential use of this property—a narrow strip of grass between two commercial businesses."

Case Questions

1. Was 2 North's use of the land strip "notorious" given the fact that it is likely that Getty didn't realize that the strip was on its property? What does one have to do to use property in a notorious fashion?
2. Because 2 North operated a shopping center and parking lot that were open to the public, how did 2 North satisfy the exclusive requirement?
3. *Focus on Critical Thinking:* Should Getty be compensated for the strip of land taken by adverse possession? If so, should there be an offset for all of the money invested by 2 North in maintenance?

SALE OF REAL ESTATE

The most common way for commercial real estate to be transferred is through a sale.[10] Typically, the seller and buyer agree on essential terms about the purchase and sale and enter into an agreement of sale. The agreement usually provides for a period of time devoted to due diligence, specifies a tentative settlement date (also called the *closing date*), and is supported by a cash deposit to be held by an escrow agent.

---

[10]Other methods used to transfer (mainly noncommercial) real estate are through a tax sale (for nonpayment of taxes), inheritance, gift, and adverse possession.

Legal Speak >))

Escrow Agent
A neutral third party designated to hold a sum of money while the parties fulfill conditions in a contract.

LO 23-7

Give examples of two types of laws that regulate the use of real property by its owners.

The due diligence time period varies based on the complexity of the transaction. During this time the buyer will (1) arrange for financing through a financial institution or a private lender (such as a relative); (2) conduct an inspection of the property to be sure that the parties are aware of any physical defects, zoning issues, and other items that may affect the use or price of the property; and (3) have an attorney or title agent verify that the seller has clear title to the property and is able to convey the property "free and clear," or without any legal obstacles.

The agreement of sale also spells out the timelines as well as the rights and obligations of the parties during the due diligence period. After the due diligence period has expired, the parties attend a settlement meeting at which the buyer presents payment and the seller conveys title to the property via a deed.

REGULATION OF COMMERCIAL LAND USE

State and local governments frequently pass statutes and ordinances that impose regulations on how a landowner may use a particular parcel of real estate. These regulations come in several forms, but the two types of regulations that are most crucial in business planning and operations are *zoning* ordinances and *environmental* regulations.

Zoning Ordinances

Zoning is generally done at the local level in the form of local ordinances passed by the county or municipal government. Counties, cities, boroughs, townships, villages, parishes, and the like are all forms of local government that pass ordinances. For better or worse, the power to pass zoning ordinances is well established in the law. Recall our discussion in Chapter 2, "Business and the Constitution," about each state's *police powers*. When a local government passes a zoning ordinance, it is exercising its police powers to advance legitimate objectives, such as health and safety. The Supreme Court has recognized such a power,[11] but at the same time, the Court has also set limits on the government's interference with private property rights.

Use Regulation   From a business perspective, ordinances that establish various districts for particular uses of property are one of the most important types of zoning regulation. A municipality is typically divided into zones, in each of which only certain uses of the land are permitted. These zones include areas for industrial, retail, and residential uses. Some municipalities divide their land uses further, specifying such uses as light industrial, warehouse, and so on.

Enforcement and Appeals   A local administrative agent, such as a zoning officer or building inspector employed by the municipality, typically enforces local use ordinances. A zoning board or commission is often appointed by the local government to handle appeals from decisions of the zoning officer and to consider applications for parties who wish to have an exception to one of the zoning laws. These exceptions are known as *variances*. Local governments vary greatly in their guidelines for permitting a variance, but, typically, if the variance does not harm the surrounding neighborhood or interfere with any local interests, the board has discretion to grant the variance.

Limits on Zoning Regulations   Courts have ruled that the law sets limits on a local government's right to regulate private property usage through a variety of constitutional protections of property owners.

---

[11]*Village of Euclid v. Ambler Realty Co.*, 272 U.S. 365 (1926).

First, if the zoning is so overreaching that it deprives the owner of all economic value of her property, the zoning will be categorized as a *taking* and the government is required to pay the owner the market value of the property as required in the Constitution's *Takings Clause*.[12] This power is known as *eminent domain* and is discussed in more detail in the next section.

Second, those parties who are adversely affected by a zoning ordinance are generally entitled to some form of procedural due process, such as a hearing by the local government.[13]

Finally, a zoning law may not discriminate in an arbitrary manner because doing so violates the Equal Protection Clause of the Fourteenth Amendment. Courts in most states have also generally allowed zoning related to *aesthetics* so long as aesthetics is only one factor, not the sole factor, in a municipality's zoning decision.

Environmental Regulation

Another major concern for business firms is federal, state, and local regulation of land use based on the government's interest in advancing sound environmental policy. In general, governments may impose environmentally based land use regulations so long as they advance some substantial and legitimate state interest.

For example, statutes aimed at preservation of open land areas have been found to be a legitimate government regulation of private property. Courts have generally held that wetland and coastland preservation ordinances that restrict the owner's right to develop, fill, or dredge the land are a legal use of the government's police powers.

The U.S. Supreme Court, however, curtailed this type of regulation by ruling that if the regulation completely depleted all economic value from the property, that act would constitute a government *taking* under the eminent domain power and trigger the government's obligation to pay compensation to the property owner.

For example, suppose that Developer purchases 20 acres of Florida beachfront property with the intent to develop the acreage into a resort. In response to concerned environmental groups, the state of Florida then passes a statute that restricts development along the coast running from the ocean to 1,000 yards inland. In Developer's case, this would amount to a loss of two prime acres of beachfront property, but Developer would have use of the remaining 18 acres. Developer sues for compensation because its partial loss of revenue was due to the state regulation. Most courts would rule against Developer because the government interest in preserving coastland has been held legitimate in the past and because Developer lost only part of the revenue stream and additional revenue is too speculative. On the other hand, if the state's statute had been more overreaching and resulted in Developer losing *all* economic value of the property, Developer would be entitled to compensation from the government.[14]

Of course, apart from understanding environmentally based land use regulations, business owners and managers must also be knowledgeable about a separate body of federal and state law aimed at broader environmental policies. These broad-based concerns, such as laws that regulate pollution, the operation of factories, and the disposal of solid waste and toxic chemicals, are discussed in detail in Chapter 18, "Environmental Law."

EMINENT DOMAIN

The authority of state and federal governments to take a person's private property is called the power of *eminent domain*. This power is derived from the Takings Clause of the Fifth Amendment, which states: "[N]or shall private property be taken for public use without just compensation."

LO 23-8

Articulate the government's power of eminent domain and the main limits to this power.

---

[12]*Lucas v. South Carolina Coastal Council*, 505 U.S. 1003 (1992).

[13]U.S. Const. amend. XIV, § 1 (Due Process Clause).

[14]Based on the facts in *Nollan v. California*, 483 U.S. 825 (1987).

But what is the difference between a government *taking* of property and a legitimate government land use or environmental *regulation*? A taking triggers the constitutional requirement of just compensation. In brief, the government is required to pay the landowner when there is a taking of property.

Procedure

Eminent domain is traditionally invoked using a *condemnation proceeding*. Once a government has decided that certain real estate is necessary for public use, the government typically begins to negotiate a sales agreement with the private property owner of the area or areas to be taken. If the negotiations fail, the government will formally institute a judicial proceeding to "condemn" the land. The court is required to respect the procedural rights of the property owner by giving her an opportunity to be heard. The court will then determine the fair market value of the land, and once it has entered its order, the condemnation is complete; the government now holds legal title to the real estate.

Public Use

Note that the text of the Constitution mentions the words *public use*. Traditionally, public use refers to the building of a public road, a public school, a public hospital, and other traditional public government functions. More recently, however, the U.S. Supreme Court has construed the public use language very broadly to include uses outside these traditional government functions so long as the government can demonstrate that the taking is rationally related to some conceivable public purpose.

This broad construction of the public use requirement has proved to be controversial. For example, suppose that the government condemns a blighted area of a city in hopes of developing the condemned area into a thriving example of urban renewal, one that brings along new retail and office buildings. What if the plan calls for the condemnation of some areas adjacent to the blight that have single-family houses and thriving, small, neighborhood businesses. Because the government does not intend to build any facilities for public use such as a public road or school, is the taking constitutional? The U.S. Supreme Court took up this very issue in Landmark Case 23.5. It was perhaps the most important eminent domain decision in our nation's history.[15]

CASE 23.5 Kelo v. City of New London, 545 U.S. 469 (2005)

FACT SUMMARY The city of New London devised an economic development plan that was projected to create more than 1,000 jobs and increase tax and other revenue. The plan called for a waterfront conference hotel; a marina; and various retail, commercial, and residential properties. The city's development authority designated a large area composed of adjacent parcels of real estate to be condemned in order to redevelop the property consistent with the overall redevelopment plan.

The city purchased some of the property from willing sellers and gave notice that the city would institute condemnation proceedings via the power of eminent domain to acquire the remaining property from unwilling owners. The city purchased all but nine parcels of real estate and brought condemnations against nine properties, including the house of Susette Kelo on 8 East Street. Although the city conceded that the condemned properties were not part of the blighted areas (in fact, some of

(continued)

---

[15]The urban renewal interest was first sanctioned by the Supreme Court in *Berman v. Parker,* 348 U.S. 26 (1954).

the houses had recently been renovated), they were condemned simply because of their location in the proposed redevelopment area. The lower courts' decisions were mixed, and the U.S. Supreme Court accepted the case on appeal to decide the question of whether the city's plan qualified as a public use within the meaning of the Takings Clause of the Fifth Amendment to the U.S. Constitution.

SYNOPSIS OF DECISION AND OPINION In a controversial 5-4 decision, the Court ruled in favor of the city. Although the Court affirmed the principle that the government is not permitted to take one party's private property for the sole purpose of transferring it to another private party, acknowledging that the city would not be able to take Kelo's house if the city had planned on bestowing it to a private development company or if any benefits from the plan would be realized only by private individuals, the Court concluded that the city's development plan did not contemplate any direct bestowment of property rights upon private individuals or companies. Moreover, even though some of the uses would be private in nature, the Court interpreted the public use requirement broadly, ruling that the standard to be used in these cases is the broader interpretation of the property being used for a *public purpose*. The Court found that the overall elimination of blight is a legitimate public purpose and thus held that the city's plan was a valid exercise of the city's eminent domain power.

WORDS OF THE COURT: Public Purpose
"[T]his 'Court long ago rejected any literal requirement that condemned property be put into use for the general public.' Indeed, while many state courts . . . endorsed 'use by the public' as the proper definition of public use, that narrow view steadily eroded over time. Not only was the 'use by the public' test difficult to administer . . . , but it proved to be impractical given the diverse and always evolving needs of society. Accordingly, when this Court began applying the Fifth Amendment to the States at the end of the 19th century, it embraced the broader and more natural interpretation of public use as 'public purpose.' . . . Without exception, our cases have defined [this] concept broadly, reflecting our longstanding policy of deference to legislative judgments in this field. . . . Given the comprehensive character of the plan [and] the thorough deliberation that preceded its adoption . . . [it] unquestionably serves a public purpose . . . ."

Case Questions

1. How does the Court define "public use"?
2. Would the case have been decided differently if the proposed project was for a large industrial park? Why or why not?
3. *Focus on Critical Thinking:* In dissenting opinions, members of the Court argued that this decision makes all private property vulnerable to being taken and transferred to another private owner so long as the property is improved in some way that serves a public purpose. Moreover, they argued that this decision is advantageous to large corporations or individuals with political power or connections, while those with few resources are disadvantaged. Do you agree with either of these criticisms? Why or why not?

KEY TERMS

Transaction costs p. 743   The costs of defining, monitoring, and enforcing property rights.

Personal property p. 743   Any movable or tangible object that can be owned or leased (e.g., computers, inventory, furniture, jewelry); includes everything except real property.

Real property p. 743   Land, or anything growing on, attached to, or erected on the land. Examples of real property include parcels of land, homes, warehouses, stores, and crops.

Title p. 744   The legal term for ownership in property; confers on the titleholder the exclusive use of personal property and the rights to sell, lease, or prohibit another from using the property.

Actual owner p. 744   The individual who is recognized as having primary or residual title to the property and is, therefore, the ultimate owner of the property.

Ownership interests p. 750   The various forms of real property ownership. Some forms limit the rights that owners of real estate have.

Fee simple p. 751   The broadest property interest in land, which endures until the current holder dies without heirs.

Life estate p. 751   An ownership interest in real estate that lasts for the lifetime of a particular person.

Leasehold estate p. 752   The qualified right to use real estate in an exclusive manner for a limited period of time. The most common form is a landlord-tenant agreement.

Lease p. 752   An agreement between a landlord and a tenant for the rental of property.

Easement p. 753   The privilege to use real estate owned by another.

CHAPTER REVIEW QUESTIONS

1. Osterman buys a metal detector and takes it to a public beach. He finds a shiny diamond bracelet near the picnic tables, but there is no one else in sight except a lifeguard. He asks the lifeguard if she owns the bracelet, and the lifeguard replies, "no." Who has title to the bracelet?
    a. Osterman, because title is a bundle of rights.
    b. Osterman, except against the true owner.
    c. The lifeguard, except against the true owner.
    d. The lifeguard, as a baileee.

2. A _____ relationship is created when the owner of personal property entrusts another to temporarily hold the property for the parties' mutual benefit.
    a. Lease
    b. Title
    c. Possession
    d. Bailment

3. Tanner is the owner of Whiteacre. In order to access the public road, he must cross through Greenacre, a parcel owned by Farmer. Tanner is granted access through a 10-foot-wide strip through Greenacre. What is this access called?
    a. Trespass
    b. Adverse possession
    c. Tenant right
    d. Easement

4. Fassett is a business executive who travels extensively for her work. Harris, her neighbor, often mows Fassett's lawn while she is traveling. Over the course of 20 years, Harris takes care of Fassett's property for periods as long as 11 consecutive months. In a lawsuit by Harris to take Fassett's property through adverse possession, who prevails?
    a. Harris, because the possession is open, notorious, and visible.
    b. Harris, because the possession is in excess of 15 years.
    c. Fassett, because Harris is a tenant.
    d. Fassett, because the possession is not continuous.

5. Which of the following is *not* true concerning zoning ordinances?
    a. They exist at the federal level.
    b. Exceptions to zoning ordinances are called variances.
    c. Zones typically include areas for industrial and retail use.
    d. They are an exercise of the government's police powers.

Answers and explanations are provided at the end of this chapter.

THEORY TO PRACTICE

Restaurant Supply Inc. (RSI) is a wholesale supplier of food and nonfood kitchen products for restaurants and hotels. Last year, RSI signed up a large hotel chain as a new client. In order to fill the needs of their new client, the principals of RSI decided to expand by constructing a new warehouse in an industrially zoned section of the city. RSI also received a tax credit for installing alternative energy sources in its new warehouse, so it invested $50,000 in a new solar panel system to be placed on the roof of the warehouse to serve as a source of power, with traditional gas and electric as a backup system.

RSI eventually finished construction of the warehouse and the solar panels and immediately moved its food and nonfood inventory into the warehouse. A few months after RSI moved into its new warehouse, the property adjacent to RSI's was sold to a glue factory.

1. Assume the glue factory runs 24 hours per day on a seven-day schedule and produces noxious fumes. Eventually, RSI begins to suspect that the fumes are tainting the taste of the food that is being stored in RSI's warehouse. RSI then files suit to stop the glue factory from discharging the noxious fumes. What is RSI's possible legal theory against the glue factory? What factors will a court use to analyze RSI's claim? Does the glue factory have any defenses?

2. Assume that the glue factory shuts down its operations in order to expand and upgrade its facilities to prevent the emission of the noxious fumes. In the process, the glue factory adds several stories to its building. The additional stories result in a blockage of sun, which subsequently results in RSI's solar panels being rendered useless. RSI files suit against the glue factory for interference in RSI's property rights. What property right violation has RSI alleged? What case in the text gives you some guidance on this question? Is the RSI case distinguishable from that case? Who prevails in the RSI–glue factory case, and why?

3. Assume that in preparation for the building renovation, the glue factory conducts a survey and finds that RSI's driveway has been built 15 feet too wide and encroaches on the glue factory's property. Since the time it built the warehouse, RSI has maintained the road, removed snow, and so on. One day RSI gets a letter from the owner of the glue factory demanding that the driveway be ripped up and repaved consistent with the correct property line. Can RSI use the doctrine of adverse possession to refuse the demand? What are the standards that courts use to analyze ownership via adverse possession?

4. Suppose that RSI is owned by Abel and that his son, Abel Jr., is the top manager in charge of business operations. When planning how the business will pass from Abel to his son upon Abel's death, Abel wishes to have the ownership of the warehouse pass to his spouse for her lifetime and then to Abel Jr. What type of ownership interest could Abel use to accomplish this objective? What restrictions will his spouse have once she inherits the warehouse?

5. Assume that RSI wishes to increase its solar panel usage by purchasing large brand A panels and installing them on the rooftop of the warehouse. However, a city ordinance exists that bans the use of brand A panels because they tend to make a building look less attractive. What is this type of ordinance called? Is this type of ordinance legal? Why or why not? Assuming that the ordinance is legal, are there any alternatives that RSI could pursue with local authorities?

LEGAL STRATEGY 101

How to Buy 27,000 Acres of Land without Anyone Noticing

The world-famous Walt Disney World Resort in Central Florida consists of 47 square miles of land, or about 30,000 acres. It is twice the size of Manhattan and the same size as San Francisco, California![16] So, how was Walt Disney originally able to buy up so

---

[16] *See generally* Lou Mongello, *WDW History 101— "How to Buy 27,000 Acres of Land and No One Notice,"* Walt Disney World Radio (Feb. 11, 2005).

Mickey Mouse. Margaret M. Savino/Alamy

many thousands of acres of land without the current landowners holding out for exorbitant prices? How did he pull off this remarkable feat?

Instead of buying the land he needed in his own company's name, Disney set up dozens of "dummy" corporations with low-key or unassuming names—shell companies with names like Tomahawk Properties, Latin-American Development and Management Corporation, and (our favorite) M.T. Lott. Acting on Disney's behalf but without disclosing their connection to Disney, these dummy companies then purchased hundreds of parcels of land ranging from swampland to cattle pastures.[17]

Eventually, a small local newspaper confirmed that over 27,000 acres in Orange and Osceola counties (just southwest of Orlando) had been bought up in a short period of time. Who was buying all this land? After enterprising reporter Emily Bavar Kelly conducted further investigations behind the scenes, she broke the biggest story of her career: It was Walt Disney himself who was secretly behind the purchases of all this land.[18]

Once Walt Disney publicly confirmed that he was behind these massive land purchases, the price of land jumped more than 1,000 percent! In particular, Walt was able to buy his first acre of land in Central Florida for Walt Disney World for $80, but the last acre of land cost him $80,000! Today, some of the windows above the shops along Main Street in the Magic Kingdom pay tribute to the pivotal role that Walt Disney's dummy corporations played in making his theme park dream a reality.

CRITICAL THINKING QUESTIONS

Using the concepts you have learned in Chapter 5, "Business Ethics, Corporate Social Responsibility, and Law," analyze the first two questions:

1. Is it ethical to use a dummy corporation for a lawful business transaction? Why or why not?
2. Suppose you are a manager for a residential real estate developer assigned to find a parcel of land for development. Would you follow Disney's strategy? Why or why not?
3. What if the government had decided to condemn the land on behalf of Walt Disney? Would the theme parks have met the public use requirement as broadly interpreted by the Supreme Court in *Kelo*?

---

[17]*See, e.g.,* Ryan P. Wilson, *A Friend in Deeds,* Main St. Gazette (Nov. 25, 2011).

[18]*See, e.g.,* Emily B. Kelly: *Reporter Broke News of Disney World Land Buys,* Sarasota Herald-Trib. (July 30, 2003).

MANAGER'S CHALLENGE

Managers provide valuable input and analysis for business operation expansion planning efforts. We've seen how various legal issues related to ownership and use of property can impact those planning efforts. Assume that, in this chapter's Theory to Practice problem, you are part of a three-person management team for RSI and have received the following e-mail from your senior manager:

> RSI is developing expansion plans that include new facilities in the southwestern United States. At this time, we are considering leasing office and operational space in several large cities but are interested in a particular 25,000-square-foot facility that has an ideal location and rental rate. However, at this time, we need only 10,000 square feet. The landlord has said that she is willing to negotiate lease terms but that we must lease the entire 25,000-square-foot space. RSI wants to expand but keep risk and financial exposure at a minimum.
>
> Research alternatives for possible subleasing or assigning of the unused space to third parties, and

develop a short presentation (no more than three to five PowerPoint slides) that could be presented to the landlord on proposed lease terms that would help RSI accomplish its objectives. Be sure to include a listing of the advantages of this arrangement for the landlord and for RSI.

See Connect for Manager's Challenge sample answers.

CASE SUMMARY 23.1 Singer Co. v. Stott & Davis Motor Express, Inc. & Stoda Corp., 79 A.2d 227 (N.Y. App. Div. 1981)

BAILMENTS

Stoda Corporation operated a warehouse used by Singer to store 133 air-conditioner units. Upon storing the goods in the warehouse, officers and managers of Singer inspected the warehouse and observed that it had a network of sprinkler systems. A fire broke out at Stoda's warehouse, the sprinkler system failed to activate, and the fire destroyed all of Singer's goods. Singer sued, claiming Stoda's negligence in storing goods in a warehouse without adequate fire protection breached its bailment duties.

CASE QUESTIONS

1. Who prevails and why?
2. What is the standard that the bailee (Stoda) owes to the bailor (Singer)?

CASE SUMMARY 23.2 Chaplin v. Sanders, 676 P.2d 431 (Wash. 1984)

ADVERSE POSSESSION

In 1957, Hibbard decided to clear his land in order to open a trailer park. Because there was no clear boundary between Hibbard's property and the adjoining property to the east, Hibbard cleared the property up to a large drainage ditch and installed an access road to the left of the ditch to signify the property line. Hibbard opened a trailer park facility, and later that year, McMurray, the owner of the eastern parcel, had a survey conducted. McMurray informed Hibbard that the access road encroached on his property by 20 feet. Subsequently, Hibbard sold the trailer park to Gilbert and noted in the sales contract that (1) the driveway encroached 20 feet on McMurray's property, (2) Gilbert agreed not to claim ownership of the property, and (3) Gilbert agreed he would remove the blacktop if ever requested to do so. From 1967 to 1976, the property changed ownership several times, but no mention was made of the encroachment or contract provision from the Hibbard-Gilbert sale. In 1976, however, when Sanders purchased the trailer park, he was given notice of the encroachment and provision, but he mistook the road to which the notice referred. Since the development of the trailer park, the road had been continuously used, and the area between the drainage ditch and road had been maintained by the various trailer park property owners (through means such as planting flowers and mowing the grass) and used by residents for picnics. Sanders also installed underground wiring and surface poles in the area. Two years later, Chaplin purchased the eastern lot from McMurray, had a survey conducted, and had architects design buildings for development based on the true property line from the survey. Washington requires a 10-year period of use in order to establish adverse possession.

CASE QUESTIONS

1. Are all of the elements for adverse possession met so that Sanders now has title to the disputed parcel? Why or why not?
2. What is the appropriate starting time from which to measure ownership in order to satisfy Washington's statutory requirement for 10 years of possession?

CASE SUMMARY 23.3 Jackson v. Wyndham Destinations, Inc., Case No. 71CV-19-36 (Ark. Cir. Ct., Van Buren Cty., filed Mar. 19, 2019)

CLUB MEMBERSHIP

Gordon Jackson purchased a lot at the Fairfield Bay Ozark Mountain Lake Resort & Community, a resort property owned by Wyndham Destinations, Inc. (Wyndham). Upon purchasing his property in the resort community, Gordon was required to join a "club" and pay a monthly fee of $30. In reality, however, Gordon alleges in his complaint that nothing accrues from club membership. Class members pay monthly assessments and receive absolutely nothing of value for their money. When they request an accounting, no accounting is provided. When they ask to withdraw from club membership, they are threatened with ruination of their credit rating if they try.

CASE QUESTIONS

1. What type of property right is Gordon's club membership? In particular, is it real or personal property? Explain.
2. What if Gordon had purchased a "timeshare" instead of a lot. A timeshare (sometimes called vacation ownership) is a form of property in which ownership or use rights are divided among many owners. What type of property is a timeshare?

CASE SUMMARY 23.4 Casino Reinvestment Development Authority v. Birnbaum, 203 A.3d 939 (N.J. Super. Ct. App. Div. 2019)

EMINENT DOMAIN

The Casino Reinvestment Development Authority (CRDA) sought to exercise its powers of eminent domain to condemn Charlie Birnbaum's three-story family home for a future tourism project in Atlantic City. At the time his house was condemned, however, the CRDA had only a "redevelopment concept" in mind, but it had no specific plans under consideration for the area. In fact, the CRDA had not even issued a request for proposals to prospective developers, and no developer had committed to redeveloping within the area in which Birnbaum's house was located. Birnbaum therefore decided to bring a lawsuit challenging the CRDA's exercise of its eminent domain powers. The CRDA defended its action by arguing it was entitled to "bank" land for a future public use.

CASE QUESTIONS

1. Does the *Kelo* case, discussed in this chapter, control the outcome of this case?
2. What if no one were living in Birnbaum's house at the time, or what if the agency had already issued a request for proposals to potential developers to redevelop the area in which Birnbaum's house was located? Who should prevail, and why?

✓ Self-Check ANSWERS Ownership Interests

1. Swineburne owns the property in fee simple absolute and is permitted to use the property for any lawful use, including a luxury resort.
2. Swineburne's ownership was in fee simple defeasible (restricted by Carroll's "provided that" language in the agreement). When he violated the restriction, the ownership rights reverted back to Carroll.
3. Swineburne's interest is in the form of a periodic (month-to-month) tenancy. Therefore, Carroll must give Swineburne at least one month's notice before terminating the lease.
4. Swineburne was a life tenant, so all ownership interests are extinguished upon his death. Carroll Jr. is then the owner in fee simple absolute and has the right to terminate Swineburne Jr.'s use of the real estate.
5. Swineburne has an express easement to use the driveway. Blago had reason to know of the easement at the time of purchase (via the easement statement recorded on the deed); therefore, he must honor Swineburne's easement.

CHAPTER REVIEW QUESTIONS: Answers and Explanations

1. **b.** The bracelet is mislaid and not abandoned. Thus, the finder has title against everyone except the true owner. Answer choice (a) is incorrect because a bundle of rights only attaches to the title holder. Answer choices (c) and (d) are incorrect because the lifeguard has no claim of ownership.

2. **d.** A bailment relationship is created when the owner of real property entrusts a merchant or repair shop with the property (e.g., dropping off a suit at the dry cleaner's). Answer choices (a), (b), and (c) are incorrect because they are unrelated to a bailment relationship.

3. **d.** An easement is a privilege to use the real estate owned by another. Answer choices (a) and (b) are incorrect because access was granted. Answer choice (c) is incorrect because this is not a landlord-tenant relationship.

4. **d.** In order for adverse possession to occur, the possession must be continuous. Therefore, Fassett prevails. Answer choices (a) and (b) are incorrect because elements of adverse possession are not met. Answer choice (c) is incorrect because there is no landlord-tenant relationship.

5. **a.** Zoning ordinances exist at the county and municipal government level only. Answer choices (b), (c), and (d) are incorrect because each is true.

CHAPTER 24
Intellectual Property

©philsajonesen/Getty Images

Learning Objectives

After studying this chapter, students who have mastered the material will be able to:

24-1 Define what a trade secret is and identify the elements of misappropriation of trade secrets.
24-2 Classify trademarks based on their level of distinctiveness and give examples of trademarks, service marks, and trade dress.
24-3 Understand how federal laws aimed at regulating trademarks in cyberspace apply to domain names.
24-4 Explain how trademarks are enforced and distinguish between trademark infringement and trademark dilution.
24-5 Define what a copyright is.
24-6 Identify the remedies for acts of copyright infringement, describe the impact of technology on copyright law, and apply the fair use defense.
24-7 Define what a patent is and explain how patents are obtained.
24-8 Identify the remedies for acts of patent infringement.

The protection of intellectual property has been a cornerstone of U.S. law since the ratification of the Constitution. Specifically, Article I, Section 8 of the U.S. Constitution authorizes Congress to protect intellectual property "by securing for limited Times to Authors and Inventors the exclusive Right to their respective Writings and Discoveries." Today, intellectual property has become more essential to business than ever before. A study published in the *Harvard Business Review,* for example, found that intellectual property represents approximately 70 percent of an average firm's value.[1] Broadly speaking, intellectual property protections not only help business firms create value; such protections also help firms capture that value. So, have you ever created any intellectual property?

This chapter explains the legal concepts of intellectual property that are most relevant to business owners and managers, who must know how to make informed decisions on how best to protect their own intellectual property and how to avoid infringing upon the intellectual property rights of others. In this chapter, we discuss

- Legal protections for trade secrets and other business information.
- Statutory and common law requirements for the protection of trademarks, service marks, and trade dress.
- Requirements for protection under federal copyright laws, consequences of infringement, and application of the fair use test.
- Protections for inventors through patent law and the statutory requirements for obtaining a patent.

---
[1] K. Rivet and D. Kline, "Discovering New Value in Intellectual Property," *Harvard Business Review,* January 2000, p. 58.

TRADE SECRETS AND THE PROTECTION OF BUSINESS INFORMATION

Among the most valuable assets of any business firm are its secret processes, formulas, methods, procedures, and lists that allow the firm to have a competitive advantage in its trade. Business firms from a wide variety of industries rely on trade secret laws to protect some or all of their valuable creative ideas. Examples of technical and business information material that can be protected by trade secret law include customer lists, designs, instructional methods, manufacturing processes, product formulas and recipes, and document-tracking processes.

It's also worth noting that many types of trade secrets, business information, and business methods may *not* be protectable by patent or copyright laws. Most patent applicants, for example, generally rely on trade secret law to protect their inventions while their patent applications are in progress.

Trade secret law is based on the common law. Courts apply several factors to determine whether certain material or information constitutes a protectable trade secret:

- The extent to which the information is known outside the business of the claimant (the firm claiming that the information is a trade secret).
- Measures taken by the claimant to guard the confidentiality of the information.
- The value of the information to competitors.
- The amount invested (in terms of time and money) in developing the information.
- The efforts taken to maintain trade secret confidentiality among the claimant's employees, potential investors, and third-party vendors (such as auditing firms).

LO 24-1

Define what a trade secret is and identify the elements of misappropriation of trade secrets.

TRADE SECRET PROTECTIONS

Trade secret protections are provided by state statutes and state common law principles. The Uniform Trade Secrets Act (UTSA)[2] defines trade secrets as information or articles that are to be kept secret because of their particular value. Broadly speaking, the UTSA defines a **trade secret** as a formula, pattern, compilation, program, device, method, technique, or process that meets the following criteria:

- Derives *independent economic value,* actual or potential, from not being generally known to and not being readily ascertainable by proper means by other persons who can obtain economic value from its disclosure or use; and
- Is the subject of efforts that are reasonable under the circumstances to maintain its secrecy. Economic value must be identified by the owner, and secrecy must be kept.

Misappropriation

Most state statutes use the following definition of **misappropriation** from the UTSA: (1) the acquisition of a trade secret of another by a person who knows or has reason to know that the trade secret was acquired by improper means or (2) any disclosure or use of a trade secret of another without express or implied consent.

In short, misappropriation is defined broadly to include not only improper acquisition of a trade secret, but also any disclosure of a trade secret without consent. Although misappropriation of a trade secret can be the result of industrial or foreign espionage, as Case 24.1 illustrates, many trade secret cases involve people who have taken their former employer's trade secrets for use in a new start-up business or by a new employer.

---

[2] The UTSA is a model law drafted by the American Law Institute (ALI) for use by state legislatures. For more information on the ALI and model laws, see Chapter 1, "Legal Foundations."

CASE 24.1 IBM v. Johnson, 629 F. Supp. 2d 321 (S.D.N.Y. 2009)

FACT SUMMARY Until his resignation in May of 2009, David L. Johnson had worked for IBM for more than 27 years, and during his tenure at IBM, he directed IBM's mergers, acquisitions, and divestitures strategy, and, according to IBM, he had access to IBM's most sensitive and confidential strategic information. In late 2008, before Johnson had resigned from IBM, a recruiter contacted Johnson concerning an employment opportunity at Dell. After several rounds of negotiations, Johnson agreed to join Dell as Senior Vice President of Strategy. In that capacity, Johnson agreed to help Dell set a strategic vision, mission, and goals based upon its existing resources and internal capabilities. As a result, IBM commenced an action in federal court requesting a preliminary injunction to prevent Johnson from working for Dell.

SYNOPSIS OF DECISION AND OPINION The District Court for the Southern District of New York denied IBM's request for a preliminary injunction, holding that Johnson did not have access to any actual trade secrets of IBM.

WORDS OF THE COURT: Trade Secret "According to IBM, Mr. Johnson is aware of IBM's past, present, and future business strategies as well as the acquisitions, transactions, and divestitures that IBM is considering. . . . In addition, IBM contends that Mr. Johnson is aware of its assessment of its clients' needs, its competitors' strategies, its opportunities, and its strategies for carrying out its business objectives. Mr. Johnson knows in which areas, companies, and technologies IBM will invest, at what times, and with what expected rates of return. Mr. Johnson, in short, has inside strategic business information about IBM, and disclosure of that information would harm the Company.

"The Court nevertheless believes that IBM has overstated its case. Mr. Johnson does not have the sort of information that is considered quintessential trade secret information—detailed technical know-how, formulae, designs, or procedures. . . . What is more, IBM's submissions regarding Mr. Johnson's knowledge of its technological information is long on generalities and rather short on details. This makes it extraordinarily difficult to determine whether and, if so, how much of, the information that Mr. Johnson possesses is public and readily available to its competition."

Case Questions
1. Why did IBM lose this case?
2. Would this case have been decided differently if IBM had plans to acquire or merge with Dell and if Johnson knew about the details of these plans? Why or why not?
3. *Focus on Critical Thinking:* Did Johnson act ethically? Did IBM?

Trade secret owners have recourse only against acts of misappropriation (i.e., improper acquisition or disclosure). Discovery of protected information through independent research or *reverse engineering* (taking a product apart to see how it works) is *not* misappropriation.

Criminal Sanctions

While the UTSA does not provide for any criminal penalties, because misappropriation is considered a private wrong or "tort," the **Economic Espionage Act** is a federal statute enacted by Congress in 1996 providing criminal penalties for domestic and foreign theft of U.S. trade secrets.

In addition, many states have enacted a separate set of statutes that make certain forms of trade secret misappropriation a criminal offense. For example, prosecutors in California filed charges against several executives and employees of Avant! Corporation, a firm that designed software related to semiconductor chips. The prosecutor was alerted to the case after a competitor of Avant! sued the firm in an action brought under California's Trade Secret Act, alleging that Avant! employees stole computer code from one of Avant!'s primary competitors.[3] Ultimately, Avant! accepted a plea bargain from the prosecutor that forced the company and seven individuals to pay $35 million in fines and resulted in incarceration for five of the defendants.

Exclusive Rights for Unlimited Duration

Perhaps the most significant advantages of trade secret protection over other forms of intellectual property (such as patents) are twofold: (1) no formal registration is required and (2) protection for trade secrets does not expire after a fixed period of time. *A trade secret owner thus has the right to keep others from misappropriating and using the trade secret for the duration of the firm's existence!*

Nevertheless, although trade secret protection endures so long as the requirements for protection continue to be met, the protection is lost if the owner of the trade secret fails to take reasonable steps to keep the information secret. For example, Tyler and Cameron discover a new idea for a social network website. They share their new idea with Mark at a party. Tyler and Cameron may have lost their trade secret protection for their idea because they failed to take appropriate steps to keep their method secret.

 Self-Check Trade Secrets

Which of the following are protectable as a trade secret?

1. A list of customers compiled by a firm that includes buying patterns, purchaser contact information, and preferred products of each customer.
2. A system used by a medical practice for scheduling patients for doctor's office visits.
3. The formula for a new brand of fruit drink at a beverage supply company.
4. The process used by an accounting firm to draft financial statements in accordance with generally accepted accounting principles (GAAP).
5. New software that helps a manufacturer speed up the design process for new products.

Answers to this Self-Check are provided at the end of the chapter.

TRADEMARKS, SERVICE MARKS, AND TRADE DRESS

Take out your smartphone and see how many registered trademarks you can find. You may see Apple's registered trademark for the iPhone or Samsung's registered trademark for the Galaxy S. As you begin to check your social media, you may see logos, words, and shapes that allow consumers to distinguish Facebook from Instagram and Snap from Tumblr in an instant. Want to listen to some music? You can choose between Pandora and Spotify with no difficulty because you recognize their trademarks.

In other words, trademarks are a daily part of a consumer's life.

LO 24-2

Classify trademarks based on their level of distinctiveness and give examples of trademarks, service marks, and trade dress.

---

[3]*Cadence Design Systems, Inc. v. Avant!*, 253 F.3d 1147 (9th Cir. 2002). The parties settled the civil suit for $265 million.

A **trademark** is a nonfunctional distinctive word, name, shape, symbol, phrase, or a combination of words and symbols that helps consumers to distinguish one product from another.[4] One court put it concisely:

> Generally speaking, a [trademark is a] distinctive mark of authenticity, through which the products of particular manufacturers or . . . commodities of particular merchants may be distinguished from those of others.
>
> *Koppers Co., Inc. v. Krupp-Koppers*, 517 F. Supp. 836, 840 (W.D. Pa. 1981).

For example, the name and logo of Coca-Cola comprise one of the most famous trademarks in the world. Consumers have confidence in the product, and the Coca-Cola trademark distinguishes the product from competing soda pops. Other world-famous marks include McDonald's golden arches and Nike's swoosh. While trademarks are typically associated with products, **service marks** are used to identify business services. Examples of famous service marks include Hilton Hotels (accommodation) and Greyhound Lines (transportation).

Most caselaw and legal texts refer to both trademarks and service marks simply as a *mark*. Owners of a mark are called *holders*. The key requirement for creating a protectable trademark is its *distinctiveness*—the mark's ability to indicate the product's source.

In addition to caselaw, the Lanham Act[5] is the federal statute that protects an owner's registered trademark from use without the owner's permission.

Trade Dress

Businesses are increasingly eager to extend trademark protection beyond words and symbols in order to gain protection for a product's shape or the color combination of its packaging. These beyond-the-mark features are called **trade dress**. Traditionally, courts have allowed trade dress protection for both product design features and product packaging, including textures, shapes, and color combinations, for businesses such as restaurants.[6] More recently, the U.S. Patent and Trademark Office (USPTO) has granted protection to trade dress characteristics so long as the mark holder proves that the trade dress provides an exclusive link to the source of the product in the consumer's mind. Notable examples include the shade of red used in Christian Louboutin red-bottomed shoes and the brown color (called Pullman brown) that UPS uses on its vehicles and uniforms.

Christian Louboutin red-bottomed shoes. EQRoy/Shutterstock

Product Design A recent trend in strategic business planning is to trademark product design as a form of trade dress. Protecting product design through trademark laws is challenging because the applicant must overcome any notion that the design purpose was to allow the product to function properly rather than as a distinctive trademark.

For example, Figure 24.1 contains a sketch of a seemingly generic row of rectangles. In its trademark application, the holder describes these rectangles as "a configuration of a chocolate bar that consists of 12 equally-sized recessed rectangular panels arranged in a four panel by three panel format with each panel having its own raised border within a large rectangle." The configuration is the

---

[4]15 U.S.C. § 1127.
[5]15 U.S.C. § 1052.
[6]*Two Pesos, Inc. v. Taco Cabana, Inc.*, 505 U.S. 763 (1992).

FIGURE 24.1 Hershey Chocolate Bar Trademark Registration

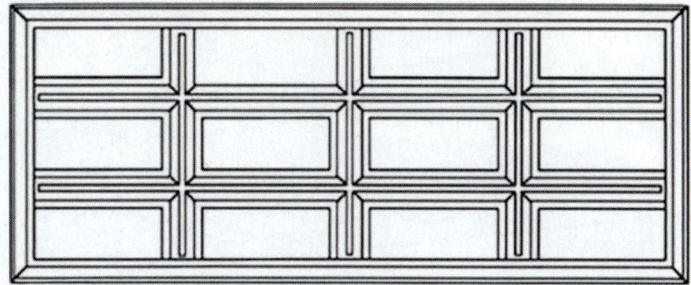

Source: U.S. Patent and Trademark Office, Application No. 77809223, filed August 20, 2009.

product design of the famous Hershey chocolate bar, and the USPTO granted the mark to Hershey Chocolate and Confectionary Corporation in 2012. Hershey was able to convince the USPTO that the rectangles were not essential to the use or purpose of the article. Figure 24.1 shows the actual sketch that was submitted by Hershey with its trademark application. Apple is also aggressively registering product designs as trademarks and has successfully protected the design of the iPod, iPhone, and iPad, among many others.

Trademarks as a Business Asset

In business terms, marks are typically referred to as *brands*. The primary objective of trademark protection is to provide the mark holder with a means of preventing others from fooling consumers into buying a product that they erroneously believe is produced by the mark holder. Businesses thus invest significant time and resources in their trademarks to build consumer loyalty to a particular brand. Designs, color schemes, shapes, and other features all play a role in creating a link in the buying public's mind.

Trademarks allow consumers to quickly identify a product and distinguish it from similar or competing products. One of the main purposes of the Lanham Act is to prevent business competitors from getting a "free ride" on the shoulders of a more famous brand. For example, if a small economy-car manufacturer could use the name or symbols associated with Tesla or Rolls-Royce, the smaller company would deprive the mark holder of its investments in the mark and gain name recognition at no cost.

Classifications of Trademarks

As discussed earlier, trademark protection is based on distinctiveness. For a trademark to be distinctive, it must identify the source of a particular product (or service for service marks). Courts classify marks based on their level of distinctiveness, and this classification determines their level of protection. Nevertheless, there is no clear line of demarcation between these classifications. Rather, courts analyze a mark on a case-by-case basis. A good rule of thumb is this: the more distinctive the mark, the more protection the mark has under the Lanham Act.

Arbitrary or Fanciful Marks A mark that has no direct connection to the product is categorized as arbitrary or fanciful. An *arbitrary* mark is a real word being used as part of a mark that has nothing to do with the word's literal meaning (e.g., Apple, Uber, or Amazon). A *fanciful* mark is one that centers upon a word made up with the intention of being used as a distinctive term. For example, Spotify's name and symbol were created by the company's founders and have no obvious connection to streaming music. Therefore, Spotify fits into the fanciful category. Which type of mark is Google? Arbitrary or fanciful?

Spotify is an example of a fanciful trademark.
Jeffrey Blackler/Alamy Stock Photo

Suggestive Marks Marks that suggest the product or service without literally describing it are considered highly distinctive. Courts classify a mark as suggestive if imagination, thought, and perception are required to understand how it is tied to the underlying product or service. For example, the trademark "Under Armour" suggests a product used under something for protection. "Netflix" suggests a web-based movie service. "Coppertone" suggests a suntan lotion. Understanding the actual product, however, requires a leap of imagination, thought, or perception. Suggestive marks are similar to arbitrary marks in that they tend to be highly distinctive and are given a high level of protection.

Descriptive Marks A descriptive mark is one that makes specific reference to features, qualities, or characteristics of a product or service and is not inherently distinctive. Courts have held marks such as After Tan (moisturizing lotion for use after sunbathing), Tender Vittles (cat food), and Car Freshener (air deodorizer for cars) are descriptive marks because no leap of imagination is required to connect the mark with the product. Because descriptive marks are not inherently distinctive, they are not protected under the Lanham Act unless they have acquired a **secondary meaning**. Descriptive-mark holders must provide evidence that the general public connects the mark with the mark holder's product or service rather than with the ordinary meaning of the term.

Standards for Secondary Meaning A secondary meaning is created when the consuming public primarily associates a mark with a *particular* product rather than any alternate meaning. For example, Microsoft attempted to protect the term *Windows* as a mark for its revolutionary operating system for many years. In order to attain that right, Microsoft was required to show that, for much of the consuming public, the term *Windows* was more often associated with Microsoft's operating system rather than with panes of glass. Similarly, Twitter's initial application in 2009 to trademark the term *tweet* was rejected because of insufficient evidence of secondary meaning. However, by 2012, Twitter acquired full trademark rights to the term "tweet."

Recall our discussion of the product design trademark for a Hershey chocolate bar. Once Hershey overcame the hurdle of proving that the rectangular design was not essential to its function, it still had to prove that the design was part of a distinctive link to its product in the minds of consumers. Case 24.2 provides insight into an analysis of the secondary meaning requirement.

CASE 24.2 *In re* Hershey Chocolate & Confectionery Corp., Serial No. 77809223 (T.T.A.B. June 28, 2012)

FACT SUMMARY The Hershey Chocolate and Confectionery Corporation (Hershey) filed an application with the USPTO for a trademark to protect the product design of its chocolate bar. The application described the configuration of the candy bar as "twelve (12) equally-sized recessed rectangular panels arranged in a four panel by three panel format with each panel having its own raised border within a large rectangle." The USPTO's Examining Attorney refused registration on two grounds: (1) that applicant's proposed mark is a functional configuration of the goods and (2) it consists of a nondistinctive configuration of the goods that does not function as a mark under existing trademark law. Hershey appealed the decision, arguing that the candy bar's configuration had nothing to do with functionality and cited marketing surveys as evidence that a sufficient percentage of the consuming public connected the design with the Hershey product.

SYNOPSIS OF DECISION AND OPINION The Trademark Trial and Appeal Board ruled in favor of Hershey and reversed the Examiner's refusal to register the mark. In terms of functionality, the board held that the prominent decorative recessed rectangle and raised border design didn't fall into the functional category because its sole purpose was as a unique branding design. With respect to secondary meaning, the board pointed to several factors that indicate a secondary meaning has been created. First, in a consumer recognition survey where respondents were shown the "four by three" panel candy bar configuration in the application, 44 percent of participants correctly identified Hershey's as the maker of the candy bar. That percentage is higher compared to other cases in which survey results were used to establish secondary meaning. Second, Hershey's offered evidence that it had used the mark for over 40 years and spent $186 million in advertising products embodying the candy bar configuration.

WORDS OF THE COURT: Secondary Meaning "There is no clear standard as to the amount of evidence necessary for allowing a mark to register [as descriptive with a secondary meaning.] . . . '[T]he exact kind and amount of evidence necessarily depends on the circumstances of the particular case, and Congress has chosen to leave the exact degree of proof necessary to qualify a mark for registration to the judgment of the Patent Office and the courts.' . . . While it is well settled that sales and advertising expenditures alone do not always amount to a finding of acquired distinctiveness, these are compelling numbers, particularly when viewed in the larger context of applicant's evidence of acquired distinctiveness. Similarly, while there is no evidence that applicant has promoted the candy bar configuration via 'look for' advertisements, we note that at least some of the advertisements submitted with the [application] display the candy bar configuration prominently."

Case Questions

1. What were the major factors used by the board in determining secondary meaning?
2. Why does Hershey's have to show a secondary meaning to obtain trademark protection?
3. *Focus on Critical Thinking:* Has the board interpreted the trademark requirements too broadly? Should Congress step in and provide clear statutory guidelines? What guidelines would be fair? What other similar types of product designs might qualify given the standard used by the board?

> **KEY POINT**
>
> Courts determine mark protection eligibility based on a classification of the mark. The more distinctive the mark, the higher the chances of obtaining protection under the Lanham Act.

LO 24-3

Understand how federal laws aimed at regulating trademarks in cyberspace apply to domain names.

Generic Marks If the mark does not fall into the arbitrary, fanciful, suggestive, or descriptive with a secondary meaning categories, it is considered generic and cannot be registered as a trademark. For example, the U.S. Patent and Trademark Office has denied trademark protection of terms such as "smartphone" or "e-mail."

Sometimes, however, a distinct mark can become so synonymous with a general class of product or service that it becomes generic and thus loses its trademark protection! Perhaps the most famous case of genericide is Bayer's loss of the right to protect the mark "aspirin" in 1921.

Other well-known mark holders that lost rights to their marks include Otis Elevator in 1950 ("escalator"), King-Seely Thermos Co. in 1963 ("thermos"), and Duncan in 1965 ("yo-yo"). Typically, genericide occurs once the consuming public uses the mark's terminology as a noun or a verb rather than as an adjective to describe a good, but not always. Case 24.3, for example, considers whether Google has become so synonymous with Internet search that it has become generic.

CASE 24.3 Elliott v. Google, Inc., 860 F.3d 1151 (9th Cir. 2017)

FACT SUMMARY Between February 29, 2012, and March 10, 2012, Chris Gillespie used a domain name registrar to acquire 763 domain names that included the word "google." Each of these domain names paired the word "google" with some other term identifying a specific brand, person, or product—for example, "googledisney.com," "googlebarackobama.net," and "googlenewtvs.com."

Google, Inc. ("Google"), however, objected to these registrations and promptly filed a complaint with the National Arbitration Forum, which has authority to decide certain domain name disputes under the registrar's terms of use. Shortly thereafter, David Elliott filed—and Chris Gillespie later joined—an action in the Arizona District Court. The plaintiffs petitioned for cancellation of the Google trademark under the Lanham Act, which allows cancellation of a registered trademark if it is primarily understood as a "generic name for the goods or services, or a portion thereof, for which it is registered." This district court ruled in favor of Google. Elliott and Gillespie appealed.

SYNOPSIS OF DECISION AND OPINION The U.S. Court of Appeals for the Ninth Circuit affirmed the lower court's decision, holding that the plaintiffs failed to present sufficient evidence to support a jury finding that the relevant public primarily understands the word "google" as a generic name for Internet search engines and not as a mark identifying the Google search engine in particular.

WORDS OF THE COURT: Genericide "We conclude that [the plaintiffs'] proposed inquiry is fundamentally flawed for two reasons. First, Elliott fails to recognize that a claim of genericide must always relate to a particular type of good or service. Second, he erroneously assumes that verb use automatically constitutes generic use. . . .

"Even if we assume that the public uses the verb 'google' in a generic and indiscriminate sense, this tells us nothing about how the public primarily understands the word itself, irrespective of its grammatical function, with regard to internet search engines. As explained below, we also agree that Elliott's admissible evidence only supports the favorable but insufficient inference already drawn by the district court—that a majority of the public uses the verb 'google' in a generic sense. Standing in isolation, this fact is insufficient to support a jury finding of genericide. The district court therefore properly granted summary judgment for Google."

(continued)

Case Questions

1. This case was decided in 2017. Do you think it would be decided differently if it were brought today?
2. What affirmative steps, if any, could Google take to avoid the genericide of its mark?
3. *Focus on Critical Thinking:* Why did both the district court and the court of appeals conclude that a jury could not make a finding of genericide in this case? Why not let the jury decide this issue?

LEGAL IMPLICATIONS IN CYBERSPACE

Domain Names, Trademarks, and Cybersquatting

The explosive growth of the Internet has caused concern among trademark holders on a number of fronts. Chief among them is the practice of individuals, so-called *cybersquatters,* who register domain names that are also words associated with a famous trademark. Once the domain name is secured, the individual would then turn around and offer the domain name at an extraordinarily inflated rate to the trademark owner.

Cybersquatting was the subject of considerable media attention in the 1990s and early 2000s. Congress eventually responded to this practice by enacting a federal statute designed to curb some of the most unscrupulous cybersquatters. That law, the Anticybersquatting Consumer Protection Act (ACPA),[7] provides specific statutory remedies to trademark owners to recover trademark-related domain names from users who act in bad faith. **Bad faith** is a dishonesty of belief or purpose. In this context, the bad-faith requirement may be met in a number of ways but is typically satisfied when the registrant has no legitimate reason for the use of the domain name or the registrant is using the domain name to profit or confuse consumers.

In Case 24.4, a federal court outlines nine examples of bad faith under the ACPA.

CASE 24.4 People for the Ethical Treatment of Animals v. Doughney, 113 F. Supp. 2d 915 (E.D. Va. 2000)

FACT SUMMARY People for the Ethical Treatment of Animals (PETA) is the high-profile nonprofit organization devoted to educating the public at large and attempting to prevent the abuse of animals for corporate gain. Doughney registered the domain name peta.org, claiming he was head of an organization called "People Eating Tasty Animals" and, thus, was entitled to use the name. Doughney's website contained links to furriers and others antithetical to PETA's mission. PETA filed suit against Doughney, alleging, among other things, that his use of peta.org violated the ACPA.

SYNOPSIS OF DECISION AND OPINION The U.S. District Court for the Eastern District of Virginia ruled in favor of PETA. The court pointed out nine examples of bad-faith action taken by Doughney and held that his actions violated the ACPA. The court rejected Doughney's claim that the website was merely a parody of the PETA organization because of the likelihood of confusion. In fact, Doughney admitted that "many people" would initially assume that they were accessing an authentic site sponsored by PETA.

WORDS OF THE COURT: Bad Faith "[Under the ACPA], there are nine factors a court must

(continued)

---

[7] 15 U.S.C. § 1125(d).

consider in making a determination of whether the Defendant had a bad faith intent. Applying these factors, it appears that Doughney had the requisite bad faith intent.

"First, Defendant possessed no intellectual property rights in 'PETA.ORG' when he registered the domain name in 1995. Second, the 'PETA.ORG' domain name is not the Defendant, Michael T. Doughney's legal name or any name that is otherwise used to identify the Defendant. Third, Defendant had not engaged in prior use of the 'PETA.ORG' domain name in connection with the bona fide offering of any goods or services prior to registering 'PETA.ORG.' Fourth, Defendant used the PETA mark in a commercial manner. Fifth, Defendant clearly intended to confuse, mislead and divert internet users into accessing his web site which contained information antithetical and therefore harmful to the goodwill represented by the PETA Mark. Sixth, on Doughney's 'PETA.ORG' web site, Doughney made reference to seeing what PETA would offer him if PETA did not like his web site. Seventh, Defendant, when registering the domain name 'PETA.ORG,' falsely stated that 'People Eating Tasty Animals' was a non-profit educational organization and that this web site did not infringe any trade mark. Eighth, Defendant has registered other internet domain names which are identical or similar to either marks or names of famous people or organizations he opposes. Ninth, the PETA Mark used in the 'PETA.ORG' domain name is distinctive and famous and was so at the time Defendant registered this site in September 1995."

Case Questions

1. Was there any indication that Doughney was cybersquatting?
2. Could Doughney have avoided liability by making changes to his website or business model? What changes might have shielded him from liability?
3. *Focus on Critical Thinking:* Because there is no evidence that Doughney earned any money off of his registration, should the law impose a ban on his use of the domain name? Are there any First Amendment issues involved?

BUSINESS ETHICS PERSPECTIVE

Name for a King's Ransom

1. Do you think that registering a domain name with the sole intent of selling the domain name is ethical? If not, what ethical norm does cybersquatting violate? Isn't this practice exactly how a market economy is supposed to work?
2. What if one individual buys a domain name from another person with the intent of reselling it to a third party? Does that transaction merit a different ethical standard than in Question 1?
3. Are there any circumstances in which a party could ethically obtain the domain name of a famous trademark?
4. Was it ethical for trademark owners to lobby Congress to pass a law against cybersquatters?

LO 24-4

Explain how trademarks are enforced and distinguish between trademark infringement and trademark dilution.

ENFORCING THE MARK

If a mark is distinctive enough to be protected, the holder's attention turns to preventing others from using it without the holder's consent. In order to enforce the holder's rights to exclusive use of the mark, a holder must acquire rights over the mark and must be vigilant in policing and maintaining the mark. If the mark holder's rights have attached, she may prevent a third party from using it without consent and collect damages from the infringer.

Acquiring Rights

Holders acquire rights to trademark protection either through (1) use in commerce or (2) registration of the mark with the U.S. Patent and Trademark Office (USPTO). Acquiring rights through use in commerce carries a significant risk that the mark holder's rights will not be fully realized nationwide, so most holders opt to register the mark (see the Strategic Legal Solutions feature later in this section).

> **KEY POINT**
>
> Trademark holders may acquire rights in the mark through use in commerce or through USPTO registration.

A mark holder typically uses the symbol^{TM} (or^{SM}) to indicate that the mark is not yet registered with the USPTO. However, use of this symbol also indicates that the mark holder considers the mark distinctive enough to be protected and, in some cases, that the application for registration is pending. Once the mark has been approved by the USPTO, it is considered registered, and the mark holder now uses the symbol$^®$ to indicate completed registration.

A mark may be registered with USPTO only if the holder has a bona fide intent to use the mark in commerce. Once the mark is registered, the mark holder has nationwide rights to its use. However, even with registration, the mark may still be used by anyone who used the mark in commerce *prior* to registration.

As a result, depending on the timing of the holder's registration, different parties can have trademark protection simultaneously. For example, if Robert begins to use a trademark for a specialty coffee in his coffee shop in Boston but does not use it in any other market, he has acquired the right to use it in *Boston only* because he was the first to use his mark in commerce. If, however, National Brand Coffee (NBC) wants to use the very same trademark, NBC may register it with the USPTO and be entitled to nationwide rights except the right to use it in the Boston geographic market. So both Robert and NBC would have rights to the same trademark, but their rights would extend only to their respective geographic areas.

Applications and the USPTO

Registration of a mark is not automatic. A mark holder must undergo an approval process through the USPTO, which examines the mark for distinctiveness, checks for any similar marks that are already registered, and ensures compliance with trademark registration standards (such as secondary meaning for descriptive marks).

The Lanham Act also allows the USPTO to reject a mark if it is "immoral, deceptive, or scandalous matter" or may be disparaging to "people, institutions, beliefs, or national symbols."[8] This section of the statute, commonly referred to as Section 2a, provides broad authority to the USPTO in evaluating the content of a mark for scandalous material. Some recent rejections under this section include

- "Stop the Islamisation of America" (*In re Geller,* 751 F.3d 1355 [Fed. Cir. 2014]).
- "Heeb" (*In re Heeb Media, LLC,* 89 U.S.P.Q.2d 1071 [T.T.A.B. Nov. 26, 2008]).
- "Sex Rod" (*Bos. Red Sox Baseball Club L.P. v. Sherman,* 88 U.S.P.Q.2d 1581 [T.T.A.B. Sept. 9, 2008]).
- "Cocaine" in a label for a highly caffeinated soft drink (*In re Kirby,* Serial No. 77006212 [T.T.A.B. Sept. 22, 2008]), as depicted in Figure 24.2.

First Amendment Issues In a landmark case that has changed the trademark landscape, the U.S. Supreme Court unanimously affirmed a federal appellate court's decision to reverse the USPTO's rejection of an application for the name "The Slants" by

---

[8]15 U.S.C. § 1052.

FIGURE 24.2 "Cocaine" Mark Rejected by USPTO under Section 2a

ZUMA Press, Inc./Alamy Stock Photo

an Asian-American rock band. In its 2017 decision, *Matal v. Tam*,[9] the Supreme Court addressed First Amendment concerns in holding that Section 2a was unconstitutional. The case arose after the USPTO rejected the application for "The Slants" based on the examiner's conclusion that the term was a highly disparaging term for Asian-Americans. The trial court agreed with the USPTO and affirmed its ruling that the mark was appropriately rejected as scandalous. However, the Federal Circuit Court of Appeals then reversed the decision, and the Supreme Court affirmed the appellate court's decision. The Supreme Court analyzed Section 2a under the *Central Hudson*[10] test for government restriction of commercial speech and concluded that because no substantial government interest exists, the section is unconstitutional. The Court then summed up its First Amendment analysis as follows:

> [The Slants] contend that many, if not all, trademarks have an expressive component. In other words, these trademarks do not simply identify the source of a product or service but go on to say something more, either about the product or service or some broader issue. The trademark in this case illustrates this point. The name "The Slants" not only identifies the band but expresses a view about social issues. . . .
>
> There is also a deeper problem with the argument that commercial speech may be cleansed of any expression likely to cause offense. The commercial market is well stocked with merchandise that disparages prominent figures and groups, and the line between commercial and non-commercial speech is not always clear, as this case illustrates. If affixing the commercial label permits the suppression of any speech that may lead to political or social "volatility," free speech would be endangered.
>
> *Matal v. Tam (137 S. Ct. 1744 [2017]).*

---

[9]137 S. Ct. 1744 (2017).

[10]The *Central Hudson* test is explored in detail in Chapter 2, "Business and the Constitution."

In light of the Supreme Court's unanimous decision in the *Tam* case, Pro-Football, Inc., the corporation that owns the Washington Redskins NFL team, was able to keep its registered mark for "Redskins," which the USPTO had previously found disparaging.[11]

Mark Maintenance

After an initial registration period of 10 years, marks registered through the USPTO may be renewed an unlimited number of times so long as the holder continues to pay the registration fee and continues to use the mark in commerce. Holders that do not maintain the mark through registration renewal may risk losing the rights to the mark and may no longer prevent the mark's use by a third party. Additionally, even when the registration is renewed, if the holder stops using the mark in commerce for a period of three years, the rights to the mark are lost through abandonment.

Policing the Mark

Mark holders have the primary obligation to protect their rights by policing their mark. A primary threat to a mark's distinctiveness is the use of the mark by competitors and other third parties. Of particular concern to business owners and managers should be the use of the mark as a noun or verb in trade and nontrade publications. If a word becomes too generic to the point where it has lost its distinctiveness, the rights are lost through *genericide,* as we discussed earlier in this chapter.

In addition, when holders of a mark misuse the mark or allow the mark to be misused by others (such as advertising agencies), such misuse can contribute to the demise of the mark's distinctiveness and therefore its protectability. To combat the growth of any linguistic re-characterization of their mark in the media or pop culture, mark holders have focused their efforts on the source of words: writers. For decades, Xerox Corporation has used advertising campaigns in publications such as *Writer's Digest* and *The Hollywood Reporter* intended to caution writers about the use of Xerox's mark "only as an adjective to identify our products and services, such as Xerox copiers, not a verb, 'to Xerox' or a noun 'Xeroxes.'"

STRATEGIC LEGAL SOLUTIONS

Trademark Registration

PROBLEM: *The common law and statutory law protections in the area of trademark result in too much uncertainty regarding a business's ability to use the mark.*

SOLUTION: *Register your trademark as soon as possible with the USPTO.*

Although this may require attorney fees, the return on investment may well be worth it. The major advantages to registration are

- Registration gives the mark holder the right to use the mark nationwide, subject to any geographic exceptions.
- Registration constitutes nationwide constructive notice to the public of trademark ownership.

(continued)

---

[11]The decision in *Pro Football, Inc. v. Blackhorse,* 112 F. Supp. 3d 439 (E.D. Va. 2015) (granting petition requesting cancellation of "Redskins" mark on disparagement grounds), was subsequently vacated by the U.S. Court of Appeals for the Fourth Circuit in an unpublished per curiam opinion. *See also* Ian Shapira & Ann E. Marimow, *Washington Redskins Win Trademark Fight over the Team's Name,* Wash. Post, June 29, 2017.

- Registration enables a party to bring an infringement suit in federal court.
- Registration allows a party to potentially recover treble (triple) damages, attorney fees, and other remedies.
- Registered trademarks may, after five years, become "incontestable," at which point the exclusive right to use the mark is conclusively established.

Registering a trademark with the USPTO provides maximum nationwide protection and gives the mark holder the right to enforce its rights in federal court. Paul J. Richards/AFP/Getty Images

Trademark Infringement

Infringement occurs when a party uses a protected mark without the mark holder's consent. For a mark holder to prevail on a claim of trademark infringement under the Lanham Act, she has the burden of proving that the infringement would likely cause confusion among reasonable consumers. (This burden is called the *likelihood of confusion* standard.)

In determining whether a likelihood of confusion exists, many courts apply a balancing test that has largely grown from a model set out by the U.S. Court of Appeals for the Second Circuit in the landmark infringement case *Polaroid Corp. v. Polarad Electronics Corp.*[12] The factors considered are (1) strength of the mark (how famous is it?), (2) similarity between marks, (3) proximity of the products and their competitiveness with each other, (4) evidence that the mark holder may be preparing to launch a product for sale in the market of the alleged infringer's product (a technique known in trademark law as *bridging the gap*), (5) evidence of actual consumer confusion, (6) evidence of bad faith

> **KEY POINT**
>
> For a trademark holder to prevent another from using the holder's mark, the holder must prove that use of the mark by another is likely to cause consumer confusion as to the source of the goods. Courts use the eight-factor *Polaroid* test to assess likelihood of confusion.

---

[12] 287 F.2d 492 (2d Cir. 1961).

by the infringer, (7) respective quality of the products, and (8) sophistication of consumers in the relevant market. The application of the *Polaroid* test is not mechanical but rather focuses on the ultimate question of whether, looking at the products in their totality, consumers are likely to be confused.

In Case 24.5, a case that received considerable media attention, an appellate court analyzes whether the use of a trademark in a song's title and lyrics constitutes infringement.

CASE 24.5 Mattel v. MCA Records, 296 F.3d 894 (9th Cir. 2002)

FACT SUMMARY Barbie is the famous doll manufactured by Mattel with roots beginning in the 1950s. Mattel has invested significant resources in the worldwide marketing and development of the doll, and it has used the Barbie trademark on a variety of accessories for decades. This included development of a Ken doll, and the toy couple went on to become a common reference in pop culture. In 1997, the Danish band Aqua produced a song called "Barbie Girl" in which one band member impersonated Barbie by singing in a high-pitched, doll-like voice in a musical conversation with another band member called Ken. The song's lyrics included details that are typical of the iconic Barbie doll sold by Mattel: plastic, changeable, and modern wardrobe.

Mattel brought an action against Aqua's record label, MCA, for trademark infringement (among other claims) for use of the Barbie mark. The trial court granted summary judgment to MCA, ruling that no infringement had occurred.

SYNOPSIS OF DECISION AND OPINION The Court of Appeals for the Ninth Circuit ruled in favor of MCA. The court distinguished between use of a mark on a product and use of a mark in a song title and explained that although consumers frequently look to the title of a work to determine what it is about, they do not regard titles of artistic works in the same way as they do the names of ordinary commercial products. The court adopted a rule that literary titles do not violate the Lanham Act unless the title has no artistic relevance to the underlying work whatsoever or, if it has some artistic relevance, unless the title explicitly misleads as to the source or the content of the work.

WORDS OF THE COURT: No Infringement "Applying [the literary title rule] to our case, we conclude that MCA's use of Barbie is not

Barbie doll. Keith Homan/Shutterstock

an infringement of Mattel's trademark. Under the first prong of [the rule], the use of Barbie in the song title clearly is relevant to the underlying work, namely, the song itself. As noted, the song is about Barbie and the values Aqua claims she represents. The song title does not explicitly

(continued)

mislead as to the source of the work; it does not, explicitly or otherwise, suggest that it was produced by Mattel. The *only* indication that Mattel might be associated with the song is the use of Barbie in the title[.]"

Counterclaim Dismissed: "After Mattel filed suit, Mattel and MCA employees traded barbs in the press. . . . MCA filed a counterclaim for defamation based on the Mattel representative's use of the words 'bank robber,' 'heist,' 'crime' and 'theft.' . . . In context, all these terms are nonactionable rhetorical hyperbole. The parties are advised to chill."

CASE QUESTIONS

1. Given the rule adopted by the court, can you think of an example in which a literary title would violate the Lanham Act?
2. Why did the court distinguish between use of a mark on a product and use of a mark in a song title?
3. *Focus on Critical Thinking:* Note the court's admonition of the attorneys in the case. Why did the court feel it was necessary to comment on the trial tactics used by the attorneys? Was the court's admonition appropriate?

Trademark Dilution

In addition to bringing an infringement claim under the Lanham Act, holders of famous marks may also enforce their rights via the **Federal Trademark Dilution Act** of 1995,[13] as amended by the Trademark Dilution Revision Act of 2006.[14]

In a dilution claim, evidence of consumer confusion is *not* necessary in order for the mark holder to prevail. Dilution occurs through either *blurring* or *tarnishment*. Blurring dilutes the distinctive quality of the mark through its identification with goods that are not alike. Dilution by blurring may be found regardless of the presence or absence of actual or likely confusion, of competition, or of actual injury. For example, consider the hypothetical products of Red Bull brand pianos or Google brand tennis shoes. Consumers would not necessarily be confused about the origin, but each dilutes the distinctive quality of a famous mark.

By contrast, dilution by tarnishment occurs when an association arising from the similarity between a mark or trade name and a famous mark harms the reputation of the famous mark with something that a consumer might find objectionable or unflattering (e.g., Apple brand cigarettes).[15]

The Trademark Dilution Revision Act now specifies six nonexhaustive factors for courts to consider in determining whether there is dilution by blurring:[16]

- The degree of similarity between the mark and the famous mark.
- The degree of inherent or acquired distinctiveness of the mark.
- The extent to which the owner of the famous mark is engaging in substantially exclusive use of the mark.
- The degree of recognition (fame) of the mark.
- Whether use of the mark by the alleged infringer was intended to create an association with the famous mark.
- Any actual association between the mark and the famous mark.

In addition to setting out statutory blurring standards, the Trademark Dilution Revision Act also requires the mark holder to prove that his mark is famous by offering evidence that it is widely recognized by the general consuming public of the United States.

---

[13] 15 U.S.C. § 1125.
[14] 15 U.S.C. § 1125.
[15] 15 U.S.C. § 1125(c)(2)(C).
[16] 15 U.S.C. § 1125(c)(2)(B)(i)–(vi).

The Trademark Dilution Revision Act thus provides a powerful legal weapon for trademark holders who cannot prove infringement through consumer confusion. For example, in a case where Facebook sued to prevent Teachbook, a social networking site for secondary school teachers, from using the mark "Teachbook," the court made clear that consumer confusion was not relevant in a dilution claim:

> Thus, despite what Teachbook says, not all of Facebook's claims turn on the likelihood of consumer confusion. Rather, Facebook's trademark dilution claim presents an alternative avenue for relief even if Facebook is unable to prove the likelihood of confusion necessary to sustain its trademark infringement and related claims. The allegations in the complaint are also sufficient to state a claim for trademark dilution. . . . Facebook also alleges that Teachbook's use of the TEACHBOOK mark "impairs the distinctiveness of the FACEBOOK Marks and weakens the connection in consumers' minds between the Facebook Marks and Facebook's services." . . . These allegations are sufficient to state a claim for trademark dilution.
>
> *Facebook, Inc. v. Teachbook.com, LLC*, 819 F. Supp. 2d 764 (N.D. Ill. 2011).

CONCEPT SUMMARY *Trademarks*

- A trademark is a word, symbol, or phrase used to identify a seller's product and distinguish it from other products.
- Businesses invest significant time and resources in trademark design; trademarks are among a company's most valuable assets.
- Trademark protection is a combination of state law and a federal statute known as the Lanham Act.
- Trademark protection is obtained through either initial use in commerce or registration with the USPTO.
- Managers should focus special attention on maintaining and policing their firm's mark by having a policy in place and taking steps to prevent others from using the mark.
- In order to prove infringement, the mark owner must prove that use of the mark by another could cause consumer confusion or that use of the mark dilutes or tarnishes the mark.

COPYRIGHT LAW: PROTECTIONS OF ORIGINAL EXPRESSIONS

LO 24-5
Define what a copyright is.

Go ahead and take a picture on your smartphone. Congratulations. You have quite possibly created some intellectual property! The moment you took that photo, you most likely created an original work and became the copyright owner of that work, for copyright protection extends automatically to a work as soon as it is created.

A **copyright** protects the rights of creators of original works for a defined period of time during which the holder has the exclusive rights to copy, distribute, display, or perform the work.

In the U.S., copyright protection is an intangible right granted by the Copyright Act of 1976[17] (a federal statute) to the author or originator of an *original* literary or artistic

---
[17] 17 U.S.C. § 101 et seq.

TABLE 24.1 Copyright Protection Periods

Copyright Owner	Copyright Duration
Sole author or originator	70 years from death of the author or originator
Publisher or other party (works for hire)	The earlier of either (1) 120 years from the date of creation or (2) 95 years from the date of publication
More than one author or originator	70 years from the death of the last-surviving author or originator

> **KEY POINT**
>
> A copyright protects the rights of creators of original works for a defined period of time during which the holder has the exclusive rights to copy, distribute, display, or perform the work.

production, whereby the artist is invested, for a specified period (see Table 24.1), with the sole and exclusive privilege of reproduction (copying) of the work and with the right to profit from its publication, performance, or display.

Copyright laws apply to works made for hire (or *works for hire*), which are works created by an employee as part of her job. When a work is made for hire, the employer—not the employee—is considered the legal owner of the work, in the absence of an agreement to the contrary.

Before proceeding any further, a key clarification is in order: Copyright law protects the *expression* of ideas, not ideas themselves. As a result, works that *cannot* be protected under copyright law include underlying ideas, facts, raw data, procedures, processes, systems, methods of operation, concepts, principles, and discoveries, no matter how they are explained, illustrated, or described.[18]

So, how does copyright law protect the expression of ideas? Specifically, the Copyright Act allows creators of original works to obtain a copyright by having an "original work of authorship fixed in any tangible medium of expression, not known or later developed, from which [it] can be perceived, reproduced, or otherwise communicated, either directly or with the aid of a machine or device."[19] As a result, protected works include such things as literary works, musical works, dramatic works, choreographic works, motion pictures, sound recordings, and pictorial or graphical works.

Fundamentally, in order to obtain copyright protection, a work must pass the following three-part test: (1) **originality**, (2) some degree of **creativity**, and (3) fixation in a **durable medium**.

Originality and Creativity Requirements

The meaning of the word *original* has generated the most controversy in interpreting the requirements of the Copyright Act. What is to be considered original, and what guidelines should be used to determine creativity? The courts have ruled that an original work of authorship is a work that is original to the *author,* which means that the author must use *her own creative capabilities* to create the work or medium.

Does this definition of originality mean that a compilation of raw data or other non-copyrightable facts (such as a list of names and telephone numbers) can be copyrighted as

---

[18] Note that ideas, procedures, systems, and the like may be covered by intellectual property protections other than copyright law, such as trade secret law or patent law.

[19] 17 U.S.C. § 102(a).

long as the creator of the list was the first to put the list together? In *Feist Publications, Inc. v. Rural Telephone Service*,[20] a landmark case on copyright originality and creativity, the U.S. Supreme Court addressed this issue head on. In brief, the Court unanimously ruled that compilations of facts could be copyrightable only if the compilation contained some element of creativity. In the words of the Court: "copyright protects only those constituent elements of a work that possess more than a *de minimis* quantum of creativity." As a result, the White Pages of a telephone directory do not meet the creativity requirement because they are simply arranged alphabetically. One federal appellate court has even gone as far as to hold that the Yellow Pages listings of a telephone directory do not meet the originality requirement.[21]

Durable Medium

To be protected, a work must not only be original and creative; it must also be fixed in a *durable medium*. This requirement underscores the general principle that copyright law protects the expression of ideas, not ideas themselves. A work must be more than just an idea or thought process. In fact, the work must be fixed in a tangible form, such as writing, digital, video, and so forth.

REGISTRATION AND NOTICE

Although works may be registered with the U.S. Copyright Office, registration is not required for the creator to own the rights. *The creation of the work itself automatically confers a copyright on the material.* Registration of the copyright, however, affords the owner legal methods for enforcing the copyright, including the right to bring an infringement action in federal court, the right to collect statutory damages from infringers, and the right to obtain injunctive relief against infringers.

The copyright notice is the familiar © symbol or the abbreviation "Copr." or the word "Copyright" accompanied by the year of first publication and the copyright owner's name. For works created after 1989, no copyright notice is necessary in order to preserve the rights of the owner. Still, placing a copyright notice on the work is a wise practice because it limits any defense by an infringer who might claim innocent infringement.

COPYRIGHT INFRINGEMENT

When a copyright holder sues a party that it believes has infringed on its copyright, the copyright owner will generally pursue one of three *theories of infringement*. These theories have been developed by the federal courts to analyze copyright infringement cases. These theories are *direct infringement*, *indirect infringement* (also known as *contributory infringement*), and *vicarious infringement*.

> **LO 24-6**
>
> Identify the remedies for acts of copyright infringement, describe the impact of technology on copyright law, and apply the fair use defense.

Direct Infringement

Direct infringement occurs when the copyright owner can prove that she has legal ownership of the work in question and that the infringer copied the work without permission.

While the first element is straightforward, the second element is more complex than appears at first glance. In the context of the copyright protections afforded by law, the word *copied* must have an expansive definition rather than a narrow one (i.e., *copy* means more

---

[20]499 U.S. 340 (1991). This case was the beginning of the phone book battles. Once *Feist* was decided, several different publication companies began to compete with telephone companies for Yellow Pages advertising. This one decision spurred a new niche in the publishing industry.

[21]*BellSouth Advertising v. Donnelley Information Publishing*, 999 F.2d 1436 (11th Cir. 1993).

than "exact replica"), but at the same time, the definition of copy cannot be so expansive as to foreclose any works of the same category.

Given this tension, courts have developed the *substantial similarity standard* to guide the definition of *copy* under copyright law. Thus, a copyright holder need prove only that the infringer copied plots, structures, or organizations that made the infringing work substantially similar to the copyrighted work.

Indirect Infringement

Indirect infringement (also known as *contributory infringement*) involves three parties: the copyright owner, the direct infringer, and the *facilitator* of the infringement. Under this theory of indirect infringement, it is the facilitator who is liable for damages. Therefore, before pursuing a theory of indirect infringement, the copyright owner must first identify the direct infringer.

Normally, for a facilitator to be liable, that party must either have direct or imputed knowledge of the infringement or contribute to the infringement in some material way. In the famous case of *A&M Records, Inc. v. Napster, Inc.*,[22] a federal appeals court held that Napster's business model of facilitating a peer-to-peer community for the sharing of digital music files constituted contributory infringement because Napster had the ability to locate infringing material listed on its search engines as well as the ability to terminate users' access to the system. Digital file sharing is discussed more extensively later in this section (see the Legal Implications in Cyberspace feature).

Vicarious Infringement

The third copyright infringement theory, **vicarious infringement**, is similar to the indirect infringement theory in that they both involve third parties not involved in actual direct infringement. Vicarious infringement most often occurs in an employer-employee context in which the employee is acting with authority from the employer and commits an act of infringement that benefits the employer. The copyright owner is entitled to remedies against the employer to the same extent as against the direct infringer.

Vicarious liability is based on agency law (see Chapter 10, "Agency") and can be used as a theory of liability not only in the employer-employee context but whenever an infringing party (the agent) is acting on behalf of or for the benefit of another party (the principal). When such a vicarious infringement occurs, the principal party can be held vicariously liable for the acts of the agent.

Criminal Sanctions for Infringement

In addition to providing for civil remedies such as money damages for acts of infringement, copyright law also provides for criminal penalties as well. In particular, the controversial **No Electronic Theft (NET) Act** of 1997[23] increased the criminal penalties for violations of the Copyright Act. The NET Act imposes criminal liability on anyone infringing on a copyright by making a reproduction or distribution, including by electronic means, of one or more copies of a copyrighted work with a total retail value of more than $1,000. Penalties include maximum fines of $250,000 and potential incarceration.[24]

Legal Speak >))

Direct and Imputed Knowledge
Direct knowledge implies that a party has firsthand, actual knowledge of a fact. Imputed knowledge is gained from circumstances or a relationship with a third party in which a diligent party "should have known" about the fact at issue.

---

[22]239 F.3d 1004 (9th Cir. 2001).

[23]17 U.S.C. § 506.

[24]A catalyst for this law was a criminal case brought against an MIT student who posted copyrighted software on the Internet free of charge for anyone to download. The government could not obtain a conviction in the case because the existing law (prior to the NET Act) imposed criminal liability only when the infringement was undertaken for private *financial* gain. The NET Act eliminated the financial gain requirement for a criminal conviction. *See United States v. LaMacchia*, 871 F. Supp. 535 (D. Mass. 1994).

DEFENSES TO INFRINGEMENT CLAIMS

Copyright owners do not enjoy unlimited rights to their work. Rather, the law attempts to balance competing public interests with the property rights of copyright owners. Specifically, infringement claims in copyright cases are subject to three major defenses: the public domain, the first sale doctrine, and the fair use test.

Public Domain

A work that is in the *public domain* is not protectable under copyright laws. Works fall into the public domain either because the copyright has expired or because federal or state governments publish the work. By way of example, reproductions of classical works in literature such as Homer's *The Odyssey* or Tolstoy's *War and Peace* do not require permissions because those works are now part of the public domain. Similarly, court cases, government agency correspondence, and statutes are all in the public domain and do not require permission for use.

First Sale

The first sale doctrine enables a lawful purchaser of a copyrighted work to resell, transfer, or gift her copy of the work to anyone else without the permission of the copyright owner. The first sale doctrine does not allow the purchaser of the work to copy the work itself; instead, it prevents the copyright owner from exercising *distribution* rights over a copyrighted work after the work enters the market.

Fair Use

The most common and powerful defense in copyright infringement cases is **fair use**. A landmark case on the fair use defense is *Sony Corp. of America v. Universal City Studios*,[25] in which the U.S. Supreme Court ruled that Sony's manufacturing and selling of Betamax (the first videocassette tape recording format for use in home videocassette recorders, or VCRs) was *not* **per se** infringement.

After Sony had started producing videotape recorders (sold under the brand name Betamax) in a price range that many consumers could afford, Universal saw the mass distribution of this product as a threat to its business model and market share. Universal sued Sony on an indirect infringement theory, claiming that consumers were using the Sony product to record its copyrighted movies and TV programs.

The U.S. Supreme Court, however, made clear that Congress did not give absolute control over all uses of copyrighted materials. Some uses were *permitted,* and because the device could still be used for "substantial non-infringing uses," the Court held that Sony was not liable for contributory infringement.

Napster unsuccessfully attempted to invoke this *fair use exception,* known as the *Sony defense* or the *Betamax doctrine,* in the *A&M Records v. Napster* case (discussed previously in this chapter), and this exception was subsequently reexamined by the Supreme Court in the *MGM v. Grokster* case (discussed later in the chapter).[26]

The term *fair use* has now been codified in the Copyright Act with four general factors or guideposts: (1) the *purpose* and *nature* of the use, (2) the nature of the *work* itself, (3) the *amount* and *substantiality* of the material used, and (4) the *effect* of the use on the market.

---

[25] 464 U.S. 417 (1984).

[26] See Legal Implications in Cyberspace: Copyrights in the Digital Age.

Purpose and Nature of the Use The first factor is often called the *transformative* factor because courts first analyze whether the work in question has added a new expression or new meaning to the copyrighted work. If a work is centered on the original but has created new information, aesthetics, or insights, the work does not infringe on the copyrighted work.[27]

By way of example, entertainers may use parody for purposes of mocking a particular work (e.g., song lyrics). At the same time, however, transformative use has its limits. In *Warner Bros. Entertainment, Inc. v. RDR Books*,[28] a court held that a Harry Potter encyclopedia may qualify as "slightly transformative" but that fair use did not apply because so much of the encyclopedia's text was taken directly from the Harry Potter book series.

Moreover, if the use of the work is to promote education or scholarship, courts are more likely to be sympathetic to an assertion of fair use. Nevertheless, just because the use of a work is educational or scholarly or otherwise noncommercial in nature does not always make it a fair use. Entire sections of textbooks or copied videotapes may not be used without the copyright holder's permission. Also, if the use is for some commercially profitable purpose, this fact will weigh heavily against the infringer.

Nature of the Work The second factor in the fair use determination is the nature of the work that is being copied, that is, whether the copyrighted material is a work of fiction (such as a novel or play) or a work of nonfiction or factual work (such as a biography). Generally speaking, all other things being equal, a judge is more likely to find a determination of fair use if material was copied from a factual work than from a fictional work.

Amount and Substantiality Used How much of the original work did the infringer take? A single sentence of a book, a whole paragraph, or an entire chapter? Courts analyze the totality of the circumstances regarding the amount of copyrighted material used compared to the entire work at issue. Short phrases and limited use of the copyrighted work are often protected by the fair use defense.

Market Effect The fourth factor in a fair-use determination is the effect of the use on the potential market for the work that was copied. Courts are reluctant to allow fair use as a defense (even if the use meets the other three factors) if a copyright holder demonstrates that the *value* of a copyrighted work will be diminished by allowing its use. Fair use cannot impair the marketability or economic success of the copyrighted work.

 Self-Check Fair Use

Which of these situations would constitute fair use?

1. A manager photocopies an article of interest from *The Wall Street Journal* and distributes it to three co-workers who also may be interested.
2. A company buys one copy of a training manual from a publisher and then distributes photocopies of several chapters to its workforce.

(continued)

---

[27]*Campbell v. Acuff-Rose Music, Inc.*, 510 U.S. 569 (1994).
[28]575 F. Supp. 2d 513 (S.D.N.Y. 2008).

3. An executive rents a DVD on motivation from her local video/DVD store. The next day, she shows the DVD during work hours to her management team in order to inspire the team members to adopt certain leadership practices.

4. A firm that arranges corporate training sessions buys a DVD that features former General Electric CEO Jack Welch speaking on problem-solving skills for executives. The firm shows 30 minutes of this DVD at the beginning of each of its eight-hour training sessions called "Solutions for Solving," for which it charges $500 per person for the entire session.

Answers to this Self-Check are provided at the end of the chapter.

LEGAL IMPLICATIONS IN CYBERSPACE

Copyrights in the Digital Age

Technology has created new challenges for legislatures and courts struggling with applying copyright law in the digital age.

Computer Software In order to settle uncertainty in the computer science field about the ability to copyright computer software, Congress amended the Copyright Act with the Computer Software Copyright Act.[29] This law, enacted in 1980, specifically defines computer software programs as literary works and, thus, works entitled to protection.

Nevertheless, the nebulous nature of computer software still brings with it a good deal of uncertainty in terms of copyright protection. *Whelan v. Jaslow,*[30] decided in 1986, was the first case to address the issue of copyright protection for software. That landmark case extended broad protection to computer programs, including both the "look and feel" of a program's displays and also the program's structure, sequence, and organization. More recently, however, courts have been scaling back this broad protection and adopting a more sophisticated test. One appellate court has even suggested that patents, not copyrights, would be the most suitable form of intellectual property protection to protect the dynamic aspects of computer software programs.[31]

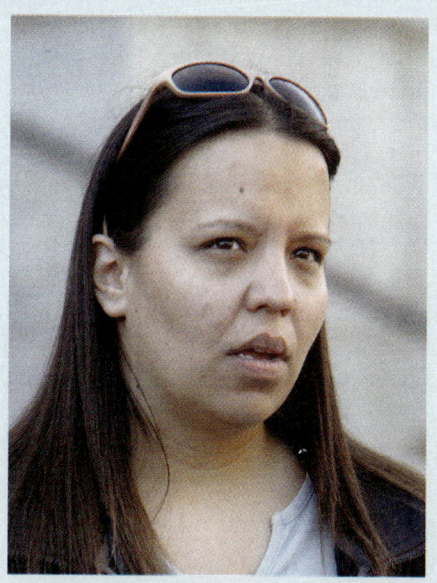

Jammie Thomas-Rasset. Julia Cheng/AP Images

Evolution of Copyright Law and Technology The revolutionary technological gains and the increasing popularity of the Internet have led to significant threats to such copyright holders as record labels and movie studios. In the past, copyright infringement of movies and music was limited

(continued)

---

[29]17 U.S.C.A. § 117.

[30]797 F.2d 1222 (3d Cir. 1986).

[31]*Computer Associates International v. Latai, Inc.*, 982 F.2d 693 (2d Cir. 1992).

because the technology that existed to copy these media was not capable of producing mass copies, except through a sophisticated criminal network. In short, when the average consumer was limited in what he could copy and distribute, copyright holders had little fear that day-to-day consumer infringement would impact their revenue stream from sales of the original. But when the digital age truly arrived, copyright holders responded by lobbying Congress for additional protections in the area of copyright laws.

Digital Millennium Copyright Act Congress enacted the Digital Millennium Copyright Act (DMCA) in 1998 in an attempt to modernize copyright law to deal with the new challenges that had emerged in the digital age. The DMCA was controversial because it extended copyright law to the Internet and created a cumbersome *notice and takedown* procedure for policing copyrights on the Internet.

In summary, in order to pursue a copyright infringement claim against an Internet service provider (ISP), the copyright owner must first provide the ISP with written notification of the claimed infringement. Moreover, the copyright owner's notification must comply with the following requirements:

- Identification of the copyrighted work claimed to have been infringed and information reasonably sufficient to permit the Internet service provider to locate the material.
- Information reasonably sufficient to permit the Internet service provider to contact the complaining party, such as an address, telephone number, and e-mail address.
- A statement that the complaining party has a good faith belief that use of the material in the manner complained of is not authorized by the copyright owner, its agent, or the law.
- A statement that the information in the notification is accurate and, under penalty of perjury, that the complaining party is authorized to act on behalf of the owner of an exclusive right that is allegedly infringed.

In addition, the DMCA provides a *safe harbor* (legal immunity) to Internet service providers who comply with the notice and takedown procedure.

File Sharing Technology changed the status quo rapidly. The late 1990s saw the introduction of two very important technological advances: (1) the popular music file format known as MP3 (essentially, compressed digital files) and (2) the increasing speed advancements of the Internet. These two technological advances changed the once hours-long process of transferring music and movies over the Internet into a process that took just a few minutes or even seconds.

The MP3 file, in particular, grew in popularity very quickly and enabled consumers to upload and download music and video files from one private personal computer to another. The ability to upload and download hundreds of files a day led to the establishment of peer-to-peer (P2P) networking and, of course, entrepreneurs who have leveraged this technology into profit. The pioneer of P2P file-sharing communities was Napster. As discussed, the Ninth Circuit Court of Appeals effectively shut down Napster after the court ruled that Napster's business model was inherently illegal because Napster had imputed knowledge of copyright infringement.

RIAA Lawsuits In addition to aggressively pursuing file-sharing services such as Napster and Grokster, the motion picture and music recording industries have filed thousands of infringement lawsuits against individuals engaged in file sharing. The Recording Industry Association of America (RIAA) in particular has invested substantial resources in tracking down and recovering damages from individual infringers.

In a 2009 federal case out of Minnesota that garnered national media attention, a jury imposed damages of $1.92 million against Jammie Thomas-Rasset. The award was the result of a lawsuit filed by RIAA against Thomas-Rasset alleging she personally downloaded more than 1,700 copyrighted songs over a file-sharing service. Despite this jury award, other Napster-like sharing services began to thrive under a business model whereby the P2P provider could not have any actual knowledge of copyright infringement. The motion picture industry also doggedly pursued each of these companies by suing them under a contributory infringement theory. Ultimately, the issue of what level of intent is necessary to constitute infringement was decided by the U.S. Supreme Court in Landmark Case 24.6.

LANDMARK CASE 24.6 Metro-Goldwyn-Mayer Studios v. Grokster, Ltd., 545 U.S. 913 (2005)

FACT SUMMARY After the *Napster* decision, a number of other P2P file-sharing communities emerged with a slightly different business model. One famous firm, Grokster, used a business model whereby it would be *impossible* for Grokster to know if the files being shared were an infringing use. Thus, Grokster argued, no Napster-like imputed liability could attach and no contributor infringement existed. According to Grokster (and many other such firms that were emerging), its business was precisely the same business that Sony was in when selling the Betamax and, thus, Grokster was entitled to the same type of fair use exception—"capable of substantial non-infringing uses"—as was articulated by the Supreme Court in the *Sony* case. When MGM Studios sued Grokster (and others, including StreamCast, the distributor of Morpheus software), both the federal trial court and the federal court of appeals *agreed* with Grokster and allowed Grokster to use the *Sony* exception in its rulings against MGM.[32]

SYNOPSIS OF DECISION AND OPINION The U.S. Supreme Court unanimously held that Grokster *could* be liable for inducing copyright infringement and reversed the court of appeals ruling. The Court specifically ruled that anyone who distributes a device with the intent to promote its use to infringe copyright is liable for the resulting acts of infringement (contributory) by third parties. Although there was some disagreement among the justices about the *Sony* defense, ultimately the Court held that the lower courts had misapplied the *Sony* exception because there was ample evidence that Grokster had acted with intent to cause copyright infringement via the use of its software.

WORDS OF THE COURT: Evidence of Intent "Three features of this evidence of intent are particularly notable. First, each company showed itself to be aiming to satisfy a known source of demand for copyright infringement, the market comprising former Napster users. StreamCast's internal documents made constant reference to Napster, it initially distributed its Morpheus software through an OpenNap program compatible with Napster, it advertised its OpenNap program to Napster users, and its Morpheus software functions as Napster did except that it could be used to distribute more kinds of files, including copyrighted movies and software programs. Grokster's name is apparently derived from Napster, it too initially offered an OpenNap program, its software's function is likewise comparable to Napster's, and it attempted to divert queries for Napster onto its own Web site. Grokster and StreamCast's efforts to supply services to former Napster users, deprived of a mechanism to copy and distribute what were overwhelmingly infringing files, indicate a principal, if not exclusive, intent on the part of each to bring about infringement."

Case Questions

1. Why was the Court so concerned about the OpenNap program offered by StreamCast and Grokster?
2. Why do you think the Court refused to apply the *Sony* exception in this case?
3. *Focus on Critical Thinking:* Is it ethical to obtain music through digital file sharing? Have you ever illegally downloaded music or movies? Does the Court's ruling stifle innovation?

CONCEPT SUMMARY Copyrights

- Copyright protection is an intangible right granted by the Copyright Act to the author or originator of an original literary or artistic work.

(continued)

---

[32]*Metro-Goldwyn-Mayer Studios v. Grokster, Ltd.*, 380 F.3d 1154 (9th Cir. 2004).

- In order to obtain copyright protection, the work must be original and have some degree of creativity, and it must be fixed in a durable medium (such as in writing).
- There are three theories of infringement: direct, indirect (contributory), and vicarious.
- Fair use is the primary defense against infringement of copyrighted material. Courts examine the purpose and nature of the use, the nature of the work, the amount used, and the market effect of the use.
- Other defenses include public domain and first sale.

STRATEGIC LEGAL SOLUTIONS

Avoiding Intellectual Property Liability: Landmines on the Web

PROBLEM: *Managers who oversee an Internet-based marketing model are often barraged with conflicting information and advice about trademark and copyright law.*

By taking simple and inexpensive precautions, managers can help protect their company from infringement liability.

SOLUTION 1: *Limit your linking.*

Courts have allowed the use of a typical hypertext link so long as the use is reasonable under the circumstances. Inline imaging, framing, and even deep linking have all been given legal protection so long as the essence of the copyright and trademark laws is protected. However, an attempt to use a link to create confusion of the consumer that ultimately could result in the consumer's being directed to a competing business would constitute infringement.

For example, let's suppose that MuseumTicketsRUs is a registered trademark of a company that sells tickets to museum exhibits in major cities and that it hosts a website, MuseumTicketsRUs.com. A second firm, Artists.com, hosts a website that provides links to all museum websites, all museum online stores, art supply stores, and the like. If Artists.com simply provides a link to MuseumTicketsRUs, then no copyright or trademark infringement has taken place. However, if Artists.com uses MuseumTicketsRUs's logo, similar name, or other similar identifying characteristics and uses the link to direct a consumer-user to a competing site with which Artists.com has a commission-based agreement, this would clearly constitute infringement and expose Artists.com to significant legal liability. Thus, it is a good idea to take steps to avoid any consumer confusion by, for example, displaying a disclaimer stating that the originating site with the link is *not* related to or a part of the linked site.

Deep linking (i.e., linking to an embedded site) may be cause for additional concerns if the embedded site skips through advertising that the web page host has placed on the original site. It is a good practice to use links only to originating web pages (home pages) or at the very least to offer links to *both* the originating home page and the deep-linked page in close proximity, with labels for the user that describe the content of the page. Moreover, if the linked site has taken technical steps to prevent linking or given notice that it does not sanction deep linking, this should give managers pause because they may be crossing the line of reasonableness into infringement.

The ultimate protection against infringement, of course, is obtaining express permission to deep link. The owner of the site will often give you permission so long as your site is not a competitor or a site that may tend to tarnish its image (such as adult-content sites). A simple form for this permission follows.

(continued)

Agreement and Permission to Use

This Agreement, made this _____ day of January, 2020, between MuseumTicketsRUs (Owner) and Artists.com (User), acknowledging sufficient consideration, the parties agree as follows:

1. Owner permits User to link, deep link, inline image, or frame Owner's website (www.MuseumTicketsRUs.com) from User's website (www.Artists.com).
2. User shall be entitled to use this permission until such time as Owner gives User 48 hours' notice via e-mail to cease the use of the link. Owner has the absolute and unconditional power to revoke this permission at any time and for any reason.
3. Upon such notice, User agrees to cease the use of any and all links to Owner's website as soon as possible.
4. Owner shall not be entitled to any compensation under this Agreement.

Signed: _____ (Owner)   Date:

_____ (User)   Date:

SOLUTION 2: *Make copyrighted images thumbnail size.*

A significant amount of litigation has ensued over the use of copyrighted photos in thumbnail size as a means of providing a website-content preview for consumers using an Internet search engine or linking to another page via the thumbnail image. The idea, of course, is to allow consumers who are searching for a particular image to scan multiple images and choose the appropriate one, rather than having to link to the actual pages to view the photos, thus saving the consumer user time.

Copying the image of another is clearly infringement. For example, if Best Furniture, a large retailer of patio furniture, takes photographs of its products and displays them on its website, the use of those photos by a competing retailer on the retailer's own website (or in a catalog for that matter) is clearly illegal. However, let's suppose that a website that is hosted by Patio and Deck Contractors Inc. provides thumbnail images of Best Furniture's patio furniture photos on its website with a link to Best Furniture's site as a service to Patio and Deck Contractors's customers. In this instance, the use of the images is legal under the fair use exception to the Copyright Act.

An overwhelming majority of courts have ruled that the use of thumbnail photograph images by Internet websites has "transformed" the original photograph in such a way as to make the use of the images legal.

PATENTS: LEGAL PROTECTION OF INVENTIONS AND PROCESSES

LO 24-7

Define what a patent is and explain how patents are obtained.

A **patent** is a statutorily created monopoly right that confers on an inventor the *exclusive right* to make, use, license, and sell her invention for a limited period of time.

Patent rights are especially vital in the manufacturing, technology, and pharmaceutical industries. Patents are often an important part of these firms' planning because their business models depend on the benefits of obtaining a patent—the full legal protection of their ideas, methods, and inventions. Once a patent is obtained, a competitor is barred from profiting off the patented device or process during the life of the patent. Thus, a patent can be a firm's most important and valuable asset.

Patents are expensive. Osman Vector/Shutterstock

Business owners and managers, however, need to have a good working understanding of the fundamentals of patent law and need to be aware of the most common myths surrounding patents. The most common myth is the assumption that nearly any new idea or invention is "patentable" (able to obtain patent law protection). This assumption is *not* true. In fact, the patent process is a lengthy and costly one, for in order to be patented, the idea or invention must meet stringent criteria set forth in federal statutes.

Cost Considerations

To begin with, the patent application procedure itself is expensive because an inventor must almost always obtain legal counsel that specializes in patent law, and because of their specialized nature, such law firms—known colloquially as *intellectual property* (or simply IP) *firms*—are often more expensive than expert counsel in other areas of the law. By way of example, one intellectual property law firm estimates that legal fees and application fees related to obtaining a patent range from $20,000 for a mechanical tool invention to $30,000 for a software patent.[33]

In addition, even if one is successful in obtaining a patent, enforcing a patent via an infringement lawsuit is an even more expensive and daunting undertaking. According to one report, the median cost for enforcing a patent claim (assuming an infringement lawsuit is necessary) is around $650,000 for claims worth less $1 million.[34] Although it is not always necessary to go all the way to trial to enforce a patent, litigation outcomes are often uncertain, so a company's patent management strategy must weigh such significant cost and risk factors ahead of time.

FUNDAMENTALS OF PATENT LAW

Patent law in the United States dates back to the founding era. It is governed by the Patent Act, which was enacted by the First Congress in 1790, the same Congress that proposed the Bill of Rights. Inventors will typically seek help from a patent attorney who is skilled and experienced in the patent application process. The application process is called *prosecuting* a patent.

Patent Prosecution

Although patent prosecution varies based on the invention, the process typically has three stages.

First, the inventor and patent counsel perform a database search in an attempt to ensure that a similar invention is not protected by an existing patent (known as *prior art*).

Second, the inventor files a *provisional application* with the U.S. Patent and Trademark Office (USPTO). A provisional patent application discloses the invention in a general way and does not require the formalities necessary for a full (nonprovisional) application.

---

[33]"How much does a patent cost?" Richards Patent Law (not dated), https://www.richardspatentlaw.com/faq/how-much-does-a-patent-cost/.

[34]*See* Gene Quinn, *The Cost of Obtaining a Patent in the US,* IP Watchdog (Apr. 4, 2015), www.ipwatchdog.com/2015/04/04/the-cost-of-obtaining-a-patent-in-the-us/id=56485/.

In addition, a provisional application protects the invention and allows the inventor to work on improving the invention for 12 months before a full patent application.

Third, once the parties are satisfied that the invention is patentable, the inventor's counsel files a full nonprovisional application with the USPTO that is much more comprehensive and typically includes sketches or other supplementary materials. An attorney employed by the USPTO acts as an *examiner* and reviews the application in order to determine whether the application describes an invention that meets the legal standards for patentability.

If the examiner concludes that the invention *is* patentable, he will issue the patent and the inventor then has full rights to enforce the patent against third parties. If the examiner determines that the invention is *not* patentable, the inventor may appeal to the Patent Trial and Appeal Board (PTAB).

Categories

There are three different categories of patents:

- *Utility patents* constitute a broad category that covers the invention of any new and useful process, machine, article of manufacture, or composition of matter or any new and useful improvement. An important subcategory of utility patents is the *business method patent*, which is discussed in more detail later in this section. Utility patents also cover software and hardware. The overwhelming majority of patents fall into this category.
- *Design patents* cover primarily the invention of new ornamental designs on articles of manufacture. This category covers how a product looks rather than how it functions; it is therefore increasingly common for business firms to obtain both trademark protection and a design patent for the same product.
- *Plant patents* are the least frequently issued type of patent and cover the invention or discovery of asexually or sexually reproducible plants (such as flowers).

Patent Duration

A patent for inventions or processes (utility and business method patents) lasts for a period of 20 years from the date of filing the application with the USPTO. A design patent lasts for 14 years.

Patentability Standards

In order to be patented, an invention must be *novel* and *nonobvious* and must be a *proper subject matter* for protection under the patent law.

Novelty
An invention or process must be unique and original, and a patent applicant must show that no other identical invention or process exists. The statute delineates the guidelines for this **novelty standard** based on a three-prong test.

The first prong is the public use test and requires that the invention or process *not already be* in public use. The second prong governs priority for inventors of the same invention or process. The United States recognizes the first inventor-to-file rule, in which patent rights are granted to the first inventor to file a patent application. The first inventor to file then has priority over other inventors of the same product. The final prong requires a determination by the USPTO that the applicant filed the patent within a reasonable time of the invention.

In *Dunlop Holdings Ltd. v. RAM Golf Corporation*,[35] a landmark case on the issue of public use, a federal appellate court invalidated a patent held by the manufacturer of a specially

---

[35] 524 F.2d 33 (7th Cir. 1975).

coated golf ball. The court held that Dunlop's patent on the specially coated ball did not meet the novelty test because there was evidence that the same product had been used by a sole proprietor golf pro 10 years prior to when the patent was issued. The court remarked

> The only novel feature of this case arises from the fact that [the golf pro] was careful not to disclose to the public the ingredient that made his golf ball so tough. . . . But in this case, although [he] may have failed to act diligently to establish his own right to a patent, there was no lack of diligence in his attempt to make the benefits of his discovery available to the public. . . . [T]he evidence clearly demonstrates that [the golf pro] endeavored to market his golf balls as promptly and effectively as possible. The balls themselves were in wide public use.
>
> 524 F.2d 33 (7th Cir. 1975).

Nonobviousness The **nonobviousness standard** requires that an invention must be something more than that which would be obvious, in light of publicly available knowledge, to one who is skilled in the relevant field. In other words, a patent cannot be granted for minimal or marginal improvements that were already apparent to those in the field. For example, Joanna adds a small extender switch to her lawn mower (an existing patented invention) that will make it easier for taller people to kill the engine. Joanna is not entitled to a new patent because the invention is essentially a minimal (also called *de minimis*) improvement and relatively obvious.

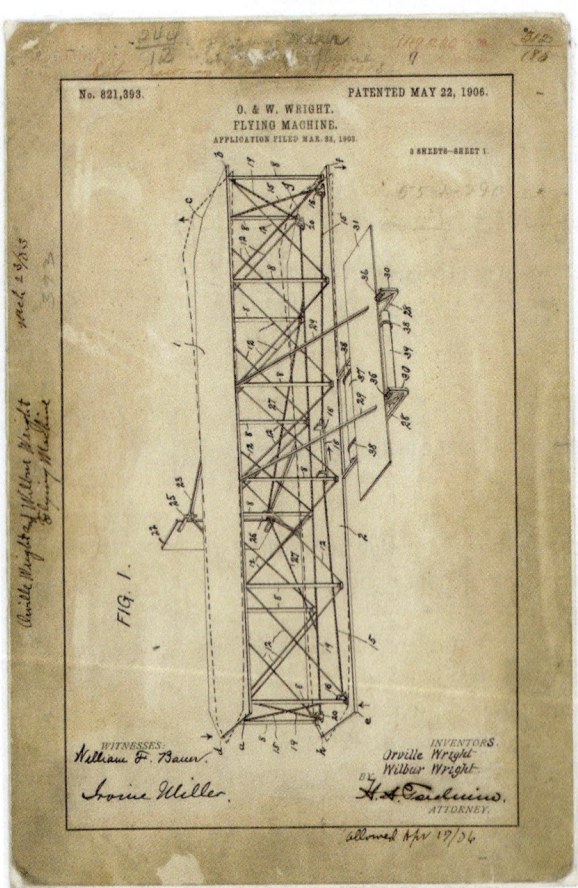

The patent issued to the Wright brothers in 1906 for their flying machine began a new era in global commerce.
U.S. National Archives Records Administration/AP Images

Patentable Subject Matter Not all processes and inventions that are nonobvious and novel are patentable. The **patentable subject matter standard** bars laws of nature, natural phenomena, and abstract ideas from being patentable. Albert Einstein's theory of relativity was groundbreaking. It was new and nonobvious beyond question. But should this natural phenomenon be patentable? The patent system was not intended to cover every novel and nonobvious idea. Courts have consistently held that mathematical algorithms, materials common to nature (such as penicillin), and unapplied or abstract ideas are not patentable.

Requirements for Design Patents

Patent laws also protect inventors of any new, original, and ornamental design for an article of manufacture. Design patents are subject to the same requirements as those for utility or business method patents (novelty and nonobvious); in addition, the design must be primarily ornamental (not primarily functional).

Design patents are thus concerned with protecting the appearance of an article. For example, in Figure 24.3, the head dress popularized by the *Dark Knight* movie series received a design patent based on its appearance and not any particular function.

Business Method Patents

Because of the patentable subject matter standard (discussed earlier), courts have historically struggled with the notion of extending patent protection to processes and methods developed by business firms to improve efficiency or generate some other form of competitive advantage.

In an attempt to provide guidance to inventors and business firms, the USPTO issued a directive in 1996 that recognizes business method patents and that instructs examiners to treat business method applications like any other process claims, and in 1998, a federal appeals court helped settle many issues related to business method patents and provided guidance for other courts in the landmark case of *State Street Bank & Trust Co. v. Signature Financial Group*.[36] The *State Street* case ruled that business methods are patentable so long as they accomplish something practically useful in a novel and nonobvious way. After the *State Street* case, the number of applications for business method patents increased nearly sixfold.

However, in Case 24.7, the U.S. Supreme Court significantly narrowed the scope of business method patents.

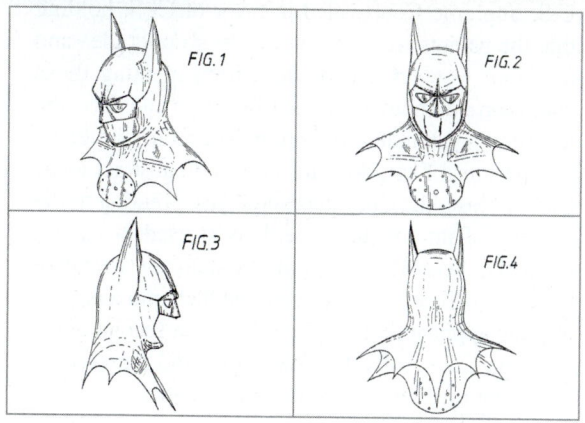

FIGURE 24.3 Dark Knight Head Dress

Source: U.S. Patent and Trademark Office, Patent No. D329,321, filed Oct. 18, 1989, and issued Sept. 15, 1992.

CASE 24.7 Alice Corporation Pty. Ltd. v. CLS Bank International, 573 U.S. 208 (2014)

FACT SUMMARY Alice Corporation (Alice) holds several patents that disclose plans to manage certain forms of financial risk. According to the specification disclosed in the patents, the invention "enables the management of risk relating to specified, yet unknown, future events." The claims at issue relate to a computerized scheme for mitigating "settlement risk"—that is, the risk that only one party to an agreed-upon financial exchange will satisfy its obligation. In particular, the claims are designed to facilitate the exchange of financial obligations between two parties by using a computer system as a third-party intermediary. The intermediary creates "shadow" credit and debit records (i.e., account ledgers) that mirror the balances in the parties' real-world accounts at "exchange institutions" (e.g., banks). The intermediary updates the shadow records in real time as transactions are entered, allowing "only those transactions for which the parties' updated shadow records indicate sufficient resources to satisfy their mutual obligations." At the end of the day, the intermediary instructs the relevant financial institutions to carry out the permitted transactions in accordance with the updated shadow records, thus mitigating the risk that only one party will perform the agreed-upon exchange.

CLS Bank International (CLS) operates a global network that facilitates currency transactions. CLS filed suit against Alice, seeking a declaratory judgment that Alice's patents were invalid. The trial court ruled that the processes were ineligible for a patent because they are directed to the abstract idea of employing a neutral intermediary to facilitate simultaneous exchange of obligations in order to minimize risk. A divided panel of the U.S. Court of Appeals for the Federal Circuit reversed, holding that it was not "manifestly evident" that the petitioner's claims were directed to an abstract idea. The parties appealed to the U.S. Supreme Court.

(continued)

---

[36]149 F.3d 1368 (Fed. Cir. 1998). The case involved a challenge to a patent issued to Signature for a process that facilitated a method whereby several mutual funds pooled their investments into a single fund that achieved management cost savings over many other funds.

SYNOPSIS OF DECISION AND OPINION The U.S. Supreme Court ruled in favor of CLS, holding that the patents were directed to an abstract idea and therefore were invalid because implementing those claims on a computer was insufficient to transform the idea into a patentable invention. The Court applied a two-part test. First, do claims cover an abstract idea? For this case, the Court answered yes, pointing to the concept of intermediated settlement used in Alice's methods. Second, do claims contain an inventive concept sufficient to transform the idea into a patent-eligible application of the idea? On the second question, the Court ruled that the claims did not contain sufficient inventive concept to be patented.

WORDS OF THE COURT: No Evidence of Transformation "Viewed as a whole, [Alice's] method claims simply recite the concept of intermediated settlement as performed by a generic computer. The method claims do not, for example, purport to improve the functioning of the computer itself. Nor do they effect an improvement in any other technology or technical field. Instead, the claims at issue amount to 'nothing significantly more' than an instruction to apply the abstract idea of intermediated settlement using some unspecified, generic computer. Under our precedents, that is not '*enough*' to transform an abstract idea into a patent-eligible invention."

Case Questions

1. What was the specific reason for the Court's determination that Alice's business methods were not patentable?
2. What does the Court mean when it states that Alice's methods "simply recite the concept of intermediated settlement as performed by a generic computer"? Why is that relevant?
3. *Focus on Critical Thinking:* Are there any ways that Alice could modify its methods in order to make them patent-eligible?

LEGAL IMPLICATIONS IN CYBERSPACE

Computer Software and Internet Business Methods

Computer Programs Advances in technology generate new challenges as to what is and what is not patentable material. In the early 1970s, the Supreme Court took the view that computer programs and the machines that process them are nothing more than glorified algorithms and, therefore, not patentable. But in 1981, the Court decided *Diamond v. Diehr*[37] and "clarified" (some would say reversed) its position, ruling that some computer programs *could* be patented. Eventually, the courts developed a test to determine whether algorithm-based computer programming was patentable. This test was designed to investigate whether a computer-related process was applied in some fashion to physical elements or processes. In other words, did the algorithm allow a certain physical transformation to take place? If the computer programs were accompanied by some physical transformation, then they were patentable.

It is interesting to note that Larry Page, one of the founders of Google, originally patented his idea for his PageRank algorithm for Internet search (the first page of which is pictured on the next page).[38] But does this patent satisfy the physical transformation test?

Internet Business Method Patents After the Court opened the door to business method patents in

(continued)

---

[37] 450 U.S. 175 (1981). This case involved a patent application for a computer program that facilitated molding uncured synthetic rubber into cured rubber. According to the patent application, the process differed from the previously employed method because of the use of specific mathematical formulas, which would allow for more accurate measuring of material heating and feeding times. The patent was rejected by the USPTO because the patent examiner did not find that the process met the subject matter requirements of the Patent Act.

[38] U.S. Patent No. US6285999B1. Larry Page's patent is available at https://patents.google.com/patent/US6285999B1/en.

(12) United States Patent
Page

(10) Patent No.: **US 6,285,999 B1**
(45) Date of Patent: **Sep. 4, 2001**

(54) **METHOD FOR NODE RANKING IN A LINKED DATABASE**

(75) Inventor: **Lawrence Page**, Stanford, CA (US)

(73) Assignee: **The Board of Trustees of the Leland Stanford Junior University**, Stanford, CA (US)

(*) Notice: Subject to any disclaimer, the term of this patent is extended or adjusted under 35 U.S.C. 154(b) by 0 days.

(21) Appl. No.: **09/004,827**

(22) Filed: **Jan. 9, 1998**

Related U.S. Application Data

(60) Provisional application No. 60/035,205, filed on Jan. 10, 1997.

(51) Int. Cl.[7] **G06F 17/30**
(52) U.S. Cl. **707/5**; 707/7; 707/501
(58) Field of Search 707/100, 5, 7, 707/513, 1–3, 10, 104, 501; 345/440; 382/226, 229, 230, 231

(56) **References Cited**

U.S. PATENT DOCUMENTS

4,953,106	*	8/1990	Gansner et al.	345/440
5,450,535	*	9/1995	North	395/140
5,748,954		5/1998	Mauldin	395/610
5,752,241	*	5/1998	Cohen	707/3
5,832,494	*	11/1998	Egger et al.	707/102
5,848,407	*	12/1998	Ishikawa et al.	707/2
6,014,678	*	1/2000	Inoue et al.	707/501

OTHER PUBLICATIONS

S. Jeromy Carriere et al, "Web Query: Searching and Visualizing the Web through Connectivity", Computer Networks and ISDN Systems 29 (1997). pp. 1257–1267.*

Wang et al "Prefetching in Worl Wide Web", IEEE 1996, pp. 28–32.*

Ramer et al "Similarity, Probability and Database Organisation: Extended Abstract", 1996, pp. 272.276.*

Craig Boyle "To link or not to link: An empirical comparison of Hypertext linking strategies". ACM 1992, pp. 221–231.*

L. Katz, "A new status index derived from sociometric analysis," 1953, Psychometricka, vol. 18, pp. 39–43.

C.H. Hubbell, "An input–output approach to clique identification sociometry," 1965, pp. 377–399.

Mizruchi et al., "Techniques for disaggregating centrality scores in social networks," 1996, Sociological Methodology, pp. 26–48.

E. Garfield, "Citation analysis as a tool in journal evaluation," 1972, Science, vol. 178, pp. 471–479.

Pinski et al., "Citation influence for journal aggregates of scientific publications: Theory, with application to the literature of physics," 1976, Inf. Proc. And Management, vol. 12, pp. 297–312.

N. Geller, "On the citation influence methodology of Pinski and Narin," 1978, Inf. Proc. And Management, vol. 14, pp. 93–95.

P. Doreian, "Measuring the relative standing of disciplinary journals," 1988, Inf. Proc. And Management, vol. 24, pp. 45–56.

(List continued on next page.)

Primary Examiner—Thomas Black
Assistant Examiner—Uyen Le
(74) Attorney, Agent, or Firm—Harrity & Snyder L.L.P.

(57) **ABSTRACT**

A method assigns importance ranks to nodes in a linked database, such as any database of documents containing citations, the world wide web or any other hypermedia database. The rank assigned to a document is calculated from the ranks of documents citing it. In addition, the rank of a document is calculated from a constant representing the probability that a browser through the database will randomly jump to the document. The method is particularly useful in enhancing the performance of search engine results for hypermedia databases, such as the world wide web, whose documents have a large variation in quality.

29 Claims, 3 Drawing Sheets

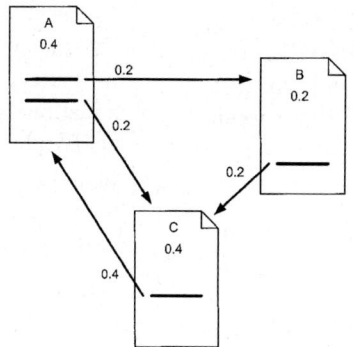

Patent for Larry Page's PageRank algorithm.
Source: United States Patent and Trademark Office

(continued)

the 1998 *State Street case* (discussed earlier), many Internet-based businesses applied for patents. One of the most famous Internet business method patents was granted to Amazon for its "One-Click" ordering system that stores a customer's billing and shipping information so that such information does not have to be reentered on subsequent visits to the site.

In a highly publicized case during the technology boom of the late 1990s, Amazon (which was still a relative newcomer in the bookselling business at the time) sued mega-bookseller Barnes & Noble over Barnes & Noble's use of an "Express Lane" option on its website that allowed consumers to "buy it now with just 1 click." Barnes & Noble's defense was that Amazon's patent should not have been issued in the first place because the invention was too obvious.

After a preliminary defeat in the federal courts for Amazon,[39] the parties settled their dispute out of court. Although Amazon lost on a procedural issue, it did *not* lose the patent on the basis of nonobviousness. What if, however, the case had not settled out of court? Given the *Alice* case (discussed earlier), how would the *Amazon* case come out if it were decided today?

INFRINGEMENT, NOTICE, AND REMEDIES

LO 24-8

Identify the remedies for acts of patent infringement.

Infringement is defined in the Patent Act as "whoever without authority makes, uses or sells any patented invention, within the United States during the term of the patent therefore, infringes the patent."[40] In addition, anyone who "actively induces infringement" of a patent is also considered an infringer as well.[41]

Infringement can occur in one of two ways: as *literal infringement* or through *equivalence*.

BUSINESS ETHICS PERSPECTIVE

Patent Trolls

A *patent troll* refers to a party who owns a patent (typically by acquiring it from the inventor for less than market value) for the sole purpose of collecting licensing fees. Patent trolls use their patent rights to search for potential infringers and assert their patents even though they are not actually using the patented invention. Once a potential infringer is identified, patent trolls demand licensing fees and threaten costly litigation. Patent trolls are not interested in producing or selling any goods. Rather, their sole objective is to maximize their profits by asserting their patent rights.

Discussion Questions

1. Critics of patent trolls argue that they stifle innovation and promote litigation. Do you agree? Why or why not?

2. Are patent trolls an example of conduct that is legal but not necessarily ethical? Is there any difference?

3. Should Congress step in to prevent patent trolls? If Congress amended the Patent Act to require that patent holders actually use the invention before they can assert their rights, would that step effectively eliminate patent trolls?

4. Are there any arguments that patent trolls actually spur innovation? If an inventor holds a patent but can't afford to halt infringement through litigation, isn't selling the rights to a patent troll a viable alternative?

5. Would you ever sell your rights to a patent troll? Would you ever buy rights and become a patent troll? Why or why not?

---

[39]*Amazon.com, Inc. v. Barnesandnoble.com, Inc.*, 239 F.3d 1343 (Fed. Cir. 2001).

[40]35 U.S.C. § 271.

[41]35 U.S.C. § 271(b).

Literal Infringement

The courts have developed three rules for determining whether **literal patent infringement** has occurred. The **rule of exactness** applies when the infringer makes, uses, or sells an invention that is exactly the same as the patent holder's claims in the patent application, thus infringing on the patent.

An infringement also occurs if the infringing device does *more* than is described in the patent application of the protected invention. This second type of literal infringement is known as the **rule of addition**. Under the **rule of omission**, by contrast, when the alleged infringing invention lacks an essential element of the patent holder's claims in the patent application, infringement has *not* occurred.

Equivalence

The rule of omission is subject to abuse because individuals may avoid infringement liability by omitting an element of the patented device and substituting another element that is substantially similar, but not exactly the same, to the one described in the patent. To prevent this abuse, the U.S. Supreme Court developed a doctrine that allows courts to find infringement if the invention performs *substantially the same function* in substantially the same way to achieve the same result. Under this doctrine, known as the **doctrine of equivalence**, courts must evaluate whether any of the key elements of a patent claim have been interchanged with known equivalents.

Notice and Enforcement

The Patent Act sets forth appropriate measures that individuals and business firms who own patents must take to properly inform users that an article is patented. This notice is often done by placing the word *patent* or the abbreviation *pat.* or the patent number on the specific article. If no marking is identifiable, then the patentee may not collect damages from infringers unless they have been properly warned and nonetheless continue to infringe.

Remedies

Patent infringers are liable for the following damages:

- *Actual damages:* Examples include profits from lost sales and royalties for any sale made by the infringer.
- *Prejudgment interest:* It is not uncommon for years to pass before an infringer is spotted; thus, revenue from possible sales may have been withheld from the patentee for a long period of time.
- *Attorney fees:* The prevailing party may receive reasonable attorney fees when the infringer has acted in bad faith (i.e., has received notice that the invention is patented and yet continues his infringing conduct).

CONCEPT SUMMARY *Patents*

- A patent is a government-sanctioned monopoly right that confers on an inventor the exclusive rights over an invention for a limited period of time.
- In order to be patented, the invention or method must be novel and nonobvious and must be of proper subject matter (laws of nature and natural phenomena are not protected under patent laws).

(continued)

- Some business methods are patentable so long as they accomplish something practically useful in a novel and nonobvious way.
- Infringement may occur either through literal means or through equivalence.

We began this chapter noting the importance of intellectual property to business firms and by asking if you have ever created any intellectual property. Check out Table 24.2 summarizing the main forms of intellectual property. Based on this table and your review of the chapter, what kinds of intellectual property have you created?

TABLE 24.2 Intellectual Property Protections

Type	Coverage	Source of Law	Example	Duration
Trade secrets	Secret processes, formulas, methods, procedures, and lists that provide the owner with economic advantage.	State statutes based on Uniform Trade Secret Act and/or state common law	Customer lists with contact information, buying patterns, and credit histories	Life of the owner (entity or individual)
Trademarks, service marks, trade dress	Words, symbols, or phrases that identify a particular seller's product or service and distinguish it from other products and services. Trade dress extends trademark protection to the shape or color scheme of a product.	Federal statute (Lanham Act) and some state and federal common law	Google (trademark); Hilton Hotels (service mark); Hershey chocolate bar's shape (trade dress)	Unlimited so long as the owner actively protects ("polices") the use of the mark
Copyrights	Authors and originators of literary or artistic production.	Federal statute (Copyright Act of 1976, as amended) and state and federal common law	Rights of a recording artist and writer of a song	*Author:* 70 years from death of the author *Work for hire:* 120 years from date of creation or 95 years from publication
Patents	Inventors, for exclusive rights to make, use, license, or sell an invention.	Federal statute (Patent Act)	Rights to a newly discovered pharmaceutical product	20 years from date of filing, except for design patents (14 years)

KEY TERMS

Trade Secret p. 767 A formula, pattern, compilation, program, device, method, technique, or process that meets the following criteria: Derives *independent economic value*, actual or potential, from not being generally known to and not being readily ascertainable by proper means by other persons who can obtain economic value from its disclosure or use; and is the subject of efforts that are reasonable under the circumstances to maintain its secrecy. Economic value must be identified by the owner, and secrecy must be kept.

Misappropriation p. 767 (1) The acquisition of a trade secret of another by a person who knows or has reason to know that the trade secret was acquired by improper means or (2) the disclosure of a trade secret to another without express or implied consent.

Economic Espionage Act p. 768 A federal statute passed in 1996 that provides criminal penalties for domestic and foreign theft of trade secrets.

Trademark p. 770   A nonfunctional, distinctive word, name, shape, symbol, phrase, or combination of words and symbols that helps consumers to distinguish one product from another.

Service mark p. 770   A word, symbol, or phrase used to identify a particular seller's services and distinguish them from other services.

Trade dress p. 770   A product's distinctive design, packaging, color, or other characteristic that makes it unique from other products or goods.

Secondary meaning p. 772   A requirement for a descriptive trademark to gain protection; acquired when the consuming public primarily associates the mark with a particular product or service rather than with the ordinary meaning of the term.

Bad faith p. 775   A dishonesty of belief or purpose; in the legal context, a concept in which a malicious motive on the part of the defendant in a lawsuit is necessary in order for the plaintiff to recover. Under the Anticybersquatting Consumer Protection Act, the court looks to nine factors in making a determination of bad-faith intent.

Federal Trademark Dilution Act p. 782   A federal law enacted in 1995 and amended in 2006 that permits mark holders to recover damages and prevent others from diluting distinctive trademarks.

Copyright p. 783   A copyright protects the rights of creators of original works for a defined period of time during which the holder has the exclusive rights to copy, distribute, display, or perform the work.

Originality p. 784   For copyright protection, the requirement that the author must use his own creative capabilities to create the work or medium.

Creativity p. 784   For copyright protection of a compilation, the requirement that there must be some creative element used that makes the compilation an original work.

Durable medium p. 784   For copyright protection, the requirement that the work must be in a tangible form, such as writing, digital, video, and so forth.

Direct infringement p. 785   A theory of copyright infringement under which the copyright owner proves that she has legal ownership of the work in question and that the infringer copied the work in a substantially similar manner without permission.

Indirect infringement p. 786   A theory of copyright infringement under which a third-party facilitator is liable for damages when the facilitator has knowledge of the infringement and/or contributes to the infringement in some material way. Also called *contributory infringement*.

Vicarious infringement p. 786   A theory of copyright infringement that applies when there has been a direct infringement and a third-party facilitator is in a position to control that infringement and benefits financially from it.

No Electronic Theft (NET) Act p. 786   A federal law enacted in 1997 that provides for criminal liability for anyone who willfully infringes on a copyright.

Fair use p. 787   A defense against copyright infringement under which the court examines the purpose and nature of the use, the nature of the work, the amount used, and the market effect of the use to determine whether the use is permitted.

Per se p. 787   (Latin for "of, in, or by itself") A standard used by courts when no additional facts are needed to prove a point.

Patent p. 793   A statutorily created monopoly right that confers on an inventor the *exclusive right* to make, use, license, and sell her invention for a limited period of time.

Novelty standard p. 795   A standard requiring that an invention or process must be unique and original to be patented and that the patent applicant must show that no other identical invention or process exists.

Nonobviousness standard p. 796   A standard requiring that to be patented, an invention must be something more than that which would be obvious, in light of publicly available knowledge, to one who is skilled in the relevant field.

Patentable subject matter standard p. 796   A standard that bars laws of nature, natural phenomena, and abstract ideas from being patentable subject matter.

Literal patent infringement p. 801   Patent infringement in which the invention or process violates either the rule of exactness or the rule of addition.

Rule of exactness p. 801   The principle that literal patent infringement has occurred when the infringer makes, uses, or sells an invention that is exactly the same as the patent holder's claims in the patent application.

Rule of addition p. 801   The principle that literal patent infringement has occurred when the infringing device does more than is described in the patent application of the protected invention.

Rule of omission p. 801   The principle that infringement has not occurred when the alleged patent-infringing invention lacks an essential element of the patent holder's claims in the patent application.

Doctrine of equivalence p. 801   A doctrine that allows courts to find patent infringement when an invention, compared with a patented device, performs substantially the same function in substantially the same way to achieve the same result.

CHAPTER REVIEW QUESTIONS

1. **Which of the following elements is/are necessary to protect a trade secret?**
   a. Independent economic value
   b. Efforts to maintain secrecy
   c. Fixed medium
   d. a and b

2. **Which of the following is an example of the arbitrary or fanciful trademark?**
   a. Uber
   b. Netflix
   c. Smartphone
   d. Hilton Hotels

3. **A start-up venture begins to market a new online service called "Foodbook" that targets consumers looking for a particular dish at a restaurant. If Facebook sues the venture under trademark laws, what will be its strongest theory of the case?**
   a. Direct infringement
   b. Blurring
   c. Tarnishment
   d. Consumer confusion

4. **One year after Fitzgerald completes his manuscript and begins to submit his novel to publishers, he notices an exact copy of the novel for sale on Amazon. What step must Fitzgerald complete prior to enforcing his copyright?**
   a. Send a cease and desist letter.
   b. Register with the Copyright Office.
   c. Obtain authorization from a court.
   d. None of the above.

5. **Which of the following is *not* required in order for an invention to receive a patent?**
   a. Novelty
   b. Nonobvious
   c. Used in commerce
   d. Proper subject matter

Answers and explanations are provided at the end of this chapter.

THEORY TO PRACTICE

WidgetCo is a manufacturer and wholesaler of a line of widgets with annual revenue of $50 million. Maurice, a midlevel manager at WidgetCo, supervises a work team responsible for assessing the quality of the widgets before they are shipped to various retailers around the United States. Maurice has developed a highly effective quality assurance process, and he has produced a training manual, a video for new employees, and a specific checklist of procedures for employees to follow to ensure that any defective or substandard widgets are detected and repaired prior to shipping.

1. Who owns the legal rights to Maurice's ideas: WidgetCo or Maurice?
2. Which forms of intellectual property protections are available to Maurice or to WidgetCo to protect the quality assurance process and materials developed by Maurice?
3. What are the major advantages and disadvantages of each protection?
4. Compare the facts of the hypothetical in this Theory to Practice with trade secret law. Could the quality assurance process be considered a trade secret under these standards?
5. What steps should the company take to achieve its objective of having this process protected under trade secret law?
6. Could WidgetCo obtain copyright protection for its manual, training video, and checklist under the Copyright Act? Or are its manuals simply a compilation of facts known in the industry and thus not protectable?

LEGAL STRATEGY 101

Mike Tyson's Tattoo

Can you copyright a tattoo? The tattoo artist who gave boxer Mike Tyson his distinctive facial tattoo, S. Victor Whitmill, thinks so. The movie studio Warner Bros., not so much.

In April 2011, the tattoo artist sued Warner Bros. for copyright infringement. Specifically, the complaint alleges that "Warner Bros. Entertainment, Inc.—without attempting to contact Whitmill, obtain his permission, or credit his creation—has copied Whitmill's Original Tattoo and placed it on the face of another actor."[42] (In the film *The Hangover Part II,* Stu wakes up with a copy of Mike Tyson's tattoo after a night of revelry in Bangkok.) In his lawsuit, the tattoo artist attached his copyright registration for the Mike Tyson Tattoo as well as Tyson's signed release granting him the legal rights in the work.

Moreover, Whitmill not only demanded substantial compensation for the infringement of his tattoo design; he also asked a judge to issue an *injunction* to stop the release of the highly anticipated comedy sequel. The movie was scheduled to be released over the Memorial Day weekend, one of the biggest box office weekends for the movie industry.

If you were the head of the movie studio, what would you do? Take your chances in court or settle out of court with the tattoo artist? On the one hand, Warner Bros. could roll the litigation dice and argue to the judge that the copyright isn't valid; or that the studio changed the design just enough to escape infringement; or that the use of the tattoo in the film constitutes a "transformative" use or that it's a parody.

But on the other hand, the tattoo artist could argue that tattoos are original and creative works that are deserving of copyright protection, regardless whether they are painted on canvases or on the faces of former heavyweight champions. Furthermore, the tattoo on the Stu character in *The Hangover Part II* appears to be a direct comedic reference to Mike Tyson, who appeared extensively in the first film, so this fact might make it difficult for the movie studio to argue that the designs are merely coincidentally similar.

In June 2011, Warner Bros. decided to settle the lawsuit with Whitmill, the tattoo artist, though the terms of the out-of-court settlement were not disclosed. In January 2013, the *University of Illinois Law Review* published a 40-page legal article addressing this case and discussing in detail the implications of applying copyright law to tattoos.[43]

> Everyone has a plan until they get punched in the face
> —Mike Tyson

Mike Tyson. Jemal Countess/WireImage/Getty Images

CRITICAL THINKING QUESTIONS

Does a tattoo qualify for copyright protection? In the absence of an agreement specifying who the owner is, who should own the legal rights to a tattoo: the tattoo artist or the person who paid for the tattoo? Draft a one-page document that could be used as a starting point for settlement negotiations between Warner Bros. and Whitmill.

---

[42]Matthew Belloni, "Mike Tyson Tattooo Artist Sues Warner Bros. to Stop Release of Hangover 2," The Hollywood Reporter (Apr. 29, 2011).

[43]David Cummings, *Creative Expression and the Human Canvas: An Examination of Tattoos as a Creative Art Form,* 2013 U. Ill. L. Rev. 279 (Jan. 2013).

MANAGER'S CHALLENGE

One major consideration in protecting a trade secret is the efforts by the company to keep the secret confidential. Develop a written policy for WidgetCo (in this chapter's Theory to Practice problem) to help ensure that its trade secrets and other materials will be protected and kept confidential under the Uniform Trade Secrets Act. What considerations should management take into account when developing a policy on trade secrets? Be sure to think about primary stakeholders (such as employees who may depart with the trade secrets) and secondary stakeholders (such as third-party visitors or outside auditors that may be privy to the processes and materials). Note that this exercise is not intended to generate a formal legal document. Rather, the firm's policy should be thought of as a draft statement of the firm's internal controls over its trade secrets, processes, and materials.

See Connect for Manager's Challenge sample answers.

CASE SUMMARY 24.1 Bennett v. Shidler, 338 F.3d 1125 (10th Cir. 2003)

TRADE SECRET

Harvey Bennett, Inc., is a company that developed a swimming technique that is designed to be taught to infants. The company developed a course for teaching this technique, called *swim-float-swim,* and generates revenue by training and certifying swim instructors, who then teach the technique to the public at large for a fee. The instructors are trained extensively on the nearly 2,000 procedures necessary to accomplish the technique. All instructors must sign a nondisclosure form and an agreement not to compete. When several of the instructors resigned and formed a venture called Aquatic Survival, Bennett filed suit claiming, among other allegations, misappropriation of the swim-float-swim system.

CASE QUESTIONS

1. Does the swim-float-swim technique qualify as a trade secret?
2. What factors would the court use to assess whether the technique is a trade secret? Discuss.

CASE SUMMARY 24.2 *In re* Reed Elsevier Props., 482 F.3d 1376 (Fed. Cir. 2007)

TRADEMARKS/SERVICE MARKS

Reed Elsevier operates a website that allows users to identify an attorney by using a variety of criteria, including geographic location, practice expertise, and so forth. Its website www.lawyers.com was first used in commerce by Reed Elsevier in 1998. A few years later, Reed Elsevier applied to have lawyers.com registered as a service mark.

CASE QUESTIONS

1. Is the mark too generic for protection?
2. If the court determines the mark is primarily descriptive, what further obstacle must Reed Elsevier overcome in order to obtain protection for the mark?

CASE SUMMARY 24.3 KSR International v. Teleflex, 550 U.S. 398 (2007)

PATENTS

KSR designs and manufactures auto parts and sells them to auto manufacturers (not consumers). KSR developed a pedal device for Ford vehicles and also received a patent on the pedal device. KSR also sold products to General Motors (GM), and, in order to make the pedal device compatible for GM cars, KSR added an electronic throttle control to the pedal device. Teleflex claimed to have a patent for the pedal device that could be connected to such a throttle and, therefore, sued KSR for patent infringement. KSR defended on the basis that the device produced for GM was simply a combination of two existing products and was not patentable.

CASE QUESTIONS

1. What do you think Teleflex's specific theory of infringement was?
2. Which element of patentability does KSR claim Teleflex is missing in the combined device?

CASE SUMMARY 24.4 Darden v. Peters, 488 F.3d 277 (4th Cir. 2007)

COPYRIGHT

Darden filed an application with the Copyright Office seeking to register his website, which he titled APPRAISERSdotCOM. He described his website as a derivative work based on "U.S. Census black and white outline maps" and "clip art." Darden's application also identified "graphics, text, colors, and arrangement" as the material that he added to the preexisting work and for which he claimed copyright protection. Additionally, Darden filed a separate application for registration of the work "Maps for APPRAISERSdotCOM." Darden described his "maps" work as a derivative work that, similar to the APPRAISERSdotCOM work, was based on preexisting U.S. Census black-and-white outline maps.

CASE QUESTIONS

1. Determine whether Darden's compilation is protectable using the *Feist* doctrine.
2. Does Darden's work contain the necessary elements for copyright protection? Discuss.

CASE SUMMARY 24.5 Rentmeester v. Nike, 883 F.3d 1111 (9th Cir. 2018), *cert. denied*, 139 S. Ct. 1375 (2019)

COPYRIGHT

Jacobus Rentmeester is a professional photographer whose iconic photo of basketball star Michael Jordan soaring in the air toward an outdoor basketball hoop, with his left arm extended and the sun setting in the background, first appeared in *LIFE* magazine in 1984. Many years later, Rentmeester alleged that Nike stole key aspects of his famous photo when it created its famous "Jumpman" logo. (The original Nike photo on which the Jumpman logo is based was taken from a similar angle and shows Michael Jordan leaping to dunk a basketball with the Chicago skyline in the background.) Nike has sold tens of billions of dollars in sneakers and other "Air Jordan" merchandise with the Jumpman logo.

CASE QUESTIONS

1. What legal standard will the courts use to determine whether Nike engaged in copyright infringement?
2. Assume Rentmeester had trademarked his photo and had then brought a trademark infringement action against Nike. Would his chances of success against Nike be higher or lower? Discuss.

CASE SUMMARY 24.6 ConnectU v. Zuckerberg, 522 F.3d 82 (1st Cir. 2008)

TRADE SECRET

When they were still in college, Tyler and Cameron Winklevoss (the Winklevoss twins), along with their business partner and fellow student Divya Narendra, came up with an idea for a new and exclusive social networking website for Harvard students. Lacking the computer programming skills necessary to bring their idea to fruition, the Winklevoss twins and Narendra hired college sophomore Mark Zuckerberg to help them complete their proposed social network's "source code." The rest is history, as they say. The Winklevoss twins and Narendra now allege that Zuckerberg misappropriated their trade secrets when he stole their idea and source code in order to launch a competing social networking website behind their backs called "The Facebook."

CASE QUESTIONS

1. What evidence will the Winklevoss twins and Divya Narendra need to produce in order to enforce their trade secrets?
2. Although this case was ultimately settled out of court, which side would have been most likely to win on the merits of the trade secret claim had this case gone to a jury?

✓ Self-Check ANSWERS Trade Secrets

1. This type of customer data is protectable as a trade secret because of its potential value to a competitor.
2. The system is probably not protectable unless it is something highly unique. But the basis of scheduling medical appointments is not typically protectable.
3. Formulas are protectable.
4. Unless the process is highly unique, it is not protectable because it is based on a public source.
5. Software source coding is protectable.

Fair Use

1. Covered by fair use. Limited amount used, noncommercial use, and minimal market effect support the fair use defense.
2. Not covered by fair use. Market effect and commercial nature of the use would exclude it from the fair use defense.
3. Probably not fair use. The market effect would determine this question, but the commercial nature and the fact that it is the entire DVD would weigh against fair use as a defense.
4. Not fair use. Commercial nature, profit motive, amount and substantiality used, and market effect would bar any use of the fair use defense in this case.

CHAPTER REVIEW QUESTIONS: Answers and Explanations

1. **d.** The Uniform Trade Secrets Act defines a trade secret as information that is to be kept secret because of its particular value. Therefore, in order to protect a trade secret, it must have independent economic value and involve efforts to keep the information secret. Answer (c) is incorrect because fixed medium is only relevant in a copyright.

2. **a.** Uber has no direct connection to the product and, therefore, it is categorized as arbitrary or fanciful. Answer choice (b) is incorrect because it suggests the underlying product. Answer choice (c) is incorrect because it is generic. Answer choice (d) is incorrect because it is directly connected with the underlying service.

3. **b.** Because there is little chance for consumer confusion, Facebook's best theory would be blurring because the Foodbook venture is deluding the distinctive quality of the mark through identification with goods that are not alike. Answer choice (a) is wrong because there is no direct infringement indicated. Answer choice (c) is wrong because there was no harm to the reputation of the famous mark. Answer choice (d) is wrong because consumer confusion is an element of direct infringement, not a theory.

4. **b.** Although Fitzgerald has the copyright as soon as he puts his work in a fixed medium, registration with the copyright office is a prerequisite to filing suit. The remaining answers are incorrect because they are nonsensical.

5. **c.** There is no requirement that the invention must be used in commerce in order for it to receive a patent. The remaining answers are incorrect because they are all requirements under the Patent Act.

CHAPTER 25
International Law and Global Commerce

©philsajonesen/Getty Images

Learning Objectives

After studying this chapter, students who have mastered the material will be able to:

25-1 Distinguish between international public law and international private law.

25-2 Give examples of and explain the various sources of international law.

25-3 Explain the role of the various international courts.

25-4 List the different categories of national legal systems used in the world and give an example of a country in each category.

25-5 Apply the standards of the Convention on the Recognition and Enforcement of Foreign Arbitral Awards.

25-6 Explain the various methods of alternate dispute resolution in an international context.

25-7 Articulate several specific laws that regulate international commercial law and understand when each law applies.

25-8 Identify the methods used to enforce the rights of intellectual property holders in foreign countries.

Rapid developments in technology, improvements in export logistics, and the creation of additional transportation lines have all been catalysts spurring the growth of our modern global economy. Although large multinational firms have had international business relationships and systems for decades, the new global marketplace has expanded dramatically to include midsize and smaller firms that see international markets as an accessible vehicle for market share growth. Of course, while the potential return may be significant, the risks, especially legal risks, increase substantially in an international business transaction. A working knowledge of international law helps business owners and managers with global interests to reduce risk and increase profits. In this chapter, we discuss

- The definition and sources of international law.
- International dispute resolution methods.
- Commercial and intellectual property regulation in an international context.

DEFINITION, SOURCES, AND SYSTEMS OF INTERNATIONAL LAW

International law has traditionally been defined in very broad terms; it is not limited simply to rules that are applied to settle disputes in court. Rather, international law is influenced by a combination of law, religious tenets, and diplomatic relations between nations. This broad definition makes enforcement of international laws challenging, and adherence to international law is sometimes based on expectations of reciprocal behavior rather than legal sanctions.

Most legal sources define modern international law as a body of *rules* and *principles* of action binding on countries, international organizations, and individuals in their relations with one another.[1]

LO 25-1
Distinguish between international public law and international private law.

Public Law versus Private Law

One important distinction necessary to an understanding of international law is that it may be categorized as either **public international law**, which primarily addresses relations between individual countries and international organizations, and **private international law**, which focuses on the regulation of private individuals and business entities.

SOURCES OF INTERNATIONAL LAW

In one sense, the primary source of international law is the body of law in each individual country. However, international law can also provide individual countries with some degree of harmonized standards that increase reliability and encourage fairness, due process, and barrier-free trade among nations. Therefore, treaties, customs, and judicial decisions are also considered to be sources of international law.

LO 25-2
Give examples of and explain the various sources of international law.

Treaties A treaty is any agreement between two or more nations to cooperate in a certain manner. Treaties may be related to defense, trade, extradition, and other matters between countries. Although treaties have been in use since before the Roman Empire, most existing modern-day treaties were created after World War II. More recently, the **Vienna Convention on the Law of Treaties**, effective in 1980, has become one of the standards used by courts and other tribunals when interpreting treaty law.[2]

Customs Along with treaty law, customary international law is a primary source of law affecting individuals and businesses engaged in international transactions. Customary law follows the basic principle of international law that individual conduct is permitted unless expressly forbidden. Therefore, prohibitions as well as affirmative practices must be proved by the state relying on them.

Judicial Decisions Most treaties and national laws recognize both an international tribunal, such as the International Court of Justice (discussed later), and a ruling by a national court applying international law principles. One important concept related to judicial decisions as a source of international law is *comity*. **Comity** is the general notion that nations will defer to and give effect to the laws and court decisions of other nations. However, comity is not a legal doctrine that requires courts to

> **KEY POINT**
>
> The three primary sources of international law are treaties, customs, and judicial decisions.

---

[1] Restatement (Third) of the Foreign Relations Law of the United States § 102.

[2] The United States has not yet ratified the Vienna Convention, but the U.S. government has recognized it as an authoritative source to guide tribunals in matters related to treaty law.

accept the judgments of foreign courts. Rather, it is rooted in the idea that reciprocal treatment is a necessary element of international relations.

One court summarized the concept succinctly:

> [According to our federal law,] [n]o legal judgment has any effect, of its own force, beyond the limits of the sovereignty from which its authority is derived. However, the United States Constitution and implementing legislation require that full faith and credit be given to judgments of sister states, territories, and possessions of the United States. The extent to which the United States, or any state, honors the judicial decrees of foreign nations is a matter of choice, governed by "the comity of nations." Comity "is neither a matter of absolute obligation, on the one hand, nor of mere courtesy and good will, upon the other."
>
> *Yahoo! v. La Ligue Contre Le Racisme, 169 F. Supp. 2d 1181 (N.D. Cal. 2001).*

INTERNATIONAL ORGANIZATIONS

International organizations play a unique role in the development of international law. These organizations are typically structured through use of multinational representation and are created and regulated by treaty. Perhaps the most famous organization is the **United Nations (U.N.)**, which was created after World War II to facilitate common international concerns on defense, trade, the protection of human rights, and other matters. From a business perspective, the U.N. has made significant achievements in harmonizing laws related to the sale of goods between businesses in different countries and other international business transactions. The U.N. Commission on International Trade Law developed the **U.N. Convention on Contracts for the International Sale of Goods (CISG)**, which is used to set rules for certain business transactions. The CISG is discussed in more detail later in this chapter.

Other important international organizations include

- The World Trade Organization (WTO), which promotes and has certain authority over disputes involving trade barriers.
- The International Monetary Fund (IMF), which is intended to promote stability of world currencies and provide temporary assistance for countries to help prevent the collapse of their economies.
- The Organization for Economic Cooperation and Development (OECD), which coordinates aid to developing countries and takes steps toward eliminating bribery and other corruption from developing economies.

INTERNATIONAL COURTS

LO 25-3

Explain the role of the various international courts.

International courts play a role in the development and interpretation of international law, but their power to enforce a ruling on sovereign nations can be tenuous and their jurisdiction may be limited.

The **International Court of Justice** (also known as the *World Court*) is the judicial branch of the United Nations. It is based in the Netherlands and its main functions are to settle legal disputes submitted to it by member states and give advisory opinions on legal questions submitted to it by duly authorized international organs, agencies, and the U.N. General Assembly. This court should not be confused with the International Criminal Court, which also potentially has global jurisdiction. Established in 1945 by the U.N. Charter, the World Court began work in 1946 as the successor to the Permanent Court of International Justice. The Statute of the International Court of Justice, similar to that of its predecessor, is the main constitutional document constituting and regulating the Court.

The World Court, seen here in session in The Hague, Netherlands, is one of the principal international courts. PETER DEJONG/AP Images

The Court's workload is characterized by a wide range of judicial activity. The Court has dealt with relatively few cases in its history, but there has clearly been an increased willingness to use the Court since the 1980s, especially among developing countries. The United States withdrew from compulsory jurisdiction in 1986, and so it accepts the court's jurisdiction only on a case-by-case basis. The U.N. Charter authorizes the U.N. Security Council to enforce rulings, but such enforcement is subject to the veto power of the five permanent members of the Security Council.

The **European Court of Justice** sits in Luxembourg and is the final arbiter of the codes governing European Union (EU) member countries. The court is composed of judges from each EU member country and is structured in a civil law tradition, so most of its procedures and decisions are based on treaties governing EU countries regarding commercial regulations, protections, and guarantees. National courts of EU members are obliged by treaty to honor the decisions of the court and are obligated to apply EU laws (known as *community laws*).

Sovereign Immunity

One of the oldest doctrines of international law is that of **sovereign immunity**. In general, this doctrine holds that, with some exceptions, nations are exempt from jurisdiction by other nations' courts. The **Foreign Sovereign Immunities Act (FSIA)** is a federal statute that incorporates this concept by explicitly prohibiting U.S. courts from rendering judicial actions against foreign nations or their government officials unless (1) the foreign nation has waived its immunity either explicitly or by implication, (2) the foreign nation is engaged in some commercial enterprise on U.S. soil, or (3) the foreign nation's actions have a direct effect on U.S. interests.

One implication of the FSIA for U.S. businesses occurs in the context of companies that provide services to foreign governments. To what extent are they protected by federal law, such as employment discrimination protection, when they are carrying out their contractual obligations to the foreign government? A federal appeals court considers that question in Case 25.1.

CASE 25.1 Butters v. Vance International, Inc., 225 F.3d 462 (4th Cir. 2000)

FACT SUMMARY Vance International is a U.S. company that provides security services to corporations and foreign sovereigns, including the Kingdom of Saudi Arabia. Vance was hired to augment the security provided to a princess of the Saudi royal family while the princess underwent medical treatments in California. The Saudi military was responsible for protection, and Saudi military officers supervised all security at the site.

Butters, a woman employed by Vance as a security officer, was assigned to the Saudi detail, and, on several occasions, Butters temporarily worked as an acting supervisor in a security command post. Vance managers recommended to the Saudis that Butters be promoted to serving a full rotation in the command post, but the Saudi authorities rejected that recommendation. Their rejection was based on the Saudi military supervisor's contention that the appointment of a woman for that post was unacceptable under Islamic law and that Saudis would consider it inappropriate for their officers to spend long periods of time in a command post with a woman present.

Butters brought suit against Vance for gender discrimination in the loss of the promotion, and Vance asserted immunity under the Federal Sovereign Immunities Act because it was carrying out orders of the Saudi government. Butters argued that Vance fell under one of the exceptions to the FSIA because the company was engaged in a commercial activity.

SYNOPSIS OF DECISION AND OPINION The Fourth Circuit Court of Appeals ruled in favor of Vance. The court reasoned that Vance was entitled to immunity from suit under the Foreign Sovereign Immunities Act because Vance's client, the Kingdom of Saudi Arabia, was responsible for Butters not being promoted. The court held that the action here was not exempt from the FSIA as "commercial activities" because the relevant act was quintessentially an act peculiar to sovereigns and that Vance was entitled to derivative immunity under the FSIA because it was following Saudi Arabia's orders not to promote Butters.

WORDS OF THE COURT: Impact of Sovereign Immunity "Any type of governmental immunity reflects a trade-off between the possibility that an official's wrongdoing will remain unpunished and the risk that government functions will be impaired. ('The resolution of immunity questions inherently requires a balance between the evils inevitable in any available alternative.') FSIA immunity presupposes a tolerance for the sovereign decisions of other countries that may reflect legal norms and cultural values quite different from our own. Here Saudi Arabia made a decision to protect a member of its royal family in a manner consistent with Islamic law and custom. The Act requires not that we approve of the diverse cultural or political motivations that may underlie another sovereign's acts, but that we respect them."

Case Questions

1. What was the theory that Butters advanced as to why the lawsuit fell into an FSIA exception?
2. How far does the FSIA immunity go? If one of Vance's employees was ordered by Saudi officials to physically detain Butters and she was injured, would Vance still be protected by the FSIA against any liability resulting from Butters's injury?
3. *Focus on Critical Thinking:* When the court states that the "FSIA immunity presupposes a tolerance for the sovereign decisions of other countries that may reflect legal norms and cultural values quite different from our own," what legal norms and cultural values is it referring to?

LEGAL SYSTEMS OF NATIONS

Legal systems of the world may be thought of as falling into one of the following broad categories: civil law, common law, religious-based law (such as Sharia law or Talmudic law), and mixed law systems (which refers not to a single system but to a combination of systems).

Civil Law Systems

Countries using **civil law systems** have drawn their body of law largely from the Roman law heritage, which uses written law as the highest source, and have opted for a systematic codification of their general law. They rely heavily on written codes to define their laws and do not favor the notion of courts filling in any gaps in the statutes. Rather, these courts apply the code law to individual cases without the mandate of following cases that have been decided by previous courts considering the same questions. Most European, Latin American, African, and Asian countries use civil law systems.

Common Law Systems

The common law system takes on a variety of cultural and legal forms throughout the world. Although there are differences from country to country, this category generally includes countries whose law, for the most part, is technically based on English common law concepts and legal organizational methods that strongly favor the use of case law, as opposed to legislation/statutes, as the ordinary means of expressions of general law. If there is no case law to guide the court, common law systems allow courts to fill in the gaps not covered by statutes and create new law consistent with public policy. Common law jurisdictions adhere to the concept of judicial review, whereby a court may strike down a law passed by the legislature if the law is found to violate some other overriding principle of law (such as the U.S. Constitution). As you may imagine, the common law tradition is used by countries that were once colonies or protectorates of Great Britain, including the United States, Canada, and Australia.

Religious-Based Legal Systems

Religious-based legal systems are legal doctrines and guidelines directly based on certain religious tenets. For example, the Sharia, derived from the Qur'an (the sacred text of Islam), regulates many aspects of life for Muslims, including crime, politics, business transactions, family, sexuality, and hygiene. The Sharia is the centerpiece of Islamic law, which is now the most widely used religious-based legal system. Islamic law is interpreted by religious leaders and is carried out by a government body.

Mixed Legal Systems

Mixed legal systems (also known as *hybrid* or *composite legal systems*) include not only political entities in which two or more systems apply cumulatively or interactively but also entities in which there is a combination of systems as a result of more or less clearly defined fields of application. For example, Saudi Arabia uses an Islamic-based set of laws to regulate the personal conduct of its citizens and visitors and a civil law system to regulate business transactions and other areas of the law.

INTERNATIONAL DISPUTE RESOLUTION

The parties to an international dispute are typically corporations or government entities, rather than private individuals, while domestic dispute resolution can involve relatively small claims by individuals. Many countries, recognizing that different considerations

---

LO 25-4

List the different categories of national legal systems used in the world and give an example of a country in each category.

LO 25-5

Apply the standards of the Convention on the Recognition and Enforcement of Foreign Arbitral Awards.

LO 25-6

Explain the various methods of alternate dispute resolution in an international context.

apply to international disputes, have provided for a separate legal regime to govern international dispute resolution.

Arbitration

Arbitration is considered international if the parties to the arbitration are of different nationalities or the subject matter of the dispute involves a state other than the country in which the parties are nationals. An international arbitration usually has no connection with the country in which the arbitration is being held, other than the fact that it is taking place on its territory.

The major difference between international and domestic arbitrations is that international arbitration awards have very wide enforceability in many countries. This is largely attributable to the acceptance of international treaties such as the 1958 **Convention on the Recognition and Enforcement of Foreign Arbitral Awards**, which allows for the enforcement of arbitration awards in many major countries, provided that the arbitration is international.

International Arbitration Forums

Prominent bodies that administer arbitrations include the International Chamber of Commerce's (ICC's) International Court of Arbitration in Paris; the London Court of International Arbitration (LCIA); and the American Arbitration Association (AAA). Each of these institutions has formulated its own arbitration rules; namely, the ICC Rules of Arbitration, the LCIA Rules, and the AAA International Arbitration Rules. Except for the AAA, which provides that its International Arbitration Rules apply only in the absence of any designated rules, the other two sets of institutional rules are applied to the arbitrations administered by the arbitration bodies.

All the institutional rules govern the commencement of the arbitration, the exchange of arbitration pleadings, the appointment and removal of arbitrators, and the hearing and interim measures of protection, among other rules. If the parties have not agreed on the number of arbitrators, one arbitrator is appointed, although the arbitration institution may appoint three arbitrators if it appears that the dispute warrants it.

In terms of the choice of arbitrator, the LCIA Rules provide that it, alone, is empowered to appoint arbitrators, although arbitrators will be appointed with due regard to any criteria for selection agreed to by the parties in writing. The ICC Rules of Arbitration allow parties to nominate, by agreement, an arbitrator for the ICC court's confirmation, while the AAA International Arbitration Rules require only that parties notify the AAA of any *designation* of an arbitrator.

When the forum of the arbitration has not been agreed to, the LCIA generally determines this according to the parties' contentions and the circumstances of the arbitration. However, the LCIA Rules provide that in such situations, the seat of the arbitration will be London unless, on the basis of the parties' written comments, the LCIA deems another seat more appropriate in view of the circumstances.

Under the ICC Rules of Arbitration, a document known as the *Terms of Reference*— containing a summary of the parties' claims, a list of issues to be determined, and applicable procedural rules—must be drafted and submitted to the arbitrator and the opposing party. Although time-consuming, discussion of agreed issues is designed to encourage settlement. Also, arbitration awards must be submitted to the ICC court for approval. There are no similar requirements under the LCIA Rules and the AAA International Arbitration Rules.

Ad Hoc Arbitration Rules

Rules such as those set out in the U.N. Commission on International Trade Law (UNCITRAL) Arbitration Rules serve to bridge the gap for parties who are unwilling to incur the additional expense involved in using the services of an arbitration body but who do not wish to spend time agreeing to the details of a procedure to govern their arbitration.

ALTERNATIVES TO THE ICC: THE WORLD INTELLECTUAL PROPERTY ORGANIZATION

There are arbitration institutions other than the ICC, some with regional specialization and some with subject matter specialization. The World International Property Organization (WIPO) in Geneva, Switzerland, created an arbitration center for arbitration related to intellectual property such as patents, trademarks, and copyrights. Some advantages of the WIPO center are

- The WIPO lists best practices regarding nomination of arbitrators, including a list system, thus encouraging the parties to agree on arbitrators based on their *qualifications*.
- The WIPO explicitly states that, when nominating arbitrators, it will take into account any preferences expressed by the parties *and* it has created a mechanism to implement this in practice: a database of names and detailed qualifications.
- The WIPO rules explicitly cater to multiparty arbitrations.

INTERNATIONAL MEDIATION

The growing popularity of mediation and conciliation, both of which first took root in the United States but have gained increasing support in other jurisdictions, reflects a high degree of frustration with the cost and delays often associated with traditional dispute resolution procedures. Mediation and conciliation both involve a consensual (rather than adjudicative) process, often with the involvement of a neutral third party. Such forms of dispute resolution may be loosely described as third-party-assisted negotiation.

Mediation and conciliation are now widely used in many countries, including the United States, Canada, Australia, South Africa, New Zealand, Germany, Holland, and Switzerland, as well as in the Hong Kong region of China. These forms of dispute resolution are also gaining acceptance in the United Kingdom through the establishment of organizations dedicated to their promotion and use, such as the London-based Center for Dispute Resolution; however, conciliation has long been practiced in the United Kingdom by the Advisory Conciliation and Arbitration Service in the field of employment-law disputes.

INTERNATIONAL COMMERCIAL LAW

Although this chapter has focused thus far on the sources and processes for a broad-based category of international law disputes, *commercial transactions and trade practices* are also governed by various sources of international (and U.S.) law.

LO 25-7

Articulate several specific laws that regulate international commercial law and understand when each law applies.

Foreign Corrupt Practices Act (FCPA)

The **Foreign Corrupt Practices Act (FCPA)** of 1977[3] was enacted principally to prevent corporate bribery of foreign officials. This act has three major parts: (1) It requires corporations to keep accurate books, records, and accounts; (2) it requires issuers registered with the Securities and Exchange Commission (i.e., publicly traded companies) to maintain a responsible internal accounting control system; and (3) it prohibits bribery by American corporations of foreign officials.

The FCPA was amended by Congress in 1988 in response to numerous criticisms. One of the changes enacted a *knowing* standard in order to find violations of the act. A person's state of mind is determined to be *knowing* with respect to conduct, a circumstance, or a result if the person is aware that he is engaging in the conduct, that the circumstance exists, or that the result is substantially certain to occur or if the person has a firm belief that the

---

[3]28 U.S.C. § 1602 et seq.

circumstance exists or that the result is substantially certain to occur. The 1998 amendment to the FCPA brought it into compliance with the Organization for Economic Cooperation and Development's agreement on bribery.

The centerpiece of the FCPA is its *antibribery* provision. The law prohibits a company and its officers, employees, and agents from giving, offering, or promising anything of value to any foreign (non-U.S.) official with the intent to obtain or retain business or any other advantage. This prohibition is interpreted broadly in that companies may be held liable for violating the antibribery provisions of the FCPA whether or not they take any action in the United States. Thus, a U.S. company can be liable for the conduct of its overseas employees or agents even if no money is transferred from the United States and no American citizen participates in any way in the foreign bribery.

Specifically,

> The FCPA prohibits "any domestic concern" from "mak[ing] use of the mails or any means . . . of interstate commerce corruptly in furtherance of" a bribe to "any foreign official," or to "any person, while knowing that all or a portion of such money or thing of value will be offered, given, or promised, directly or indirectly, to any foreign official," for the purpose of "influencing any act or decision of such foreign official . . . in order to assist such domestic concern in obtaining or retaining business for or with, or directing business to, any person."
>
> 15 U.S.C. 78dd-2(a)(1)(3).

Foreign officials include any officers or employees of a foreign government, regardless of rank; employees of government-owned or government-controlled businesses; foreign political parties and party officials; candidates for political office; and employees of public international organizations (such as the United Nations or the World Bank). This can include owner-employees as well. Even if the improper payment is not consummated, just offering it violates the FCPA. Likewise, instructing, authorizing, or allowing a third party to make a prohibited payment on a company's behalf, ratifying a payment after the fact, and making a payment to a third party knowing or having reason to know that it will likely be given to a government official all constitute FCPA violations. This includes not only cash and cash equivalents but also gifts, entertainment, travel expenses, accommodations, and anything else of tangible or intangible value.

The FCPA defines a *foreign official* as any officer or employee of a foreign government or any department, agency, or *instrumentality* thereof. One of the recent controversies surrounding the FCPA centers on the meaning of "instrumentality" because it is not defined in the statute. In Case 25.2, a federal appellate court considers the appeal of a U.S. business executive convicted in a bribery scheme with a foreign telephone company.

> **KEY POINT**
>
> The FCPA's antibribery provisions are interpreted very broadly and cover anything of value that is offered or given to a foreign official for purposes of influencing any act or decision by the official.

CASE 25.2 United States v. Esquenazi, 752 F.3d 912 (11th Cir. 2014)

FACT SUMMARY Esquenazi was a co-owner/president of Terra Telecommunications Corp. (Terra), a Florida company that purchased phone time from foreign vendors and resold the minutes to customers in the United States. One of Terra's main vendors was Telecommunications D'Haiti, S.A.M.

(continued)

(Teleco). In 2001 Terra contracted to buy minutes from Teleco directly. At that time, Teleco's Director General was Patrick Joseph (appointed by then-President Jean-Bertrand Aristide), and its Director of International Relations was Robert Antoine. In October 2001, Terra contacted Teleco about $400,000 in past due accounts. According to testimony at trial, Antoine agreed to reduce Terra's future bills to Teleco in exchange for receiving from Terra 50 percent of what the company saved. Antoine suggested that Terra disguise the payments by making them to sham companies, which Terra ultimately did. According to Terra employees, Esquenazi was fully aware of the arrangement and shared details of the deal in a meeting with executive management. The following month, Terra began funneling personal payments to Antoine using the subterfuge of sham consulting agreements. All told, while Antoine remained at Teleco, Terra paid him and his associates approximately $822,000. During that time, Terra's bills were reduced by over $2 million.

Soon after, the U.S. Internal Revenue Service (IRS) began to investigate Terra and its relationship with vendors, including Teleco. As part of the investigation, Esquenazi admitted he had bribed Teleco officials. The government charged Esquenazi and other Terra officials with several counts of violating the Foreign Corrupt Practices Act (FCPA). Esquenazi pleaded not guilty, proceeded to trial, and was found guilty on all counts. On appeal, Esquenazi argued that his conviction should be reversed because the FCPA did not apply to the Terra-Teleco payments because they were paid directly to Teleco officials. Esquenazi claimed that Teleco officials did not meet the FCPA definition for "foreign official." The government countered that Haiti Teleco was an "instrumentality" of the Haitian government and therefore Terra's acts of bribery were prohibited by the FCPA.

SYNOPSIS OF DECISION AND OPINION The U.S. Court of Appeals for the 11th Circuit affirmed Esquenazi's conviction. The court rejected Esquenazi's narrow definition of foreign official. Instead, the court adopted the fact-based approach looking to questions such as who runs the company, who appoints the management, where the company's profits come from, and the extent to which the government is involved in day-to-day decisions. The court cited evidence that 97 percent of the ownership of Teleco was held by the Haitian government and that Teleco was considered a de facto government entity because the Haitian government invests in the enterprise, appoints the board of directors, hires and fires the principals, and exercises a monopoly function.

WORDS OF THE COURT: Evidence of Teleco as Instrumentality "From Teleco's creation, Haiti granted the company a monopoly over telecommunications service and gave it various tax advantages. Beginning in early 1970s, and through the years [Esquenazi was] involved, Haiti's national bank owned 97 percent of Teleco. The company's Director General was chosen by the Haitian President with the consent of the Haitian Prime Minister and the ministers of public works and economic finance. And the Haitian President appointed all of Teleco's board members. The government's expert testified that Teleco belonged 'totally to the state' and 'was considered . . . a public entity.' Although the expert also testified that '[t]here was no specific law that . . . decided that at the beginning that Teleco is a public entity,' he maintained that 'government, officials, everyone consider[ed] Teleco as a public administration.' Construed in the light most favorable to the jury's verdict, that evidence was sufficient to show Teleco was controlled by the Haitian government and performed a function Haiti treated as its own, namely, nationalized telecommunication services."

Case Questions

1. Why is it important to the court's analysis that Antoine set up a sham company and consulting agreements?

2. If Esquenazi had not known about the bribes, would he still be guilty under the FCPA?

3. *Focus on Critical Thinking:* This case was controversial because it was the first time that an appellate court had interpreted the term "foreign official" in the FCPA so broadly. Critics contend that the court inserted its own broad definition instead of using the more narrow definition intended by Congress. Did the court go too far? If Congress had meant to include public/private partnerships in the definition of a foreign official, wouldn't they have added it into the statute? Is this good public policy?

Self-Check Foreign Corrupt Practices Act

Which proposed transactions violate the FCPA?

1. WidgetCo applies for a permit to do business in Venezuela. The government official denies the permit, and a WidgetCo executive pays for a lavish meal at a four-star restaurant while discussing the permit application with the official.
2. WidgetCo applies for a permit to do business in Venezuela. The government official denies the permit, so WidgetCo hires a consultant in Venezuela who is the brother of the government official. WidgetCo pays the consultant $100,000 to handle the permit process although the permit itself costs only $1,000.
3. WidgetCo applies for a permit to do business in Venezuela. A government official denies the permit, so WidgetCo hires a consultant in Venezuela who is the brother of the government official and pays a reasonable fee for services plus reimbursement of traveling expenses. The consultant submits a handwritten invoice for the reimbursements totaling $100,000.
4. WidgetCo applies for a permit to do business in Venezuela. A government official denies the permit, so WidgetCo hires a consultant in Venezuela who is the brother of the government official and pays a reasonable fee for services plus reasonable reimbursement of traveling expenses. When the permit is finally approved, WidgetCo executives send the consultant a case of California wine as a thank-you gift.

Answers to this Self-Check are provided at the end of the chapter.

U.N. Convention on Contracts for the International Sale of Goods (CISG)

Legal Speak >))

Choice of Law and Forum Clauses
Terms of a contract that predetermine what nation's laws and court system will be used in a potential lawsuit under that contract.

In 1988, the United States became a signatory nation to a U.N. treaty that attempts to establish an international commercial code. The *U.N. Convention on Contracts for the International Sale of Goods (CISG)* governs transactions between any of its 91 ratifying countries (as of March 2013). Much like America's Uniform Commercial Code, the CISG exists to fill in the terms of a sale of goods contract when the parties haven't otherwise reached agreement. Parties are free to negotiate the allocation of risk, insurance requirements, delivery, payment terms, choice of law, and the like to displace the CISG principles. It is particularly important for managers to understand *choice of law and forum* principles in international contracts because risk and expense of enforcement become increasingly important factors that must be considered in arriving at appropriate pricing and delivery proposals. If one party will have to travel significant distances or hire special counsel to enforce an agreement or recover for damages suffered, adjusting the price or delivery terms accordingly may sometimes help to reduce the risks.

Coverage and Major Provisions of the CISG The CISG operates on the same fundamental principle as many commercial codes around the world (including the Uniform Commercial Code, or UCC,[4] followed by most American states) in that the law favors the completion of a transaction as agreed upon but also provides relief when one party has breached. The CISG covers parties that maintain a place of business in one of

---
[4]The Uniform Commercial Code was covered in Chapter 8, "Contracts for the Sale of Goods."

the signatory countries. Note that the citizenship of shareholders, directors, or officers is not a factor under the CISG. Generally, the CISG covers contracts for the sale of goods between *merchants*. This is perhaps the biggest difference between the UCC and the CISG. The CISG provisions do *not* apply to transactions in which one party is a nonmerchant. Other major important provisions are discussed below.

No Writing Required The CISG has no formal writing requirement (such as the UCC's statute of frauds) and specifically provides that contracts are not subject to requirements as to format. A totality of the circumstances, such as course of past dealing, evidence of oral or written negotiations between the parties, and industry practice, may be sufficient to prove that an enforceable contract exists.

Although the CISG eliminates any formal writing requirement, it still allows individual countries to impose a writing requirement through an Article 96 declaration. The United States has not made such a declaration. In Case 25.3, a federal court grapples with a dispute in which one country has made an Article 96 declaration and the other country has not.

CASE 25.3 Forestal Guarani S.A. v. Daros International, Inc., 613 F.3d 395 (3d Cir. 2010)

FACT SUMMARY Forestal Guarani S.A. is an Argentina-based manufacturer of various lumber products, including wood finger joints. Daros International, Inc., is a New Jersey–based import-export corporation. In 1999, Forestal and Daros entered into an oral agreement for Daros to sell Forestal's wood finger joints to third parties in the United States. Pursuant to that agreement, Forestal sent Daros the finger joints along with an invoice for $1.86 million. However, Daros paid Forestal a total of only $1.46 million. When Forestal sued to recover the amount owed, Daros admitted that it had paid Forestal $1.46 million in exchange for the finger joints but denied that it owed Forestal any additional money. Daros argued that under the CISG, which governed its relationship with Forestal, there was no liability because the absence of any written contract precluded Forestal's claims because Argentina had exercised its rights in an Article 96 declaration. The trial court granted a summary judgment claim in favor of Daros, finding that Argentina's declaration was sufficient to extinguish Forestal's claim.

SYNOPSIS OF DECISION AND OPINION The U.S. Court of Appeals for the Third Circuit reversed the decision of the trial court and ruled in favor of Forestal. Although the court acknowledged that the issue of whether a contract must be in writing under these circumstances was a case of first impression, it rejected the trial court's conclusion that Forestal's claim was extinguished by virtue of the Article 96 declaration. The court held that when one country has adopted an Article 96 declaration and the other country has not, choice of law principles must be considered and the trial court should have taken the course of past conduct into account before granting a summary judgment motion.

WORDS OF THE COURT: Evidence of a Contract "Daros contended that Forestal had submitted no 'credible evidence' of a contract with Daros. The [trial court] agreed with that contention, concluding that there was no evidence that the parties ever had any contract at all. It is undisputed, however, that Forestal sold wooden finger-joints to Daros and that Daros gave Forestal money in exchange. Indeed, Daros nowhere denies that the parties at the very least had a verbal contract for those sales. Furthermore, Forestal submitted an accountant's certification, with supporting documentation, as well as invoices in an effort to substantiate its claim that it is owed money. There is also deposition testimony indicating that the parties had a contract. The [trial court] did not expressly refer to some of these materials in its opinion, and we do not know why it evidently disregarded them. . . . In short, we cannot

(continued)

say at this stage that there is no genuine question of material fact as to whether the parties had or did not have some sort of contractual relationship and whether Forestal can prove as much under whatever law actually controls this case."

Case Questions

1. What evidence does the court cite that tends to show that a contract existed?

2. Do the advantages of a statute of frauds rule (e.g., certainty) outweigh the advantages of a no-writing requirement (e.g., flow of commerce)?

3. *Focus on Critical Thinking:* After reading this case, do you think that the United States should opt for an Article 96 declaration? Why or why not?

Offer and Acceptance   A contract for the sale of goods between businesses located in different CISG signatory countries begins with offer and acceptance. As with the UCC, the offer need not have complete terms in order to be valid. The offer requires only a brief description of the goods, quantity, and price. Beyond those three terms, so long as there is some evidence that the parties intended to form a contract, nothing more is needed for a valid offer. Acceptance may be made within a reasonable time and is effective only when it is received by the offeror (thus, the offer may be withdrawn at any point prior to that time).

Remedies   The CISG provides for a party that has delivered nonconforming goods to be given an adequate opportunity to cure the problem. In general, the CISG gives sellers an absolute right and obligation to cure, and buyers must allow the seller the opportunity to cure even if the time for performance is past due. Of course, a buyer must give notice of the nonconformance in a timely manner in order to trigger the seller's cure obligations. If the seller does not cure, the CISG provides a right for the buyer to pursue remedies.

INCO: International Chamber of Commerce Terms

With respect to title, risk of loss, and delivery terms, sometimes the language barrier can lead to confusion among the parties and to disputes regarding a loss. The International Chamber of Commerce provides international abbreviations, known as **INCO terms**, to designate many of the responsibilities. INCO terms are generally used in conjunction with the CISG. For example, in the absence of any agreement between the parties, the CISG provides that risk passes at the point at which the seller has delivered the goods to a carrier. If the goods are not to be delivered, the risk of loss passes in accordance with the INCO term *EXW ("ex works")*. The INCO term EXW has the universal meaning that the parties understand the goods will not be delivered or transported by the seller. Rather, the seller need only make the goods available to the buyer at the seller's place of business and provide the buyer with appropriate documentation of title. There are 11 INCO terms in all. Some of the more common ones are

- *FCA ("free carrier"):* This term means that the seller provides transportation at the seller's expense only to the carrier named by the buyer.
- *FOB ("free on board"):* This term is always accompanied by the name of a port (e.g., FOB New York) and applies only when transportation is via freighter ship. It means that the seller's expense and risk of loss *end* when the seller delivers goods "over the ship's rail" to the freighter ship. The buyer is responsible for the freighter delivery charges and any losses occurring en route to delivery.

> **CONCEPT SUMMARY** *Contracts for International Sales of Goods*
>
> - The CISG, the international counterpart to the UCC, is a treaty that governs sales contracts between businesses located in signatory countries.
> - Four major differences between the CISG and the UCC are that (1) it does not apply to nonmerchants, (2) it has no writing requirement, (3) offers can be withdrawn at any point prior to the offeror's receiving the acceptance, and (4) the right to cure exists even after the performance period is over.
> - INCO terms are standardized contractual terms and designations used in international sales contracts to avoid confusion due to language barriers and differing legal systems.

ENFORCING INTELLECTUAL PROPERTY RIGHTS ABROAD

LO 25-8
Identify the methods used to enforce the rights of intellectual property holders in foreign countries.

While the laws of intellectual property protection are well settled in the United States, as U.S. companies become increasingly dependent on foreign sales and operations, global agreements have become increasingly important as well. The international law protection of intellectual property rights has primarily taken the form of multilateral agreements. However, as a practical matter, while many countries have improved intellectual property rights protection significantly over the past several decades, these agreements are still voluntary. Even when the government of a country agrees to abide by them (sometimes to avoid trade sanctions), the agreements are sometimes difficult to enforce in certain parts of the world. At the very least, the enforcement of rights abroad significantly impacts the cost-benefit analysis of pursuing infringement claims in terms of additional fees and expenses related to foreign litigation.

Comprehensive Agreements

While U.S. firms are motivated to be committed to stronger intellectual property protection abroad, some countries' intellectual property trade agreements often lack a meaningful mechanism to ensure that signatory countries are actually fulfilling their obligations. Thus, the United States and other similarly situated countries have backed the adoption of multinational minimal standards for intellectual property protection and an enforcement structure empowered with the ability to allow trade embargoes and other remedies designed to ensure that signatory countries comply with the agreement. As part of the **General Agreement on Tariffs and Trade (GATT)**, administered by the multinational World Trade Organization (WTO), the agreement to set these standards is known as the **Agreement on Trade-Related Aspects of Intellectual Property (TRIPS)**. TRIPS covers minimum requirements and standards for all areas of intellectual property protection and also provides an infrastructure for enforcement and dispute resolution.

Agreements on Trademarks

International trademark policy is governed primarily by two agreements: the *Paris Convention* and the *Madrid Protocol*. The Paris Convention (discussed below) was the first multinational agreement to establish minimum requirements for trademark protection, and a general agreement by its signatories established protections against unfair competition. The **Madrid Protocol**, a 2003 agreement that was a descendant of the earlier Madrid Agreement, aims to help reduce the burden of multinational companies that desire

The WTO (also called OMC, the abbreviation for its French name) plays an important role in the protection of intellectual property in global commerce. KEYSTONE/Fabrice Coffrini/AP Images

multinational protection of their trademarks by providing a uniform, single-source process. Although important, these international agreements are not so specific as to actually require fundamental enforcement from signatory countries, and thus trademark protection may still be dubious and uneven in certain regions. Efforts to harmonize trademark laws on a regional level have been more successful.[5]

Agreement on Copyrights

Copyright protection in foreign countries is covered in the **Berne Convention** agreement. Fundamentally, this agreement requires that foreigners from signatory countries must be granted protection via reciprocity (known as *national treatment*) under the copyright laws of any other member country. For example, if Samuel, an American, distributes his novel in Great Britain (or in any signatory country), British courts are bound by the convention agreement to protect Samuel's rights under British law in the same way as would apply if Samuel were a citizen of Great Britain.

As the international business community became more concerned with the advances in information technology and the impact on copyright protection, the WTO passed the **World Intellectual Property Organization Copyright Treaty (WCT)**, which became effective in 2002. The primary purpose of the WCT was to provide uniform copyright protection to computer programs and to certain protectible databases. It also affords authors with specific rights over the sale and distribution of their works that they may not have under the Berne Convention alone.

---

[5]The European Union established the Community Trademark System to make trademark registration and protection more uniform in member states.

Agreement on Patents

The most important multilateral agreement on patents is the **Paris Convention** agreement. This agreement requires the approximately 160 member countries that signed the agreement to protect the same inventor rights under *any* member country's patent laws as those enjoyed by citizens of that member country. That is, each member agrees to extend national rights (or give full protection) to foreign inventors. However, risks still remain for the foreign inventor because the Paris Convention does not specify common standards for patentability. Also, some jurisdictions may not allow certain inventions, which are patentable in the United States, to obtain patent protection in their own country due to noncompliance with domestic law.

KEY TERMS

Public international law p. 811   Category of international law principles that primarily addresses relations between individual countries and international organizations.

Private international law p. 811   Category of international law principles that focuses on the regulation of private individuals and business entities.

Vienna Convention on the Law of Treaties p. 811
One of the standards used by courts and other tribunals when interpreting treaty law.

Comity p. 811   The general notion that nations will defer to and give effect to the laws and court decisions of other nations.

United Nations (U.N.) p. 812   An international organization created after World War II to facilitate common international concerns on defense, trade, protection of human rights, and other matters.

U.N. Convention on Contracts for the International Sale of Goods (CISG) p. 812   A trade agreement developed by the U.N. Commission on International Trade Law to establish uniform rules for drafting certain international sales contracts.

International Court of Justice p. 812   The judicial branch of the United Nations, charged with settling legal disputes submitted to it by member states and giving advisory opinions on legal questions submitted to it by duly authorized international organs, agencies, and the U.N. General Assembly. Also known as *World Court*.

European Court of Justice p. 813   The court that functions as the final arbiter of the codes governing European Union member states.

Sovereign immunity p. 813   Long-standing doctrine of international law that holds that, with some exceptions, nations are exempt from jurisdiction by other nations' courts.

Foreign Sovereign Immunities Act (FSIA) p. 813
A federal statute that incorporates the concept of sovereign immunity by explicitly prohibiting U.S. courts from rendering judicial actions against foreign nations or their government officials unless the foreign nation has waived its immunity, is engaged in a commercial enterprise on U.S. soil, or has taken actions that have a direct effect on U.S. interests.

Civil law systems p. 815   Systems of law that are drawn largely from the Roman law heritage, which uses written law as the highest source, and opt for a systematic codification of general law principles.

Convention on the Recognition and Enforcement of Foreign Arbitral Awards p. 816   An international treaty established in 1958 that allows for the enforcement of arbitration awards in many major countries, provided that the arbitration is international.

Foreign Corrupt Practices Act (FCPA) p. 817   Federal legislation enacted in 1977 that prohibits corporate bribery of foreign officials; requires corporations to keep accurate books, records, and accounts; and requires issuers registered with the Securities and Exchange Commission to maintain a responsible internal accounting control system.

INCO terms p. 822   Standardized contractual terms and designations used in international and some domestic sales contracts to avoid confusion due to language barriers and differing legal systems.

General Agreement on Tariffs and Trade (GATT) p. 823   A treaty designed to facilitate international trade; administered by the World Trade Organization.

Agreement on Trade-Related Aspects of Intellectual Property (TRIPS) p. 823   A multinational agreement that covers minimum requirements and standards for all areas of intellectual property protection and provides an infrastructure for enforcement and dispute resolution.

Madrid Protocol p. 823 A multinational agreement that aims to facilitate multinational protection of trademarks through the use of a uniform, single-source process.

Berne Convention p. 824 A multinational agreement covering copyright protection; requires that foreigners from signatory countries be granted protection, via reciprocity, under the copyright laws of any other member country.

World Intellectual Property Organization Copyright Treaty (WCT) p. 824 Supplement to the Berne Convention intended primarily to address copyright protection related to technology (e.g., computer programs).

Paris Convention p. 825 A multinational agreement covering patents; requires signatory countries to protect the same inventor rights under any member country's patent laws as those enjoyed by citizens of that member country.

CHAPTER REVIEW QUESTIONS

1. **What term is used to describe the general notion that nations will defer to and give effect to the laws and court decisions of all nations?**
   a. Comity
   b. Mutual aid
   c. Benefit doctrine
   d. Equal protection

2. **The Foreign Corrupt Practices Act (FCPA) includes which of the following provisions?**
   a. Anti-bribery
   b. Record keeping
   c. Dispute resolution
   d. Both (a) and (b)

3. **Ahab, a U.S. citizen, orders a whale harpoon from Ishmael Corporation, which is located in the United Kingdom. When the harpoon arrives, Ahab discovers it is defective and seeks relief under the provisions of the Contracts for the International Sale of Goods (CISG). Who prevails?**
   a. Ahab, because the CISG requires the contract to be in writing.
   b. Ahab, because Ishmael Corporation delivered nonconforming goods.
   c. Ishmael Corporation, because the CISG only applies when both parties are merchants.
   d. Ishmael Corporation, because they have the right to cure.

4. **When the seller is to provide transportation at the seller's expense only to the carrier named by the buyer, the correct INCO term is**
   a. FOB
   b. EXW
   c. FCA
   d. WTO

5. **International trademark policy is primarily governed by the**
   a. Berne Convention
   b. Paris Convention
   c. Madrid Protocol
   d. Both (b) and (c)

Answers and explanations are provided at the end of this chapter.

THEORY TO PRACTICE

Cold Call Company (CCC) is a cellular phone manufacturer and distributor based in Miami, Florida. The firm has a significant market share in the southeastern United States and began to expand into South America as a natural supplement to its existing market. CCC entered into a written distribution agreement with Telefonica, a Brazil-based provider of cell phone service and retailer of cell phone units with stores throughout Latin America. Telefonica agreed to buy 25,000 units over 12 months at US$5 per unit. The agreement also contained a provision whereby the parties agreed to ICC dispute resolution in the event of a dispute arising out of the distribution agreement. After several months, a dispute developed, and Telefonica filed suit against CCC in a federal district court in Miami.

1. What source(s) of international law(s) would generally govern this international business relationship?
2. When CCC asks the court to dismiss the case due to the ICC clause, Telefonica claims that the clause is invalid because it will have to travel to Europe to resolve the dispute and that is too burdensome. How will the federal court rule, and what case have you studied in this chapter that supports your answer?
3. Assume further that the CCC-Telefonica agreement provides that all shipments are "FOB Port of Rio de Janeiro, Brazil." During one shipment, a batch of 1,000 units is accidentally destroyed when being loaded on the freighter in Miami. Under the CISG, who bears the risk of this loss? When did title pass?
4. Assume that an executive at Telefonica arranges a golf outing with a politician in Argentina on behalf of the distribution manager of CCC. The Telefonica executive explains that it is customary in Argentina for business owners to entertain local politicians and that it is a necessary part of securing appropriate licenses for the CCC-Telefonica distribution relationship in Argentina. One day after the golf outing, the Telefonica executive sends a bill to CCC for the golf expenses, including equipment, food, and drinks ordered by the group. If CCC pays the bill, will the company potentially violate any U.S. laws? If so, does the law apply to these circumstances? Will CCC be at a competitive disadvantage if it follows the law?
5. Suppose that CCC refuses to pay the bill (see Question 4) and that the Argentinean government prohibits CCC from exporting any products to Argentina. CCC loses a significant portion of its investment with Telefonica as a result of the ban. Does CCC have recourse against the Argentinean government in U.S. courts? Why or why not? What legal doctrine controls this question? Could this be an exception?

LEGAL STRATEGY 101

China versus the United States

Until June 2010, the Chinese government pegged (i.e., dictated) the value of its currency, the yuan (see photo), against the dollar. Although China claims to have abandoned this pegging strategy, the Chinese government still manages the value of the yuan within a narrow range. In fact, according to many estimates, Chinese government intervention keeps the yuan approximately 20 percent below its free market value against the dollar.[6] So, is currency manipulation legal?

Nations like the United States and China enjoy *monetary sovereignty* under public international law: the right to manage their currencies as they see fit.[7] At the same time, a country can limit its rights through international agreements. Both China and the United States, for example, are members of the International Monetary Fund (IMF), and membership in the IMF requires member governments to "avoid manipulating exchange rates . . . in order to prevent effective balance of payments adjustment or to gain an unfair competitive advantage over other members."[8]

Is China breaking its solemn pledge to the IMF? China says no. Specifically, the Chinese government claims that it manages its national currency to ensure "domestic stability," not to cheat trading partners. Furthermore, even if the United States could prove that China is indeed manipulating its currency, there's no legal venue or international tribunal for the United States to effectively challenge China's domestic stability claim.

Dissatisfied with such weak international enforcement options, Congress passed its own law in 2011 that requires the Treasury Department to publish

---

[6]*See generally* Rebecca M. Nelson, Congressional Research Service, R43242, *Current Debates over Exchange Rates: Overview and Issues for Congress* (Sept. 27, 2015).

[7]*See* F. A. Mann, *The Legal Aspect of Money* 460–78 (Oxford University Press 5th ed. 1992).

[8]*See* Article IV of the "Articles of Agreement of the International Monetary Fund."

Chinese yuan. Thomas Ruecker/Getty Images

semiannual reports on suspected currency manipulators.[9] If the United States deems a country to be a currency manipulator, the president may impose tariffs against its imports to offset the effects of the depressed currency. So, should the U.S. government retaliate against China?

Advocates for direct retaliation argue that the mere threat of sanctions would force China to change its monetary policies. But would China call our bluff? If not, direct retaliation against China might impact our own economy because import tariffs on Chinese products would raise the prices of Chinese products to American consumers.[10]

CRITICAL THINKING QUESTIONS

1. Should the IMF Articles of Agreement be amended to include specific penalties against member governments that manipulate their currencies?
2. Alternatively, should the IMF Articles of Agreement be amended to allow countries to manipulate their currencies under the doctrine of "monetary sovereignty"?

---

[9]*See, e.g.,* Office of International Affairs, U.S. Dep't of Treasury, *Report to Congress on International Economic and Exchange Rate Policies* (May 25, 2012).

[10]*See, e.g.,* Brian Palmer, *If Currency Manipulation Is So Great for Imports, Why Don't We Do It?* Slate (Oct. 17, 2012).

MANAGER'S CHALLENGE

One important responsibility of a manager is to be vigilant about protecting his company from liability. One such liability in the international law context is a potential violation of the Foreign Corrupt Practices Act (FCPA). Individually or in small groups, take on the role of a CCC manager (from this chapter's Theory to Practice problem) and draft a two-page memorandum to your senior manager on a proposed policy for CCC employees to help them avoid any violations of the FCPA. The policy should contain at least five red-flag situations in which CCC may be in danger of violating the act. For example, paying for entertainment of a government official when the official has some decision-making role is a red-flag situation in which CCC employees must recognize potential FCPA violations and act with restraint.

See Connect for Manager's Challenge sample answers.

CASE SUMMARY 25.1 TermoRio S.A. v. Electrificadora Del Atlantico S.A., 421 F. Supp. 2d 87 (D.D.C. 2006)

ARBITRATION ENFORCEMENT

Electranta is a power company owned by the Colombian government. Electranta became involved in a dispute with TermoRio, a U.S. company doing business in Colombia. The dispute was arbitrated consistent with International Chamber of Commerce rules, and TermoRio was awarded US$60 million in damages. However, TermoRio could not convince the Colombian courts to enforce the award, and the government of Colombia refused to pay. TermoRio then filed suit in the United States, attempting to have a federal court declare the acts of the Colombia courts unlawful and recognize the arbitration award.

CASE QUESTIONS

1. Under the Convention on the Recognition and Enforcement of Foreign Arbitral Awards, do the U.S. courts have authority to decide this case?
2. What do the ICC rules provide?

CASE SUMMARY 25.2 Plaintiffs A, B, C v. Zemin, 224 F. Supp. 2d 52 (N.D. Ill. 2003)

SOVEREIGN IMMUNITY

Several Chinese ex-patriots now living in the United States are members of a religious movement, Falun Gong, which is outlawed in China, and they brought suit against the Chinese government. Members of this movement are subject to arrest by Chinese government officials in the Falun Gong Control Office without any further charge, and the lawsuit maintained that they were subject to severe torture resulting in permanent physical damage. The suit named the former president of China and officials of the Control Office as defendants, but the defendants never responded to the lawsuit.

CASE QUESTIONS

1. May the federal court issue a default judgment against the defendants?
2. What role does the doctrine of sovereign immunity play in this case?

CASE SUMMARY 25.3 Chateau des Charmes Wines Ltd. v. Sabate USA Inc., 328 F.3d 528 (9th Cir. 2003)

CONTRACTS FOR THE INTERNATIONAL SALE OF GOODS

Sabate, a France-based company, sold wine corks to Chateau, a Canadian winery, via Sabate's U.S. subsidiary. The parties made the agreement by telephone, and no written contracts existed. After several transactions and the sale of over 1.2 million corks, Sabate began to send an invoice with each shipment that included a forum selection clause naming France as the agreed-upon location to resolve disputes. Chateau sued Sabate in a U.S. court over the poor quality of the corks. Sabate moved to dismiss because the forum selection clause required the dispute to be litigated in France. Chateau claimed that the forum selection clause was added after the terms were agreed upon and, thus, was invalid and not part of the original contract.

CASE QUESTIONS

1. Is Chateau's silence upon receiving the invoices binding on the company under the Convention on Contracts for the International Sale of Goods?
2. Would your answer be the same under the UCC?

CASE SUMMARY 25.4 Republic of Austria v. Altmann, 541 U.S. 677 (2004)

FOREIGN SOVEREIGN IMMUNITIES ACT

Altmann, a U.S. resident, filed suit in a federal district court against the Republic of Austria to recover a series of paintings that Altmann claims were wrongfully appropriated from her uncle just prior to World War II. The paintings had been held in her uncle's Vienna home until the German annexation of Austria in 1938. Altmann's uncle fled Austria, fearing persecution, and left half of his estate to Altmann in his will. The paintings were discovered by an Austrian journalist who alerted Altmann to the fact that her uncle's paintings were being held by the Austrian government in its art gallery archives. The Austrian government moved to dismiss the case based on the FSIA, but Altmann contended (among other arguments) that because the Austrian government's actions were taken *prior* to passage of the FSIA, they were outside the scope of the statute's immunity protection.

CASE QUESTIONS

1. Do sovereigns have immunity protection for actions prior to the FSIA's enactment?
2. Is it fair to allow Austria protection under these circumstances? Why or why not?

CASE SUMMARY 25.5 DiMercurio v. Sphere Drake Insurance PLC, 202 F.3d 71 (1st Cir. 2000)

DISPUTE RESOLUTION

DiMercurio was a fisherman who was injured when a commercial shipping vessel owned by a Massachusetts company, Rosalie & Matteo Corporation, sank. DiMercurio prevailed in a personal injury suit against Rosalie & Matteo, but the company was without assets and could not pay the $350,000 judgment. Rosalie & Matteo subsequently assigned to DiMercurio all rights it had against its London-based insurance company, Sphere Drake, under an insurance policy issued to Rosalie & Matteo Corporation. DiMercurio then took his claim directly to Sphere Drake, demanding that the insurer pay the $350,000 judgment. Sphere Drake sought to invoke the arbitration process specified in the policy, which called for arbitration of all coverage disputes to be held in London under convention rules. DiMercurio challenged the validity of the arbitration provision, contending that it was overly burdensome on the arbitrating parties given that he would have to travel to London.

CASE QUESTIONS

1. Recall that in the *Brower v. Gateway* case in Chapter 4, "Resolving Disputes: Litigation and Alternative Dispute Resolution," the court held that Gateway's inclusion of an arbitration clause in a terms and conditions agreement was invalid because of the choice of ICC as the arbitration forum. Is this case distinguishable?
2. Give examples of types of agreements that you would consider too one-sided to be valid.

Self-Check ANSWERS Foreign Corrupt Practices Act

1. Violates FCPA's prohibition of offering anything of value (a meal at a four-star restaurant) with intent to obtain the permit.
2. Violates FCPA's prohibition of paying a third party to pay off the government official (a consultant).
3. Violates FCPA's prohibition of paying cash equivalents (travel) in connection with the permit.
4. Violates FCPA's prohibition of after-the-fact (ratification) payments related to the permit application.

CHAPTER REVIEW QUESTIONS: Answers and Explanations

1. **a.** Comity is an important concept related to judicial decisions as a source of international law. Answer choices (b), (c), and (d) are incorrect because they are unrelated to international law.

2. **d.** The FCPA includes anti-bribery provisions and also requires companies to keep accurate records in order to help government investigators identify corruption. Answer choice (c) is incorrect because no dispute resolution provisions are included in the statute.

3. **c.** Unlike the UCC, the CISG does not cover contracts for the sale of goods unless both parties are merchants. Because Ahab is not a merchant, he may not get relief under the CISG. Therefore answer choices (a), (b), and (d) are incorrect because they are all related to provisions that cover merchants only.

4. **c.** FCA is the INCO term for "free carrier" and issues when the seller is required to deliver only to the carrier. Answer choices (a) and (b) are incorrect because those INCO terms do not apply. Answer choice (d) is incorrect because it is not an INCO term.

5. **d.** International trademark policy is primarily governed by two agreements. The Paris Convention was the first multinational agreement on trademarks and the Madrid Protocol added important protections for trademark holders. Answer choice (a) is incorrect because the Berne Convention covers copyright protection.

©philsajonesen/Getty Images

BUSINESS LAW SIMULATION EXERCISE 3

Trademarks in Cyberspace: Cool Runnings v. BigBuy.com

Learning Objectives

After participating in this simulation, students who have mastered the material will be able to:

1. Explain the legal doctrines that govern trademark protection and infringement.
2. Interpret and apply the rules set forth in current case law.
3. Articulate a cogent argument for each party/side in the dispute.
4. Negotiate a tenable solution as an alternative to a judicial forum.

This simulation is designed to help you understand how the various topics covered in Chapter 24, "Intellectual Property," connect. By focusing on a simulated legal dispute, you will gain real-world experience in applying legal doctrines and using analytical and critical-thinking skills. This simulation is a sequential decision-making exercise structured around a model in which the participants assume a role in managing tasks and work toward a tenable solution.

The simulation is structured in three parts:

- Part 1 is a hypothetical fact pattern describing events leading up to a legal dispute in the hypothetical U.S. state of Longville.
- Part 2 is a statutory excerpt and a set of two hypothetical case summaries from two federal trial courts, both situated in Longville. Each summary provides a brief set of facts, several legal points, and short excerpts from the opinion itself. While these cases are hypothetical, they are based on actual cases from federal courts in various circuits.
- Part 3 is an assignment sheet handout that will be provided to you by your instructor for use in conjunction with this simulation.

Part 1: Stipulated Facts

1. BigBuy.com Inc. is a company with a website that facilitates a web-based discount wholesaler business model that targets consumers wishing to buy products in bulk. In early 2015, BigBuy.com began developing a new marketing device that featured pop-up advertising. In 2016, the company launched "BargainNow" as integrated software for BigBuy users.

2. BigBuy.com made the BargainNow software available to computer users, at no charge, as part of a larger package of software that users downloaded from BigBuy's website. The BargainNow software uses an internal directory of website addresses, search terms, and keyword algorithms to generate pop-up advertisements in response to a user's Internet activity.

3. The advertisements generated are randomly drawn from a list of BigBuy's advertising clients. In essence, BigBuy's software operates behind the scenes monitoring a user's Internet activity and then responds according to keywords the software identifies as part of a user's activity, such as words entered in an Internet search engine query or websites visited whose domain names match information contained in the BigBuy internal directory.

4. The pop-ups occur only a few seconds after the user has reached a retail website and, thus, present the user with a choice: to close the pop-up and continue navigating the website or to click on the promotion and navigate away from the original retailer's website to a competitor's website.

5. Cool Runnings Corporation is a large retailer of skateboards and snowboards with a USPTO registered trademark for "Cool Runnings" and sole and exclusive use of the mark. The company sells its products both from a catalog system with a 1-800 number and via its website at www.coolrunnings.com.

6. In January 2017, BigBuy landed an advertising client that is a major competitor to Cool Runnings and, pursuant to its business model, BigBuy installed www.coolrunnings.com and keywords such as *snowboards* and *skateboards* into its internal directory. Note that it did *not* install the keywords *Cool Runnings* in the directory.

This simulation exercise involves a trademark dispute between a snowboard retailer and an Internet advertising company. Ipatov/Shutterstock.com

Part 2: Statutory and Case Law

Statute: United States Code
Excerpt from the Lanham Act

Section 1: False designations of origin, false descriptions, and dilution forbidden

Any person who, on or in connection with any goods or services, or any container for goods, uses in commerce any word, term, name, symbol, or device, or any combination thereof, or any false designation of origin, false or misleading description of fact, or false or misleading representation of fact, which—

(A) is likely to cause confusion, or to cause mistake, or to deceive as to the affiliation, connection, or association of such person with another person, or as to the origin, sponsorship, or approval of his or her goods, services, or commercial activities by another person, or

(B) in commercial advertising or promotion, misrepresents the nature, characteristics, qualities, or geographic origin of his or her or another person's goods, services, or commercial activities,

—shall be liable in a civil action by any person who believes that he or she is or is likely to be damaged by such act.

Excerpt from Trademark Dilution Revision Act

Section 1: The owner of a famous mark . . . shall be entitled to an injunction against another person who, at any time after the owner's mark has become famous, commences use of a mark or trade name in commerce that is likely to cause dilution by blurring or dilution by tarnishment of the famous mark, regardless of the presence or absence of actual or likely confusion, of competition, or of actual economic injury.

Section 2: There are six nonexhaustive factors for courts to consider in determining whether there is dilution by blurring:

- The degree of similarity between the mark and the famous mark.
- The degree of inherent or acquired distinctiveness of the mark.
- The extent to which the owner of the famous mark is engaging in substantially exclusive use of the mark.
- The degree of recognition (fame) of the mark.
- Whether use of the mark by the alleged infringer was intended to create an association with the famous mark.
- Any actual association between the mark and the famous mark.

Case Law

1-800 Lenses, Inc., v. WhenU.com Federal District Court, Eastern District of Longville (2017)

Facts

- 1-800 Lenses, Inc. (800-Lenses) sells and markets replacement lenses and related products through its website, located at www.1800Lenses.com, and also through telephone and mail orders. 800-Lenses obtained USPTO registration for the mark "1-800 LENSES" and the 1-800 LENSES logo.
- 800-Lenses has expended considerable sums on marketing these marks; in 2001, 800-Lenses spent $27,118,000 on marketing. Since the founding of 800-Lenses in 1995, the company has continuously used its service marks to promote and identify its products and services in the United States and abroad.
- 800-Lenses is the sole owner of the 1800-Lenses.com website.
- WhenU.com is a software company that has developed and distributes, among other products, the "SaveNow" program, a proprietary software application.
- The SaveNow program is computer software that operates only on the Microsoft Windows operating system. The SaveNow software, when installed, resides on individual computer users' computer desktops. When a computer user who has installed the SaveNow software browses the Internet, the SaveNow software scans activity conducted within the SaveNow user's Internet browser, comparing URLs, website addresses, search terms, and web-page content accessed by the SaveNow user with a proprietary directory, using algorithms contained in the software.
- Entering a URL into the browser will trigger the SaveNow software to deliver a pop-up advertisement. When a user types in "1800-Lenses.com," the URL for 800-Lenses's owned website, the SaveNow software recognizes that the user is interested in the eye-care category, and it retrieves from an Internet server a pop-up advertisement from that category.
- 800-Lenses filed a trademark infringement claim after discovering that the SaveNow software produced pop-up advertising for Lenses Warehouse, a WhenU.com customer and competitor of 800-Lenses.

POINTS OF LAW AND OPINION EXCERPTS

Point (a)

The Lanham Act, a federal statute, prohibits the *use in commerce,* without consent, of any registered mark in connection with the sale, offering for sale, distribution, or advertising of any goods in a way that is likely to cause confusion.

Excerpt (a1)

"A trademark is 'used in commerce' for purposes of the Lanham Act when it is used or displayed in the sale or advertising of services and the services are rendered in commerce, or the services are rendered in more than one state or in the United States and a foreign country and the person rendering the services is engaged in commerce in connection with the services."

Excerpt (a2)

"WhenU (defendant) *uses* 1-800 Lenses (plaintiff) mark in commerce. First, in causing pop-up advertisements for a competitor to appear when SaveNow users have specifically attempted to access plaintiff's website—on which plaintiff's trademark appears—defendants are displaying plaintiff's mark in the advertising of a competitor's services. SaveNow users that type plaintiff's website address into their browsers are clearly attempting to access plaintiff's website because of prior knowledge of the website, knowledge that is dependent on plaintiff's reputation and goodwill. SaveNow users that type 1-800 Lenses into a search engine in an attempt to find the URL for plaintiff's website are exhibiting a similar knowledge of plaintiff's goods and services, and pop-up advertisements that capitalize on this are clearly using plaintiff's mark. Thus, by causing pop-up advertisements to appear when SaveNow users have specifically attempted to find or access plaintiff's website, defendants are 'using' plaintiff's marks that appear on plaintiff's website."

Excerpt (a3)

"WhenU.com also *uses* the mark by including Plaintiff's URL, www.1800Lenses.com, in the proprietary WhenU.com directory of terms that triggers pop-up advertisements on SaveNow users' computers. In so doing, WhenU.com 'uses' Plaintiff's mark by including a version of Plaintiff's 1-800 LENSES mark, to advertise and publicize companies that are in direct competition with the Plaintiff."

Point (b)

Confusion for purposes of the Lanham Act is shown when there is a likelihood that an appreciable number of ordinarily prudent purchasers are likely to be misled, or indeed simply confused, as to the source of the goods in question or when consumers are likely to believe that the challenged use of a trademark is somehow sponsored, endorsed, or authorized by its owner. Thus, "confusion" for purposes of the Lanham Act includes confusion of any kind, including confusion as to source, sponsorship, affiliation, connection, or identification.

Excerpt (b1)

"It is black letter law that actual confusion need not be shown to prevail under the Lanham Act, since actual confusion is very difficult to prove and the Act requires only a likelihood of confusion as to source. In order to support a claim of infringement, a plaintiff must show a probability, not just a possibility, of confusion; a likelihood of confusion is actionable even absent evidence of actual confusion."

Excerpt (b2)

"Confusion that occurs prior to a sale may be actionable under the Lanham Act. For example, *initial interest confusion* occurs when a consumer, seeking a particular trademark holder's product, is instead lured away to the product of a competitor because of the competitor's use of a similar mark, even though the consumer is not actually confused about the source of the products or services at the time of actual purchase."

Excerpt (b3)

"Federal courts assess the likelihood of consumer confusion by examining (1) the strength of plaintiff's mark, (2) the similarity between the plaintiff's and defendant's marks, (3) proximity of the parties' services, (4) the likelihood that one party will 'bridge the gap' into the other's product line, (5) the existence of actual confusion between the marks, (6) the good faith of the defendant in using the mark, (7) the quality of the defendant's services, and (8) the sophistication of the consumers."

Point (c)

A mark holder may also be entitled to an injunction if it dilutes a famous mark under the Trademark Dilution Revision Act.

Excerpt (c1)

"The TDRA outlines several nonexclusive factors the court may consider in determining whether a mark is famous such as (1) the duration, extent, and geographic reach of advertising and publicity of the mark, and (2) the amount, volume, and geographic extent of sales of goods or services offered under the mark, and (3) whether the mark is registered."

Excerpt (c2)

"For a dilution claim to succeed under TDRA, the mark used by the alleged diluter must be identical, or nearly identical, to the protected mark. Although [it] no longer requires actual dilution, the new law does not eliminate the requirement that the mark used by the alleged diluter be identical, nearly identical, or substantially similar to the protected mark. For marks to be nearly identical to one another, they must be similar enough that a significant segment of the target group of customers sees the two marks as essentially the same."

Excerpt (c3)

"In the dilution context, the 'similarity of the marks' test is more stringent than in the infringement context."

Held

WhenU.com infringed the 1-800 Lenses trademark by using the 1-800 LENSES mark or confusingly similar terms as an element in the SaveNow proprietary directory. Ruling in favor of 800-Lenses.

Truck Rental International Inc. v. Web Marketing LLC Federal District Court, Western District of Longville (2018)

Facts

- Truck Rental International (TRI) Inc. claimed that Web Marketing LLC's pop-up advertising model infringed upon TRI's trademark. TRI alleged that Web Marketing's pop-up advertisements, which crowd the computer user's screen and block out TRI's website display, in effect, infringe on TRI's registered trademark.

- The SuperSavings program is computer software that operates only on the Microsoft Windows operating system. The SuperSavings software, if installed, resides on individual computer users' computer desktops. When a computer user who has installed the SuperSavings software browses the Internet, the SuperSavings software scans activity conducted within the SuperSavings user's Internet browser, comparing URLs, website addresses, search terms, and web-page content accessed by the SuperSavings user with a proprietary directory, using algorithms contained in the software.

- The average computer user who conducts a web search for the TRI website would expect the TRI website to appear on her computer screen; however, in this case, the computer screen fills with the advertisement of a TRI competitor.
- The user must then click and close the pop-up advertisement window in order to get to her destination, the TRI website. While at first blush this detour in the user's web search seems like a siphoning off of a business opportunity, the fact is that the computer user consented to this detour when the user downloaded Web Marketing's computer software from the Internet. In other words, the user deliberately or unwittingly downloaded the pop-up advertisement software.

POINTS OF LAW AND OPINION EXCERPTS

Point (a)

A fundamental prerequisite for claims of trademark infringement pursuant to unfair competition is proof that the defendant used one of the plaintiff's protected marks in commerce.

Excerpt (a1)

"Web Marketing's pop-up advertisement software resides in individual computers as a result of the invitation and consent of the individual computer user and, thus, the advertisements do not use, alter, or interfere with TRI's trademarks and copyrights. Alas, computer users must endure pop-up advertising along with her ugly brother unsolicited bulk e-mail, 'spam,' as a burden of using the Internet."

Excerpt (a2)

"Domain names, like trade names, do not act as trademarks when they are used to identify a business entity; in order to infringe they must be used to identify the source of goods or services and 'where . . . the pure machine-linking function is the only use at issue, there is no trademark use and there can be no infringement.' Likewise in the instant case, Web Marketing's incorporation of TRI's URL and 'Truck Rental International' in the SuperSavings program is not a trademark use because Web Marketing merely uses the marks for the 'pure machine-linking function' and in no way advertises or promotes TRI's web address or any other TRI trademark."

Point b

In order to have a claim for trademark infringement under the Lanham Act, the mark owner must show that the defendant used the mark in a manner likely to confuse consumers.

Excerpt (b1)

"Consumer confusion is *not* established merely because trademarks are simultaneously visible to a consumer. Such comparative advertising does not violate trademark law, even when the advertising makes use of a competitor's trademark. A use of a rival's mark that does not engender confusion about origin or quality is permissible. For example, previous cases have held that the use of *'If You Like ESTEE LAUDER . . . You'll Love BEAUTY USA'* on a product's packaging and point of sale advertising is lawful comparative advertising. Thus, the appearance of Web Marketing's ads on a user's computer screen at the same time as the TRI web page is a result of how applications operate in the Windows environment and not consistent with evidence of intent to confuse the consumer."

Excerpt (b2)

"The SuperSavings program does not hinder or impede Internet users from accessing TRI's website. The SuperSavings program resides within the user's computer and does not interact or communicate with TRI's website, its computer servers, or its computer systems. Further, the SuperSavings program does not change the underlying appearance of the TRI website. In addition, the SuperSavings program is installed by the computer user who can decline to accept the licensing agreement or decline to download the program. Thus, the user controls the computer display the moment the Web Marketing ad pops up, and the user may also have other programs with pop-up windows notifying the user of an event within the computer system. The SuperSavings program is, therefore, no different than an e-mail system that pops a window up when the registered user receives a new e-mail message."

Held

In favor of Web Marketing. While pop-up advertisements seize the user's computer screen with a window of advertisement, blocking out the object of his search and his document and requiring the user to click several times to clear the computer screen, the advertisements do not meet the use and consumer confusion requirements necessary to prove trademark infringement.

capstone case study 1
COFFEE WARS: STARBUCKS V. CHARBUCKS[1]

OVERVIEW AND OBJECTIVES

Two years after opening their family-owned coffee bean roastery, Jim and Annie Clark had become accustomed to long workweeks and bootstrap financing. By 1997, their Black Bear Micro Roastery was finally growing, and the Clarks were hopeful that their new specialty blend, Charbucks, would give their uniquely dark-roasted coffee bean a catchy name to remember. Soon after launching the new blend, Annie Clark received a phone call from an insistent in-house lawyer at coffee giant Starbucks that threatened the very existence of the Clarks' company. Starbucks claimed that the Charbucks name and label infringed on its trademark, and it demanded that the Clarks cease the use of the name Charbucks and that any existing products with that name be removed from supermarket shelves. But the Clarks insisted that they had been careful to design the label with Black Bear Micro Roastery logos and that the name was tied to the dark-roasting process and not to anything related to the name Starbucks. Despite their beliefs that no infringement had taken place, the Clarks entered into settlement negotiations to avoid the legal costs associated with defending a trademark lawsuit. After the settlement negotiations failed, Starbucks sued Black Bear Micro Roastery, and the stage was set for a coffee war that pitted a multinational powerhouse against a Main Street merchant. This case study emphasizes use of legal insight and business strategy, gives context for evaluating business ethics, and requires the application of trademark law.

Review Legal Concepts

Prior to reading the case, briefly review the following legal concepts that were covered in the textbook: legal insight and business strategy (Chapter 1); business, societal, and ethical contexts of law (Chapter 5); and trademark law (Chapter 24). Think of these areas of the law as you read the case study facts and questions.

---

[1] An earlier version of this case study appeared in the *Journal of Legal Studies Education* (29 J. Legal Stud. Educ. 27 (2012)). Permission by Sean P. Melvin.

THE BLACK BEAR MICRO ROASTERY

Jim and Annie Clark were native New Englanders who shared a passion for coffee and an entrepreneurial spirit. After three years of research, they launched Black Bear Micro Roastery in 1995 with a mission of creating a unique methodology for roasting gourmet coffee beans through use of advanced technology and the "traditional Yankee work ethic." The company was situated in the lakes region of New Hampshire and targeted connoisseur coffee drinkers, primarily in the New England area, who appreciated the micro-roastery approach of producing small, high-quality batches of coffee beans. The beans were sold via mail order, from the Black Bear website, and through New England specialty stores and supermarkets. Eventually, Black Bear also sold its products through its own retail outlet and café in Portsmouth, New Hampshire.

True to their belief in the micro-roastery concept and their entrepreneurial courage, the Clarks invested their life savings in the company. In order to start the business, the couple sold many of their assets and refinanced the mortgage on their home for extra cash. They enlisted their teenage daughters as their labor force and committed to seven-day workweeks. The family business was the centerpiece of their family's livelihood.

As with many start-ups, business for Black Bear was slow and rocky at first. The price of green coffee beans had fluctuated unexpectedly, and the 1997 Teamsters strike at United Parcel Service had eaten into profit margins. Undeterred, Jim and Annie Clark kept the company going until it began to grow ever so slowly. In order to develop a niche in the gourmet coffee market, Black Bear began to develop unique blends with catchy names that were easy to remember. This included blends such as "Country French," "Kenya Safari," and "Mocha Java."

Charbucks

By April 1997, Black Bear had developed a loyal following from which it often solicited feedback and suggestions for new products. One common theme from customers was a desire for a blend with a darker-roasted bean that yielded a richer taste. Responding to that customer demand, Black Bear developed a darker-roasted blend and named it "Charbucks Blend." The *Char* was a reference to the new, darker-roasted coffee bean blend.

Charbucks Blend was sold in packaging that showed a picture of a black bear above the large-font printed words "Black Bear Micro Roastery." The label also informed consumers that the coffee was roasted and "Air Quenched" in New Hampshire, and it contained the catchphrase "You wanted it dark . . . You've got it dark!" There was no similarity between the Starbucks famous logo, a circular shape with the graphic of a mermaidlike siren encompassed by the phrase "Starbucks Coffee," and the Charbucks label except for the partial word *bucks*.

A CALL FROM GOLIATH

It didn't take long for Starbucks to get word of Charbucks Blend. Just four months after making their first sale of their new blend, the Clarks received a call from Starbucks' in-house counsel. In what Annie Clark described as an unmistakably threatening phone call, Starbucks' counsel insisted that Charbucks Blend was a violation of Starbucks' trademark rights and demanded that Black Bear cease the use of the name and take steps to completely remove Charbucks from the marketplace. Starbucks followed up with a formal demand to cease and desist and alleged that Black Bear's use of *Charbucks* was disparaging, diluted Starbucks' mark, and violated federal trademark law.

The Clarks held a family meeting to discuss the matter. While they agreed that they had done nothing wrong, they decided that a trademark battle with Starbucks could bankrupt their family business even if they eventually prevailed in court. The risk was too high, so they decided to pursue negotiations for settlement. They hired an attorney who sent Starbucks a letter on behalf of Black Bear denying any liability for trademark infringement but also offering to engage in settlement negotiations given the limited time and financial resources that the Clarks had at their disposal. Starbucks hired outside counsel to negotiate a settlement agreement. In the event that settlement negotiations failed, Starbucks made it clear to Black Bear that it intended to file suit for trademark infringement. The negotiations dragged on for three years, and Black Bear's legal bills were soaring. Starbucks offered to compensate Black Bear for some of its legal expenses and costs of compliance (e.g., changing advertising, removing the products), but the parties could not agree on the amount or on a mutually acceptable public statement. On July 2, 2001, nearly four years after the first phone call about

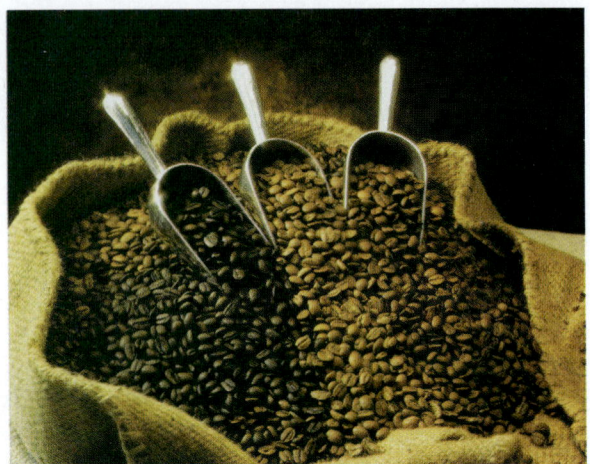

Starbucks sued a small company in a battle over the use of the word "Charbucks." Greg Kuchik/Getty Images

the dispute, Starbucks filed suit against Black Bear in the U.S. District Court for the Southern District of New York, alleging trademark dilution, trademark infringement, and violation of Section 43(a) of the Lanham Act (the federal trademark law). Starbucks demanded both damages and injunctive relief.

Starbucks' Strategy

The Clarks breathed a sigh of relief after learning that Zurich, the insurance carrier that issued Black Bear's general commercial liability insurance policy, determined that their company was covered under the policy for this particular lawsuit and that coverage for their legal defense costs against Starbucks would be provided. This allowed them the opportunity to have their day in court without the fear that Starbucks would use the litigation process to drive Black Bear out of business. Both sides were ordered to mediation, but little progress was made and the case looked headed for the courtroom.

However, soon after the mediation attempts failed, Starbucks employed a more aggressive litigation strategy. Its outside counsel notified Black Bear's counsel that unless the case was resolved, Starbucks would move to amend the lawsuit to drop a claim for certain damages listed in the original complaint. The impact of this amendment was that Zurich would be able to withdraw coverage for Black Bear's defense on the basis that the remaining claims in the lawsuit were exempt from Black Bear's policy. Still, the Clarks would not settle the claim. Three months later, Starbucks followed through on its promise to amend the complaint, and Zurich soon notified the Clarks of its decision to terminate coverage for defense of the Starbucks case once the amendment was approved by the court. Ultimately, however, the court denied Starbucks' attempt to amend the complaint, finding that the amendment was designed primarily for affecting settlement negotiation leverage. Zurich was therefore compelled to continue covering the costs of Black Bear's defense.

In March 2005, a two-day trial was held in the matter of *Starbucks Corp. v. Wolfe's Borough Coffee, Inc., dba Black Bear Micro Roastery* in the U.S. District Court for the Southern District of New York. Starbucks relied primarily on the testimony of its expert, Warren Mitofsky, a scientist who had conducted a consumer survey and concluded that the number-one association of the nature of the name Charbucks in the mind of the consumers was with the brand Starbucks. However, Mitofsky also conceded that his survey had been conducted entirely by telephone and that any measurement of reaction to the familiarity with other visual cues, such as the Charbucks Blend label, could not be accomplished through a telephone survey. The trial court issued an opinion and order ruling in favor of Black Bear and dismissed all of the counts of Starbucks' complaint. The court held that Starbucks did not meet its burden of proving that *actual dilution* had taken place and that Starbucks could not prevail on the trademark infringement claim because there was no likelihood that consumers would confuse the Charbucks mark with the Starbucks mark.

For the time being, David had battled back Goliath—but the giant continued the fight in the appellate courts.

The Trademark Dilution Revision Act (TDRA)

In January 2006, Starbucks filed an appeal of the trial court's decision. While the appeal was pending, Congress amended the trademark laws by passing the Trademark Dilution Revision Act (TDRA) of 2006. The TDRA was passed primarily in response to the U.S. Supreme Court's decision in *Moseley v. V Secret Catalogue, Inc.*, in which the Court established the burden of proof for trademark holders by requiring evidence of *actual dilution*. Starbucks then argued that under the TDRA the test for dilution was substantially easier to meet because the statute rejects actual dilution in favor of a more relaxed *likelihood of dilution* standard. In its appeal, Starbucks contended that the TDRA definition of dilution by blurring and/or tarnishment was directly related to its claims against Black Bear and that the case should now be evaluated in light of changes made by the TDRA.

The appellate wheels of justice were grinding slowly in this case. The appellate court ordered a rehearing by the trial court in light of the TDRA. The trial court again entered a judgment in favor of Black Bear for substantially the same reasons detailed in the first opinion. Not surprisingly, Starbucks appealed.

In a December 2009 opinion, the U.S. Court of Appeals for the Second Circuit handed down its decision and affirmed much of the trial court's ruling. Specifically

- Although the appellate court agreed with the trial court's conclusion that the Charbucks package design was significantly different in imagery, color, and format from Starbucks' logo and signage, the appellate court also held that the trial court had used the incorrect analytical framework for dilution by blurring as set out in the TDRA. Therefore, the appellate court remanded this one issue back to the trial court.

- The appellate court affirmed the trial court's ruling that Starbucks did not provide sufficient evidence that dilution had occurred through tarnishment because Black Bear's intent was clearly to promote a positive image for its brand of coffee rather than referring to it as a way to harm the reputation of Starbucks' coffees.

- The appellate court also affirmed the trial court's ruling that no infringement had occurred under the federal trademark statute and agreed with Black Bear's argument that the coexistence of the Starbucks mark and Charbucks Blend for 11 years with no report of a single customer becoming confused is a powerful indication that there is no confusion or likelihood of confusion.

Connecting Legal and Ethical Concepts: Questions for Discussion

Chapter 1, "Legal Foundations"

1. What lessons can managers learn from this case in terms of avoiding trademark liability and of decision making when enforcing a trademark?

2. Consider the Charbucks dispute from a cost-benefit perspective. What was the return on Starbucks' investment to pursue Black Bear for trademark infringement? Even if Black Bear's defense was covered by insurance, did the investment of time by the Clarks yield a sufficient return?

3. Apply a strategy that you learned in "Strategic Legal Solutions: The Big Picture." What strategy would be helpful in preventing or resolving this dispute?

Chapter 5, "Business Ethics, Corporate Social Responsibility, and Law"

1. Consider Starbucks' litigation strategy. When it used legal maneuvering to attempt to get Zurich to withdraw, was that ethical? Was it a legitimate hard-nosed business practice, or did Starbucks use its resources in an attempt to force Black Bear into settlement?
2. Starbucks invests substantial resources into its theme of being a responsible company. On its website, the company announces, "We've always believed that businesses can—and should—have a positive impact on the communities they serve." How does that statement square with its strategy in the Charbucks litigation? Is there any ethical conflict between a company's stated objective to be a good corporate neighbor and its obligation to its stakeholders to protect its intellectual property?
3. Even if Black Bear was legally entitled to use *Charbucks*, is it ethical to use a name that sounds so close to someone else's famous coffee trademark?

Chapter 24, "Intellectual Property"

1. The TDRA defines blurring as an "association arising from the similarity between a mark and a famous mark that impairs the distinctiveness of the famous mark." How should the trial court rule on the issue of dilution by blurring given the new language in the TDRA?
2. Should the court have given more weight to the testimony of Starbucks' expert? Although the survey was conducted by telephone, shouldn't consumer confusion in the similar sounds (*Charbucks* versus *Starbucks*) be sufficient to show blurring?
3. What legal issues must a famous-mark holder consider in preserving its trademark?

ASSIGNMENT: Find Black Bear a Trademark

Think of several names and a mark that Black Bear could have used for dark-roasted coffee beans instead of Charbucks. Conduct a preliminary search on the USPTO's website (www.uspto.gov) and on a commercial domain name website such as www.register.com to see if the name or mark is available. Use your knowledge of dilution law to be sure that your trademark is viable and protectable.

capstone case study 2
THE ODWALLA JUICE COMPANY CRISIS

OVERVIEW AND OBJECTIVES

In 1996, a deadly strain of bacteria broke out among residents of some West Coast states and eventually spread into western Canada. When the bacteria was traced to juice products made by the Odwalla Juice Company in California, the company's loyal customers and market analysts were shocked in disbelief. Odwalla had prided itself on being a socially responsible company that was passionate about producing the healthiest juice on the market.

The events that followed the outbreak provide an example of how vastly different areas of the law impact corporate strategy during a corporate crisis and how business ethics principles help drive the decision-making process. The objective of this case study[1] is to attempt to understand legal and ethical implications using a comprehensive and practical approach. In analyzing this case, students hone skills in constructing a business strategy for handling a crisis by (1) spotting the multifaceted legal and ethical challenges of the crisis, (2) recognizing the strengths and weaknesses in Odwalla's responses, and (3) using legal insight and ethical decision-making models to craft a response.

Review Legal Concepts

Prior to reading the case, briefly review the following legal concepts that were covered previously in this textbook: food and drug safety (Chapter 21), products liability (Chapter 9), negligence (Chapter 9), criminal law (Chapter 22), and business ethics (Chapter 5). Think of these areas of the law as you read the case study facts and questions.

THE ODWALLA JUICE COMPANY'S ORIGINS

Odwalla Juice Company was started in 1986 by a group of health-conscious friends living together in the San Francisco Bay area. Starting with a hand juicer and organically grown fruit, the owners produced fresh juice in the back shed of one of the founders' homes and sold their juice by delivering it daily to area restaurants. Perhaps the most essential part of their business model was their claim that their juice was fresh from the fruit, without the pasteurization process that was used by other juice producers. In fact, Odwalla was one of the pioneers of a wider movement in the United States favoring more organic food consumption. Odwalla's founders held the belief that pasteurization—the process of heating the juice to a certain temperature for purposes of killing any bacteria that had developed during growing, picking, or processing—affected the taste of the juice and was unnecessary. Instead, Odwalla used an acid-based rinsing process to kill bacteria. Producing fresh organic fruit juice as a central component of its business model, Odwalla developed a loyal following of consumers who desired the freshest juice possible, and its sales grew exponentially. By the mid-1990s, Odwalla was selling nearly $90 million worth of juice per year.

"SOIL TO SOUL"

Odwalla's founders were at the forefront of the corporate social responsibility movement that can be traced to the mid-1980s. Indeed, as one of the founders was fond of saying, they embraced a "Zen-like philosophy" in all of their dealings, and community was an important factor in the equation. The company employed a *soil to soul* metaphor to describe its commitment to using fresh organic fruit (soil) to nurture the "body whole" (soul) of its consumers. Odwalla's reputation as a socially responsible, growth-oriented company flourished as it received awards from *Business Ethics* magazine in 1995 for Outstanding Corporate Environmentalism and from *Inc.* magazine in 1996 as Employer of the Year.

CRISIS ON THE COAST

In early October 1996, an outbreak of *E. coli*[2] struck several West Coast states, including California and Washington, and reached into western Canada as well. *E. coli* is a potentially deadly bacterium that develops as a result

---

[1] A complete bibliography for this case study may be found in Connect.

[2] For purposes of this case study, *E. coli* is shorthand for *E. coli 0157:H7*, which is the name of a strain of bacteria that lives in the digestive tracts of humans and animals. *E. coli* has been found in uncooked meat, raw milk or dairy products, and raw fruits and vegetables that have not been properly pasteurized or processed.

The Odwalla juice company faced a corporate crisis, which included legal issues and ethical questions, after its product was tied to an *E. coli* outbreak. Michael Neelon/Alamy Stock Photo

of contamination of food products or processing. On October 30, 1996, health officials in the state of Washington notified Odwalla that they were investigating a possible link between the *E. coli* outbreak and Odwalla apple and carrot juice. After learning of the potential link, Odwalla's executive management team had an emergency meeting to discuss their response. Although there was no demonstrable link at this point, Odwalla's executive management team decided to mobilize a voluntary recall of products containing apple or carrot products. This was a major financial commitment involving the removal of Odwalla products from nearly 4,600 retail outlets in seven states in just 48 hours. Odwalla claimed that it spent $6.5 million on the recall effort.

Odwalla's corporate crisis took a tragic turn when, in November 1996, a 16-month-old child died from *E. coli* after drinking Odwalla apple juice. As many as 60 other consumers were hospitalized with *E. coli*–related illnesses in a period of just one month. At the height of the outbreak, government investigators confirmed that the Odwalla products were in fact the source of the *E. coli* contamination. Odwalla implemented a media strategy that included issuing daily statements to the press, holding internal conference calls whereby managers were informed of updates, and setting up a website to disseminate information. Odwalla publicly promised to pay for all medical expenses of injured consumers and to reevaluate its manufacturing process immediately.

FALLOUT

Odwalla's brand name was decimated by the crisis. Immediately after the outbreak, Odwalla's stock price dropped 34 percent and sales of its juice products fell 90 percent in one month. The outbreak triggered numerous investigations by federal and state authorities. Customers filed negligence lawsuits, claiming that Odwalla had known that the acid-rinse method was ineffective and that scientific studies had shown that the method was effective in killing bacteria that caused *E. coli* only 8 percent of the time. After it had been shown that pasteurization was a widely used practice in the industry (although not required by federal or state laws) and that Odwalla management had ignored its own head of quality assurance's warning about potential contamination sources in the factory, the Food and Drug Administration levied a $1.5 million fine, the largest in the agency's history at that time.

Immediately after the recall, Odwalla was widely praised by the media and commentators for its handling of the crisis. The company decided that, despite mounting financial pressures from lawsuits and fines, no employees would be laid off and that it would continue to donate to community charities. Odwalla hired a public relations firm that constructed a standard explanation that the contamination was unforeseeable and that all appropriate safety measures were in place. The public largely believed Odwalla's explanations because its reputation for social responsibility was ironclad in its consumers' minds. Even the parents of the child whose *E. coli*–related death had ignited the crisis were quoted as saying that they didn't blame the company for her death and that Odwalla had done everything it could have under the circumstances.

However, during the discovery process in one of the lawsuits filed by an injured consumer, it was revealed that Odwalla had more knowledge of a potential health hazard prior to the outbreak than had been previously reported. A report surfaced that indicated that the U.S. Army had rejected Odwalla's proposal to sell its juice in U.S. Army commissaries after an army inspector found uncommonly high levels of bacteria in a sample and concluded that the risk of contamination was extraordinarily high. The army rejection had taken place four months prior to the *E. coli* outbreak. Responding to the army's findings, Odwalla's head of quality assurance recommended that the company add an additional layer of contamination protection by employing a chlorine-based washing system for the fruit. His recommendations were rejected, however, due to management's concern that the chlorine wash would affect the taste of the juice. After the army disclosures were made public, Odwalla settled several lawsuits despite its earlier resistance to a nonlitigation solution.

Soon after the settlement, *The Seattle Times* wrote a scathing editorial about Odwalla's course of action. The editorial predicted that Odwalla would forever be known as "the careless provider of poisoned fruit juice." Odwalla's stock was now trading at its lowest level ever, and the company was incurring massive debt to cover litigation costs and technology upgrades.

ODWALLA TODAY

After the fallout from the *E. coli* crisis, Odwalla invested heavily in quality assurance technology and eventually became an innovator of a "flash-pasteurization" process that killed all bacteria but kept the fresh taste and quality of the juice intact. Just two years after the crisis began, the readers of *San Francisco Magazine* voted Odwalla "Best Brand." Although the company looked poised for a comeback, it had accrued substantial debt and was forced to begin exploring the possibility of merger opportunities. After a merger with East Coast juice maker Fresh Samantha in 2000, Odwalla ended up as part of a large acquisition by the Minute Maid division of the Coca-Cola Company in October 2001. Today, Odwalla remains a subsidiary of Coca-Cola and has over 650 employees. Its management continues to focus on its "soil to soul" model, and Odwalla now features 25 organic products within eight product lines, including smoothies, soy shakes, and food bars.

Connecting Legal and Ethical Concepts: Questions for Discussion

Chapter 5, "Business Ethics, Corporate Social Responsibility, and Law"

1. Is there a disconnect between Odwalla's corporate social responsibility model and its actions or course of conduct? In what ways did Odwalla's course of conduct differ from its stated social goals?
2. Because Odwalla was not specifically required to use the pasteurization process at the time, what ethical considerations factor into the decision on whether or not to use pasteurization?
3. Does the fact that the industry standard at the time was to subject juice to pasteurization impact the ethical decision-making analysis?

Chapter 9, "Torts and Products Liability"

1. Did the manufacturing or *design process* of the juice render it an unreasonably dangerous product under the Restatements? Why or why not?
2. Are there any other ways in which the product could have been defective aside from manufacturing or design?
3. What defenses, if any, could Odwalla use to rebut a claim of a defective product?

Chapter 9, "Torts and Products Liability"

1. Are there any incidents of negligence indicated in the case (either pre- or postcontamination)?
2. In the context of a negligence analysis, what legal duties did Odwalla owe to its consumers? Does it owe any special duty to consumers?
3. Does failing to comply with industry standards at the time of the contamination constitute a breach of duty?

Chapter 21, "Warranties and Consumer Protection Law"

1. What federal statute regulates Odwalla's processes and procedures?
2. Because the FDA required no specific pasteurization standards at the time, should Odwalla be fined for failing to use such a system?
3. If Odwalla had not voluntarily recalled the juice, what options did the FDA have in response to the outbreak?

Chapter 22, "Criminal Law and Procedure in Business"

1. Apply the Model Penal Code sections on criminal liability for business entities to the Odwalla case. Do the facts in the case indicate that Odwalla's action rose to the level of criminal culpability? If yes, what defense, if any, is available to Odwalla?
2. Odwalla's managers consistently issued statements denying that they had any actual or constructive knowledge that Odwalla's processing systems were dangerous. Do any facts in the case study contradict those statements? Are these facts sufficient to establish the elements of criminal intent on the part of the executives who made the denials?

ASSIGNMENT: Devise Odwalla's Strategy

Odwalla ordered a voluntary recall that was expensive and potentially devastating to the company before an affirmative link was found. Assume you were one of the managers at the Odwalla emergency meeting held after the *E. coli* outbreak. What were Odwalla's options? Using what you have learned in "Strategic Legal Solutions: The Big Picture" in Chapter 1, "Legal Foundations," and the ethical decision-making paradigm in Chapter 5, "Business Ethics, Corporate Social Responsibility, and Law," as a starting point, devise a strategy that includes the appropriate balance between (1) representing the best interests of the primary and secondary stakeholders, (2) protecting the company's future, (3) minimizing the risk of public harm, and (4) fulfilling the corporation's commitment to corporate social responsibility.

©philsajonesen/Getty Images

capstone case study 3
FRAUD UNDER THE ARCHES: THE MCDONALD'S GAME PIECE SCANDAL

OVERVIEW AND OBJECTIVES

In August 2001, the Federal Bureau of Investigation arrested eight individuals involved in a nationwide scheme to defraud the McDonald's Corporation and its customers by fraudulently manipulating McDonald's promotional prize contests over a period of five years. Although no McDonald's employees were implicated in the scam, the arrests sparked class action litigation by customers and competitors against McDonald's under a variety of legal theories. The events that led up to the arrests and the legal and ethical implications of McDonald's response to the revelations of the fraud are examined in this case study.[1]

Review Legal Concepts

Prior to reading the case, briefly review the following legal concepts that were covered in the textbook: standing (Chapter 4), arbitration (Chapter 4), consumer fraud (Chapter 21), contracts agreement (Chapter 6), unjust enrichment (Chapter 6), agency (Chapter 10), criminal law (Chapter 22), and business ethics (Chapter 5). Think of these areas of the law as you read the case study facts and questions.

MCDONALD'S PROMOTIONAL GAMES

McDonald's is perhaps the most familiar fast-food restaurant name in the world. The business began in 1940 with a restaurant opened by brothers Richard and Maurice McDonald in San Bernardino, California. Their introduction of the "Speedee Service System" in 1948 established the principles of the modern fast-food restaurant. The present company dates its founding to the opening of one of the first McDonald's franchises by Ray Kroc. Eventually, Mr. Kroc purchased the McDonald brothers' shares and began a worldwide expansion. The company was listed on the public stock market in 1965, and there are now more than 32,000 McDonald's restaurants around the world.

---

[1] A complete bibliography for this case study may be found in Connect.

Marketing Strategies

One of McDonald's most successful marketing strategies has been to use various cash games of chance based on themes from popular television shows such as *Who Wants to Be a Millionaire?* and another promotional cash game based on the popular board game *Monopoly.* McDonald's operates these games as part of a consolidated national and international advertising and marketing effort. Industry experts have lauded McDonald's games as highly effective in attracting more customers and encouraging more visits by offering the opportunity to win instant prizes ranging from food to cash prizes of $1 million. Each of the promotional games has low-value, midvalue, and high-value prizes. In order to win a prize, a McDonald's customer obtains a game piece, which may be (1) received at a restaurant, either attached to food containers (such as french fry boxes and drink cups) or unattached and handed out separately; (2) found in an advertising insert of a newspaper; (3) received by direct mail; or (4) obtained by requesting a game piece via the mail. Customers have the opportunity to become instant winners or to win by collecting specific game pieces. Low-value prizes include food items and low-dollar cash prizes. High-value prizes include vehicles and cash prizes up to $1 million. Customers can win the cash prize either by obtaining an instant $1 million–winner game piece or by collecting a sufficient number of certain game pieces.

Simon Marketing

Simon Marketing, Inc., an international marketing company headquartered in Los Angeles, was originally hired by McDonald's to develop its highly successful Happy Meals prize and promotional campaigns in the 1980s. Simon eventually became the exclusive company handling McDonald's promotional games, including "Monopoly Game at McDonald's," "Hatch, Match and Win," "When the USA Wins, You Win," and "Who Wants to Be a Millionaire?" In order to claim a high-value prize, the winner was required to redeem the winning game piece through Simon's security procedures. After receiving a game piece claim,

The Department of Justice's announcement of arrests related to a fraud scheme involving game pieces from McDonald's *Monopoly* promotional game sparked legal and ethical challenges for the fast-food giant.
Tim Boyle/Getty Images

Simon would confirm the legitimacy of the game piece and notify McDonald's that the claim was legitimate. McDonald's then distributed the prize to the winner.

In addition to verifying winning game pieces, Simon was also responsible for the printing and distribution of game pieces. As part of its agreement with McDonald's, Simon provided security measures to ensure the integrity of promotional games. Simon entrusted its security chief, retired police officer Jerome Jacobson, with the responsibility of ensuring the games' integrity and with disseminating the high-value pieces through legitimate channels.

Arrests and Indictments

In August 2001, the U.S. Attorney's Office filed criminal charges against eight people in Georgia, South Carolina, Florida, Texas, Indiana, and Wisconsin as part of a nationwide investigation into a plot to defraud the public by diverting winning game pieces from various McDonald's cash award giveaways. Dubbed "Operation Final Answer" by government investigators, the Department of Justice alleged that the group had been responsible for more than $20 million worth of winning game pieces that were diverted from proper delivery and then fraudulently claimed by winners pretending to be legitimate. The ringleader of the plot was 58-year-old Jerome Jacobson, the director of security at Simon Marketing. Jacobson devised a way to remove high-price game pieces prior to their distribution to retail McDonald's restaurants. Jacobson concocted a system of recruiters (none of whom were Simon or McDonald's employees) who solicited others willing to falsely claim that they were legitimate winners of the McDonald's games. Prosecutors alleged that Jacobson sold $1 million prize pieces from the games and charged the fake winner $50,000 in cash plus a commission for the recruiter. On midvalue prizes and luxury vehicle prizes, the recruiters would sell the winning game pieces to other family members or friends. Among those arrested were a husband and wife whose son acted as one of Jacobson's recruiters.

After Jacobson agreed to cooperate with federal authorities in exchange for leniency, the government announced criminal indictments of 51 more individuals involved in the scam. Eventually, Jacobson pled guilty and was sentenced to 37 months in prison, assessed $750,000 in fines, and ordered to pay $13.4 million in restitution.

Civil Suits

Two weeks after the government announced the indictment, the first civil lawsuit was filed against McDonald's. By October 2001, so many civil suits had been filed against it that McDonald's asked the federal courts to consolidate all of the litigation into a single proceeding. Lawsuits alleged various claims, including violation of consumer fraud protection laws, unjust enrichment, and breach of contract. In many cases, the plaintiff sought class action[2] status.

In one case filed in an Illinois trial court, a customer sued McDonald's and Simon under the state consumer fraud statute and sought class action status. The plaintiffs alleged that McDonald's and Simon's actions constituted deceptive conduct and omissions of material terms from their promotional games. They pointed to

---
[2]A class action lawsuit is a method for conducting a lawsuit in which a large group of persons with a well-defined common interest (class) has a representative of the group litigate the claim on behalf of the larger group, without the need to join every individual member of the class.

evidence that McDonald's had been made aware of the fraud being conducted by Jacobson but had continued to market its promotional games, including publishing the odds of winning, for at least an additional eight months. However, because of Jacobson's scheme, the plaintiffs alleged that their actual odds of winning a substantial prize were zero.

Other cases centered on a theory of unjust enrichment. In these cases, plaintiffs alleged that McDonald's promotional games were highly successful and resulted in increased revenue for McDonald's and Simon. The plaintiffs pointed to evidence that McDonald's had a spike in sales during certain promotions. They alleged that McDonald's continued to use the promotion even after it knew that the integrity of the game was compromised and, therefore, that any profits made were caused by the fraud. Because customers were induced to purchase McDonald's products through the promotion, McDonald's was unjustly enriched by retaining the profits from the products.

McDonald's was also sued by its competitors over the scandal. In *Phoenix of Broward, Inc. v. McDonald's Corporation*,[3] the owner of a Burger King franchise in Fort Lauderdale, Florida, filed suit against McDonald's for false advertising and unfair competition. The owner alleged that McDonald's had enticed customers away from Burger King by employing the promotional game. Because the promotional materials represented that each customer had a fair chance to win the high-value prizes, Phoenix alleged that McDonald's actual knowledge that the game was rigged and its course of conduct, after learning of the FBI investigation, in continuing the promotion constituted unfair competition. Phoenix also claimed that the fraudulent game promotion yielded an unnatural spike in profits for McDonald's and that the Burger King franchise suffered damages as a result of McDonald's conduct.

MCDONALD'S STRATEGY

On the day the Justice Department announced the arrest of Jacobson and seven others, McDonald's announced that it was suspending the game entirely pending an internal investigation of the matter. It also announced a campaign to regain any lost public trust by launching an immediate $10 million promotional giveaway. The promotion allowed customers to win prizes of up to $1 million from promotional game pieces during a weeklong period beginning in late August 2001.

Immediately after the arrests, McDonald's terminated its 25-year relationship with Simon by unilaterally canceling its contract with the agency. The move was devastating to Simon because McDonald's represented two-thirds of the agency's annual revenue.[4] After the revelations of fraud, Simon's other major client, Philip Morris,[5] which contracted with Simon to run promotional campaigns for its Kraft and Marlboro brands, also terminated its relationship with Simon. In less than one week, the value of Simon's public shares plunged 78 percent, and the company was facing dozens of lawsuits and a criminal investigation.

Aggressive Litigation

McDonald's employed what can aptly be described as an aggressive litigation strategy by vigorously defending lawsuits while also pursuing Simon for reimbursement of the costs being incurred by McDonald's because of the fraudulent act of Simon's employee.

For each case that it defended that was related to the fraud, either McDonald's challenged the *standing* of the plaintiffs to bring an action against McDonald's based on the fraud or it sought a court order to compel *arbitration* based on the published rules of the game.

Phoenix Case

In the *Phoenix* case, McDonald's asserted that Phoenix did not have standing in a case alleging unfair competition because McDonald's actions were unrelated to any provable harm suffered by Phoenix's restaurant. Phoenix alleged that McDonald's misrepresented customers' chances to win high-value prizes but also alleged that as a result of this false advertising, the fraudulent promotion induced customers who would have eaten at Phoenix's Burger King restaurants (and not any other fast-food restaurants) to eat at McDonald's. Ultimately the courts agreed with McDonald's and dismissed the lawsuit, holding that Phoenix's allegations of the link between the false advertising (McDonald's games) and the injury suffered by Phoenix (decrease in Burger King's sales) was too vague to have standing to sue.

Customer Lawsuits

While McDonald's was successful at repelling suits by competitors, its attempts to halt lawsuits by its customers had mixed results. The stakes for customer lawsuits were becoming increasingly high as each plaintiff requested class action status. In each customer case, McDonald's argued that the plaintiff was bound by

---

[3] 489 F.3d 1156 (11th Cir. 2007).

[4] In the year prior to the scandal, Simon's annual revenue was $768 million.

[5] Philip Morris changed its name to Altria in 2003.

the terms of the Official Contest Rules published by McDonald's in conjunction with each of its promotional cash giveaway games. The rules included an arbitration clause whereby participants in the game promotion agreed to resolve any disputes by final and binding arbitration. The clause called for the arbitration to be held at the regional office of the American Arbitration Association (AAA) located closest to the participant.

In *Popovich v. McDonald's*,[6] a federal district court ruled that the arbitration clause included in the official rules was invalid because the arbitration costs were too prohibitive. Popovich argued that the fees associated with an arbitration proceeding rendered the arbitration agreement an ineffective way to enforce his statutory rights of recovery from McDonald's for its fraudulent conduct. Popovich submitted evidence that, under the AAA rules, his claim would have to be arbitrated using the high-fee *commercial* procedures instead of the much lower-cost *consumer* procedures. In ruling in favor of Popovich, the court held that because Popovich sought $20 million in damages for his potential class action, the fees required by the AAA would be between $48,000 and $126,000. The court concluded that, in the context of this claim, the arbitration costs were prohibitive and the clause was thus unenforceable.

An alternate theory was advanced by the plaintiff in *James v. McDonald's Corp.*[7] In that case, James argued that she should not be forced to arbitrate her claims because she never entered into an agreement to arbitrate her dispute. The plaintiff claimed that she was not aware of the rules, much less any rules that deprived her of a jury trial. She maintained that customers cannot be expected to read every container of food they purchase in order to know that they are entering into a contract. She also argued that, even if she was found to be bound by the rules, the arbitration clause in the rules was invalid because it was overly burdensome due to the high up-front costs required to pursue a claim through the AAA. However, the court ultimately ruled against James, found the arbitration clause to be valid, and refused to allow her lawsuit to go forward in the courts. In rejecting James's claim that the costs were too burdensome, the court pointed out that James had not submitted evidence that she considered applying for a fee waiver from the AAA that could have reduced the fees significantly.

SIMON LAWSUIT AND COUNTERSUIT

Two months after McDonald's terminated its relationship with Simon, its parent company filed a $1.9 billion lawsuit against McDonald's in which the company alleged breach of contract, fraud, and defamation. Simon alleged that, after learning of the nearly year-long FBI investigation, McDonald's ran a fraudulent campaign to intentionally destroy Simon for its own public relations and financial benefit. The lawsuit also accused McDonald's of orchestrating a smear campaign through McDonald's representatives' contacting other Simon clients and urging them to quit doing business with Simon. Simon alleged that McDonald's abrupt termination of their contract was unwarranted and unlawful and resulted in substantial losses.

McDonald's responded with a $105 million countersuit against Simon for negligence in failing to detect the fraud scheme and for breach of contract. McDonald's contended that its contract with Simon required Simon to repay McDonald's for any losses it incurred as a result of Simon's conduct. Given the losses from the embezzlement and the subsequent giveaway that was required to restore public confidence, McDonald's argued that it was entitled to be reimbursed by Simon.

SETTLEMENTS AND AFTERMATH

After aggressively battling litigants in the courtroom for a year, McDonald's reevaluated its two-front litigation strategy. The company engaged in settlement negotiations with customer lawsuit plaintiffs and was able to structure an agreement with Simon's insurance carrier that ultimately helped settle the class action claims filed against it by various customers. One year later, McDonald's agreed to a final settlement with Simon.

Customer Class Actions

The uncertainties surrounding the arbitration clause and expenses of litigating a class action case resulted in a change in McDonald's strategy. Beginning in April 2002, McDonald's and Simon began to settle the various class action complaints filed by consumers by tapping the proceeds from Simon's liability insurance policies. Eventually, McDonald's settled a similar class action consumer suit filed in Canada.

Simon Litigation

In an August 2003 filing with the Securities and Exchange Commission, McDonald's reported that it had agreed to pay Simon $16.6 million to settle all claims that were raised in the lawsuit.[8] However, in the

---

[6]189 F. Supp. 2d 772 (N.D. Ill. 2002).
[7]417 F.3d 672 (7th Cir. 2005).

[8]Simon also sued Philip Morris and Simon Marketing's auditing firms (KPMG, PricewaterhouseCoopers, and Ernst & Young). Each case was settled before trial with a favorable outcome for Simon.

meantime, Simon had effectively eliminated a majority of its ongoing promotion business operations and was in the process of disposing of its assets and settling liabilities related to the fraud. During the second quarter of 2002, the company ceased operations altogether except for attempting to find a buyer for its remaining assets. A September 2009 filing indicated that the company had reduced its workforce to 4 employees (from 136 employees in 2001). Although the company was not successful in finding a buyer for many years, in December 2009, Simon's remaining directors issued public disclosures that they had formed a committee to investigate the potential of an acquisition or combination with another company.

Connecting Legal and Ethical Concepts: Questions for Discussion

Chapter 4, "Resolving Disputes: Litigation and Alternative Dispute Resolution"

1. In the *Phoenix* case, the court ruled that competitors didn't have standing to sue McDonald's for fraud in the promotional games. Would competitors have standing to sue McDonald's? Would customers have standing?

2. Could the arbitration clause used by McDonald's in its rules fit into any of the four grounds for unenforceability under the Federal Arbitration Act?

Chapter 5, "Business Ethics, Corporate Social Responsibility, and Law"

1. Consider the ethical dilemma of McDonald's if it was approached by government authorities and informed that the promotion's integrity was suspect because of possible embezzlement. However, in order to gather additional evidence, investigators requested that McDonald's take no action until arrests were made. What was McDonald's ethical duty at this point? If it continued to run the game with knowledge of the fraud, no matter what its motives, wouldn't that expose the company to significant liability?

2. Is there a conflict in this case between McDonald's duties to primary stakeholders and its duties to secondary shareholders?

3. Was McDonald's decision not to discontinue the promotion in the face of ongoing fraud more of a principles-based approach or a consequences-based approach to ethical decision making?

4. Was the use of class action litigation ethically justified in this case? Were the civil suits an attempt to redress harm or a boon for law firms that specialize in class action litigation? Were the plaintiffs more interested in shaking down McDonald's or in justice?

Chapter 6, "Overview and Formation of Contracts"

1. Why did trial courts consider the rules' contractual language binding on participants of the games when it was obvious that most customers hadn't actually read the rules? Had the customers agreed to the terms of the rules contract simply by purchasing a soft drink? Why or why not?

2. Assuming that offer and acceptance are satisfied, what consideration supports a customer-McDonald's contract?

3. Could the inclusion of an arbitration clause by McDonald's in an advertisement amid logos and trademarks be considered bad faith and held invalid as unconscionable?

Chapter 10, "Agency"

1. What were the agency status and relationship between McDonald's and Simon? Based on your answer, what duties did the parties owe each other? Were any duties breached?

2. To what extent was Simon liable for the embezzlement scheme of its employee Jacobson? Were Jacobson's actions within the scope of his employment? Why or why not?

Chapter 21, "Warranties and Consumer Protection Law"

1. Could McDonald's conduct, specifically its continuing operations after being informed of possible fraud in its promotional games, constitute deceptive advertising and a deceptive sales practice under FTC regulations?

2. Suppose that one lawsuit that was brought against McDonald's was in New Jersey and the state court applied the New Jersey Consumer Fraud Act in the same way the appellate court applied it in *Vagias v. Woodmont Properties* (Case 22.1). Would McDonald's be liable under the state law? Why or why not?

3. Would your answers to Questions 1 and 2 above be the same if McDonald's halted the promotion as soon as it learned of the FBI investigation?

Chapter 22, "Criminal Law and Procedure in Business"

1. Do Jacobson's actions amount to fraud? Embezzlement? Theft?

2. Ultimately, the government charged Jacobson and his co-conspirators with mail fraud and wire fraud. Why do you think the government did not charge them with embezzlement?

3. Could the executives of Simon be held criminally liable for the embezzlement perpetrated by Jacobson? Why or why not?

ASSIGNMENT: Devise a Strategy for McDonald's

Assume you are one of the managers called to a confidential meeting to discuss McDonald's strategy after notification by government authorities that its promotional games were being rigged by a Simon insider. What are McDonald's options? Using what you have learned from "Strategic Legal Solutions: The Big Picture" in Chapter 1, "Legal Foundations," and the ethical decision-making paradigm in Chapter 5, "Business Ethics, Corporate Social Responsibility, and Law" as a starting point, devise a strategy that includes the appropriate balance between (1) representing the best interests of its primary and secondary stakeholders, (2) protecting the future of the company, (3) minimizing the risk of public harm, and (4) addressing factors related to corporate social responsibility. Memorialize your strategy in a two-page memorandum.

APPENDIX A

The Constitution of the United States of America

Preamble

We the People of the United States, in Order to form a more perfect Union, establish Justice, insure domestic Tranquility, provide for the common defense, promote the general Welfare, and secure the Blessings of Liberty to ourselves and our Posterity, do ordain and establish this Constitution for the United States of America.

Article I

Section 1 All legislative Powers herein granted shall be vested in a Congress of the United States, which shall consist of a Senate and House of Representatives.

Section 2 The House of Representatives shall be composed of Members chosen every second Year by the People of the several States, and the Electors in each State shall have the Qualifications requisite for Electors of the most numerous Branch of the State Legislature.

No Person shall be a Representative who shall not have attained to the age of twenty five Years, and been seven Years a Citizen of the United States, and who shall not, when elected, be an Inhabitant of that State in which he shall be chosen.

Representatives and direct Taxes shall be apportioned among the several States which may be included within this Union, according to their respective Numbers, which shall be determined by adding to the whole Number of free Persons, including those bound to Service for a Term of Years, and excluding Indians not taxed, three fifths of all other Persons.[1] The actual Enumeration shall be made within three Years after the first Meeting of the Congress of the United States, and within every subsequent Term of ten Years, in such Manner as they shall by Law direct. The Number of Representatives shall not exceed one for every thirty Thousand, but each State shall have at Least one Representative, and until such enumeration shall be made, the State of New Hampshire shall be entitled to choose three, Massachusetts eight, Rhode-Island and Providence Plantations one, Connecticut five, New York six, New Jersey four, Pennsylvania eight, Delaware one, Maryland six, Virginia ten, North Carolina five, South Carolina five, and Georgia three.

When vacancies happen in the Representation from any State, the Executive Authority thereof shall issue Writs of Election to fill such Vacancies.

The House of Representatives shall chuse their Speaker and other Officers; and shall have the sole Power of Impeachment.

Section 3 The Senate of the United States shall be composed of two Senators from each State, chosen by the Legislature thereof,[2] for six Years; and each Senator shall have one Vote.

Immediately after they shall be assembled in Consequence of the first Election, they shall be divided as equally as may be into three Classes. The Seats of the Senators of the first Class shall be vacated at the Expiration of the second Year, of the second Class at the Expiration of the fourth Year, and of the third Class at the Expiration of the sixth Year, so that one third may be chosen every second Year; and if Vacancies happen by Resignation, or otherwise, during the Recess of the Legislature of any State, the Executive thereof may make temporary Appointments until the next Meeting of the Legislature, which shall then fill such Vacancies.[3]

---

[1] Changed by the Fourteenth Amendment.

[2] Changed by the Seventeenth Amendment.
[3] Changed by the Seventeenth Amendment.

No Person shall be a Senator who shall not have attained to the Age of thirty Years, and been nine Years a Citizen of the United States, and who shall not, when elected, be an Inhabitant of that State for which he shall be chosen.

The Vice President of the United States shall be President of the Senate, but shall have no Vote, unless they be equally divided.

The Senate shall chuse their other Officers, and also a President pro tempore, in the Absence of the Vice President, or when he shall exercise the Office of President of the United States.

The Senate shall have the sole Power to try all Impeachments. When sitting for that Purpose, they shall be on Oath or Affirmation. When the President of the United States is tried, the Chief Justice shall preside: And no Person shall be convicted without the Concurrence of two thirds of the Members present.

Judgment in Cases of Impeachment shall not extend further than to removal from Office, and disqualification to hold and enjoy any Office of honor, Trust or Profit under the United States: but the Party convicted shall nevertheless be liable and subject to Indictment, Trial, Judgment and Punishment, according to Law.

Section 4 The Times, Places and Manner of holding Elections for Senators and Representatives, shall be prescribed in each State by the Legislature thereof; but the Congress may at any time by Law make or alter such Regulations, except as to the Places of chusing Senators.

The Congress shall assemble at least once in every Year, and such Meeting shall be on the first Monday in December, unless they shall by Law appoint a different Day.[4]

Section 5 Each House shall be the Judge of the Elections, Returns and Qualifications of its own Members, and a Majority of each shall constitute a Quorum to do Business; but a smaller Number may adjourn from day to day, and may be authorized to compel the Attendance of absent Members, in such Manner, and under such Penalties as each House may provide.

Each House may determine the Rules of its Proceedings, punish its Members for disorderly Behaviour, and with the Concurrence of two thirds, expel a Member.

Each House shall keep a Journal of its Proceedings, and from time to time publish the same, excepting such Parts as may in their Judgment require Secrecy; and the Yeas and Nays of the Members of either House on any question shall, at the Desire of one fifth of those Present, be entered on the Journal.

Neither House, during the Session of Congress, shall, without the Consent of the other, adjourn for more than three days, nor to any other Place than that in which the two Houses shall be sitting.

Section 6 The Senators and Representatives shall receive a Compensation for their Services, to be ascertained by Law, and paid out of the Treasury of the United States. They shall in all Cases, except Treason, Felony and Breach of the Peace, be privileged from Arrest during their Attendance at the Session of their respective Houses, and in going to and returning from the same; and for any Speech or Debate in either House, they shall not be questioned in any other Place.

No Senator or Representative shall, during the Time for which he was elected, be appointed to any civil Office under the Authority of the United States, which shall have been created, or the Emoluments whereof shall have been encreased during such time; and no Person holding any Office under the United States, shall be a Member of either House during his Continuance in Office.

Section 7 All Bills for raising Revenue shall originate in the House of Representatives; but the Senate may propose or concur with Amendments as on other Bills.

Every Bill which shall have passed the House of Representatives and the Senate, shall, before it becomes a Law, be presented to the President of the United States; If he approves he shall sign it, but if not he shall return it, with his Objections to that House in which it shall have originated, who shall enter the Objections at large on their Journal, and proceed to reconsider it. If after such Reconsideration two thirds of that House shall agree to pass the Bill, it shall be sent, together with the Objections, to the other House, by which it shall likewise be reconsidered, and if approved by two thirds of that House, it shall become a Law. But in all such Cases the Votes of both Houses shall be determined by Yeas and Nays, and the Names of the Persons voting for and against the Bill shall be entered on the Journal of each House respectively. If any Bill shall not be returned by the President within ten Days (Sundays excepted) after it shall have been presented to him, the Same shall be a Law, in like Manner as if he had signed it, unless the Congress by their Adjournment prevent its Return, in which Case it shall not be a Law.

Every Order, Resolution, or Vote to which the Concurrence of the Senate and House of Representatives may be necessary (except on a question of Adjournment) shall be presented to the President of the United States; and before the Same shall take Effect, shall be approved by him, or being disapproved by him,

---

[4]Changed by the Twentieth Amendment.

shall be repassed by two thirds of the Senate and House of Representatives, according to the Rules and Limitations prescribed in the Case of a Bill.

Section 8 The Congress shall have Power To lay and collect Taxes, Duties, Imposts and Excises, to pay the Debts and provide for the common Defence and general Welfare of the United States; but all Duties, Imposts and Excises shall be uniform throughout the United States.

To borrow Money on the credit of the United States;

To regulate Commerce with foreign Nations, and among the several States, and with the Indian Tribes;

To establish an uniform Rule of Naturalization, and uniform Laws on the subject of Bankruptcies throughout the United States;

To coin Money, regulate the Value thereof, and of foreign Coin, and fix the Standard of Weights and Measures;

To provide for the Punishment of counterfeiting the Securities and current Coin of the United States;

To establish Post Offices and post Roads;

To promote the Progress of Science and useful Arts, by securing for limited Times to Authors and Inventors the exclusive Right to their respective Writings and Discoveries;

To constitute Tribunals inferior to the supreme Court;

To define and punish Piracies and Felonies committed on the high Seas, and Offences against the Law of Nations;

To declare War, grant Letters of Marque and Reprisal, and make Rules concerning Captures on Land and Water;

To raise and support Armies, but no Appropriation of Money to that Use shall be for a longer Term than two Years;

To provide and maintain a Navy;

To make Rules for the Government and Regulation of the land and naval Forces;

To provide for calling forth the Militia to execute the Laws of the Union, suppress Insurrections and repel Invasions;

To provide for organizing, arming, and disciplining, the Militia, and for governing such Part of them as may be employed in the Service of the United States, reserving to the States respectively, the Appointment of the Officers, and the Authority of training the Militia according to the discipline prescribed by Congress;

To exercise exclusive Legislation in all Cases whatsoever, over such District (not exceeding ten Miles square) as may, by Cession of particular States, and the Acceptance of Congress, become the Seat of the Government of the United States, and to exercise like Authority over all Places purchased by the Consent of the Legislature of the State in which the Same shall be, for the Erection of Forts, Magazines, Arsenals, dock-Yards, and other needful Buildings;—And

To make all Laws which shall be necessary and proper for carrying into Execution the foregoing Powers, and all other Powers vested by this Constitution in the Government of the United States, or in any Department or Officer thereof.

Section 9 The Migration or Importation of such Persons as any of the States now existing shall think proper to admit, shall not be prohibited by the Congress prior to the Year one thousand eight hundred and eight, but a Tax or duty may be imposed on such Importation, not exceeding ten dollars for each Person.

The Privilege of the Writ of Habeas Corpus shall not be suspended, unless when in Cases of Rebellion or Invasion the public Safety may require it.

No Bill of Attainder or ex post facto Law shall be passed.

No Capitation, or other direct, Tax shall be laid, unless in Proportion to the Census of enumeration herein before directed to be taken.[5]

No Tax or Duty shall be laid on Articles exported from any State.

No Preference shall be given by any Regulation of Commerce or Revenue to the Ports of one State over those of another: nor shall Vessels bound to, or from, one State, be obliged to enter, clear, or pay Duties in another.

No Money shall be drawn from the Treasury, but in Consequence of Appropriations made by Law; and a regular Statement and Account of the Receipts and Expenditures of all public Money shall be published from time to time.

No Title of Nobility shall be granted by the United States: And no Person holding any Office of Profit or Trust under them, shall, without the Consent of the Congress, accept of any present, Emolument, Office, or Title, of any kind whatever, from any King, Prince, or foreign State.

Section 10 No State shall enter into any Treaty, Alliance, or Confederation; grant Letters of Marque and Reprisal; coin Money; emit Bills of Credit; make any Thing but gold and silver coin a Tender in Payment of Debts; pass any Bill of Attainder, ex post facto Law, or Law impairing the Obligation of Contracts, or grant any Title of Nobility.

---

[5]Changed by the Sixteenth Amendment.

No State shall, without the Consent of the Congress, lay any Imposts or Duties on Imports or Exports, except what may be absolutely necessary for executing its inspection Laws: and the net Produce of all Duties and Imposts, laid by any State on Imports or Exports, shall be for the Use of the Treasury of the United States; and all such Laws shall be subject to the Revision and Controul of the Congress.

No State shall, without the consent of Congress, lay any Duty of Tonnage, keep Troops, or Ships of War in time of Peace, enter into any Agreement or Compact with another State, or with a foreign Power, or engage in War, unless actually invaded, or in such imminent Danger as will not admit of delay.

Article II

Section 1 The executive Power shall be vested in a President of the United States of America. He shall hold his Office during the Term of four Years, and, together with the Vice President, chosen for the same Term, be elected, as follows

Each state shall appoint, in such Manner as the Legislature thereof may direct, a Number of Electors, equal to the whole Number of Senators and Representatives to which the State may be entitled in Congress: but no Senator or Representative, or Person holding an Office of Trust or Profit under the United States, shall be appointed an Elector.

The Electors shall meet in their respective States, and vote by Ballot for two Persons, of whom one at least shall not be an inhabitant of the same State with themselves. And they shall make a List of all the Persons voted for, and of the Number of Votes for each; which List they shall sign and certify, and transmit sealed to the Seat of the Government of the United States, directed to the President of the Senate. The President of the Senate shall, in the Presence of the Senate and House of Representatives, open all the Certificates, and the Votes shall then be counted. The Person having the greatest Number of Votes shall be the President, if such Number be a Majority of the whole Number of Electors appointed; and if there be more than one who have such Majority, and have an equal Number of Votes, then the House of Representatives shall immediately chuse by Ballot one of them for President; and if no Person have a Majority, then from the five highest on the List the said House shall in like Manner chuse the President. But in chusing the President, the Votes shall be taken by States, the Representation from each State having one Vote; A quorum for this purpose shall consist of a Member or Members from two thirds of the States, and a Majority of all the States shall be necessary to a Choice. In every Case, after the Choice of the President, the Person having the greatest Number of Votes of the Electors shall be the Vice President. But if there should remain two or more who have equal Votes, the Senate shall chuse from them by Ballot the Vice President.[6]

The Congress may determine the Time of chusing the Electors, and the Day on which they shall give their Votes; which Day shall be the same throughout the United States.

No Person except a natural born Citizen, or a Citizen of the United States, at the time of the Adoption of this Constitution, shall be eligible to the Office of President; neither shall any Person be eligible to that Office who shall not have attained to the Age of thirty five Years, and been fourteen Years a Resident within the United States.

In Case of the Removal of the President from Office, or of his Death, Resignation, or Inability to discharge the Powers and Duties of the said Office, the Same shall devolve on the Vice President, and the Congress may by Law provide for the Case of Removal, Death, Resignation or Inability, both of the President and Vice President, declaring what Officer shall then act as President, and such Officer shall act accordingly, until the Disability be removed, or a President shall be elected.[7]

The President shall, at stated Times, receive for his Services, a Compensation, which shall neither be encreased nor diminished during the Period for which he shall have been elected, and he shall not receive within that Period any other Emolument from the United States, or any of them.

Before he enter on the Execution of his Office, he shall take the following Oath or Affirmation:—"I do solemnly swear (or affirm) that I will faithfully execute the Office of President of the United States, and will to the best of my Ability, preserve, protect, and defend the Constitution of the United States."

Section 2 The President shall be Commander in Chief of the Army and Navy of the United States, and of the Militia of the several States, when called into the actual Service of the United States; he may require the Opinion, in writing, of the principal Officer in each of the executive Departments, upon any Subject relating to the Duties of their respective Offices, and he shall have Power to grant Reprieves and Pardons for Offences against the United States, except in Cases of Impeachment.

He shall have Power, by and with the Advice and Consent of the Senate, to make Treaties, provided two

---

[6]Changed by the Twelfth Amendment.
[7]Changed by the Twenty-Fifth Amendment.

thirds of the Senators present concur; and he shall nominate, and by and with the Advice and Consent of the Senate, shall appoint Ambassadors, other public Ministers and Consuls, Judges of the supreme Court, and all other Officers of the United States, whose Appointments are not herein otherwise provided for, and which shall be established by Law; but the Congress may by Law vest the Appointment of such inferior Officers, as they think proper, in the President alone, in the Courts of Law, or in the Heads of Departments.

The President shall have Power to fill up all Vacancies that may happen during the Recess of the Senate, by granting Commissions which shall expire at the End of their next Session.

Section 3 He shall from time to time give to the Congress Information of the State of the Union, and recommend to their Consideration such Measures as he shall judge necessary and expedient; he may, on extraordinary Occasions, convene both Houses, or either of them, and in Case of Disagreement between them, with Respect to the Time of Adjournment, he may adjourn them to such Time as he shall think proper; he shall receive Ambassadors and other public Ministers; he shall take Care that the Laws be faithfully executed, and shall Commission all the Officers of the United States.

Section 4 The President, Vice President and all civil Officers of the United States, shall be removed from Office on Impeachment for, and Conviction of, Treason, Bribery, or other high Crimes and Misdemeanors.

Article III

Section 1 The judicial Power of the United States, shall be vested in one supreme Court, and in such inferior Courts as the Congress may from time to time ordain and establish. The Judges, both of the supreme and inferior Courts, shall hold their Offices during good Behaviour, and shall, at stated Times, receive for their Services, a Compensation, which shall not be diminished during their Continuance in Office.

Section 2 The judicial Power shall extend to all Cases, in Law and Equity, arising under this Constitution, the Laws of the United States, and Treaties made, or which shall be made, under their Authority;—to all Cases affecting Ambassadors, other public Ministers and Consuls;—to all Cases of admiralty and maritime Jurisdiction;—to Controversies to which the United States shall be a party;—to Controversies between two or more States;—between a State and Citizens of another State;[8]—between Citizens of different States;—between Citizens of the same State claiming Lands under Grants of different States, and between a State, or the Citizens thereof, and foreign States, Citizens or Subjects.

In all Cases affecting Ambassadors, other public Ministers and Consuls, and those in which a State shall be Party, the supreme Court shall have original Jurisdiction. In all the other Cases before mentioned, the supreme Court shall have appellate Jurisdiction, both as to Law and Fact, with such Exceptions, and under such Regulations as the Congress shall make.

The Trial of all Crimes, except in Cases of Impeachment, shall be by Jury: and such Trial shall be held in the State where the said Crimes shall have been committed; but when not committed within any State, the Trial shall be at such Place or Places as the Congress may by Law have directed.

Section 3 Treason against the United States, shall consist only in levying War against them, or in adhering to their Enemies, giving them Aid and Comfort. No Person shall be convicted of Treason unless on the Testimony of two Witnesses to the same overt Act, or on Confession in open Court.

The Congress shall have Power to declare the Punishment of Treason, but no Attainder of Treason shall work Corruption of Blood, or Forfeiture except during the Life of the Person attainted.

Article IV

Section 1 Full Faith and Credit shall be given in each State to the public Acts, Records, and judicial Proceedings of every other State. And the Congress may by general Laws prescribe the Manner in which such Acts, Records and Proceedings shall be proved, and the Effect thereof.

Section 2 The Citizens of each State shall be entitled to all Privileges and Immunities of Citizens in the several States.

A Person charged in any State with Treason, Felony, or other Crime, who shall flee from Justice, and be found in another State, shall on Demand of the executive Authority of the State from which he fled, be delivered up, to be removed to the State having Jurisdiction of the Crime.

No Person held to Service or Labour in one State, under the Laws thereof, escaping into another, shall, in Consequence of any Law or Regulation therein, be discharged from such Service or Labour, but shall be delivered up on Claim of the Party to whom such Service or Labour may be due.[9]

---

[8] Changed by the Eleventh Amendment.

[9] Changed by the Thirteenth Amendment.

Section 3 New States may be admitted by the Congress into this Union; but no new State shall be formed or erected within the Jurisdiction of any other State; nor any State be formed by the Junction of two or more States, or Parts of States, without the Consent of the Legislatures of the States concerned as well as of the Congress.

The Congress shall have Power to dispose of and make all needful Rules and Regulations respecting the Territory or other Property belonging to the United States; and nothing in this Constitution shall be so construed as to Prejudice any Claims of the United States, or of any particular State.

Section 4 The United States shall guarantee to every State in this Union a Republican Form of Government, and shall protect each of them against Invasion; and on Application of the Legislature, or of the Executive (when the Legislature cannot be convened) against domestic Violence.

Article V

The Congress, whenever two thirds of both Houses shall deem it necessary, shall propose Amendments to this Constitution, or, on the Application of the Legislatures of two thirds of the several States, shall call a Convention for proposing Amendments, which, in either Case, shall be valid to all Intents and Purposes, as Part of this Constitution, when ratified by the legislatures of three fourths of the several States, or by Conventions in three fourths thereof, as the one or the other Mode of Ratification may be proposed by the Congress; Provided that no Amendment which may be made prior to the Year One thousand eight hundred and eight shall in any Manner affect the first and fourth Clauses in the Ninth Section of the first Article; and that no State, without its Consent, shall be deprived of its equal Suffrage in the Senate.

Article VI

All Debts contracted and Engagements entered into, before the Adoption of this Constitution, shall be as valid against the United States under this Constitution, as under the Confederation.

The Constitution, and the Laws of the United States which shall be made in Pursuance thereof; and all Treaties made, or which shall be made, under the Authority of the United States, shall be the supreme Law of the Land; and the Judges in every State shall be bound thereby, any Thing in the Constitution or Laws of any State to the Contrary notwithstanding.

The Senators and Representatives before mentioned, and the Members of the several State Legislatures, and all executive and judicial Officers, both of the United States and of the several States, shall be bound by Oath or Affirmation, to support this Constitution; but no religious Test shall ever be required as a Qualification to any Office or public Trust under the United States.

Article VII

The Ratification of the Conventions of nine States, shall be sufficient for the Establishment of this Constitution between the States so ratifying the Same.

Done in Convention by the Unanimous Consent of the States present the Seventeenth Day of September in the Year of our Lord one thousand seven hundred and eighty seven and of the Independence of the United States of America the Twelfth. In witness whereof We have hereunto subscribed our Names.

Amendments

[The first 10 amendments are known as the "Bill of Rights."]

Amendment 1 (Ratified 1791)

Congress shall make no law respecting an establishment of religion, or prohibiting the free exercise thereof; or abridging the freedom of speech, or of the press; or the right of the people peaceably to assemble, and to petition the Government for a redress of grievances.

Amendment 2 (Ratified 1791)

A well regulated Militia, being necessary to the security of a free State, the right of the people to keep and bear Arms, shall not be infringed.

Amendment 3 (Ratified 1791)

No Soldier shall, in time of peace be quartered in any house, without the consent of the Owner, nor in time of war, but in a manner to be prescribed by law.

Amendment 4 (Ratified 1791)

The right of the people to be secure in their persons, houses, papers, and effects, against unreasonable searches and seizures, shall not be violated, and no Warrants shall issue, but upon probable cause, supported by Oath or affirmation, and particularly describing the place to be searched, and the persons or things to be seized.

Amendment 5 (Ratified 1791)

No person shall be held to answer for a capital, or otherwise infamous crime, unless on a presentment or indictment of a Grand Jury, except in cases arising in the land or naval forces, or in the Militia, when in actual service in time of War or public danger; nor shall any person be subject for the same offence to be twice put in jeopardy of life or limb; nor shall be compelled in any criminal case to be a witness against himself, nor be deprived of life, liberty, or property, without due process of law; nor shall private property be taken for public use, without just compensation.

Amendment 6 (Ratified 1791)

In all criminal prosecutions, the accused shall enjoy the right to a speedy and public trial, by an impartial jury of the State and district wherein the crime shall have been committed, which district shall have been previously ascertained by law, and to be informed of the nature and cause of the accusation; to be confronted with the witnesses against him; to have compulsory process for obtaining Witnesses in his favor, and to have assistance of counsel for his defence.

Amendment 7 (Ratified 1791)

In Suits at common law, where the value in controversy shall exceed twenty dollars, the right of trial by jury shall be preserved, and no fact tried by a jury, shall be otherwise re-examined in any Court of the United States, than according to the rules of the common law.

Amendment 8 (Ratified 1791)

Excessive bail shall not be required, nor excessive fines imposed, nor cruel and unusual punishments inflicted.

Amendment 9 (Ratified 1791)

The enumeration in the Constitution, of certain rights, shall not be construed to deny or disparage others retained by the people.

Amendment 10 (Ratified 1791)

The powers not delegated to the United States by the Constitution, nor prohibited by it to the States, are reserved to the States respectively, or to the people.

Amendment 11 (Ratified 1795)

The Judicial power of the United States shall not be construed to extend to any suit in law or equity, commenced or prosecuted against one of the United States by Citizens of another State, or by Citizens or Subjects of any Foreign State.

Amendment 12 (Ratified 1804)

The Electors shall meet in their respective states, and vote by ballot for President and Vice-President, one of whom, at least, shall not be an inhabitant of the same state with themselves; they shall name in their ballots the person voted for as President, and in distinct ballots the person voted for as Vice-President, and they shall make distinct lists of all persons voted for as President, and of all persons voted for as Vice-President, and of the number of votes for each, which lists they shall sign and certify, and transmit sealed to the seat of the government of the United States, directed to the President of the Senate;—The President of the Senate shall, in the presence of the Senate and House of Representatives, open all the certificates and the votes shall then be counted;—The person having the greatest number of votes for President, shall be the President, if such number be a majority of the whole number of Electors appointed; and if no person have such majority, then from the persons having the highest numbers not exceeding three on the list of those voted for as President, the House of Representatives shall choose immediately, by ballot, the President. But in choosing the President, the votes shall be taken by states, the representation from each state having one vote; a quorum for this purpose shall consist of a member or members from two-thirds of the states, and a majority of all the states shall be necessary to a choice. And if the House of Representatives shall not choose a President whenever the right of choice shall devolve upon them, before the fourth day of March next following, then the Vice-President shall act as president, as in the case of the death or other constitutional disability of the President.[10] —The person having the greatest number of votes as Vice-President, shall be the Vice-President, if such number be a majority of the whole number of Electors appointed, and if no person have a majority, then from the two highest numbers on the list, the Senate shall choose the Vice-President; a quorum for the purpose shall consist of two-thirds of the whole number of Senators, and a majority of the whole number shall be necessary to a choice. But no person constitutionally ineligible to the office of President shall be eligible to that of Vice-President of the United States.

---

[10]Changed by the Twentieth Amendment.

Amendment 13 (Ratified 1865)

Section 1 Neither slavery nor involuntary servitude, except as a punishment for crime whereof the party shall have been duly convicted, shall exist within the United States, or any place subject to their jurisdiction.

Section 2 Congress shall have power to enforce this article by appropriate legislation.

Amendment 14 (Ratified 1868)

Section 1 All persons born or naturalized in the United States, and subject to the jurisdiction thereof, are citizens of the United States and of the State wherein they reside. No State shall make or enforce any law which shall abridge the privileges or immunities of citizens of the United States; nor shall any State deprive any person of life, liberty, or property, without due process of law; nor deny to any person within its jurisdiction the equal protection of the laws.

Section 2 Representatives shall be apportioned among the several States according to their respective numbers, counting the whole number of persons in each State, excluding Indians not taxed. But when the right to vote at any election for the choice of electors for President and Vice President of the United States, Representatives in Congress, the Executive and Judicial officers of a State, or the members of the Legislature thereof, is denied to any of the male inhabitants of such State, being twenty-one[11] years of age, and citizens of the United States, or in any way abridged except for participation in rebellion, or other crime, the basis of representation therein shall be reduced in the proportion which the number of such male citizens shall bear to the whole number of male citizens twenty-one years of age in such State.

Section 3 No person shall be a Senator or Representative in Congress, or elector of President and Vice President, or hold any office, civil or military, under the United States, or under any State, who, having previously taken an oath, as a member of Congress, or as an officer of the United States, or as a member of any State legislature, or as an executive or judicial officer of any State, to support the Constitution of the United States, shall have engaged in insurrection or rebellion against the same, or given aid or comfort to the enemies thereof. But Congress may by a vote of two-thirds of each House, remove such disability.

Section 4 The validity of the public debt of the United States, authorized by law, including debts incurred for payment of pensions and bounties for services in suppressing insurrection or rebellion, shall not be questioned. But neither the United States nor any State shall assume or pay any debt or obligation incurred in aid of insurrection or rebellion against the United States, or any claim for the loss or emancipation of any slave; but all such debts, obligations and claims shall be held illegal and void.

Section 5 The Congress shall have power to enforce, by appropriate legislation, the provisions of this article.

Amendment 15 (Ratified 1870)

Section 1 The right of citizens of the United States to vote shall not be denied or abridged by the United States or by any State on account of race, color, or previous condition of servitude.

Section 2 The Congress shall have power to enforce this article by appropriate legislation.

Amendment 16 (Ratified 1913)

The Congress shall have power to lay and collect taxes on incomes, from whatever source derived, without apportionment among the several States, and without regard to any census or enumeration.

Amendment 17 (Ratified 1913)

The Senate of the United States shall be composed of two Senators from each State, elected by the people thereof, for six years; and each Senator shall have one vote. The electors in each State shall have the qualifications requisite for electors of the most numerous branch of the State legislatures.

When vacancies happen in the representation of any State in the Senate, the executive authority of such State shall issue writs of election to fill such vacancies: *Provided,* That the legislature of any State may empower the executive thereof to make temporary appointments until the people fill the vacancies by election as the legislature may direct.

This amendment shall not be so construed as to affect the election or term of any Senator chosen before it becomes valid as part of the Constitution.

Amendment 18 (Ratified 1919; Repealed 1933)

Section 1 After one year from the ratification of this article the manufacture, sale, or transportation of intoxicating liquors within, the importation thereof into, or the exportation thereof from the United States and all territory subject to the jurisdiction thereof for beverage purposes is hereby prohibited.

---

[11]Changed by the Twenty-Sixth Amendment.

Section 2 The Congress and the several States shall have concurrent power to enforce this article by appropriate legislation.

Section 3 This article shall be inoperative unless it shall have been ratified as an amendment to the Constitution by the legislatures of the several States, as provided in the Constitution, within seven years from the date of the submission hereof to the States by the Congress.[12]

Amendment 19 (Ratified 1920)

The right of citizens of the United States to vote shall not be denied or abridged by the United States or by any State on account of sex.

Congress shall have power to enforce this article by appropriate legislation.

Amendment 20 (Ratified 1933)

Section 1 The terms of the President and Vice President shall end at noon on the 20th day of January, and the terms of Senators and Representatives at noon on the 3d day of January, of the years in which such terms would have ended if this article had not been ratified; and the terms of their successors shall then begin.

Section 2 The Congress shall assemble at least once in every year, and such meeting shall begin at noon on the 3d day of January, unless they shall by law appoint a different day.

Section 3 If, at the time fixed for the beginning of the term of the President, the President elect shall have died, the Vice President elect shall become President. If a President shall not have been chosen before the time fixed for the beginning of his term, or if the President elect shall have failed to qualify, then the Vice President elect shall act as President until a President shall have qualified; and the Congress may by law provide for the case wherein neither a President elect nor a Vice President elect shall have qualified, declaring who shall then act as President, or the manner in which one who is to act shall be selected, and such person shall act accordingly until a President or Vice President shall have qualified.

Section 4 The Congress may by law provide for the case of the death of any of the persons from whom the House of Representatives may choose a President whenever the right of choice shall have devolved upon them, and for the case of the death of any of the persons from whom the Senate may choose a Vice President whenever the right of choice shall have devolved upon them.

Section 5 Sections 1 and 2 shall take effect on the 15th day of October following the ratification of this article.

Section 6 This article shall be inoperative unless it shall have been ratified as an amendment to the Constitution by the legislatures of three-fourths of the several States within seven years from the date of its submission.

Amendment 21 (Ratified 1933)

Section 1 The eighteenth article of amendment to the Constitution of the United States is hereby repealed.

Section 2 The transportation or importation into any State, Territory, or possession of the United States for delivery or use therein of intoxicating liquors, in violation of the laws thereof, is hereby prohibited.

Section 3 This article shall be inoperative unless it shall have been ratified as an amendment to the Constitution by conventions in the several States, as provided in the Constitution, within seven years from the date of the submission hereof to the States by the Congress.

Amendment 22 (Ratified 1951)

Section 1 No person shall be elected to the office of the President more than twice, and no person who has held the office of President, or acted as President, for more than two years of a term to which some other person was elected President shall be elected to the office of the President more than once. But this Article shall not apply to any person holding the office of President when this Article was proposed by the Congress, and shall not prevent any person who may be holding the office of President, or acting as President, during the term within which this Article becomes operative from holding the office of President or acting as President during the remainder of such term.

Section 2 This Article shall be inoperative unless it shall have been ratified as an amendment to the Constitution by the legislatures of three-fourths of the several States within seven years from the date of its submission to the States by the Congress.

Amendment 23 (Ratified 1961)

Section 1 The District constituting the seat of Government of the United States shall appoint in such manner as the Congress may direct:

A number of electors of President and Vice President equal to the whole number of Senators and Representatives in Congress to which the District would be entitled if it were a State, but in no event more than the least populous State; they shall be in addition to

---

[12]Repealed by the Twenty-First Amendment.

those appointed by the States, but they shall be considered, for the purposes of the election of President and Vice President, to be electors appointed by a State; and they shall meet in the District and perform such duties as provided by the twelfth article of amendment.

Section 2 The Congress shall have power to enforce this article by appropriate legislation.

Amendment 24 (Ratified 1964)

Section 1 The right of citizens of the United States to vote in any primary or other election for President or Vice President, for electors for President or Vice President, or for Senator or Representative in Congress, shall not be denied or abridged by the United States or any State by reason of failure to pay any poll tax or other tax.

Section 2 The Congress shall have power to enforce this article by appropriate legislation.

Amendment 25 (Ratified 1967)

Section 1 In case of the removal of the President from office or of his death or resignation, the Vice President shall become President.

Section 2 Whenever there is a vacancy in the office of the Vice President, the President shall nominate a Vice President who shall take office upon confirmation by a majority vote of both Houses of Congress.

Section 3 Whenever the President transmits to the President pro tempore of the Senate and the Speaker of the House of Representatives his written declaration that he is unable to discharge the powers and duties of his office, and until he transmits to them a written declaration to the contrary, such powers and duties shall be discharged by the Vice President as Acting President.

Section 4 Whenever the Vice President and a majority of either the principal officers of the executive departments or of such other body as Congress may by law provide, transmit to the President pro tempore of the Senate and the Speaker of the House of Representatives their written declaration that the President is unable to discharge the powers and duties of his office, the Vice President shall immediately assume the powers and duties of the office as Acting President.

Thereafter, when the President transmits to the President pro tempore of the Senate and the Speaker of the House of Representatives his written declaration that no inability exists, he shall resume the powers and duties of his office unless the Vice President and a majority of either the principal officers of the executive department or of such other body as Congress may by law provide, transmit within four days to the President pro tempore of the Senate and the Speaker of the House of Representatives their written declaration that the President is unable to discharge the powers and duties of his office. Thereupon Congress shall decide the issue, assembling within forty-eight hours for that purpose if not in session. If the Congress, within twenty-one days after receipt of the latter written declaration, or, if Congress is not in session, within twenty-one days after Congress is required to assemble, determines by two-thirds vote of both Houses that the President is unable to discharge the powers and duties of his office, the Vice President shall continue to discharge the same as Acting President; otherwise, the President shall resume the powers and duties of his office.

Amendment 26 (Ratified 1971)

Section 1 The right of citizens of the United States, who are eighteen years of age or older, to vote shall not be denied or abridged by the United States or by any State on account of age.

Section 2 The Congress shall have power to enforce this article by appropriate legislation.

Amendment 27 (Ratified 1992)

No law, varying the compensation for the services of the Senators and Representatives, shall take effect, until an election of Representatives shall have intervened.

Source: United States Courts.

APPENDIX B

Excerpts from the Sarbanes-Oxley Act of 2002

©philsajonesen/Getty Images

15 U.S.C. § 7241. Corporate Responsibility for Financial Reports

(a) **Regulations required**

The Commission shall, by rule, require, for each company filing periodic reports under section 78m(a) or 78o(d) of this title, that the principal executive officer or officers and the principal financial officer or officers, or persons performing similar functions, certify in each annual or quarterly report filed or submitted under either such section of this title that—

(1) the signing officer has reviewed the report;

(2) based on the officer's knowledge, the report does not contain any untrue statement of a material fact or omit to state a material fact necessary in order to make the statements made, in light of the circumstances under which such statements were made, not misleading;

(3) based on such officer's knowledge, the financial statements, and other financial information included in the report, fairly present in all material respects the financial condition and results of operations of the issuer as of, and for, the periods presented in the report;

(4) the signing officers—

   (A) are responsible for establishing and maintaining internal controls;

   (B) have designed such internal controls to ensure that material information relating to the issuer and its consolidated subsidiaries is made known to such officers by others within those entities, particularly during the period in which the periodic reports are being prepared;

   (C) have evaluated the effectiveness of the issuer's internal controls as of a date within 90 days prior to the report; and

   (D) have presented in the report their conclusions about the effectiveness of their internal controls based on their evaluation as of that date;

(5) the signing officers have disclosed to the issuer's auditors and the audit committee of the board of directors (or persons fulfilling the equivalent function)—

   (A) all significant deficiencies in the design or operation of internal controls which could adversely affect the issuer's ability to record, process, summarize, and report financial data and have identified for the issuer's auditors any material weaknesses in internal controls; and

   (B) any fraud, whether or not material, that involves management or other employees who have a significant role in the issuer's internal controls; and

(6) the signing officers have indicated in the report whether or not there were significant changes in internal controls or in other factors that could significantly affect internal controls subsequent to the date of their evaluation, including any corrective actions with

regard to significant deficiencies and material weaknesses.

(b) **Foreign reincorporations have no effect**

Nothing in this section shall be interpreted or applied in any way to allow any issuer to lessen the legal force of the statement required under this section, by an issuer having reincorporated or having engaged in any other transaction that resulted in the transfer of the corporate domicile or offices of the issuer from inside the United States to outside of the United States.

(c) **Deadline**

The rules required by subsection (a) of this section shall be effective not later than 30 days after July 30, 2002.

15 U.S.C. § 7262. Management Assessment of Internal Controls

(a) **Rules required**

The Commission shall prescribe rules requiring each annual report required by section 78m(a) or 78o(d) of this title to contain an internal control report, which shall—

(1) state the responsibility of management for establishing and maintaining an adequate internal control structure and procedures for financial reporting; and

(2) contain an assessment, as of the end of the most recent fiscal year of the issuer, of the effectiveness of the internal control structure and procedures of the issuer for financial reporting.

(b) **Internal control evaluation and reporting**

With respect to the internal control assessment required by subsection (a) of this section, each registered public accounting firm that prepares or issues the audit report for the issuer shall attest to, and report on, the assessment made by the management of the issuer. An attestation made under this subsection shall be made in accordance with standards for attestation engagements issued or adopted by the Board. Any such attestation shall not be the subject of a separate engagement.

18 U.S.C. § 1519. Destruction, Alteration, or Falsification of Records in Federal Investigations and Bankruptcy

Whoever knowingly alters, destroys, mutilates, conceals, covers up, falsifies, or makes a false entry in any record, document, or tangible object with the intent to impede, obstruct, or influence the investigation or proper administration of any matter within the jurisdiction of any department or agency of the United States or any case filed under title 11, or in relation to or contemplation of any such matter or case, shall be fined under this title, imprisoned not more than 20 years, or both.

Source: U.S. Government Publishing Office.

glossary

©philsajonesen/Getty Images

ABC test Statutory standard used by many states to determine agency status.

Absolute privilege A defense to a defamation claim whereby the defendant need not proffer any further evidence to assert the defense; provided to government officials, judicial officers and proceedings, and state legislatures.

Acceptance The offeree's expression of agreement to the terms of the offer. The power of acceptance is created by a valid offer.

Accord and satisfaction A doctrine that allows one party to create an agreement, or accord, with the other party to accept a substitute performance in order to satisfy the original performance; the completion of the new duty discharges the old one.

Account A subduty of fiduciary duty that requires that the agent keep records such as a written list of transactions, noting money owed and money paid, and other detailed statements of mutual demands.

Acknowledgment form A form commonly used in sales contracts as an acceptance from the seller in response to a purchase order; contains preprinted provisions and has blanks to accommodate the specifics of the transaction. Also referred to as an *invoice*.

Act requirement For criminal liability, the requirement that the government prove that a defendant's actions objectively satisfied the elements of a particular offense. Also called *actus reus*.

Actual authority A source of the agent's authority that occurs either when the parties expressly agree to create an agency relationship or when the authority is implied based on custom or the course of past dealings.

Actual damages A fundamental element that must be proved to recover in a negligence lawsuit against a tortfeasor: The injured party must prove that she suffered some physical harm that resulted in identifiable losses.

Actual owner The individual who is recognized as having primary or residual title to the property and is, therefore, the ultimate owner of the property.

Adjudication (Administrative) The judicial function of administrative agencies, whereby the agencies make policy. Administrative law judges hear cases brought before the specific agency.

Adjudication (Criminal) A phase of the criminal justice system in which the prosecutor, after investigation, elects to proceed with the charges.

Administrative agencies Governmental bodies, including department, nondepartment, and independent agencies, that have the authority to implement and administer particular regulations.

Administrative law Refers to both the law made by administrative agencies and the laws and regulations that govern the creation, organization, and operation of administrative agencies.

Administrative law judge (ALJ) An individual, typically an attorney, who is employed by an agency to adjudicate disputes.

Affirmative action An action plan designed to maintain equal employment opportunities and to remedy past employment discrimination of women, persons of color, persons with disabilities, and other underutilized protected classes.

Age Discrimination in Employment Act (ADEA) of 1967 A federal statute that prohibits employers from discriminating against employees on the basis of their age once employees have reached age 40.

Agency law The body of laws that govern the relationships created when one party hires another party to act on the hiring party's behalf.

Agent One who agrees to act and is authorized to act on behalf of another, a principal, to legally bind the principal in particular business transactions with third parties pursuant to an agency relationship.

Agreement Any meeting of the minds resulting in mutual assent to do or refrain from doing something.

Agreement on Trade-Related Aspects of Intellectual Property (TRIPS) A multinational agreement that covers minimum requirements and standards for all areas of intellectual property protection and provides an infrastructure for enforcement and dispute resolution.

Ambiguous terms Contract terms that are vague and indefinite. In contract law, these terms are construed by the court against the interest of the side that drafted the agreement.

Amendments Changes made to the Constitution since its ratification.

American Recovery and Reinvestment Act of 2009 Federal legislation that created a loan program and underlying mandates for corporations most acutely impacted by the financial crisis that began in 2008; also established the Troubled Assets Relief Program (TARP) to administer the loans.

Americans with Disabilities Act (ADA) of 1990 A federal statute that seeks to eliminate discriminatory employment practices against persons with disabilities; requires that employers with 15 or more employees make reasonable accommodations for an employee with disabilities in the workplace as long as the accommodations do not cause the employer to suffer an undue hardship.

Answer Defendant's formal response to each paragraph of the complaint.

Anticipatory repudiation Doctrine under which, when one party makes clear that he has no intention to perform as agreed, the nonbreaching party is entitled to recover damages in anticipation of the breach rather than waiting until performance is due. Also called *anticipatory breach.*

Apparent authority A source of the agent's authority that occurs when there is an appearance of legitimate authority to a third party rather than express authorization by the principal.

Arbitrary and capricious standard The broad judicial benchmark used to determine whether an agency's actions were a result of a reasoned decision-making process.

Arbitration Method of alternative dispute resolution in which the parties present their sides of the dispute to one or more neutral parties who then render a decision; often involves a set of rules designed to move from dispute to decision quickly.

Article I, Section 8 The main provision of the Constitution that enumerates the limited powers of Congress.

Articles The main provisions of the Constitution that set out the government's structure, power, and procedures.

Articles of incorporation The document filed with a state authority that sets in motion the incorporation process; includes the corporation's name and purpose, the number of shares issued, and the address of the corporation's headquarters.

Articles of organization Document filed to create an LLC; in most states, requires only basic information such as the name of the entity, the location of its principal place of business, and the names of its members. Also called *certificate of organization.*

Assignment A tenant's transfer of his interests to a third party for the entire term remaining on the lease.

Assignment The transfer of one party's current rights under a contract to a third party, thereby extinguishing the original party's rights.

Assignment for the benefit of creditors A form of liquidation that is an alternative to bankruptcy and is provided either by state statute, state common law, or a combination of both.

Assumption of the risk A defense to claims of negligence in which the injured party knew that a substantial and apparent risk was associated with certain conduct and the party went ahead with the dangerous activity anyway.

Assurance A pledge or guarantee that gives confidence to one party that the other party is able to complete performance under a contract.

At-will employee Any employee who is not a contractual employee; may be terminated at any time and for any reason except in cases where public policy is violated or the termination is illegally discriminatory or is prohibited by statutory or common law exceptions.

Authorization cards Signed statements by employees indicating that they wish to unionize and/or are electing to be represented by an existing union.

Automatic stay A legal prohibition whereby creditors may neither initiate nor continue any debt collection action against the debtor or her property.

Bad faith A dishonesty of belief or purpose; in the legal context, a concept in which a malicious motive on the part of the defendant in a lawsuit is necessary in order for the plaintiff to recover. Under the Anticybersquatting Consumer Protection Act, the court looks to nine factors in making a determination of bad-faith intent.

Bankruptcy A procedure by which a debtor's assets are reorganized and liquidated by a court order to pay off creditors and free the debtor from obligations under existing contracts.

Bankruptcy estate The debtor's available assets in a bankruptcy proceeding.

Bankruptcy trustee An individual, often an attorney highly skilled in bankruptcy law, appointed in Chapter 7 or Chapter 13 cases and charged with the duty of taking control of the bankruptcy estate and reducing it to cash for distribution, preserving the interests of both the debtor and the creditors.

Bargained-for exchange The aspect of consideration that differentiates contracts from illusory promises by holding that a performance or return promise is bargained for only if it was exchanged for another promise.

Battle of the forms The conflict between the terms written into standardized purchase (offer) and acknowledgment (acceptance) forms that differ in that one form favors the buyer and the other the seller. The UCC attempts to broker a truce in this battle while keeping the contract of sale intact.

Bench trial Trial without a jury, in which the judge is both the finder of law and the finder of fact.

Berne Convention A multinational agreement covering copyright protection; requires that foreigners from signatory countries be granted protection, via reciprocity, under the copyright laws of any other member country.

Beyond a reasonable doubt The heightened burden of proof used in criminal cases, under which a fact finder must be convinced that the defendant's criminal liability is not in doubt to a reasonable person.

Bilateral contract A contract involving two promises and two performances.

Bill of Rights The first 10 amendments to the Constitution that preserve the rights of the people from unlawful acts of government officials, establish and protect freedom of speech and religion, and so on.

Black's Law Dictionary The leading legal dictionary.

Blue-sky laws State securities laws intended to cover purely intrastate securities offerings.

Bona fide occupational qualification (BFOQ) A provision in certain federal antidiscrimination statutes that allows discrimination based on religion, gender, or national origin when it can be shown that such discrimination is reasonably necessary to the business operation.

Borrower The party to whom credit is extended and who owes the debt.

Breach Condition that exists when one party has failed to perform her obligation under the contract. If the breach is material, the nonbreaching party is excused from his performance and can recover monetary damages.

Breach of duty A fundamental element that must be proved to recover in a negligence lawsuit against a tortfeasor: The injured party must prove that the tortfeasor failed to exercise reasonable care in fulfilling her obligations.

Burden of proof The responsibility of producing sufficient evidence in support of a fact or issue and favorably convincing the fact finder of that fact or issue.

Business corporation law Often the title for a specific state law that covers such matters as the structure of the corporation, oversight of the activity of the corporation's managers, rights of the principals in the case of the sale of assets or ownership interests, annual reporting requirements, and other issues that affect the internal rules of the business venture.

Business ethics Recognizing right and wrong business behavior and acting responsibly toward the business's stakeholders.

Business judgment rule A principle that protects corporate officers and directors from liability when they have made an unwise decision that results in a loss to the corporation, but they have acted in good faith, had no private financial self-interest, and used diligence to acquire the best information related to the decision.

Business necessity test A defense used to rebut disparate impact claims when a business can prove that a certain skill, ability, or procedure is absolutely necessary to the operation of the business. Discrimination is permitted even if a protected class is adversely affected.

Capacity For the formation of a valid contract, the requirement that both parties have the power to contract. Certain classes of persons have only limited powers to contract, including minors and those with mental incapacity.

Cause in fact A fundamental element that must be proved to recover in a negligence lawsuit against a tortfeasor: The injured party must prove that, except for the breach of duty by the tortfeasor, he would not have suffered damages.

Celler-Kefauver Antimerger Act A federal antitrust law enacted in 1950 that amends the Clayton Act provisions by severely restricting anticompetitive mergers resulting from the acquisition of assets.

Certificate of limited partnership The document filed with the state government authority by the general partner to form a limited partnership; requires routine information such as the name, address, and capital contribution of each partner.

Certify In labor law, to recognize a collective bargaining unit as a union. The NLRB's certification process occurs when a legally sound election reveals a simple majority of pro-union votes.

Charging of the jury Instructions given from the judge to the jury explaining how to work through the process of coming to a factual decision in the case.

Circuit split Occurs when two or more different federal circuit courts of appeal offer conflicting rulings on the same issue.

Citation The special format used by the legal community to express where a statute or case law can be found.

Citizen suit provisions Laws that authorize private individuals or watchdog groups to file environmental enforcement lawsuits.

Citizen suits Lawsuits initiated by members of the public who are directly affected by an agency action and brought against violators of the regulation and/or the administrative agency itself for failing to fulfill a duty imposed upon it.

Civil cases Cases in which one party seeks a remedy, such as an award of money damages, for a private wrong committed by another party.

Civil law systems Systems of law that are drawn largely from the Roman law heritage, which uses written law as the highest source, and opt for a systematic codification of general law principles.

Civil laws Laws designed to compensate parties for money lost as a result of another's conduct.

Civil litigation A dispute resolution process in which the parties and their counsel argue their views of a civil controversy in a court of law.

Clayton Act A federal antitrust law enacted in 1914 as a preventive statute that deals with specific types of trade restraints, including exclusive dealing arrangements, tie-in sales, price discrimination, mergers and acquisitions, and interlocking directorates.

Clean Air Act (CAA) Federal legislation enacted in 1963 to improve, strengthen, and accelerate programs for the prevention and abatement of air pollution; focuses on stationary and mobile sources in the United States.

Clean hands An equitable doctrine whereby a party seeking to enforce a breach of contract against the opposing party must prove that he has no fault in causing the breach. Clean hands are shown by proving that you are prepared to tender performance.

Clean Water Act (CWA) Federal legislation that regulates water quality standards and aims to stem water pollution from industrial, municipal, and agricultural sources; implemented and enforced by the EPA.

Closing arguments Attorneys' summations of the case, during which each attorney tries to convince the jury to decide the case in her party's favor; occurs after testimony is completed and evidence has been submitted.

Collective bargaining The process of negotiating terms and conditions of employment for employees in the collective bargaining unit.

Collective bargaining unit An employee group that, on the basis of a mutuality of interests, is an appropriate unit for collective bargaining.

Comity The general notion that nations will defer to and give effect to the laws and court decisions of other nations.

Commerce Clause The constitutional clause giving Congress the exclusive power to regulate foreign commerce, interstate commerce, and commerce with the Indian Tribes.

Commercially impracticable Rule applied by the UCC when a delay in delivery or nondelivery has been made impracticable by the occurrence of an unanticipated event so long as the event directly affected a basic assumption of the contract.

Common law Law that has not been passed by the legislature but rather is made by the courts; based on the fundamentals of previous cases with similar facts.

Common stock (common shares) A form of equity instrument that entitles the equity owner to payments based on the current profitability of the company.

Communications Decency Act (CDA) of 1996 Federal legislation that extends immunity to Internet service providers (ISPs) by protecting them from any defamation liability as a "publisher or speaker of any information provided by another information content provider."

Comparative negligence A defense to claims of negligence in which the injured party's conduct has played a factor in the harm suffered and, thus, the proportion of negligence should be divided.

Compensatory damages Damages that are meant to make the injured party whole again. In contract law, they are an attempt to place the nonbreaching party in the position he would have been in had the contract been executed as agreed. Also called *direct* or *actual damages*.

Complaint The first formal document filed with the local clerk of courts when the plaintiff initiates a lawsuit claiming legal rights against another.

Complaint (Discrimination) A form that an aggrieved employee files against his employer with the EEOC that details how the employee was discriminated against.

Comprehensive Environmental Response Compensation and Liability Act (CERCLA) Federal legislation enacted in 1980 to create a tax on the chemical and petroleum industries and provide broad federal authority to respond directly to releases or threatened releases of hazardous substances that may endanger public health or the environment. Also called *Superfund*.

Computer Fraud and Abuse Act (CFAA) Federal legislation that prohibits unauthorized use of computers to commit espionage, the accessing of unauthorized information or of a nonpublic government computer, fraud by computer, damage to a computer, trafficking in passwords, and extortionate threats to damage a computer.

Conciliation negotiations The required attempts by the EEOC to settle a discrimination case instead of filing a lawsuit.

Concurrent jurisdiction Situation in which two different courts each has subject matter jurisdiction to hear a case.

Condition An event that must occur before a contract obligation is triggered.

Confirmation memorandum A written verification of an agreement. Under the statute of frauds section of the UCC, a merchant who receives a signed confirmation memorandum from another merchant will be bound by the memorandum just as if she had signed it, unless she promptly objects.

Consent An agent's agreeing to act for the principal. In the context of agency law, courts apply an objective standard to determine whether the agent did in fact agree to the agency relationship.

Consequential damages Damages that repay the injured party for any foreseeable but indirect losses that flow from the breach of contract.

Consideration The mutual exchange of benefits and detriments; for the formation of a valid contract, the requirement that each party receives something of value (the benefit) from the other and that each party gives up something of value (the legal detriment) to the other, resulting in a bargained-for exchange.

Constitutional law The body of law interpreting state and federal constitutions.

Consumer Credit Protection Act (CCPA) Federal legislation that regulates credit transactions between a creditor and a borrower and provides consumer protections in the areas of disclosure of credit terms, credit reporting, antidiscrimination laws, and collection of debts from consumers; serves as the centerpiece of federal statutory regulation of credit transactions.

Consumer Financial Protection Bureau (CFPB) Independent agency created by the Wall Street Reform and Consumer Protection Act responsible for consumer education, regulation of credit and loan companies, and enforcement of consumer protection laws.

Consumer law The statutory and administrative body of law that protects consumers engaging in transactions with merchants and creditors.

Consumer Leasing Act (CLA) Federal legislation that regulates lessors engaged in leasing or arranging leases for consumers in the ordinary course of business.

Consumer Product Safety Act (CPSA) The federal statute that created the Consumer Product Safety Commission, with the aim of making consumer products safer.

Consumer Review Fairness Act (CRFA) Federal legislation that protects people's ability to share their honest opinions about a business's products, services, or conduct in any forum, including social media.

Contractual employee An employee who works under an agreement that defines when the employee begins employment and when the employment ends.

Controlling the Assault of Non-Solicited Pornography and Marketing Act of 2003 A federal statute that regulates the sending of unsolicited e-mail (spam) by prohibiting certain practices, such as falsifying the "from" name and information in the subject line, and requiring the sender to provide a physical address of the producer of the e-mail. Also called *CAN-SPAM Act*.

Convention on the Recognition and Enforcement of Foreign Arbitral Awards An international treaty established in 1958 that allows for the enforcement of arbitration awards in many major countries, provided that the arbitration is international.

Copyright A copyright protects the rights of creators of original works for a defined period of time during which the holder has the exclusive rights to copy, distribute, display, or perform the work.

Corporate governance The process used by corporate officers and directors to establish lines of responsibility, approval, and oversight among key stakeholders and set out rules for making corporate decisions.

Corporate veil The liability protection afforded to shareholders, directors, and officers of a corporation whereby they are insulated from personal liability in the event that the corporation runs up large debts or suffers some liability.

Corporation A fictitious legal entity that exists as an independent "person" separate from its principals.

Counsel Another term for *attorney*.

Counterclaim A claim filed by a defendant who believes that the plaintiff has caused her damages arising out of the very same set of facts as articulated in the complaint.

Counteroffer An action terminating an offer whereby the offeree rejects the original offer and proposes a new offer with different terms.

Country of origin principle General agreement between the United States, Canada, and the European Union governments to apply the law of the country in which the defendant's servers are located.

Court A judicial tribunal duly constituted for the hearing and adjudication of cases.

Covenant not to compete Type of contract in which one party agrees not to compete with another party for a specified period of time.

Cover A nonbreaching buyer's right to purchase substitute goods on the open market after a delivery of nonconforming goods from the original seller and to sue for the difference.

Covered (nonexempt) employees Employees who are protected by the FLSA and other statutes.

Cram-down provision A term used in reference to the Chapter 11 provision that allows the debtor to request that the court force the creditors to accept a plan that is fair, equitable, and feasible.

Creativity For copyright protection of a compilation, the requirement that there must be some creative element used that makes the compilation an original work.

Credit Card Accountability Responsibility and Disclosure Act of 2009 (CARD Act) Federal legislation that protects consumers from unreasonable interest rate increases and credit card fees and requires card issuers to give a 45-day advance notice of any impending rate increase.

Creditor Any party that regularly extends credit and to which a debt becomes owed.

Criminal cases Cases in which the accused party is charged by the government with committing a crime.

Criminal law The body of law that, for the purpose of preventing harm to society, defines the boundaries of behavior and prescribes sanctions for violating those boundaries.

Criminal laws Laws designed to protect society that result in penalties to the violator such as fines or imprisonment.

Criminal procedure The body of constitutional protections afforded to individuals and business entities during criminal investigations, arrests, trials, and sentencing.

Cross-claim A claim filed by a defendant who believes that a third party is either partially or fully liable for the damages that the plaintiff has suffered and, therefore, should be involved as an indispensable party in the trial.

Cross-examination The opportunity for an attorney to ask questions in court, limited to issues brought out on direct examination, of a witness who has testified for the opposing party.

Cure The right of a seller to replace nonconforming goods before final contract performance is due. If nonconforming goods were delivered in good faith and were considered equal to or superior to what was ordered, the seller may cure after final contract performance is due if the buyer will not suffer injury.

Damages Money lost as a result of another's conduct.

Debt A common tool for raising capital; includes promissory notes, bonds, and debentures that offer investors a fixed rate of return, regardless of the profitability of the corporation, and repayment after a certain period of years. Debt is senior in priority to equity instruments.

Debtor The borrower in a secured transaction.

Debtor in possession (DIP) A Chapter 11 bankruptcy process in which the debtor generally remains in control of assets and business operations in an attempt to rehabilitate the business entity.

Defendant The party responding to a lawsuit and alleged by the plaintiff to have caused a wrongful act.

Delegation The transfer of one party's current duties under a contract to a third party to perform, with the original party remaining liable for any breach.

Deliberations The process in which jurors discuss, in private, the testimony and evidence presented at trial and vote to reach their verdict.

Deposition Method of discovery in which a party or witness gives sworn testimony prior to trial.

Destination contract A contract in which the seller is required to deliver the goods to a chosen destination and not just to the carrier. When the goods have been tendered at the destination, the seller has fulfilled his duty and the buyer takes title and risk of loss.

Detour Conduct classified as a small-scale deviation that is normally expected in the workday and, therefore, is within the ambit of respondeat superior.

Detrimental reliance Situation in which the offeree acts, based on a reasonable promise made by the offeror, and would be injured if the offeror's promise is not enforced.

Direct examination The first questioning of a witness during a trial, in which the witness is questioned by the attorney for the party presenting the witness.

Direct infringement A theory of copyright infringement under which the copyright owner proves that she has legal ownership of the work in question and that the infringer copied the work in a substantially similar manner without permission.

Directors Individuals responsible for oversight and management of the corporation's course of direction.

Disability A physical or mental impairment that substantially limits a person's ability to participate in major life activities.

Discharge In contract law, the removal of all legal obligations under the agreement.

Disclaim To renounce a legal right or claim.

Disclosure The process in which companies are to release all information, positive or negative, that might bear on an investment decision; serves as the underlying premise of all securities regulation and is required by the Securities and Exchange Commission to protect investors and ensure public confidence in the integrity of the securities market.

Discovery Process for the orderly exchange of information and evidence between the parties involved in litigation prior to trial.

Disparate impact Theory of employment discrimination in which employee evaluation techniques that are not themselves discriminatory have a different and adverse impact on members of a protected class.

Disparate treatment Theory of employment discrimination predicated on overt and intentional discrimination; includes being treated differently because of one's membership in a protected class.

Dissociation Term used in the RUPA to describe the act of separation of a partner from the partnership. Also, the process in which an individual member of an LLC exercises the right to withdraw from the partnership.

Dissolution In the context of an LLC, a liquidation process triggered by an event that is specified in the operating agreement (such as the death of a key member) or by the decision of the majority of membership interests (or the percentage called for in the operating agreement) to dissolve the company.

Diversity of citizenship Situation in which opposing parties in a lawsuit are citizens of different states or one party is a citizen of a foreign country; the case is placed under federal court jurisdiction if the amount in controversy exceeds $75,000 and does not involve a decree for divorce, alimony, or child custody.

Doctrine of equivalence A doctrine that allows courts to find patent infringement when an invention, compared with a patented device, performs substantially the same function in substantially the same way to achieve the same result.

Doctrine of stare decisis The principle that similar cases with similar facts under similar circumstances should have similar outcomes.

Dodd-Frank Wall Street Reform and Consumer Protection Act of 2010 Federal legislation designed to overhaul the regulation of U.S. financial services and markets.

Double jeopardy Situation in which a defendant could be subject to prosecution twice for the same offense; prohibited by the Fifth Amendment.

Due care A subduty of fiduciary duty that requires that the agent act in the same careful manner when conducting the principal's affairs as a reasonable person would in conducting her own personal affairs.

Due Process Clause The constitutional clause protecting individuals from being deprived of "life, liberty, or property" without due process of law.

Due process of law The constitutional principle that the government must respect the legal rights that are owed to a person according to the law.

Durable medium For copyright protection, the requirement that the work must be in a tangible form, such as writing, digital, video, and so forth.

Duress The use of any form of unfair coercion by one party to induce another party to enter into or modify a contract; basis for avoiding a contract.

Duty A fundamental element that must be proved to recover in a negligence lawsuit against a tortfeasor: The injured party must prove that the tortfeasor owed him a duty of care.

Duty of care A fiduciary duty owed to shareholders by officers and directors; requires that the fiduciaries exercise the degree of skill, diligence, and care that a reasonably prudent person would exercise under the same circumstances, acting in good faith and in a manner that is reasonably calculated to advance the best interests of the corporation.

Duty of loyalty A fiduciary duty owed to shareholders by officers, directors, and controlling shareholders; requires that the fiduciaries put the corporation's interests ahead of their own and do not engage in self-dealing or conflicts of interest.

Easement The privilege to use real estate owned by another.

Economic Espionage Act A federal statute passed in 1996 that provides criminal penalties for domestic and foreign theft of trade secrets.

Election A vote to elect or reject unionization by the entire bargaining unit.

Electronic Communications Privacy Act (ECPA) A federal law enacted in 1986 that extends legal protection against wiretapping and other forms of unauthorized interception and explicitly allows employers to monitor employee communications on company equipment as long as this is done in the ordinary course of business or the employee consents to the monitoring.

Employee agents One of three broad categories of agents; includes, generally, anyone who performs services for a principal who can control what will be done and how it will be done.

Employee Polygraph Protection Act A federal law that prohibits most private sector employers from requiring a polygraph test as a condition of employment.

Employee Retirement Income Security Act (ERISA) A federal law enacted in 1974 consisting of a comprehensive set of laws and regulations that requires employers to make certain disclosures related to investment risk, thus providing transparency for plan beneficiaries.

Employment discrimination Workplace-related discrimination in the hiring process and treatment of employees; encompasses everything from promotions and demotions to work schedules, working conditions, and disciplinary measures.

Employment-at-will Deep-seated common law principle that employers have the right to terminate an employee with or without advance notice and with or without just cause, subject to certain exceptions.

Enabling statute A law passed by Congress when it is establishing an administrative agency; serves as the source of the agency's authority and describes the agency's scope and jurisdiction over certain matters.

Endangered Species Act (ESA) Federal legislation enacted in 1973 that established a procedure for identifying imperiled species and preserving them from extinction.

Enforceability The ability of a properly formed contract to be enforceable in a court of law; determined by examining whether the contract is a product of genuine assent and is in writing (under certain circumstances).

Enforcement The function of administrative agencies whereby they investigate alleged violations of their administrative regulations and recommend enforcement actions; generally carried out through an agency's Office of General Counsel. In deciding when and whom to regulate, the agencies have prosecutorial discretion that is practically unreviewable by the judiciary.

Enumerated powers Those powers that are explicitly granted to the three branches of government in the Constitution.

Equal Credit Opportunity Act Federal legislation, passed in 1974, that prohibits discrimination of a credit applicant based on the applicant's race, religion, national origin, color, gender, age, or marital status.

Equal Employment Opportunity Commission (EEOC) A five-member federal administrative agency that administers congressional mandates that ensure adequate protection for victims of discrimination; accepts and investigates worker complaints and, in certain cases, will sue on behalf of employees.

Equal Pay Act of 1963 A federal statute that makes it illegal for employers to pay unequal wages to men and women who perform substantially equal work.

Equitable maxims Common law rules that guide courts in deciding cases and controversies and are intended to be broad statements of rules based on notions of fairness and justice.

Equitable relief Relief granted in the form of either specific performance ("do it") or an injunction ("stop doing it") when monetary damages are insufficient due to the unique or irreversible consequence of the breach.

Equity Ownership interest in a corporation whereby financial return on the investment is based primarily on the performance of the venture.

Ethics A conscious system used for deciding moral dilemmas.

European Court of Justice The court that functions as the final arbiter of the codes governing European Union member states.

Executive branch Established under Article II of the Constitution; consists of the president and vice president.

Executive order An order made by the president and that carries the full force of law; issued to enforce or interpret federal statutes and treaties.

Exempt employees Classification of employees who are not covered by FLSA protections; generally consists of employees whose responsibilities are primarily executive, administrative, or professional.

Exemptions For smaller issuers of securities, types of offerings or transactions in selling a security that are not subject to certain Securities and Exchange Commission regulations on registration; intended to assist business ventures seeking smaller amounts of capital from the public investment community.

Expert evaluation Method of alternative dispute resolution in which an independent expert acts as the neutral fact-finder; particularly useful for parties involved in a business dispute where the issues are somewhat complex and related to the intricacies of a certain industry or profession.

Expert evaluator The neutral fact-finder in expert evaluation who reviews documents and evidence provided by each party and draws on her range of experience and expertise in the industry to offer an opinion on the merits and value of the claim and recommend a settlement amount.

Expiration Method of ending an agency relationship whereby the parties agree to a fixed term for the relationship.

Express acts Acts by which an agency relationship is terminated; can be either simple communication of the desire to terminate the relationship, the expiration of a fixed term, or satisfaction of purpose.

Express contract A contract that is created when the parties have knowingly and intentionally agreed on the promises and performances.

Express partnership Partnership formed when the parties have agreed to conduct a partnership on certain terms and conditions.

Express warranty A warranty that arises when a seller makes a representation of fact about a product.

Fair and Accurate Credit Transactions (FACT) Act Federal legislation that requires credit bureaus to stop reporting any fraudulent account information from the time a consumer alleges identity theft until the conclusion of the investigation.

Fair Credit Reporting Act (FCRA) Federal legislation that sets privacy rights for consumer credit reports and requires that the credit bureaus give individual consumers complete and timely access to their own credit reports.

Fair Debt Collection Practices Act (FDCPA) A federal statute that regulates agents of the creditor involved in debt collection for consumer debts and that requires the collection agency to make known certain rights of the debtor.

Fair Labor Standards Act (FLSA) A federal law enacted in 1938 and intended to cover all employers engaged in interstate commerce; mandates payment of a minimum wage, a maximum 40-hour workweek, overtime pay, and restrictions on children working in certain occupations and during certain hours.

Fair use A defense against copyright infringement under which the court examines the purpose and nature of the use, the nature of the work, the amount used, and the market effect of the use to determine whether the use is permitted.

Family and Medical Leave Act (FMLA) A federal law enacted in 1993 that requires certain employers to give time off to employees to take care of their own or a family member's illness or to care for a newborn or adopted child.

Federal courts Courts that adjudicate matters dealing primarily with national laws, federal constitutional issues, and other cases (such as cases involving diversity jurisdiction).

Federal Odometer Act A law that makes it a crime to change vehicle odometers and requires that any faulty odometer be plainly disclosed in writing to potential buyers.

Federal question Some issue arising from the Constitution, a federal statute or regulation, or federal common law.

Federal system System in which a national government coexists with state governments.

Federal Trade Commission (FTC) An agency charged with the broad mandate of preventing unfair and deceptive acts or practices in commercial transactions.

Federal Trade Commission Act (FTCA) A federal law enacted in 1914 that established the Federal Trade Commission, which administers the act; intended as a catchall statute that has been construed as including all the prohibitions of the other antitrust laws.

Federal Trademark Dilution Act A federal law enacted in 1995 and amended in 2006 that permits mark holders to recover damages and prevent others from diluting distinctive trademarks.

Federal Unemployment Tax Act (FUTA) A federal law enacted in 1935 that established a state-administered fund to provide payments to workers who have suffered sudden job loss; funded through employment taxes shared by employer and employee.

Fee simple The broadest property interest in land, which endures until the current holder dies without heirs.

Felonies Crimes that generally carry one year or more of incarceration as the penalty.

Fiduciary duties Under the Revised Uniform Partnership Act, general partners' duties of loyalty, care, and good faith; intended to ensure that the partners are acting in the best interest of the partnership.

FOB point *Domestic:* A shipping term that indicates the place to which the seller must deliver goods. In the absence of a contract provision to the contrary, title and risk of loss pass to the buyer at this point. *International:* An INCO term indicating that goods are to be shipped via freighter ship and that title and risk of loss transfer to the buyer when the goods are delivered to the named ship.

Food and Drug Administration (FDA) The federal agency that regulates the testing, manufacturing, and distributing of foods, medications, and medical devices.

Food, Drug and Cosmetic Act (FDCA) The federal statute that created the Food and Drug Administration and that requires the makers of certain food ingredients, additives, drugs, or medical devices to obtain formal FDA approval before selling the product to the general public.

Forbearance The giving up of a legal right as consideration in a contract.

Foreign Corrupt Practices Act (FCPA) A federal criminal statute enacted principally to prevent corporate bribery of foreign officials in business transactions.

Foreign Sovereign Immunities Act (FSIA) A federal statute that incorporates the concept of sovereign immunity by explicitly prohibiting U.S. courts from rendering judicial actions against foreign nations or their government officials unless the foreign nation has waived its immunity, is engaged in a commercial enterprise on U.S. soil, or has taken actions that have a direct effect on U.S. interests.

Fourth Amendment Protects individual citizens' rights to be secure in their "persons, houses, papers, and effects."

Franchise A business arrangement (not a form of business entity) of continuing commercial relationship for the right to operate a business pursuant to the franchisor's trade name or to sell the seller's branded goods.

Franchisee Individual or business with the legal right to operate a franchised business and use the business's trademarks and trade secrets.

Franchisor A business entity that has a proven track record of success and ability to franchise its products.

Fraudulent misrepresentation Situation in which one party has engaged in conduct that meets the standards for misrepresentation and that party has actual knowledge that the representation is not true; basis for avoiding a contract.

Frolic An exception to the respondeat superior doctrine that occurs when an agent, during a normal workday, does something purely for her own reasons that are unrelated to her employment.

Frustration of purpose Doctrine that excuses a party from performance if, before a breach, a state of things that was the basis for forming the contract no longer exists, by no fault of either party.

Fully disclosed agency A type of agency relationship in which the third party entering into the contract is aware of the identity of the principal and knows that the agent is acting on behalf of the principal in the transaction.

General Agreement on Tariffs and Trade (GATT) A treaty designed to facilitate international trade; administered by the World Trade Organization.

Genuine assent The knowing, voluntary, and mutual approval of the terms of a contract by each party; required for a contract to be enforceable.

Going-and-coming rule Rule whereby employers are generally not liable for tortious acts committed by employees while on their way to and from work.

Good faith In contract law, the duty to honestly adhere to the contract's common purpose. Under this obligation neither party can do anything to prevent the other party from enjoying the "fruits of the contract." Instead, both must try to make the deal work as written.

Goods Tangible personal property that is movable at the time of identification to a contract of sale.

Gratuitous agents One of three broad categories of agents; includes, generally, anyone who acts on behalf of a principal without receiving any compensation.

Grievance In labor law, a complaint filed with or by a union to challenge an employer's treatment of one or more union members.

Guarantor A third party that agrees to be liable to pay a loan only if the debtor actually defaults.

Horizontal restraints Per se violations of the Sherman Act in which the restraining of trade involves agreements between competitors to take action that results in the elimination or reduction of competition from other competitors.

Hostile work environment Theory of liability under Title VII for sexual harassment that is of such a severe and crude nature or is so pervasive in the workplace that it interferes with the victim's ability to do the job.

Hung jury A jury that cannot come to a consensus decision on which party should prevail in a case.

Hybrid contract A contract that involves terms for both goods and services; the source of law is established by determining the predominant thrust of the subject matter.

Illusory promise A promise that courts will not enforce because the offeror is not truly bound by his vague promise or because a party cannot be bound by his promise due to the lack of a bargained-for exchange. Promises of gifts and deathbed promises are two examples.

Implied contract A contract in which the agreement is reached by the parties' actions rather than their words.

Implied partnership Partnership formed when the parties have acted like general partners even though the parties did not agree or intend to form a partnership.

Implied warranty A warranty that exists even when the seller does not make a specific representation about the product.

Impossibility Doctrine that excuses performance when an essential part of the contract has become impossible because a crucial, irreplaceable thing has been destroyed; a crucial person has died; a crucial means of performance no longer exists; or a crucial action has become illegal.

Impracticability Doctrine that excuses performance when an extreme circumstance occurs or reveals itself that destroys the value of the performance to the party and that circumstance was not the fault of either party and was not reasonably foreseeable.

In personam jurisdiction Another term for *personal jurisdiction*.

In rem jurisdiction Jurisdiction over real or personal property when the property itself is the principal subject of the lawsuit.

Incidental beneficiary Someone who, while not a party to the contract, stands to benefit from the contract simply because she may be in the right place at the right time. The contract was not entered into to benefit her specifically and she has no enforceable rights under the contract.

INCO terms Standardized contractual terms and designations used in international and some domestic sales contracts to avoid confusion due to language barriers and differing legal systems.

Independent contractor agents One of three broad categories of agents; includes, generally, anyone who performs services for a principal who has the right to control or direct only the result of the work and not the means and methods of accomplishing the result.

Indirect infringement A theory of copyright infringement under which a third-party facilitator is liable for damages when the facilitator has knowledge of the infringement and/or contributes to the infringement in some material way. Also called *contributory infringement*.

Injunctive relief A court order to refrain from performing a particular act.

Insider trading Illegal securities trading in which a corporate insider uses information not available to the general investor public as the basis for trades in the company's stock.

Insider Trading and Securities Fraud Enforcement Act Federal legislation passed in 1988 that raised the criminal and civil penalties for insider trading, increased the liability of brokerage firms for wrongful acts of their employees, and gave the Securities and Exchange Commission more power to pursue violations of insider trading.

Insider trading laws Federal securities statutes that prohibit corporate insiders who have access to certain information that is not available to the general investment public from trading their company's stock based on the insider knowledge.

Insolvent Condition in which a business venture no longer has adequate assets to maintain its operations and can no longer pay its bills as they become due in the usual course of trade and business.

Inspection The act of monitoring a business's compliance with administrative regulations. An administrative agency ordinarily secures a warrant and then enters and inspects the business's premises.

Installment contract A contract allowing delivery of goods and payments for goods at separate times, with the goods being accepted or rejected separately.

Intended beneficiary Someone who, while not a party to the contract, stands to benefit from the contract because the contracting parties intended that he receive a benefit. He has enforceable rights under the contract.

Intentional torts A category of torts in which the tortfeasor was willful in bringing about a particular event that caused harm to another party.

Intermediate-level scrutiny The middle level of scrutiny applied by courts deciding constitutional issues through judicial review; upheld if the government shows that a regulation involves an important government objective that is furthered by substantially related means.

International Court of Justice The judicial branch of the United Nations, charged with settling legal disputes submitted to it by member states and giving advisory opinions on legal questions submitted to it by duly authorized international organs, agencies, and the U.N. General Assembly. Also known as *World Court*.

Interrogatory Method of discovery in which one party submits written questions to the opposing party to gather evidence prior to trial.

Investigation The initial phase of the criminal justice process in which authorities become aware of an alleged criminal act and begin gathering physical evidence and interviewing witnesses and potential suspects.

Involuntary bankruptcy petition A petition filed in the bankruptcy court against a debtor by a group of three or more creditors with an unsecured aggregate claim of at least $15,775 who claim that the debtor is failing to pay the debt as it comes due.

Irrevocable offers Offers that cannot be withdrawn by the offeror; include offers in the form of an option contract, offers that the offeree partly performed or detrimentally relied on, and firm offers by a merchant under the Uniform Commercial Code.

Joint venture Business relationship between two or more parties for a limited-in-time venture.

Jointly and severally liable Legal principle that imposes liability on general partners both together (jointly) and separately (severally) for debts and liabilities of the partnership.

Judicial branch Established under Article III of the Constitution; consists of the Supreme Court and other federal courts.

Judicial review The power of the judiciary to declare a legislative or executive act unconstitutional.

Judiciary The collection of federal and state courts existing primarily to adjudicate disputes and charged with the responsibility of judicial review.

Jurisdiction The legal authority that a court must have before it can hear a case.

Jurisprudence The science and philosophy of law that defines various approaches to the appropriate function of law and how legal doctrines should be developed and applied.

Jury selection The process of asking potential jurors questions to reveal any prejudices that may affect their judgment of the facts.

Knockout rule As applied in many states, the view that when a buyer and seller engage in a battle of the forms and different terms are exchanged, both the seller's and buyer's differing terms drop out and substitute UCC gap fillers complete the contract.

Labor Management Relations Act A federal law, enacted in 1947 as an amendment to the NLRA, that prohibits requiring employees to join or continue membership in a union as a condition of employment. Also known as the *Taft-Hartley Act*.

Labor-Management Reporting and Disclosure Act A federal law enacted in 1959 that established a system of reporting and checks intended to uncover and prevent fraud and corruption among union officials by regulating internal operating procedures and union matters. Also known as the *Landrum-Griffin Act*.

Lapse of time An event covered under operation of law in which a contract may be terminated once either the offeror's expressed time limit has expired or a reasonable time has passed.

Law A body of rules of action or conduct prescribed by controlling authority and having legal binding force.

Lease An agreement between a landlord and a tenant for the rental of property.

Leasehold estate The qualified right to use real estate in an exclusive manner for a limited period of time. The most common form is a landlord-tenant agreement.

Legality (Contracts) For the formation of a valid contract, the requirement that both the subject matter and performance of the contract must be legal.

Legality (Criminal) A principle of criminal law that protects individuals from being charged with some unspecified general offense; requires that crimes be specifically proscribed by law in advance of the conduct sought to be punished.

Legislative branch Established under Article I of the Constitution; consists of the House of Representatives and the Senate.

Legislative history The records kept by the legislature, including the debates, committee and conference reports, and legislative findings of fact used when creating a law, which can be used to show the legislature's intent.

Libel Written defamation, in which someone publishes in print (words or pictures), writes, or broadcasts through radio, television, or film an untruth about another that will do harm to that person's reputation or honesty or subject a party to hate, contempt, or ridicule.

Licensing The task of issuing a license authorizing a business or industry to do something.

Life estate An ownership interest in real estate that lasts for the lifetime of a particular person.

Limited liability company (LLC) A multiperson form of business entity that offers liability protection for its principals along with various tax options.

Limited liability partnership (LLP) Form of business entity that provides the same level of liability protection to a general partner in an LLP as is provided to a limited partner in a limited partnership form of entity.

Liquidated damages Reasonable estimates of the actual damages that will result if the contract is breached; agreed to by the parties ahead of time.

Literal patent infringement Patent infringement in which the invention or process violates either the rule of exactness or the rule of addition.

Lockout The shutdown of a business by the employer to prevent employees from working, thus depriving them of their employment and putting economic pressure on the union's members before the union can do the same to the employer through a strike.

Lucid Sane and thinking clearly.

Madrid Protocol A multinational agreement that aims to facilitate multinational protection of trademarks through the use of a uniform, single-source process.

Mail Fraud Act Federal legislation enacted in 1990 as a comprehensive approach to criminalizing any fraud in which the defrauding party uses the mail or any wire, radio, or television in perpetrating the fraud.

Mailbox rule Principle stating that the acceptance of an offer is effective upon dispatch of the acceptance via a commercially reasonable means and not when the acceptance is received by the offeree; governs common law contracts.

Manager-managed LLC LLC management structure in which the members name a manager (or managers) who generally has the day-to-day operational responsibilities, while the nonmanaging members are typically investors with little input on the course of business taken by the entity except for major decisions.

Manifest Apparent and evident to the senses. In the context of agency law, courts apply an objective standard to determine whether the principal intended that an agency be created.

Market-based approach An approach to pollution control that gives businesses a choice of methods based on economic incentives for complying with pollution standards; instituted by the 1990 amendments to the Clean Air Act.

Material Something that is important to the contract by being necessary and generally indispensable to the contract.

Maximizing profits A corporate ethical philosophy in which a company strives to make as much money as possible with an emphasis on not breaking the law. Ethics and corporate social responsibility are often secondary concerns.

Med-arb Method of alternative dispute resolution whereby the parties begin with mediation and agree to submit to arbitration if mediation fails in a fixed time period.

Mediation Method of alternative dispute resolution in which a mediator attempts to settle a dispute by learning the facts of the matter and then negotiating a settlement between the two adverse parties.

Member-managed LLC LLC management structure similar to that of a general partnership, with all the members having the authority to bind the business.

Mental incapacity (contract) Category of individuals who have limited capacity to enter into a contract; includes anyone who is unable to understand the nature and consequences of the contract and anyone who is unable to act in a reasonable manner in relation to the transaction when the other party has reason to know of that person's condition.

Mental incapacity (criminal) A defense to avoid criminal liability whereby the defendant's actions are related to some type of mental disease or defect.

Merchant One that is regularly engaged in the sale of a particular good.

Merchant's firm offer An offer in writing between merchants to buy or sell goods along with a promise without consideration to keep that offer for a stated amount of time or, if unstated, no longer than three months.

Merchant's privilege A narrow privilege, provided for in the Restatements, that shields a merchant from liability for temporarily detaining a party who is reasonably suspected of stealing merchandise.

Mini-trial A condensed version of the case is presented to the top management from both sides, with an expert neutral party conducting the trial, allowing them to see and hear facts and arguments so more meaningful negotiations can take place.

Minimum contacts A legal term for when it is appropriate for a court in one state (the forum state) to assert personal jurisdiction over a defendant from another state.

Minors Category of individuals who have limited capacity to enter into a contract; includes those younger than the majority age of 18. Until a person reaches her majority age, any contract that she may enter into is voidable at the minor's option.

Mirror image rule Principle stating that the offeree's response operates as an acceptance only if it is the precise mirror image of the offer.

Misappropriation (1) The acquisition of a trade secret of another by a person who knows or has reason to know that the trade secret was acquired by improper means or (2) the disclosure of a trade secret to another without express or implied consent.

Misdemeanors Crimes that carry up to one year of incarceration as the penalty.

Misfeasance An act by one party that harms or endangers another party.

Misrepresentation Situation in which one party to an agreement makes a promise or representation about a material fact that is not true; basis for avoiding a contract.

Mistake In contract law, an erroneous belief that is not in accord with the existing facts.

Mixed motives Theory of employment discrimination in which the cause of the adverse employment action was motivated by both legitimate and discriminatory motives.

Mobile sources of air pollution Nonstationary sources of air pollutants, including automobiles, buses, trucks, ships, trains, aircraft, and various other vehicles.

Model Penal Code (MPC) A statutory text adopted by the American Law Institute in 1962 in an effort to bring greater uniformity to state criminal laws by proffering certain legal standards and reforms.

Model state statutes Statutes drafted by legal experts to be used as a model for state legislatures to adopt in their individual jurisdictions in order to increase the level of uniformity and fairness across courts in all states.

Money damages Sums levied on the breaching party and awarded to the nonbreaching party to remedy a loss from breach of contract.

Moral minimum A corporate ethical philosophy in which a company strives to act as ethically as possible as long as a reasonable profit is made. Ethics and corporate social responsibility are priorities.

Morals Generally accepted standards of right and wrong in a given society or community.

Mortgage A written document that specifies the parties and the real estate being used to collateralize a loan and is filed with a state and/or local government agency.

Mortgage foreclosure A remedy against a debtor in which a creditor declares the loan in default and takes title and possession of the collateralized real estate in hopes of selling the property to pay off the debt owed.

Mortgagee The creditor in a transaction in which real estate is being used to collateralize a loan.

Mortgagor The borrower in a transaction in which real estate is being used to collateralize a loan.

Motion A request made by either party that asks the court to issue a certain order (such as a motion for summary judgment). Motions may be made before, during, and after the trial.

Mutual assent For the formation of a valid contract, the broad underlying requirement that the parties must reach an agreement using a combination of offer and acceptance and that the assent must be genuine.

Mutual consent Circumstance under which contracting parties may be discharged from their obligation although neither party has fully performed because they agree to cancel the contract.

Mutual mistake An erroneous belief held by both parties that concerns a basic assumption on which a contract was made.

National Environmental Policy Act (NEPA) Federal legislation enacted in 1969 that established a process federal agencies must follow when making decisions that have the potential to significantly impact the environment.

National Labor Relations Act (NLRA) A federal law enacted in 1935 that provides general protections for the rights of workers to organize, engage in collective bargaining, and take part in strikes and other forms of concerted activity in support of their demands. Also known as the *Wagner Act*.

National Labor Relations Board (NLRB) An independent federal agency created by the NLRA and charged with administering, implementing, and enforcing NLRA provisions, as well as monitoring union elections for fraud and setting guidelines for employers and unions in regard to fair labor practices.

Necessary and Proper Clause The constitutional clause giving Congress the general implied authority to make laws necessary to carry out its other enumerated powers.

Negligence A category of torts in which the tortfeasor was without willful intent in bringing about a particular event that caused harm to another party.

Negligent hiring doctrine A tort-based theory of liability for employers for negligent or intentional torts of employees when the employer had reason to know that the employee may cause harm within his scope of employment.

Net neutrality The principle that all movement and content on the Internet should receive equal treatment.

No Electronic Theft (NET) Act A federal law enacted in 1997 that provides for criminal liability for anyone who willfully infringes on a copyright.

Nominal consideration Consideration that is stated in a written contract even though it is not actually exchanged.

Nonfeasance The failure to act or intervene in a certain situation.

Nonobviousness standard A standard requiring that to be patented, an invention must be something more than that which would be obvious, in light of publicly available knowledge, to one who is skilled in the relevant field.

Novation A type of substitute agreement in which the duties of the contract remain the same but a new, third party assumes the duties of an original party, discharging the original party from further obligations. (*Note:* Many courts use novation for new parties and new terms or substitute agreements.)

Novelty standard A standard requiring that an invention or process must be unique and original to be patented and that the patent applicant must show that no other identical invention or process exists.

Nuisance A common law legal action for redressing harm arising from the misuse of one's property that is based on the aggrieved party's right to enjoy his property without interference from a third party.

Objective intent For an offer to have legal effect, the requirement that, generally, the offeror must have a serious intention to become bound by the offer and that the terms of the offer must be reasonably certain.

Occupational Safety and Health Act (OSHA) A federal law enacted in 1970 that sets forth workplace rules and regulations to promote the safety of workers and prevent workplace injuries.

Offer A promise or commitment to do (or refrain from doing) a specified activity. In contract law, the expression of a willingness to enter into a contract by the offeror's promising an offeree that she will perform certain obligations in exchange for the offeree's counterpromise to perform.

Officers Individuals appointed by the board of directors to carry out the directors' set course of direction through management of the day-to-day operations of the business.

Oil Pollution Act (OPA) Federal legislation enacted in 1990 to streamline and strengthen the Environmental Protection Agency's ability to prevent and respond to catastrophic oil spills in water sources.

Omitted terms Contract terms that are left out or absent. In contract law, courts may supply a reasonable term in a situation where the contract is silent.

Open terms Unspecified terms in a sales contract that do not detract from the validity of the contract so long as the parties intended to make the contract and other specified terms give a basis for remedy in case of breach.

Opening statements Attorneys' presentations of their theories of the case and what they hope to prove to the jury; made at the onset of the trial.

Operating agreement Document that governs an LLC; sets out the structure and internal rules for operation of the entity.

Operating permits Licenses issued by authorities to existing stationary sources, permitting pollution emission at certain levels.

Operation of law (Agency) Method whereby an agency relationship is terminated as provided for in a statute or through certain common law doctrines covering the destruction of essential subject matter, death, bankruptcy, or lack of requisite mental capacity.

Operation of law (Contracts) Termination of an offer by the occurrence of certain happenings or events, which generally include lapse of time, death or incapacity of the offeror or offeree, destruction of the subject matter of the contract prior to acceptance, and supervening illegality.

Ordinances Local statutes passed by local legislatures.

Original jurisdiction Jurisdiction that enables a court to be the trial court to hear the case. The case must be filed first in this court.

Originality For copyright protection, the requirement that the author must use his own creative capabilities to create the work or medium.

Output contract A contract in which the buyer agrees to buy all the goods that the seller produces for a set time and at a set price and the seller may sell only to that one buyer. The quantity for the contract is the seller's output.

Overtime compensation A higher rate of pay for the hours that nonexempt employees work in excess of 40 hours in one seven-day workweek; calculated at one and one-half times the employee's hourly base rate.

Ownership interests The various forms of real property ownership. Some forms limit the rights that owners of real estate have.

Paris Convention A multinational agreement covering patents; requires signatory countries to protect the same inventor rights under any member country's patent laws as those enjoyed by citizens of that member country.

Parol evidence rule Interpretation rule stating that any writing intended by the parties to be the final expression of their agreement may not be contradicted by any oral or written agreements made prior to the writing.

Partially disclosed agency A type of agency relationship in which the third party knows that the agent is representing a principal but does not know the actual identity of the principal.

Partnership Multiple-person business entity in which the partners conduct an ongoing business relationship and share profits and losses.

Partnership at will A partnership in which the partners have not agreed to remain partners until the expiration of a definite term or the completion of a particular undertaking.

Party A person or entity making or responding to a claim in a court.

Pass-through entity A business entity that does not pay corporate taxes, such as a partnership. Rather, any profits are taxed at individual rates after they pass through the business and are distributed to the partners.

Past consideration A promise made in return for a detriment previously made by the promisee; does not meet the bargained-for exchange requirement.

Patent A statutorily created monopoly right that confers on an inventor the *exclusive right* to make, use, license, and sell her invention for a limited period of time.

Patentable subject matter standard A standard that bars laws of nature, natural phenomena, and abstract ideas from being patentable subject matter.

Pension A retirement benefit in which the employer promises to pay a monthly sum to employees who retire from the company after a certain number of years of service. The amount is ordinarily based on the length of service and the employee's final salary rate.

Per se standard (*per se:* Latin for "of, in, or by itself," i.e., without any additional facts needed to prove a point) A standard used by federal courts in deciding whether a certain transaction or action violates the Sherman Act; applied in cases of concerted activities that are blatantly anticompetitive.

Perfect tender rule Rule that requires the seller to deliver her goods exactly as the contract requires in quantity, quality, and all other respects or risk the buyer's lawful rejection of the goods.

Perfecting Procedure by which the secured party establishes priority in the collateral over other creditors, as provided by Article 9 of the Uniform Commercial Code.

Personal guarantee Pledge from LLC members of personal assets to guarantee payment obligations of the business venture.

Personal guaranty In a business loan, a pledge given by the principals of a business to repay the loan with their personal assets if the assets of the business are insufficient to do so in the event of a default by the business entity debtor; serves as a safeguard for creditors.

Personal jurisdiction The court's authority over the parties involved in the dispute.

Personal property Any movable or tangible object that can be owned or leased (e.g., computers, inventory, furniture, jewelry); includes everything except real property.

Picketing A union's patrolling alongside the premises of a business to organize the workers, to gain recognition as a bargaining agent, or to publicize a labor dispute with the owner or whomever the owner deals with.

Piercing the corporate veil Action in which a court discards the corporate veil and holds some or all of the shareholders personally liable because fairness demands doing so in certain cases of inadequate capitalization, fraud, and failure to follow corporate formalities.

Plain meaning rule The principle that if the words in a statute have clear and widely understood meanings, the court applies the statute; used as the initial guideline in statutory interpretation to determine how a rule should be applied.

Plain view doctrine A doctrine stating that authorities generally do not commit a Fourth Amendment violation when a government agent obtains evidence by virtue of seeing an object that is in plain view of the agent.

Plaintiff The party initiating a lawsuit.

Portal-to-Portal Act Provides guidelines for what constitutes compensable work under the FLSA's wage and hour requirements.

Preamble The introductory part of the Constitution that states its broad objectives.

Precedent Applying the law made in previous appellate court opinions to current cases with similar facts; binding on the trial courts.

Preemption The concept that primary sources of law are applied consistent with a hierarchy and that a law higher in the hierarchy will overrule and make void a conflicting law lower in the hierarchy. Federal law preempts conflicting state law.

Preexisting duty A duty that one is already legally obligated to perform and, thus, that is generally not recognized as a legal detriment.

Preferred stock A form of equity instrument that has less risk than common stock because it has certain quasi-debt features. Preferred stockholders have preference rights over common stockholders in receiving dividends from the corporation.

Preliminary adjudication A hearing at which the prosecutor presents evidence of the defendant's guilt and the decision maker (either the grand jurors or a magistrate) determines whether sufficient probable cause exists to hold the defendant over for trial.

Preponderance of the evidence The standard used to decide a civil case whereby the jury is to favor one party when the evidence is of greater weight and more convincing than the evidence that is offered in opposition to it (i.e., more likely than not). The preponderance standard is a substantially lower standard of proof than that used in a criminal case.

Presidential proclamation Statement issued by the president on a ceremonial occasion or to elaborate an issue of public or foreign policy.

Pretext A false reason offered to justify an action.

Pretrial conference A meeting between the attorneys for the parties and the judge in the case several weeks prior to trial, with the objectives of encouraging settlement and resolving any outstanding motions or procedural issues that arose during the pleadings or discovery stage.

Principal An agent's master; the person from whom an agent has received instruction and authorization and to whose benefit the agent is expected to perform and make decisions pursuant to an agency relationship.

Principals Owners of a business entity.

Private international law Category of international law principles that focuses on the regulation of private individuals and business entities.

Private laws Laws recognized as binding between two parties even though no specific statute or regulation provides for the rights of the parties.

Private placement A securities law provision that exempts an issuer from registration when the issuer accepts investments only from those who meet the standards for accredited investors.

Private Securities Litigation Reform Act of 1995 (PSLRA) Federal legislation making it more difficult to pursue litigation under the securities laws that is based solely on commentary by company executives; intended to protect publicly held companies from frivolous litigation.

Privately held corporation A corporation that does not sell ownership interests through sales via a broker to the general public or to financial institutions or investors.

Probable cause A reasonable amount of suspicion supported by circumstances sufficiently strong to justify a belief that a person has committed a crime.

Procedural laws Laws that provide a structure and set out rules for pursuing substantive rights.

Product disparagement statutes Statutes intended to protect the interest of a state's major industries, such as agriculture, dairy, or beef.

Promissory estoppel Theory allowing for the recovery of damages by the relying party if the promisee actually relied on the promise and the promisee's reliance was reasonably foreseeable to the promisor.

Promissory note A contract in which the borrower promises to pay back the creditor at a certain rate of interest over a specified period of years.

Prospectus The first part of the security registration statement prescribed by Securities and Exchange Commission regulations; intended to give investors a realistic view of the issuer's business, risk factors, financial position, financial statements, and disclosures concerning directors, officers, and controlling shareholders.

Protected classes The classifications of individuals that are specified in Title VII, including color, race, national origin, religion, gender, and pregnancy.

Proximate (legal) cause A fundamental element that must be proved to recover in a negligence lawsuit against a tortfeasor: The injured party must prove a legally recognized and close-in-proximity link between the breach of duty and the damages suffered.

Public international law Category of international law principles that primarily addresses relations between individual countries and international organizations.

Public laws Laws derived from a government entity.

Public policy Part of the legality requirement for a valid contract; necessitates that the terms be consistent with public policy objectives.

Punishment A principle of criminal law that imposes a hardship in response to misconduct; based on the concepts that criminal law acts as a deterrent, it removes dangerous criminals from the population, and rehabilitation is an important part of the criminal justice system.

Purchase order A form commonly used in sales contracts as an offer from the buyer; contains preprinted clauses along with blanks to accommodate the specifics of the transaction.

Qualified privilege A defense to a defamation claim whereby the defendant must offer evidence of good faith and be absent of malice to be shielded from liability; provided for the media and employers.

Quasi in rem jurisdiction Jurisdiction over real or personal property when the lawsuit has to do with personal liabilities not directly associated with the property.

Quasi-contract A classification that permits a contract to be enforceable in cases where no express or implied contract exists and one party suffers losses as a result of another party's unjust enrichment.

Ratification A retroactive source of the agent's authority that occurs when the principal affirms a previously unauthorized act by either (1) expressly ratifying the transaction or (2) not repudiating the act (i.e., the principal retains the benefits while knowing that they resulted from an unauthorized act by the agent).

Rational basis The lowest level of scrutiny applied by courts deciding constitutional issues through judicial review; upheld if the government shows that the law has a reasonable connection to achieving a legitimate and constitutional objective.

Real property Land, or anything growing on, attached to, or erected on the land. Examples of real property include parcels of land, homes, warehouses, stores, and crops.

Reasonable accommodations Accommodations, required under the Americans with Disabilities Act, that allow disabled individuals to adequately perform essential job functions.

Reformation Contract modification in which the court rewrites the contract to conform to the parties' actual intentions when the parties have imperfectly expressed their agreement and the imperfection results in a dispute.

Regulation A rule that is in effect, is published in the Code of Federal Regulations, and has the force of a law.

Regulation D A securities law provision that exempts an issuer from registration on the basis of certain transactions; applies to limited offers that involve a relatively small amount of money or offers that are made in a limited manner.

Regulation Z The part of the Truth in Lending Act requiring that certain written disclosures be made prior to the time that a credit transaction is consummated.

Rejection An action terminating an offer whereby the offeree rejects the offer outright prior to acceptance.

Remand When an appellate court sends a case back to the lower court from which it came for further action consistent with the opinion and instructions of the higher court.

Remedial Under the Superfund law, an approach to handling hazardous substance cleanup whereby the Environmental Protection Agency identifies the most hazardous waste sites and generates a National Priorities List.

Remedies Judicial actions, which can be monetary or equitable, taken by courts that are intended to compensate an injured party in a civil lawsuit.

Removal Under the Superfund law, an approach to handling hazardous substance cleanup whereby authorization is given for actions to address releases or imminent releases of hazardous materials.

Reorganization plan A plan, generally filed by the debtor, that articulates a specific strategy and financial plan for emerging from financial distress; serves as the keystone of a Chapter 11 case.

Replacement workers Nonunion employees hired by a company in order to continue its operations during a strike.

Request for admissions A set of statements sent from one litigant to an adversary for the purpose of determining what facts are in dispute and which facts both parties accept as true.

Request for production A request aimed at producing specific items to help one party discover some important fact in the case.

Requirements contract A contract in which the buyer agrees to buy whatever he needs from the seller during a set period and the buyer may buy only from that one seller. The quantity for the contract is what the buyer requires.

Rescission Cancellation of a contract that occurs when both parties agree to discharge each other from all duties under the contract and end the agreement, no matter what has been done or left undone.

Resource Conservation and Recovery Act (RCRA) Federal legislation enacted in 1976 to regulate active and future facilities that produce solid waste and/or hazardous materials.

Respondeat superior (Latin for "let the master answer") A common law doctrine under which a principal (employer) is liable for the tortious action of the servant or agent (employee) when that act resulted in physical harm or injury and occurred within the agent's scope of employment.

Restatement (Third) of Agency A set of principles, issued by the American Law Institute, intended to clarify the prevailing opinion of how the law of agency stands.

Restatement of Torts An influential document issued by the American Law Institute that summarizes the general principles of U.S. tort law and is recognized by the courts as a source of widely applied principles of law. ALI has amended the Restatements twice, resulting in the *Restatement (Second) of Torts* and the *Restatement (Third) of Torts*.

Restatements of the Law A collection of uniform legal principles focused in a particular area of the law, which contains statements of common law legal principles and rules in a given area of law.

Restitution A remedy that restores to the plaintiff the value of the performance that he has already rendered to the breaching party and by which the breaching party has been unjustly enriched.

Revised Model Business Corporation Act (RMBCA) Model act drafted by the American Law Institute and adopted by over half of the states as a template for compiling their own statutes governing corporations.

Revocation An action terminating an offer whereby the offeror decides to withdraw the offer by expressly communicating the revocation to the offeree prior to acceptance.

Revoking acceptance Remedy whereby the buyer, even after accepting the goods, can still revoke acceptance if the goods are nonconforming in a way that substantially affects their value and he notifies the seller of the revocation in a timely fashion.

Right-to-work law A state law prohibiting employers from requiring that employees join a union to continue working and that nonunion employees contribute to certain union costs such as the cost related to collective bargaining.

Rightful rejection The justified refusal to accept nonconforming goods under a sales contract.

Risk of loss The risk of one party's having to bear the loss due to damage, destruction, or loss of goods bargained for under a sales contract.

Robinson-Patman Act A federal antitrust law enacted in 1936 that amends the Clayton Act provisions by providing for broader regulatory authority to curb price discrimination.

Rule of addition The principle that literal patent infringement has occurred when the infringing device does more than is described in the patent application of the protected invention.

Rule of exactness The principle that literal patent infringement has occurred when the infringer makes, uses, or sells an invention that is exactly the same as the patent holder's claims in the patent application.

Rule of omission The principle that infringement has not occurred when the alleged patent-infringing invention lacks an essential element of the patent holder's claims in the patent application.

Rule of reason standard A second standard used by federal courts in deciding whether or not a certain transaction or action violates the Sherman Act; the rule contemplates a scale in which the court weighs any anticompetitive harm suffered against the marketwide benefit of the action.

Rulemaking The legislative function of administrative agencies, whereby they create legally enforceable rules in order to fill in the details of a statute.

Safe Drinking Water Act (SDWA) Federal legislation that sets minimum quality and safety standards for every public water system and every source of drinking water in the United States.

Sales contracts Agreements to transfer title to real property or tangible assets at a given price.

Sarbanes-Oxley (SOX) Act of 2002 Amendments to the 1933 and 1934 Securities Acts that impose stricter regulation and controls on how corporations do business, through regulation of auditing, financial reporting, and internal corporate governance.

Scienter Specific intent to deceive, manipulate, or defraud.

Secondary meaning A requirement for a descriptive trademark to gain protection; acquired when the consuming public primarily associates the mark with a particular product or service rather than with the ordinary meaning of the term.

Secondary sources Sources of law that have no independent authority or legally binding effect but can be used to illustrate a point or clarify a legal issue.

Section 16 Provision of the Securities Exchange Act of 1934 that imposes restrictions and reporting requirements on ownership positions and stock trades made by certain corporate insiders named in the statute.

Secured creditor A creditor that extends credit based on collateral pledged by the borrower.

Secured party The creditor in a secured transaction.

Securities Act of 1933 Federal legislation that covers the processes of issuing and reissuing securities to the public; requires registration and certain disclosures and authorizes the Securities and Exchange Commission to oversee the transactions.

Securities and Exchange Commission (SEC) The independent federal administrative agency charged with rulemaking, enforcement, and adjudication of federal securities laws.

Securities Exchange Act of 1934 Federal legislation that regulates the sale of securities between investors after an investor has purchased them from a business entity issuer.

Securities law The body of federal and state laws governing the issuance and trading of equity and debt instruments to public investors.

Securities Litigation Uniform Standards Act of 1998 An amendment to the Securities Exchange Act of 1934 that prevents private parties from instituting certain lawsuits in federal or state court that are based on the statutory or common law of any state that punishes "a misrepresentation or omission of a material fact" or the use of "any manipulative device or contrivance" concerning the purchase or sale of a covered security.

Security interest The rights of the secured party in a transaction.

Self-defense A defense to avoid criminal liability whereby the defendant's actions are related to the necessity of using deadly force to repel an attack in which the defendant reasonably feared that death or substantial harm was about to occur either to the defendant or to a third party.

Sentencing guidelines Statutorily prescribed standards for determining the punishment that a convicted criminal should receive on the basis of the nature of the crime and the offender's criminal history.

Separation of powers The system of checks and balances created by the Constitution whereby the three branches have unique powers that allow them to resolve conflicts among themselves, thus ensuring no one branch exceeds its constitutional authority.

Service mark A word, symbol, or phrase used to identify a particular seller's services and distinguish them from other services.

Shareholders The owners of a corporation; act principally through electing and removing directors and approving or withholding approval of major corporate decisions.

Sherman Act The centerpiece of the statutory scheme of federal antitrust law; prohibits contracts, combinations, and conspiracies in restraint of trade and prohibits monopolization.

Shipment contract A contract in which the seller is required to send the goods to the buyer via a carrier. When the carrier receives the goods, the seller has fulfilled his duty and the buyer assumes title and bears the risk of loss.

Slander Oral defamation, in which someone tells one or more persons an untruth about another that will harm the reputation or honesty of the person defamed or subject a party to hate, contempt, or ridicule.

Social Security Act (SSA) of 1935 A federal law providing a broad set of benefits for workers, including a retirement income; funded by mandatory employment taxes paid into a trust fund by both employer and employee and administered by the federal government.

Soft per se analysis An approach developed by the courts for determining the legality of a tying arrangement: An arrangement in which a seller ties a second product to the first product is illegal per se if the seller possesses sufficient market power to render the tie-in coercive.

Sole proprietorship One-person business entity with minimal filing requirements.

Sovereign immunity Long-standing doctrine of international law that holds that, with some exceptions, nations are exempt from jurisdiction by other nations' courts.

Special relationship In tort law, a heightened duty created between certain parties, such as that of a common carrier to its passengers, innkeepers to guests, employers to employees, businesses to patrons, a school to students, and a landlord to tenants and landowners.

Specific performance An equitable remedy whereby a court orders the breaching party to render the promised performance by ordering the party to take a specific action.

Speedy Trial Act A federal statute that sets out specific time periods in which an accused must be brought to trial.

Stakeholder Any individual or entity affected by a business's operations, including the business's owners, investors, employees, customers, suppliers, and the wider community.

Standing Requirement that, to maintain a lawsuit against another party, the party asserting the claim must have suffered an injury in fact; the harm must be direct, concrete, and individualized; and an appropriate legal remedy must be available.

State appellate courts State-level courts of precedent, concerned primarily with reviewing the decisions of trial courts.

State common law The body of law governing contracts for services or real estate.

State courts Courts that adjudicate matters dealing primarily with cases arising from state statutory, state common, or state constitutional law.

State Implementation Plan (SIP) A mandated state plan for complying with the federal Clean Air Act that is submitted to the Environmental Protection Agency; consists of a collection of regulations that help to achieve a reduction in pollution.

State long-arm statutes State statutes intended to allow a court to reach into another state and exercise jurisdiction over a nonresident defendant due to the defendant's activities or other conduct affecting the state in which the court sits.

State statutory law The body of law governing contracts for goods or products; based on the Uniform Commercial Code.

State trial courts The first courts at the state level before which the facts of a case are decided.

Statement of qualification Document filed to form a limited liability partnership by converting a general partnership.

Stationary sources of air pollution Fixed-site emitters of air pollutants, including fossil-fueled power plants, petroleum refineries, petrochemical plants, food processing plants, and other industrial sources.

Statute of frauds The law governing which contracts must be in writing in order to be enforceable.

Statute of limitations The time limit within which a lawsuit must be filed or the lawsuit will be barred forever *(ch. 4)*. State law that places a time limit on the enforcement of certain contracts in order to ensure diligent enforcement *(ch. 7)*.

Statutory law The body of law created by the legislature and approved by the executive branch of state and federal government.

Statutory scheme The structure of a statute and the format of its mandates.

Strict liability A category of torts in which a tortfeasor may be held liable for an act regardless of intent or willfulness; applies primarily to cases of defective products and abnormally dangerous activities.

Strict scrutiny The most stringent standard of scrutiny applied by courts deciding constitutional issues through judicial review when the government action is related to a fundamental right or is based on a suspect classification; upheld if the government shows a compelling need that justifies the law being enacted and no less-restrictive alternatives exist.

Strike A concerted and sustained refusal by workers to perform some or all of the services for which they were hired in order to induce the employer to concede certain contract terms during collective bargaining or to engage in fair labor practices.

Strong-arm clause Provision of the Bankruptcy Code that allows the debtor in possession to avoid any obligation or transfer of property that the debtor would otherwise be obligated to perform.

Structural-offense laws Antitrust laws designed to combat the problem of monopolization by outlawing affirmative action toward monopolizing or attempting to monopolize a part of trade or commerce.

Subject matter jurisdiction The court's authority over the dispute between the parties.

Sublease A tenant's transfer of her interests to a third party for anything less than the term remaining on the lease.

Substantial performance Performance of the essential terms of the contract such that performance can be considered complete less damages for anything still unperformed.

Substantive laws Laws that provide individuals with rights and create certain duties.

Substitute agreement (modification) An agreement that replaces the original contract when the two parties agree to different duties. The new duties then replace and dissolve the obligations of the original contract.

Summary jury trial An abbreviated trial conducted before a jury and a sitting or retired judge at which attorneys present oral arguments without witness testimony and the decision is nonbinding.

Summons Formal notification to the defendant that she has been named in the lawsuit and that her answer must be filed within a certain period of time.

Superfund Another name for the CERCLA, derived from that act's main provisions whereby cleanup operations for abandoned toxic waste sites are to be funded by a self-sustaining quasi-escrow fund to be administered by the federal government.

Superfund Amendments and Reauthorization Act (SARA) A 1986 amendment to the CERCLA that requires that states establish emergency response commissions to draft emergency procedures for a hazardous chemical accident and implement them in the event of such an accident; requires that businesses disclose the presence of certain chemicals within a community; and imposes an obligation on businesses to notify authorities of any spills or discharges of hazardous materials.

Supremacy Clause The constitutional clause that makes clear that federal law is always supreme to any state law that is in direct conflict.

Surety A third party that agrees to be primarily liable to pay a loan.

Tax-deferred retirement savings account A retirement savings plan in which the employee commits to saving a certain percentage of base pay in an account that is controlled directly by the employee. The funds grow tax-free until they are withdrawn.

Telephone Consumer Protection Act and **Telemarketing and Consumer Fraud and Abuse Prevention Act** Two statutes that regulate telemarketing firms and practices; allow consumers to opt out of unwanted calls from telemarketers, ban the use of unsolicited recorded calls and faxes, and prohibit telemarketers from making false representations.

Tenant remedies The legal alternatives available to tenants as compensation in the event a landlord breaches a lease, including termination of the lease, a suit for damages, and withholding of rent.

Tender An unconditional performance of the seller by delivering the purchased goods or otherwise making them available to the buyer.

Tender of delivery Seller's obligation under which, for delivery of goods, tender occurs when the seller produces goods conforming to the contract and provides adequate notice of their delivery to the buyer.

Tender of performance An offer or attempt to perform what is required under a contract.

Termination Method of ending an agency relationship whereby either the principal (revocation) or the agent (renunciation) simply communicate the desire to dissolve the relationship.

Third-party beneficiary Someone who, while not a party to a contract, stands to benefit from the existence of the contract. (See *Incidental beneficiary* and *Intended beneficiary* in this glossary.)

Title The legal term for ownership in property; confers on the titleholder the exclusive use of personal property and the rights to sell, lease, or prohibit another from using the property.

Title VII The section of the Civil Rights Act of 1964 that serves as the centerpiece of antidiscrimination law; covers a comprehensive set of job-related transactions and prohibits discrimination in the workplace on the basis of an employee's race, color, national origin, gender, religion, or pregancy. The law applies to any private sector employer with 15 or more full-time employees and to unions, employment agencies, state and local governments, and most of the federal government.

Tort A civil wrong in which one party's action or inaction causes a loss to be suffered by another party.

Tortfeasor One who commits a civil wrong against another that results in injury to person or property.

Tortious conduct The wrongful action or inaction of a tortfeasor.

Toxic Substances Control Act (TSCA) Federal legislation that gives the Environmental Protection Agency jurisdiction to control risks that may be posed by the manufacturing, processing, using, and disposing of chemical compounds.

Trade dress A product's distinctive design, packaging, color, or other characteristic that makes it unique from other products or goods.

Trade libel A tort in which a competitor has made a false statement that disparaged a competing product.

Trade secret A formula, pattern, compilation, program, device, method, technique, or process that meets the following criteria: Derives *independent economic value,* actual or potential, from not being generally known to and not being readily ascertainable by proper means by other persons who can obtain economic value from its disclosure or use; and is the subject of efforts that are reasonable under the circumstances to maintain its secrecy. Economic value must be identified by the owner, and secrecy must be kept.

Trademark A nonfunctional, distinctive word, name, shape, symbol, phrase, or combination of words and symbols that helps consumers to distinguish one product from another.

Transaction costs The costs of defining, monitoring, and enforcing property rights.

Treble damages Triple damages; often awarded in fraud cases.

Trial Stage of litigation that occurs when the case cannot be settled, generally taking place in front of a judge as the finder of law and with a jury as the finder of fact.

Trial de novo A completely new trial.

Truth in Lending Act (TILA) The part of the Consumer Credit Protection Act that requires lenders to disclose to borrower applicants certain information about the loan or terms of credit and mandates uniform methods of computation and explanation of the terms of the loan or credit arrangements.

Two-sided markets In use when an organization creates value primarily by enabling direct interactions between two (or more) distinct types of affiliated customers.

U.N. Convention on Contracts for the International Sale of Goods (CISG) A trade agreement developed by the U.N. Commission on International Trade Law to establish uniform rules for drafting certain international sales contracts.

U.S. courts of appeal The intermediate appellate courts in the federal system, frequently referred to as the *circuit courts of appeal.* There are 13 circuits or geographical areas, each of which reviews the decisions of the federal district courts in the state or several states within its circuit.

U.S. district courts Trial courts at the federal level.

U.S. Supreme Court The highest federal court that not only reviews decisions of the lower federal courts but also reviews decisions of state courts that involve some issue of federal law.

Unconscionability A defense that may allow a party to potentially avoid a contract on the grounds that she suffered a grossly unfair burden that shocks the objective conscience.

Undisclosed agency A type of agency relationship in which a third party is completely unaware that an agency relationship exists and believes that the agent is acting on her own behalf in entering a contract.

Undue influence A defense that gives legal relief to a party who was induced to enter into a contract through the improper pressure of a trusted relationship.

Unenforceable contract A contract that meets the elements required by law for an otherwise binding agreement but is subject to a legal defense.

Unilateral contract A contract involving one promise followed by one performance, which then triggers a second performance from the offeror.

Unilateral mistake An erroneous belief held by only one party about a basic assumption in the terms of an agreement.

Unilaterally altered Term pertaining to a contract in which one party changes a term of the offer or acceptance after the contract was made and without the consent of the other party, who is then discharged from performing.

United Nations (U.N.) An international organization created after World War II to facilitate common international concerns on defense, trade, protection of human rights, and other matters.

Unsecured debt Credit that is not collateralized.

Utilitarian Model of moral philosophy that holds that an action is ethically sound if it produces positive results for the most people.

Valid contract A contract that has the necessary elements and, thus, can be enforceable.

Validation disclosure A notice in which a collection agency, when making initial contact with a debtor, makes known certain rights of the debtor, including the fact that he has 30 days to dispute the debt; required under the Fair Debt Collection Practices Act.

Values management Managerial system that emphasizes prioritizing moral values for the organization and ensuring that behaviors are aligned with those values.

Venue A determination of the most appropriate court location for litigating a dispute.

Verdict The final decision of a jury in a case.

Vertical price-fixing Price-fixing in which a seller attempts to control the resale price of a product at a lower level in the supply chain.

Vertical restraints Violations of the Sherman Act (judged by the rule of reason) in which the restraining of trade involves agreements between noncompetitors on different distributional levels in the chain of commercial supply.

Vicarious infringement A theory of copyright infringement that applies when there has been a direct infringement and a third-party facilitator is in a position to control that infringement and benefits financially from it.

Vienna Convention on the Law of Treaties One of the standards used by courts and other tribunals when interpreting treaty law.

Void contract A contract that lacks one or more of the basic required elements of a contract or that has not been formed in conformance with the law from the outset of the agreement and, thus, cannot be enforced by either party.

Voidable contract A contract that one party may, at its option, either disaffirm or enforce.

Voidable transfers In bankruptcy proceedings, certain transfers that are considered an unfair advantage of one creditor over another.

Voluntary bankruptcy petition A petition filed in the bankruptcy court by the debtor that includes the names of creditors, a list of debts, and a list of the debtor's assets, income, and expenses.

Warranty A seller's (or lessor's) legally enforceable promise to a consumer concerning the quality and/or functionality of a product.

Whistleblower An employee or agent who reports illegal misconduct or a statutory violation by his or her employer to the authorities.

Winding up After dissolution, the process of paying the debts of the partnership and liquidating and/or distributing the remaining assets.

Withdrawal Term used by the RULPA to describe the act of separation of one partner from the partnership.

Workers' compensation State statutes that provide an employee who is injured in the course of employment with a partial payment in exchange for mandatory relinquishment of the employee's right to sue the employer for the tort of negligence; funded through employer-paid insurance policies.

Workout The process in which a debtor meets a loan commitment by satisfying altered repayment terms; intended to turn around a business when the principals wish to continue operations and the business is underperforming and is in poor financial condition.

World Intellectual Property Organization Copyright Treaty (WCT) Supplement to the Berne Convention intended primarily to address copyright protection related to technology (e.g., computer programs).

Written express warranty A warranty whose terms are put in writing for the consumer.

case index

A

A&M Records, Inc. v. Napster, Inc. (2001), 786, 787
Aaris v. Las Virgenes Unified School District (1998), 317
Abbot v. Payne (1984), 346–347
Abolin v. Farmers American Mutual Life Insurance (1931), 216n
Accettura & Wozniak v. Vacationland, Inc. (2018), 261–262
ACLU v. Reno (1997), 733–734
Adams v. Salt River Master Carvers (2014), 448–450
Adarand Constructors, Inc. v. Pena (1995), 433
AK-Feel, LLC v. NHAOCG, LLC (2012), 486–487
Akin Bay Company, LLC v. Von Kahle (2015), 659–660
Alice Corporation Pty. Ltd. v. CLS Bank International (2014), 797–798
ALS Scan, Inc. v. Digital Serv. Consultants, Inc. (2002), 108
Amazon.com, Inc. v. Barnesandnoble.com, Inc. (2001), 800n
American Express v. Italian Colors Restaurant (2013), 136
American Medical Association v. U.S. Internal Revenue Service (1989), 595
American Needle, Inc. v. National Football League (2010), 641
American Shipbuilding Company v. NLRB (1965), 395n
American Suzuki Motor Corp. v. Carney (1995), 706
Angel v. Murray (1974), 191n
Aquino v. Honda of America, Inc. (2005), 440
Arizona Cartridge Remanufacturers Association v. Lexmark (2005), 202
Arizona v. United States (2012), 29
Armory v. Delamirie (1722), 744n
Arthur Andersen LLP v. United States (2005), 721–722
Asahi Metal Industrial Co., Ltd. v. Superior Court of California (1987), 89
Ashcroft v. American Civil Liberties Union (2002), 734n
Associated Rubber Co. v. NLRB (2002), 390n
Association of Private Sector Colleges and Universities v. Duncan and the U.S. Department of Education (2012), 575–576
Augstein v. Leslie and NextSelection, Inc. (2012), 172–173
AutoNation USA Corp. v. Leroy (2003), 137
Avanti Press v. Employment Department Tax Section (2012), 331–332

B

Bad Frog Brewery, Inc. v. N.Y. State Liquor Authority (1998), 57–58
Bammert v. Don's Super-Valu, Inc. (2002), 368
Barrer v. Chase Bank USA (2009), 704–705
Barr v. Matteo (1959), 286n
Bartus v. Riccardi (1967), 260n
Baxter v. Ford Motor Co. (1932), 679n
Bear Sterns & Co. v. Wyler (2002), 739
BellSouth Advertising v. Donnelley Information Publishing (1993), 785n
Bennett v. American Electric Power Services Corp. (2001), 190
Bennett v. Shidler (2003), 806
Bennett v. Spear (1997), 588n
Berman v. Parker (1954), 758n
Best Van Lines, Inc. v. Walker (2007), 108
Beverly E. Black & James A. Black v. George Weston & Stroehmann Bakeries, Inc. (2008), 625
Bickford v. Onslow Memorial Hospital Foundation (2004), 104
Biller v. Snug Harbor Jazz Bistro of Louisiana, LLC (2012), 455–456
Biomedical Systems Corp. v. GE Marquette Medical Systems, Inc. (2002), 202
Birdsong v. Apple, Inc. (2009), 681–682
Bishop v. Texas A&M University (2002), 361
Blumenthal v. Drudge and America Online, Inc. (1998), 290
Bonilla v. Baker Concrete Construction (2007), 402
Bos. Red Sox Baseball Club L.P. v. Sherman (2008), 777
Bosse v. Brinker Restaurant Corp. d/b/a Chili's Grill and Bar (2005), 337–338
Bradley v. Pizzaco of Nebraska, Inc. (1993), 441
Branch v. Mullineaux (2010), 503–504
Brayton Purcell, LLP v. Recordon & Recordon (2010), 96n
Bristol-Myers Squibb Co. v. Superior Court of California (2017), 107
Brooks Brothers Group, Inc. v. Bubbles by Brooks, LLC (2013), 159
Brower v. Gateway (1998), 137–138, 211n, 830
Brown v. Board of Education (1954), 70
Brown v. Entertainment Merchants Association (2011), 47, 64
Buckley v. Valeo (1976), 582n
Bunch v. Hoffinger Industries (2004), 308
Burdick v. Koerner (1998), 526
Burton v. MDC PGA Plaza Corp. (2012), 318
Butters v. Vance International, Inc. (2000), 814
Buttrick v. Intercity Alarms (2009), 367–368
Byrne v. Boadle (1863), 299n

C

Cadence Design Systems, Inc. v. Avant!, 769n
Calder v. Jones (1984), 90, 97
Campbell v. Acuff-Rose Music, Inc. (1994), 788n
Cargill v. Monfort of Colorado, Inc. (1986), 29
Carlill v. Carbolic Smoke Ball Co. (1893), 181n
Carnival Cruise Lines v. Shute (1991), 92
Carpenter v. United States (2018), 71
Carroll Management Group, LLC v. A Carpet & Paint, LLC (2015), 342–343
Casino Reinvestment Development Authority v. Birnbaum (2019), 764
Casserly v. State (1992), 403
Central Hudson Gas v. Public Service Commission (1980), 56
Chambers v. Travelers Companies (2012), 200
Chaplin v. Sanders (1984), 763
Chateau des Charmes Wines Ltd. v. Sabate (2003), 829
Chevron USA, Inc. v. NRDC (1984), 582n
Cipollone v. Liggett Group, Inc. (1992), 71–72
Citizens to Preserve Overton Park, Inc. v. Volpe (1971), 586n
Citizens United v. Federal Election Commission (2010), 59–60
City of Philadelphia v. Fleming Companies, Inc. (2001), 565
Clancy v. King (2008), 478
Clemens v. McNamee (2010), 91
Coker v. Wal-Mart Stores, Inc. (1994), 316–317
Coleman v. Donahoe (2012), 432n
Comcast Corp v. FCC (2010), 584
Communications v. Merola d/b/a NY Telecom Supply (2013), 270
Computer Associates International v. Latai, Inc. (1992), 789n
Conklin v. Holland (2003), 475
ConnectU v. Zuckerberg (2008), 808
Consulting Engineers Corp. v. Geometric Ltd. (2009), 95
Consumer Federation of America v. Department of Agriculture (2006), 590
Continental T.V. v. GTE Sylvania (1977), 636
Cool Runnings v. BigBuy.com (simulation exercise), 832–833
Corning Glass Works v. Brennan (1974), 429n
Costar Realty Information v. Meissner (2009), 95
Covad Communications Co. v. BellSouth Corp. (2002), 649
CSX Transportation, Inc. v. Surface Transportation Board (1996), 576
Cubby Inc. v. CompuServe, Inc. (1991), 290

D

Dalton v. Educational Testing Service (1995), 241
Darden v. Peters (2007), 807
Data General Corporation, et al. v. Grumman Systems Support Corporation (1994), 649
Day v. Case Credit Corp. (2007), 28
Del Monte Corp. v. Martin (1978), 243
Deutsche Bank Sec., Inc. v. Mont. Bd. of Invs. (2006), 108
Diamond v. Diehr (1981), 798
Diaz v. Pan Am World Airways, Inc. (1971), 432
DiFolco v. MSNBC (2010), 242
Digital Realty Trust v. Somers (2018), 558–559
Dillard Department Stores, Inc. v. Chargois & Ernster (2010), 490–491
DiMercurio v. Sphere Drake Insurance PLC (2000), 830
Doctors Hospital at Renaissance v. Andrade (2016), 463
Dodge v. Ford Motor Co. (1919), 166
Dollar S.S. Co. v. United States (1939), 739
Dorton v. Collins & Aikman Corp. (1972), 251n
Dow Chemical Co. v. United States (1986), 727, 741
Drennan v. Star Paving (1958), 184n
Dumas v. Union Pacific Railroad Co. (2008), 438–439

Dunlop Holdings Ltd. v. RAM Golf Corporation (1975), 795–796
Dynamex Operations West, Inc. v. Superior Court (2018), 332

E

Ebenezer United Methodist Church v. Riverwalk Development Phase II (2012), 517–518
Edgewater Motels, Inc. v. A. J. Gatzke & Walgreen Co. (1979), 362
Ellerth v. Burlington Industries (1998), 418n
Elliott v. Google, Inc. (2017), 774–775
Ellison v. Comm'r of Internal Revenue Service (2008), 675
Elsroth v. Johnson & Johnson (1988), 309
Emmelyn Logan-Baldwin et al. v. L.S.M. General Contractors, Inc. (2012), 234–235
Emprise v. Rumisek (2009), 496
Enriquez v. West Jersey Health Systems (2001), 434–435, 437
Estrada v. Fedex Ground Package System, Inc. (2007), 362

F

Facebook, Inc. v. Teachbook.com, LLC (2011), 783
Faragher v. City of Boca Raton (1998), 417, 418n
Federal Baseball Club v. National League (1922), 639n
Federal Express Corporation v. Holowecki (2008), 595–596
Feist Publications, Inc. v. Rural Telephone Service (1991), 785
Fernandez v. Wynn Oil Co. (1981), 432n
First American Title v. Lawson (2003), 497
First National Bank of Boston v. Bellotti (1978), 58
Fisherman Surgical Instruments, LLC v. Tri-anim Health Services, Inc. (2007), 277–278
Flagiello v. Pennsylvania Hospital (1965), 12
Flood v. Kuhn (1972), 640
Florence Cement Co. v. Vittraino (2011), 521
Florida v. Georgia (2018), 107–108
Fontainebleau Hotel Corp. v. Forty-Five Twenty-Five, Inc. (1959), 750
Forest Park Pictures v. Universal Television Network, Inc. (2012), 201
Forestal Guarani S.A. v. Daros International, Inc. (2010), 821–822
14 Penn Plaza LLC v. Pyett (2009), 129
Franklin v. Facebook (2015), 93–94
Friends of the Earth v. Gaston Copper Recycling Corp. (2011), 601–602
Frostifresh Corp. v. Reynoso (1966), 211n

G

Gardner v. Loomis Armored, Inc. (1996), 369
Gardner v. U.S. Bureau of Land Management (2011), 596–597
Geier v. American Honda Motor Company (2000), 48
General Dynamics Land Systems v. Cline (2004), 425n
General Motors Corp. v. Acme Refining Co. (2007), 278
George v. Jordan Marsh Co. (1971), 292n
Georges v. Pacific Telephone & Telegraph Co. (1960), 243
GGNSC Batesville, LLC d/b/a Golden Living Center v. Johnson (2013), 339–340
Gilmer v. Interstate/Johnson Lane Corporation (1991), 129
Glenn Distributors Corp. v. Carlisle Plastics, Inc. (2002), 278
Goldman v. Chapman & Region Associates (2007), 525
Goldstein v. California (1973), 709n
Gonzales v. Krueger (1990), 318
Gonzalez v. Raich (2005), 48–49, 52
Goodrich Corp. v. Town of Middlebury (2002), 616–617
Goodyear Dunlop Tires Operation v. Brown (2011), 89–90
Gorran v. Atkins Nutritionals, Inc. (2006), 317
Goswami v. American Collections Enterprise, Inc. (2004), 164–165
Grand River Enters. Six Nations, Ltd. v. Pryor (2005), 96n
Grande, as Personal Representative of the Estate of Robert A. Spann v. Jennings (2012), 745
Graves v. Warner Brothers (2002), 295n
Greenen v. Washington State Board of Accountancy (2005), 165
Greenman v. Yuba Power Products, Inc. (1963), 306–307
Greyhound v. International Business Machines Corporation (1977), 649
Griggs v. Duke Power Co. (1971), 411n, 415
Grimshaw v. Ford Motor Company (1981), 160–161
Grindle v. Watkins Motor Lines (2012), 446–448
Griswold v. Connecticut (1965), 66
Grobow v. Perot (1988), 526

Grouse v. Group Health Plan, Inc. (1981), 193
Gruttinger v. Bollinger (2003), 433n

H

Hadley v. Baxendale (1854), 229
Hammer v. Sidway (1891), 190n
Hannington v. University of Pennsylvania (2002), 361
Harley-Davidson Motor Co. v. PowerSports, Inc. (2003), 240
Harris v. Forklift Systems, Inc. (1993), 417n
Hauter v. Zogarts (1975), 706
Haynes v. Zoological Society of Cincinnati (1995), 404
Headfirst Baseball LLC v. Elwood (2017), 488–489
Heart of Atlanta Motel v. United States (1964), 50
Hebberd-Kulow Enterprises v. Kelomar (2016), 252–253
Heintz v. Jenkins (1995), 698n
Hemlock Semiconductor Operations v. SolarWorld Industries Sachsen (2017), 263–264
Henningsen v. Bloomfield Motors, Inc. (1960), 211
Henry Schein, Inc. v. Archer & White Sales, Inc. (2019), 128
Herring v. United States (2009), 733
Hickman v. Taylor (1947), 138
Holder Construction Group v. Georgia Tech Facilities, Inc. (2006), 223–224
Holloway v. Dekkers and Twin Lakes Golf Course (2012), 212–213
Hooters of America, Inc. v. Phillips (1999), 136–137
Hope v. California Youth Authority (2005), 440
Hornbeck Offshore Services LLC v. Salazar (2010), 586n

I

IBM v. Johnson (2009), 768
IBP, Inc. v. Alvarez (2005), 372n
Infinite Energy, Inc. v. Thai Heng Chang (2008), 136
In re Brightful (2001), 677
In re Cardizem CD Antitrust Litigation (2003), 650
In re Drive-In Development Corporation (1966), 513n
In re Exxon Valdez (2004), 166
In re Fedderson (2001), 675
In re Fehrs (2008), 675
In re Geller (2014), 777
In re Heeb Media, LLC (2008), 777
In re Hershey Chocolate & Confectionery Corp. (2012), 773
In re Jones (2008), 676–677
In re Kirby (2008), 777
In re Northwest Airlines Corp. (2006), 676
In re Oil Spill by the Oil Rig "Deepwater Horizon" in the Gulf of Mexico, on April 20, 2010 (2014), 610–611
In re Reed Elsevier Props. (2007), 806
In re Richie (2006), 676
In re Sosa (2005), 669n
In re Spree.com Corp. (2001), 477
In re Subway Sandwich Marketing & Sales Practices Litigation, T. Frank, Objector (2017), 113–114
In re the Appeal from the Civil Penalty Assessed for Violations of the Sedimentation Pollution Control Act (1989), 29–30
In re Vantive Corporation Securities Litigation (2000), 564
INS v. Chadha (1983), 582, 582n
Integrity Staffing Solutions v. Busk (2014), 373
International Shoe v. Washington (1945), 89n
International Transportation Service v. NLRB (2006), 390n
Int'l Union, United Mine Workers of America v. Mine Safety & Health Admin. (2005), 595
Italian Cowboy Partners, Ltd. v. The Prudential Company of America (2011), 208–209

J

Jackson v. Wyndham Destinations, Inc. (2019), 764
Jacob & Youngs v. Kent (1921), 219, 226
James v. McDonald's Corp. (2005), 850
Jasper v. H. Nizam, Inc. (2009), 401
Jaszczyszyn v. Advantage Health Physician Network (2012), 384
John Flastaff v. Paul Revere Furniture Company (simulation exercise), 443–450
Jones v. R. R. Donnelley & Sons Co. (2004), 28

Case Index 891

K

Kamilewicz v. Bank of Boston Corporation (1996), 113
Katzenbach v. McClung (1964), 50–51
Kaufman v. Trump's Castle Funding (1993), 544–545
Kaycee Land & Livestock v. Flahive (2002), 496
Keeton v. Hustler Magazine (1984), 90n
Kelley v. Cypress Financial Trading Co., L.P. (2014), 664
Kelo v. City of New London (2005), 758–759
Koppers Co., Inc v. Krupp-Koppers (1981), 770
Krell v. Henry (1903), 225n
KSR International v. Teleflex (2007), 807
Kyllo v. United States (2001), 727n

L

Lamb v. Phillip Morris, Inc. (1990), 740
Lamprecht v. Jordan, LLC (2003), 496–497
Lange v. National Biscuit Company (1973), 346n
Lechmere, Inc. v. NLRB (1992), 390n
Ledbetter v. Goodyear Tire & Rubber Co. (2007), 429
Leegin Creative Leather Products v. PSKS, Inc. (2007), 636
Leon v. IDX Systems Corporation (2006), 565
Leonard v. PepsiCo, Inc. (2000), 181–182
Leonel v. American Airlines, Inc. (2005), 387–388
Lieberman v. Wyoming.com LLC (2004), 497
Lucy v. Zehmer (1954), 179–180, 194
Luther v. Countrywide Home Loans Servicing (2008), 165
Luttinger v. Rosen (1972), 216

M

MacPherson v. Buick (1916), 306
Madden v. Lumber One Home Center (2014), 375–376
Maher v. Best Western Inn (1998), 316
Marbury v. Madison (1803), 43–44, 44n, 77n
Mark v. FSC Securities Corporation (1989), 564
Masterpiece Cakeshop, Ltd. v. Colorado Civil Rights Commission (2018), 55–56, 64
Matal v. Tam (2017), 778–779
Mattel v. MCA Records (2002), 781–782
Matthias v. United Pacific Ins. Co. (1968), 318
McCown v. International Harvester Co. (1975), 318
McDonald v. Santa Fe Train (1976), 409
McDonnell Douglas Corp. v. Green (1973), 411n, 413–414, 447
McKennon v. Nashville Banner Publishing Co. (1995), 432n
McLaurin v. Oklahoma (1950), 70
McQueary v. The Pennsylvania State University (2016), 370–371
McWane, Inc. v. Federal Trade Commission (2015), 643–644
MediaNews Group v. McCarthey (2007), 240
Meinhard v. Salmon (1928), 476
Metro-Goldwyn-Mayer Studios v. Grokster, Ltd. (2005), 787, 791
Micallef v. Miehle Co. (1976), 311n
Midtown, Ltd. v. Urban Storage, LP (2008), 349–350
Miner v. Fashion Enterprises, Inc. (2003), 525
Miranda v. Arizona (1966), 730
Missouri ex rel. Gaines v. Canada (1938), 70
Mitchell v. King Packing Co. (1956), 372n
Moradi v. Marsh USA, Inc. (2013), 345–346
Morris v. City of Colorado Springs d/b/a Memorial Health System (2012), 417–418
Morrison v. Gugle (2001), 525
Morrow v. Hallmark Cards, Inc. (2008), 201–202
Moseley v. V Secret Catalogue, Inc. (2003), 841
Motor Vehicle Manufacturing Association v. State Farm Mutual Automobile Association (1983), 586
Movado Group, Inc. v. Mozaffarian et al. (2012), 279
M/S Bremen v. Zapata Off-Shore Co. (1972), 104
Murray v. Maryland (1936), 70
Myers v. LHR, Inc. (2008), 705

N

National Federation of Independent Business v. Sebelius (2012), 52
National Football League Management Council v. Brady (2016), 129–130
Nelson v. Tradewind Aviation (2015), 287–288, 316
Ner Tamid Congregation of North Town v. Krivoruchko (2009), 279
Neurology Associates, LLP v. Elizabeth Blackwell, M.D. (simulation exercise), 320–325
New York Times v. Sullivan (1964), 285
NLRB v. Midwestern Personnel Services, Inc. (2003), 393–394, 405
No Spray Coalition, Inc. v. City of New York (2000), 625
Noldi v. Grunberg (2010), 213n
Nollan v. California (1987), 757n
North Street Corp. v. Getty Saugerties Corp. (2009), 755
Nursing Home Pension Fund v. Oracle Corp. (2004), 564

O

O'Bannon v. National Collegiate Athletic Association (2015), 638–639
Office Depot, Inc. v. Zuccarini (2010), 106
Ohio v. American Express Co. (2018), 632–633
Oncale v. Sundowner Offshore Services, Inc. (1998), 418
1-800 Lenses, Inc. v. WhenU.com (2017), 834–836

P

Pagan v. Fruchey and Village of Glendale (2007), 73–74
Palmer v. Champion Mortgage (2006), 694–695
Palsgraf v. Long Island Railroad Co. (1928), 300–301
Patel v. Zillow, Inc. (2019), 74
Pennoyer v. Neff (1877), 88
Pennzoil v. Colelli (1998), 105
People v. Defore (1926), 733n
People for the Ethical Treatment of Animals v. Doughney (2000), 775–776
Pepsi-Cola Co. v. Steak 'n Shake, Inc. (1997), 242
PGA Tour, Inc. v. Martin (2001), 439
Phoenix of Broward, Inc. v. McDonald's Corp. (2007), 705, 849
Pitasi v. Gartner Group, Inc. (1999), 424n
Plaintiffs A, B, C v. Zemin (2003), 829
Plessy v. Ferguson (1896), 69
Polaroid Corp. v. Polarad Electronics Corp. (1961), 780
Popovich v. McDonald's (2002), 850
PriceWaterhouse v. Hopkins (1989), 411n, 414–415
Pro Football, Inc. v. Blackhorse (2015), 779n
Public Citizen, Inc. v. Mineta (2003), 597

R

Radovich v. National Football League (1957), 641n
Raffles v. Wichelhaus (1864), 189
Rahemtulla v. Hassam (2008), 477
Ranchers Cattlemen Action Legal Fund United Stockgrowers of America v. U.S. Department of Agriculture (2007), 596
Ransom v. FIA Card Services (2011), 669
Reed's Photo Mart, Inc. v. Monarch (1971), 203
Regents of the University of California v. Bakke (1978), 433n
Regional General Hospital v. Anesthesiology Associates, Inc. (2007), 324–325
Rentmeester v. Nike (2019), 807
Republic of Austria v. Altmann (2004), 830
Revell v. Lidov (2002), 96n
Ricci v. DeStefano (2009), 416
Riley v. California (2014), 728–729
R.J. Reynolds Tobacco Company v. Food and Drug Administration (2012), 57
Robertson v. Mauro (2013), 467–468
Robin v. Espo Engineering Corp. (2000), 424n
Rochon Corp. v. City of Saint Paul (2012), 200–201
Roe v. Wade (1973), 66
Romanelli v. Citibank (2009), 352–353
Rosenfeld v. Basquit (1996), 211n, 254

S

Sally Beauty Company v. Nexxus Products Co., 233n
Samson v. Federal Express Corporation (2014), 427–428
Sauer Inc. v. Lawson (2015), 667–668
SEC v. Alliance Leasing Corp. (2000), 566
SEC v. Gemstar-TV Guide International, Inc. (2005), 554
SEC v. SG, Ltd. (2001), 532
SEC v. W. J. Howey Co. (1946), 530–531
Seeger v. Cincinnati Bell Tel. Co., LLC (2012), 383n
Seidel v. Greenberg (1969), 318
Sierra Club v. El Paso Gold Mines, Inc. (2005), 624

Silverthorne Lumber Company v. United States (1920), 732n
Singer Co. v. Stott & Davis Motor Express, Inc. & Stoda Corp. (1981), 763
Sisco v. Quicker Recovery, Inc. (2008), 402
Smith v. City of Jackson, Miss. (2005), 425
Smith v. Gross (1979), 566
Smith v. Van Gorkom (1985), 515–516
Sokoloff v. Harriman Estate Development Corp. (2001), 28
Sons of Thunder v. Borden (1997), 259
Sony Corp. of America v. Universal City Studios (1984), 787
Soto v. Bushmaster Firearms (2015), 310
South Dakota v. Dole (1987), 53
South Dakota v. Wayfair, Inc. (2018), 13–14
Sparrow v. Demonico (2012), 194–195
Starbucks Corp. v. Wolfe's Borough Coffee, Inc., dba Black Bear Micro Roastery (2005), 841
State v. DeAngelo (2007), 72
State Farm Mutual v. Campbell (2003), 73
State Street Bank & Trust Co. v. Signature Financial Group (1998), 797
State v. Yenzer (2008), 740
Steiner v. Mitchell (1956), 372n
Stewart v. Happy Herman's Cheshire Bridge, Inc. (1997), 428n
Stratton Oakmont v. Prodigy Services Company (1995), 290
Sullivan v. U.S. Postal Service (2012), 403–404
Sutton v. United Airlines (1999), 426n
S.W.B. New England, Inc. v. R.A.B. Food Group, LLC (2008), 278
Sweatt v. Painter (1950), 70
Symbiotics, L.L.C. v. FERC (2004), 597

T

Tafel v. Lion Antique Investments & Consulting Services (2011), 241
Tanka v. University of Southern California (2001), 650
Taylor v. Palmer (1966), 242
Tellabs v. Makor Issues and Rights, Ltd. (2007), 551
Tempur-Pedic International v. Go Satellite Inc. (2010), 107
TermoRio v. Electricrificadora Del Atlantico S.A. (2006), 829
Terry v. Ohio (1968), 726n
Texaco, Inc. v. Dagher, et al. (2006), 635
Texas Beef Group v. Winfrey (2000), 288n
Texas Oil & Gas Ass'n v. United States EPA (1998), 597
Thomas v. Montelucia Villas, LLC (2013), 227–228
Toms v. Links Sports Management Group, L.P. (2006), 361–362
Toolson v. New York Yankees (1953), 639
Toyota Motor Manufacturing v. Williams (2002), 426n
Toys "R" Us, Inc. v. Step Two, S.A. (2003), 105–106
Tracy v. Solesky (2011), 284
Trinity Marine Products v. Secretary of Labor Elaine Chao (2007), 579
Truck Rental International Inc. v. Web Marketing LLC (2018), 836–838
Trump v. Hawaii (2018), 70–71
Turner v. Summit Treestands, LLC (2011), 119n
Turner v. Wells (2018), 285–286
20/20 Financial Consulting, Inc. v. John Does 1–5 (2010), 119–120
Two Pesos, Inc. v. Taco Cabana, Inc. (1992), 770n

U

United States v. Alderman (2009), 72
United States v. Alvarez (2012), 44–45
United States v. American Library Association (2003), 72–73
United States v. Bhagat (2006), 563
United States v. Caceres (1979), 732n
United States v. Causby (1946), 749n
United States v. Colgate (1919), 635
United States v. Correa (2016), 722n
United States v. DeCoster (2016), 714–715
United States v. Doe (1984), 731n
United States v. Esquenazi (2014), 818–819
United States v. Grinnell (1966), 641
United States v. Hudson & Goodwin (1812), 709n
United States v. Jones (2012), 62–63
United States v. LaMacchia (1994), 786n
United States v. Lopez (1995), 51
United States v. Martoma (2017), 548n
United States v. McGee (2014), 546–547
United States v. Microsoft (2001), 642
United States v. Morrison (2000), 51
United States v. Newman (2014), 548n
United States v. O'Hagan (1997), 546
United States v. Park (1975), 713–714, 741
United States v. Shaffer (2007), 691n
United States v. Southeastern Pennsylvania Transportation Authority (2000), 624
United States v. Stewart (2004), 739
United States v. Ulbricht (2014), 9–10, 33–35
U.S. Airways, Inc. v. Barnett (2002), 439
U.S. Consumer Financial Protection Bureau v. Pressler & Pressler LLP (2016), 699–700
U.S. Equal Employment Opportunity Commission v. Albercombie & Fitch Stores, Inc. (2015), 412–413
U.S. Steel v. Fortner Enterprises (1977), 637

V

Vagias v. Woodmont Properties (2006), 689–690, 851
Van Hollen v. Federal Elections Commission (2016), 586–587
Vance v. Ball State University (2013), 419, 431n
Vaughn v. Edel (1990), 411n
Verizon v. FCC (2014), 585
Vernon v. Schuster (1997), 476
Village of Euclid v. Ambler Realty Co. (1926), 756n
Virginia State Board of Pharmacy v. Virginia Citizens Consumer Council (1976), 56
Vokes v. Arthur Murray, Inc. (1968), 207n

W

Waddell v. Rustin (2011), 457–458
Waremart Foods v. NLRB (2004), 402–403
Warner Bros. Entertainment, Inc. v. RDR Books (2008), 788
Waters v. Min Limited (1992), 210–211
Wellspan Hospital and Medical Group v. Phillip Bayliss, M.D. (2005), 322–324
Whelan v. Jaslow (1986), 789
Whirlpool v. Marshall (1980), 382
Wilcox Investment, L.P. v. Brad Wooley Auctioneers, Inc. (2015), 19–20
William Paxton v. Wal-Mart Stores, Inc. (2008), 624
World-Wide Volkswagen Corp. v. Woodson (1980), 105
Wurtz v. Beecher Metro District (2014), 369
Wurtzel v. Starbucks Coffee Co. (2003), 316
Wygant v. Jackson Board of Education (1986), 433n

Y

Yahoo! v. La Ligue Contre Le Racisme (2001), 812
Yost v. Wabash College, Phi Kappa Psi Fraternity (2014), 297–298
Ypsilanti Township v. General Motors Corporation (1993), 144

Z

Zarda v. Altitude Express (2018), 410
Zeidman v. Fisher (2009), 303–304
Zippo Manufacturing Co. v. Zippo Dot Com, Inc. (1997), 96
Ziva Jewelry v. Car Wash Headquarters (2004), 746–747

subject index

A

AAA (American Arbitration Association), 126, 130, 816
A/B testing, 155–157
Abandoned toxic waste sites. *see* Superfund
ABC test, 330–333, 357
Abortion rights, 66
Absolute privilege, 286, 313
Acceptance
 case summary, 202
 CISG on, 272, 822
 defined, 182, 196
 mailbox rule and, 185–187
 in merchant transactions, 250–253
 mutual assent and, 178
 in nonmerchant transactions, 250
 revocation of, 269, 274
 in sales contracts, 250–254, 264–265, 269, 272
 UCC on, 250–254
Accord and satisfaction, 220, 221, 236
Account, duty to, 351, 357
Accounting industry reforms, 553
Acid rain, 604, 604n
Acknowledgment forms (invoices), 250, 274
ACPA (Anticybersquatting Consumer Protection Act of 1999), 775
Acquisitions, 643
Acquittals, 725
Act requirement, 710–711, 735
Actual authority, 339, 357
Actual damages, 302, 313
Actual owner of property, 744, 760
Actual possession, 754
Actus reus, 710–711, 735
ADA. *see* Americans with Disabilities Act of 1990
ADAAA (Americans with Disabilities Amendments Act of 2008), 426, 446
ADEA (Age Discrimination in Employment Act of 1967), 407, 424–425, 435
Ad hoc arbitration rules, 816
Adhesion contracts, 211
Adjudication, 76–77, 569, 580, 580n, 591, 724–725, 735
Administrative agencies. *see also* Administrative law
 adjudication by, 569, 580, 580n, 591
 defined, 407n, 569, 591
 disclosure statutes and, 589–591
 enforcement by, 569, 578–580, 591
 functions of, 14, 569–570
 inspection by, 578–579, 591
 licensing by, 570, 578, 591
 limits on, 581–588
 organizational structure, 571, 583
 overview, 568
 public accountability of, 588–591
 rulemaking by, 569, 572–578, 591, 595
 scope of power, 572–581
Administrative law, 568–597. *see also* Administrative agencies
 case summaries, 595–597
 citizen suit provisions in, 588–589, 592, 596–597
 concept summaries, 578, 580–581
 defined, 25, 569, 591
 enabling statutes, 570, 572, 591
 function of, 14

overview, 568
 sources of, 570, 572
 at state level, 591
Administrative law courts (ALCs), 719
Administrative law judges (ALJs), 580, 591, 719
Administrative Procedures Act of 1946 (APA)
 amendments to, 582, 582n
 defined, 570
 on final publication rules, 575–576
 on judicial review, 582, 586
 on public comment, 573
 rulemaking under, 572–573, 595
Administrative warrants, 729
Admission, requests for, 120–121, 132
ADR. *see* Alternative dispute resolution
Adulterated food, 692
Adverse possession, 746, 754–755, 763
Advertisements
 bait-and-switch, 180n, 686–687
 as contract offers, 180–182
 false, 686–691
 greenwashing, 622–623
 obscenity regulation in, 57–58
 online, 690–691
 pricing in, 687
 puffery in, 679
Affirmative action programs, 432–433, 436
Affordable Care Act. *see* Patient Protection and Affordable Care Act of 2010 (PPACA)
AFL-CIO (American Federation of Labor–Congress of Industrial Organizations), 388, 390
Age Discrimination in Employment Act of 1967 (ADEA), 407, 424–425, 435
Agency law, 328–363. *see also* Agents; Principals
 authority in, 339–341
 case summaries, 361–362
 classification of agents in, 329–335
 concept summaries, 338, 347–348, 356
 creation of relationships in, 336–338
 defined, 357
 duty and obligation in, 348–351, 353
 employee agents in, 329–335, 357
 gratuitous agents in, 329, 350, 357
 independent contractors in, 329–335, 347, 357
 IRS three-prong test in, 333
 liability in, 339–348
 misclassification liability in, 333–335
 overlay with other areas of law, 338
 overview, 328
 ratification in, 340–341, 357
 remedies in, 351–354
 respondeat superior and, 343, 357
 sources of, 329
 strategic use of, 359–360
 termination of relationship in, 354–356, 358
 tort liability to third parties in, 343–346
 transactions in, 336–338
Agents
 classification of, 329–335
 contract liability to third parties, 341–343
 defined, 328–329, 357
 duties to principals, 348–351
 employee, 329–335, 357
 gratuitous, 329, 350, 357
 independent contractors, 329–335, 357
 principal's duties to, 353
 principal's liability for acts of, 339–348
 unauthorized acts of, 352
Agreement on Trade-Related Aspects of Intellectual Property (TRIPS), 823, 825
Agreements, 171, 196. *see also* Contracts
AI (artificial intelligence), 153–154
AIG (American International Group), 556, 557
Air pollution
 acid rain, 604, 604n
 Clean Air Act and, 14, 604–607, 620, 625

economic incentive theory and, 605
 fuel composition and distribution and, 607
 fuel economy standards and, 606
 market-based approaches to mitigation, 604–605, 621
 mobile sources of, 604, 606–607, 620
 performance standards and, 606
 State Implementation Plans (SIP) for, 604, 621
 stationary sources of, 604, 620
 tailpipe emissions, 606
Airspace rights, 749–750
Alcohol testing, 387
ALCs (administrative law courts), 719
ALI. *see* American Law Institute
Alien corporations, 502
Alimony, 670
ALJs (administrative law judges), 580, 591, 719
Alternative dispute resolution (ADR), 124–131
 advantages of, 125
 arbitration, 126–131, 133, 135, 816
 in business environment, 111, 125
 case summaries, 136–138
 in contracts, 136, 137
 costs of, 125
 defined, 124
 expert evaluation, 125, 130–131, 133
 formal, 125–131
 hybrid form of, 131
 informal, 125
 international, 815–817, 830
 med-arb, 131, 133
 mediation, 130, 131, 133, 135, 817
 mini-trials, 131, 133
 online, 134–135
 overview of options for, 112
 privacy issues and, 125
 summary jury trials, 131, 133
 time considerations, 125
Amazon, 647–648, 800
Ambiguous terms, 215, 236
Amendments to U.S. Constitution, 41, 42, 67. *see also specific amendments*
American Arbitration Association (AAA), 126, 130, 816
American Federation of Labor–Congress of Industrial Organizations (AFL-CIO), 388, 390
American International Group (AIG), 556, 557
American Law Institute (ALI), 16, 247, 283, 501, 501n, 709, 767n
American Recovery and Reinvestment Act of 2009, 556, 560
Americans with Disabilities Act of 1990 (ADA)
 amendments to, 407, 425, 426, 446
 case law, 446–450
 case summary, 439
 defined, 435
 documented-disability requirement, 425–426
 medical testing and, 387–388
 qualified individuals under, 427–428
 reasonable accommodations under, 425, 428, 435, 439
 "regarded-as" test and, 426
 simulation exercise, 443–450
Americans with Disabilities Amendments Act of 2008 (ADAAA), 426, 446
Annual percentage rate (APR), 693–694
Answer, in civil litigation, 115, 117–118, 132
Anticipatory repudiation, 226–228, 237, 242, 266
Anticybersquatting Consumer Protection Act of 1999 (ACPA), 775
Antitrust Criminal Penalty Enhancement and Reform Act of 2004, 637
Antitrust law, 628–651. *see also* Sherman Act of 1890
 boycotts and, 635
 case summaries, 649–650
 Celler-Kefauver Antimerger Act, 629, 646

894 Subject Index

Clayton Act, 629, 642–643, 646
   criminal liability for violations, 637
   exclusive dealing and, 643
   Federal Trade Commission Act, 629, 643–646
   Hart-Scott-Rodino Antitrust Improvements Act, 645
   history of, 629
   market allocation and, 635
   meeting of the minds in, 634
   mergers and acquisitions in, 643
   monopolies and, 641–642, 647–648
   nonprice restraints and, 636–637
   overview, 628
   predatory pricing and, 649
   price discrimination and, 645
   price-fixing and, 631, 634–636, 646
   purpose of, 629
   restraint of trade in, 633–638, 646, 650
   Robinson-Patman Act, 629, 645, 646
   sports and, 638–641
   structural-offense laws, 641, 646
   two-sided markets in, 631–633, 646
   tying agreements and, 637, 643, 649
APA. *see* Administrative Procedures Act of 1946
Apparent authority, 339–340, 357, 361
Appeals
   in administrative law, 580
   circuit courts of, 79, 80, 100
   in civil litigation, 123–124
   in criminal law, 725
   discretionary, 78
   in land use regulation, 756
Appellants, 78
Appellate courts, 11, 78–80, 78n, 100
Apple, 315, 771
Appointments Clause, 581
APR (annual percentage rate), 693–694
Aquinas, Thomas, 145
Arbitrary and capricious standard, 577, 584, 586–588, 592, 596
Arbitrary marks, 771
Arbitration
   case summaries, 136–138, 829
   contract provisions for, 136
   defined, 133
   employment, 129–130
   enforceability of arbitration clauses, 137–138
   Federal Arbitration Act, 127–128
   international, 816–817
   legally mandated, 126
   med-arb, 131, 133
   online, 135
   process for, 126
   public policy and, 136–137
Arbitrators, 126
Aristotle, 145
Army Corps of Engineers, U.S., 607
Arrests, 724, 726–728, 730
Arrest warrants, 724
Arthur Andersen, 721–722
Articles of incorporation, 502–503, 522
Articles of organization, 482–484, 493
Articles of U.S. Constitution, 41–44, 67
Artificial intelligence (AI), 153–154
Assent. *see* Mutual assent
Assignment
   for the benefit of creditors, 658–660, 671
   of contract rights, 232–233, 237, 242
Associate counsel, 6
Assumption of duty, 296–298
Assumption of risk, 303–304, 311, 313, 317
Assurances, 262–263, 274
Attorneys, 5–7
At-will employees, 365–371, 396
Audit lottery, 593
Audit reforms, 553, 554

Authority
   in agency law, 339–341
   in corporations, 511–512
Authorization cards, 390, 397
Automatic stay, 661, 663, 671, 675
Avant! Corporation, 768–769
Avoidance strategy, 22

B

Bad faith, 775–776, 803
Bail, 724
Bailments, 746–747, 763
Bait-and-switch advertisements, 180n, 686–687
Bajarin, Tim, 648
Ballot initiatives, 58n
Ballot propositions, 58
Bankruptcy, 660–671
   administration of estate in, 664–665
   alimony and support in, 670
   automatic stay and, 661, 663, 671, 675
   case summaries, 675–677
   Chapter 7: liquidation and discharge, 663–665
   Chapter 11: reorganization, 666–667, 676
   Chapter 13: repayment plan, 667
   concept summary, 670–671
   contract performance and, 225
   cram-down provision in, 666, 672
   credit counseling and, 670
   defined, 236
   DIP powers in, 666
   distribution and discharge in, 665
   fraud and, 662, 667–668
   liquidation and discharge (Chapter 7), 663–665
   means test in, 663, 668–669, 676
   meeting of creditors in, 664–665
   orders for relief in, 663
   overview, 660–661
   proof of income and, 670
   reorganization (Chapter 11), 666–667, 676
   repayment plan (Chapter 13), 667
   strategic, 673–674
   strong-arm clause in, 666, 672
   trustee appointment and, 661–664, 671
   voidable transfers in, 661–662, 671, 675
Bankruptcy Abuse Prevention and Consumer Protection Act of 2005 (BAPCPA), 661, 668–670
Bankruptcy Code, 225, 660–661
Bankruptcy estate, 661, 671
Bankruptcy petitions, 663, 671
Bankruptcy trustees, 661–664, 671
Bargained-for exchange, 189–191, 197
Barnes & Noble, 800
Battle of the forms, 250–253, 274, 276–277, 279
Bench trials, 123, 132
Benefit corporations, 502
Bentham, Jeremy, 146n
Berne Convention, 824, 826
Bespeaks caution doctrine, 544
Betamax doctrine, 787
Beyond a reasonable doubt standard, 123n, 710, 735
Bezos, Jeff, 647–648
BFOQ (bona fide occupations qualification), 431–432, 436
Bilateral contracts, 171–172, 196
Bill of Rights, 42, 54–64, 67
Bills, 8
Binding rulings, 78–80
Bipartisan Campaign Reform Act of 2002, 59
Black Bear Micro Roastery, 839–842
Black's Law Dictionary, 3n, 4, 25, 283n, 655n
Blue-sky laws, 551, 560
Blurring, 782
Board of directors, 506, 509–511, 522, 526

Bona fide occupations qualification (BFOQ), 431–432, 436
Bonds, 534
Borrowers (debtors), 654, 671, 692, 701
Boycotts, 395, 635
BP (British Petroleum), 586, 609–611
Branches of government
   executive, 14, 41, 43, 67, 70–71, 581–582
   judicial, 41, 43–44, 67
   legislative, 41, 42, 52–53, 67
Brands. *see* Trademarks
Breach of contract
   anticipatory repudiation and, 226–228, 266
   defined, 17, 19, 225, 236–237, 266, 274
   partial breach, 226
   sales contracts, 266–271
   statute of limitations for, 115
   total breach, 226
Breach of duty, 298–299, 313, 351–354
Breach of fiduciary duty, 519
Breach of warranty, 681–682
Brennan, William J., Jr., 415n
Brexit, 152
Bribery, 720–721, 723, 817–820
Bridging the gap technique, 780
Briefs, 78
Brin, Sergey, 23–24, 474
British common law, 11
British Petroleum (BP), 586, 609–611
Bundle of rights, 744, 749
Burden of proof
   in criminal law, 710, 735
   in employment law, 413–414, 435
Bureau of Justice Statistics, 111
Business corporation law, 501, 521
Business entities
   case summaries, 475–478
   common forms of, 453
   corporations (*see* Corporations)
   criminal law and, 712–715, 739
   franchises, 470–471
   joint ventures, 458, 471
   LLCs (*see* Limited liability companies)
   LLPs (*see* Limited liability partnerships)
   overview, 452
   partnerships (*see* Partnerships)
   selection of, 453
   sole proprietorships, 454–456, 465–466, 471, 476
   trusts, 629, 630
Business environment
   Bill of Rights in, 54–64
   congressional powers and, 42
   contracts in (*see* Contracts)
   counsel's role in, 5–7
   dispute resolution in, 111, 125
   environmental law in, 599
   executive powers and, 43
   expansion options in, 5, 6
   insight and strategy in, 5
   intentional torts in, 284–294
   jurisdiction and, 85
   laws impacting business, 14, 15
   legal decisions in, 4–7
   model laws in, 15–16
   stare decisis in, 12
   strategic nature of, 21–25
Business ethics
   case studies, 153–157
   case summaries, 164–166
   codes of ethics and conduct in, 149–150
   corporate social responsibility and, 157–161, 165, 166
   in debt collection, 164–165
   decision making in, 152–157
   defined, 142, 161
   domain names and, 776

Subject Index   895

Business ethics—*Cont.*
  Facebook's secret psychology experiment and, 155–157
  good faith and nuclear condition option, 217
  Google's Project Maven and, 153–154
  insider trading and, 718–720
  moral minimum and, 143, 161
  patent trolls, 800
  professional, 165
  profit maximization and, 143, 161
  stakeholders and, 142, 154, 161, 166
  strategic, 163–164
  values management and, 148–152, 162
Business judgment rule, 504, 513–516, 522, 526
Business lawyers, 7
Business method patents, 795–800
Business necessity test, 431, 436
Business organizations. *see* Business entities
Business records, production of, 731, 739
But-for test, 299–300
Bylaws, corporate, 505–506

C

CAA (Clean Air Act of 1963), 14, 604–607, 620, 625
CAFA (Class Action Fairness Act of 2005), 113
CAFE (Corporate Average Fuel Economy) standards, 606
Calder effects test, 96–97
California independent contractor law, 332–333
CAN-SPAM (Controlling the Assault of Non-Solicited Pornography and Marketing) Act of 2003, 690–691, 701
Capacity, in contract formation, 185, 193–194, 197
Cap and trade plans, 604
Capital call, 491–492
Capitalization
  of corporations, 505
  of general partnerships, 459
  of limited liability companies, 485
  of limited liability partnerships, 491–492
  of limited partnerships, 464
Capital One Financial, 556
Card Check Act. *see* Employee Free Choice Act of 2009
CARD (Credit Card Accountability Responsibility and Disclosure) Act of 2009, 696–697, 701
Cardozo, Benjamin, 733n
Care, duty of
  in corporations, 513–514, 522
  due care, 350, 357
  in limited liability companies, 486
Case of first impression, 12
Case precedent. *see* Precedent
Case studies
  coffee wars (Starbucks and Charbucks), 839–842
  fraud (McDonald's promotional games), 847–851
  juice contamination (Odwalla), 843–845
Categorical exclusion (CE), 602–603
Categorical imperative, 146
Cause in fact, 299–300, 313
CBAs (collective bargaining agreements), 366, 392, 666, 676
C corporations, 508
CCPA (Consumer Credit Protection Act of 1968), 693–694, 701
CDA (Communications Decency Act of 1996), 290, 290n, 313, 733–734
Cease and desist orders, 536, 536n
Celler-Kefauver Antimerger Act of 1950, 629, 646
Central Hudson test, 56–57, 73–74
CERCLA (Comprehensive Environmental Response Compensation and Liability Act of 1980), 614–619, 621

Ceremonial proclamations, 43
Certificates of limited partnership, 461, 462, 471
Certificates of organization, 482–484, 493
Certification, of collective bargaining units, 391, 397
CFAA (Computer Fraud and Abuse Act of 1986), 722, 735
CFPB. *see* Consumer Financial Protection Bureau
CFR (Code of Federal Regulations), 577
Chancery courts, 78, 524
Change of venue, 93
Changes to Win Federation, 388
Chapter 7 bankruptcy, 663–665
Chapter 11 bankruptcy, 666–667, 676
Chapter 13 bankruptcy, 667
Charging of the jury, 123, 132
Checks and balances system, 41–42, 45
Child labor laws, 377–378
Child Online Protection Act of 1998, 734
Child Protection and Toy Safety Act of 1969, 685
Child support, 670
China, currency pegging strategy of, 827
Choice of law, 271, 820
Christie's International, 634
Circuit courts of appeal, 79, 80, 100
Circuit split, 81, 96–97, 101
CISG. *see* U.N. Convention on Contracts for the International Sale of Goods
Citations, 10, 25, 724
Citigroup, 556
Citizen suits
  in administrative law, 588–589, 592, 596–597
  in environmental law, 600–602, 620, 625
Civil cases, 78, 100
Civil law, 11, 18, 26, 709–710, 815, 825
Civil litigation, 111–124
  answer in, 115, 117–118, 132
  appeals in, 123–124
  charging the jury in, 123, 132
  class action lawsuits, 111–114
  closing arguments in, 123, 132
  collecting the judgment in, 124
  complaint in, 115, 116, 132
  corporate social responsibility and, 159–160
  counterclaims (countersuits) in, 118, 132
  cross-claims in, 118, 132
  cross-examination in, 123, 132
  defined, 111, 132
  deliberations and verdict in, 123, 132
  demand in, 114
  depositions in, 120, 132
  direct examination in, 123, 132
  discovery stage of, 118–122, 132
  ethics in, 166
  forum shopping in, 102–103
  interrogatories in, 120, 132, 138
  jury selection in, 123, 132
  motions in, 118, 123, 132
  opening statements in, 123, 132
  pleadings stage of, 115–118
  prelawsuit stage of, 114–115
  pretrial conferences in, 122, 132
  prevalence of, 111
  requests for admission in, 120–121, 132
  requests for production in, 121, 132, 136
  settlements in, 113–115, 122
  stages of, 114–124
  standing in, 115, 132
  statute of limitations in, 115, 132
  submission of evidence in, 123
  summons in, 115, 132
  testimony in, 123
  trial stage of, 122–124
Civil Rights Act of 1964, 50–51, 407–424, 435
Civil Rights Act of 1991, 407
CLA (Consumer Leasing Act of 1976), 698, 701
Clarity of offers, 178

Class Action Fairness Act of 2005 (CAFA), 113
Class action lawsuits, 111–114
Clawback provision, 554
Clayton Act of 1914, 629, 642–643, 646
Clean Air Act of 1963 (CAA), 14, 604–607, 620, 625
"Clean hands" doctrine, 20, 28, 232, 237
Clean Water Act of 1970 (CWA), 607–608, 621, 624
Clerk of courts, 115, 115n
Clinton, Hillary, 59–60
Closely held corporations, 501
Closing arguments, 123, 132
Closing date, 755
Club membership, 764
COBRA (Consolidated Omnibus Budget Reconciliation Act of 1985), 379–380
Coca-Cola, 7–8, 770
Code of Federal Regulations (CFR), 577
Codes of conduct, 150
Codes of ethics, 150
Codes (statutes), 10
Codified law, 332, 572
Coffee wars (case study), 839–842
Collateral, 653–655
Collecting the judgment, 124, 454, 454n
Collective bargaining
  authorizing legislation for, 389
  defined, 391–392, 397
  good faith requirements for, 392
  grievances in, 392, 397
Collective bargaining agreements (CBAs), 366, 392, 666, 676
Collective bargaining units, 390–391, 397
Comfort letters, 538
Comity, 811–812, 825
Commerce Clause
  application of, 48, 50–51
  case summary, 72
  civil rights and, 50–51
  defined, 42, 67
  on interstate vs. intrastate activity, 48
  on limits of congressional power, 51
  on noncommercial activities, 51
  on state regulatory power, 51
Commercial impracticability, 263–264, 274, 279
Commercial land use regulation, 756–757
Commercial reasonableness, 259
Commercial speech, 56–58, 72, 74
Committees, corporate, 511
Commonality, vertical vs. horizontal, 531
Common law
  administrative, 572
  contract law and, 175
  defined, 11, 25
  development of, 83
  employment-at-will exceptions and, 366–369
  international systems of, 815
  Internet and, 11
  standards of behavior and, 299
  state, 175, 196, 299
Common property, 743
Common stock, 533–534, 559
Communication of offers, 178
Communications Decency Act of 1996 (CDA), 290, 290n, 313, 733–734
Community laws, 813
Community Trademark System, 824n
Commuting compensation, 402
Comparative negligence, 303, 313, 318
Compel discovery, motion to, 118
Compensatory damages, 228–229, 237, 423
Competition regulation. *see* Antitrust law
Competitive advantage, 23–24
Complaint
  in civil litigation, 115, 116, 132
  employment discrimination, 430, 436

Composite legal systems, 815
Comprehensive Environmental Response Compensation and Liability Act of 1980 (CERCLA), 614–619, 621
Computer Fraud and Abuse Act of 1986 (CFAA), 722, 735
Computer Software Copyright Act of 1980, 789
Concealment of material fact, 209–210
Concept summaries
   administrative law, 578, 580–581
   agency law, 338, 347–348, 356
   alternative dispute resolution, 131
   bankruptcy and alternatives, 670–671
   breach of contract, 228, 271
   business ethics, 144
   business-related intentional and competition torts, 294
   class action lawsuits, 114
   Clean Air Act, 607
   conditions, 216
   constitutional protections, 65
   contract law, 171, 174–176, 196, 225, 266
   copyrights, 791–792
   corporations, 161, 507–509, 519
   creditors' rights, 656–657
   criminal justice process, 725
   criminal law, 715
   criminal procedure, 734
   employment discrimination statutes, 429–430
   employment regulation laws, 385
   employment relationships, 371
   environmental law, 603, 607, 611–613, 619
   federal powers in U.S. Constitution, 53–54
   Howey test, 531
   international sale of goods, 273, 823
   Internet and e-mail jurisdiction, 97
   judiciary, role and structure of, 81–82
   jurisdiction, 92–93
   limited liability companies and partnerships, 492
   litigation stages, 124
   minimum contacts on the Internet, 99–100
   moral philosophy and ethical decision making, 147
   mutual assent, 187
   National Environmental Policy Act, 603
   negligence analysis, 304
   partner dissociation/dissolution or withdrawal, 469
   patents, 801–802
   personal property, 747
   precedent, 84
   principal and agent liability to third parties, 347–348
   products liability, 312
   remedies and damages, 232
   restraints of trade, 637–638
   rulemaking process, 578
   sales contracts, 255, 258, 266, 271, 273
   Sarbanes-Oxley Act, 555
   scope of administrative agency power, 580–581
   securities law, 531
   sole proprietorships vs. partnerships, 465–466
   solid waste and hazardous materials regulation, 613
   sources of law, 16–17
   strict liability, 312
   Superfund response, 619
   third-party rights, 234
   title and allocation of risk, 258
   Title VII, 423–424
   trademarks, 783
   unfair and deceptive trade practices, 691
   U.S. Constitution, 53–54, 65
   values management, 161
   warranties and product safety, 684
   water pollution control, 611–612
Conciliation negotiations, 430, 436
Concurrent conditions, 216
Concurrent jurisdiction, 87, 100
Condemnation proceeding, 758
Condition precedent, 215, 216
Condition subsequent, 215–216
Conditions, in contracts, 215–216, 236
Conduct, codes of, 150
Confidentiality. *see* Privacy
Confirmation memorandum, 254, 274
Congressional powers, 42, 582
Consent
   in agency law, 336, 357
   for dissolution of partnerships, 469
   mutual, 220–221, 236
   unanimous consent resolutions, 501
Consent decrees, 616
Consent orders, 642, 699
Consequences-based approach to ethics, 146
Consequential damages, 229, 237, 268
Consideration
   amount and type of, 190
   bargained-for exchange aspect of, 189–191, 197
   defined, 189, 197
   legal detriment and, 189, 190
   nominal, 190, 197
   in option contracts, 183
   past, 191–192, 197
   preexisting duty rule for, 191, 191n, 197
   promissory estoppel and, 192–193, 197
   in sales contracts, 253–254
   UCC on, 253–254
Consolidated Omnibus Budget Reconciliation Act of 1985 (COBRA), 379–380
Consolidated statutes, 10
Conspiracy, 555, 717
Constitution, U.S., 40–75. *see also specific amendments and clauses*
   on administrative law, 570
   amendments to, 41, 42, 67
   articles of, 41–44, 67
   case summaries, 70–74
   checks and balances in, 41–42, 45
   commerce powers in, 42, 48, 50–51
   concept summaries, 53–54, 65
   due process in, 64
   enumerated powers in, 8, 42–44, 67
   federal powers in, 42–48
   functions of, 41
   on intellectual property, 766
   interpretation of, 29
   on jurisdiction, 43, 85
   overview, 40
   preamble to, 41, 67
   privacy rights and, 66
   protections provided by, 54–65
   on separation of powers, 45, 67
   structure of, 41–42
   Takings Clause, 757
   tax and spend powers in, 42, 52–53
   text of, 853–862
Constitutional interpretation, 29
Constitutional law
   characteristics of, 8
   defined, 25
   functions of, 8
   judicial review and, 43–44, 65
   privacy in, 66
Consumer Credit Protection Act of 1968 (CCPA), 693–694, 701
Consumer Financial Protection Bureau (CFPB), 557, 685, 693, 695, 699, 701
Consumer Fraud Acts (state statutes), 689–690, 705
Consumer law, 678–707
   case summaries, 704–706
   consumer reviews and, 686
   credit transactions and, 692–698
   debt collection and, 698–700, 705
   defined, 678, 700
   enforcement of, 685
   false advertisements and, 686–691
   for food and drug safety, 692
   warranties (*see* Warranties)
Consumer Leasing Act of 1976 (CLA), 698, 701
Consumer Product Safety Act of 1972 (CPSA), 684–685, 700
Consumer Product Safety Commission, 684–685
Consumer Review Fairness Act of 2016 (CRFA), 686, 701
Continuous possession, 754
Contract-based approach to ethics, 147
Contract enforceability, 206–215
   concealment of material fact and, 209–210
   defined, 235
   duress and, 210, 210n, 235
   as element of transactions, 177
   fraud and, 207–210
   genuineness of assent and, 206–211, 235
   historical, 170
   interpretation rules and, 214–215
   misrepresentation and, 207–210, 235
   of quasi-contracts, 174
   statute of frauds and, 171, 211–213, 236, 240, 752n
   unconscionability and, 210–211, 236
   undue influence and, 210, 236
   of unilateral contracts, 172
   of written contracts, 171, 211–215
Contract formation, 178–196
   acceptance in (*see* Acceptance)
   agreements to agree in, 188
   capacity in, 185, 193–194, 197
   concept summary, 196
   consideration in (*see* Consideration)
   detrimental reliance and, 184, 197
   indefinite terms in, 188
   insufficient agreement, 187–189
   legality requirement for, 195, 197, 202
   mailbox rule and, 185–187, 197
   mistakes in, 188–189, 197, 203
   mutual assent and, 178, 187, 196, 202
   objective intent and, 178–180, 196
   offers in (*see* Contract offers)
   partial performance, 183–184
   performance (*see* Contract performance)
   public policy and, 195, 197
Contract offers, 178–187
   acceptance of, 178, 182, 185–187, 196, 202
   advertisements as, 180–182
   CISG on, 272, 822
   counteroffers, 184–185, 197
   death of offerors/offerees and, 185
   defined, 178, 196
   destruction of, 185
   detrimental reliance and, 184, 197
   incapacity of offerors/offerees and, 185
   irrevocable, 183, 184, 197, 250
   lapse of time and, 185, 197
   merchant's firm, 250, 273–274
   mirror image rule and, 184–185, 197
   objective intent and, 178–180, 196
   open terms in, 249, 273
   in option contracts, 183
   partial performance and, 183–184
   rejection of, 184–185, 197
   revocation of, 182–183, 196
   in sales contracts, 248–250, 272
   supervening illegalities and, 185
   termination of, 182–185
   UCC on, 248–250

Contract performance, 215–235. *see also* Breach of contract
  anticipatory repudiation and, 226–228, 237, 242, 266
  assignment of rights and, 232–233, 237, 242
  assurances and, 262–263, 274
  bankruptcy and, 225
  "clean hands" doctrine and, 232, 237
  conditions and, 215–216, 236
  damages and, 228–232
  delegation of duties and, 233, 237
  discharge of contract, 217, 220–225
  good faith and, 217–218, 236, 241
  impossibility of, 222, 236
  impracticability of, 223, 236, 263–264
  material (deviation from contract), 218, 236
  perfect performance, 217
  remedies and, 228–231, 242
  restitution and, 229–230, 237
  sales contracts and, 259–266
  statute of limitations and, 225
  substantial performance, 218–219, 236
  tender of performance, 232, 237
  third-party rights and, 232–235, 242
Contracts
  adhesion, 211
  arbitration provision in, 136
  bilateral, 171–172, 196
  categories of, 171–175
  defined, 171
  destination, 257, 274
  dispute resolution in, 136, 137
  enforceability of (*see* Contract enforceability)
  express, 173, 196, 365–366
  formation of (*see* Contract formation)
  hybrid, 175, 196
  implied, 173, 196, 201, 366–368
  installment, 265–266, 274
  legal strategy and, 239
  option contracts, 183, 250
  oral, 171
  output, 249, 273
  performance of (*see* Contract performance)
  predominant thrust of, 175
  quasi-contracts, 173–174, 196
  requirements contracts, 249, 273, 277–278
  restrictive covenants in, 195, 214–215, 291, 320–325
  sales (*see* Sales contracts)
  shipment, 256–257, 274
  sources of contract law, 175–176
  strategic, 199
  tortious interference with, 291–293
  transaction elements, 176–177
  unenforceable, 174, 196, 201–202, 241
  unilateral, 172–173, 180, 196, 200
  unilaterally altered, 225, 236
  valid, 174, 196
  void, 174, 196, 200–201
  void per se, 194
  voidable, 174, 194, 196
  written, 171, 190, 211–215
Contractual employees, 365–366, 396
Contract with America Advancement Act of 1996, 582n
Contributory infringement, 786, 803
Contributory negligence, 303
Controlling the Assault of Non-Solicited Pornography and Marketing (CAN-SPAM) Act of 2003, 690–691, 701
Convention on Contracts for the International Sale of Goods. *see* U.N. Convention on Contracts for the International Sale of Goods (CISG)
Convention on the Recognition and Enforcement of Foreign Arbitral Awards, 816, 825
Convictions, 725
Cooling-off periods, 395

Copyright, 783–792
  case summaries, 807
  concept summary, 791–792
  creativity requirement for, 784–785, 803
  criminal sanctions for infringement, 786
  defenses to infringement, 787–789
  defined, 783, 803
  in digital age, 789–791
  durable medium requirement for, 785, 803
  infringement, 785–789
  international agreement on, 824
  notice of, 785
  originality requirement for, 784–785, 803
  protection periods, 784
  registration of, 785
  sources of law for, 783–784
  for tattoos, 805
Copyright Act of 1976, 783–784, 787
Corporate Average Fuel Economy (CAFE) standards, 606
Corporate charters, 502n
Corporate citizenship, 158
Corporate governance, 502, 551–554, 560
Corporate lawyers, 7
Corporate opportunity doctrine, 517–519
Corporate social responsibility (CSR), 157–161, 165, 166
Corporate veil, 506–507, 520–522, 525
Corporations, 500–527. *see also* Shareholders
  accounting reforms for, 553
  alien, 502
  articles of incorporation, 502–503, 522
  audit reforms and, 553, 554
  benefit, 502
  breach-of-fiduciary-duty lawsuits and, 519
  business judgment rule and, 504, 513–516, 522, 526
  bylaws for, 505–506
  C corporations, 508
  capitalization of, 505
  case summaries, 525–526
  categories of, 501–502
  choice of state incorporation, 504
  closely held, 501
  commencement of business, 506–507
  concept summaries, 161, 507–509, 519
  debt and, 505
  defined, 500, 501, 521
  directors of, 506, 509–511, 522, 526
  domestic, 502
  equity and, 505
  family-held, 501
  fiduciary duties in, 513–519
  financial reporting by, 553
  foreign, 502
  formalities in, 506
  formation of, 502–503, 507
  governance of, 502, 551–554, 560
  initial organizational meetings, 505–506
  initial public offerings and, 502, 505
  issuance of shares by, 506, 510
  liability in, 503, 506–507, 519, 526
  management and operation of, 509–521
  officers in, 506, 509, 511–513, 522
  piercing the corporate veil, 507, 520–522, 525
  political speech and spending by, 58–60
  preincorporation activity, 503–504
  presidents of, 512
  privately held, 501–502, 522
  professional, 502
  publicly held, 502, 504
  S corporations, 508
  secretaries for, 512–513
  state laws and, 501
  taxation of, 507–508
  treasurers of, 512

  venture capital firms, 505
  vice presidents of, 512
Cosco, Inc., 684–685
Cosigning, 655
Cost-benefit analysis, 85, 111
Council on Environmental Quality, 602
Counsel, 5–7, 25
Counterclaims (countersuits), 118, 132
Counteroffers, 184–185, 197
Country of origin principle, 99, 101
Country of reception approach, 99
Coupon settlements, 113
Courts, 76–84. *see also* Jurisdiction
  adjudicatory function of, 76–77
  authority of, 76–81
  defined, 100
  development of law through, 83–84
  district, 79, 83, 100
  federal (*see* Federal courts)
  of general authority, 78
  inferior, 78
  in international law, 812–814
  levels of, 77–81
  of limited authority, 78
  local, 78
  parties in cases, 77, 78, 86, 88, 100
  state (*see* State courts)
  venue and, 84, 93–94
Covenants not to compete, 214–215, 236
Cover, 268, 274, 278
Covered (nonexempt) employees, 376–377, 396
CPSA (Consumer Product Safety Act of 1972), 684–685, 700
Cram-down provision, 666, 672
Creativity requirement for copyright, 784–785, 803
Credit Card Accountability Responsibility and Disclosure (CARD) Act of 2009, 696–697, 701
Credit cards, 696–697
Credit counseling, 670
Credit freeze, 698
Creditors. *see also* Debt
  assignment for the benefit of, 658–660, 671
  defined, 692, 692n, 701
  overview, 652
  real property and, 655
  rights of, 653–654, 656–657
  secured, 617, 653, 654, 671
  secured transactions under UCC, 654
  sureties and guarantors, 655–656, 671
  unsecured, 653, 665
Credit reports, 698
Credit transactions, 692–698
  actors involved in, 692
  antidiscrimination policies for, 695
  consumer credit regulation, 693–694
  credit cards, 696–697
  credit reports, 698
  disclosures, 693–698
  identity theft and, 697–698
  leases, 698
  mortgages, 695
CRFA (Consumer Review Fairness Act of 2016), 686, 701
Criminal cases, 78, 100
Criminal justice system, 724–725
Criminal law, 708–723
  act requirement in, 710–711, 735
  burden of proof in, 710, 735
  business entities and, 712–715, 739
  case summaries, 739–740
  civil law vs., 709–710
  classification of crime in, 712
  concept summary, 715
  criminal procedure vs., 709, 725–726
  defenses in, 711–712
  defined, 18, 26, 735

898 Subject Index

felonies in, 712, 735
general principles of, 710
infractions in, 712
legality principle in, 710, 735
liability in, 710–712
mental requirement in, 711
misdemeanors in, 712, 735
Model Penal Code and, 709, 712, 713, 717, 735
property crime in, 712
public order crime in, 712
punishment principle in, 710, 735
purpose of, 18
sentencing guidelines and, 710, 725, 735
sources of, 708–709
summary offenses in, 712
violent crime in, 712
white-collar crime in, 712, 715–723
Criminal procedure, 725–734
arrests and, 726–728, 730
business records production in, 731, 739
concept summary, 734
criminal law vs., 709, 725–726
defined, 709, 735
double jeopardy and, 731, 735
exclusionary rule in, 731–733, 740
expectation of privacy in, 726–727
plain view doctrine in, 727, 735
searches and, 726–729
self-incrimination and, 729–730
trials in, 731
The Critique of Practical Reason (Kant), 146
Cross-claims, 118, 132
Cross-examination, 123, 132
Crowdfunding, 532–533, 542
CSR (corporate social responsibility), 157–161, 165, 166
Cuban, Mark, 719–720
Culpability, 709
Cure, 260–261, 274
Currency values, 827–828
Curt Flood Act of 1998, 640
Customs, 811
CWA (Clean Water Act of 1970), 607–608, 621, 624
Cybersecurity, 552
Cyberspace. *see* Internet
Cybersquatting, 775

D

Damages
actual, 302, 313
avoidance of, 231
compensatory, 228–229, 237, 423
consequential, 229, 237, 268
contract performance and, 228–232
in defamation suits, 284
defined, 18, 26
for imperfect performance, 218
incidental, 267, 268
liquidated, 230, 237
mitigation of, 231–232
money, 18, 226, 228, 237, 268–269
nominal, 228n
products liability and, 311
punitive, 73, 228n, 302n, 303, 423
treble, 207, 235, 290, 291
DBA ("doing business as"), 454
Death of offerors/offerees, 185
Debentures, 534
Debt. *see also* Bankruptcy; Creditors
bonds, 534
collection of, 698–700, 705
corporate, 505
debentures, 534
defined, 559

ethics in collection of, 164–165
insolvent borrowers, 657–660, 671
mortgages, 655, 671, 692n, 695
nondischargeable, 665, 675
peer-to-peer lending, 534–535
promissory notes, 534, 655, 671
secured loans, 454n
unsecured, 653, 671
Debtor in possession (DIP), 666, 672
Debtors (borrowers), 654, 671, 692, 701
Deceptive trade practices. *see* Unfair and deceptive trade practices
Decision making, ethics in, 52, 145–147, 152–157
Declaration of Independence, U.S., 145
Declaratory judgment, 324
Deeds, property, 749
Deepwater Horizon oil spill (2010), 586, 609–611
Defamation
defenses to, 286–288
defined, 90
effects test and, 90–91, 97
elements of, 284
international jurisdiction and, 99
libel, 284, 288–290, 313
online content providers and, 289–290
public figure standard and, 284–286
slander, 284, 313
truth, 286
Defamatory statements, 284
Default judgment, 118
Defeasible, 751
Defective products, 307
Defendants, 77, 100, 115, 724–725
Defenses
copyright infringement, 787–789
in criminal law, 711–712
defamation, 286–288
employment discrimination claims, 431–432
negligence, 302–304
price discrimination, 645
products liability, 311
securities law, 543–544, 550–551
Superfund liability, 617
workers' compensation claims, 381
Delaware
chancery courts in, 78, 524
incorporation in, 504
Delegation of duties, 233, 237
Deliberations, 123, 132
Demand, in civil litigation, 114
Department of Labor, 372, 374, 376–377, 379, 382, 383
Depositions, 120, 132
Derivative action, 519
Derivative evidence, 732
Descriptive marks, 772
Desegregation, 69–70
Design defects, 307
Design patents, 795, 796
Destination contracts, 257, 274
Detours, 344, 357
Detrimental reliance, 184, 197
DIF (Discriminant Function System), 593
Differentiation, 23
Digital Millennium Copyright Act of 1998 (DMCA), 790
Dilution of trademarks, 782–783, 840, 841
DIP (Debtor in possession), 666, 672
Direct copyright infringement, 785–786, 803
Direct examination, 123, 132
Direct and imputed knowledge, 786
Direct power, 581–582
Directed verdict, motion for, 118
Directors, corporate, 506, 509–511, 522, 526
Disabilities, defined, 425, 436. *see also* Americans with Disabilities Act of 1990 (ADA)

Discharge of contracts
accord and satisfaction in, 220, 221, 236
defined, 217, 236
frustration of purpose and, 224–225, 236
impossibility of performance and, 222, 236
impracticability of performance and, 223, 236
mutual consent and, 220–221, 236
novation and, 221, 236
by operation of law, 222–225
rescission and, 220, 236
substitute agreements and, 220, 236
Disclaimers
legal risk management and, 315
as prevention strategy, 22–23
warranties and, 680–681, 683, 700
Disclosure
administrative agencies and, 589–591
in agency law, 350–351
credit transactions and, 693–698
cybersecurity and, 552
debt collection and, 699
in employment law, 389–390
by franchises, 470, 471
of genetically modified organisms, 703–704
securities law and, 535, 559
Discovery, 118–122, 132
Discretionary appeals, 78
Discriminant Function System (DIF), 593
Discrimination. *see also* Employment discrimination
in commerce regulation, 51
in credit transactions, 695
racial, 50, 69–70, 142, 441
Disgorgement, 352
Dismiss, motion to, 118
Disney, Walt, 761–762
Disparate impact, 415–416, 425, 435
Disparate treatment, 411–414, 435
Dispute resolution. *see* Alternative dispute resolution (ADR); Civil litigation
Dissociation/dissolution
of limited liability companies, 487–488, 493
of partnerships, 466–469, 471
District courts, 79, 83, 100
Diversity-of-citizenship cases, 83, 86, 100
Dividends, 510, 533–534
DMCA (Digital Millennium Copyright Act of 1998), 790
Doctrine of equivalence, 801, 803
Doctrine of stare decisis, 11–12, 25, 79n5
Document destruction rules, 555
Dodd-Frank Wall Street Reform and Consumer Protection Act of 2010, 555, 557–560
"Doing business as" (DBA), 454
Domain names, 775–776
Domestic corporations, 502
Do Not Call Registry, 688
Double jeopardy, 731, 735
Dram shop laws, 298
Drinking water safety, 611, 621
Drug safety, 692
Drug testing, 387
Duces tecum subpoenas, 120
Due care, duty of, 350, 357
Due Process Clause, 64, 67, 73, 85
Due process of law, 64, 67
Durable medium, 785, 803
Duress, 210, 210n, 235, 712
Duty
to account, 351, 357
in agency law, 348–351, 353
assumption of, 296–298
breach of, 298–299, 313, 351–354
of care, 350, 357, 486, 513–514, 522
defined, 313
of disclosure, 350–351
of due care, 350, 357

Duty—Cont.
    fiduciary (see Fiduciary duties)
    general duty of reasonable conduct, 295
    of landowners, 296
    of loyalty, 348–350, 477, 486, 516–519, 522
    negligence and, 295–298
    no general duty to act, 295–296
    of obedience, 350
Duty-based ethics, 146
Duty to accept, 265

E

E. coli outbreak (case study), 843–845
EA (environmental assessment), 603
Easements, 753, 760
Economic Espionage Act of 1996, 768, 802
Economic Growth, Regulatory Relief, and Consumer Protection Act of 2018, 697–698
Economic incentive theory, 605
EDGAR database, 537
EEOC. *see* Equal Employment Opportunity Commission
Effects test, 90–91, 90n
EIS (environmental impact statement), 603
Elections
    for board of directors, 510–511
    in labor unions, 390, 397
Electronic Communications Privacy Act of 1986 (ECPA), 386–387, 397
Electronic searches and seizures, 62
E-mail
    jurisdictional issues, 95–98
    statute of frauds and, 213
    workplace monitoring of, 386
Embezzlement, 716
Eminent domain, 757–759, 764
Emission trading, 604
Emotional contagion, 155
Employee agents, 329–335, 357
Employee Free Choice Act of 2009, 391, 391n
Employee Polygraph Protection Act of 1988, 388, 397
Employee Retirement Income Security Act of 1974 (ERISA), 379, 397
Employment arbitration, 129–130
Employment-at-will doctrine, 365–371
    collective bargaining agreements and, 366
    common law exceptions to, 366–369
    defined, 365, 396
    express contract exception to, 365–366
    implied contracts and, 366–368
    public policy exception to, 368–369, 401
    statutory exceptions to, 369–371
    whistleblower statutes and, 369–371
Employment discrimination, 406–450
    affirmative action programs and, 432–433, 436
    age discrimination, 407, 424–425
    case summaries, 438–441
    claims procedures, 430–431
    defenses for employers, 431–432
    defined, 407, 435
    disabilities and (*see* Americans with Disabilities Act of 1990 (ADA))
    federal antidiscrimination statutes, 407–408
    filing complaints with EEOC, 430–431, 436
    overview, 406
    pay equality and fairness, 407, 408, 428–429, 437–438
    remedies for, 423
    sexual harassment, 416–421
    simulation exercise, 443–450
    state statutes, 433–435, 440
    Title VII and (*see* Title VII)

Employment law, 364–405
    affirmative action programs and, 432–433, 436
    case summaries, 401–404
    child labor laws, 377–378
    commuting compensation, 402
    concept summaries, 371, 385
    covenants not to compete in, 214–215
    covered (nonexempt) employees in, 376–377, 396
    discrimination and (*see* Employment discrimination)
    drug and alcohol testing in, 387
    employment-at-will doctrine and, 365–371, 396, 401
    exempt employees in, 374–377, 396
    family and medical leave in, 383–385, 397, 403–404
    health care and, 379–380
    hours of work and, 372–374, 378
    medical testing in, 387–388
    minimum wage and, 372
    on-call time compensation, 403
    origins of, 365
    overtime compensation and, 373–374, 396
    overview, 364
    polygraph testing and, 388
    privacy issues in, 66, 386–388
    promissory estoppel in, 192–193
    retirement plans in, 378–379
    Social Security and, 379
    unemployment benefits in, 380
    unfair labor practices and, 402–403
    unions and (*see* Labor unions)
    wages and, 372–374, 378
    whistleblowers and, 369–371, 396, 404
    workers' compensation in, 380–381, 397, 402
    workplace safety and, 381–382
Enabling statutes, 570, 572, 591
Endangered Species Act of 1973 (ESA), 620, 621
Enforcement
    by administrative agencies, 569, 578–580, 591
    of arbitration clauses, 137–138
    of contracts (*see* Contract enforceability)
    of environmental law, 599–602
    in land use regulation, 756
    SEC mechanisms for, 535–536, 558
    in securities law, 554–555
Enron Corporation, 553, 721
Entourage (television show), 239
Enumerated powers, 8, 42–44, 67
Environmental assessment (EA), 603
Environmental impact statement (EIS), 603
Environmental law, 598–626. *see also* Air pollution; Water pollution
    in business environment, 599
    case summaries, 624–625
    citizen suit provisions in, 600–602, 620, 625
    Clean Air Act, 14, 604–607, 620, 625
    Clean Water Act, 607–608, 621, 624
    concept summaries, 603, 607, 611–613, 619
    Endangered Species Act, 620, 621
    enforcement of, 599–602
    greenwashing and, 622–623
    hazardous materials disposal, 612–613
    land acquisitions in, 618–619
    land use regulation, 757
    major statutes summary, 620
    National Environmental Policy Act, 602–603, 620
    Oil Pollution Act, 608–611, 621
    origins of, 599
    overview, 598–599
    Resource Conservation and Recovery Act, 612–613, 621, 624
    Safe Drinking Water Act, 611, 621
    solid waste disposal, 612–613
    sources of, 599
    Superfund, 614–619, 621, 624

Toxic Substances Control Act, 613, 621
watchdog groups and, 600
wildlife protection, 620
Environmental Protection Agency (EPA)
    air pollution regulation, 604, 606–607
    establishment of, 599
    functions of, 14, 599–600
    hazardous materials regulation, 612–613
    solid waste regulation, 612–613
    water pollution regulation, 607–608, 611
Equal Credit Opportunity Act of 1974, 695, 701
Equal Employment Opportunity Commission (EEOC)
    conciliation negotiations with, 430, 436
    defined, 435
    filing complaints with, 430–431, 436
    functions of, 407
    right-to-sue letters issued by, 430–431
    on sexual orientation as protected class, 409
    Uniform Guidelines on Employee Selection Criteria, 415
Equalization strategy, 69
Equal Pay Act of 1963, 407, 408, 428–429, 435, 437–438
Equal Protection Clause, 64–65, 64n, 70, 757
Equipment leases, 747–748
Equitable maxims, 20, 26
Equitable relief. *see also* Specific performance
    case summary, 29
    defined, 26, 237
    injunctive relief, 18, 231, 237
    reformation, 231, 237
Equity
    common stock, 533–534
    corporate, 505
    defined, 529, 559
    fairness and, 20, 28
    law vs., 18–20
    preferred stock, 534
Equity aids the vigilant, 20
Equivalence doctrine, 801, 803
ERISA (Employee Retirement Income Security Act of 1974), 379, 397
ESA (Endangered Species Act of 1973), 620, 621
Escrow agents, 756
Escrow funds, 554–555
Estate, 302
Ethical-sourcing program, 164
Ethics. *see also* Business ethics
    codes of, 150
    coffee wars case study and, 839–842
    consequences-based approach to, 146
    contract-based approach to, 147
    in decision making, 52, 145–147, 152–157
    defined, 141, 145, 162
    fraud case study, 847–851
    judicial speculation and, 52
    juice contamination case study, 843–845
    law and, 141–143
    in litigation, 166
    moral philosophy and, 145–147
    principles-based approach to, 145–146
    products liability and guns, 309–311
    professional, 165
    strategic, 163–164
    trolley problem in, 146
    UCC contract rules and, 255
    witness testimony and, 121
European Court of Justice, 813, 825
Evidence
    derivative, 732
    exculpatory, 119
    extrinsic, 188
    inculpatory, 119
    parol evidence rule, 214, 236
    preponderance of, 123, 132, 415, 710, 735
    submission of, 123

Examination of witnesses, 123
Exclusionary rule, 61, 731–733, 740
Exclusive dealing, 643
Exclusive possession, 754
Exculpatory evidence, 119
Execute the judgment, 454
Executive branch, 14, 41, 43, 67, 70–71, 581–582
Executive orders, 43, 67
Exempt assets, 454n, 663, 665
Exempt employees, 374–377, 396
Exempt securities, 539–541, 560
Expansion of businesses, legal impact of, 5, 6
Expedited discovery, 119–120
Expert evaluation, 125, 130–131, 133
Expert evaluators, 125, 131, 133
Expiration, termination by, 355–356, 358
Express acts, termination by, 354–358
Express authority, 511–512
Express contracts, 173, 196, 365–366
Express partnerships, 456, 471
Express warranties, 306, 679, 682, 700
Expulsion of members from LLCs, 488–489
Extrinsic evidence, 188
Exxon Valdez oil spill (1989), 608

F

FAA (Federal Arbitration Act of 1925), 127–128
Face amount of bonds, 534
Facebook
 forum selection clause, 92, 102–103
 founding of, 474, 494–495, 523–524
 jurisdictional issues and, 85, 92
 secret psychology experiment, 155–157
Fair and Accurate Credit Transactions (FACT) Act of 2003, 697, 701
Fair Credit Billing Act of 1974, 697n
Fair Credit Reporting Act of 1970 (FCRA), 698, 701
Fair Debt Collection Practices Act of 1977 (FDCPA), 698–699, 701, 705
Fair Labor Standards Act of 1938 (FLSA), 10, 371–377, 372n, 396
Fair use defense, 787–789, 803
Fairness and equity, 20, 28
False advertisements, 686–691
False Claims Act of 1863, 371
False imprisonment, 291
Family and Medical Leave Act of 1993 (FMLA), 383–385, 397, 403–404
Family-held corporations, 501
Family limited partnerships, 465
Fanciful marks, 771
Faragher/Ellerth defense, 431
FCA (free carrier), 273, 822
FCPA. *see* Foreign Corrupt Practices Act of 1977
FCRA (Fair Credit Reporting Act of 1970), 698, 701
FDA. *see* Food and Drug Administration
FDCA. *see* Food, Drug, and Cosmetic Act of 1938
FDCPA (Fair Debt Collection Practices Act of 1977), 698–699, 701, 705
Federal Arbitration Act of 1925 (FAA), 127–128
Federal Bureau of Investigation (FBI), 64
Federal cause of action, 682–683
Federal Communications Commission (FCC), 578, 584–585
Federal courts. *see also* Supreme Court, U.S.
 appellate, 79, 80, 100
 defined, 77, 100
 district, 79, 83, 100
 jurisdiction of, 86
 structure of, 83
Federal Insurance Contributions Act of 1935 (FICA), 379
Federalism, 8
Federalist Papers, 41–42, 44n

Federal Odometer Act of 1972, 688, 701
Federal powers, 42–48
Federal questions, 86, 100
Federal Register, 572–576
Federal Reserve, 556
Federal system of government, 41, 67, 77
Federal Trade Commission Act of 1914 (FTCA), 629, 643–646, 685, 700
Federal Trade Commission (FTC)
 antitrust law and, 629, 643–645
 debt collection and, 699
 defined, 701
 establishment of, 685
 franchise regulation and, 470–471
 jurisdiction of, 556
 Magnuson-Moss Act and, 681–683
Federal Trademark Dilution Act of 1995, 782, 803
Federal Unemployment Tax Act of 1935 (FUTA), 380, 397
Fee simple, 751, 760
Fee tail, 751n
Felonies, 712, 735
FICA (Federal Insurance Contributions Act of 1935), 379
Fictitious names, 454
Fiduciary duties
 in agency law, 348–351, 361–362
 breach of, 519
 in corporations, 513–519
 in limited liability companies, 486–487
 in partnerships, 460–461, 471, 476, 478
Fiduciary relationships, 336
Fifth Amendment, 64, 66, 85, 729–731, 757
50 Cent (Curtis James Jackson III), 673–674
File sharing, 790
Finance charges, 693–694
Financial crisis (2008), 152, 556–557, 652, 692n
Financial market regulation, 556
Financial reporting, 553
Financial Stability Oversight Council (FSOC), 557
Finder of fact role, 123
Finder of law role, 123
First Amendment, 55–60, 66, 777–778
First sale doctrine, 787
Fish and Wildlife Service, U.S., 599–600
Fit for a particular purpose warranty, 680
Fixtures, 749
Flammable Fabrics Act of 1953, 685
Flood, Curt, 640
FLSA (Fair Labor Standards Act of 1938), 10, 371–377, 372n, 396
FMLA (Family and Medical Leave Act of 1993), 383–385, 397, 403–404
FOB (free on board) point, 257, 273, 274, 822
FOIA (Freedom of Information Act of 1966), 66, 589–590
Food, Drug, and Cosmetic Act of 1938 (FDCA), 613, 613n, 692, 701, 713
Food and Drug Administration (FDA), 583, 600, 692, 701, 703, 713, 844
Food safety, 692
Forbearance, 190, 197
Force majeure, 223–224
Foreclosure, 655, 671
Foreign corporations, 502
Foreign Corrupt Practices Act of 1977 (FCPA), 723, 735, 740, 817–820, 825
Foreign Sovereign Immunities Act of 1976 (FSIA), 813–814, 825, 830
Foreseeability, 295, 300, 301
Formal rulemaking, 572
Forum choice, 87, 92, 102–104
Forum clauses, 271, 820
Forum selection clause, 92, 102–104
Forum shopping, 102–103
Found articles, 744–745
401(k) plans, 378, 378n

Fourteenth Amendment, 64–65, 70, 85, 757
Fourth Amendment, 18, 60–64, 66, 67, 726–729
Franchise agreements, 470
Franchisees, 470, 471
Franchises, 470–471
Franchisors, 470, 471
Fraud. *see also* Statute of frauds
 bankruptcy and, 662, 667–668
 case summary, 240
 computer, 722, 735
 conspiracy to commit, 555
 Consumer Fraud Acts (state statutes), 689–690, 705
 contract enforceability and, 207–210
 McDonald's promotional games, 847–851
 securities regulation, 545
 telemarketing and, 688, 701
 white-collar crime and, 715–716
Fraudulent misrepresentation, 207–210, 235, 289–291
Fraudulent transfers, 662
Freedom of Information Act of 1966 (FOIA), 66, 589–590
Freedom of speech, 55–60
Friedman, Milton, 157
Frolics, 344, 357
Fruit of the poisonous tree, 732
Frustration of purpose, 224–225, 236
FSIA (Foreign Sovereign Immunities Act of 1976), 813–814, 825, 830
FSOC (Financial Stability Oversight Council), 557
FTC. *see* Federal Trade Commission
FTCA (Federal Trade Commission Act of 1914), 629, 643–646, 685, 700
Fuel economy standards, 606
Fully disclosed agency, 341, 357
FUTA (Federal Unemployment Tax Act of 1935), 380, 397

G

Gag orders, 63
GE Capital Corporation, 557
Gender wage gap, 437–438
General Agreement on Tariffs and Trade (GATT), 823, 825
General Assembly, 8
General authority, 78
General counsel, 5–6
General partnerships
 capitalization of, 459
 case summaries, 475, 477
 fiduciary duties in, 460–461, 471
 formation of, 457–458
 governance of, 456–457
 liability of principals, 458–459, 475
 management and operation of, 460
 taxation of, 459–460
 withdrawal from, 468
Generic marks, 774–775
Genetically modified organisms (GMOs), 703–704
Genuine assent, 206–211, 235
Global Crossing, 553
Going-and-coming rule, 344–346, 357
Good faith
 collective bargaining and, 392
 contract performance and, 217–218, 236, 241
 defined, 236
 in partnerships, 460–461, 477
 personal property and, 746
 sales contracts and, 259, 277–278
 in securities law, 565
 UCC requirement for, 259, 265n
Goods, defined, 247, 273
Goodwill, 214
Google, 23–24, 153–154, 474, 645

"Government hand" approach, 158, 160
Government in the Sunshine Act of 1976, 591
Grand jury, 724
Gratuitous agents, 329, 350, 357
Greenwashing, 622–623
Greyhound Lines, 770
Grievances, 392, 397
Grimmelmann, James, 155
Grokster, 787, 791
Guarantors, 655–656, 671
Guilty knowledge, 207
Gun-Free School Zones Act of 1990, 51
Guns, products liability and, 309–311

H

Hamilton, Alexander, 41
Hammurabi's Code, 170
Harassment, sexual, 416–421
Hart-Scott-Rodino Antitrust Improvements Act of 1976, 645
Hazardous materials disposal, 612–613
Health Care and Education Reconciliation Act of 2010 (HCERA), 380
Health Insurance Portability and Accountability Act of 1996 (HIPPA), 66, 379
HealthSouth, 553
Heirs, 751
Hershey Chocolate and Confectionery Corporation, 771, 773
Hillary: The Movie (film), 59–60
Hilton Hotels, 770
Holdings, 11
Holmes, Oliver Wendell, 55
Horizontal commonality, 531
Horizontal restraints, 633–636, 646, 650
Hostile work environments, 416–417, 435
Hours of work, 372–374, 378
Houston, Charles Hamilton, 69, 70
Hung juries, 123, 133
Hybrid contracts, 175, 196
Hybrid legal systems, 815

I

ICC (International Chamber of Commerce), 272–273, 816, 822
Identity theft, 697–698
Illusory promises, 191, 197
IMF (International Monetary Fund), 812, 827
Implied authority, 339, 340, 511–512
Implied contracts, 173, 196, 201, 366–368
Implied-in-law recovery, 174
Implied partnerships, 457–458, 471
Implied warranties, 306, 679–680, 700, 706
Impossibility of contract performance, 222, 236
Impracticability of contract performance, 223, 236, 263–264
Improper distribution, 485
Improper packaging, 309
Inadequate warnings, 307–308
Incapacity, in contract formation, 185, 193–194, 197
Incidental beneficiaries, 234, 237
Incidental damages, 267, 268
INCO terms, 272–274, 822, 825
Inculpatory evidence, 119
Indemnification, 342, 353
Independent agencies, 14
Independent contractors
  in California, 332–333
  case summary, 362
  defined, 329, 357
  direction and control criterion for, 330–332, 335
  employee agents vs., 329–335

peculiar risk doctrine and, 347
state law and, 330–331
Indictments, 724
Indirect copyright infringement, 786, 803
Induce, defined, 293
Industrial Revolution, 365, 629
Inferior trial courts, 78
Informal rulemaking, 572
Information, filing of, 724
Infractions, 712
Infringement
  copyright, 785–789
  patents, 800–801
  trademark, 780–782, 832–842
In-house counsel, 5–6
Initial public offerings (IPOs), 502, 505, 529
Injunctive relief, 18, 231, 237
Injurious effects, 90–91
Innocent misrepresentation, 207, 208
In personam jurisdiction. *see* Personal jurisdiction
In rem jurisdiction, 88, 101, 106
Insanity defense, 712
Insiders. *see* Shareholders
Insider trading, 546–548, 560, 563, 718–720, 735, 739
Insider Trading and Securities Fraud Enforcement Act of 1988, 546, 560, 718
Insolvent, 485, 657–660
Inspection by administrative agencies, 578–579, 591
Installment contracts, 265–266, 274
In-state defendants, 88
Intellectual property, 766–809
  Agreement and Permission to Use (sample form), 793
  case summaries, 806–808
  constitutional protections for, 766
  copyright (*see* Copyright)
  international agreements on, 823–825
  liability avoidance, 792–793
  patents (*see* Patents)
  service marks, 770, 771
  summary of protections, 802
  trade dress, 770–771
  trademarks (*see* Trademarks)
  trade secrets (*see* Trade secrets)
Intended beneficiaries, 233–234, 237
Intentional torts, 283–294
  in agency law, 346
  business competition, 291–293
  concept summary, 294
  defamation, 90–91, 97, 99, 284–290
  defined, 283, 312
  false imprisonment, 291
  fraudulent misrepresentation, 289–291
  product disparagement, 288, 313
Interbrand competition, 636–637
Intermediaries, 533
Intermediate-level scrutiny, 45, 46, 65, 67
Internal Revenue Service (IRS)
  defined, 12n
  limited liability companies and, 480–481
  risk of tax avoidance strategies, 593
  stare decisis and, 12
  tax payments to, 52
  three-prong test, 333
  20-point test, 333n
International Chamber of Commerce (ICC), 272–273, 816, 822
International Court of Arbitration, 816
International Court of Justice, 812–813, 825
International law, 810–831
  antibribery provisions, 723, 817–820
  case summaries, 829–830
  CISG (*see* U.N. Convention on Contracts for the International Sale of Goods)
  civil law systems, 815, 825

comity in, 811–812, 825
commercial law, 817–823
common law systems, 815
courts in, 812–814
customs, 811
defined, 811
dispute resolution in, 815–817, 830
Foreign Corrupt Practices Act, 723, 735, 740, 817–820, 825
intellectual property in, 823–825
Internet and, 98–100
judicial decisions, 811–812
legal systems of nations, 815
mixed legal systems, 815
organizations and, 812
overview, 810
public vs. private, 811, 825
religion-based legal systems, 815
sales contracts and, 271–273, 822–823
sources of, 811–812
sovereign immunity and, 813–814, 825, 829
treaties, 811
International Monetary Fund (IMF), 812, 827
Internet
  advertisements on, 690–691
  business method patents, 798–800
  common law and, 11
  computer fraud, 722
  copyright in digital age, 789–791
  country of origin principle and, 99, 101
  cybersecurity and disclosures, 552
  disclaimers and, 315
  domain names, 775–776
  e-mail jurisdiction, 95–98
  e-mail and statute of frauds, 213
  international jurisdiction, 98–100
  jurisdictional issues, 95–100, 105–107
  legal research on, 32, 36–38
  minimum contacts and, 95–98, 105–106
  net neutrality, 584–585, 592
  obscenity regulation, 733–734
  online dispute resolution, 134–135
  protections for online content providers, 289–290
  trademarks and, 775, 832–838
  Uniform Electronic Transactions Act and, 175–176
  workplace monitoring of, 386
Interrogatories, 120, 132, 138
Interstate vs. intrastate commercial activity, 48
Intoxication, as defense, 712
Intrabrand competition, 636
Investigation, 569, 724, 735
Investment games, 532
Investors, 533. *see also* Securities law
"Invisible hand" approach, 158, 160
Invoices (acknowledgment forms), 250, 274
Involuntary bankruptcy petitions, 663, 671
IPOs (initial public offerings), 502, 505, 529
Irrevocable offers, 183, 184, 197, 250
IRS. *see* Internal Revenue Service
Issuers, 533

J

Jackson, Curtis James, III (50 Cent), 673–674
James, LeBron, 359–360
Jargon, 4
Jay, John, 41
JOBS (Jumpstart Our Business Startups) Act of 2012, 542
Johnson, Lyndon B., 50, 432
Johnson & Johnson, 309
Joint ventures, 458, 471
Jointly and severally liable, 458–459, 471, 615
JPMorgan Chase, 556
Judges, 79, 81, 123

Judgment
    business judgment rule, 504
    collecting, 124, 454, 454n
    declaratory, 324
    default, 118
    summary, 118
Judgment creditors, 124
Judgment as a matter of law, motion for, 118
Judicial branch, 41, 43–44, 67
Judicial review. *see also* Appellate courts
    of administrative agency regulations, 582, 584–587, 595–596
    constitutional law and, 43–44, 65
    defined, 43, 67, 77
    establishment of, 43–44, 77n
    standards of, 45–46
    Supreme Court's authority for, 43–44, 44n
Judiciary, 76–82, 100. *see also* Courts
Juice contamination crisis (case study), 843–845
Jumpstart Our Business Startups (JOBS) Act of 2012, 542
The Jungle (Sinclair), 365n
Juries, 123, 132, 133
Jurisdiction, 84–100
    authority and, 76, 77
    business strategy and, 85
    Calder effects test and, 96–97
    case summaries, 104–108
    concept summary, 92–93
    concurrent, 87, 100
    constitutional basis for, 43, 85
    country of origin principle and, 99, 101
    defined, 67, 84, 85, 100
    diversity-of-citizenship cases and, 83, 86, 100
    effects test and, 90, 90n
    e-mail and, 95–98
    federal questions and, 86, 100
    forum choice and, 87, 92, 102–104
    in rem, 88, 101, 106
    in-state defendants and, 88
    Internet and, 95–100, 105–107
    long-arm statutes and, 88–89, 101
    minimum contacts and, 89, 95–98, 101, 105–106
    original, 86–87, 100, 107–108
    out-of-state defendants and, 88–92
    personal (*see* Personal jurisdiction)
    quasi in rem, 88, 101, 106
    subject matter (*see* Subject matter jurisdiction)
    two-part analysis of, 85–86
    of U.S. Supreme Court, 80
    Zippo standard and, 96–98, 108
Jurisprudence, 3, 25
Jury, 123, 132, 133
Justice, defined, 141
Justice-of-the-peace courts, 78
Justinian Code, 170

K

Kant, Immanuel, 146
Kennedy, John F., 428, 438
Key employees, 385
King, Martin Luther, Jr., 50
Knockout rule, 252, 274

L

Labeling requirements for warranties, 683
Labor arbitration, 129–130
Labor law. *see* Employment law
Labor Management Relations Act of 1947, 389, 389n, 397
Labor-Management Reporting and Disclosure Act of 1959, 389–390, 390n, 397
Labor Management Services Administration, 379

Labor unions, 388–395
    authorization cards for, 390, 397
    boycotts by, 395
    certification in, 391, 397
    collective bargaining and, 389, 391–392, 397
    elections in, 390, 397
    formation of, 390–391
    governing law, 388–389
    illegal work stoppages by, 395
    lockouts and, 395, 398, 400–401
    management relations with, 389–390
    membership trends, 388
    origins of, 365
    reform efforts, 391
    reporting and disclosure requirements for, 389–390
    right-to-work laws and, 389, 397
    strikes and, 392–395, 397, 400–401
Land acquisitions, 618–619
Landlord-tenant agreements, 748, 752–753
Landowners, 296, 617
Landrum-Griffin Act. *see* Labor-Management Reporting and Disclosure Act of 1959
Lanham Act of 1946, 770, 833, 840
Lapse of time, termination of contract offers by, 185, 197
Law
    administrative (*see* Administrative law)
    agency (*see* Agency law)
    antitrust (*see* Antitrust law)
    in business environment, 4–7, 21–25
    categories of, 17–21
    civil, 11, 18, 26, 709–710, 815, 825
    common (*see* Common law)
    constitutional (*see* Constitutional law)
    consumer (*see* Consumer law)
    contract (*see* Contracts)
    criminal (*see* Criminal law)
    defined, 3, 25
    development through courts, 83–84
    employment (*see* Employment law)
    environmental (*see* Environmental law)
    equity vs., 18–20
    ethics and, 141–143
    international (*see* International law)
    language of, 4
    natural, 145
    operation of (*see* Operation of law)
    primary sources of, 7–12, 14, 15
    private, 20–21, 26
    procedural, 18, 26
    public, 20–21, 26
    purposes of, 3
    research strategies, 37–38
    restatements of, 15, 16, 25–26
    secondary sources of, 14–16, 25
    securities (*see* Securities law)
    state (*see* State law)
    statutory, 8–11, 17, 25, 175, 196
    substantive, 18, 26
    tort (*see* Torts)
Law firms, 6–7
Lawyers, 5–7
LCIA (London Court of International Arbitration), 816
Leasehold estate, 752–753, 760
Leases, 698, 747–748, 760
Legal competitive advantage, 23–24
Legal detriment, 189, 190
Legal (proximate) cause, 300–302, 313
Legal research strategies, 37–38
Legal risk management, 315
Legalese, 4
Legality
    in contract formation, 195, 197, 202
    in criminal law, 710, 735
Legislative branch, 41, 42, 52–53, 67

Legislative history, 9, 25
Legislative veto, 582n
Lemon laws, 689
Lenders. *see* Creditors
Letters of intent, 538
Liability
    in agency law, 339–348
    for business crimes, 713–715
    corporate, 503, 506–507, 519, 526
    in criminal law, 710–712
    in general partnerships, 458–459, 475
    intellectual property and, 792–793
    jointly and severally liable, 458–459, 471, 615
    in limited liability companies, 485, 496
    in limited liability partnerships, 489–491
    in limited partnerships, 461, 463
    for misclassification in agency law, 333–335
    personal, 461, 463, 503
    products (*see* Products liability)
    for securities law violations, 542–543, 548
    strict (*see* Strict liability)
    Superfund, 617
    tipper-tippee, 548
    vicarious, 343, 361, 418–419
Libel, 284, 288–290, 313
Licensing, 570, 578, 591
Lie detector tests, 388
Life estate, 751–752, 760
Life tenants, 751
Lights-out option, 657
Likelihood of confusion standard, 780
Lilly Ledbetter Fair Pay Act of 2009, 429
Limited authority, 78
Limited liability companies (LLCs)
    capitalization of, 485
    case summaries, 496–497
    certificates of organization for, 482–484, 493
    characteristics of, 482
    concept summary, 492
    defined, 493
    dissociation/dissolution of, 487–488, 493
    expulsion of members from, 488–489
    fiduciary duties in, 486–487
    formation of, 482–485
    innocent partners in, 497
    liability of members, 485, 496
    management and operation of, 486
    manager-managed, 486, 493
    member-managed, 486, 493
    operating agreements for, 482, 493
    overview, 480–481
    personal guarantee from members, 485, 493, 496
    state laws and, 480–481
    taxation of, 485
    withdrawal of members from, 496–497
Limited liability partnerships (LLPs)
    capitalization of, 491–492
    characteristics of, 489
    concept summary, 492
    defined, 493
    formation of, 489
    liability of partners, 489–491
    management and operation of, 492
    state laws and, 481
    statement of qualification for, 489, 493
    taxation of, 491
Limited partnerships
    capitalization of, 464
    case summaries, 477, 478
    certificates of limited partnership, 461, 462, 471
    family, 465
    formation of, 461, 462
    governance of, 461
    management and operation of, 464–465
    personal liability of principals, 461, 463
    taxation of, 464
    withdrawal from, 468–469

Subject Index   903

Liquidated damages, 230, 237
Liquidation process, 487, 487n
Literal patent infringement, 801, 803
Litigants, 88
Litigation. *see* Alternative dispute resolution (ADR); Civil litigation
Litigators, 6
LLCs. *see* Limited liability companies
LLPs. *see* Limited liability partnerships
Loan origination fees (points), 694, 694n
Local regulations, 8–9
Lockouts, 395, 398, 400–401
Logical-outgrowth test, 575–576, 595
London Court of International Arbitration (LCIA), 816
Long-arm statutes, 88–89, 101
Loss
   of consortium, 302
   risk of, 256–258, 269–270, 274
   of trademarks, 774, 779
Lost property, 744
Loyalty, duty of
   in agency law, 348–350
   in corporations, 516–519, 522
   in limited liability companies, 486
   in limited partnerships, 477
Lucidity, 194, 197

M

Mackey, John, 164
Madison, James, 41–42
Madoff, Bernie, 562–563, 717
Madrid Protocol, 823–824, 826
Magna Carta (1215), 64
Magnuson-Moss Warranty–Federal Trade Commission Improvement Act of 1975, 681–683
Mail Fraud Act of 1990, 716, 735
Mailbox rule, 185–187, 197
Major League Baseball (MLB), 638–640
Malice, 284
Manager-managed LLCs, 486, 493
Manifestation, in agency law, 336, 357
Manifestation of intent, 178
Manufacturing defects, 307
Marine Mammal Protection Act of 1972, 620
Market allocation, 635
Market-based approaches, 604–605, 621
Marshall, Thurgood, 69, 70
Mass tort action, 111
Master-servant relationship, 329
Material (deviation from contract), 218, 236
Material misstatements, 564
Materiality defense, 543–544
Maturity date, 505
Maximin strategy, 147
Maximizing profits, 143, 157, 161
McCain-Feingold Act of 2002, 59
McDonald's, 770, 847–851
MCI WorldCom, 553
Means test, 663, 668–669, 676
Measure of judicial action, 18
Med-arb, 131, 133
Mediation, 130, 131, 133, 135, 817
Medical leave, 383–385
Meeting of the minds, 178, 634
Meetings, corporate, 511
Member-managed LLCs, 486, 493
Mens rea, 711
Mental incapacity, 193–194, 197, 712, 735
Mental requirement, 711
Merchantability, implied warranty of, 679–680
Merchant's firm offers, 250, 273–274
Merchant's (shopkeeper's) privilege, 291, 313
Merchants, 247, 251–253, 273

Mergers, 643
MetLife, 557
#MeToo movement, 419
Microsoft Corporation, 642, 772
Migratory Bird Conservation Act of 1929, 620
Milano, Alyssa, 419
Minimum contacts
   case summaries, 105–106
   defined, 101
   e-mail and, 95–98
   Internet business and, 95–98
   out-of-state defendants and, 89
Minimum wage, 372
Mini-trials, 131, 133
Minors
   capacity to contract, 193, 197
   child labor laws, 377–378
Miranda, Ernesto, 730, 730n
Mirror image rule, 184–185, 197
Misappropriation, 546–548, 767–768, 802
Misclassification in agency law, liability for, 333–335
Misconduct of employee defense, 432
Misdemeanors, 712, 735
Misfeasance, 295, 313
Mislaid property, 744
Misrepresentation, 207–210, 235, 289–291
Mistake (criminal law), 711
Mistakes in contract formation, 188–189, 197, 203
Mistrial, 118, 725
Mitigating circumstances, 710
Mixed legal systems, 815
Mixed motives, 414–415, 435
MLB (Major League Baseball), 638–640
Mobile sources of air pollution, 604, 606–607, 620
Model Business Corporation Act, 16
Model Penal Code (MPC), 709, 712, 713, 717, 735
Model state statutes, 15–16, 26. *see also specific statutes*
Modifications (substitute agreements), 220, 236
Monetary sovereignty, 827
Money damages, 18, 226, 228, 237, 268–269
Monopolies, 641–642, 647–648
Moral minimum, 143, 161
Moral philosophy, 145–147
Morals, defined, 145, 161
Mortgage foreclosure, 655, 671
Mortgage Forgiveness Debt Relief Act of 2007, 655
Mortgagees, 655, 671
Mortgages, 655, 671, 692n, 695
Mortgagors, 655, 671
Moskovitz, Dustin, 495
Motions, in civil litigation, 118, 123, 132
MPC. *see* Model Penal Code
Multidistrict litigation, 610
Municipal courts, 78
Murray, Donald Gaines, 69
Mutual assent
   acceptance and, 178
   case summary, 202
   concept summary, 187
   defined, 196
   genuineness of, 206–211, 235
Mutual consent, 220–221, 236
Mutual mistakes, 189, 197

N

Napster, 786, 787, 790
National Ambient Air Quality Standards (NAAQS), 604
National Association for the Advancement of Colored People (NAACP), 69–70

National Collegiate Athletic Association (NCAA), 638
National Commission on Reform of Federal Criminal Laws, 709
National Conference of Commissioners on Uniform State Laws (NCCUSL), 15–16, 175n, 247, 456, 744n
National Environmental Policy Act of 1969 (NEPA), 602–603, 620
National Football League (NFL), 129, 400–401, 638, 641
National Football League Players Association (NFLPA), 400
National Highway Traffic Safety Administration, 606
National Labor Relations Act of 1935 (NLRA), 388–392, 389n, 394, 395, 397
National Labor Relations Board (NLRB), 389–392, 397
National Pollution Discharge Elimination System, 608
National Security Letters, 63–64
Natural law, 145
NCAA (National Collegiate Athletic Association), 638
NCCUSL. *see* National Conference of Commissioners on Uniform State Laws
Necessary and Proper Clause, 42, 52–53, 67, 72–73
Negligence, 294–304
   actual damages and, 302
   analysis of, 302, 304
   assumption of risk and, 303–304, 313, 317
   breach of duty and, 298–299
   but-for test and, 299–300
   cause in fact and, 299–300, 313
   common law standards of behavior and, 299
   comparative, 303, 313, 318
   contributory, 303
   defenses to, 302–304
   defined, 85, 283, 312
   duty and, 295–298
   elements of, 294–302
   misfeasance, 295, 313
   nonfeasance, 295, 313
   products liability and, 306
   proximate (legal) cause and, 300–302, 313
   res ipsa loquitur and, 299, 316
   safety statute violations and, 298
   superseding causes and, 301
Negligence per se, 298, 316–317
Negligent hiring doctrine, 346–347, 357
Negligent retention, 347
Negotiated Rulemaking Act of 1990, 577
NEPA (National Environmental Policy Act of 1969), 602–603, 620
Net neutrality, 584–585, 592
NET (No Electronic Theft) Act of 1997, 786, 803
NFL (National Football League), 129, 400–401, 638, 641
NFLPA (National Football League Players Association), 400
Nike, 770
Ninth Amendment, 66
NLRA. *see* National Labor Relations Act of 1935
NLRB (National Labor Relations Board), 389–392, 397
No Electronic Theft (NET) Act of 1997, 786, 803
Nolo contendere, 725n
Nominal consideration, 190, 197
Nominal damages, 228n
Noncompliance, 21–22, 562–563
Nondischargeable debt, 665, 675
Nonexempt (covered) employees, 376–377, 396
Nonfeasance, 295, 313
Nonobviousness standard, 796, 803
Nonpecuniary settlements, 113

Nonprice restraints, 636–637
Nonvoting stock, 510, 534
Notorious possession, 754
Novation, 221, 236
Novelty standard, 795–796, 803
Nuclear condition, 217
Nuclear Regulatory Commission (NRC), 600
Nuisance, common law doctrine of, 599, 620

O

Obama, Barack, 43, 142
Obamacare. *see* Patient Protection and Affordable Care Act of 2010 (PPACA)
Obedience, duty of, 350
Objective intent, 178–180, 196
Obscenity regulation, 57–58, 733–734
Obstruction of justice, 721–722
Occupational licenses, 578
Occupational Safety and Health Act of 1970, 381–382, 397, 570
Occupational Safety and Health Administration (OSHA), 382, 570, 579
Odometer rollback, 688
ODR (online dispute resolution), 134–135
Odwalla Juice Company, 692, 843–845
OECD (Organization for Economic Cooperation and Development), 812, 818
Offers. *see* Contract offers
Office of Management and Budget (OMB), 582
Office of the Comptroller of the Currency, 556
Officers, corporate, 506, 509, 511–513, 522
Oil Pollution Act of 1990 (OPA), 608–611, 621
Oil Spill Liability Trust Fund, 609
Oil spills, 586, 608–611
Omitted terms, 215, 236
On-call time compensation, 403
Online advertisements, 690–691
Online dispute resolution (ODR), 134–135
Open-access property, 743
Opening statements, 123, 132
Open possession, 754
Open terms, 249, 273
Operating agreements, 482, 493
Operating permits, 604, 621
Operation of law
  defined, 197, 236, 358
  discharge of contracts by, 222–225
  termination by, 185, 356
Option contracts, 183, 250
Oral arguments, 78–79
Oral contracts, 171
Orders for relief, 663
Ordinances, 8–9, 25
Organization for Economic Cooperation and Development (OECD), 812, 818
Organized crime, 717–718
Originality requirement for copyright, 784–785, 803
Original jurisdiction, 86–87, 100, 107–108
Original Position, 147
OSHA (Occupational Safety and Health Administration), 382, 570, 579
Out-of-existence option, 657
Out-of-state defendants, 88–92
Output contracts, 249, 273
Overtime compensation, 373–374, 396
Ownership interests, 750–754, 760

P

Packaging, improper, 309
Page, Larry, 23–24, 474, 798
Paris Convention, 823, 825, 826
Park, John, 713–714
Park doctrine, 713–715
Parks, Rosa, 142
Parol evidence rule, 214, 236
Partial breach of contract, 226
Partial performance, 183–184
Partially disclosed agency, 341, 357
Parties, in court cases, 77, 78, 86, 88, 100
Partnerships
  at will, 458, 471
  capitalization of, 459, 464
  case summary, 475
  defined, 456, 471
  dissociation/dissolution of, 466–469, 471
  express, 456, 471
  fiduciary duties and, 460–461, 471, 476, 478
  formation of, 457–458, 461, 462
  general (*see* General partnerships)
  good faith in, 460–461, 477
  implied, 457–458, 471
  liability in, 458–459, 461, 463, 475
  limited (*see* Limited partnerships)
  limited liability (*see* Limited liability partnerships (LLPs))
  management and operation of, 460, 464–465
  as pass-through entities, 459–460, 471
  sole proprietorships vs., 465–466
  taxation of, 459–460, 464
  winding up, 468, 471
  withdrawal from, 466, 468–469, 471
Partnerships at will, 458, 471
Pass-through entities, 459–460, 471
Past consideration, 191–192, 197
Patent Act of 1790, 794, 800, 801
Patentable subject matter standard, 796, 803
Patents, 793–802
  business method patents, 795–800
  case summary, 807
  categories of, 795
  concept summaries, 801–802
  cost considerations, 794
  defined, 793, 803
  design patents, 795, 796
  duration of protection, 795
  enforcement of, 801
  infringement, 800–801
  international agreement on, 825
  nonobviousness standard for, 796, 803
  notice of, 801
  novelty standard for, 795–796, 803
  patentable subject matter standard for, 796, 803
  prosecution of, 794–795
  remedies for infringement, 801
  sources of law for, 794
  standards for, 795–796
  utility patents, 795–798
Patent Trial and Appeal Board (PTAB), 795
Patent trolls, 800
Paterno, Joe, 151
Patient Protection and Affordable Care Act of 2010 (PPACA), 9, 52, 379, 380
PATRIOT Act of 2001, 63–64
"Pay secrecy" policies, 438
PCAOB (Public Company Accounting Oversight Board), 553
Peculiar risk doctrine, 347
Pecuniary harm, 284
Peer-to-peer lending (P2PL), 534–535
Penalty clause, 354
Pennsylvania State University, 150–151
Pensions, 378, 379, 397
Perfecting security interests, 654, 671
Perfect performance, 217
Perfect tender rule, 260, 274
Permanence of constitutional law, 8
Permitting, 570, 608
Per se, defined, 631
Per se infringement, 787, 803
Per se standard, 631, 633, 646, 650
Personal benefit test, 548
Personal guarantee
  of business loans, 656, 671
  from corporate shareholders, 506–507
  from LLC members, 485, 493, 496
Personal jurisdiction
  case summaries, 104, 107
  concept summary, 92–93
  defined, 76, 85, 88, 100
  forum choice and, 92
  injurious effects and, 90–91
  in-state defendants and, 88
  out-of-state defendants and, 88–92
  physical presence and, 91–92
  voluntary, 92
Personal liability, 461, 463, 503
Personal property, 743–748
  actual owner of, 744, 760
  adverse possession, 746
  bailments and, 746–747, 763
  characteristics of, 743–744
  concept summary, 747
  defined, 759
  found articles, 744–745
  good faith purchasers, 746
  leased, 747–748
  ownership rights, 744
Petitioning parties, 78, 78n
Petitions, for writ of certiorari, 81
Pharmaceutical industry, 142–143
Picketing, 394, 397–398
Piercing the corporate veil, 507, 520–522, 525
Plain meaning rule, 9, 25
Plain view doctrine, 727, 735
Plaintiffs, 77, 100, 115
Plant patents, 795
PLCAA (Protection of Lawful Commerce in Arms Act of 2005), 310
Pleadings stage of civil litigation, 115–118
Pleas, 724–725, 725n
Points (loan origination fees), 694, 694n
Poison Prevention Packaging Act of 1970, 685
Police power of states, 41n, 51, 64, 756
Political speech/spending by corporations, 58–60
Pollution. *see* Air pollution; Water pollution
Polygraph testing, 388
Ponzi, Charles, 716
Ponzi schemes, 562–563, 663–665, 716–717
Portal-to-Portal Act of 1947, 372, 396
PPACA (Patient Protection and Affordable Care Act of 2010), 9, 52, 379, 380
Preamble to U.S. Constitution, 41, 67
Prebankruptcy petitions, 661
Precedent
  case summary, 29–30
  in civil law, 11
  concept summary, 84
  defined, 11, 25, 84, 100
  departing from, 12
  stare decisis and, 11–12, 79n5
  in state appellate courts, 79
Predatory pricing, 649
Predominant thrust, 175
Preemption
  case summary, 71–72
  constitutional law and, 8
  criminal law and, 709
  defined, 14, 67
  Supremacy Clause and, 48
Preexisting duty rule, 191, 191n, 197
Preferential transfers, 661–662
Preferred stock, 533, 559
Pregnancy Discrimination Act of 1978, 408n
Prelawsuit stage of civil litigation, 114–115
Preliminary adjudication, 724, 735
Preoperating permits, 604

Preponderance of the evidence standard, 123, 132, 415, 710, 735
Presidential proclamations, 43, 67
Presidents of corporations, 512
Pretext, 414, 435, 440
Pretrial conferences, 122, 132
Prevention strategy, 22–23, 102, 315
Price discrimination, 645
Price-fixing, 631, 634–636, 646
Prima facie case, 413, 413n, 425
Primary securities market, 529
Primary sources of law, 7–12, 14, 15
Primary stakeholders, 142
Principally responsible parties (PRPs), 615–616
Principals
   agent's duties to, 348–351
   in business entities, 453, 471, 656
   defined, 328–329, 357, 471
   duties to agents, 353
   liability for acts of agents, 339–348
   in partnerships, 458–461, 463, 464
   remedies for breach of duty, 351–353
   taxation of, 459–460, 464
Principles-based approach to ethics, 145–146
Prior art, 794
Prisoner's dilemma, 737–738
Privacy
   in constitutional law, 66
   dispute resolution and, 125
   expectations of, 61
   federal statutes on, 66
   searches and, 61, 726–727
   in workplace, 66, 386–388
Private arbitration, 126
Private international law, 811, 825
Private law, 20–21, 26
Private placements, 540–541, 560
Private property, 743
Private Securities Litigation Reform Act of 1995 (PSLRA), 543–544, 550, 560, 565
Privately held corporations, 501–502, 522
Privilege defenses, 286–288
Privity of contract, 306n, 307
Probable cause, 61, 67, 724, 735
Procedural due process, 64
Procedural law, 18, 26
Product disparagement statutes, 288, 313
Product safety, 684–685
Production, requests for, 121, 132, 136
Productivity, 152
Products liability, 306–312
   assumption of risk and, 311, 313
   concept summary, 312
   damages and, 311
   defenses to, 311
   defined, 306
   design defects and, 307
   guns and, 309–311
   improper packaging and, 309
   inadequate warnings and, 307–308
   manufacturing defects and, 307
   misuse of product and, 311
   negligence and, 306
   strict liability and, 306–311, 317
   substantial change and, 311
   unavoidably unsafe products and, 309
   warranties and, 306
Professional corporations, 502
Professional ethics, 165
Profit maximization, 143, 157, 161
Project Maven, 153–154
Promissory estoppel, 192–193, 197
Promissory notes, 534, 655, 671
Promoters, 503–504, 531
Property
   categories of, 743
   intellectual (*see* Intellectual property)
   overview, 742
   personal (*see* Personal property)
   physical seizures of, 62
   real (*see* Real property)
   subject matter jurisdiction and, 88
   types of, 743
Property crime, 712
Prosecution of patents, 794–795
Prosecutorial discretion, 578
Prospective advantage, tortious interference with, 293
Prospectus, 538, 560
Protected classes, 408–410, 435
Protection of Lawful Commerce in Arms Act of 2005 (PLCAA), 310
Proximate (legal) cause, 300–302, 313
PRPs (principally responsible parties), 615–616
Prudential Financial, 557
PSLRA (Private Securities Litigation Reform Act of 1995), 543–544, 550, 560, 565
PTAB (Patent Trial and Appeal Board), 795
P2PL (peer-to-peer lending), 534–535
Public benefits, distribution of, 570
Public Company Accounting Oversight Board (PCAOB), 553
Public domain, 787
Public figure standard, defamation and, 284–286
Public image, 152
Public international law, 811, 825
Public law, 20–21, 26
Public order crime, 712
Public policy
   arbitration clauses and, 136–137
   contract formation and, 195, 197
   employment-at-will exceptions and, 368–369, 401
Public property, 743
Public use requirement, 758
Publicly held companies, 153n
Publicly held corporations, 502, 504
Puffery, 679
Punishment, 710, 735
Punitive damages, 73, 228n, 302n, 303, 423
Purchase orders, 250, 251, 274
Purposeful availment, 89, 105

Q

Qualified privilege, 286, 287, 313
Quasi-contracts, 173–174, 196
Quasi in rem jurisdiction, 88, 101, 106
Quasi-suspect classifications, 65
Quid pro quo theory, 416
Quorum requirement, 511

R

Racial discrimination, 50, 69–70, 142, 441
Racketeer Influenced and Corrupt Organizations (RICO) Act of 1970, 717–718
Rakoff, Jed S., 719
Ratification, in agency law, 340–341, 357
Rational basis standard, 45, 46, 65, 67
Rawls, John, 147
RCRA (Resource Conservation and Recovery Act of 1976), 612–613, 621, 624
Reagan, Ronald, 581
Real estate. *see* Real property
Real Estate Settlement Procedures Act of 1974 (RESPA), 695
Real property, 748–759
   adverse possession, 754–755, 763
   airspace rights, 749–750
   commercial land use regulation, 756–757
   continuous possession, 754
   creditors and, 655
   defined, 759
   easements and, 753, 760
   eminent domain and, 757–759, 764
   environmental regulation and, 757
   exclusive and actual possession, 754
   fee simple and, 751, 760
   home equity loan notice of right to cancel, 696
   leasehold estate and, 752–753, 760
   leases, 698, 747–748, 760
   life estate and, 751–752, 760
   loans collateralized with, 654, 655
   open, notorious, and visible possession, 754
   ownership interests, 750–754, 760
   ownership rights, 749–750
   sale of real estate, 755–756
   sources of law for, 748
   subsurface rights, 749
   use and enjoyment of land, 749
   water rights, 749
   zoning ordinances and, 756–757
Reasonable accommodations, 425, 428, 435, 439
Reasonable conduct, general duty of, 295
Reasonableness requirement, 61, 259–260
Reasonable suspicion, 726, 726n
Recording Industry Association of America (RIAA), 790
Referendum, 58n
Reformation, 231, 237
Refrigerator Safety Act of 1956, 685
Refusal orders, 538
"Regarded-as" test, 426
Regulation, defined, 577, 591
Regulation A exemptions, 541
Regulation D exemptions, 540, 560
Regulation Z, 693–694, 701
Regulatory Flexibility Act of 1980 (RFA), 575
Reimbursement, 353
Religion-based legal systems, 815
Religious tenets, 145
Remand, 79, 100
Remedial approach of Superfund, 614, 621
Remedies. *see also* Damages; Equitable relief
   in agency law, 351–354
   for buyers, 267–269
   case summary, 242
   CISG on, 272, 822
   contract performance and, 228–231, 242
   cover, 268, 274, 278
   defined, 18, 26, 226, 237, 266, 274
   employment discrimination, 423
   lawsuits, 268–269
   patent infringement, 801
   for principals, 351–353
   restitution, 229–230, 237
   rightful rejection, 268, 274
   for sellers, 267
   warranty limitations, 681, 683
Removal approach of Superfund, 614, 621
Removal of corporate directors, 511
Renunciation, 354
Reorganization plans, 666–667, 672
Replacement workers, 395, 398
Requests for admission, 120–121, 132
Requests for production, 121, 132, 136
Required-vehicle exception, 344
Requirements contracts, 249, 273, 277–278
Res ipsa loquitur, 299, 316
Res nullius, 743
Rescission, 220, 236, 352
Resource Conservation and Recovery Act of 1976 (RCRA), 612–613, 621, 624
RESPA (Real Estate Settlement Procedures Act of 1974), 695
Respondeat superior, 343, 357
Responsible corporate officer doctrine, 713–715
Restatement (Second) of Contracts, 16, 188
Restatement (Second) of Torts, 283, 307, 311, 312

Restatements of the law, 15, 16, 25–26
Restatement (Third) of Agency, 329, 357
Restatement (Third) of Torts, 283, 312
Restitution, 229–230, 237
Restraining orders, 18
Restraint of trade, 633–638, 646, 650
Restrictive covenants, 195, 214–215, 291, 320–325
Retirement plans, 378–379
Reverse engineering, 768
Revised Model Business Corporation Act (RMBCA), 501, 509, 513–514, 521
Revised Uniform Limited Liability Company Act (RULLCA), 481, 485, 486
Revised Uniform Limited Partnership Act (RULPA), 461, 464–466, 468–469
Revised Uniform Partnership Act (RUPA), 456–458, 460, 466–468
Revocation of acceptance, 269, 274
Revocation of contract offers, 182–183, 196
RFA (Regulatory Flexibility Act of 1980), 575
RIAA (Recording Industry Association of America), 790
RICO (Racketeer Influenced and Corrupt Organizations) Act of 1970, 717–718
Rightful rejection, 268, 274, 278
Right-to-sue letters, 430–431
Right-to-work laws, 389, 397
Riparian (water) rights, 607n, 749
Risk
    assumption of, 303–304, 311, 313, 317
    of loss, 256–258, 269–270, 274
    management of, 315
RMBCA (Revised Model Business Corporation Act), 501, 509, 513–514, 521
Robinson-Patman Act of 1936, 629, 645, 646
Rockefeller, John D., 474, 629, 630
Roosevelt, Franklin D., 432
Roosevelt, Theodore, 629, 630
Rudder, Christian, 157
Rule 504 exemptions, 540–541
Rule 506 exemptions, 540–541
Rulemaking by administrative agencies, 572–578
    case summary, 595
    concept summary, 578
    defined, 569, 591
    final publication process, 575–577
    formal vs. informal, 572
    judicial challenges, 577
    publication of proposed rules, 572–574
    public comment period, 573, 575
    revision of rules, 575–576
    small business owner considerations, 575
    study and research in, 572
Rule of addition, 801, 803
Rule of exactness, 801, 803
Rule of omission, 801, 803
Rule of reason standard, 631–633, 646
Rules of Civil Procedure, 119
RULLCA (Revised Uniform Limited Liability Company Act), 481, 485, 486
RULPA (Revised Uniform Limited Partnership Act), 461, 464–466, 468–469
RUPA (Revised Uniform Partnership Act), 456–458, 460, 466–468

S

S corporations, 508
Safe and Accurate Food Labeling Act of 2015, 703
Safe Drinking Water Act of 1974 (SDWA), 611, 621
Safe harbor (securities regulation), 539, 543–544
Safer Affordable Fuel-Efficient (SAFE) Vehicle Rules, 606
Safety in workplace, 381–382

Safety statute violations, 298
Sales contracts, 246–281. *see also* U.N. Convention on Contracts for the International Sale of Goods (CISG); Uniform Commercial Code (UCC)
    acceptance in, 250–254, 264–265, 269, 272
    agreement in, 248–254
    anticipatory repudiation and, 266
    battle of the forms and, 250–253, 274, 276–277, 279
    breach and remedies for, 266–272
    buyer's rights and obligations in, 264–265
    case summaries, 277–279
    commercial impracticability of, 263–264, 274, 279
    consideration in, 253–254
    defined, 247, 253, 273
    delivery requirements in, 249
    destination contracts and, 257, 274
    good faith and, 259, 277–278
    good faith provision for, 259
    goods picked up by buyer and, 257–258
    inspection of goods and, 264–265
    installment contracts, 265–266, 274
    international, 271–273, 822–823
    knockout rule and, 252, 274
    for merchant transactions, 251–253
    nonconforming goods and, 269
    for nonmerchant transactions, 250
    obligations of all parties in, 259
    offers in, 248–250, 272
    open terms in, 249, 273
    payment requirements in, 249, 264
    performance of, 259–266
    price requirements in, 249
    quantity requirements in, 249
    rejection of goods and, 264–265, 268, 278
    risk of loss and, 256–258, 269–270, 274
    seller's rights and obligations in, 259–263
    shipment contracts and, 256–257, 274
    statute of frauds and, 254–255
    title and, 256, 274
    writing requirements for, 254, 272
Same sex harassment, 418
Sandburg, Sheryl, 156
Sandusky, Jerry, 150–151
SARA (Superfund Amendments and Reauthorization Act of 1986), 614, 621
Sarbanes-Oxley (SOX) Act of 2002
    accounting industry reforms under, 553
    concept summary, 555
    corporate governance and, 502, 551–554
    defined, 560
    enforcement under, 554–555
    excerpts from, 863–864
    financial reporting requirements of, 553
    major provisions of, 553–554
    penalties for violators, 555
    whistleblower protections in, 371
Saverin, Eduardo, 474, 495
SBREFA (Small Business Regulatory Enforcement Fairness Act of 1996), 575
Scienter, 207n, 550–551, 560, 564
Scope of employment, 343–346, 362
Script settlements, 113
SDWA (Safe Drinking Water Act of 1974), 611, 621
Searches
    of business premises, 61, 729
    of cellphone location data, 71
    in criminal procedure, 726–729
    of electronic devices, 728–729
    Fourth Amendment on, 18, 60–62, 726–729
    physical, 62
    plain view doctrine and, 727, 735
    privacy expectations and, 61, 726–727
    probable cause for, 61

    reasonableness requirement for, 61
    USA PATRIOT Act and, 63–64
Search incident to arrest exception, 727–728
Seasonable notice, 260, 268
SEC. *see* Securities and Exchange Commission
Secondary boycotts, 395
Secondary meaning, 772–773, 803
Secondary securities market, 529
Secondary sources of law, 14–16, 25
Secondary stakeholders, 142
Secretaries, corporate, 512–513
Section 10b (Securities Exchange Act of 1934), 545–549
Section 16 (Securities Exchange Act of 1934), 549, 560
Secured creditors, 617, 653, 654, 671
Secured loans, 454, 454n
Secured party, 654, 671
Secured-party relationships, 654
Securities. *see also* Securities law
    categories of, 533–535
    concept summary, 535
    debt instruments, 534–535
    defining, 530–531
    equity instruments, 533–534
    parties involved with, 533
    primary market for, 529
    secondary market for, 529
Securities Act of 1933, 537–539, 542, 560
Securities and Exchange Commission (SEC)
    crowdfunding regulation, 533, 542
    defined, 535, 560
    Dodd-Frank and, 557
    EDGAR database, 537
    enforcement mechanisms of, 535–536, 558
    executive powers of, 535
    as independent agency, 535, 538
    insider trading cases and, 718–720
    jurisdiction of, 556, 557
    organizational structure, 536–537
    refusal orders issued by, 538
    stop orders issued by, 538
Securities Exchange Act of 1934, 545–549, 560
Securities law, 529–554. *see also* Securities; Securities and Exchange Commission (SEC)
    anti-fraud provisions, 543–545
    blue-sky laws, 551, 560
    case summaries, 563–565
    comfort letters in, 538
    concept summaries, 531, 541
    crowdfunding and, 532–533, 542
    defenses in, 543–544, 550–551
    defined, 529, 559
    disclosure and, 535, 559
    enforcement under SOX Act, 554–555
    exemptions in, 539–542, 560, 564
    good faith in, 565
    Howey test in, 530–532
    insider trading and, 546–548, 560, 563
    letters of intent in, 538
    liability for violations, 542–543, 548
    overview, 529
    preregistration documentation in, 538
    prospectus in, 538, 560
    registration phases in, 538–539
    safe harbor and, 539, 543–544
    statutes for, 537–539, 545–551
    stock market games and, 532
    underwriting agreements in, 538
Securities Litigation Uniform Standards Act of 1998, 551, 560
Security agreements, 654
Security interest, 654, 671
Segregation, 69–70, 142
Seizures, 18, 60–63
Self-dealing, 348, 516–517
Self-defense, 711, 735

Self-incrimination, 729–730
Semi-suspect classifications, 65
Senior in priority, 534
Seniority defense, 432
Sentencing guidelines, 710, 725, 735
"Separate but equal" doctrine, 69
Separation of powers, 45, 67
Seriousness of offers, 178
Service marks, 770, 771, 803, 806
Settlements
    coupon settlements, 113
    prelitigation negotiations, 114–115
    pretrial conference on, 122, 132
Sexual harassment, 416–421
Sexual orientation, as protected class, 409–410
Shareholders
    case summary, 525
    defined, 506, 522
    lawsuits by, 519
    personal guarantee from, 506–507
    rights of, 509–510, 525, 534
Sharia law, 815
Sheriff's sale, 653n
Sherman Act of 1890
    case summaries, 649–650
    criminal liability for violations, 637
    defined, 646
    horizontal restraints and, 633–636, 646, 650
    on monopolies, 641–642
    overview, 629–630
    per se standard and, 631, 633, 646, 650
    rule of reason standard and, 631–633, 646
    sports and, 638–641
    vertical restraints and, 633, 636–637, 646
Shipment contracts, 256–257, 274
Shopkeeper's (merchant's) privilege, 291, 313
Short-swing profits, 549
SIFIs (systemically risky financial institutions), 557
Silence as contract acceptance, 187
Silent partners, 464
Simon Marketing, Inc., 847–848
Simulation exercises
    employment discrimination, 443–450
    restrictive covenants in contracts, 320–325
    trademarks in cyberspace, 832–838
Sinclair, Upton, 365n
SIPs (State Implementation Plans), 604, 621
Sit-in strikes, 395
Sixth Amendment, 731
Slander, 284, 313
Small Business Liability Relief Act of 2002, 617
Small Business Regulatory Enforcement Fairness Act of 1996 (SBREFA), 575
Small-claims courts, 78
Smith, Adam, 158, 634
Sneak-and-peak warrants, 63
Social responsibility, corporate, 157–161
Social Security Act of 1935 (SSA), 379, 397
Soft per se analysis, 637, 646
Sole proprietorships, 454–456, 465–466, 471, 476
Solid waste disposal, 612–613
Sony defense, 787
Sotheby's Holding, Inc., 634
Sovereign immunity, 813–814, 825, 829
SOX. *see* Sarbanes-Oxley Act of 2002
Spam, 690–691
Spanier, Graham, 151
Special relationships, in tort law, 295, 313, 316
Specific performance
    case summaries, 241, 278
    defined, 18, 230, 237, 274
    example of, 18–19
    personal-service contracts and, 230–231
    real estate contracts and, 230
    sales contracts and, 230, 269
Speech, freedom of, 55–60

Speedy Trial Act of 1974, 731, 735
Spitzer, Eliot, 690
Sports and antitrust law, 638–641
SSA (Social Security Act of 1935), 379, 397
Stakeholders, 142, 154, 161, 166
Standard Oil Trust, 629, 630
Standing, 115, 132
Starbucks, 163–164, 839–842
Stare decisis, 11–12, 25, 79n5
State courts
    appellate, 78–79, 78n, 100
    defined, 77, 100
    jurisdiction of, 86
    structure of, 83
    trial, 77–78, 100
State Implementation Plans (SIPs), 604, 621
State law
    administrative, 591
    air pollution and, 604
    antidiscrimination statutes, 433–435, 440
    blue-sky laws, 551, 560
    commerce regulation and, 51
    common law, 175, 196, 299
    constitutional law, 8
    corporations and, 501
    diversity-of-citizenship cases and, 83
    federal district courts and, 79
    franchises and, 471
    independent contractor status and, 330–331
    leased personal property and, 748
    limited liability companies and, 480–481
    limited liability partnerships and, 481
    long-arm statutes, 88–89, 101
    model laws (*see* Model state statutes)
    primary sources of, 14, 15
    right-to-work laws, 389, 397
    for sale of goods, 247
    securities regulation, 551
    statutory law, 8–11, 175, 196
    on unfair and deceptive trade practices, 688–690
    workers' compensation and, 380–381, 397
State long-arm statutes, 88–89, 101
Statement of qualification, 489, 493
State supreme courts, 79
State trial courts, 77–78, 100
Stationary sources of air pollution, 604, 620
Statute of frauds
    applicability of, 213
    case summary, 240
    contract enforceability and, 171, 211–213, 236, 752n
    defined, 211, 236
    e-mail and, 213
    sales contracts and, 254–255
Statute of limitations
    case summary, 28
    in civil litigation, 115
    contract performance and, 225
    defined, 115, 132, 141, 236
Statutory law, 8–11, 17, 25, 175, 196
Statutory scheme, 9, 25
Stevens, John Paul, 641
Stock, 510, 533–534, 559
Stock market games, 532
Stolen Valor Act of 2005, 44
Stop orders, 538
Strategic bankruptcy, 673–674
Strategic contracts, 199
Strategic ethics, 163–164
Strategic Legal Solutions
    Avoiding Environmental Liability in Land Acquisitions, 618–619
    Avoiding Intellectual Property Liability, 792–793
    Cybersecurity and Disclosures, 552
    Developing Codes of Ethics and Conduct, 149–150

    Eliminating Lingering Liability, 355
    Enforcing Covenants Not to Compete, 214–215
    Limiting Liability for Misclassification, 334–335
    Performance Assurances, 262–263
    Proactive Harassment Prevention Framework, 419–421
    Trademark Registration, 779–780
    Understanding Check Deposits as Accord and Satisfaction, 221
Strategy, defined, 21
Stress tests, 557
Strict liability
    abnormally dangerous activities, 305–306
    concept summary, 312
    in criminal law, 711
    defined, 283–284, 312–313
    for harassment by supervisors, 419
    overview, 304–305
    products liability, 306–311, 317
Strict scrutiny, 45, 46, 58, 65, 67, 433
Strikes, 392–395, 397, 400–401
Strong-arm clause, 666, 672
Structural-offense laws, 641, 646
Subchapter S, 508
Subject matter jurisdiction
    concept summary, 93
    concurrent, 87, 100
    defined, 76, 85, 100
    forum choice and, 87
    original, 86–87, 100, 107–108
    property and, 88
Subordinate position, 534
Subpoenas, 120
Substance over form, 20, 330, 330n
Substantial evidence test, 584
"Substantially younger" requirement, 424–425
Substantial performance, 218–219, 236
Substantial similarity standard, 786
Substantive due process, 64
Substantive law, 18, 26
Substantive proclamations, 43
Substitute agreements, 220, 236
Subsurface rights, 749
Suggestive marks, 772
Summary judgment, motion for, 118
Summary jury trials, 131, 133
Summary offenses, 712
Summons, 115, 132
Superfund, 614–619, 621, 624
Superfund Amendments and Reauthorization Act of 1986 (SARA), 614, 621
Superseding causes, 301
Supervening illegalities, 185, 222
Supremacy Clause, 47–48, 67
Supreme Court, U.S.
    authority of, 79
    case acceptance rate, 81
    defined, 100
    judicial review function of, 43–44, 44n
    jurisdiction of, 80
    petitions for review, 81
    racial equality and, 69–70
    selection of justices for, 81
Supreme courts (state), 79
Sureties, 655–656, 671
SUR system, 32–37
Suspect classifications, 65
Systemically risky financial institutions (SIFIs), 557

T

Tables
    Agency Transaction Overview, 336
    Articles in the U.S. Constitution, 42
    Bankruptcy Options, 670

Challenges and Realities in Business Ethics, 149
Checks and Balances, 45
Child Labor Restrictions, 378
Common Forms of Business Entities, 453
Comparative Negligence Formula, 303
Constitutional Checks and Balances, 45
Copyright Protection Periods, 784
Dispute Resolution Options, 112
Environmental Laws, 620
Equitable Maxims, 20
Expansion Options and Potential Legal Impacts, 6
Forming a Union, 391
Fourth Amendment Warrant Requirement, 729
Insider-Trading Theories, 548
Intellectual Property Protections, 802
Intentional Torts, 292
Investor Limits on Crowdfunding, 542
Laws That Impact Business, 14, 15
Liabilities and Penalties under Securities Act of 1933, 542–543
Motions Used during Litigation, 118
Order of Priority for Unsecured Creditors, 665
Overview of Contract Transactions, 177
Phases of Security Registration, 539
Reliable Sources for Legal Research on the Internet, 36
Research Strategy Using Internet Sources, 37
Special Relationship Duties Owed by Landowners, 296
Subject Matter Jurisdiction, 87
Supreme Court Case Acceptance Rate, 81
When Is Acceptance Effective?, 186
Taft-Hartley Act. *see* Labor Management Relations Act of 1947
Tailpipe emissions, 606
Takings Clause, 757
Talmudic law, 815
Tangible property. *see* Personal property; Real property
Tarnishment, 782
TARP (Troubled Assets Relief Program), 556
Taubman, Alfred, 634
Tax and spend powers, 42, 52–53
Taxation
    of corporations, 507–508
    of general partnerships, 459–460
    of limited liability companies, 485
    of limited liability partnerships, 491
    of limited partnerships, 464
    risk of tax avoidance strategies, 593
    stare decisis and, 12
Tax-deferred retirement savings accounts, 378–379, 397
TDRA (Trademark Dilution Revision Act of 2006), 782–783, 833, 841
Teamwork, 152
Telemarketing, 688
Telemarketing and Consumer Fraud and Abuse Prevention Act of 1994, 688, 701
Telephone calls, workplace monitoring of, 386–387
Telephone Consumer Protection Act of 1991 (TCPA), 94, 688, 701
Tender of delivery, 259–260, 274
Tender of goods, 217, 257, 274
Tender of performance, 232, 237
Tennant, Anthony, 634
Termination
    of agency relationships, 354–356, 358
    of contract offers, 182–185
    of sole proprietorships, 455–456, 476
    of whistleblowers, 369–371
Testimony, 123
A Theory of Justice (Rawls), 147

Thiel, Peter, 524
Third Amendment, 66
Third parties
    agent's contract liability to, 341–343
    assignment to, 242
    contracts and rights of, 232–235
    sureties and guarantors, 655–656
    tort liability to, 343–346
Third-party beneficiaries, 232–234, 237
Thomas-Rasset, Jammie, 790
Three-prong test, 333
Threshold requirement, 323
Ticketmaster, 199
TILA-RESPA Integration Disclosure (TRID) rule, 695
TILA (Truth in Lending Act of 1968), 693–695, 697, 701, 704–705
Tipper-tippee liability, 548
Title, 256, 274, 744, 759–760
Title VII (Civil Rights Act of 1964), 407–424
    amendments to, 407
    case summary, 441
    concept summary, 423–424
    defined, 435
    disparate impact under, 415–416, 435
    disparate treatment under, 411–414, 435
    liability analysis under, 422
    mixed motives under, 414–415, 435
    protected classes under, 408–410, 435
    remedies under, 423
    sexual harassment under, 416–421
    theories of discrimination under, 411–416
Tortfeasor, 283, 312
Tortious conduct, 283, 312
Torts, 283–319
    case summaries, 316–318
    categories of, 283–284
    defined, 283, 283n, 312
    intentional (*see* Intentional torts)
    negligence (*see* Negligence)
    products liability (*see* Products liability)
    sources of law for, 283
    strict liability (*see* Strict liability)
    third party liability and, 343–346
Total breach of contract, 226
Toxic Substances Control Act of 1976 (TSCA), 613, 621
Trade dress, 770–771, 803
Trade libel, 288, 313
Trademark Dilution Revision Act of 2006 (TDRA), 782–783, 833, 841
Trademarks, 770–783
    acquiring rights for, 777
    applications for registration, 777–778
    arbitrary, 771
    as business assets, 771
    case summary, 806
    classifications of, 771–775
    in coffee wars case study, 839–842
    concept summary, 783
    defined, 770, 803
    descriptive, 772
    dilution, 782–783, 840, 841
    enforcement of, 776–783
    fanciful, 771
    generic, 774–775
    infringement, 780–782, 832–842
    international agreement on, 823–824
    Internet and, 775, 832–838
    loss of, 774, 779
    maintenance of, 779
    policing, 779
    product design and, 770–771
    registration of, 777–780
    secondary meaning of, 772–773, 803
    sources of law for, 770
    suggestive, 772

Trade secrets
    case summaries, 806, 808
    criminal sanctions and, 768–769
    defined, 7n, 214n, 767, 802
    eligibility for protection, 767
    exclusive rights for unlimited duration, 769
    misappropriation of, 767–768, 802
    sources of law for, 7–8, 767
Traditional insider trading, 546–548
Transaction costs, 743, 759
Treasure trove property, 744
Treasurers, corporate, 512
Treaties, 811
Treble damages, 207, 235, 290, 291
Trial courts, 77–79, 83, 100
Trial de novo, 78, 100
Trials
    bench trials, 123, 132
    in civil litigation, 122–124
    in criminal procedure, 731
    defined, 132
    mini-trials, 131, 133
    summary jury, 131, 133
Tribunal administrators, 126
TRID (TILA-RESPA Integration Disclosure) rule, 695
Triple bottom line, 158
TRIPS (Agreement on Trade-Related Aspects of Intellectual Property), 823, 825
Trojan horse (virus), 722, 722n
Trolley problem, 146
Troubled Assets Relief Program (TARP), 556
Trusts, 629, 630
Truth, as defense, 286
Truth in Lending Act of 1968 (TILA), 693–695, 697, 701, 704–705
TSCA (Toxic Substances Control Act of 1976), 613, 621
Turnaround specialists, 657–658
20-point test, 333n
Twitter, 772
Two-sided markets, 631–633, 646
Tyco, 553
Tying agreements, 637, 643, 649
Tylenol, 309
Tyson, Mike, 805

U

Uber, 332
UCC. *see* Uniform Commercial Code
UETA (Uniform Electronic Transactions Act), 175–176
ULLCA (Uniform Limited Liability Company Act), 481
U.N. Convention on Contracts for the International Sale of Goods (CISG)
    case summary, 829
    coverage and major provisions, 272, 820–822
    defined, 271, 274, 825
    function of, 271, 812
    INCO terms and, 272–273, 822
    on offer and acceptance, 272, 822
    remedies under, 272, 822
Unanimous consent resolutions, 501
Unavoidably unsafe products, 309
Unconscionability, 210–211, 236
Underwriting agreements, 538
Undisclosed agency, 342–343, 357
Undue hardship, 428, 676–677
Undue influence, 210, 236
Unemployment benefits, 380
Unenforceable contracts, 174, 196, 201–202, 241

Unfair and deceptive trade practices
    bait-and-switch, 686–687
    concept summary, 691
    odometer rollback, 688
    pricing in advertisements, 687
    spam, 690–691
    state statutes on, 688–690
    telemarketing, 688
Unfair labor practices, 402–403
Uniform Commercial Code (UCC). *see also* Sales contracts
    on acceptance, 250–254
    adoption of, 175n, 247
    anticipatory repudiation in, 266
    on breach and remedies, 266–271
    on consideration, 253–254
    on contract offers, 248–250
    coverage and definitions, 247
    ethical issues, 255
    function of, 16, 247–248
    as gap filler, 247, 249
    good faith requirement of, 259, 265n
    incidental damages under, 267
    on leased personal property, 747–748
    overview, 175, 246, 744n
    on passing of title, 256
    on performance, 259–266
    on risk of loss, 256–258, 269–270
    secured transactions under, 654
    on warranties, 306, 679–681
    writing requirements, 254
Uniform Electronic Transactions Act (UETA), 175–176
Uniform Guidelines on Employee Selection Criteria (EEOC), 415
Uniform Interstate and International Procedure Act, 89n
Uniform Limited Liability Company Act (ULLCA), 481
Uniform model laws. *see* Model state statutes
Uniform Partnership Act (UPA), 16, 456–457
Uniform Residential Landlord-Tenant Act (URLTA), 748
Uniform Trade Secrets Act (UTSA), 767, 767n
Unilateral contracts, 172–173, 180, 196, 200
Unilateral mistakes, 189, 197
Unilaterally altered contracts, 225, 236
Unions. *see* Labor unions
United Nations (U.N.), 812, 825
United States Code (U.S.C.), 10
Universalization test, 146
Unreported Income DIF (URDIF), 593
Unsecured creditors, 653, 665
Unsecured debt, 653, 671
UPA (Uniform Partnership Act), 16, 456–457
URLTA (Uniform Residential Landlord-Tenant Act), 748
U.S. Patent and Trademark Office (USPTO), 770–774, 777–779, 794–797
USA PATRIOT Act of 2001, 63–64
Usurp, 517
Utilitarianism, 146, 146n, 162
Utility patents, 795–798
UTSA (Uniform Trade Secrets Act), 767, 767n

V

Validation disclosure, 699, 701
Valid contracts, 174, 196
Value creation, 23–24

Values management
    challenges to business ethics and, 148
    clarity of operations and, 152
    common traits for effectiveness, 148–151
    concept summary, 161
    crises and, 152
    defined, 148, 162
    productivity and, 152
    public image and, 152
    strategic advantages of, 151–152
    teamwork and, 152
Variances, 756
VAWA (Violence Against Women Act of 1994), 51
Veil of ignorance, 147
Venture capital firms, 505
Venue, 84, 93–94, 100
Verdict, 123, 132
Vertical commonality, 531
Vertical price-fixing, 636, 646
Vertical restraints, 633, 636–637, 646
Vesting, 379
Veto power, 8, 582n
Vicarious copyright infringement, 786, 803
Vicarious liability, 343, 361, 418–419
Vice presidents of corporations, 512
Vienna Convention on the Law of Treaties, 811, 811n, 825
Violence Against Women Act of 1994 (VAWA), 51
Violent crime, 712
Virtual stock exchanges, 532
Virtue ethics, 145
Visible possession, 754
Voice mail, workplace monitoring of, 386–387
Void contracts, 174, 196, 200–201
Void per se contracts, 194
Voidable contracts, 174, 194, 196
Voidable transfers, 661–662, 671, 675
Voir dire, 123, 123n
Voluntary bankruptcy petitions, 663, 671
Voluntary personal jurisdiction, 92
Voting stock, 510, 534
Voucher settlements, 113

W

Wages, 372–374, 378
Wagner Act. *see* National Labor Relations Act of 1935 (NLRA)
Walmart, 647, 648
Walt Disney Company, 24
Walt Disney World, 761–762
Warnings, inadequate, 307–308
Warranties, 678–684
    breach of, 681–682
    case summaries, 706
    concept summary, 684
    defined, 678, 700
    disclaimers and, 680–681, 683, 700
    express, 306, 679, 682, 700
    implied, 306, 679–680, 700, 706
    labeling requirements for, 683
    limitation of remedies, 681, 683
    Magnuson-Moss Act and, 681–683
    sources of law for, 679
Warrants, 18, 60–63, 724, 726, 729
Waste disposal, 612–613
Watchdog groups, 600

Water pollution
    case summary, 624
    Clean Water Act and, 607–608, 621, 624
    oil spills, 586, 608–611
    permitting and, 608
    Safe Drinking Water Act and, 611, 621
    water quality regulation, 608
Water (riparian) rights, 607n, 749
WCT (World Intellectual Property Organization Copyright Treaty), 824, 826
The Wealth of Nations (Smith), 634
Web. *see* Internet
Whirlpool Corporation, 142
Whistleblower Protection Act of 1989, 371
Whistleblowers
    case summary, 404, 565
    defined, 369, 396, 555n
    Dodd-Frank provisions on, 558
    federal statutes, 371, 555
    separate and independent defense for termination of, 369–371
    state statutes, 369–371
White, Mary Jo, 718–719
White-collar crime, 715–723
    bribery, 720–721, 723
    computer fraud, 722
    conspiracy, 717
    defined, 712
    fraud, 715–716
    insider trading, 718–720, 739
    obstruction of justice, 721–722
    Ponzi schemes, 716–717
    RICO Act violations, 717–718
White-collar employees, 374
Whole Foods, 164
Wildcat strikes, 395
Wildlife protection, 620
Willful conduct, 283
Winding up, 468, 471
Winfrey, Oprah, 288
WIPO (World International Property Organization), 817
Withdrawal from partnerships, 466, 468–469, 471
Witnesses, 120–121, 123
Workers' compensation, 380–381, 397, 402
Working papers, 377
Workouts, 657–658, 671
Workplace privacy, 66
Workplace safety, 381–382
Works for hire, 784
World Court (International Court of Justice), 812–813
World Intellectual Property Organization Copyright Treaty (WCT), 824, 826
World International Property Organization (WIPO), 817
World Trade Organization (WTO), 812, 823
Writ of certiorari, 81
Written contracts, 171, 190, 211–215
Written express warranties, 682, 700

X

Xerox Corporation, 779

Z

Zippo standard, 96–98, 108
Zoning ordinances, 756–757
Zuckerberg, Mark, 474, 494–495, 523–524